Oil Paintings in Public Ownership in Hampshire: Southampton & the Isle of Wight

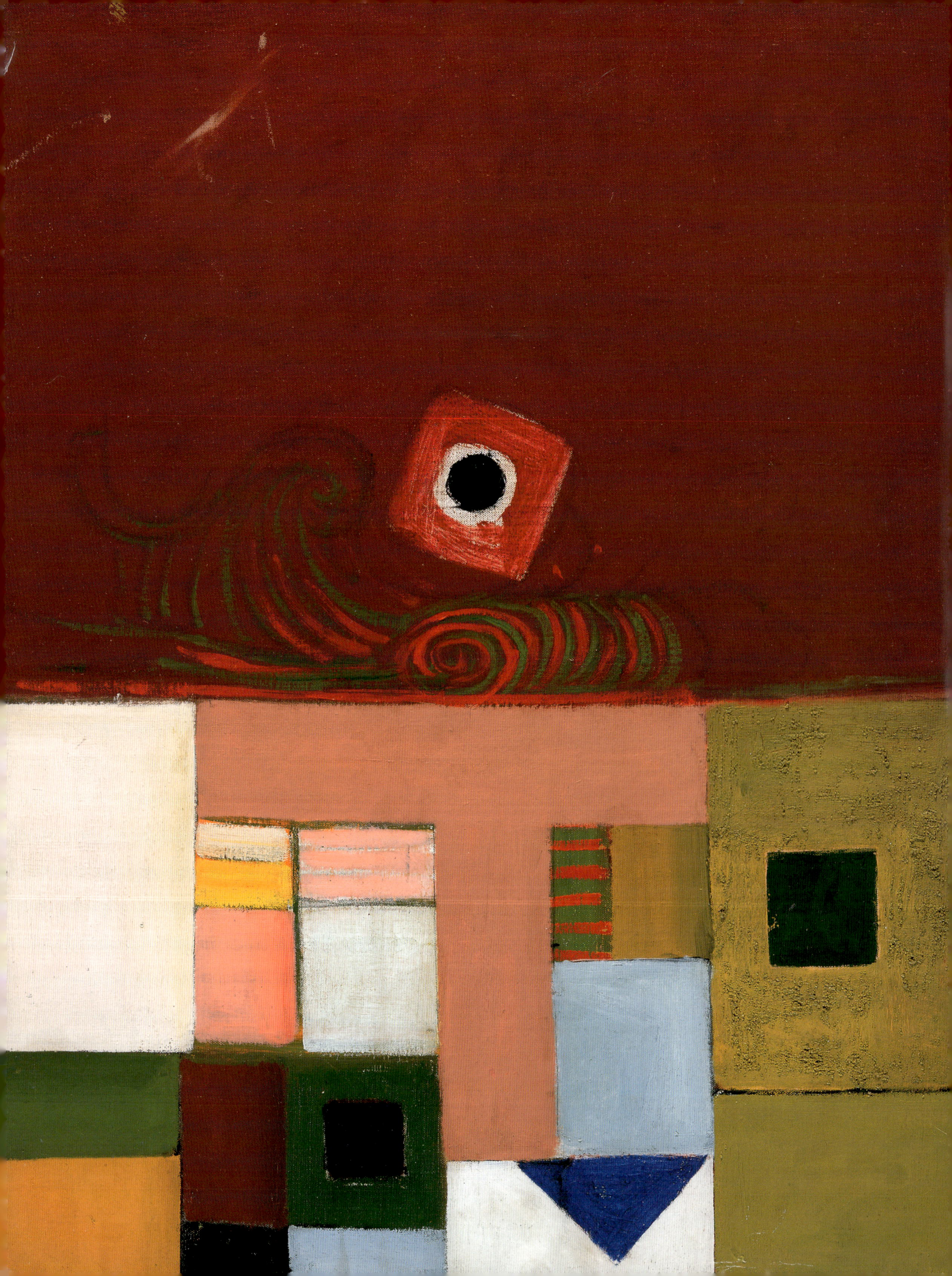

Oil Paintings in Public Ownership in Hampshire: Southampton & the Isle of Wight

The Public Catalogue Foundation

Andrew Ellis, Director
Sonia Roe, Editor
Georgina Dennis, Catalogue Coordinator
Elizabeth Vickers, Photography

First published in 2007 by the Public Catalogue Foundation, St Vincent House, 30 Orange Street, London, WC2H 7HH

We wish to thank the individual artists and all the copyright holders for their permission to reproduce the works of art. Exhaustive efforts have been made to locate the copyright owners of all the images included within this catalogue and to meet their requirements. Any omissions or mistakes brought to our attention will be duly attended to and corrected in future publications. Owners of copyright in the paintings illustrated who have been traced are listed in the Further Information section.

The responsibility for the accuracy of the information presented in this catalogue lies solely with the holding collections. Suggestions that might improve the accuracy of the information contained in this catalogue should be sent to the relevant collection and emailed to info@thepcf.org.uk.

ISBN 1-904931-18-9 (hardback)
ISBN 1-904931-19-7 (paperback)

Southampton photography: Elizabeth Vickers

Designed by Jeffery Design, London

Distributed by the Public Catalogue Foundation, St Vincent House, 30 Orange Street, London, WC2H 7HH
Telephone 020 7747 5936

Printed and bound in the UK by Butler & Tanner Ltd, Frome, Somerset

Cover image:

Nevinson, Christopher 1889–1946
Loading Timber at Southampton Docks (detail), 1917
Southampton City Art Gallery (see p. 100)

Image opposite title page:

Pasmore, Victor 1909–1989
Rectangular Motif: Red and Mustard (detail), 1950
Southampton City Art Gallery (see p. 104)

Back cover images (from top to bottom):

Markey, Peter, b.1930
Copse, 1990s
Healing Arts, Isle of Wight NHS Primary Care Trust (see p. 244)

Taylor, S. M. Louisa, active 1872–1890
Mrs A. E. White, 1890
Southampton City Museums (see p. 166)

Morris, Desmond, b.1928
The Hermit Discovered, 1948
Southampton City Art Gallery (see p. 98)

Contents

* Southampton City Art Gallery, the Collections Management Centre and Southampton Maritime Museum are all managed by Southampton City Arts & Cultural Services. Cowes Maritime Museum is managed by the Isle of Wight Council Museum Service.

Foreword

We are often asked whether we have made any 'important discoveries' in the course of our work. My answer used to be 'no'. These days, it is 'yes'. I know full well though that this affirmative does not answer the question in the way it was meant. The questioner wants to know how many Titians or Van Dykes we have uncovered, the answer to which is 'none'. It is not our job to do so. That some, or possibly many, paintings in our catalogues are wrongly attributed is certainly true, and there may be Titians and Van Dykes amongst them. But it is our job to publish what is currently believed to be the case. It is your job, as reader, to identify errors and offer corrections.

Yet we have made an important discovery. That discovery is that, as this series has progressed, a truth has emerged that speaks for itself. This is not a miscellaneous assortment of county collections that we are binding together in our catalogues. It is a National Collection.

This collection is probably the finest collection of oil paintings in public ownership in the world today. It is, moreover, an important but unregistered part of our National Heritage. That is an important discovery.

Southampton and the Isle of Wight are timely witness to that. In Southampton City Art Gallery there is a collection of national importance. It reflects the distinction of a founding advisor, Kenneth Clark, and of his visionary successors. Its collection of 1970s and 1980s painting (and sculpture) is 'unequalled in Britain outside Tate Modern', to quote Mark Fisher.

Over the Solent in the Isle of Wight, Guy Eades is Art Director for the Healing Arts programme that uses paintings (and art generally) to assist patient recuperation at St Mary's Hospital in Newport. Not unique – go and see the equivalent in the Chelsea and Westminster Hospital in London – but both the City Art Gallery and the Healing Arts programme alone should persuade funders of the extraordinary worth of these parts of our National Collection.

Does it? Sadly, all I seem to hear is the depressing sound of the flow reducing as the spigot is turned remorselessly off.

There are a number of people who have made essential contributions to this catalogue. Peter Andreae, has been dedicated and tireless in his campaign to raise funds for both this catalogue and the second Hampshire catalogue that will soon follow. Without him our task would have been infinitely more difficult, if not impossible. Lady Fagan and Lord Douro have also been at the fore of the fundraising campaign and deserve my great thanks. Georgie Dennis, our Hampshire Catalogue Coordinator and Liz Vickers, our photographer, also are due an enormous debt of appreciation for their wonderful work in creating both Hampshire volumes. But above all, our thanks must go to all the Hampshire and Isle of Wight collection directors and curators. Without their enthusiasm, support and hard work nothing would have happened at all. In particular, Tim Craven and Clare Mitchell at Southampton City Art Gallery, and Guy Eades and Mike Bishop on the Isle of Wight, deserve particular praise for their contributions.

Fred Hohler, Chairman

The Public Catalogue Foundation

The United Kingdom holds in its galleries and civic buildings arguably the greatest publicly owned collection of oil paintings in the world. However, an alarming four in five of these paintings are not on view. Whilst many galleries make strenuous efforts to display their collections, too many paintings across the country are held in storage, usually because there are insufficient funds and space to show them. Furthermore, very few galleries have created a complete photographic record of their paintings, let alone a comprehensive illustrated catalogue of their collections. In short, what is publicly owned is not publicly accessible.

The Public Catalogue Foundation, a registered charity, has three aims. First, it intends to create a complete record of the nation's collection of oil, tempera and acrylic paintings in public ownership. Second, it intends to make this accessible to the public through a series of affordable catalogues and, after a suitable delay, through a free Internet website. Finally, it aims to raise funds through the sale of catalogues in gallery shops for the conservation and restoration of oil paintings in these collections and for gallery education.

The initial focus of the project is on collections outside London. Highlighting the richness and diversity of collections outside the capital should bring major benefits to regional collections around the country. The benefits also include a revenue stream for conservation, restoration, gallery education and the digitisation of collections' paintings, thereby allowing them to put the images on the Internet if they so desire. These substantial benefits to galleries around the country come at no financial cost to the collections themselves.

The project should be of enormous benefit and inspiration to students of art and to members of the general public with an interest in art. It will also provide a major source of material for scholarly research into art history.

Financial Supporters

The Public Catalogue Foundation would like to express its profound appreciation to the following organisations and individuals who have made the publication of this catalogue possible.

Donations of £10,000 or more

Peter Harrison Foundation
The Linbury Trust

Donations of £5,000 or more

Marquess of Douro
National Gallery Trust
Oakmoor Trust
Philip Gwyn
Southampton City Council
Garfield Weston Foundation

Donations of £1,000 or more

Marcus & Kate Agius
Sir Christopher Bland
The Charlotte Bonham-Carter Charitable Trust
Bramdean Asset Management LLP
The Bulldog Trust
Graeme Cottam & Gloriana Marks de Chabris
De La Rue Charitable Trust
The Friends of Southampton's Museums, Archives and Galleries
Hobart Charitable Trust
The Isle of Wight Council
The J. and S. B. Charitable Trust
Lord Lea of Crondall, OBE
Rupert Nabarro
P. F. Charitable Trust
The Pilgrim Trust
Rathbone Investment Management Ltd
Sir Miles & Lady Rivett-Carnac
Smith & Williamson
Strutt and Parker
The Bernard Sunley Charitable Foundation
Thistle Trust
Michael J. Woodhall, FRICS

Other Donations

D. A. Bailey
The Roger Brooke Charitable Trust
Sir James Butler, CBE DL
Sir Jeremiah Colman Gift Trust
Anthony R. C. B. Cooke
Desmond Corcoran
Freddie Emery-Wallis
Mrs Mary Fagan, JP
Sybilla Jane Flower
The Golden Bottle Trust
Mrs Margaret Hayter
Rear Admiral R. O. Irwin, CB
John Isherwood, CMG
Rose & Gareth Lewis
The Lilian Trust
Mr & Mrs Charles Marriott
Mr & Mrs Nigel McNair Scott
Sir Edwin & Lady Nixon
David M. Norman
J. W. Robertson Charitable Trust
Simon Robertson
Leopold de Rothschild Charitable Trust
Alicia Salter
Dr John Sargent
Savills Ltd
Joanna Selbourne
Julian Sheffield
Mr & Mrs Ronald Taylor
Edward & Katherine Wake
Mr & Mrs Hady Wakefield

National Supporters

The Bulldog Trust
The John S. Cohen Foundation
Hiscox plc
National Gallery Trust
P. F. Charitable Trust
The Pilgrim Trust
The Bernard Sunley Charitable Foundation
Garfield Weston Foundation

National Sponsor

Christie's

Acknowledgements

The Public Catalogue Foundation would like to thank the individual artists and copyright holders for their permission to reproduce for free the paintings in this catalogue. Exhaustive efforts have been made to locate the copyright owners of all the images included within this catalogue and to meet their requirements. Copyright credit lines for copyright owners who have been traced are listed in the Further Information section.

The Public Catalogue Foundation would like to express its great appreciation to the following organisations for their great assistance in the preparation of this catalogue:

Bridgeman Art Library
Flowers East
Marlborough Fine Art
National Association of Decorative & Fine Arts Societies (NADFAS)
National Gallery, London
National Portrait Gallery, London
Royal Academy of Arts, London
Tate

The participating collections included in this catalogue would like to express their appreciation to the following individuals and organisations who have contributed so generously to the county's collections and who in many cases continue to do so:

Arnolfini Collection Trust
Arthur Tilden Jeffress
Arts Council of Great Britain
Barns-Graham Charitable Trust
Lady Bonham Carter
Dr David & Liza Brown
Chipperfield Bequest Fund
Robert Chipperfield
Contemporary Art Society
Elephant Trust
Mr & Mrs W. J. Fernie
The Friends of Southampton's Museums, Archives and Galleries
Gulbenkian Foundation
Miss Annie Hicks
John Lewis Partnership
Libraries Department
National Art Collections Fund (The Art Fund)
Frederick William Smith Bequest Fund
Southampton Art Committee
Victoria & Albert Museum Purchase Grant Fund
War Artists Advisory Committee
Wessex Cancer Trust

Catalogue Scope and Organisation

Medium and Support
The principal focus of this series is oil paintings. However, tempera and acrylic are also included as well as mixed media, where oil is the predominant constituent. Paintings on all forms of support (e.g. canvas, panel, etc.) are included as long as the support is portable. The principal exclusions are miniatures, hatchments or other purely heraldic paintings and wall paintings *in situ*.

Public Ownership
Public ownership has been taken to mean any paintings that are directly owned by the public purse, made accessible to the public by means of public subsidy or generally perceived to be in public ownership. The term 'public' refers to both central government and local government. Paintings held by national museums, local authority museums, English Heritage and independent museums, where there is at least some form of public subsidy, are included. Paintings held in civic buildings such as local government offices, town halls, guildhalls, public libraries, universities, hospitals, crematoria, fire stations and police stations are also included. Paintings held in central government buildings as part of the Government Art Collection and MoD collections are not included in the county-by-county series but should be included later in the series on a national basis.

Geographical Boundaries of Catalogues
The geographical boundary of each county is the 'ceremonial county' boundary. This county definition includes all unitary authorities. Counties that have a particularly large number of paintings are divided between two or more catalogues on a geographical basis.

Criteria for Inclusion
As long as paintings meet the requirements above, all paintings are included irrespective of their condition and perceived quality. However, painting reproductions can only be included with the agreement of the participating collections and, where appropriate, the relevant copyright owner. It is rare that a collection forbids the inclusion of its paintings. Where this is the case and it is possible to obtain a list of paintings, this list is given in the Paintings Without Reproductions section. Where copyright consent is refused, the paintings are also listed in the Paintings Without Reproductions section. All paintings in collections' stacks and stores are included, as well as those on display. Paintings which have been lent to other institutions, whether for short-term exhibition or long-term loan, are listed under the owner collection. In addition, paintings on long-term loan are also included under the borrowing institution when they are likely to remain there for at least another five years from the date of publication of this catalogue. Information relating to owners and borrowers is listed in the Further Information section.

Layout
Collections are grouped together under their home town. These locations are listed in alphabetical order. In some cases collections that are spread over a number of locations are included under a single owner collection. A number of collections, principally the larger ones, are preceded by curatorial forewords. Within each collection paintings are listed in order of artist surname. Where there is more than one painting by the same artist, the paintings are listed chronologically, according to their execution date.

The few paintings that are not accompanied by photographs are listed in the Paintings Without Reproductions section.

There is additional reference material in the Further Information section at the back of the catalogue. This gives the full names of artists, titles and media if it has not been possible to include these in full in the main section. It also provides acquisition credit lines and information about loans in and out, as well as copyright and photographic credits for each painting. Finally, there is an index of artists' surnames.

Key to Painting Information

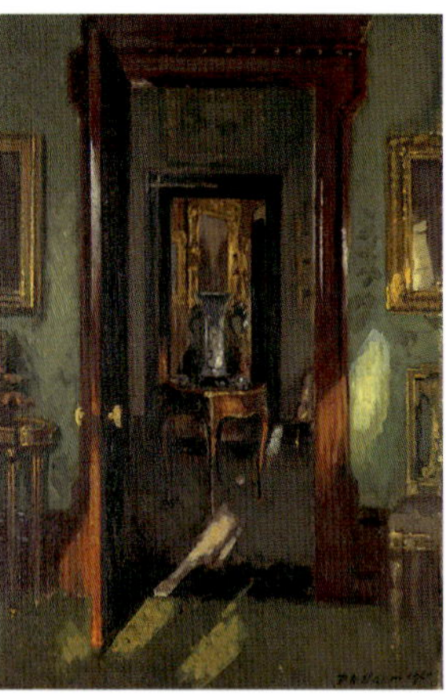

Almost all paintings are reproduced in the catalogue. Where this is not the case they are listed in the Paintings Without Reproductions section. Where paintings are missing or have been stolen, the best possible photograph on record has been reproduced. In some cases this may be black and white. Paintings that have been stolen are highlighted with a red border. Some paintings are shown with conservation tissue attached to parts of the painting surface.

Adam, Patrick William 1854–1929
Interior, Rutland Lodge: Vista through Open Doors 1920
oil on canvas 67.3 × 45.7
LEEAG.PA.1925.0671.LACF ❁

Artist name This is shown as surname first. Where the artist is listed on the Getty Union List of Artist Names (ULAN), ULAN's preferred presentation of the name is always given. In a number of cases the name may not be a firm attribution and this is made clear. Where the artist name is not known, a school may be given instead. Where the school is not known, the painter name is listed as *unknown artist*. If the artist name is too long for the space, as much of the name is given as possible followed by (…). This indicates the full name is given at the rear of the catalogue in the Further Information section.

Painting title A painting followed by *(?)* indicates that the title is in doubt. Where the alternative title to the painting is considered to be better known than the original, the alternative title is given in parentheses. Where the collection has not given a painting a title, the publisher does so instead and marks this with an asterisk. If the title is too long for the space, as much of the title is given as possible followed by *(…)* and the full title is given in the Further Information section.

Medium and support Where the precise material used in the support is known, this is given.

Artist dates Where known, the years of birth and death of the artist are given. In some cases one or both dates may not be known with certainty, and this is marked. No date indicates that even an approximate date is not known. Where only the period in which the artist was active is known, these dates are given and preceded with the word *active*.

Execution date In some cases the precise year of execution may not be known for certain. Instead an approximate date will be given or no date at all.

Dimensions All measurements refer to the unframed painting and are given in cm with up to one decimal point. In all cases the height is shown before the width. An (E) is indicated where a painting has not been measured and its size has been calculated by sight only. If the painting is circular, the single dimension is the diameter. If the painting is oval, the dimensions are height and width.

Collection inventory number In the case of paintings owned by museums, this number will always be the accession number. In all other cases it will be a unique inventory number of the owner institution. (P) indicates that a painting is a private loan. Details can be found in the Further Information section. The ❁ symbol indicates that the reproduction is based on a Bridgeman Art Library transparency (go to www.bridgeman.co.uk) or that the Bridgeman administers the copyright for that artist.

Facing page: Cooper, Eileen, b.1953, *To Steal a Wedding Ring* (detail), Southampton University Hospitals NHS Trust, (p. 191)

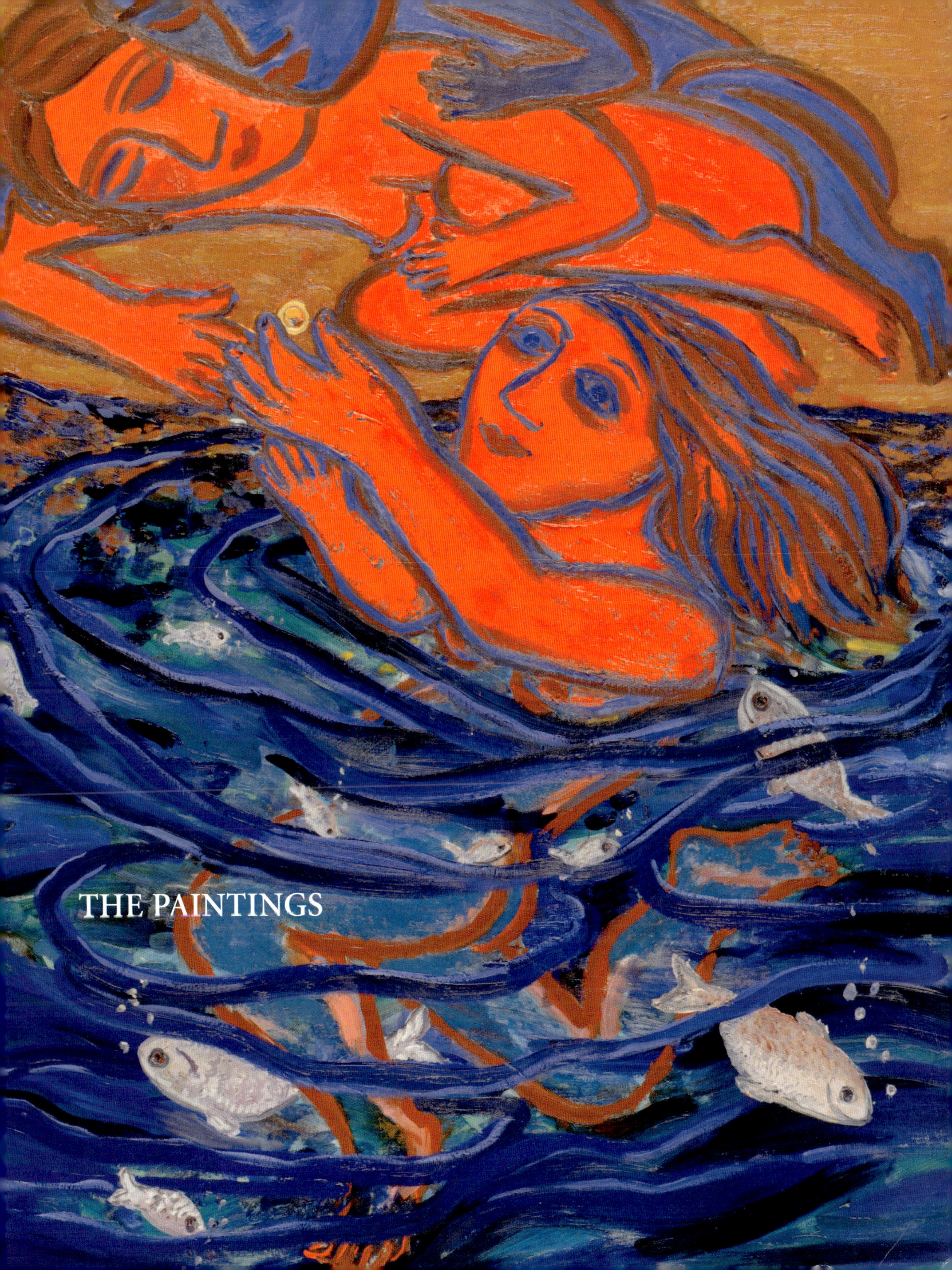

THE PAINTINGS

Solent Sky Aviation Museum

The Solent Sky Aviation Museum, formerly known as The Southampton Hall of Aviation, was first established over 30 years ago, originally to tell the story of R. J. Mitchell, the designer of the legendary aircraft the Vickers-Supermarine Spitfire.

The Solent, a relatively small geographical area, was the most important centre in the world for aircraft experimental and development work between 1908 and the late 1960s. The world-renowned Spitfire is perhaps the best known of these aircraft and is synonymous with Southampton. By the end of the Second World War, of the 22,000 spitfires manufactured, 8,000 had been built in the city.

Located in Albert Road South in Southampton, the Museum has one of the most important aircraft collections in the UK. Of the 15 aircraft on display, some are the only examples still surviving and all are relevant to this fascinating story of British aviation achievement. The Museum encompasses the history of 26 aircraft companies, as well as being the home of the largest flying boat operation in the world.

As well as the aircraft themselves, the Museum has a collection of paintings, prints and photographs and an extensive archive.

Alan Jones, Executive Director and Curator

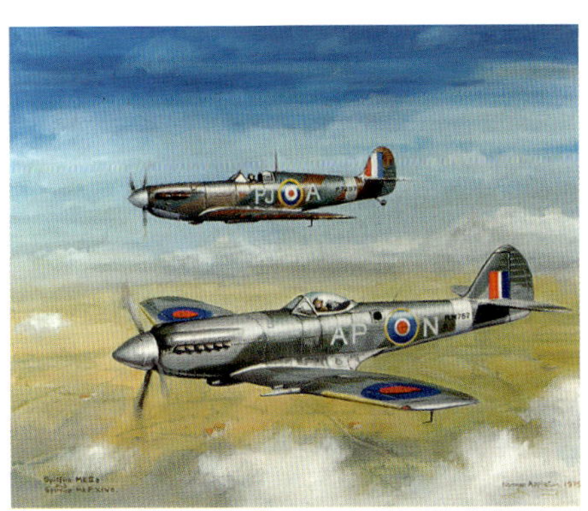

Appleton, Norman b.1926
Spitfire MkIIa and Spitfire MkFXIVe 1975
oil on canvas 44 x 54
A83.57

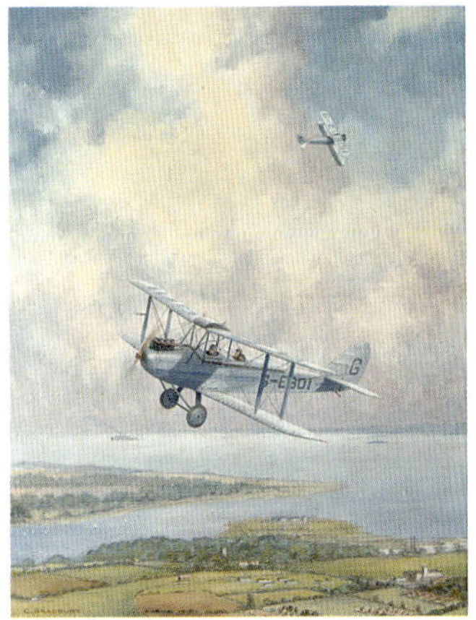

Bradbury, C.
DH Moth
oil on canvas 48.5 x 37.4
c93/004

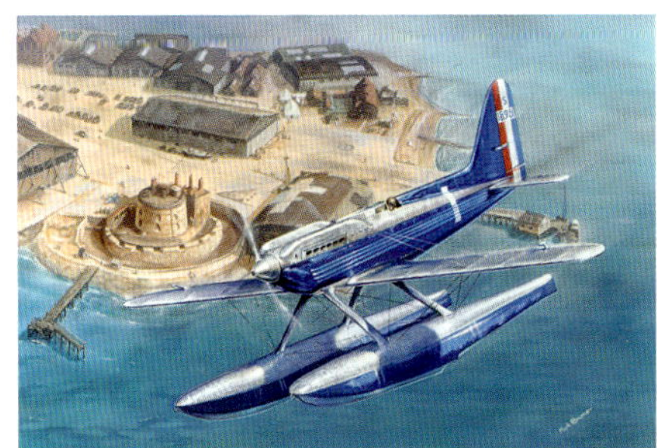

Bromley, Mark
Spirit of the Solent
oil on board 48 x 72.5
e06/15

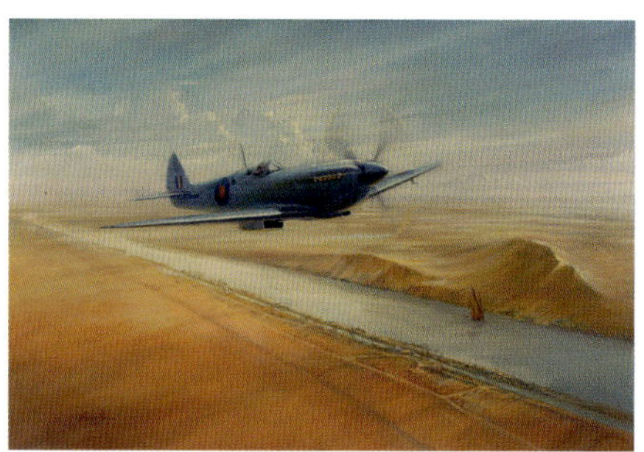

Brown, Stuart b.1966
Spitfire over Suez 1995
oil on board 49.5 x 75
c03/348/01

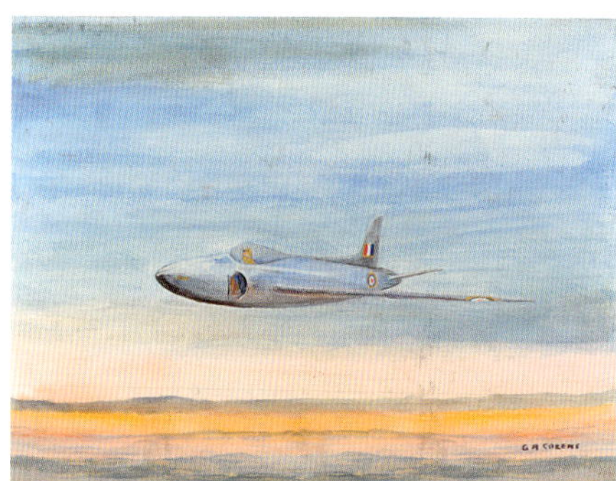

Cozens, G. A.
Supermarine Swift 1952
oil on board 30.5 x 39.7
c03/024/06

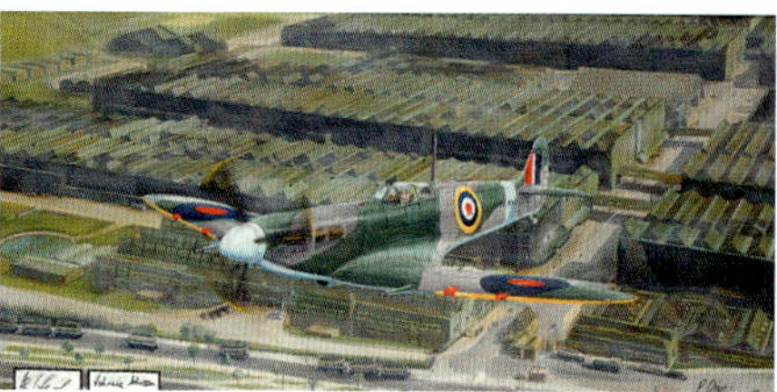

Davis, P.
Spitfire over Castle Bromwich, Birmingham
oil on canvas 44 x 91
B2294

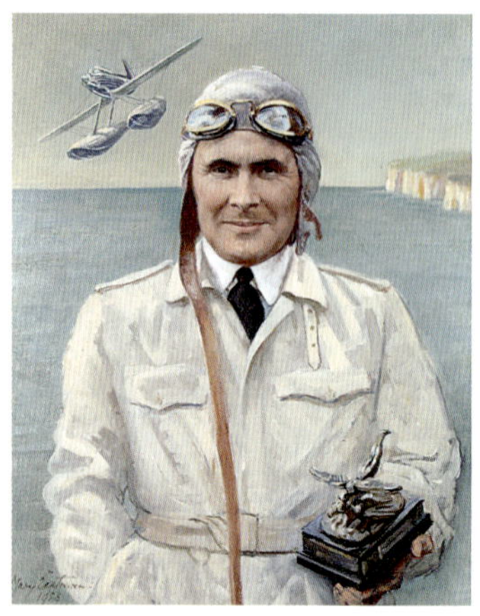

Eastman, Mary active c.1932–1979
Air Chief Marshall Sir John Boothman (1901–1957), KCB, KBE, DFC, ATC 1958
oil on canvas 74 x 62
e06/20

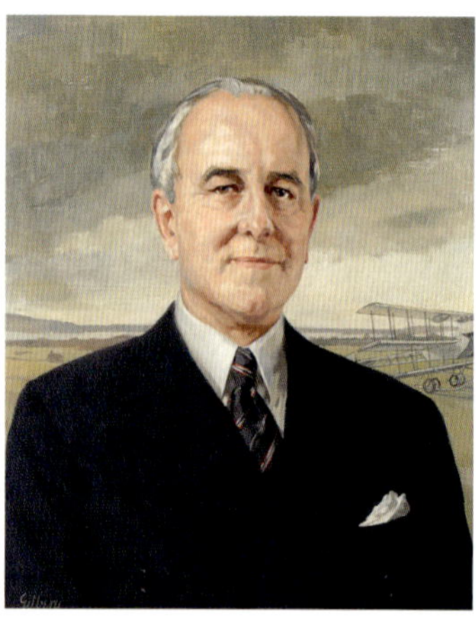

Gilbery, Michael 1913–2000
Sir Alliott Verdon-Roe OBE (1877–1958)
oil on canvas 59 x 49
c00/396

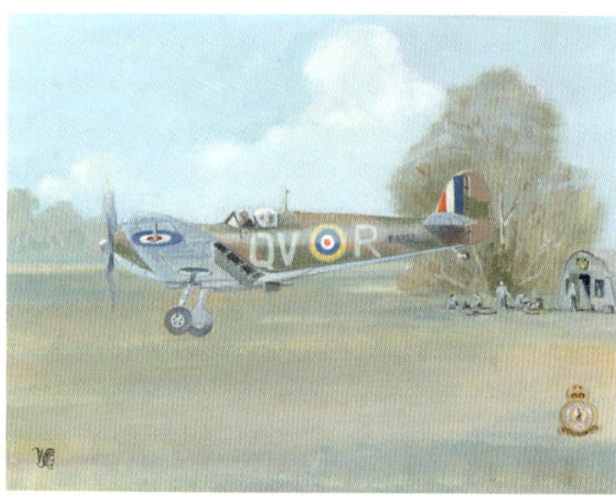

Green, W. A.
Spitfire 2 of 19 Squadron 1940
oil on canvas 29 x 39.5
c04/041/16

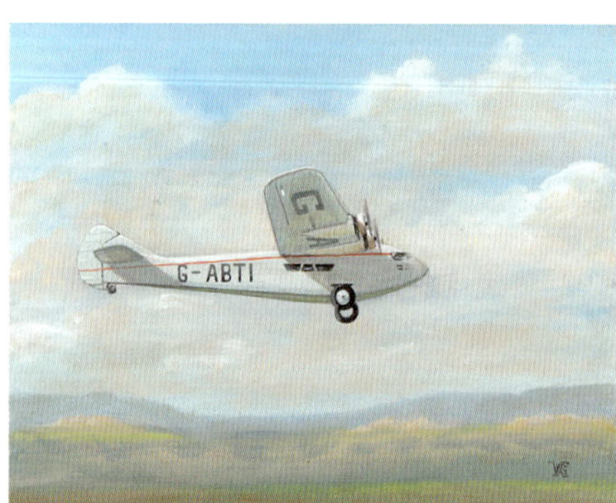

Green, W. A.
Imperial Airways Atalanta
oil on board 30.5 x 40 (E)
c04/186/29

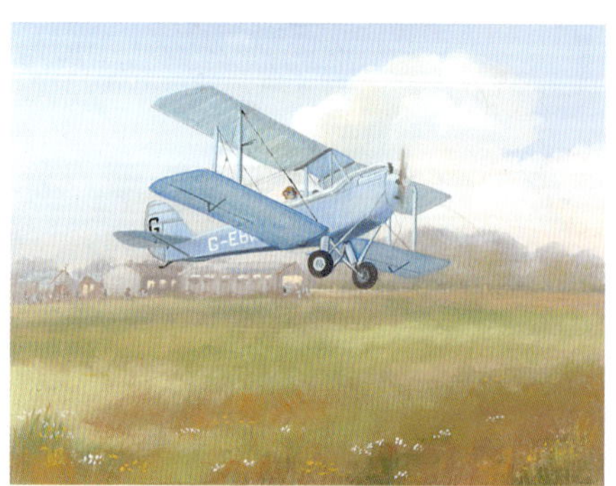

Green, W. A.
Moth
oil on board 30.5 x 40 (E)
c04/186/32

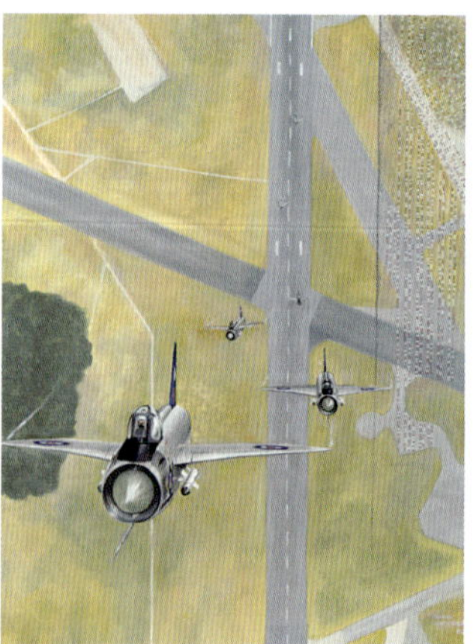

Hatchard, David b.1945
Vertical Take-off 2002
oil on board 45 x 34.5
e06/19

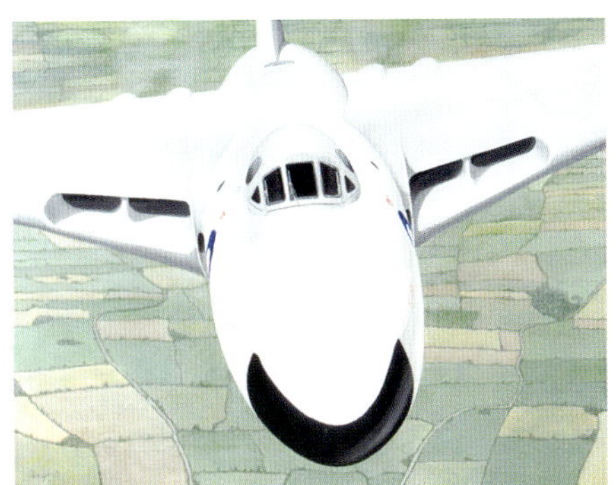

Hatchard, David b.1945
Up Close and Personal 2003
oil on board 36 x 45.5
e06/17

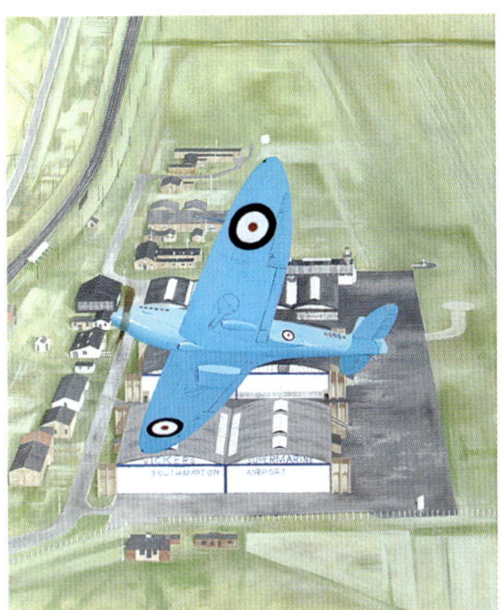

Hatchard, David b.1945
Spitfire Prototype over Southampton Airport 2005
acrylic on board 60 x 50.5
e06.18

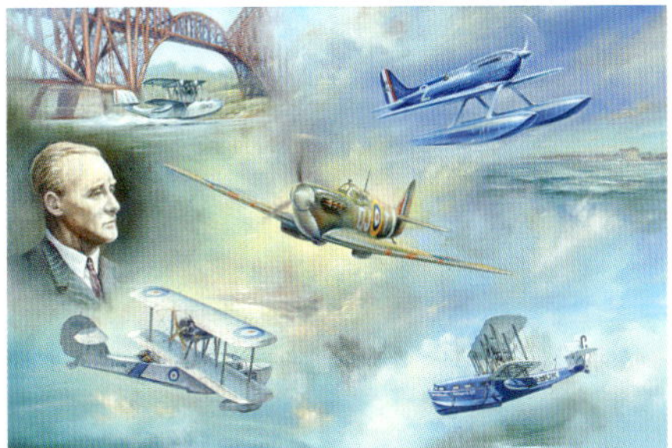

Mitchell, Jim
Aircraft Montage
oil on board 48.5 x 74
c04/074/02

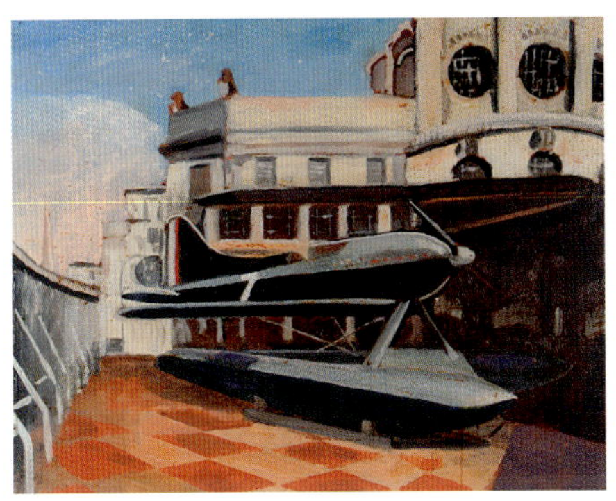

Pannell, J. P. M
Seaplane at the Pier
oil on canvas 44 x 56.5
A83.79

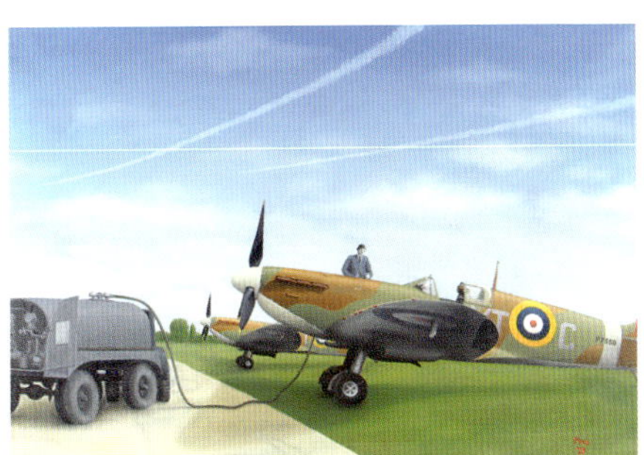

Prub
Preparing for Action 1973
oil on canvas 50 x 75
A83.66

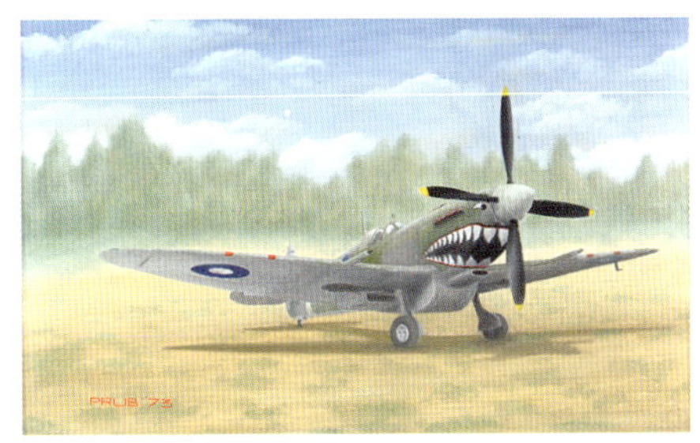

Prub
Spitfire VIII 1973
oil on board 42 x 70
A83.65

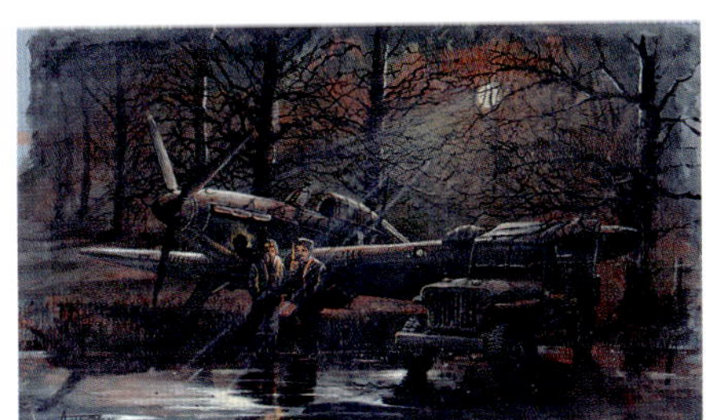

Toomer, A. J.
Spitfire 1990
oil on board 57.5 x 96
e06.14

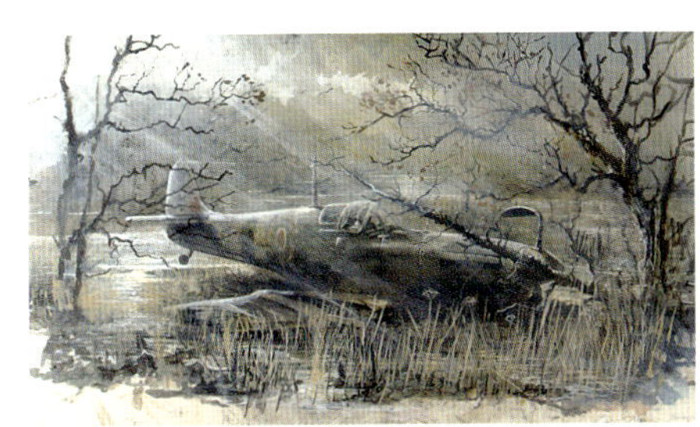

Toomer, A. J.
Plane Crash
oil on board 52.5 x 91
e06.13

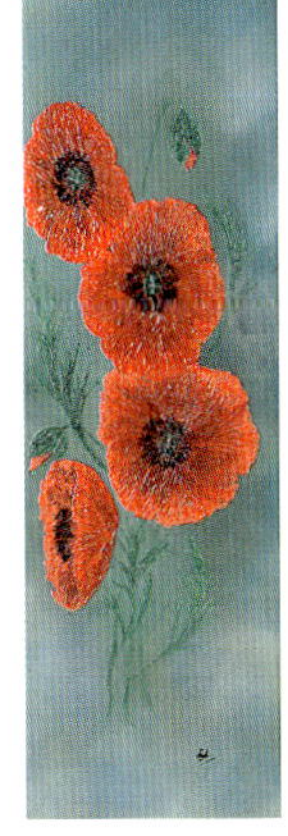

unknown artist mid-20th C
In Remembrance of 1940
acrylic on board 90.7 x 29.4
c94/205

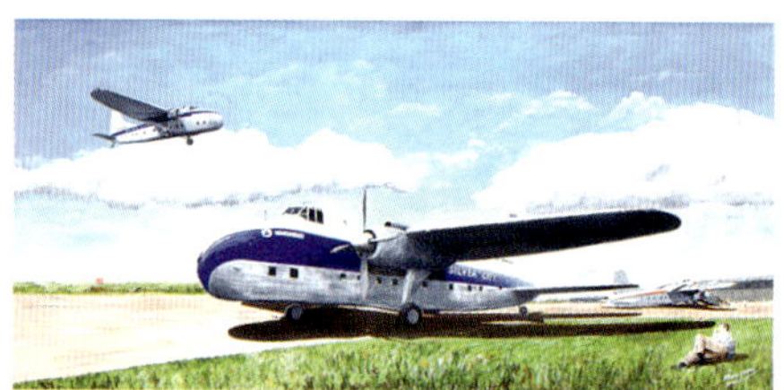

unknown artist
Bristol Freighter at Lydd Airfield
acrylic on board 61.5 x 123
e06/16

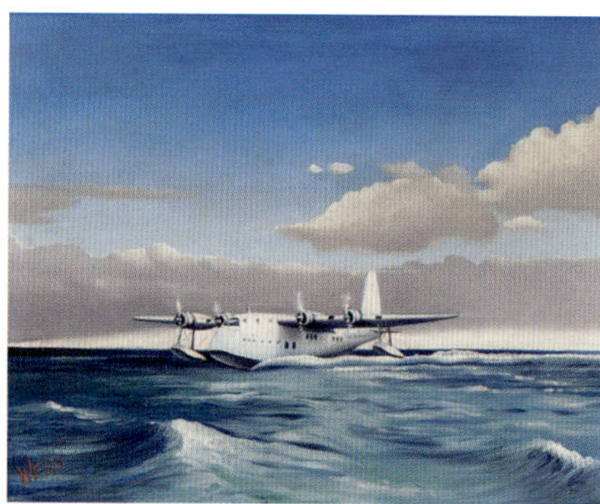

Webb
Seaplane
oil on board 34.5 x 45
co4/086/03

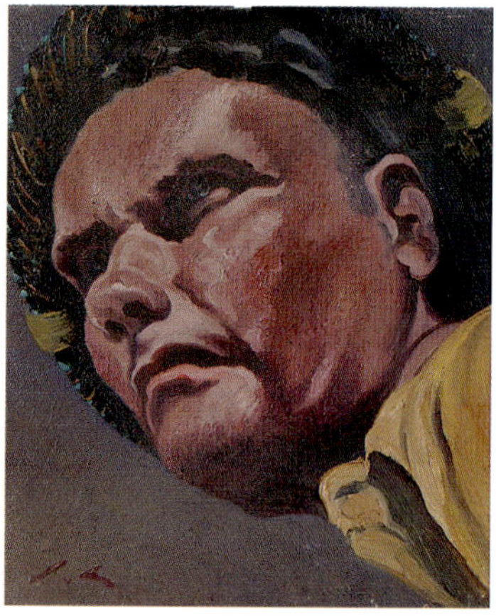

Wilson, Stanley active 1943–1944
Australian Infantryman, Halifax 1943
oil on canvas 32.5 x 27.5
c04/028/03

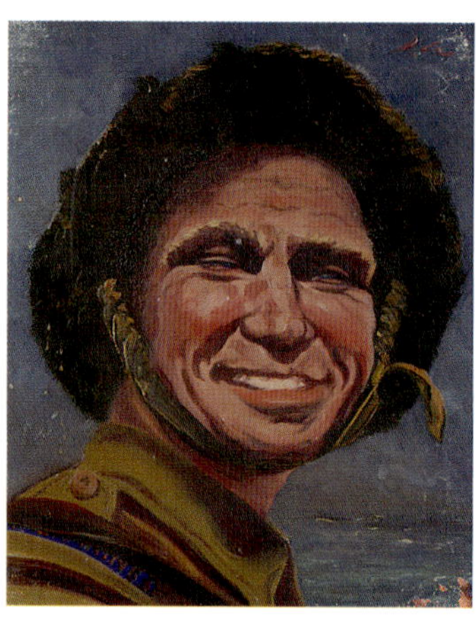

Wilson, Stanley active 1943–1944
A Devonshire Golly 1944
oil on canvas 38 x 31
c04/028/01

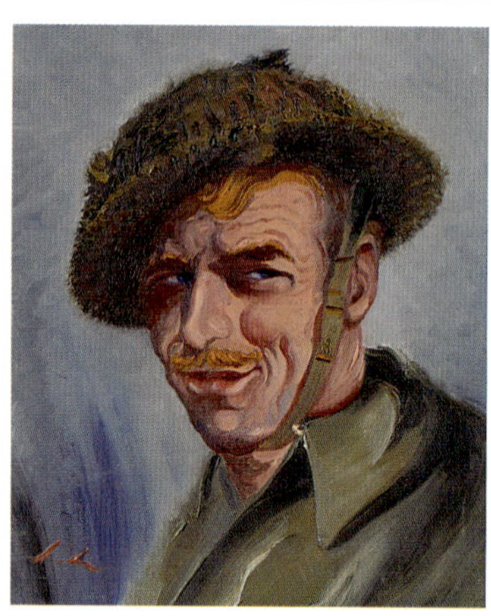

Wilson, Stanley active 1943–1944
8th Army Gunner
oil on canvas 36.5 x 31
c04/028/02

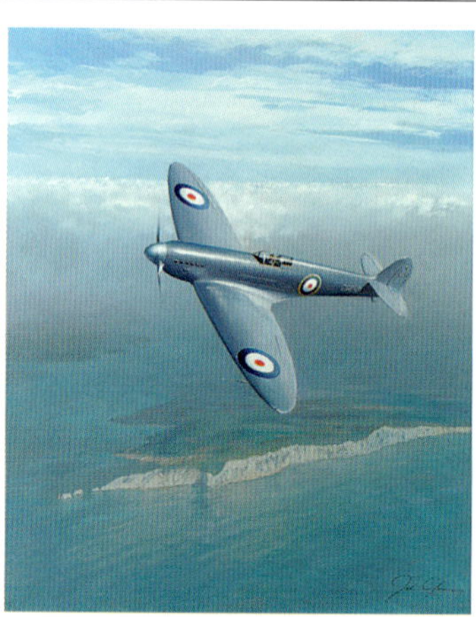

Young, John b.1930
Spitfire Prototype Over the Needles
oil on canvas 59.3 x 49
c04/074/01

Southampton City Art Gallery

Southampton is most fortunate in possessing a magnificent city art gallery which arguably houses the finest public collection of fine art south of London. Southampton's holdings of modern British art are nationally outstanding. In 1998 the Government 'designated' the Permanent Collection as having pre-eminent national significance. Most city museums and galleries are Victorian in origin but Southampton's City Art Gallery first opened its doors as late as 1939. That the Gallery's curators and advisers were able to establish a high quality collection, now of international reputation, within a few decades is remarkable and the Gallery's story is both unique and fascinating.

In 1911, Robert Chipperfield, a local pharmacist, Southampton councillor and justice of the peace, laid the foundations for an art gallery in Southampton. In his will, he clearly stated his ideas concerning the provision for visual arts in Southampton:

'My fervent desire is, and my executors aim shall be, the furtherance and encouragement of Art, in the town of my adoption – Southampton. I therefore bequeath the whole of my collection of oil paintings, watercolour drawings and engravings to my Executors for the public exhibition in Southampton … I authorise my Executors to build an Art Gallery which shall be free to the Public, as soon as funds will permit, and also establish a Southampton School of Art, which shall be worthy of the name.'

Without Chipperfield's trust fund and his sensible stipulation that money could only be spent after consultation with the director of the National Gallery, the collection would not be what it is today. At first, the Gallery was without a curator or a building and it was Lord Clark, in 1936, who advised on future policy for the Gallery and took an active role in purchasing pictures and building up a permanent collection. Another Southampton councillor, Frederick William Smith, also bequeathed a separate trust fund to the city exclusively for the purchase of paintings to be administered by a Purchasing Committee composed of representatives from the Tate Gallery and Royal Academy as well as important local organisations such as the University and Chamber of Commerce. Since Robert Chipperfield and Frederick William Smith laid the foundations for visual arts provision in Southampton, the permanent collection has grown to over 3,500 works of art and the Gallery is visited today by some 60,000 visitors per year.

The income from the two bequest funds, when combined with financial support from organisations such as the National Art Collections Fund and the Museums, Libraries and Archives Council Purchase Grant Fund, enabled the Gallery to make many important large scale acquisitions critical to the development of the collection, particularly during the 1960s and 1970s. It was during this time, for example, that the National Art Collections Fund and the MLA Purchase Grant Fund assisted the Gallery with the purchases of *Wilhem Muhlfeld* by Pierre-Auguste Renoir and *The Dunes near Haarlem* by Jacob van Ruisdael. In more recent times, the Art Fund and MLA have assisted with the purchase of works by leading British artist such as Rachel Whiteread, Michael Craig-Martin, Antony Gormley, Barry Flanagan, David Nash, and Lisa Milroy (not all of these paintings are necessarily in oils, acrylic or tempera and therefore are not included in the present volume). The Art Fund and MLA have also enabled the collection to develop by facilitating numerous donations of key works. In 1980, the Gallery accepted the work *Madonna and Child* by Giovanni Bellini from HM Government in lieu of tax through the MLA, then known as the Museums and Galleries Commission.

An important bequest of paintings was made to the Gallery in 1961 by Arthur Tilden Jeffress (1905–1961) a London gallery owner and art collector. The curator at the time, Maurice Palmer, together with the director of the Tate Gallery selected 99 paintings from the estate including eight paintings by Graham Sutherland, four works by John Piper and the Gallery's highly regarded early Lucian Freud, *Bananas.* Southampton is also uniquely privileged to own four works by the Belgian Surrealist artist Paul Delvaux through the Jeffress bequest.

In 2002 the Gallery received a magnificent bequest of 220 works of British Modern art from Dr David and Liza Brown. Dr Brown, as a Tate curator, was the Gallery's acquisition's advisor (appointed for his knowledge of contemporary art) from 1976 until his retirement in 1985. Through Dr Brown's advice the Gallery soon established a new contemporary art collection of international reputation, not usually synonymous with a local authority governed art museum. Dr Brown's legacy for the Gallery is immense and was further enhanced by his generous new bequest fund for the purchase of works of art made post 1900 for the permanent collection.

Since 1975, the Gallery has concentrated on developing its collection of contemporary art since the 1970s and today has one of the most outstanding collections of contemporary British art outside London. The policy of collecting art within two years of its making means that the Gallery has a fine group of early works by key British artists who went on to win, or were shortlisted for, the annual Turner Prize. Of the British artists awarded the prize since its inauguration in 1984, the Gallery has fine examples of work by 12 out of 21 prize winners to date. The collection holds impressive works from the post-war era including Sutherland, Ayrton, Piper and Minton as well as a group of works by St Ives based abstract artists such as Terry Frost, Peter Lanyon and Roger Hilton. A key acquisition of this period is *Miss Lynn* a prize winning work from the Festival of Britain competition and a late masterpiece by Claude Rogers. However, a major gap in the collection is the absence of work by Francis Bacon.

The multitude of schools and art philosophies which blossomed during the period between the two World Wars, such as the social realism of the Euston Road School, Surrealism, the Seven and Five Society and Unit One are well represented through paintings and drawings by some of the major artists of the era. These include William Coldstream, Eileen Agar, Sir Roland Penrose, Ben Nicholson, Christopher Wood, Frances Hodgkins and the outstanding painting *The Archer* by Paul Nash. Although the collection contains only a small number of First World War works *Loading Timber at Southampton Docks* by Christopher Nevinson and Percy Wyndam Lewis's great war drawings are superb examples of the art of the period. Another great strength in this area are the four works by Stanley Spencer.

Of equivalent stature to the contemporary collection are the Gallery's early twentieth century holdings. The Camden Town Group and associated artists form one of the richest and most representative collections of its type in the world. Of particular significance are Sickert's self portrait *The Juvenile Lead* and Drummond's Seurat-inspired *In the Park (St James' Park)*. These works are supported by outstanding paintings by artists such as Henri Gaudier-Brzeska, Mark Gertler, William Roberts, Matthew Smith, Philip Wilson Steer and the Scottish Colourist John Duncan Fergusson. The Gallery is also well known for its fine range of paintings by Duncan Grant and Vanessa Bell.

A second aspect of the original collecting policy was to build up a representative collection of nineteenth century paintings. The jewel in this crown are undoubtedly the ten works in gouache of the *Perseus Series* by Burne-Jones. Other Pre-Raphaelite works of note are *The Afterglow in Egypt* by William Holman Hunt and *Cordelia's Portion* by Ford Maddox Brown. The collection also holds significant works by William Blake, John Martin, J. M. W Turner and a small drawing by John Constable from the earlier nineteenth century.

To complement the great strength of the British collection the Gallery is fortunate enough to have acquired a small but impressive group of French Impressionist paintings. These important works contextualise the British paintings of the same era and anticipate the later British Post-Impressionist movement. The Gallery owns at least one painting by each of the most widely recognised French Impressionist painters: Claude Monet, Alfred Sisley, Eugène Boudin, Pierre-Auguste Renoir, Camille Pissaro and also a superb bronze by Edgar Degas entitled *Woman Putting on a Stocking*.

The small collection of Old Master paintings acquired by Southampton through the early collecting policy are of remarkable quality. The developments of British eighteenth century painting are exemplified by such paintings as Joseph Wright of Derby's outstanding *Landscape*, Gainsborough's *George Venables Vernon*, Reynolds' portrait of Cornet Nehemiah Winter and *The Shipwreck* by Philip de Loutherbourg. The greatest strength of the seventeenth century collection is the Dutch School. Works by Jan Davidsz. de Heem, Isack van Ostaade, Jan Hackaert, Philips de Koninck, Jacob van Ruisdael and Cesar Boetius van Everdingen are all superb examples and are complemented by contemporaneous French and Italian masterpieces such as works by de Mura, Trevisani and Ricci.

Only a few works from the Renaissance period are held by the Gallery but works by Cesare de Sesto, Bellini and Bril all serve to illustrate some of the major developments of this era. Sofonisba Anguissola's portrait of her sister is the earliest known work by this artist and Goswijn van der Weyden's impressive Flemish triptych is representative of the northern European school. The earliest work in the collection is Allegretto di Nuzio's triptych *The Coronation of the Virgin*, which dates from the 1360s. This extremely well preserved altarpiece provides a remarkable and unique introduction to the history of European art which can be effectively traced to present day in Britain through the collection as a whole.

Tim Craven, Curator

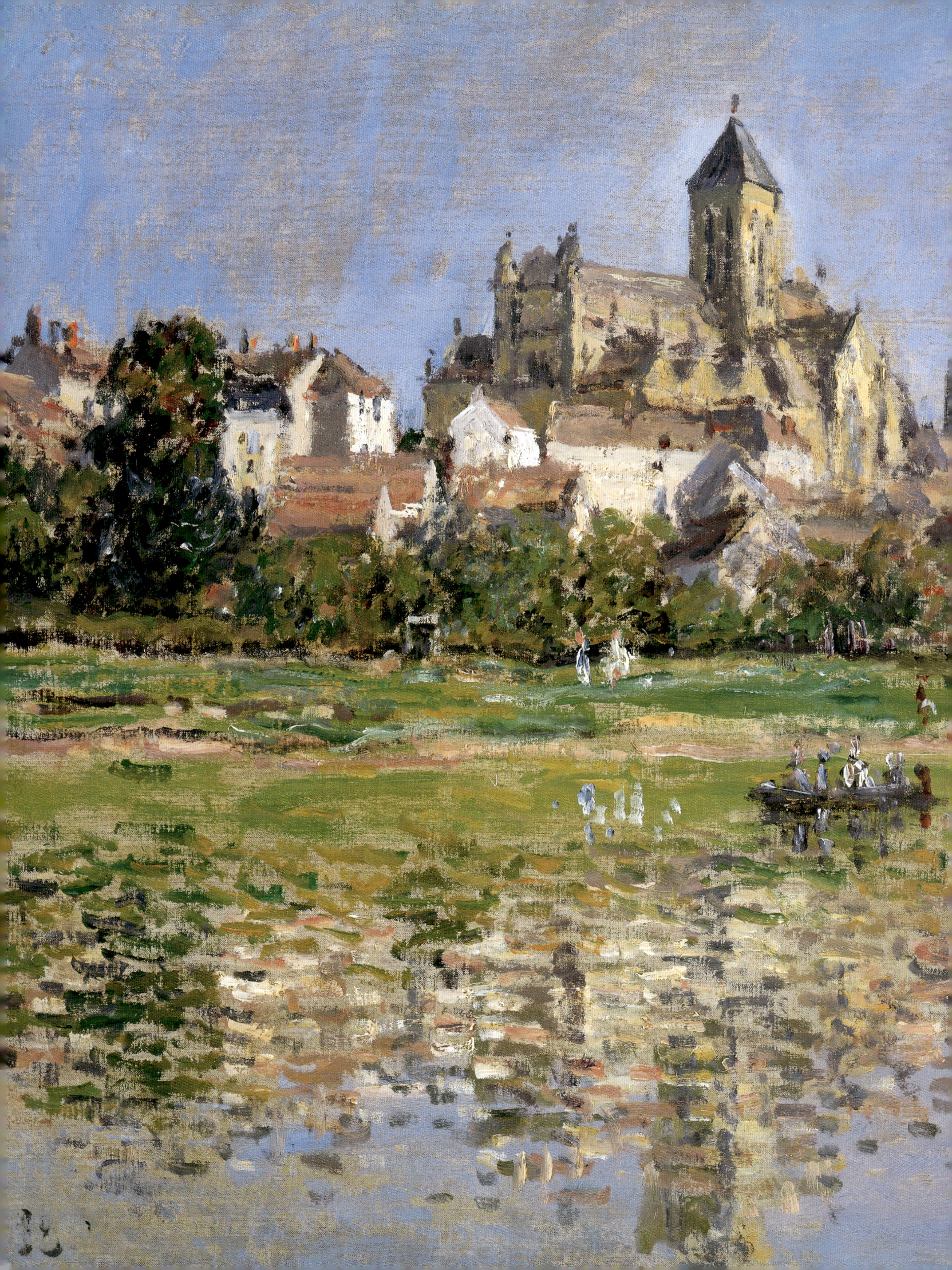

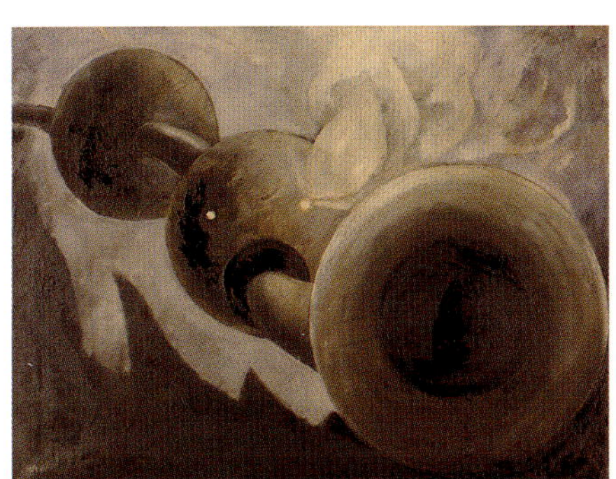

Adams, Norman 1927–2005
The Trumpet 1961
oil on canvas 76.5 x 102
3/1991

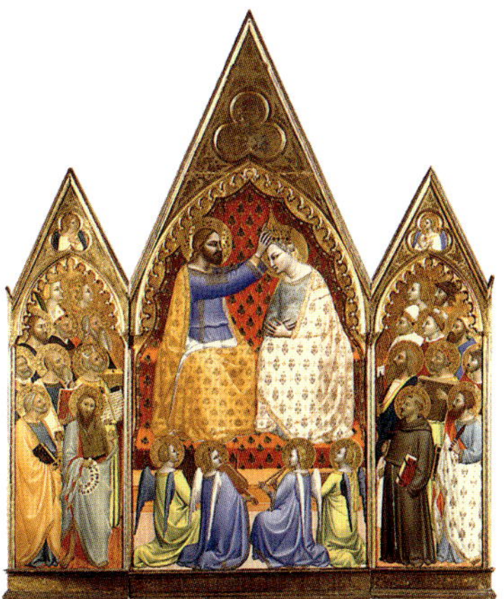

Allegretto di Nuzio c.1315–1373
The Coronation of the Virgin 1360s
tempera on board 245.7 x 102.5
1403

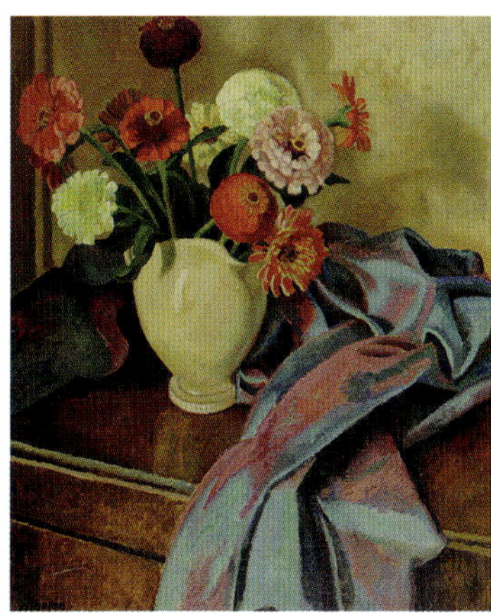

Allinson, Adrian Paul 1890–1959
Zinnias
oil on wood 68.2 x 55.5
2/1976

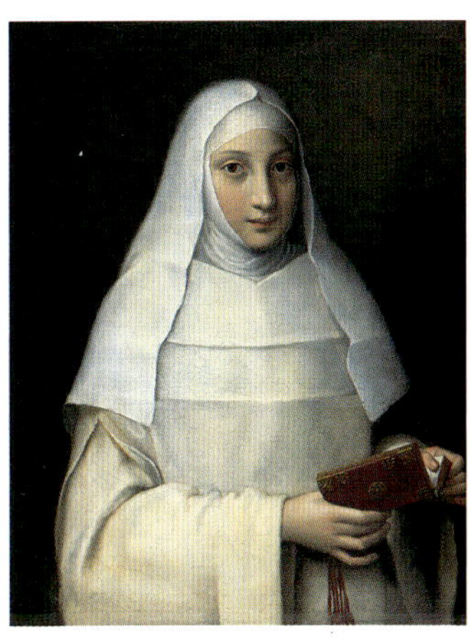

Anguissola, Sofonisba c.1532–1625
The Artist's Sister in the Garb of a Nun 1551
oil on canvas 68.5 x 53.3
3

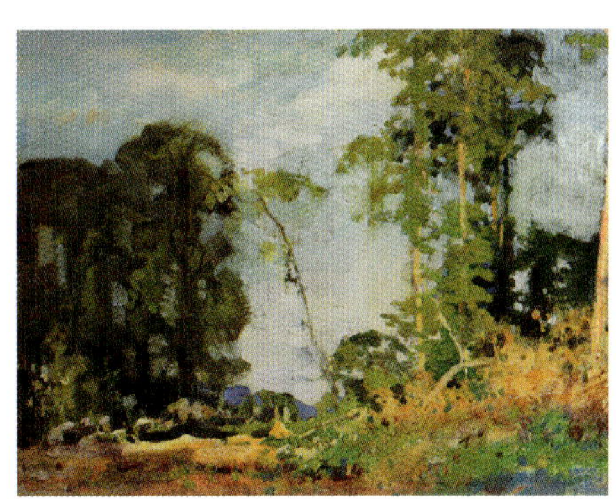

Appleyard, Frederick 1874–1963
Landscape
oil on board 29.2 x 37.9
23/1978

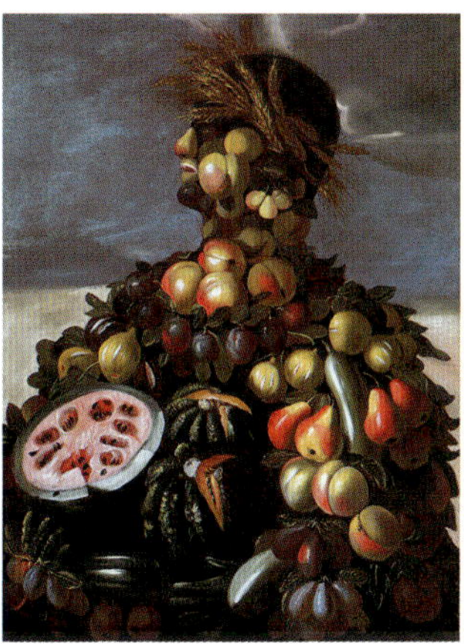

Arcimboldo, Giuseppe c.1527–1593
Summer
oil on canvas 97.7 x 73
18/1963

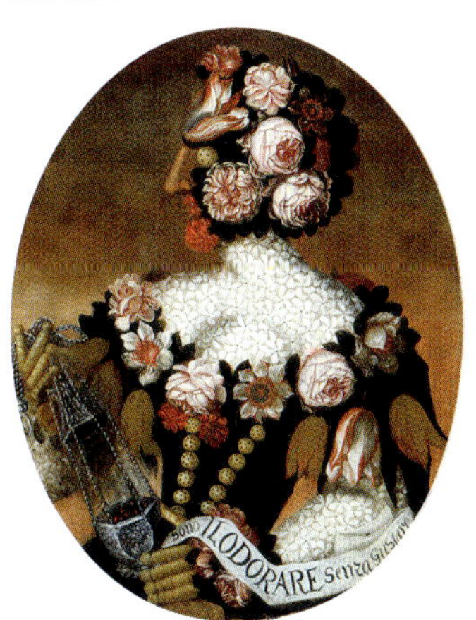

Arcimboldo, Giuseppe (follower of)
c.1527–1593
The Sense of Smell
oil on canvas 91.5 x 71.7
17/1963

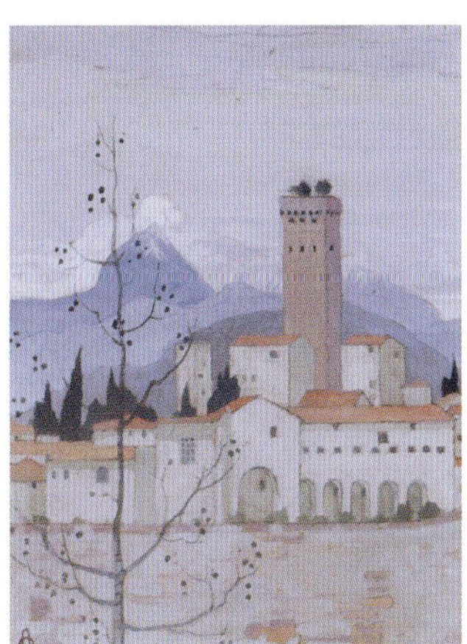

Armfield, Maxwell Ashby 1882–1972
The Tower (Trees, Lucca) 1905
tempera on panel 48.9 x 39.3
49/2002

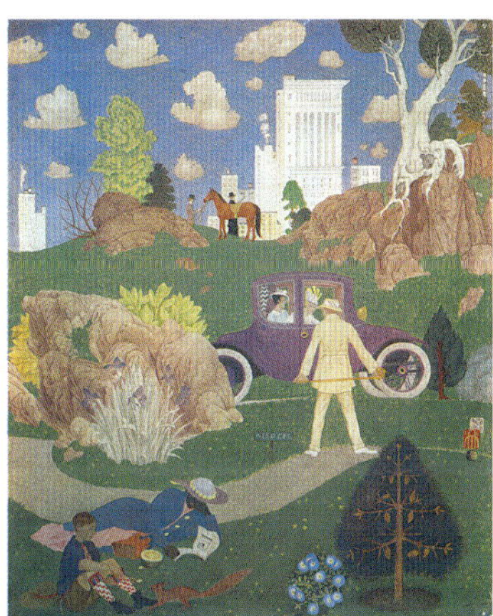

Armfield, Maxwell Ashby 1882–1972
Central Park, New York 1916
tempera on canvas 64.2 x 39
42/1976

Facing page: Monet, Claude, 1840–1926, *The Church at Vétheuil* (detail), 1880, Southampton City Art Gallery, (p. 97)

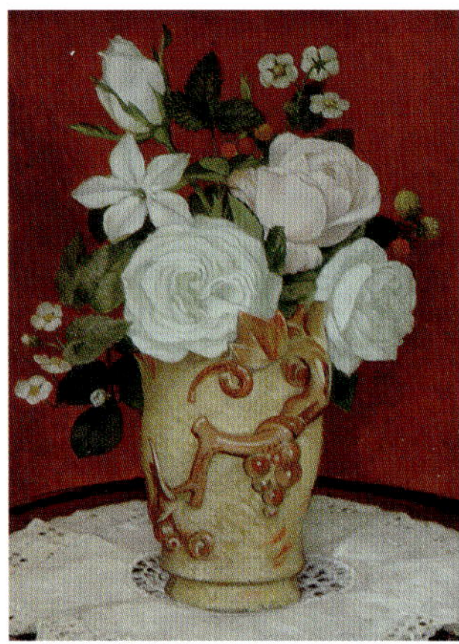

Armfield, Maxwell Ashby 1882–1972
Bunch of White 1933
oil on panel 48.9 x 39.3
101/2002

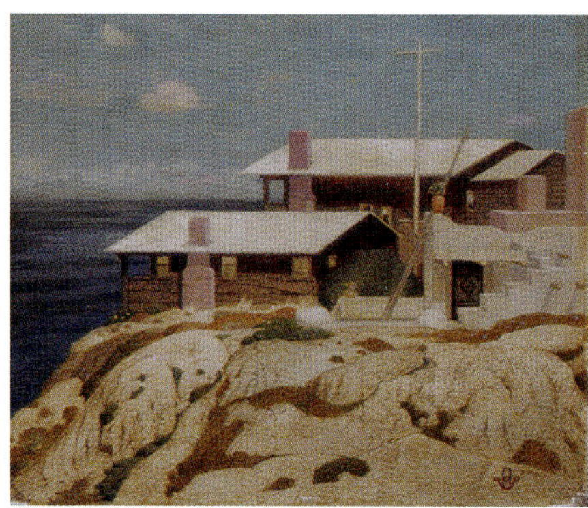

Armfield, Maxwell Ashby 1882–1972
'Pacific Patterns', the Artist's House at Berkeley, California 1940
tempera on board 34.2 x 39.2
48/2002

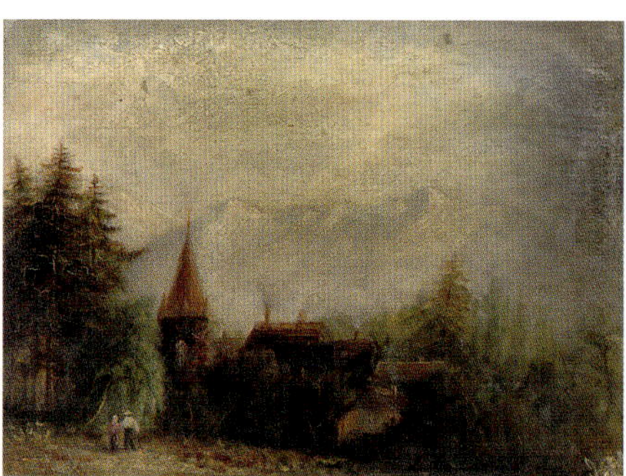

Arthur, J. D. active 1909
A Bit of Thun, Switzerland
oil on canvas 28 x 38
9

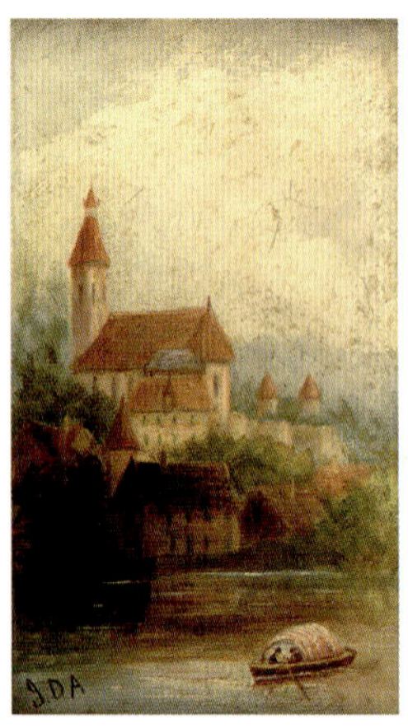

Arthur, J. D. active 1909
A Bit of Thun, Switzerland
oil on canvas 38 x 27.5 (E)
10

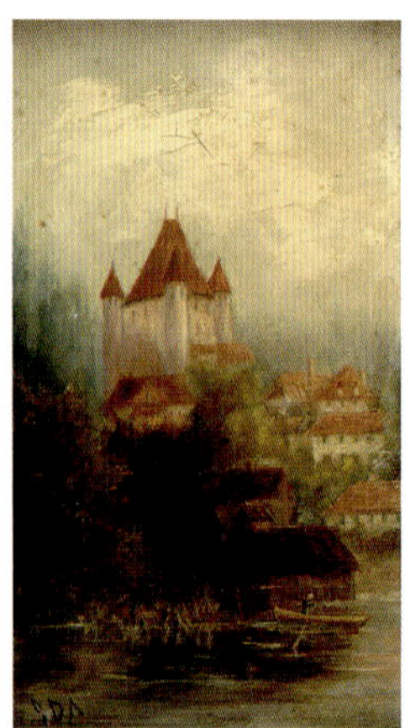

Arthur, J. D. active 1909
A River, Switzerland
oil on canvas 25.3 x 15.3
8

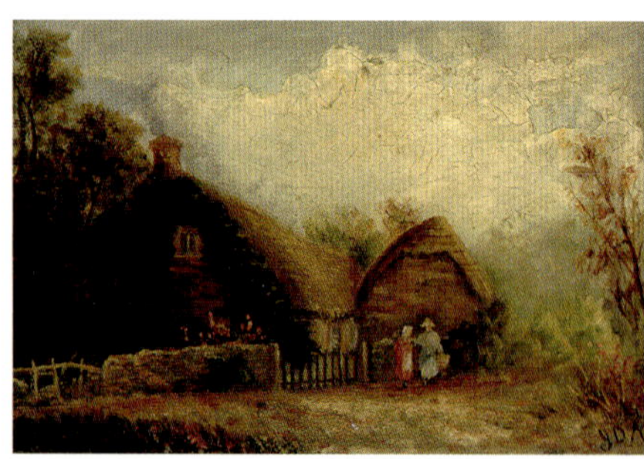

Arthur, J. D. active 1909
Cottage at Studland
oil on canvas 20.9 x 30.5
5

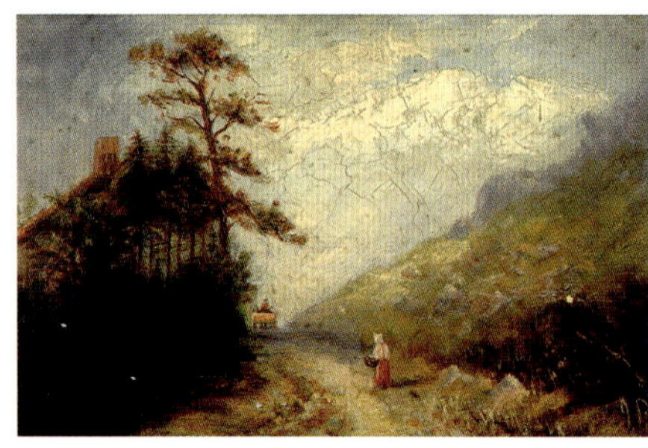

Arthur, J. D. active 1909
Landscape
oil on canvas 20.7 x 32
6

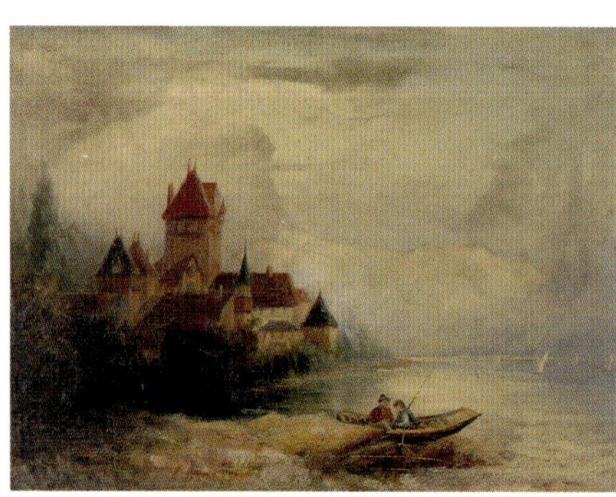

Arthur, J. D. active 1909
Old Bay
oil on canvas 30.5 x 41
7

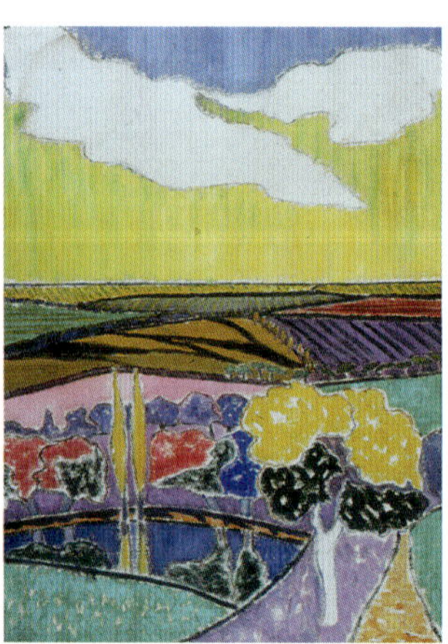

Atkinson, Lawrence 1873–1931
Landscape 1912
oil on canvas 95 x 73.3
3/1979

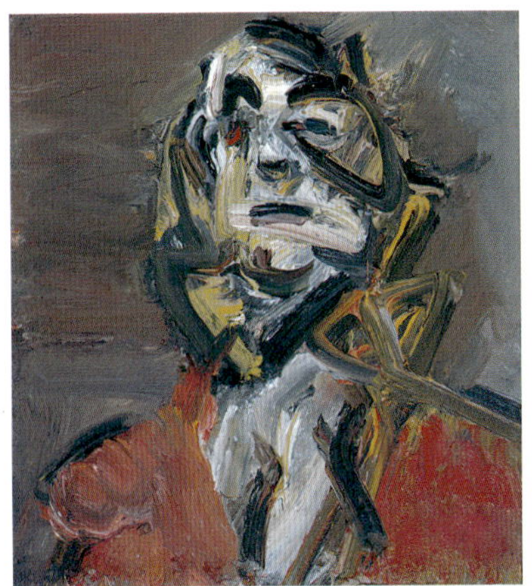

Auerbach, Frank Helmuth b.1931
JYM1 1981
oil on board 73.2 x 68.2
12/1982

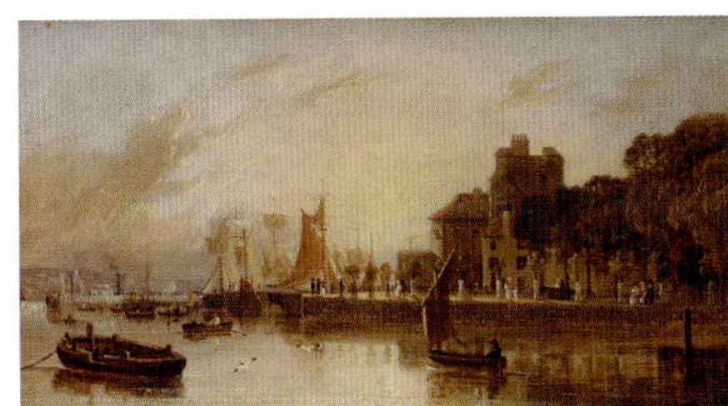

Austin, Samuel 1796–1834
View of Southampton from near the Baths
oil on canvas 20 x 34.3 (E)
13/1969

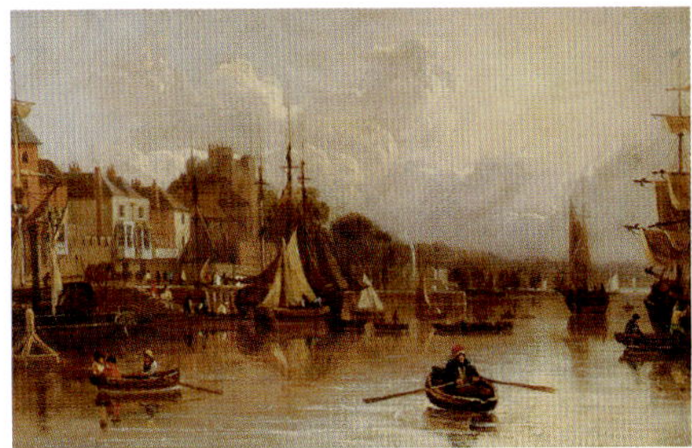

Austin, Samuel 1796–1834
View of Southampton from the End of the New Pier
oil on canvas 20 x 34.3 (E)
14/1969

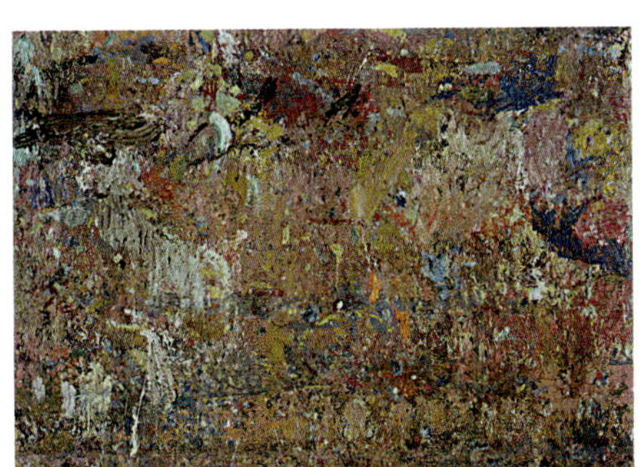

Ayres, Gillian b.1930
Hinba 1978
oil on canvas 213.3 x 304.8
15/1979

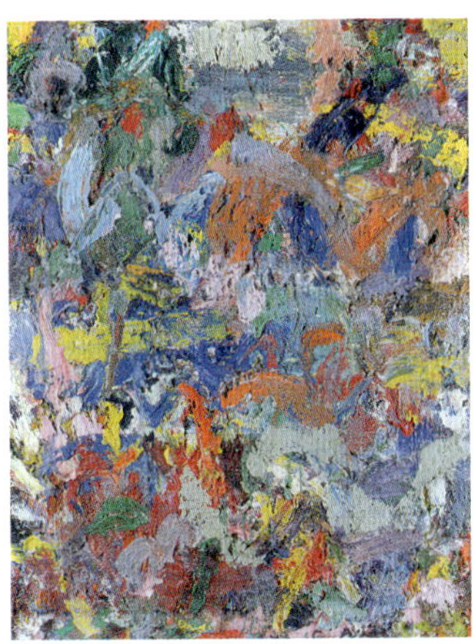

Ayres, Gillian b.1930
Kintraw
oil on board 97.5 x 78.3
45/2002

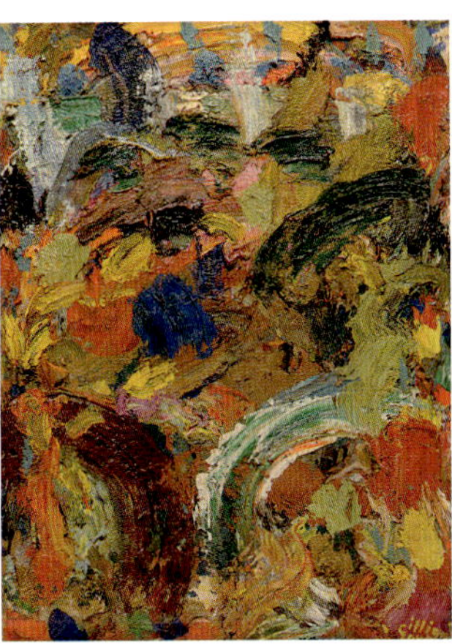

Ayres, Gillian b.1930
Untitled
oil on paper 75.2 x 55.2
111/2002

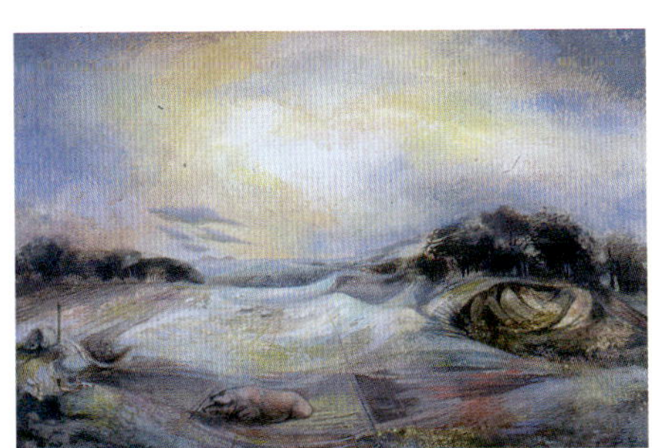

Ayrton, Michael 1921–1975
Landscape with a Pig 1946
oil on wood 51.5 x 76.6
1293

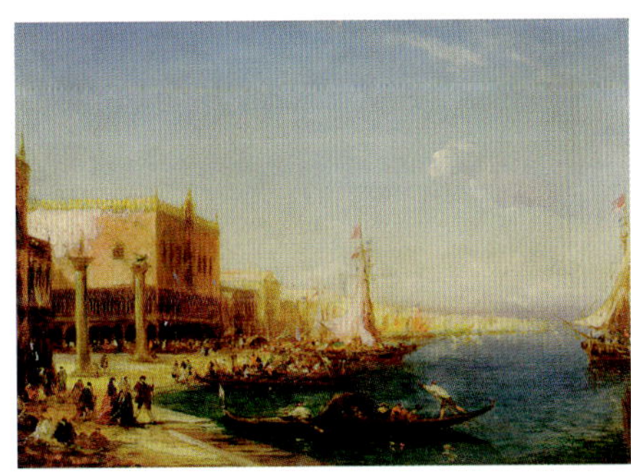

Bachmann, Adolphe b.c.1880
Venice, Riva degli Schiavoni and the Doge's Palace
oil on canvas 38.6 x 55
91/1963

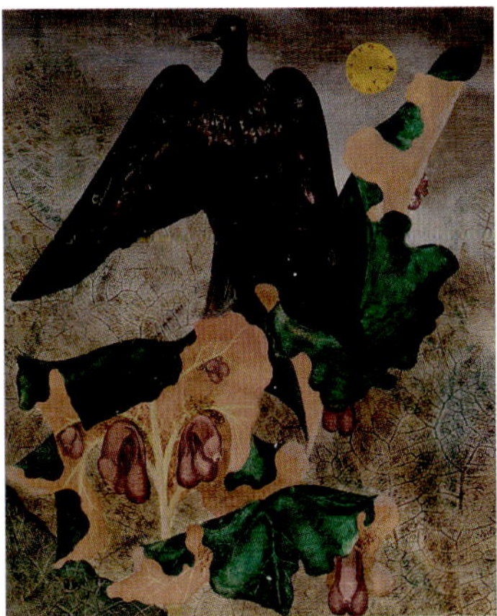

Banting, John 1902–1972
Time for Tea (Foliage Fantasy) 1934
oil on canvas 48.2 x 40
3/2002

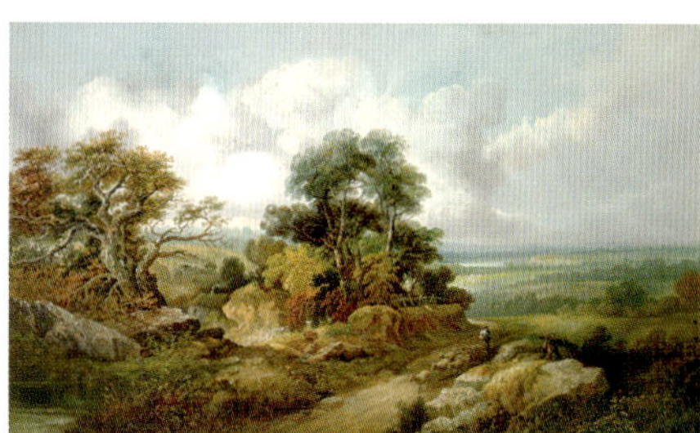

Barker, Joseph (attributed to) 1782–1809
Landscape
oil on canvas 76.5 x 127
14

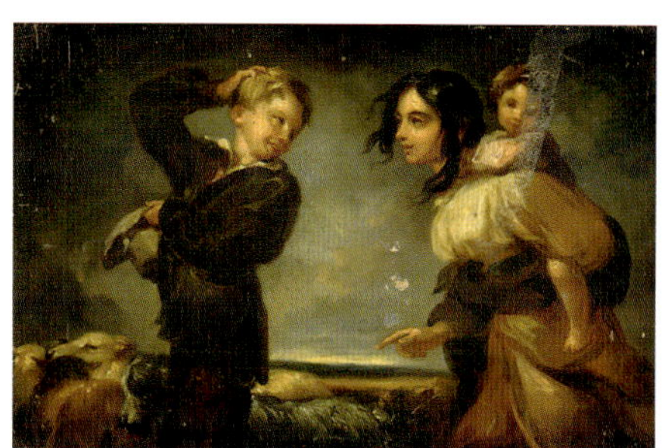

Barker, Thomas 1769–1847
Young Children 1816
oil on canvas 35.1 x 56.5
16

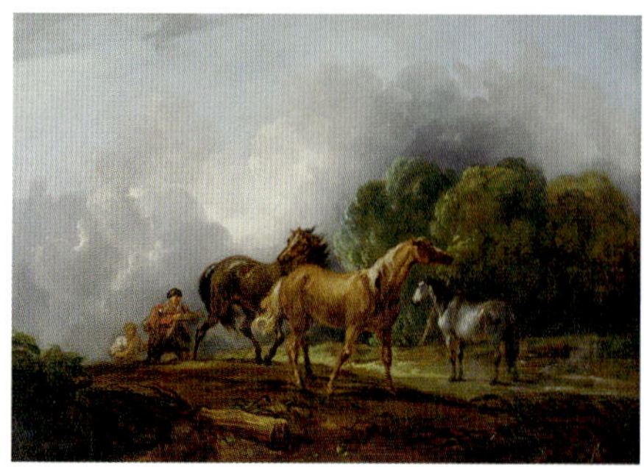

Barker, Thomas 1769–1847
Catching Colts
oil on canvas 46 x 65
15

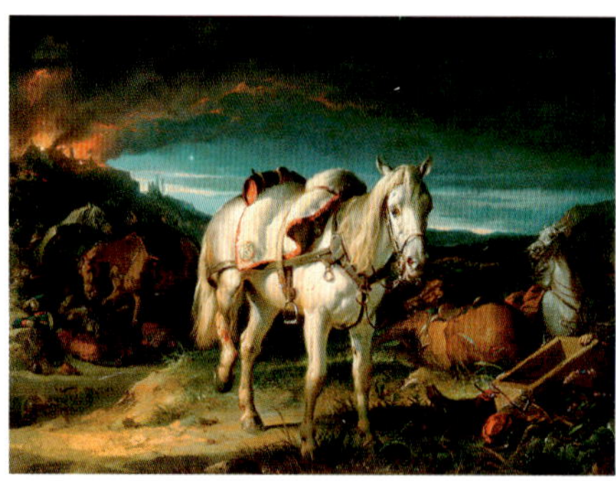

Barker, Thomas 1769–1847
Riderless Horse after the Battle of Sedan
oil on canvas 68.5 x 91.5
1279

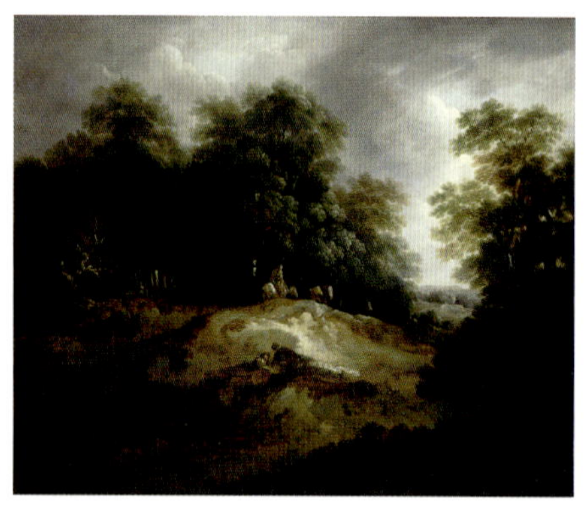

Barker, Thomas 1769–1847
The Edge of the Common
oil on canvas 85.9 x 97.9
1414

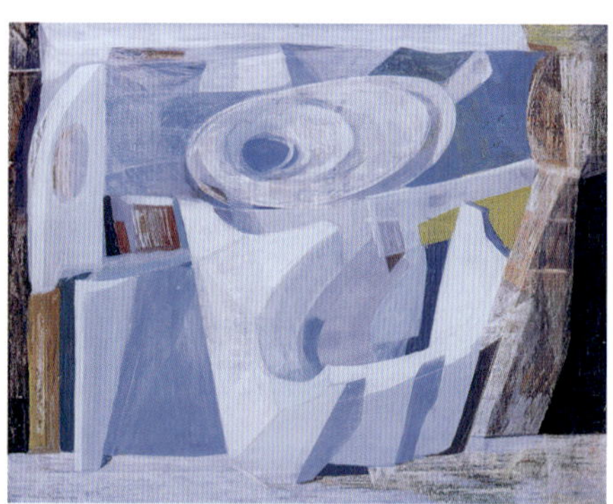

Barns-Graham, Wilhelmina 1912–2004
Glacier Vortex 1951
oil on canvas 60 x 71.5
208/2002

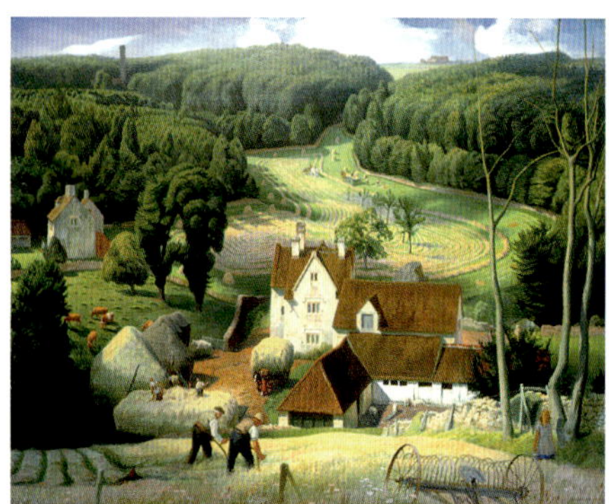

Bateman, James 1893–1959
Haytime in the Cotswolds
oil on canvas 106.8 x 133.8
20

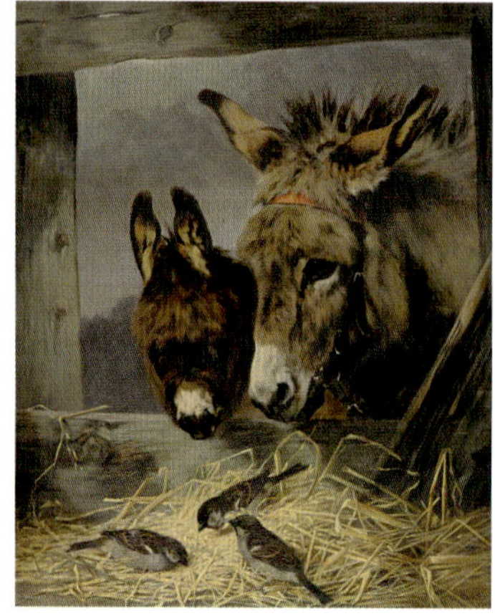

Batt, Arthur 1846–1911
Good Companions 1880
oil on canvas 61 x 50.8
22

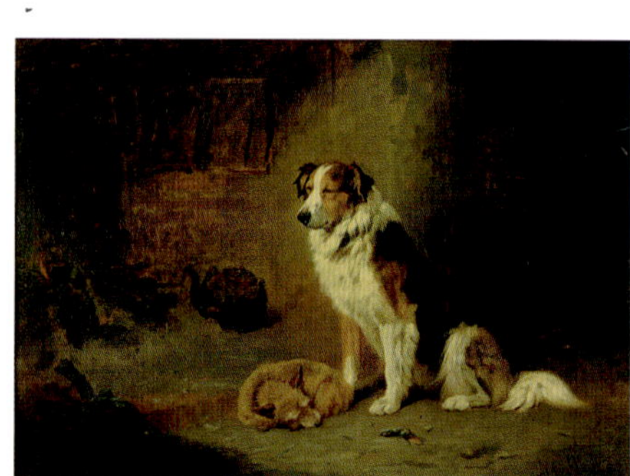

Batt, Arthur 1846–1911
Terrier Asleep and Collie Dozing before the Fire
1887
oil on canvas 25.4 x 35.2
24

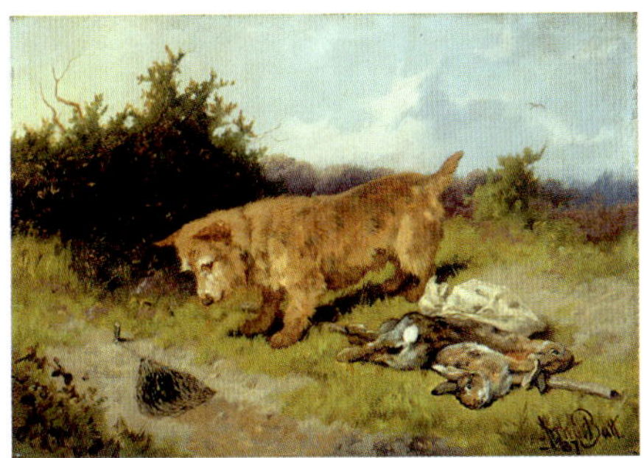

Batt, Arthur 1846–1911
Terrier Watching Rabbit Trap 1887
oil on board 22.8 x 33
25

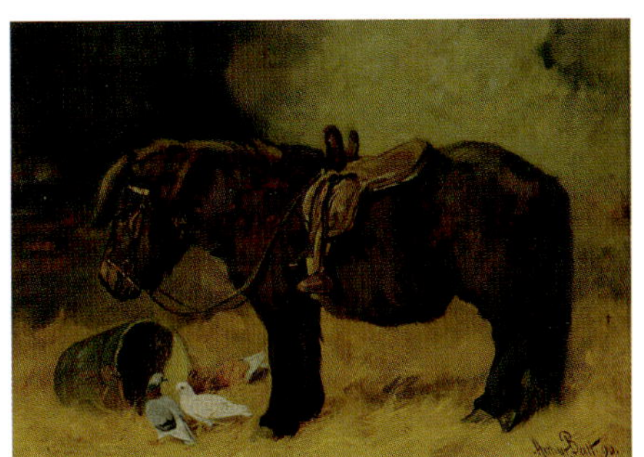

Batt, Arthur 1846–1911
The Empty Bucket 1890
oil on canvas 25.3 x 35
23

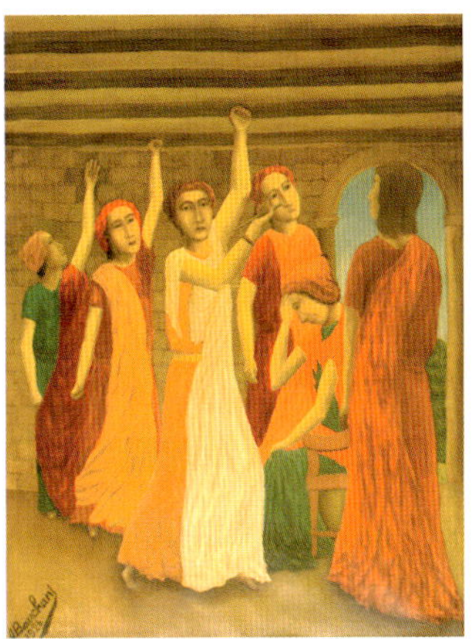

Bauchant, André 1873–1958
Lucretia 1924
oil on canvas 81.3 x 61.5
68/1963

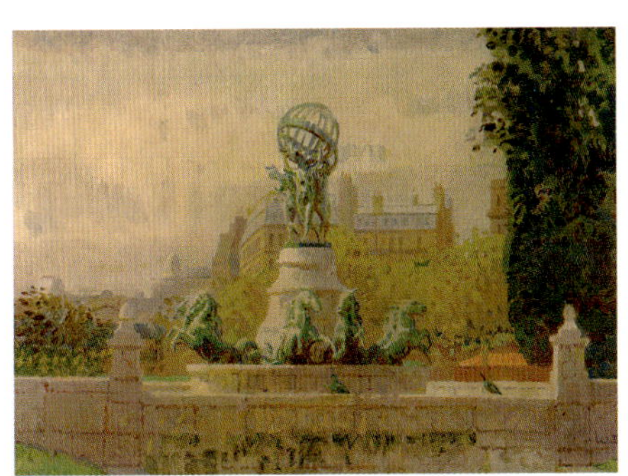

Bayes, Walter 1869–1956
Parisian Fountain 1914
oil on canvas 72.4 x 92.1
5/2000

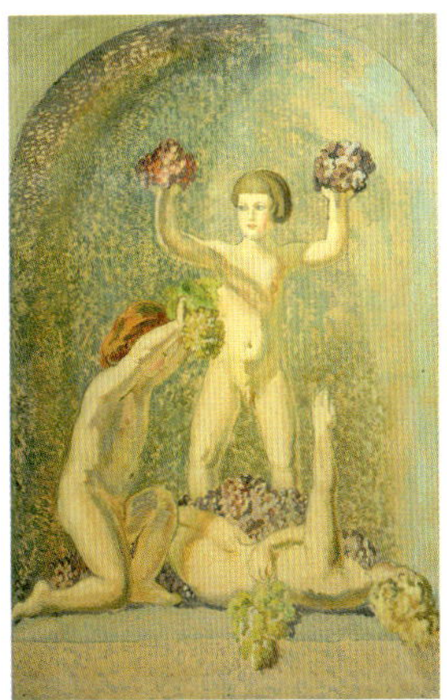

Bell, Vanessa 1879–1961 & **Grant, Duncan** 1885–1978
Bacchanale 1929
oil on canvas 213.4 x 137
11/1972

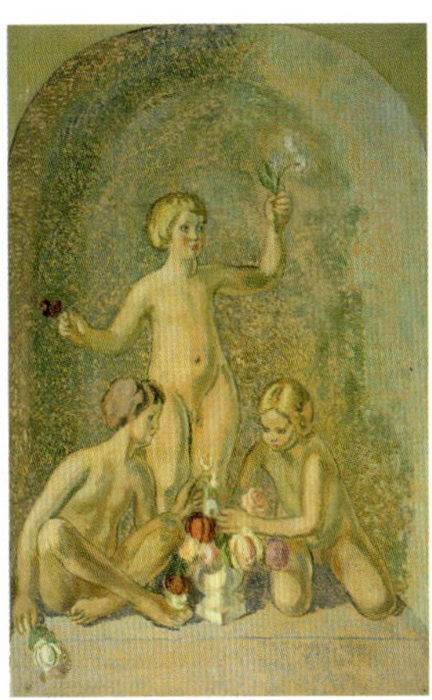

Bell, Vanessa 1879–1961 & **Grant, Duncan** 1885–1978
Children Arranging Flowers 1929
oil on canvas 213.4 x 137.2
14/1972

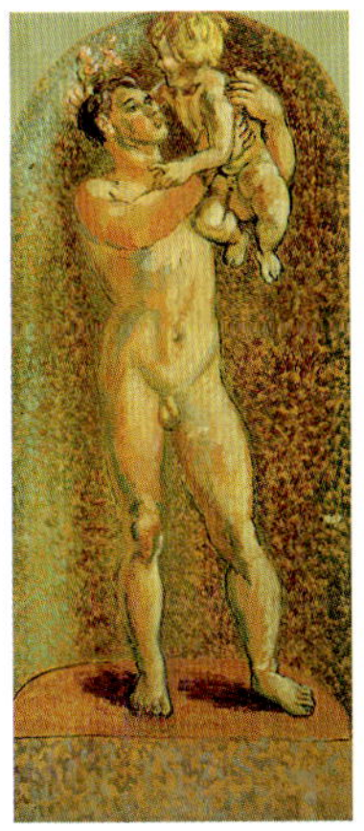

Bell, Vanessa 1879–1961 & **Grant, Duncan** 1885–1978
Father and Child 1929
oil on canvas 201.3 x 88.9
12/1972

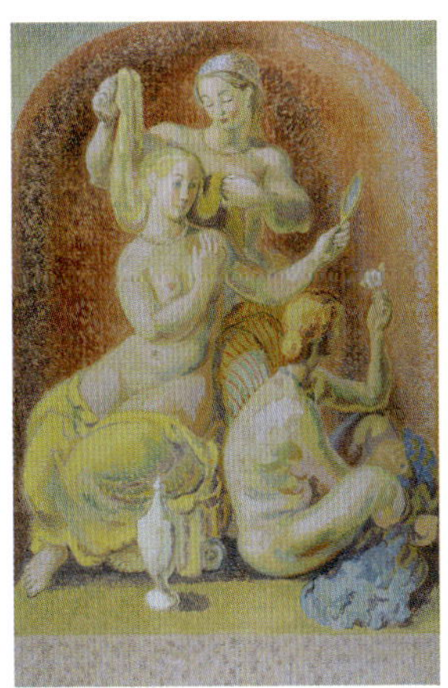

Bell, Vanessa 1879–1961 & **Grant, Duncan** 1885–1978
The Toilet of Venus 1929
oil on canvas 213.4 x 139.3
10/1972

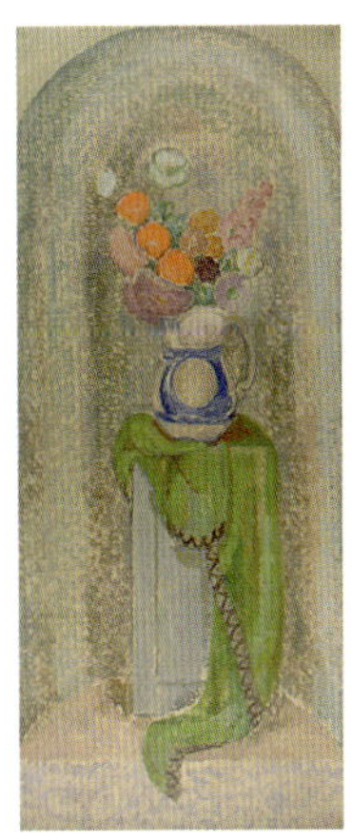

Bell, Vanessa 1879–1961 & **Grant, Duncan** 1885–1978
Vase and Flowers 1929
oil on canvas 213.4 x 91.6
13/1972

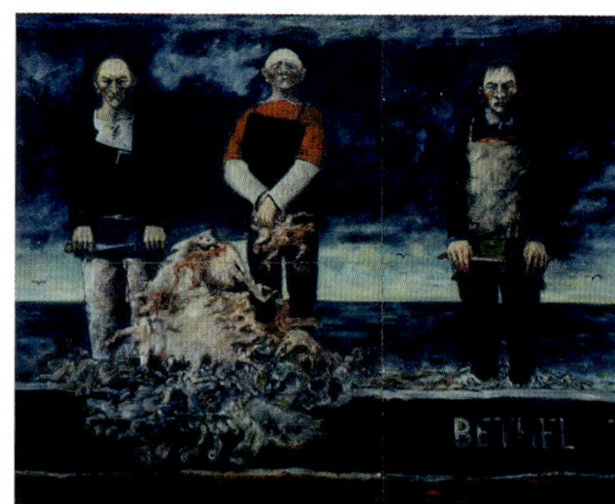

Bellany, John b.1942
Bethel 1967
oil on wood 248 x 319.7
12/1979

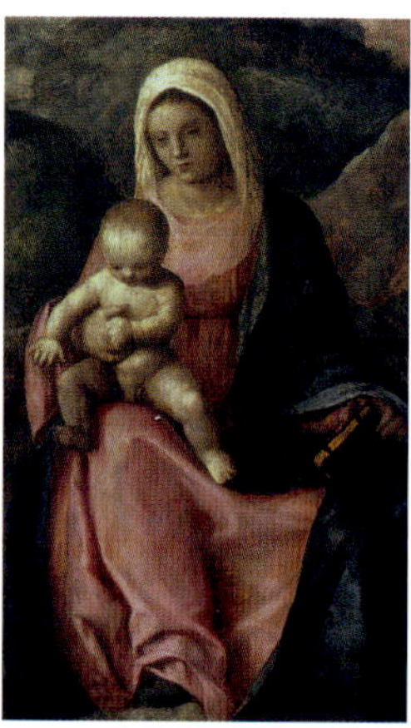

Bellini, Giovanni 1431–1436–1516
Madonna and Child 1514
oil on wood 94 x 59.7
1/1980

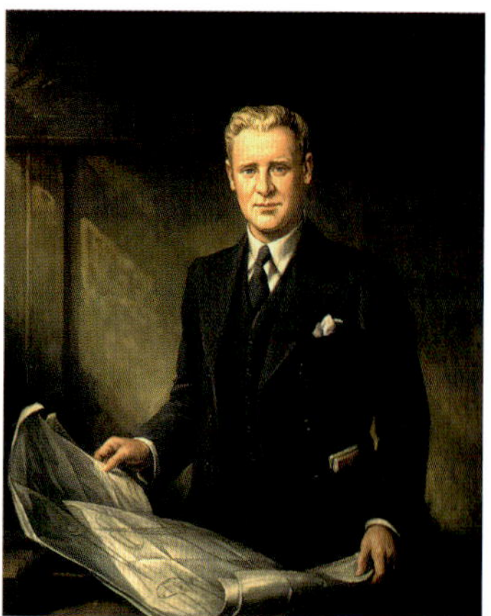

Beresford, Frank Ernest 1881–1967
Reginald Joseph Mitchell, CBE (1895–1937), Aeronautical Engineer 1942
oil on canvas 127 x 102
1405

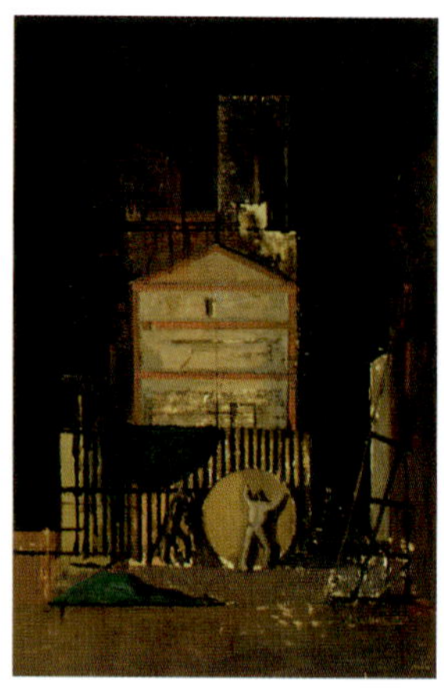

Berman, Eugene 1899–1972
Perspective Nocturne 1930
oil on canvas 81 x 54
67/1963

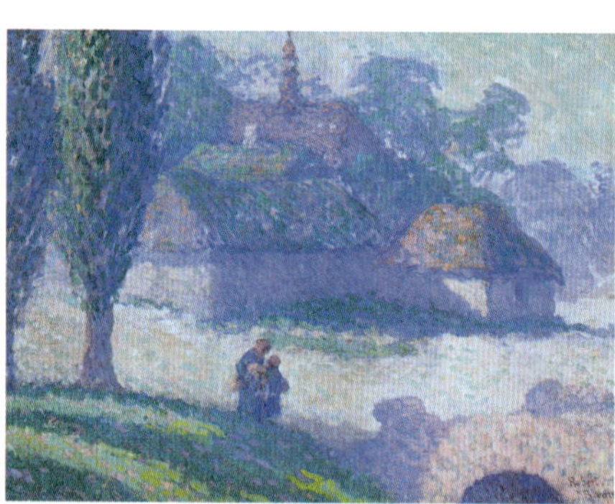

Bevan, Robert Polhill 1865–1925
Mydlow Village, Poland 1907
oil on canvas 60 x 79
1417

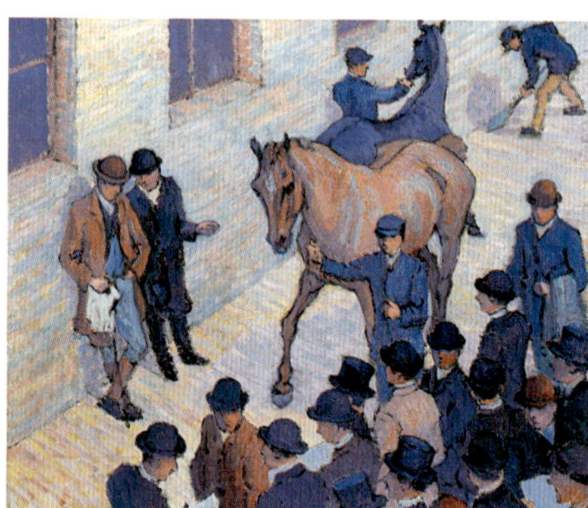

Bevan, Robert Polhill 1865–1925
A Sale at Tattersalls 1911
oil on canvas 50.8 x 61
11/1974

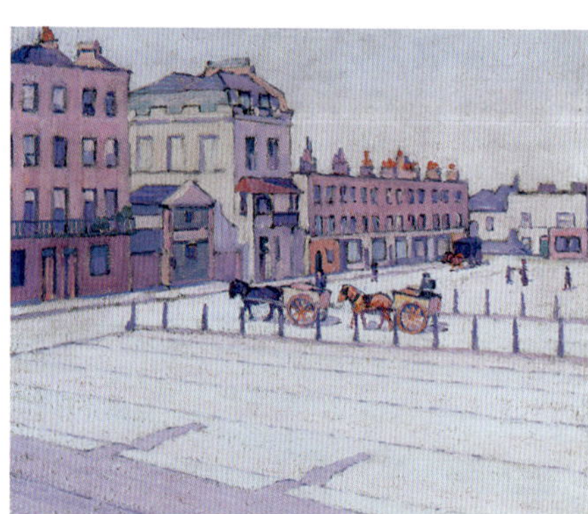

Bevan, Robert Polhill 1865–1925
Cumberland Market, North Side 1912
oil on canvas 51.1 x 61
1299

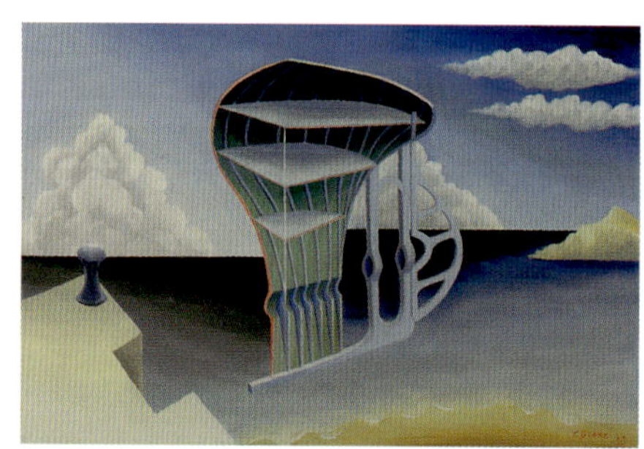

Bigge, John Selby 1892–1973
Composition 1930
oil on board 68.3 x 93.5
28/2005

Blackman, M. S. active c.1900
Robert J. Chipperfield
oil on canvas 76.5 x 63.5
988

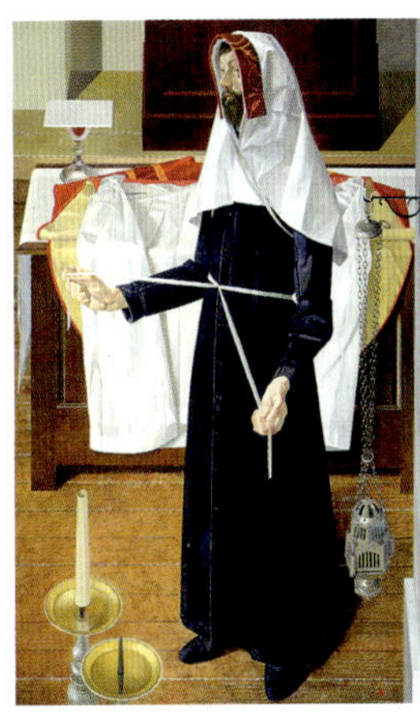

Blamey, Norman Charles 1914–1999
Vesting Priest with Apparelled Amice 1991
oil on panel 167 x 107
13/1993

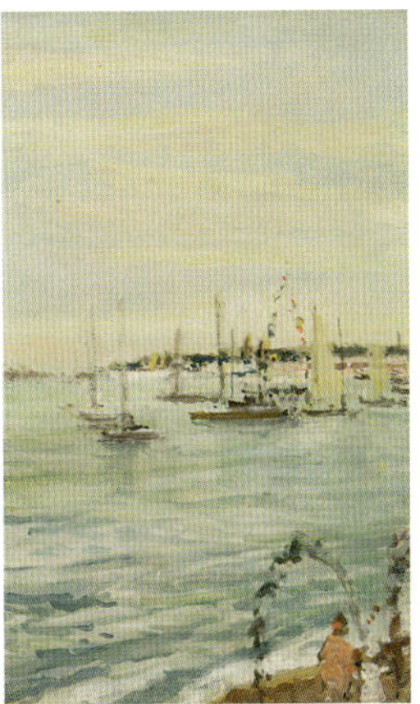

Blanche, Jacques-Emile 1861–1942
Yachts at Weymouth 1931
oil on board 32.5 x 20.1
54/1963

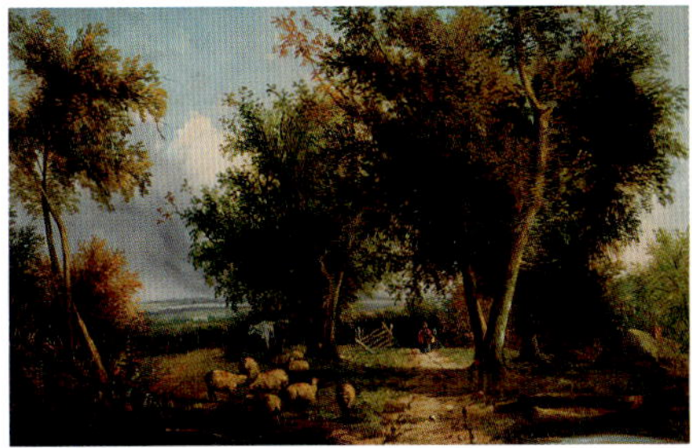

Boddington, Henry John 1811–1865
Farm Scene 1855
oil on canvas 38.4 x 61
30

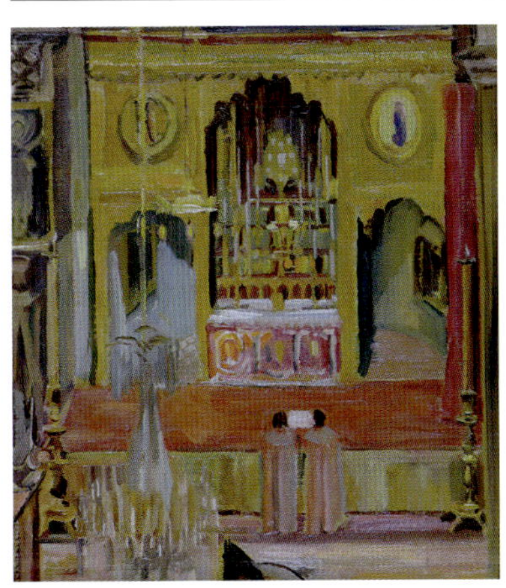

Bomberg, David 1890–1957
Interior of the Armenian Church 1925
oil on canvas 64.4 x 58
44/2002

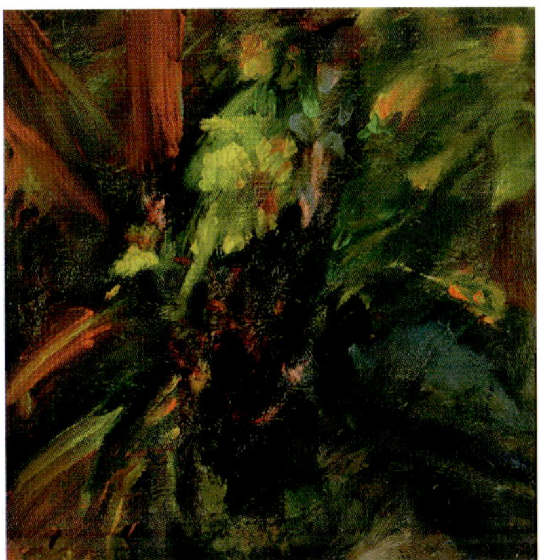

Bomberg, David 1890–1957
Flower Group 1943
oil on canvas 43.2 x 43.2
17/1982

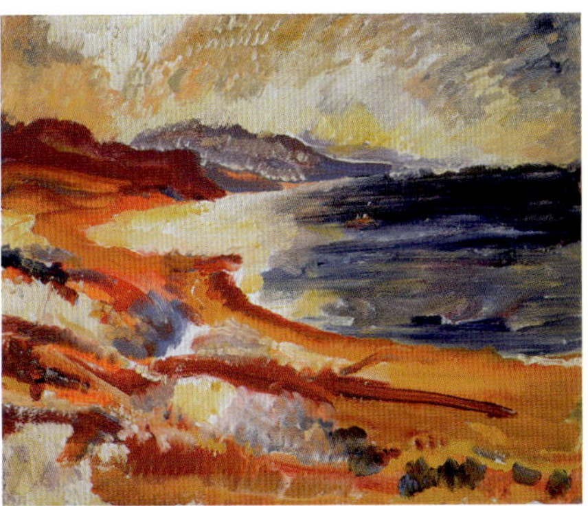

Bomberg, David 1890–1957
Cyprus 1948
oil on canvas 51 x 61
2/1960

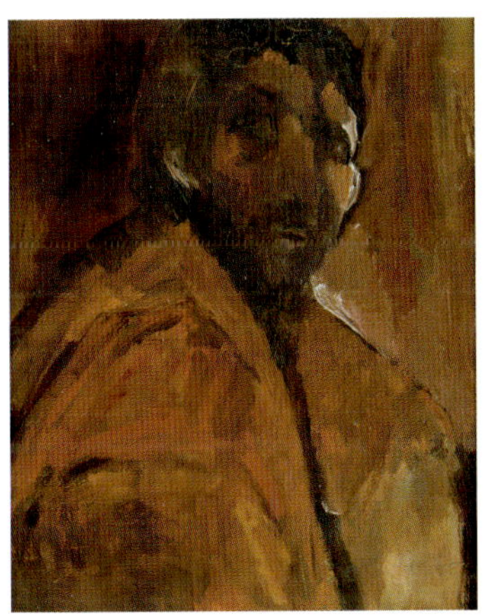

Bomberg, David 1890–1957
Spanish Gypsy Woman
oil on panel 76.9 x 66.5
40/2002

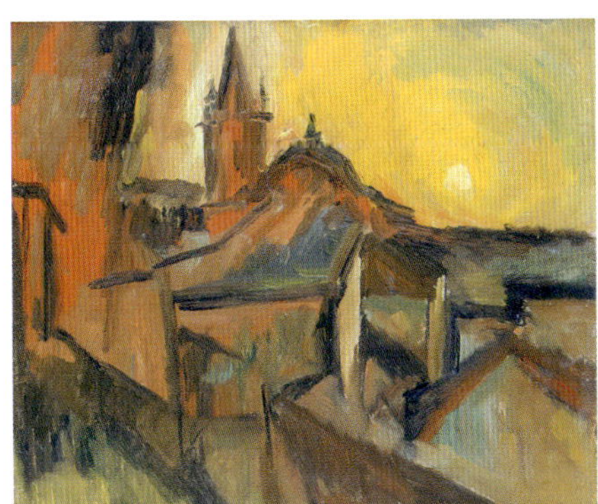

Bomberg, David 1890–1957
Zahara Evening
oil on panel 72.3 x 82.2
41/2002

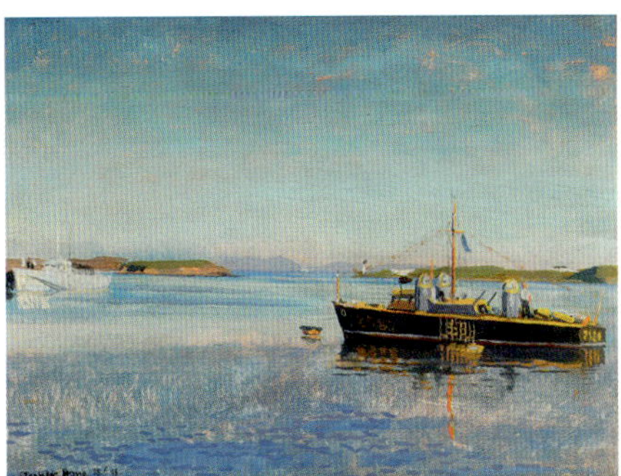

Bone, Stephen 1904–1958
Air-Sea Rescue Launch 'D' Type 1943
oil on canvas 23.5 x 35.5
1308

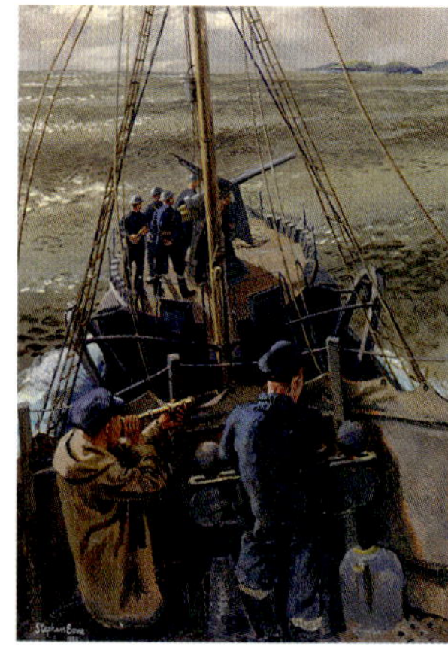

Bone, Stephen 1904–1958
Trawler's Twelve Pounder 1943
oil on wood 92 x 64.1
1309

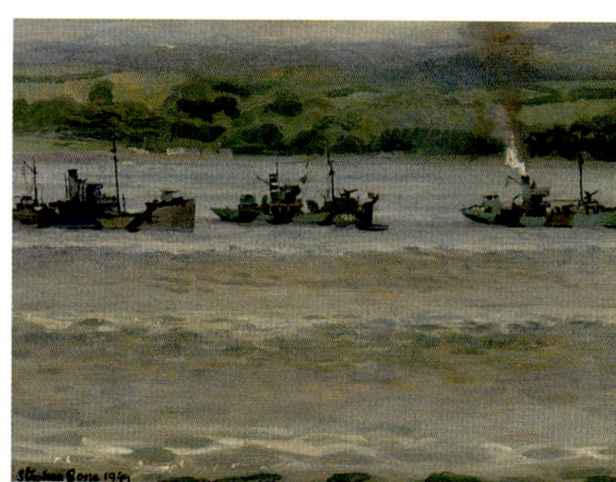

Bone, Stephen 1904–1958
Three Trawlers 1944
oil on wood 25.4 x 35.5
1310

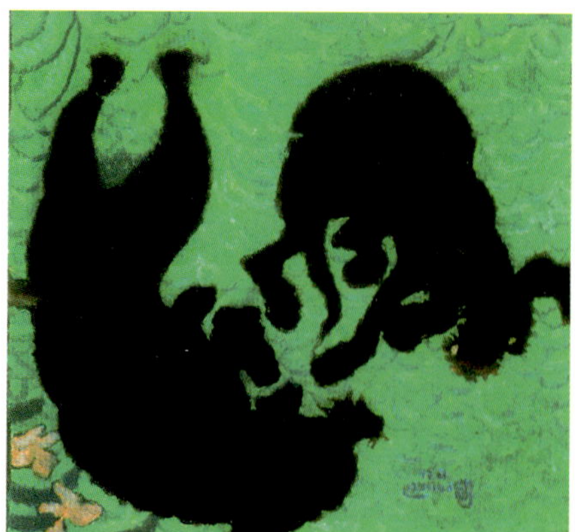

Bonnard, Pierre 1867–1947
Deux chiens 1891
oil on canvas 37 x 39.7
60/1963

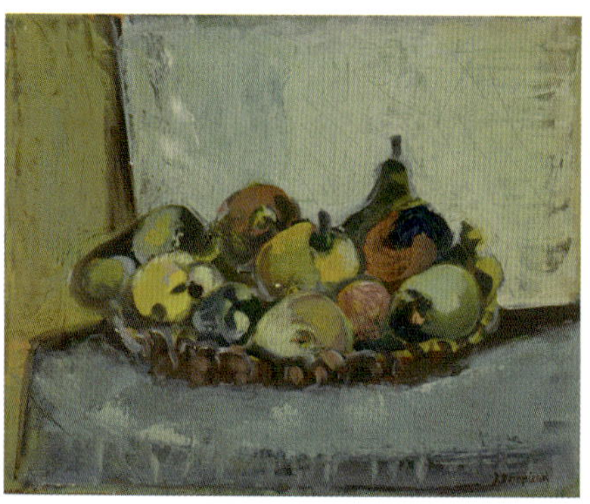

Bornfriend, Jacob 1904–1976
Fruit
oil on canvas 40.3 x 51
1443

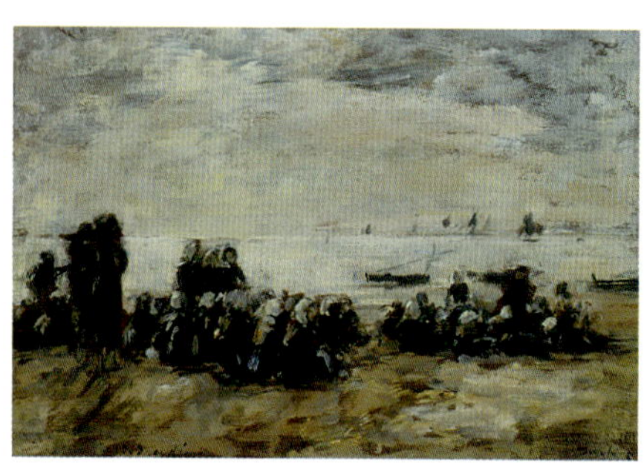

Boudin, Eugène Louis 1824–1898
Women Awaiting Fishing Boats on Berck Beach 1880
oil on canvas 21.5 x 31.1
4/1986

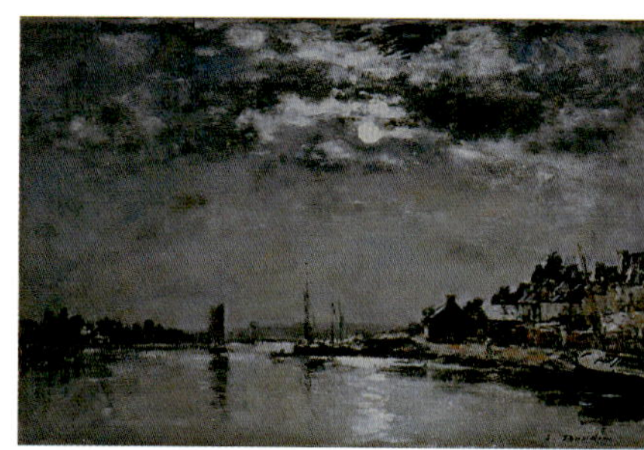

Boudin, Eugène Louis 1824–1898
Marine effet de lune
oil on canvas 30.5 x 46.5
45

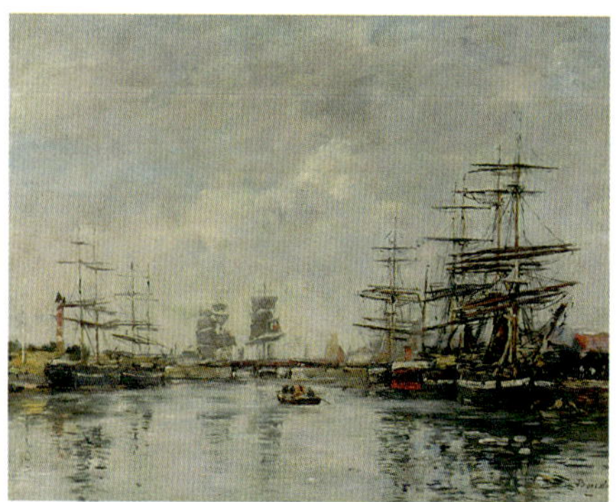

Boudin, Eugène Louis 1824–1898
Port d'Honfleur
oil on panel 31.9 x 41.1
1/2003

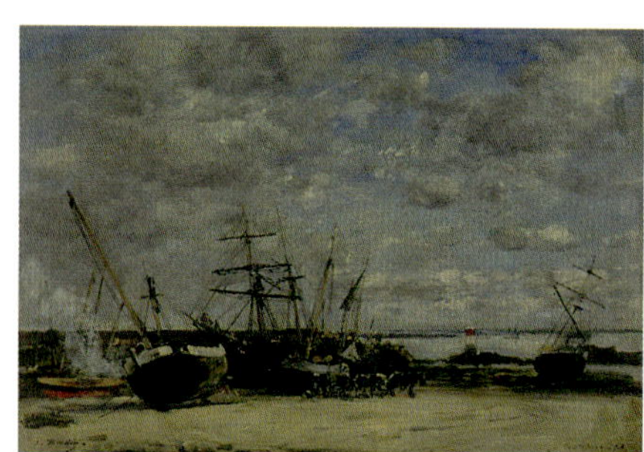

Boudin, Eugène Louis 1824–1898
Vessels and Horses on the Shoreline
oil on canvas 49 x 64
2/2003

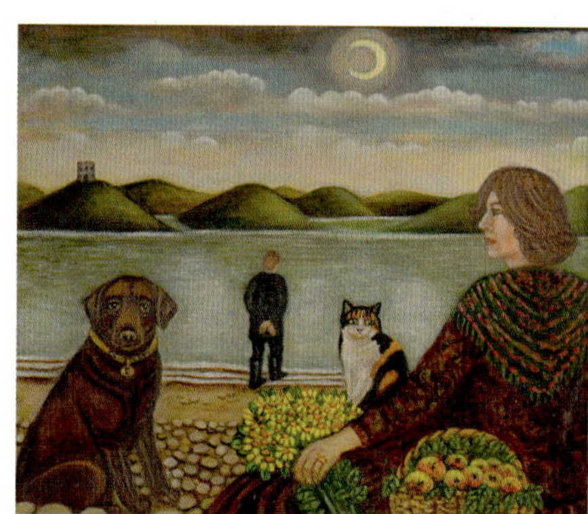

Box, Eden 1919–1988
Stranger on the Shore 1981
oil on canvas 61.4 x 71.7
41/1976

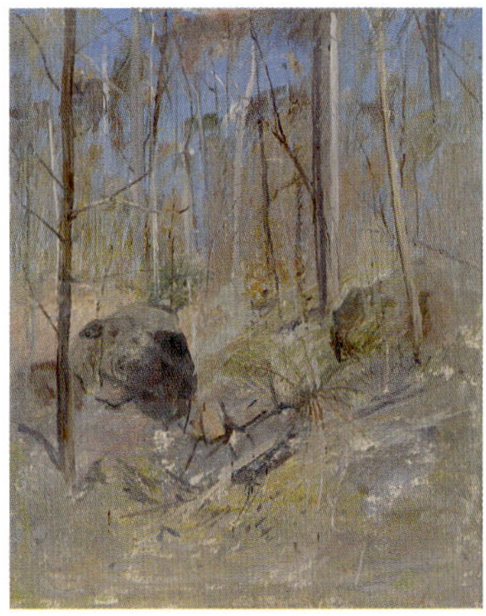

Boyd, Arthur Merric 1862–1940
Australian Landscape
oil on copper 34.4 x 28
9/2006

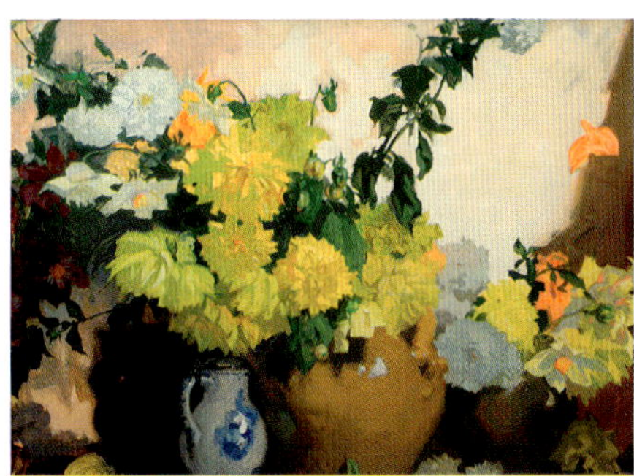

Brangwyn, Frank 1867–1956
Yellow Dahlias
oil on canvas 81 x 104.4
50

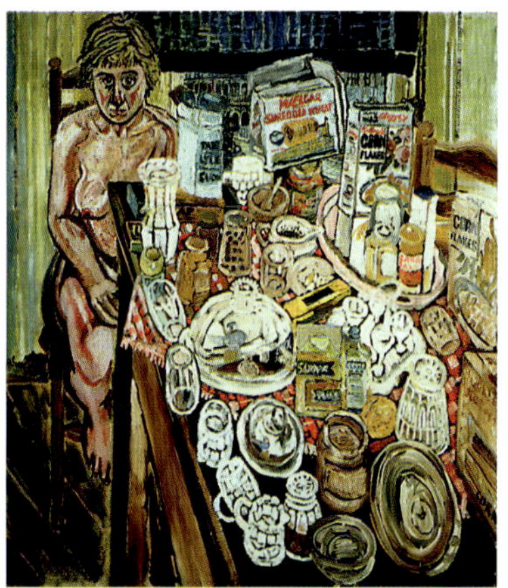

Bratby, John Randall 1928–1992
Jean and Still Life in front of a Window 1954
oil on board 122 x 108
40/1963

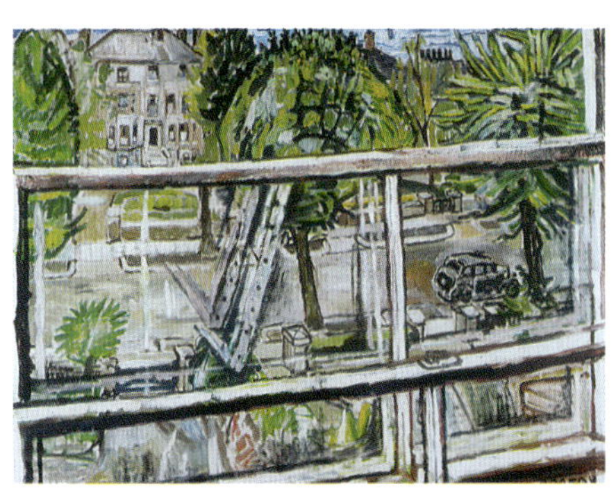

Bratby, John Randall 1928–1992
Canvas Reflected in a Window
oil on canvas 86.3 x 111.5
7/1959

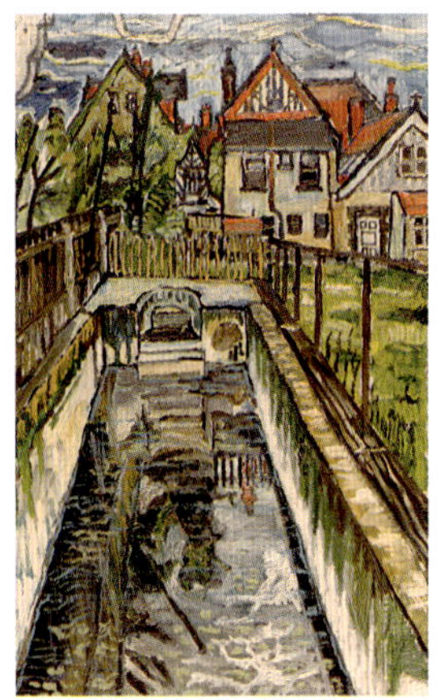

Bratby, John Randall 1928–1992
Swim Pool
oil on board 122 x 75
6/1959

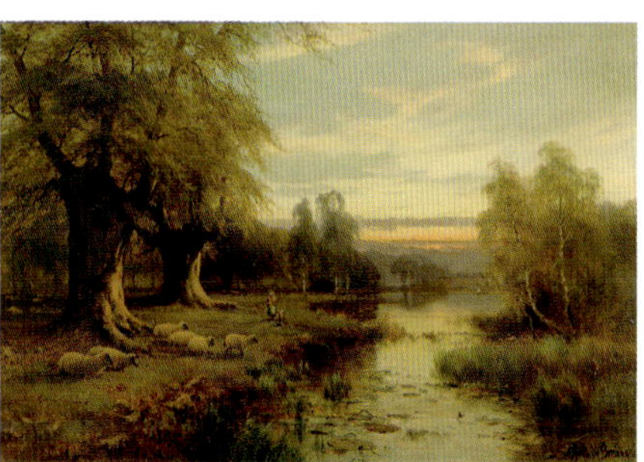

Breanski, Alfred de 1852–1928
Evening Repose, Burnham Beeches
oil on canvas 61 x 91.5
144

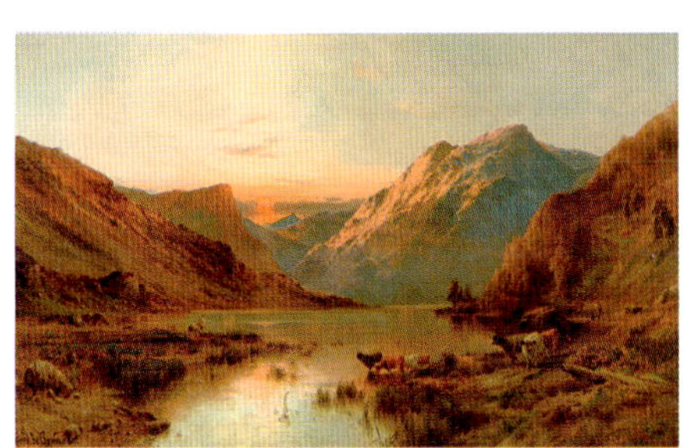

Breanski, Alfred de 1852–1928
Golden Sunset, Loch Lubnaig
oil on canvas 75.6 x 127.1
145

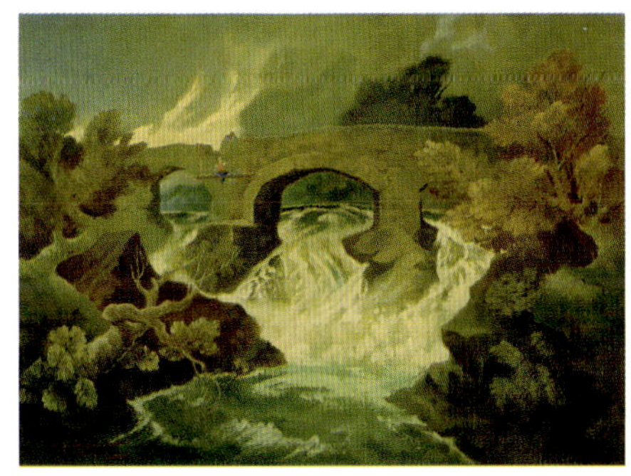

Brent, Ralph Richard Angus b.1903
Repairing the Bridge 1965
oil on board 66.8 x 91.5
31/1977

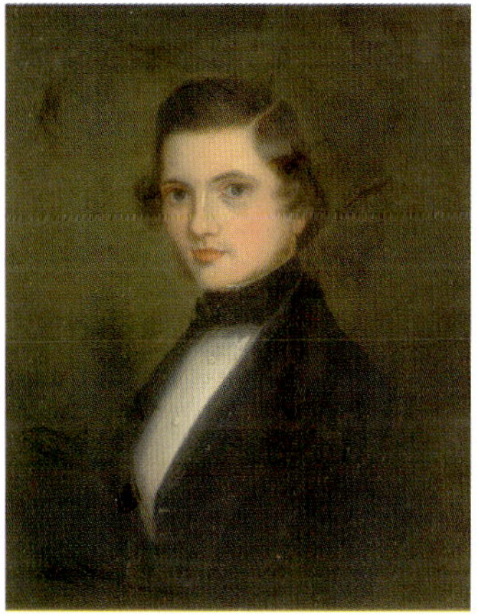

Bridell, Frederick Lee 1831–1863
Henry Rose 1848
oil on tin 18.1 x 15.2
54

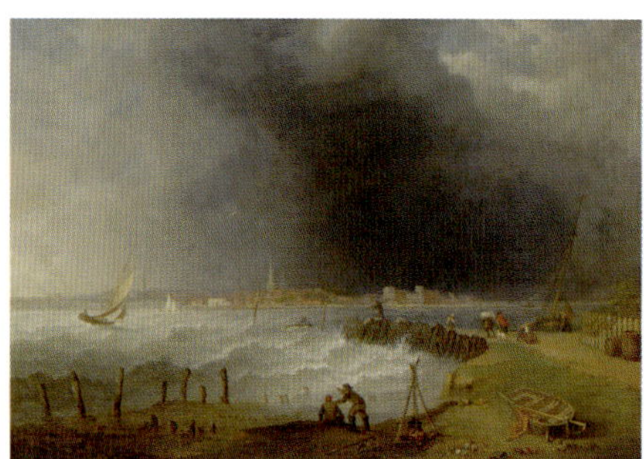

Bridell, Frederick Lee 1831–1863
View of Southampton 1849
oil on canvas 43.2 x 63.8
1380

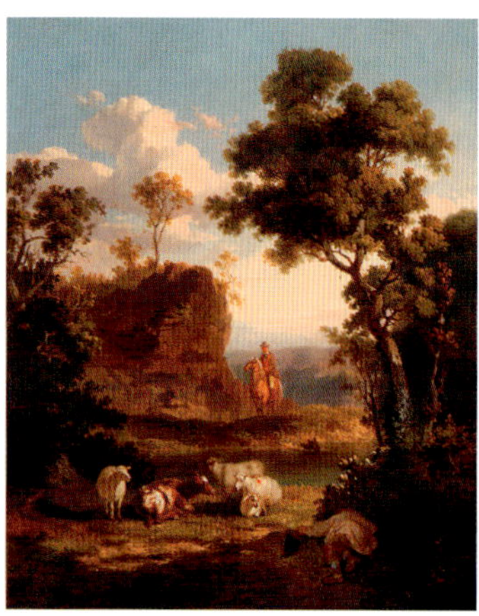

Bridell, Frederick Lee 1831–1863
Autumn Evening 1852
oil on canvas 75 x 63.2
56

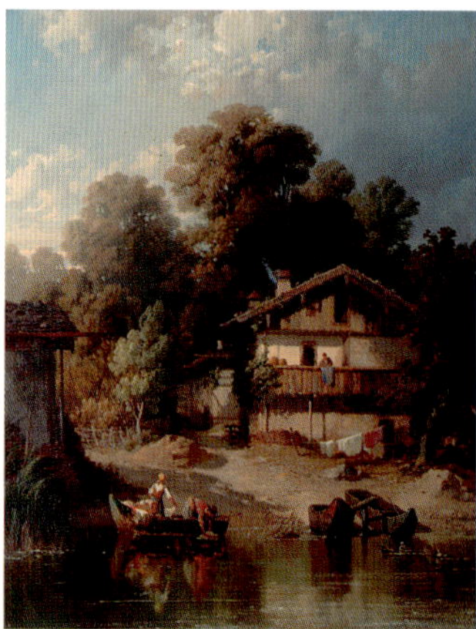

Bridell, Frederick Lee 1831–1863
The Fisherman's House 1854
oil on canvas 49 x 39.5
57

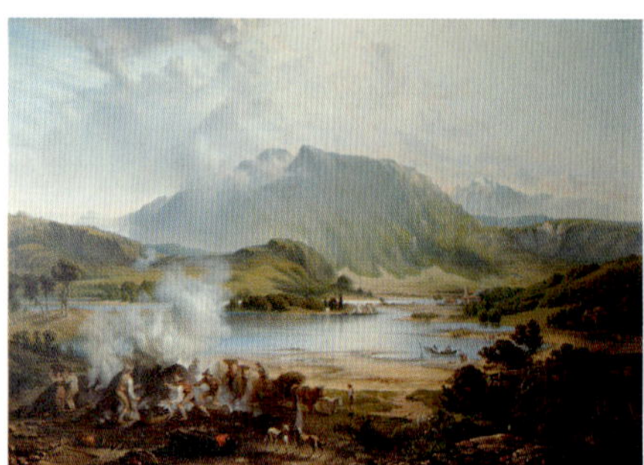

Bridell, Frederick Lee 1831–1863
The Charcoal Burners 1856
oil on canvas 106.5 x 126
55

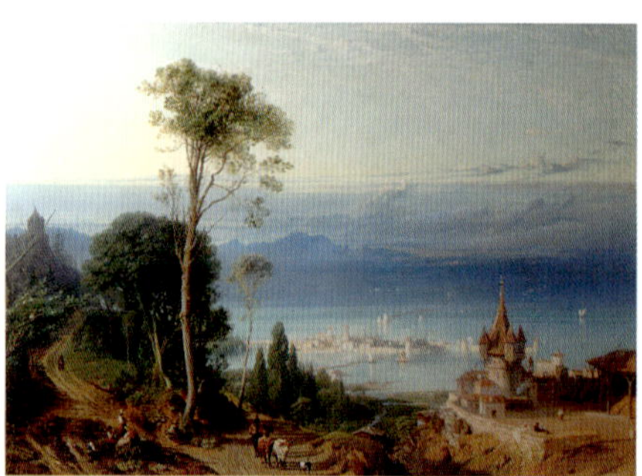

Bridell, Frederick Lee 1831–1863
The Lake of Constance 1858
oil on canvas 120 x 158.8
142/1975

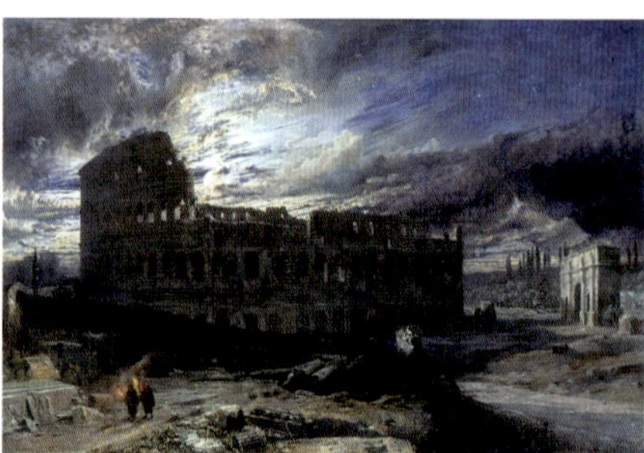

Bridell, Frederick Lee 1831–1863
The Coliseum at Rome by Moonlight 1859
oil on canvas 155 x 230.5
60

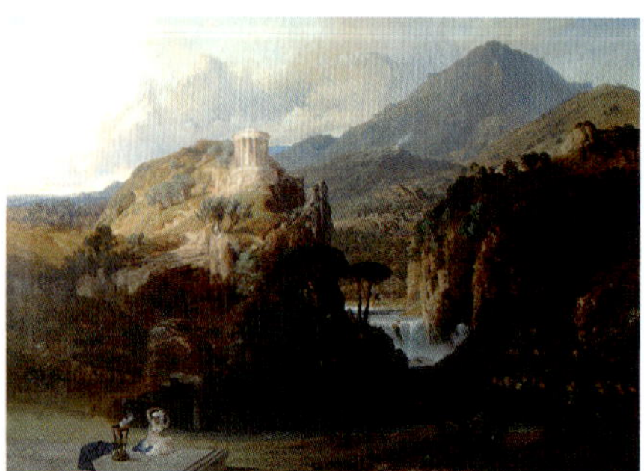

Bridell, Frederick Lee 1831–1863
The Temple of Vesta, Tivoli 1859
oil on canvas 89.6 x 128.6
62

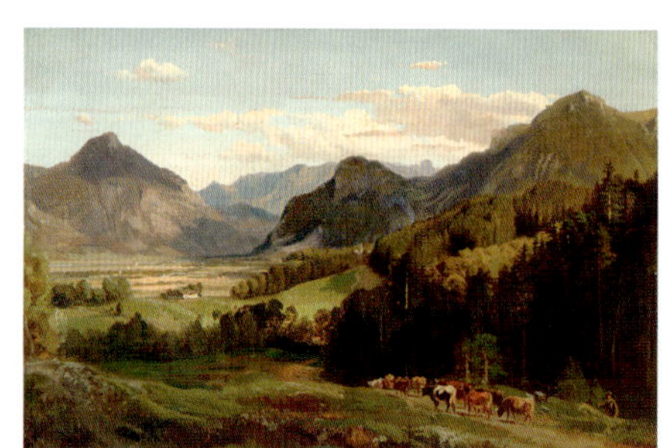

Bridell, Frederick Lee 1831–1863
In the Austrian Tyrol
oil on card 47.9 x 72.7
1107

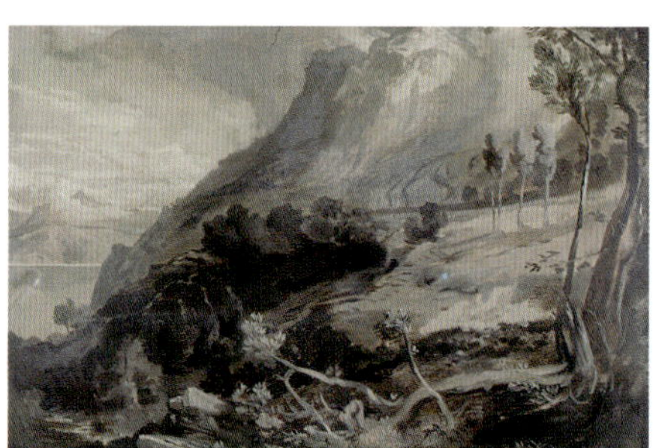

Bridell, Frederick Lee 1831–1863
Lake Como, Sweet Chestnuts
oil on paper 34.7 x 52.7
71

Facing page: Weyden, Goswijn van der, c.1465–after 1538, *St Catherine and the Philosophers* (detail), Southampton City Art Gallery, (p. 139)

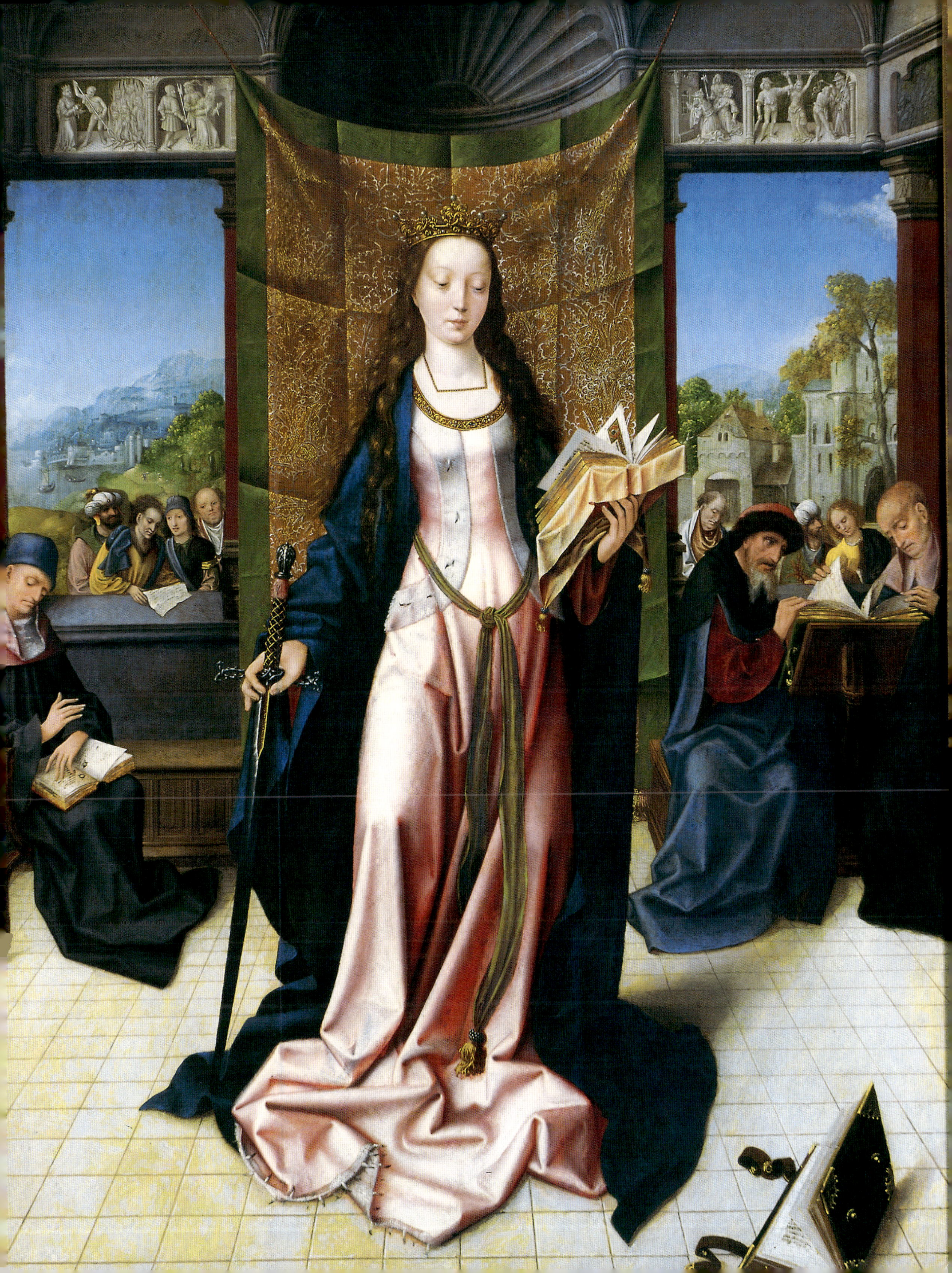

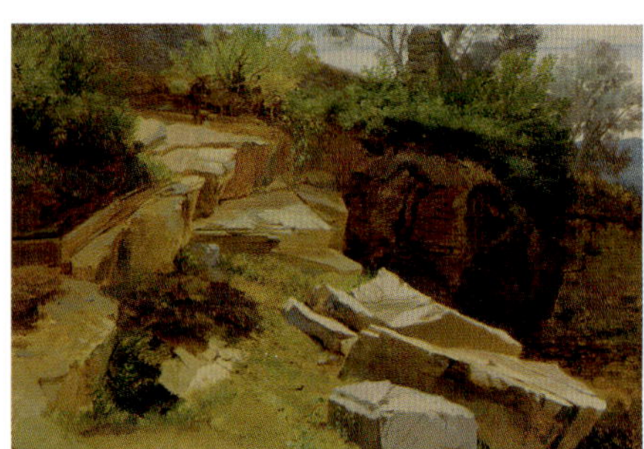

Bridell, Frederick Lee 1831–1863
Mountainside, Lake and Rocks
oil on canvas 35.7 x 52
74

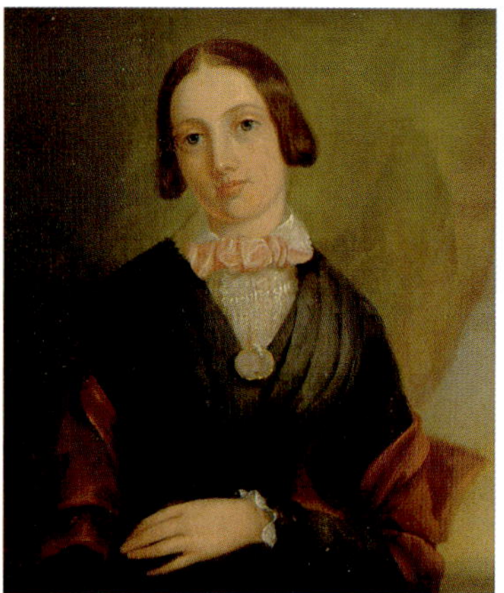

Bridell, Frederick Lee 1831–1863
Mrs Gilroy of Southampton
oil on tin 17.6 x 15.5
1066

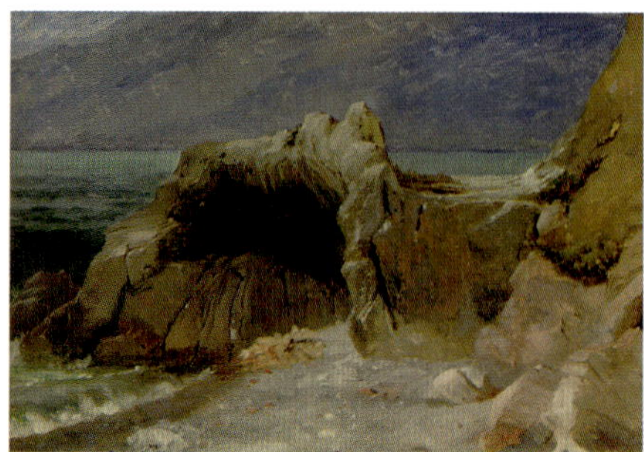

Bridell, Frederick Lee 1831–1863
Quarry, Civita Castellana
oil on paper 37.5 x 54.1
59

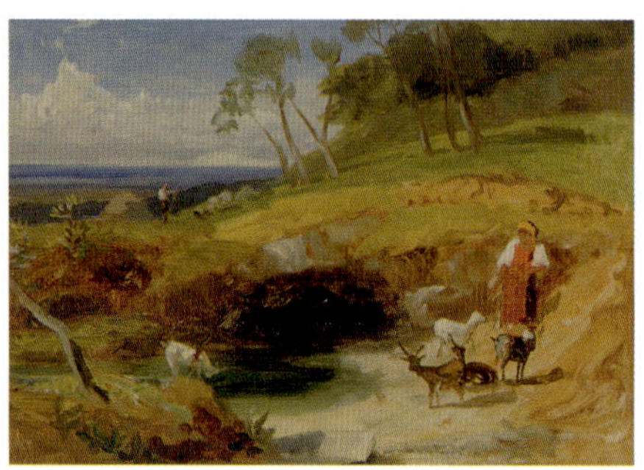

Bridell, Frederick Lee 1831–1863
Study of a Picture in the Collection of Sir Theodore Martin
oil on paper 36.5 x 53
76

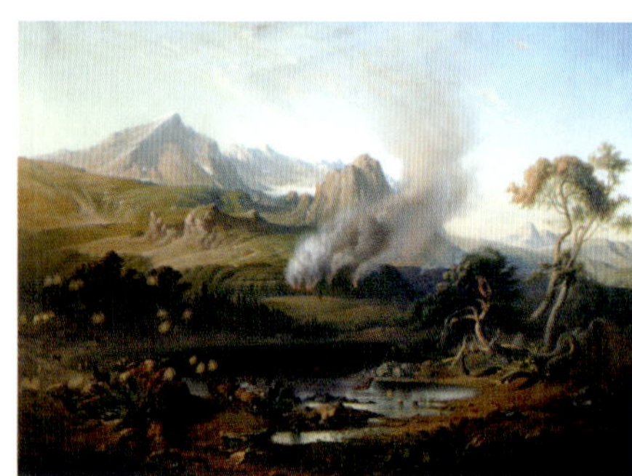

Bridell, Frederick Lee 1831–1863
The Forest on Fire
oil on canvas 71.5 x 102
58

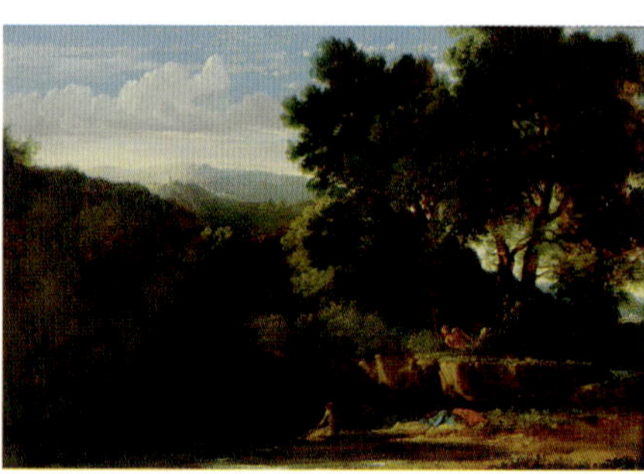

Bridell, Frederick Lee 1831–1863
Tivoli
oil on canvas 51.5 x 76.3
61

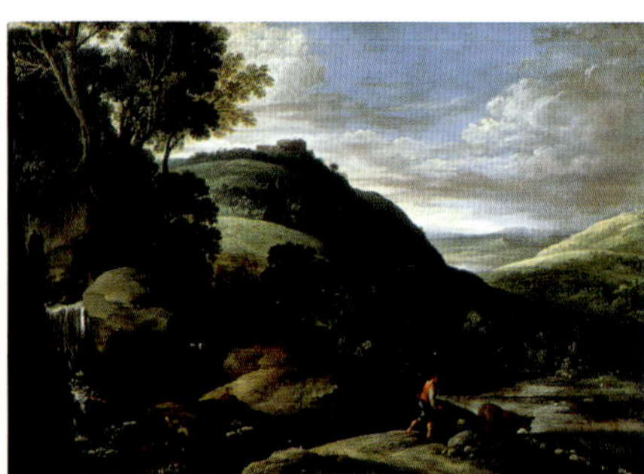

Bril, Paul 1554–1626
Hilly Landscape with a Shepherd 1619
oil on canvas 103 x 148.7
9/1967

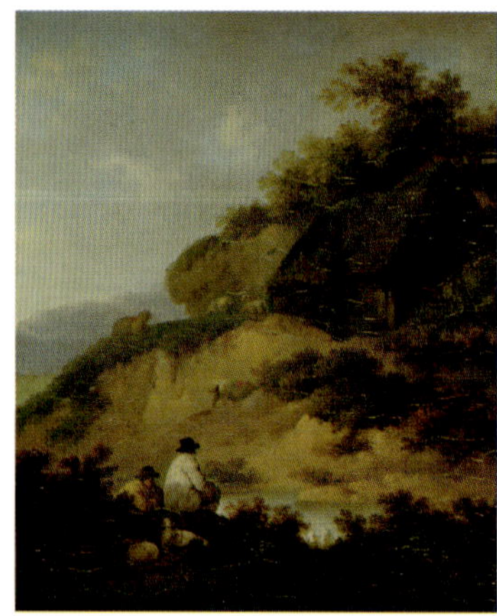

British School
Isle of Wight 1794
oil on canvas 30 x 25.4
412

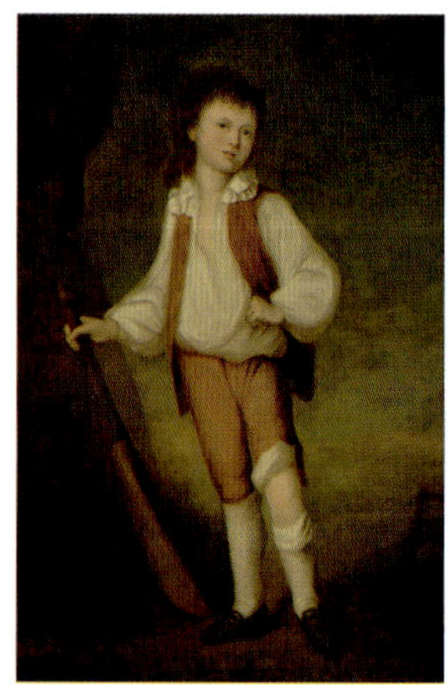

British School 18th C
Boy with Cricket Bat
oil on canvas 138 x 91.5
1477

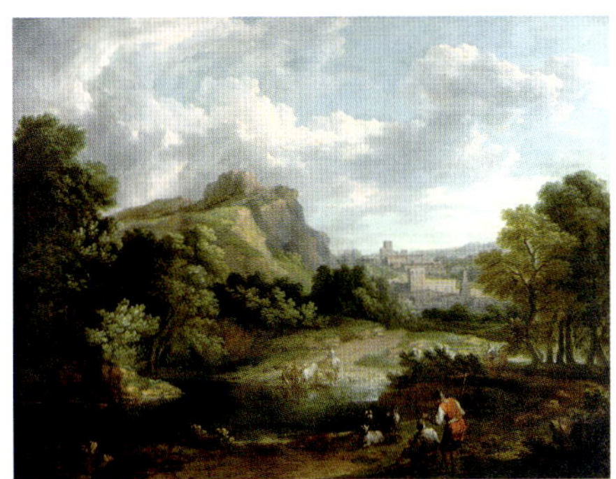

British School 18th C
Classical Landscape with Cattle
oil on canvas 112.4 x 148
404

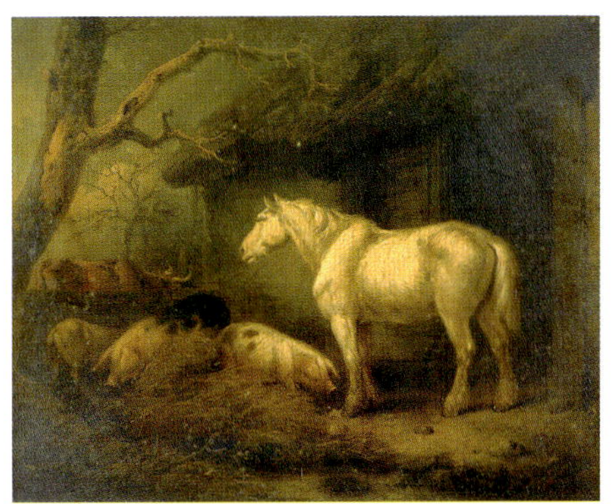

British School 18th C
Farmyard Scene (The White Horse)
oil on canvas 35.8 x 45
414

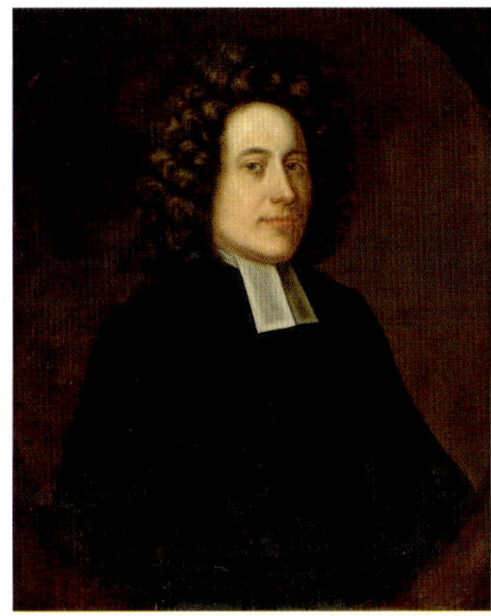

British School 18th C
Portrait of a Man
oil on canvas 77 x 63.8
180

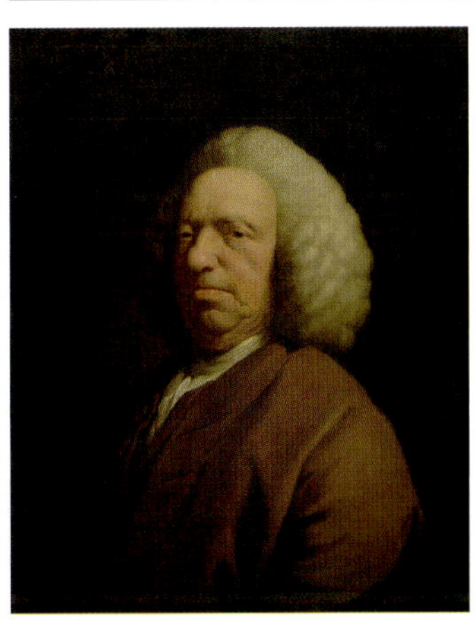

British School 18th C
Portrait of a Man
oil on canvas 74.5 x 63.5
972

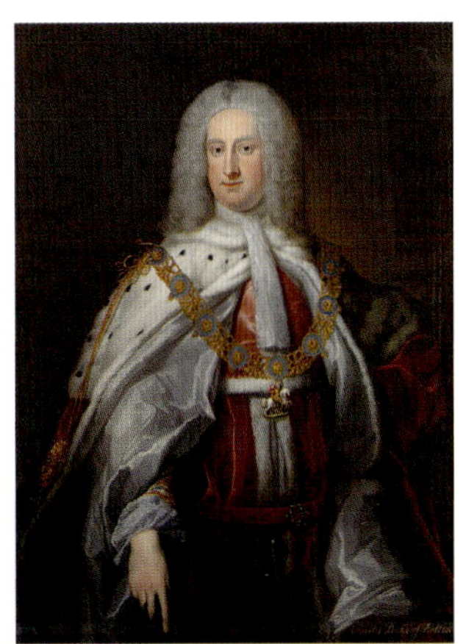

British School 18th C
Portrait of a Man
oil on canvas 127 x 101.5
1067

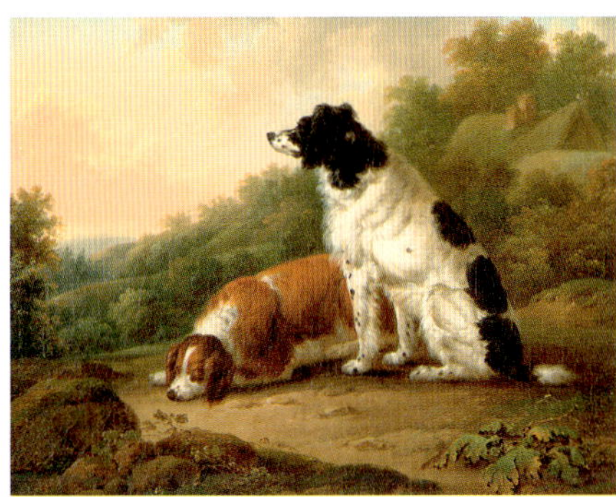

British School 18th C
The Setters
oil on canvas 39.5 x 47.5
413

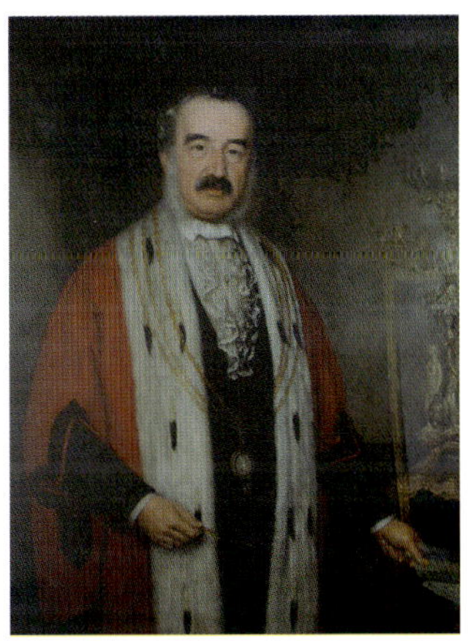

British School
Alderman Samuel Michael Emanuel 1868
oil on canvas 127 x 102.1
603

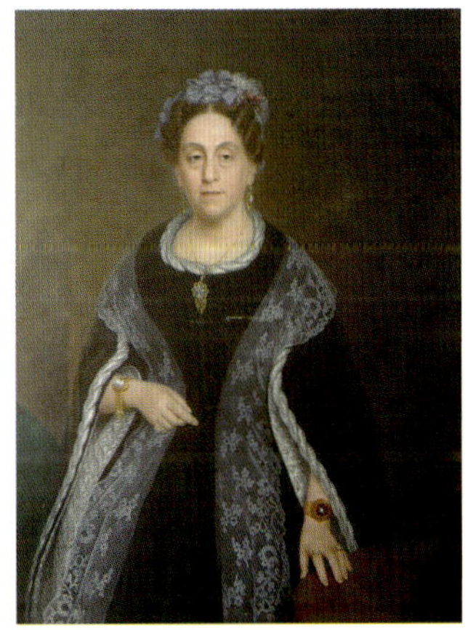

British School 19th C
Mrs Samuel Michael Emanuel
oil on canvas 127 x 101.5
604

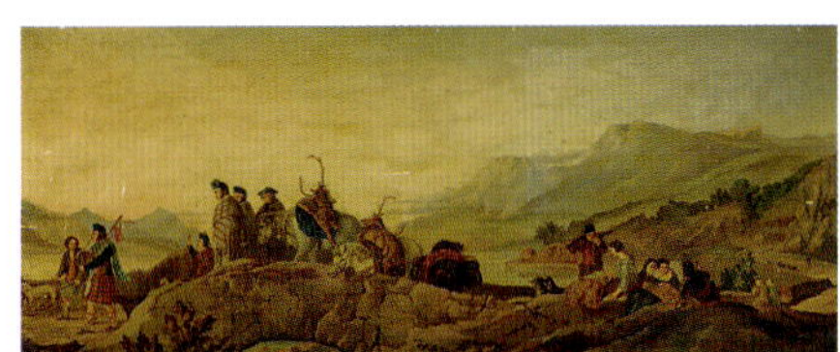

British School 19th C
After the Hunt
oil on card 47.6 x 115
272

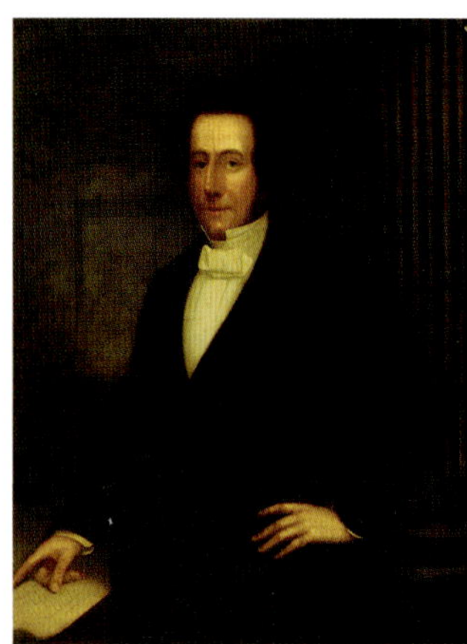

British School 19th C
Alderman Joseph Rankin Stebbing
oil on canvas 111.9 x 86.4
605

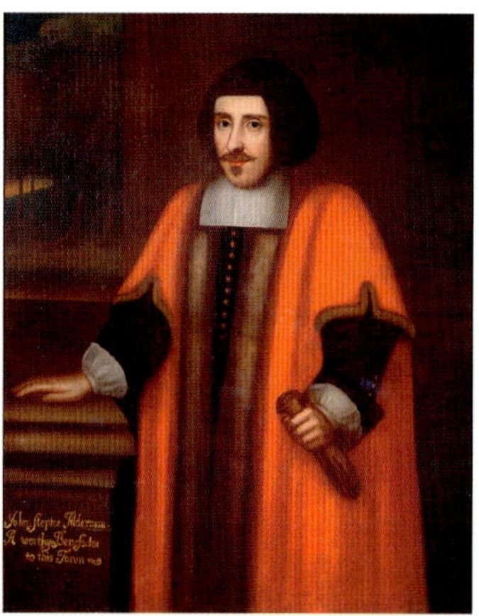

British School 19th C
Alderman Steptoe
oil on canvas 129.3 x 102.5
607

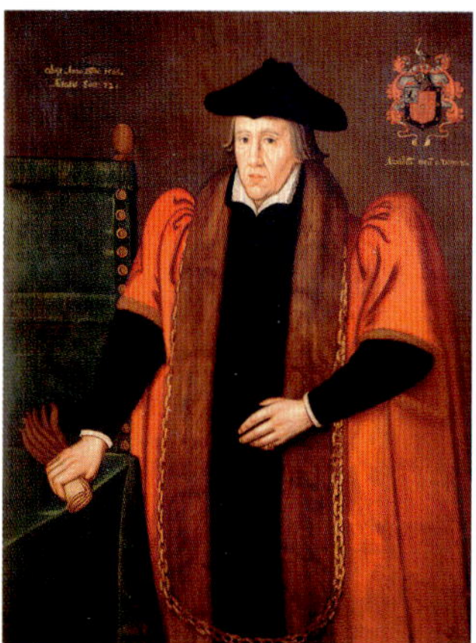

British School 19th C
Alderman Thomas White Miles
oil on canvas 127 x 101.7
608

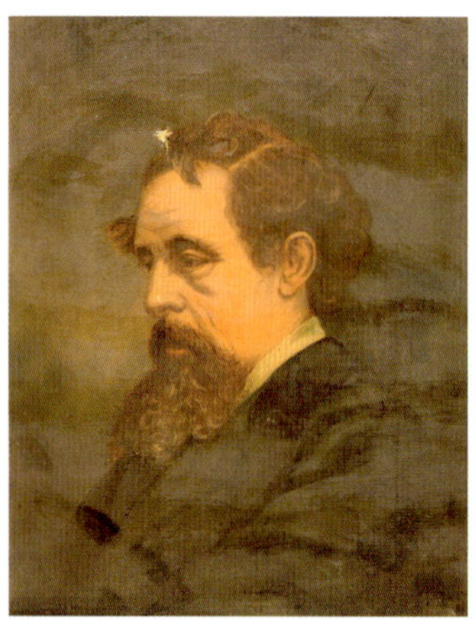

British School 19th C
Charles Dickens (1812–1870)
oil on canvas 28 x 21.7
635

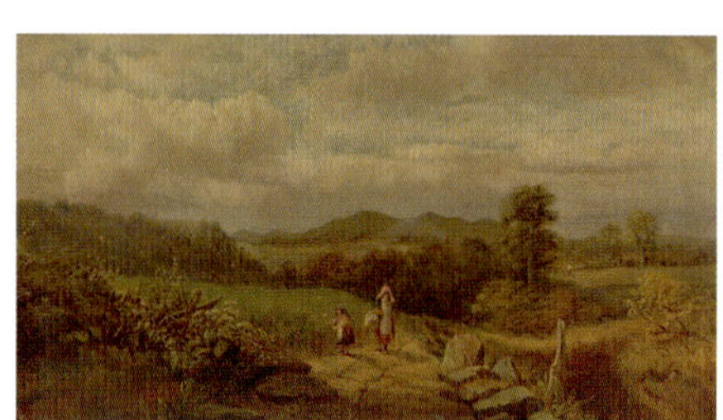

British School 19th C
Children Roaming Heath
oil on canvas 27.9 x 50.5
641

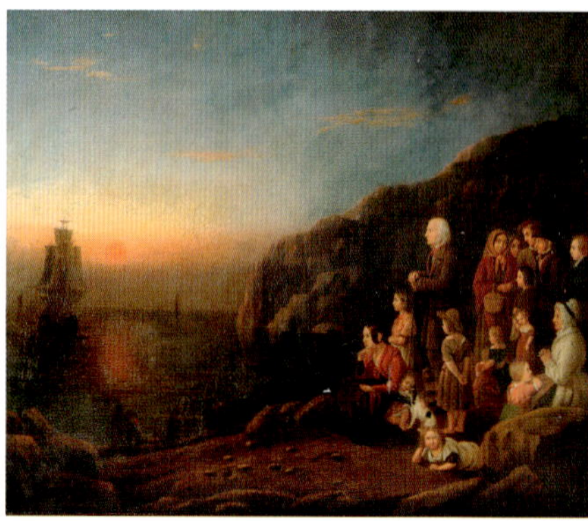

British School 19th C
Departure of the 'Mayflower', 1620
oil on canvas 96.5 x 116.5
630

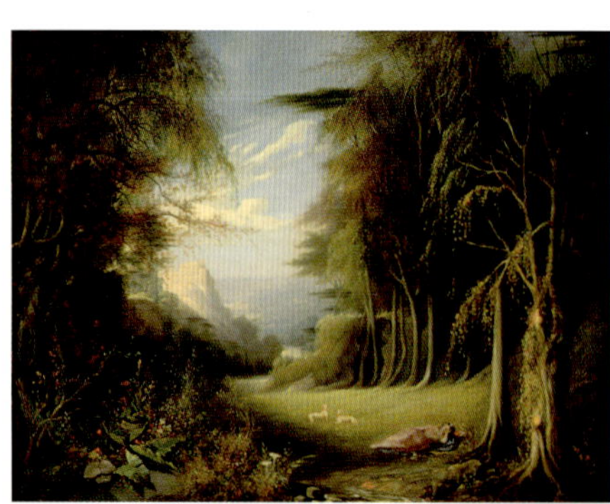

British School 19th C
Diana Asleep in a Woodland Glade
oil on canvas 71 x 91.5
58/1963

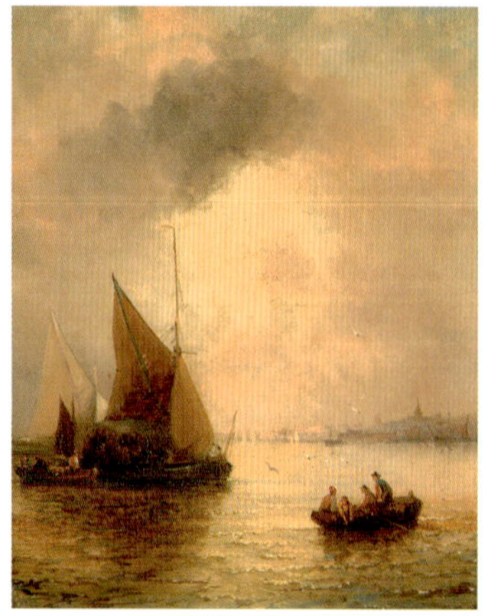

British School 19th C
Fishing Boat Scene
oil on canvas 30.5 x 25.5
644

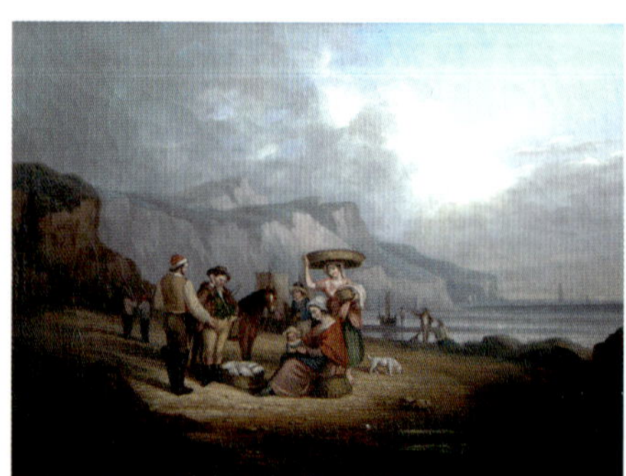

British School 19th C
Fishing Scene, Early Morning
oil on canvas 90 x 112
1384

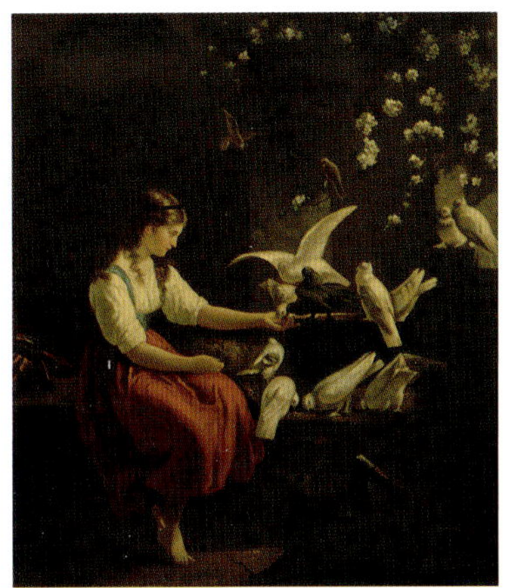

British School 19th C
Girl with Pigeons
oil on canvas 56.2 x 49.6
639

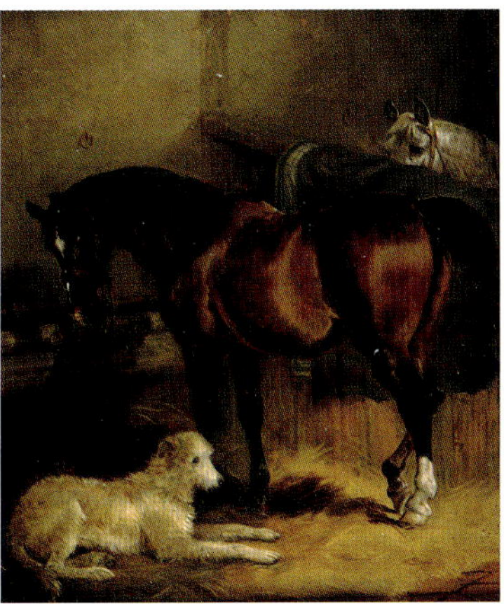

British School 19th C
Horses in Stable
oil on card 30.4 x 25.3
496

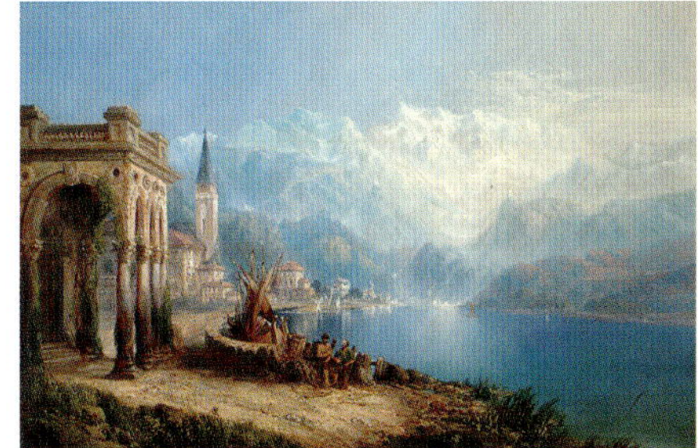

British School 19th C
Italian Landscape (Lake Como)
oil on canvas 61 x 91.5
63

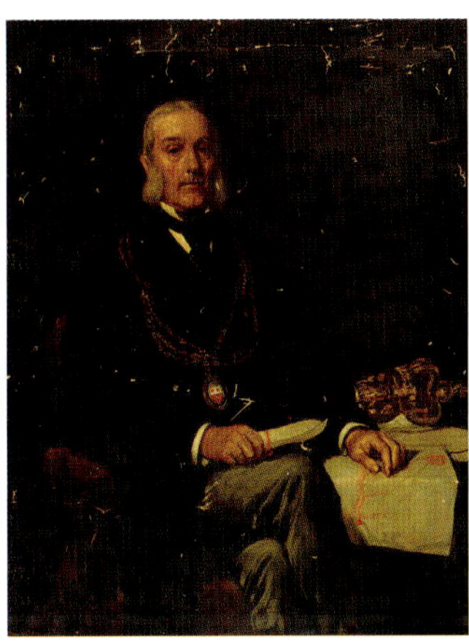

British School 19th C
John Henry Cooksey Esq.
oil on canvas 142.2 x 112.4
606

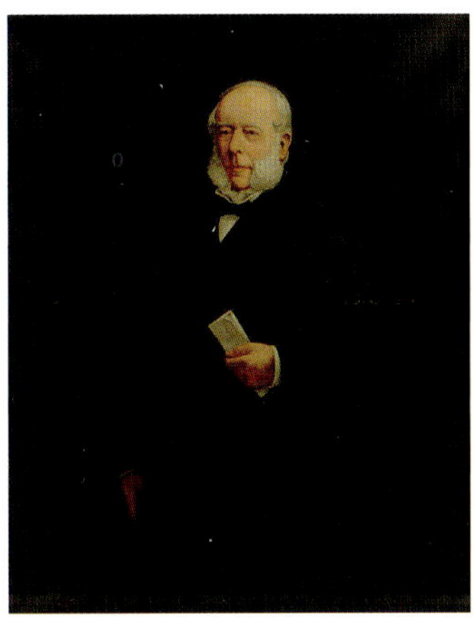

British School 19th C
John Joliffe Esq.
oil on canvas 142.2 x 111.7
598

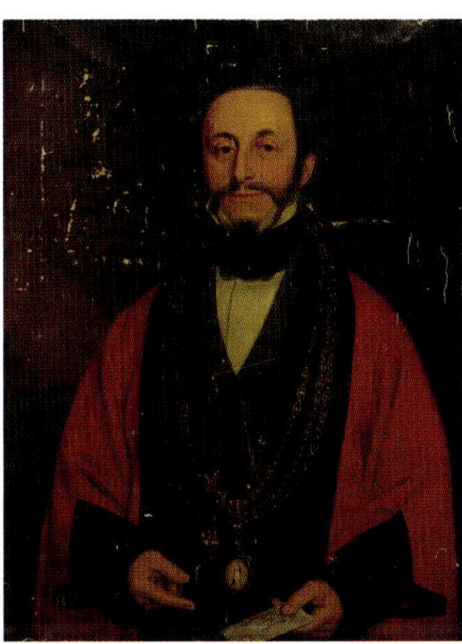

British School 19th C
John Traffles Tucker Esq., Mayor (1853)
oil on canvas 90 x 71
599

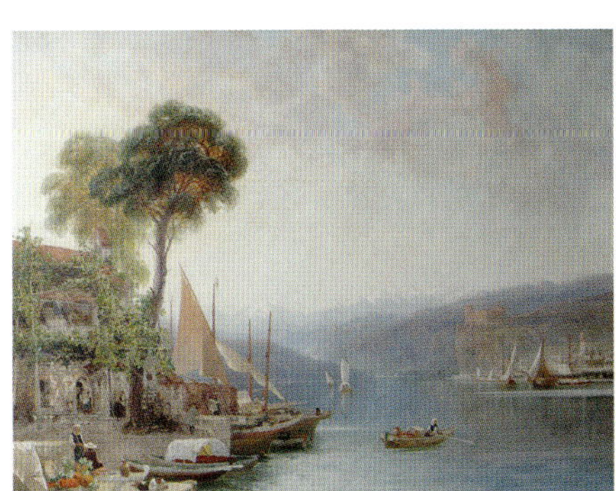

British School 19th C
Lake Como, Italy
oil on canvas 91.5 x 121.5
64

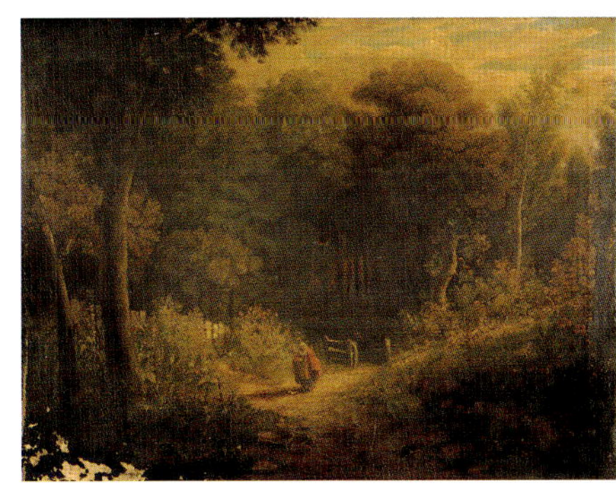

British School 19th C
Landscape with Figure of a Woman
oil on canvas 48.3 x 65.3
653

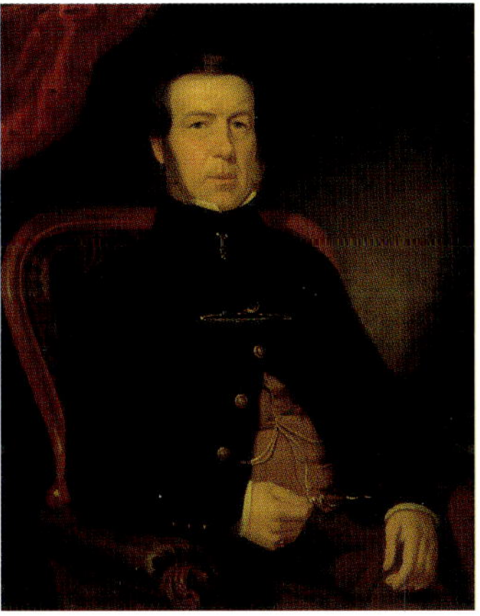

British School 19th C
Mr Andrews
oil on canvas 91.2 x 71.5
610

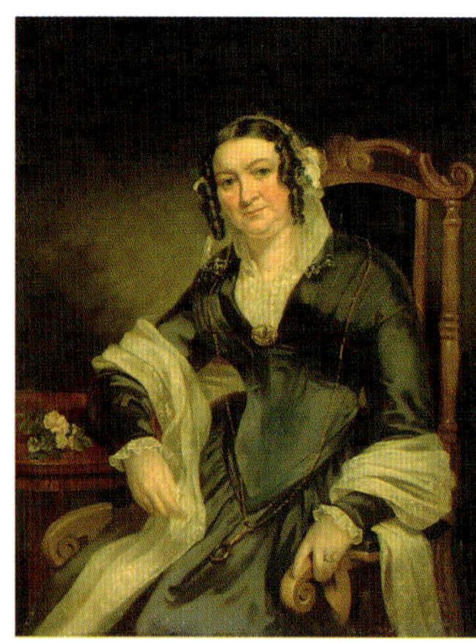

British School 19th C
Mrs Andrews
oil on canvas 91.7 x 71.7
609

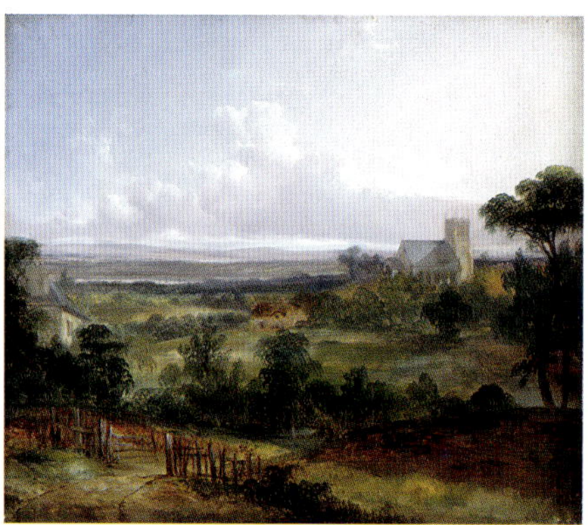

British School 19th C
Old Shirley, Southampton
oil on canvas 30.2 x 35.5
495

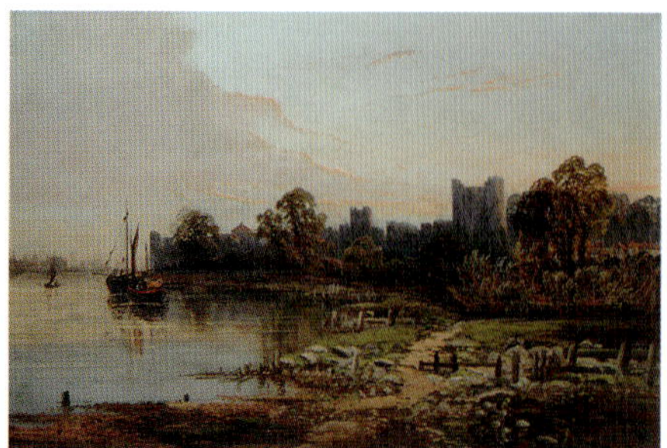

British School 19th C
Porchester Castle
oil on canvas 40.6 x 61
643

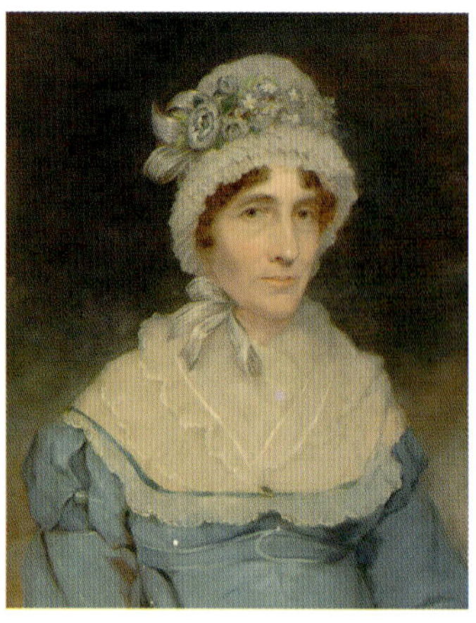

British School 19th C
Portrait of a Lady
oil on canvas 60.3 x 48.4
10/1979

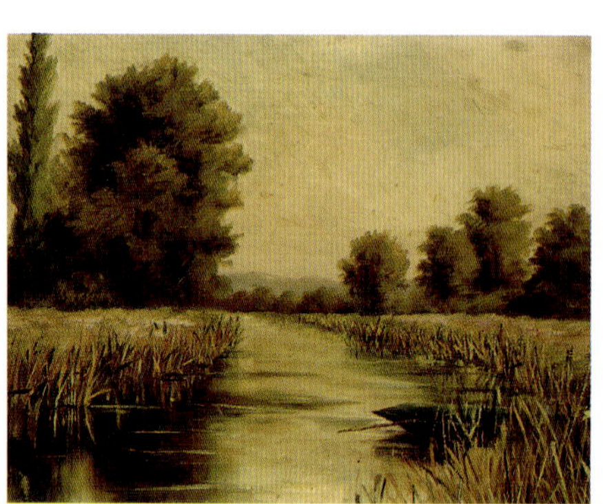

British School 19th C
River Itchen
oil on canvas 25.3 x 32.9
638

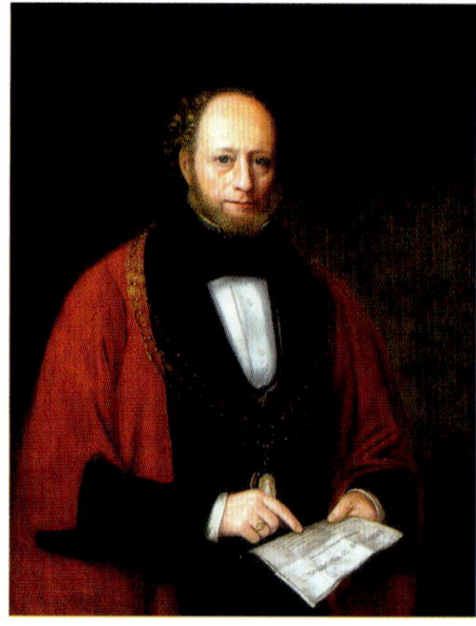

British School 19th C
Samson Payne, Mayor of Southampton
oil on canvas 91.5 x 70.5
600

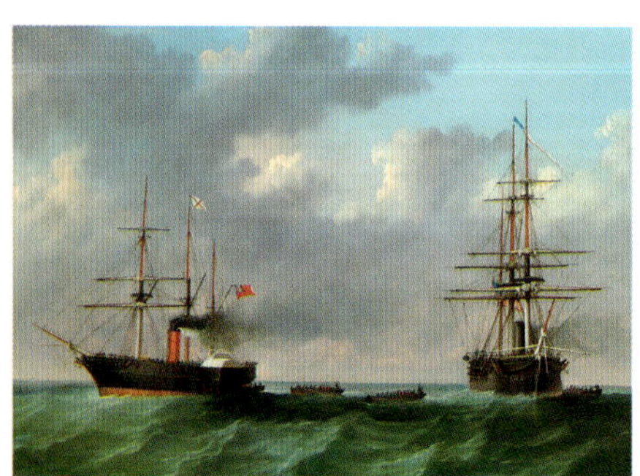

British School 19th C
'San Jacinto' and 'Trent Affair'
oil on canvas 59.4 x 77.5
636

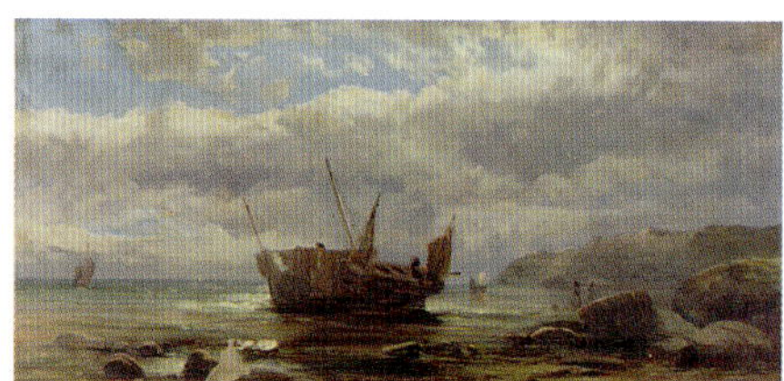

British School 19th C
Ship Ashore
oil on canvas 51.5 x 58.5
642

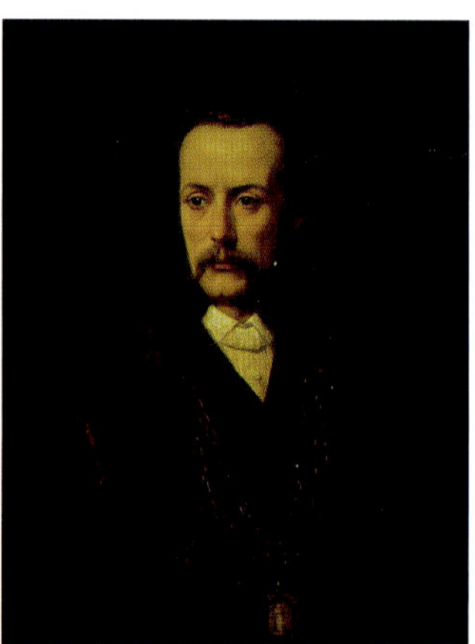

British School 19th C
Sir Frederick Perkins (detail)
oil on canvas 239.3 x 148
601

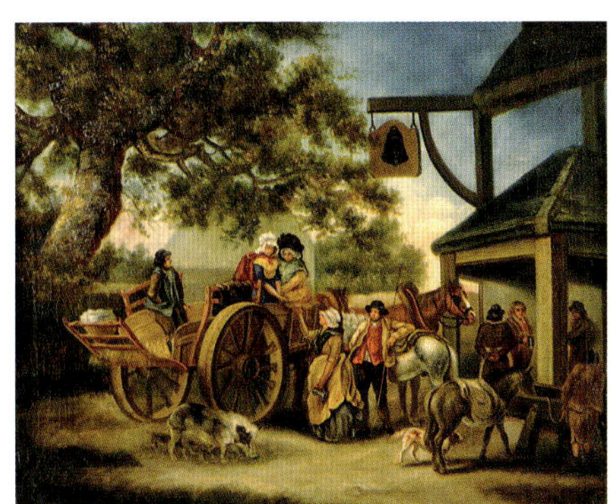

British School 19th C
'The Bell' Inn
oil on canvas 44.5 x 57
494

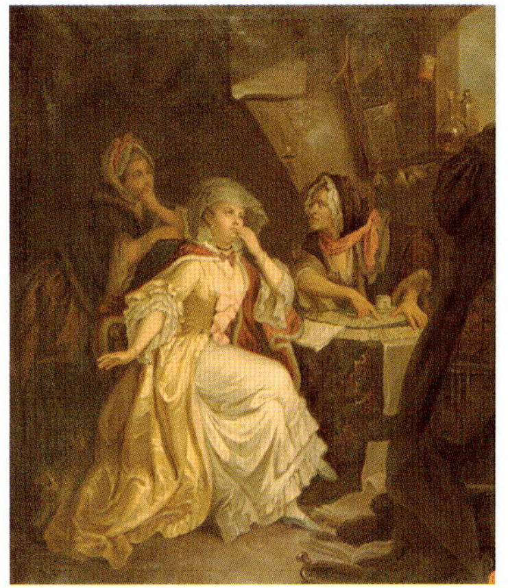

British School 19th C
The Fortune Teller
oil on canvas 56.5 x 48
640

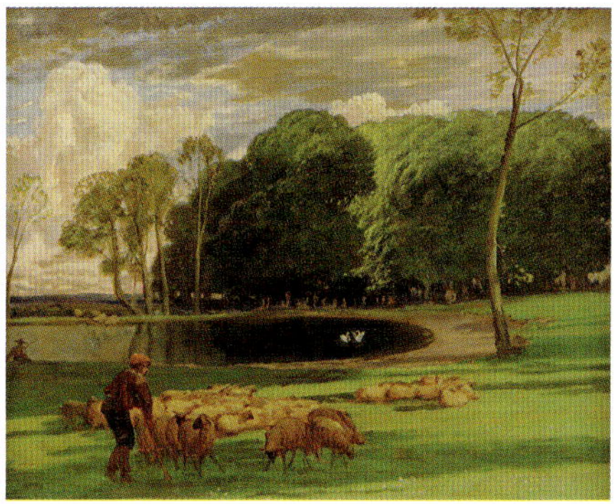

British School 19th C
The Round Pool, Kensington Gardens
oil on canvas 30 x 38.5
1063

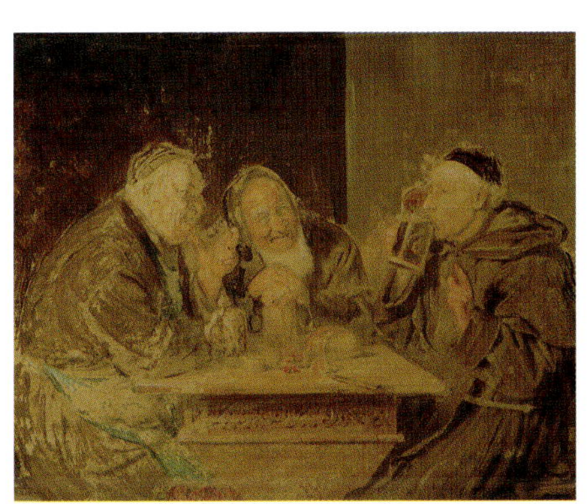

British School 19th C
Three Monks
oil on wood 19.9 x 25.3
637

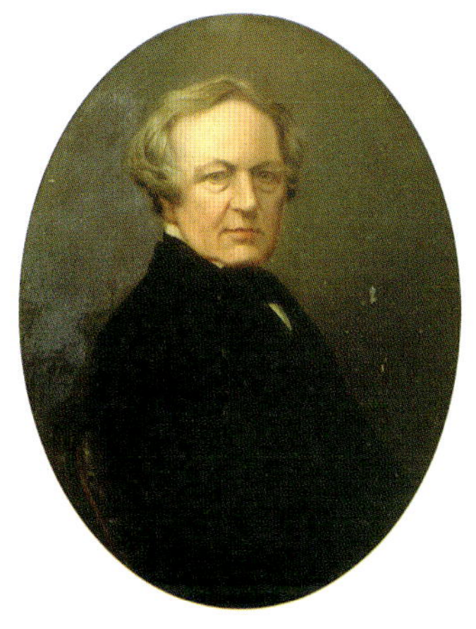

British School 19th C
William Charles Macready (1793–1873)
oil on card 26 x 21
634

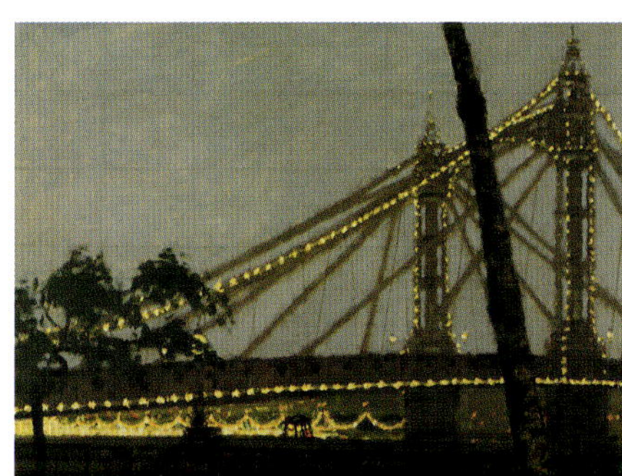

Brockhurst, Gerald Leslie 1890–1978
The Albert Bridge 1953
oil on canvas 55.9 x 76.3
1441

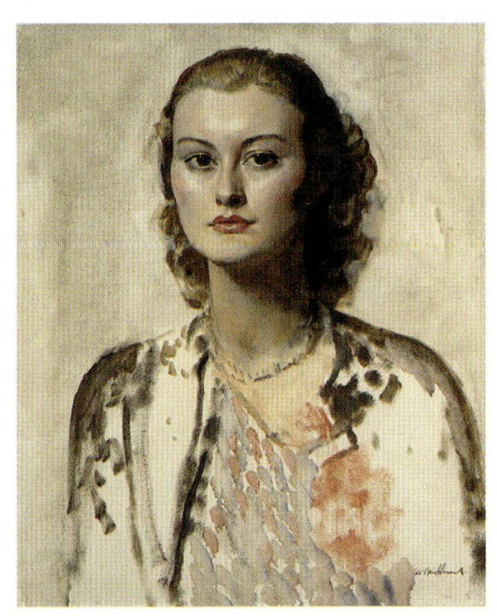

Brockhurst, Gerald Leslie 1890–1978
Portrait of a Girl
oil on canvas 52 x 41
90

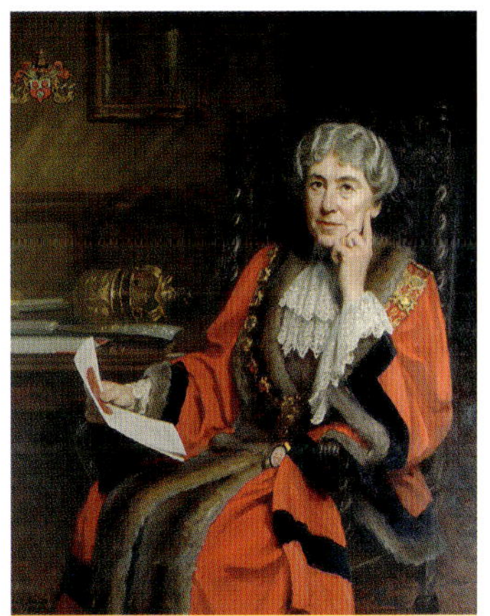

Brooks, Frank 1854–1937
Alderman Mrs L. Foster Welch, JP 1928
oil on canvas 122.3 x 101.6
93

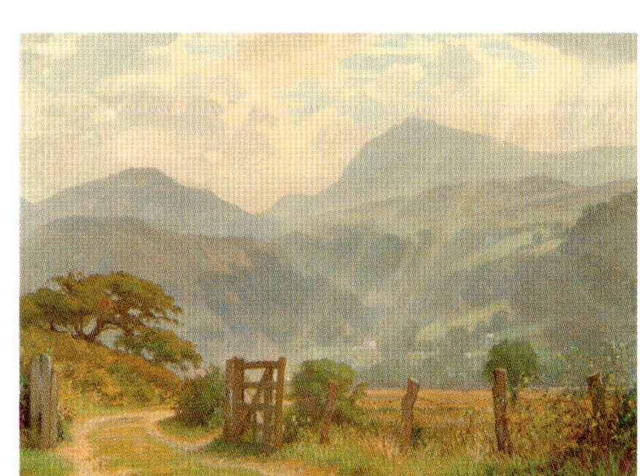

Brooks, Frank 1854–1937
Misty Morning, Cader Idris
oil on canvas 86.4 x 122.1
94

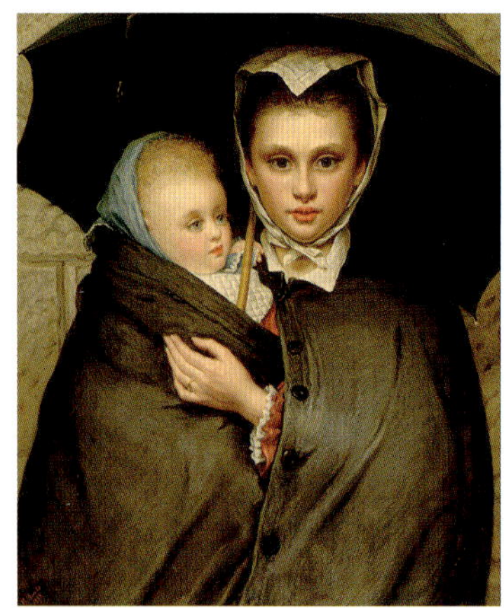

Brooks, Maria 1837–1913
Out in the Rain
oil on canvas 76.5 x 63.7
95

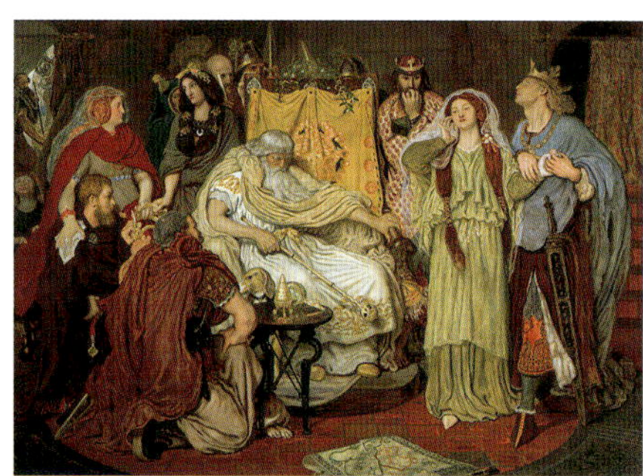

Brown, Ford Madox 1821–1893
Cordelia's Portion
oil on canvas 79.5 x 111.8
97

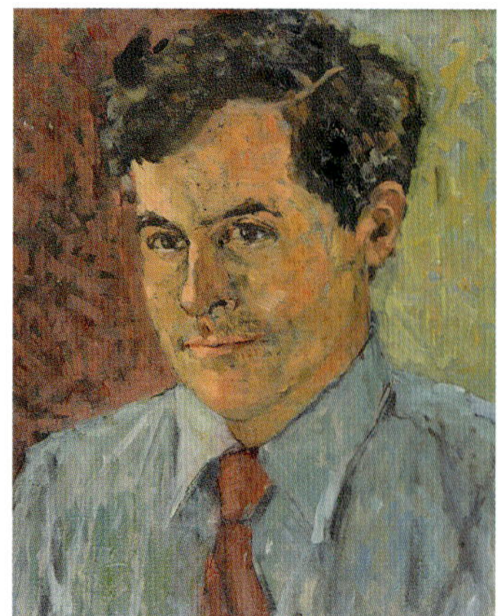

Brown, Jean
David Brown
oil on canvas 51.7 x 42.8
32/2002

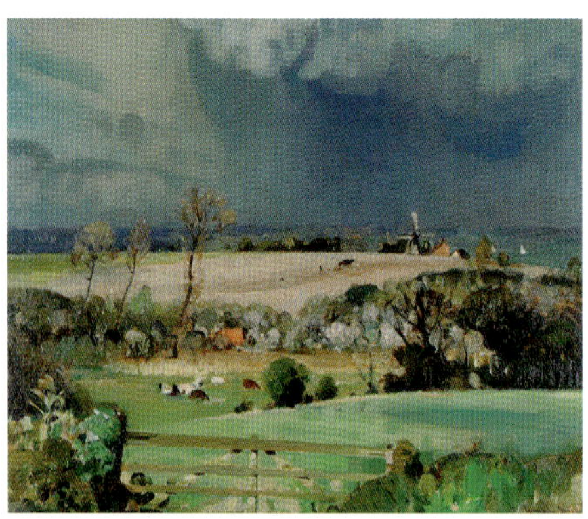

Brown, John Alfred Arnesby 1866–1955
Spring
oil on canvas 43.5 x 55.8
96

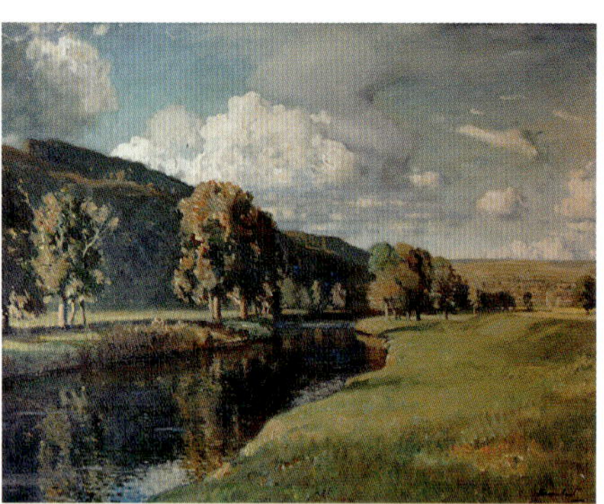

Brundrit, Reginald Grange 1883–1960
Autumn by the River
oil on canvas 76.5 x 102
98

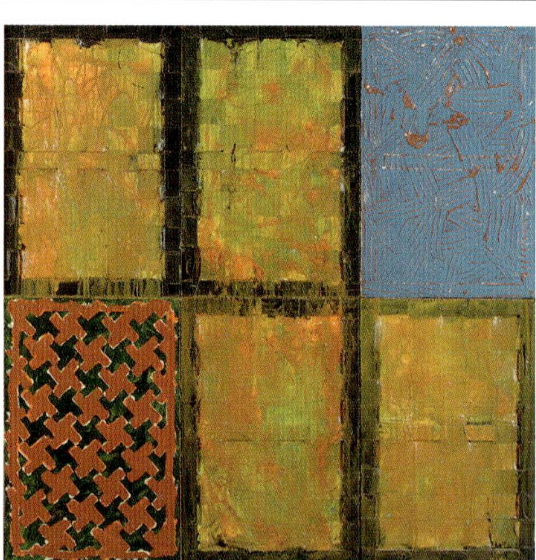

Buckley, Stephen b.1944
V S A 1973
PVA & oil on canvas 182.9 x 182.9
4/1979

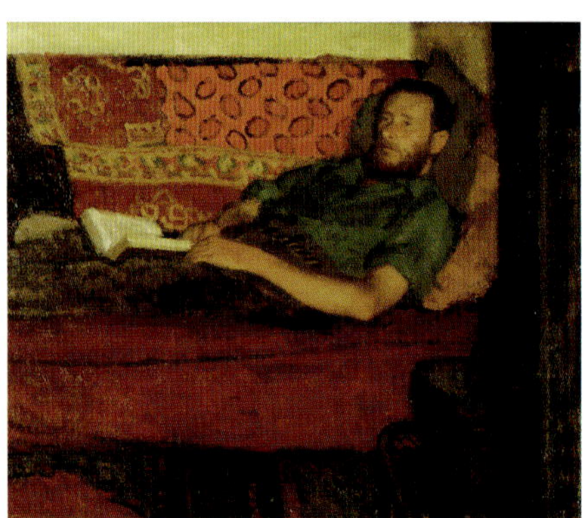

Buhler, Robert A. 1916–1989
Robert Kitchener
oil on canvas 46 x 55.5
1294

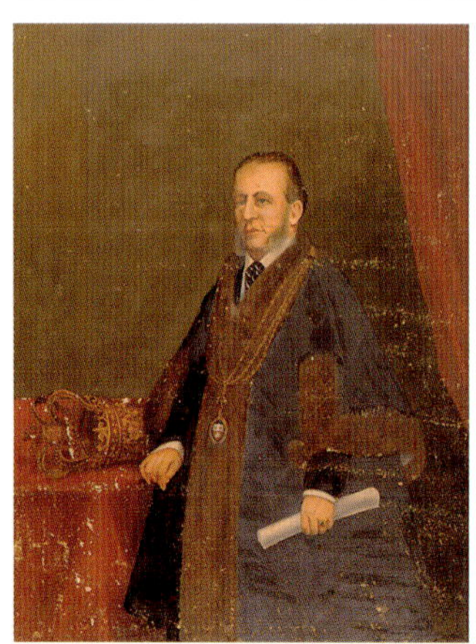

Burcher, Frank P.
H. J. Buchan, Mayor of Southampton (1871)
oil on canvas 91.3 x 71.2
99

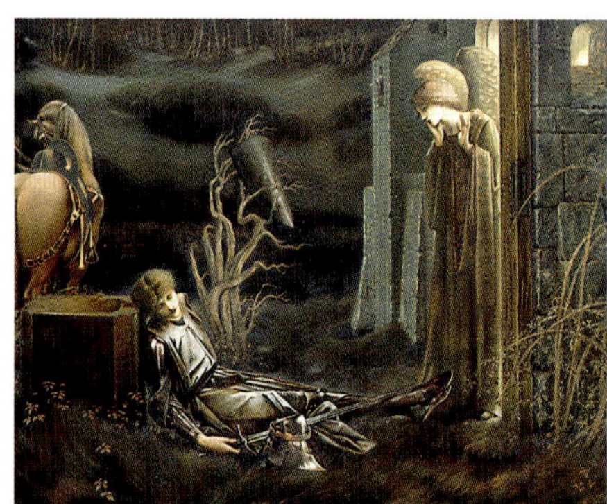

Burne-Jones, Edward 1833–1898
Lancelot at the Chapel of the Holy Grail 1896
oil on canvas 138.5 x 169.8
3/1958

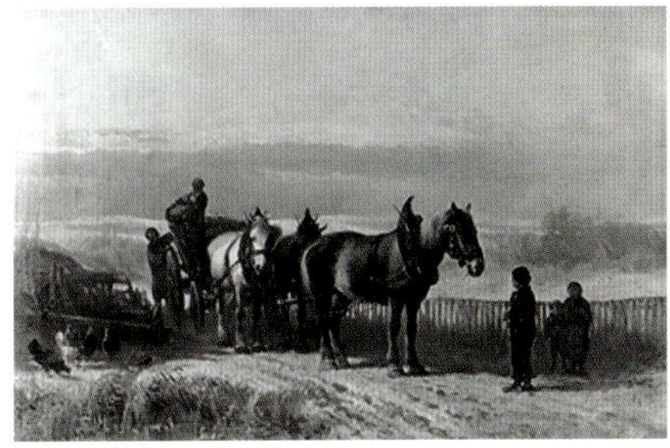

Bylandt, Alfred Edouard Agenor van 1829–1890
Wagon and Team
oil on canvas 53 x 81.5
111

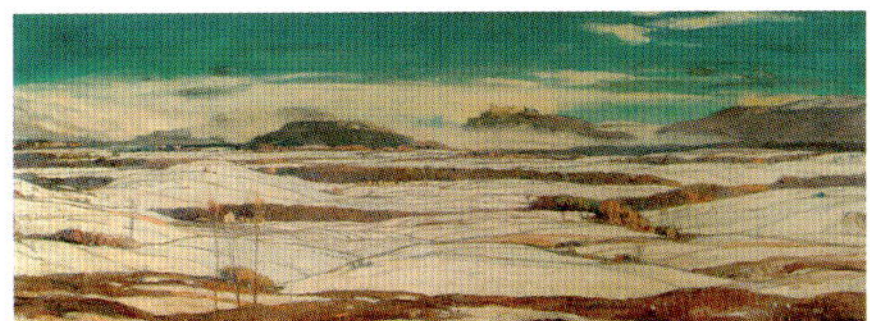

Cameron, David Young 1865–1945
Autumn Snows, Menteith
oil on canvas 66.3 x 183.2
114

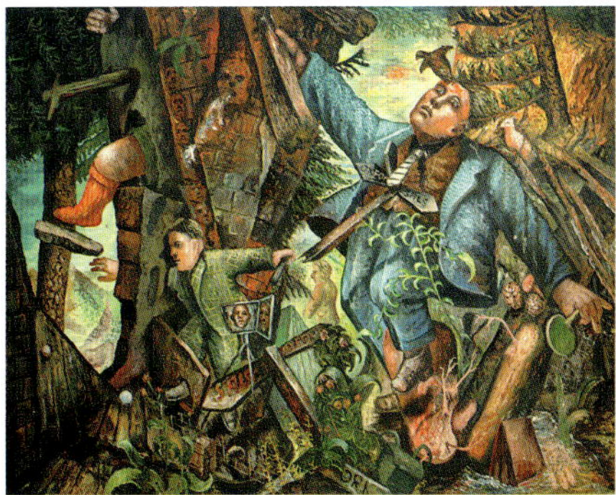

Campbell, Steven b.1953
The Fall of the House of Nook with Tree Blight 1984
oil on canvas 277.1 x 355.6
3/1985

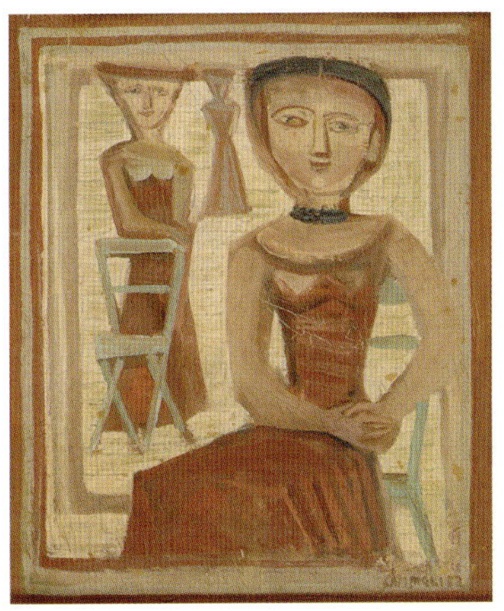

Campigli, Massimo 1895–1971
Three Figures
oil on canvas 37.2 x 31.1
92/1963

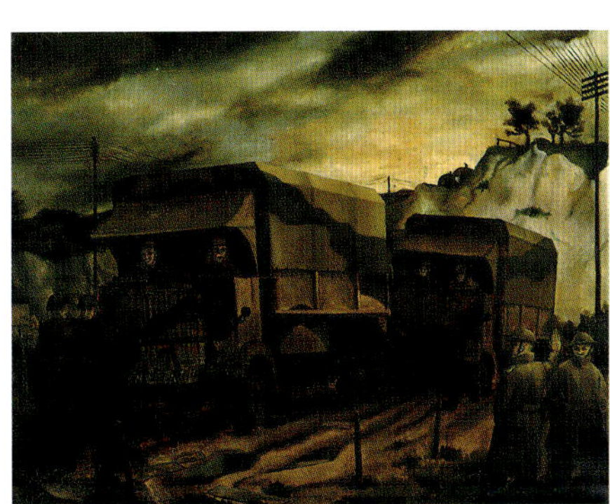

Carpenter, Patrick active 1939–1946
Ammunition Column Moving out 1942
oil on canvas 71.8 x 92.1
1312

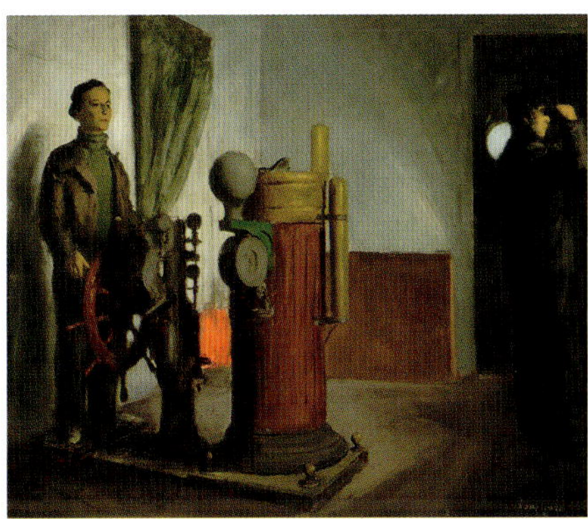

Carr, Henry Marvell 1894–1970
Merchant Navy, the Bridge
oil on canvas 62.5 x 76.2
1313

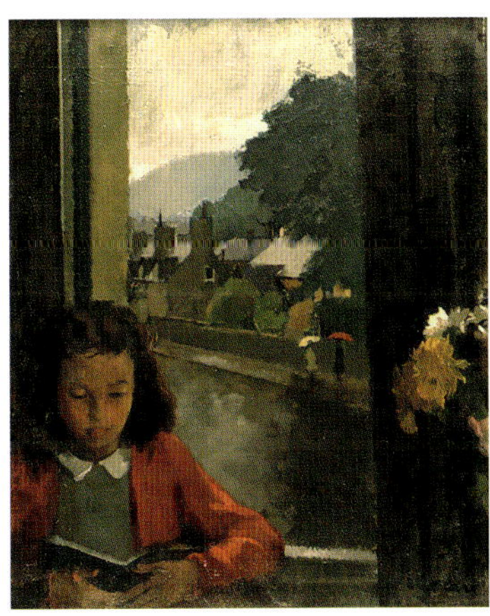

Carr, Thomas 1909–1999
Wet Day
oil on canvas 61 x 50.8
1295

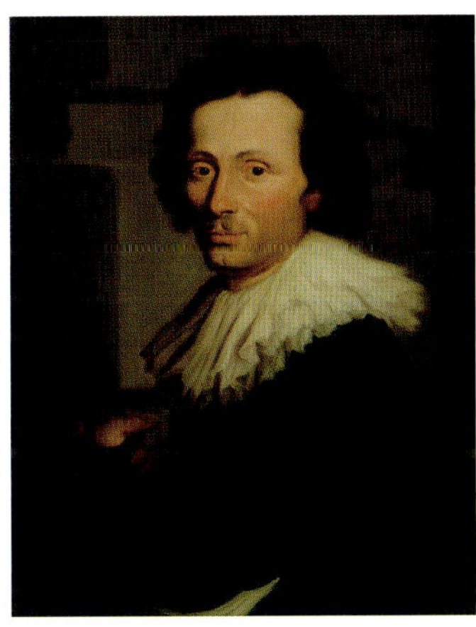

Cassana, Niccolò (copy after) 1659–1713
Portrait of an Artist 19th C
oil on canvas 73.4 x 58.8
3/1968

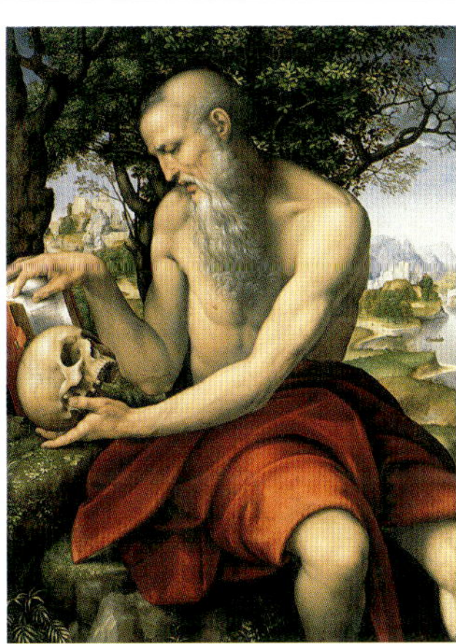

Cesare da Sesto 1477–1523
St Jerome 1520
oil on wood 80.3 x 60.7
2/1958

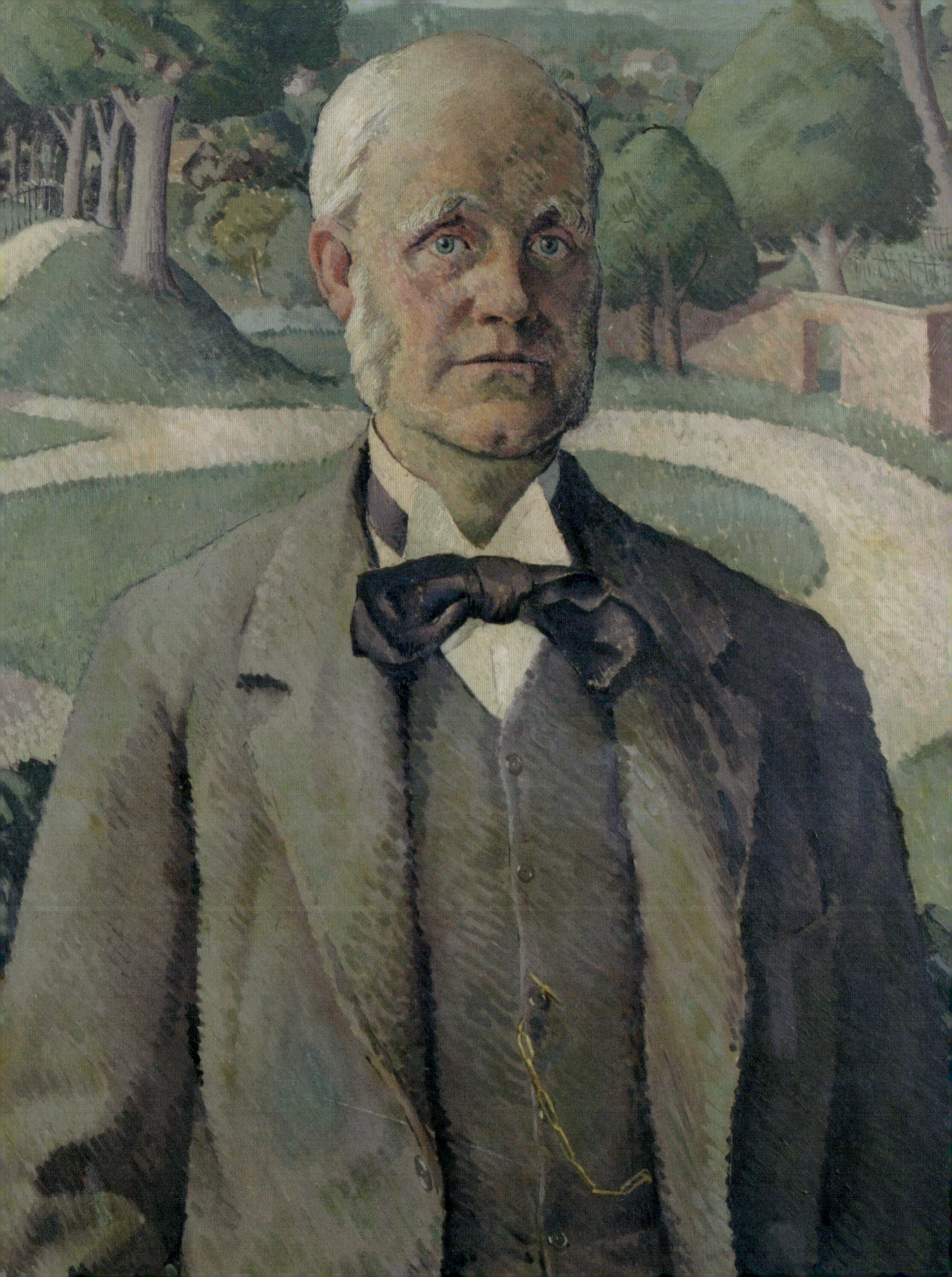

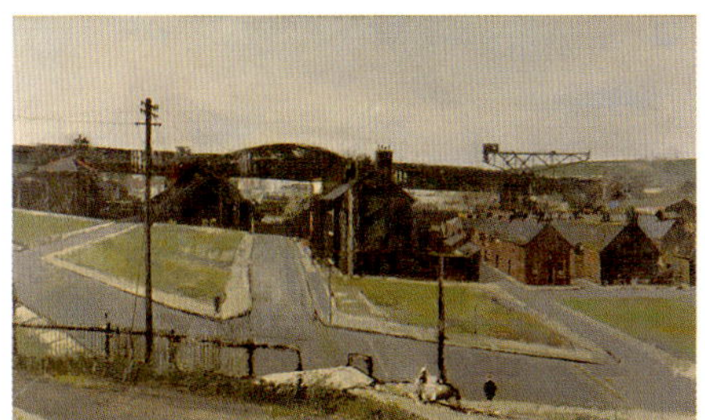

Chamberlain, Christopher 1918–1984
Middlesborough
oil on board 60 x 103
1437

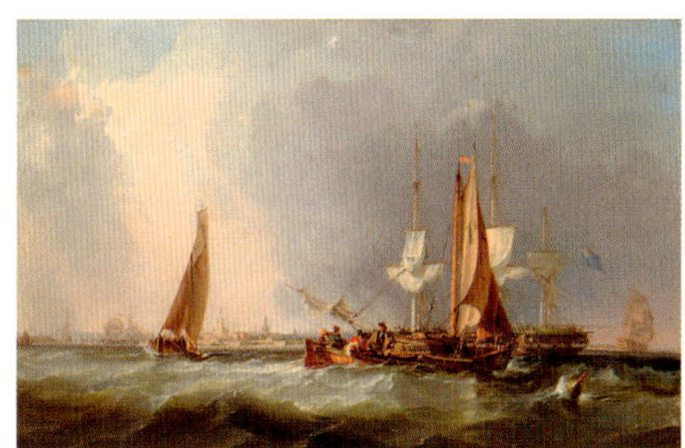

Chambers, George 1803–1840
Portsmouth
oil on canvas 46.5 x 76.3
1342

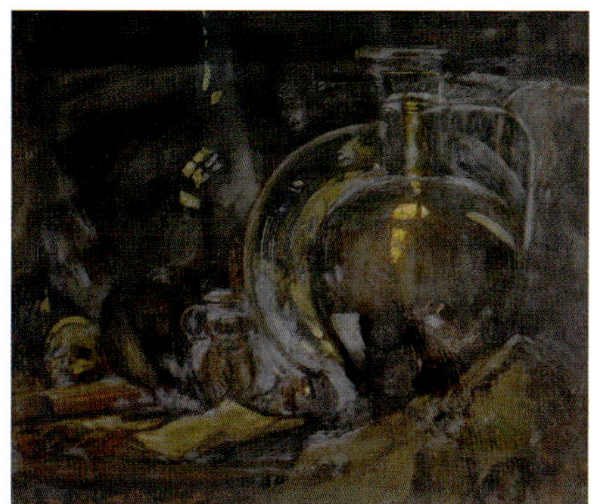

Chambers, H. P. (Mrs)
Antiques
oil on canvas 50.8 x 61
116

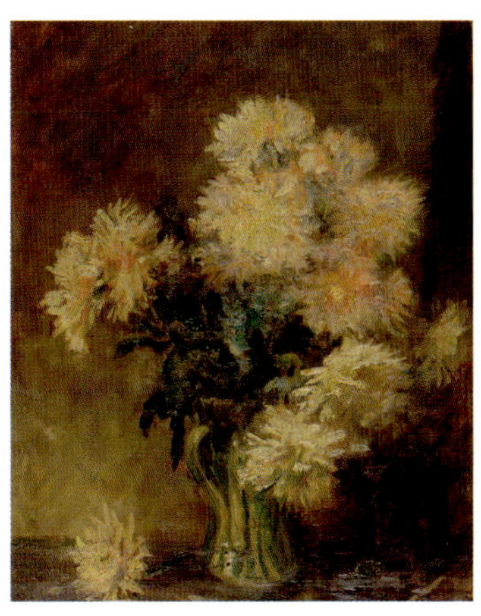

Chambers, H. P. (Mrs)
Chrysanthemums
oil on canvas 50.9 x 41.5
117

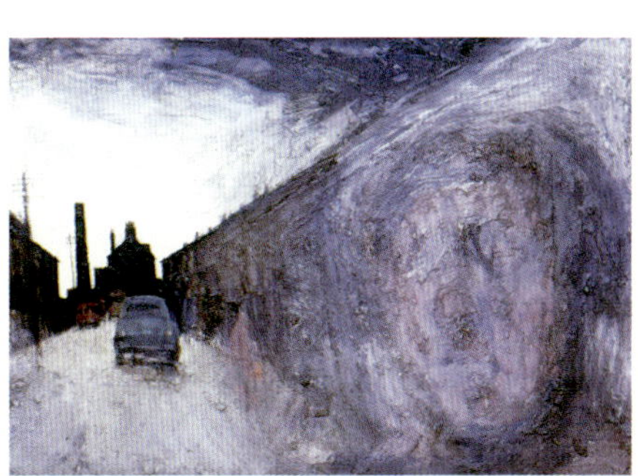

Chapman, George 1908–1993
Old Woman Passing
oil on board 61 x 75.8
2/1967

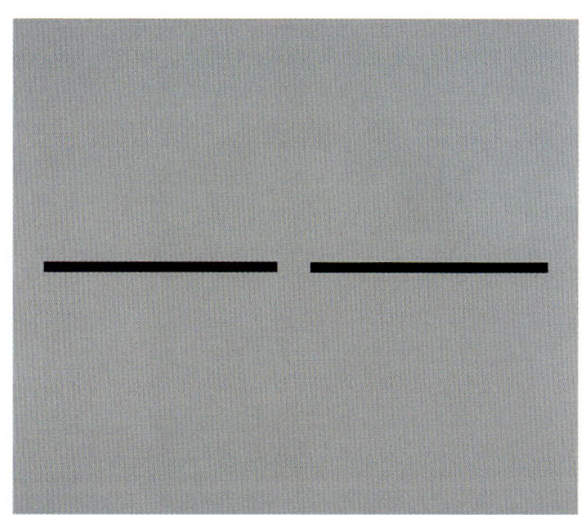

Charlton, Alan b.1948
Slot Painting
acrylic on canvas 230 x 270
1/1985

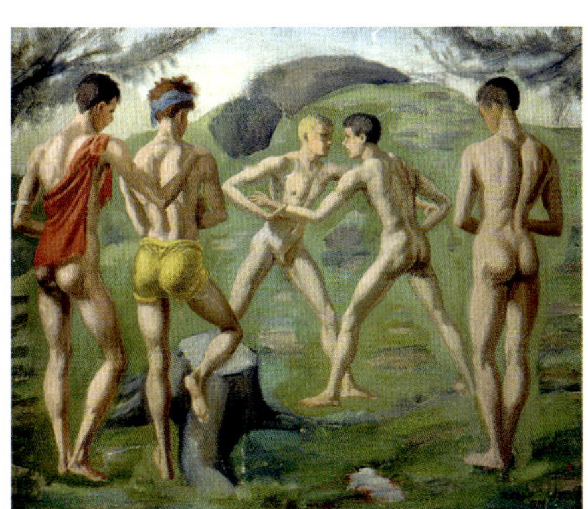

Chubb, Ralph Nicholas 1892–1960
The Bathers 1924
oil on canvas 51.5 x 61
1453

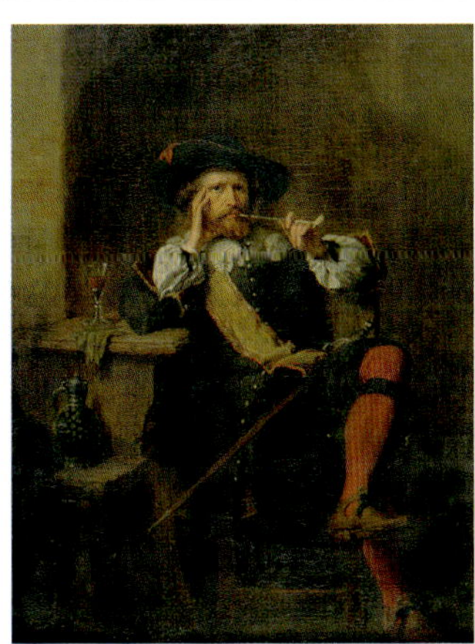

Claes, Constant Guillaume 1826–1905
Man Smoking 1853
oil on canvas 30.3 x 23
201

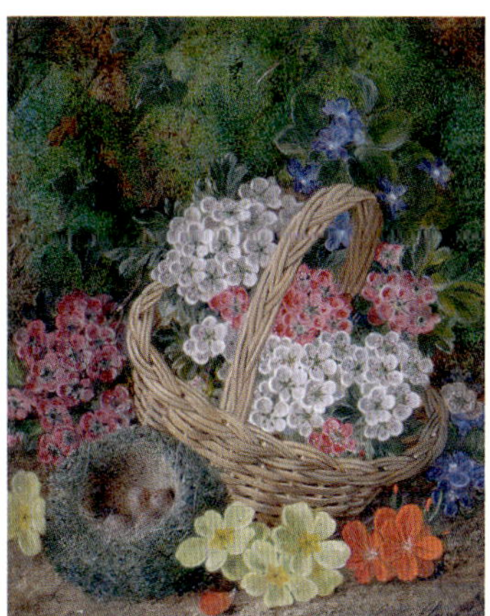

Clare, George c.1830–c.1900
Basket with Flowers
oil on canvas 30.5 x 25.5
367

Facing page: Daniels, Leonard, 1909–1998, *Portrait of an Unknown Man (possibly a headmaster of Tauntons School)* (detail), 1936, Southampton City Museums, (p. 151)

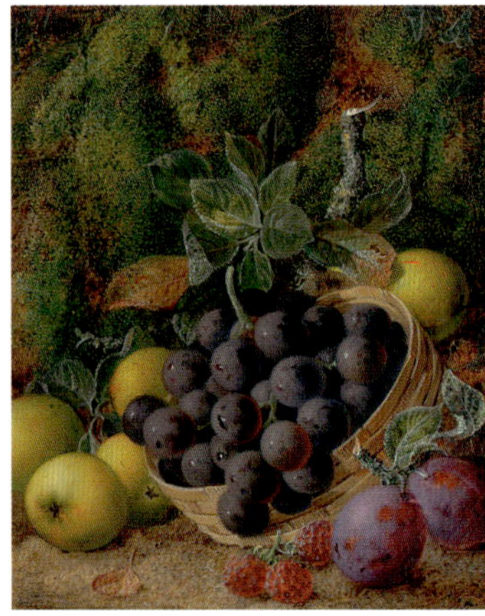

Clare, George c.1830–c.1900
Grapes
oil on canvas 30.5 x 25.5
377

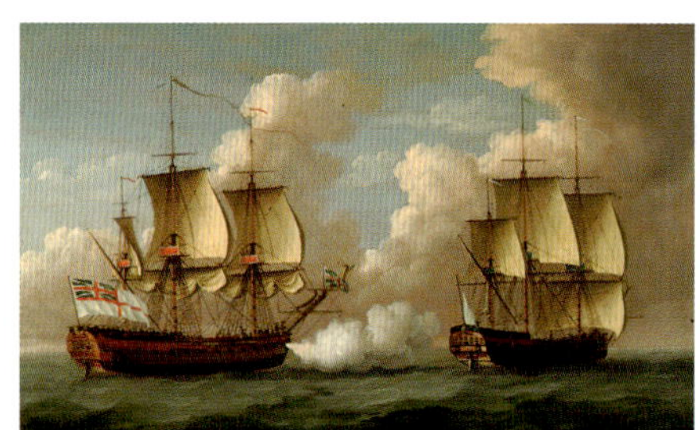

Cleveley, John c.1712–1777
'HMS Brune' Captures French Ship 'L'oiseau'
oil on canvas 74.5 x 119.8
118

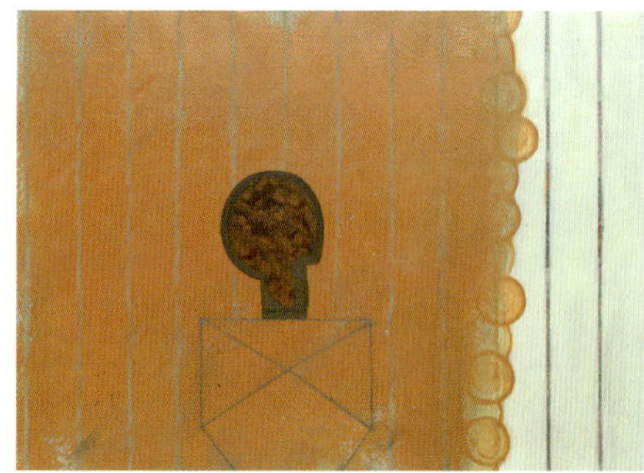

Clough, Prunella 1919–1999
Plinth 1995
oil on canvas 66.6 x 93.9
7/1996

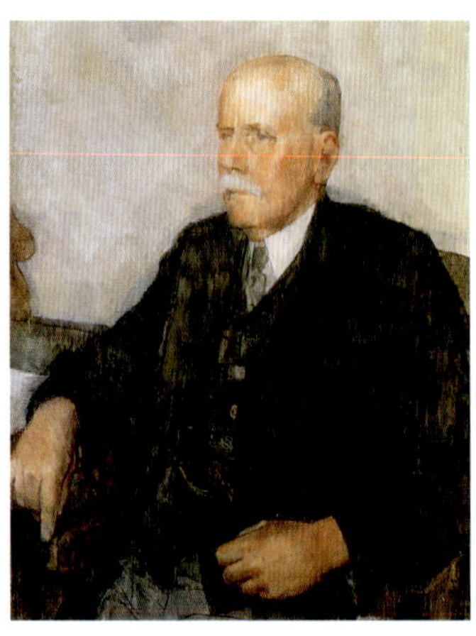

Coldstream, William Menzies 1908–1987
E. A. Smith-Rewse 1937
oil on canvas 91.5 x 71.3
1/1969

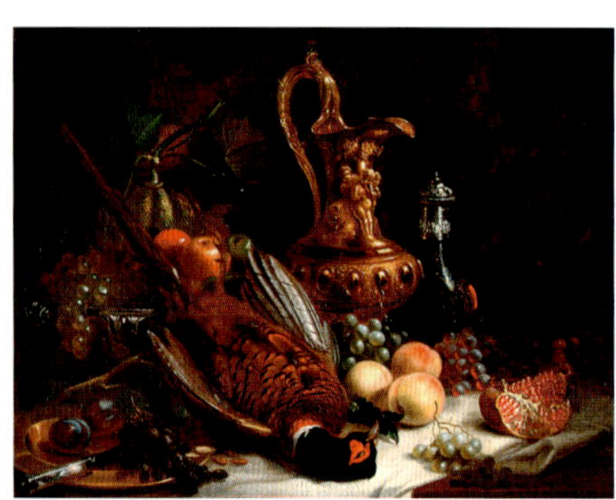

Cole, George 1810–1883
Still Life with Pheasant 1847
oil on canvas 71.8 x 92
1250

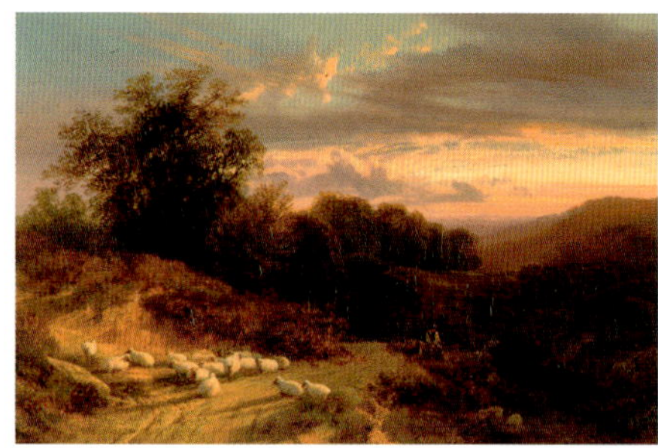

Cole, George 1810–1883
Evening in Hampshire 1872
oil on canvas 51.1 x 76.6
120

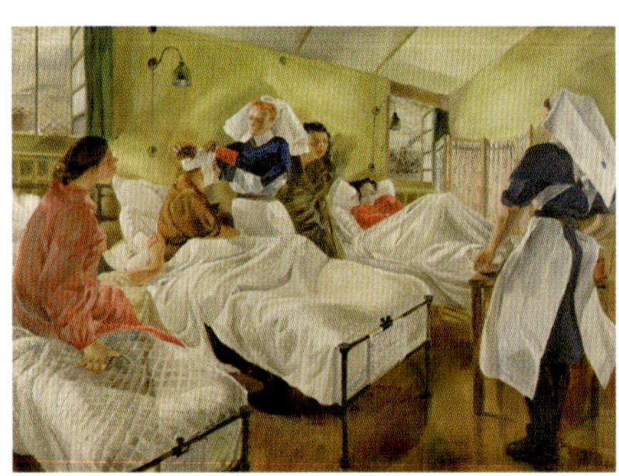

Cole, Leslie 1910–1976
Naval Base: Women's Royal Naval Service Sick Bay 1942
oil on canvas 54.5 x 77.4
1311

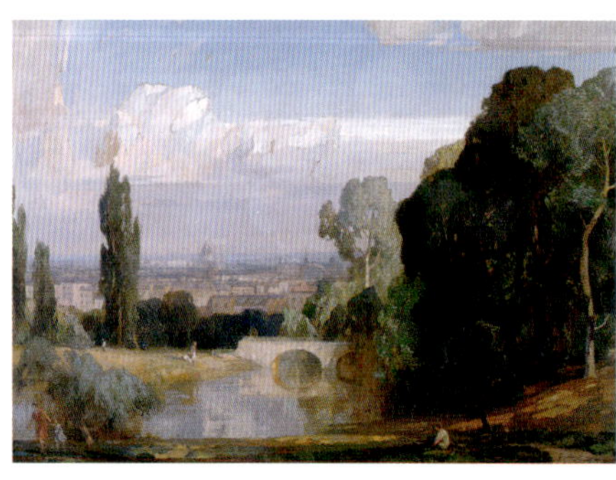

Cole, Rex Vicat 1870–1940
London from Waterloo Park, Highgate 1926
oil on canvas 91.7 x 127.5
4/1968

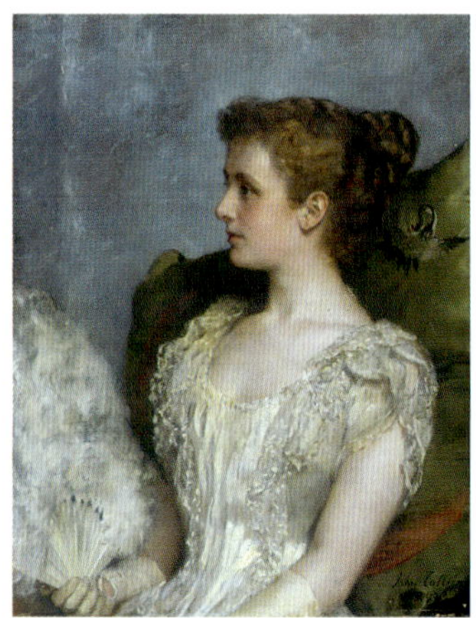

Collier, John 1850–1934
Lady Darling 1892
oil on canvas 77.1 x 64.2
1386

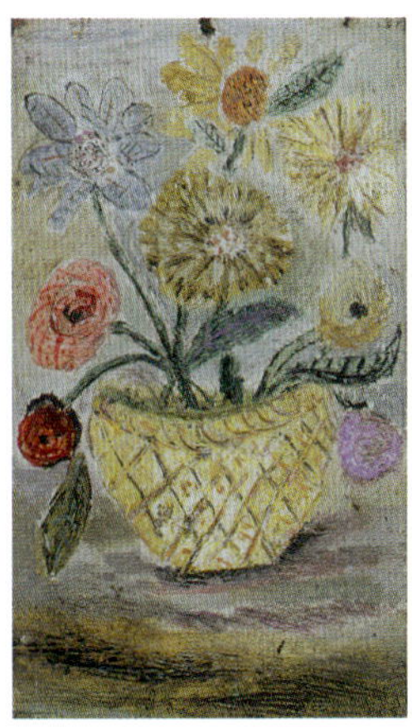

Collins, Cecil 1908–1989
Flowers 1932
oil on board 23.9 x 13.6
61/2002

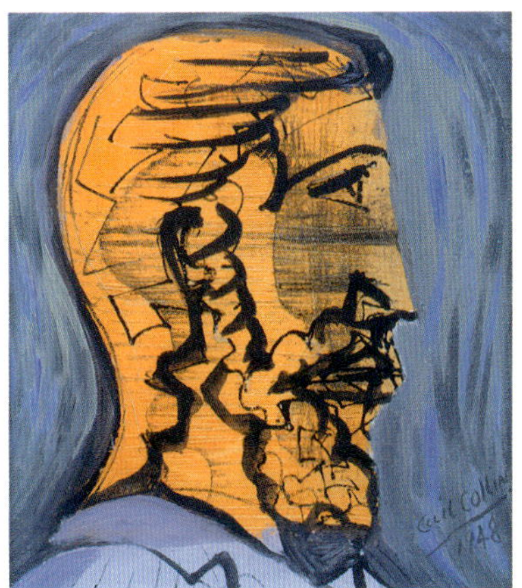

Collins, Cecil 1908–1989
Portrait of the Artist 1948
oil on canvas 37.1 x 34.2
31/2002

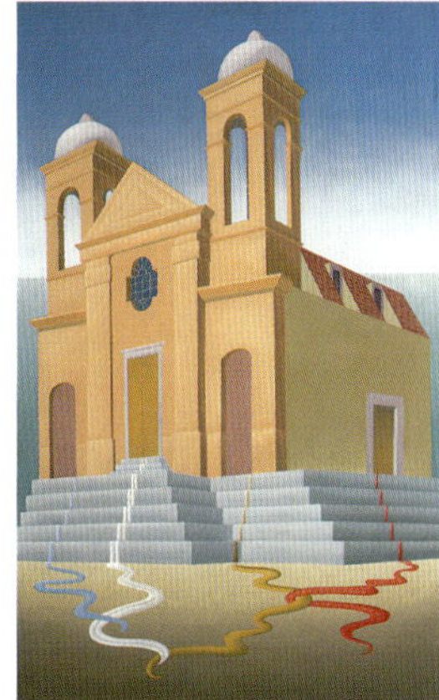

Colquhoun, Ithell 1906–1988
Rivières tièdes (Mediterranée) 1939
oil on wood 91.1 x 61.2
46/1977

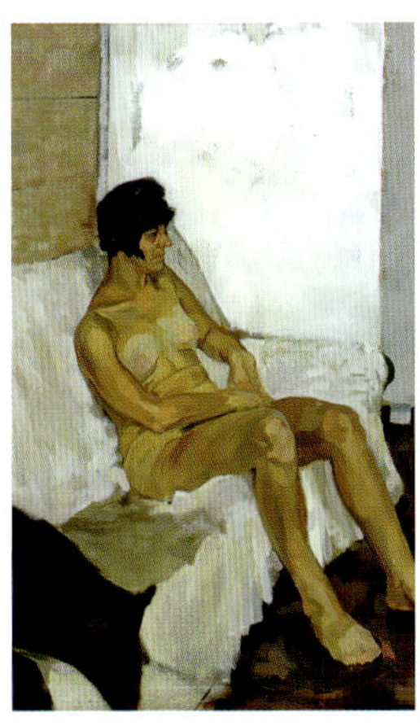

Conroy, Stephen b.1964
The Australian 1985
oil on canvas 140.3 x 89.4
107/2002

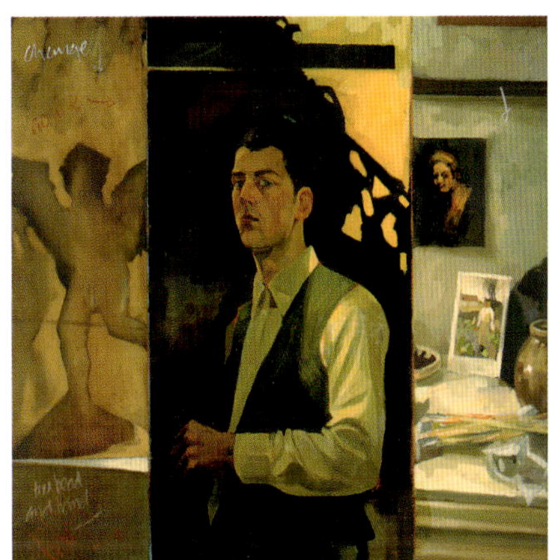

Conroy, Stephen b.1964
Self Portrait
oil on canvas 105.5 x 105.5
209/2002

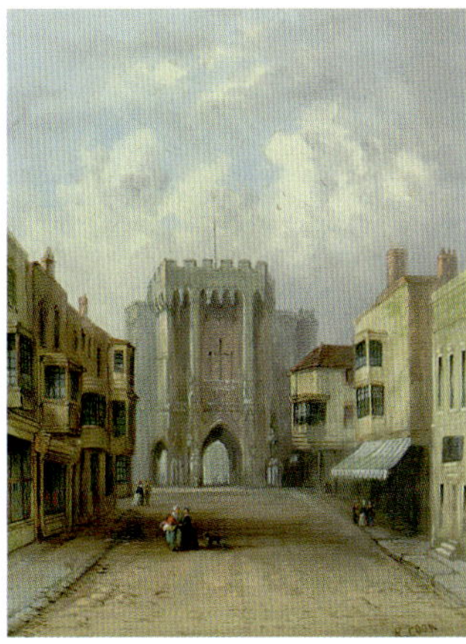

Cook, Richard 1784–1857
High Street and Bargate, Southampton
oil on canvas 41 x 30.9
1274

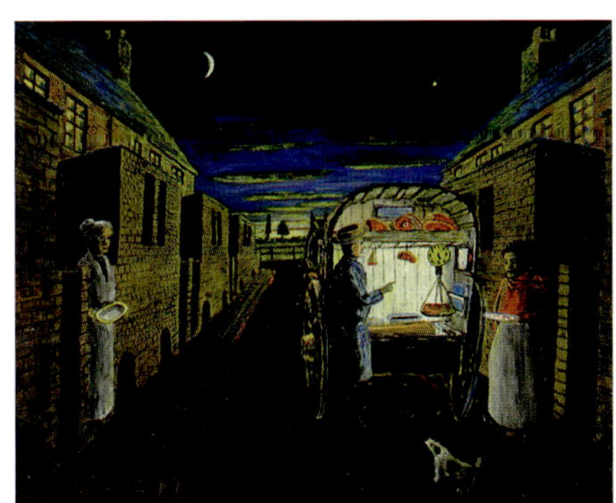

Cooper, Herbert
The Butcher's Van
oil on board 42.6 x 53
27/2002

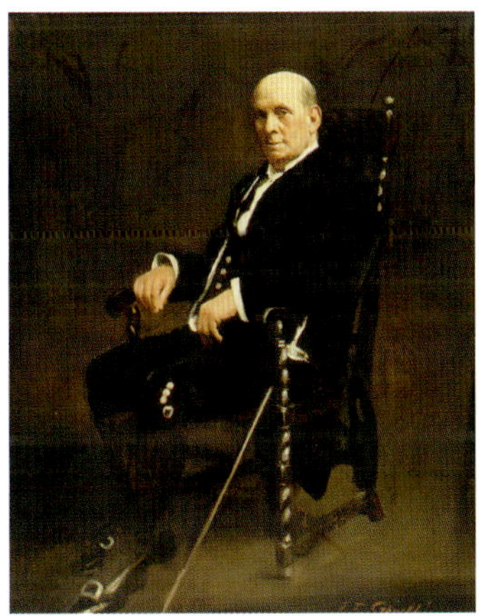

Copnall, Frank T. 1870–1949
Sir Russell Bencraft, JP
oil on canvas 127.5 x 102.3
1247

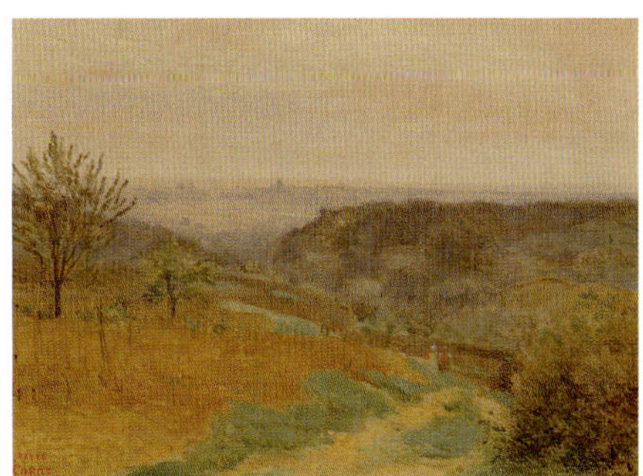

Corot, Jean-Baptiste-Camille 1796–1875
Ville d'Avray 1851
oil on canvas 23.9 x 33.7
15/1972

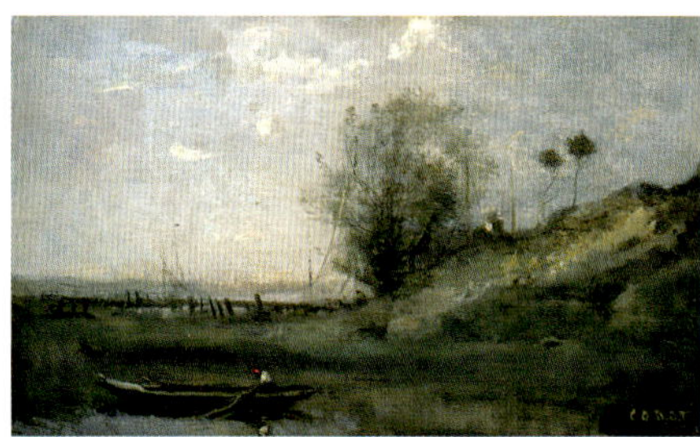

Corot, Jean-Baptiste-Camille 1796–1875
Breakwater in Normandy
oil on canvas 23.5 x 39
1288

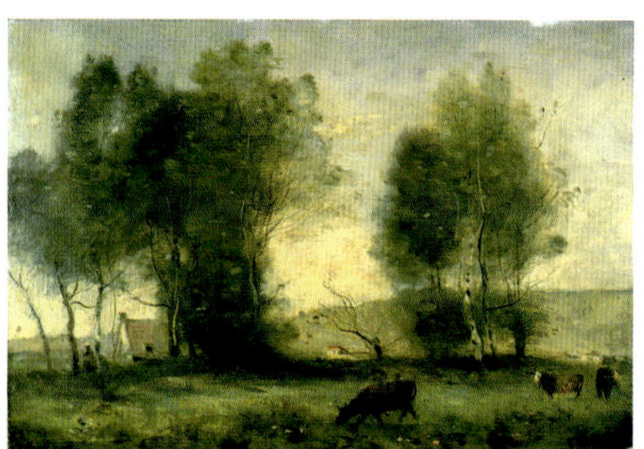

Corot, Jean-Baptiste-Camille (after)
1796–1875
Landscape
oil on canvas 24.5 x 35.5
1442

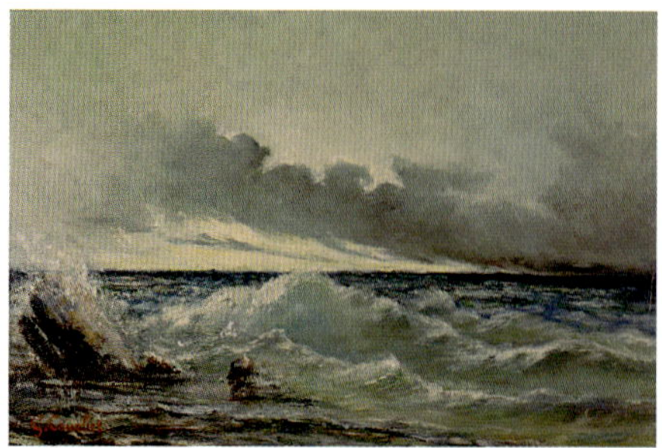

Courbet, Gustave 1819–1877
La vague
oil on canvas 43.4 x 64.9
4/2004

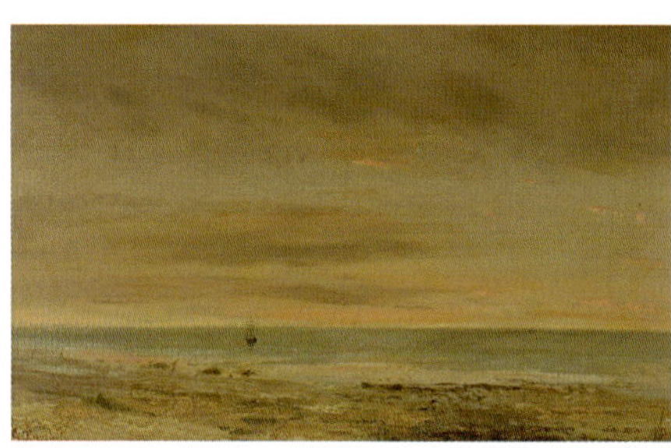

Courbet, Gustave (imitator of) 1819–1877
Seapiece at Honfleur
oil on canvas 31 x 52.8
124

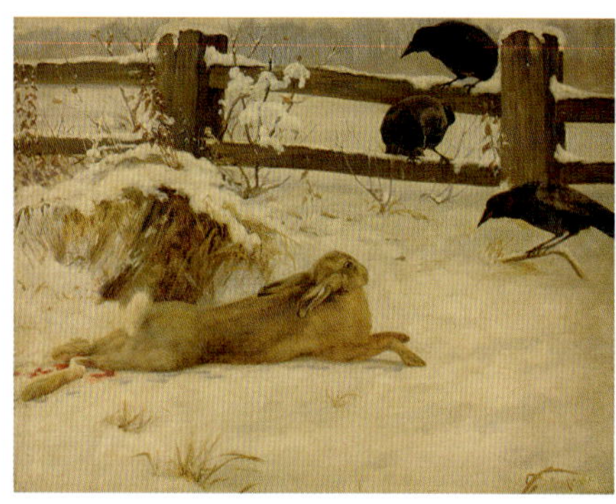

Craft, Percy Robert 1856–1934
Birds and Hare
oil on canvas 86.4 x 112
1246

Craig-Martin, Michael b.1941
Untitled Painting No.1 1976
oil on canvas 122.4 x 122.4
43/1976

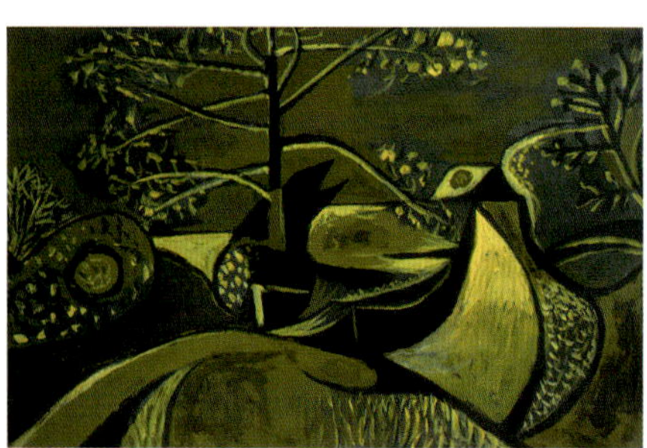

Craxton, John b.1922
Dark Landscape 1943
oil on canvas 37.5 x 55.2
1378

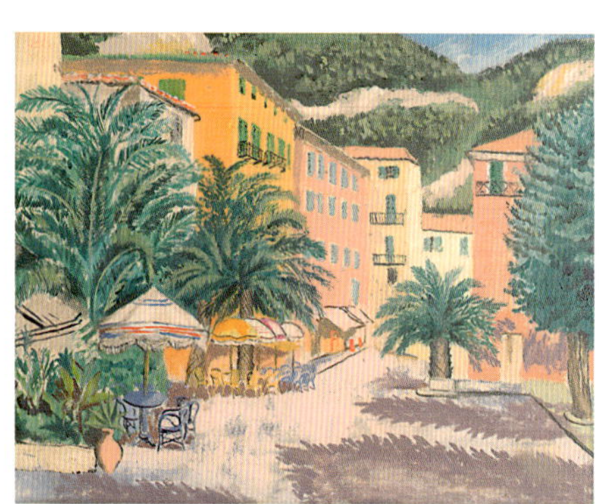

Crook, Frederick
Villefranche
oil on canvas 46 x 61
131

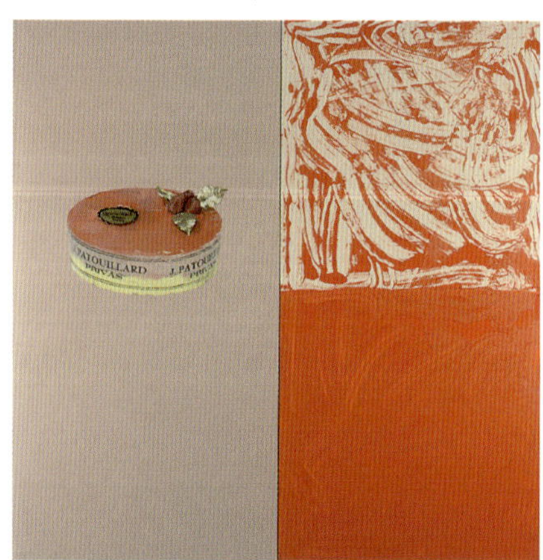

Crumplin, Colin b.1946
Cake 1992
oil on canvas 152.5 x 152.6
4/1997

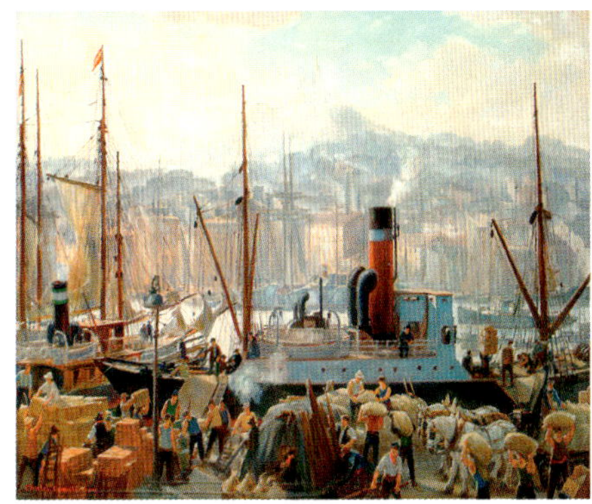

Cundall, Charles Ernest 1890–1971
Stevedores, Marseilles 1929
oil on canvas 63.8 x 76.9
134

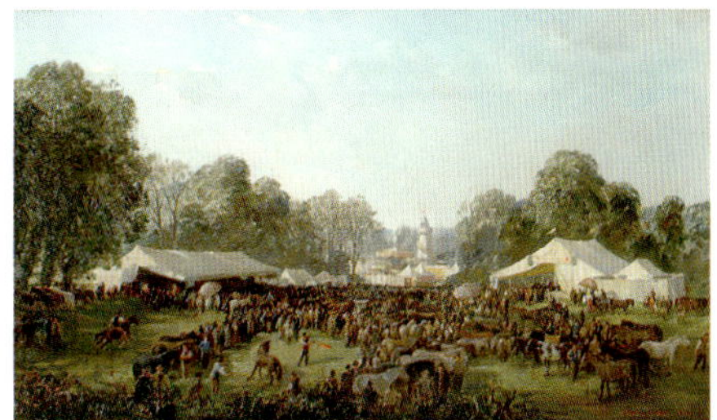

Cundall, Charles Ernest 1890–1971
Barnet Fair 1936
oil on canvas 50.2 x 81.8
132

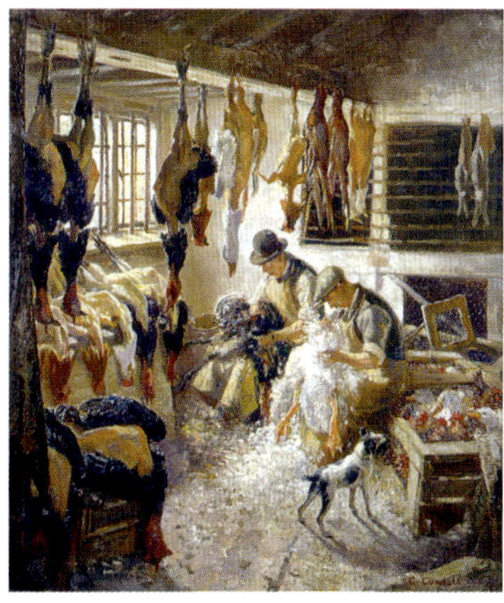

Cundall, Charles Ernest 1890–1971
Christmas Preparations at Beaulieu
oil on canvas 57.2 x 50.5
133

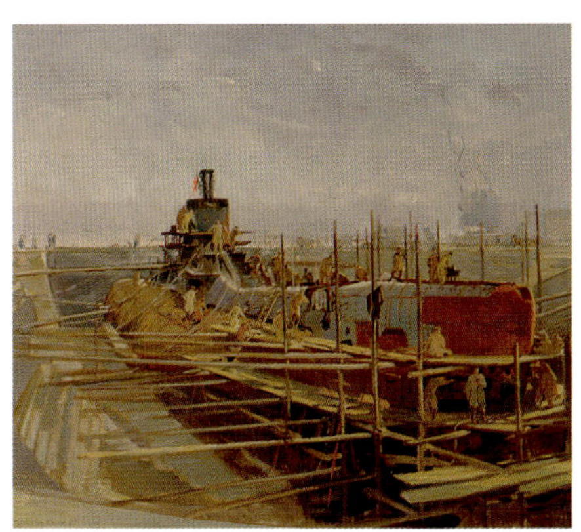

Cundall, Charles Ernest 1890–1971
Repairing a Submarine
oil on canvas 50.8 x 61.1
1315

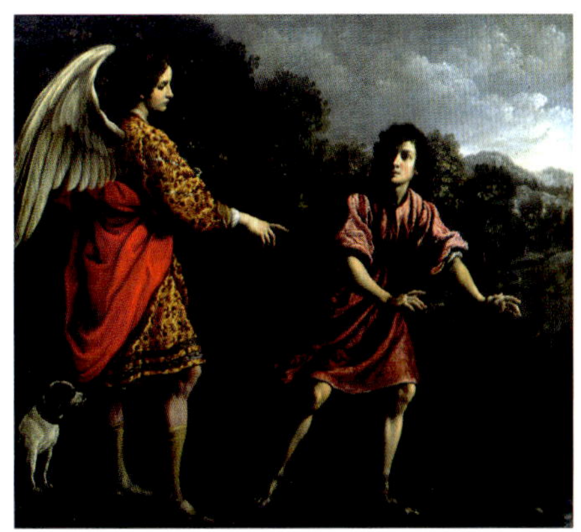

Curradi, Francesco 1570–1661
Tobias and the Angel
oil on canvas 192 x 214.5
1492

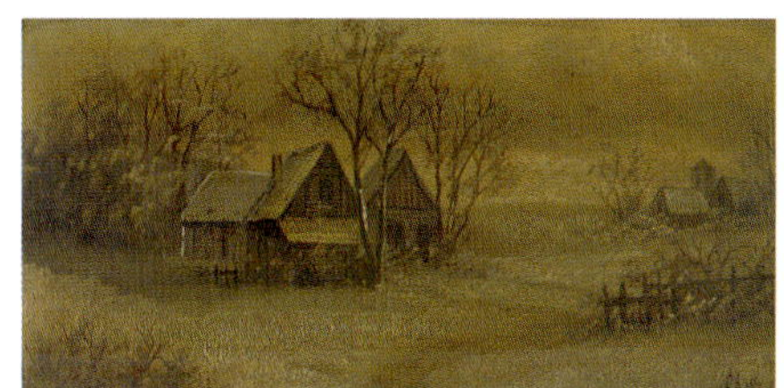

Dalton, R.
Landscape
oil on metal 15.5 x 30.5
136

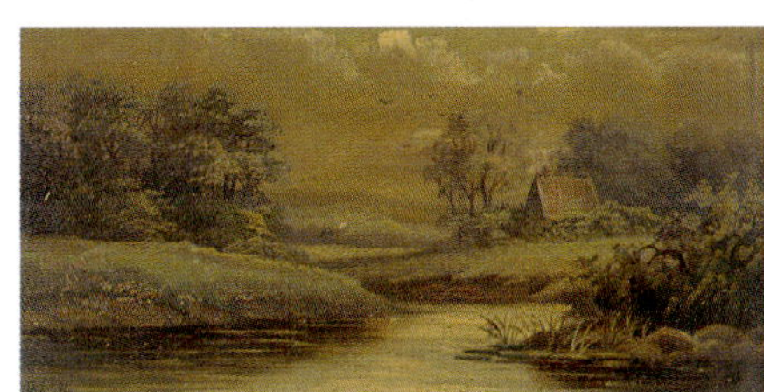

Dalton, R.
River Scene
oil on metal 15.5 x 30.5
137

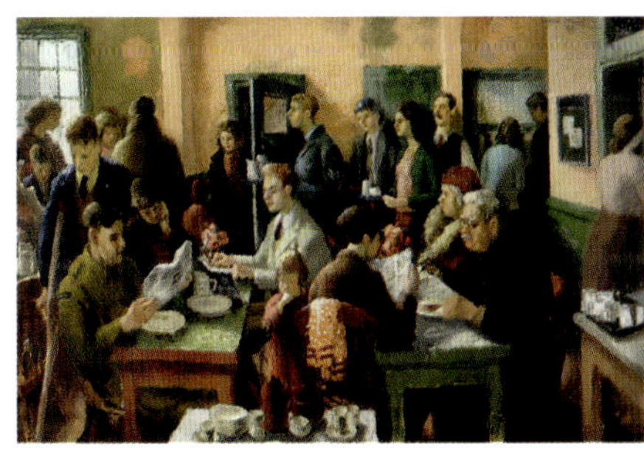

Daniels, Leonard 1909–1998
A British Restaurant at Winchester
oil on canvas 50.7 x 76.1
1316

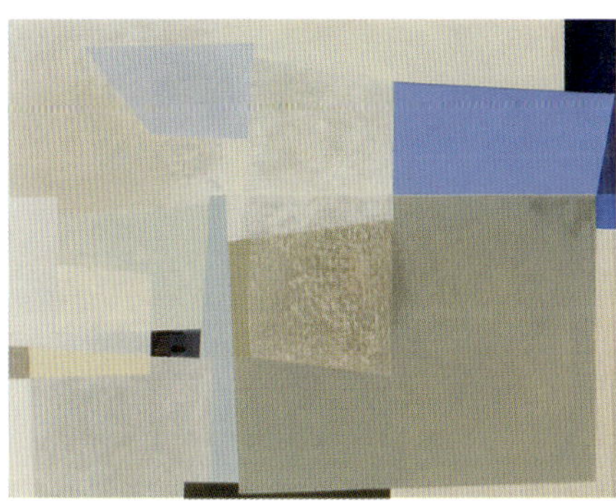

Dannatt, George b.1915
Citadel No.5 (St Malo) 1996–1997
oil on board 75 x 113.5 (E)
57/2006

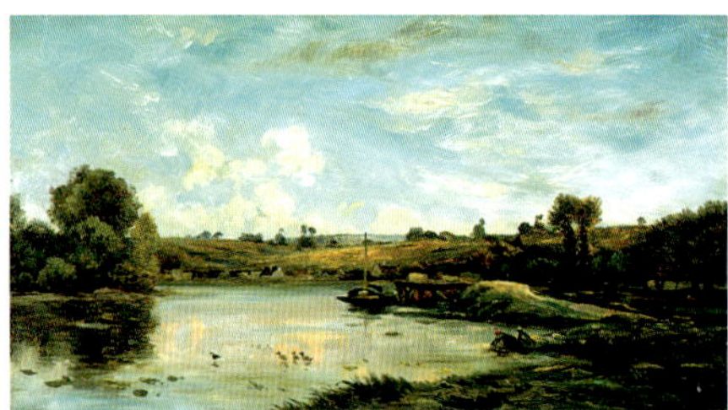

Daubigny, Charles-François 1817–1878
On the Loire
oil on wood 33.8 x 40
14/1967

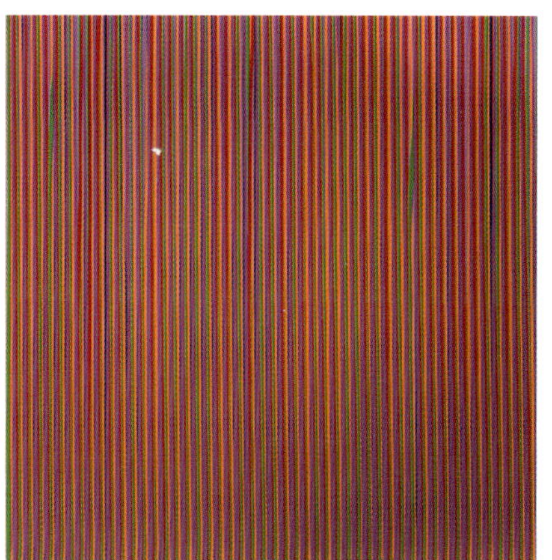

Davenport, Ian b.1966
Poured Lines Painting
acrylic on canvas 213.4 x 213.4
9/1996

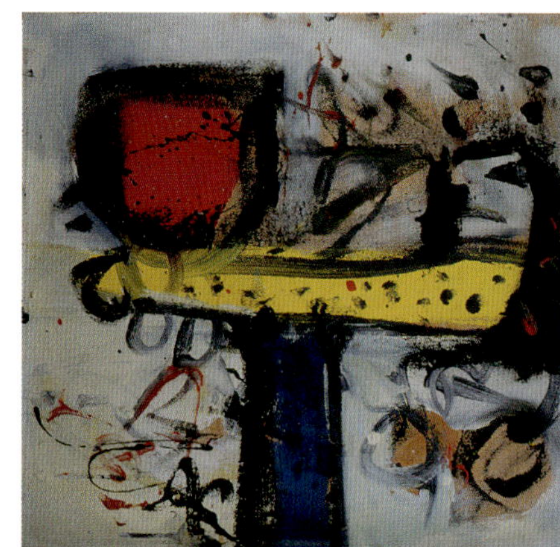

Davie, Alan b.1920
Bird Singing 1957
oil on board 53.7 x 55.2
47/2002

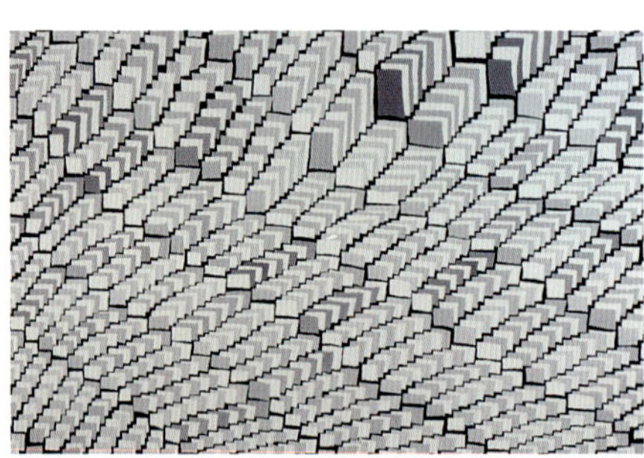

Davies, Peter b.1970
Overlapping Grey Squares Painting 1998
acrylic on canvas 213.5 x 330.6
5/1998

Davis, Peter b.1972
0626-B01G Diamante 1995
gloss paint & satin wood on canvas
155.3 x 218.8
14/1996

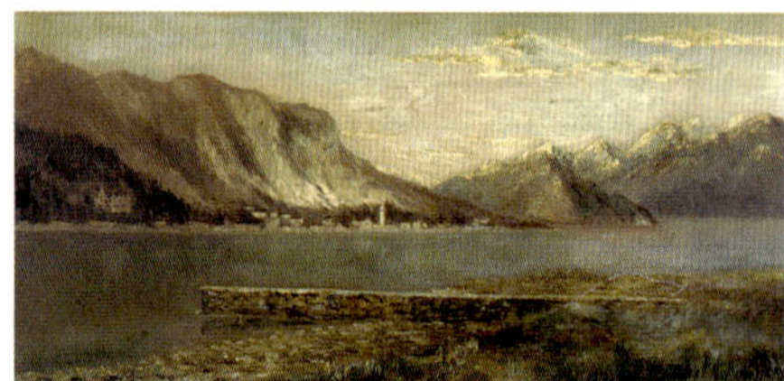

Davis, William 1812–1873
Breakwater Scene
oil on board 22.5 x 46.7
139

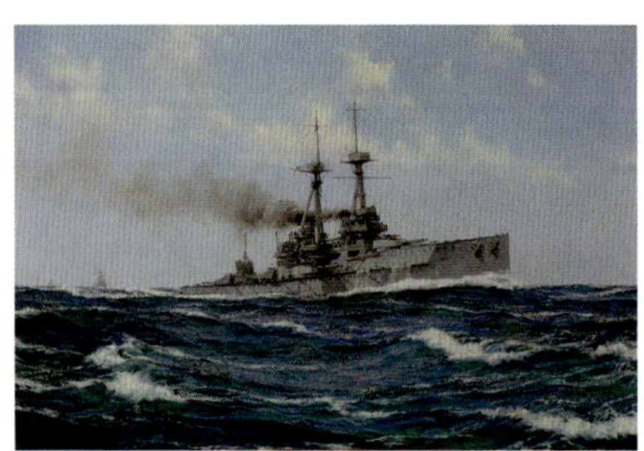

Dawson, Montague J. 1895–1973
'HMS Collingwood'
oil on canvas 71 x 106.6
141

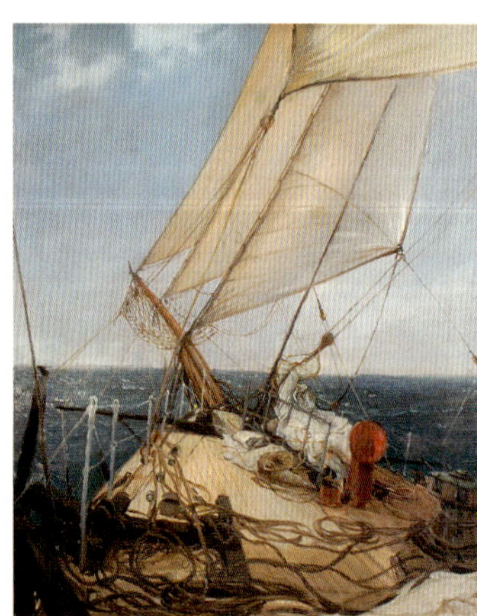

Dawson, Montague J. 1895–1973
The Forecastle Head
oil on canvas 61.2 x 50.7
142

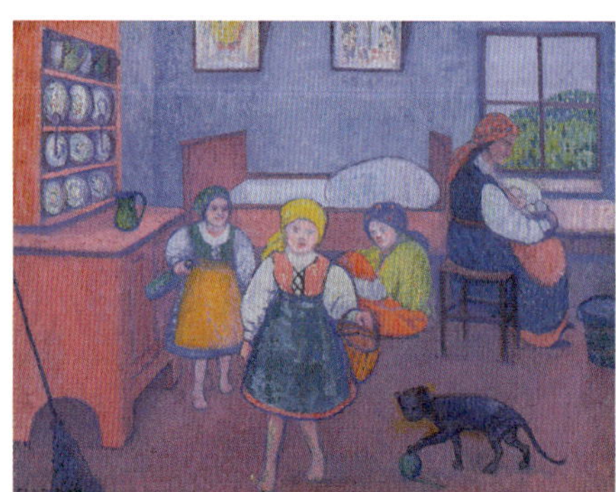

De Karlowska, Stanislawa 1876–1952
Polish Interior 1909
oil on canvas 62.8 x 80.8
1/1968

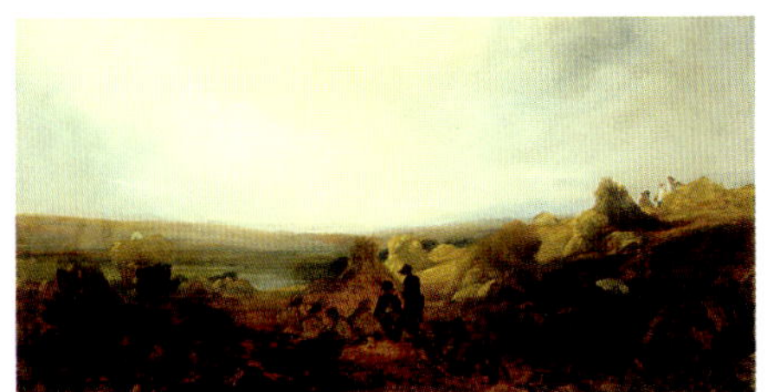

De Wint, Peter 1784–1849
A Cornfield with Figures in Sunlight
oil on canvas 58.1 x 106.4
870

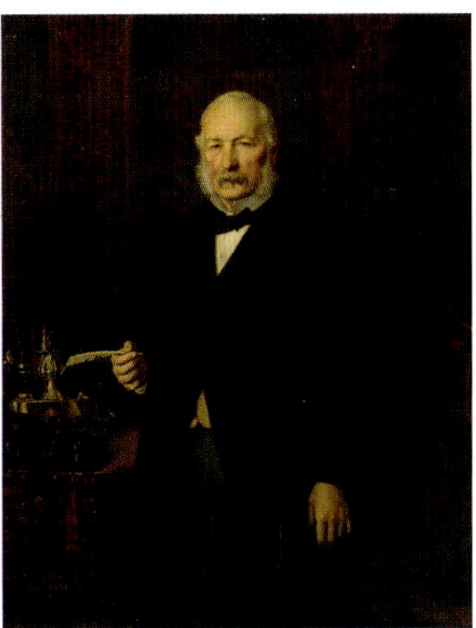

Deacon, George S. active 1860s–1879
Charles Ewens, Esq., Town Clerk (1838–1870)
1871
oil on canvas 142.5 x 112
143

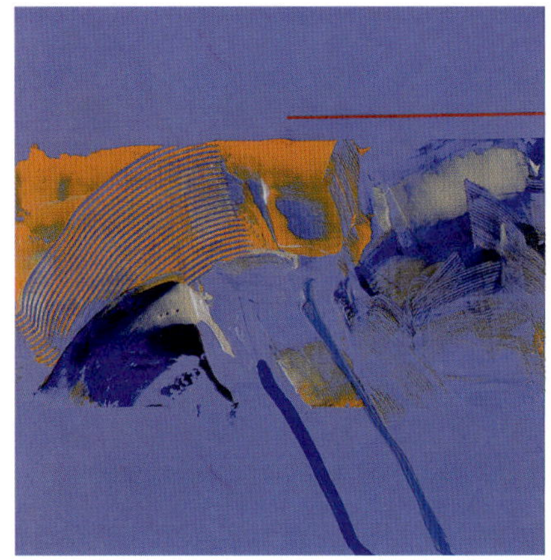

Delaney, Barbara b.1941
The Meeting of the Dragon, the Bull and the Anteater 2003
acrylic on canvas 35.5 x 35.6
4/2005

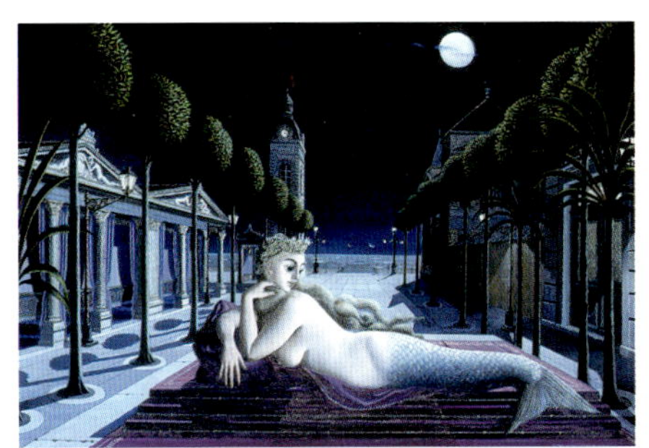

Delvaux, Paul 1897–1994
A Siren in Full Moonlight 1940
oil on panel 111.9 x 180
87/1963

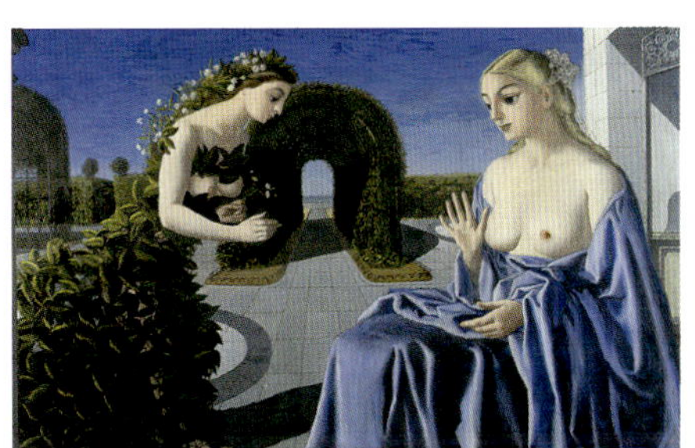

Delvaux, Paul 1897–1994
Annunciation 1949
oil on board 99.7 x 159.7
63/1963

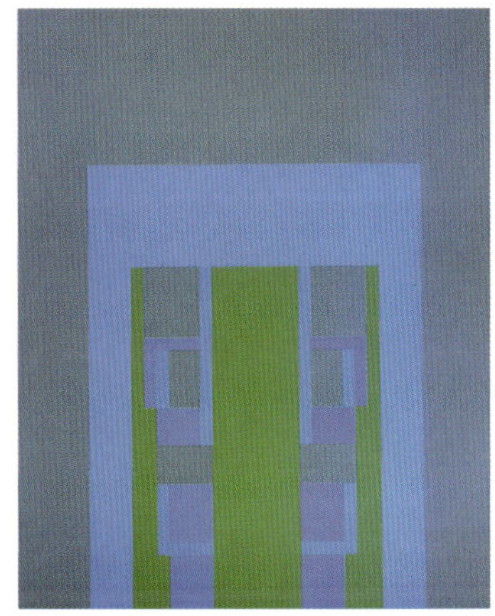

Denny, Robyn b.1930
Time of Day III
oil on canvas 243.4 x 197.8
2/2001

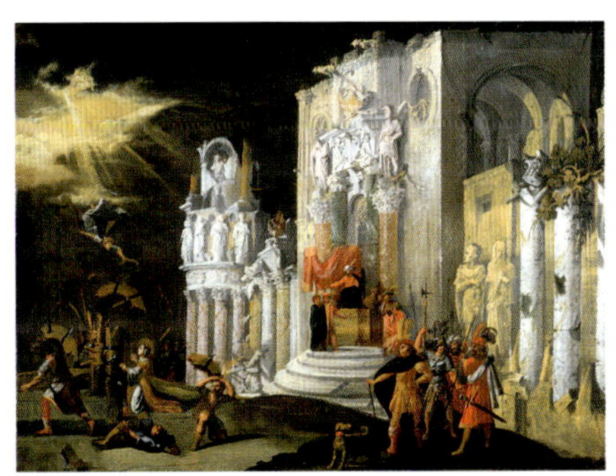

Desiderio, Monsù 1590–1644 or **Nomé, François de** c.1593–after 1644 or **Barra, Didier** c.1590–after 1652
The Martyrdom of St Catherine
oil on canvas 95.8 x 126
1359

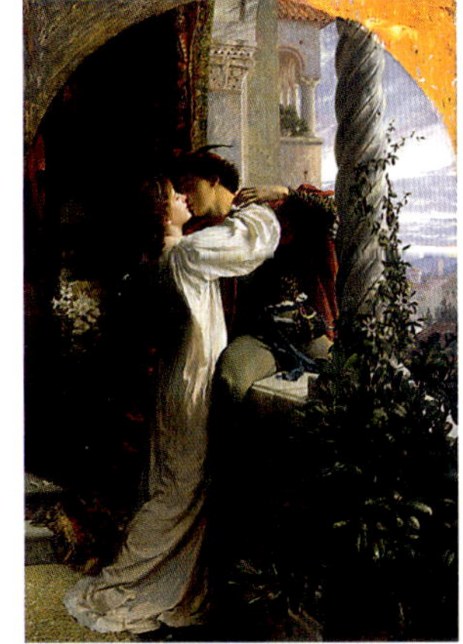

Dicksee, Frank 1853–1928
Romeo and Juliet 1884
oil on canvas 171 x 118
1006

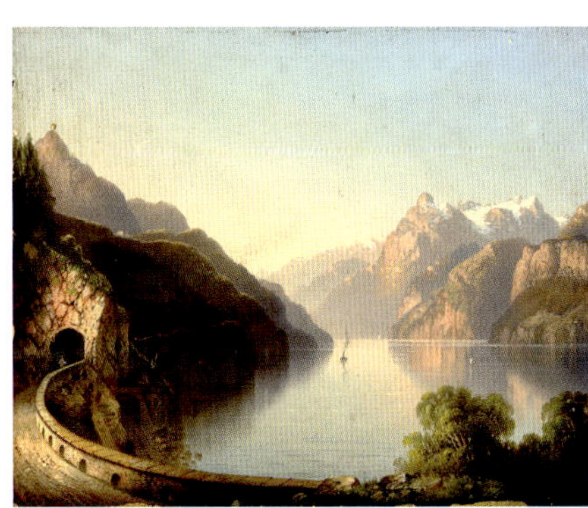

Dietrich, Gustave Otto b.1860
Lake Scene
oil on canvas 31.7 x 40.1
651

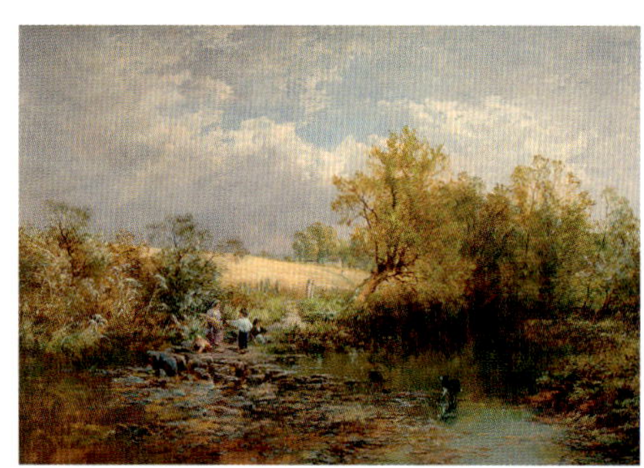

Dingle, Thomas active 1846–1888
The Nearest Way Home
oil on canvas 61 x 91.5
149

Dingwall, Kenneth b.1938
Edinburgh Blue II 1976
oil on canvas 182.6 x 122.7
11/1979

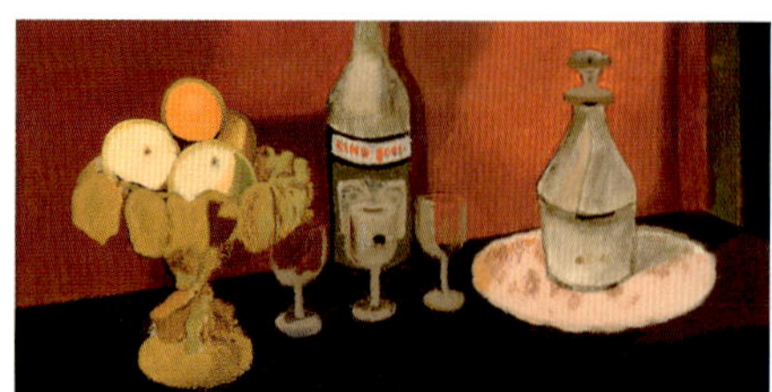

Dodgson, John Arthur 1890–1969
Still Life with Dessert 1930
oil on canvas 30.7 x 61.4
7/2000

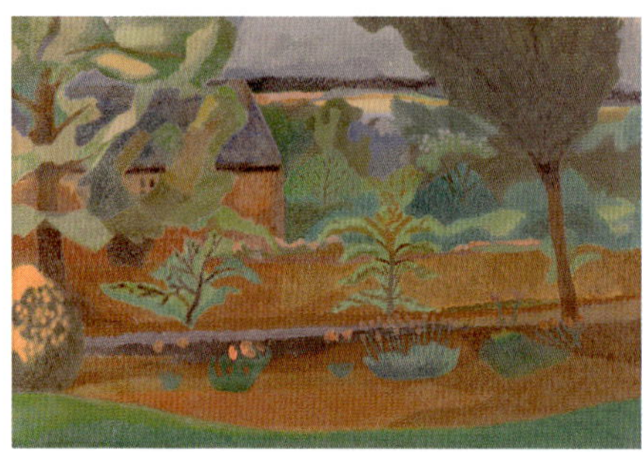

Dodgson, John Arthur 1890–1969
Berkhampstead Garden 1936
oil on canvas 51 x 76
8/2005

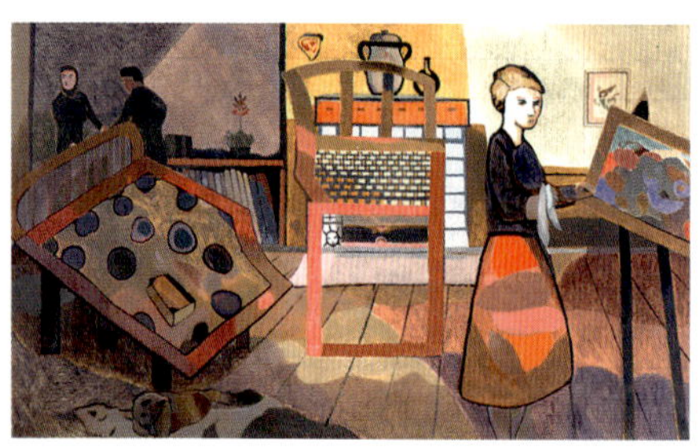

Dodgson, John Arthur 1890–1969
A Visit to the Studio 1950
oil on canvas 113.1 x 186.6
2/1996

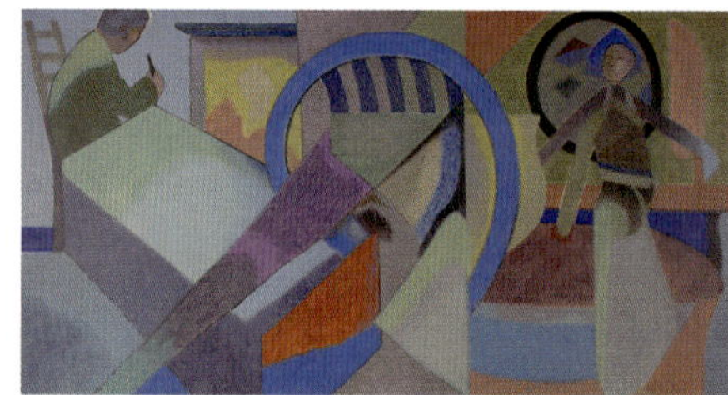

Dodgson, John Arthur 1890–1969
Untitled 1950
oil on canvas 84 x 145
1/1997

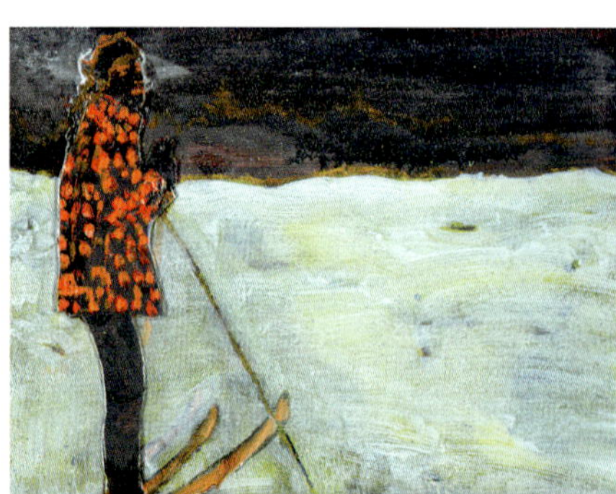

Doig, Peter b.1959
Girl on Skis 1997
oil on canvas 30.3 x 40.6
1/1999

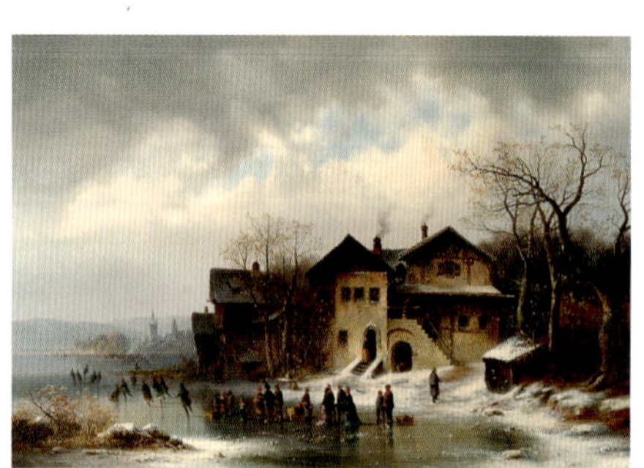

Doll, Anton Eduard 1826–1887
Skating Scene
oil on canvas 75.5 x 112
11/1984

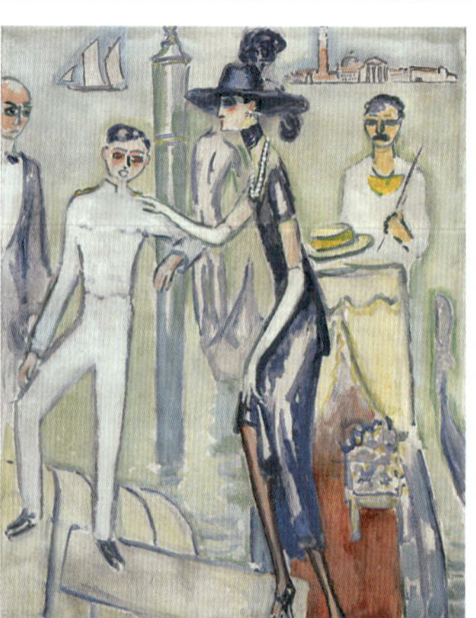

Dongen, Kees van 1877–1968
Woman in Venice
oil on canvas 92.1 x 73.7
84/1963

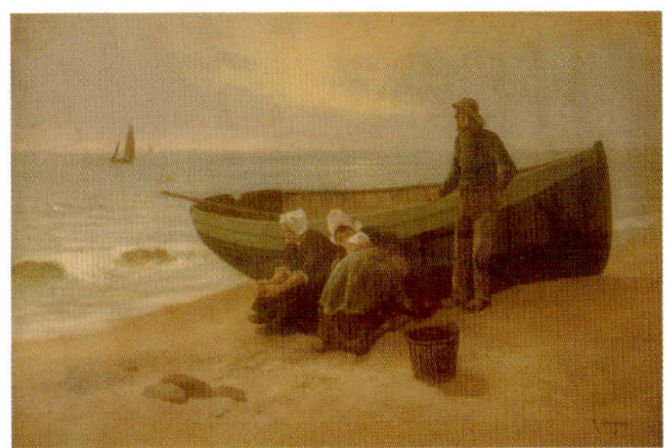

Douglas, Rose active 1893–1898
Group by Rowing Boat
oil on canvas 40.5 x 60.9
1270

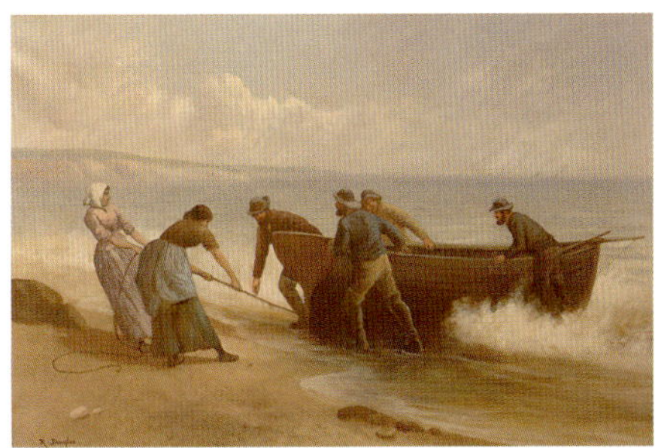

Douglas, Rose active 1893–1898
Pulling Rowboat Ashore
oil on canvas 40.5 x 60.9
1269

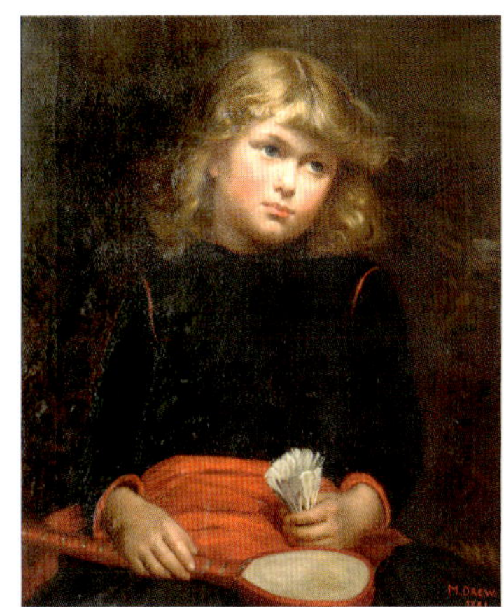

Drew, Mary active 1880–1901
I Cannot Play Alone 1881
oil on canvas 63.5 x 53.3
153

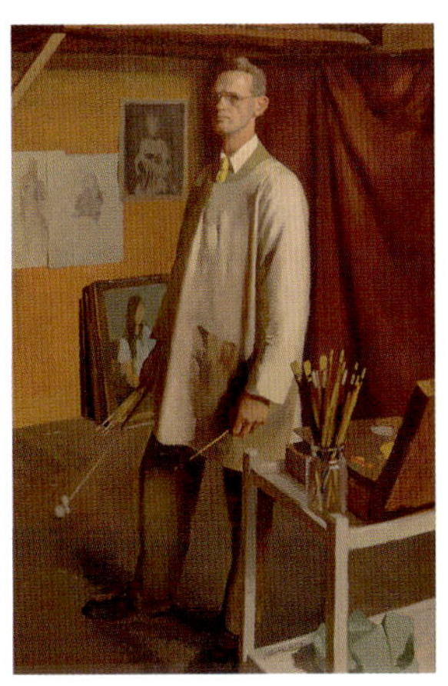

Dring, William D. 1904–1990
Self Portrait 1940
oil on canvas 91.4 x 60.8
10/2000

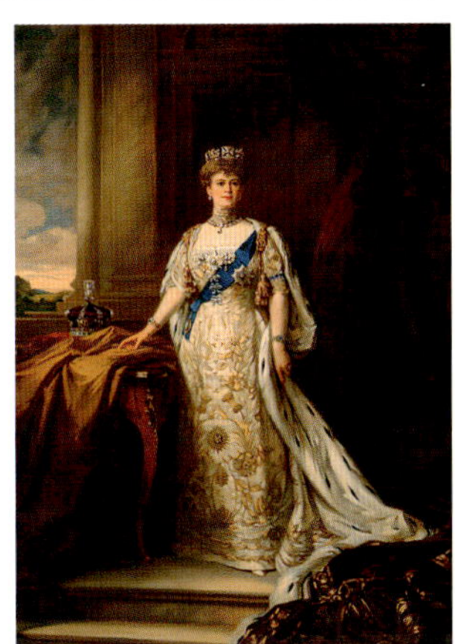

Dring, William D. 1904–1990
Queen Mary (1867–1953) (after Luke Fildes)
oil on canvas 78.3 x 61.4
154

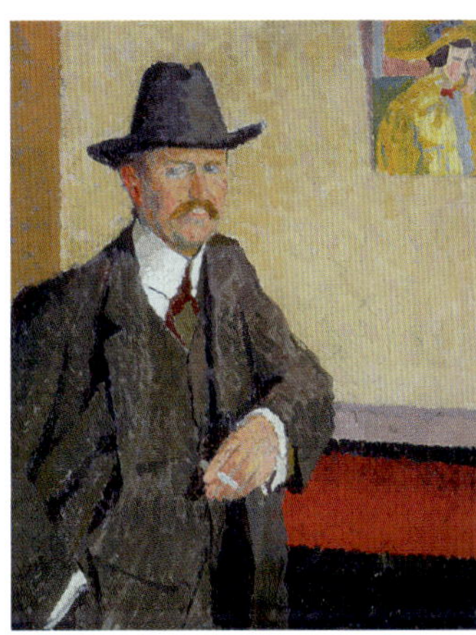

Drummond, Malcolm 1880–1945
Charles Ginner (1878–1952) 1911
oil on board 60.3 x 49
1486

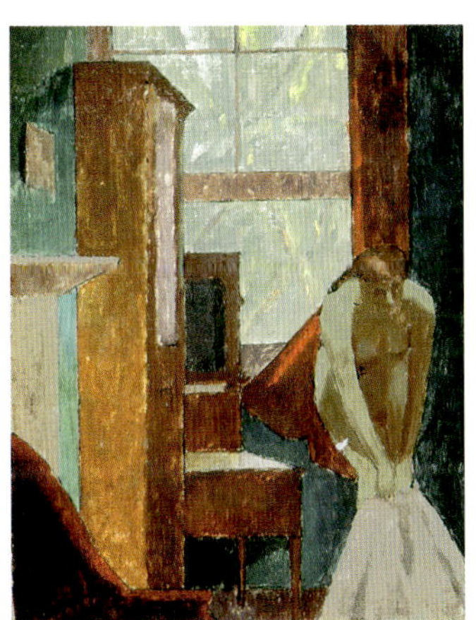

Drummond, Malcolm 1880–1945
Girl Dressing 1911
oil on canvas 45.7 x 35.5
2/1975

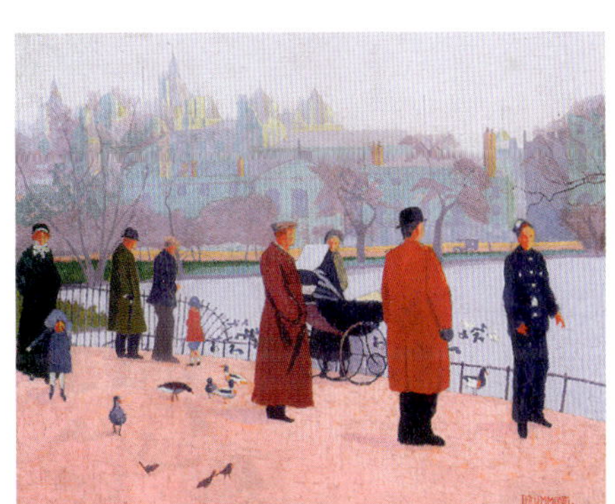

Drummond, Malcolm 1880–1945
In the Park (St James' Park) 1911
oil on canvas 72.5 x 90
1427

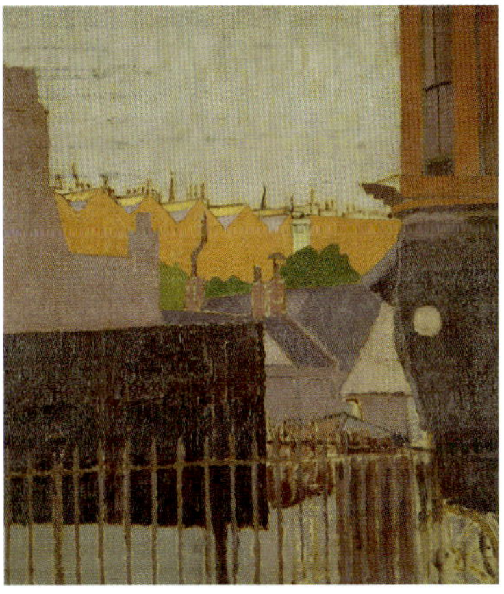

Drummond, Malcolm 1880–1945
Backs of Houses, Chelsea 1914
oil on canvas 65.1 x 57.5
1411

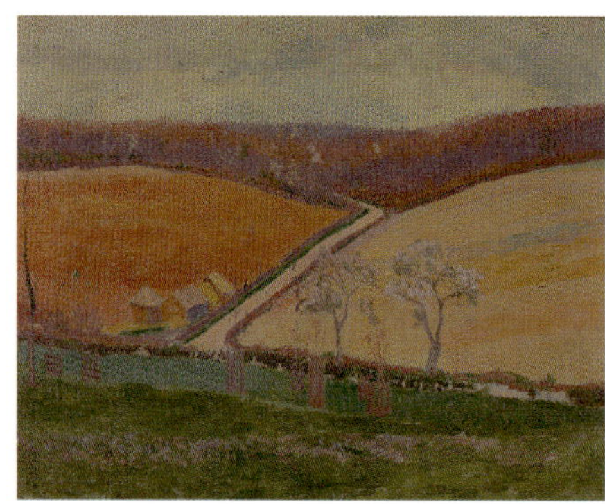

Drummond, Malcolm 1880–1945
Fields and Road, Penn Street 1918
oil on canvas 40.5 x 51
10/1998

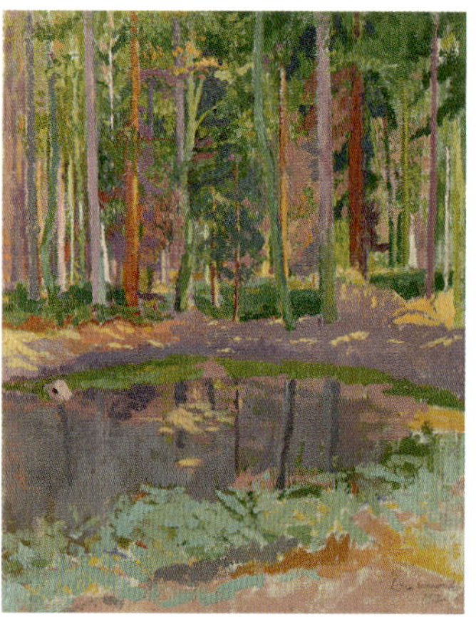

Drummond, Malcolm 1880–1945
Wooded Pond 1918
oil on canvas 51.2 x 41
9/1998

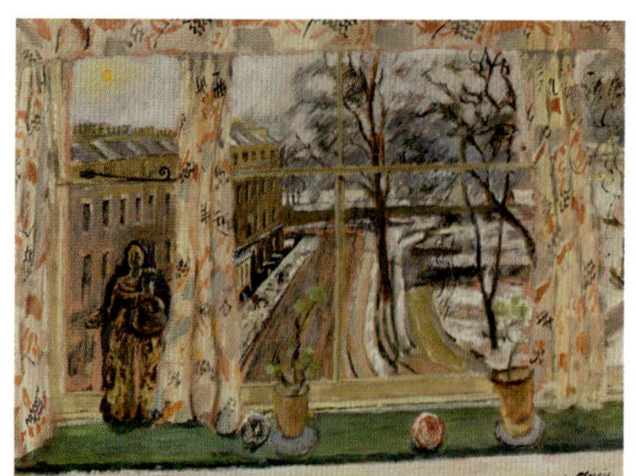

Du Plessis, Enslin 1894–1978
Mecklenburgh Square, Winter
oil on card 46.3 x 62
1291

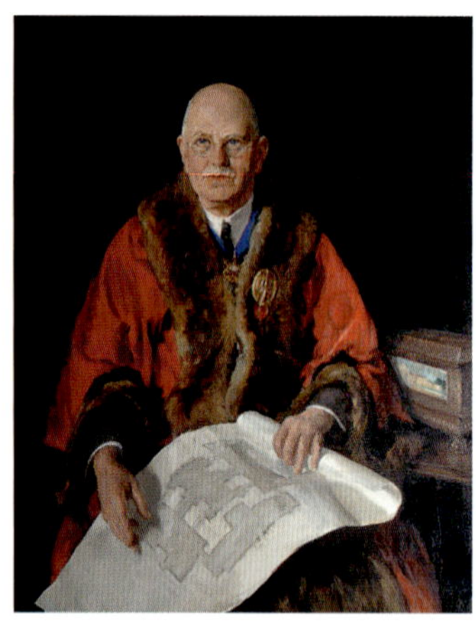

Dugdale, Thomas Cantrell 1880–1952
Alderman Sir Sidney Kimber, JP
oil on canvas 127.4 x 102.4
156

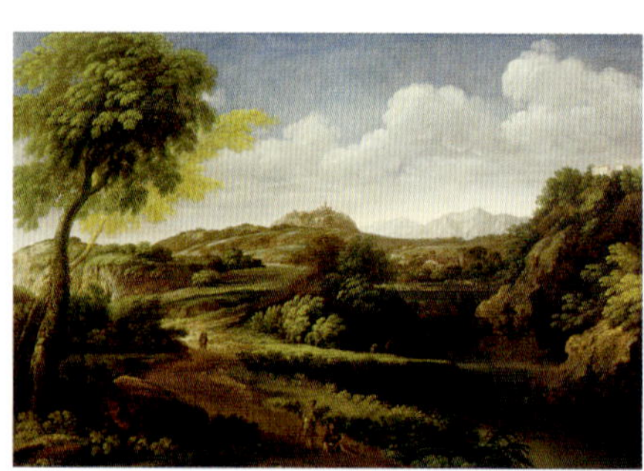

Dughet, Gaspard 1615–1675
Landscape of the Roman Campagna 1660
oil on canvas 121.2 x 168
1/1959

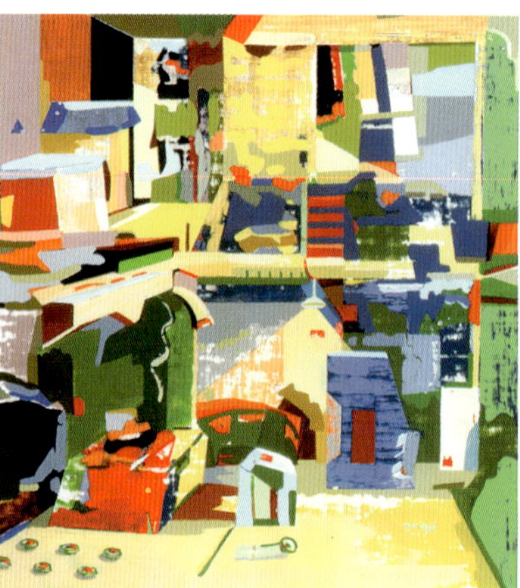

Duncalf, Stephen b.1950
The Workshop 1977
oil on board 35.9 x 33
26/2002

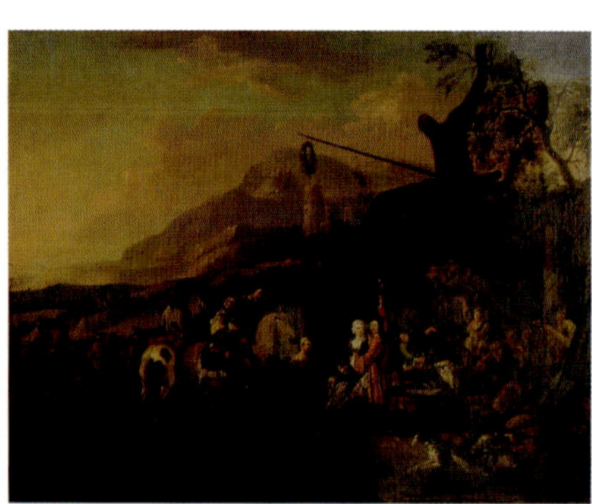

Dutch School 18th C
Dutch Wedding
oil on canvas 49.7 x 64.2
1258

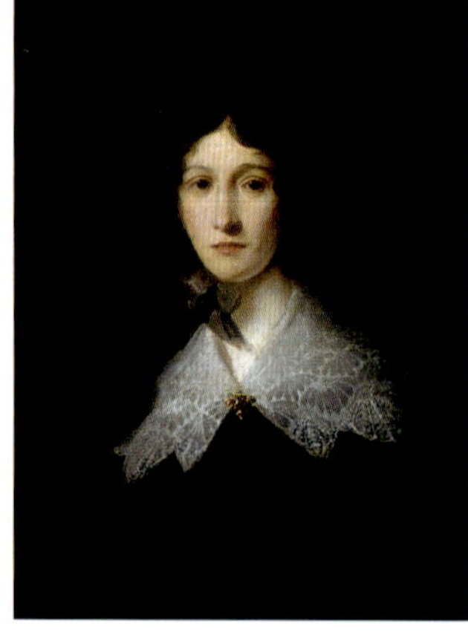

Dyce, William 1806–1864
The Honourable Charlotte Noel
oil on canvas 76.3 x 63.5
165

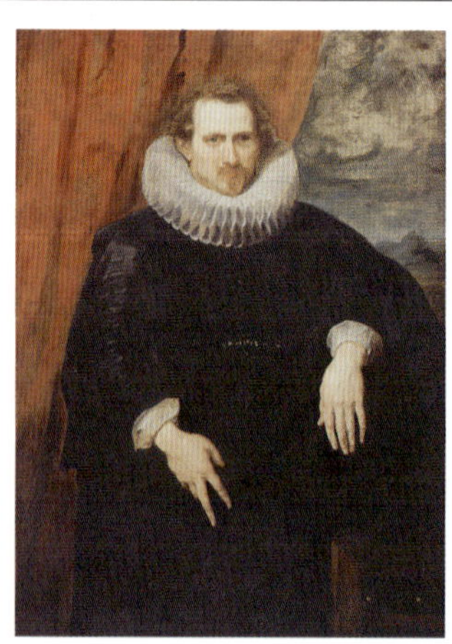

Dyck, Anthony van 1599–1641
Portrait of a Man 1618
oil on canvas 127.5 x 90.9
1430

Facing page: Nibbs, Richard Henry, 1816–1893, *The Departure from Gravesend of HRH Princess Royal on Her Marriage, 2 February 1858, to Prince Frederick, during a Snowstorm* (detail), Sir Max Aitken Museum, (p. 219)

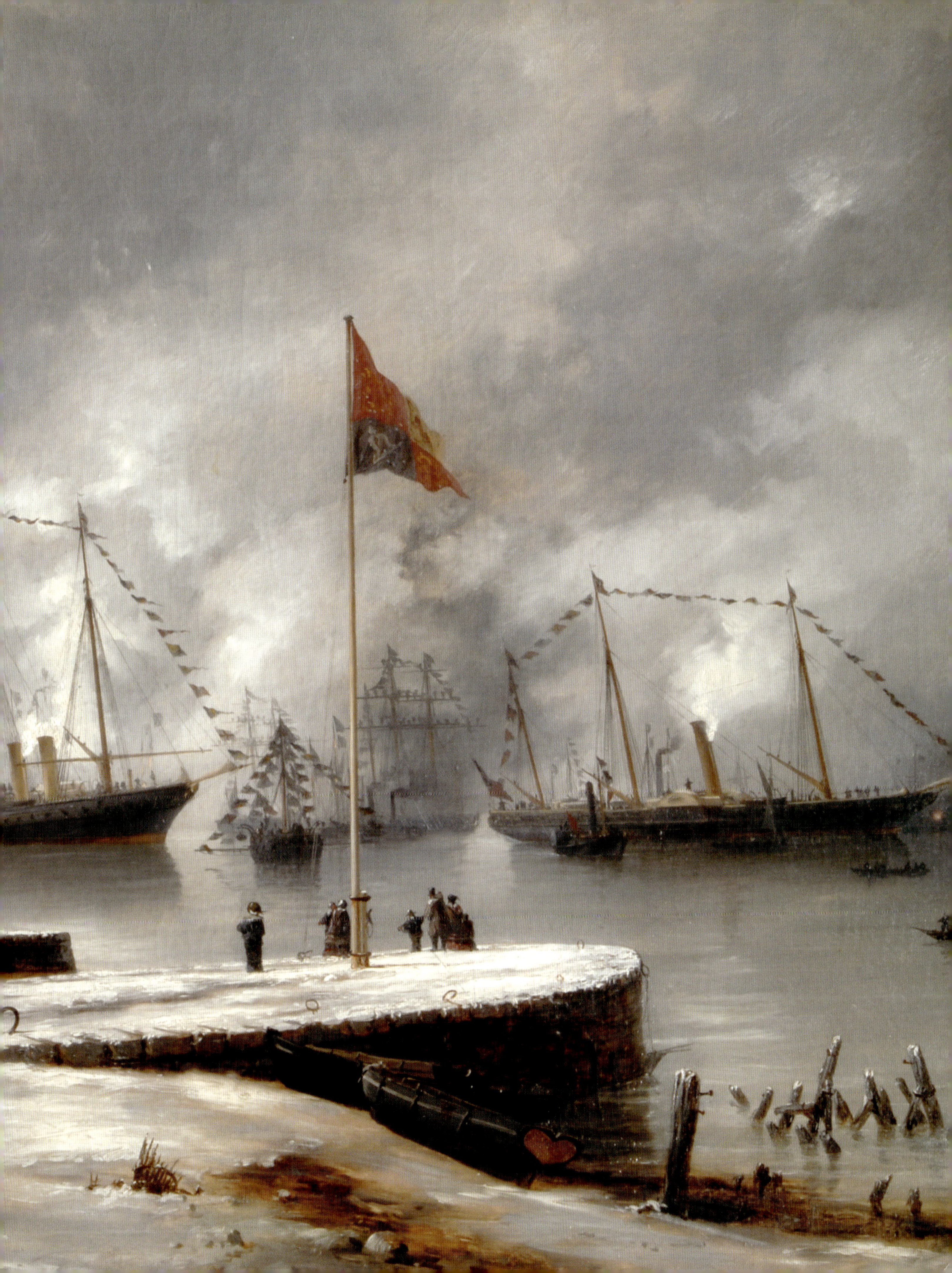

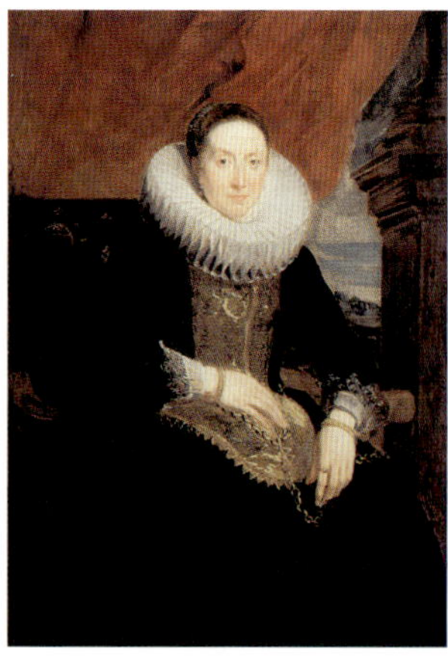

Dyck, Anthony van 1599–1641
Portrait of a Woman 1618
oil on canvas 127.5 x 90.9
1431

Eatwell, John b.1923
Blue Mystery
oil on canvas 152 x 182.5
50/1977

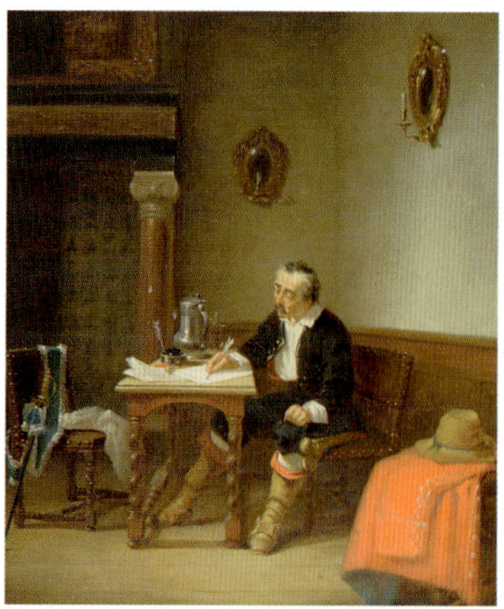

Eeckhout, Jacobus Josefus 1793–1861
Man Writing
oil on wood 41.3 x 33.3
167

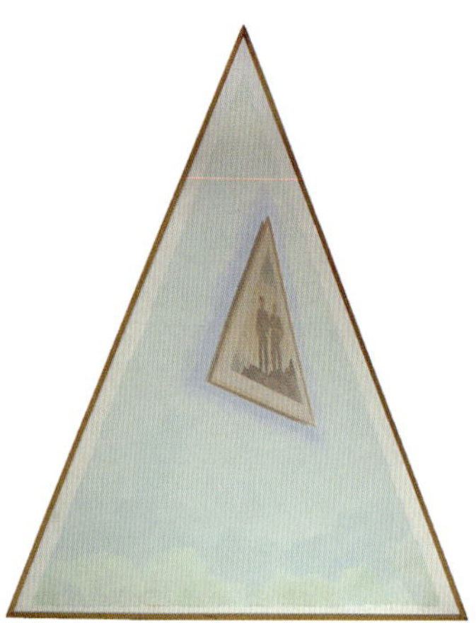

Elk, Ger van b.1941
Gilbert and George
oil on board 202.6 x 160.8
2/1985

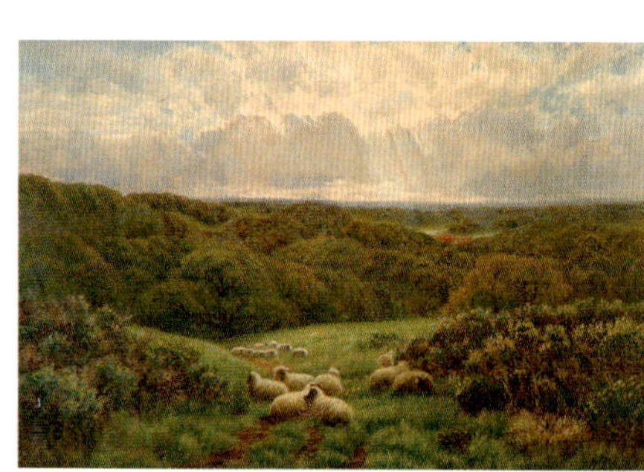

Elleby, William Alfred active 1883–1903
Early Summer
oil on canvas 51.3 x 76.6
169

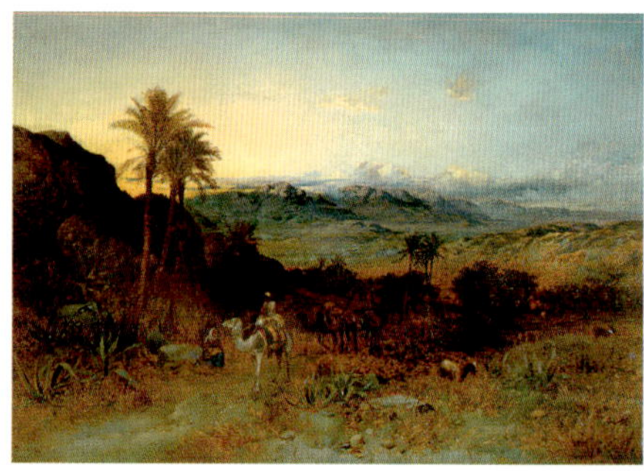

Ellis, Paul H. active 1871–1908
Eastern Sunset
oil on canvas 89 x 127.2
170

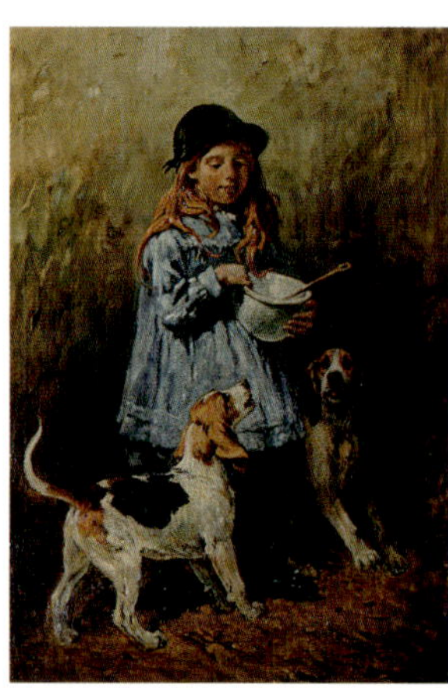

Emms, John 1843–1912
Girl with Two Hounds 1893
oil on canvas 61 x 46.6
11/1964

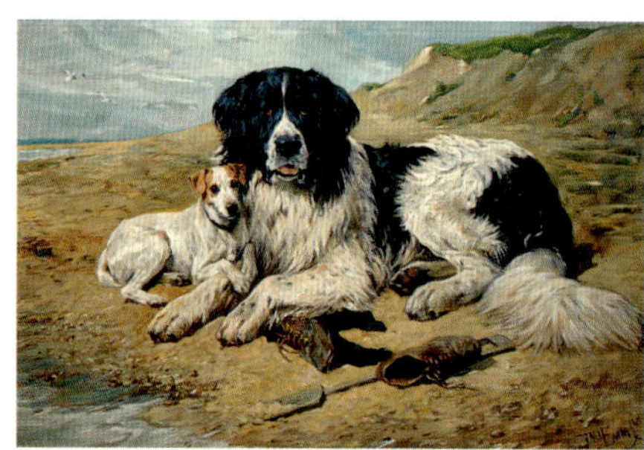

Emms, John 1843–1912
Dogs Watching Bathers
oil on canvas 61 x 91.5
171

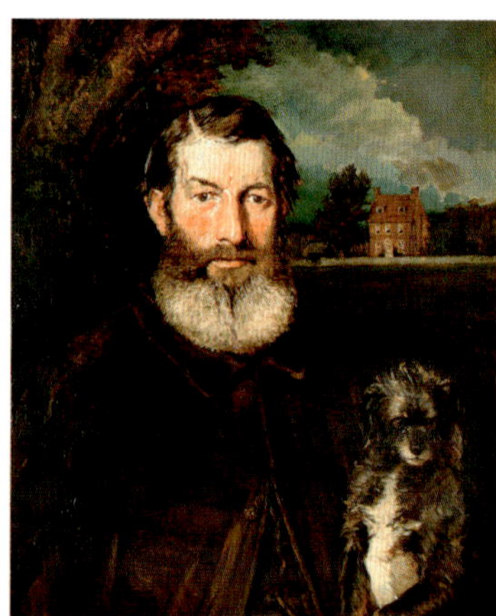

Emms, John 1843–1912
George Primmer
oil on canvas 79.1 x 66
1468

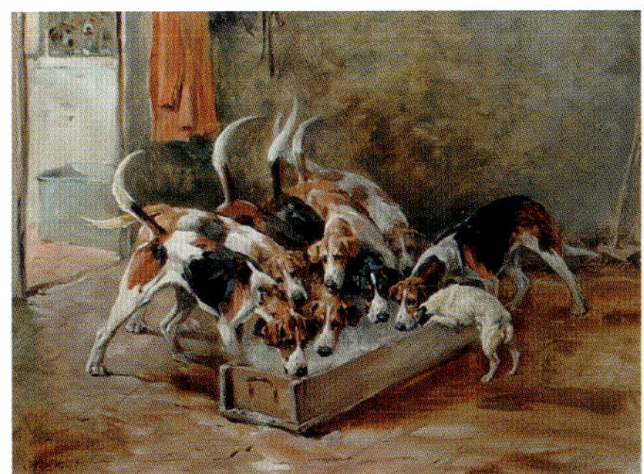

Emms, John 1843–1912
Hounds Feeding
oil on canvas 46.5 x 61.5
172

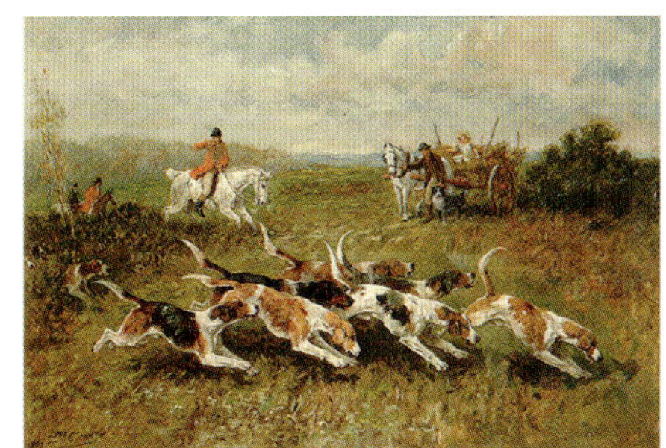

Emms, John 1843–1912
Hunting, New Forest
oil on canvas 45.8 x 66.2
173

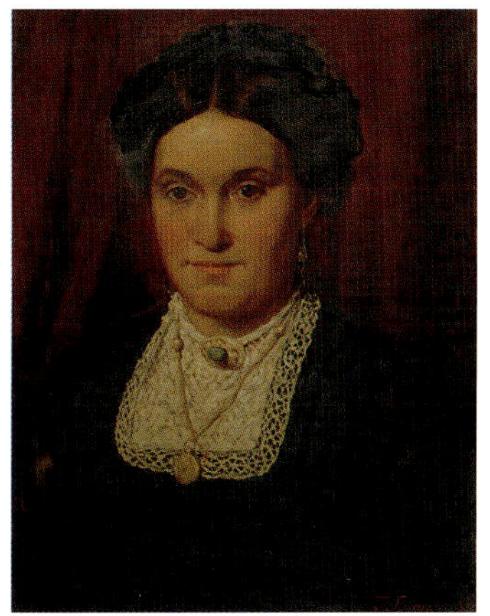

Emms, John 1843–1912
Portrait of a Lady
oil on canvas 51 x 40.7
174

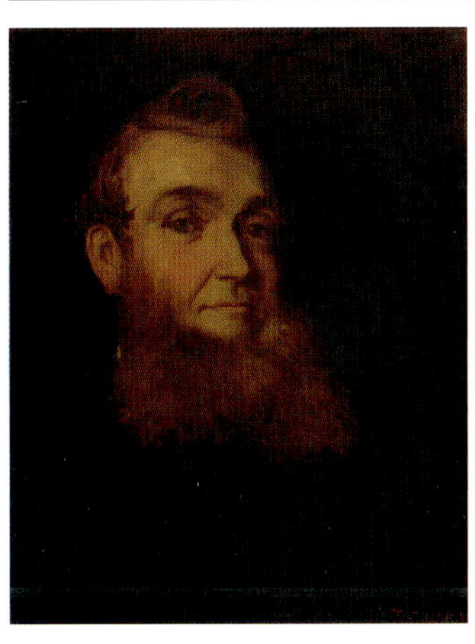

Emms, John 1843–1912
Portrait of a Man
oil on canvas 51 x 40.7
175

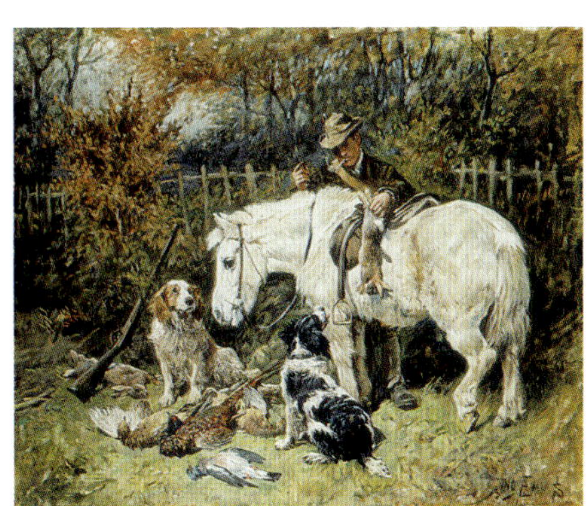

Emms, John 1843–1912
Rest after Sport
oil on canvas 63.3 x 76
176

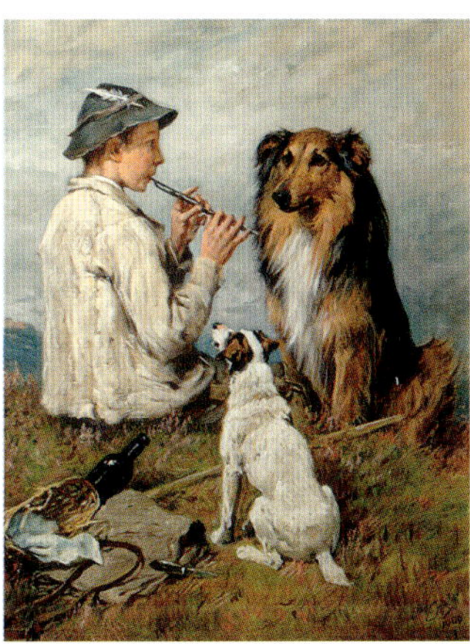

Emms, John 1843–1912
Shepherd and Dogs
oil on canvas 50.5 x 40.6
177

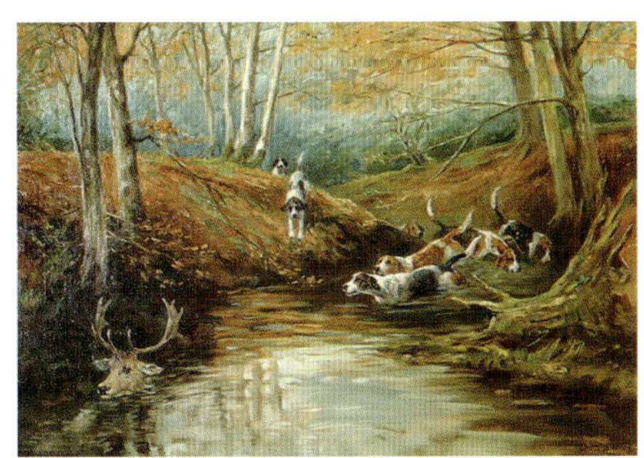

Emms, John 1843–1912
Stag Hunt, New Forest
oil on canvas 45.8 x 69
178

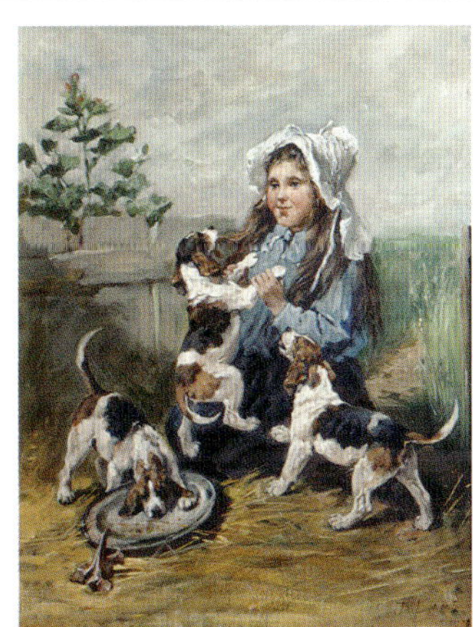

Emms, John 1843–1912
Young Hounds Playing
oil on canvas 50.5 x 40.5
179

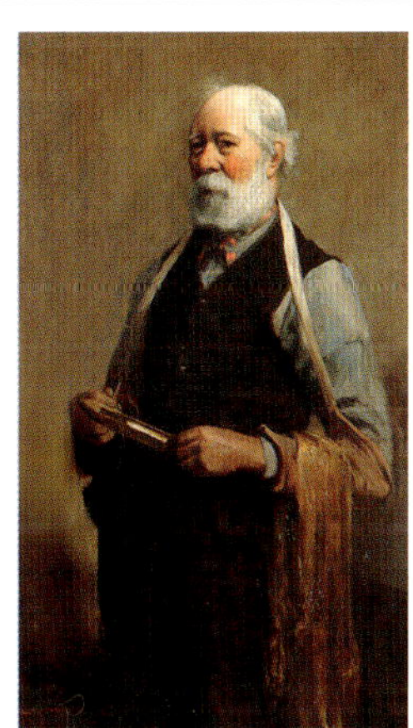

Emsley, Walter active 1883–1927
Last of the Cottage Handloom Weavers of Lancashire
oil on canvas 127.4 x 76.2
1262

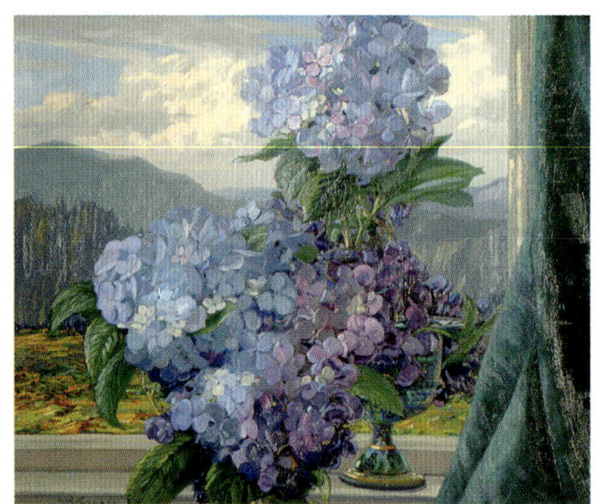

Enness, Augustus William 1876–1948
From a Lakeland Window: Hydrangeas
oil on canvas 63.8 x 76.3
182

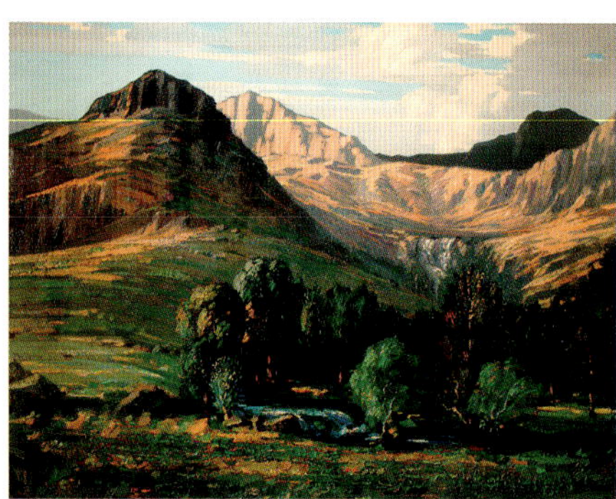

Enness, Augustus William 1876–1948
Langdale
oil on canvas 76.7 x 102.3
183

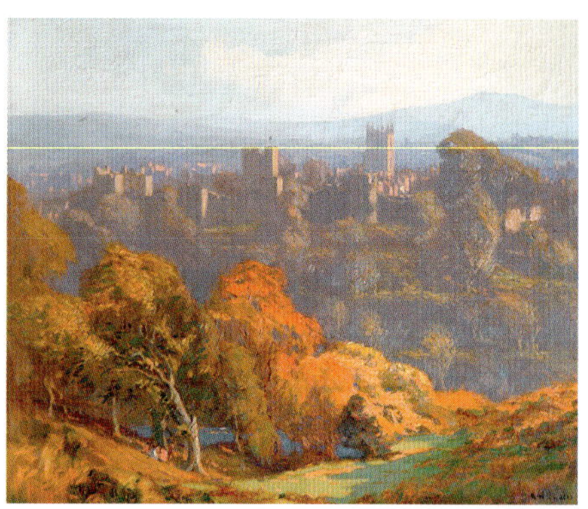

Enness, Augustus William 1876–1948
Ludlow Castle
oil on canvas 63.7 x 76.7
184

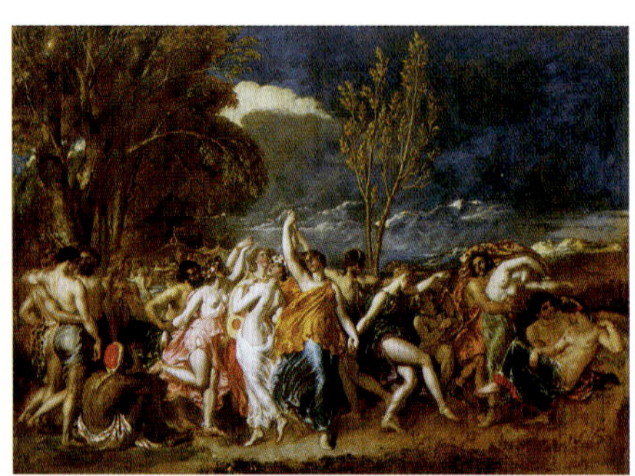

Etty, William 1787–1849
The World before the Flood
oil on canvas 141 x 202.3
186

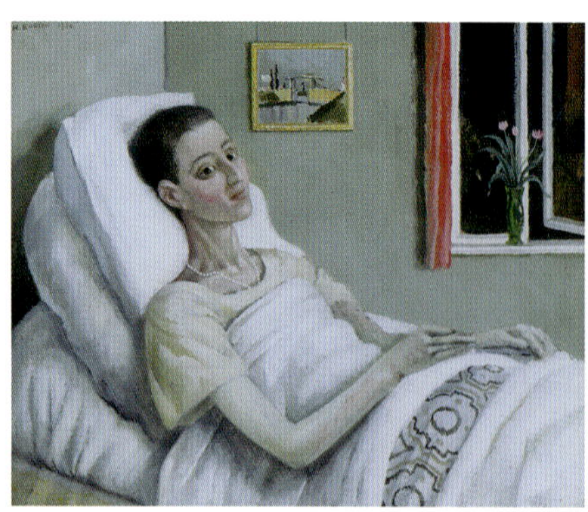

Eurich, Richard Ernst 1903–1992
Mrs Green 1930
oil on canvas 37.2 x 42.6
20/2002

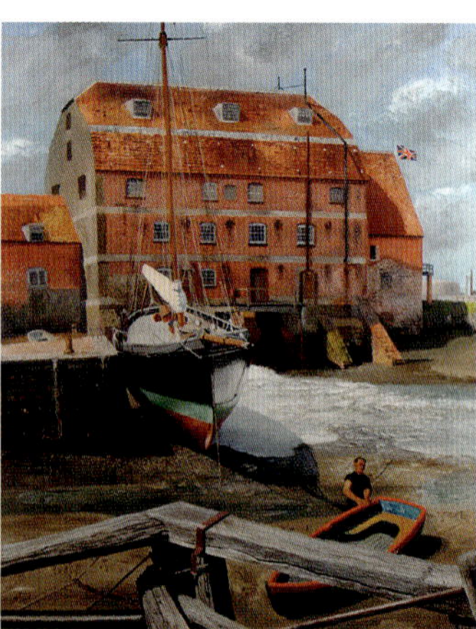

Eurich, Richard Ernst 1903–1992
Old Fawley Mill 1937
oil on canvas 76.1 x 63.4
1282

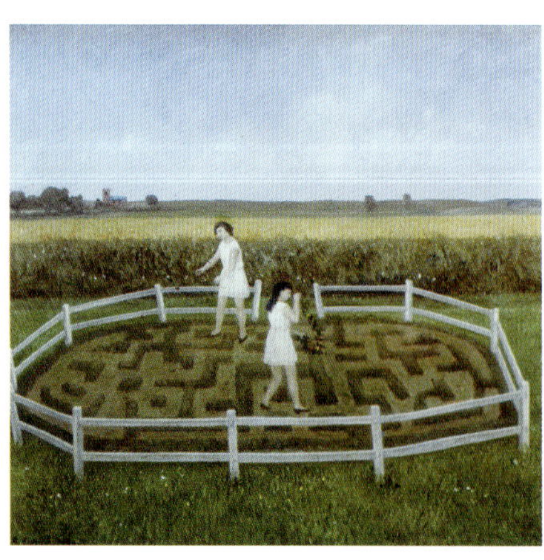

Eurich, Richard Ernst 1903–1992
The Maze 1980
oil on canvas 56 x 59.5
21/1983

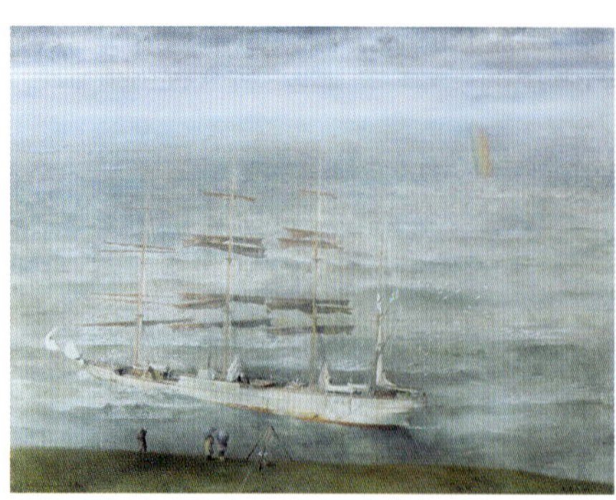

Eurich, Richard Ernst 1903–1992
The Wreck of the 'Herzogin Cecilie'
oil on canvas 76.5 x 101.7
1371

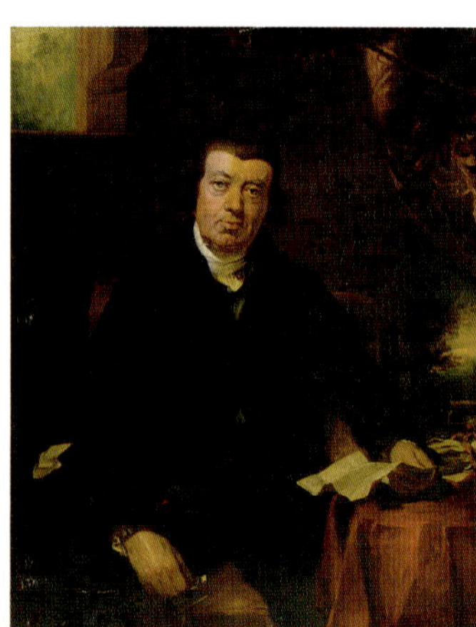

Evans, Richard 1784–1871
Portrait of a Man
oil on canvas 127 x 101.5
1306

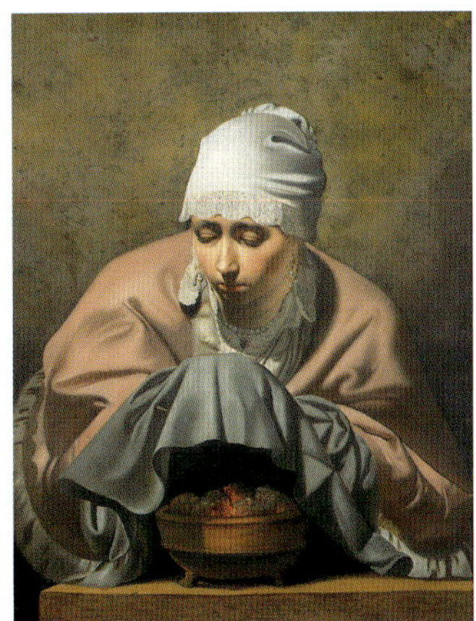

Everdingen, Cesar Boetius van c.1606–1678
Allegory of Winter 1650
oil on canvas 91.8 x 71.2
188

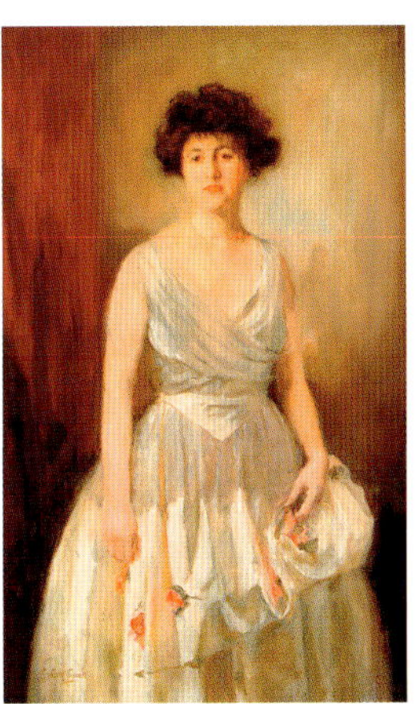

Everett, Edith M. Leeson b.1881
Lady Swaythling
oil on canvas 132.7 x 87
189

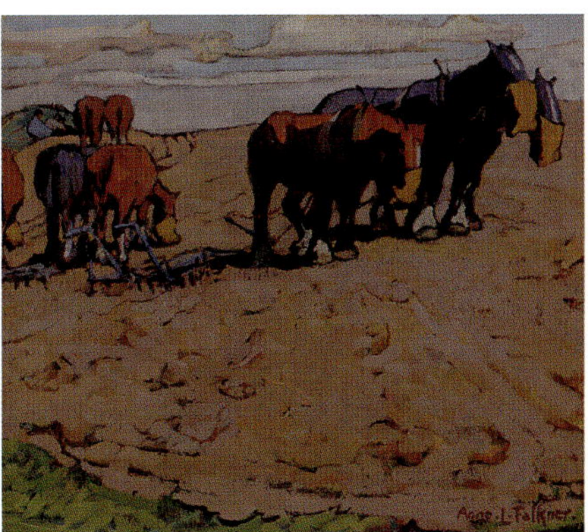

Falkner, Anne L. active 1922
The Lunch Hour
oil on canvas 50.8 x 61
191

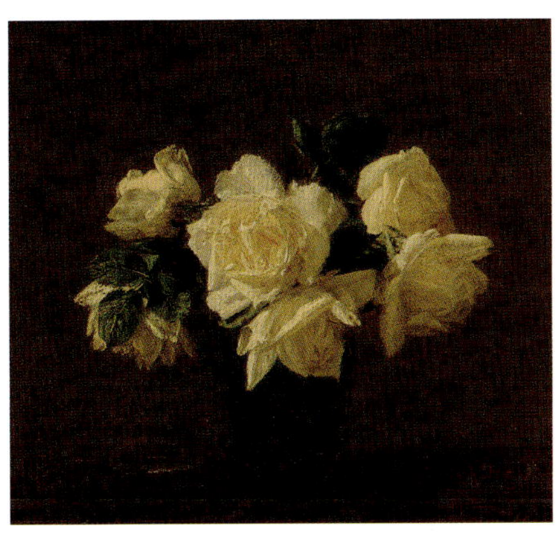

Fantin-Latour, Henri 1836–1904
Yellow Roses 1883
oil on canvas 30.4 x 34.6
2/1973

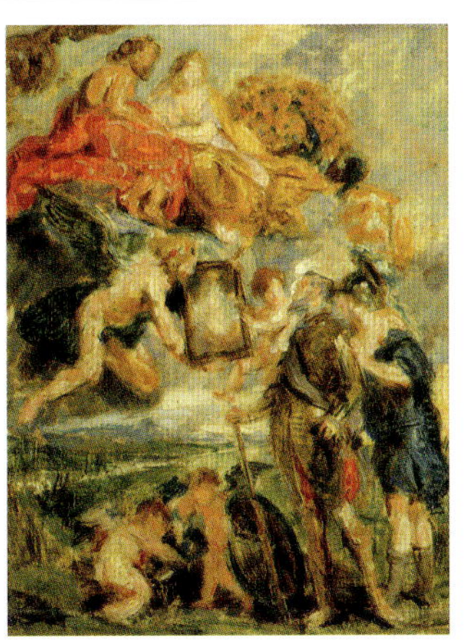

Fantin-Latour, Henri 1836–1904
Homage to Rubens
oil on canvas 40.5 x 30.2
336

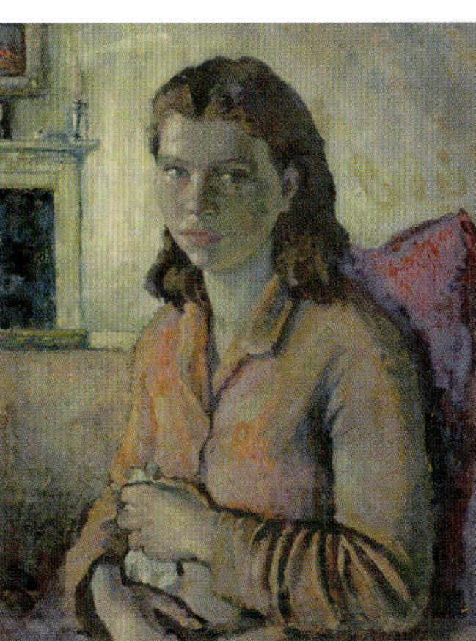

Farquharson, Jean Boswell
Portrait of a Young Girl
oil on canvas 56.5 x 45.7
190

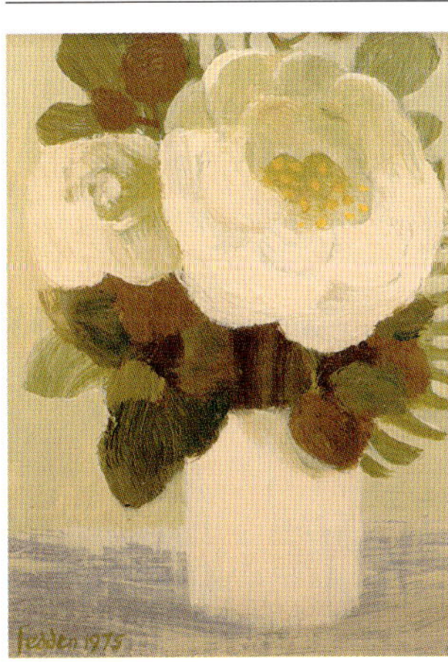

Fedden, Mary b.1915
White Roses 1975
oil on board 20.4 x 15.3
10/1988

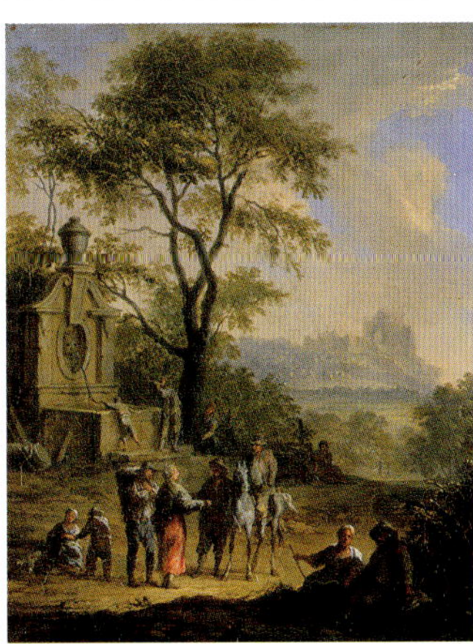

Ferg, Franz de Paula 1689–1740
Landscape
oil on copper 17 x 13.4
192

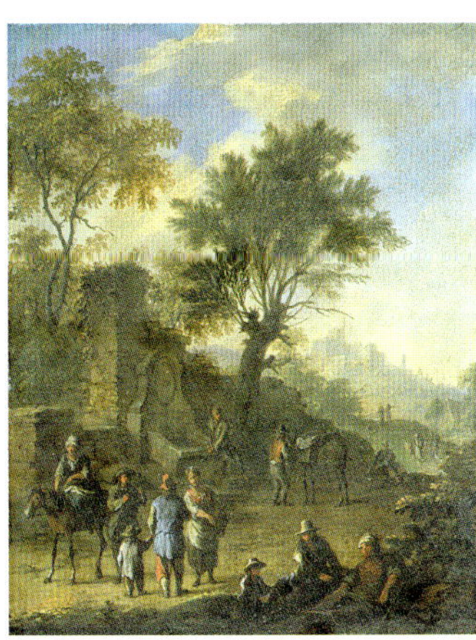

Ferg, Franz de Paula 1689–1740
Landscape
oil on copper 16.9 x 13.5
193

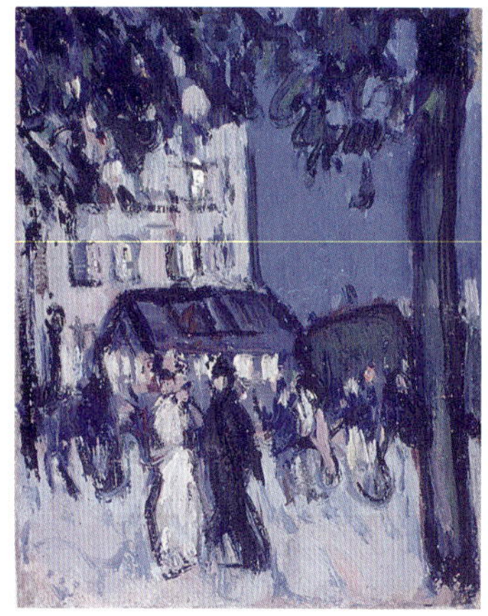

Fergusson, John Duncan 1874–1961
Street at Night 1907
oil on board 23.8 x 18.8
13/1967

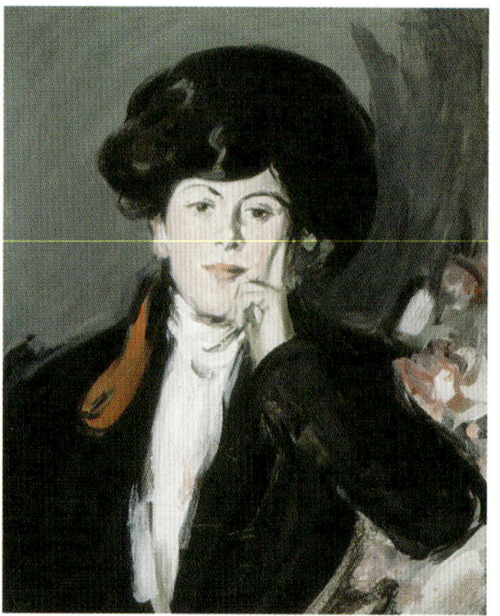

Fergusson, John Duncan 1874–1961
A Girl with Black Hair
oil on canvas 73.8 x 61
1/1972

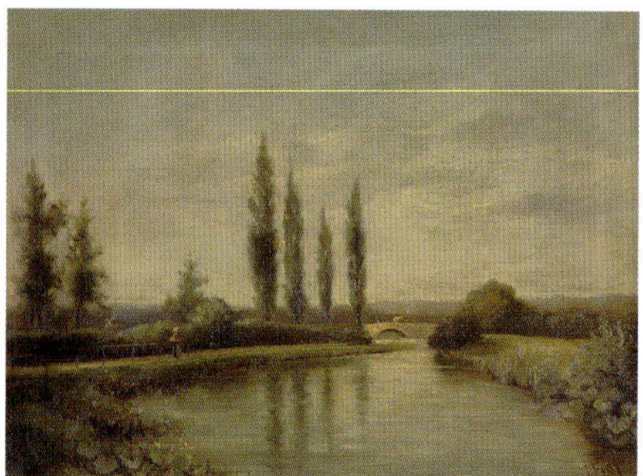

Ferry, John active 1897–1929
Woodmill 1897
oil on canvas 30.5 x 40.7
194

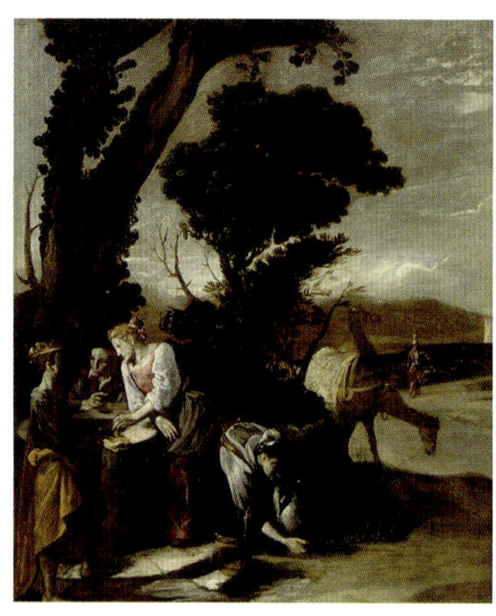

Fetti, Domenico c.1589–1623
Rebecca at the Well
oil on canvas 76.8 x 62.3
195

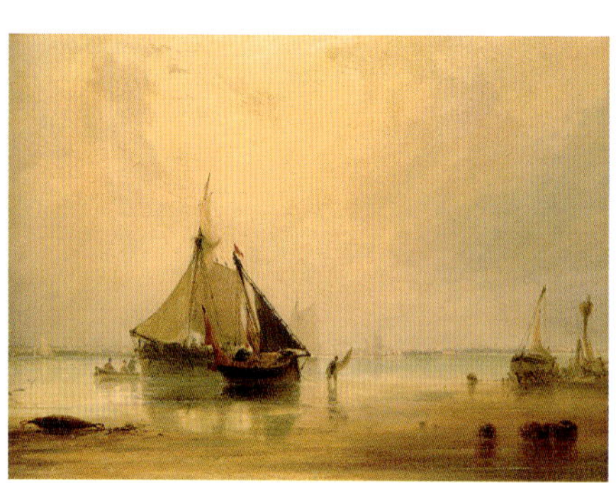

Fielding, Anthony V. C. 1787–1855
Vessels on Shore near Southampton
oil on canvas 21.5 x 30.5
1343

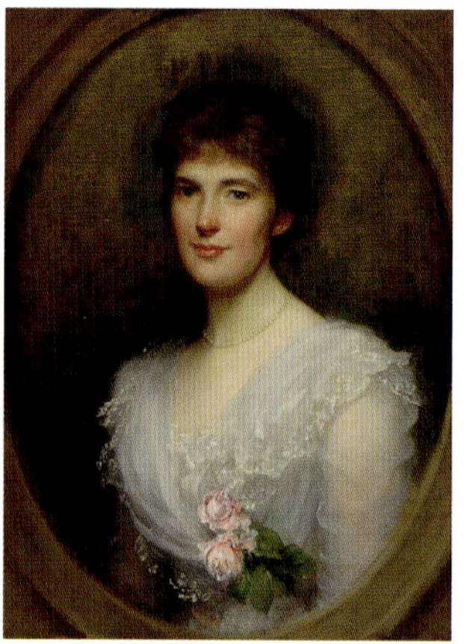

Fildes, Luke 1844–1927
Annie Winifred Marsden-Smedley 1900
oil on canvas 73.7 x 54.5
2/1999

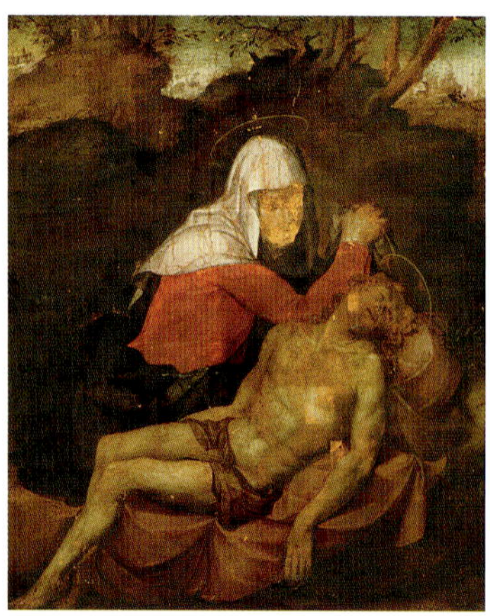

Flemish School 16th C
Pietà
oil on wood 86.4 x 72.6
666

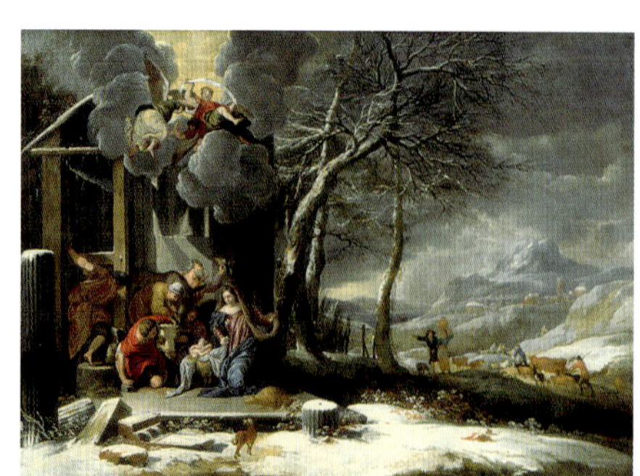

Flemish School 17th C
Winter Landscape with the Nativity
oil on canvas 123.5 x 173.5
1408

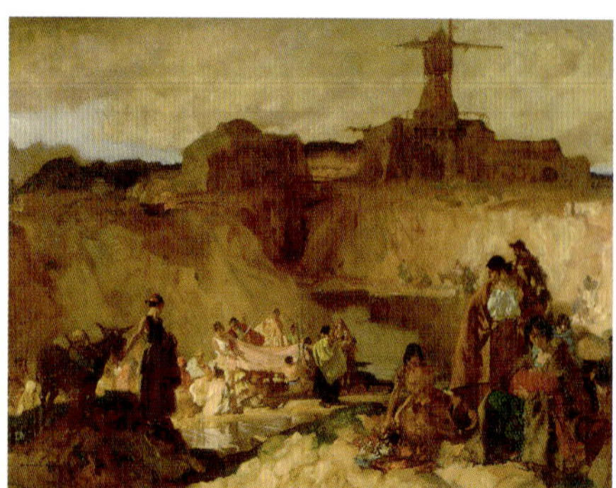

Flint, William Russell 1880–1969
Nomads' Rendezvous
oil on canvas 105.2 x 130.8
203

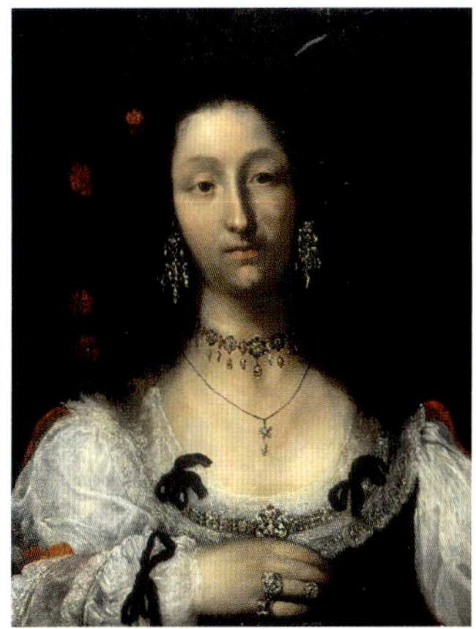

Forabosco, Girolamo c.1605–1679
Portrait of a Lady
oil on wood 66.3 x 50.5
553

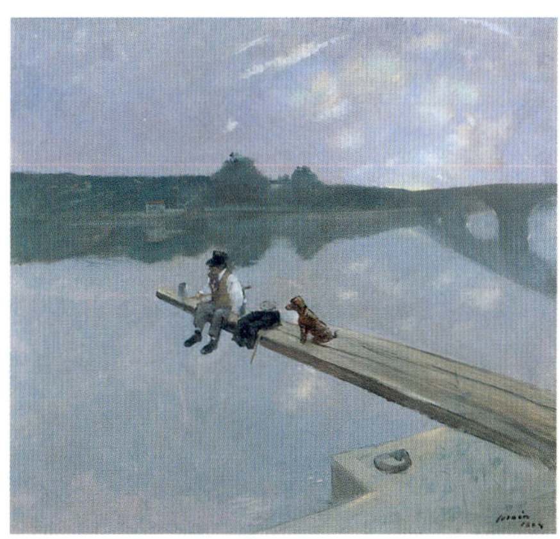

Forain, Jean Louis 1852–1931
The Fisherman 1884
oil on canvas 94.7 x 100.1
204

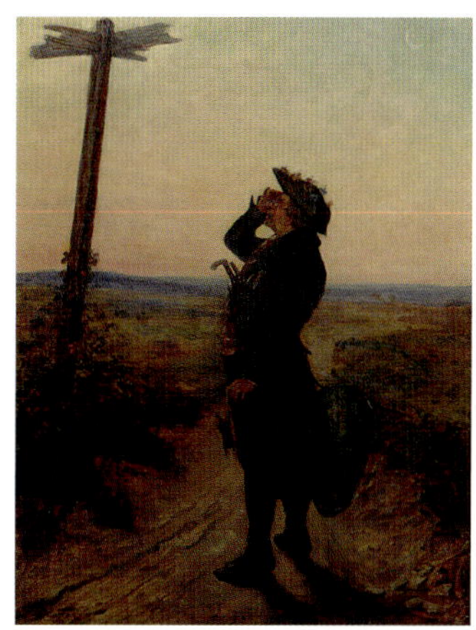

Fox, George c.1816–1910
'Many signs but nothing shown'
oil on canvas 46 x 35.9
205

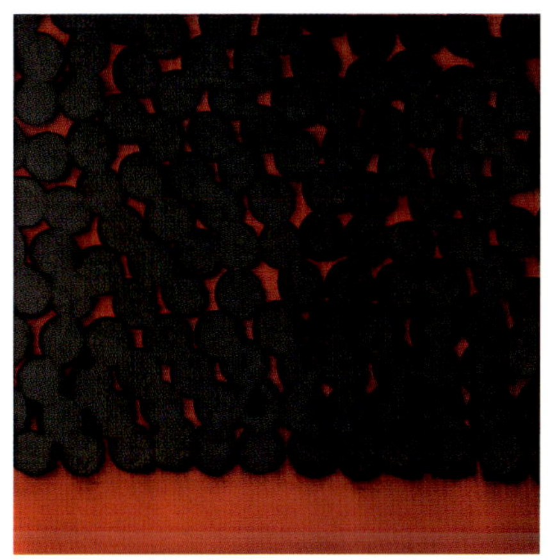

Francis, Mark b.1962
Growth Study 1991
oil on canvas 61.8 x 61.3
5/1999

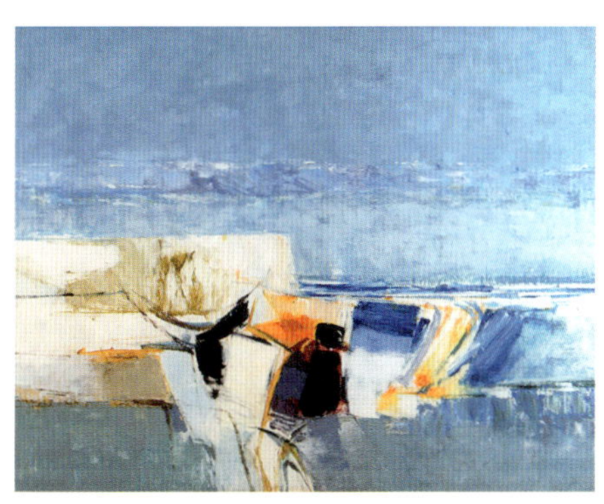

Fraser, Donald Hamilton b.1929
Beach with Cloud Banks and Cliffs 1955
oil on canvas 71 x 91
1488

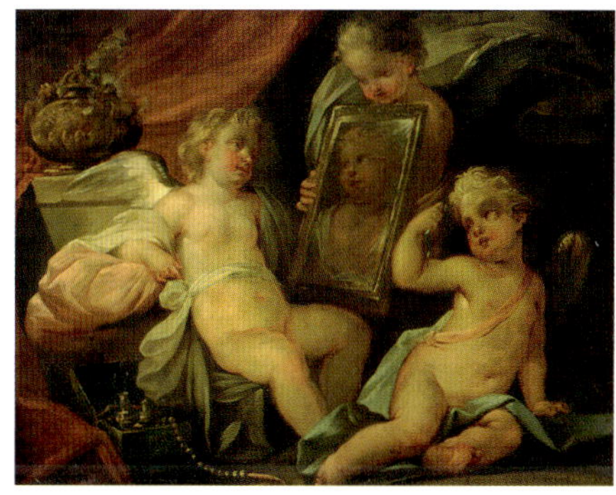

French School
The Three Cupids
oil on canvas 62.2 x 79
44

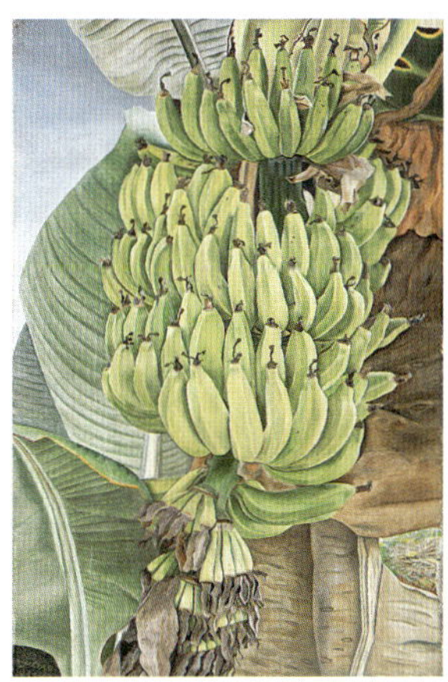

Freud, Lucian b.1922
Bananas 1952
oil on canvas 23 x 15
85/1963

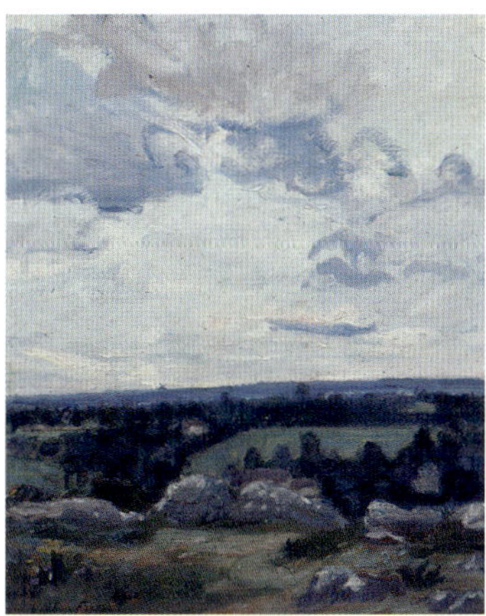

Friesz, Othon 1879–1949
Rochers de Noron 1902
oil on canvas 55.3 x 46.3
1/1960

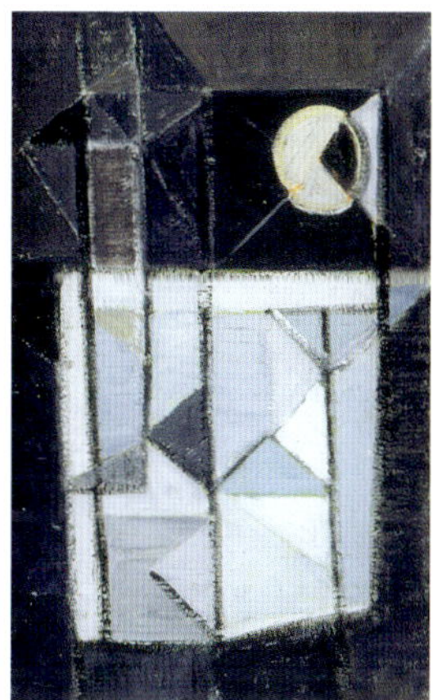

Frost, Terry 1915–2003
Silver and Grey 1953
oil on canvas 57.5 x 36.5
10/2002

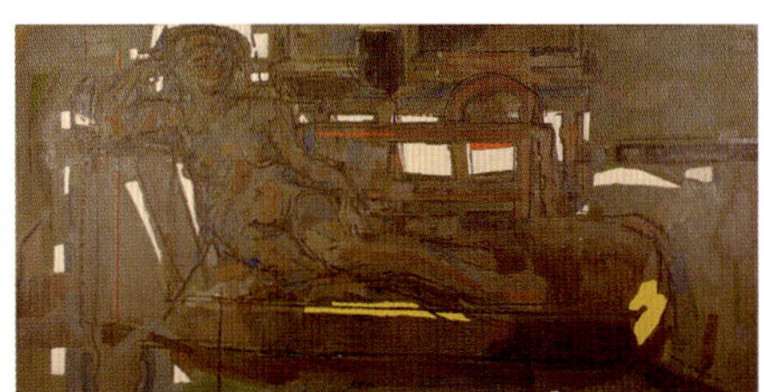

Froy, Martin b.1926
Model Resting
oil on canvas 121.9 x 244.6
3/1959

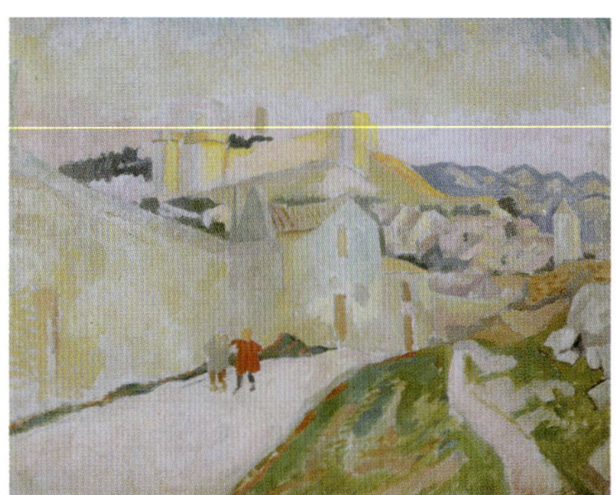

Fry, Roger Eliot 1866–1934
Fort Saint André, Villeneuve lez Avignon 1913
oil on canvas 75.1 x 92.7
52/2002

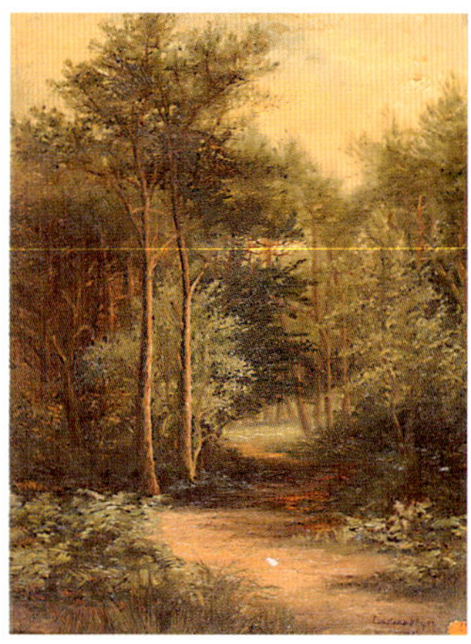

Fryer, Calvin W. 1871–1942
Talbot Woods 1894
oil on canvas 40.7 x 30.5
206

Fussell, Michael 1927–1974
Still Life 1959
oil on canvas 94.9 x 142
1/1979

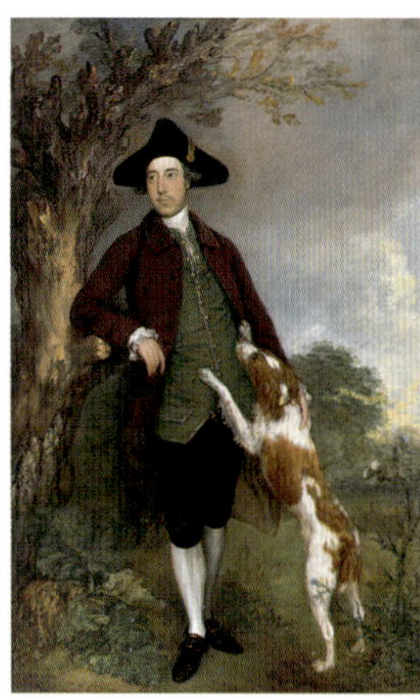

Gainsborough, Thomas 1727–1788
George Venables Vernon 1767
oil on canvas 246.3 x 150
1494

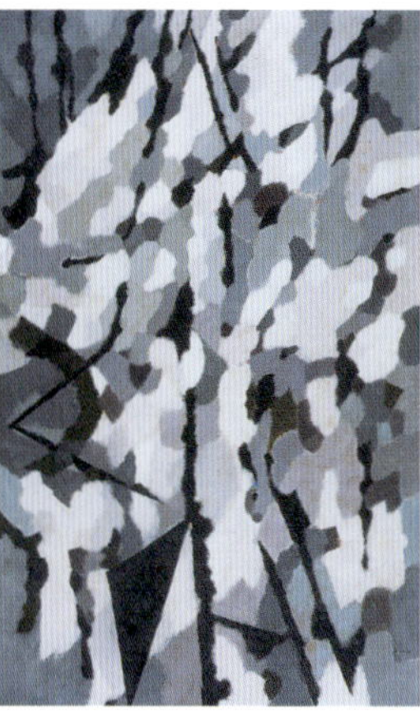

Gear, William 1915–1997
Winter Landscape 1960
oil on canvas 203.5 x 127
4/1964

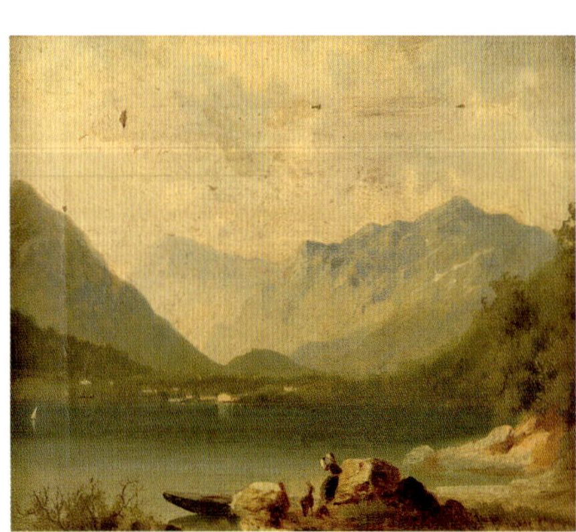

Gelb, Georg
Swiss Scene
oil on canvas 28.5 x 34.2
897

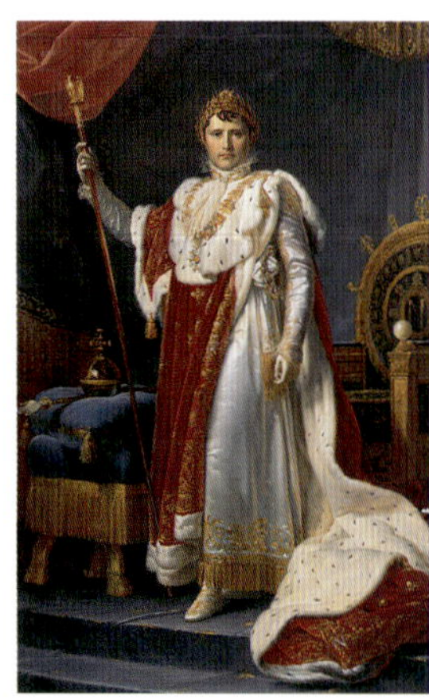

Gérard, François 1770–1837
Napoleon (1769–1821)
oil on canvas 218.5 x 141
79/1963

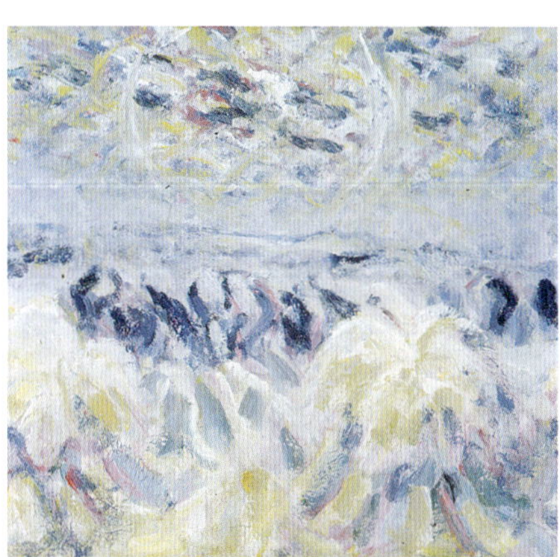

Gerrard, Kaff 1894–1970
Corn Stooks
oil on board 30.3 x 40.5
60/1991

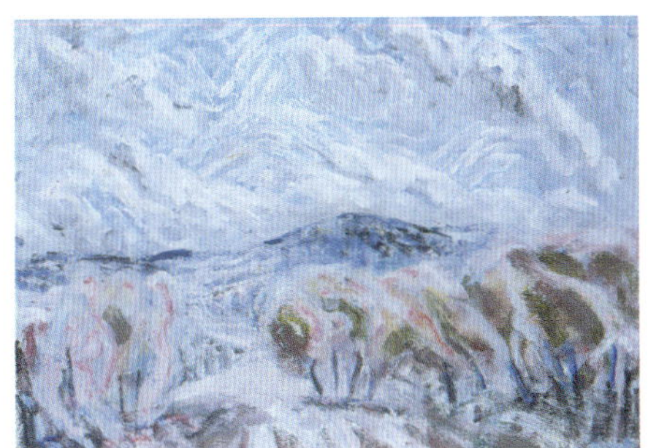

Gerrard, Kaff 1894–1970
Landscape with Pink Trees
oil on board 30.3 x 40.8
62/1991

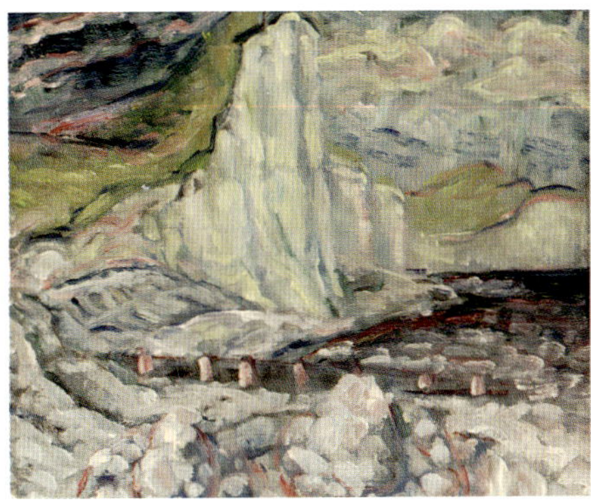

Gerrard, Kaff 1894–1970
Seascape with Cliffs
oil on board 34 x 43.4
61/1991

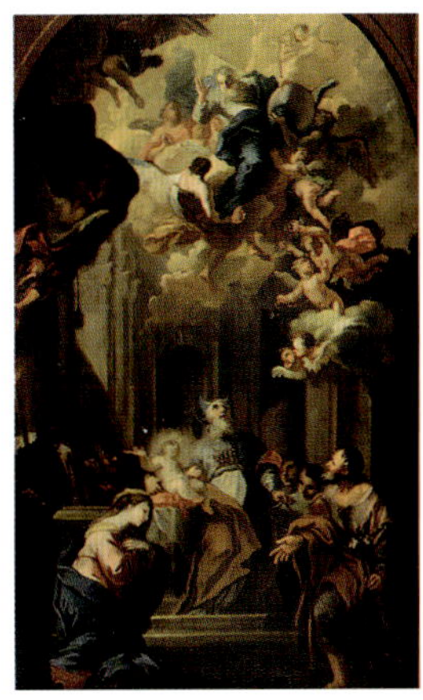

Gerrard, Kaff 1894–1970
The Circumcision
oil on canvas 89 x 55
178/1975

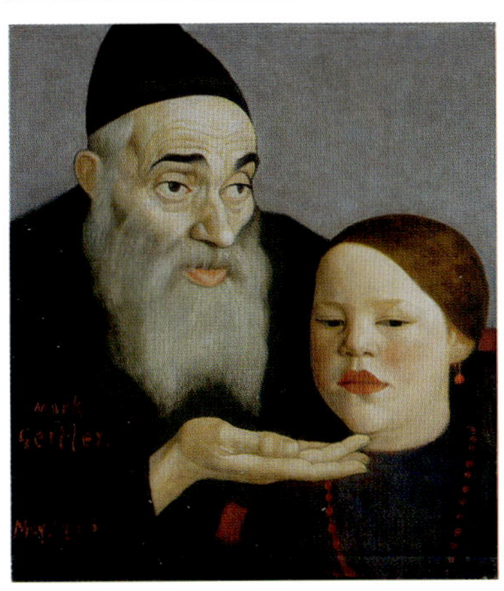

Gertler, Mark 1892–1939
The Rabbi and His Grandchild 1913
oil on canvas 50.8 x 45.9
6/1968

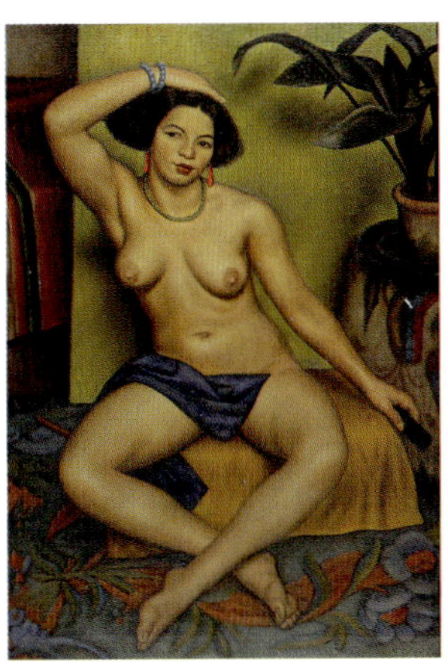

Gertler, Mark 1892–1939
Seated Nude 1924
oil on canvas 102 x 71.4
1457

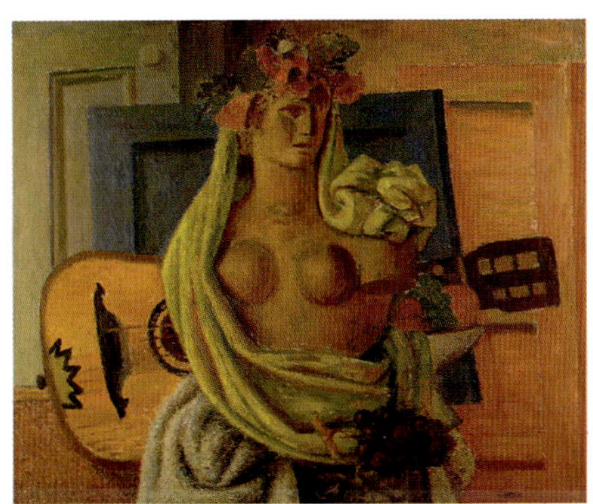

Gertler, Mark 1892–1939
Still Life with Bust 1936
oil on board 106.8 x 130.7
1420

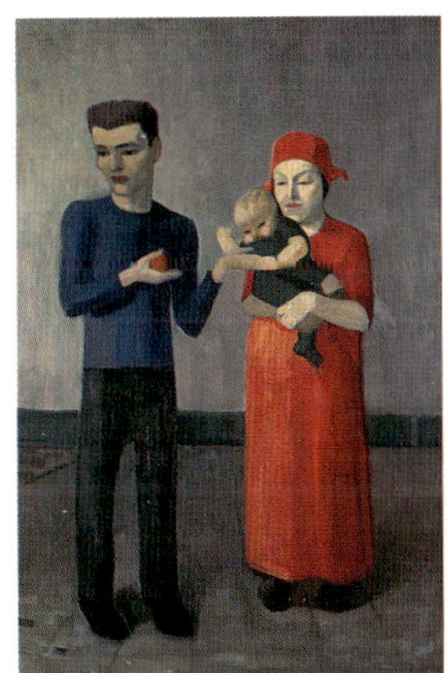

Gertler, Mark 1892–1939
Family Group
oil on canvas 92.4 x 61
1428

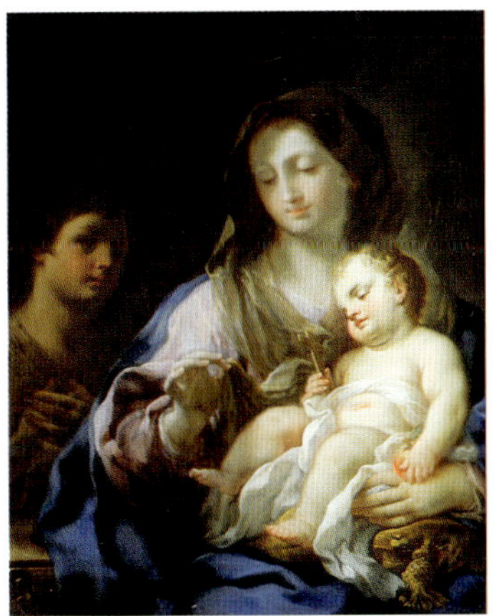

Giaquinto, Corrado 1703–1765
Virgin and Child with an Angel
oil on canvas 76.3 x 62.3
3/1970

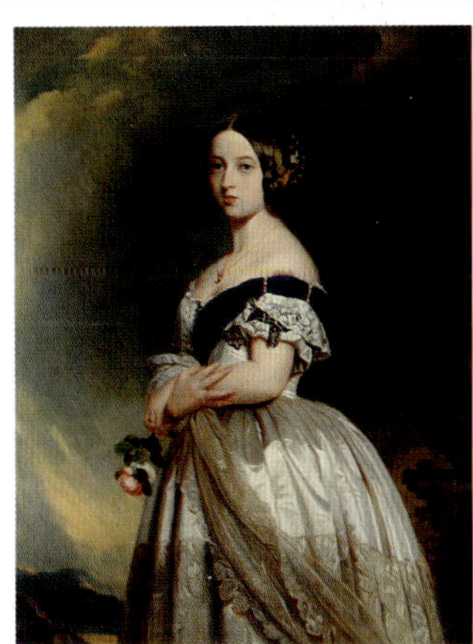

Gilbert, Joseph Marc
Queen Victoria (1819–1901)
oil on canvas 130.3 x 97.5
632

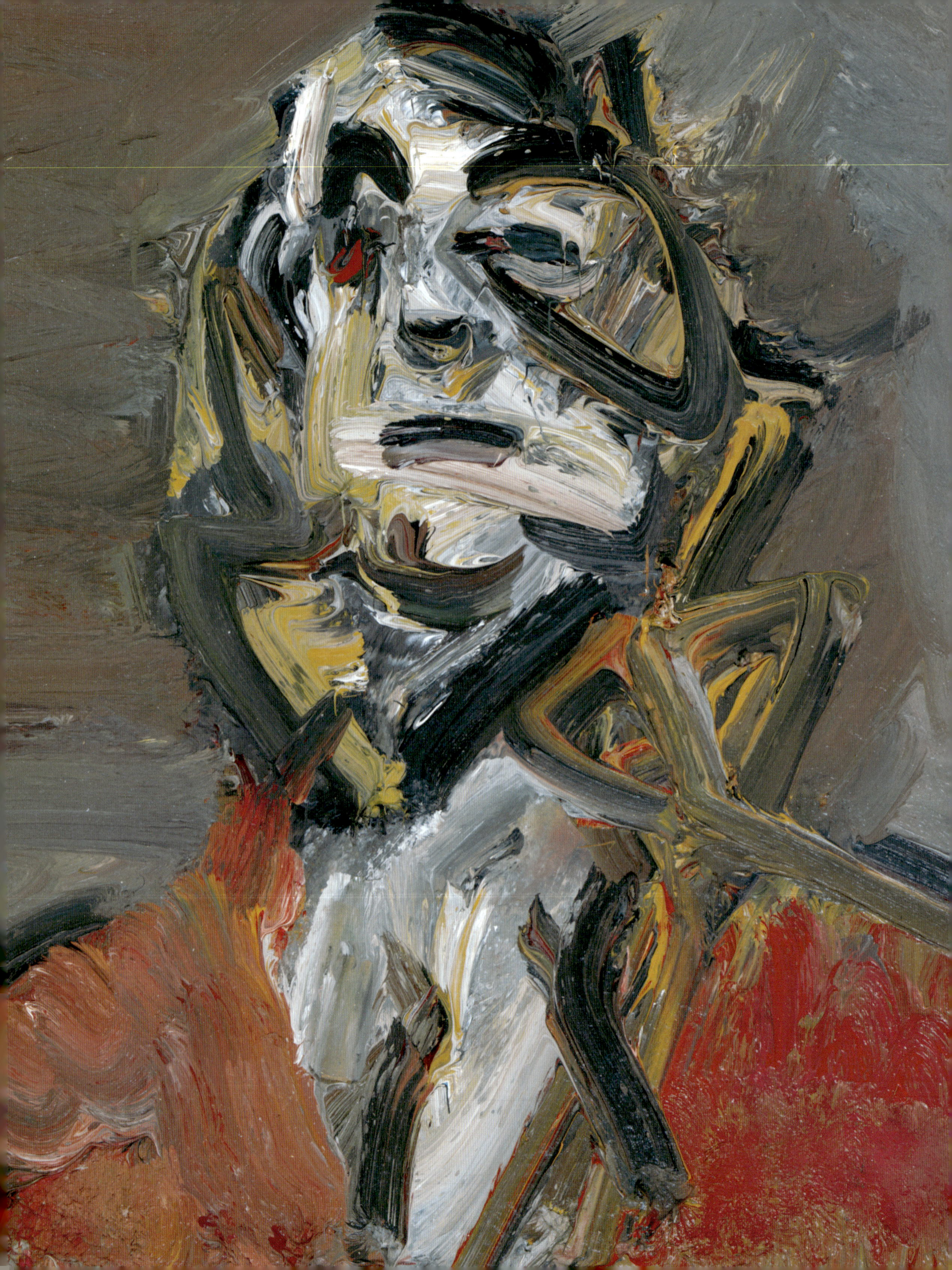

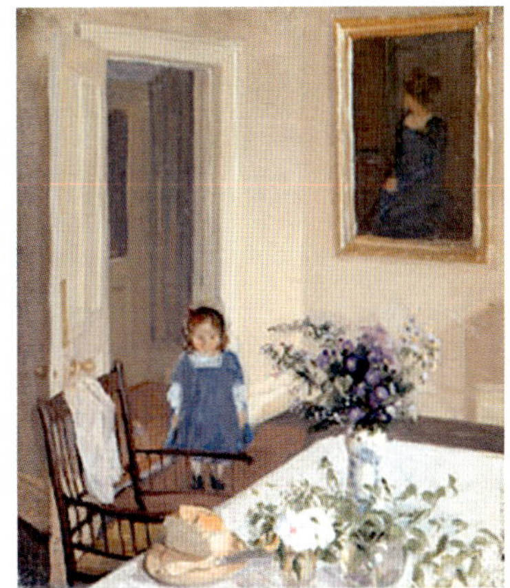

Gilman, Harold 1876–1919
Interior 1907
oil on canvas 41.5 x 32.1
208

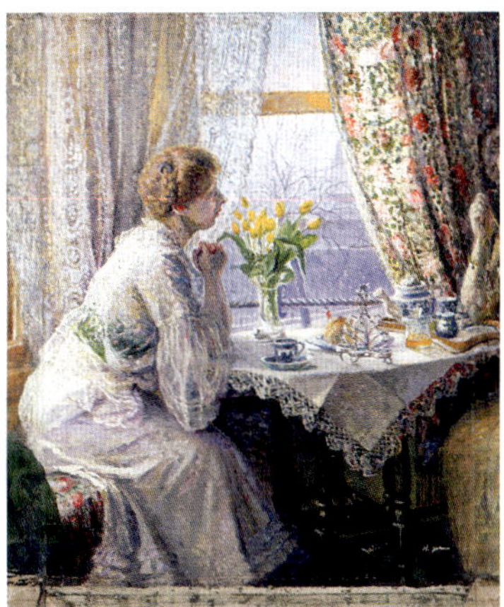

Gilman, Harold 1876–1919
The Breakfast Table 1911
oil on canvas 77 x 61
1354

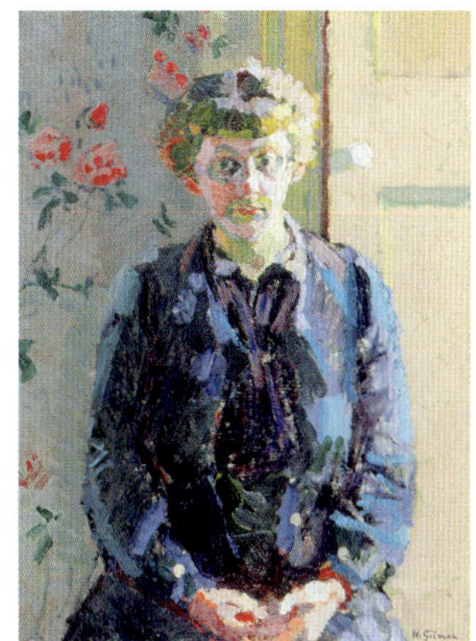

Gilman, Harold 1876–1919
Sylvia Gosse (1881–1968) 1912
oil on canvas 67 x 49
1389

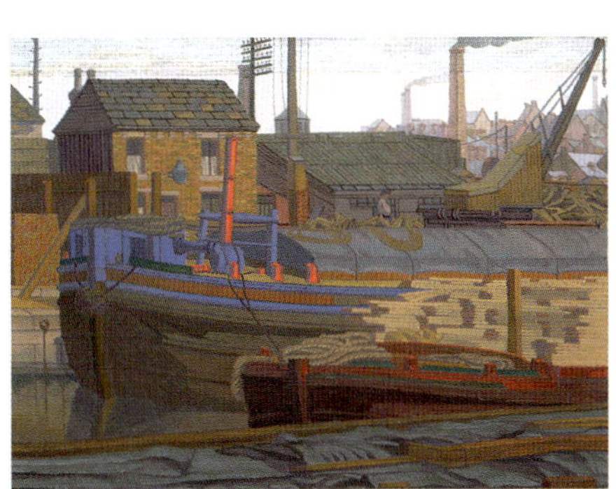

Ginner, Charles 1878–1952
The Barges, Leeds 1916
oil on canvas 51 x 68.5
9/1974

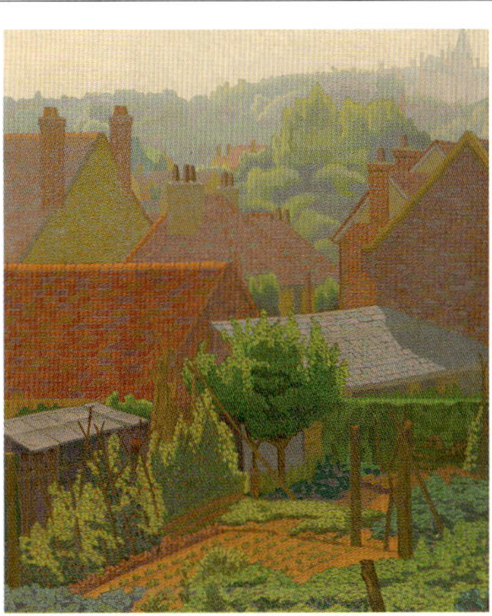

Ginner, Charles 1878–1952
Early Morning 1917
oil on canvas 61.6 x 50.2
12/1969

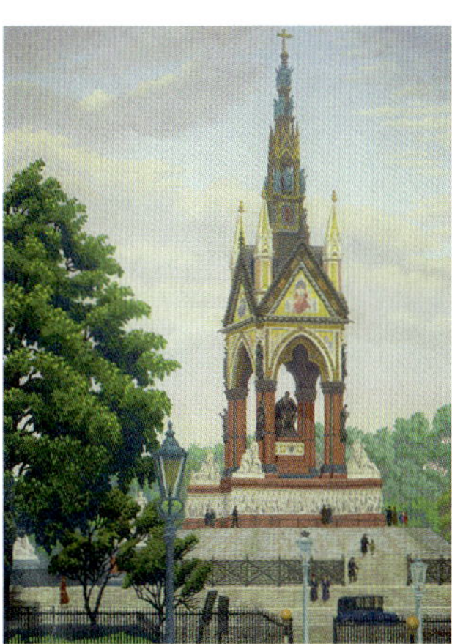

Ginner, Charles 1878–1952
The Albert Memorial 1947
oil on canvas 102 x 82.5
1304

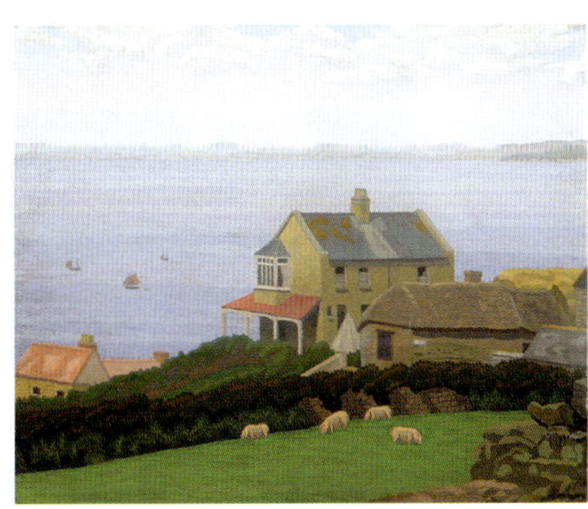

Ginner, Charles 1878–1952
Landscape
oil on canvas 50.9 x 61.3
7/1964

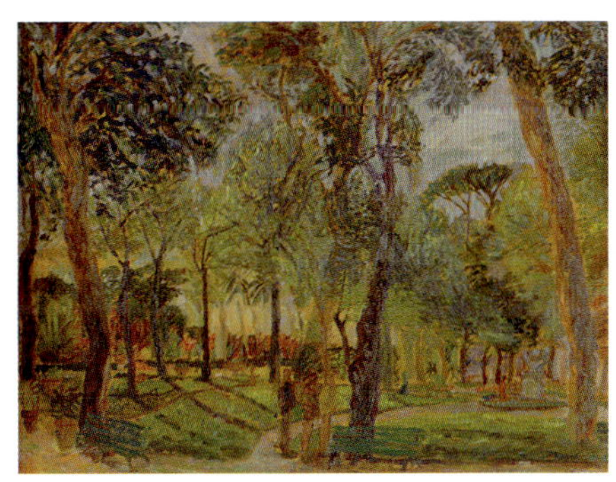

Girvin, Joy b.1961
Evening in the Borghese Gardens 1993
oil on canvas 29.1 x 39.5
106/2002

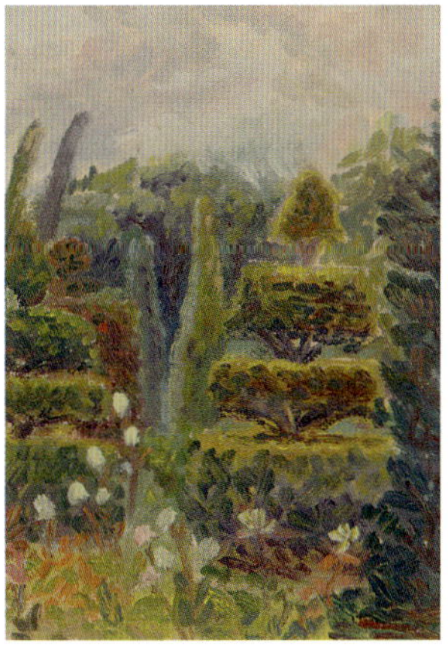

Girvin, Joy b.1961
Plas Brondanw
oil on canvas 17.5 x 12.5
34/2002

Facing page: Auerbach, Frank Helmuth, b.1931, *JYM1* (detail), Southampton City Art Gallery, (p. 13)

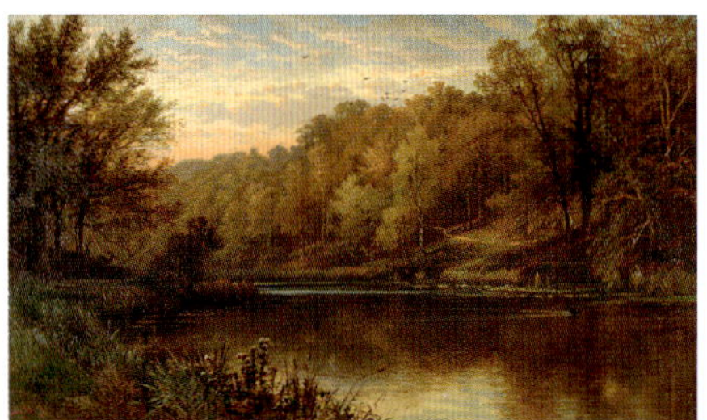

Glendening, Alfred Augustus I
c.1840–c.1910
Autumn, Arundel Park
oil on canvas 61.1 x 105.7
209

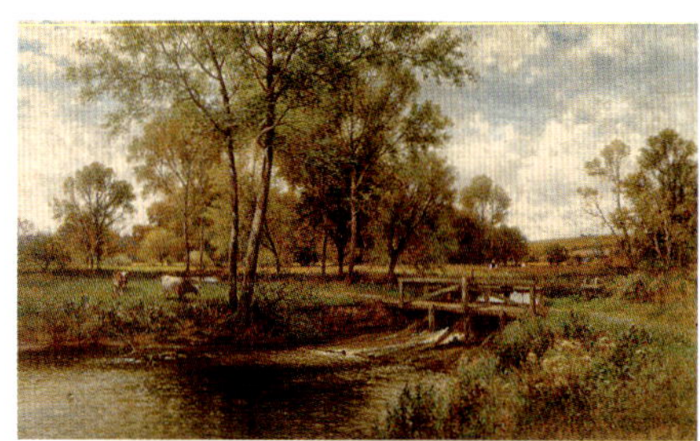

Glendening, Alfred Augustus I
c.1840–c.1910
In the Meadow, Youngsbury
oil on canvas 76.7 x 127.6
210

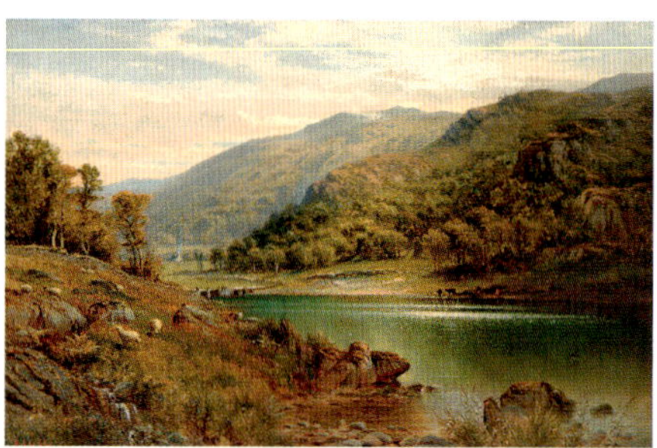

Glendening, Alfred Augustus I
c.1840–c.1910
Llyn Mymbyr, Capel Curig
oil on canvas 51.1 x 76.5
211

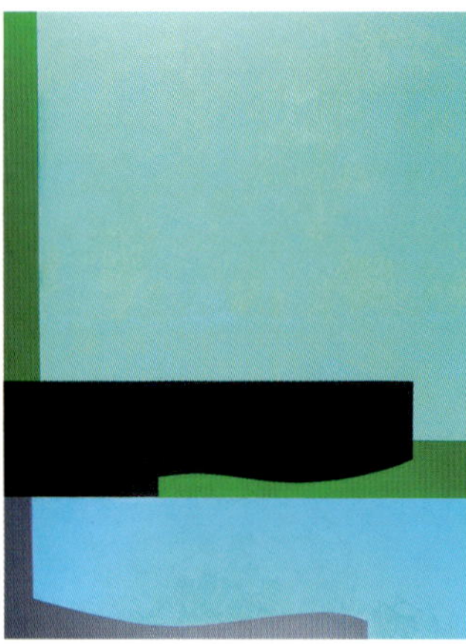

Golding, John b.1929
Asphodel
oil on canvas 183 x 142.2
6/1967

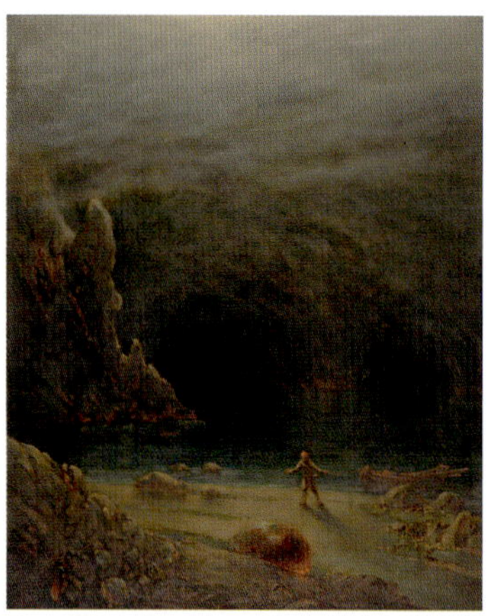

Goodwin, William Sidney 1833–1916
The Great Carbuncle
oil on canvas 48.4 x 38.2
214

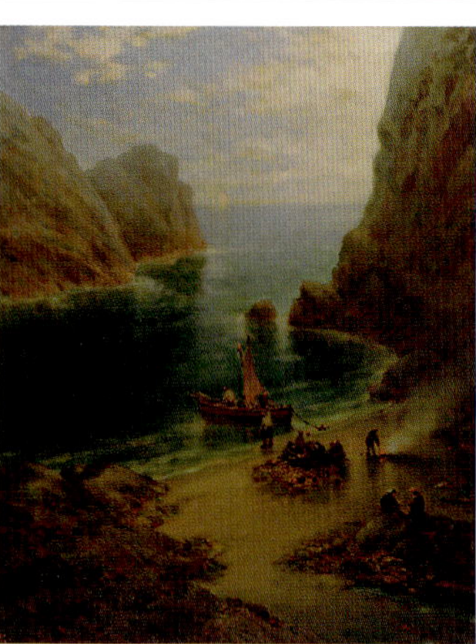

Goodwin, William Sidney 1833–1916
Landing of the Treasure
oil on canvas 48.5 x 38.1
215

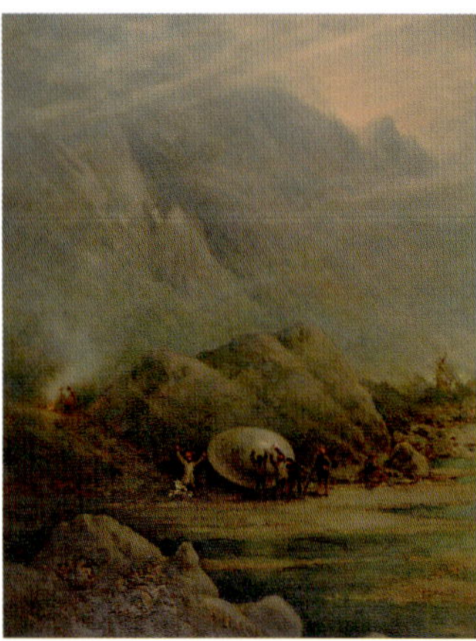

Goodwin, William Sidney 1833–1916
The Rukh's Egg
oil on canvas 48.3 x 38
216

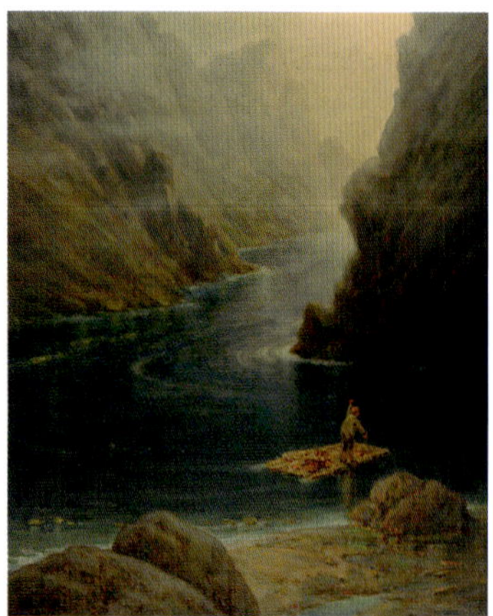

Goodwin, William Sidney 1833–1916
Sinbad on the Raft
oil on canvas 48.2 x 38.3
217

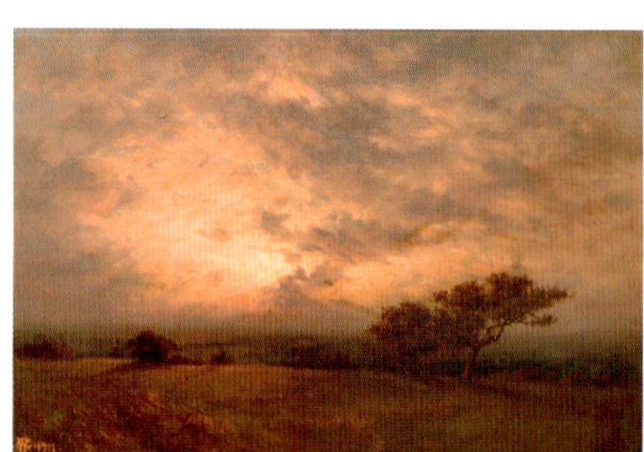

Goodwin, William Sidney 1833–1916
Stormy Sunset, New Forest
oil on canvas 51 x 76.2
218

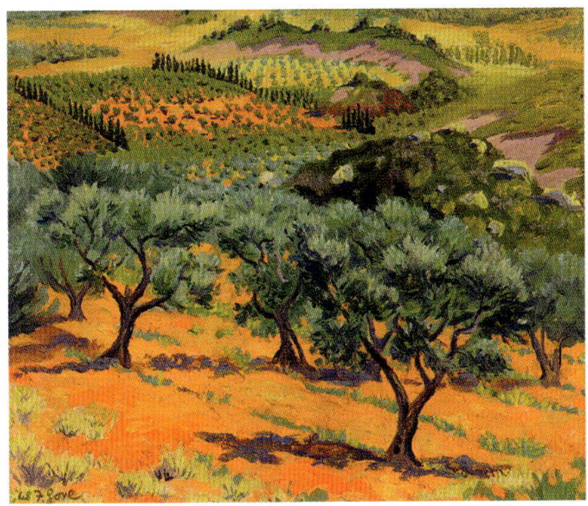

Gore, Frederick b.1913
Olive Trees, Les Baux 1948
oil on canvas 50.8 x 61
1363

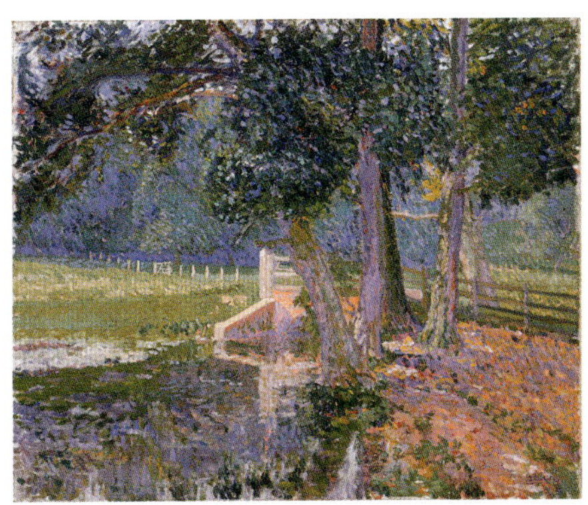

Gore, Spencer 1878–1914
Panshanger Park 1908
oil on canvas 50.8 x 61
220

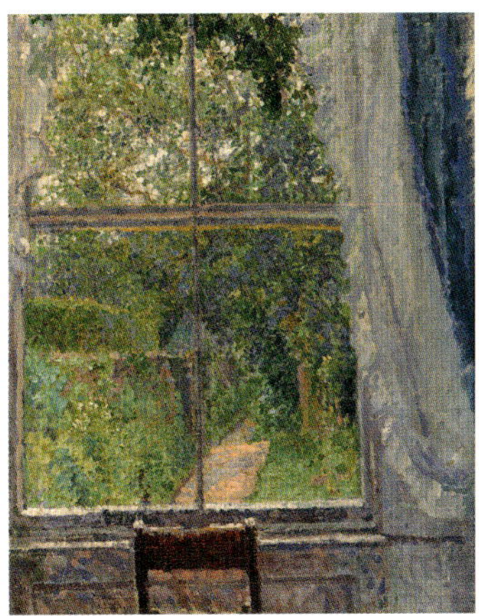

Gore, Spencer 1878–1914
View from a Window 1909
oil on canvas 50.8 x 40.3
221

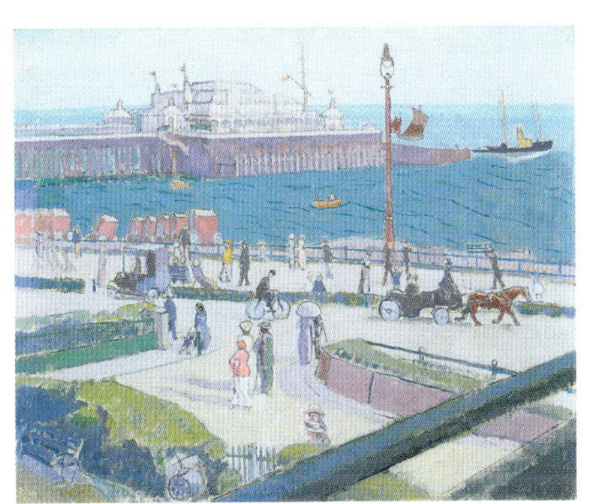

Gore, Spencer 1878–1914
Brighton Pier 1913
oil on canvas 63.5 x 76.3
1484

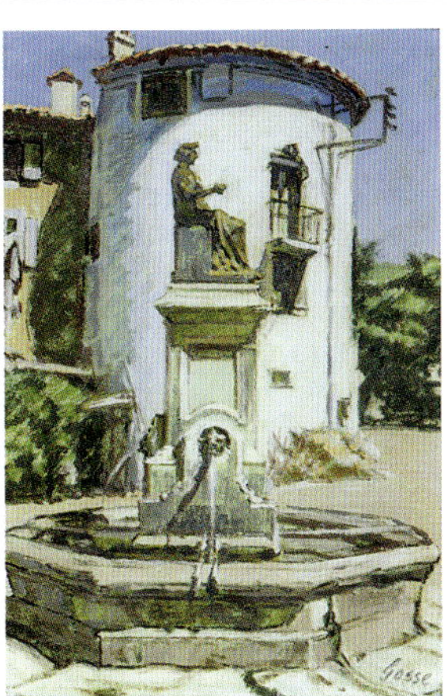

Gosse, Laura Sylvia 1881–1968
Fountain, Saule 1951
oil on canvas 65.4 x 51.3
43/2002

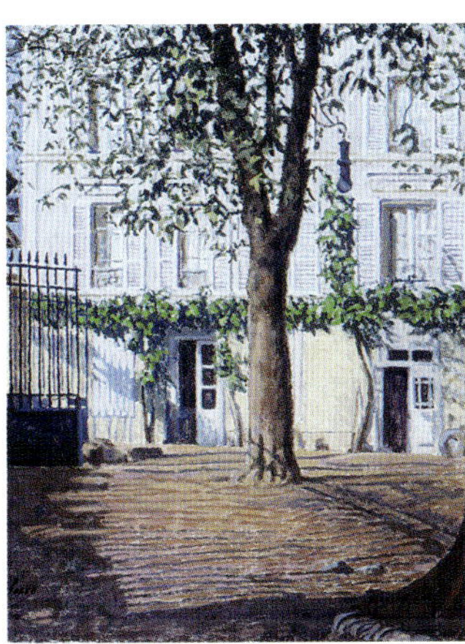

Gosse, Laura Sylvia 1881–1968
From the Garden, Morning, Dieppe
oil on canvas 55.8 x 45.8
7/1973

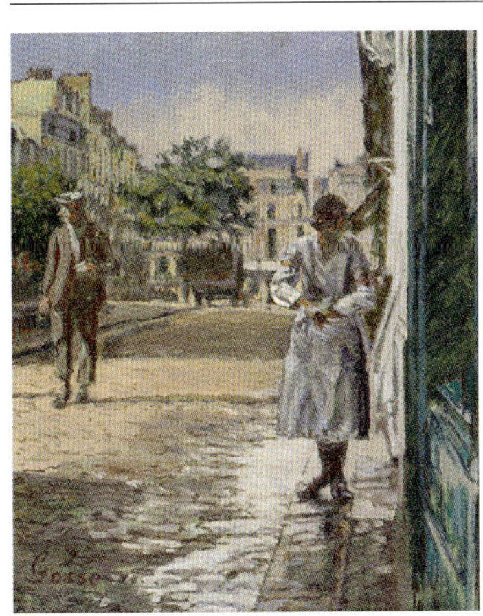

Gosse, Laura Sylvia 1881–1968
Street Scene, Dieppe
oil on canvas 55.6 x 46
6/1973

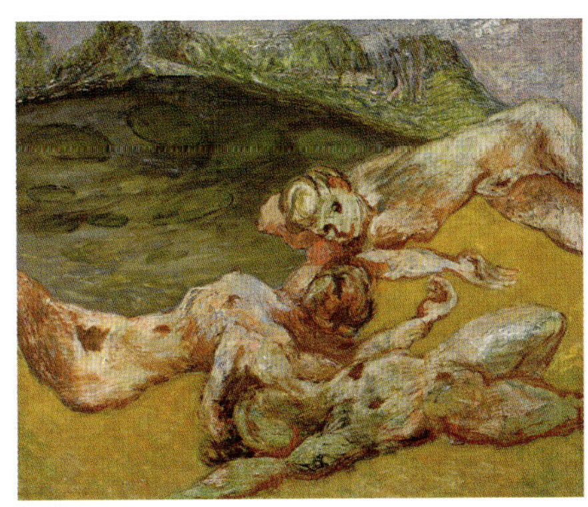

Gotlib, Henryk 1890–1966
The Lake 1952
oil on canvas 141.5 x 172.5
63/1991

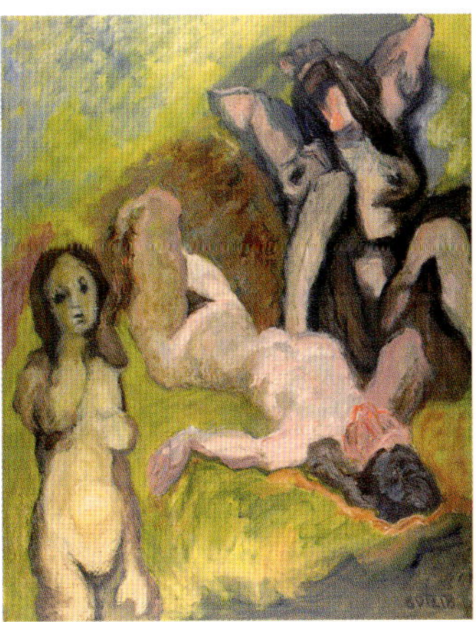

Gotlib, Henryk 1890–1966
Three Nudes 1966
oil on canvas 165 x 132
3/1996

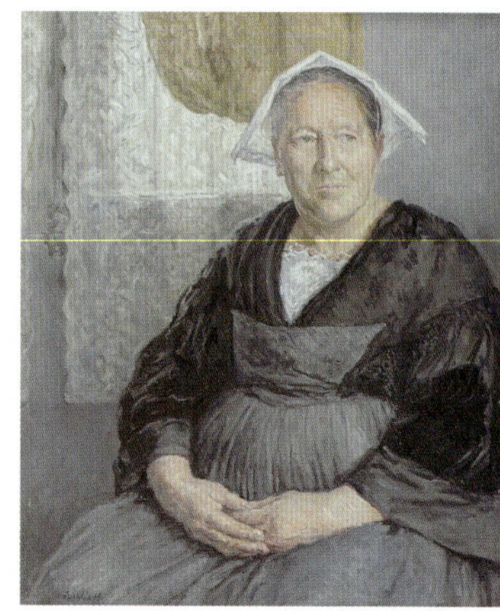

Gotto, Basil 1866–1954
Our Charlady 1938
oil on canvas 53.3 x 42.8
1008

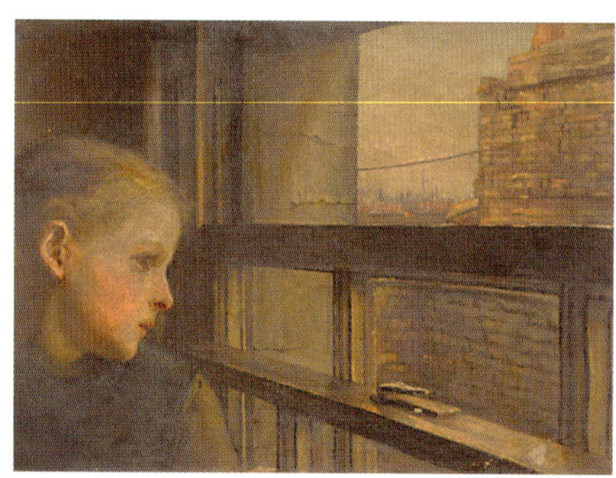

Grace, Frances Lily active 1876–1909
Watching the Birds
oil on canvas 27.6 x 38.1
222

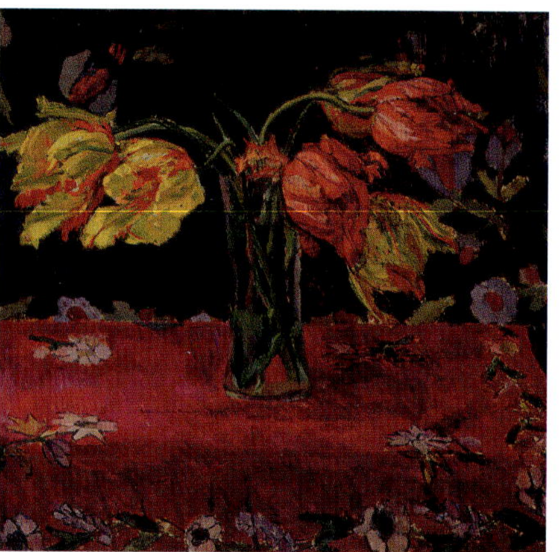

Grant, Duncan 1885–1978
Parrot Tulips 1911
oil on panel 49 x 52
1458

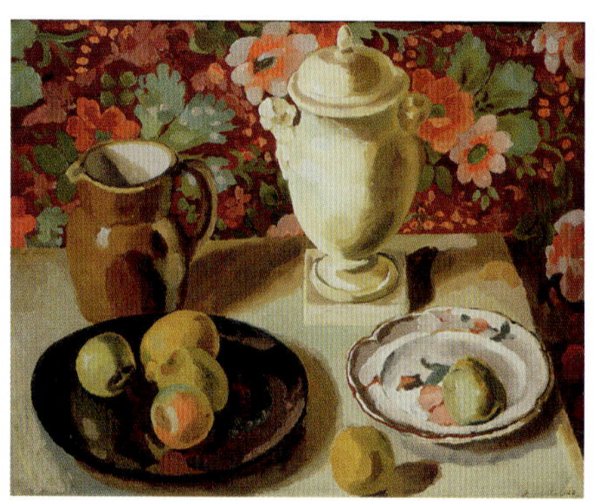

Grant, Duncan 1885–1978
Still Life 1922
oil on canvas 53.3 x 66
2/1972

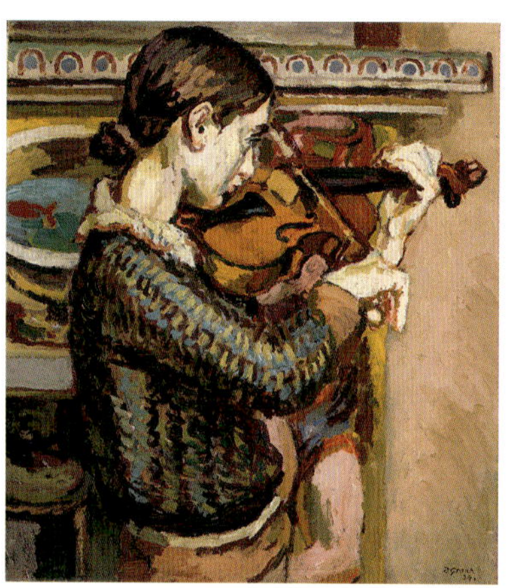

Grant, Duncan 1885–1978
Angelica Playing the Violin 1934
oil on canvas 71.5 x 65.5
2/1984

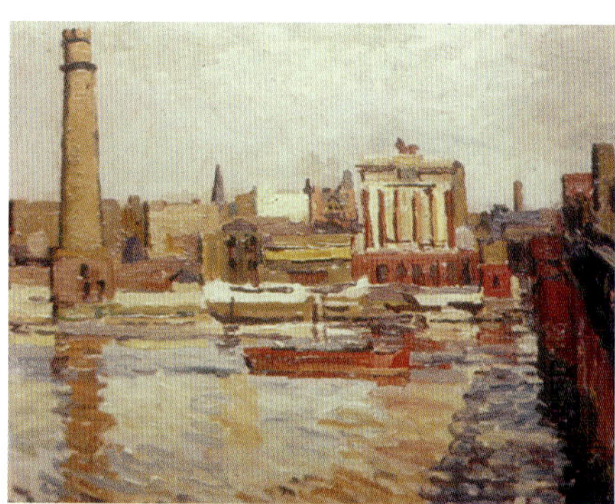

Grant, Duncan 1885–1978
Thames Wharves 1936
oil on wood 46.4 x 57.8
224

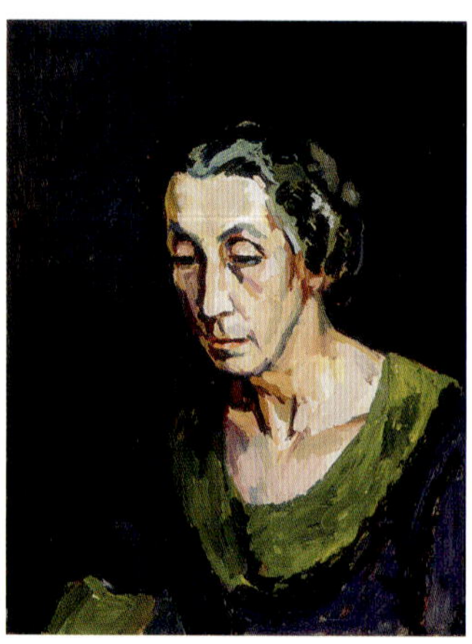

Grant, Duncan 1885–1978
Mrs Hammersley 1937
oil on board 45.7 x 35.6
223

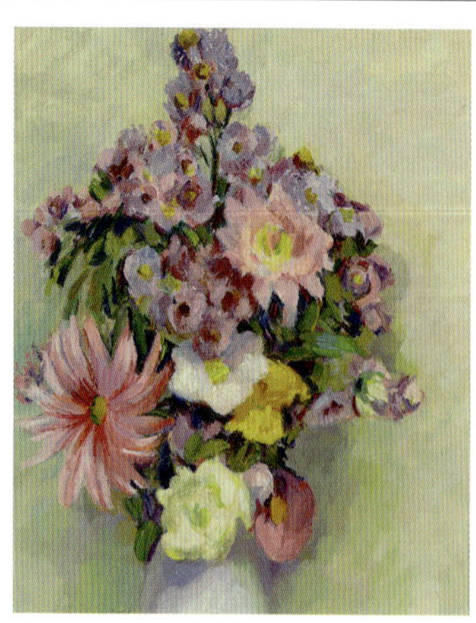

Grant, Duncan 1885–1978
Still Life, Flowers in a Vase
oil on board 47.4 x 41
3/1988

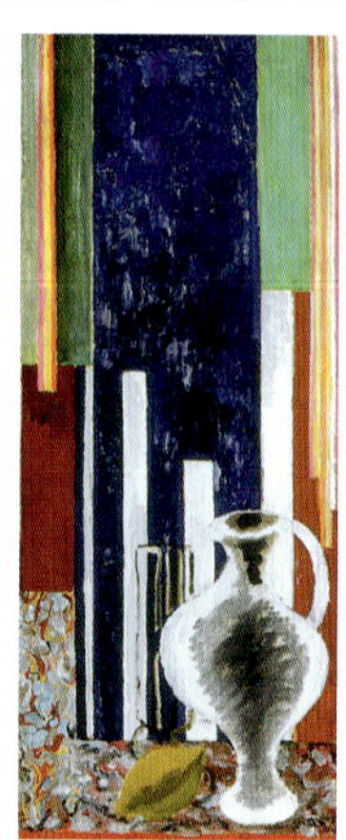

Grant, Duncan 1885–1978
The White Jug
oil on panel 106.5 x 44.3
36/2002

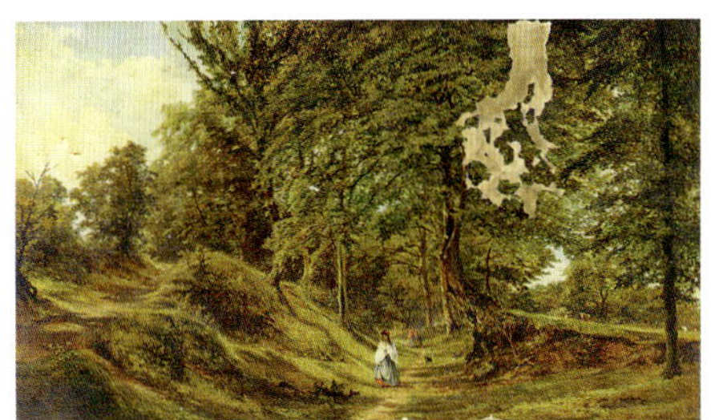

Gray, H. Barnard active 1844–1871
Lane near Kenilworth 1862
oil on canvas 45.8 x 76.3
226

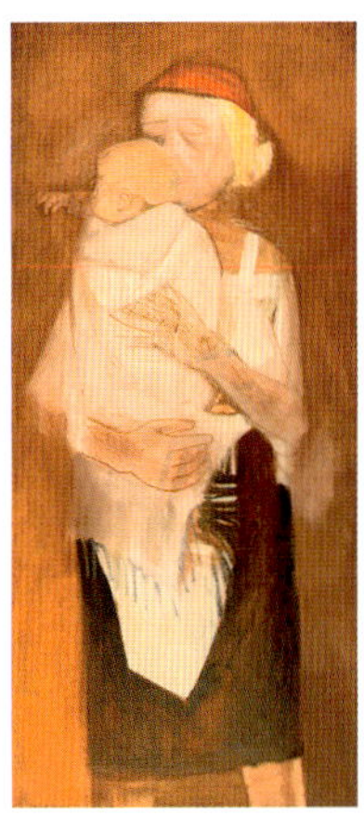

Greaves, Derrick b.1927
Woman in a Red Hat with a Baby
oil on canvas 151.7 x 68.6
9/1958

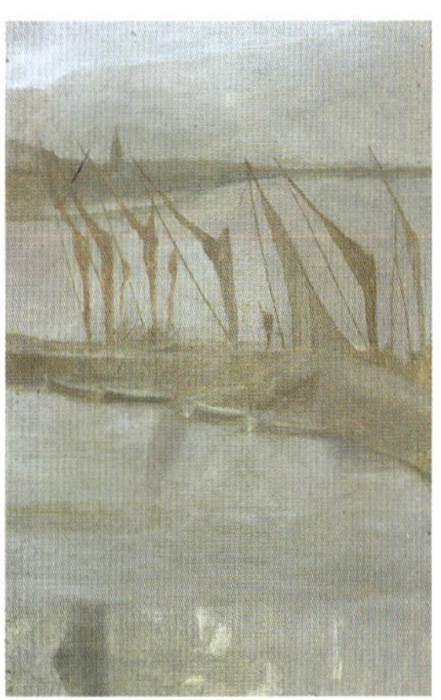

Greaves, Walter 1846–1930
Thames
oil on canvas 71.2 x 45.6
9/1979

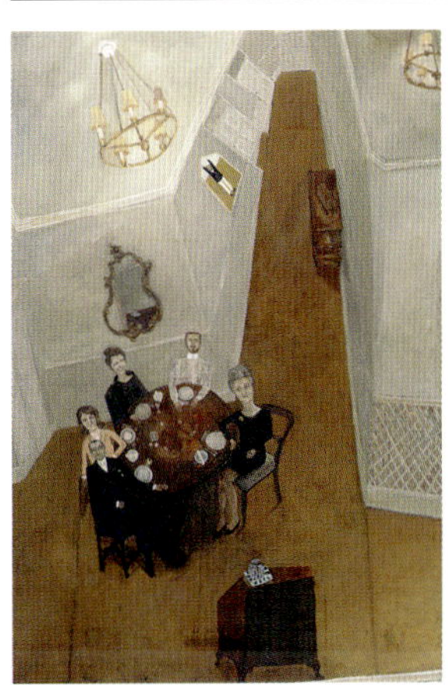

Green, Anthony b.1939
The Dinner Party 1966
oil on canvas 183.2 x 122
8/1967

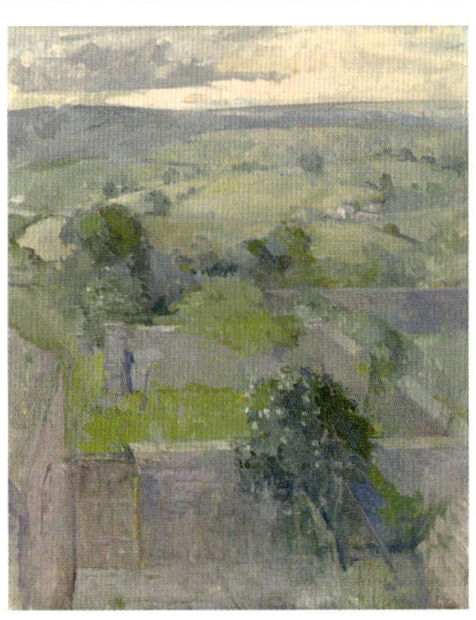

Greenham, Peter 1909–1992
The Cheviots 1977
oil on board 56.9 x 48.5
90/2002

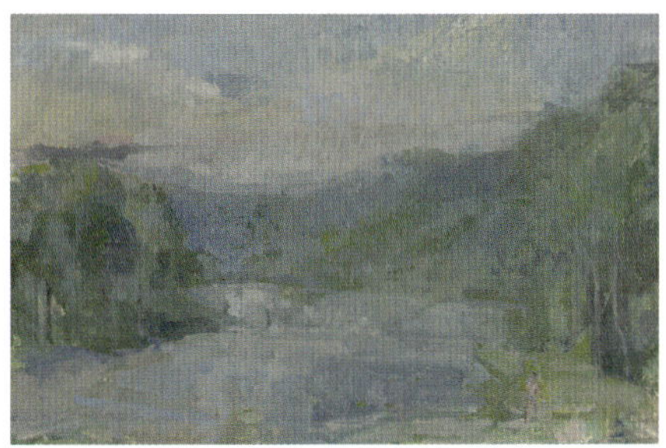

Greenham, Peter 1909–1992
Limeuil
oil on board 29.9 x 54.1
21/2002

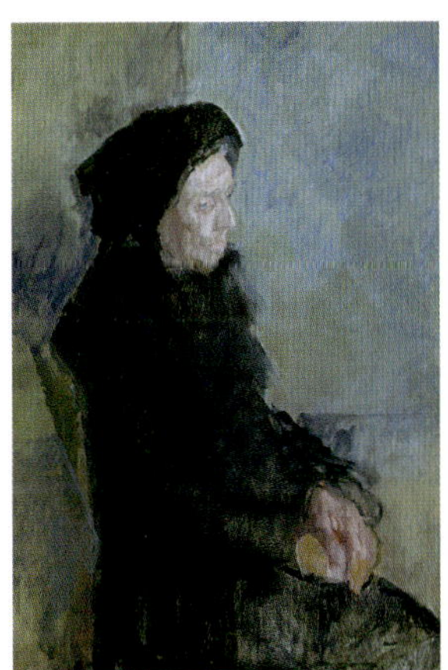

Greenham, Peter 1909–1992
Old Lady in Black
oil on canvas 88.4 x 64.1
22/2002

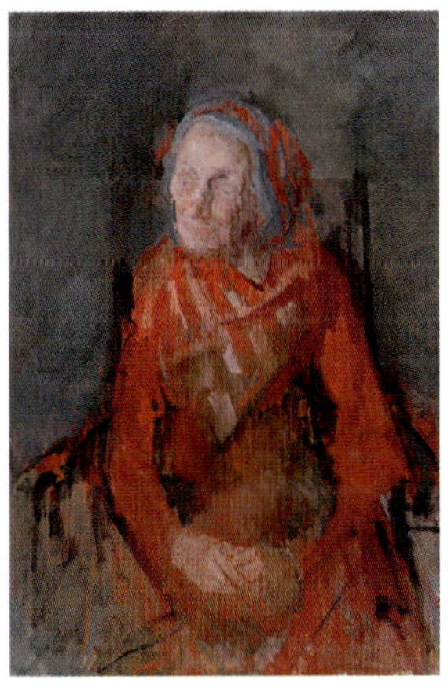

Greenham, Peter 1909–1992
Portrait of an Old Lady
oil on canvas 91.2 x 61.4
11/1982

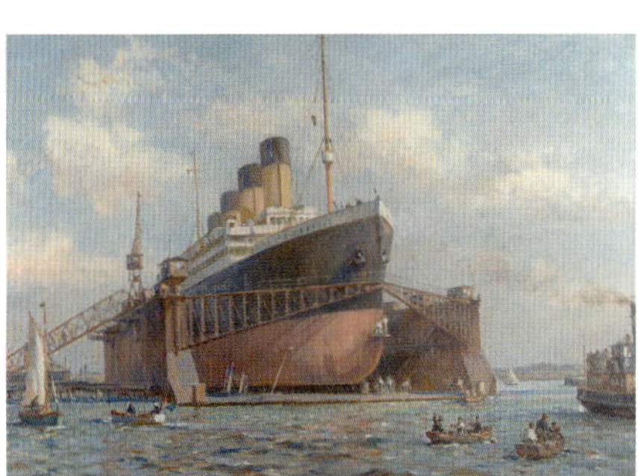

Gribble, Bernard Finegan 1873–1962
A Well-Known Subject at Southampton
oil on canvas 50.7 x 76.7
1009

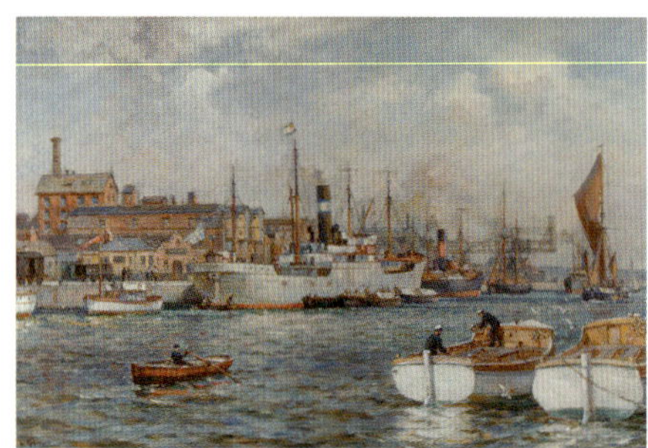

Gribble, Bernard Finegan 1873–1962
Poole Harbour
oil on canvas 45.8 x 71
227

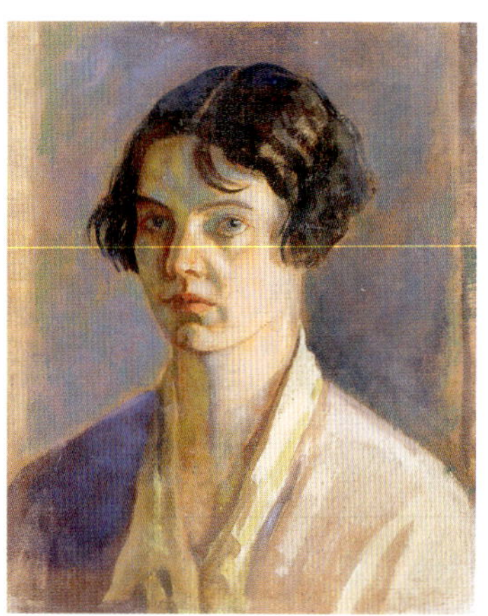

Griffith, Frank 1889–1979
Jaqueline 1930
oil on canvas 46.5 x 38.5
5/1997

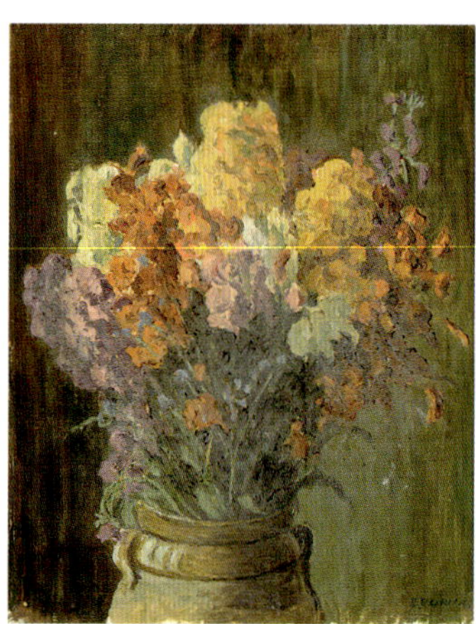

Grigg, Edgar P. active 1939–1940
Flower Study
oil on board 39.3 x 33
228

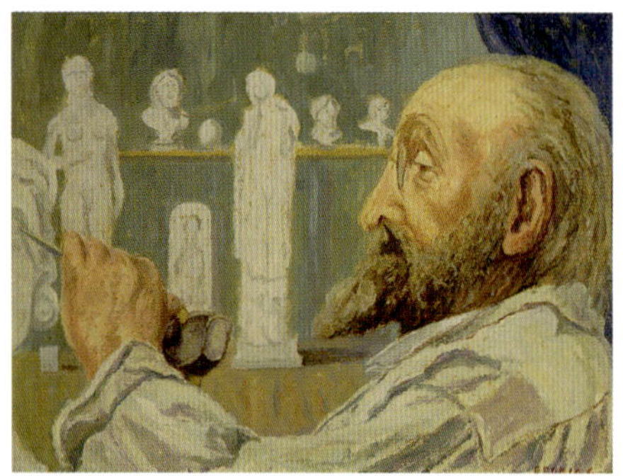

Grigg, Edgar P. active 1939–1940
The Sculptor
oil on lino 34.4 x 44.5
229

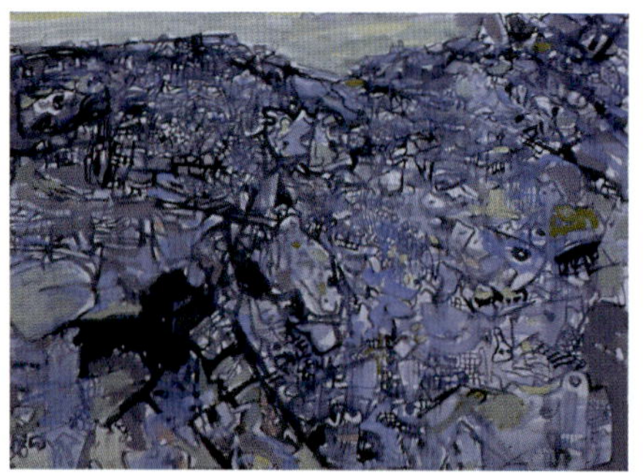

Gross, Anthony 1905–1984
Blue Rocks
oil on canvas 97.1 x 130.3
2/1966

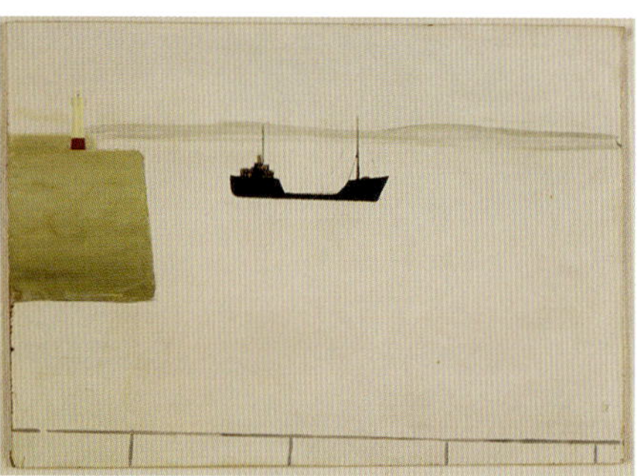

Guthrie, Derek b.1936
ICI Tanker 1962
oil on canvas 29 x 41.4
2/1965

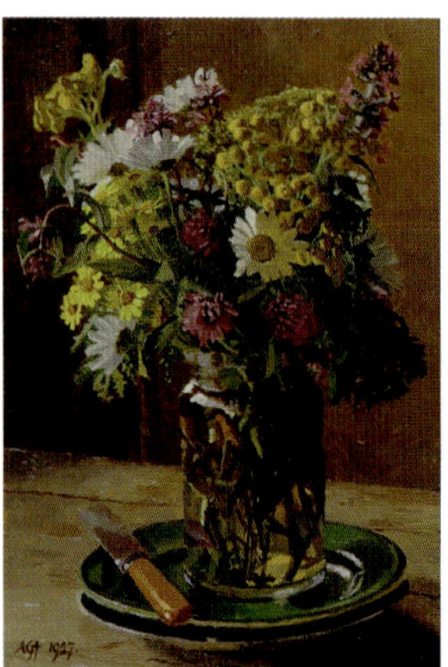

Gwynne-Jones, Allan 1892–1982
Flowers in a Jam Jar 1927
oil on board 35.4 x 25
25/2002

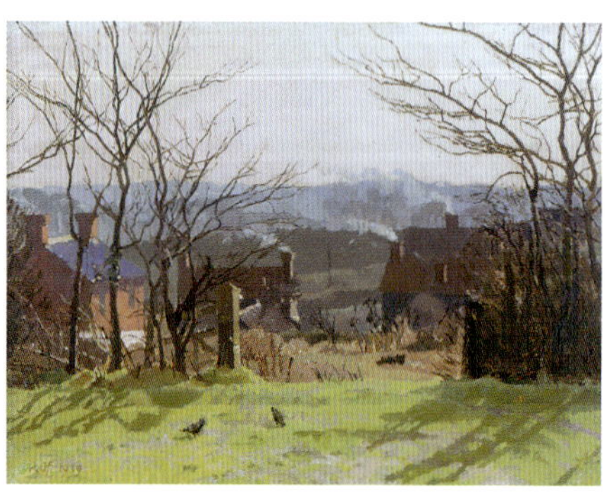

Gwynne-Jones, Allan 1892–1982
Winter Landscape, Suffolk 1939
oil on canvas 63.5 x 78.9
39/2002

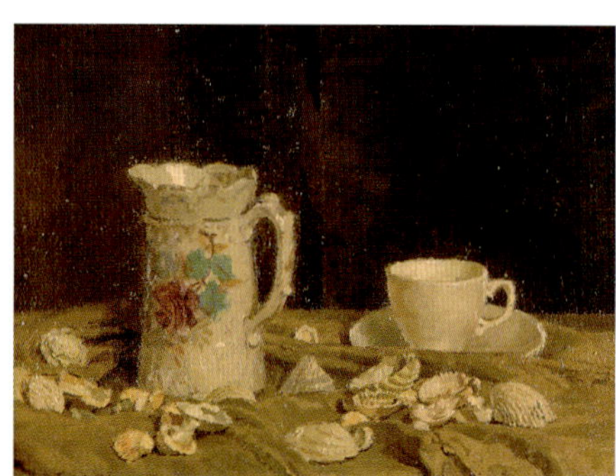

Gwynne-Jones, Allan 1892–1982
Still Life: A Jug, Teacup and Shells 1954
oil on canvas 49 x 60
29/2002

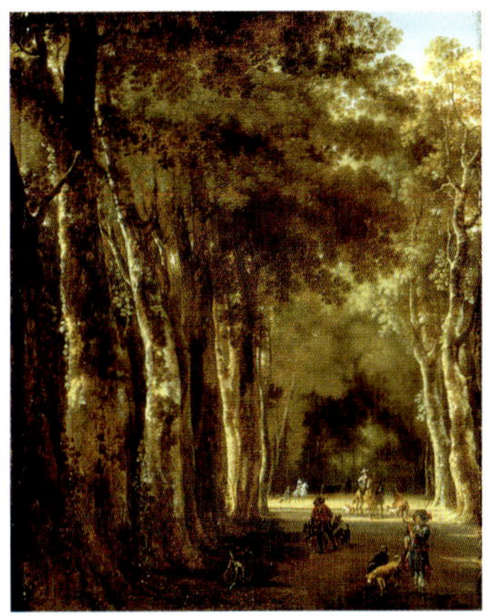

Hackaert, Jan 1629–1699
The Avenue
oil on canvas 70.2 x 56
230

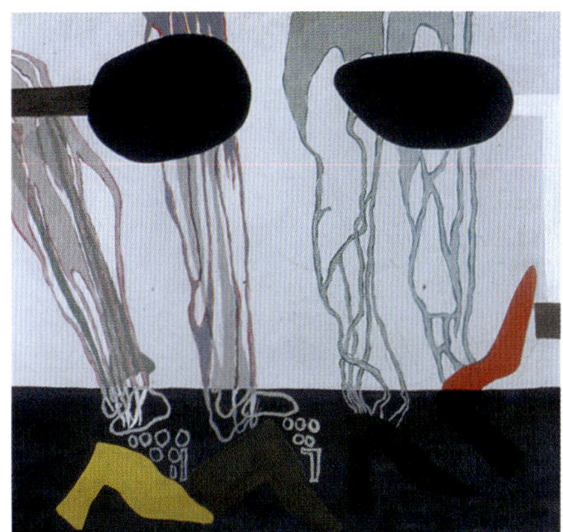

Haile, Samuel 1909–1948
Les automobilistes 1938
oil on canvas 63.5 x 76.3
7/1968

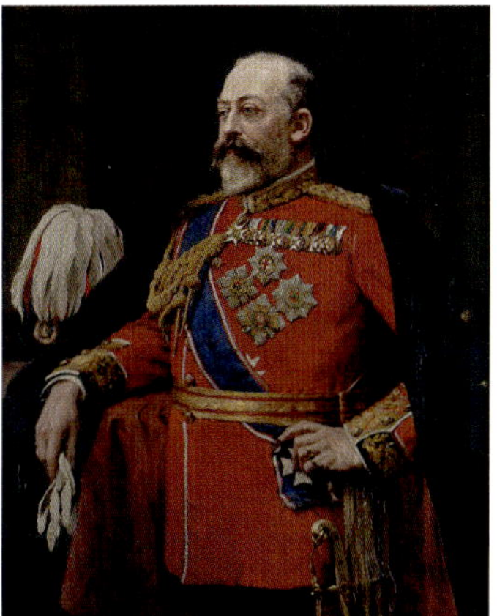

Hall, Frederick 1860–1948
King Edward VII (1841–1910) 1902
oil on canvas 122.2 x 101.7
232

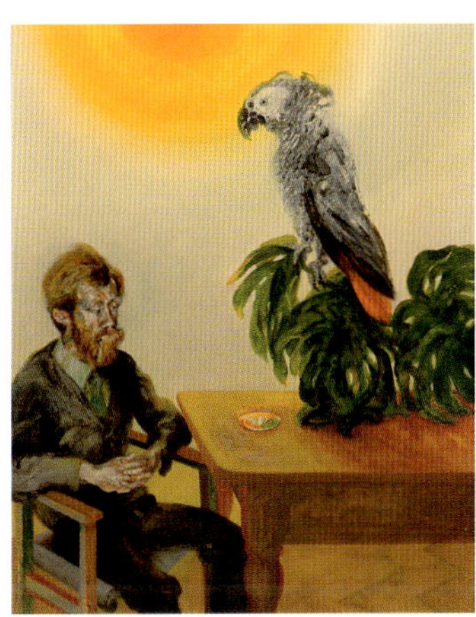

Hambling, Maggi b.1945
Untitled 1980
oil on canvas 90 x 74.8
35/2002

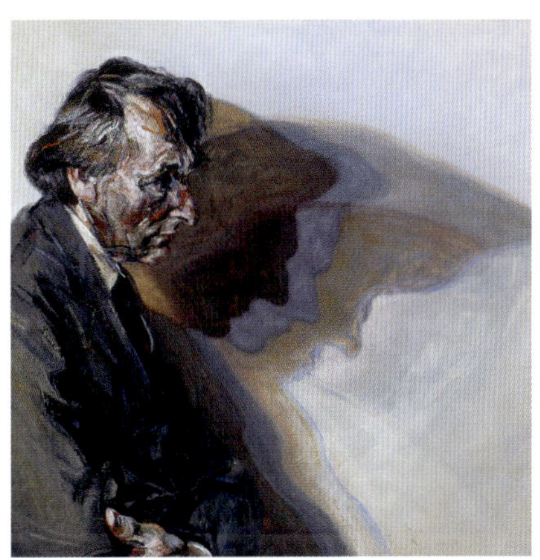

Hambling, Maggi b.1945
Mac with Shadows 1981
oil on canvas 66.9 x 66.5
13/1982

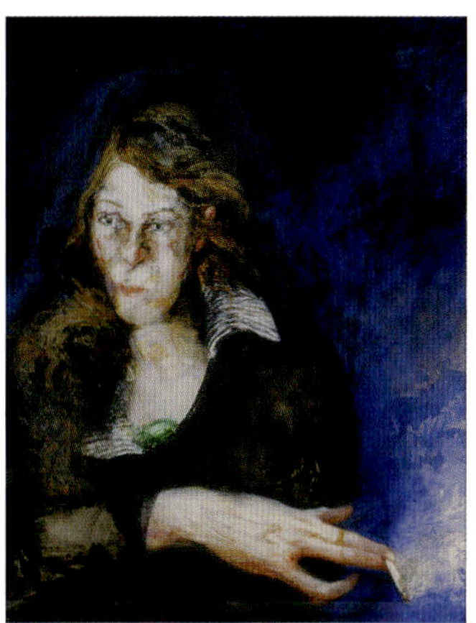

Hambling, Maggi b.1945
Catherine Parkinson
oil on canvas 82.8 x 67.7
23/2002

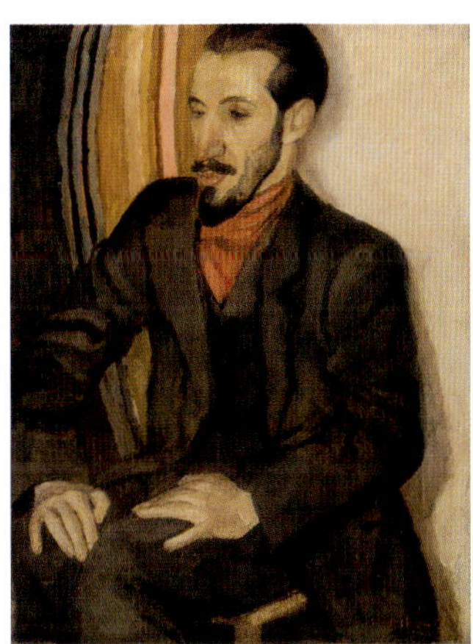

Hamnett, Nina 1890–1956
Horace Brodzky 1915
oil on canvas 89.2 x 68.9
1489

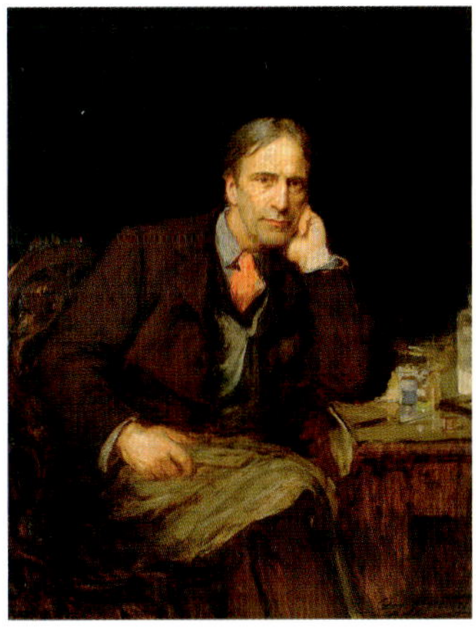

Harcourt, George 1868–1947
Sir Hubert von Herkomer, RA (1849–1914)
oil on canvas 127 x 101.5
233

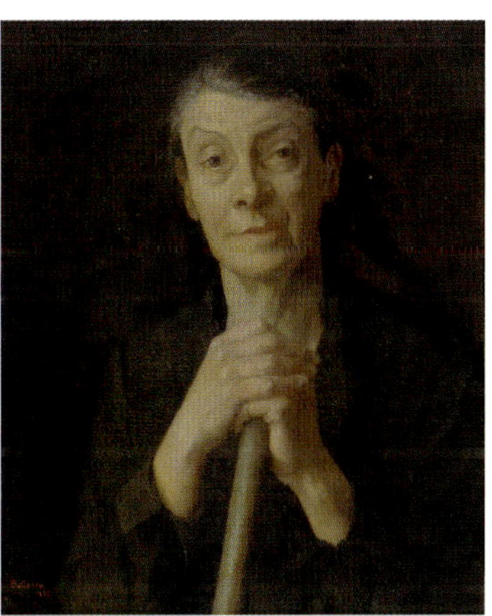

Harmar, Fairlie 1876–1945
La Bretonne
oil on canvas 76 x 63.5
1390

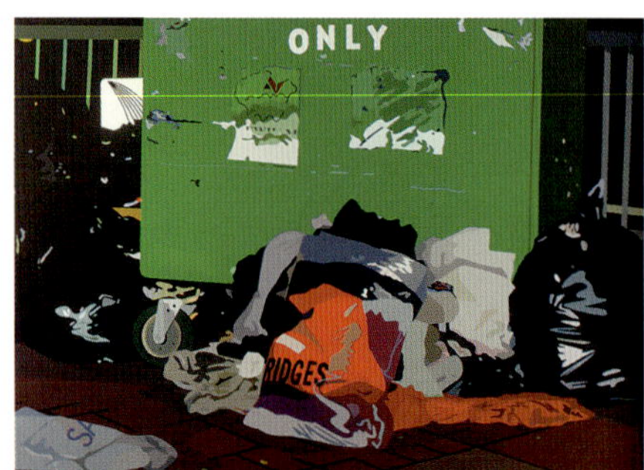

Harper, Ed b.1970
Sebert Road 2005
acrylic on canvas 152.5 x 213.5
6/2005

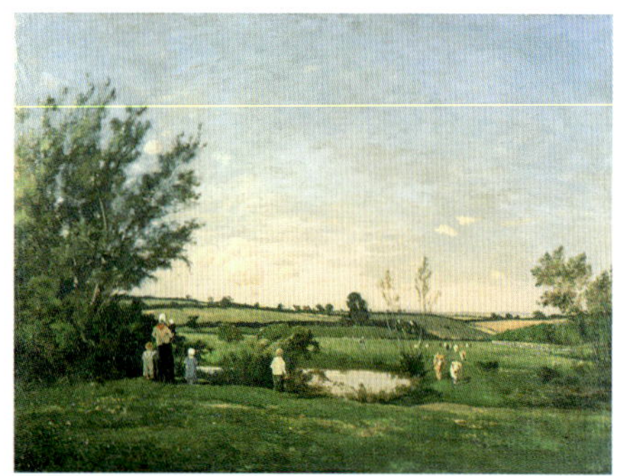

Harpignies, Henri-Joseph 1819–1916
Environs de Saint Pierre, Yonne 1886
oil on canvas 60.2 x 81.2
1462

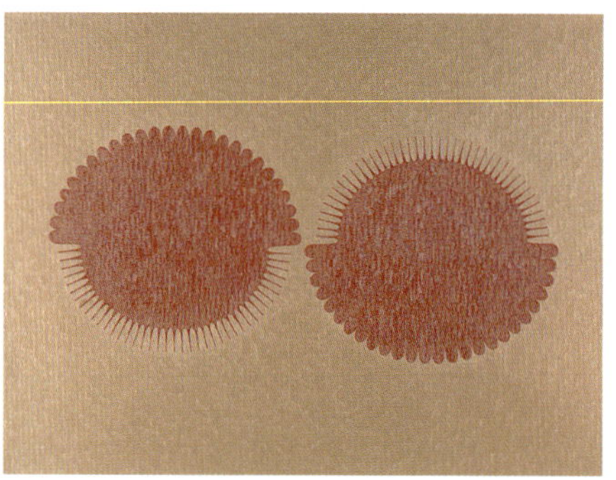

Harris, Jane b.1956
'Fandango' 2001
oil on canvas 57.5 x 76.4
1/2002

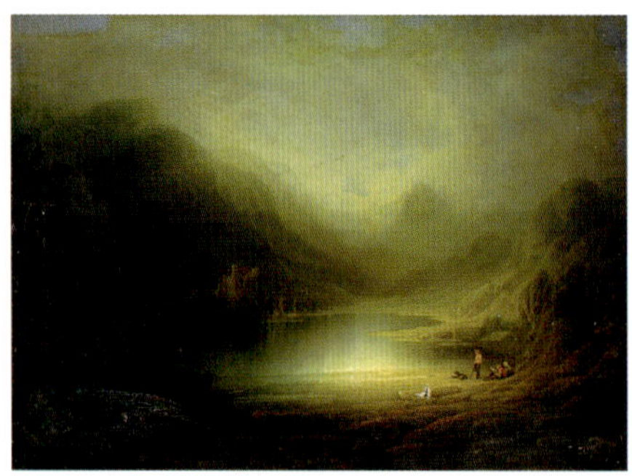

Hart, Thomas Gray 1797–1881
Kilchurn Castle
oil on canvas 66.2 x 91.5
911

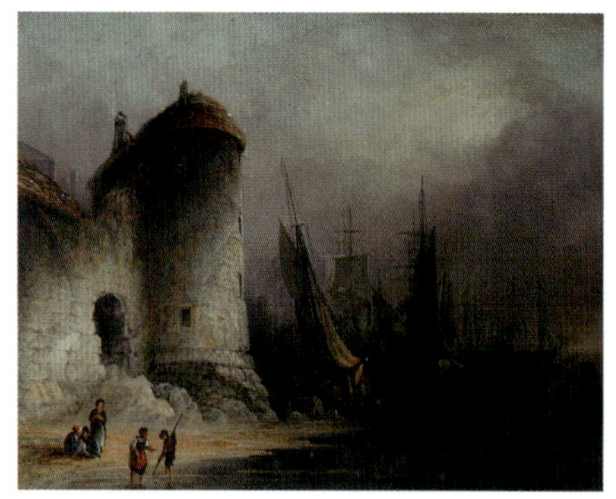

Hart, Thomas Gray 1797–1881
South-East Tower, Town Quay
oil on canvas 68.6 x 89
913

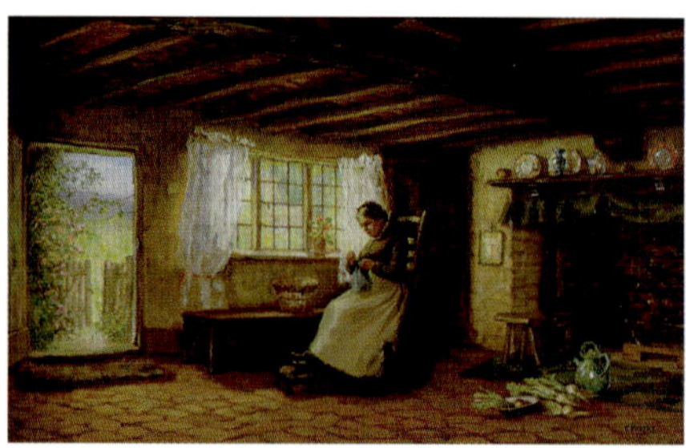

Hartry, Edith active 1883–1919
A Quiet Afternoon
oil on canvas 40.6 x 66.1
236

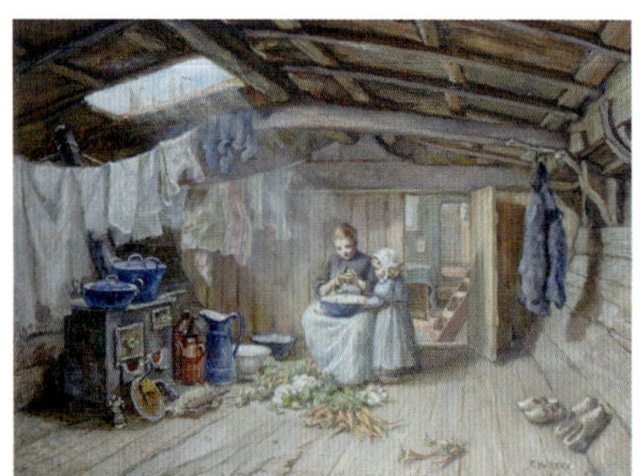

Hartry, Edith active 1883–1919
Kitchen of a Dutch Barge
oil on canvas 42.5 x 57.2
237

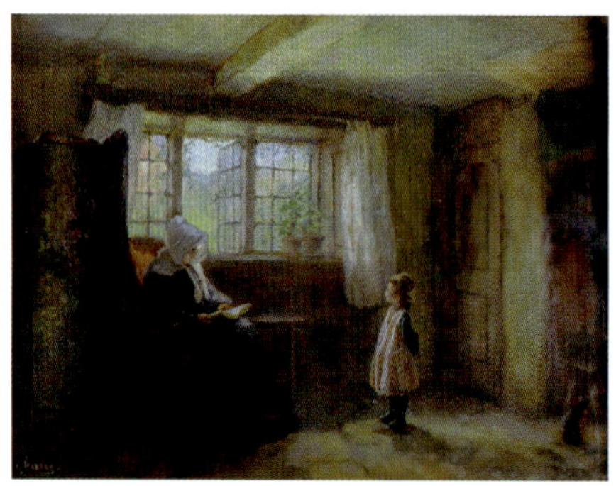

Hartry, Edith active 1883–1919
The Catechism
oil on canvas 45.6 x 61
238

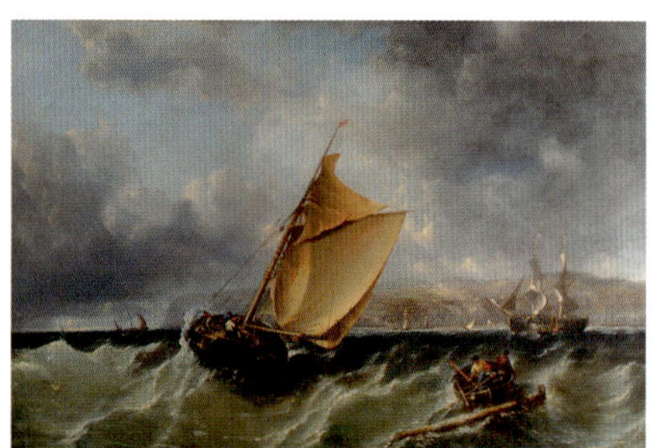

Hayes, Edwin 1820–1904
Howth Head 1854
oil on canvas 61 x 92.5
1278

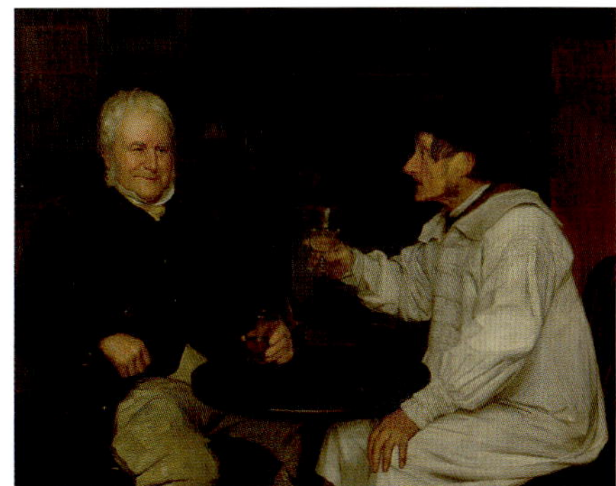

Hayllar, James 1829–1920
Rival Drinks 1881
oil on canvas 50.9 x 66.3
240

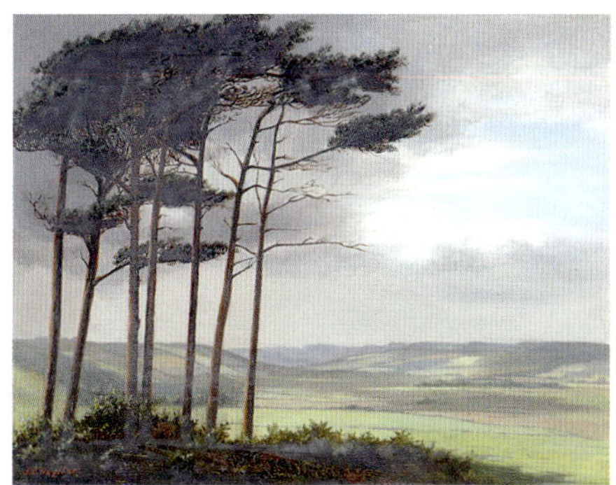

Hayllar, James 1829–1920
Old Fir Trees
oil on card 17.4 x 22.5
239

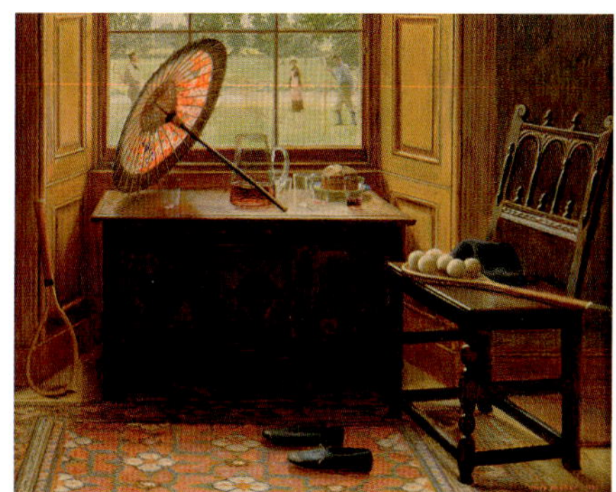

Hayllar, Mary active 1880–1885
The Lawn Tennis Season 1881
oil on canvas 19.3 x 24.3
241

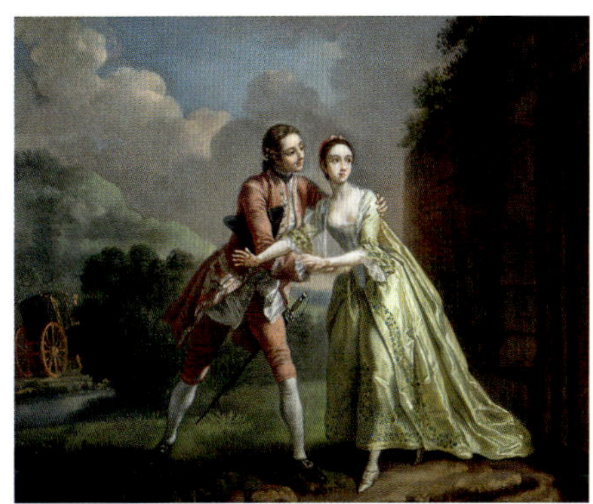

Hayman, Francis c.1708–1776
'Robert Lovelace Preparing to Abduct…' 1753
oil on canvas 63.5 x 76.3
3/1965

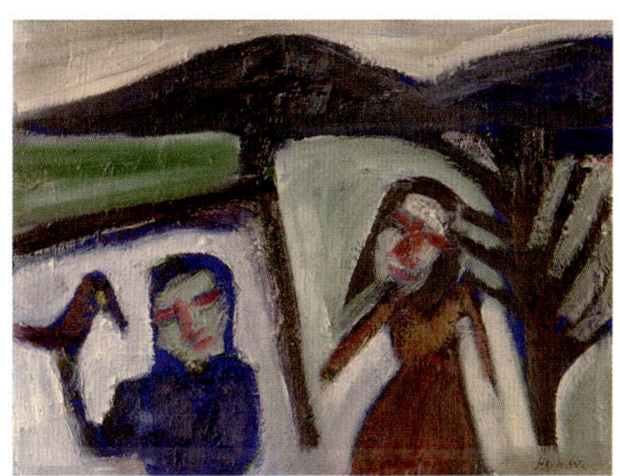

Hayman, Patrick 1915–1988
Lovers by the Sea with a Hawk 1976
oil on board 32.5 x 40
89/2002

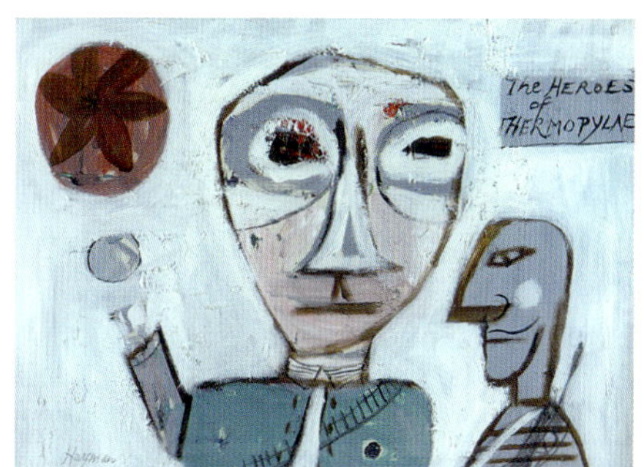

Hayman, Patrick 1915–1988
The Heroes of Thermopylae 1976
oil on board 36 x 46
57/2002

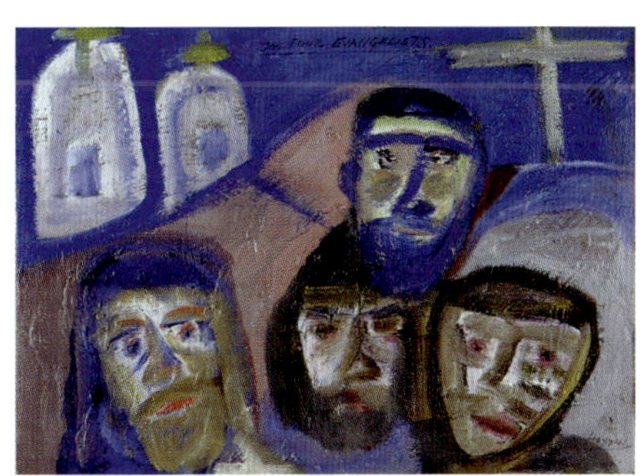

Hayman, Patrick 1915–1988
The Four Evangelists 1980
oil on board 25.4 x 36
33/2002

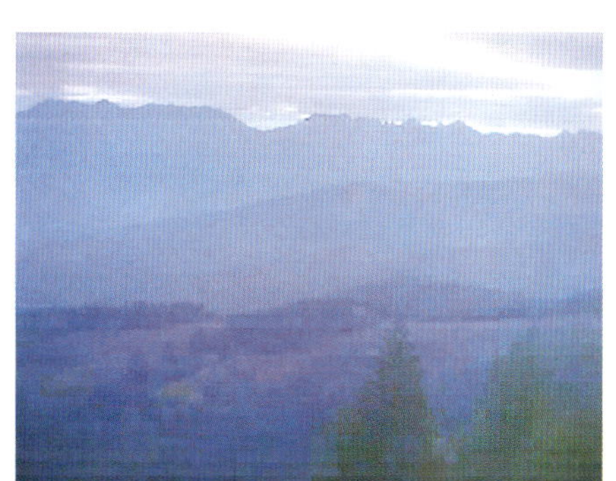

Hays, Dan b.1966
Colorado Impression 12a (Sunrise, Beaver Creek, 11 September 2002) 2002
oil on canvas 152.2 x 225.7
6/2004

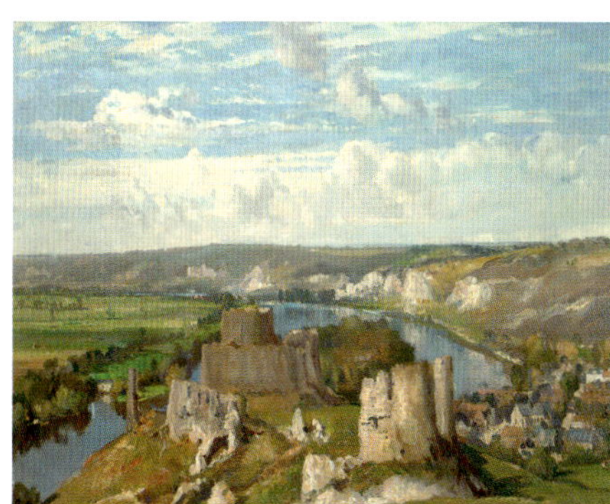

Hayward, Alfred Robert 1875–1971
Château Gaillard
oil on canvas 71.2 x 91.7
242

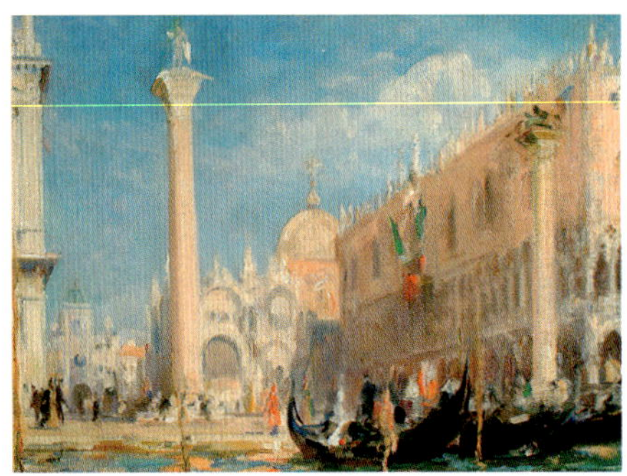

Hayward, Alfred Robert 1875–1971
St Mark's, Venice
oil on canvas 56 x 76.2
243

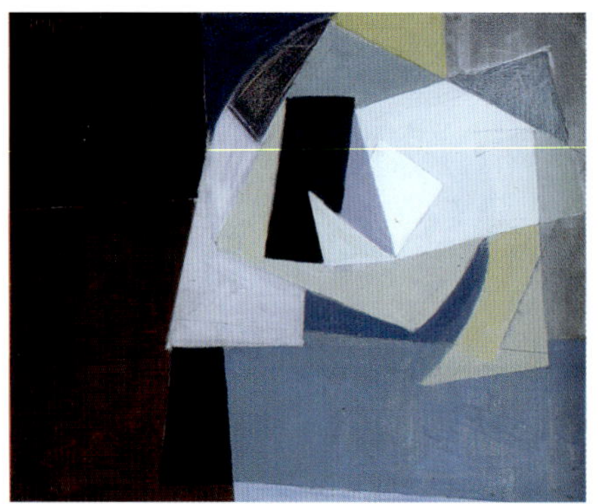

Heath, Adrian 1920–1992
Composition 1952 (Rotating Forms) 1952
oil on canvas 55.8 x 60.9
13/2002

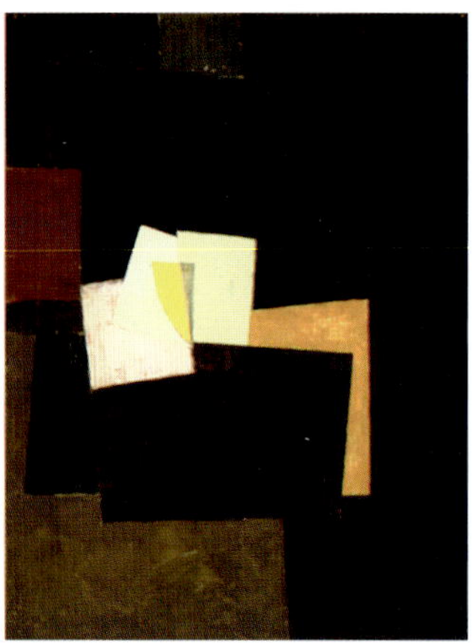

Heath, Adrian 1920–1992
Composition with Black and Purple
oil on canvas 81 x 60.6
45/1976

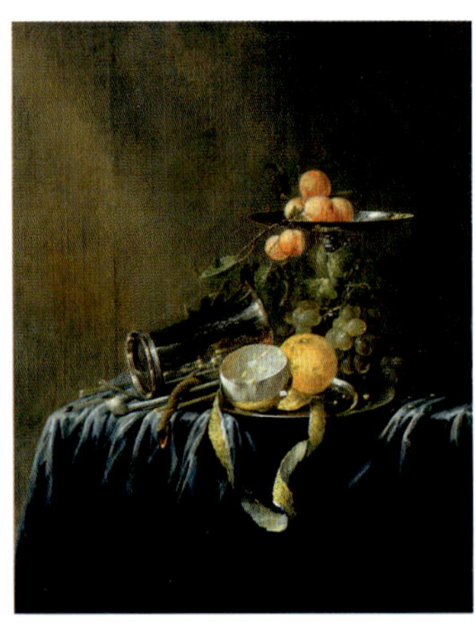

Heem, Jan Davidsz. de (attributed to)
1606–1683/1684
Still Life 1665
oil on wood 74.2 x 57.8
4/1959

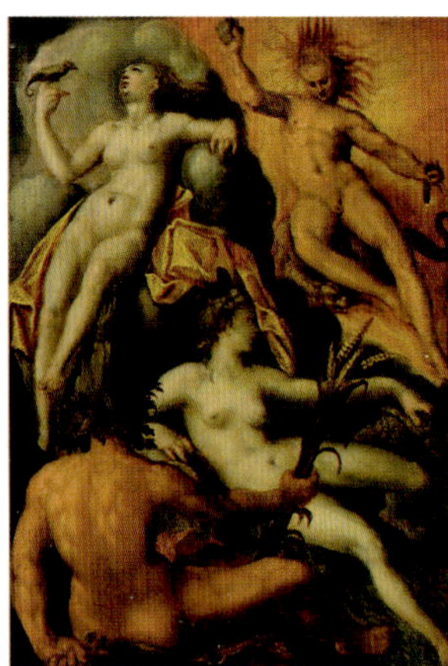

Heintz, Joseph the elder 1564–1609
The Four Elements
oil on panel 40 x 28
179/1975

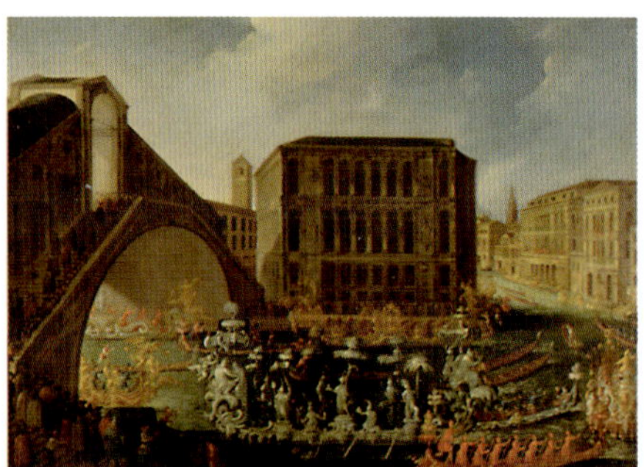

Heintz, Joseph the younger c.1600–1678
Venetian Regatta at the Rialto Bridge
oil on canvas 80.3 x 110.8
97/1963

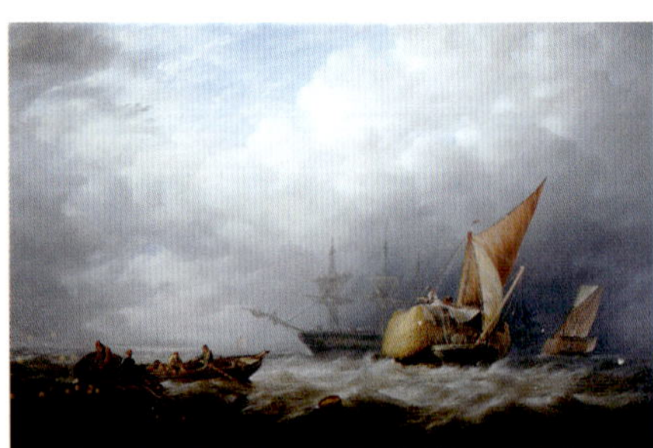

Herbert, Alfred c.1820–1861
Hay Barges in the Thames Estuary
oil on canvas 73.6 x 111.8
1110

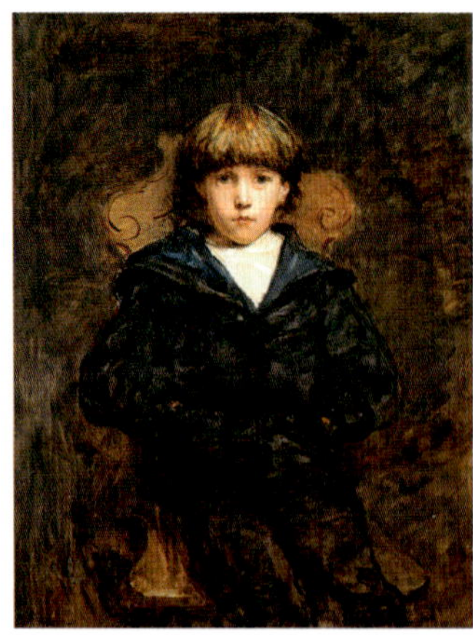

Herkomer, Hubert von 1849–1914
Portrait of a Boy 1882
oil on canvas 91.1 x 70.7
9/1964

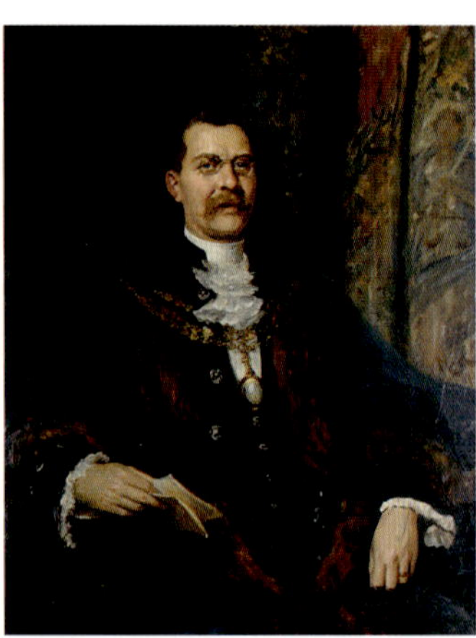

Herkomer, Hubert von 1849–1914
Alderman Sir George Hussey 1901
oil on canvas 125.7 x 99
247

Facing page: Martin, John, 1789–1854, *Sadak in Search of the Waters of Oblivion* (detail), 1812, Southampton City Art Gallery, (p. 92)

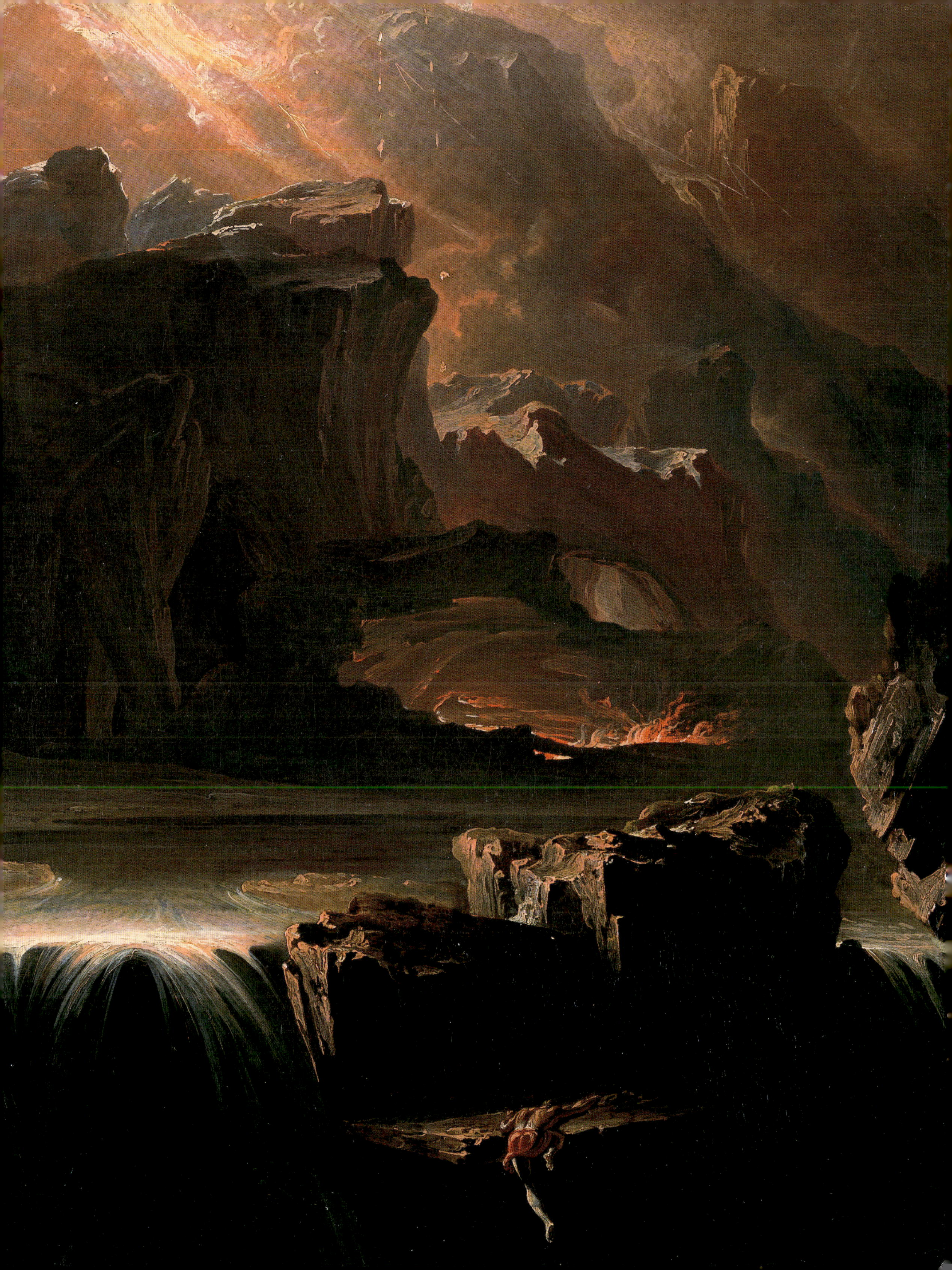

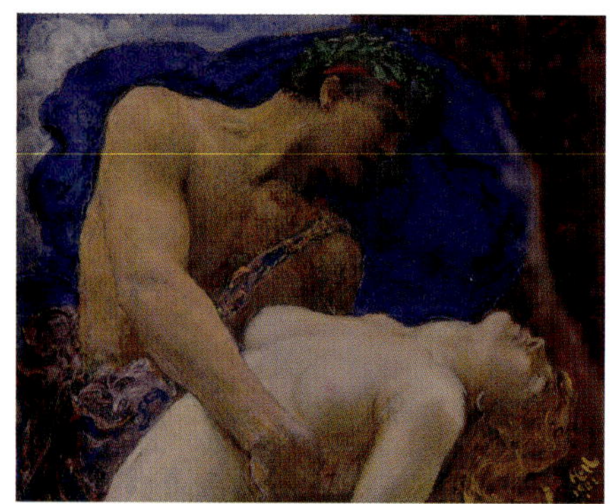

Herkomer, Hubert von 1849–1914
Souvenir of Watts 1901
oil on metal 16 x 20
271

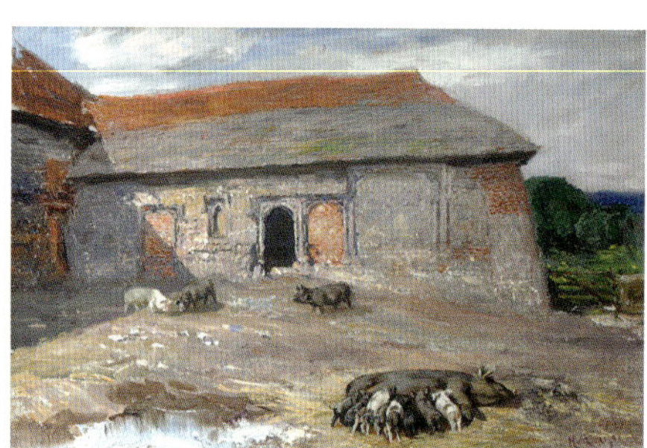

Herkomer, Hubert von 1849–1914
Farmyard 1912
oil on canvas 33 x 48.2
245

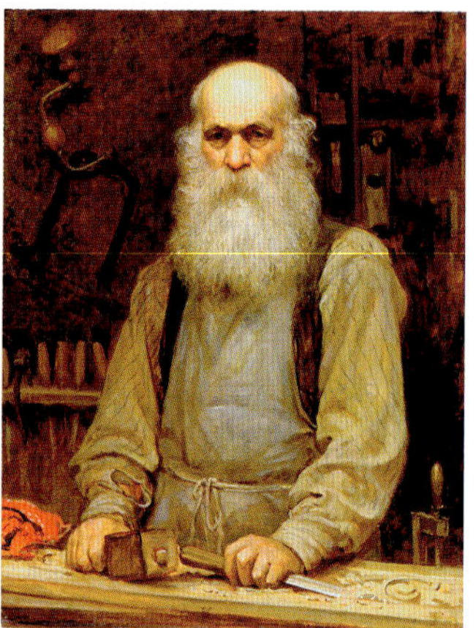

Herkomer, Hubert von 1849–1914
Lorenz Herkomer
oil on canvas 112.1 x 87.1
246

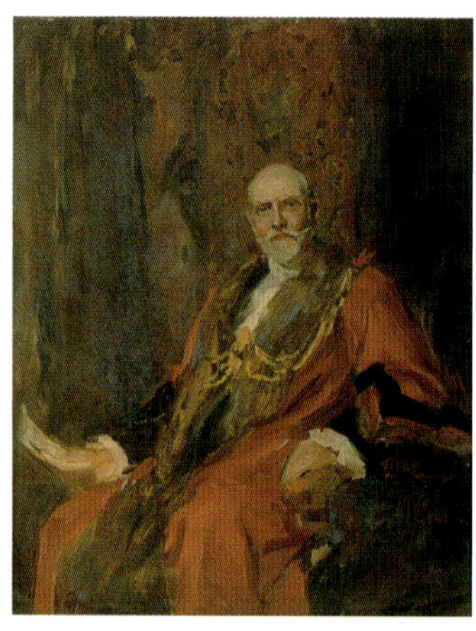

Herkomer, Hubert von 1849–1914
Study of a Lord Mayor
oil on canvas 52.7 x 43.5
248

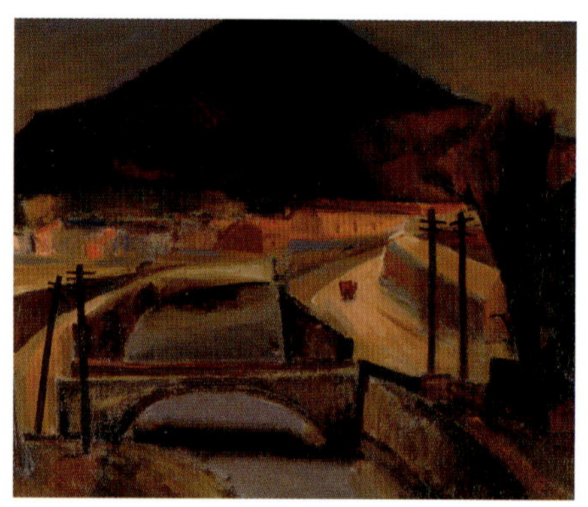

Herman, Josef 1911–2000
The Bridge, Ystradgynlais 1946
oil on canvas 62.9 x 76.5
1352

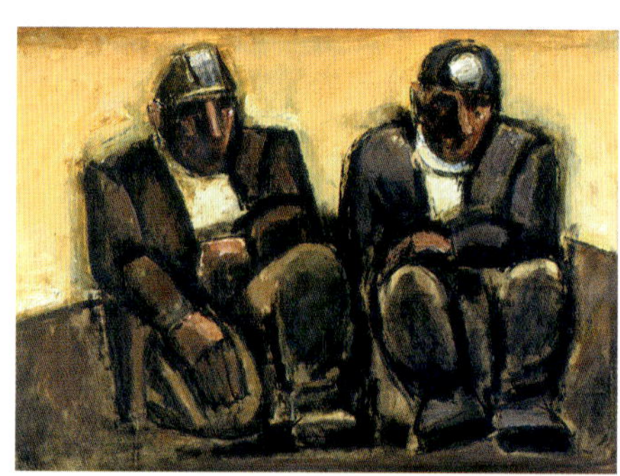

Herman, Josef 1911–2000
Miners
oil on canvas 54.7 x 73
L7B

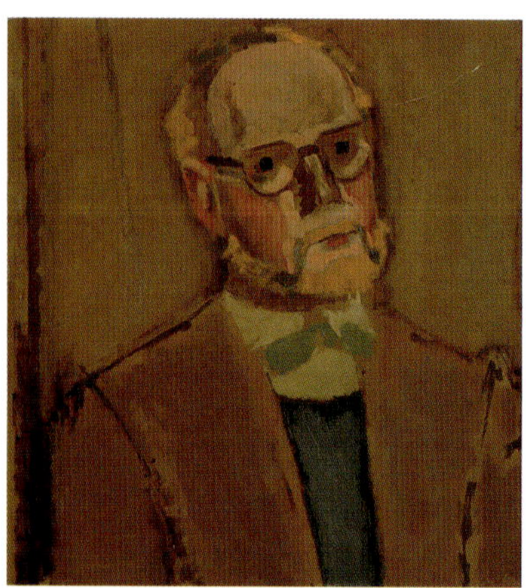

Herman, Josef 1911–2000
Reece Pemberton
oil on canvas 80 x 76
8/2006

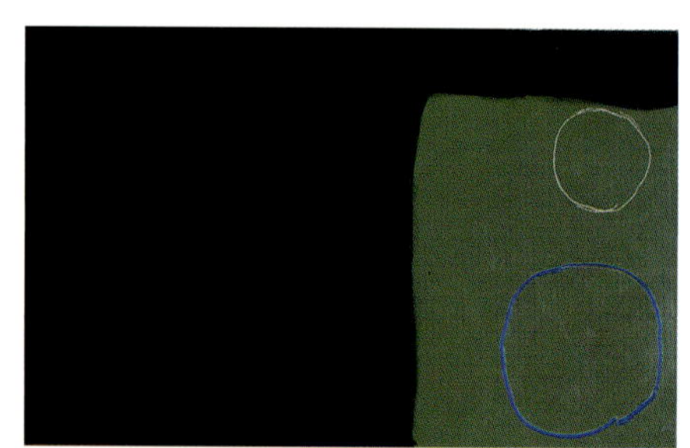

Heron, Patrick 1920–1999
Black and Dull Green with Two Circles 1962
oil on canvas 76.3 x 122
3/1972

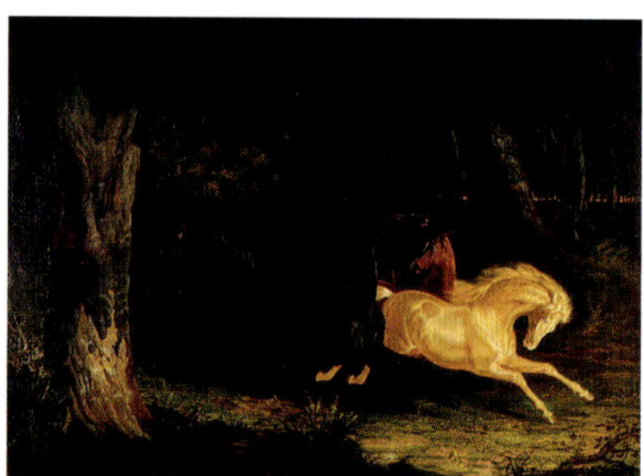

Herring, John Frederick I 1795–1865
Wild Horses 1827
oil on canvas 91.3 x 127.3
274

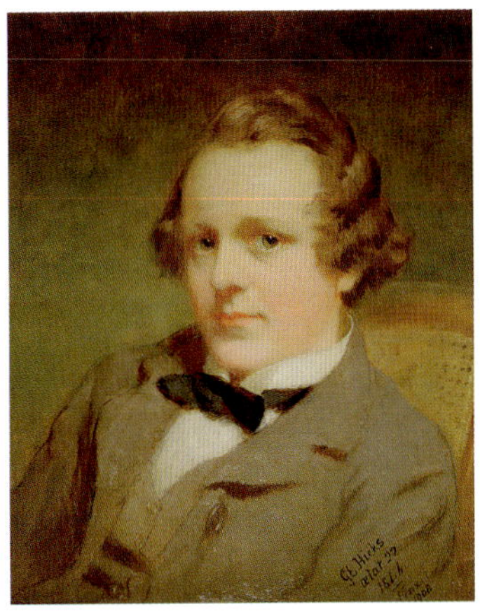

Hicks, George Elgar 1824–1914
Self Portrait, Aged 22 1846
oil on canvas 40.6 x 33
1083

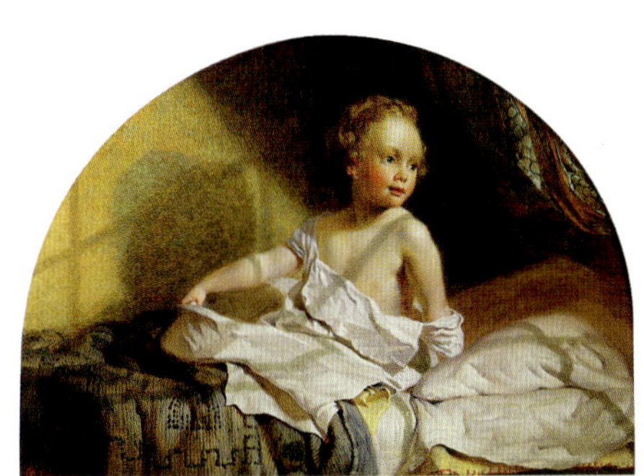

Hicks, George Elgar 1824–1914
Portrait of Second Son 1855
oil on wood 24.5 x 36
1089

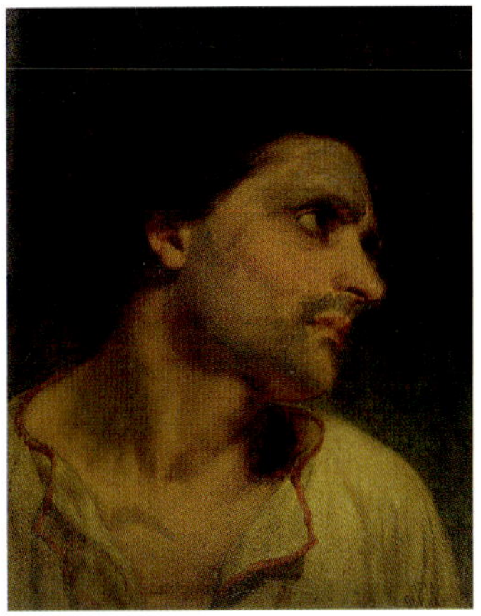

Hicks, George Elgar 1824–1914
Study of an Italian Man's Head 1873
oil on card 47.5 x 37.2
1081

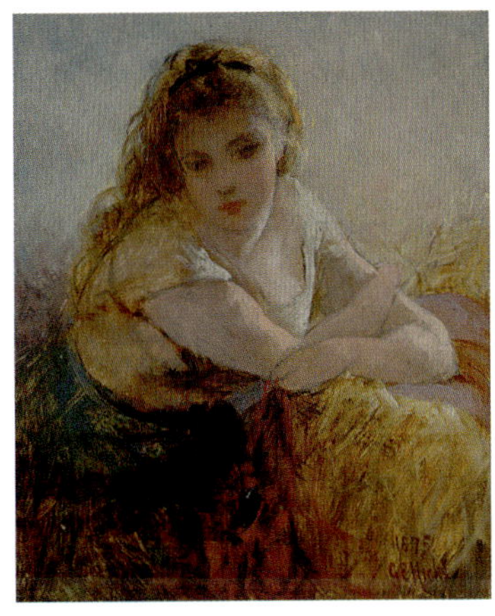

Hicks, George Elgar 1824–1914
Girl Seated 1875
oil on board 22 x 18.7
1077h

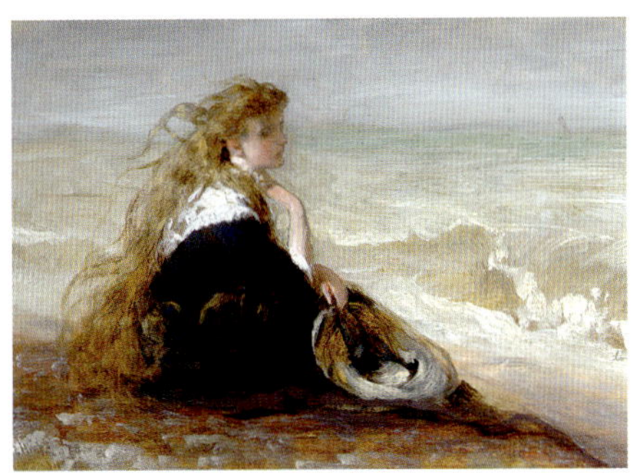

Hicks, George Elgar 1824–1914
Girl Seated by Shore 1878
oil on card 22.8 x 33
1074a

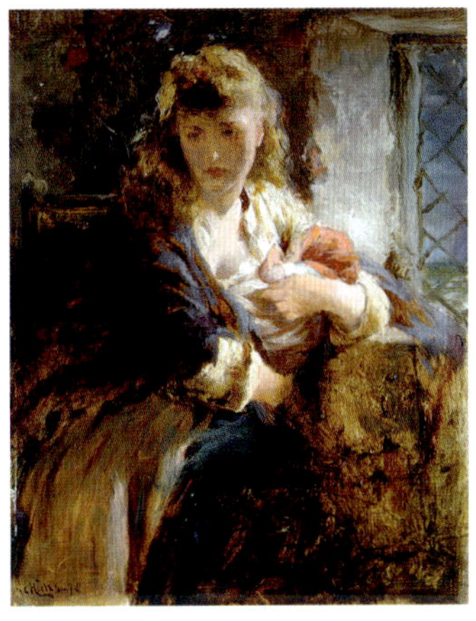

Hicks, George Elgar 1824–1914
Mother and Baby 1878
oil on board 31.1 x 23.5
1077b

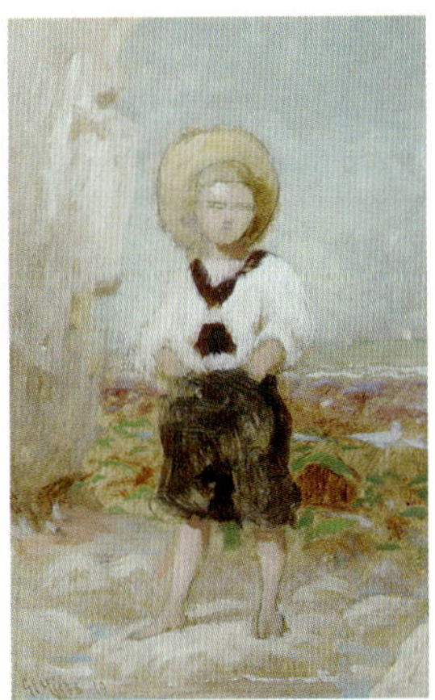

Hicks, George Elgar 1824–1914
Boy in Sailor's Costume 1879
oil on card 29.2 x 19
1074i

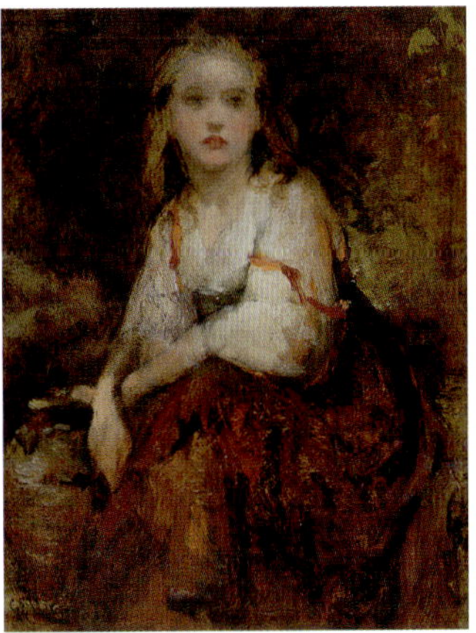

Hicks, George Elgar 1824–1914
Seated Girl 1879
oil on card 22.5 x 18.1
1077d

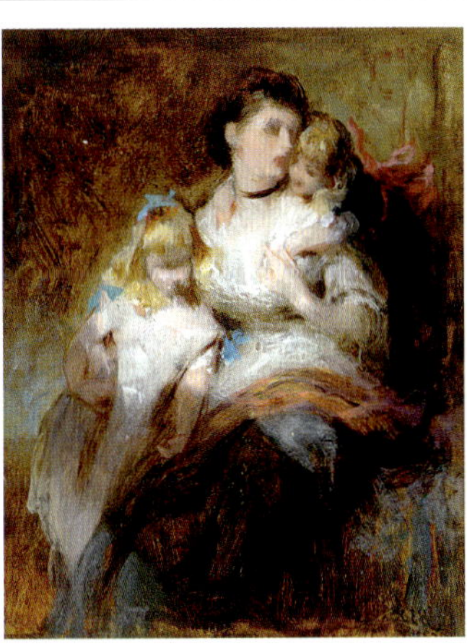

Hicks, George Elgar 1824–1914
Seated Woman and Two Children 1879
oil on card 27.2 x 21.5
1074e

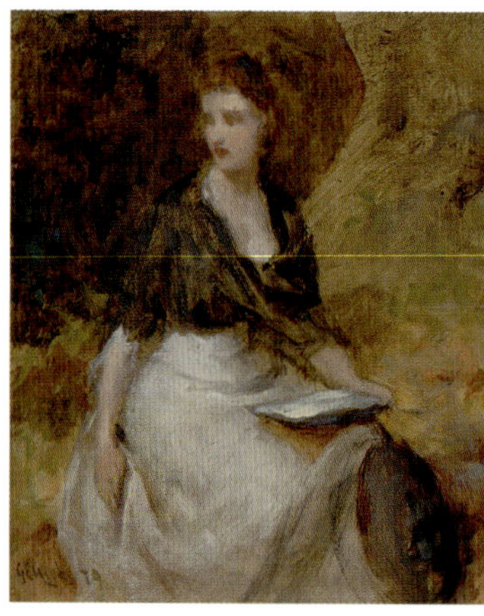

Hicks, George Elgar 1824–1914
Seated Woman Holding Dish 1879
oil on card 22 x 18.3
1074b

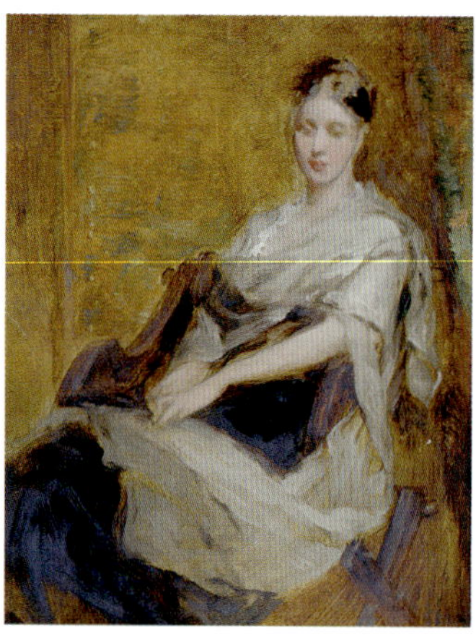

Hicks, George Elgar 1824–1914
Seated Woman in Chair 1879
oil on card 27.6 x 21.3
1074h

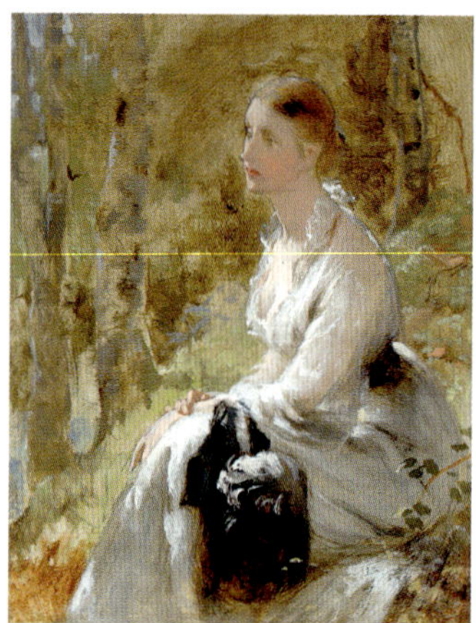

Hicks, George Elgar 1824–1914
Seated Woman in White Dress 1879
oil on card 29.2 x 23.5
1074g

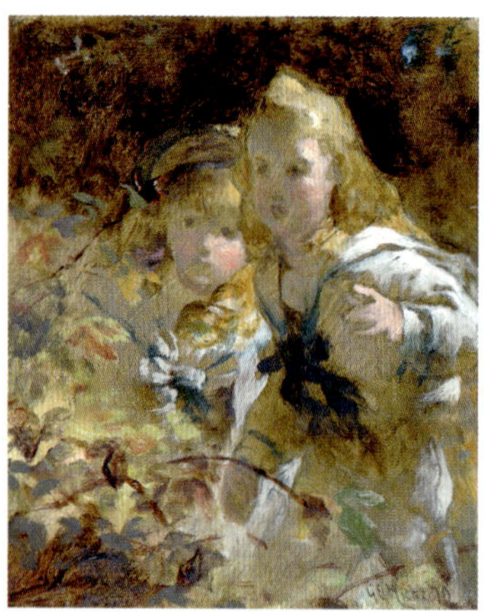

Hicks, George Elgar 1824–1914
Sketch of Mrs Chas Rose's Two Boys 1879
oil on card 23.5 x 19
1074c

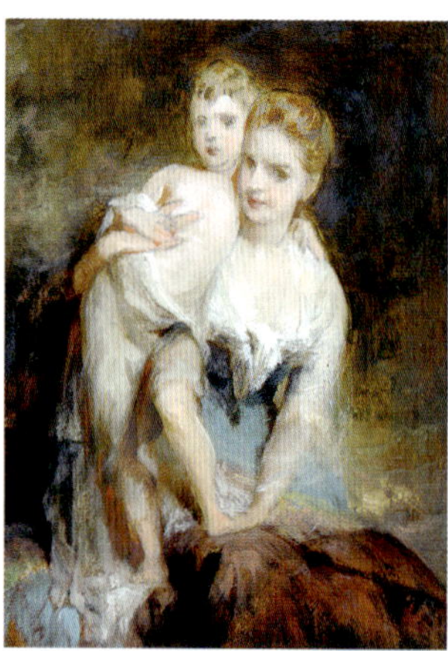

Hicks, George Elgar 1824–1914
Woman and Semi-Nude Child 1879
oil on card 27.2 x 20.6
1074d

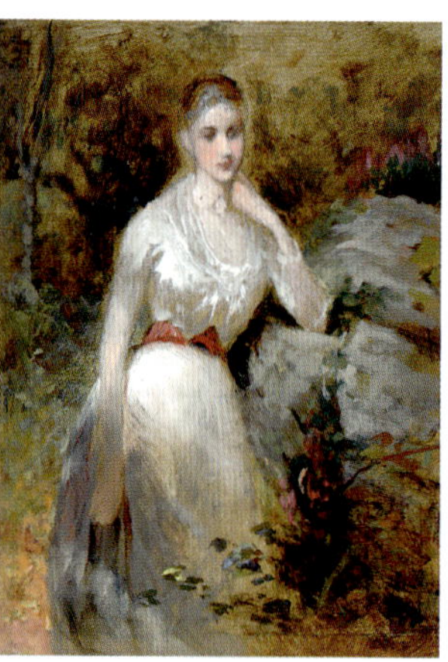

Hicks, George Elgar 1824–1914
Woman in White Dress with Red Sash 1879
oil on card 29.8 x 22.2
1074f

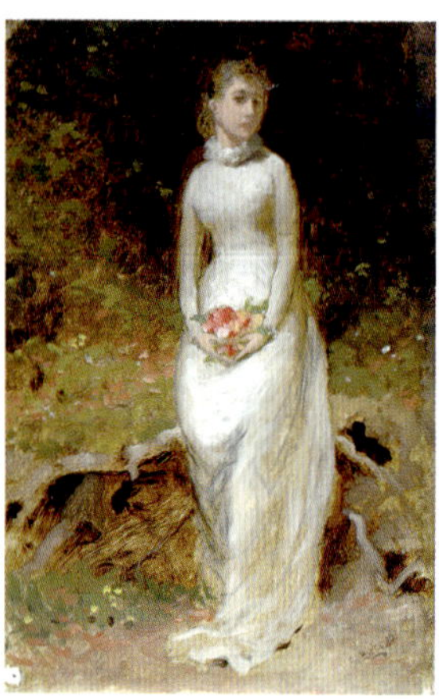

Hicks, George Elgar 1824–1914
Lady in White Dress Holding Flowers 1880
oil on card 36.8 x 26
1072i

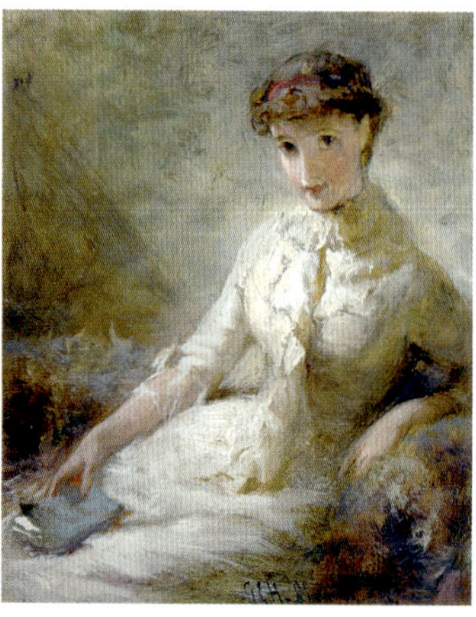

Hicks, George Elgar 1824–1914
Mrs Park Yates 1881
oil on card 21 x 17.2
1076g

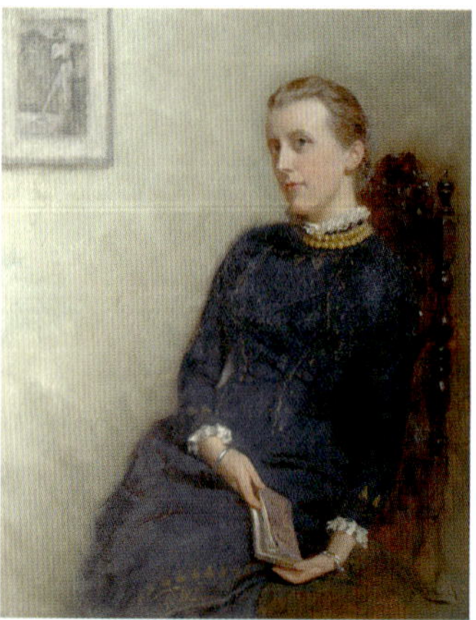

Hicks, George Elgar 1824–1914
Annie Hicks 1883
oil on canvas 50.5 x 39.5
1079

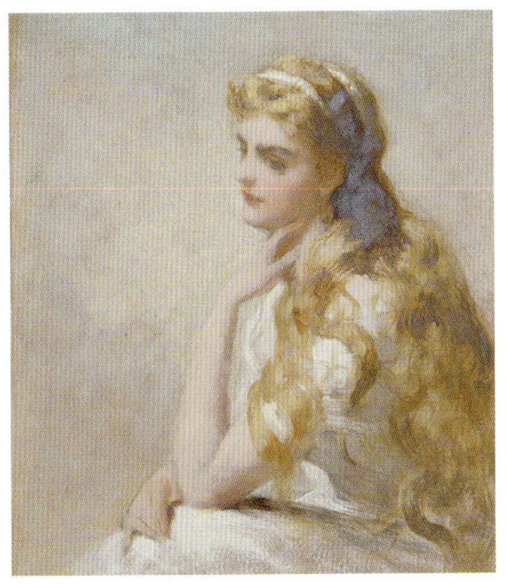

Hicks, George Elgar 1824–1914
Miss Harrison 1883
oil on card 15.8 x 13.3
1075i

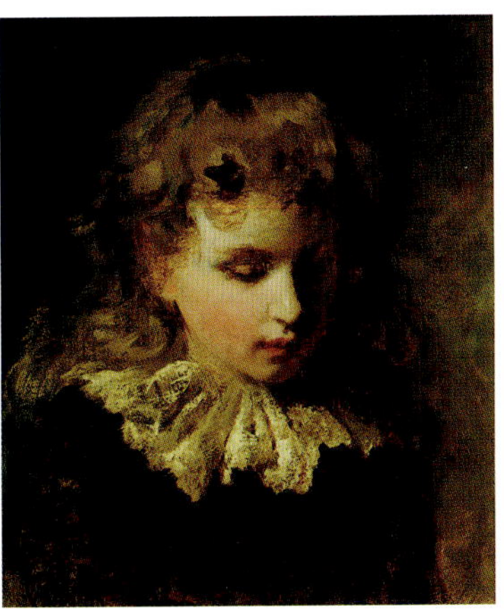

Hicks, George Elgar 1824–1914
Child's Head 1886
oil on card 42.8 x 35.8
1084

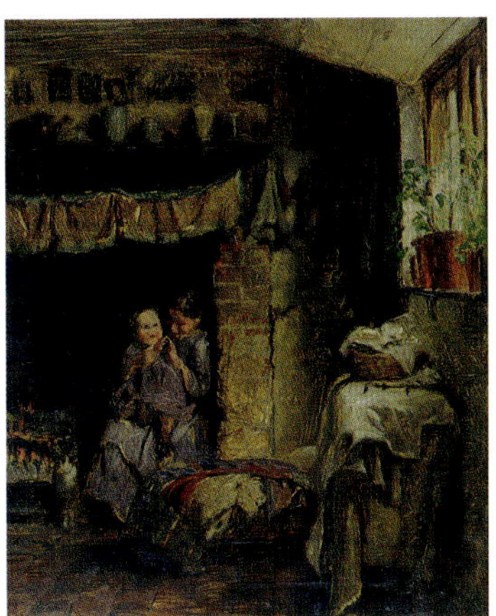

Hicks, George Elgar 1824–1914
A Sussex Interior
oil on board 22.8 x 18.8
1088

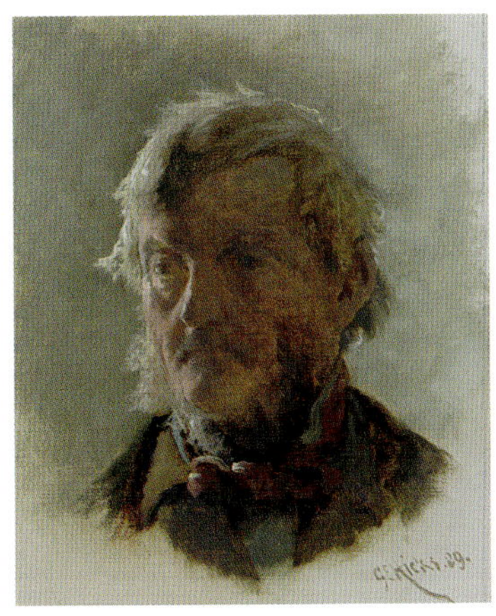

Hicks, George Elgar 1824–1914
An Old Man's Head
oil on canvas 22.7 x 18.8
1087

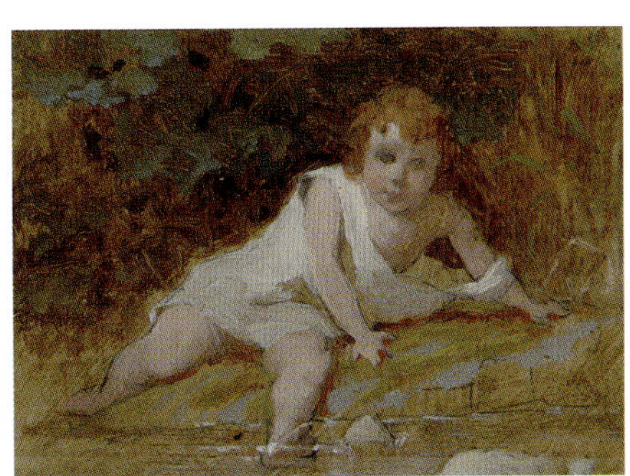

Hicks, George Elgar 1824–1914
Baby
oil on card 10.8 x 13.6
1075b

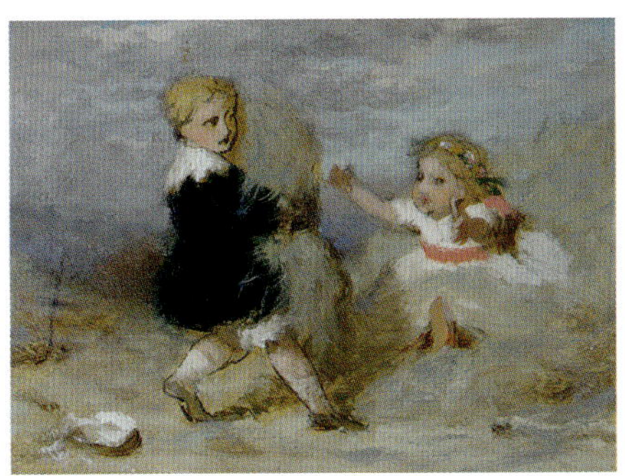

Hicks, George Elgar 1824–1914
Baby and Child Playing
oil on board 18.4 x 24.8
1076f

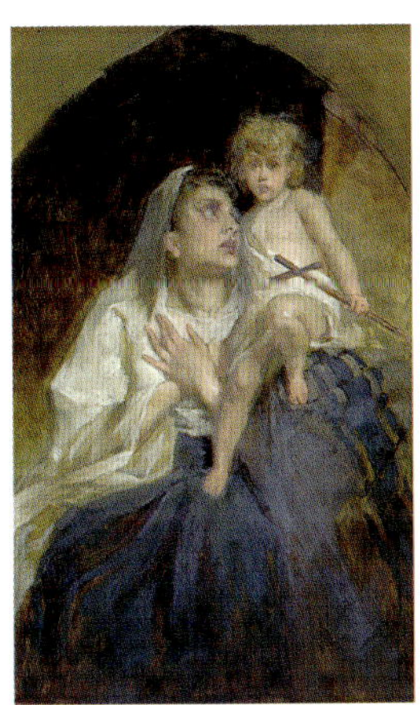

Hicks, George Elgar 1824–1914
Biblical Study
oil on card 34.2 x 23.9
1101

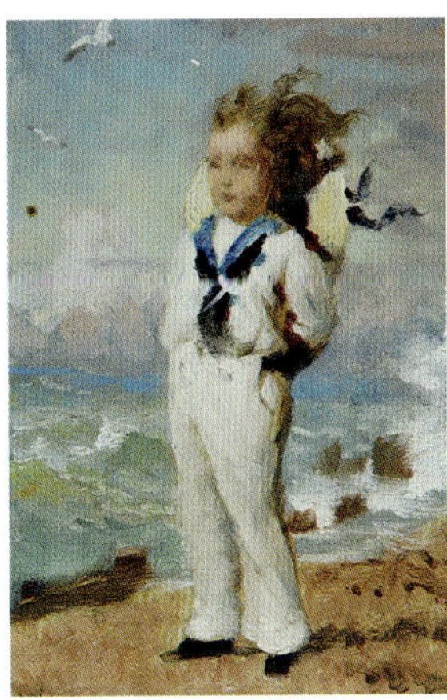

Hicks, George Elgar 1824–1914
Boy in Sailor's Uniform
oil on card 16.5 x 10.5
1073a

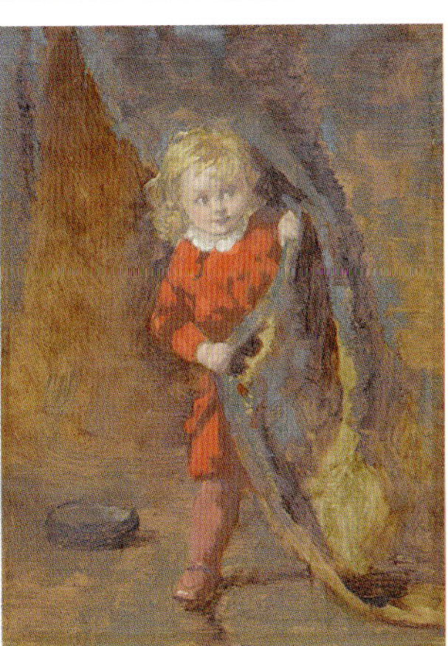

Hicks, George Elgar 1824–1914
Child in Red Costume
oil on card 21.5 x 17.8
1073i

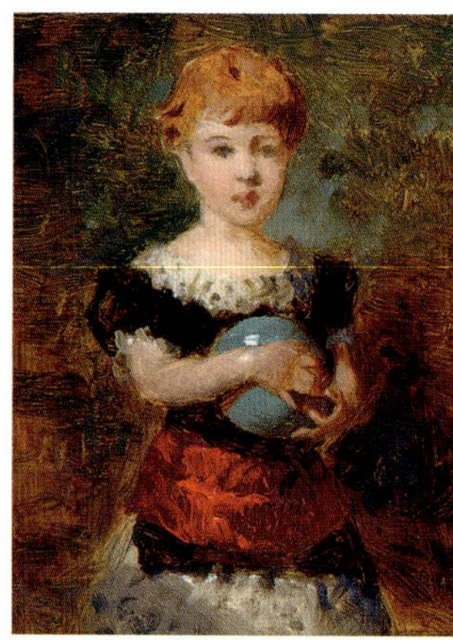

Hicks, George Elgar 1824–1914
Child with Ball
oil on card 18.1 x 14
1075ab

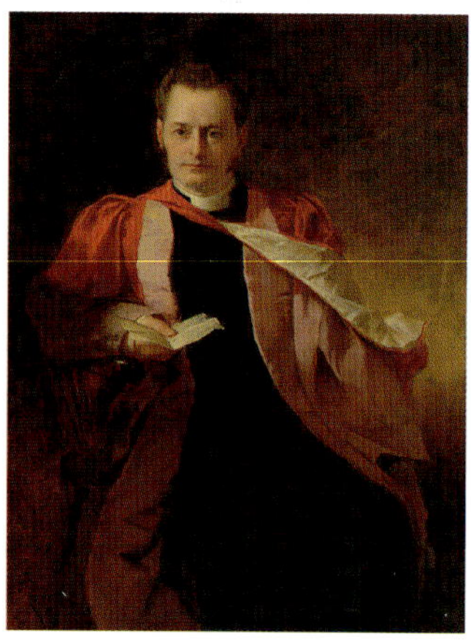

Hicks, George Elgar 1824–1914
Edward Hicks, DD, DCL
oil on canvas 109.3 x 83.8
1103

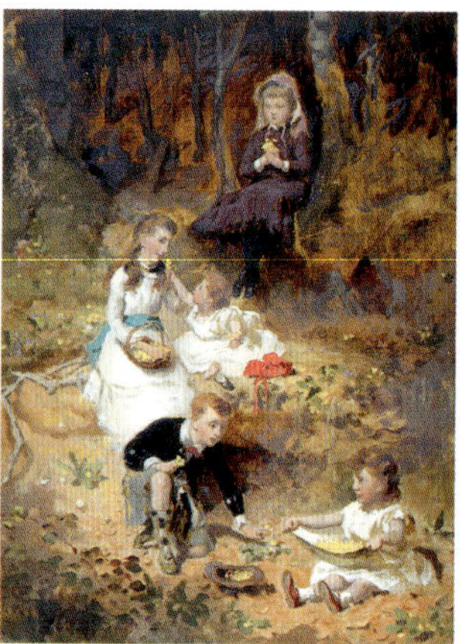

Hicks, George Elgar 1824–1914
Five Children Playing in the Forest
oil on card 41.9 x 30.5
1094

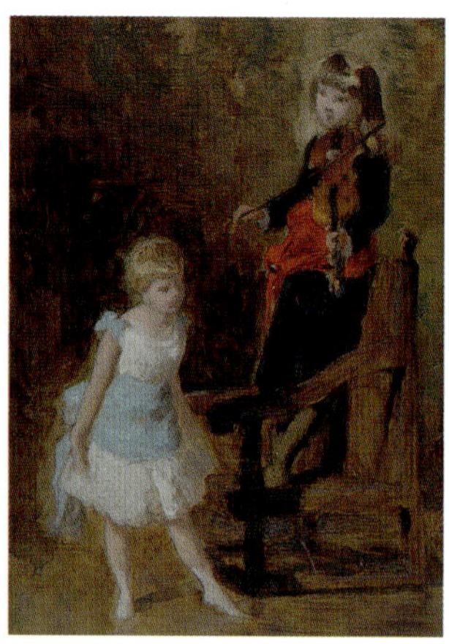

Hicks, George Elgar 1824–1914
Girl and Boy with Violin
oil on card 25 x 18.1
1075ac

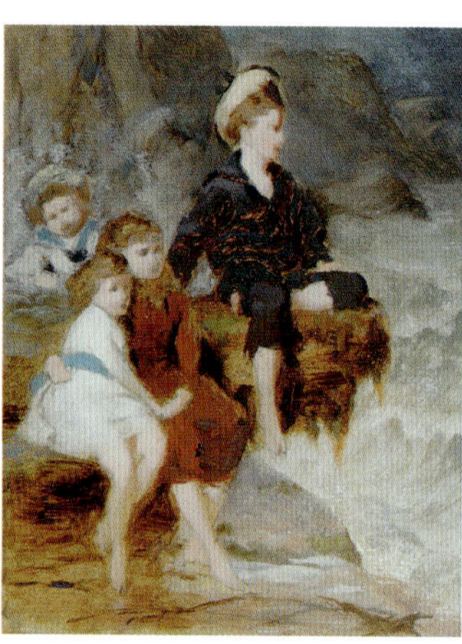

Hicks, George Elgar 1824–1914
Group of Children by Seashore
oil on card 26.6 x 21
1075af

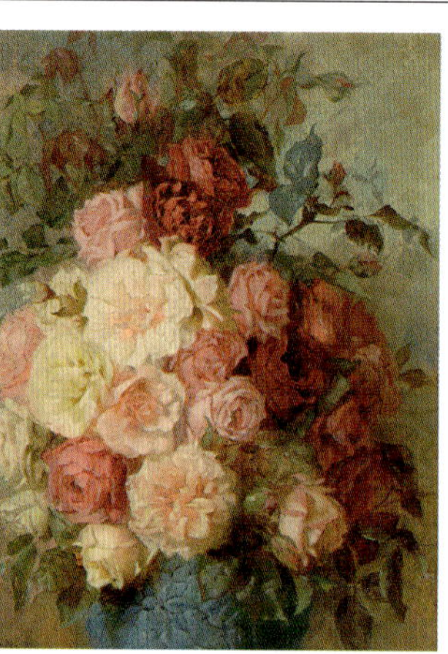

Hicks, George Elgar 1824–1914
Group of Roses
oil on board 61 x 48.2
1078

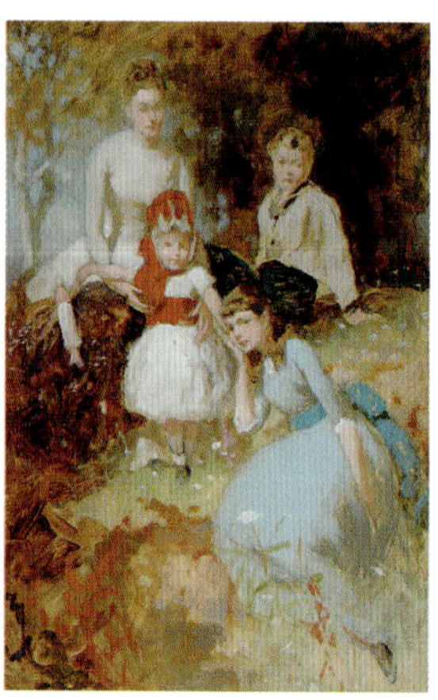

Hicks, George Elgar 1824–1914
Group with Baby
oil on card 31.8 x 21.5
1075k

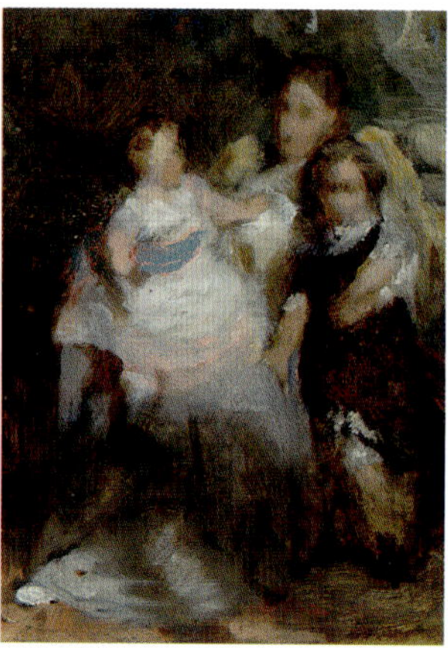

Hicks, George Elgar 1824–1914
Group with Baby
oil on card 19 x 15.2
1076a

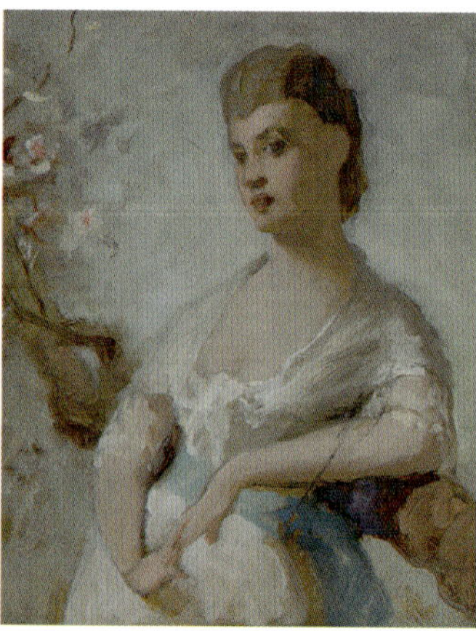

Hicks, George Elgar 1824–1914
Lady in White Dress
oil on card 19 x 15.2
1076h

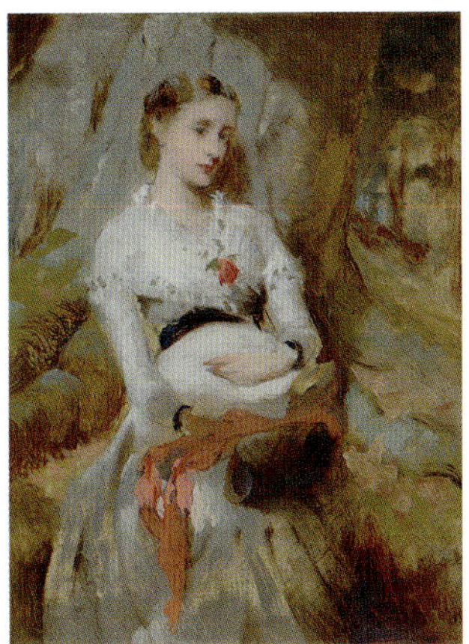

Hicks, George Elgar 1824–1914
Lady in White Dress
oil on card 27.2 x 21
1076i

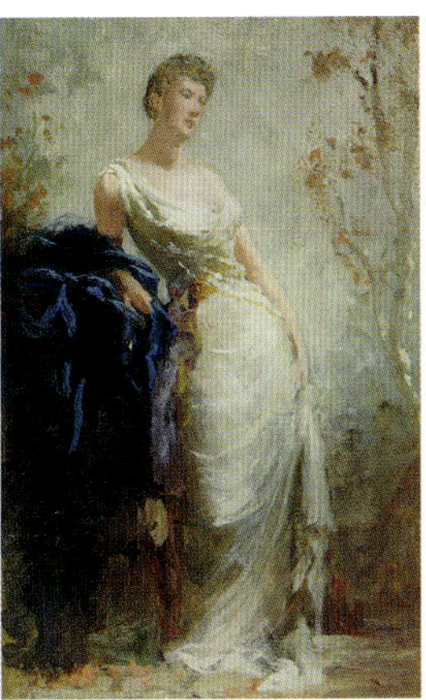

Hicks, George Elgar 1824–1914
Lady in White Dress
oil on card 21.3 x 14
1099

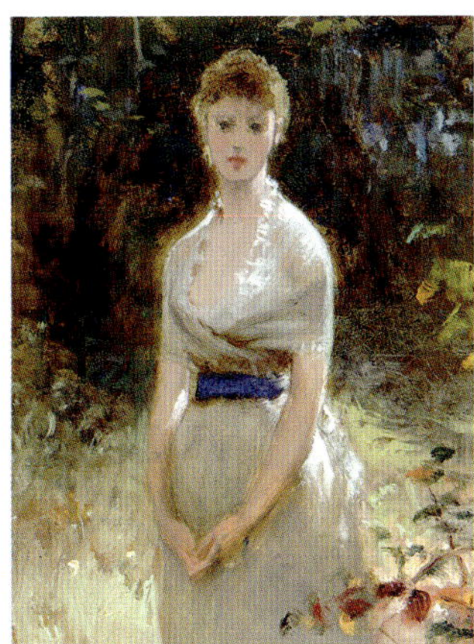

Hicks, George Elgar 1824–1914
Lady in White Dress with Blue Sash
oil on card 27.2 x 21.2
1072h

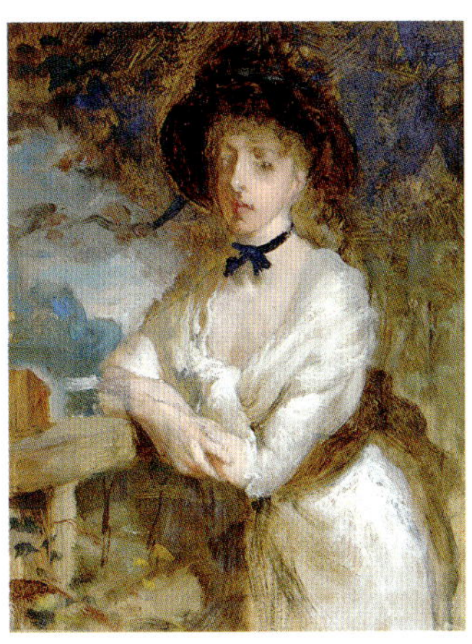

Hicks, George Elgar 1824–1914
Lady in White Dress with Hat
oil on card 27.2 x 21.5
1072g

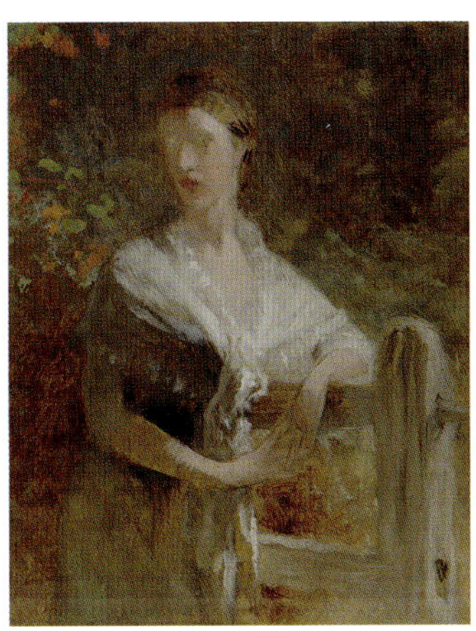

Hicks, George Elgar 1824–1914
Lady in White Shawl
oil on card 26 x 21
1072c

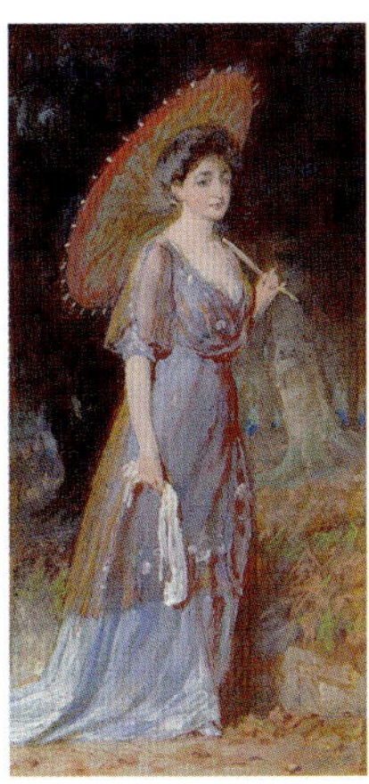

Hicks, George Elgar 1824–1914
Lady with Parasol
oil on card 21.3 x 10.8
1100

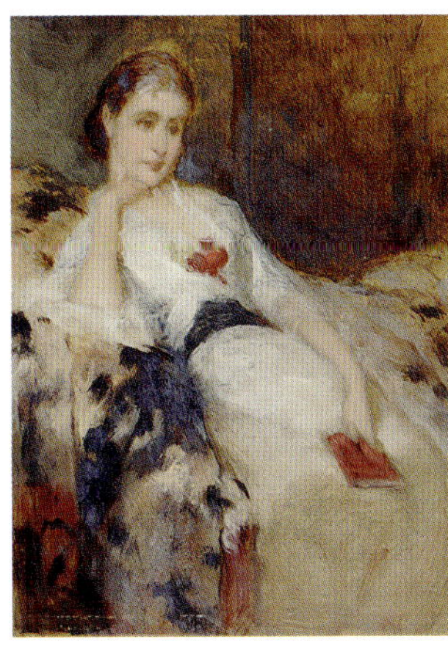

Hicks, George Elgar 1824–1914
Lady with Red Book
oil on card 28 x 20.3
1072d

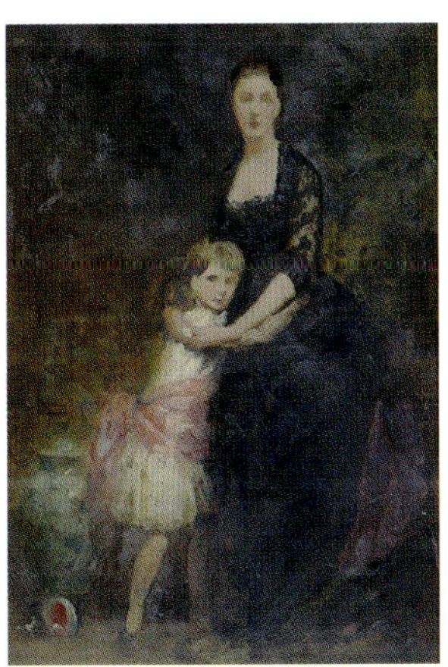

Hicks, George Elgar 1824–1914
Lady with Small Girl
oil on card 25.1 x 17.6
1097

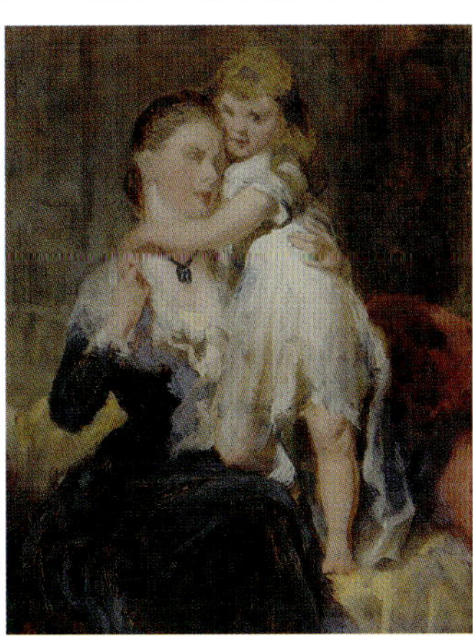

Hicks, George Elgar 1824–1914
Mother and Child
oil on card 19.6 x 15.8
1075aa

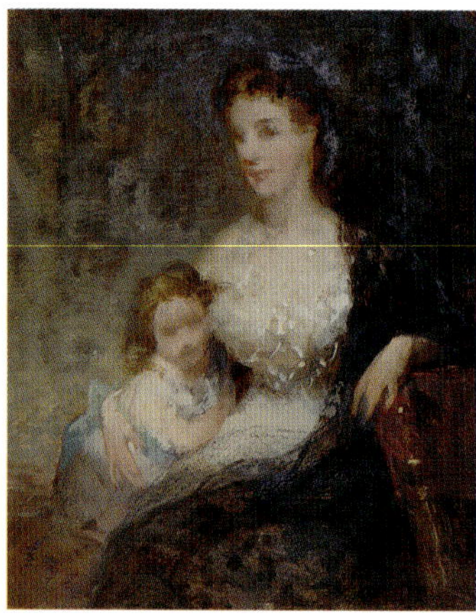

Hicks, George Elgar 1824–1914
Mother and Child
oil on card 20.3 x 16.5
1076d

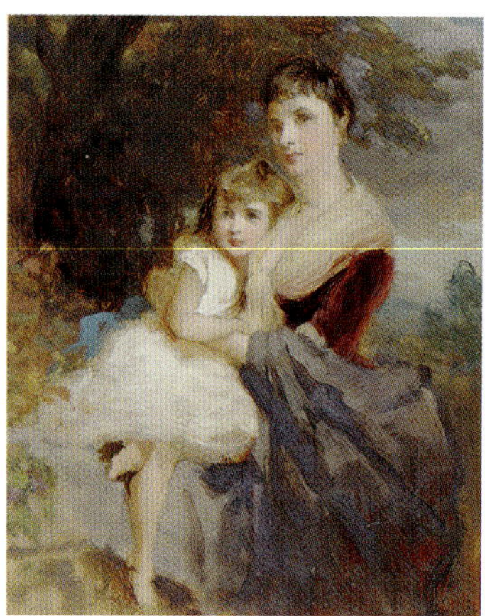

Hicks, George Elgar 1824–1914
Mother and Child
oil on card 26.6 x 22
1076j

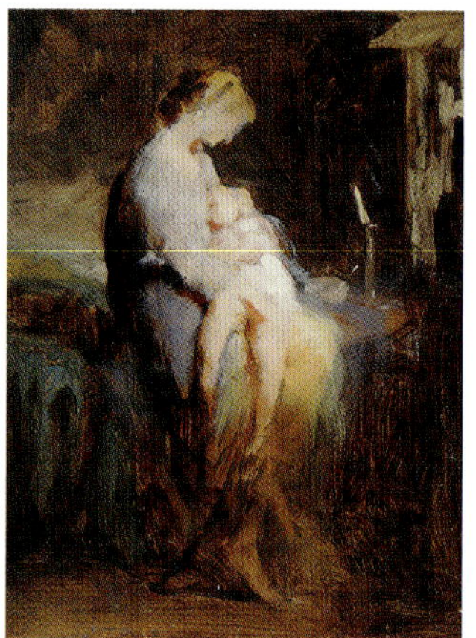

Hicks, George Elgar 1824–1914
Mother and Child
oil on board 22.2 x 17.5
1077i

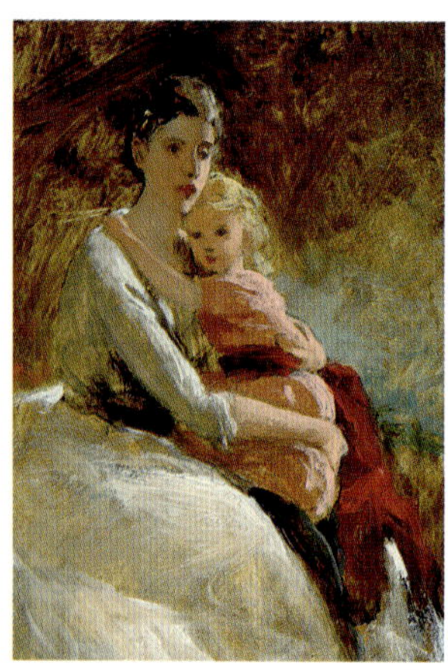

Hicks, George Elgar 1824–1914
Mother with Child in Pink Dress
oil on card 17.5 x 14
1073b

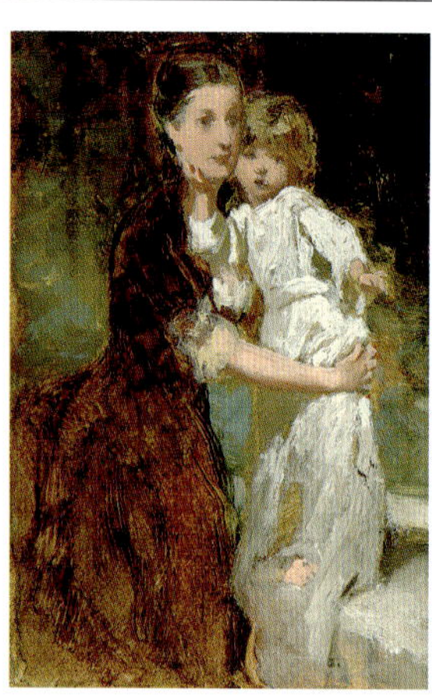

Hicks, George Elgar 1824–1914
Mother with Child in White Dress
oil on card 16.5 x 10.5
1073c

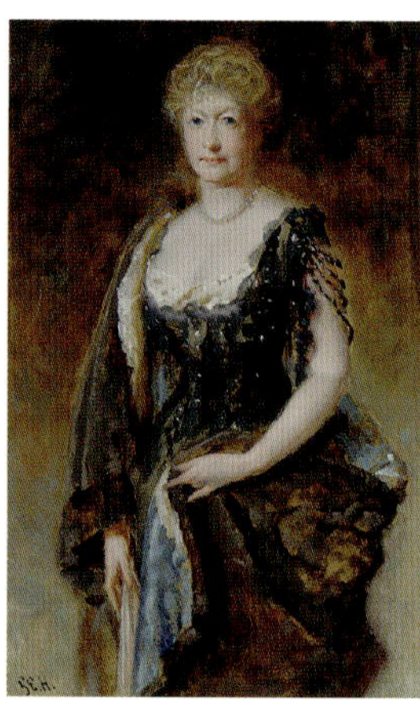

Hicks, George Elgar 1824–1914
Mrs Ridley
oil on card 29.2 x 19
1095

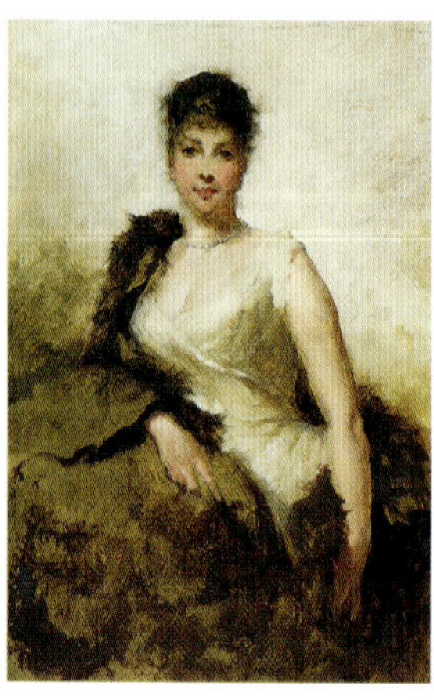

Hicks, George Elgar 1824–1914
Portrait of a Lady
oil on card 29 x 19.7
1092

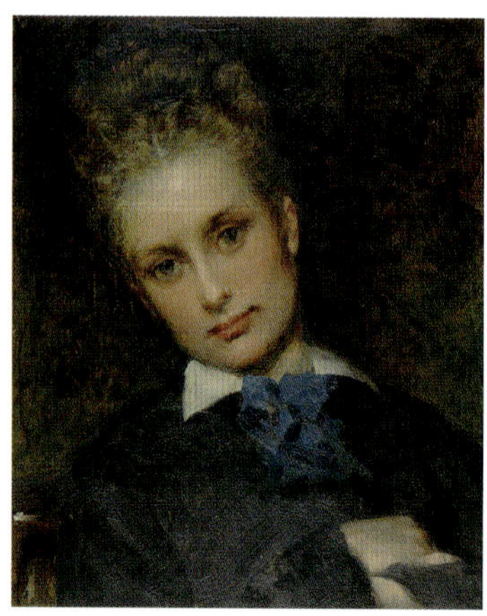

Hicks, George Elgar 1824–1914
Rose Gordon Hicks
oil on card 30 x 25.6
1082

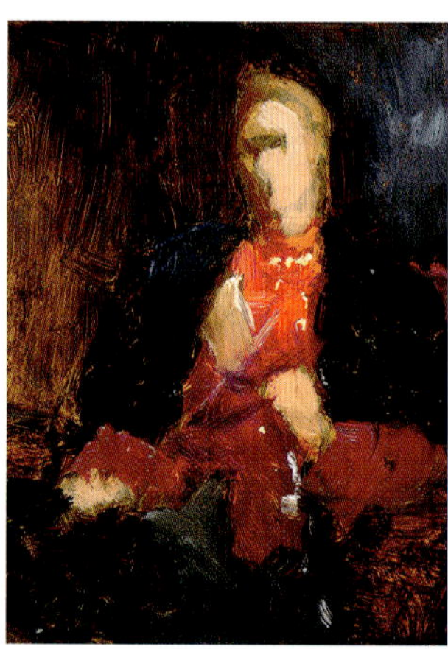

Hicks, George Elgar 1824–1914
Seated Figure in Red and Black
oil on card 15.2 x 13.6
1075e

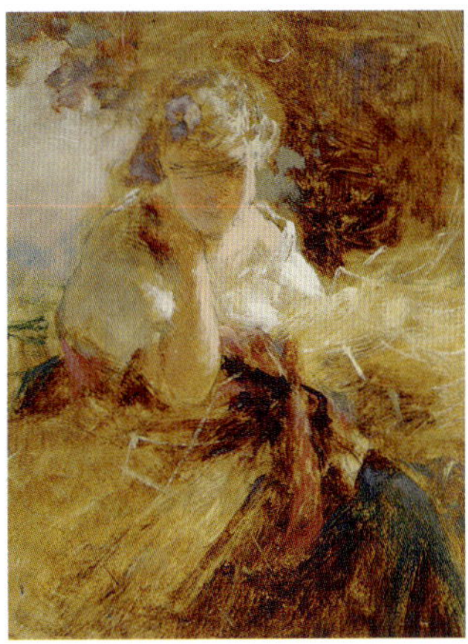

Hicks, George Elgar 1824–1914
Seated Girl
oil on card 26.6 x 20.3
1077e

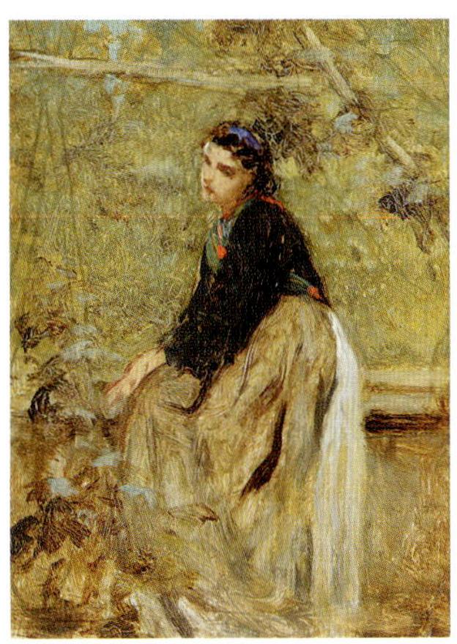

Hicks, George Elgar 1824–1914
Seated Girl
oil on board 30.5 x 22.5
1077f

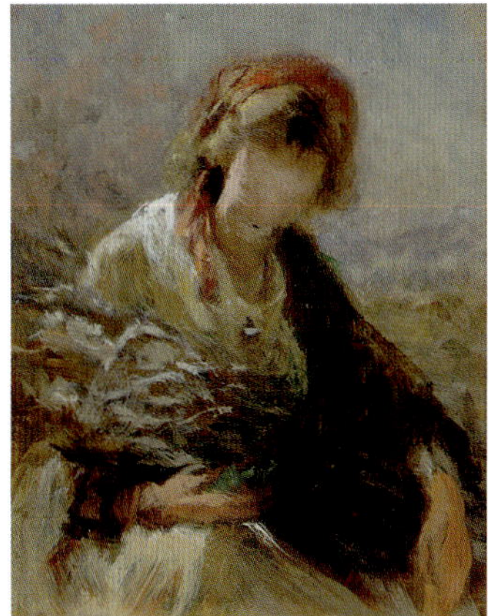

Hicks, George Elgar 1824–1914
Seated Girl
oil on board 22.8 x 19
1077g

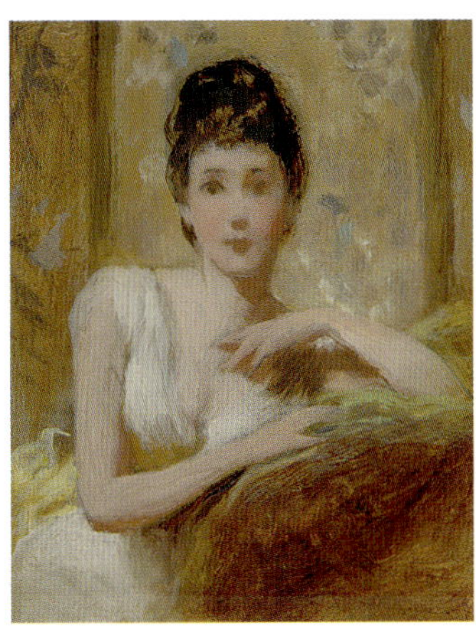

Hicks, George Elgar 1824–1914
Seated Girl in White Dress
oil on card 11.5 x 9.5
1075a

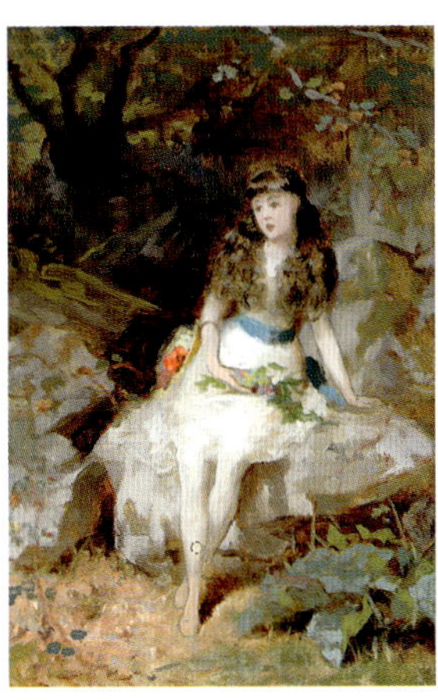

Hicks, George Elgar 1824–1914
Seated Girl in Wood
oil on card 31 x 21
1075ad

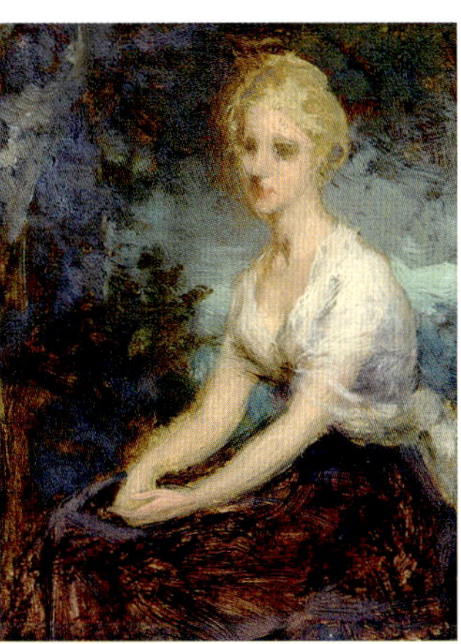

Hicks, George Elgar 1824–1914
Seated Lady
oil on card 15.2 x 10.8
1075c

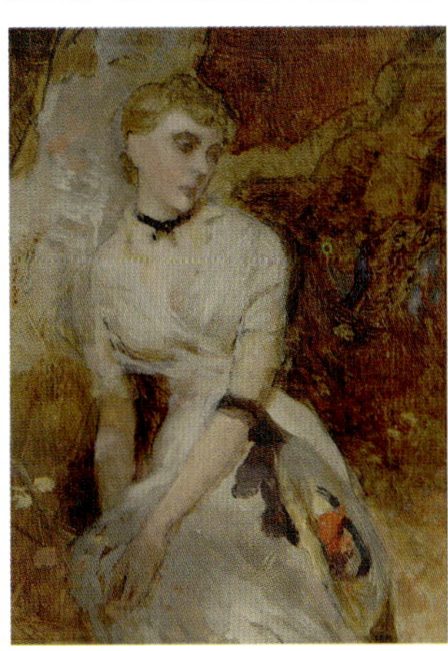

Hicks, George Elgar 1824–1914
Seated Lady by Tree
oil on card 21 x 16.2
1076c

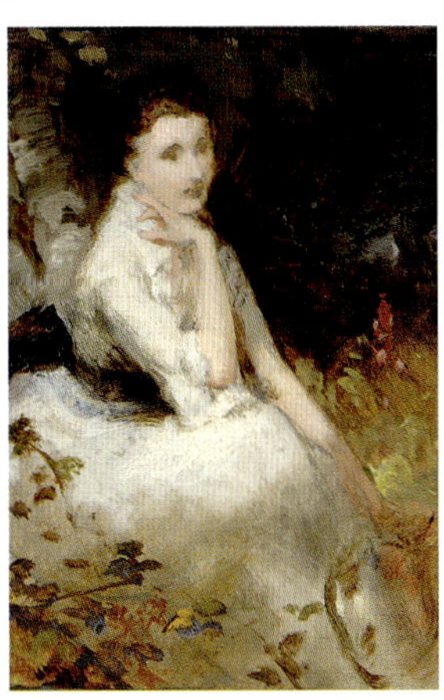

Hicks, George Elgar 1824–1914
Seated Lady in White Dress
oil on card 20.3 x 15.2
1076b

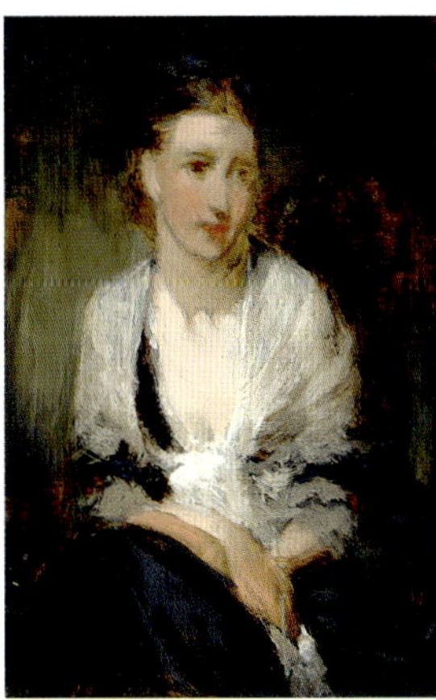

Hicks, George Elgar 1824–1914
Seated Lady in White Shawl
oil on card 22.5 x 16.5
1076e

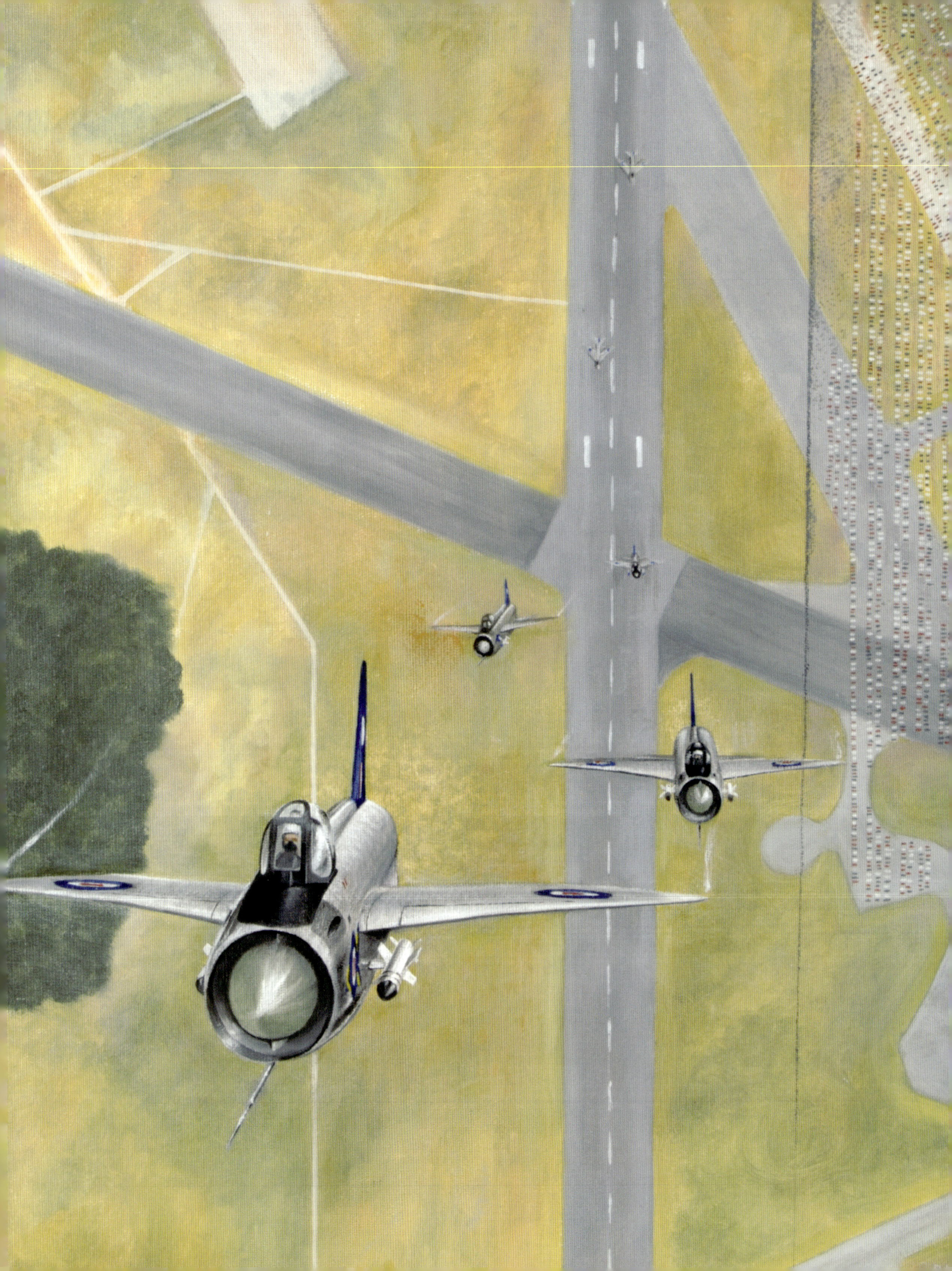

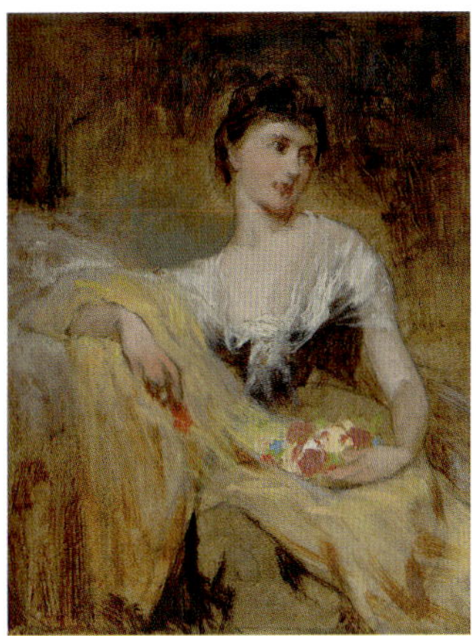

Hicks, George Elgar 1824–1914
Seated Lady with Flowers
oil on card 28.5 x 22
1072e

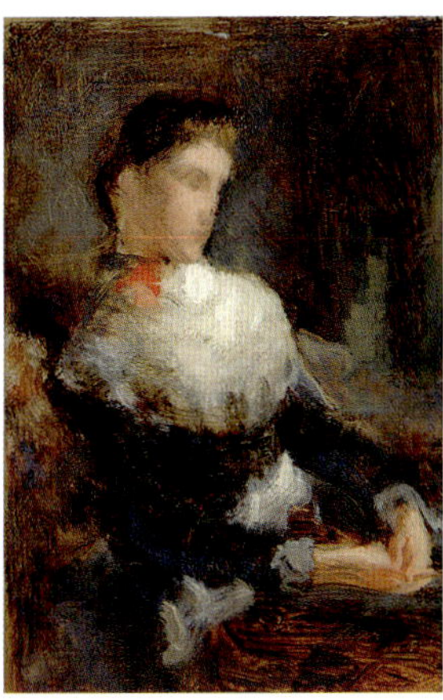

Hicks, George Elgar 1824–1914
Seated Woman
oil on card 15.8 x 11.5
1075ah

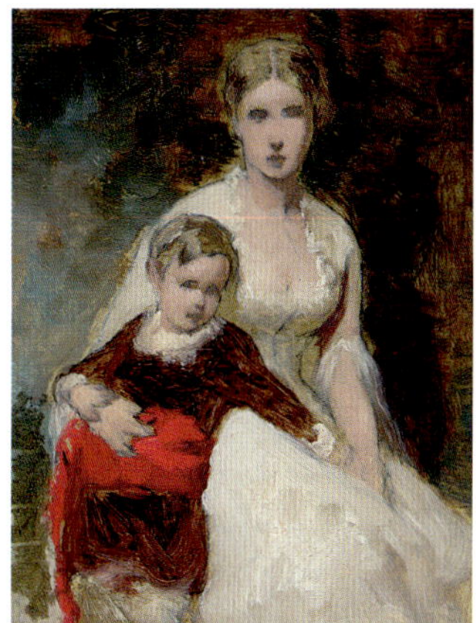

Hicks, George Elgar 1824–1914
Seated Woman and Child
oil on card 16.5 x 14
1075d

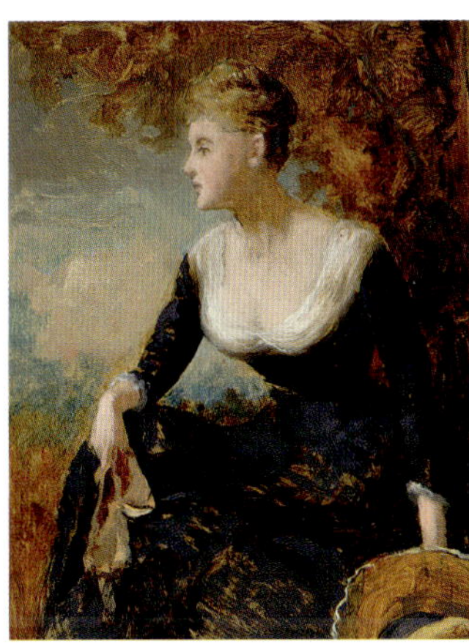

Hicks, George Elgar 1824–1914
Seated Woman in Black Dress
oil on card 19 x 14.8
1073f

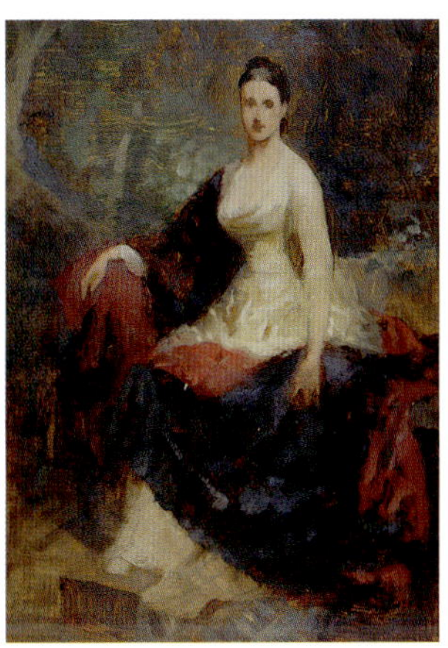

Hicks, George Elgar 1824–1914
Seated Woman in White Dress
oil on card 25.4 x 16.8
1073h

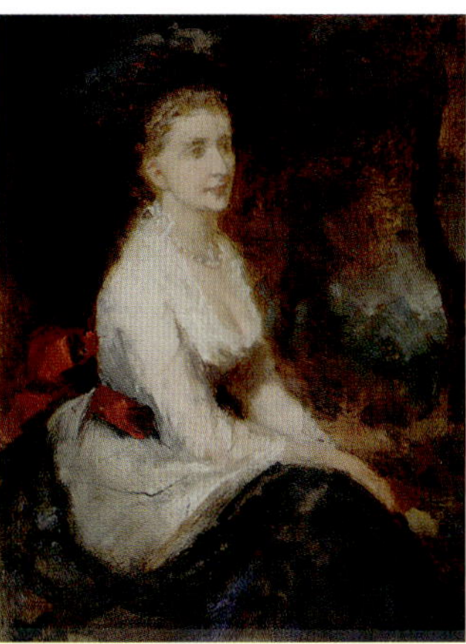

Hicks, George Elgar 1824–1914
Seated Woman in Wood
oil on card 19.6 x 15.2
1075ai

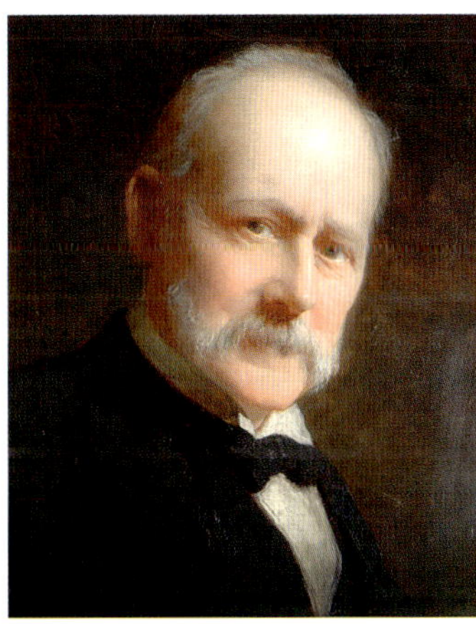

Hicks, George Elgar 1824–1914
Self Portrait at the Age of 75
oil on canvas 47 x 39.3
1080

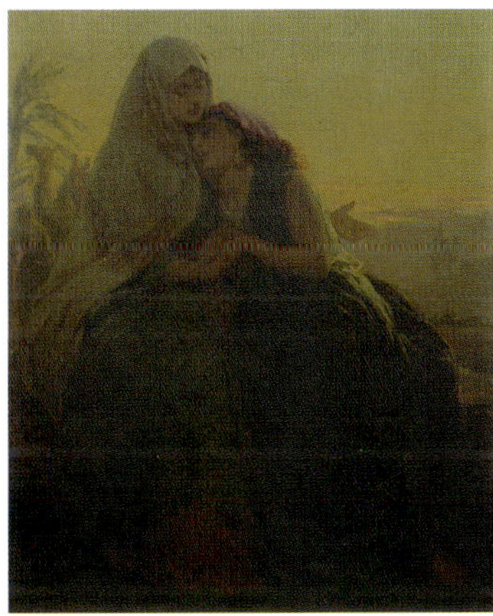

Hicks, George Elgar 1824–1914
Sketch for 'Entreat Me Not to Leave Thee'
oil on board 28 x 22.8
1085

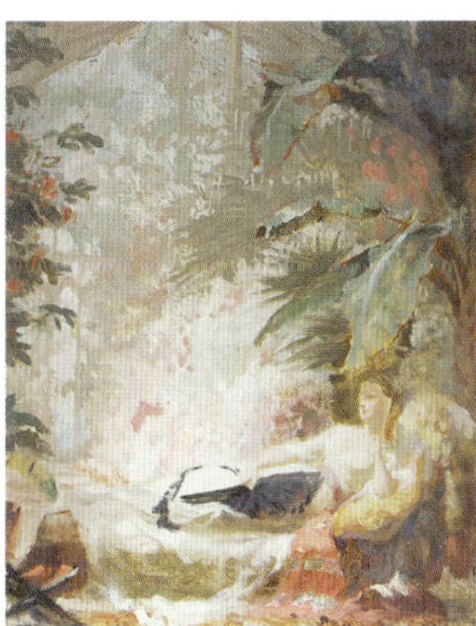

Hicks, George Elgar 1824–1914
Sketch of Reclining Woman
oil on canvas 30.5 x 23.5
1090

Facing page: Hatchard, David, b.1945, *Vertical Take-off* (detail), 2002, Solent Sky Aviation Museum, (p. 4)

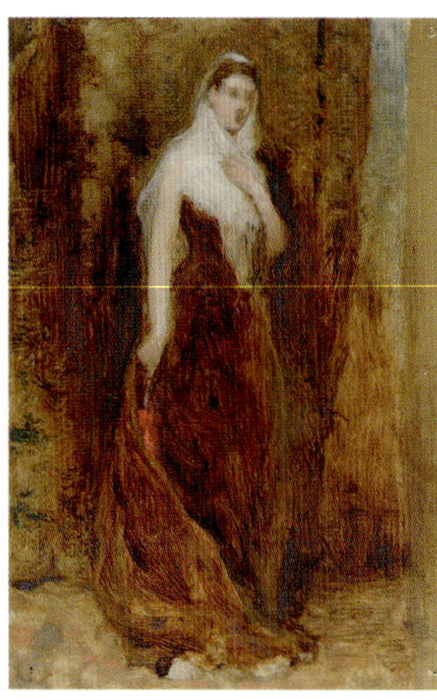

Hicks, George Elgar 1824–1914
Standing Woman
oil on card 27.2 x 16.5
1075ag

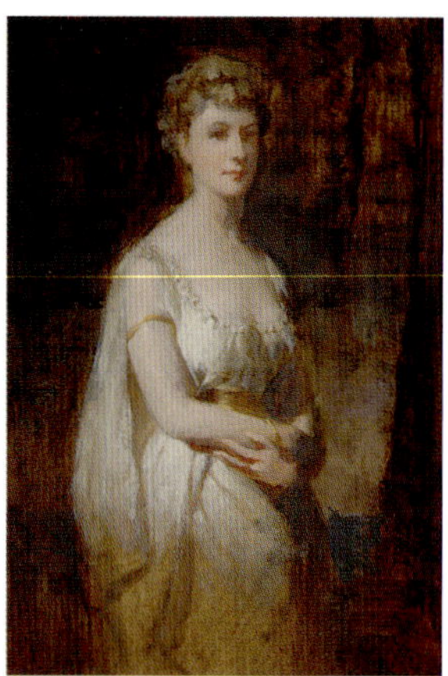

Hicks, George Elgar 1824–1914
Standing Woman in White Dress
oil on card 21.3 x 15.2
1075g

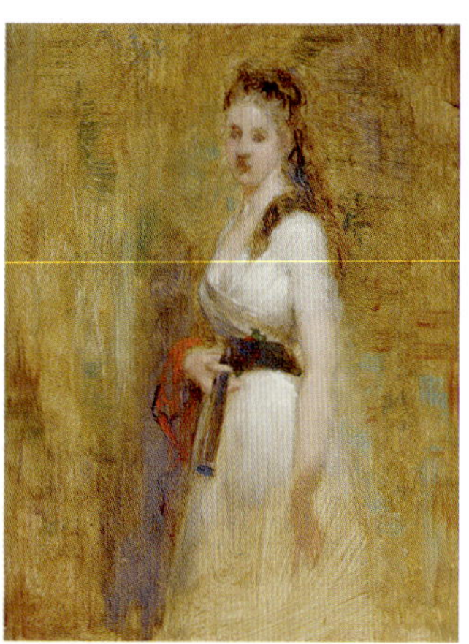

Hicks, George Elgar 1824–1914
Standing Woman with Fan
oil on card 27.2 x 21
1075aj

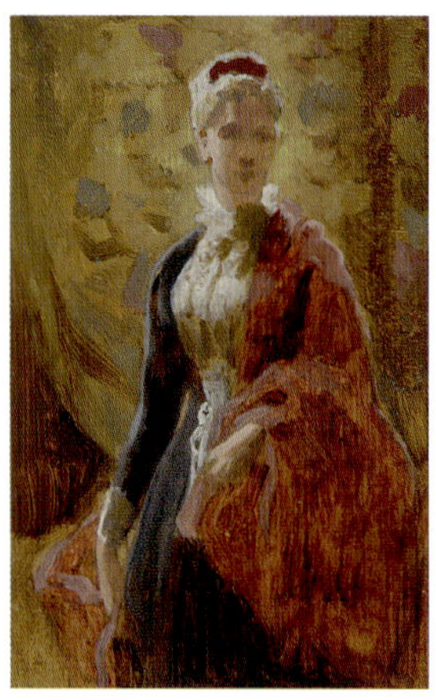

Hicks, George Elgar 1824–1914
Standing Woman with Red Cloak
oil on card 19 x 12
1075h

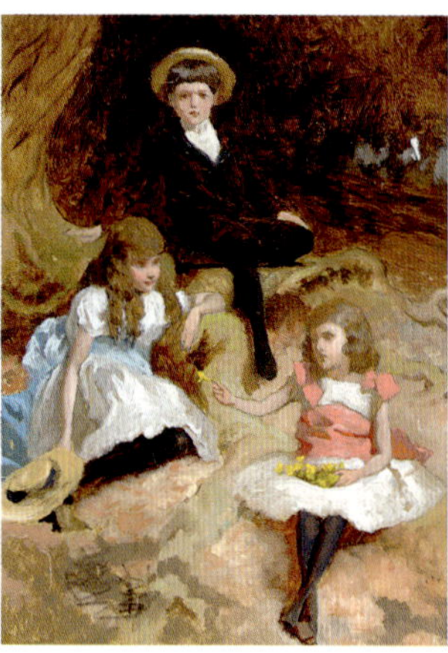

Hicks, George Elgar 1824–1914
Three Children
oil on card 35.8 x 26.3
1073k

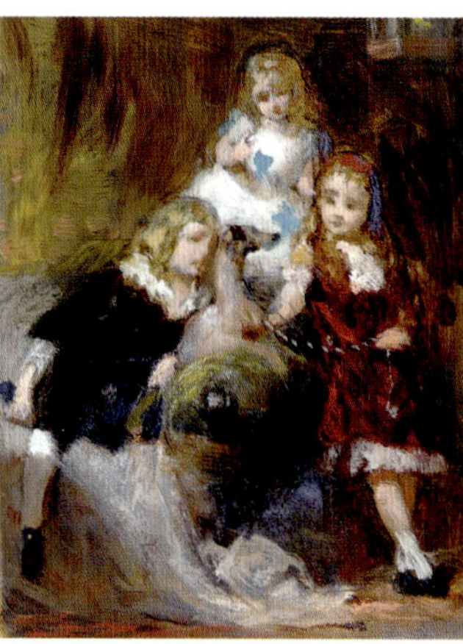

Hicks, George Elgar 1824–1914
Three Children and Dog
oil on card 26.6 x 21
1072b

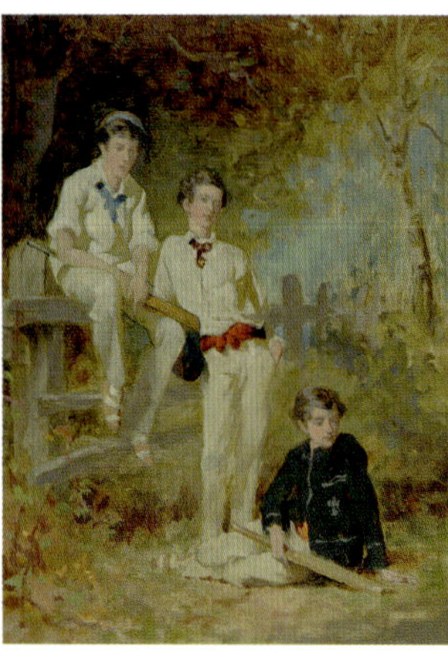

Hicks, George Elgar 1824–1914
Three Young Cricketers
oil on card 28.8 x 21.3
1093

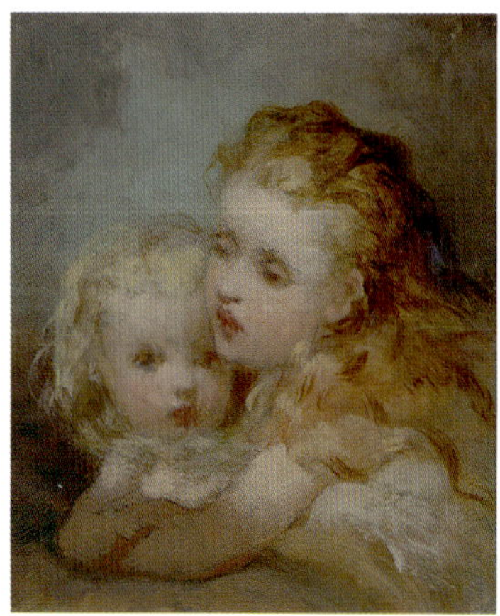

Hicks, George Elgar 1824–1914
Two Children
oil on card 23.8 x 18.4
1072f

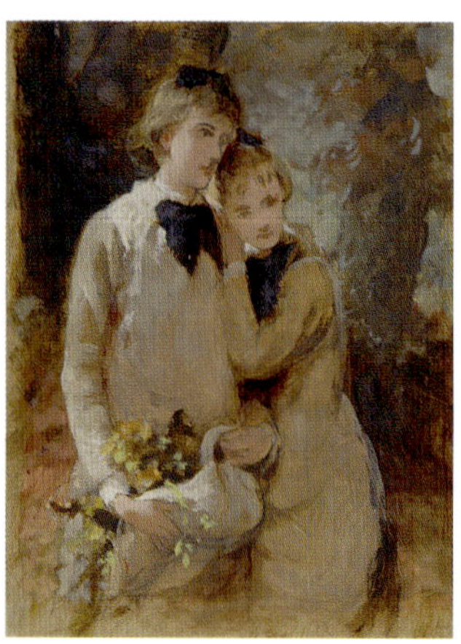

Hicks, George Elgar 1824–1914
Two Girls Standing
oil on card 24.5 x 19
1075j

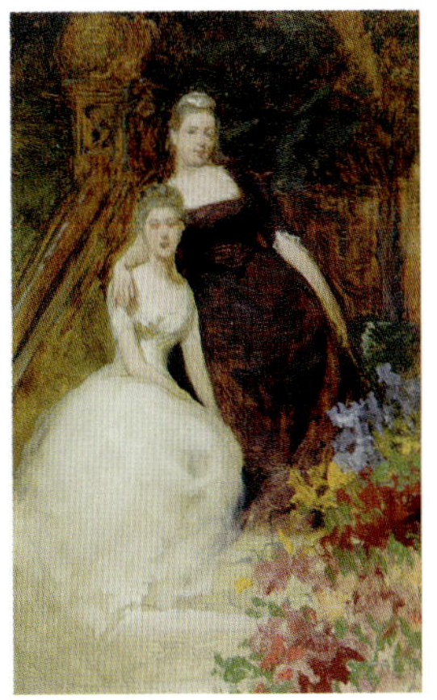

Hicks, George Elgar 1824–1914
Two Ladies
oil on card 25 x 15.7
1096

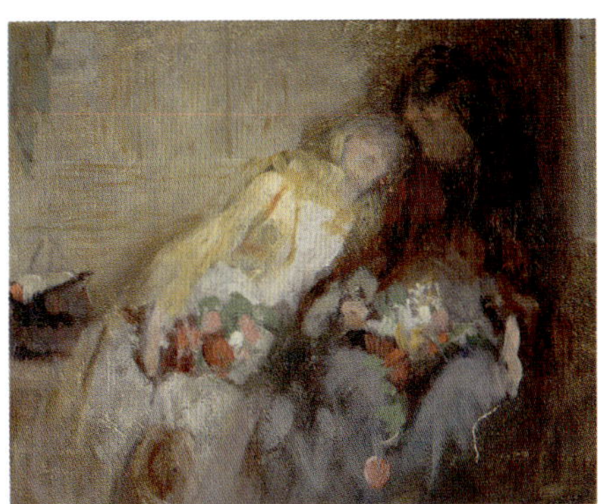

Hicks, George Elgar 1824–1914
Two Seated Figures with Flowers
oil on card 21 x 31.7 (E)
1077a

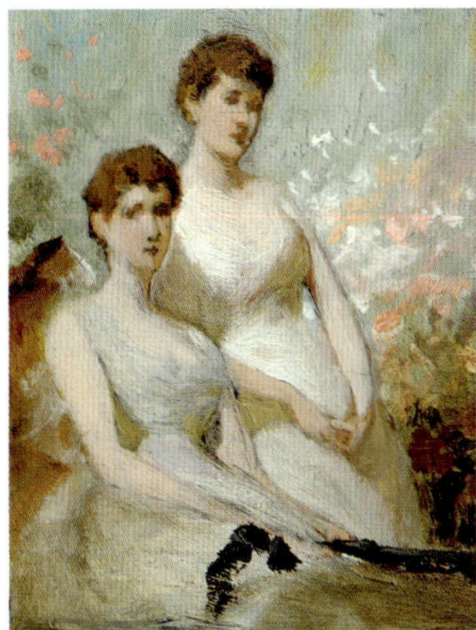

Hicks, George Elgar 1824–1914
Two Seated Ladies in White Dresses
oil on card 14 x 11.2
1075f

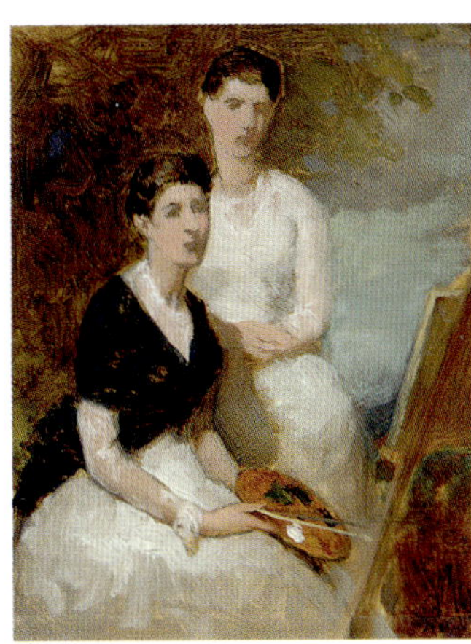

Hicks, George Elgar 1824–1914
Two Women with Easel and Palette
oil on card 17.2 x 13
1073d

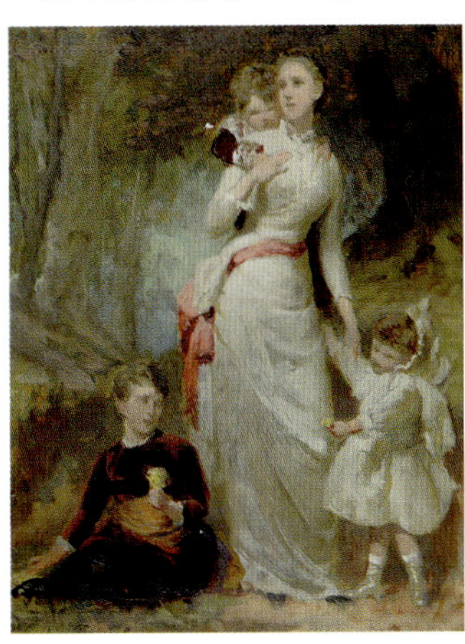

Hicks, George Elgar 1824–1914
Woman and Three Children
oil on card 22.8 x 17.6
1091

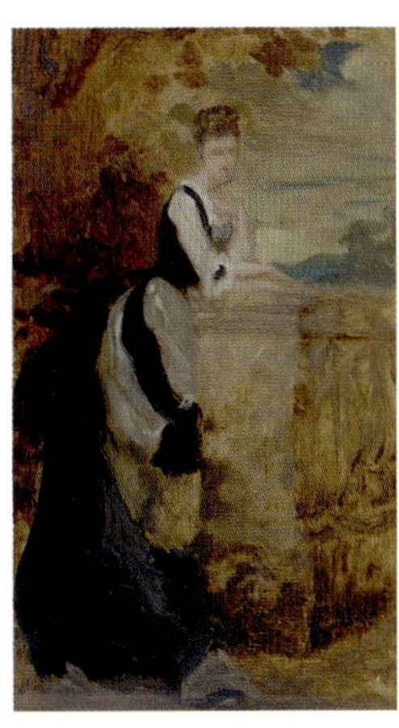

Hicks, George Elgar 1824–1914
Woman in Black and White Dress
oil on card 24.5 x 13.7
1073j

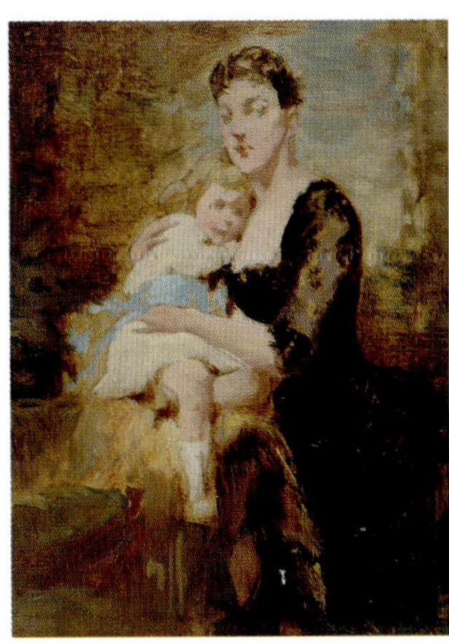

Hicks, George Elgar 1824–1914
Woman in Black Dress Holding Child
oil on card 18.4 x 14
1073g

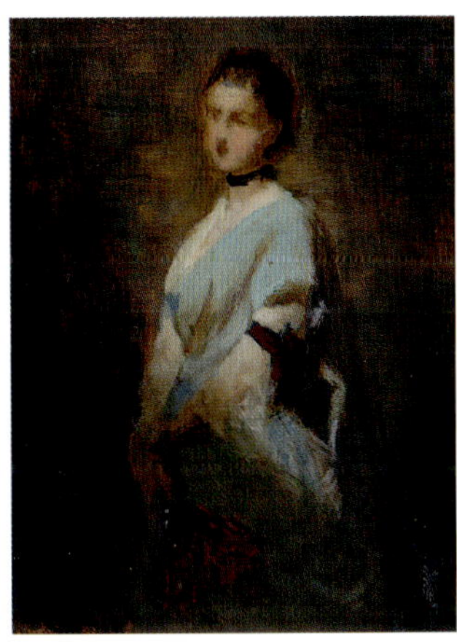

Hicks, George Elgar 1824–1914
Woman in Blue Dress with Fan
oil on card 22 x 17.2
1072a

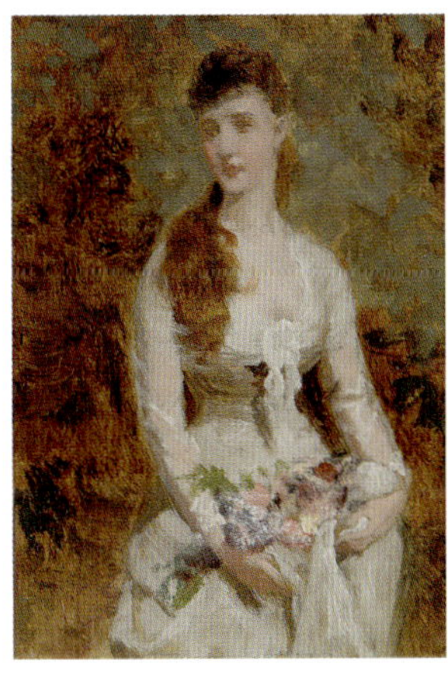

Hicks, George Elgar 1824–1914
Woman in White Dress
oil on card 17.2 x 13.3
1073e

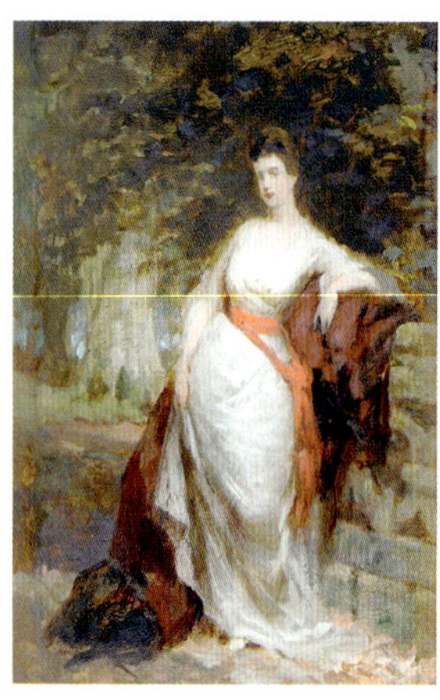

Hicks, George Elgar 1824–1914
Woman Standing by Balustrade
oil on card 31.1 x 21.5
1075ae

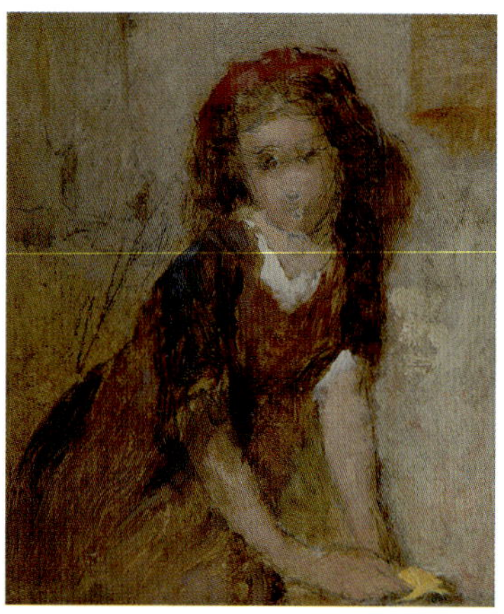

Hicks, George Elgar 1824–1914
Young Girl
oil on card 14.5 x 12.2
1077c

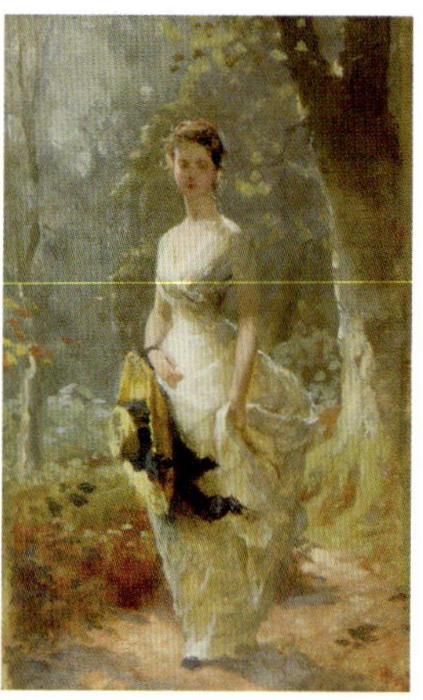

Hicks, George Elgar 1824–1914
Young Lady in the Forest
oil on card 24.6 x 15.2
1098

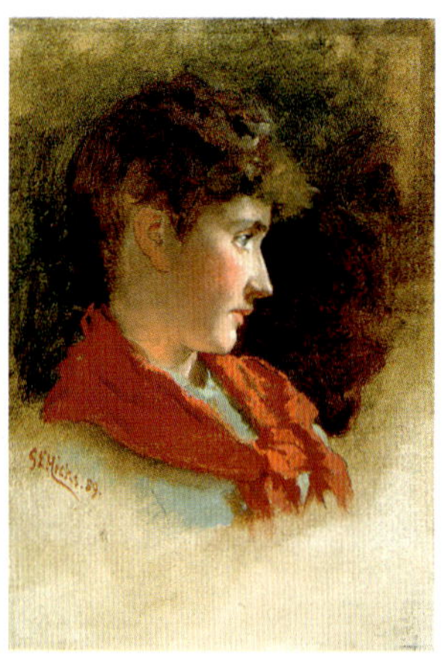

Hicks, George Elgar 1824–1914
Young Woman's Head
oil on canvas 23.5 x 20.3
1086

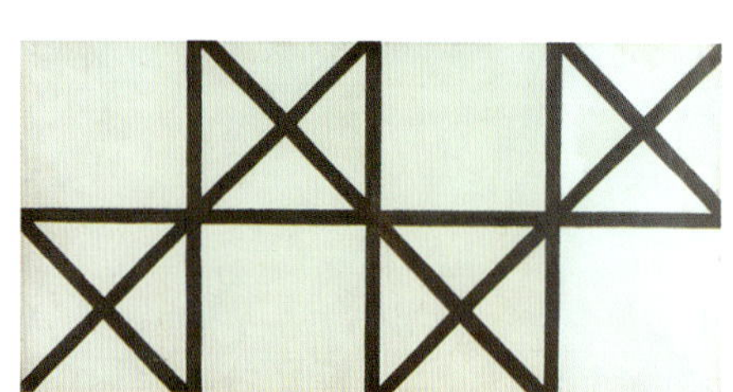

Hill, Anthony b.1930
Orthogonal/Diagonal Composition 1954
oil on canvas 39 x 69.8
11/2002

Hill, Anthony b.1930
January 1956 1956
oil on canvas 127.3 x 51.1
17/2002

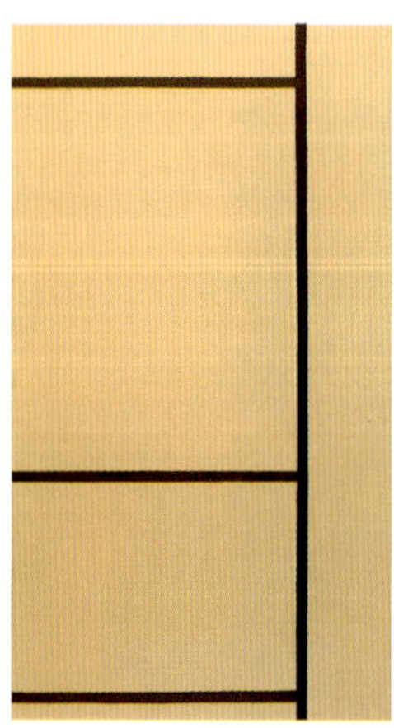

Hill, Anthony b.1930
Untitled
oil on canvas 105 x 58.3
16/2002

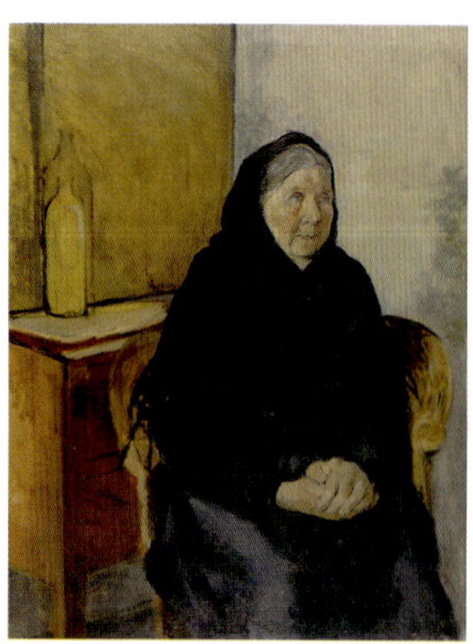

Hill, Derek 1916–2000
Mrs Mary Miley Mangan 1946
oil on canvas 91.5 x 71.8
1300

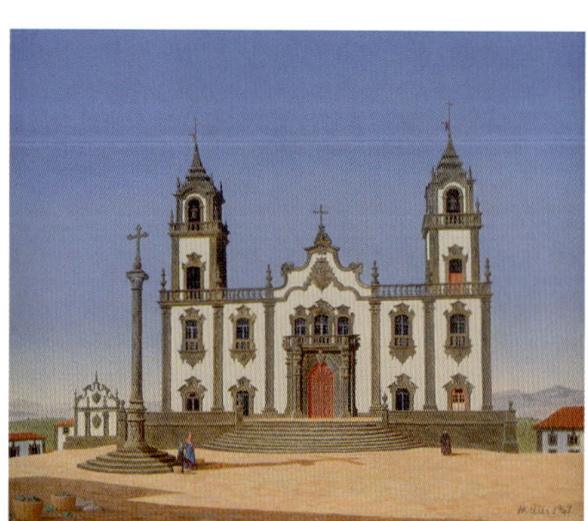

Hillier, Tristram Paul 1905–1983
Chapel of the Misericordia 1947
oil on canvas 25.4 x 29.2
76/1963

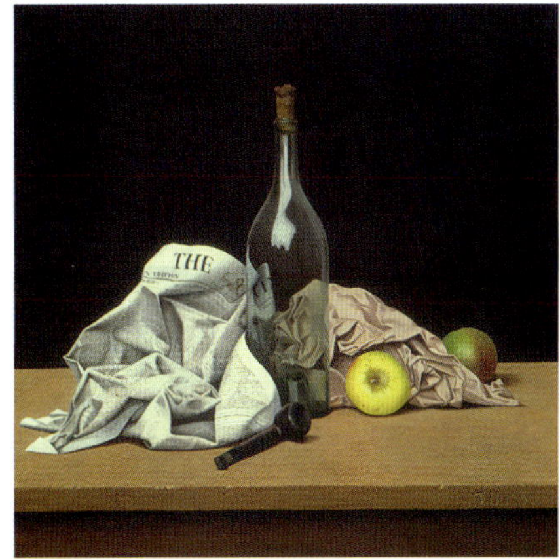

Hillier, Tristram Paul 1905–1983
The Green Bottle 1950
oil on canvas 61 x 61
1393

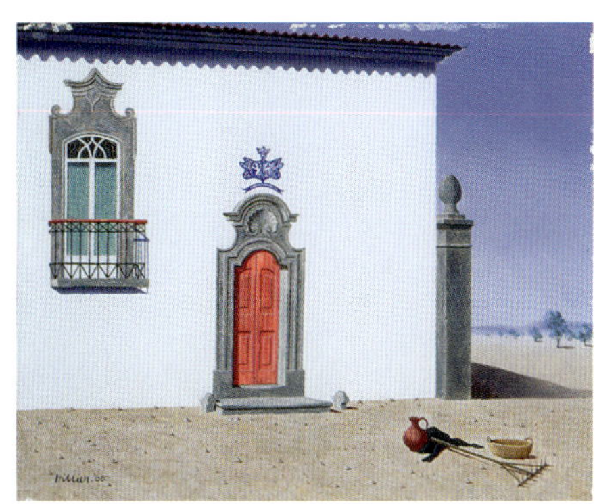

Hillier, Tristram Paul 1905–1983
Portuguese Farmhouse 1960
oil on canvas 22.9 x 28.2
28/1963

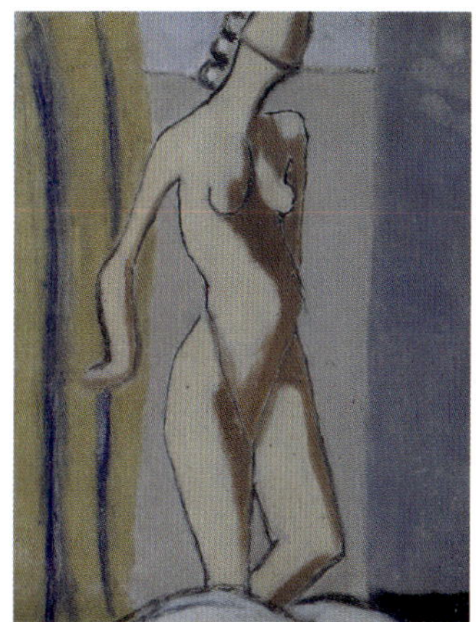

Hilton, Roger 1911–1975
Ghislaine and Grey Nude 1935
oil on board 34 x 26.4
9/2002

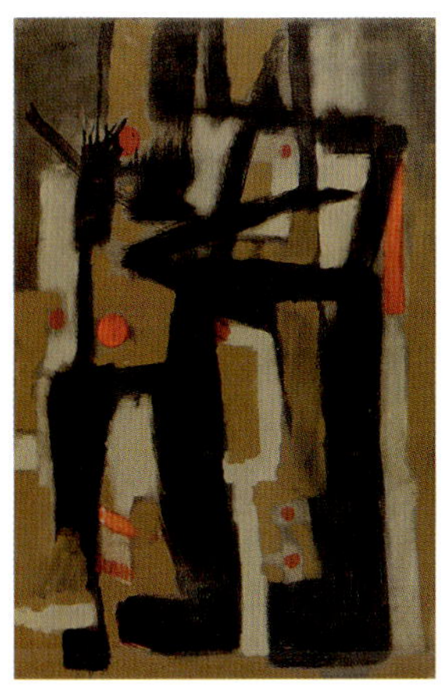

Hilton, Roger 1911–1975
Composition II 1951
oil on canvas 76.5 x 50.9
14/2002

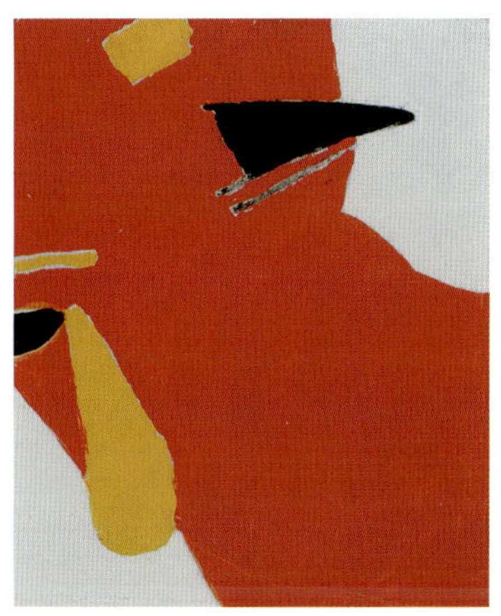

Hilton, Roger 1911–1975
August 1953 1953
acrylic on canvas 61 x 50.9
8/2002

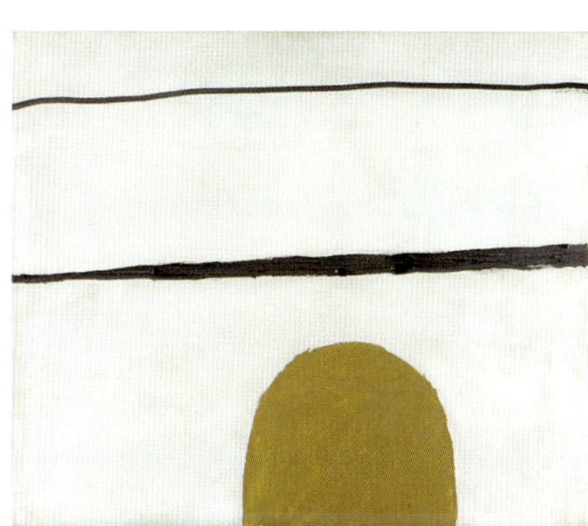

Hilton, Roger 1911–1975
October 1953 1953
oil on canvas 65.2 x 78
15/2002

Hilton, Roger 1911–1975
October 1953 1953
oil on canvas 20.4 x 61
74/2002

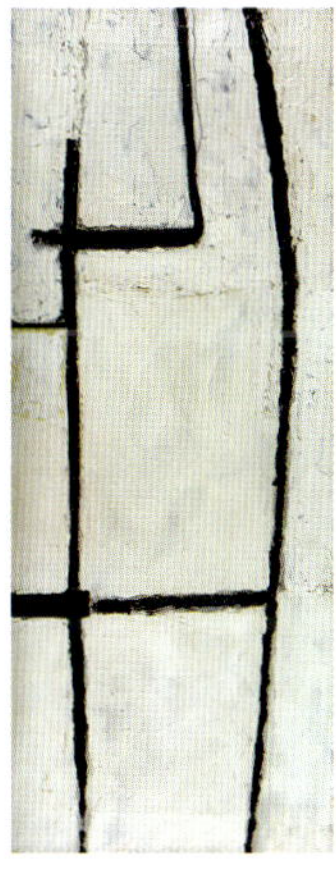

Hilton, Roger 1911–1975
Black on White, March 1954 1954
oil on canvas 76.2 x 30.6
18/2002

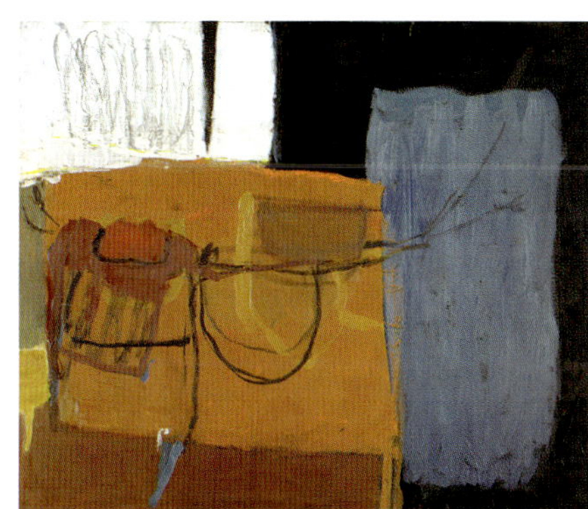

Hilton, Roger 1911–1975
October 1956 1956
oil on canvas 75 x 91
6/2002

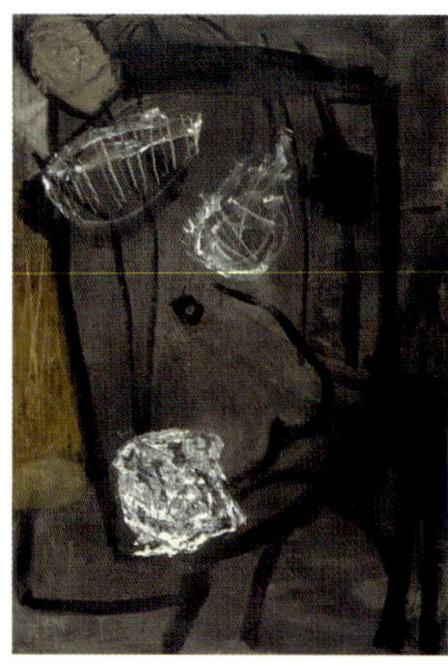

Hilton, Roger 1911–1975
Grey Figure, February 1957 1957
oil on board 174 x 122
1/1962

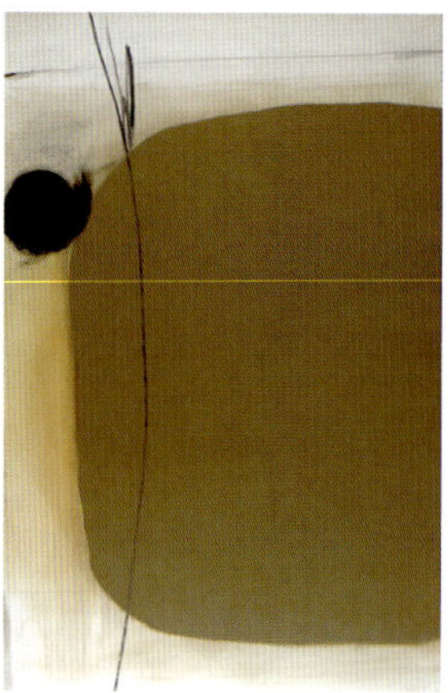

Hilton, Roger 1911–1975
May 1960 1960
acrylic on canvas 152 x 101
7/2002

Hilton, Roger 1911–1975
December 1961 1961
oil on canvas 45.9 x 35.7
46/2002

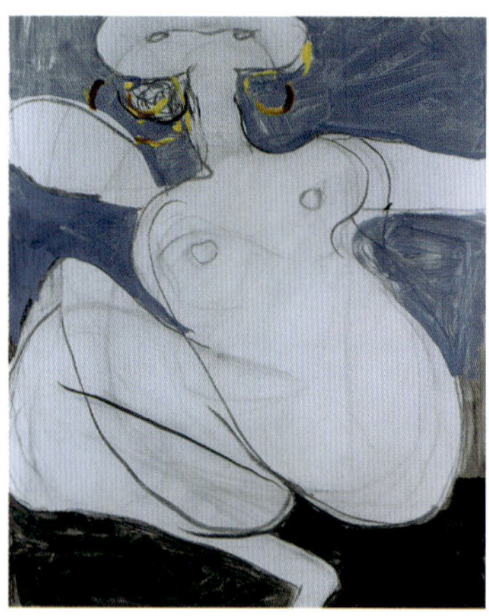

Hilton, Roger 1911–1975
Figure 61 1961
acrylic on canvas 92 x 76
5/2002

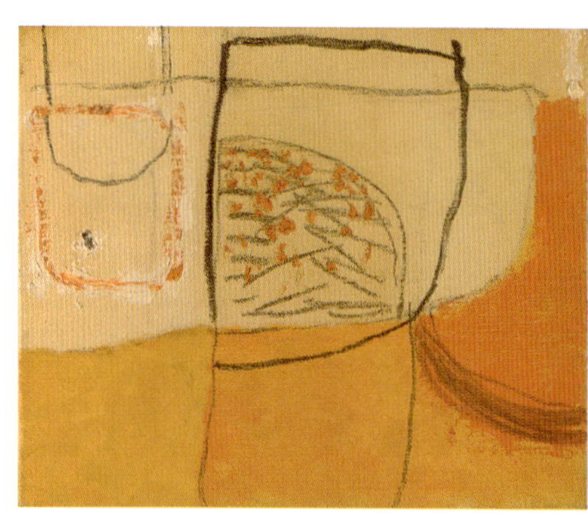

Hilton, Roger 1911–1975
July 1961 1961
oil on canvas 42.5 x 47.9
72/2002

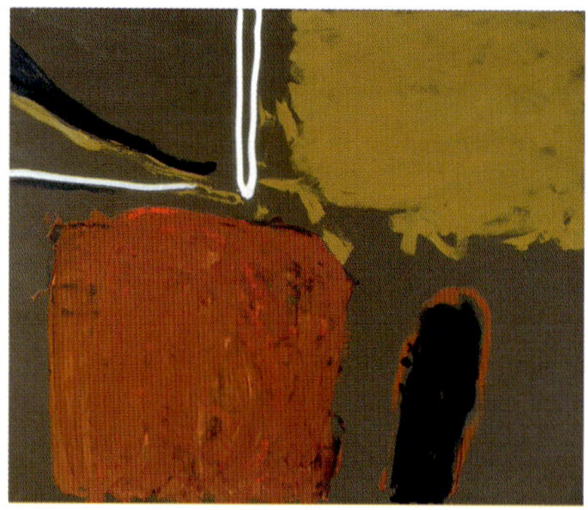

Hilton, Roger 1911–1975
January 1962 1962
oil on canvas 76.2 x 91.7
77/2002

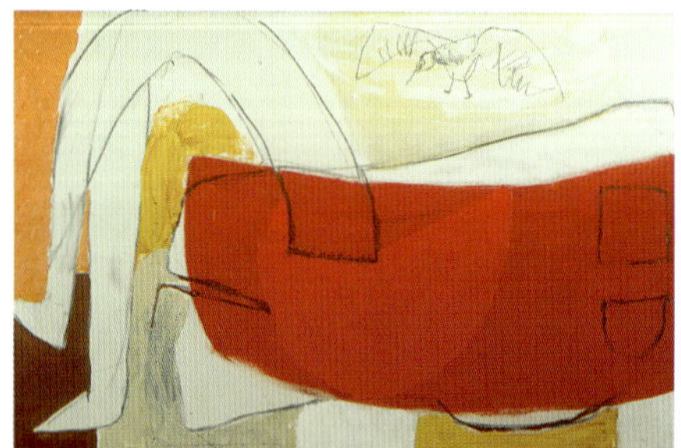

Hilton, Roger 1911–1975
Figure and Bird 1963
oil on canvas 117 x 178
L7R

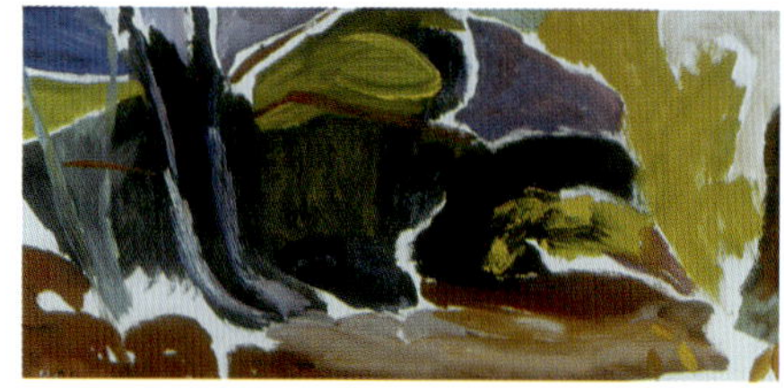

Hitchens, Ivon 1893–1979
Arched Trees No.7 1957
oil on canvas 41 x 86.4
2/1987

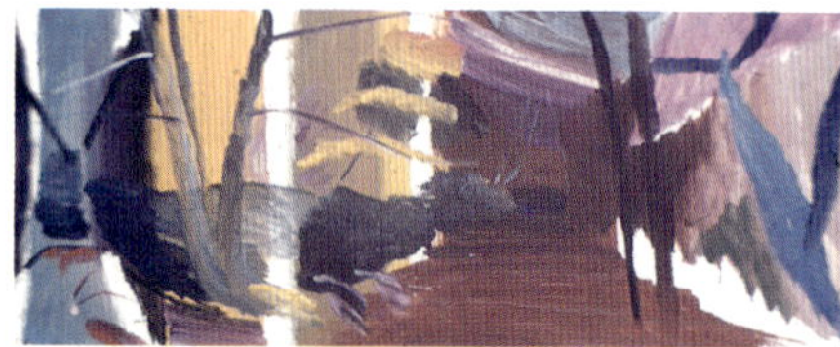

Hitchens, Ivon 1893–1979
Oak Tree in Purple Woods
oil on canvas 45.3 x 109.4
5/1959

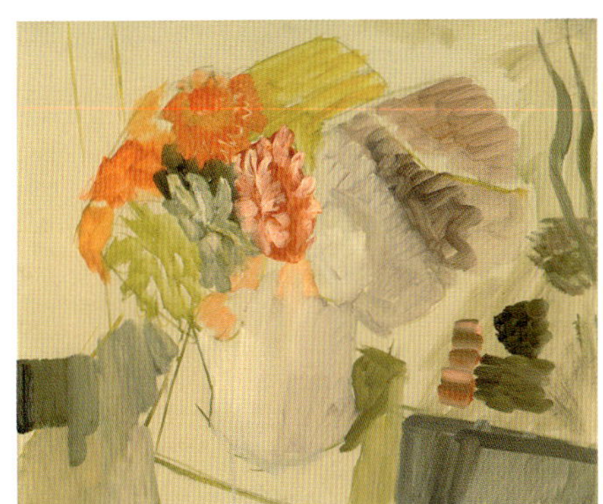

Hitchens, Ivon 1893–1979
Vase of Flowers
oil on canvas 43.2 x 51.8
189/1975

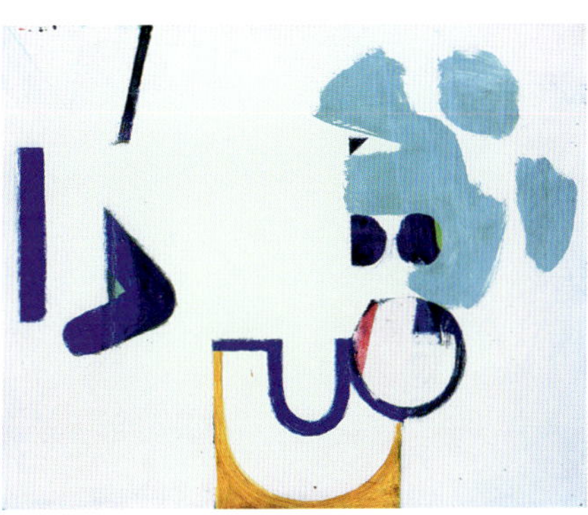

Hodgkin, Howard b.1932
The Second Visit 1963
oil on wood 40.5 x 50.7
15/2001

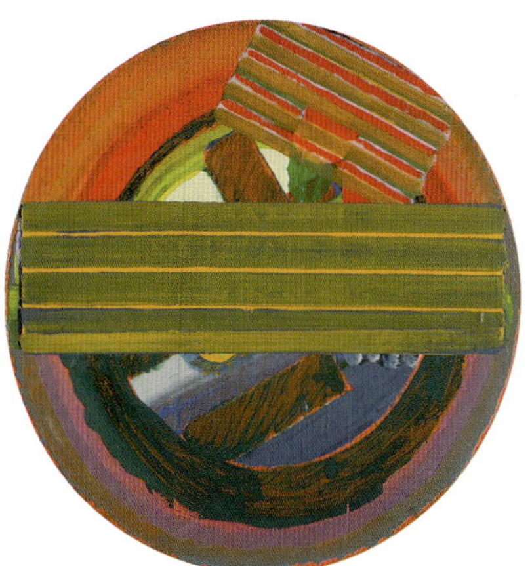

Hodgkin, Howard b.1932
Simon Digby Talking 1972–1975
oil on wood 63.2 (E)
14/1979

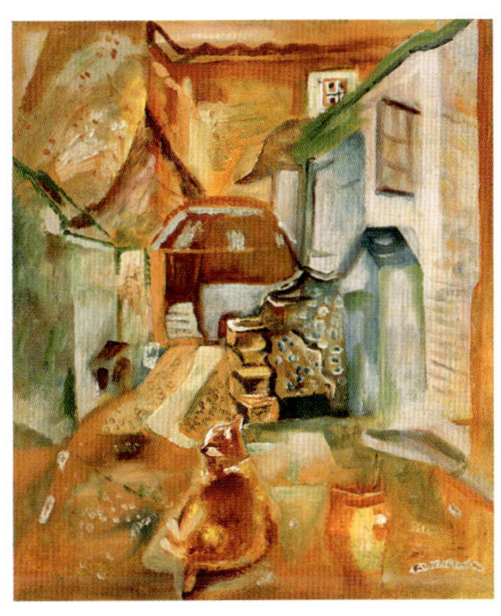

Hodgkins, Frances 1869–1947
Purbeck Courtyard Morning 1944
oil on wood 71.2 x 61
1362

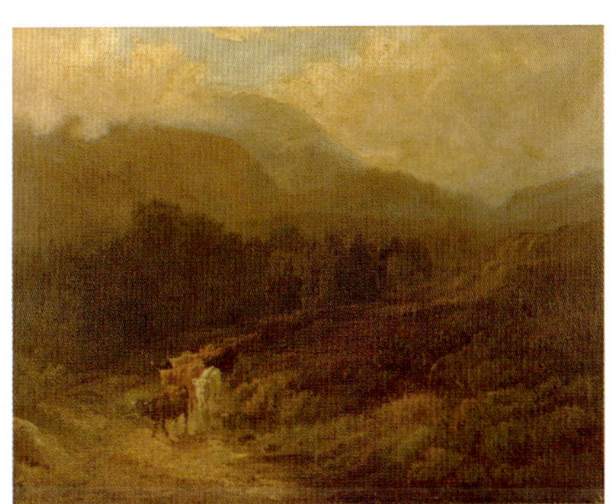

Hogley, Stephen E. active 1874–1893
Going South
oil on canvas 71.4 x 91.7
291

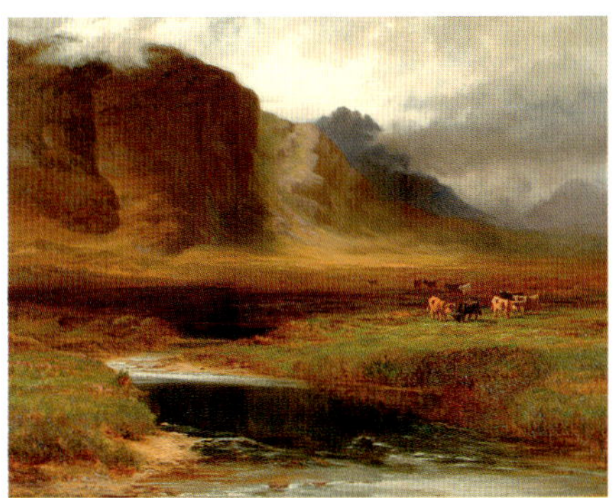

Hogley, Stephen E. active 1874–1893
In the Ogram Valley
oil on canvas 71.1 x 91.5
292

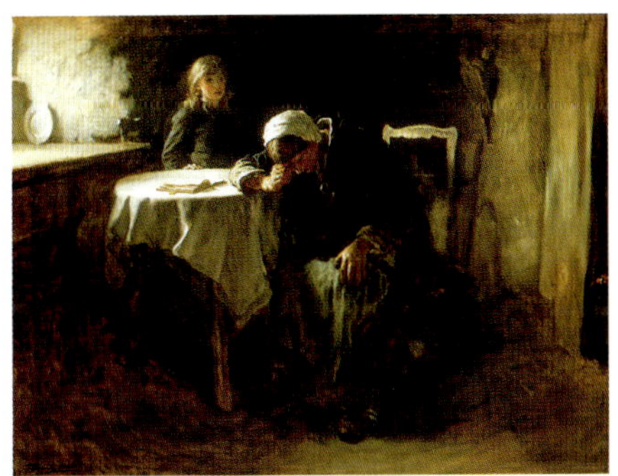

Holl, Frank 1845–1888
Despair 1881
oil on canvas 84 x 112
297

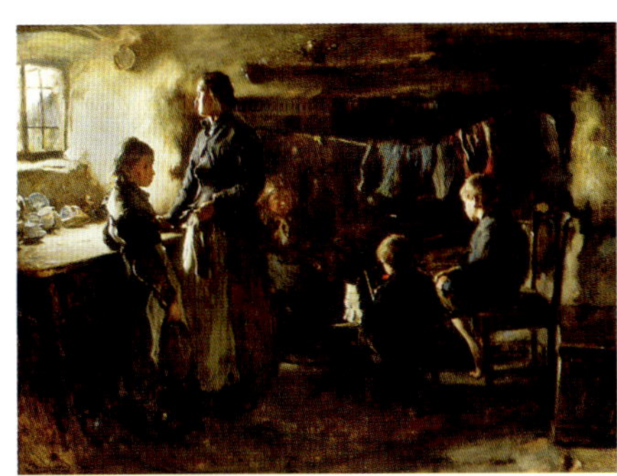

Holl, Frank 1845–1888
Hope 1883
oil on canvas 79.7 x 110
296

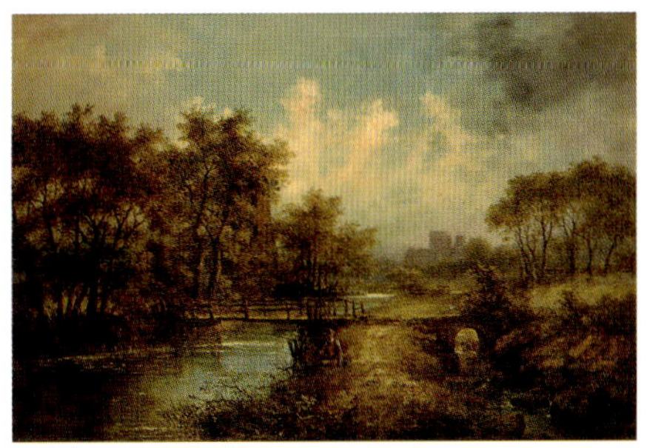

Hornibrook, George Farrington 1842–1882
York Minster from the Foss
oil on canvas 51.5 x 76.7
300

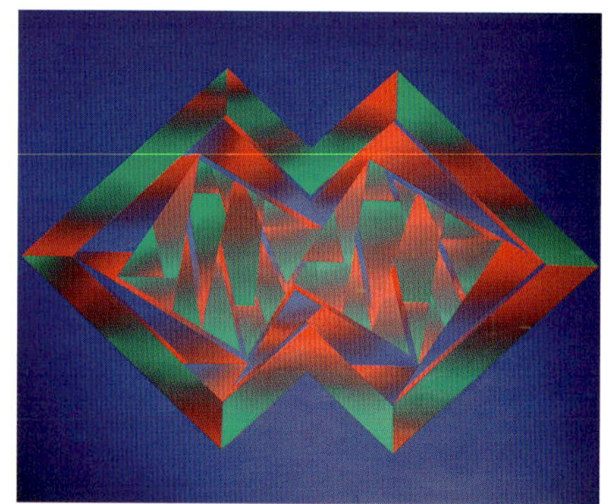

Hoskins, Ned b.1939
Double Sky Structure
acrylic on canvas 81.7 x 91.5 (E)
4/1974

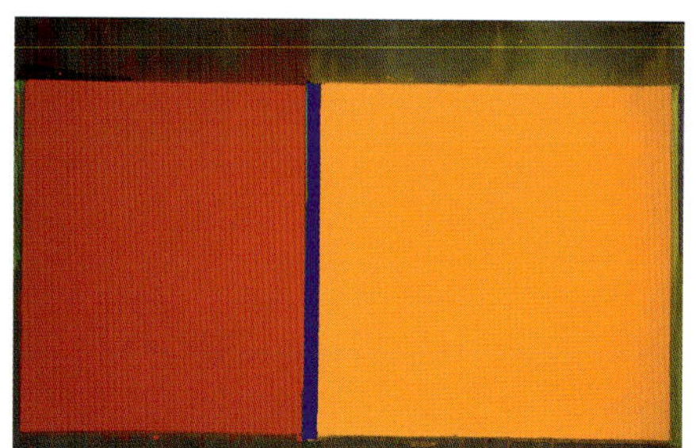

Hoyland, John b.1934
16.10.68 1968
acrylic on canvas 145 x 183.2
2/1997

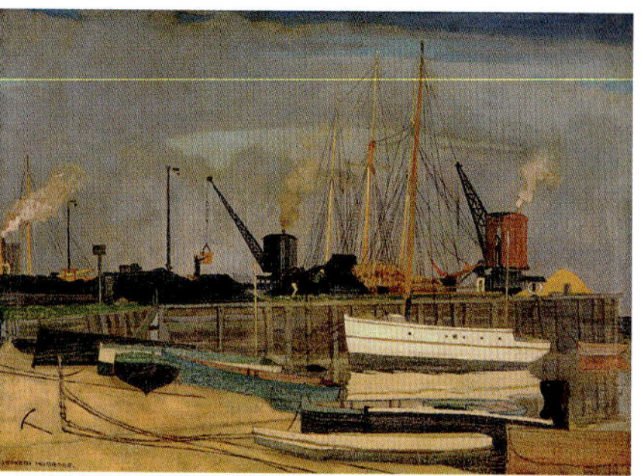

Hubbard, Eric Hesketh 1892–1957
Eling Wharf
oil on canvas 40 x 61.2
12/1989

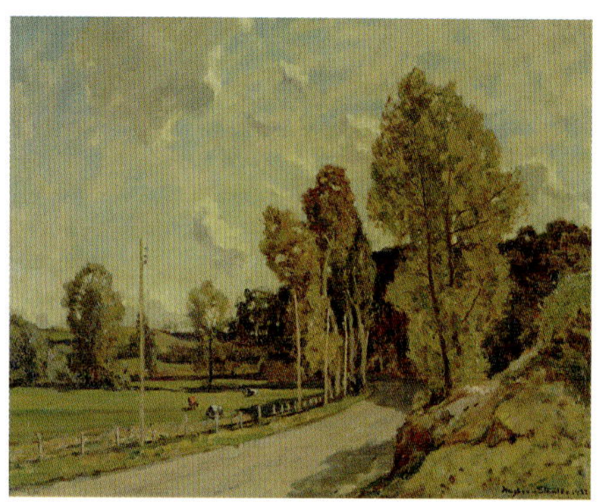

Hughes-Stanton, Herbert Edwin Pelham 1870–1937
Trépied, Pas de Calais 1932
oil on canvas 40.7 x 51.1
304

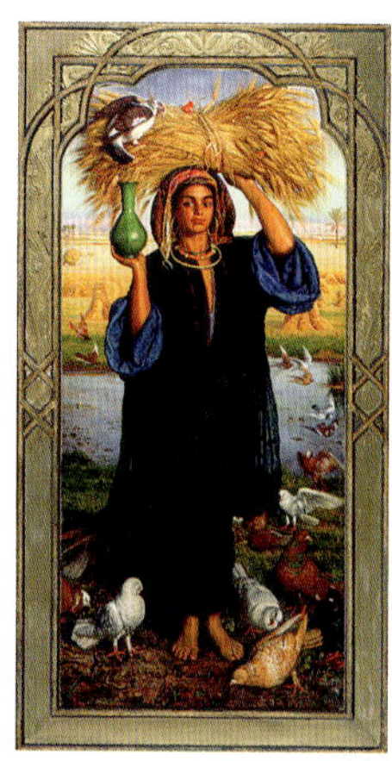

Hunt, William Holman 1827–1910
Afterglow in Egypt 1854
oil on canvas 185.4 x 86.3
1280

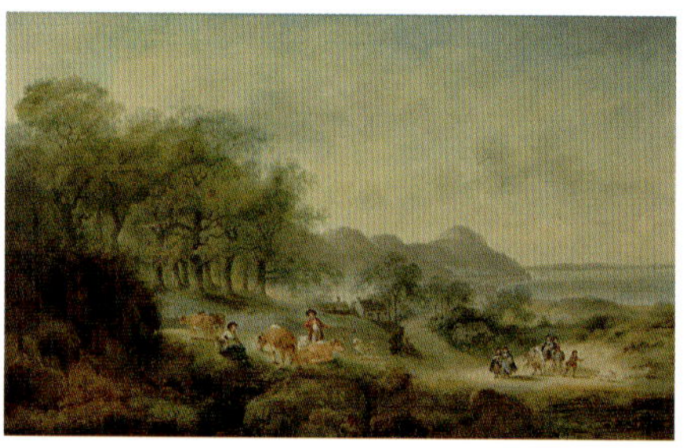

Ibbetson, Julius Caesar 1759–1817
Distant View of Anglesea
oil on canvas 85.8 x 139.3
1370

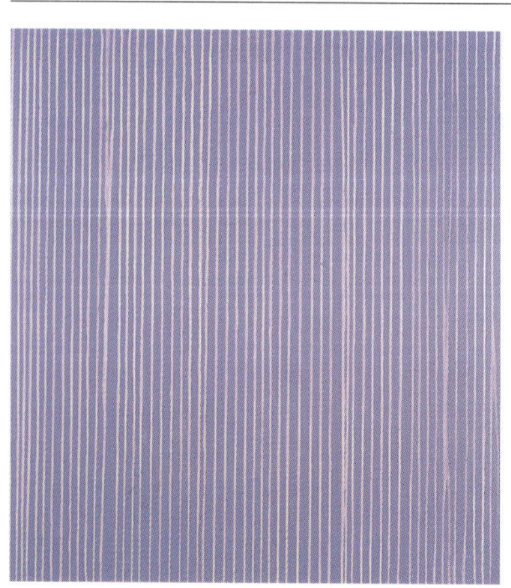

Innes, Callum b.1962
Repetition (Grey) 1995
oil on canvas 110 x 100
5/1996

Innes, Callum b.1962
Resonance 1995
oil on canvas 200.2 x 190.2
4/1996

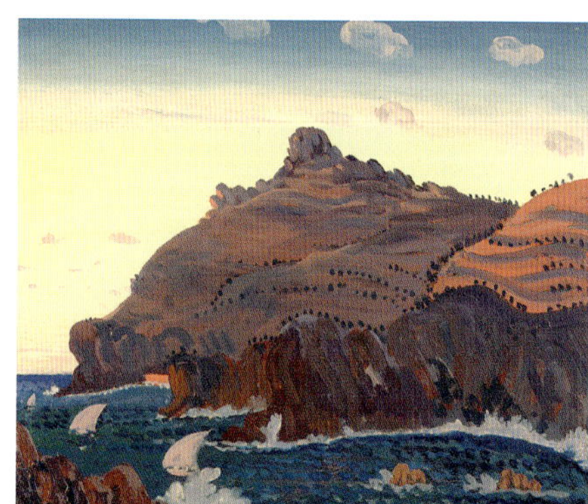

Innes, James Dickson 1887–1914
Collioure 1912
oil on canvas 38.1 x 46.3
1391

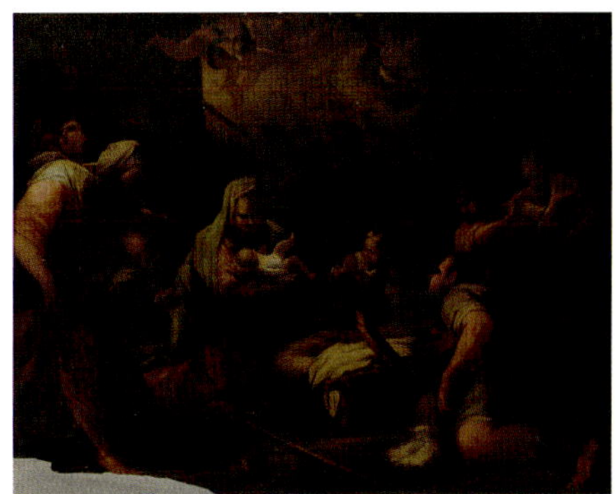

Italian School 17th C
Nativity: The Birth of Christ
oil on canvas 124.9 x 160
654

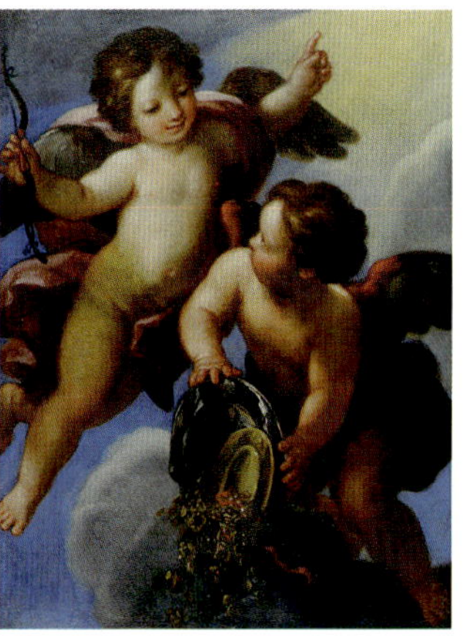

Italian School 18th C
Cupid and Putto
oil on canvas 65 x 48.6
5/1990

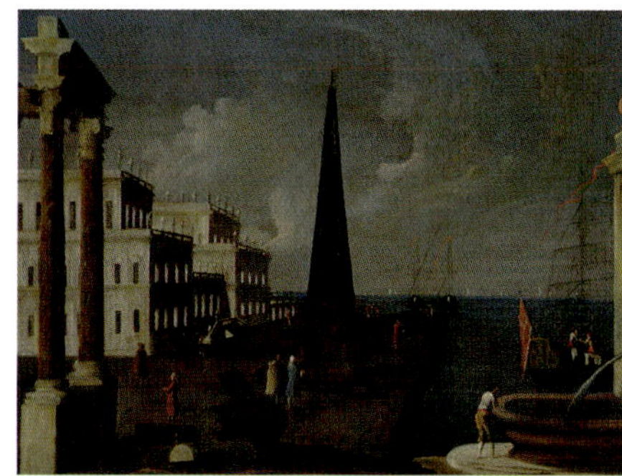

Italian School 18th C
Fantasy Architectural View
oil on canvas 65.7 x 89
94/1963

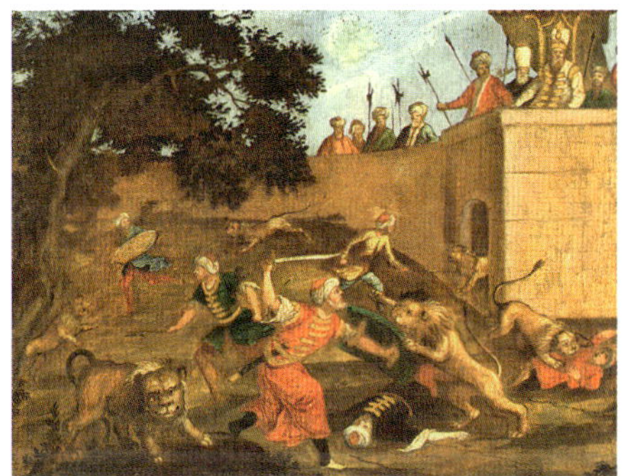

Italian School 18th C
Gladiators and Lions
oil on canvas 58.1 x 77.5
102/1963

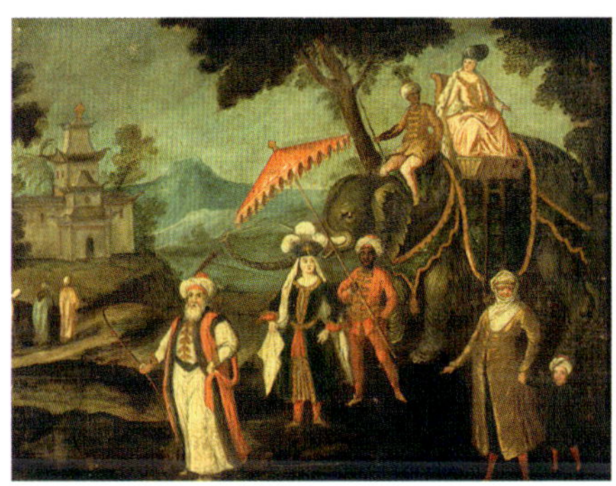

Italian School 18th C
Oriental Scene with Figures
oil on canvas 58 x 77
103/1963

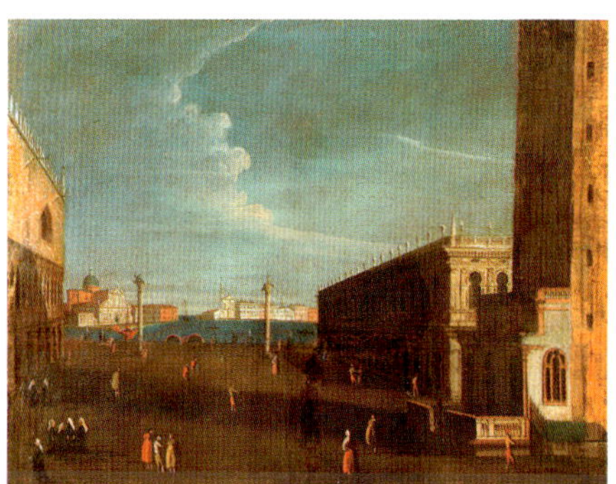

Italian School 18th C
View of Mole with San Giorgio
oil on canvas 66 x 88.7
93/1963

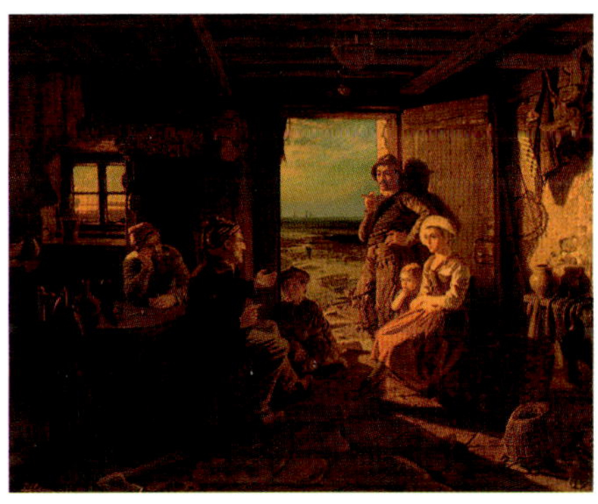

Jackman, Paul active 1864–1878
Fisherman's Cottage
oil on canvas 101.5 x 126.7
308

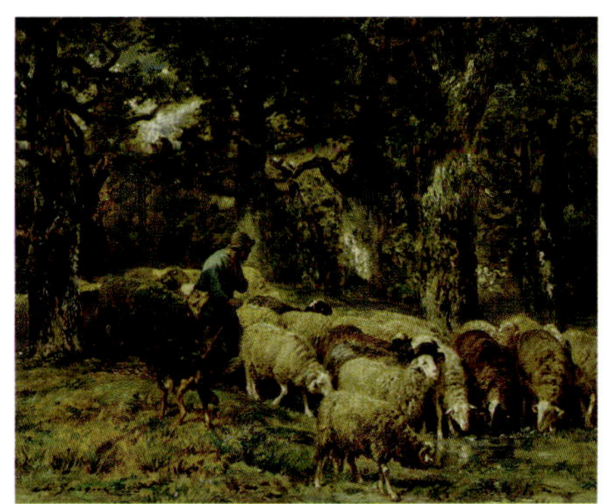

Jacque, Charles Émile 1813–1894
Shepherd and His Flock
oil on canvas 81.3 x 100
309

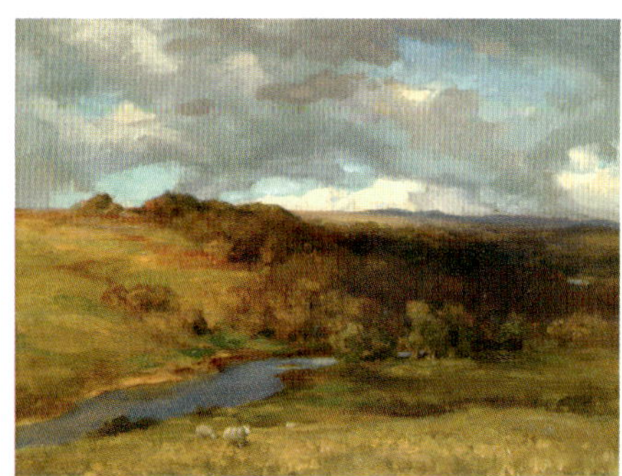

James, Walter John 1869–1932
Valley of the Rede
oil on canvas 30.6 x 41
1244

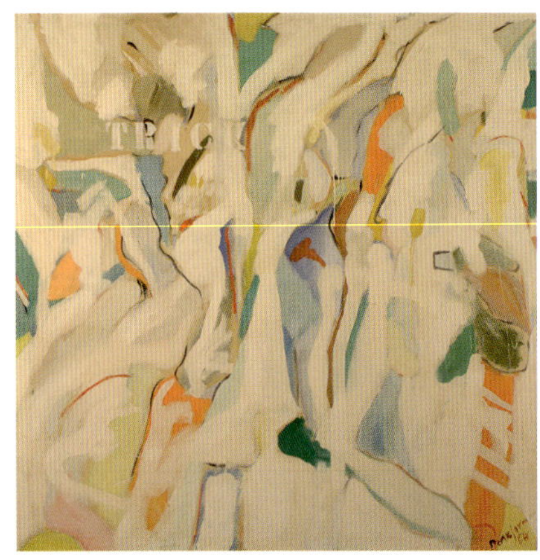

Jarman, Derek 1942–1994
Trick 1964
oil on canvas 115.3 x 115.3
12/2003

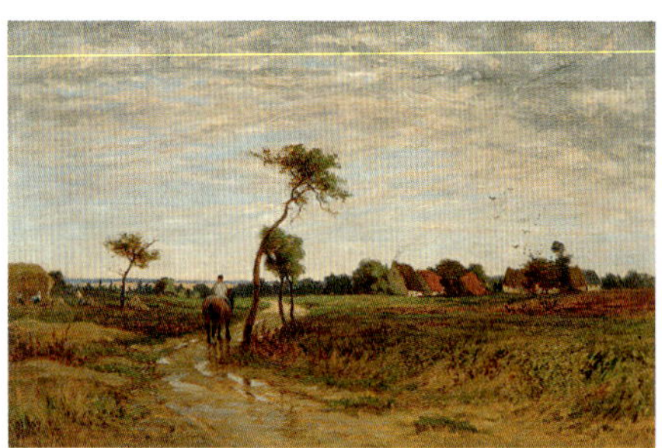

Jay, William Samuel 1843–1933
Thicket Wood
oil on canvas 43.2 x 67.1
1252

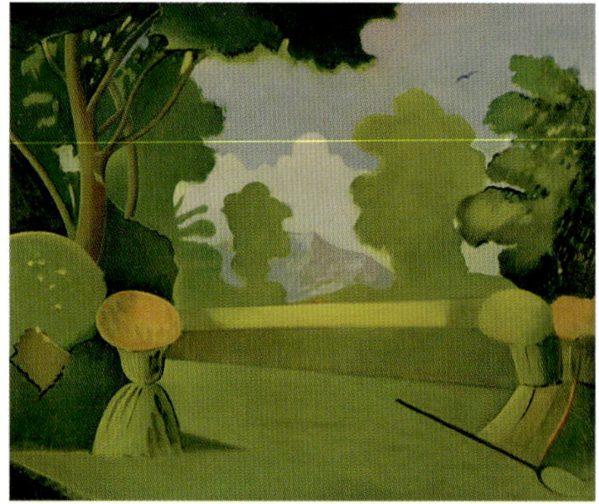

Jennings, Humphrey 1907–1950
Untitled 1941
oil on canvas 38 x 45.8
16/1982

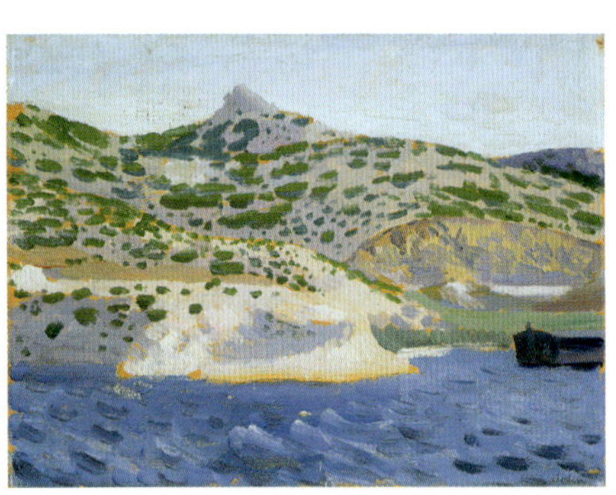

John, Augustus Edwin 1878–1961
Port de Bouc 1910
oil on wood 23.5 x 31.7
1471

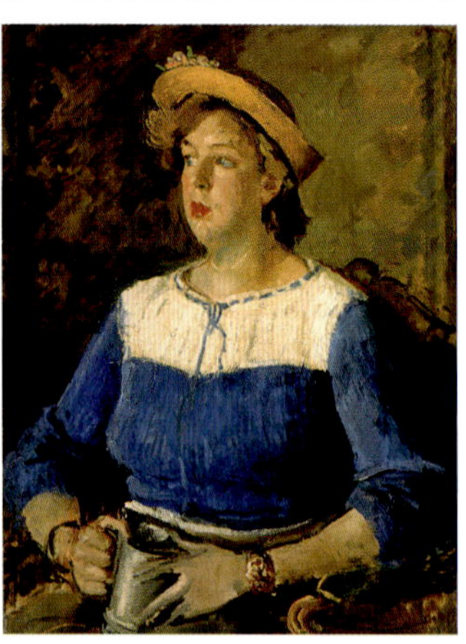

John, Augustus Edwin 1878–1961
Brigit 1937
oil on canvas 91.5 x 71.2
313

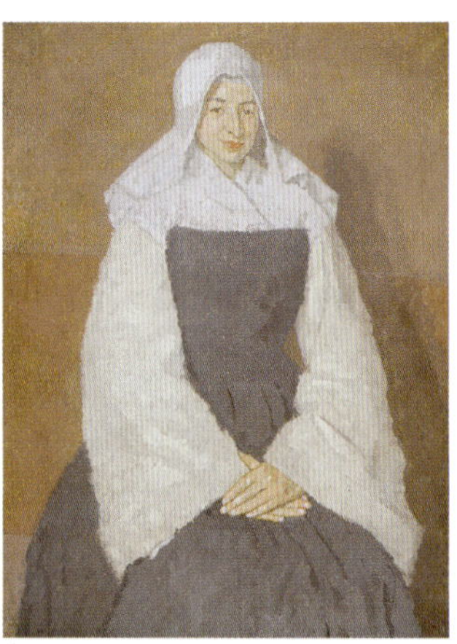

John, Gwen 1876–1939
Mère Poussepin 1920
oil on canvas 68.7 x 51.2
1456

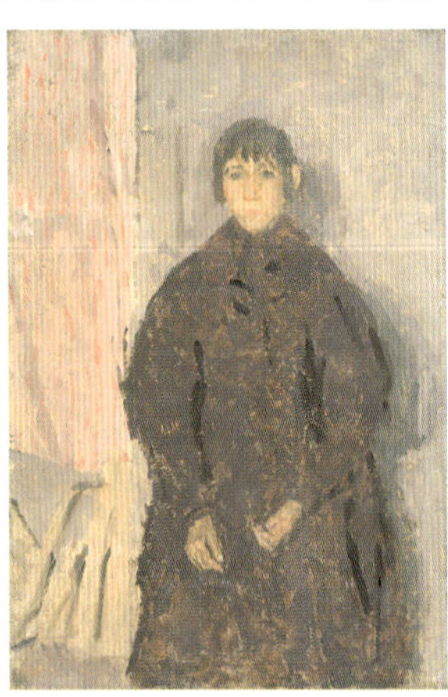

John, Gwen 1876–1939
Girl in Mulberry Dress 1923
oil on canvas 54 x 37.5
11/1962

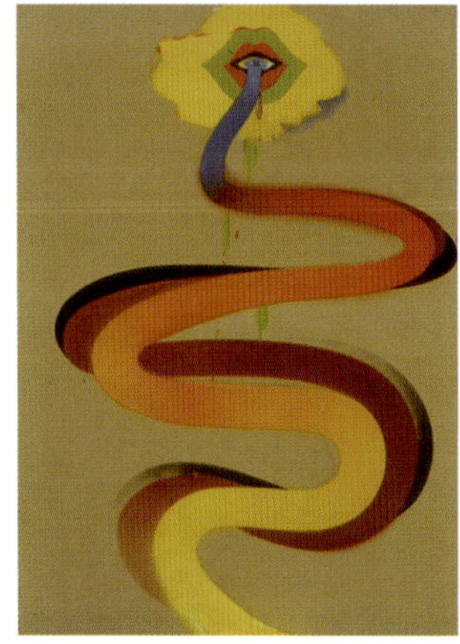

Jones, Allen b.1937
Pathway 1966
oil on canvas 127.5 x 102.2
4/1967

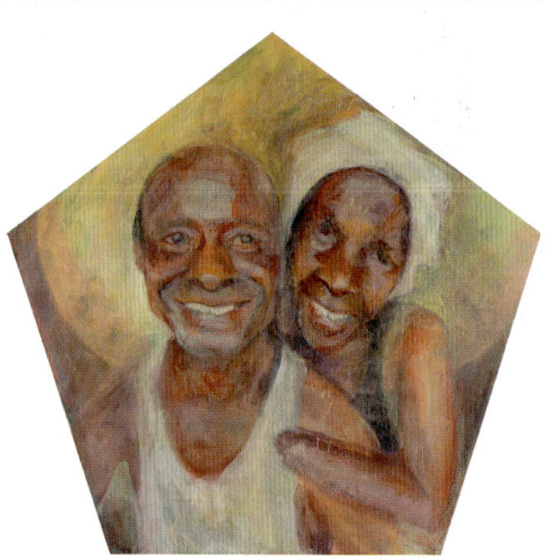

Jones, Lizzie
The Couple
acrylic & wax on canvas 107.3 x 112.8
55/2006

Facing Page: Thornton, Sue, b.1952, *Looking Sideways*, Southampton Solent University, (p. 185)

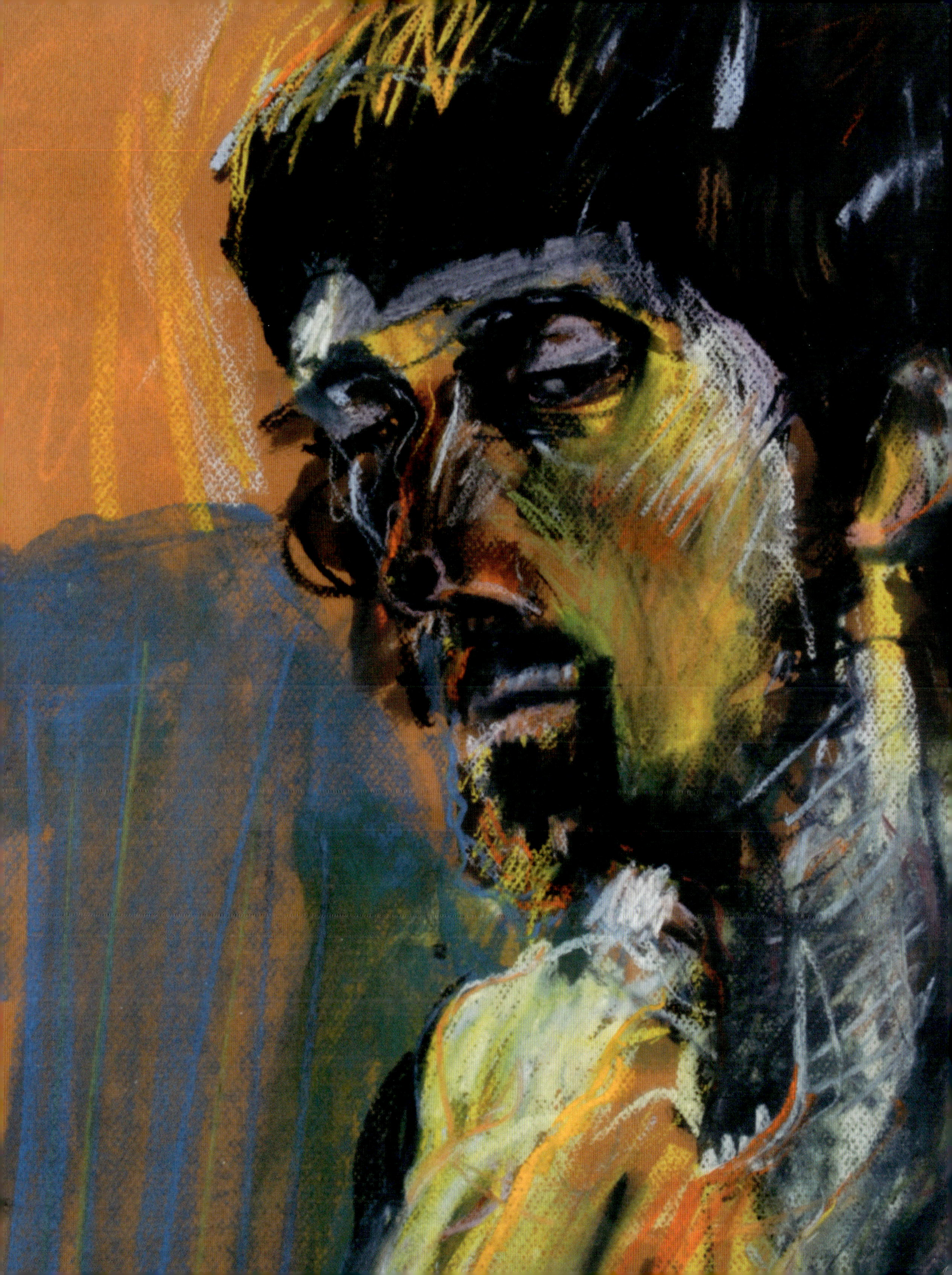

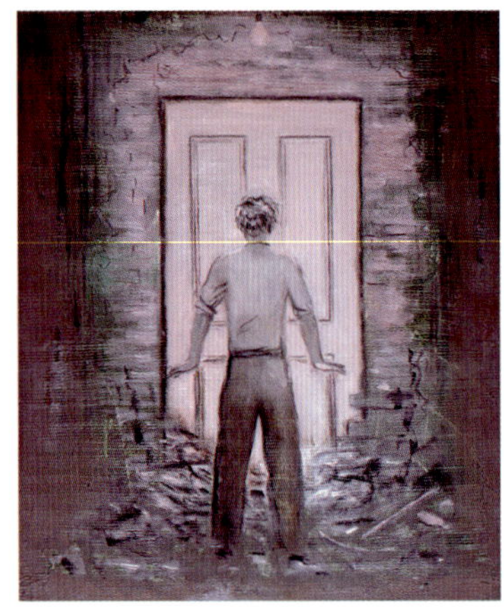

Jones, Philip b.1971
Orpheus at the Door of the Underworld 1996
oil on canvas 76 x 61
3/1997

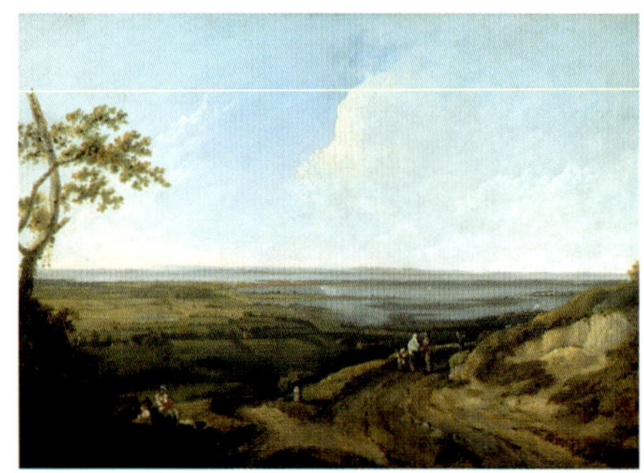

Jones, Thomas 1742–1803
View of Portsmouth from Portsdown Hill
oil on canvas 101.7 x 142.2
1469

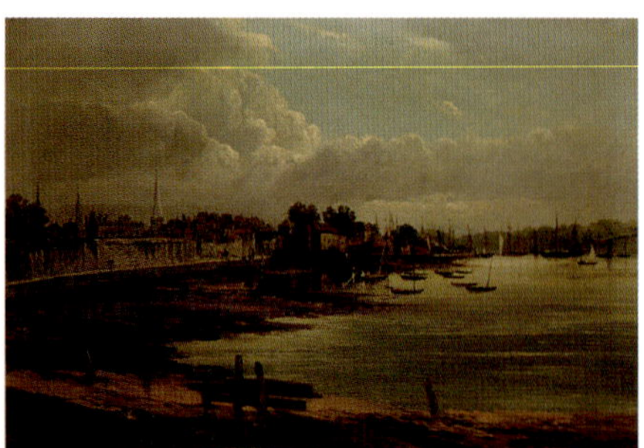

Jones, W. active before 1911
Western Shore
oil on canvas 40.9 x 61
314

Jones, Zebedee b.1970
Dark Green Gridiron 1994
oil on canvas 152.5 x 152
1/1996

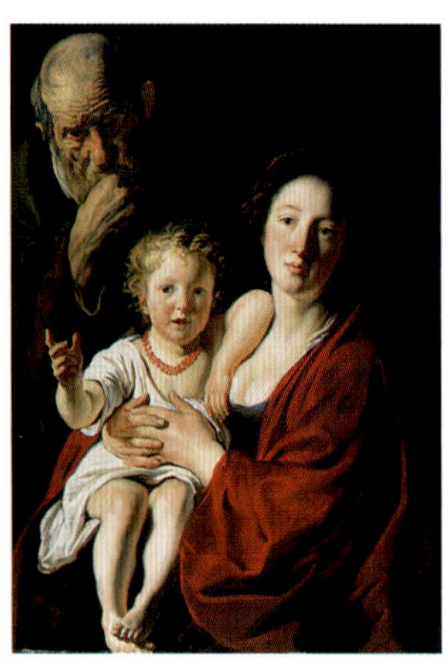

Jordaens, Jacob 1593–1678
The Holy Family
oil on canvas 105.8 x 75.5
315

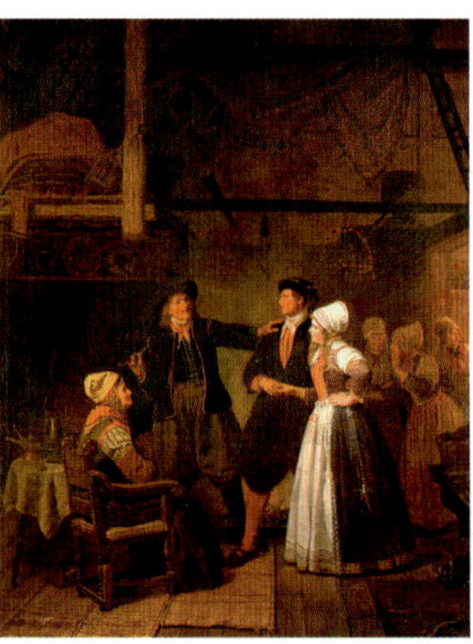

Jordan, Rudolf (attributed to) 1810–1887
The Engagement 1856
oil on canvas 125.5 x 94.5
1117

Joseph, Peter b.1929
Dark Blue/Black Border No.37 1978
oil on canvas 157.4 x 208
22/1980

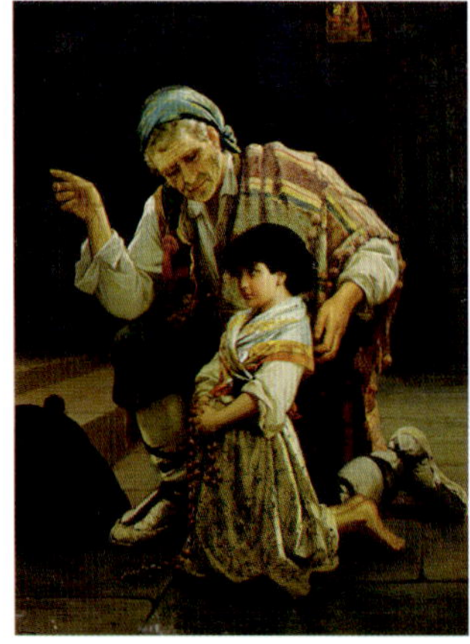

Kemm, Robert 1837–1895
At the Steps of the Altar
oil on canvas 101.7 x 76.1
316

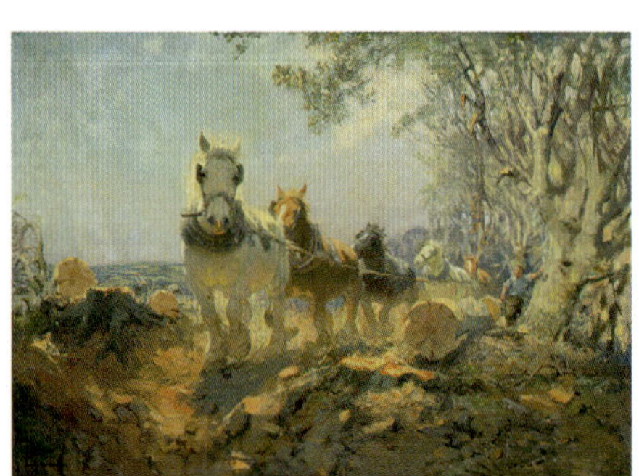

Kemp-Welch, Lucy 1869–1958
Timber Run in the Welsh Hills
oil on canvas 110.8 x 155.5
317

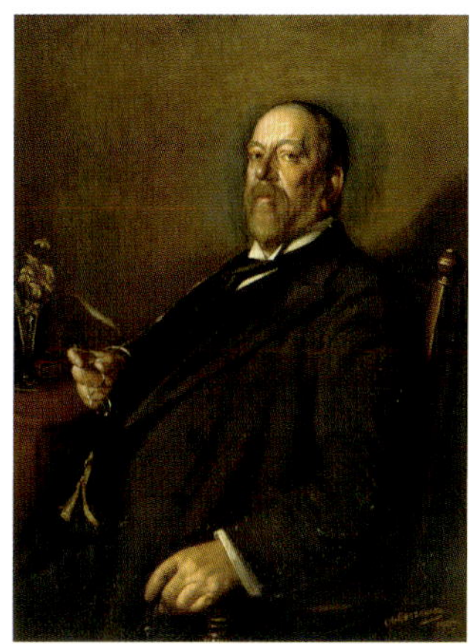

Kennaway, Charles Gray active 1860–1925
James Patrick Muir
oil on canvas 102.3 x 76.8
1069

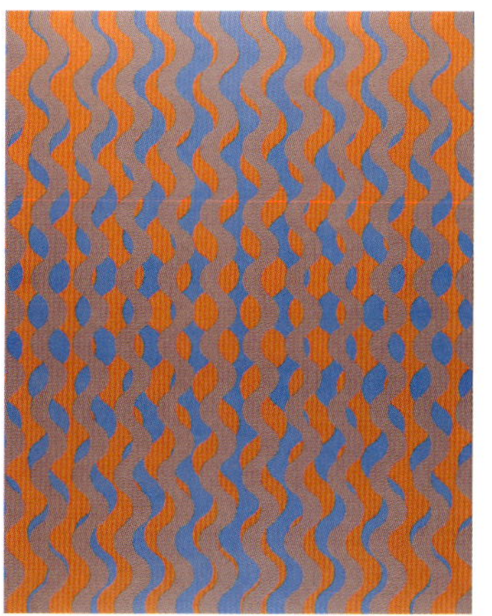

Kidner, Michael b.1917
Brown, Blue and Violet No.2
oil on canvas 126.4 x 101
5/1967

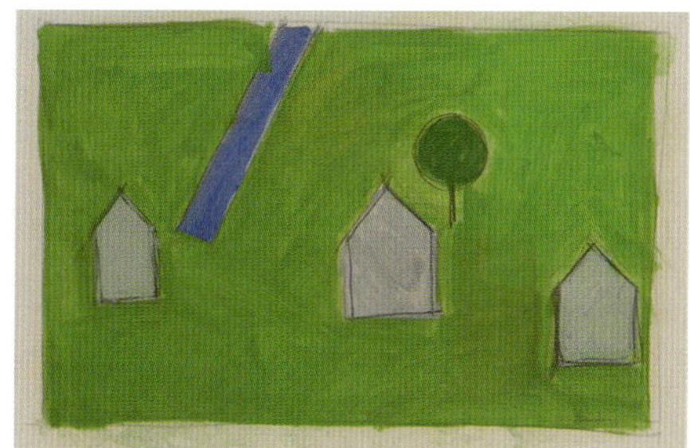

Kinley, Peter 1926–1988
Study for 'Three Houses' 1973
oil & charcoal on paper 26.5 x 40
33/2006

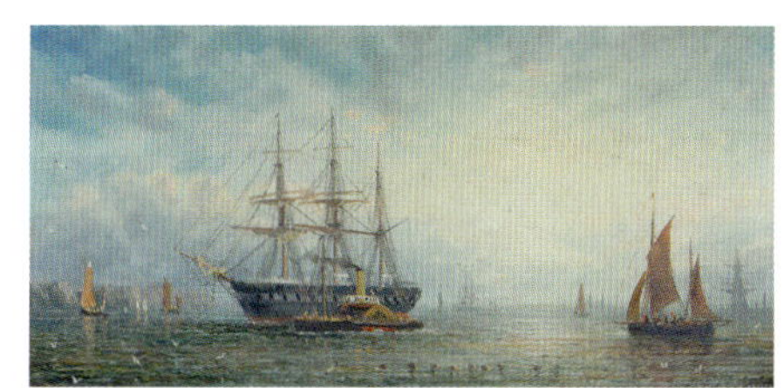

Knell, William Adolphus 1802–1875
'HMS Victory'
oil on board 17 x 34.9
320

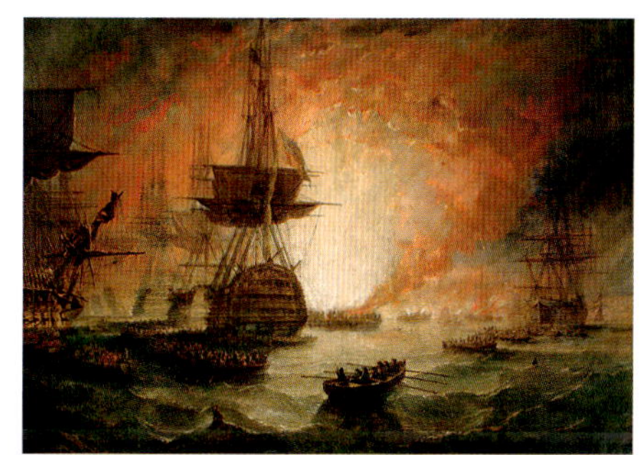

Knell, William Adolphus 1802–1875
Lord Hood at Toulon
oil on canvas 217.2 x 292.5
324

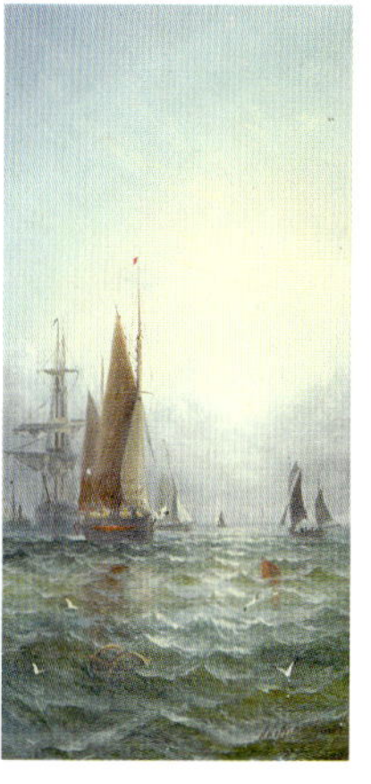

Knell, William Adolphus 1802–1875
Marine Subject
oil on board 35.6 x 17.7
322

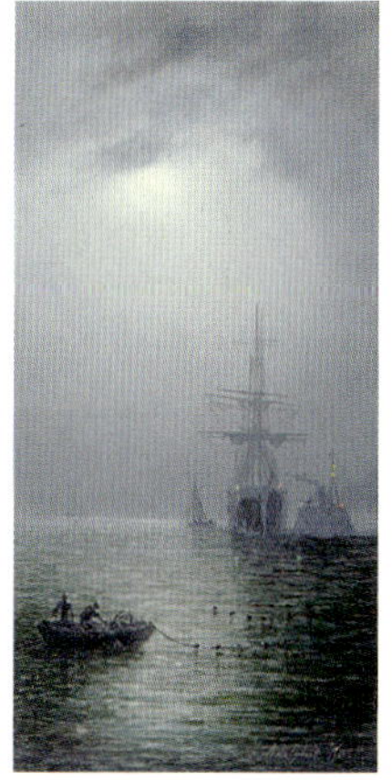

Knell, William Adolphus 1802–1875
Moonlight at Sea
oil on board 35.6 x 17.9
318

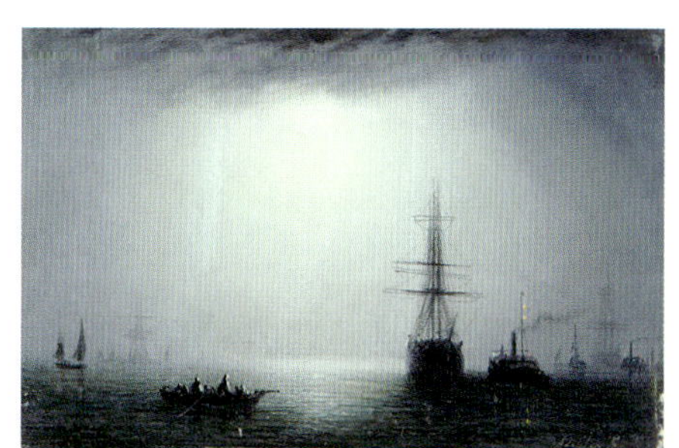

Knell, William Adolphus 1802–1875
Moonlight Scene
oil on canvas 19.7 x 30.1
323

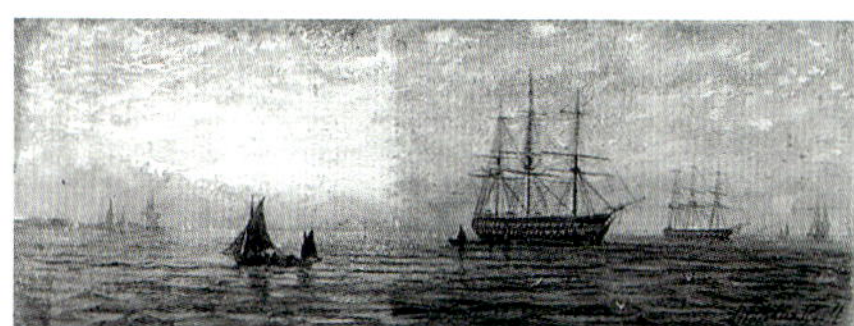

Knell, William Adolphus 1802–1875
Seascape
oil on board 10.5 x 28.5
1/1994

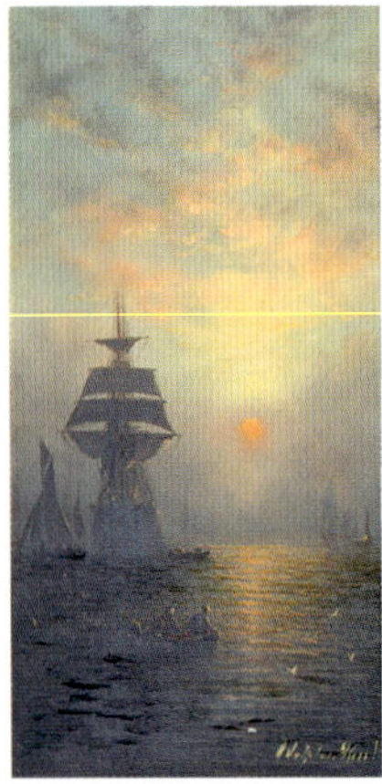

Knell, William Adolphus 1802–1875
Sunset at Sea
oil on board 35.4 x 17.7
319

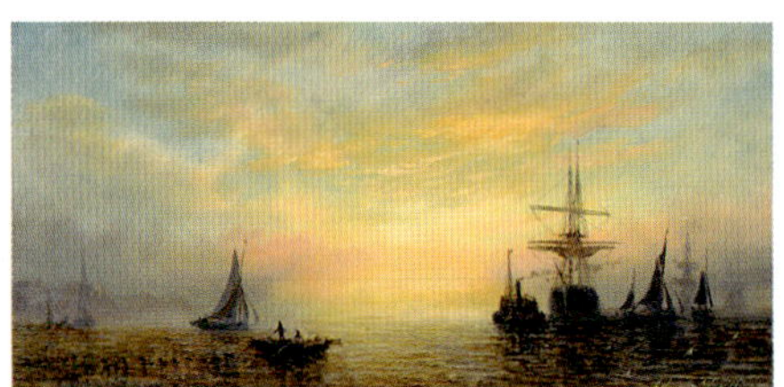

Knell, William Adolphus 1802–1875
Sunset Scene
oil on board 17.8 x 36
321

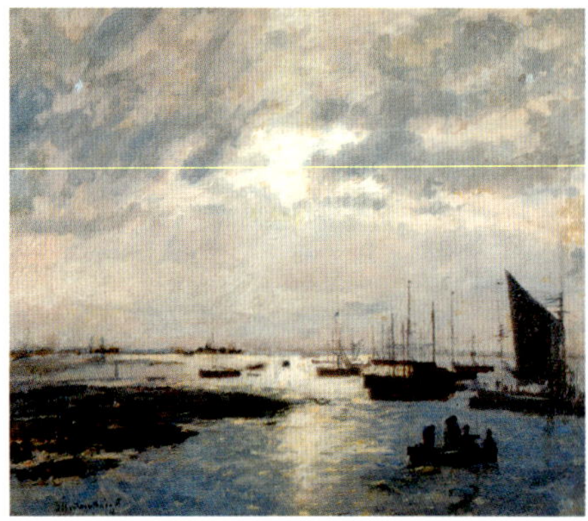

Knight, John William Buxton 1842/1843–1908
An English Port, Evening 1906
oil on canvas 64.5 x 76.4
328

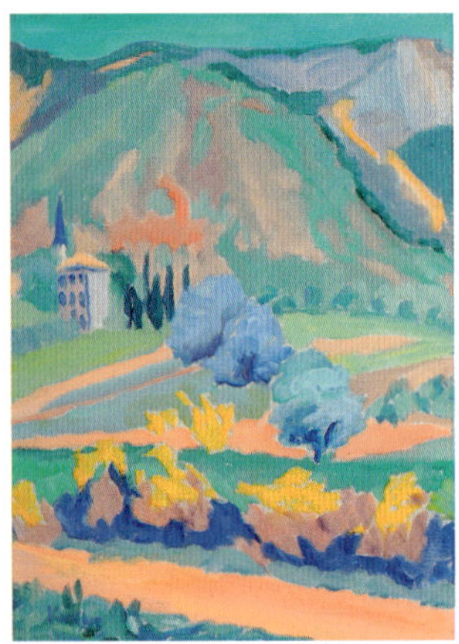

Knollys, Eardley 1902–1991
Distant Spire
oil on canvas 51.2 x 41.3
13/1988

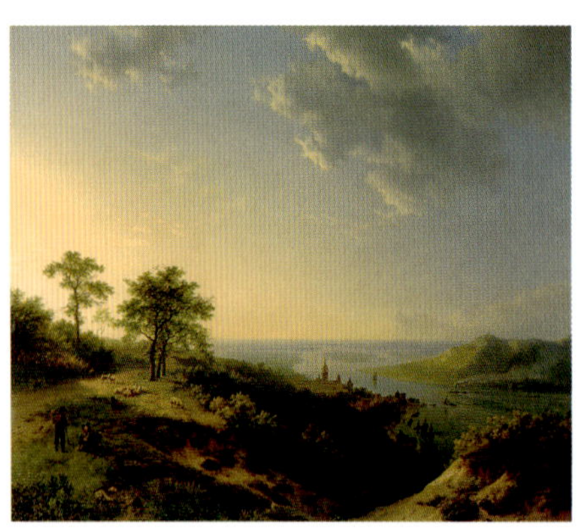

Koekkoek, Barend Cornelis 1803–1862
View over Heidelberg 1837
oil on canvas 102.9 x 120.5
1111

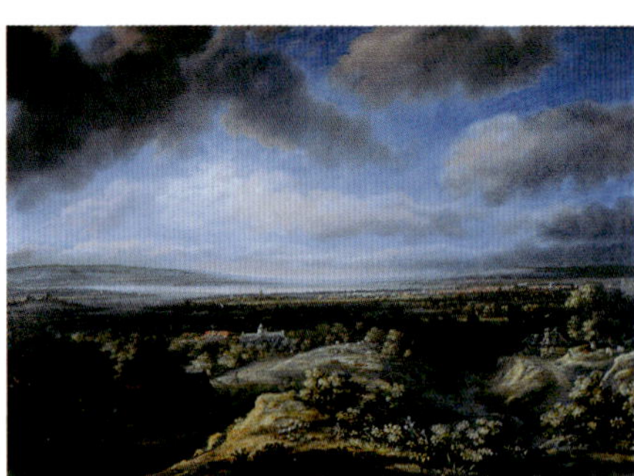

Koninck, Philips de 1619–1688
An Extensive Landscape
oil on canvas 87 x 122.4
2/1963

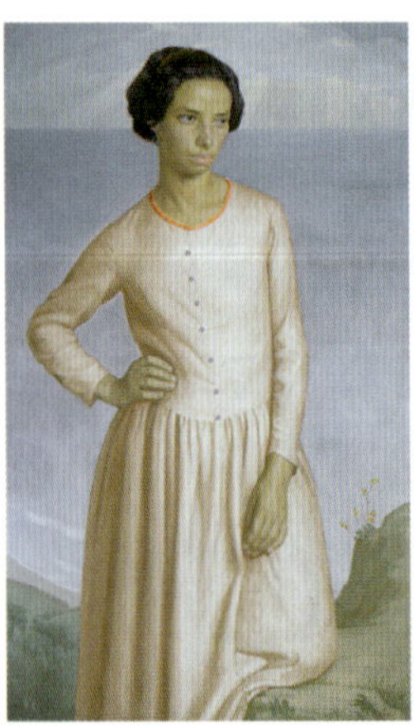

Lamb, Henry 1883–1960
Edie McNeill 1911
oil on canvas 127.5 x 76.2
330

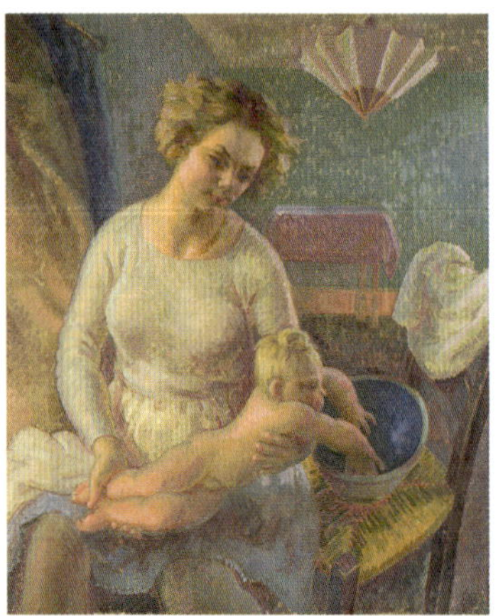

Lamb, Henry 1883–1960
Lady Mary Pakenham 1929
oil on canvas 40.8 x 30.4
22/1973

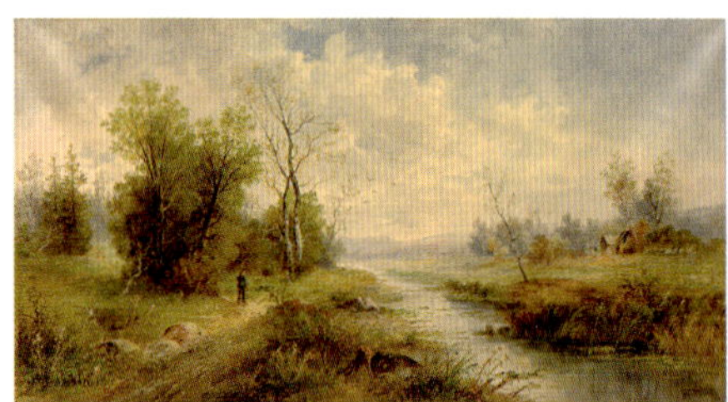

Lambert, B.
Landscape
oil on canvas 36.8 x 68.2
331

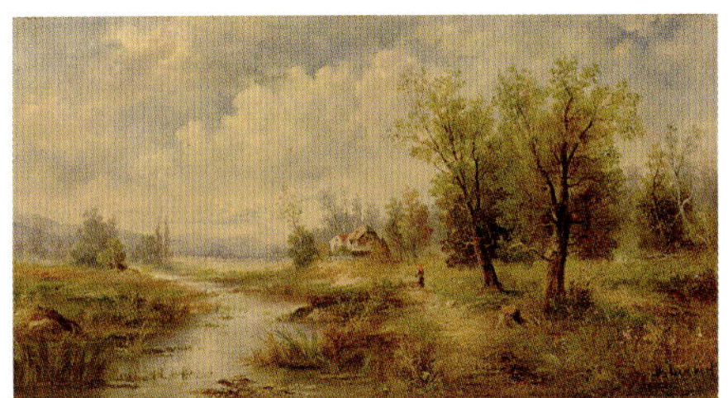

Lambert, B.
Landscape
oil on canvas 40 x 71
332

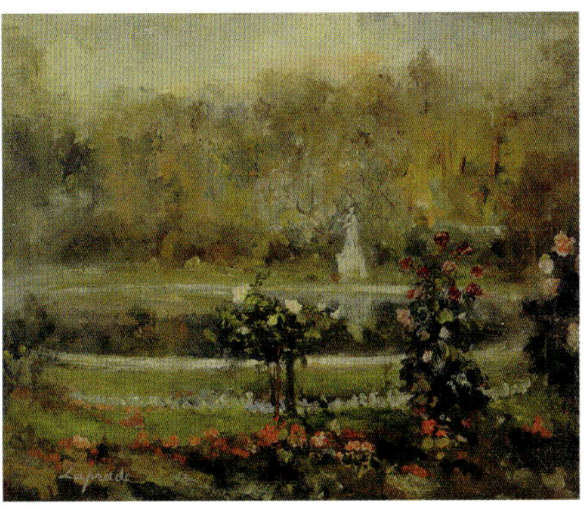

Laprade, Pierre 1875–1931
Scene in a Garden
oil on canvas 50 x 62.3
335

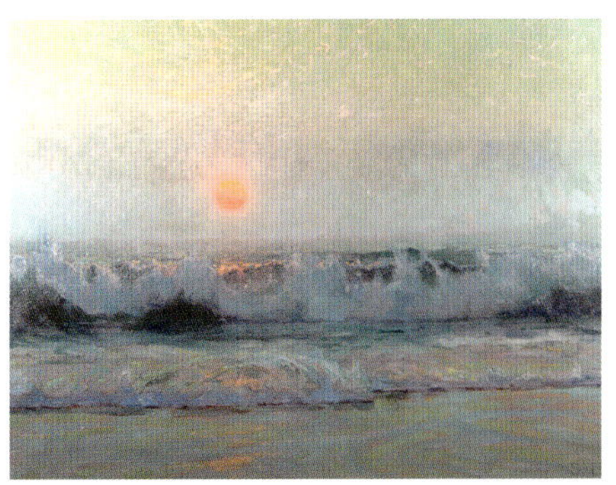

Laurence, Sydney Mortimer 1865–1940
Waves Breaking on Shore, Sunset (detail)
oil on canvas 137.2 x 274.5
348

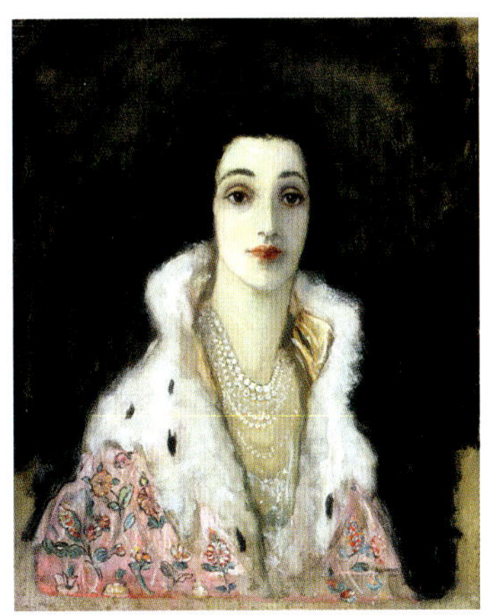

Lavery, John 1856–1941
The Countess of Rocksavage 1922
oil on canvas 75.9 x 63.2
19/1963

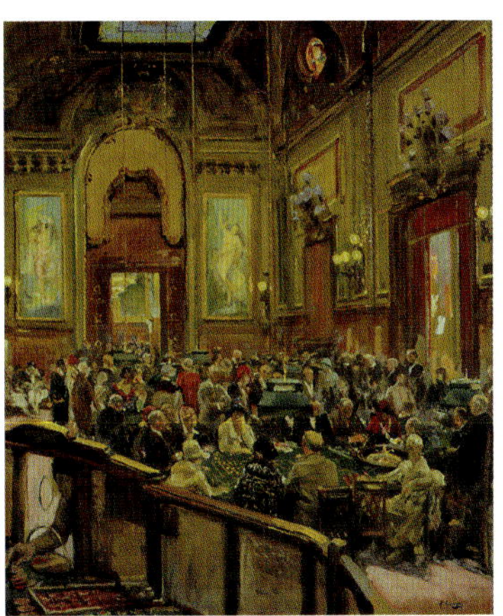

Lavery, John 1856–1941
Monte Carlo, Afternoon 1930
oil on canvas 61.6 x 51.7
337

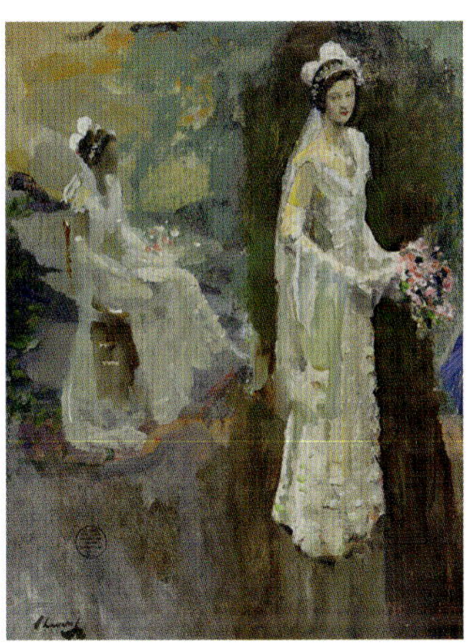

Lavery, John 1856–1941
Miss Betty Shaughnessy
oil on canvas 50.7 x 37.8
339

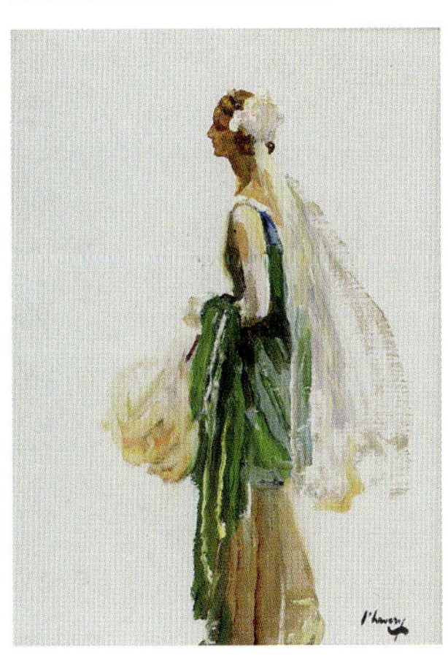

Lavery, John 1856–1941
Miss Diana Chamberlain
oil on canvas 51.6 x 35.4
338

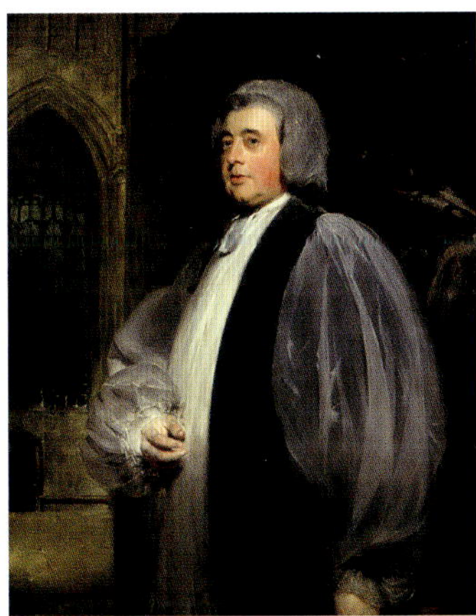

Lawrence, Thomas 1769–1830
Dr John Moore, Archbishop of Canterbury
oil on canvas 127.5 x 102.3
349

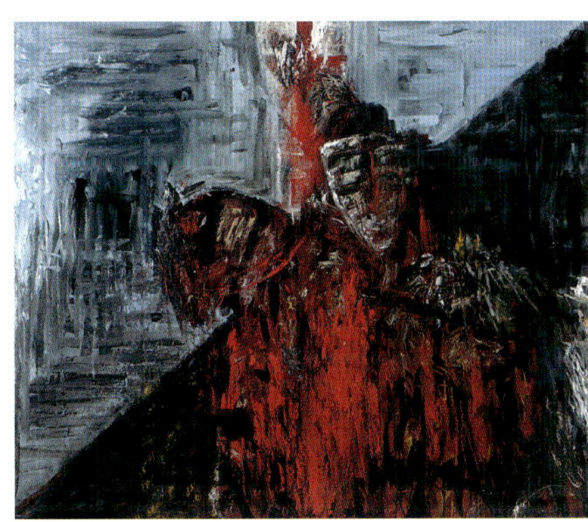

Le Brun, Christopher b.1951
Sir Tristram 1984
oil on canvas 25.4 x 29.2
10/1984

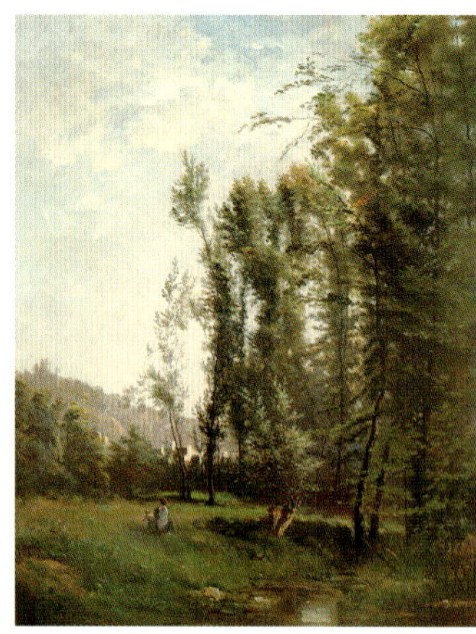

Lecocq, Adrien Louis 1832–1887
Landscape 1867
oil on canvas 100 x 81
350

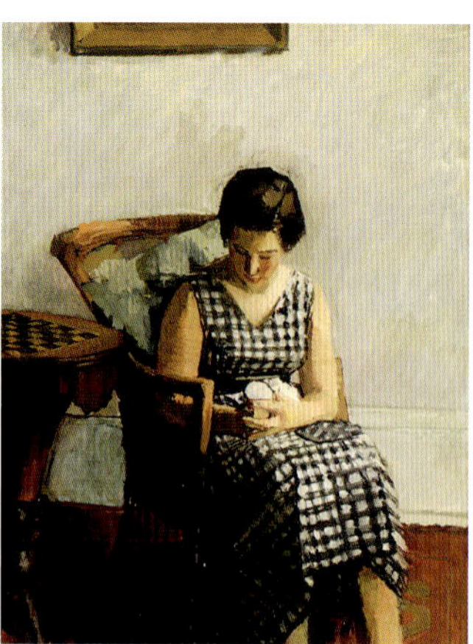

Lee, Dick 1923–2001
Gillie
oil on canvas 91.5 x 71.1
8/1958

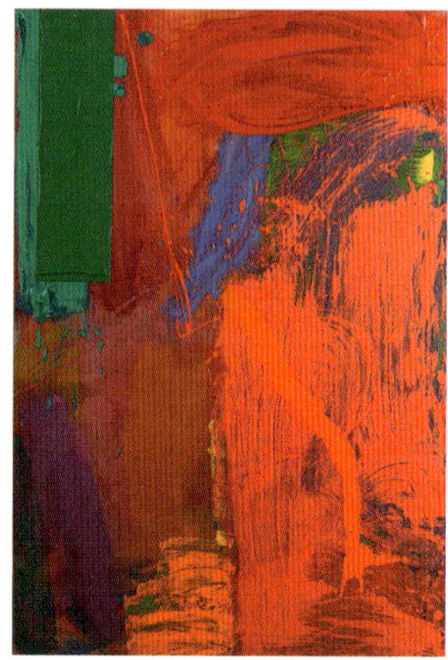

Lee, Moses 1950–1995
Untitled 1990
acrylic on canvas 86.2 x 60.4
7/1998

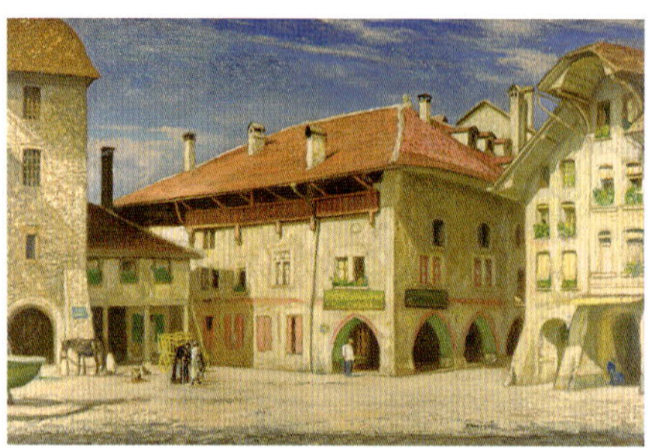

Lee, Sydney 1866–1949
The Wine Store
oil on canvas 82.5 x 128
351

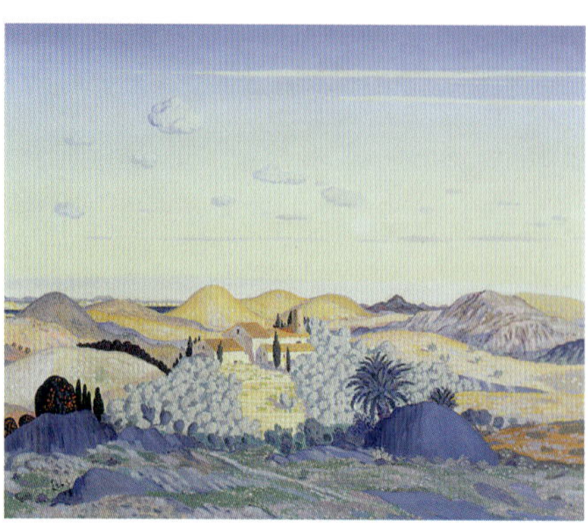

Lees, Derwent 1885–1931
Banyuls
oil on canvas 79 x 94.7
1373

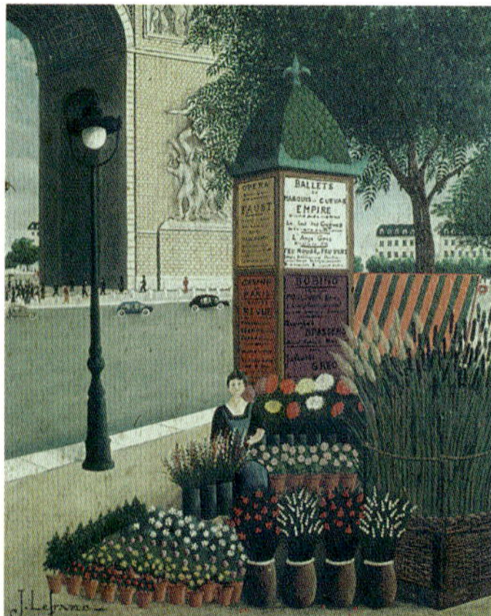

Lefranc, Jules 1887–1972
The Pretty Flowergirl
oil on panel 65 x 54
16/1963

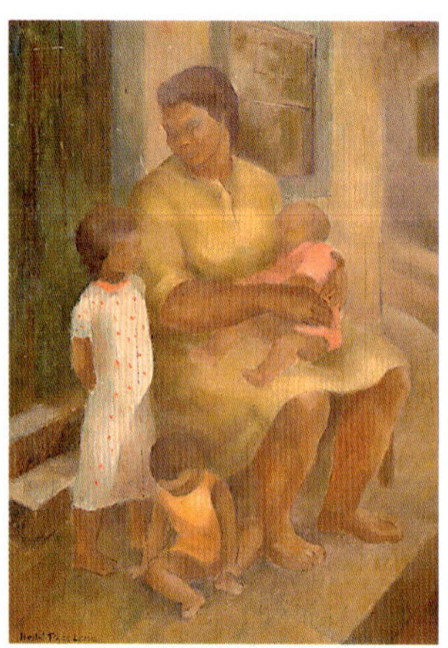

Leme, Bella Paes b.1910
Family Group
oil on canvas 46 x 33.1
1376

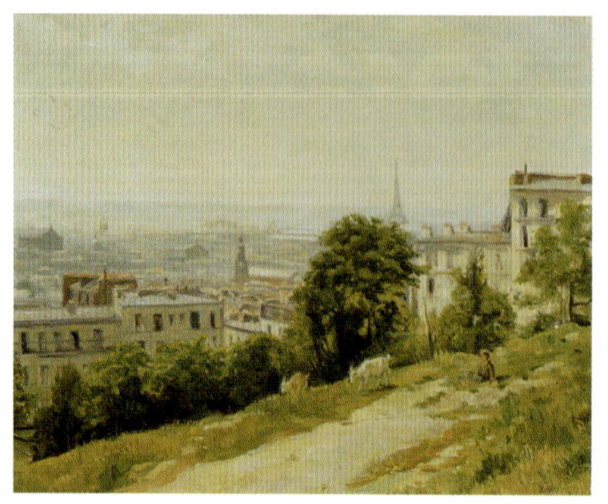

Lépine, Stanislas 1835–1892
View of Paris 1936
oil on canvas 48.8 x 65.2
359

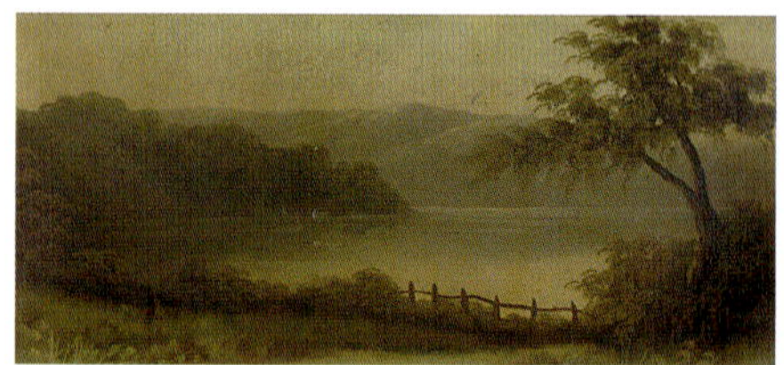

Leslie, Clayton
River Scene
oil on card 24.8 x 54
360

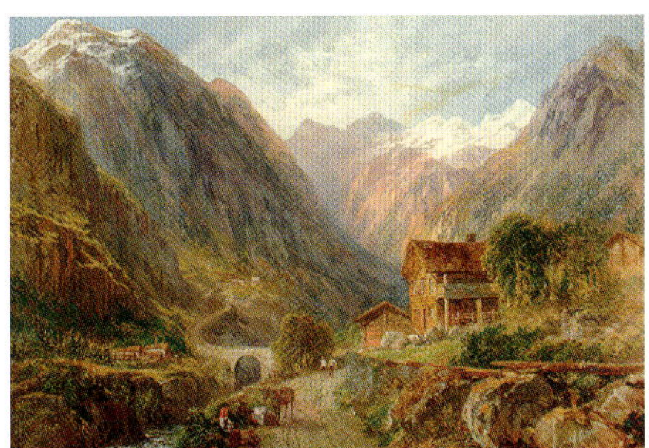

Lines, Henry Harris 1801–1889
Route of St Gotthard, Göschenen
oil on canvas 74.8 x 110.5
364

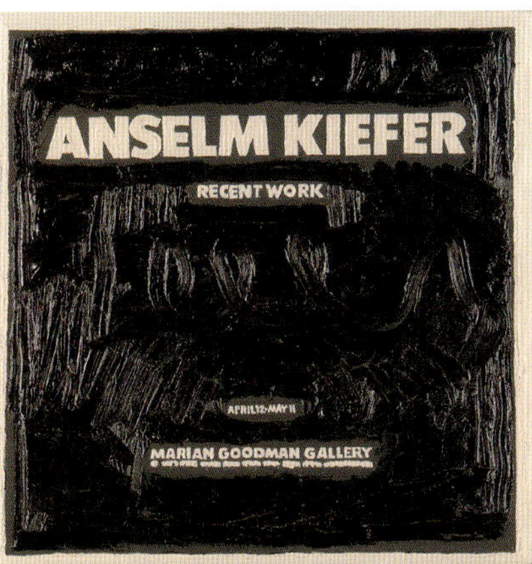

Linke, Simon b.1958
Anselm Kiefer
acrylic on canvas 26.4 x 26.4
75/2002

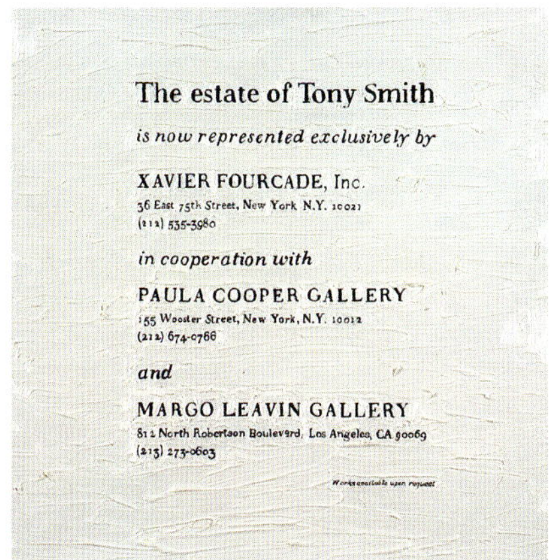

Linke, Simon b.1958
The Estate of Tony Smith
acrylic on canvas 26.3 x 26.7
55/2002

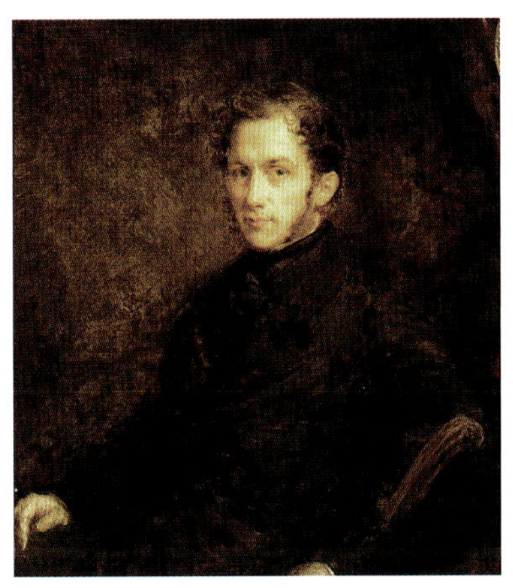

Linnell, John 1792–1882
Doctor Robert Walker
oil on wood 36.8 x 31.1
1487

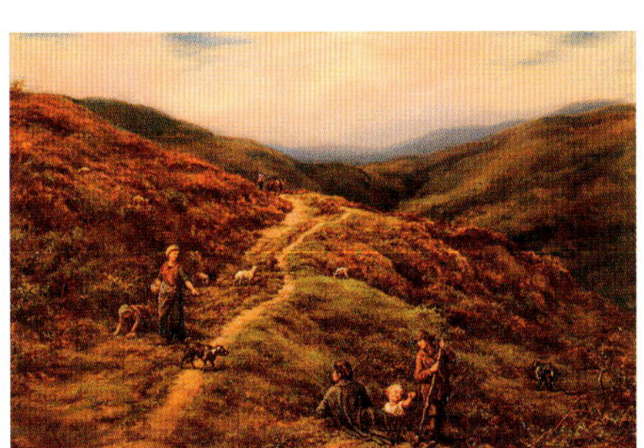

Linnell, William 1826–1906
The Old Mountain Road
oil on canvas 78.7 x 119.5
365

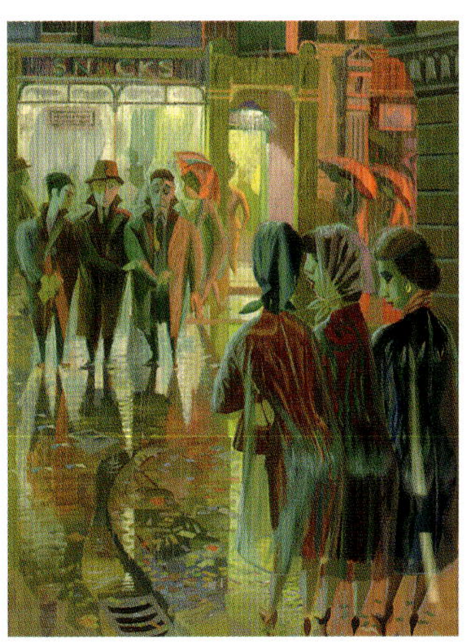

Lister, Edward d'Arcy b.1911
Saturday Night 1958
oil on board 69 x 51
6/1958

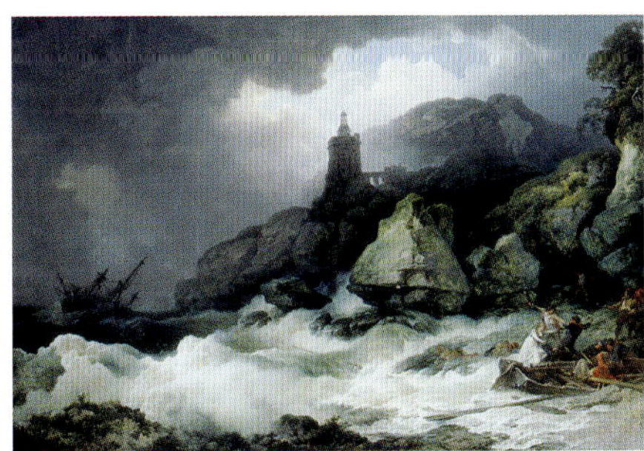

Loutherbourg, Philip James de 1740–1812
The Shipwreck 1793
oil on canvas 109.8 x 160.5
1365

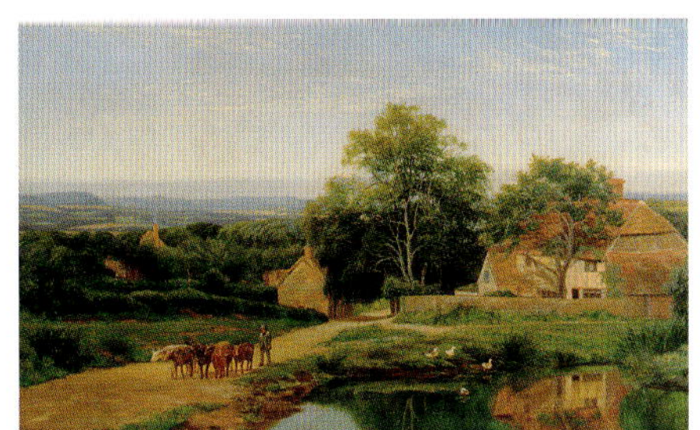

Low, Charles c.1860–c.1920
A Surrey Lane
oil on canvas 40.5 x 66.2
366

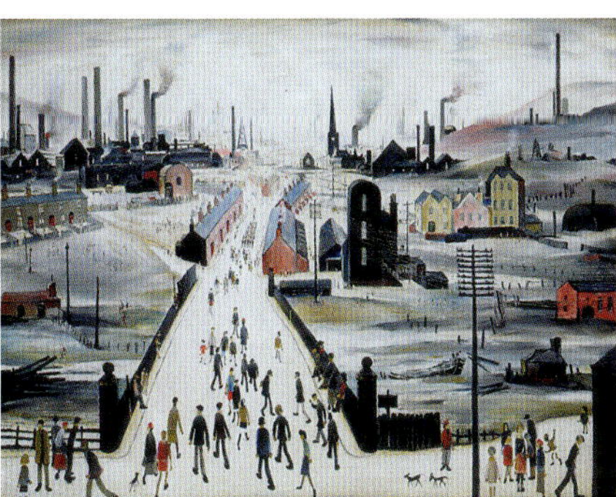

Lowry, Laurence Stephen 1887–1976
The Canal Bridge 1949
oil on canvas 71 x 91.2
1397

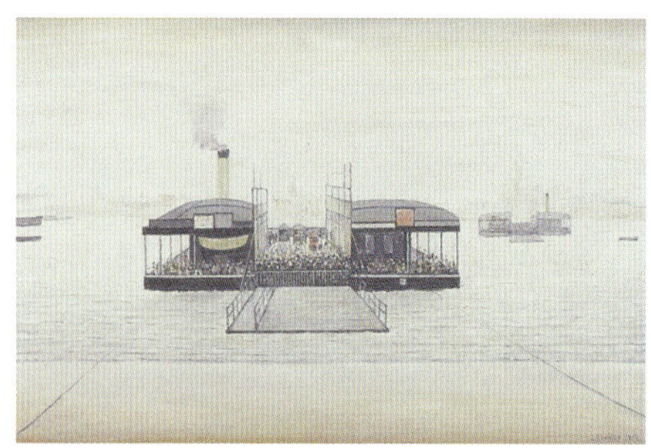

Lowry, Laurence Stephen 1887–1976
The Floating Bridge, Southampton
oil on canvas 50.8 x 76.3
1483

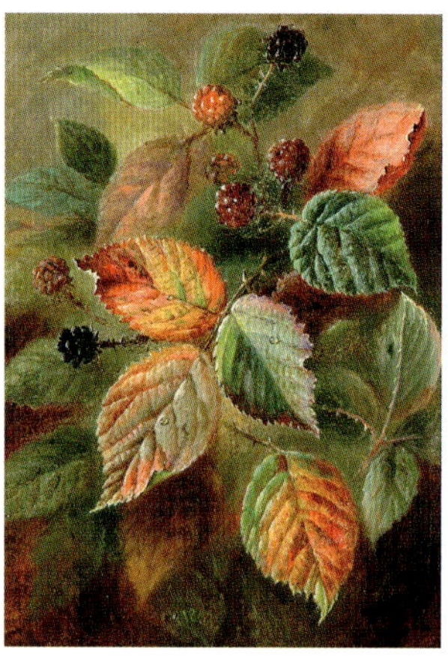

Lucas, Albert Durer 1828–1919
Blackberries
oil on canvas 20.5 x 15.5
381

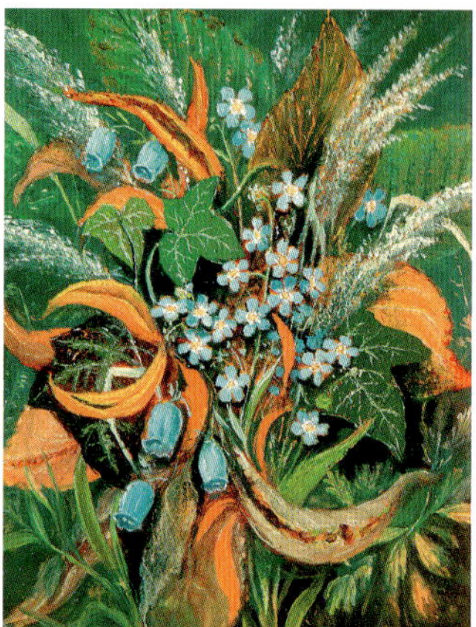

Lucas, Albert Durer 1828–1919
Forget-Me-Nots
oil on canvas 14.5 x 11.2
368

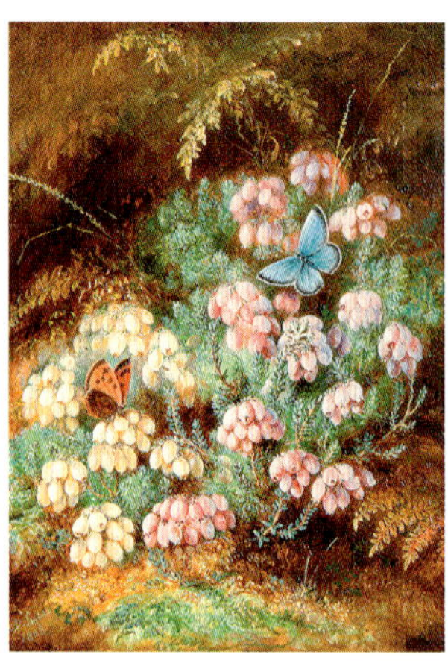

Lucas, Albert Durer 1828–1919
Heather
oil on board 20.3 x 15.2
370

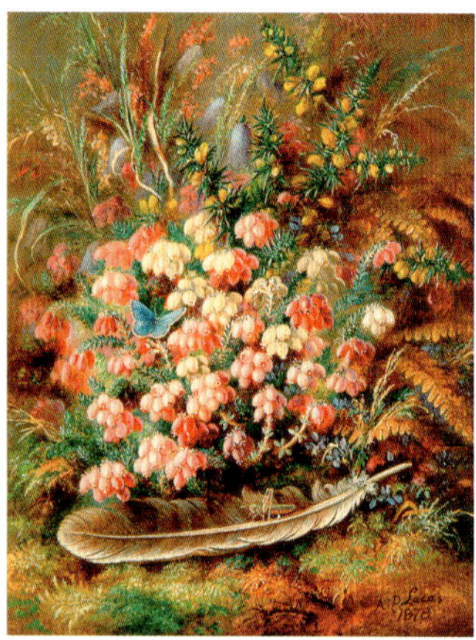

Lucas, Albert Durer 1828–1919
Heather
oil on canvas 15.1 x 12.8
372

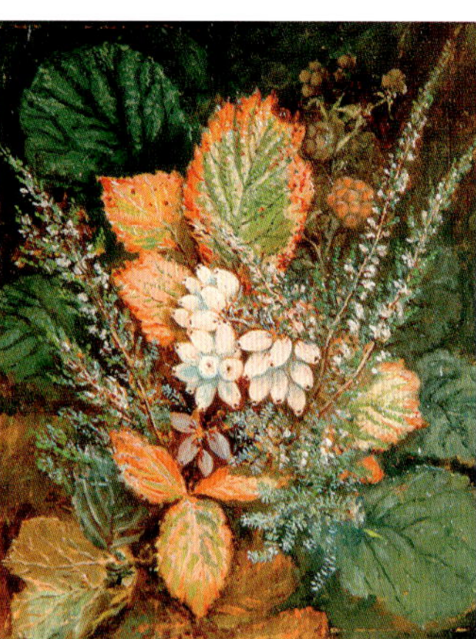

Lucas, Albert Durer 1828–1919
Heather and Gorse
oil on canvas 25.5 x 20.4
371

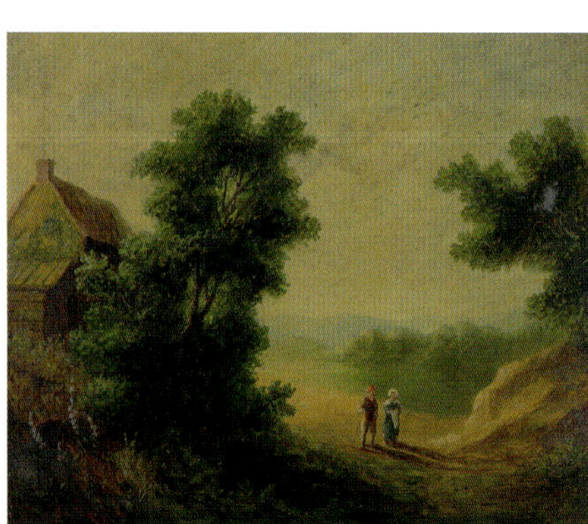

Lucas, Albert Durer 1828–1919
Landscape
oil on canvas 24.7 x 30.3
380

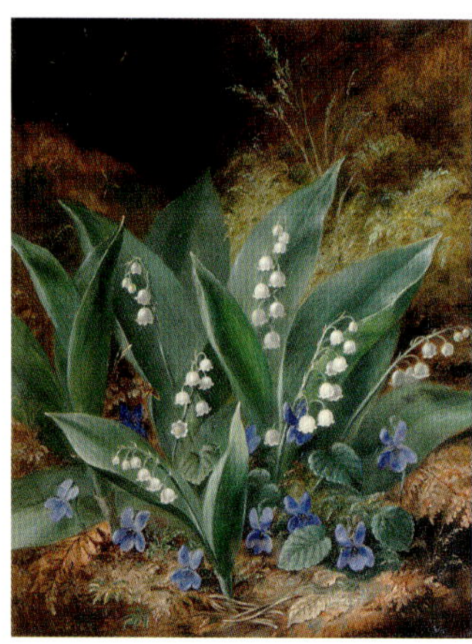

Lucas, Albert Durer 1828–1919
Lilies of the Valley
oil on canvas 25.3 x 20.4
375

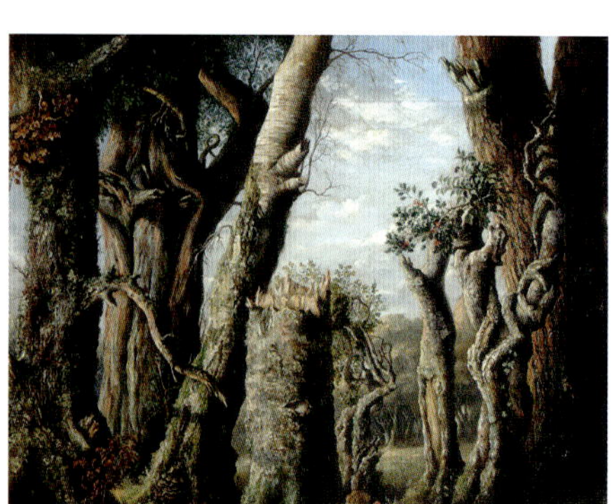

Lucas, Albert Durer 1828–1919
Oak, Holly and Other Trees
oil on canvas 35.5 x 45.7
376

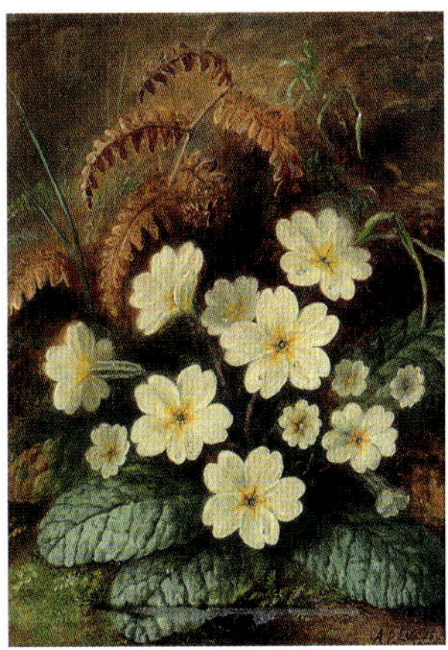

Lucas, Albert Durer 1828–1919
Primroses
oil on card 20.4 x 15.5
373

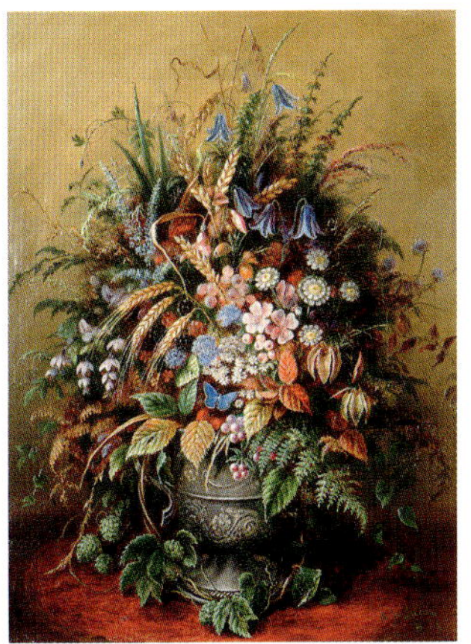

Lucas, Albert Durer 1828–1919
Vase of Flowers
oil on canvas 45 x 30.8
374

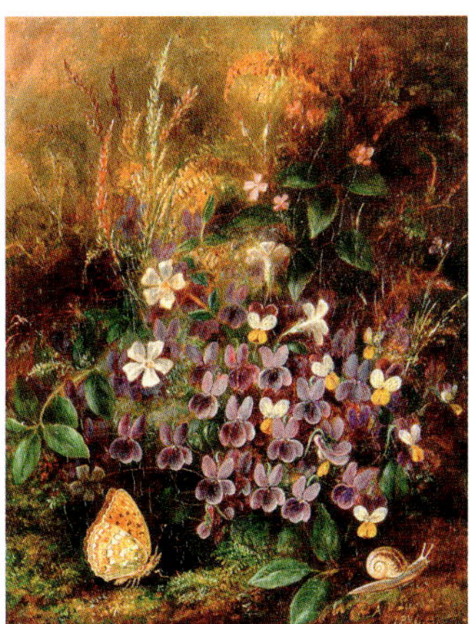

Lucas, Albert Durer 1828–1919
Violets
oil on canvas 25.5 x 20.5
369

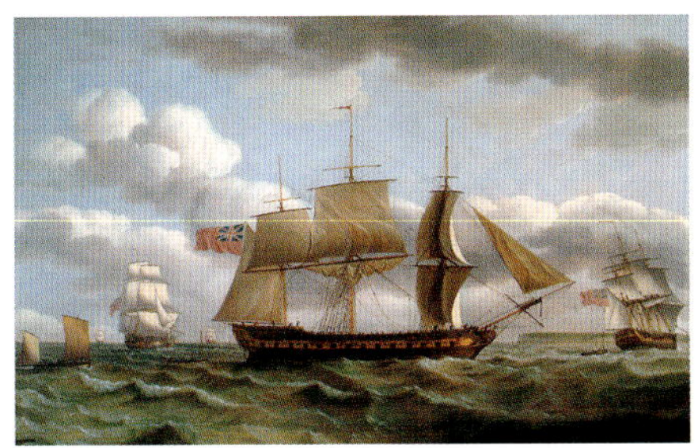

Luny, Thomas 1759–1837
East Indian 'Cumberland' off Dover, 1803
oil on canvas 108 x 168.2
1355

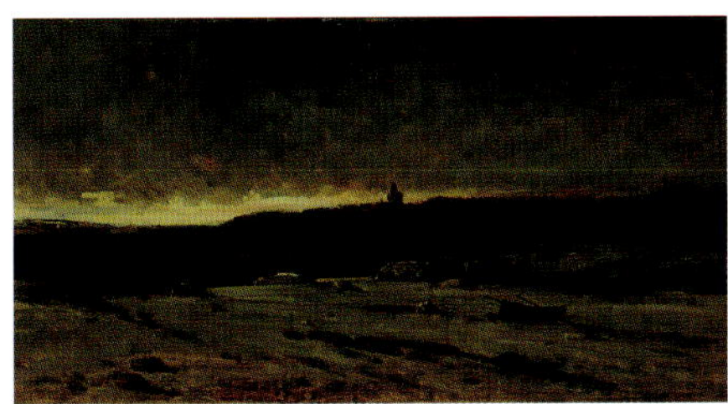

Lyoncourt, Hubert de
Château de Henat
oil on wood 30 x 51.1
384

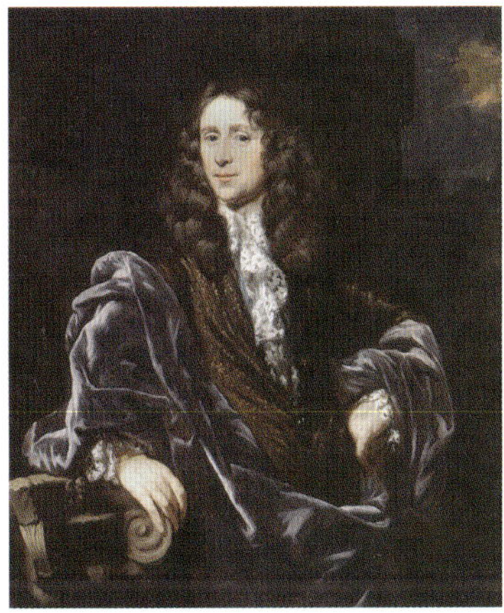

Maes, Nicolaes 1634–1693
Portrait of a Man
oil on canvas 68.5 x 58.5
385

Magill, Elizabeth b.1959
Forest Edge I 1998
oil on canvas 152.5 x 183
9/2000

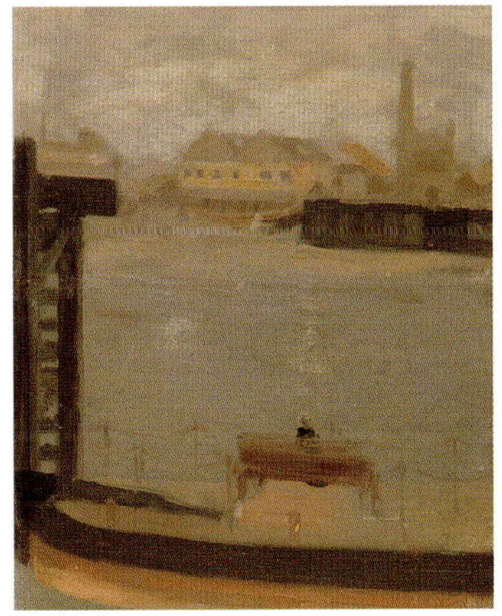

Maitland, Paul Fordyce 1863–1909
View on the Thames
oil on panel 40.4 x 34.5
28/2002

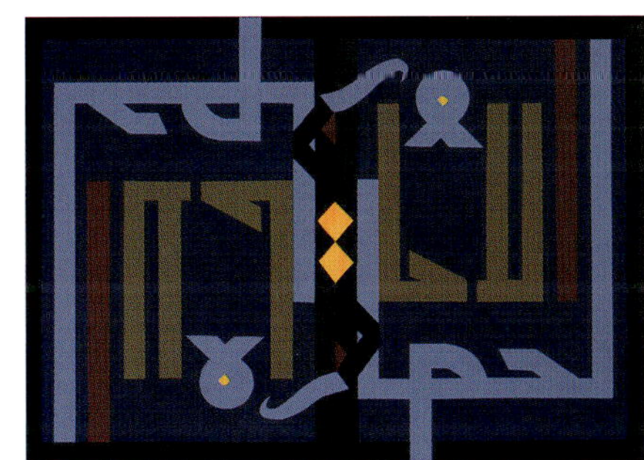

Makhoul, Bashir b.1963
Al Hadara 1993
acrylic on canvas 56.3 x 81.4
3/2005

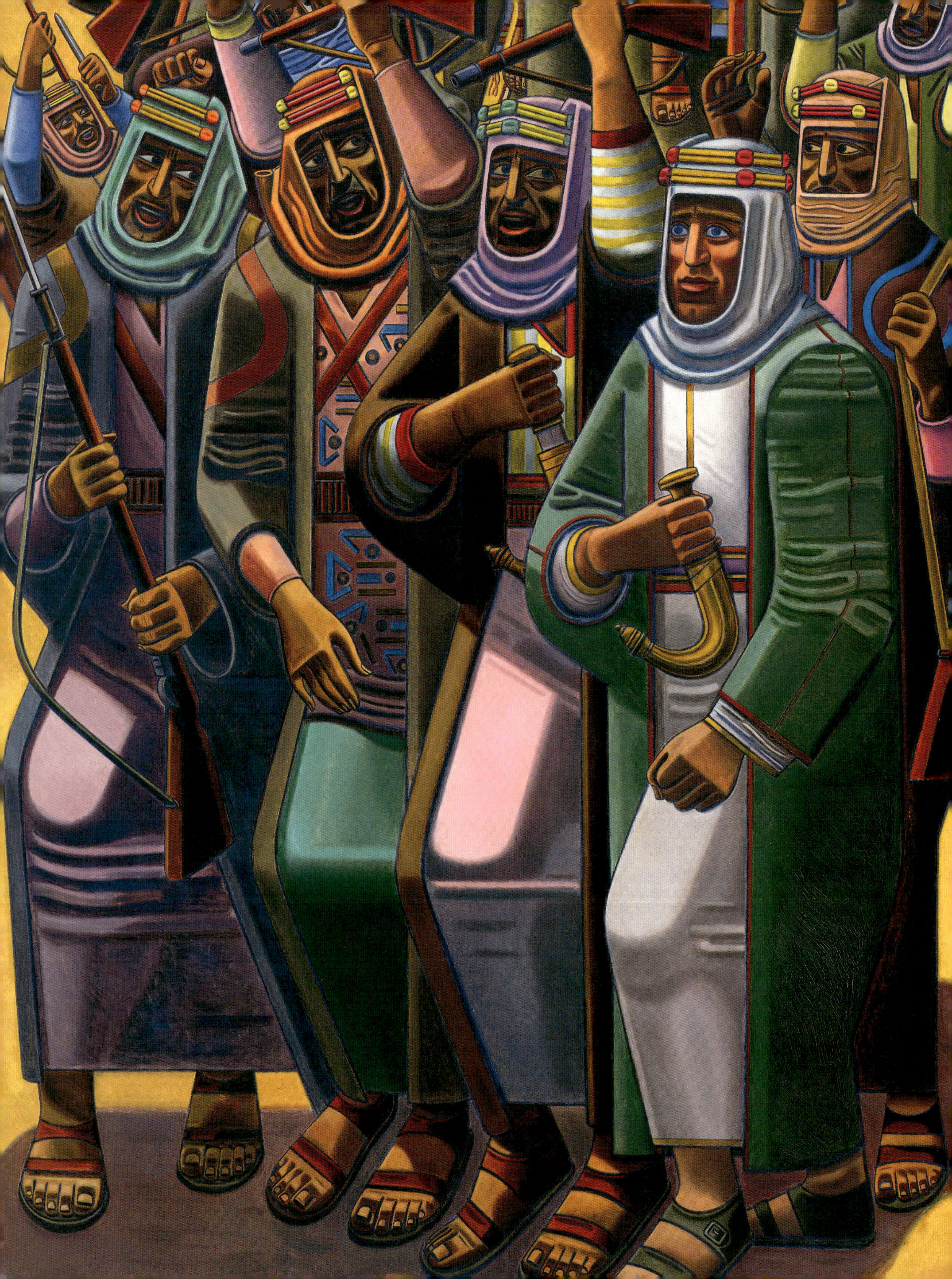

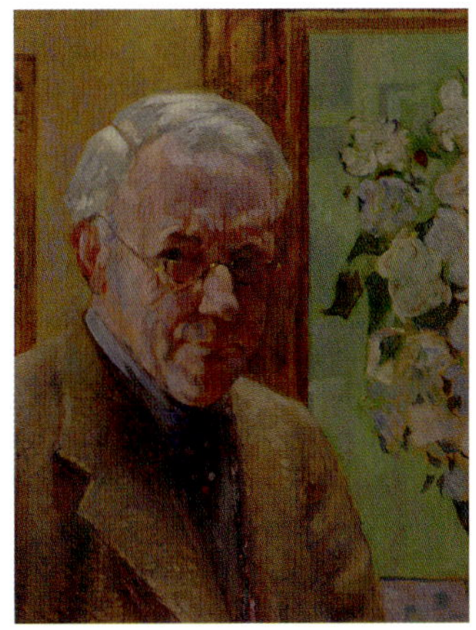

Manson, James Bolivar 1879–1945
Self Portrait 1937
oil on canvas 51.1 x 40
386

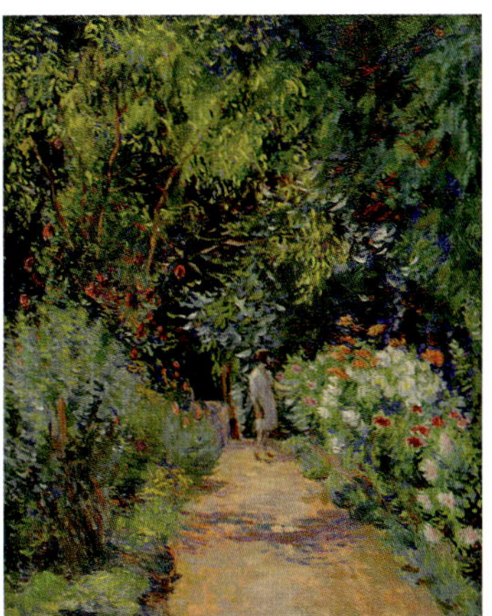

Manson, James Bolivar 1879–1945
The Garden
oil on canvas 47 x 36
387

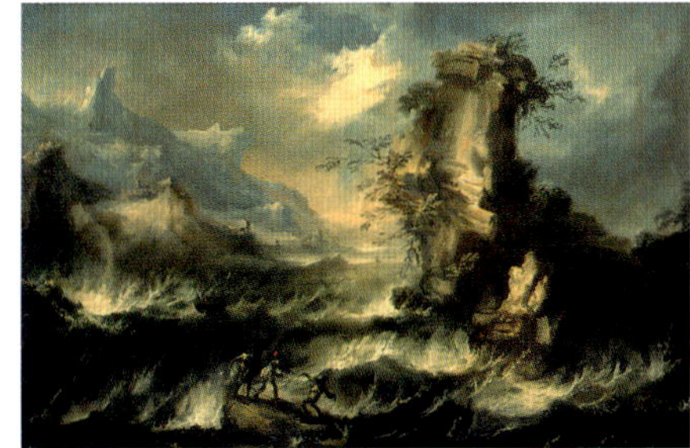

Marini, Antonio 1668–1725
Italian Seascape
oil on canvas 86.5 x 132.6
12/1967

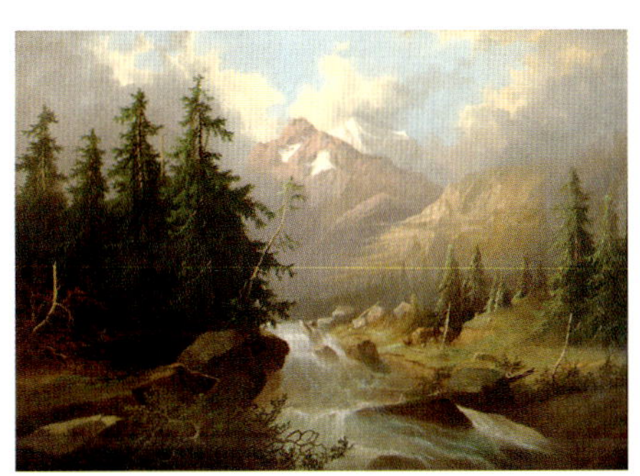

Markó, András 1824–1895
Swiss Scene
oil on canvas 73.2 x 99.7
421

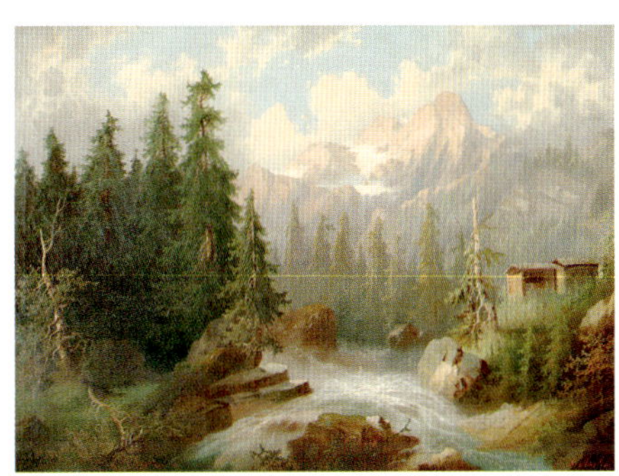

Markó, András 1824–1895
Swiss Scene
oil on canvas 73 x 100.1
422

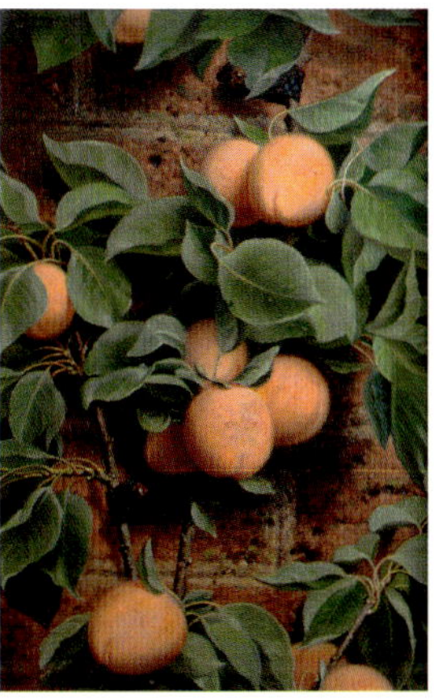

Marshall, John Fitz 1859–1932
Peaches
oil on canvas 35.9 x 25.6
378

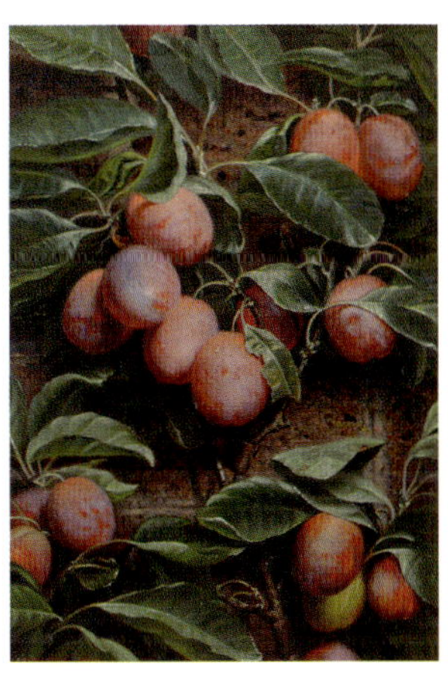

Marshall, John Fitz 1859–1932
Plums
oil on canvas 35.5 x 25.5
379

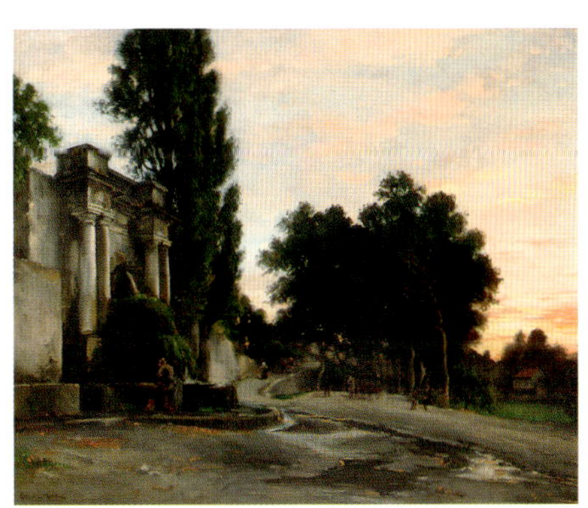

Martin, Étienne Philippe 1858–1945
The Fountain
oil on canvas 84 x 103.3
388

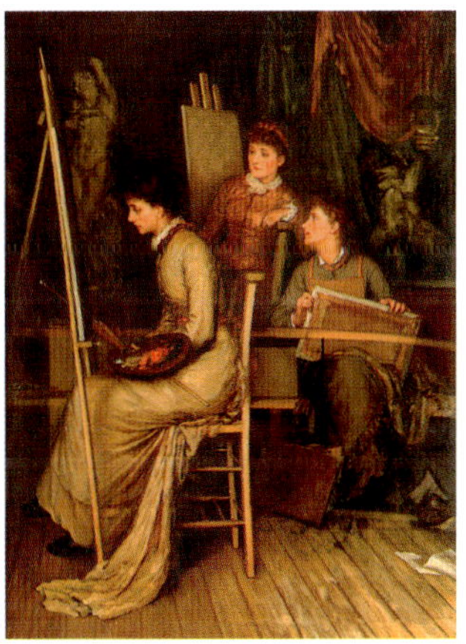

Martin, Florence active 1876–1893
The New Student
oil on canvas 89 x 67.2
389

Facing page: Roberts, William Patrick, 1895–1980, *Revolt in the Desert* (detail), 1952, Southampton City Art Gallery, (p. 112)

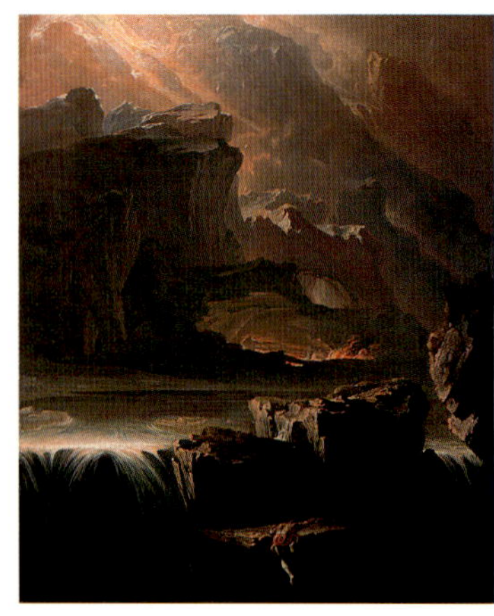

Martin, John 1789–1854
Sadak in Search of the Waters of Oblivion 1812
oil on canvas 76.2 x 63.5
1367

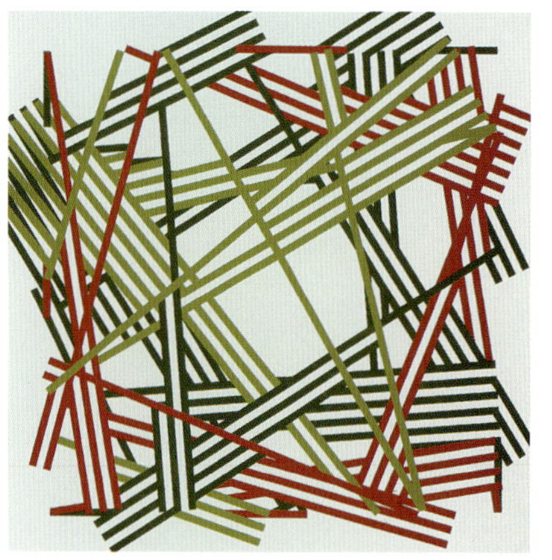

Martin, Kenneth 1905–1984
Chance Order Change 10 1980
oil on canvas 121.6 x 121.6
23/1982

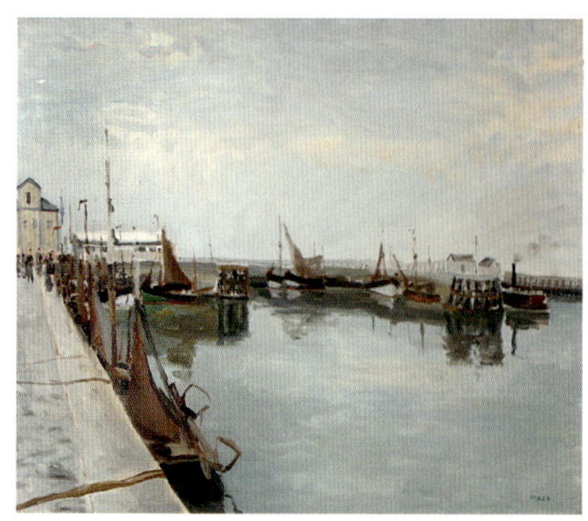

Maze, Paul Lucien 1887–1979
The Harbour, Ostende
oil on canvas 65.6 x 81
393

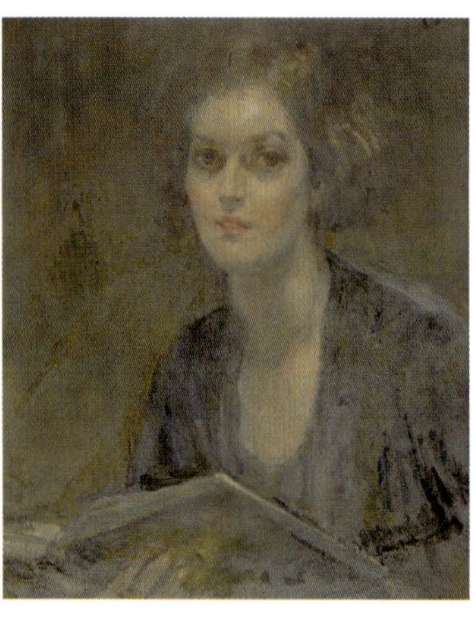

McEvoy, Mary 1870–1941
Audrey 1931
oil on canvas 58 x 51
395

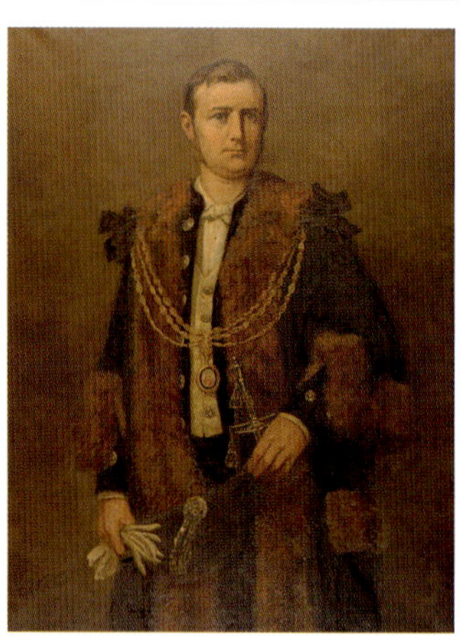

McFadden, Frank active 1879–1894
Alderman Alfred Leighton McCalmont, JP
oil on canvas 143.2 x 112
397

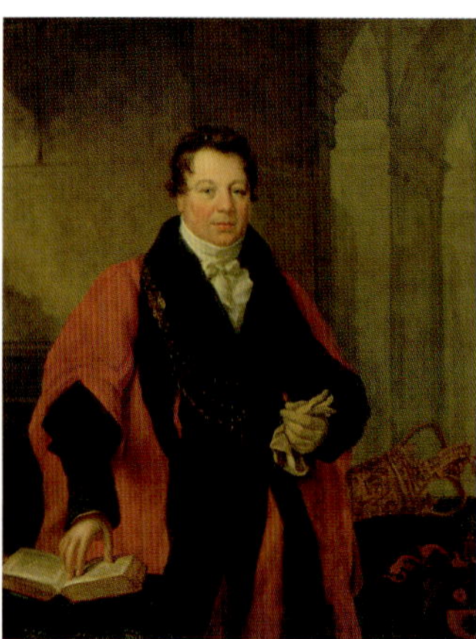

McFadden, Frank active 1879–1894
Alderman Dunlop, JP
oil on canvas 146.5 x 116.2
398

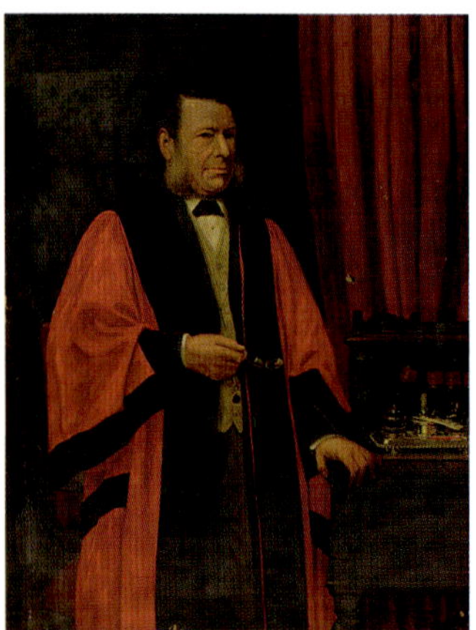

McFadden, Frank active 1879–1894
R. S. Pearce Esq.
oil on canvas 127.6 x 102
950

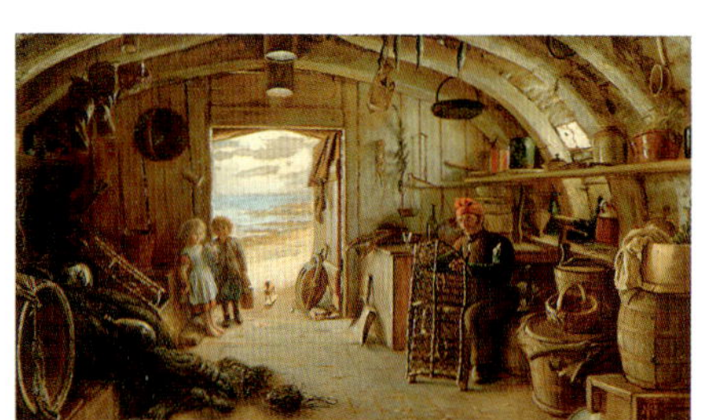

McIntyre, James active 1867–1909
Not Married Yet 1877
oil on canvas 45.5 x 81.3
399

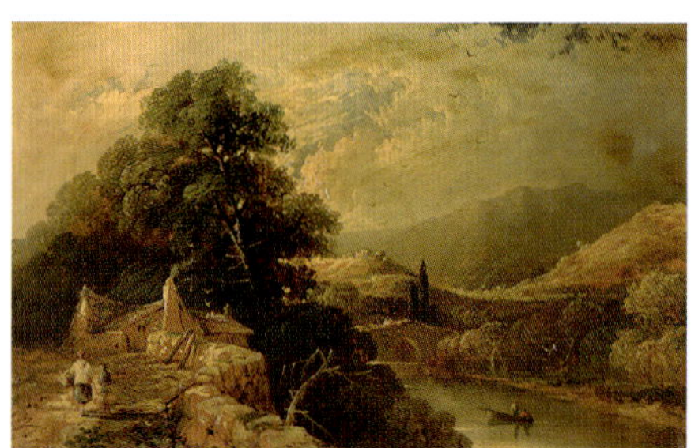

McIntyre, James active 1867–1909
Landscape
oil on board 29.3 x 47
400

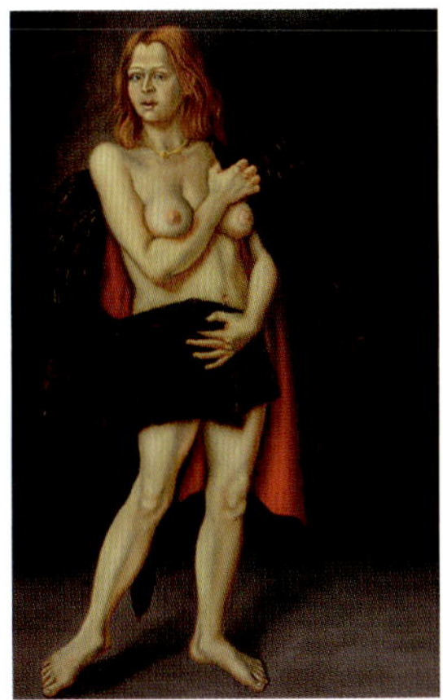

McKenna, Stephen b.1939
'Fourment' 1977
oil on canvas 12.2 x 8
24/1978

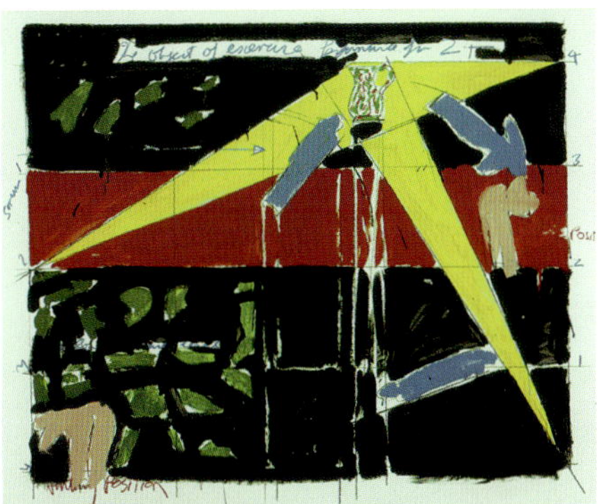

McLean, Bruce b.1944
Study for the Object of Exercise 1979
acrylic on paper 142.1 x 166.4
18/1983

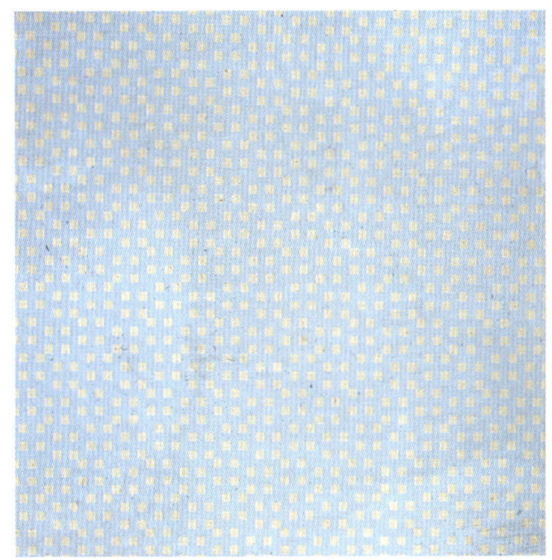

McLean, John b.1939
Quadrillion 1967
oil on board 122 x 122.2
7/1967

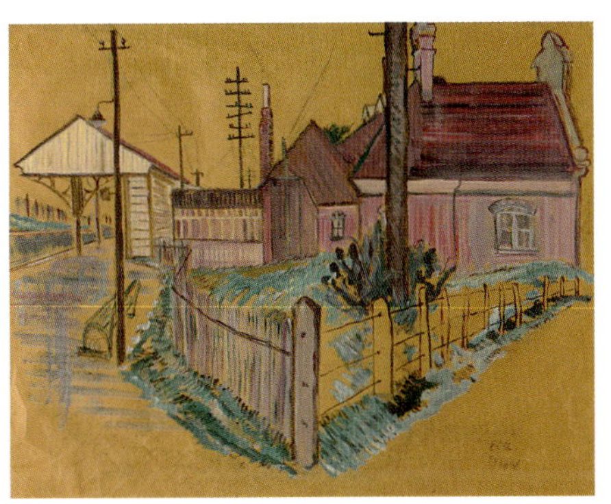

Meadus, Eric 1931–1970
Summer, Swaythling 1959
oil on paper 80.4 x 93.3
64/1991

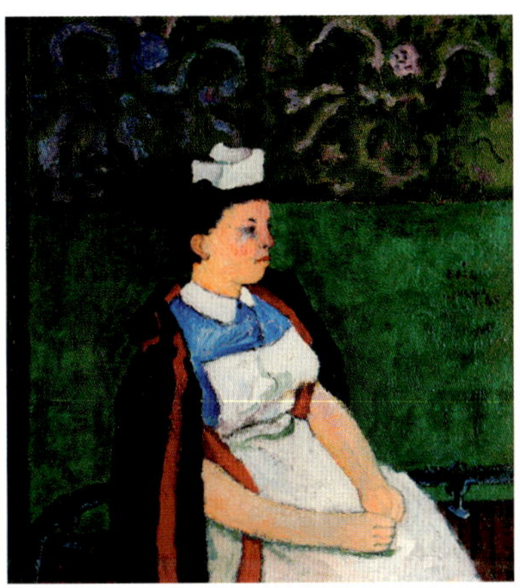

Meadus, Eric 1931–1970
Portrait of a Nurse 1965
oil on canvas 43.2 x 40.5
7/1975

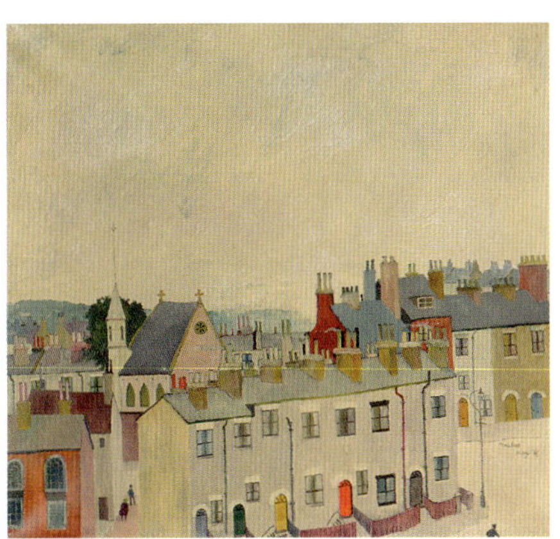

Meadus, Eric 1931–1970
Untitled (May 1967) 1967
oil on canvas 64 x 69 (E)
59/2006

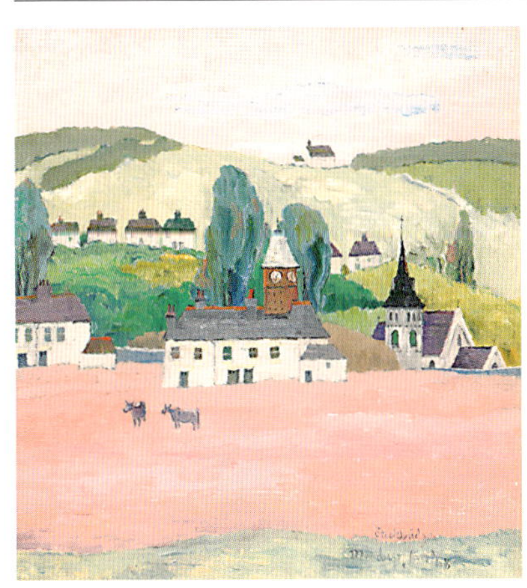

Meadus, Eric 1931–1970
Stockbridge 1968
oil on canvas 50.8 x 45.7
11/1975

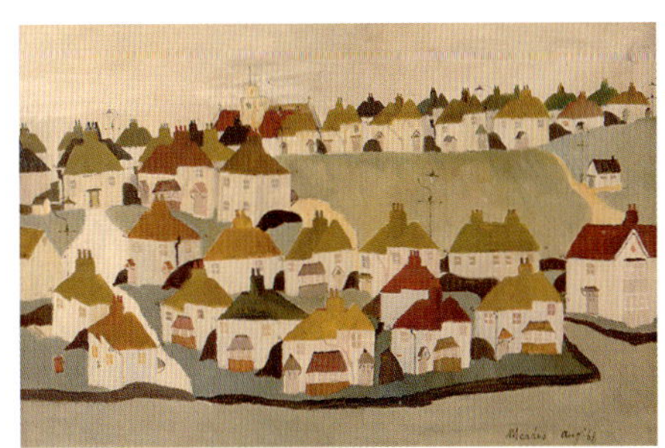

Meadus, Eric 1931–1970
Townscape 1968
oil on board 25.4 x 40.5
9/1975

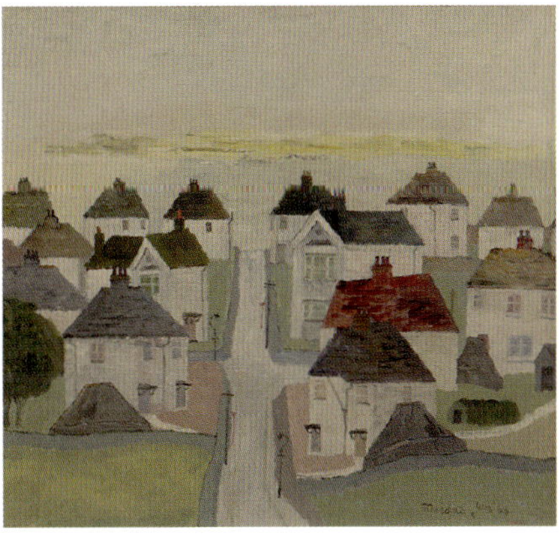

Meadus, Eric 1931–1970
Townscape by River 1968
oil on canvas 45.7 x 50.8
12/1975

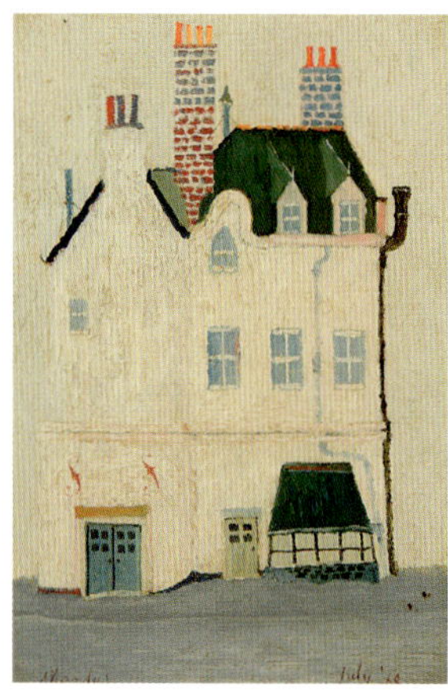

Meadus, Eric 1931–1970
Untitled (July 1968) 1968
oil on board 31 x 24.1
60/2006

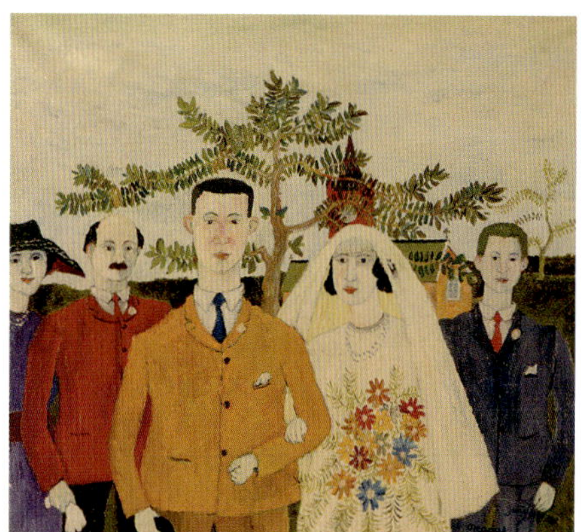

Meadus, Eric 1931–1970
Wedding 1968
oil on canvas 51.5 x 55.5
13/1975

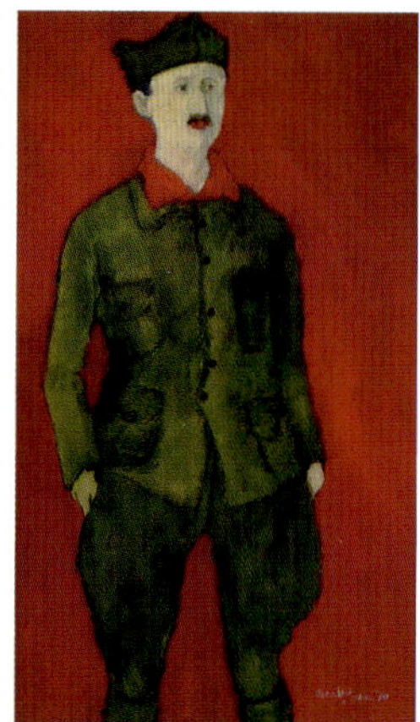

Meadus, Eric 1931–1970
Portrait of a Spanish Soldier 1970
oil on board 36.5 x 25
6/1975

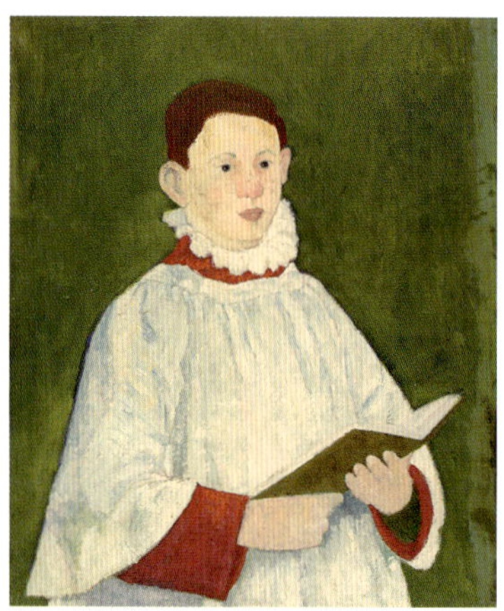

Meadus, Eric 1931–1970
Choirboy
oil on board 60.5 x 50.5
15/1975

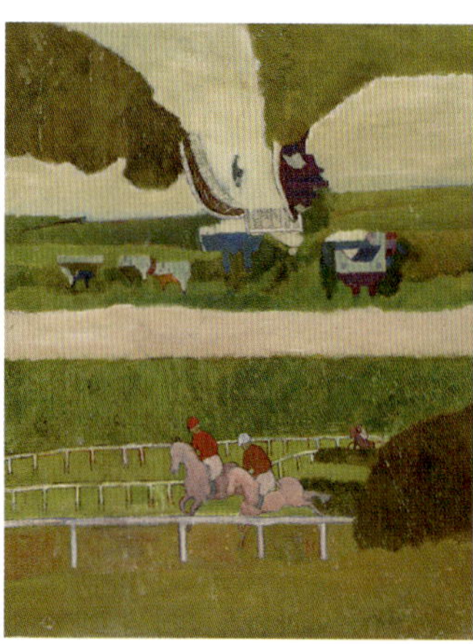

Meadus, Eric 1931–1970
Double/Inverted Landscape
oil on board 61 x 48.2
14/1975

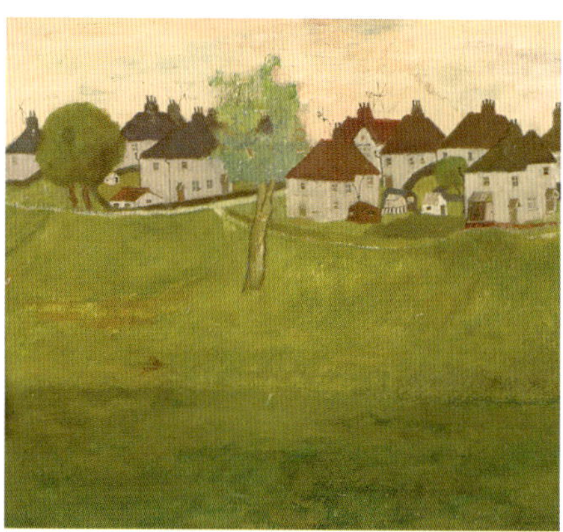

Meadus, Eric 1931–1970
Park with Houses
oil on board 40.5 x 45.7
10/1975

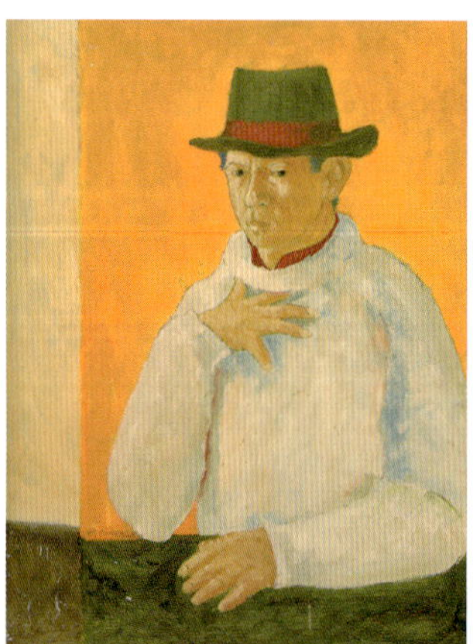

Meadus, Eric 1931–1970
Self Portrait
oil on board 61 x 45
16/1975

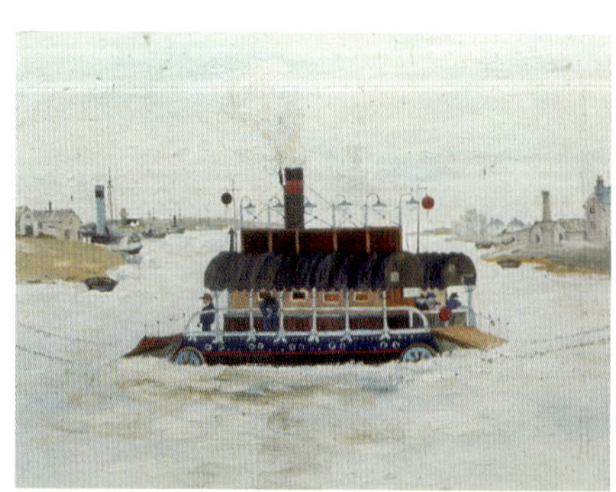

Meadus, Eric 1931–1970
The Floating Bridge
oil on board 53.5 x 71.1
21/1975

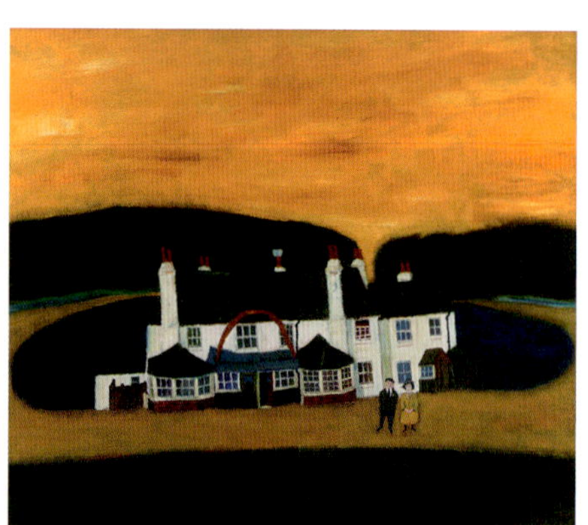

Meadus, Eric 1931–1970
The January Landscape (Cowherds)
oil on board 50.5 x 60.7
18/1975

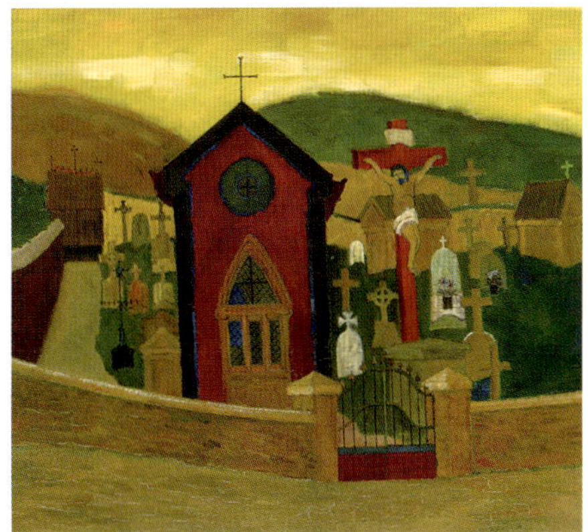

Meadus, Eric 1931–1970
The Red Church
oil on board 53.3 x 60.5
19/1975

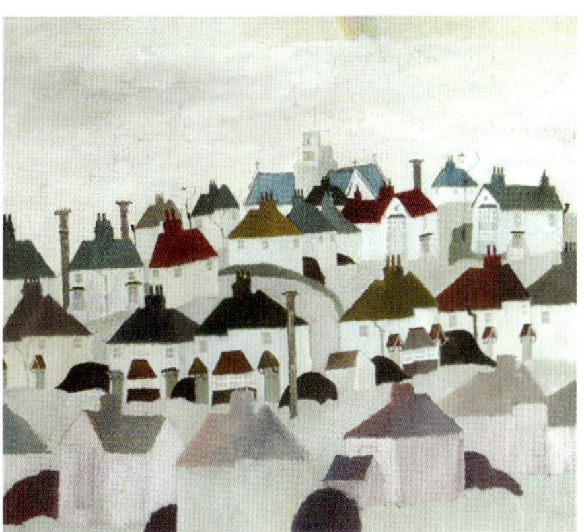

Meadus, Eric 1931–1970
Townscape
oil on board 35.5 x 40.4
8/1975

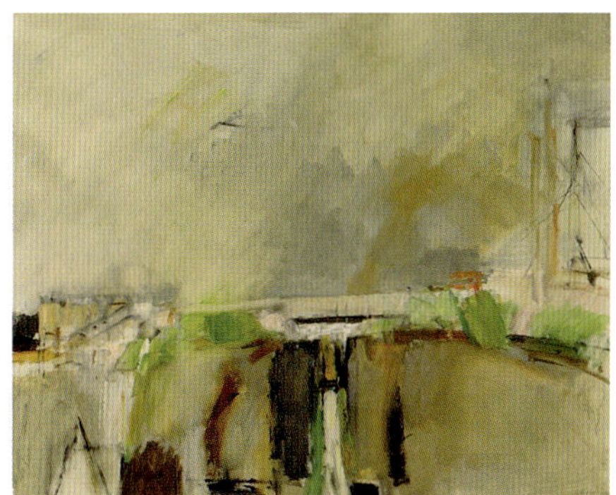

Medley, Robert 1905–1994
Path to Cement Works near Gravesend 1957
oil on canvas 71.1 x 91.5
5/1962

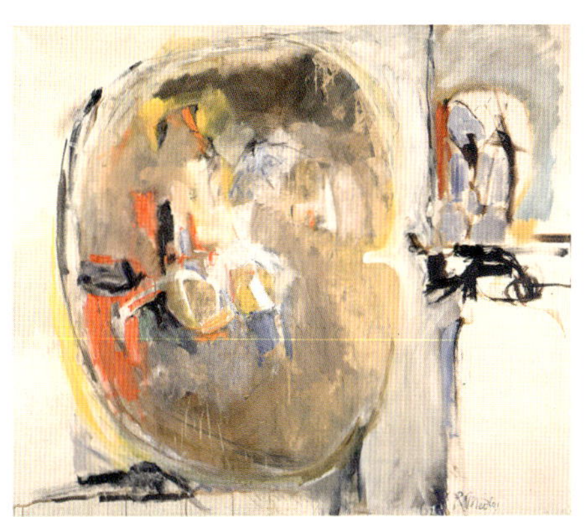

Medley, Robert 1905–1994
The Ear 1962
oil on canvas 157.6 x 182.5
2/1995

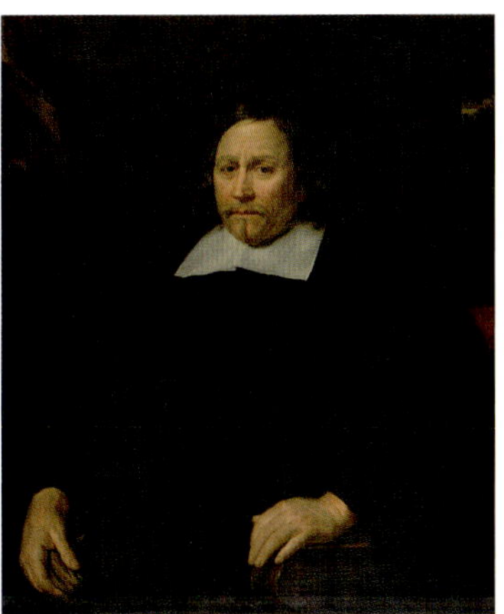

Meert, Pieter c.1610–c.1669
Portrait of a Man
oil on canvas 106 x 89
1118

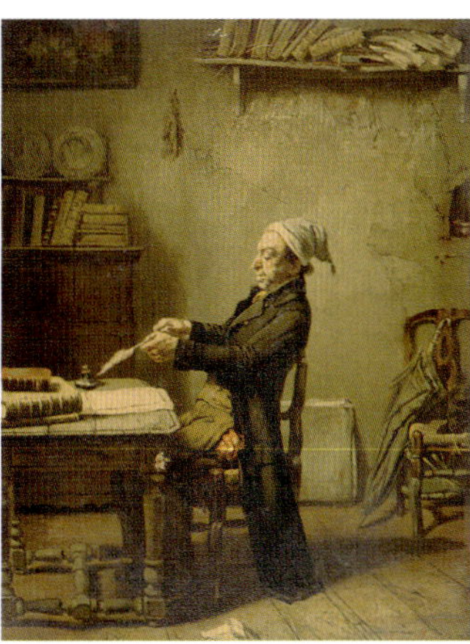

Meerts, Franz 1836–1896
The Old Attorney
oil on canvas 40.3 x 31.4
401

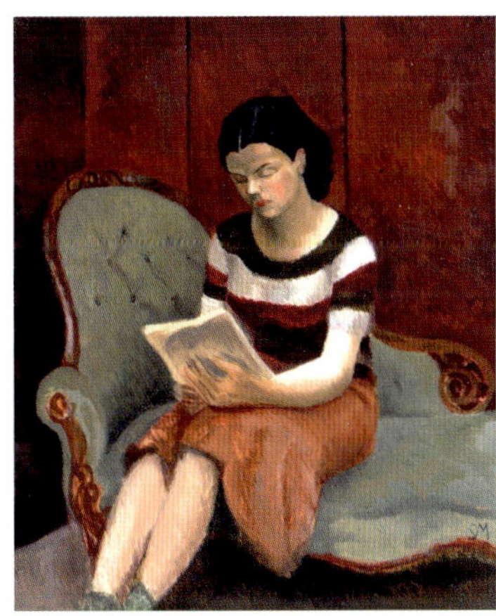

Melland, Sylvia 1906–1993
Thelma Hulbert
oil on canvas 64.8 x 54.5
4/2000

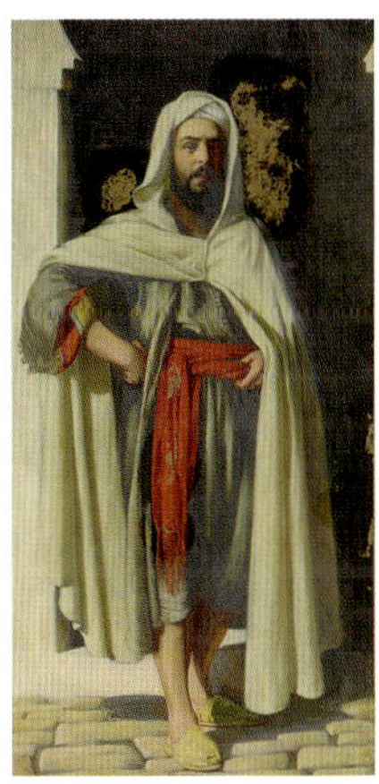

Michaelson, Assur active 1895–1915
Lord Swaythling in Moorish Costume
oil on canvas 183 x 92
402

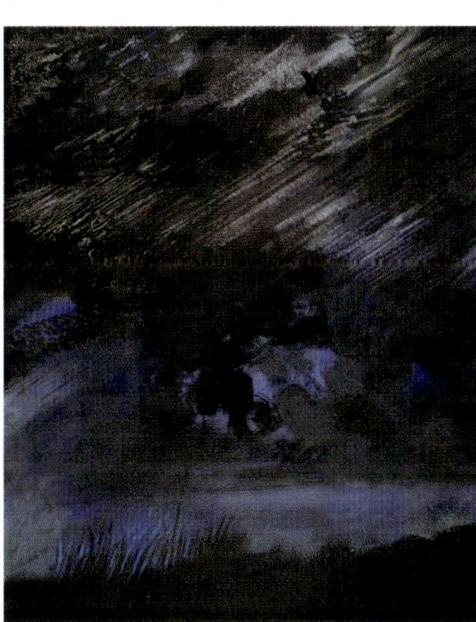

Middleditch, Edward 1923–1987
Night Sky
oil on board 120.3 x 100.9
1/2000

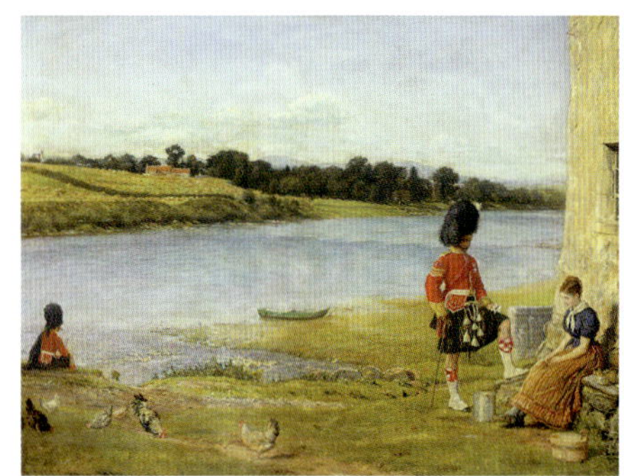

Millais, John Everett 1829–1896
Flowing to the Sea 1871
oil on canvas 143 x 188
403

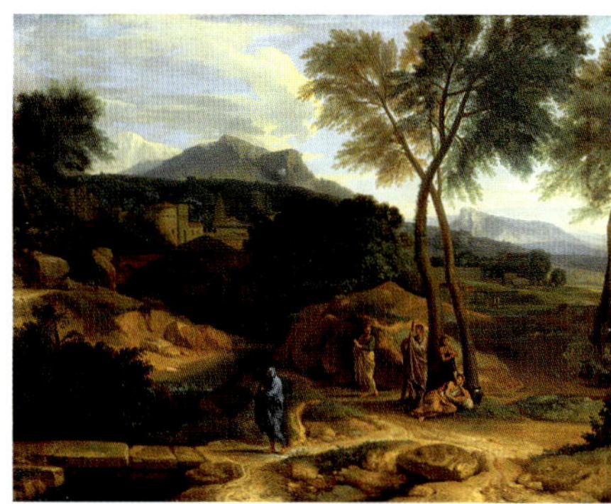

Millet, Jean-François the elder 1642–1679
Classical Landscape
oil on canvas 112 x 143.3
1490

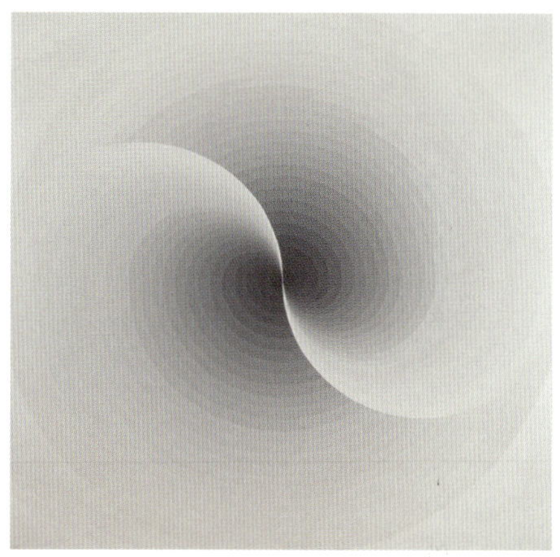

Mills, David b.1947
Twist 1974
emulsion & acrylic on canvas 122 x 122
4/1972

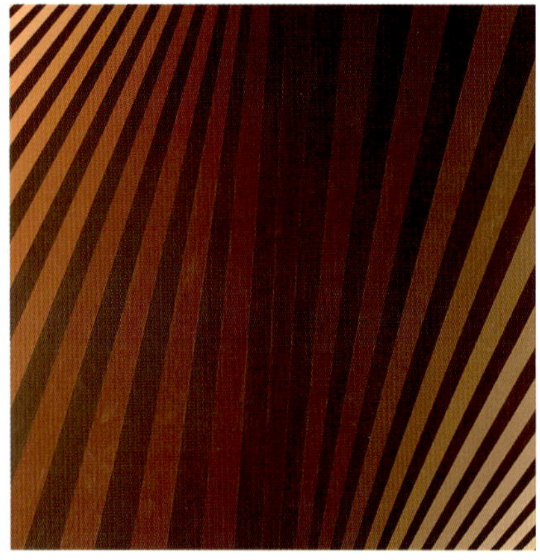

Mills, David b.1947
Chocolate Suite No.1: Chocolate Orange
acrylic on board 132 x 132
94/1975

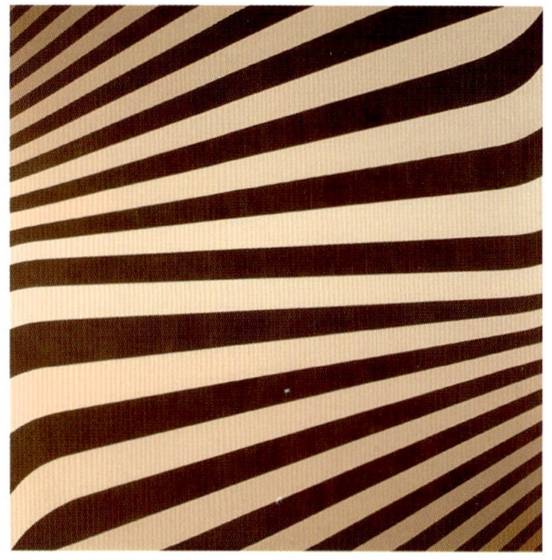

Mills, David b.1947
Chocolate Suite No.2: Coffee Humbug
acrylic on board 132 x 132
95/1975

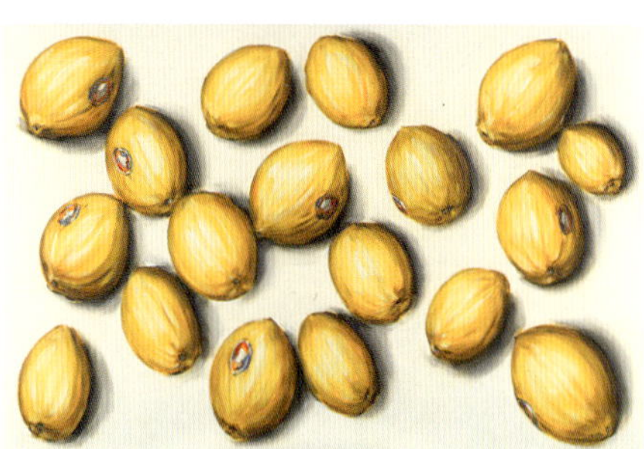

Milroy, Lisa b.1959
Melons 1986
oil on canvas 177.8 x 269.2
14/1986

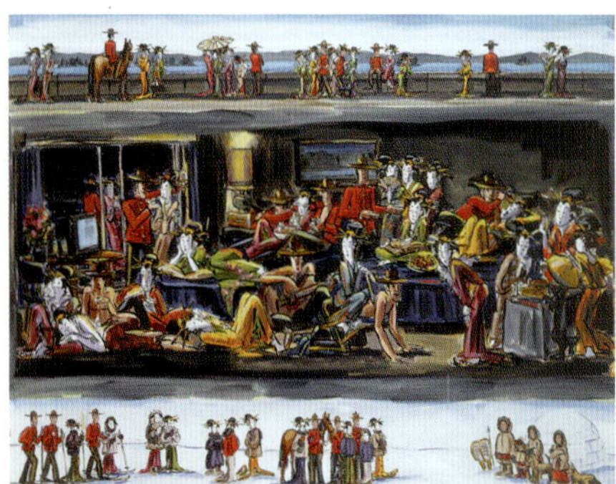

Milroy, Lisa b.1959
Togetherness 2002
oil on canvas 190.5 x 246.4
30/2005

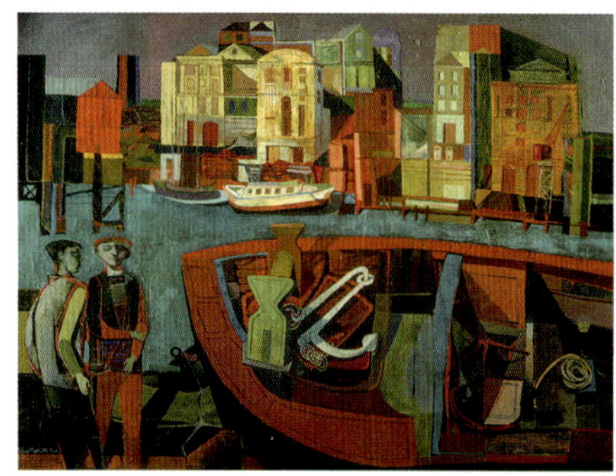

Minton, John 1917–1957
Rotherhithe from Wapping 1946
oil on board 91.5 x 122
1377

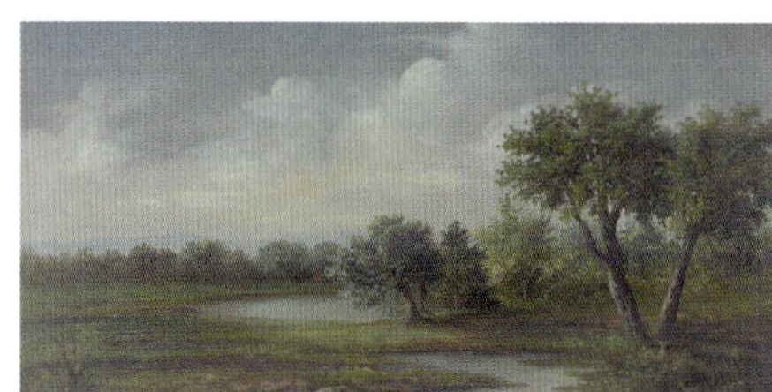

Mitchell, W. B. active 1884–1902
Near Ashford, Kent
oil on canvas 30.5 x 61
406

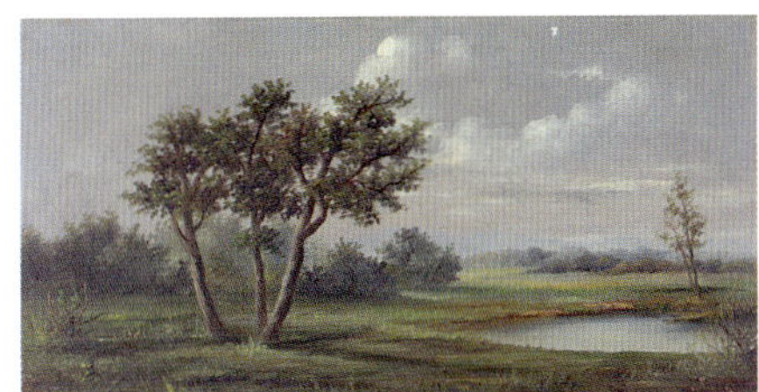

Mitchell, W. B. active 1884–1902
Near Tonbridge, Kent
oil on canvas 30.5 x 61
405

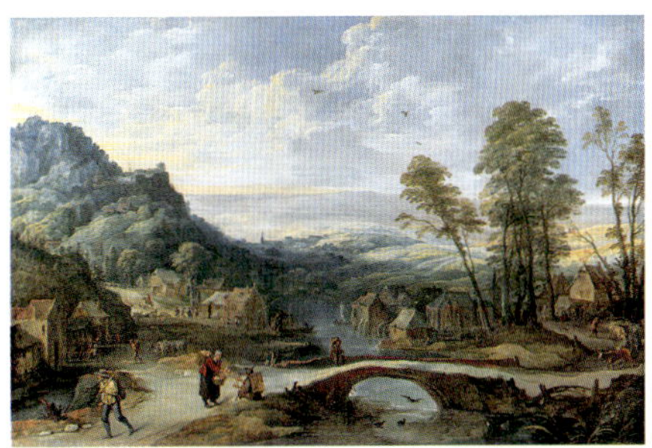

Momper, Joos de the younger 1564–1635
Landscape
oil on canvas 138 x 207.9
655

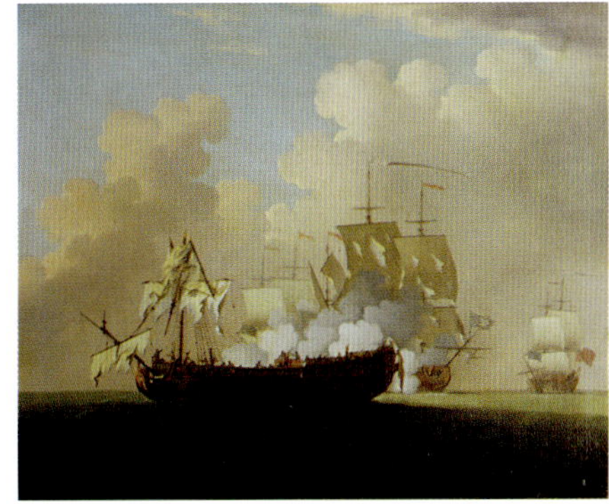

Monamy, Peter 1681–1749
The 'Princesa' Action
oil on canvas 64.4 x 77
1395

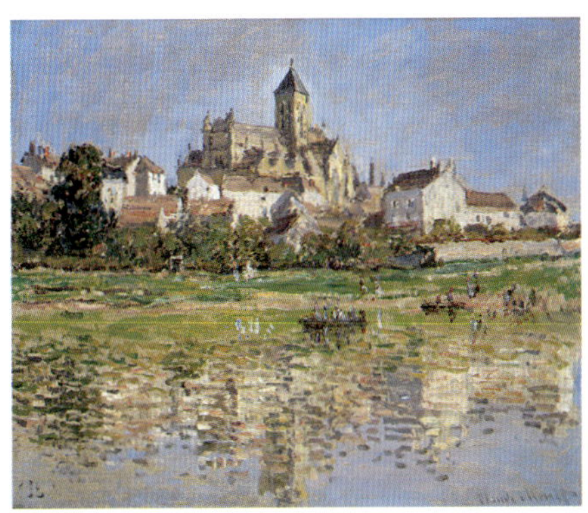

Monet, Claude 1840–1926
The Church at Vétheuil 1880
oil on canvas 50.5 x 61
183/1975

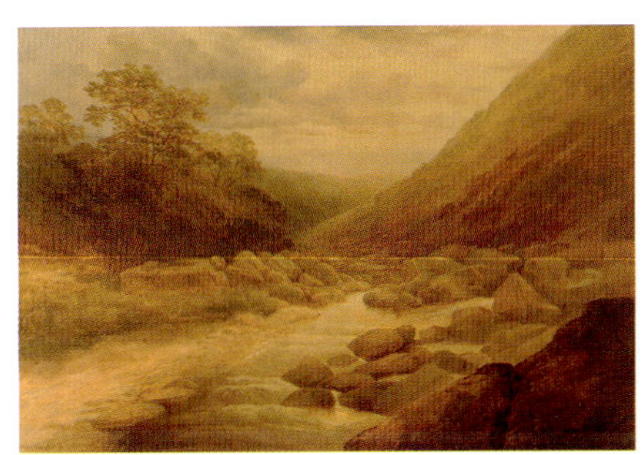

Monkhouse, W.
A Mountain Stream in Yorkshire
oil on canvas 50.7 x 76.3
407

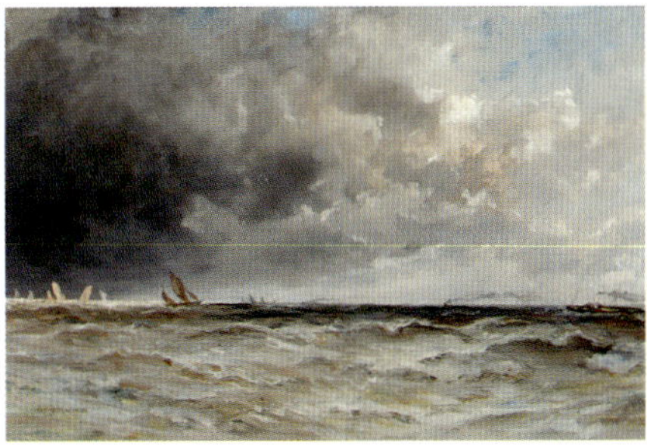

Moore, Henry 1831–1895
Coming Storm 1936
oil on canvas 61.3 x 95
408

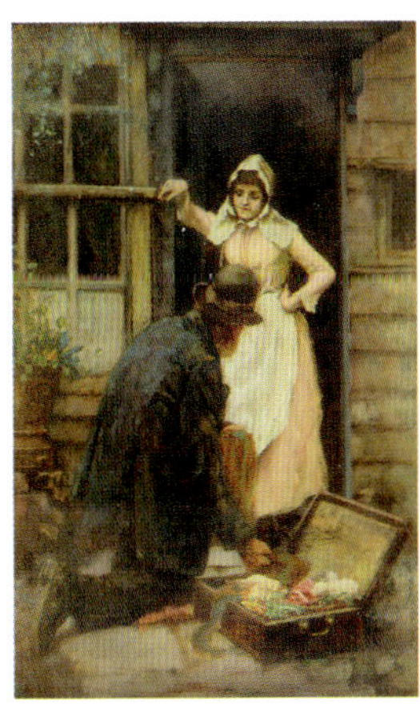

Moore, Sidney active 1880–1911
The Old Pedlar 1911
oil on canvas 50.8 x 32
411

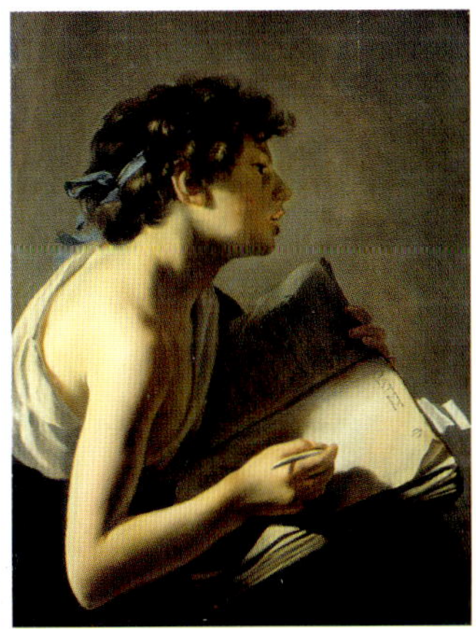

Moreelse, Johannes after 1602–1634
The Young Poet
oil on wood 70.5 x 54.3
110

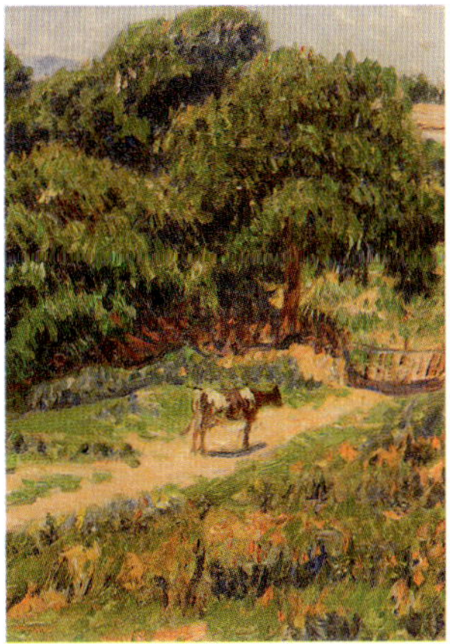

Moret, Henry 1856–1913
Landscape 1890
oil on canvas 35 x 24.2
5/1964

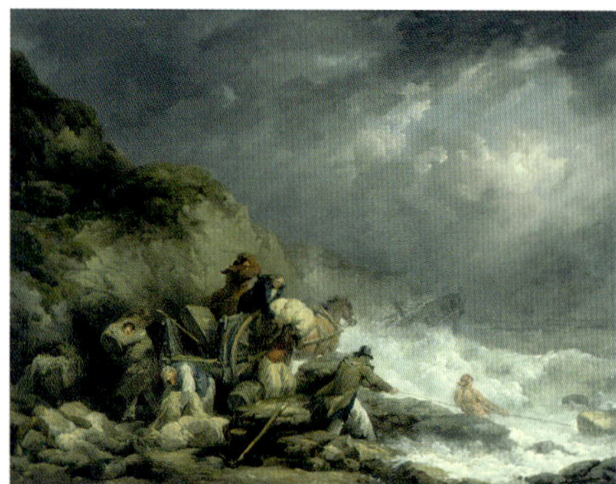

Morland, George 1763–1804
The Wreckers 1791
oil on canvas 102.8 x 138.5
1305

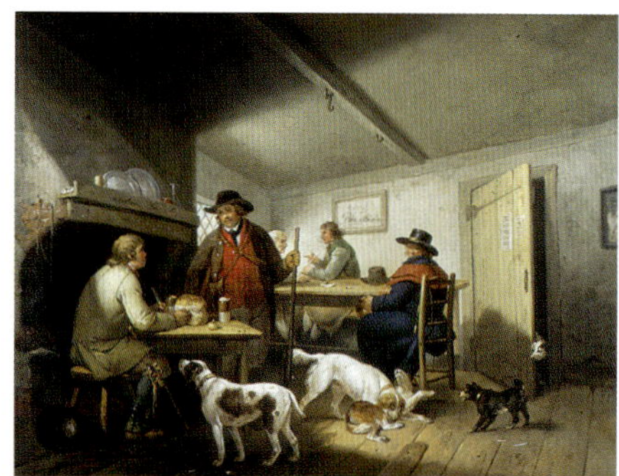

Morland, George 1763–1804
Interior of a Country Inn
oil on canvas 59.7 x 76.6
1479

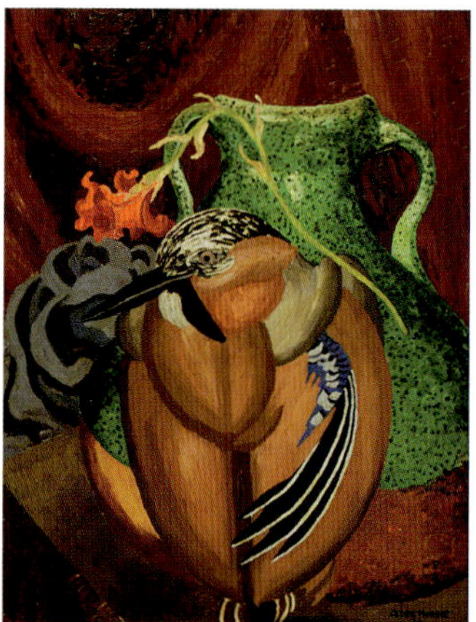

Morris, Cedric Lockwood 1889–1982
The Jay 1924
oil on board 81.8 x 68.6
5/1988

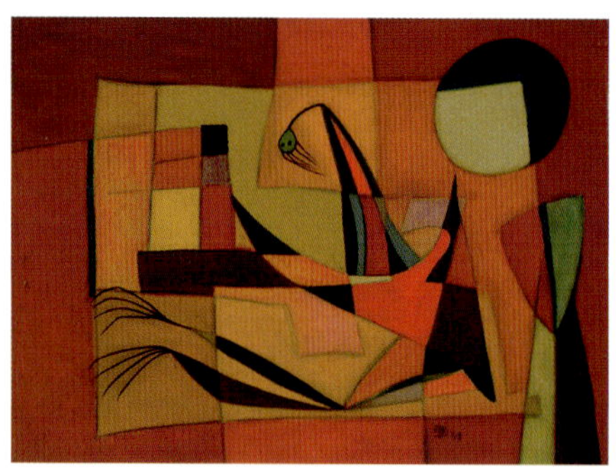

Morris, Desmond b.1928
The Hermit Discovered 1948
oil on canvas 40.8 x 56
4/2002

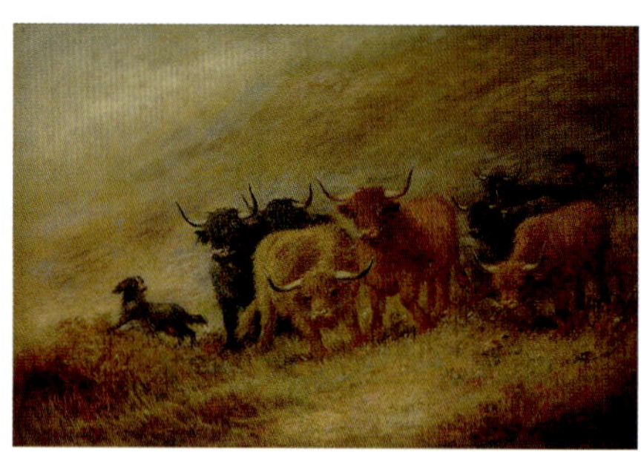

Morris, J. D.
Loch Aron 1905
oil on canvas 50.8 x 76.8
89

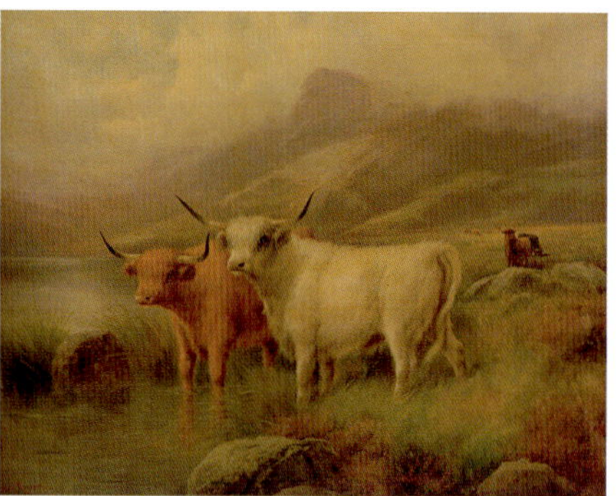

Morris, John W. 1865–1924
Cattle
oil on canvas 70.5 x 91.4
416

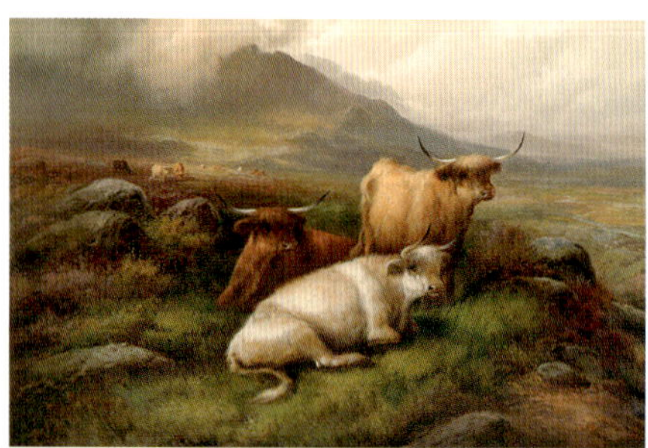

Morris, John W. 1865–1924
Cattle
oil on canvas 61 x 91.8
1265

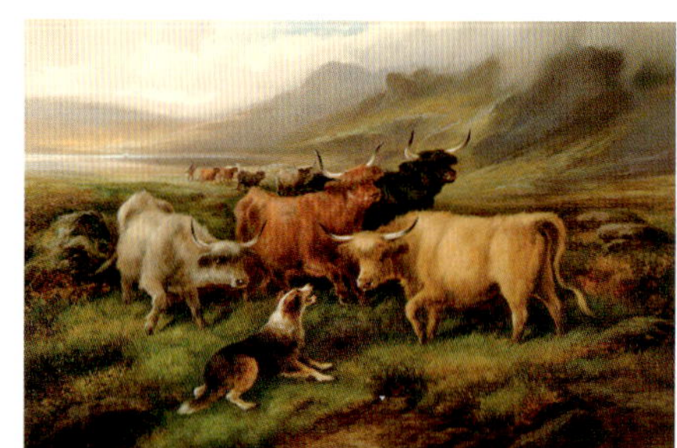

Morris, John W. 1865–1924
Highland Cattle in Mountain Scene
oil on canvas 61 x 91.5
1264

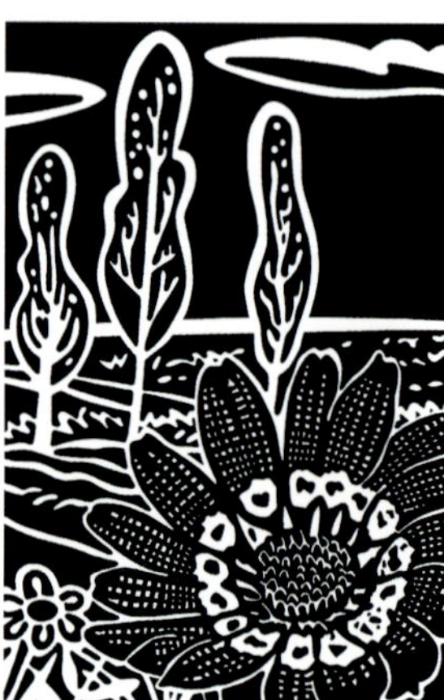

Morrison, Paul b.1966
Bast 2003
acrylic on canvas 229 x 152.4
7/2004

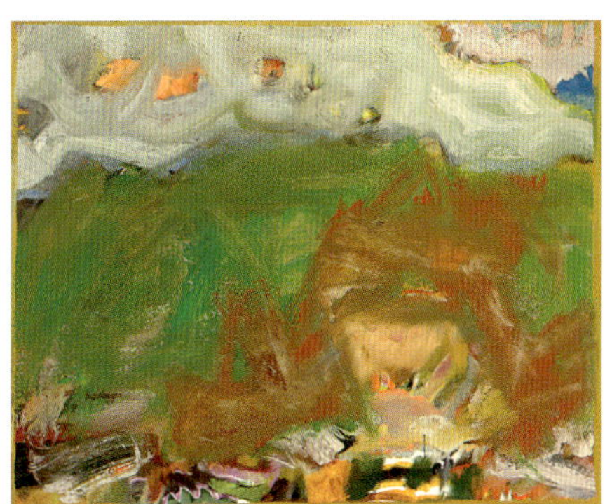

Morsberger, Philip b.1933
Untitled 1980
oil on canvas 64.9 x 80.5 (E)
38/2006

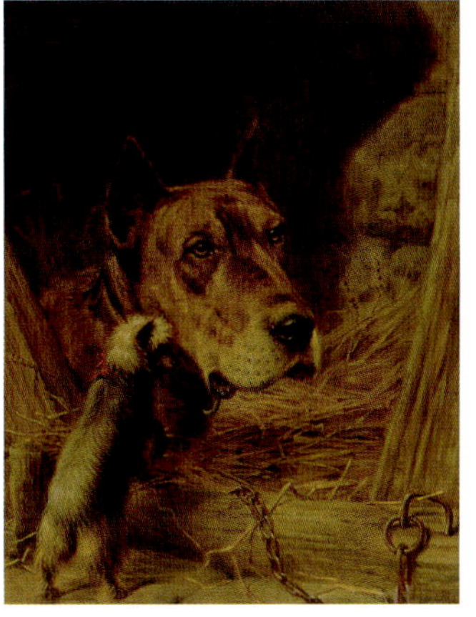

Moseley, Richard S. active 1863–1912
Telling His Big Brother 1894
oil on canvas 91.1 x 71.2
1104

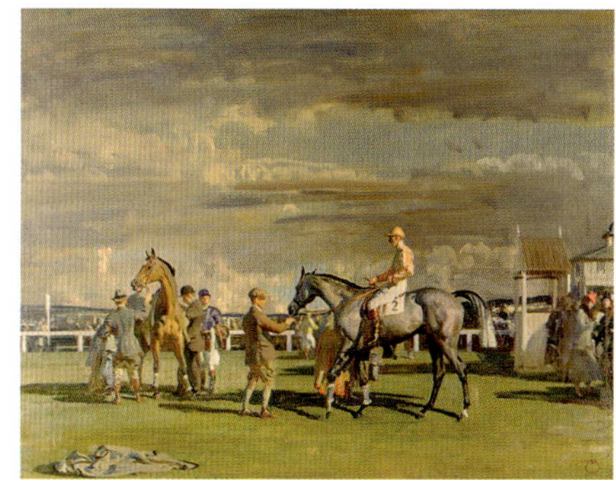

Munnings, Alfred James 1878–1959
After the Race
oil on canvas 99 x 129.6
418

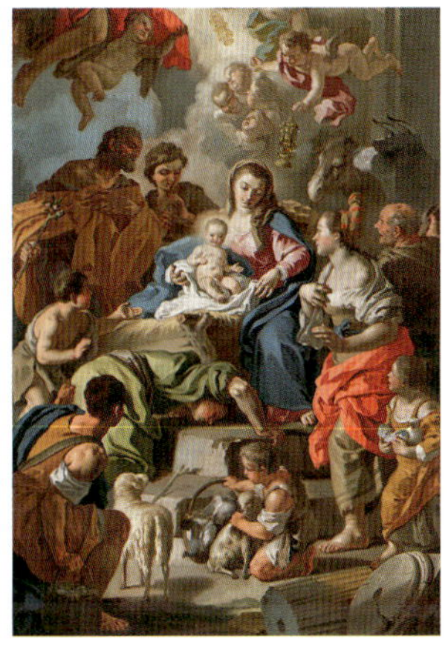

Mura, Francesco de 1696–1782
The Adoration of the Shepherds
oil on canvas 139.1 x 99.6
177/1975

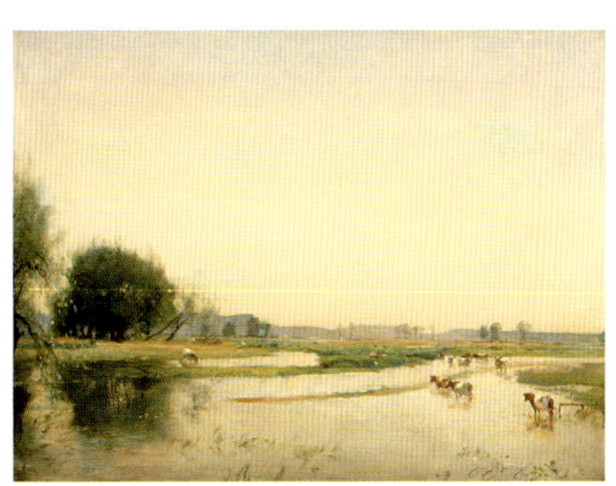

Murray, David 1849–1933
Cows in a Stream
oil on canvas 50.9 x 66.1
420

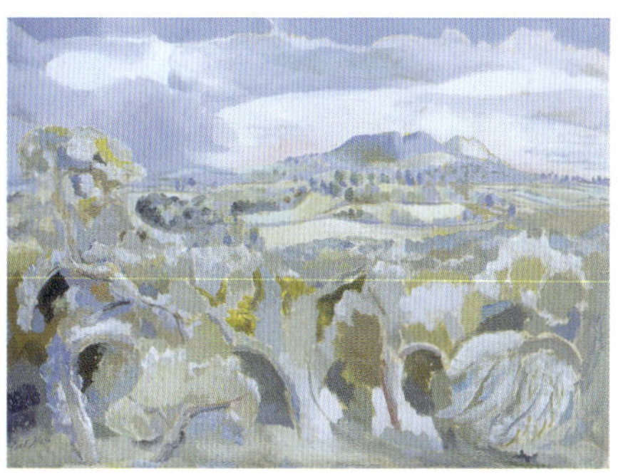

Nash, Paul 1889–1946
Landscape of the Malvern Distance 1943
oil on board 55.9 x 76.2
1353

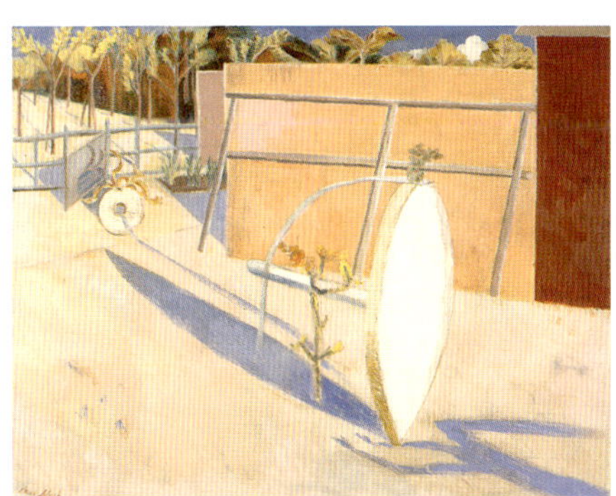

Nash, Paul 1889–1946
The Archer
oil on canvas 71 x 91.5
1415

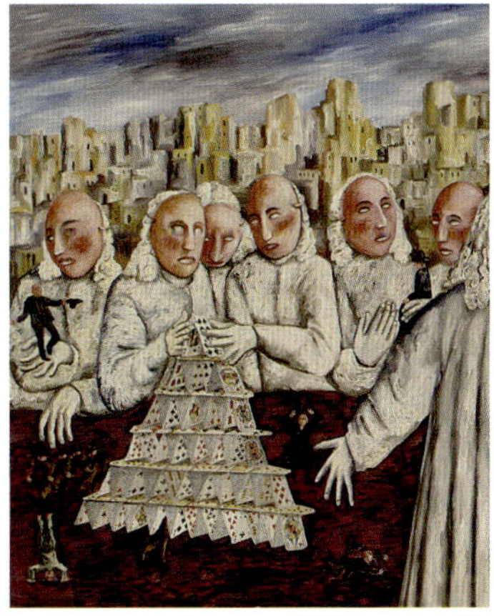

Nesterova, Natalya b.1944
Human Masks (left wing) 1989
oil on canvas 360 x 300
9/1993

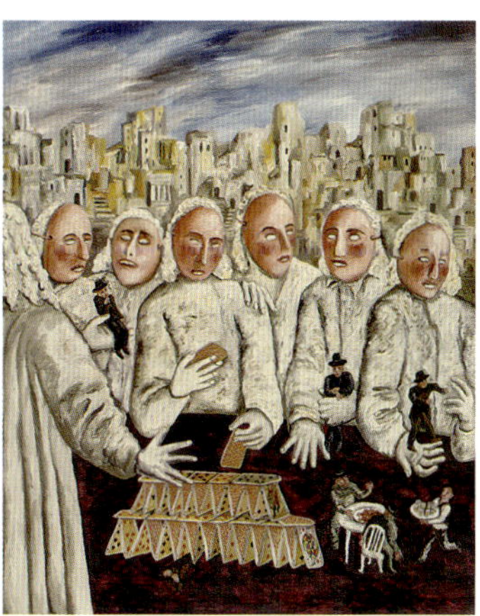

Nesterova, Natalya b.1944
Human Masks (right wing) 1989
oil on canvas 360 x 300
9/1993

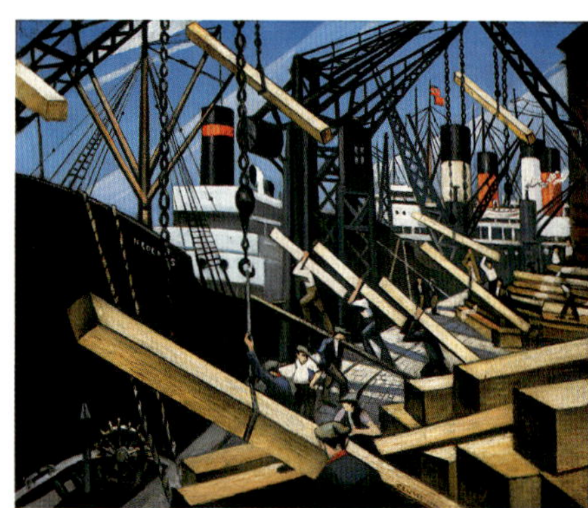

Nevinson, Christopher 1889–1946
Loading Timber at Southampton Docks 1917
oil on canvas 51 x 61
4/1962

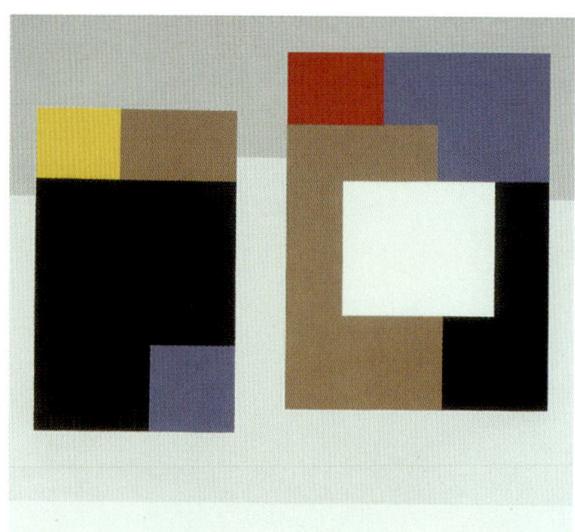

Nicholson, Ben 1894–1982
Two Forms (1940–1942) 1940–1942
oil on canvas 91 x 91.7 (E)
1/1966

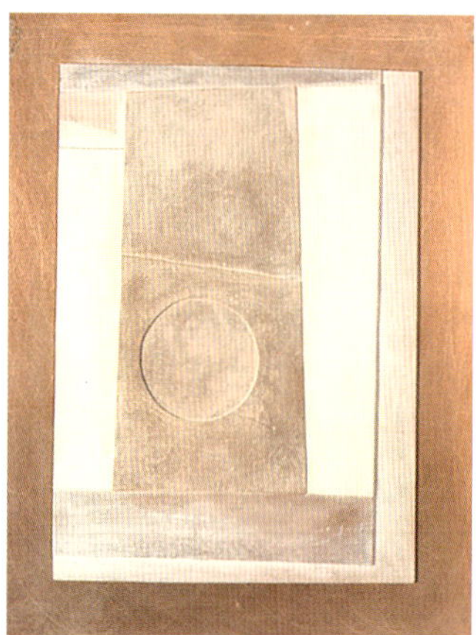

Nicholson, Ben 1894–1982
Greystone 1966
oil on board 56.5 x 43.9
10/1967

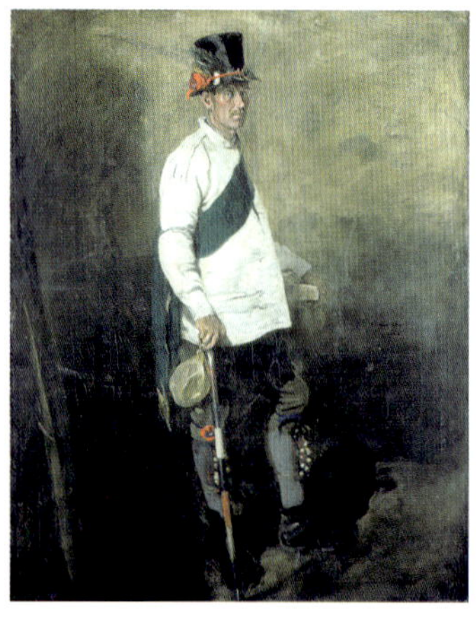

Nicholson, William 1872–1949
The Morris Dancer 1902
oil on canvas 127.5 x 102.2
425

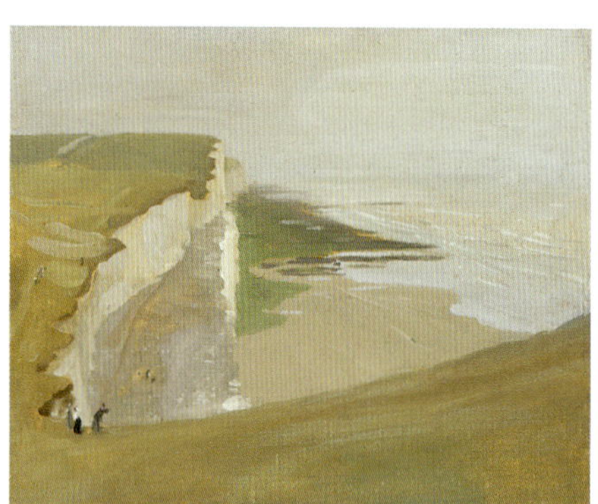

Nicholson, William 1872–1949
Cliffs at Rottingdean 1910
oil on canvas 33 x 41.5
10/1962

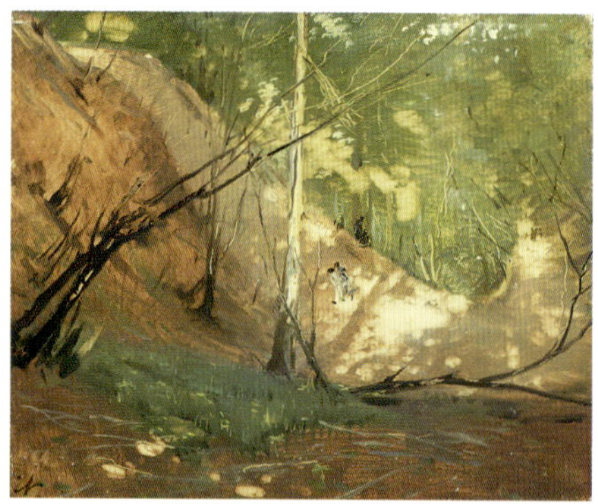

Nicholson, William 1872–1949
A Glade near Midhurst 1936
oil on wood 37.8 x 46
426

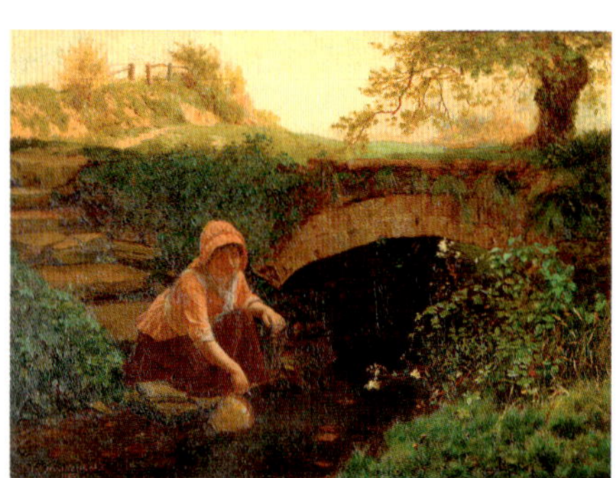

Nightingale, Leonard Charles active 1877–1913
The Dipping Place 1880
oil on canvas 51.7 x 68.8
427

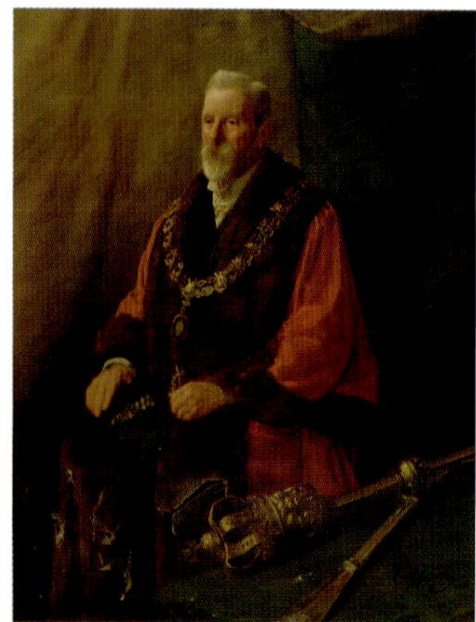

Oakley, Herbert Colborne 1869–1944
Alderman Edward Bance, DL, Mayor (1890–1904 & 1910) 1906
oil on canvas 139.8 x 108.6
429

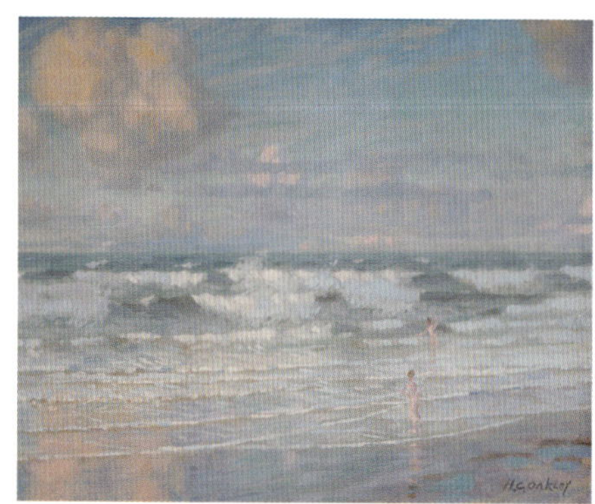

Oakley, Herbert Colborne 1869–1944
Bathers
oil on canvas 30.3 x 38.2
430

Facing page: Mura, Francesco de, 1696–1782, *The Adoration of the Shepherds* (detail), Southampton City Art Gallery, (p. 99)

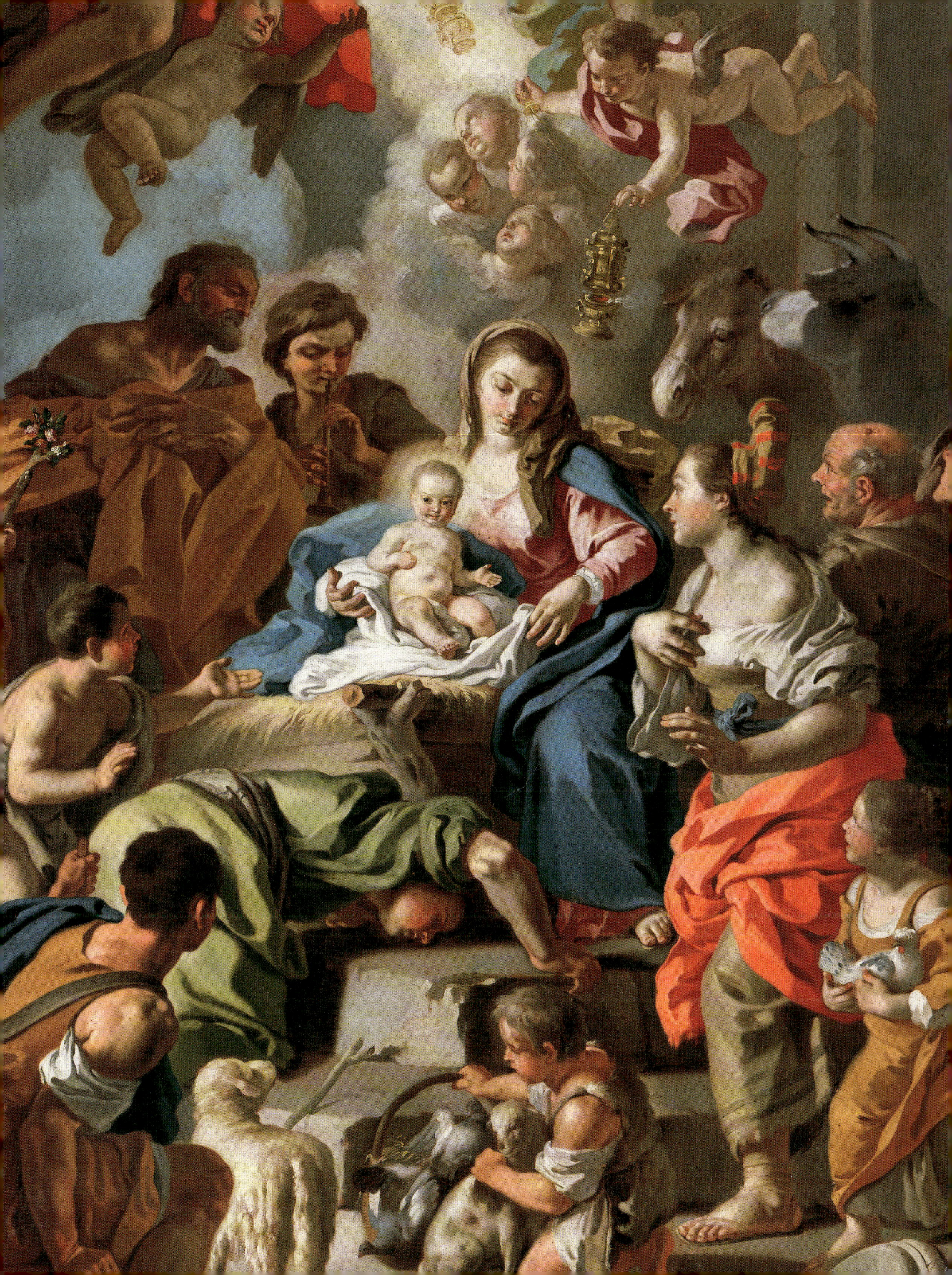

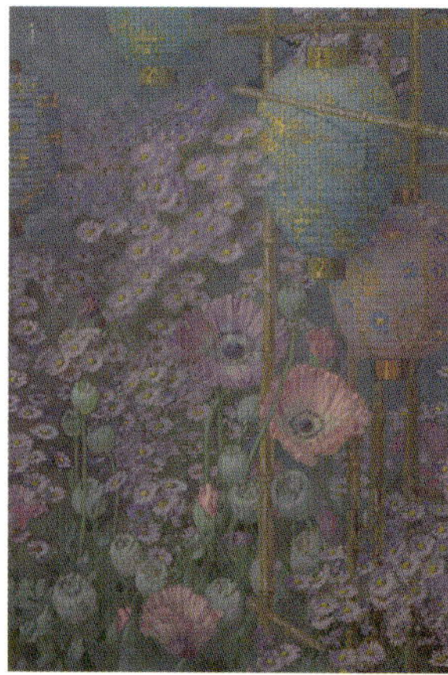

Oakley, Herbert Colborne 1869–1944
Floral Piece
oil on canvas 66 x 45.6
431

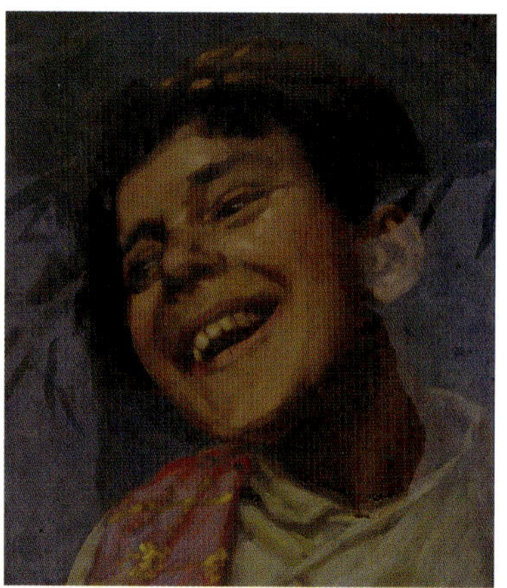

Oakley, Herbert Colborne 1869–1944
Neapolitan Boy
oil on canvas 35.7 x 31.5
432

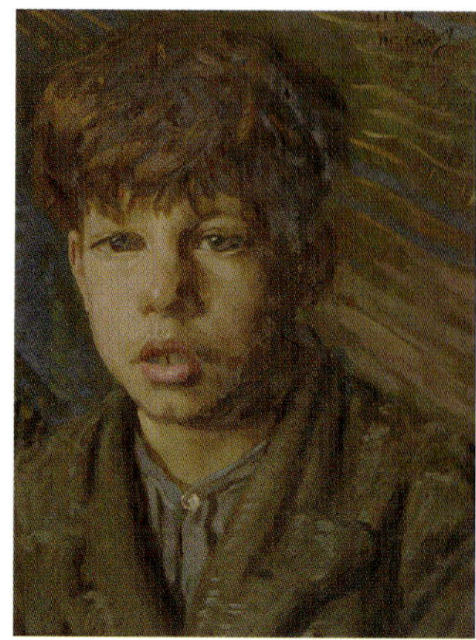

Oakley, Herbert Colborne 1869–1944
Welsh Gamin
oil on canvas 34 x 25.4
433

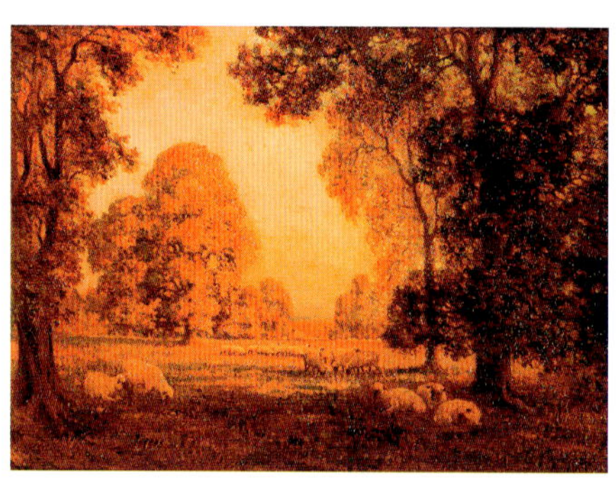

O'Dell, Alan Edmonds active c.1900
The Hour before Sunset
oil on canvas 56.2 x 81.3
434

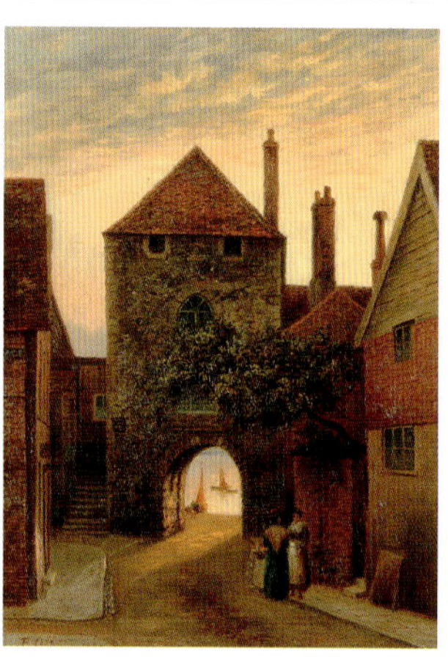

Offer, Frank Rawlings 1847–1932
West Gate, Southampton 1898
oil on canvas 56.2 x 40.7
435

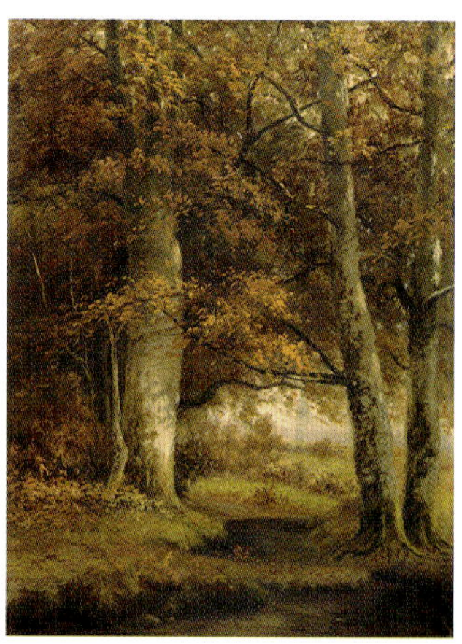

Offer, Frank Rawlings 1847–1932
Landscape
oil on canvas 40.7 x 30.5
436

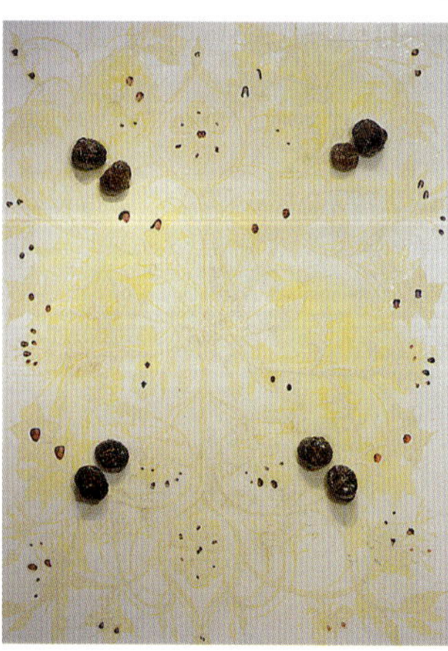

Ofili, Chris b.1968
Two Doo Voodoo 1997
acrylic, resin, oil & elephant dung on canvas
243.5 x 182.7
1/1998

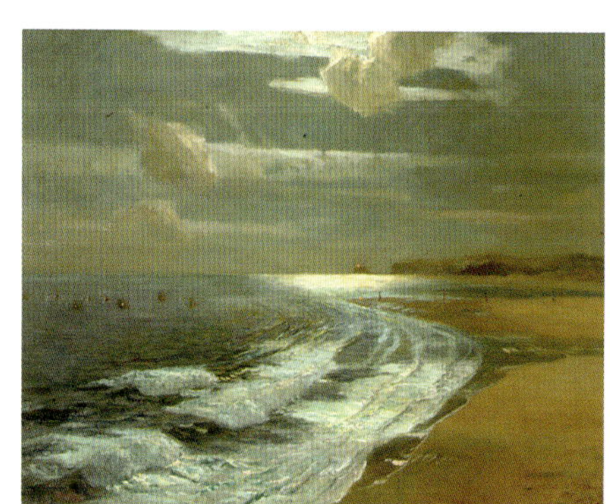

Olsson, Albert Julius 1864–1942
Silver Moonlight, St Ives Bay
oil on canvas 61.1 x 76.5
437

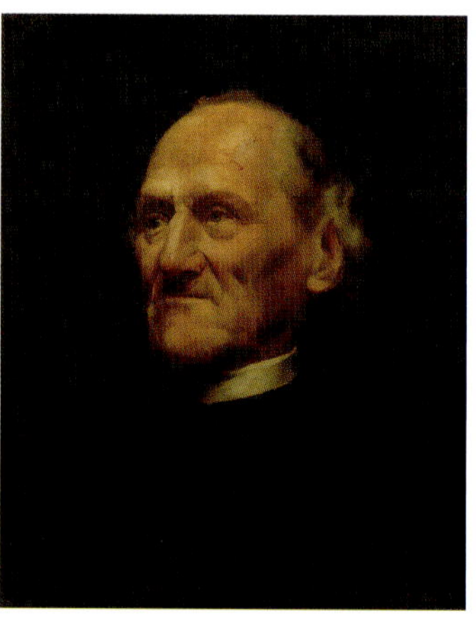

Ommanney, George active 1912–1917
Reverend Ommaney
oil on canvas 53.3 x 43.1
438

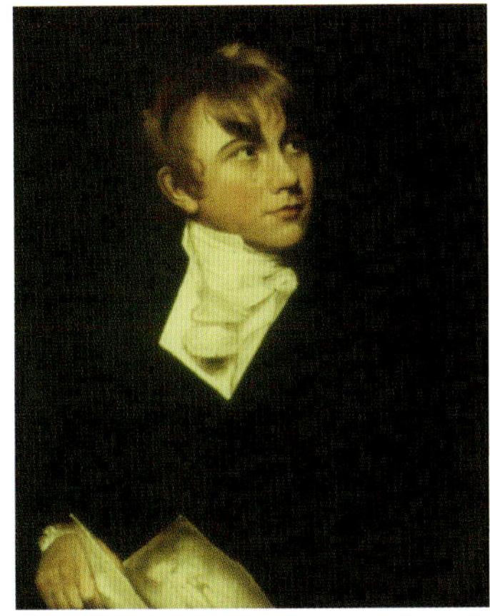

Opie, John 1761–1807
Portrait of an Artist
oil on canvas 76.5 x 64
439

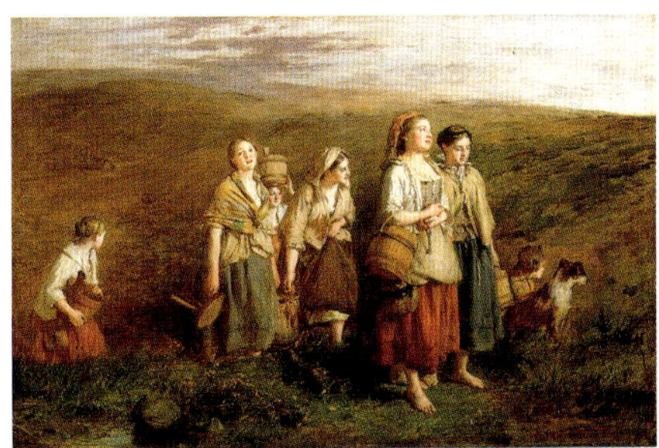

Orchardson, William Quiller 1832–1910
The Flowers of the Forest
oil on canvas 86.9 x 131.8
440

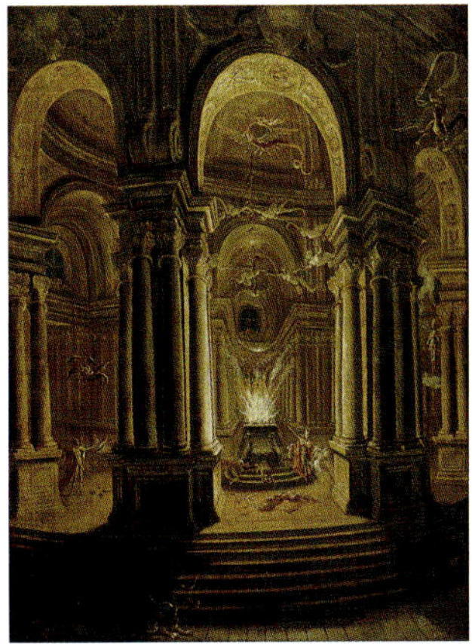

Orlandi, Stefano 1681–1760
A Church with Pagan Sacrifices at a Burning Altar
oil on canvas 94 x 71
101/1963

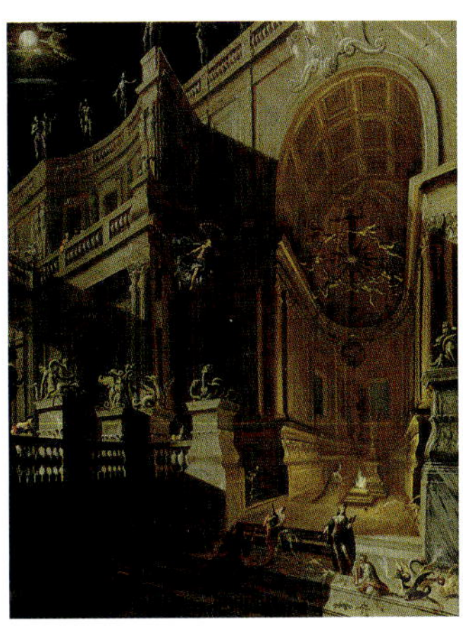

Orlandi, Stefano 1681–1760
Architectural Fantasy with Figures
oil on canvas 106.5 x 82
100/1963

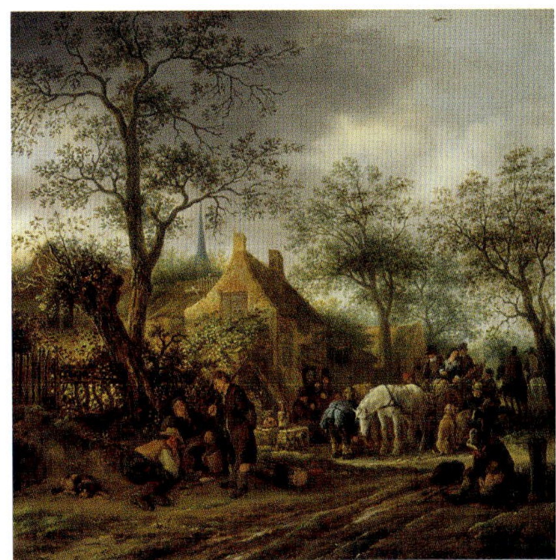

Ostade, Isack van 1621–1649
Travellers at an Inn
oil on panel 51 x 52
1478

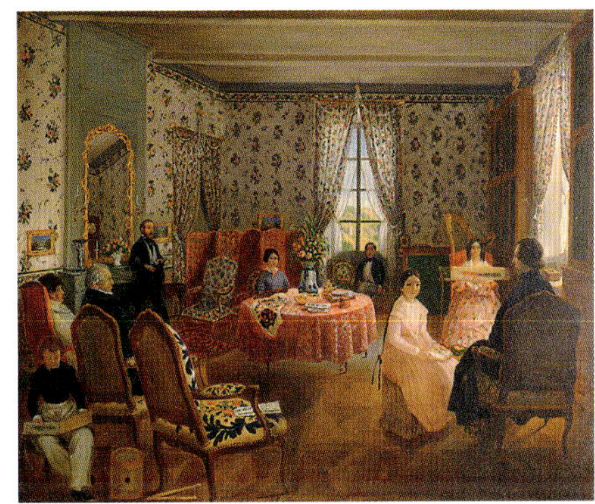

G. P.
Mexican Interior 1846
oil on canvas 38.2 x 46.4
55/1963

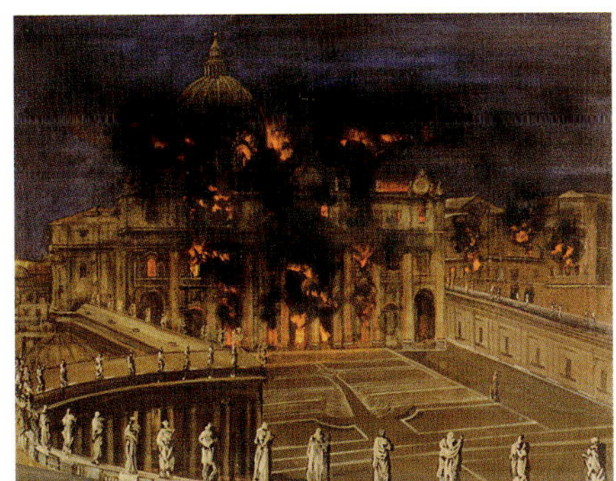

Pagliacci, Aldo 1913–1991
Exterior of a Church in Flames 1951
oil on panel 46 x 59.5
89/1963

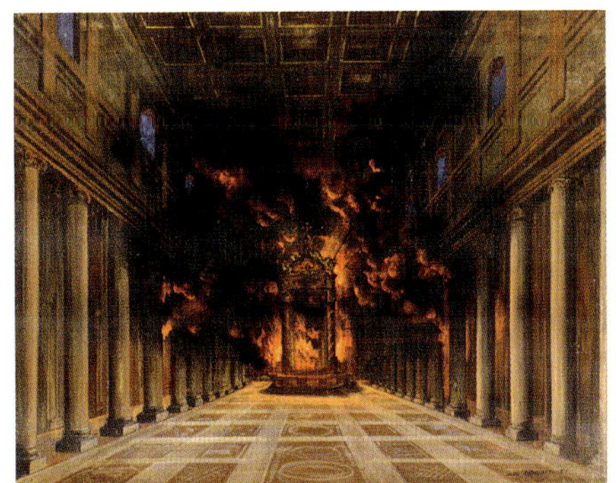

Pagliacci, Aldo 1913–1991
Interior of a Church in Flames 1951
oil on panel 46 x 59.4
88/1963

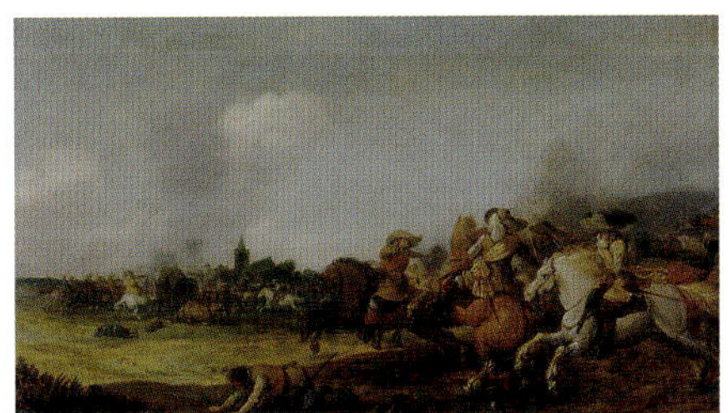

Palamedesz., Palamedes I 1607–1638
Battle Scene
oil on wood 26 x 46.4
1259

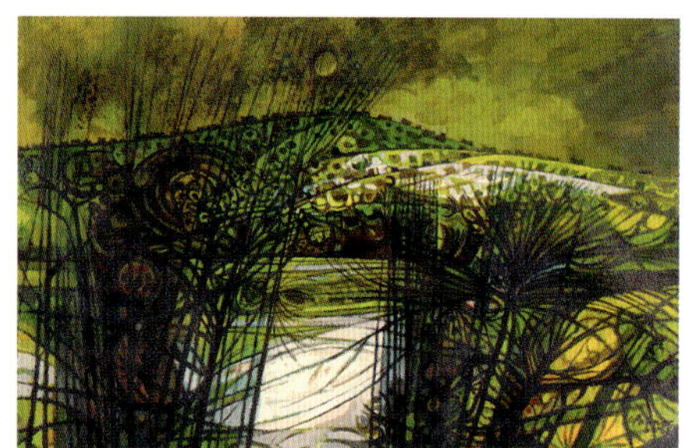

Palmer, Garrick b.1933
Winchester Landscape
oil on canvas 34 x 53
27/1975

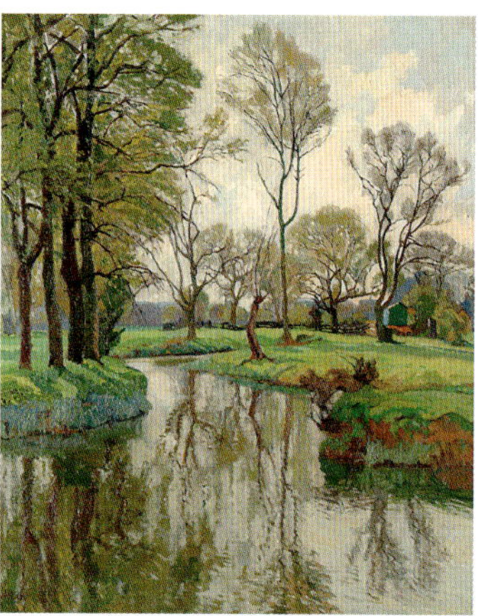

Park, John Anthony 1880–1962
Spring on the Stour
oil on canvas 76 x 62.8
441

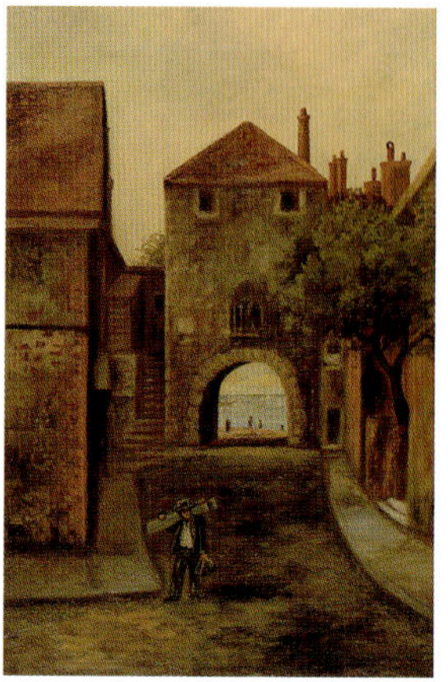

Parsons, E. J.
West Gate, Southampton
oil on canvas 76.2 x 50.8
444

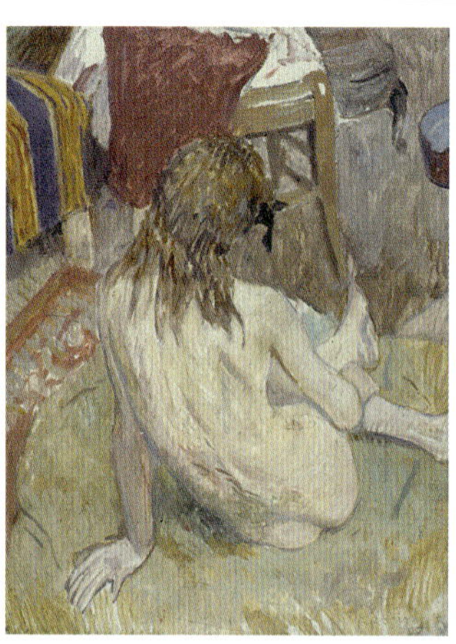

Pascin, Jules 1885–1930
Nude
oil on wood 63 x 47.6
1448

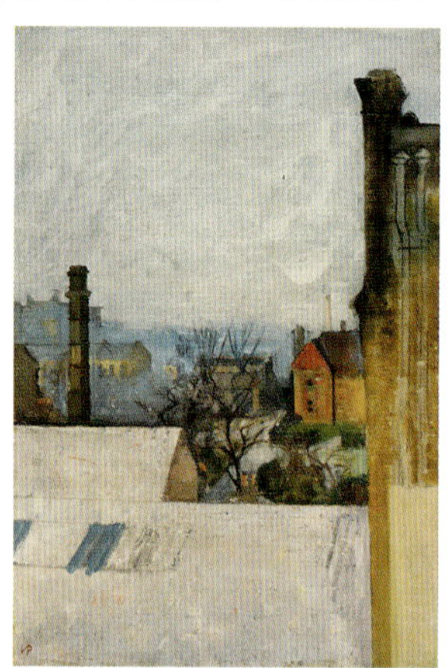

Pasmore, Victor 1909–1998
Camberwell 1943
oil on canvas 67.3 x 47
1372

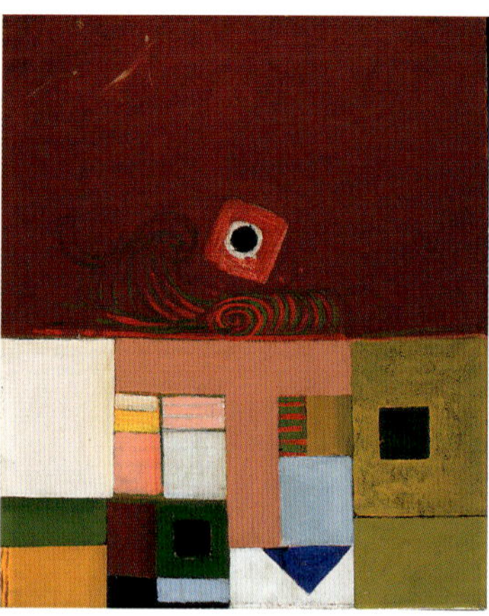

Pasmore, Victor 1909–1998
Rectangular Motif: Red and Mustard 1950
oil on canvas 61 x 50.8
1438

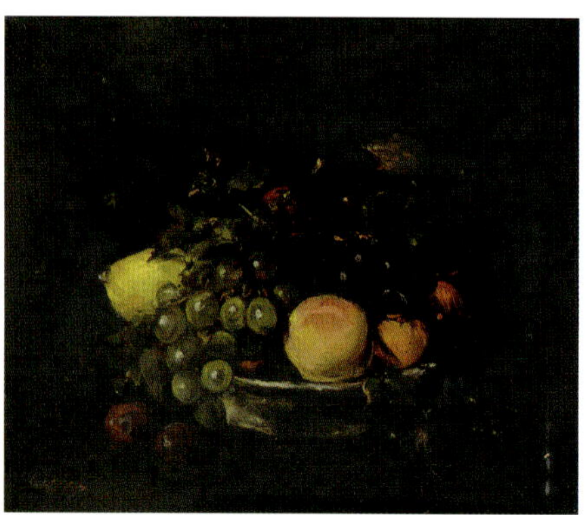

Paterson, Emil Murray 1855–1934
Bowl of Fruit
oil on wood 37.8 x 45.7
445

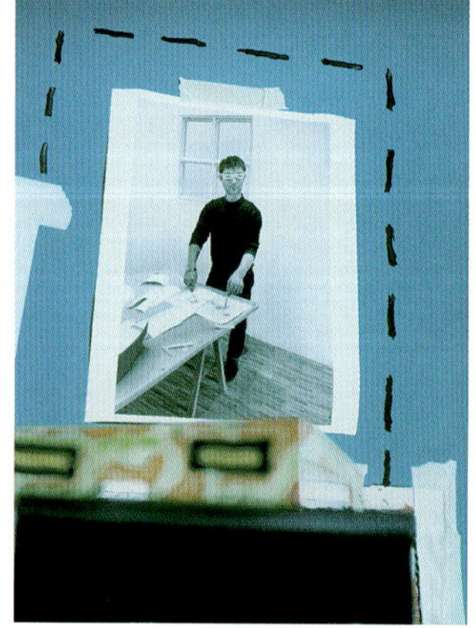

Patterson, Richard b.1963
Self Portrait 1996
oil on canvas 148 x 112
8/1996

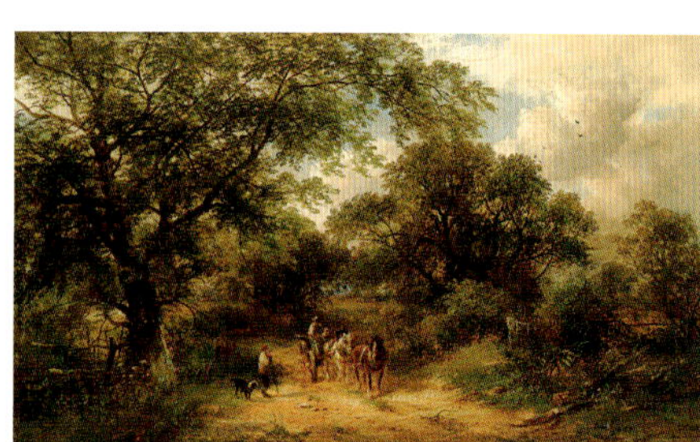

Payne, David d.1891
An English Lane
oil on canvas 61.3 x 101.7
446

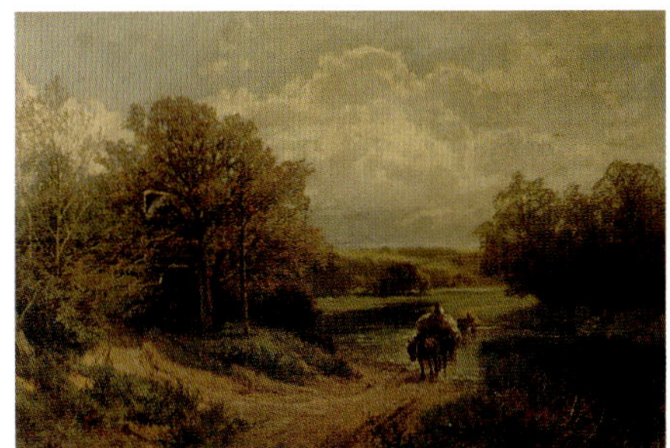

Peel, James 1811–1906
Ford-on-Trent
oil on canvas 51 x 76.3
448

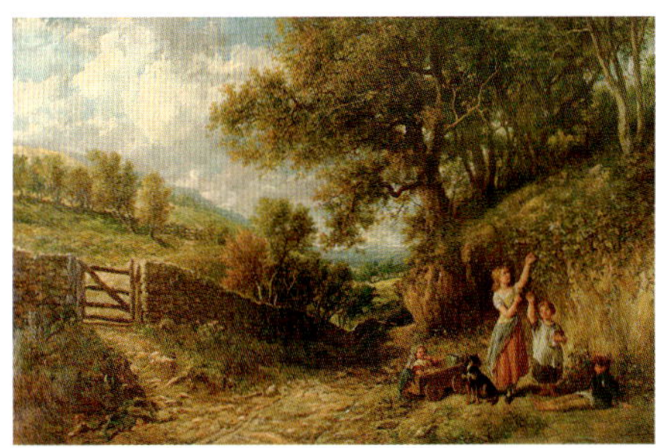

Peele, John Thomas 1822–1897
Blackberrying, Isle of Man
oil on canvas 69.3 x 106.7
447

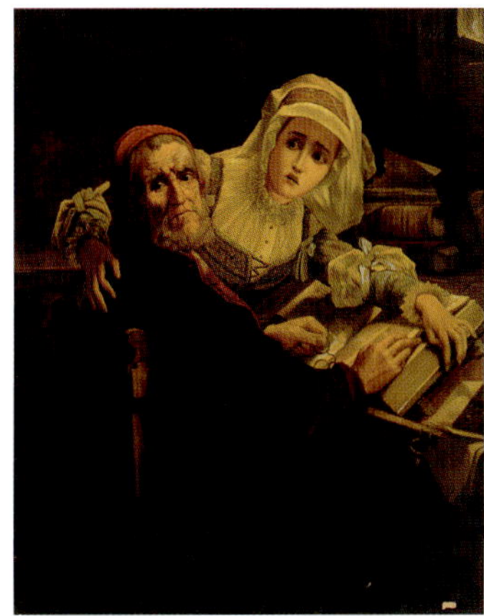

Peellaert, J.
The Forbidden Book
oil on canvas 135.5 x 108.1
665

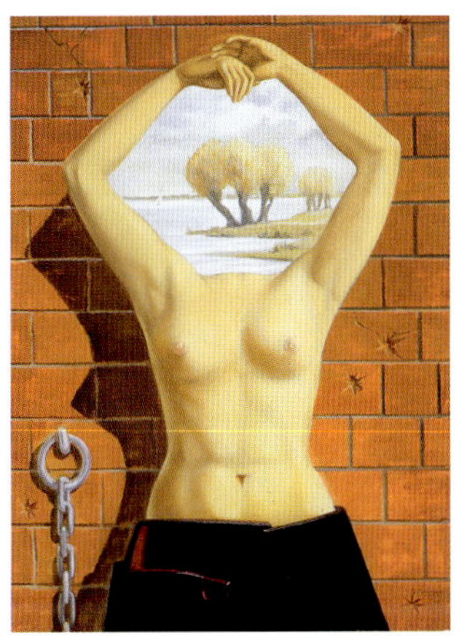

Penrose, Roland 1900–1984
Good Shooting 1939
oil on canvas 101.7 x 76.2
48/1977

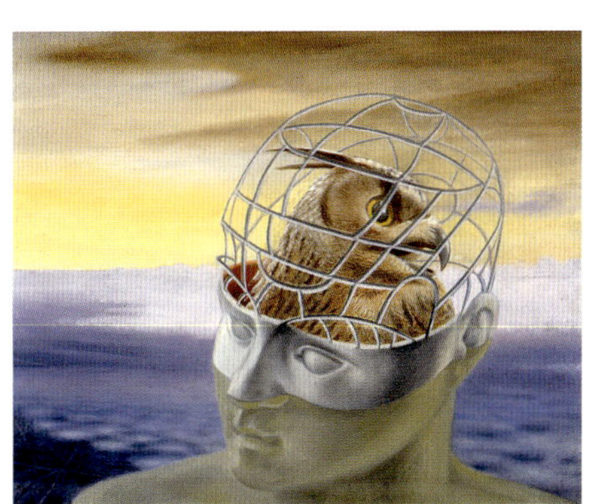

Penrose, Roland 1900–1984
The Conquest of the Air
oil on canvas 50.8 x 61.1
47/1977

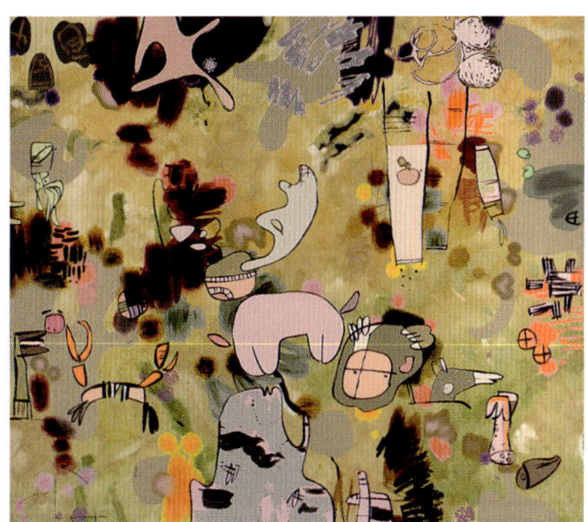

Perfect, Dan b.1965
Deerdog
oil on canvas 183 x 213
5/2006

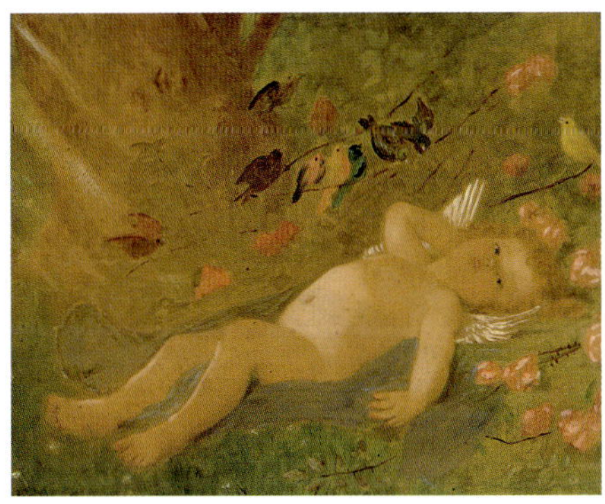

Perrault, Léon Bazile (copy after)
1832–1908
Cherub
oil on wood 21 x 27.7
443

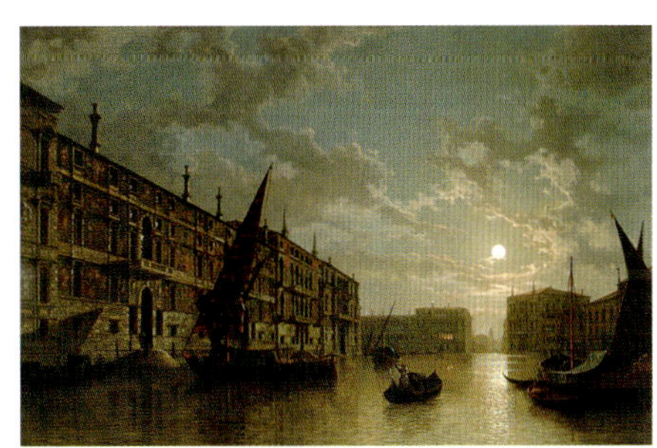

Pether, Henry active 1828–1865
Venice by Moonlight
oil on canvas 60.6 x 91.5
244

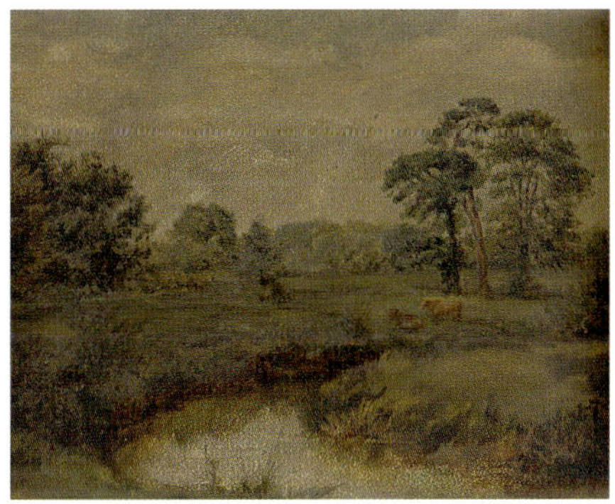

Pike, Jack
Stream and Cattle
oil on canvas 23.1 x 37.8
456

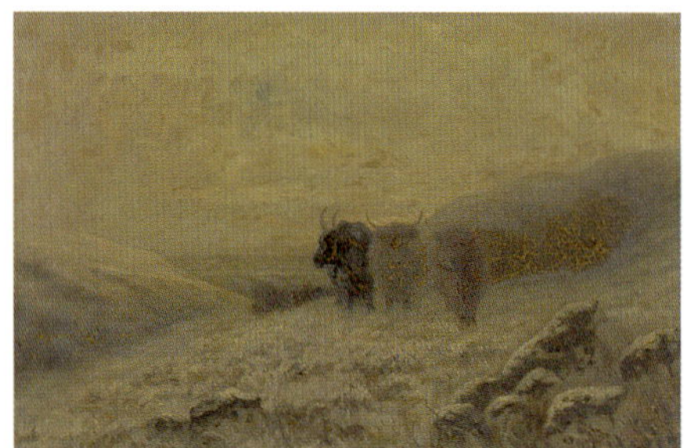

Pike, Sidney active 1880–1907
In Search of Food
oil on canvas 25.4 x 41.6
460

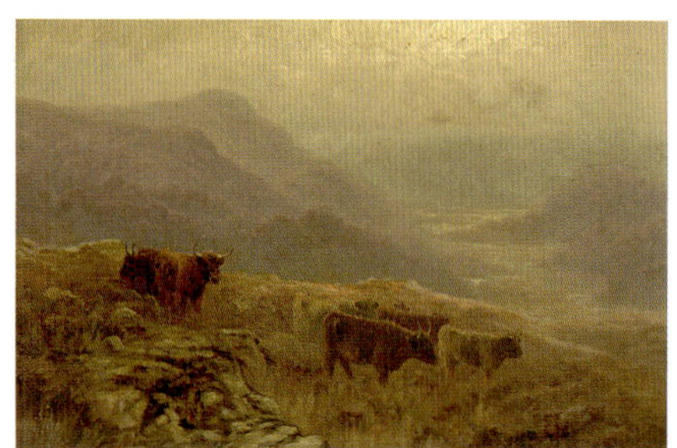

Pike, Sidney active 1880–1907
Landscape with Cattle
oil on canvas 35.5 x 40.6
457

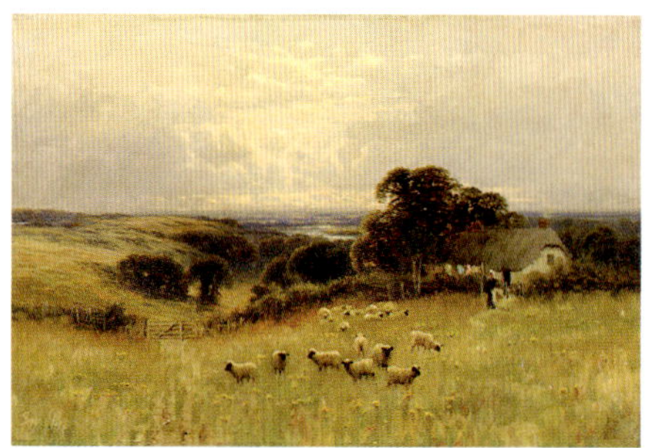

Pike, Sidney active 1880–1907
Meadow with Sheep
oil on canvas 30.5 x 45.6
458

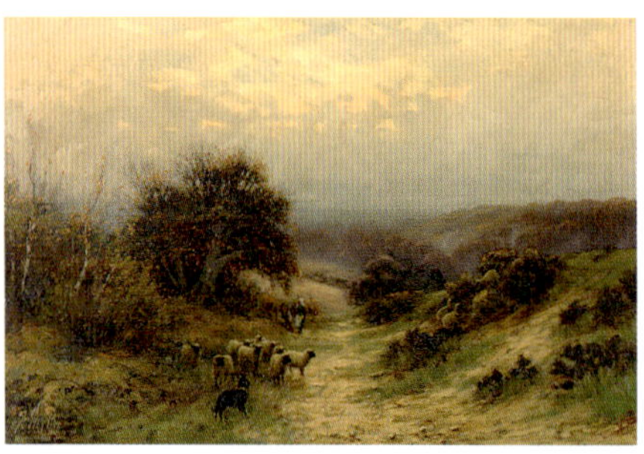

Pike, Sidney active 1880–1907
Sheep
oil on canvas 30.5 x 45.7
459

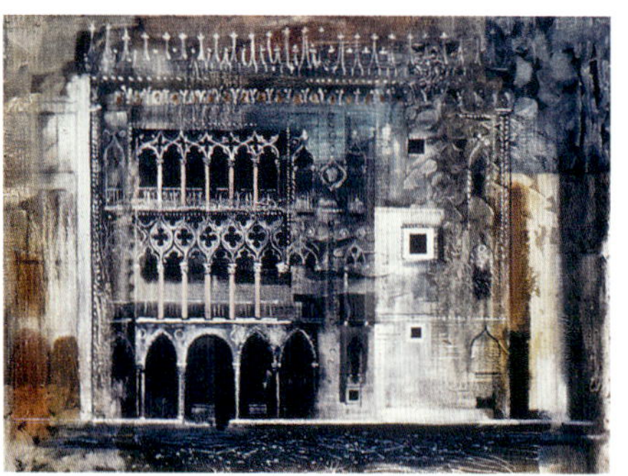

Piper, John 1903–1992
Ca' d'Oro
oil on canvas 122 x 152.5
78/1963

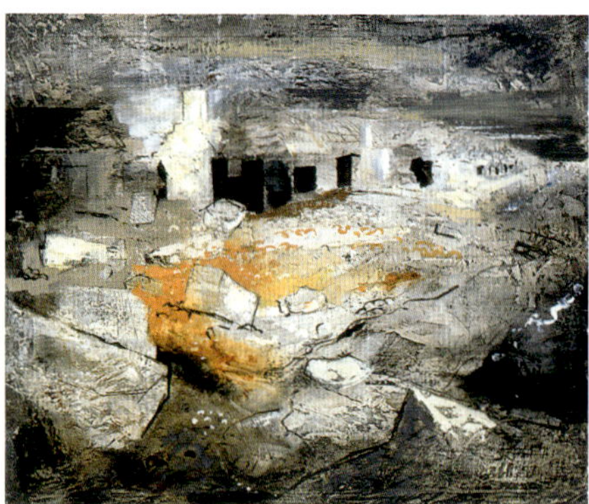

Piper, John 1903–1992
Portland Foreshore
oil on canvas 63.5 x 76.1
1361

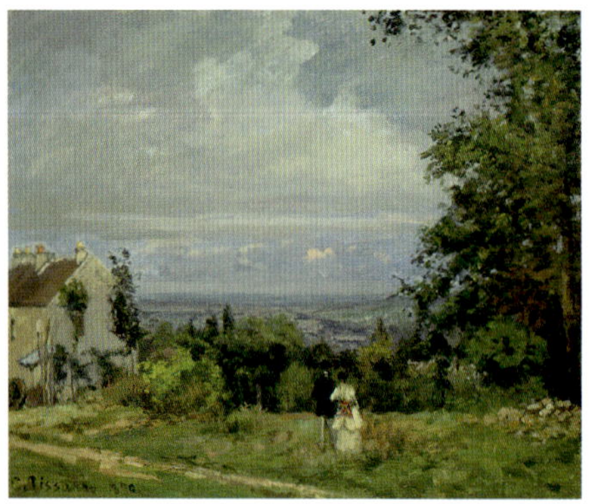

Pissarro, Camille 1830–1903
Louveciennes 1870
oil on canvas 45.8 x 55.7
461

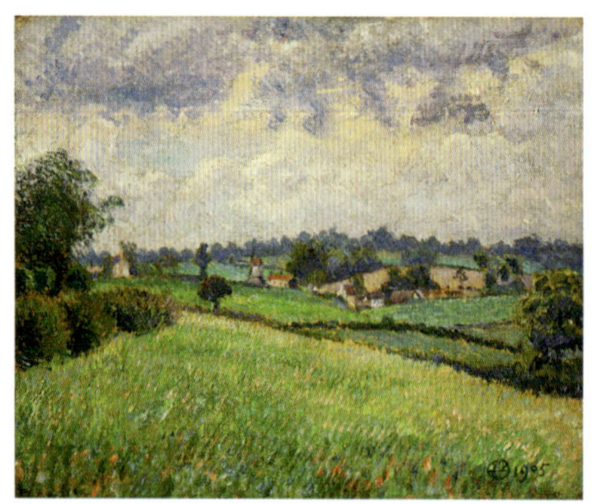

Pissarro, Lucien 1863–1944
Grey Weather, Finchingfield
oil on canvas 53.5 x 64.8
1/1975

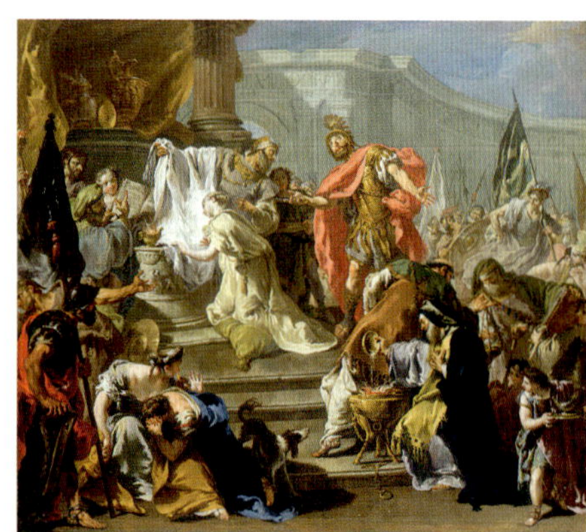

Pittoni, Giovanni Battista the younger
1687–1767
The Sacrifice of Jephtha's Daughter
oil on canvas 63.5 x 71.9
16/1969

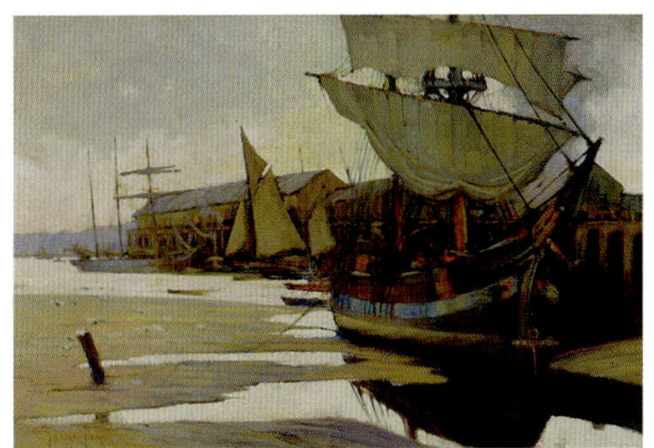

Pontin, George active 1893–1916
Town Quay, Southampton
oil on canvas 51 x 76.2
462

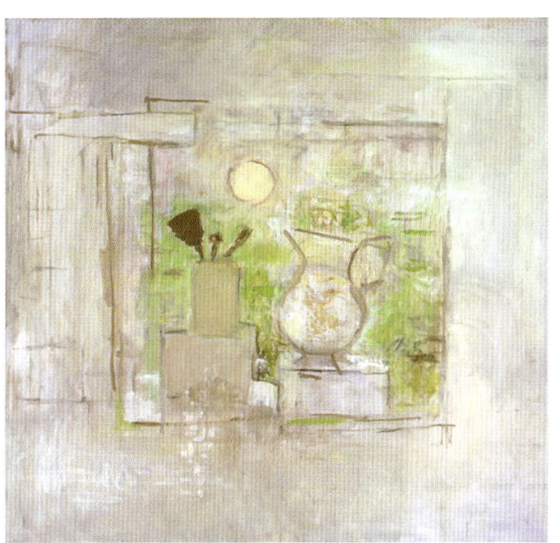

Potter, Mary 1900–1981
Studio Window 1976
oil on canvas 71 x 76
108/2002

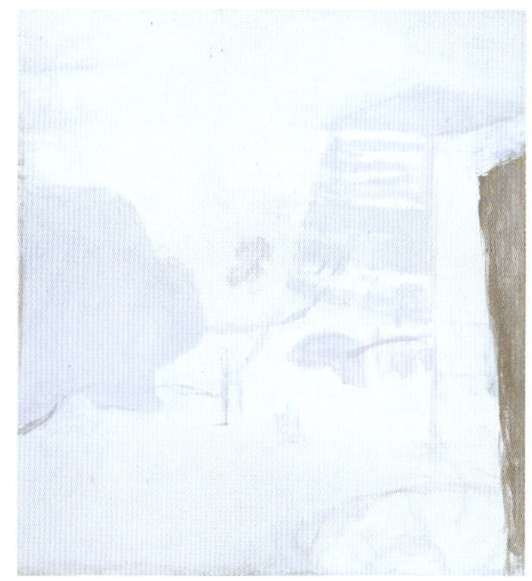

Potter, Mary 1900–1981
Little Shadow 1978
oil on board 60.6 x 55.9
51/2002

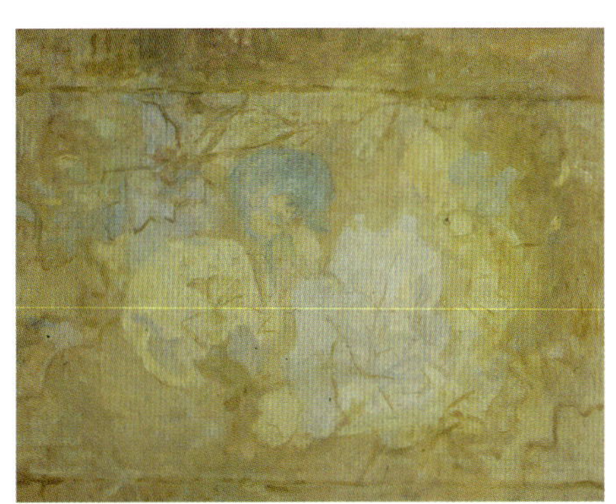

Potter, Mary 1900–1981
Frieze
oil on canvas 102 x 127
20/1978

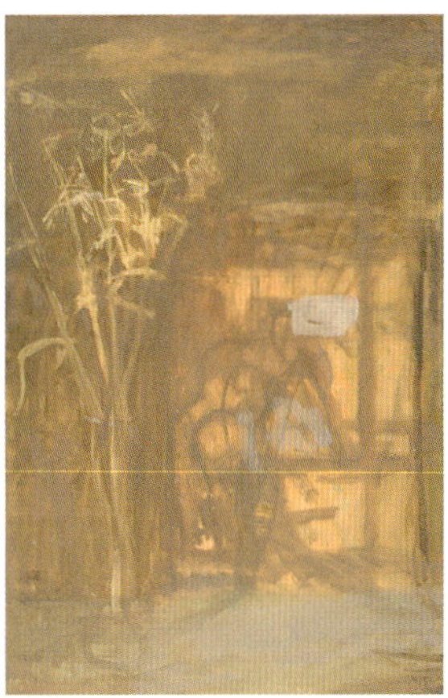

Potter, Mary 1900–1981
Grasses and Shadows 2, 1973
oil on canvas 87.6 x 62.5
7/1988

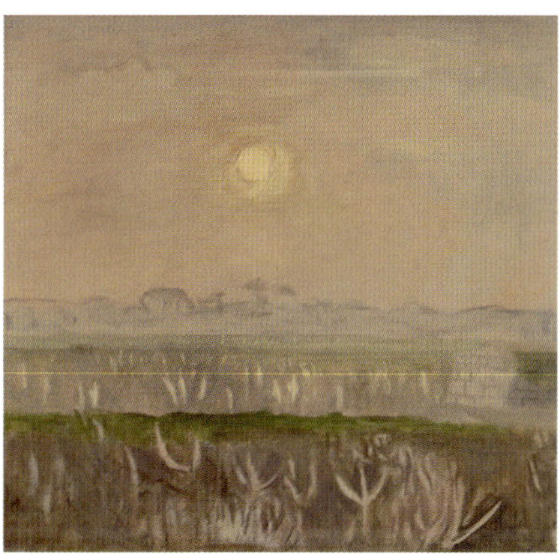

Potter, Mary 1900–1981
Setting Sun
oil on canvas 58.4 x 63.4
8/1988

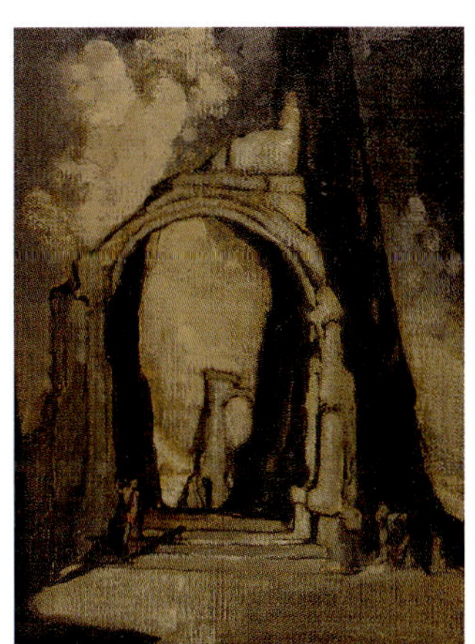

Pride, James
Ruined Arch with Figure
oil on canvas 55.1 x 42.2
110/2002

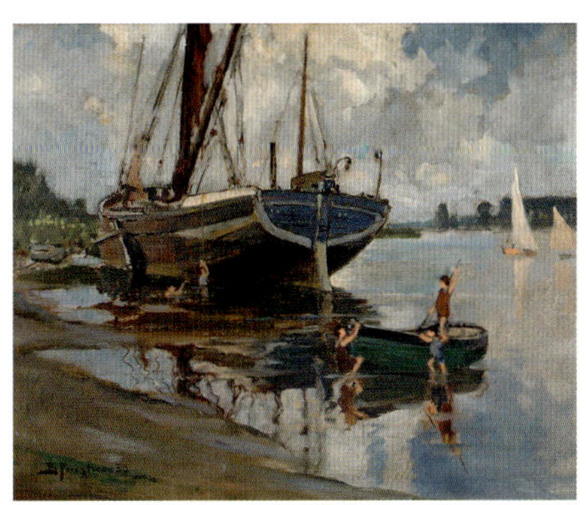

Priestman, Bertram 1868–1951
Unseaworthy
oil on canvas 40.5 x 51.8
464

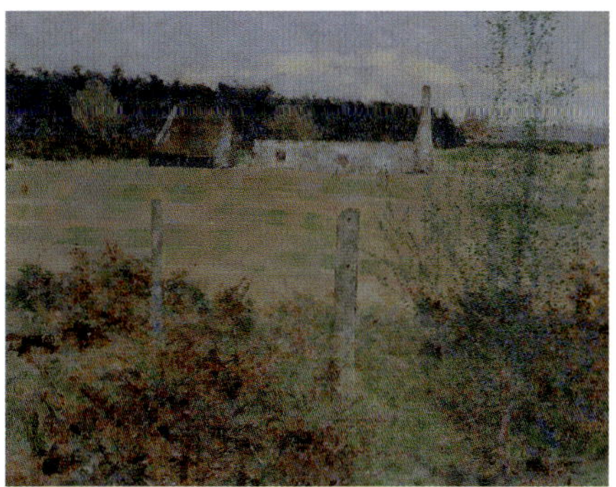

Pringle, John Quinton 1864–1925
Springtime, Ardersier (village near Inverness)
1923
oil on canvas 40 x 45.2
87/2002

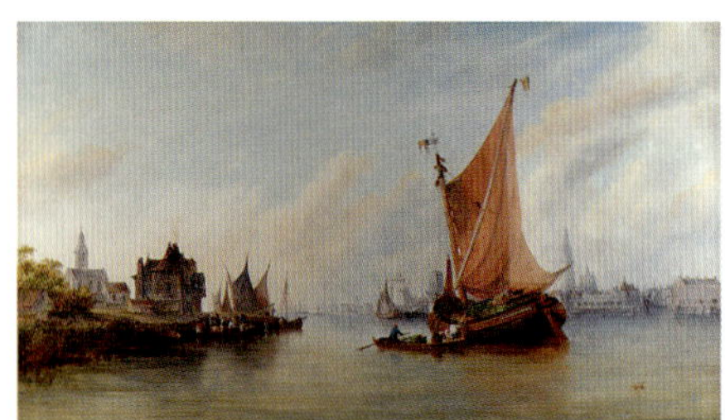

Pritchard, Edward F. D. 1809–1905
Antwerp 1864
oil on canvas 53.4 x 91.2
465

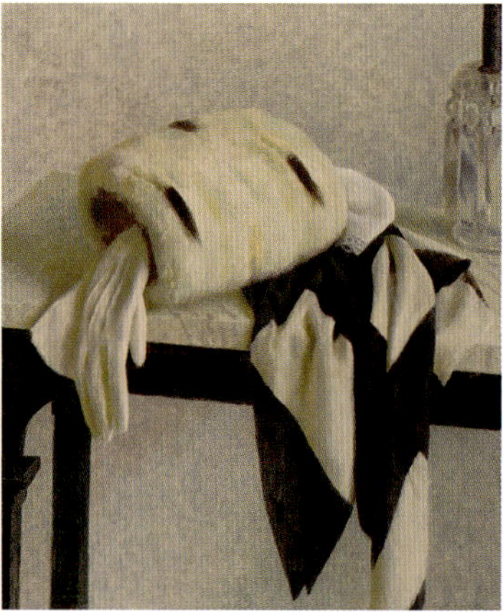

Procter, Dod 1892–1972
Black and White
oil on canvas 61 x 50.8
466

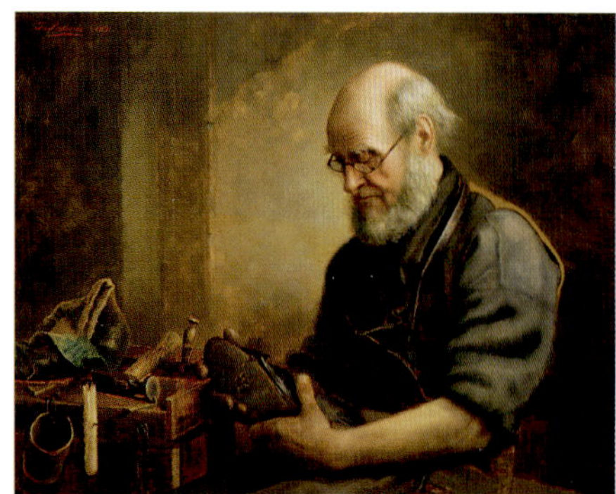

Protherore, Thomas active 1881–1904
A Sad Case before the Bench 1891
oil on canvas 56 x 71.7
467

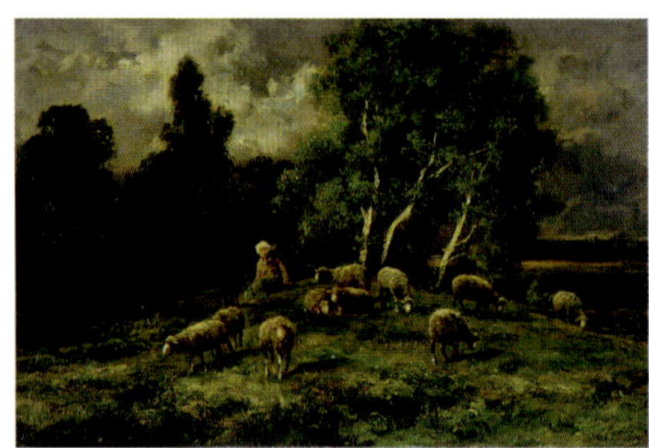

Quinton, Clément 1851–1920
Landscape with Sheep
oil on wood 28.7 x 46
469

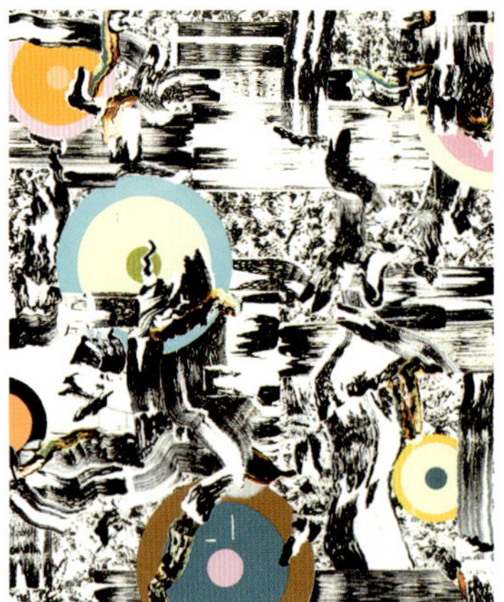

Rae, Fiona b.1963
Untitled (Fast Breeder) 1997
acrylic on canvas 152.8 x 127.1
6/1998

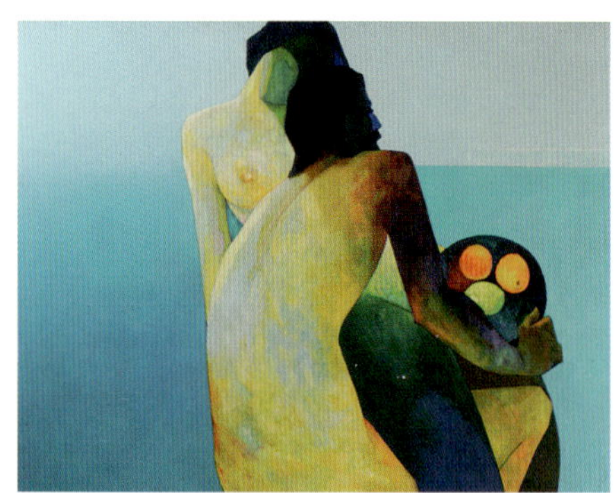

Randall, Michael 1947–2000
Daydream
oil on canvas 132.3 x 175.5
185/1975

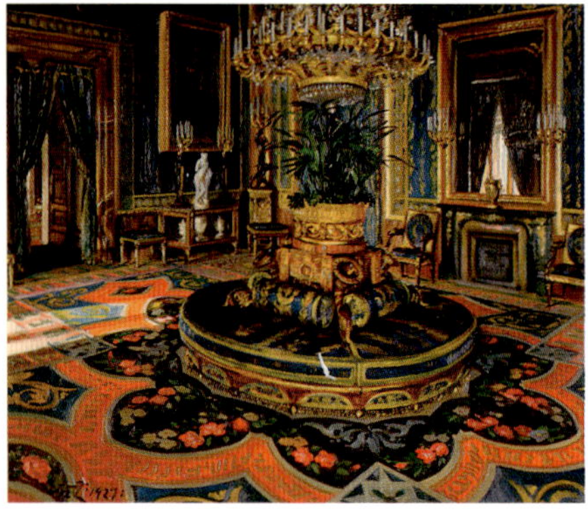

Ranken, William Bruce Ellis 1881–1941
Blue Ante Room 1927
oil on card 68 x 81.4
1285

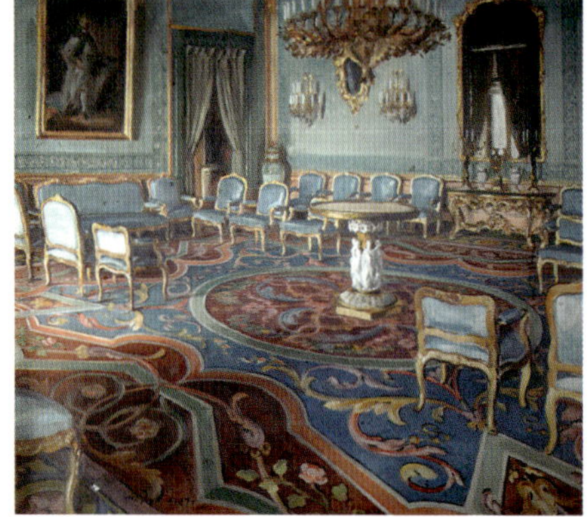

Ranken, William Bruce Ellis 1881–1941
Salon of Charles III 1927
oil on card 74.5 x 84.6
1286

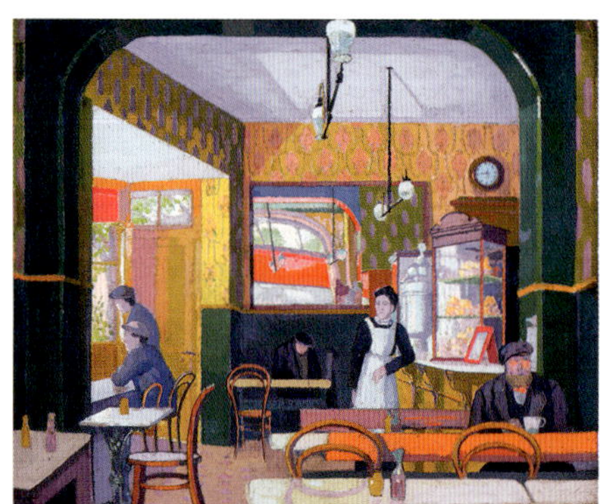

Ratcliffe, William Whitehead 1870–1955
The Coffee House 1914
oil on canvas 51 x 61.3
1436

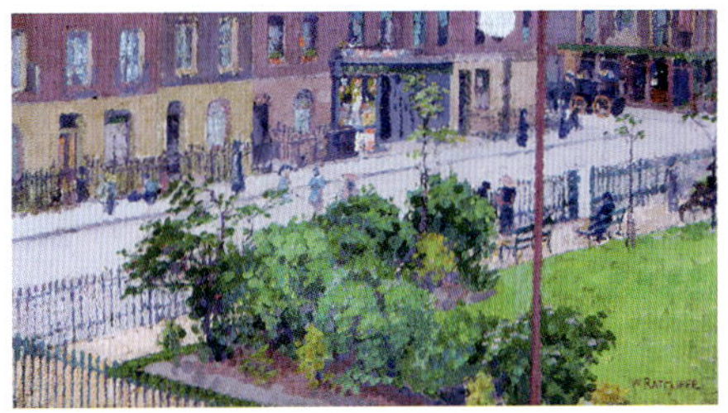

Ratcliffe, William Whitehead 1870–1955
Clarence Gardens
oil on canvas 34 x 57.2
L7Q

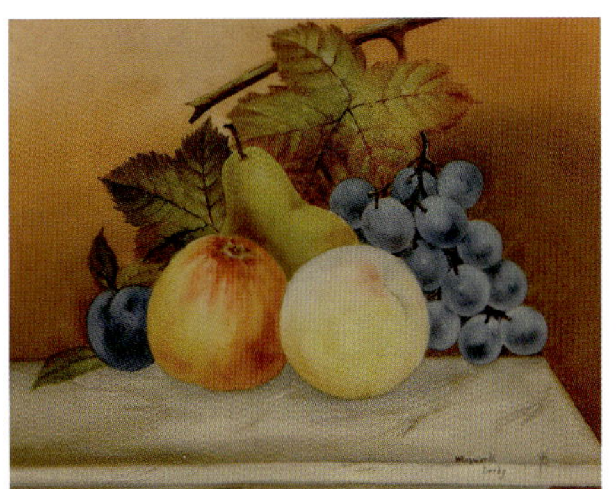

Rayworth, William
Still Life: Blue Grapes
oil on porcelain 27 x 32.5
6/1989

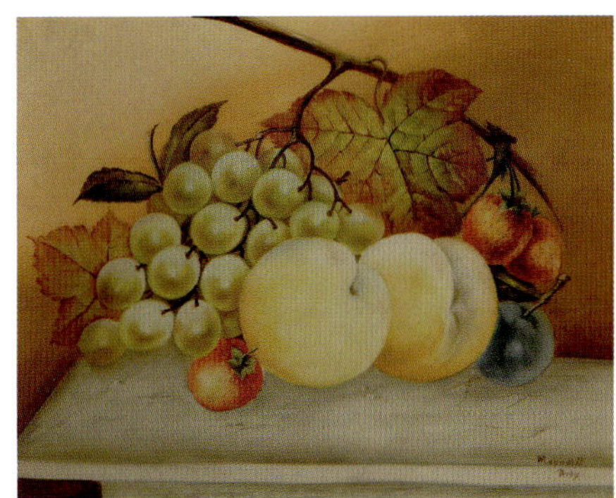

Rayworth, William
Still Life: White Grapes
oil on porcelain 27 x 32.5
7/1989

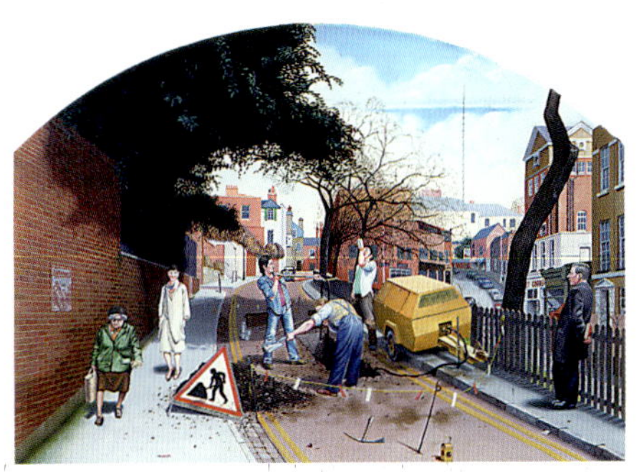

Redfern, David b.1947
Work 1977
oil on canvas 87.2 x 121.8
16/1979

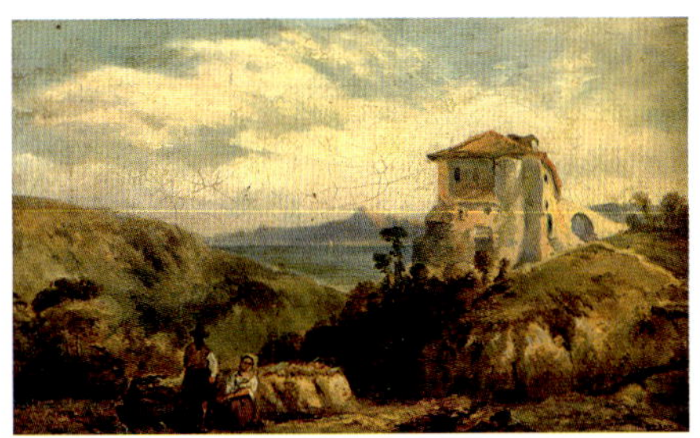

Reed, William Thomas 1845–1881
Continental Landscape 1862
oil on canvas 18.3 x 30.2
473

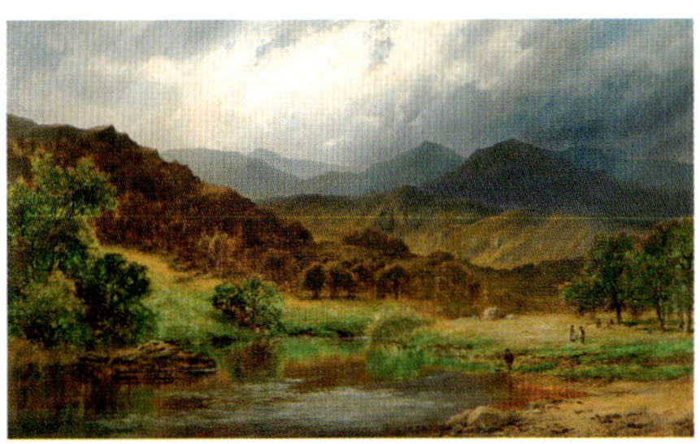

Reed, William Thomas 1845–1881
Early Morning, Epping Forest 1876
oil on canvas 45.7 x 76.2
472

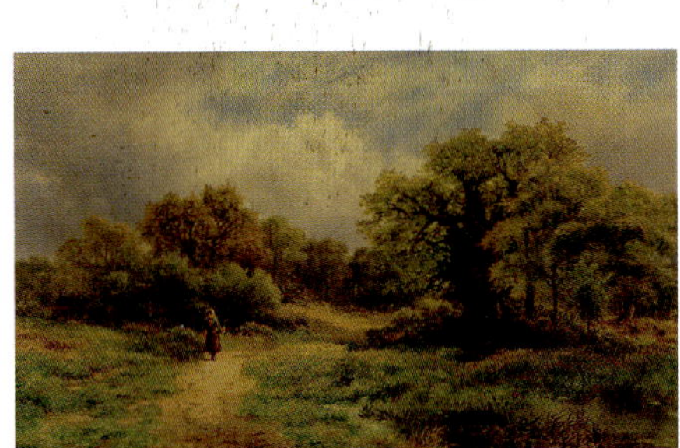

Reed, William Thomas 1845–1881
In the Dolwyddelan Valley
oil on canvas 47.1 x 77.5
471

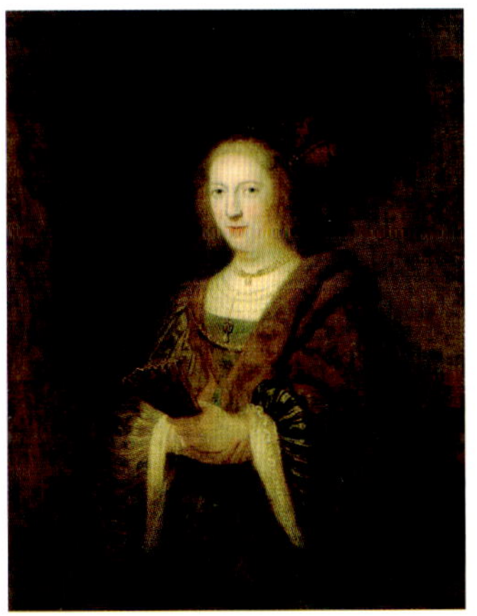

Rembrandt van Rijn (copy after) 1606–1669
Lady Holding a Fan
oil on canvas 111.3 x 85.8
1256

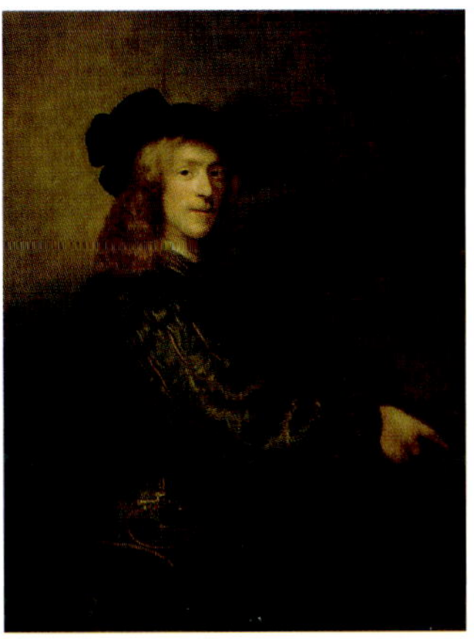

Rembrandt van Rijn (copy after) 1606–1669
Portrait of a Gentleman
oil on canvas 112.3 x 86.3
1257

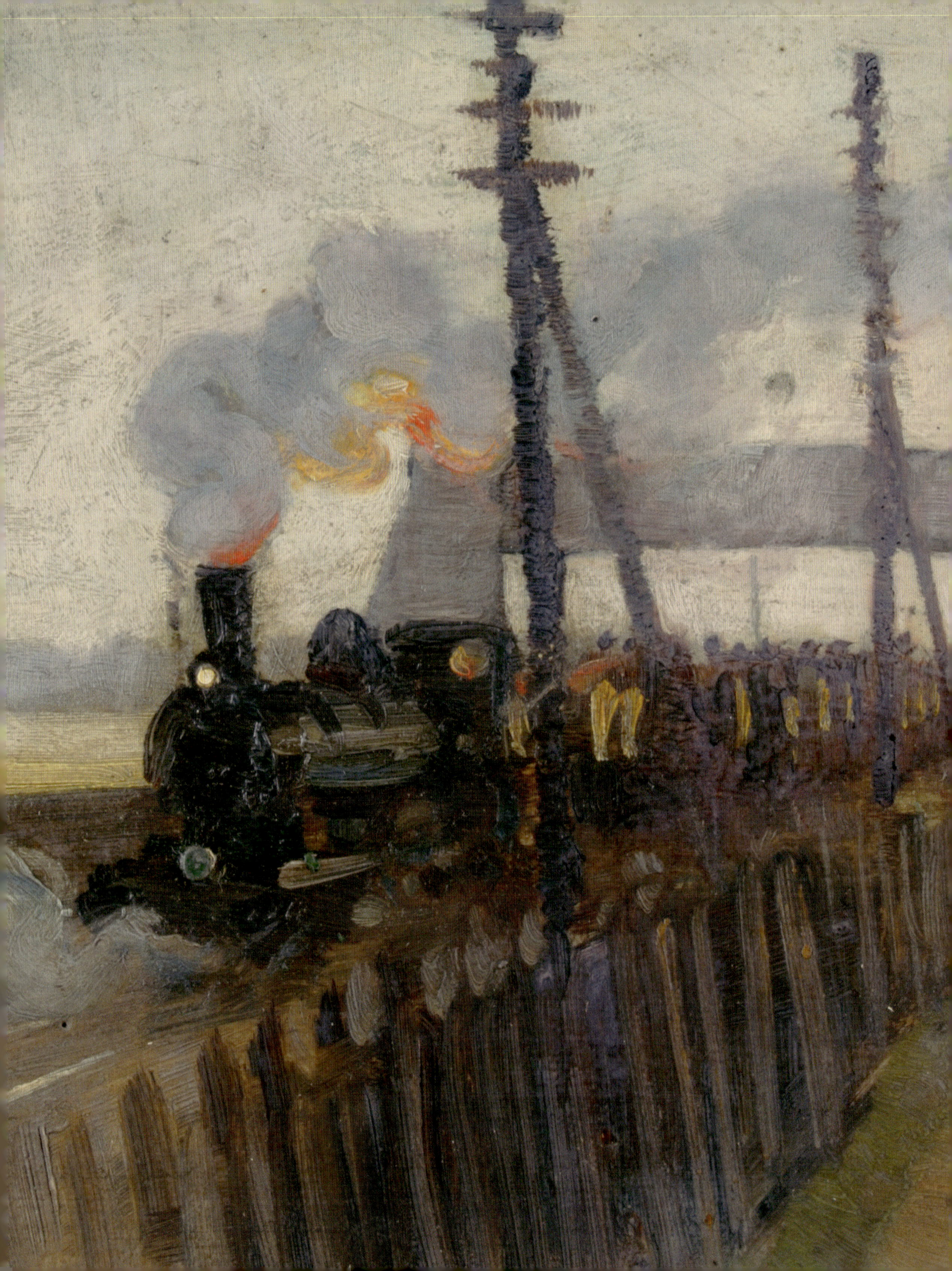

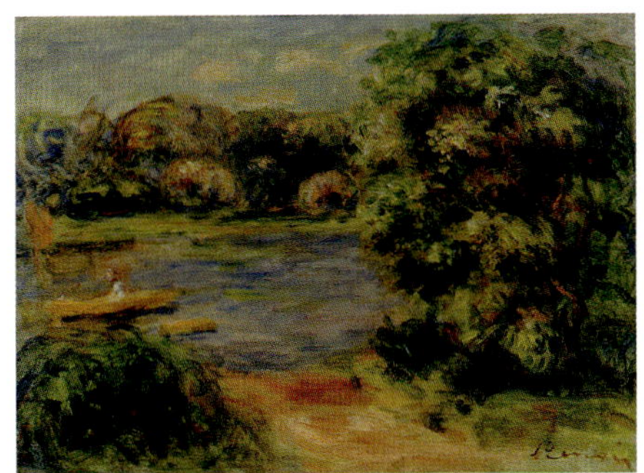

Renoir, Pierre-Auguste 1841–1919
The Boat on the Lake 1901
oil on canvas 24.3 x 33.2
54/2006

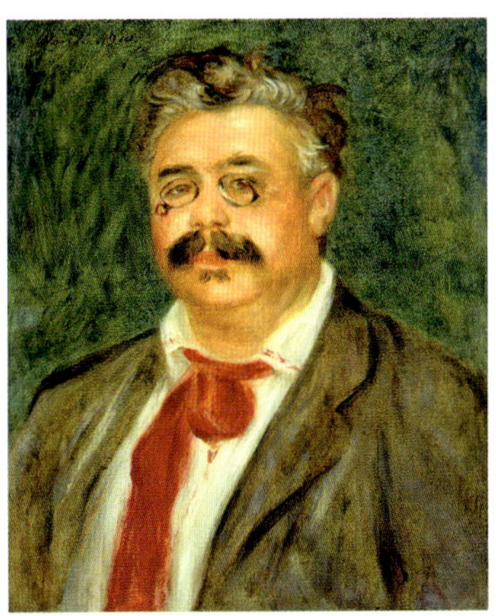

Renoir, Pierre-Auguste 1841–1919
Wilhelm Muhlfeld 1910
oil on canvas 55 x 45.8
3/1964

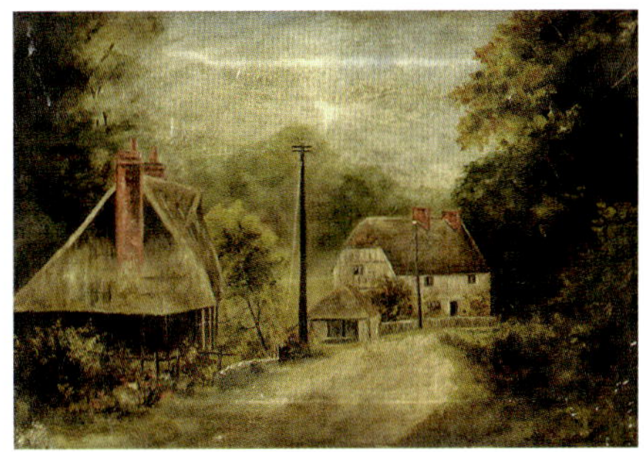

Revitt, E. M.
Fishers, Odiham
oil on canvas 25.3 x 35.5
474

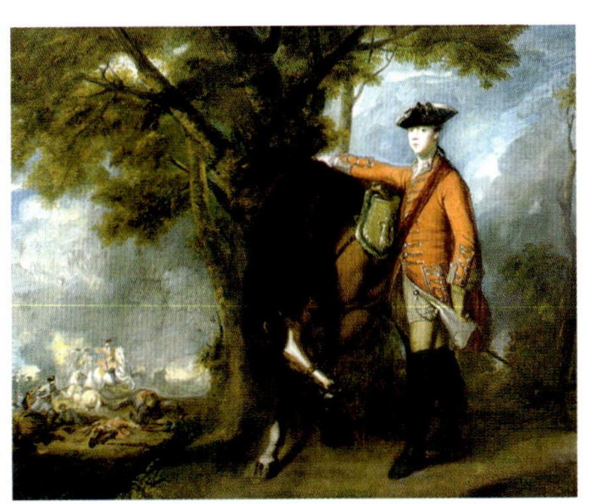

Reynolds, Joshua 1723–1792
Cornet Nehemiah Winter, 11th Dragoons 1759
oil on canvas 113.5 x 137.5
1482

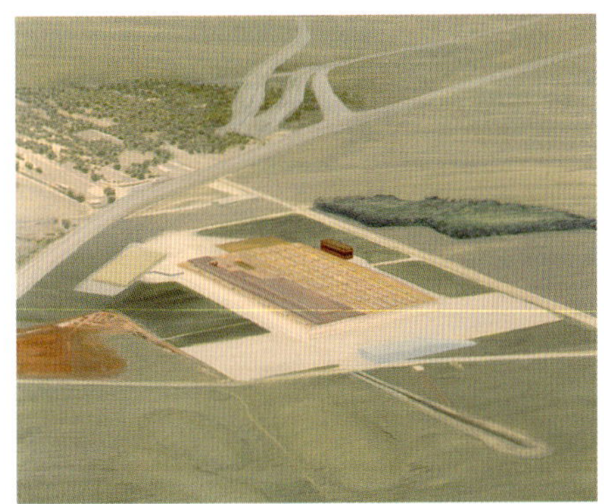

Rhodes, Carol b.1959
Factory Roof, Countryside 2002
oil on board 46.9 x 56.9
2/2004

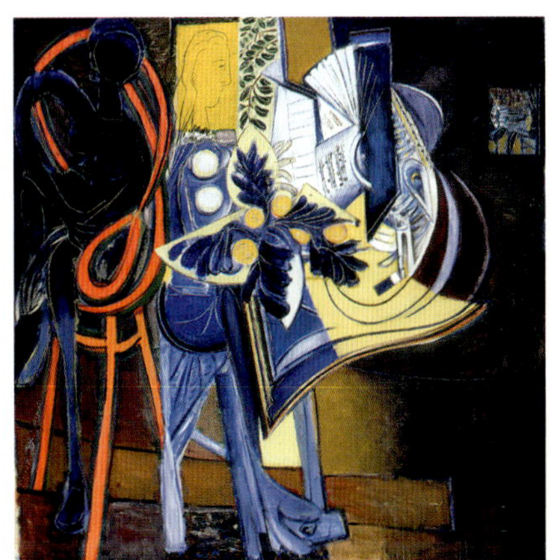

Richards, Ceri Geraldus 1903–1971
Girl at Piano 1949
oil on canvas 89 x 89
1439

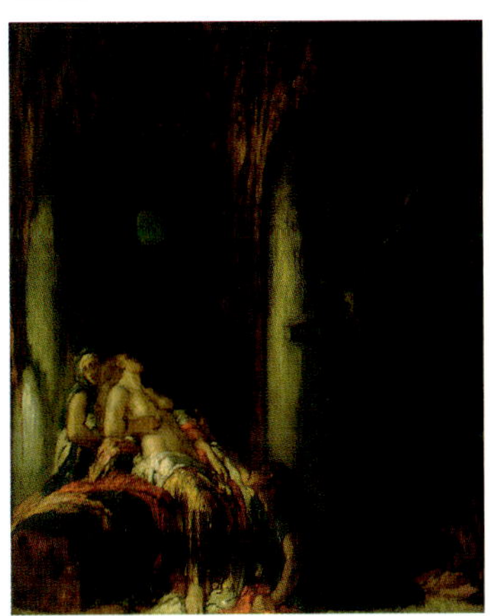

Ricketts, Charles S. 1866–1931
The Death of Cleopatra
oil on canvas 76.5 x 63.4
7/1972

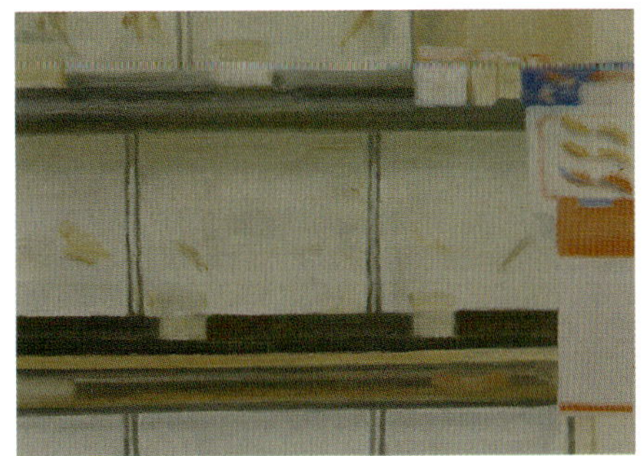

Rieck, Hellmuth
Canaries 1980
oil on card 29.3 x 31.9
82/2002

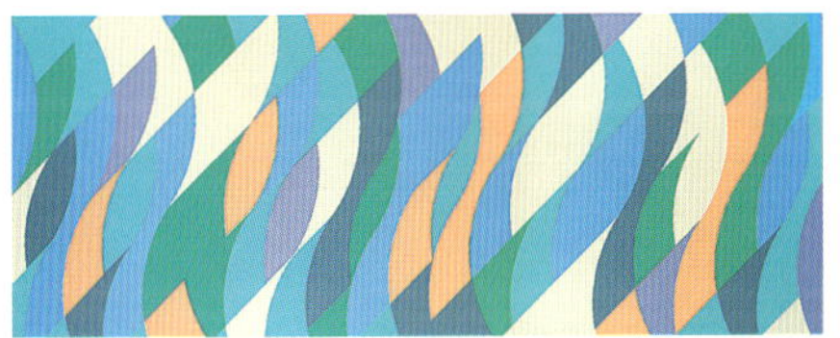

Riley, Bridget b.1931
Red Movement 2005
oil on linen 135.3 x 352.4
1/2007

Facing page: Pontin, George, active 1893–1916, *New Millbrook* (detail), 1900, Southampton City Museums, (p. 162)

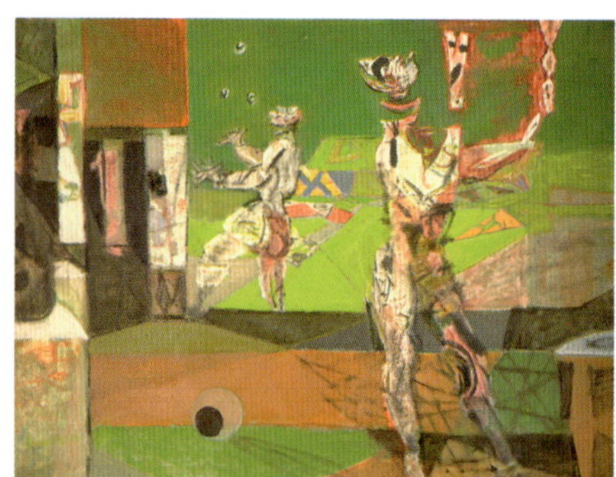

Robb, Brian 1913–1979
Jugglers
oil on canvas 96.9 x 129.7
1435

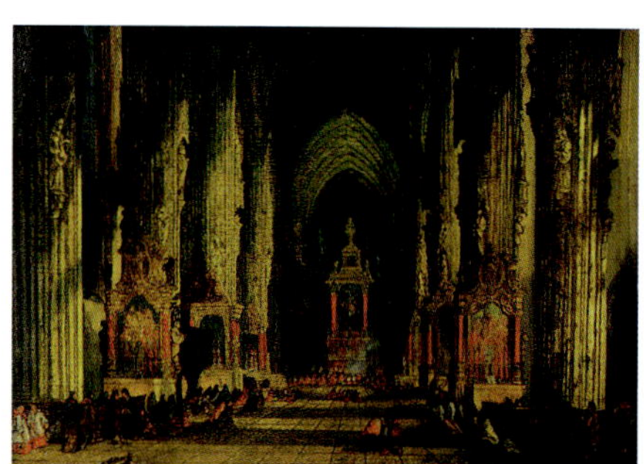

Roberts, David 1796–1864
Interior of St Stephen's Church, Vienna 1859
oil on board 21 x 30.5
25/1963

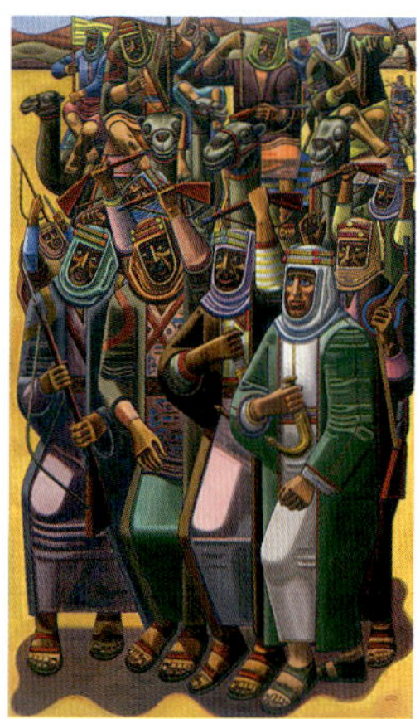

Roberts, William Patrick 1895–1980
Revolt in the Desert 1952
oil on canvas 244.7 x 144.8
7/1958

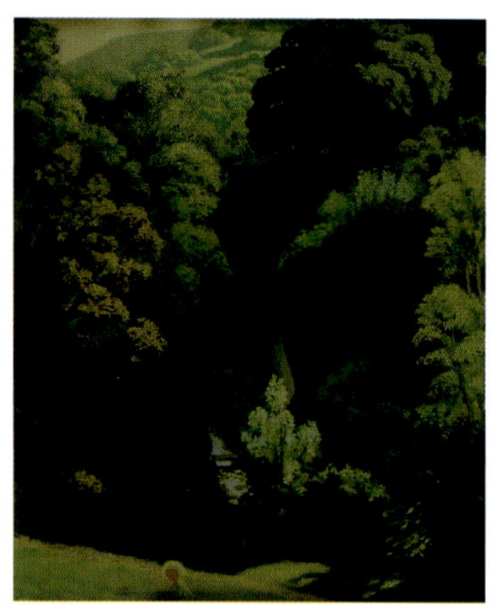

Robertson, Walford Graham 1866–1948
Fairyland, under Hindhead
oil on canvas 127.5 x 101.7
1424

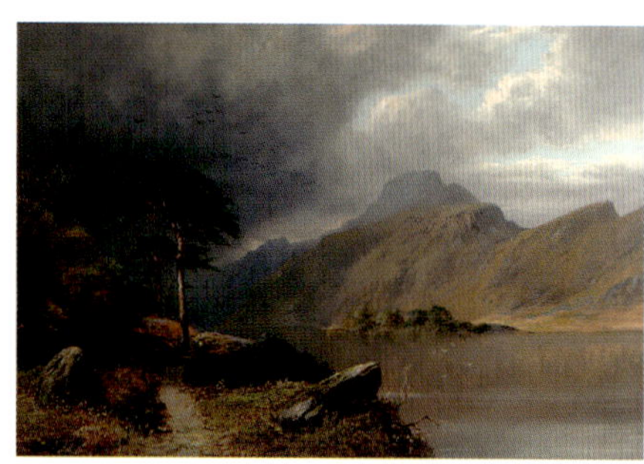

Roe, Clarence 1850–1909
Highland Landscape
oil on canvas 61 x 91.5
1003

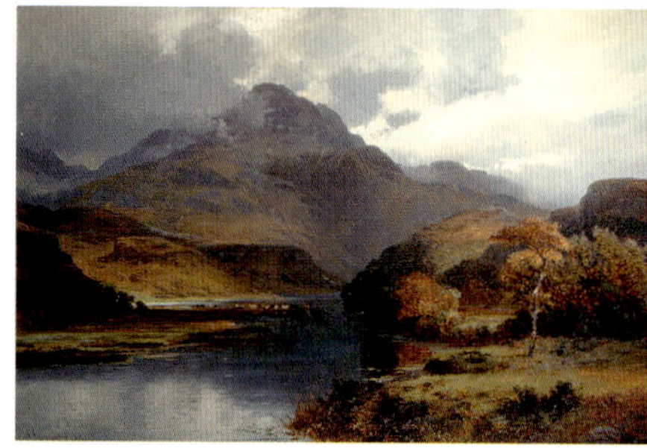

Roe, Clarence 1850–1909
Highland Landscape
oil on canvas 61 x 91.5
1004

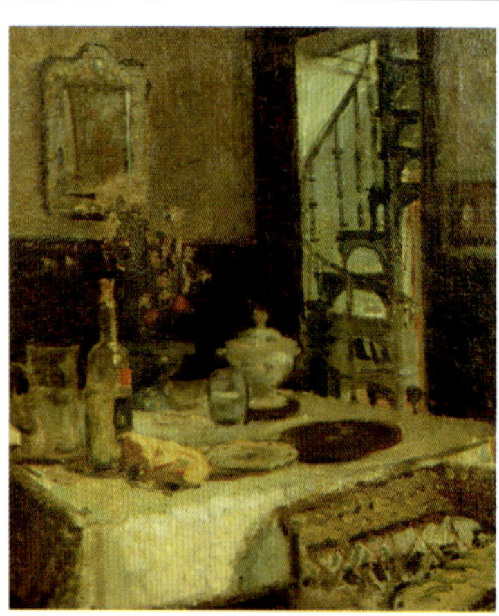

Rogers, Claude 1907–1979
Spiral Staircase 1936
oil on canvas 61.3 x 51
478

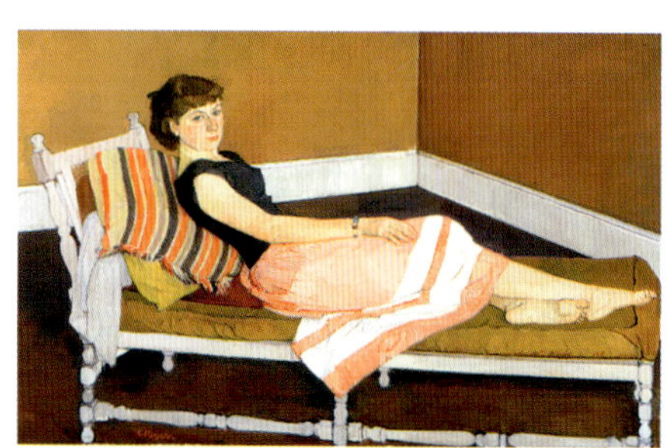

Rogers, Claude 1907–1979
Miss Lynn 1951
oil on canvas 108 x 177.3
1419

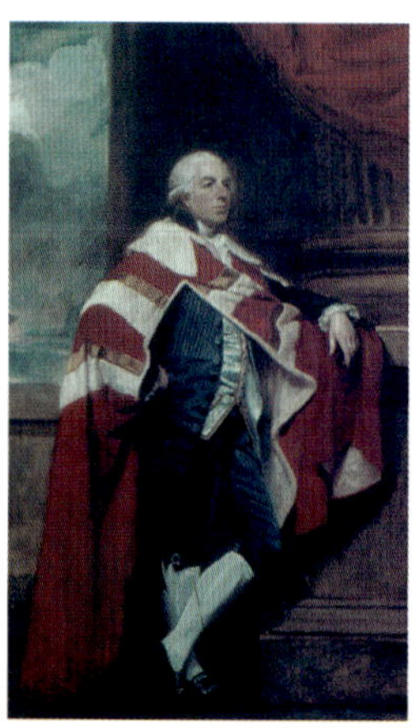

Romney, George 1734–1802
Lord Ducie 1792
oil on canvas 239.5 x 147.2
1491

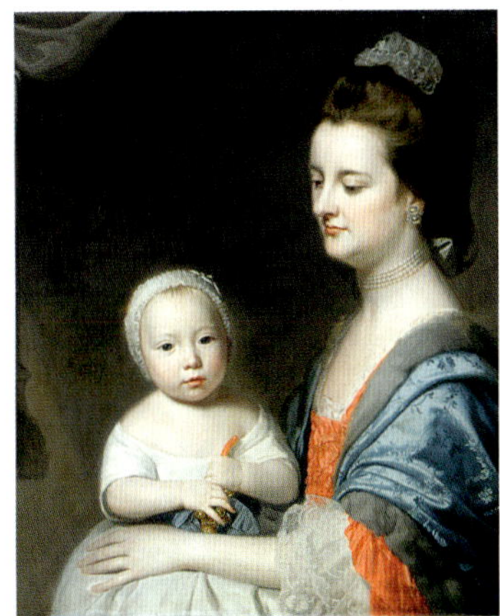

Romney, George 1734–1802
Mrs Marton and Her Son Oliver
oil on canvas 75.6 x 63.5
1421

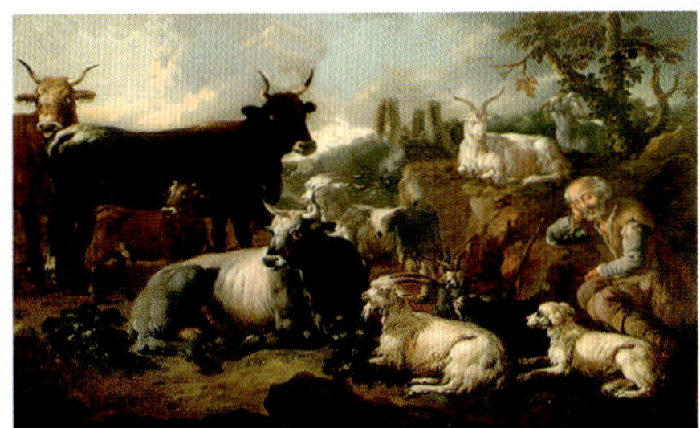

Roos, Philipp Peter 1657–1706
Landscape with Cattle
oil on canvas 122 x 170.3
582

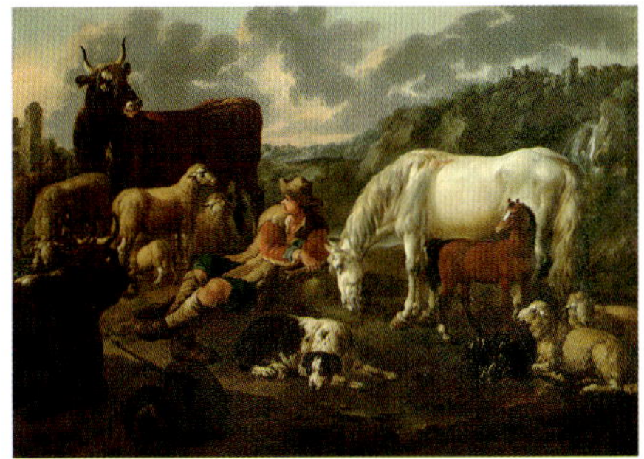

Roos, Philipp Peter 1657–1706
Landscape with Cattle
oil on canvas 122 x 172.5
583

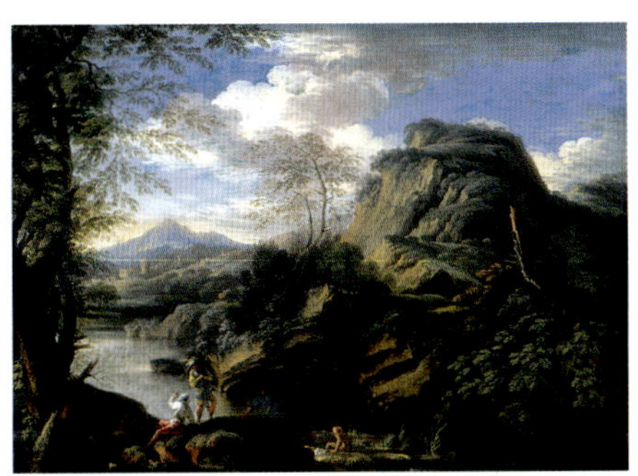

Rosa, Salvator 1615–1673
A Mountain Landscape
oil on canvas 98 x 136.5
1/1961

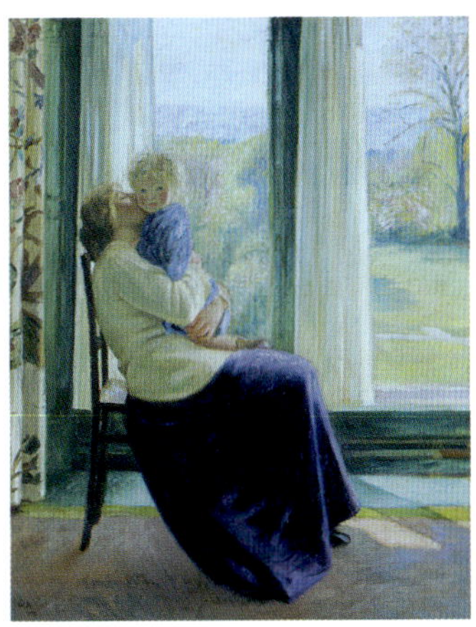

Rothenstein, William 1872–1945
Spring, the Morning Room
oil on canvas 97.3 x 76.3
481

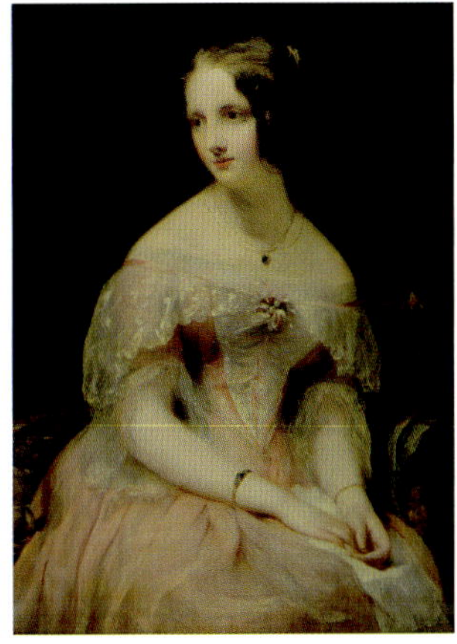

Rothwell, Richard 1800–1868
Portrait of a Lady
oil on canvas 97 x 71.8
482

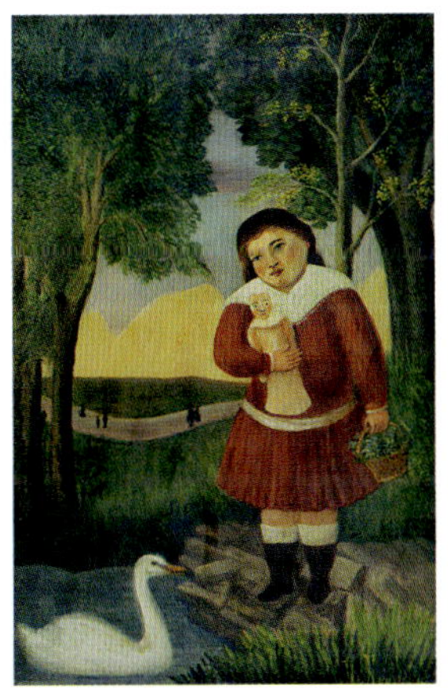

Rousseau, Henri 1844–1910
Child with a Doll in a Landscape
oil on canvas 37.8 x 23.9
82/1963

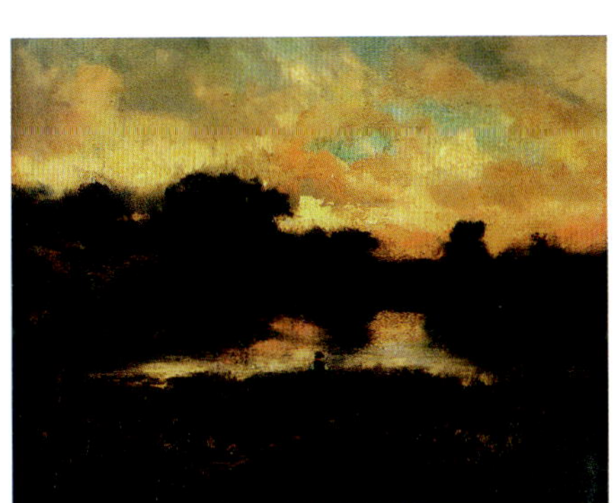

Rousseau, Théodore 1812–1867
Evening
oil on canvas 20.4 x 25.7
10/2004

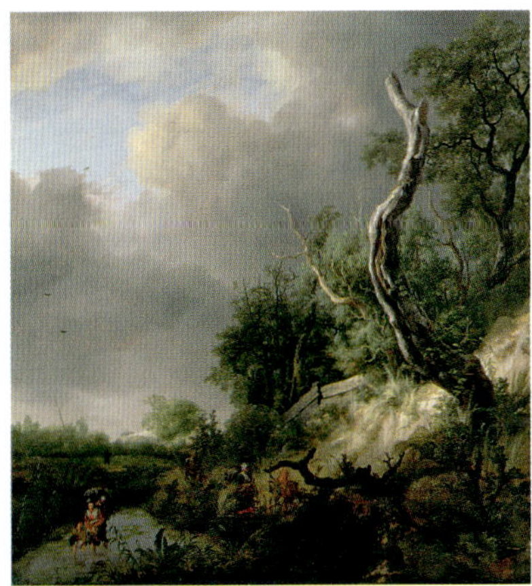

Ruisdael, Jacob van 1628/1629–1682
The Dunes near Haarlem
oil on canvas 70 x 65.6
1/1964

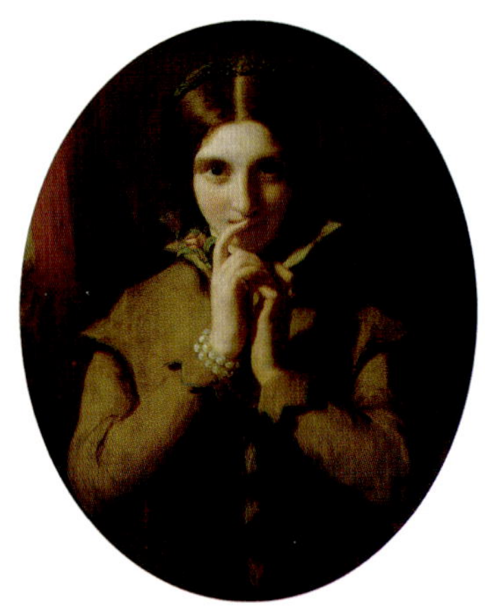

Sant, James 1820–1916
Enigma
oil on canvas 75.5 x 63.3
484

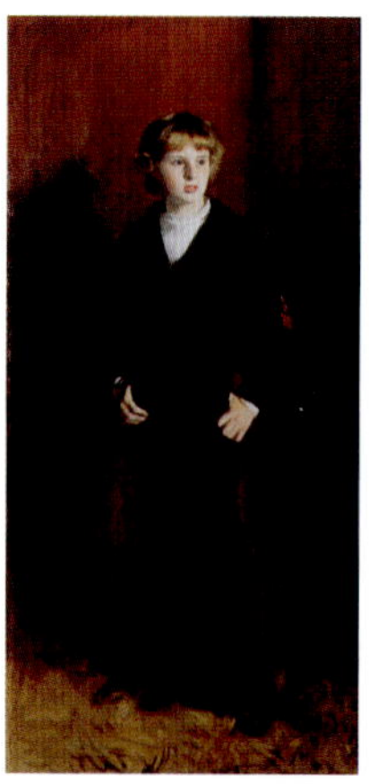

Sargent, John Singer 1856–1925
Major E. C. Harrison 1887
oil on canvas 172.8 x 83.6
485

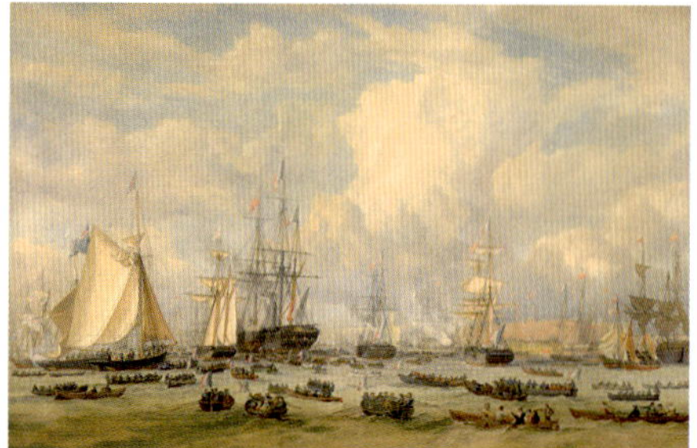

Schetky, John Christian 1778–1874
The Arrival of the King of France
oil on canvas 61 x 94.3
486

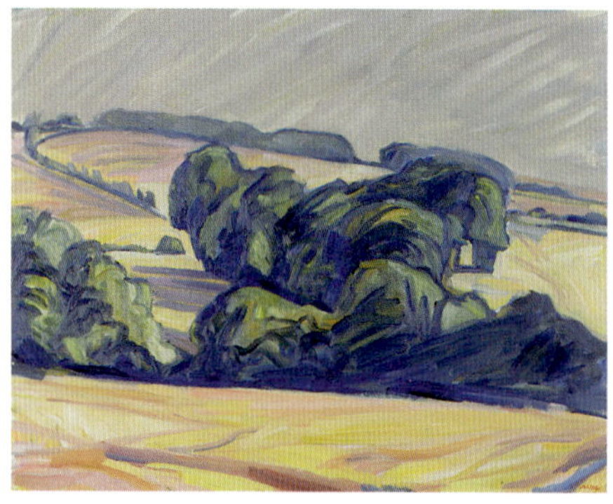

Schlee, Nick b.1931
The Ridgeway from Letcombe Basset 2004
oil on board 81 x 102
2/2005

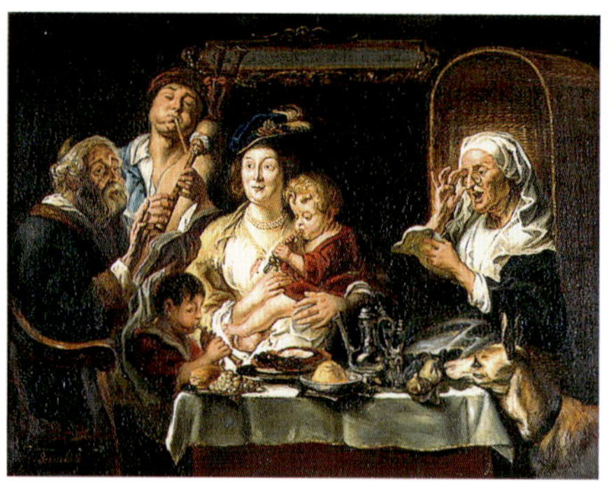

Scholowei, M.
Family Group
oil on canvas 40.8 x 53.3
487

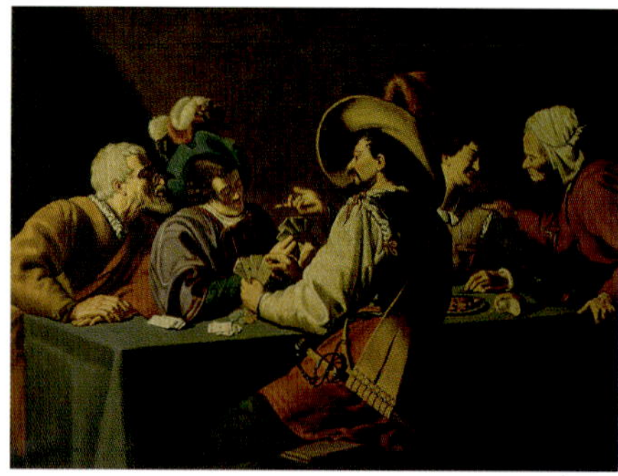

Scholowei, M.
The Cheat
oil on canvas 40.7 x 53.4
488

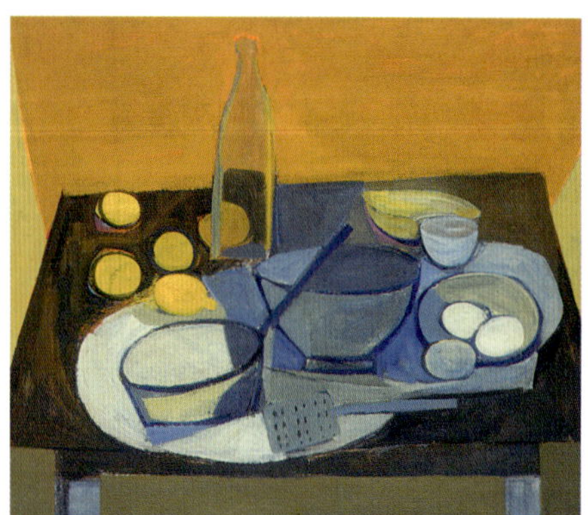

Scott, William George 1913–1989
Kitchen Still Life 1948
oil on canvas 57.9 x 65.9
L7S

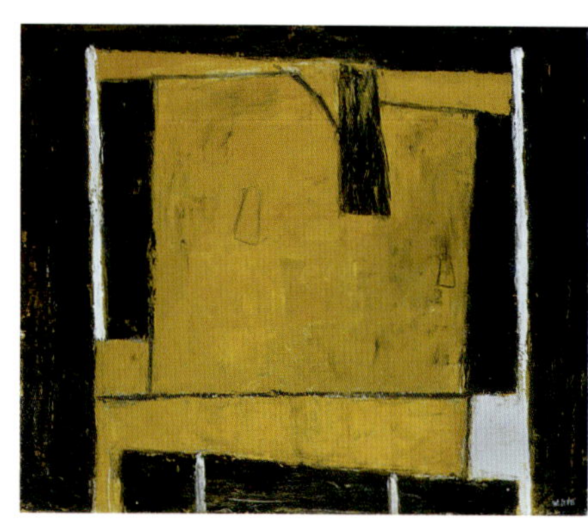

Scott, William George 1913–1989
Still Life: Coffee Pot I 1952
oil on canvas 67.2 x 81
42/2002

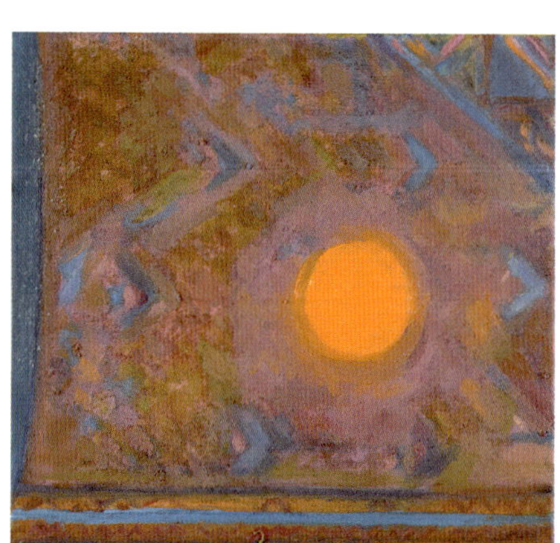

Scott Wilkie, Pamela b.1937
Trio 1 No.1, Version 2 (from the series 'In Progress') 1999
oil on linen 29 x 31.4
53/2002

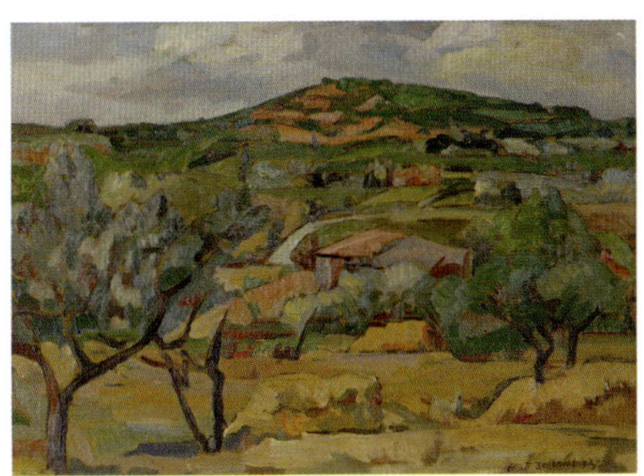

Seabrooke, Elliot 1886–1950
Landscape in the South of France 1929
oil on canvas 44.5 x 61.8
489

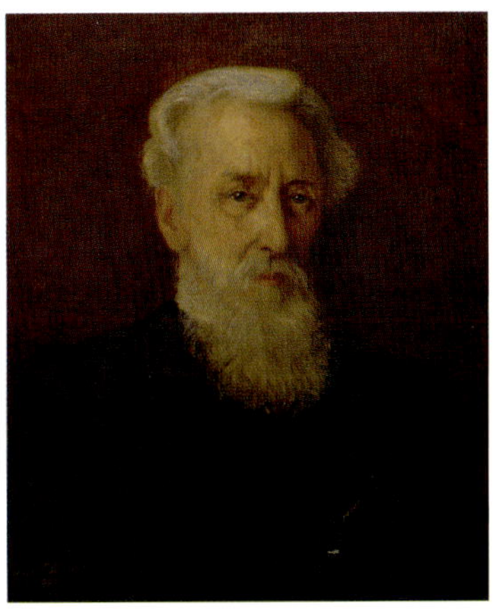

Seaward, Mary L. active 1903–1915
Robert Chipperfield, JP 1903
oil on canvas 61 x 50.8
490

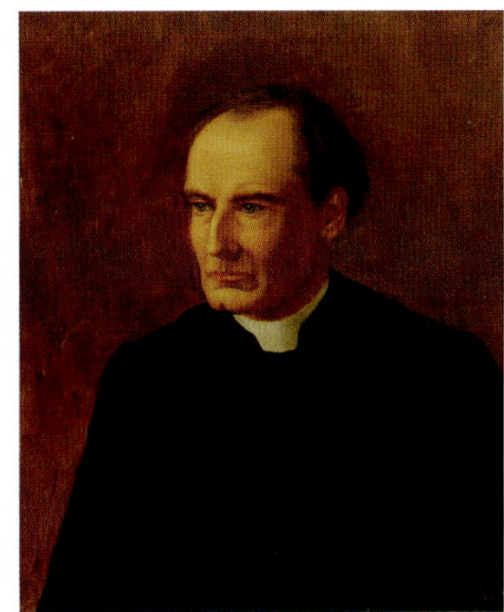

Seaward, Mary L. active 1903–1915
Canon Basil Wilberforce
oil on canvas 75.8 x 63.2
491

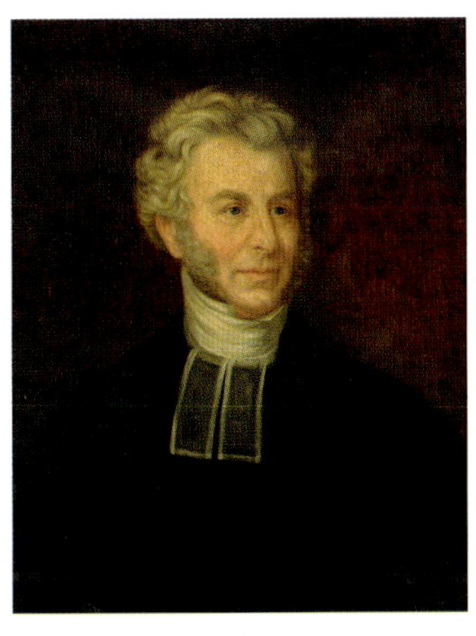

Seaward, Mary L. active 1903–1915
The Reverend Thomas Atkins
oil on canvas 77 x 64
492

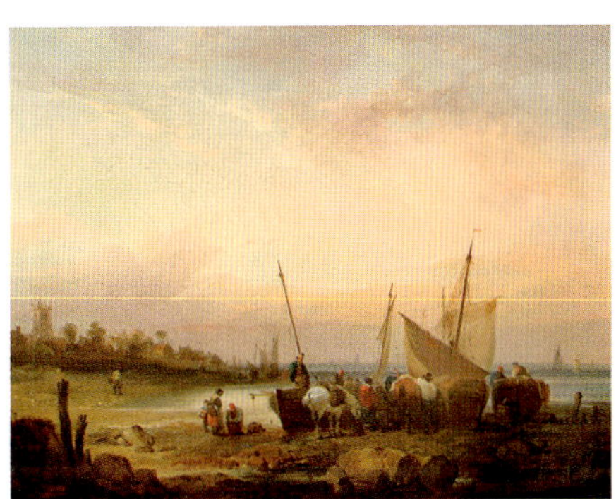

Shayer, Charles Waller 1826–1914 & **Shayer, Henry Thring** 1825–1894
Coast Scene
oil on canvas 46 x 61
1480

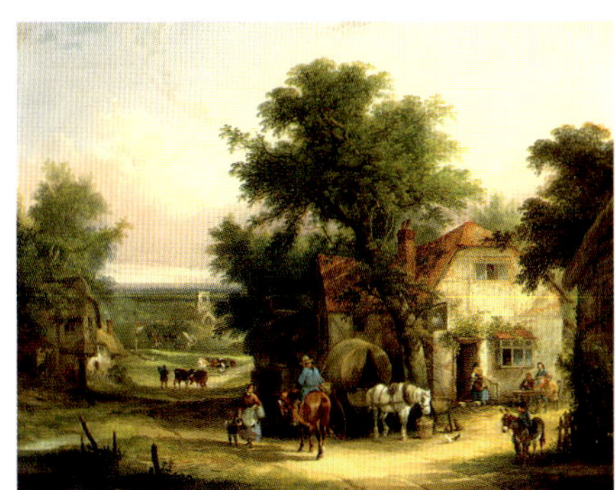

Shayer, Charles Waller 1826–1914 & **Shayer, Henry Thring** 1825–1894
The White Swan
oil on canvas 86.5 x 106.9
1302

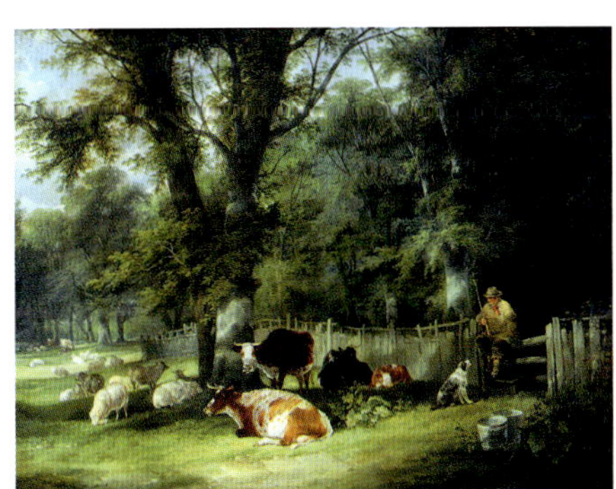

Shayer, William 1788–1879
A Shady Corner 1840
oil on canvas 103.3 x 123.3
1341

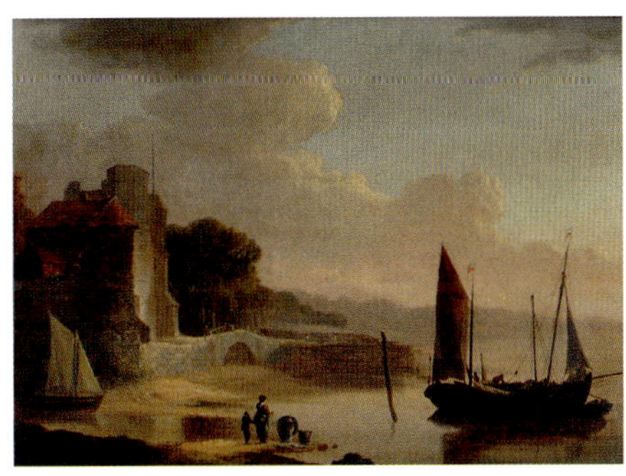

Shayer, William 1788–1879
Mouth of the Old Canal 1842
oil on canvas 42.7 x 55.5
15/1969

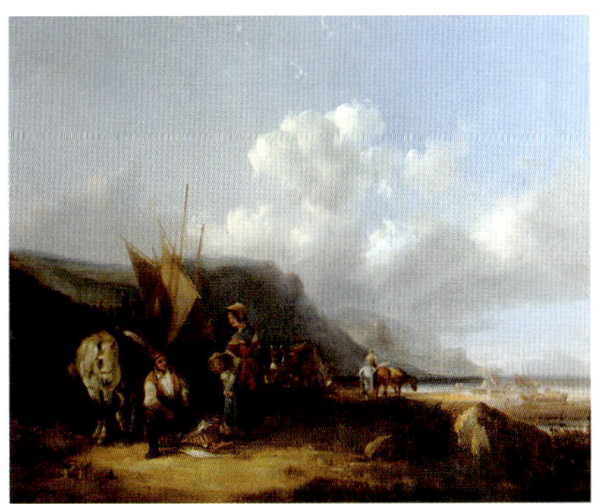

Shayer, William 1788–1879
Coast Scene
oil on canvas 102.5 x 120.4
497

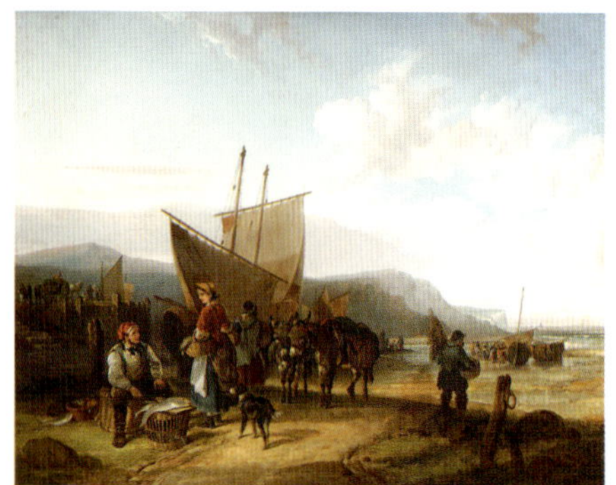

Shayer, William 1788–1879
Coast Scene
oil on canvas 110.2 x 132
498

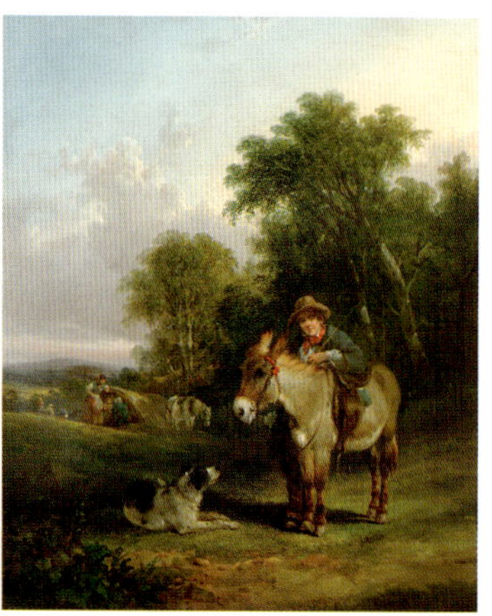

Shayer, William 1788–1879
Gypsies in Wood
oil on canvas 74.5 x 64.2
500

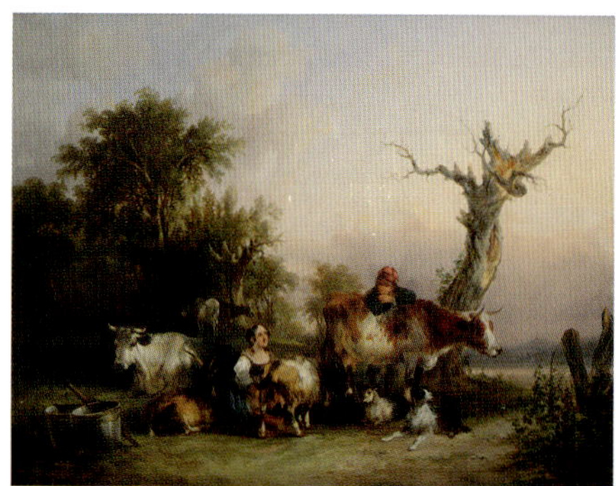

Shayer, William 1788–1879
Milking Time
oil on canvas 71 x 91.5
501

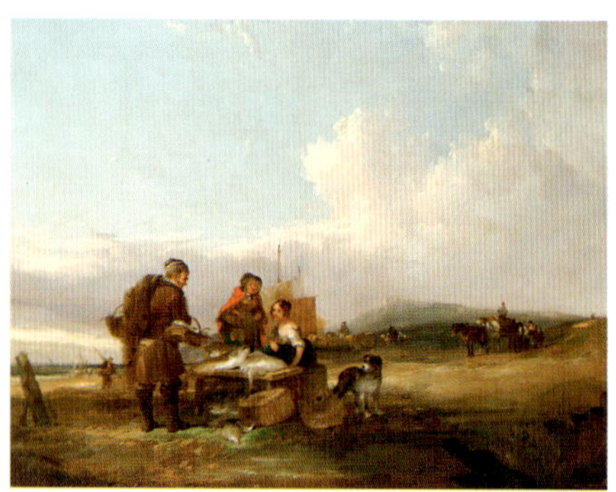

Shayer, William 1788–1879
The Fish Stall
oil on canvas 46 x 61
1248

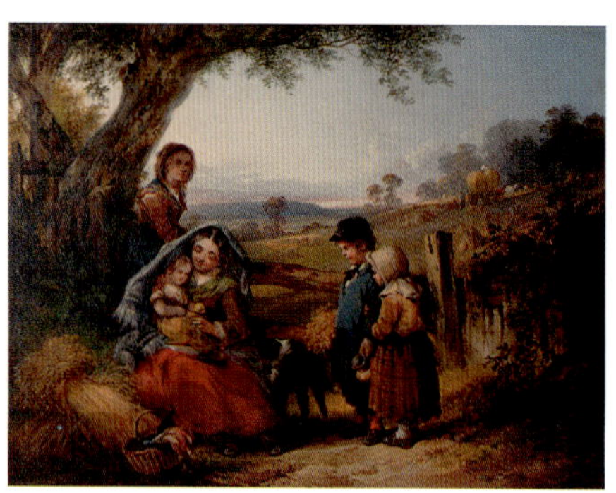

Shayer, William 1788–1879
The Gleaners
oil on canvas 63.4 x 74
1251

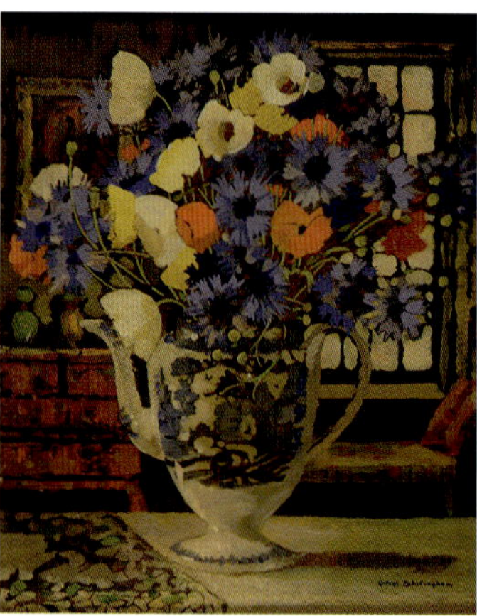

Sheringham, George 1884–1937
Flowers in a Teapot
oil on panel 41 x 33.7
4/1988

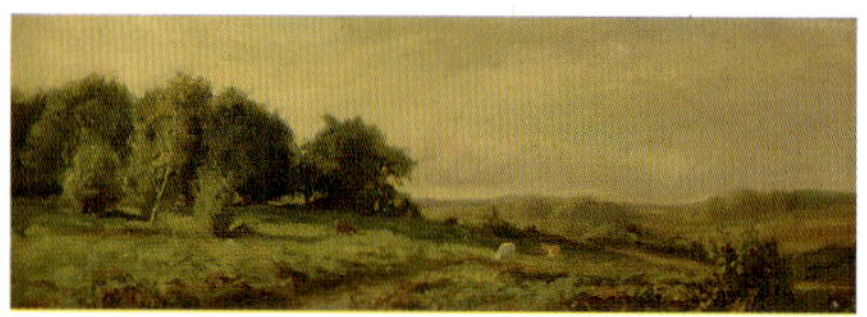

Short, Emily A.
Landscape with Cattle
oil on board 14 x 38.2
515

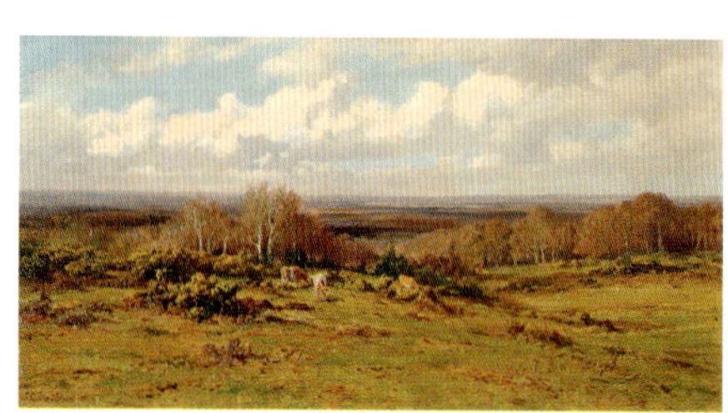

Short, Frederick Golden 1863–1936
A Distant Forest Scene 1891
oil on canvas 28 x 53.3
503

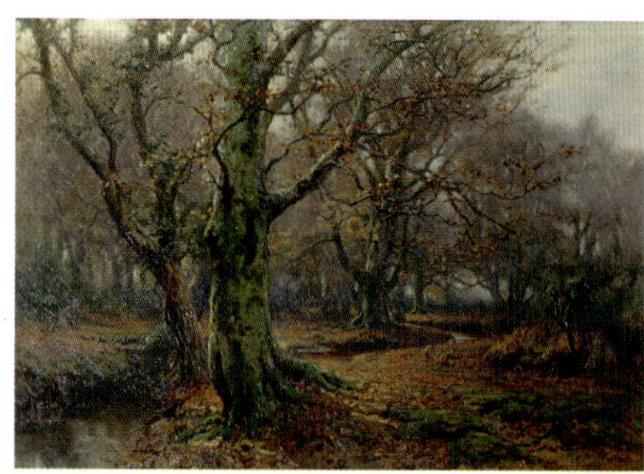

Short, Frederick Golden 1863–1936
Autumn Leaves 1895
oil on canvas 51.2 x 76.3
502

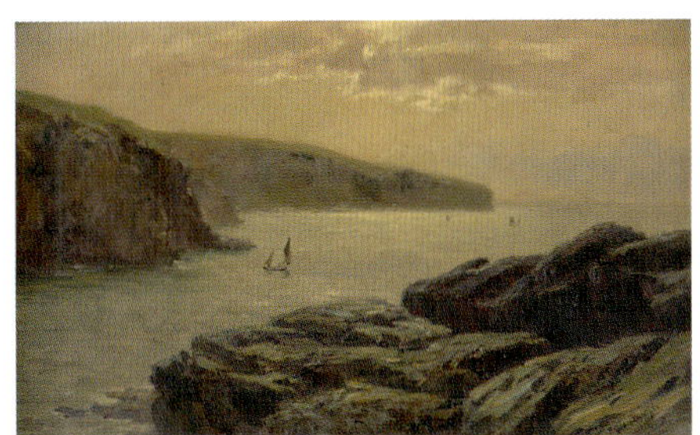

Short, Frederick Golden 1863–1936
Seascape 1896
oil on canvas 22.8 x 38.2
513

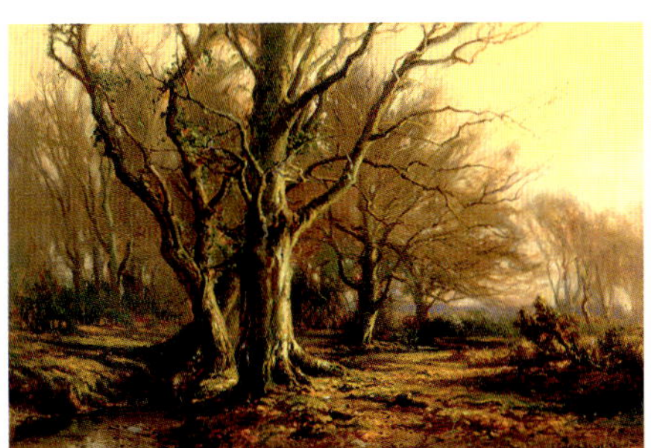

Short, Frederick Golden 1863–1936
Trees and River, New Forest 1896
oil on canvas 36 x 53.5
510

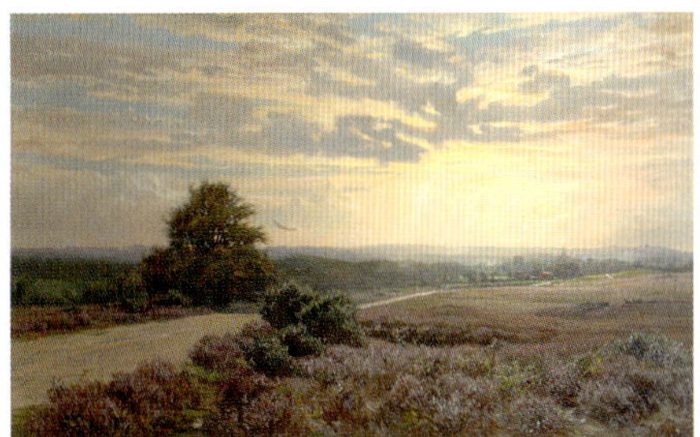

Short, Frederick Golden 1863–1936
Burley Road, New Forest 1900
oil on canvas 47.1 x 76.3
508

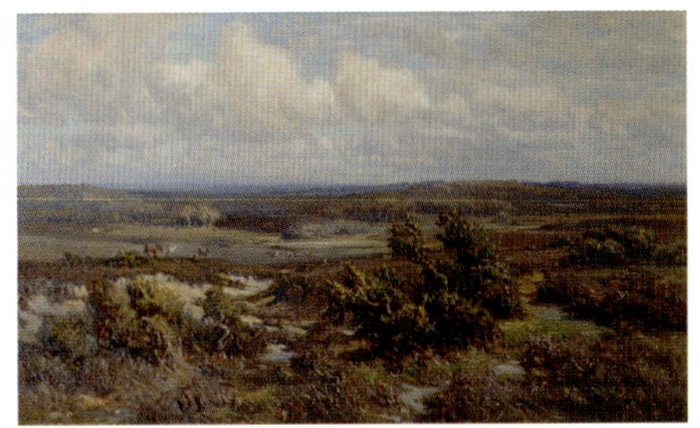

Short, Frederick Golden 1863–1936
New Forest 1900
oil on canvas 47 x 76.2
507

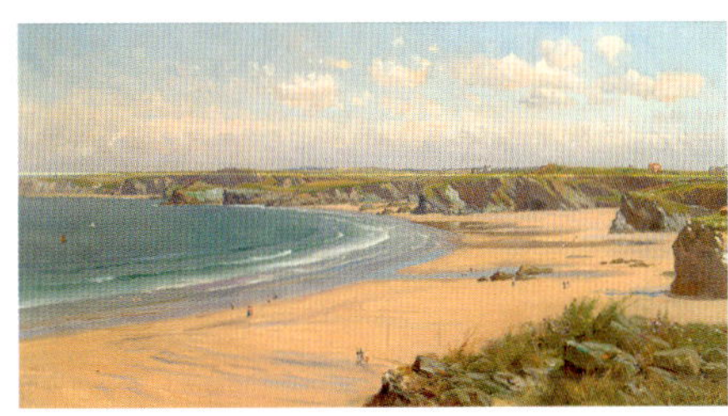

Short, Frederick Golden 1863–1936
Newquay, Cornwall 1900
oil on canvas 28.5 x 53.4
509

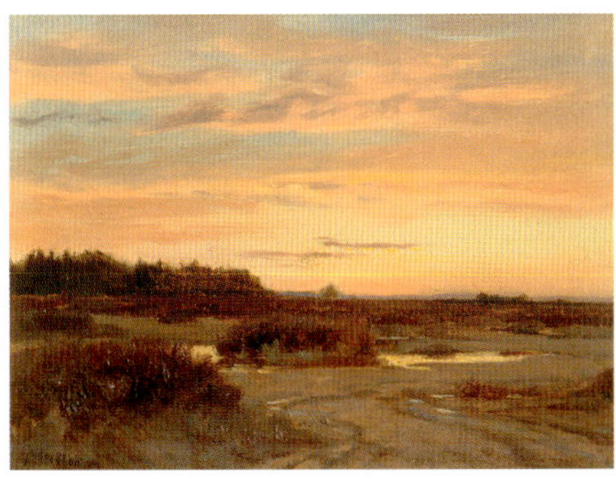

Short, Frederick Golden 1863–1936
Cloud Study, New Forest 1901
oil on canvas 12.6 x 21.5
504

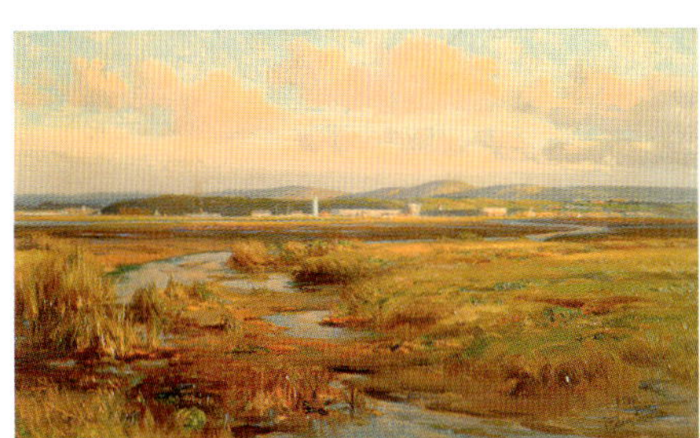

Short, Frederick Golden 1863–1936
Lymington River 1901
oil on canvas 22.9 x 38.1
506

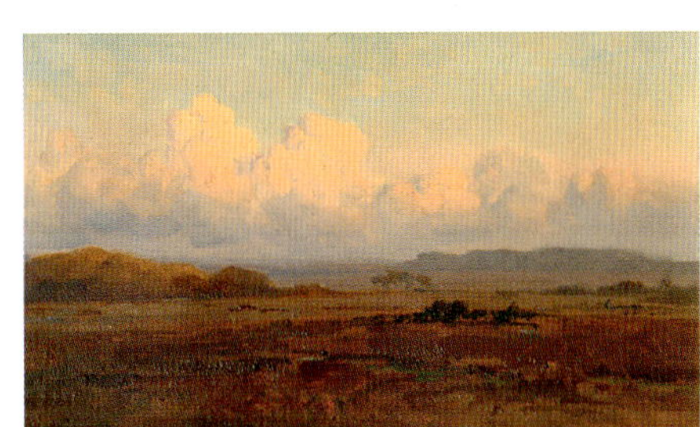

Short, Frederick Golden 1863–1936
New Forest 1901
oil on board 15.7 x 21.6
512

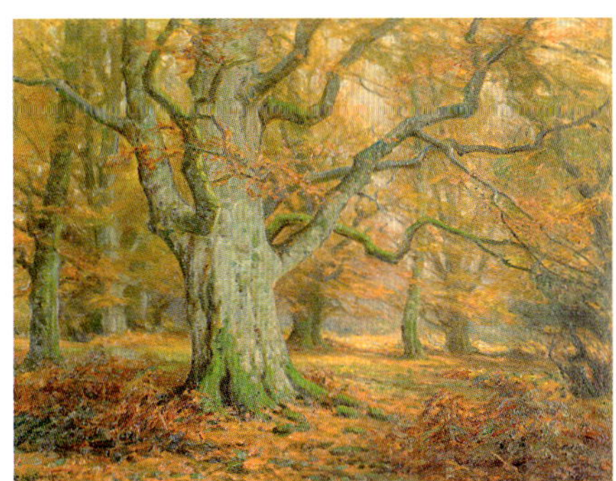

Short, Frederick Golden 1863–1936
Whitley Road 1932
oil on canvas 40.7 x 53.3
511

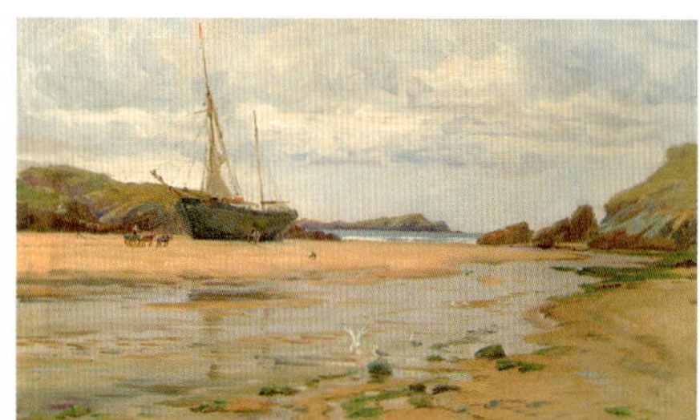

Short, Frederick Golden 1863–1936
Discharging Cargo, Lymington
oil on canvas 23 x 38.4
505

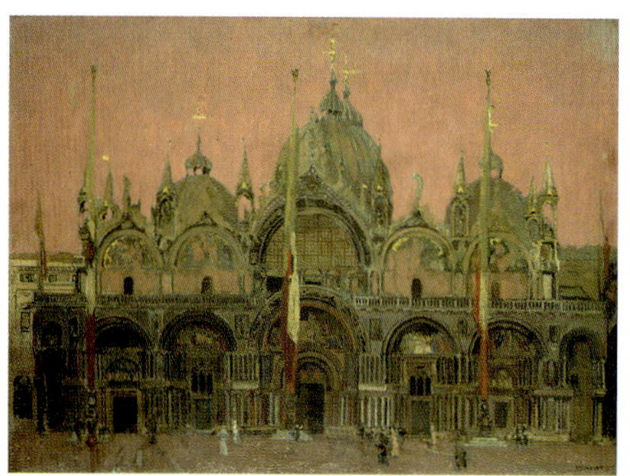

Sickert, Walter Richard 1860–1942
A Red Sky at Night 1896
oil on canvas 45.4 x 61
83/1963

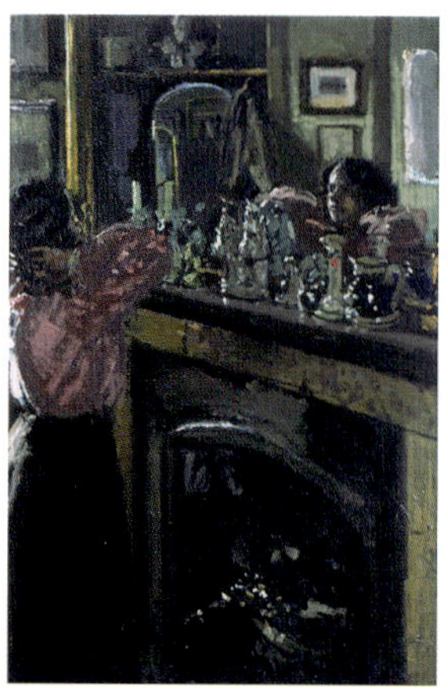

Sickert, Walter Richard 1860–1942
The Mantelpiece 1907
oil on canvas 76.2 x 50.8
517

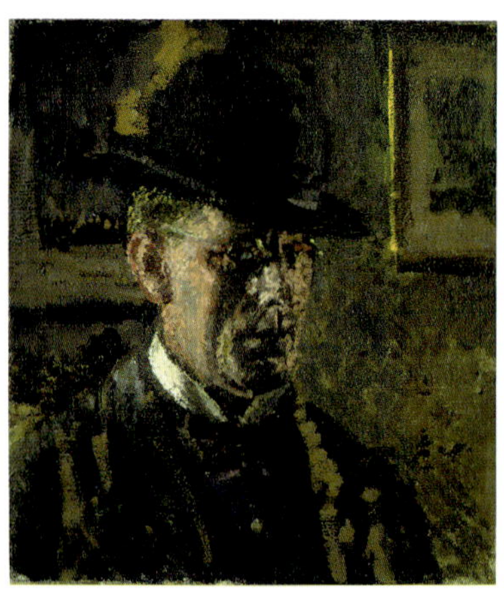

Sickert, Walter Richard 1860–1942
The Juvenile Lead 1908
oil on canvas 51 x 45.8
1402

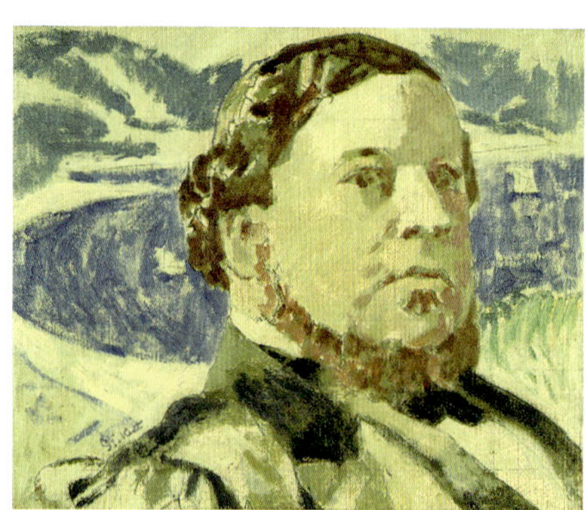

Sickert, Walter Richard 1860–1942
The Tichborne Claimant 1931
oil on canvas 50.8 x 61
516

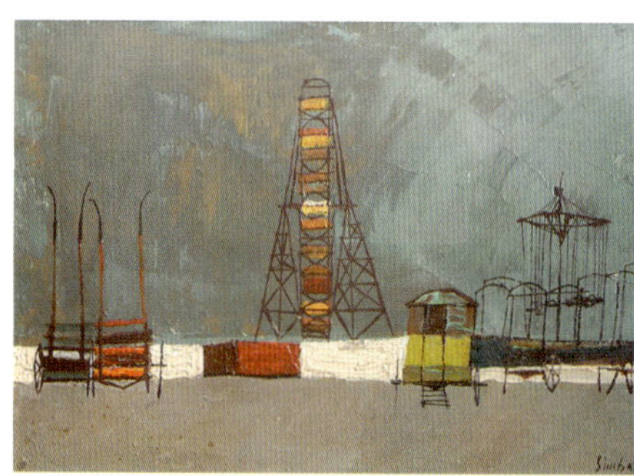

Simbari, Nicola b.1927
Luna park a sera 1957
oil on canvas 25.5 x 35
36/1963

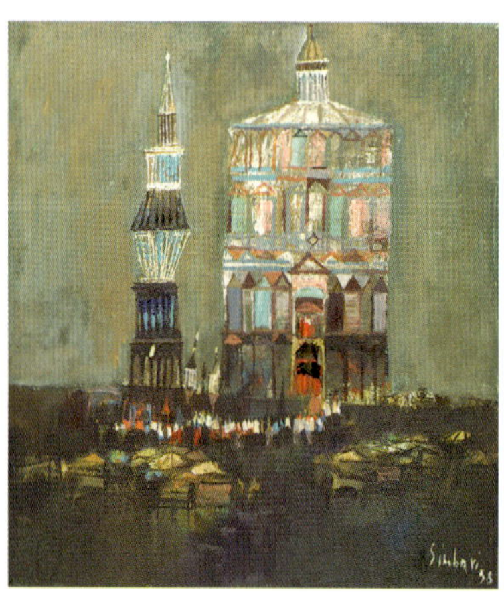

Simbari, Nicola b.1927
Battistero 1958
oil on canvas 49.9 x 44.8
34/1963

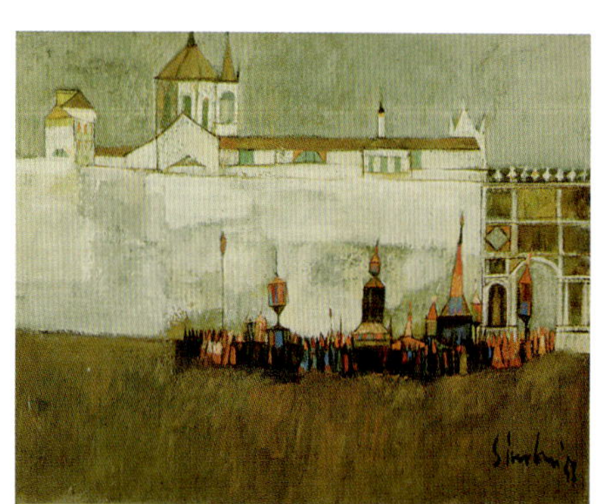

Simbari, Nicola b.1927
Processione al Flamino 1958
oil on canvas 32.8 x 41
35/1963

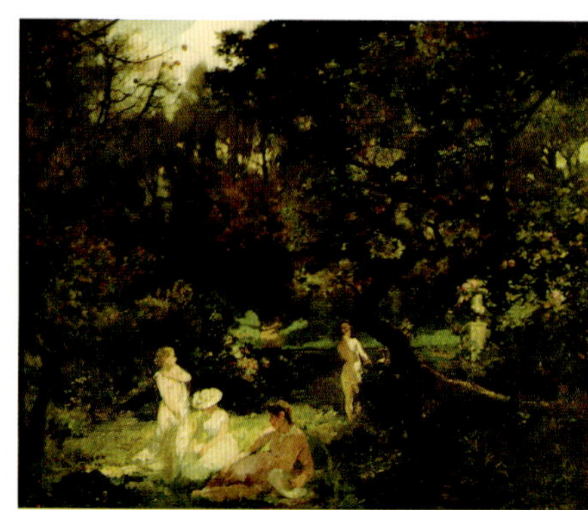

Sims, Charles 1873–1928
The Bathers
oil on canvas 55.9 x 68.8
523

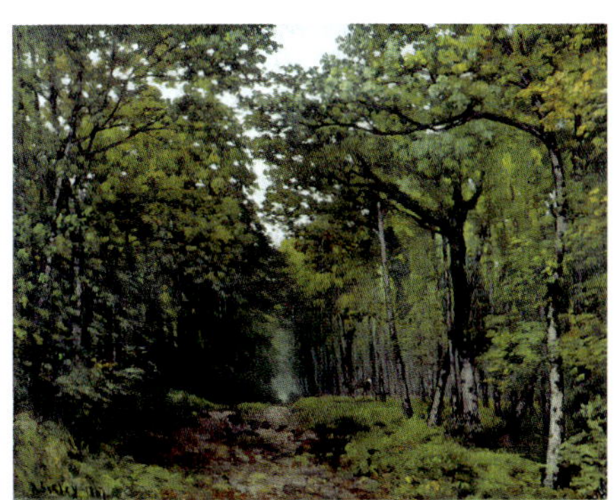

Sisley, Alfred 1839–1899
Avenue of Chestnut Trees at La Celle-Saint-Cloud 1867
oil on canvas 95.5 x 122.2
524

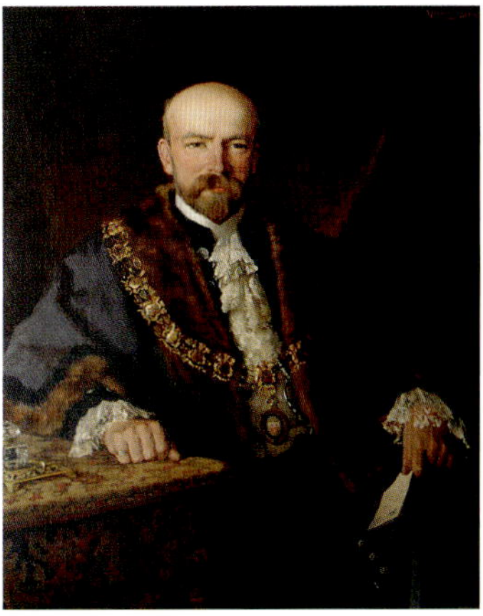

Skeats, Leonard Frank 1874–1943
Alderman Frederick A. Dunsford, JP 1902
oil on canvas 127.5 x 101.4
527

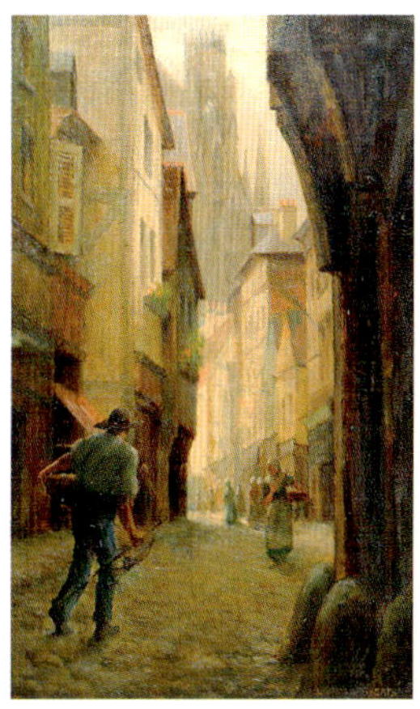

Skeats, Leonard Frank 1874–1943
Brittany
oil on canvas 40.7 x 25.4
530

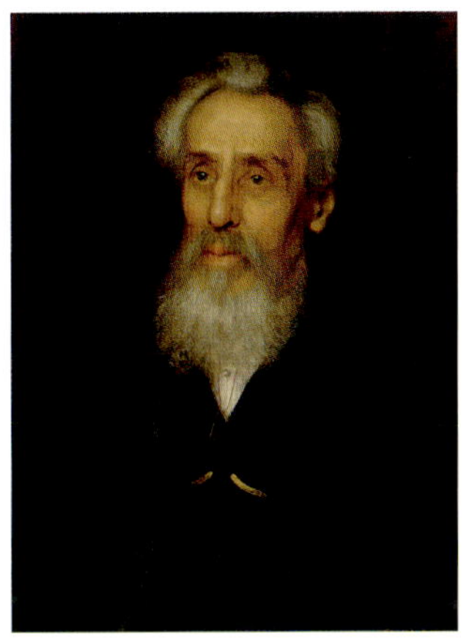

Skeats, Leonard Frank 1874–1943
Robert Chipperfield, JP
oil on canvas 60.7 x 45.8
526

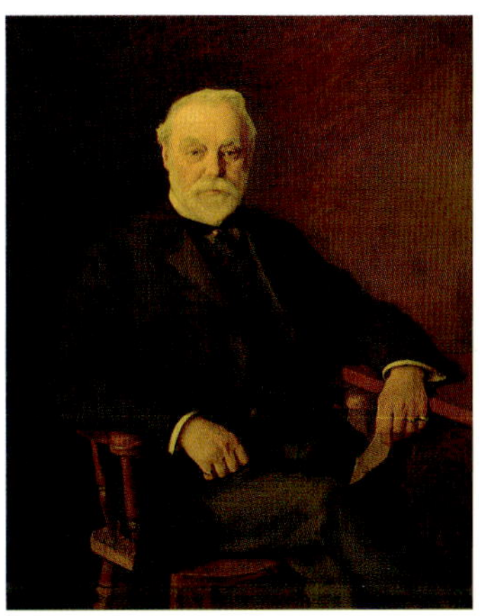

Skeats, Leonard Frank 1874–1943
Sir James Lemon, JP
oil on canvas 126.8 x 101.6
528

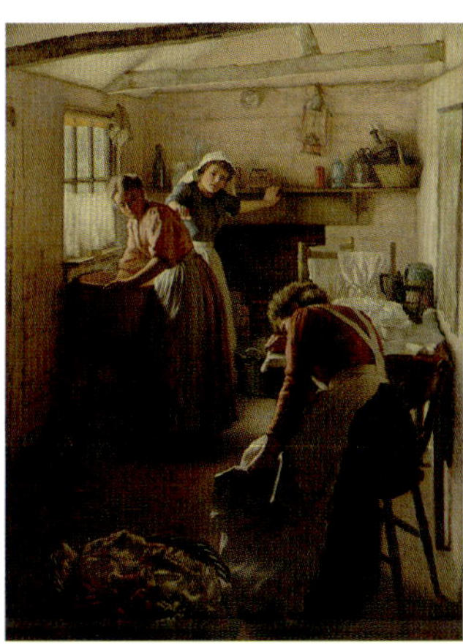

Skeats, Leonard Frank 1874–1943
The Casualty List
oil on canvas 155 x 117
1275

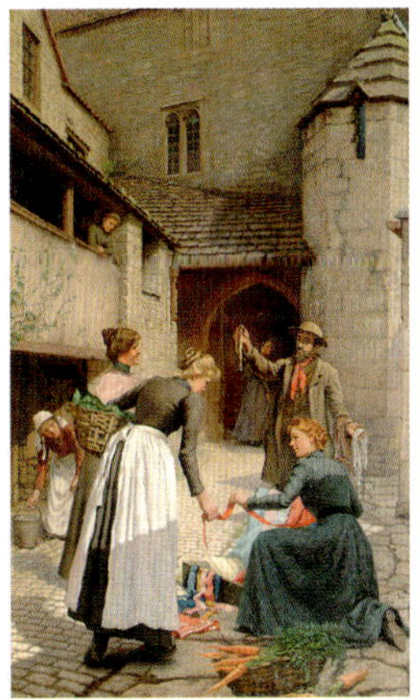

Skeats, Leonard Frank 1874–1943
The Pedlar
oil on canvas 152.8 x 94
525

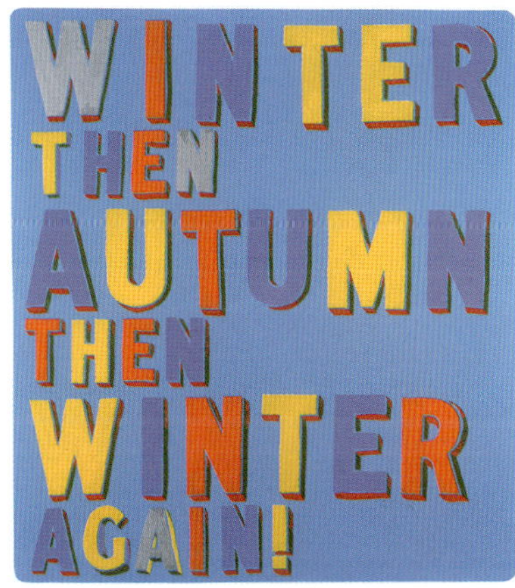

Smith, Bob & Roberta b.1963
Winter then Autumn 1999
acrylic on canvas 112.6 x 110.1
8/2000

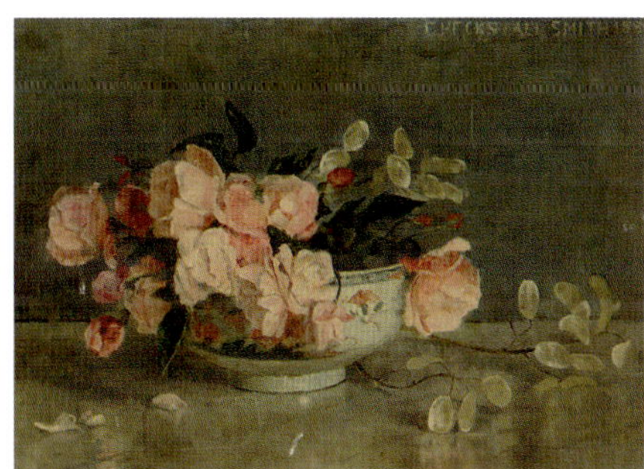

Smith, Edith Heckstall active 1884–1890
Roses 1886
oil on canvas 32.7 x 48.2
1245

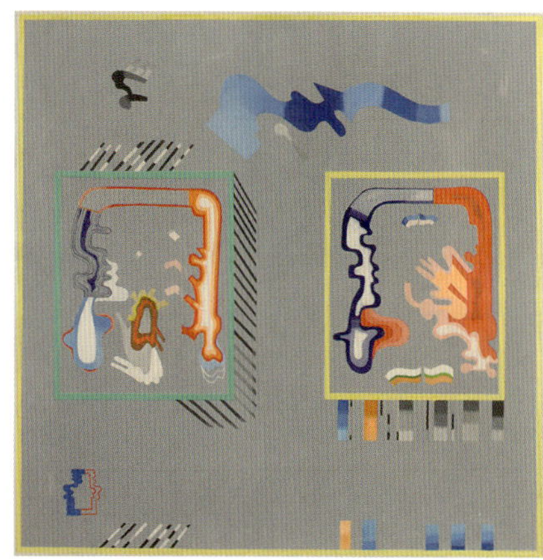

Smith, Jack b.1928
Various Activities No.4
acrylic on canvas 93.7 x 93.7
10/2006

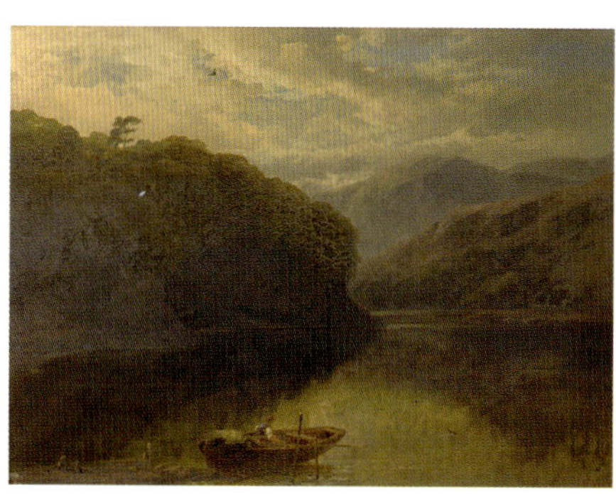

Smith, James Burrell 1822–1897
Windermere 1877
oil on canvas 50.8 x 68.5
539

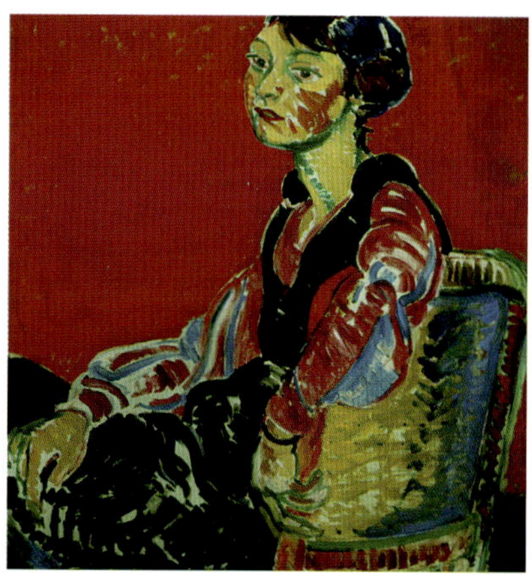

Smith, Matthew Arnold Bracy 1879–1959
Dulcie 1915
oil on canvas 82.5 x 77
1394

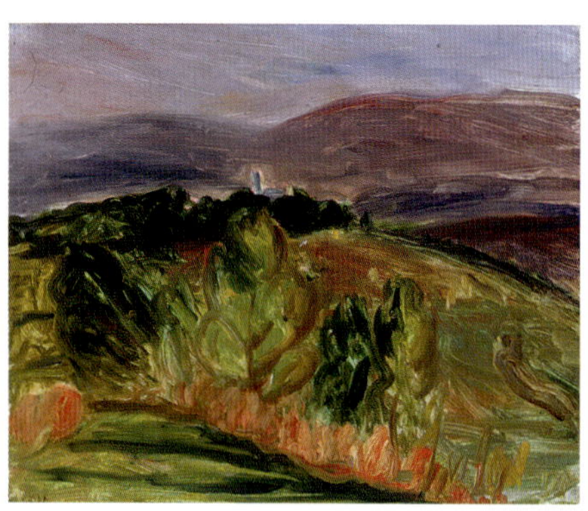

Smith, Matthew Arnold Bracy 1879–1959
Landscape at Cagnes
oil on canvas 46.3 x 55.2
1423

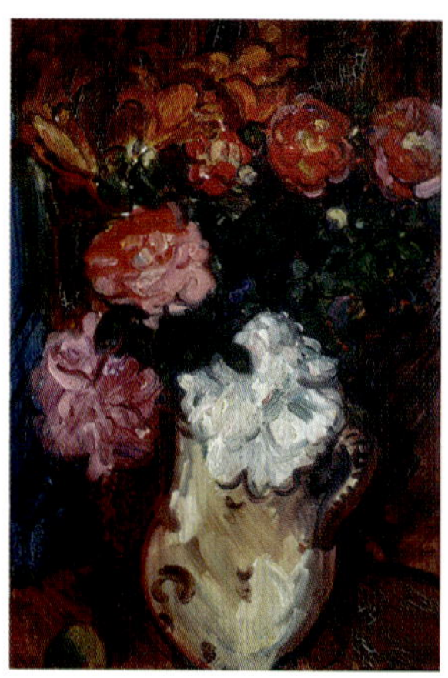

Smith, Matthew Arnold Bracy 1879–1959
Roses and Lilies
oil on canvas 65 x 46.5
531

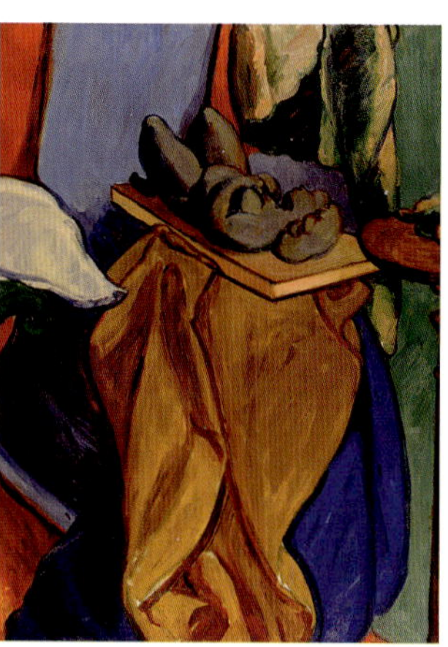

Smith, Matthew Arnold Bracy 1879–1959
Still Life with Clay Figure
oil on canvas 131.5 x 97.2
1332

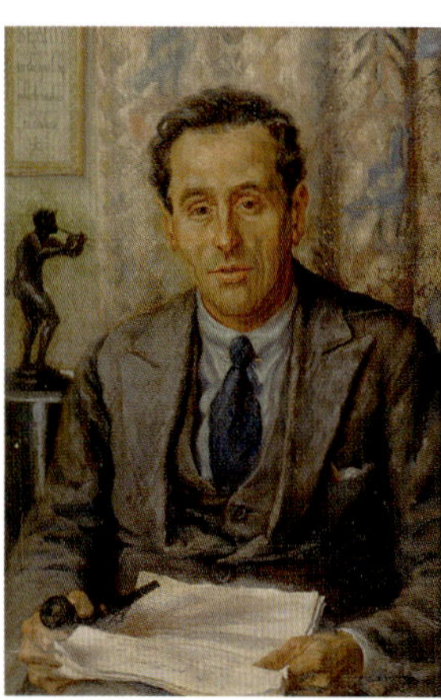

Smith, Percy John Delf 1882–1948
F. T. Murphy 1933
oil on canvas 87.5 x 62.5
6/2006

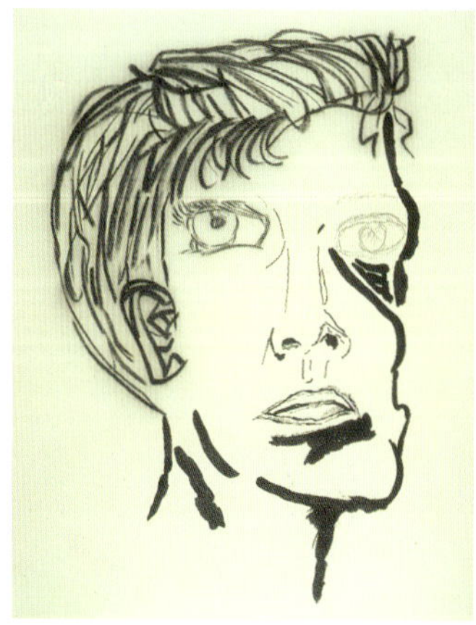

Smith, Ray b.1947
Compromise Formation
acrylic, charcoal & pencil on canvas
167 x 132
58/1992

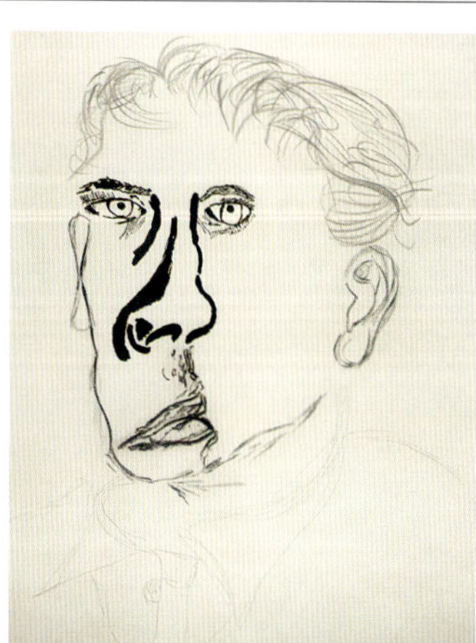

Smith, Ray b.1947
Secondary Revision
acrylic, charcoal & pencil on canvas
167 x 132
57/1992

Facing page: Momper, Joos de the younger, 1564–1635, *Landscape* (detail), Southampton City Art Gallery, (p. 97)

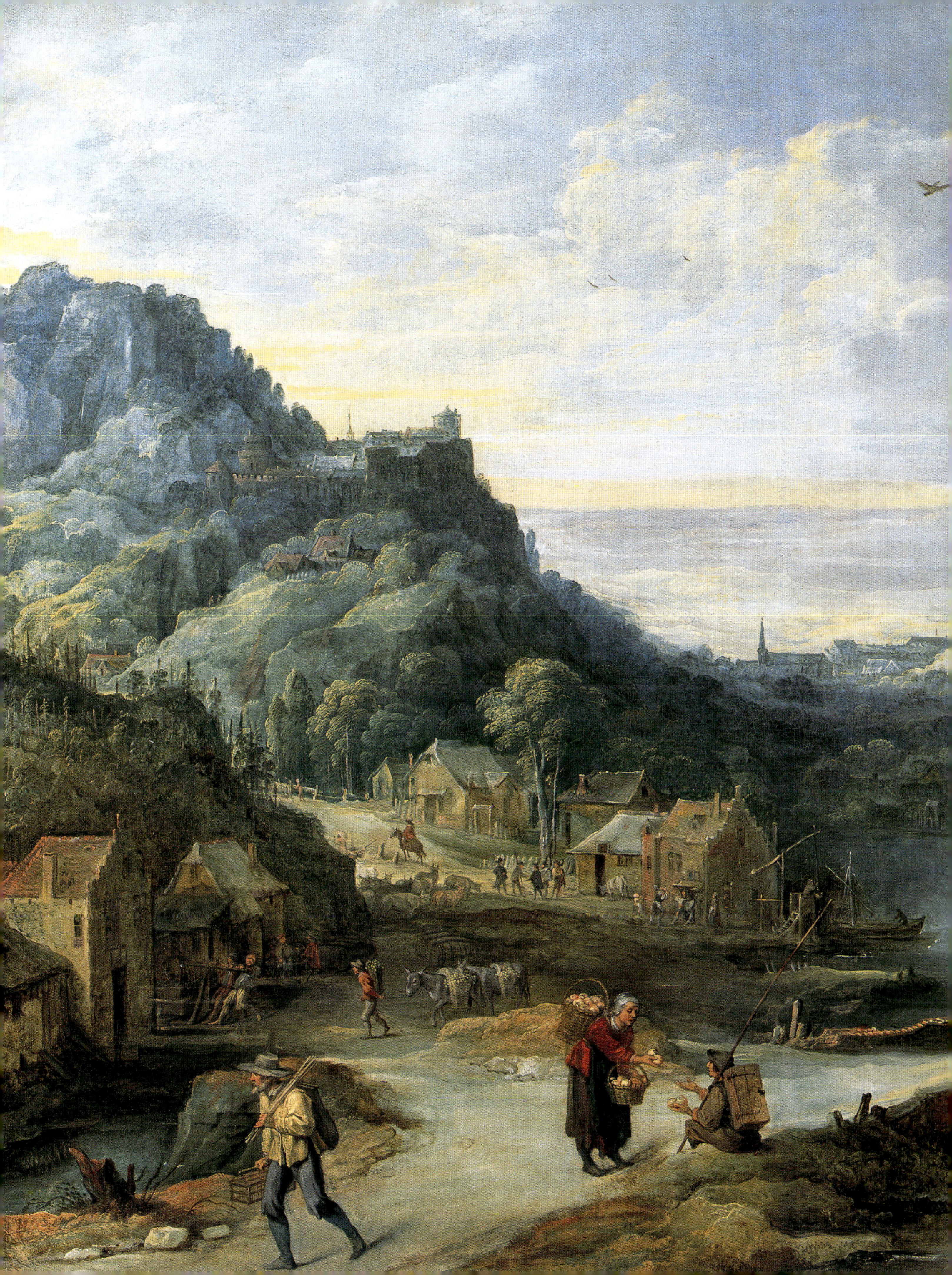

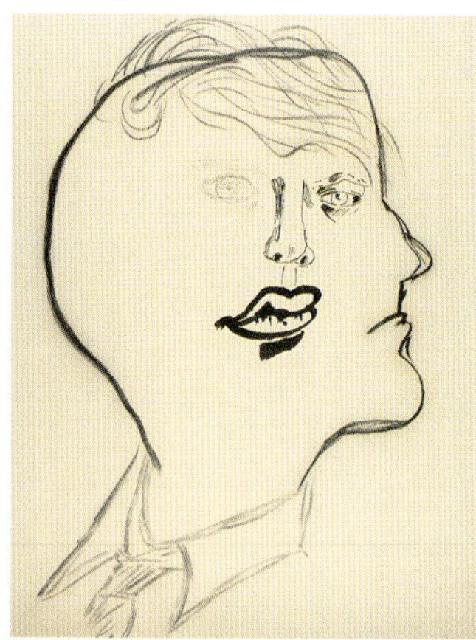

Smith, Ray b.1947
Transitional Object
acrylic, charcoal & pencil on canvas
167 x 132
56/1992

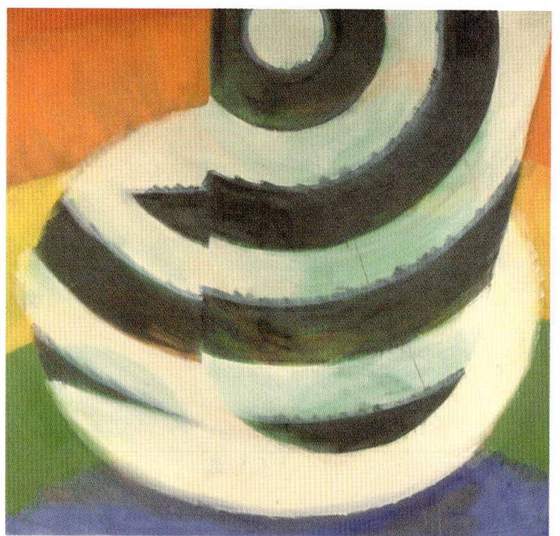

Smith, Richard b.1931
Product 1962
oil on canvas 121.8 x 129.8
L7T

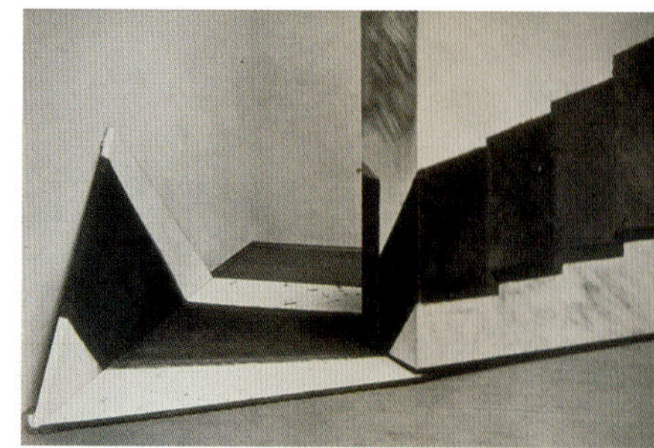

Smith, Richard b.1931
Replace 1963
oil on canvas 135 x 180
25/1977

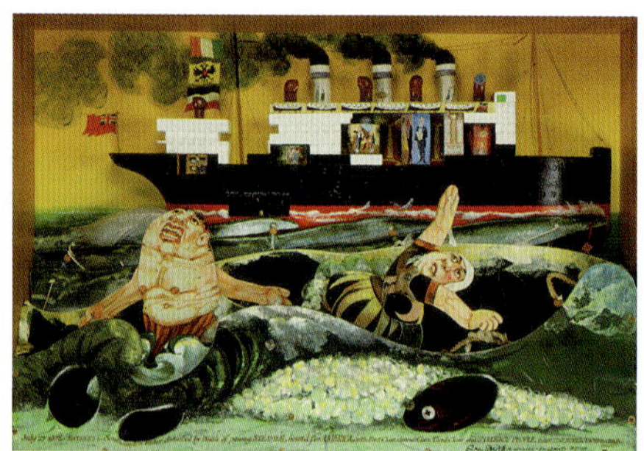

Smith, Sam 1908–1983
Bathers in Southampton Water 1979
mixed media 56.1 x 58.5
10/1982

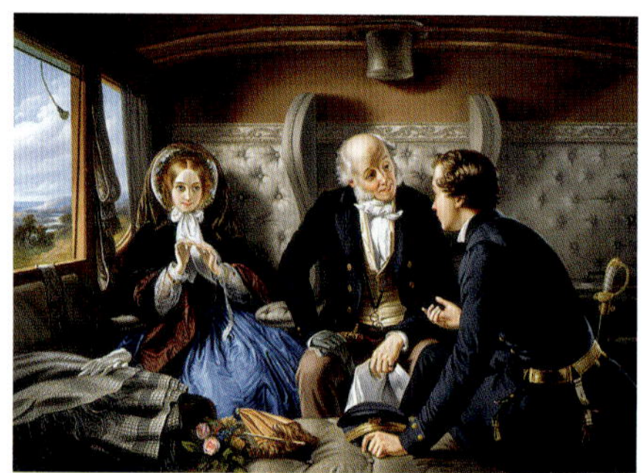

Solomon, Abraham 1824–1862
First Class, the Meeting
oil on canvas 54.5 x 76.3
541

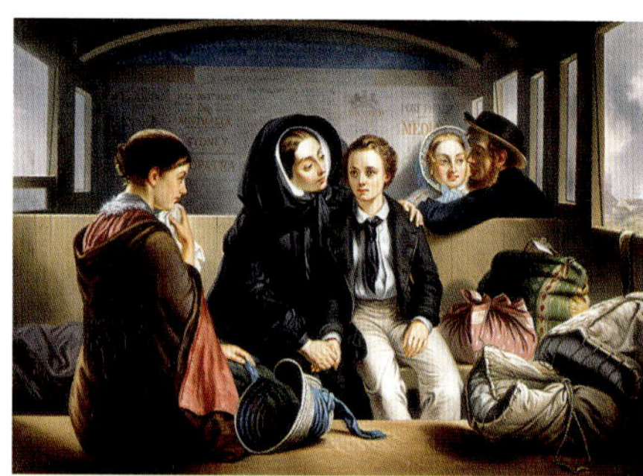

Solomon, Abraham 1824–1862
Second Class, the Parting
oil on canvas 54.5 x 76.3
540

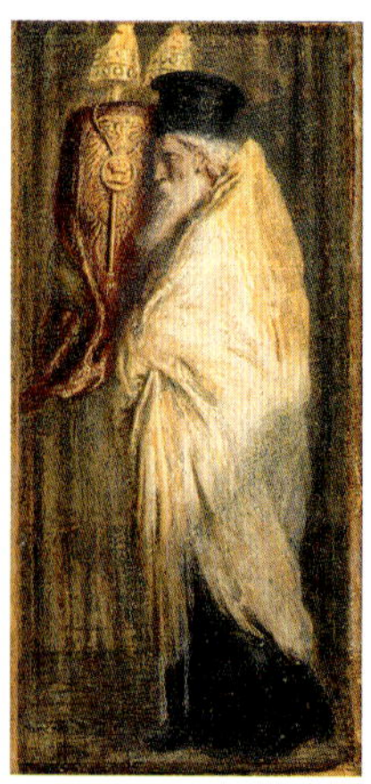

Solomon, Simeon 1840–1905
Aaron with the Scroll of the Law 1875
oil on canvas 30.9 x 15.1
1379

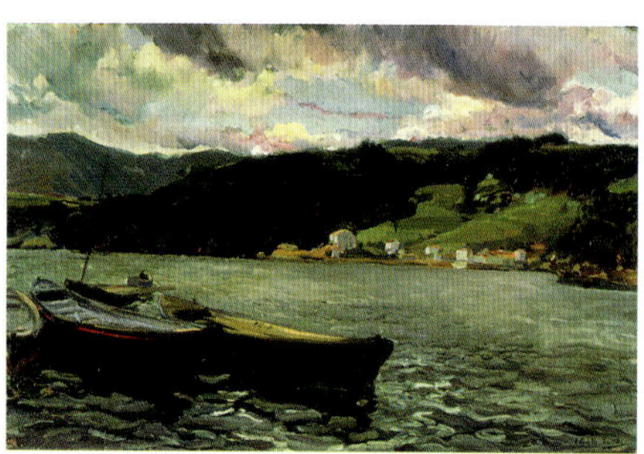

Sorolla y Bastida, Joaquín 1863–1923
Estuary of the Nalón, Asturias
oil on canvas 62 x 93.5
542

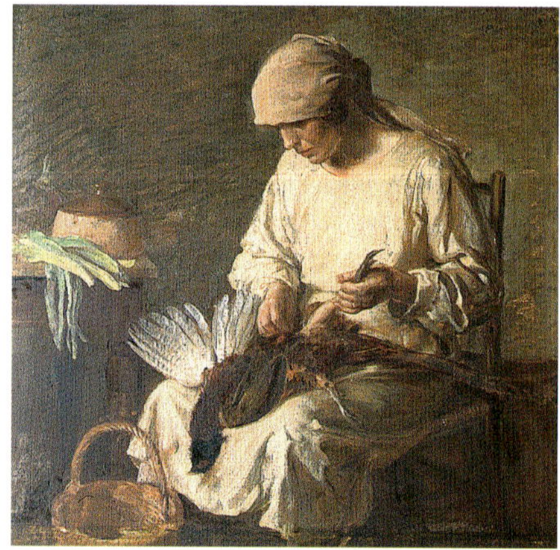

Souter, John Bullloch 1890–1972
A Kitchen Task
oil on canvas 50.7 x 53
543

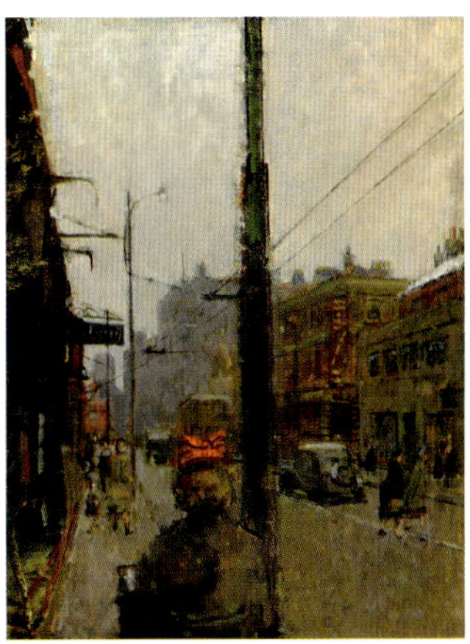

Spear, Ruskin 1911–1990
Winter
oil on canvas 77 x 58.5
1289

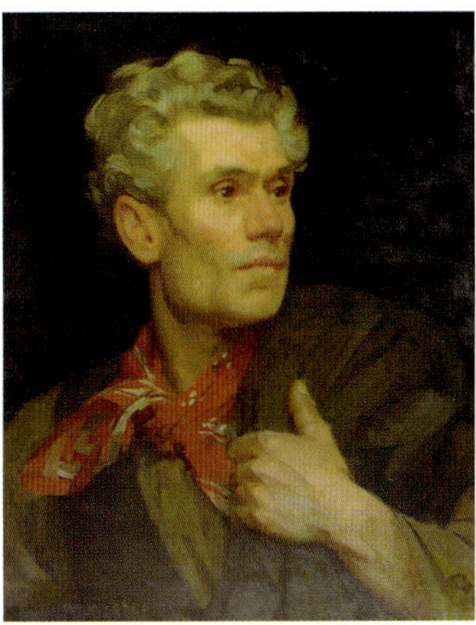

Speed, Harold 1872–1957
Old Tom
oil on canvas 63.9 x 51
545

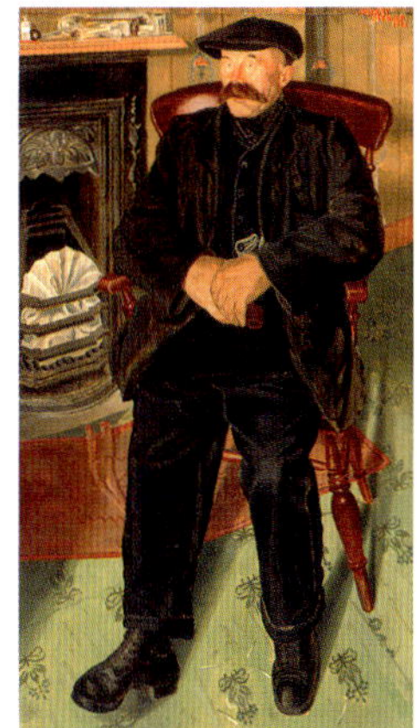

Spencer, Gilbert 1893–1979
The Rat Catcher 1922
oil on canvas 144.8 x 81.9
1426

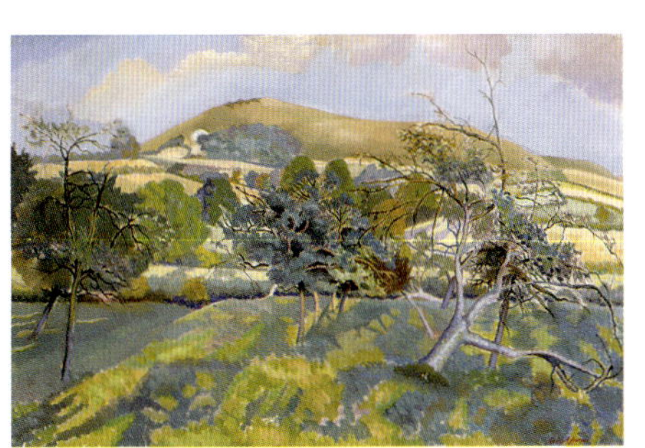

Spencer, Gilbert 1893–1979
Melbury Beacon
oil on canvas 61 x 91.5
546

Spencer, Jean 1942–1998
Four-Part Double-Square 1991
oil on linen 80 x 40
3/2003

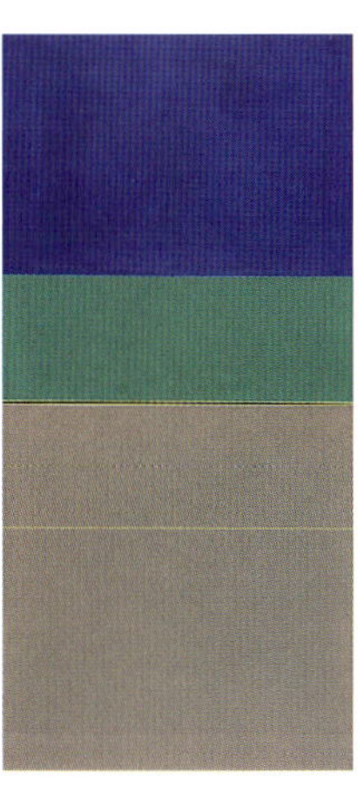

Spencer, Jean 1942–1998
Four-Part Double-Square 1991
oil on linen 80 x 40
3/2003

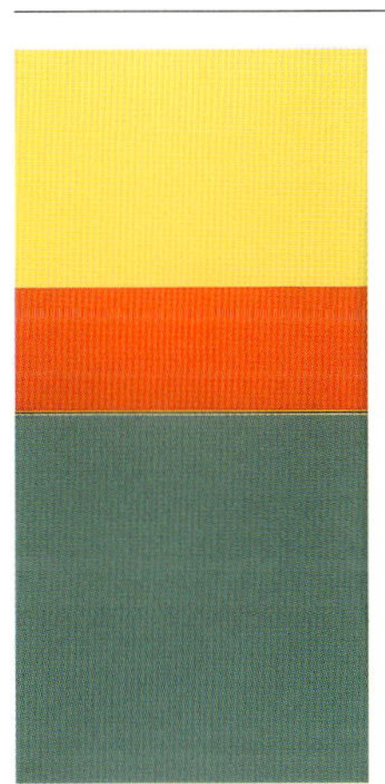

Spencer, Jean 1942–1998
Four-Part Double-Square 1991
oil on linen 80 x 40
3/2003

Spencer, Jean 1942–1998
Four-Part Double-Square 1991
oil on linen 80 x 40
3/2003

Spencer, Jean 1942–1998
White Relief
acrylic on wood 60.5 x 60.5
7/2003

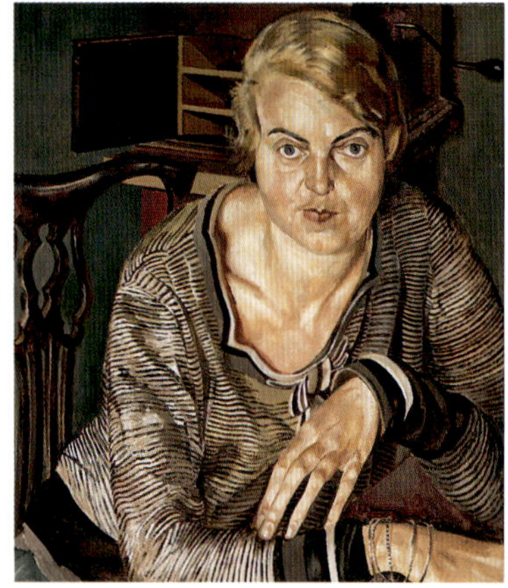
Spencer, Stanley 1891–1959
Patricia Preece 1933
oil on canvas 83.9 x 73.6
1444

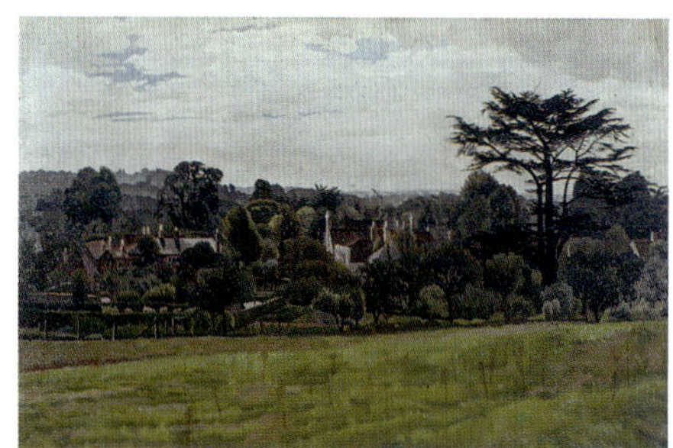
Spencer, Stanley 1891–1959
Pound Field, Cookham 1935
oil on canvas 50.8 x 76.1
547

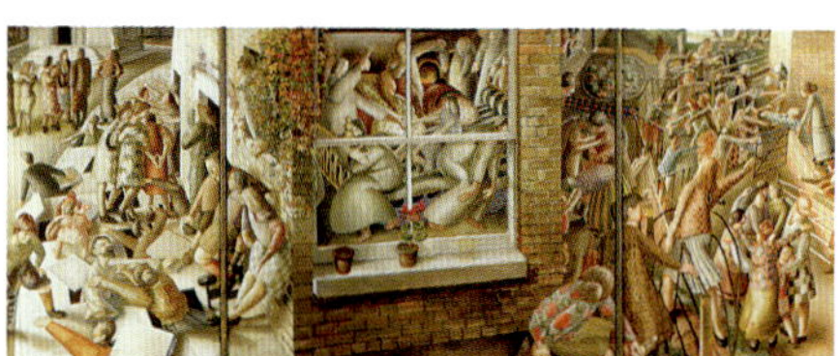
Spencer, Stanley 1891–1959
The Resurrection 1947
oil on canvas 76.8 x 189
1383

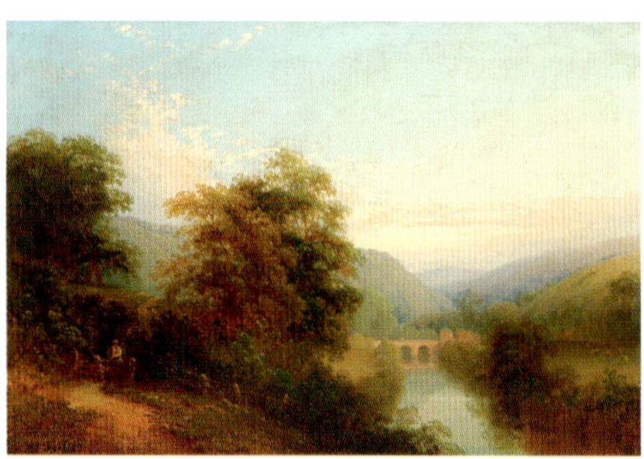
Spreat, William active c.1820–1881
Clifford Bridge on Teign 1881
oil on canvas 51.5 x 76.8
548

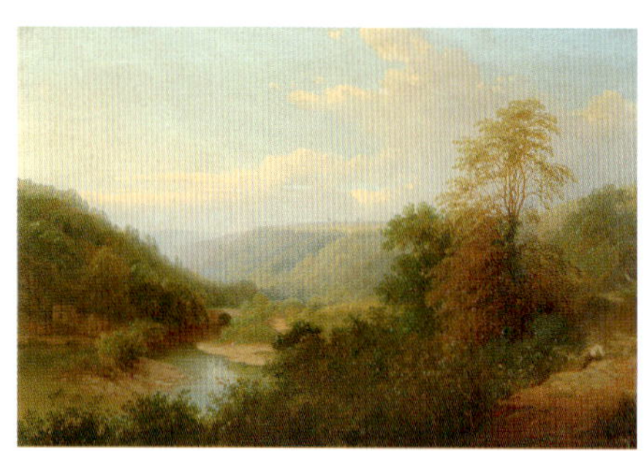
Spreat, William active c.1820–1881
Dedham Bridge on Tavy 1881
oil on canvas 51.2 x 76.5
549

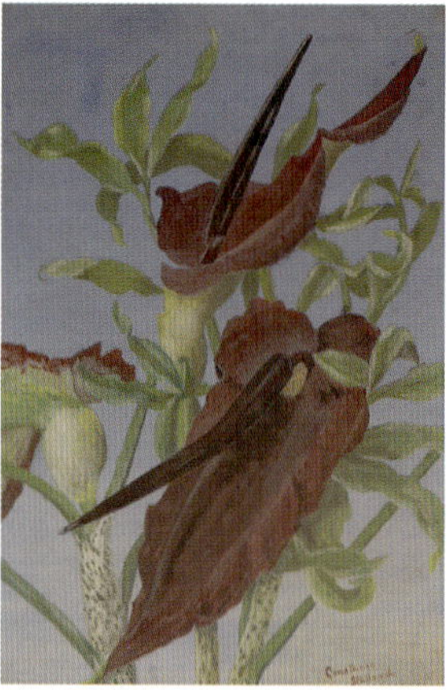
Stallard, Constance b.1870
Black Lilies
tempera on board 45.3 x 30.5
1454

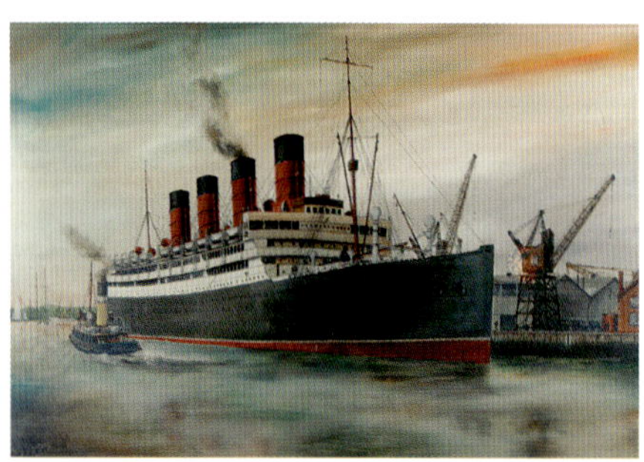
Standing, W.
'Aquitania' 1932
oil on canvas 54.8 x 80
551

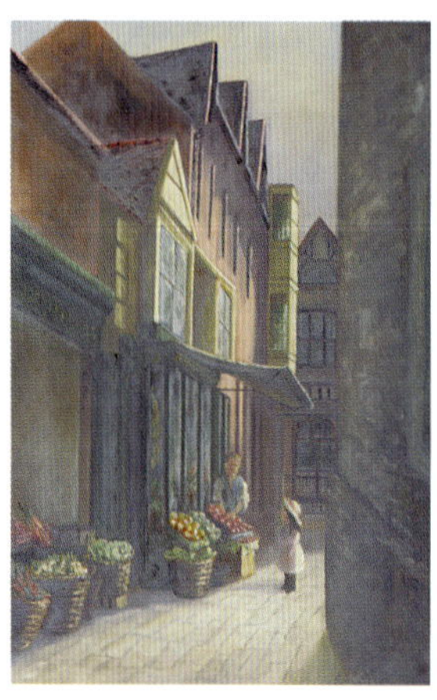
Stanley, Amy
Church Passage, St Michael's 1900
oil on canvas 61 x 41.8
552

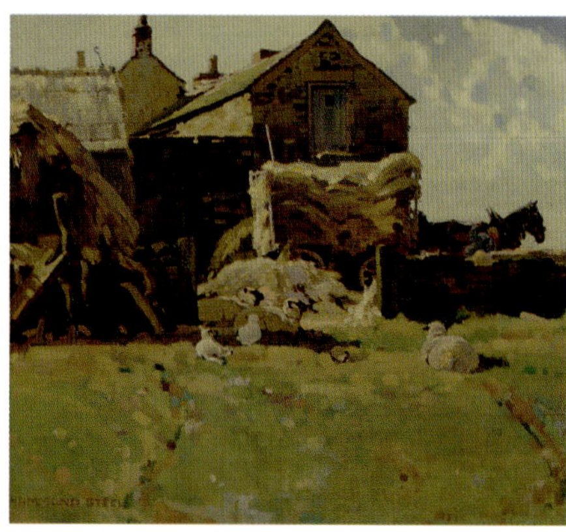
Steel, George Hammond 1900–1960
A Load from the Stack
oil on canvas 51.9 x 61.5
554

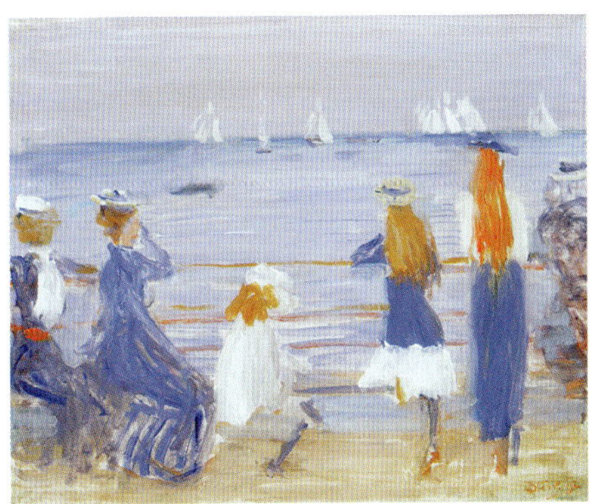

Steer, Philip Wilson 1860–1942
Watching Cowes Regatta 1892
oil on canvas 50.8 x 61
1/1963

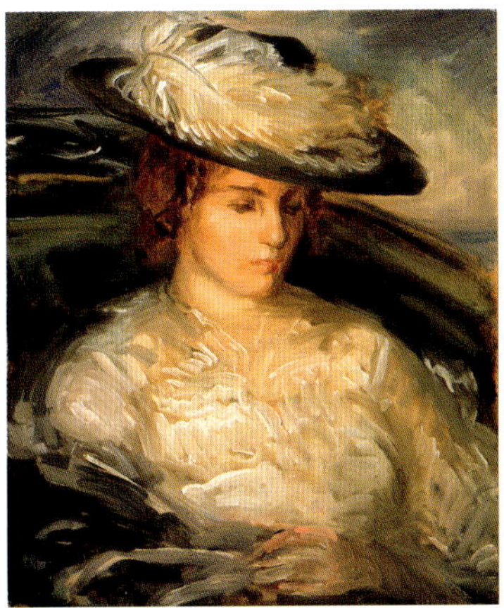

Steer, Philip Wilson 1860–1942
Convalescent 1898
oil on canvas 61.3 x 50.8
557

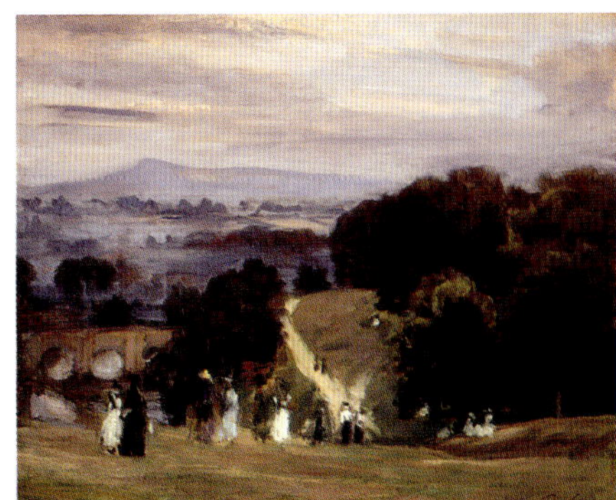

Steer, Philip Wilson 1860–1942
Ludlow Walks 1899
oil on canvas 53.3 x 66.1
556

Steer, Philip Wilson 1860–1942
Digging for Bait, Shoreham 1926
oil on canvas 50.8 x 81.2
555

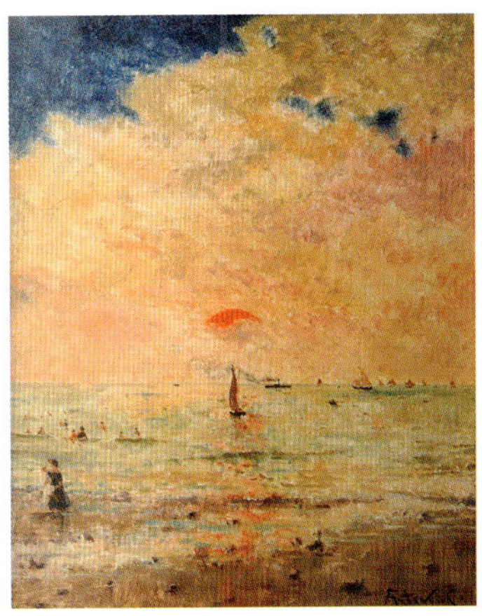

Stevens, Alfred Emile Léopold Joseph Victor 1823–1906
Off the Coast at Deauville
oil on wood 46 x 37.5
24/1963

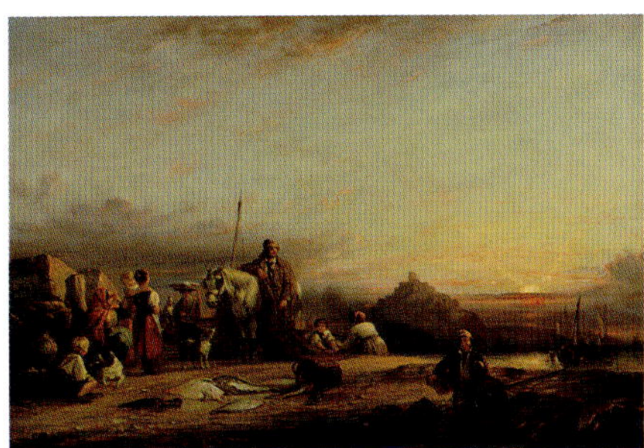

Stewart, John I 1800–after 1865
Fishing Scene
oil on canvas 60.3 x 91.1
1385

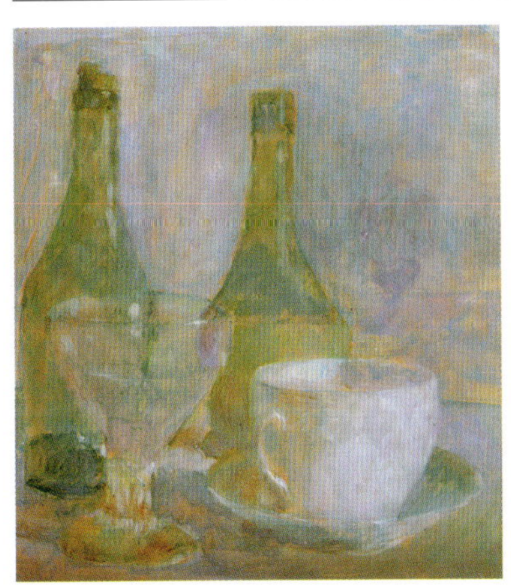

Stokes, Adrian Durham 1902–1972
Glass, Cup and Saucer with Two Wine Bottles 1959
oil on canvas 35.7 x 33.5
60/2002

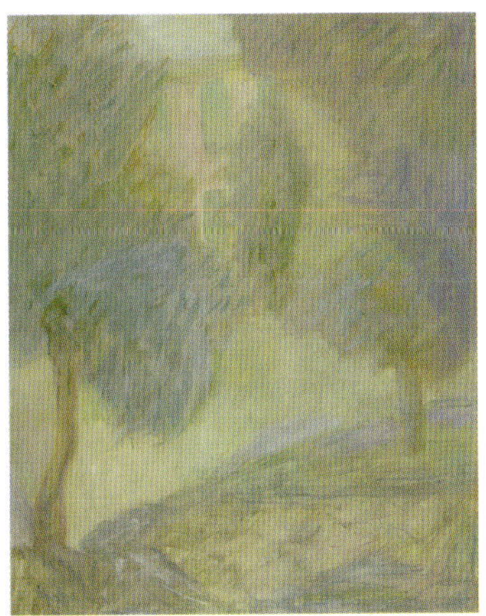

Stokes, Adrian Durham 1902–1972
Quarry at Evening, La Mortola 1959
oil on canvas 50.5 x 40.5
109/2002

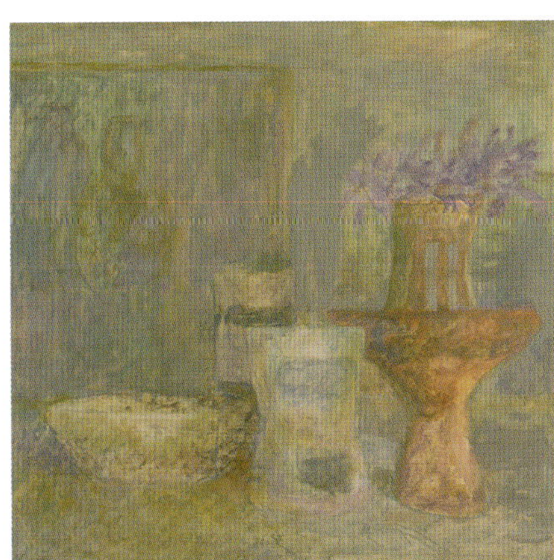

Stokes, Adrian Durham 1902–1972
Pots 1963
oil on canvas 46.2 x 49
102/2002

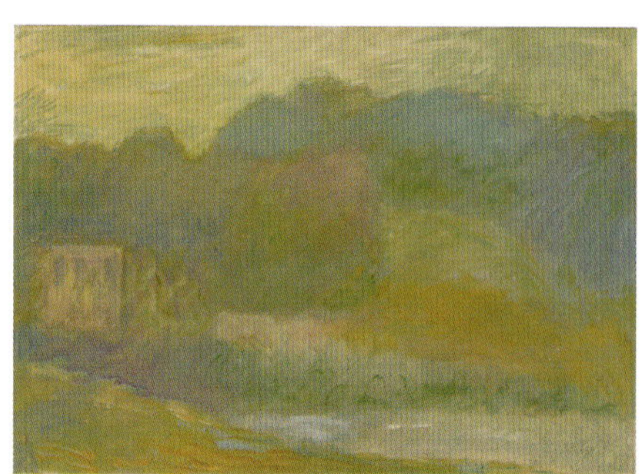

Stokes, Adrian Scott 1854–1935
Heath Pond
oil on canvas 36.6 x 51.7
91/2002

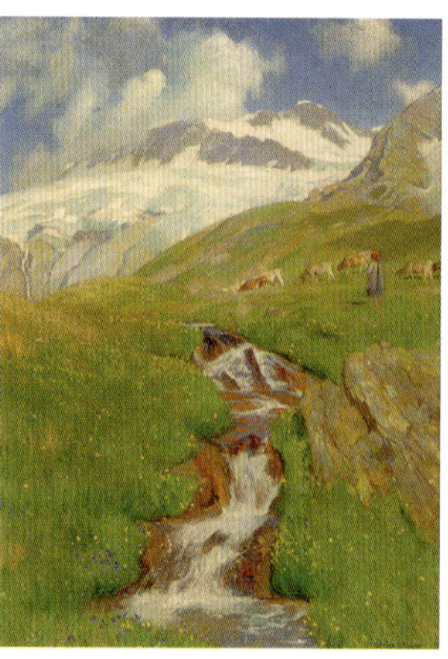

Stokes, Adrian Scott 1854–1935
Near the Simplon Pass
oil on canvas 81.7 x 61.8
563

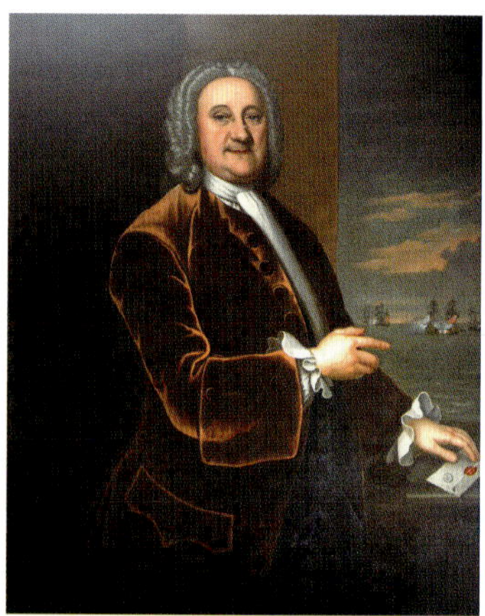

Stokes, Thomas active 1737
Richard Taunton
oil on canvas 127 x 101.5
564

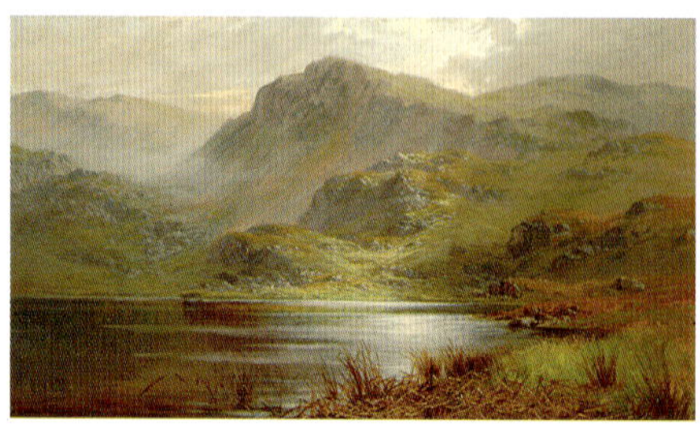

Stuart, Charles active 1880–1904
A Gleam of Sunshine 1880
oil on canvas 36 x 61.3
569

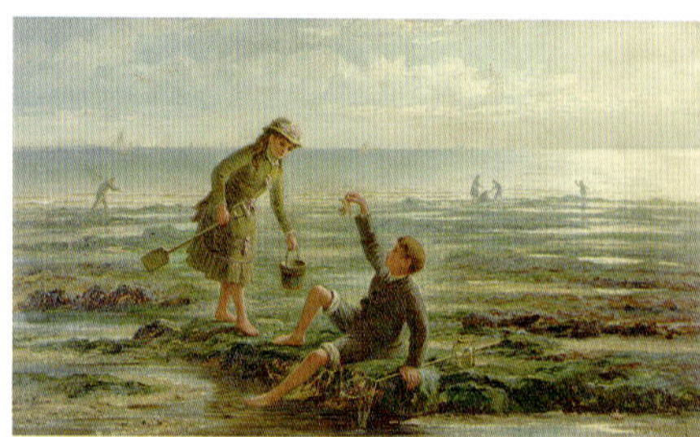

Stuart, Charles active 1880–1904
Children on a Beach 1881
oil on canvas 50.8 x 86.6
565

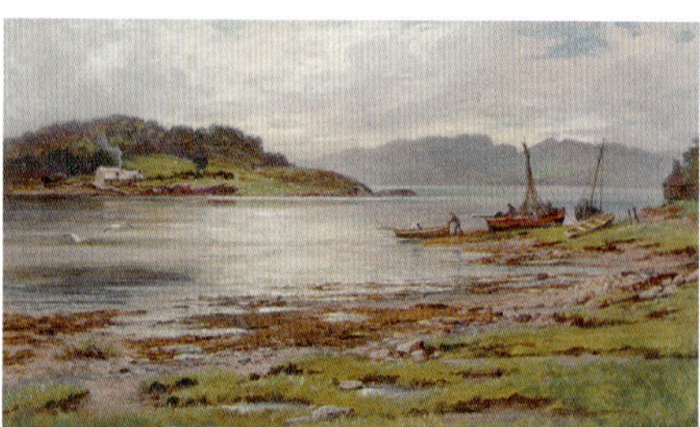

Stuart, Charles active 1880–1904
Fishing Boats 1881
oil on canvas 35.8 x 60.9
568

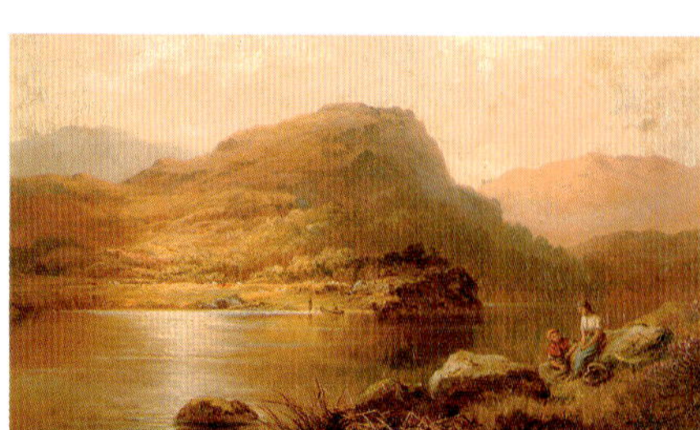

Stuart, Charles active 1880–1904
A Cumberland Lake
oil on canvas 35.7 x 61.3
567

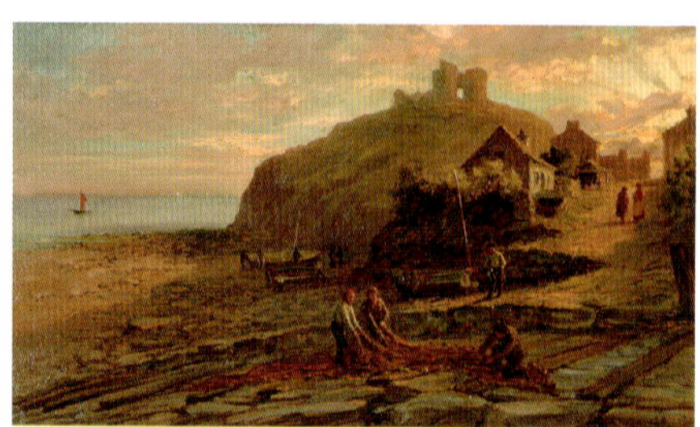

Stuart, Charles active 1880–1904
Criccieth, North Wales
oil on canvas 35 x 60.9
566

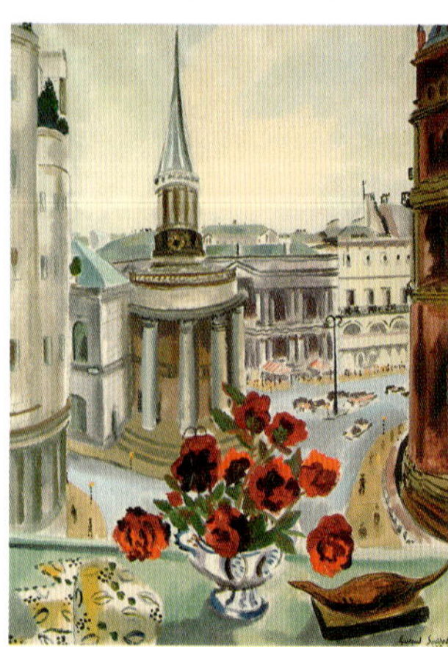

Suddaby, Rowland 1912–1972
Window at No.5 Portland Place 1938
oil on canvas 91.1 x 67.3
570

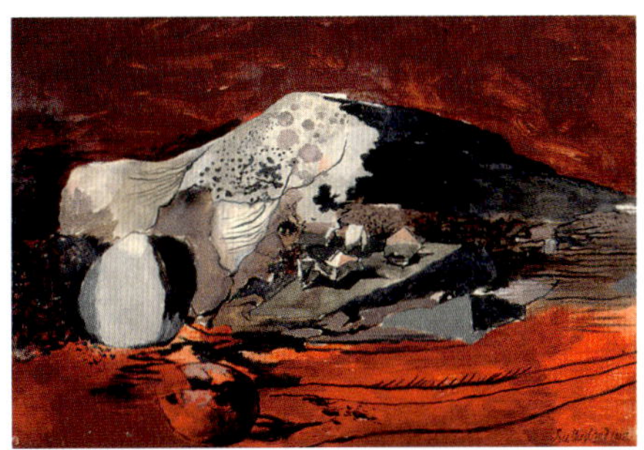

Sutherland, Graham Vivian 1903–1980
Red Landscape 1942
oil on canvas 68 x 99.8
1369

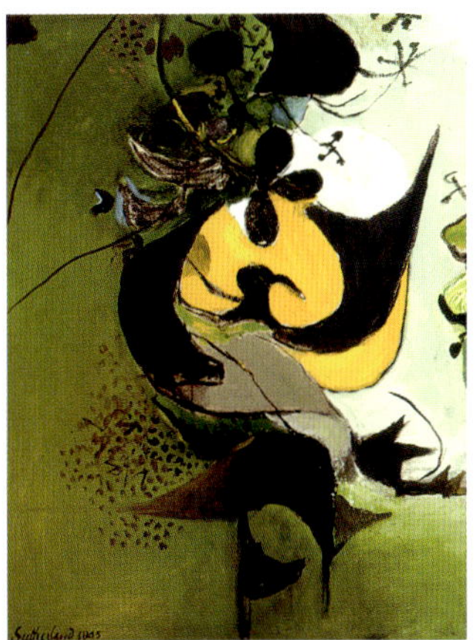

Sutherland, Graham Vivian 1903–1980
Green Lane 1945
oil on canvas 66 x 50.7
1290

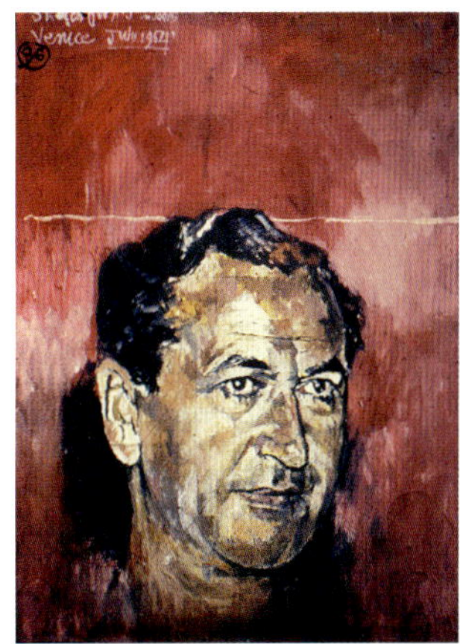

Sutherland, Graham Vivian 1903–1980
Sketch for 'Arthur Jeffress' 1954
oil on card 40.3 x 29.7
72/1963

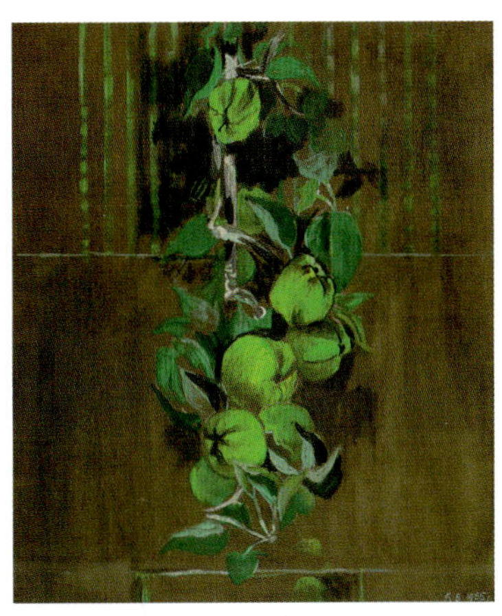

Sutherland, Graham Vivian 1903–1980
Apple Orchard 1955
oil on canvas 55 x 46
61/1963

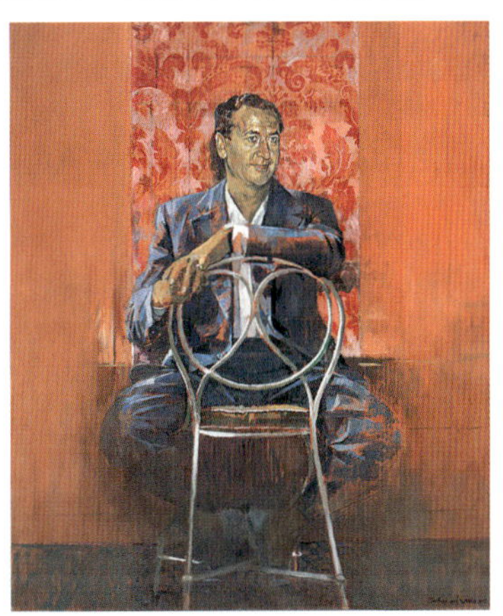

Sutherland, Graham Vivian 1903–1980
Arthur Jeffress 1955
oil on canvas 145.5 x 122
71/1963

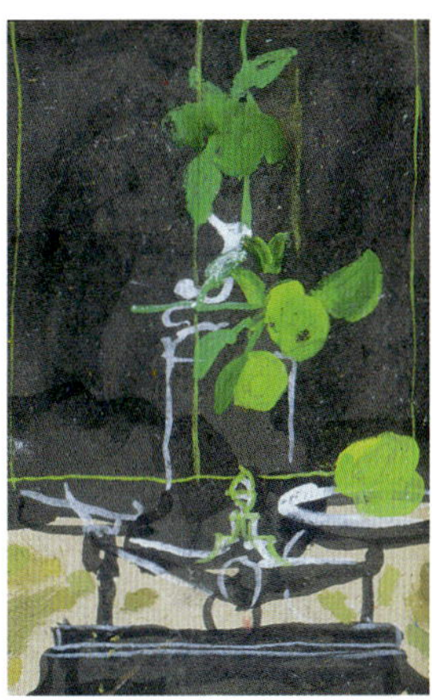

Sutherland, Graham Vivian 1903–1980
Apples and Scales 1957
oil on card 24.5 x 17
74/1963

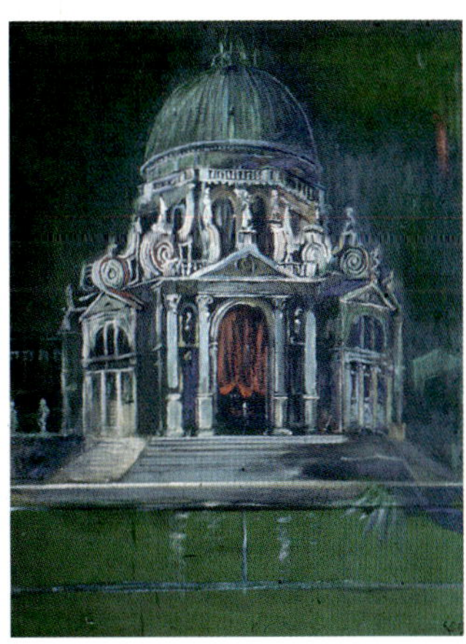

Sutherland, Graham Vivian 1903–1980
Santa Maria della Salute 1957
oil on canvas 99.5 x 80
65/1963

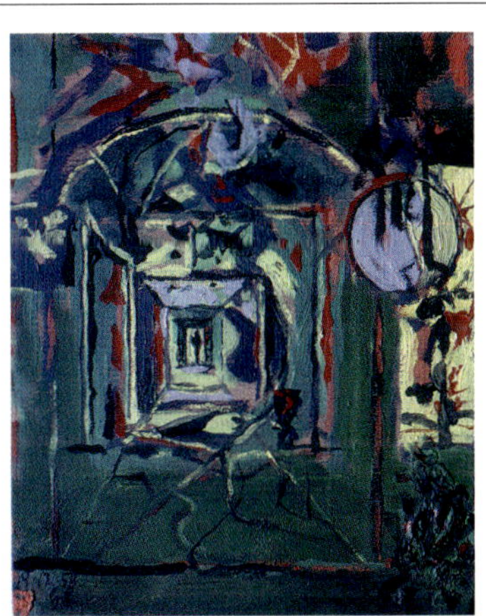

Sutherland, Graham Vivian 1903–1980
Path through Wood 1958
oil on canvas 31 x 25.4
81/1963

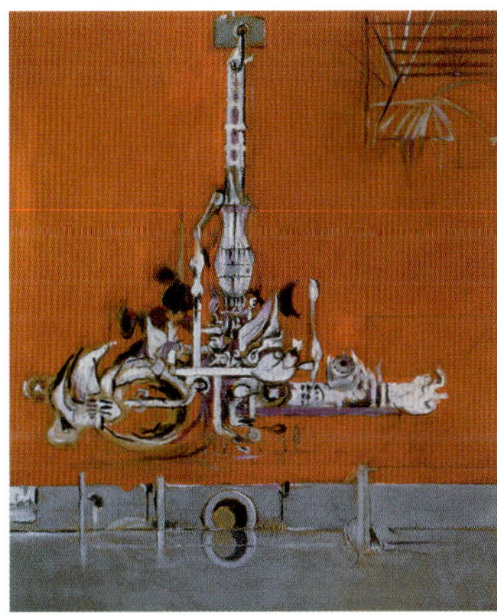

Sutherland, Graham Vivian 1903–1980
Hanging Form over Water 1959
oil on canvas 165.1 x 138.6
62/1963

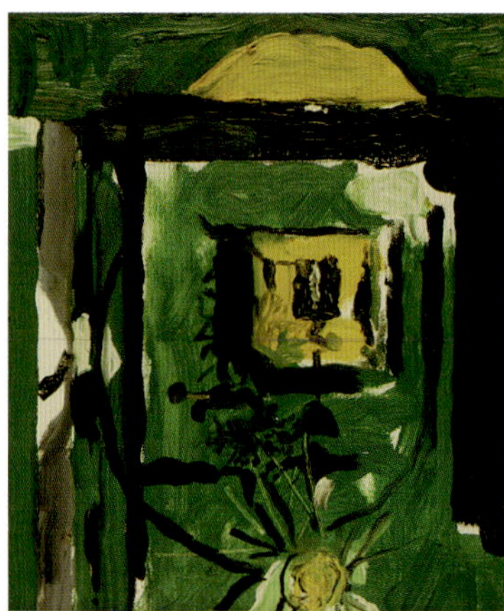

Sutherland, Graham Vivian 1903–1980
Path through Woods
oil on canvas 27 x 22.2
30/1963

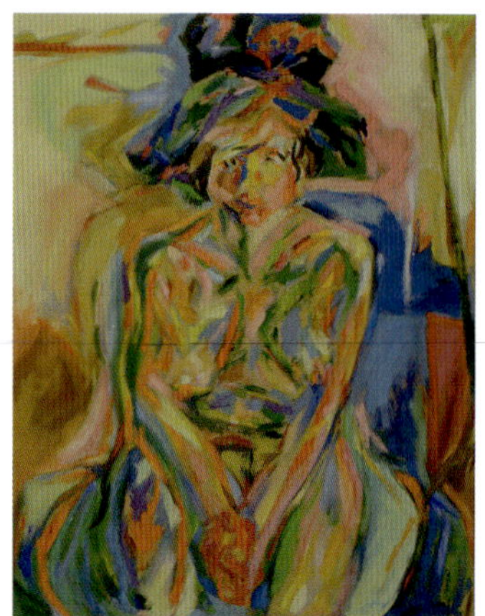

Sutton, Philip b.1928
Nude with Hat 1959
oil on canvas 91.9 x 73
7/1962

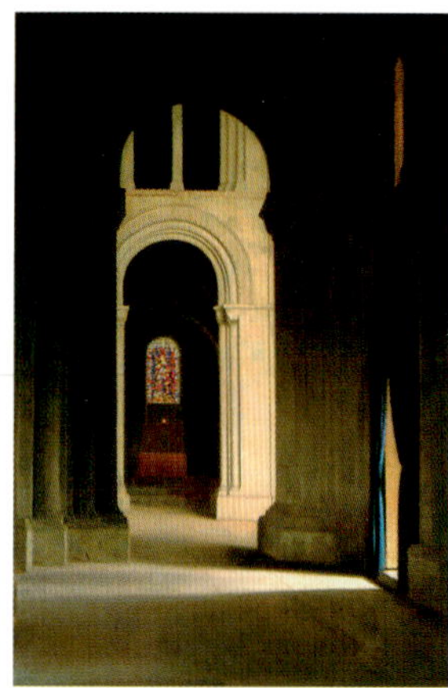

Taylor, Leonard Campbell 1874–1969
Romsey Abbey
oil on canvas 86 x 58.3
571

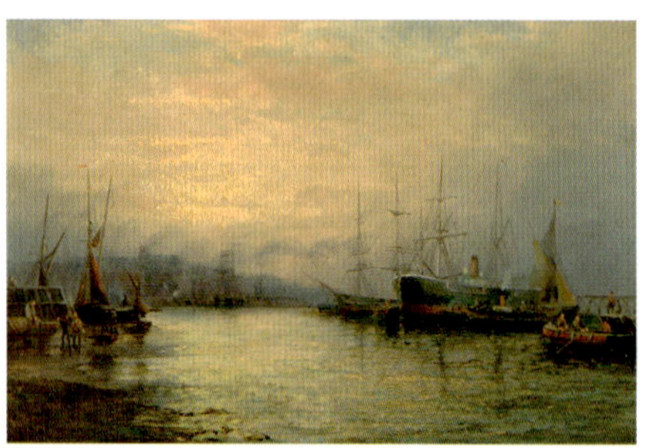

Thornbury, William Anslow
active 1858–1906
Sunset at Low Tide
oil on wood 20.2 x 30.5
576

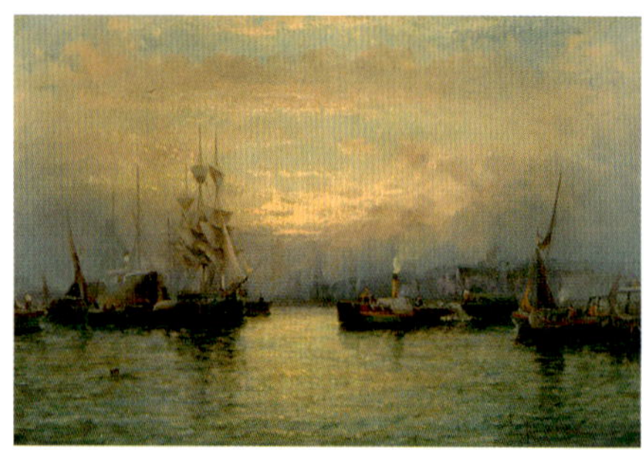

Thornbury, William Anslow
active 1858–1906
Sunset on the Thames
oil on canvas 20.2 x 30.4
577

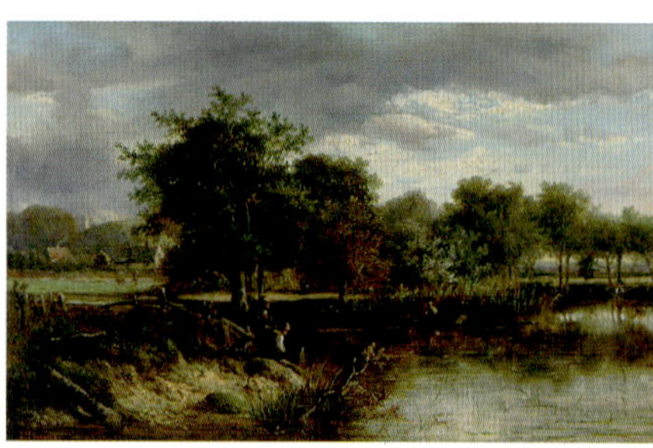

Thors, Joseph (attributed to) c.1834–1898
The Anglers
oil on canvas 22.5 x 40.8
575

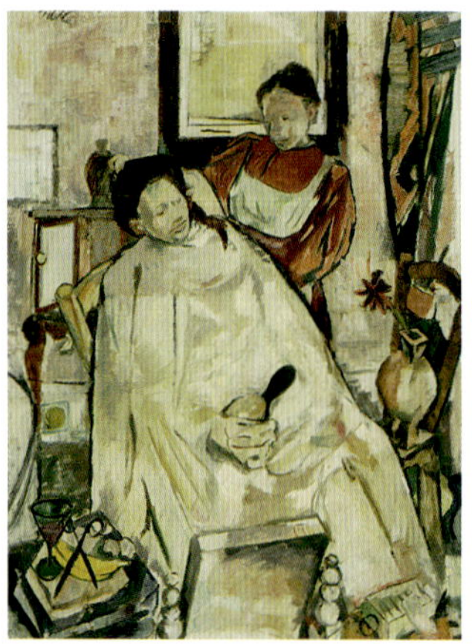

Tibble, Geoffrey Arthur 1909–1952
Hairdressing 1947
oil on canvas 100 x 73.7
1303

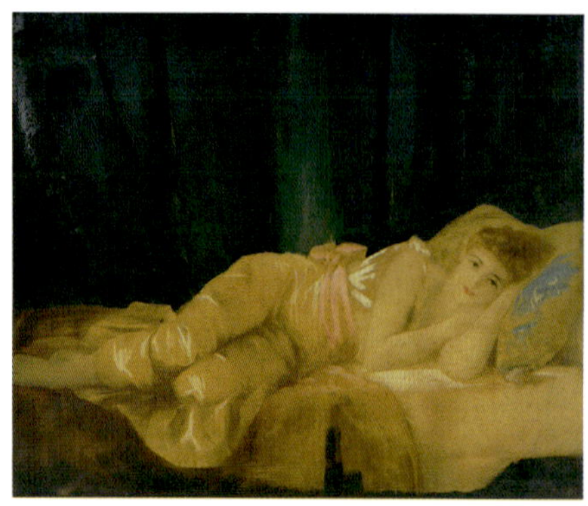

Tillier, Paul Prosper (copy after) 1834–1915
Woman in Repose
oil on wood 21 x 26.7
578

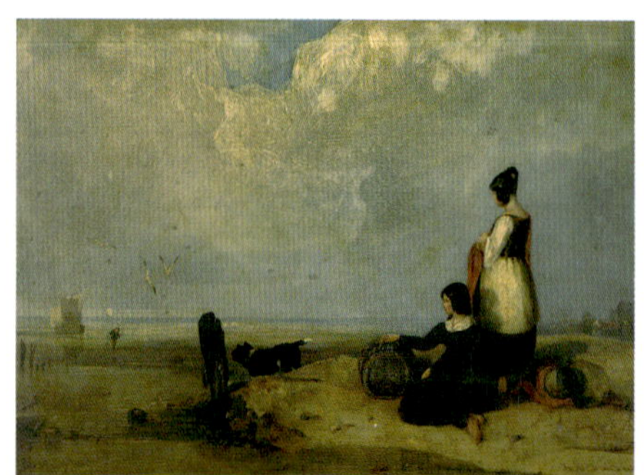

Timbrell, James Christopher 1807–1850
Watching for Boats 1834
oil on card 36.2 x 52.1
579

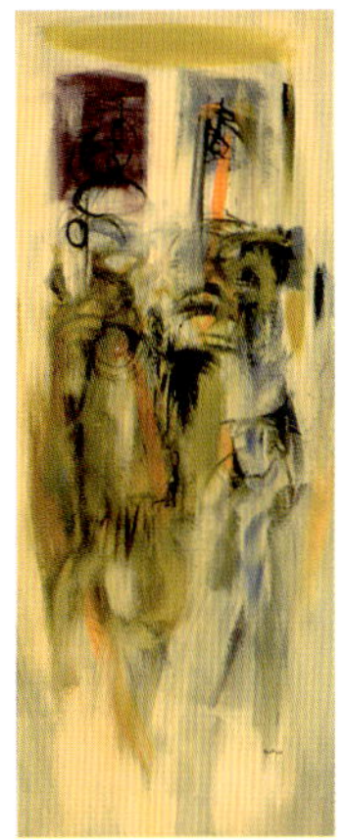

Tippett, Bruce b.1933
Abstract 1958
oil on board 154.5 x 62.7
L7E

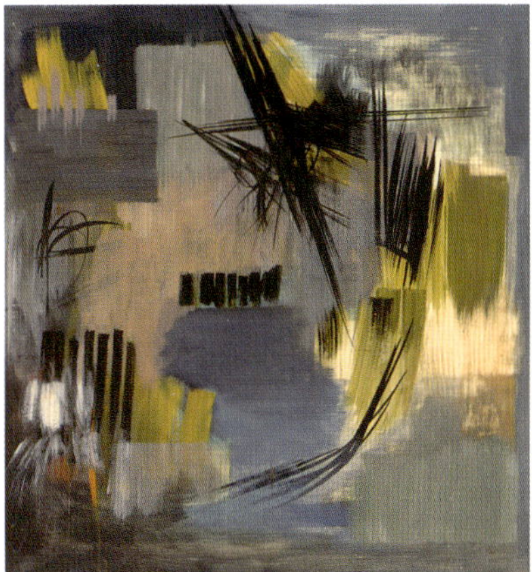

Tippett, Bruce b.1933
Abstract 3 1958
tempera on board 93.7 x 93.9
L7D

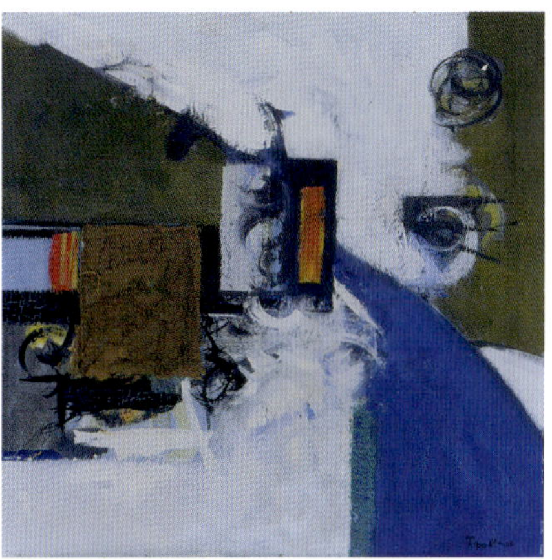

Tippett, Bruce b.1933
Untitled 1958
oil on board 71.8 x 71.8
71/2002

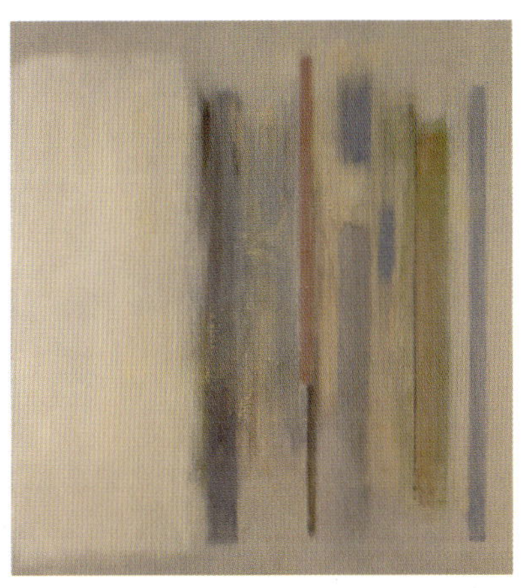

Tippett, Bruce b.1933
Mainly Blue
oil on board 124.6 x 117.2
L7G

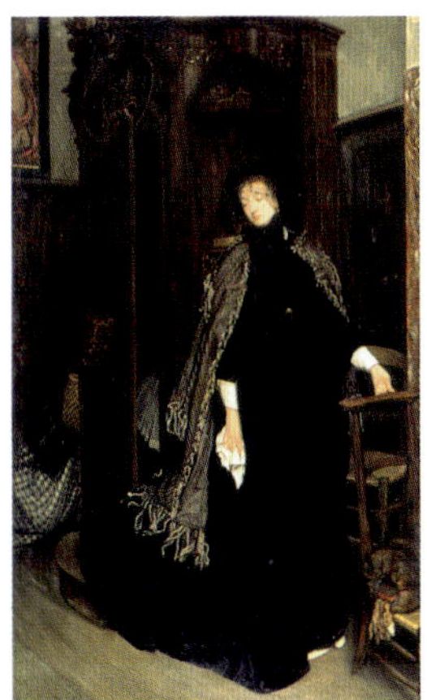

Tissot, James 1836–1902
In Church 1865
oil on canvas 115.4 x 69.2
581

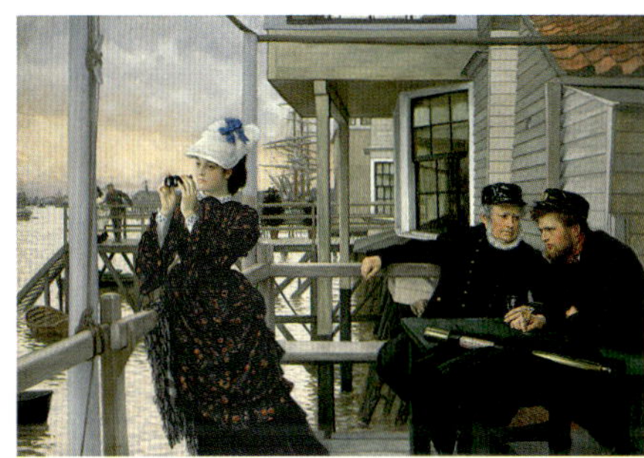

Tissot, James 1836–1902
The Captain's Daughter (The Last Evening)
1873
oil on canvas 72.4 x 104.8
580

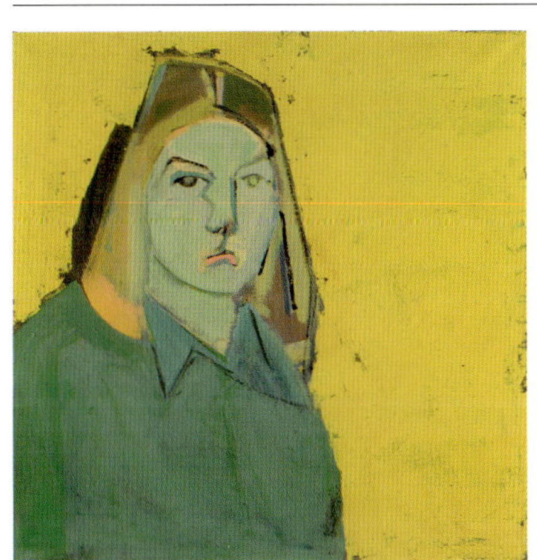

Tomkins, Riduan b.1941
Jacky
oil on canvas 95.3 x 95.5
44/2006

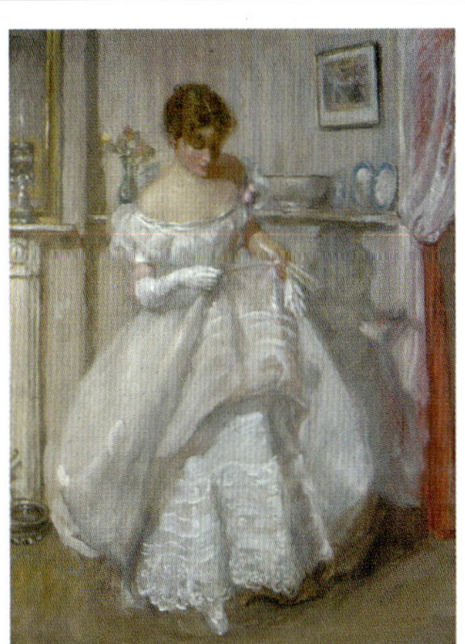

Tonks, Henry 1862–1937
The Torn Gown
oil on canvas 87.2 x 72.1
584

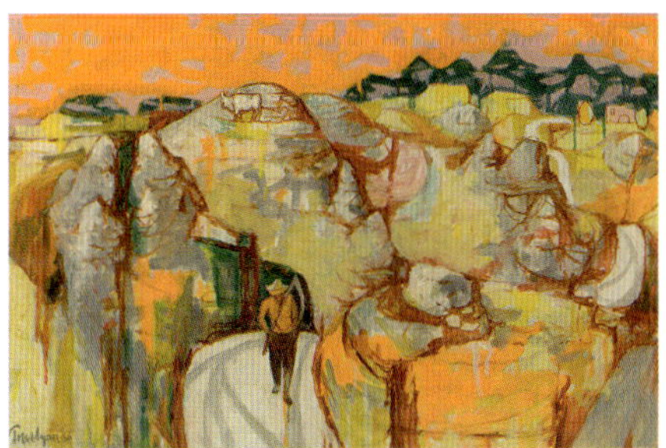

Trevelyan, Julian 1910–1989
'Siense Creti' 1956
oil on canvas 59.8 x 92.5
4/1958

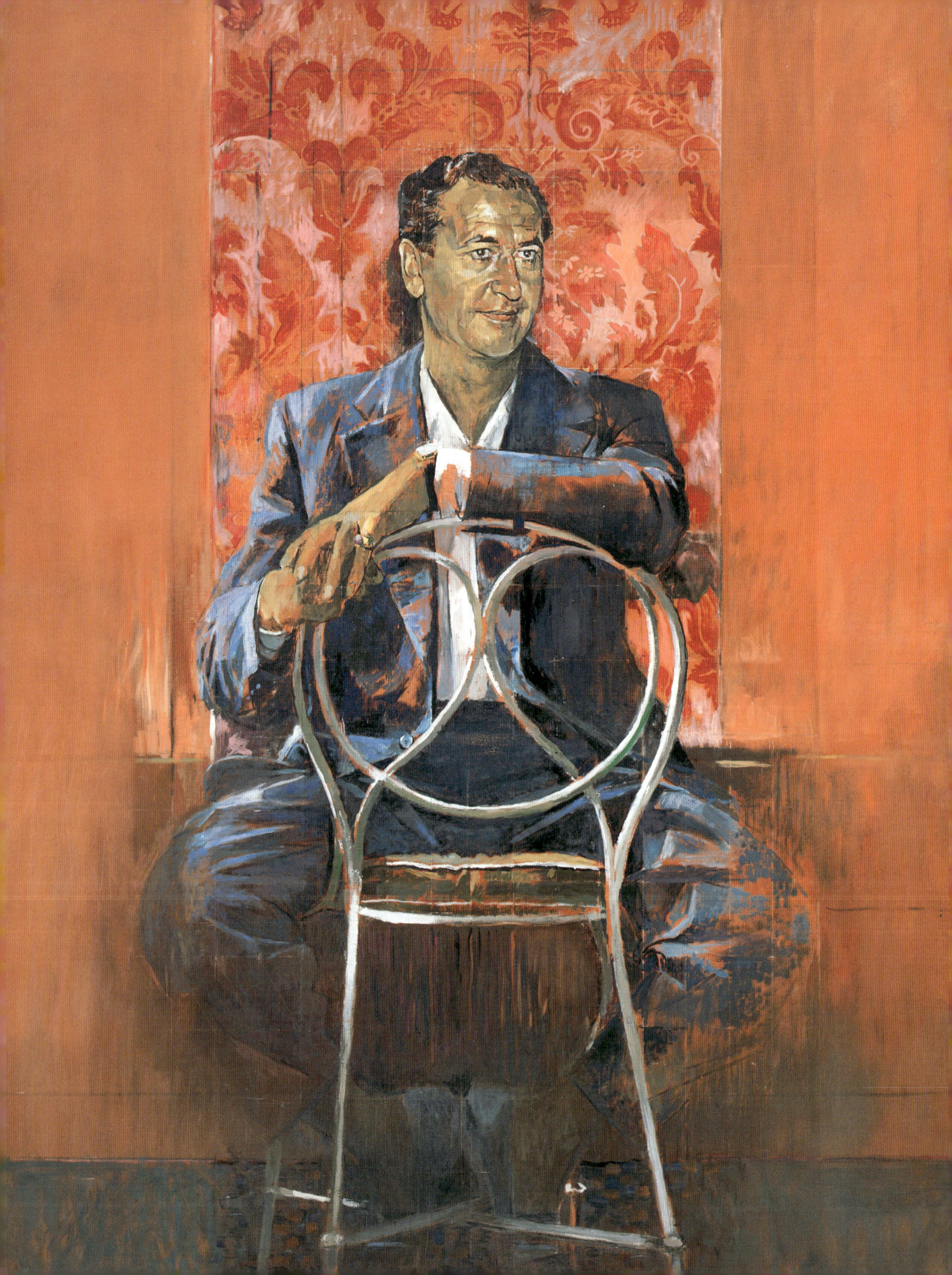

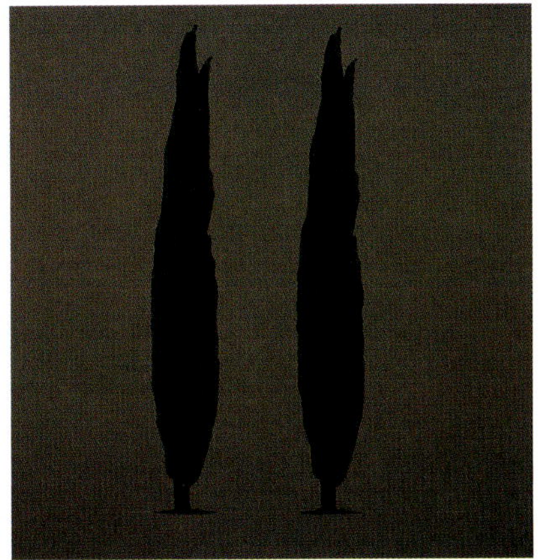

Troostwyk, David b.1929
The Funeral Cypress 2005
spectra gel & alkyd resin on canvas
169.6 x 169.6
7/2005

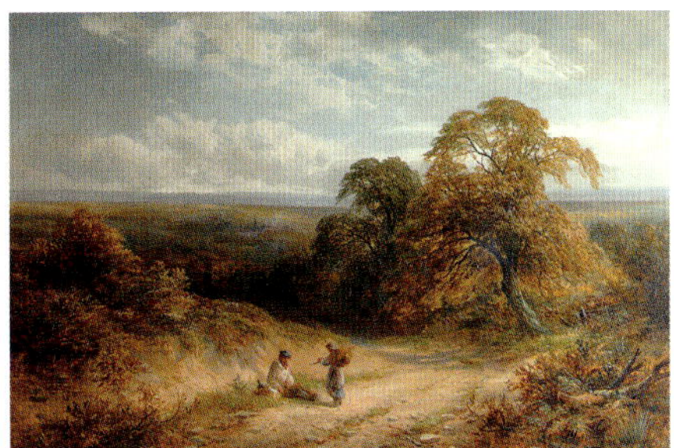

Turner, George II 1843–1910
A Lane in Surrey 1880
oil on canvas 61.2 x 91.3
587

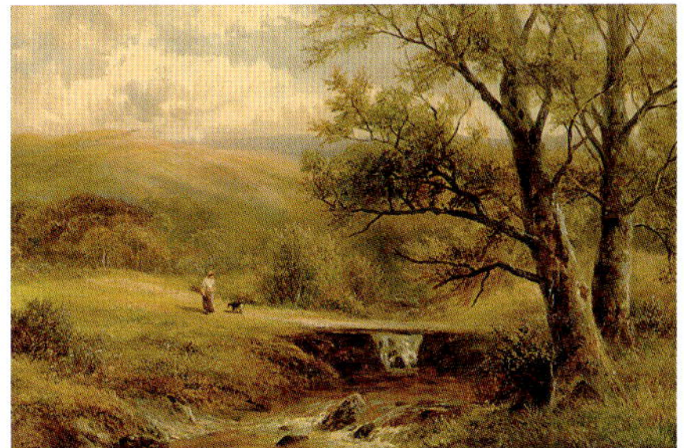

Turner, George II 1843–1910
Mountain Stream 1891
oil on canvas 40.6 x 60.6
589

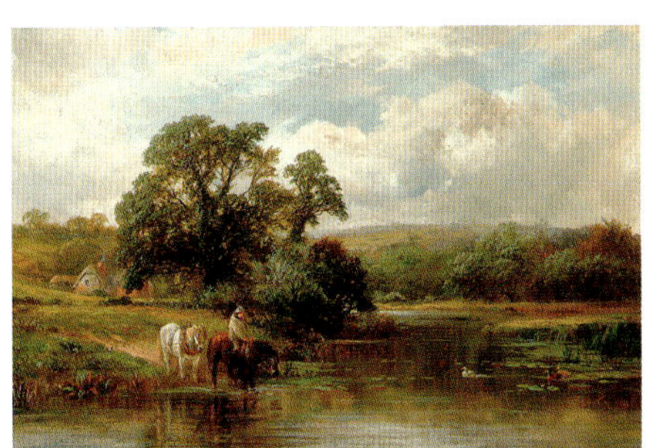

Turner, George II 1843–1910
Watering Place
oil on canvas 40.5 x 61
588

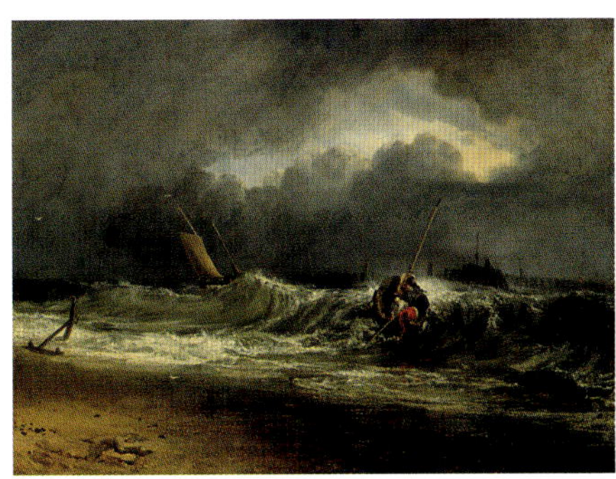

Turner, Joseph Mallord William 1775–1851
Fishermen upon a Lee Shore in Squally Weather 1802
oil on canvas 91.5 x 122
1396

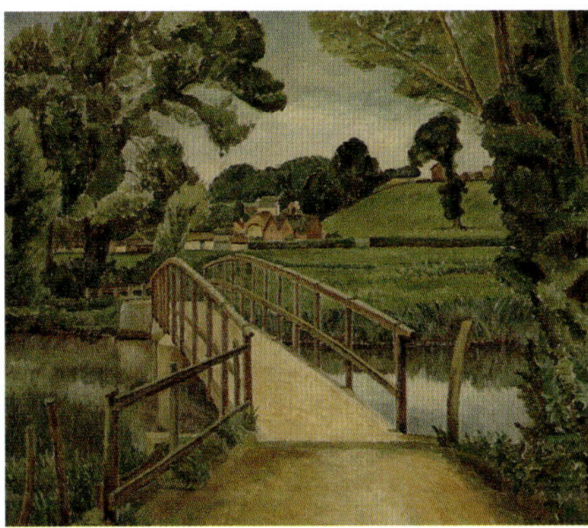

Tyson, Kathleen 1898–c.1982
Woodford
oil on canvas 63.8 x 76.5
590

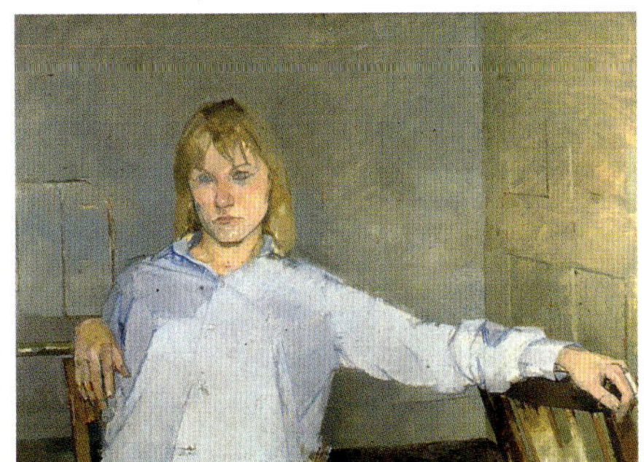

Uglow, Euan 1932–2000
Miss Benge 1961
oil on canvas 71 x 99
6/1962

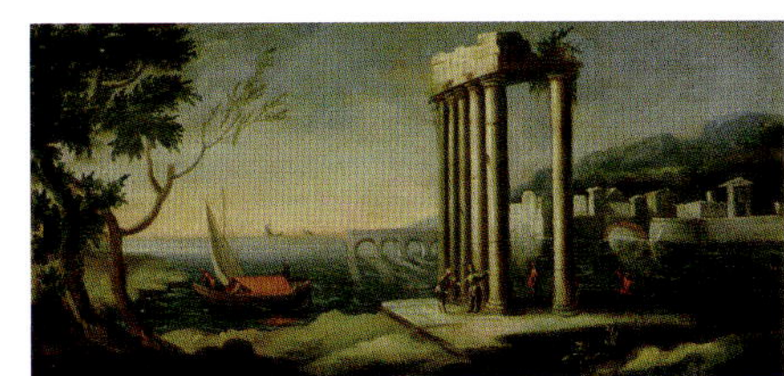

unknown artist 18th C
Coastal Town with Ruined Temple
oil on canvas 41.2 x 88.9
96/1963

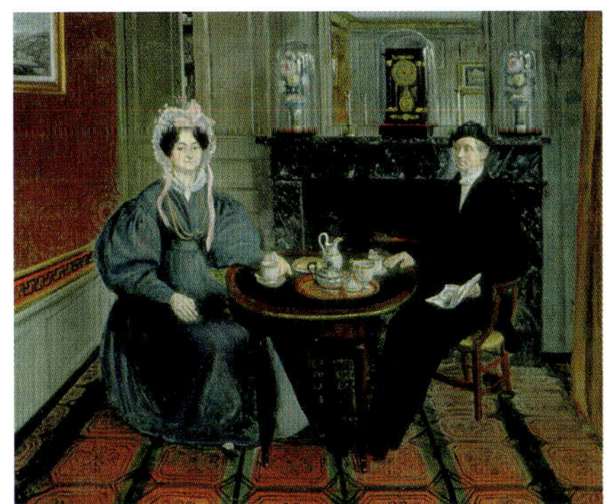

unknown artist
Couple Having Tea 1830–1840
oil on canvas 60 x 73
56/1963

Facing page: Sutherland, Graham Vivian, 1903–1980, *Arthur Jeffress* (detail), 1955, Southampton City Art Gallery, (p. 127)

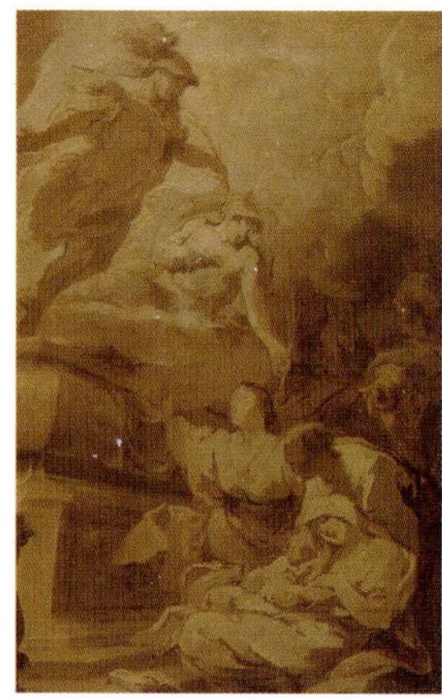

unknown artist
A Female Saint(?) in Ecstasy before 1900
oil on card 37.5 x 22.8
180/1975

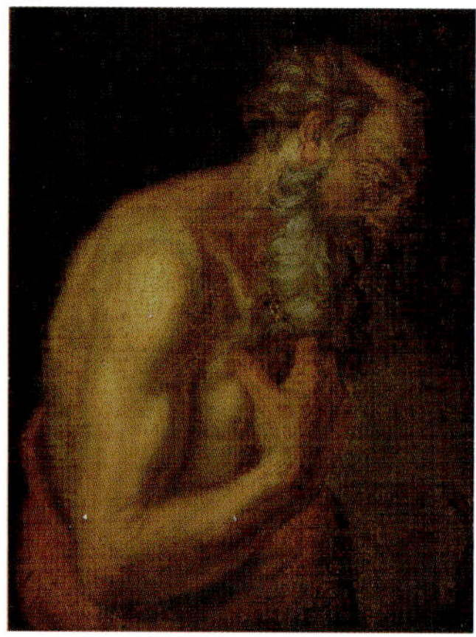

unknown artist
Figure of a Saint before 1900
oil on canvas 30.5 x 24.8
645

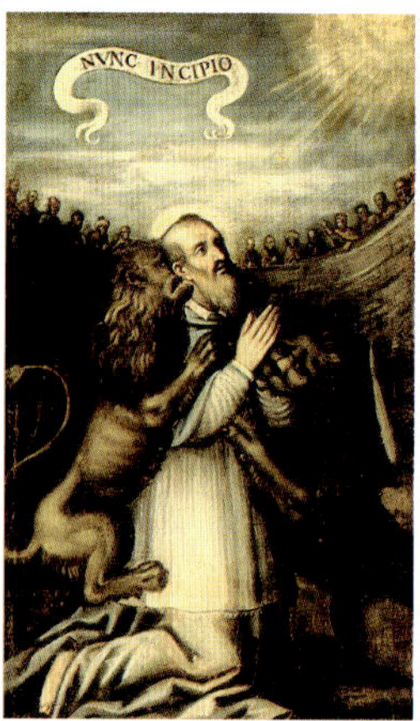

unknown artist
Martyrdom of a Saint in the Lion's Den
before 1900
oil on canvas 118 x 70.2
95/1963

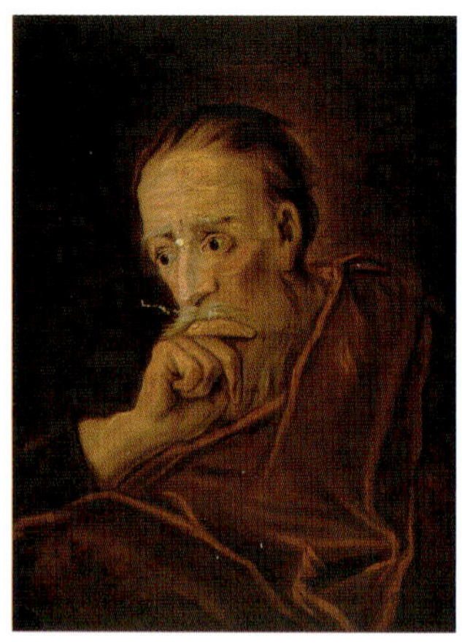

unknown artist
St Jerome before 1900
oil on canvas 72.5 x 55
646

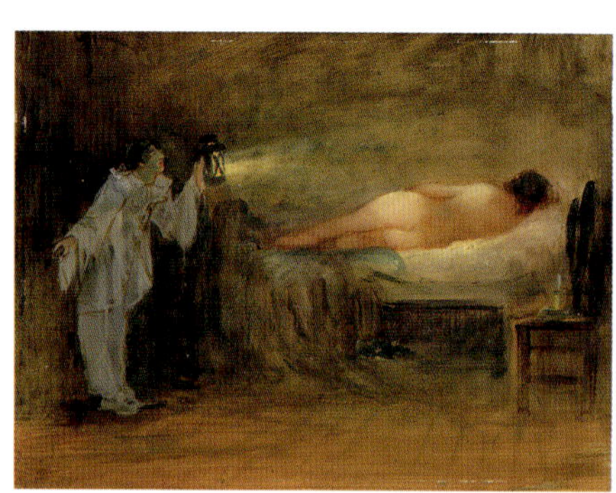

unknown artist 19th C
Carnival Scene
oil on board 29 x 39
27/1963

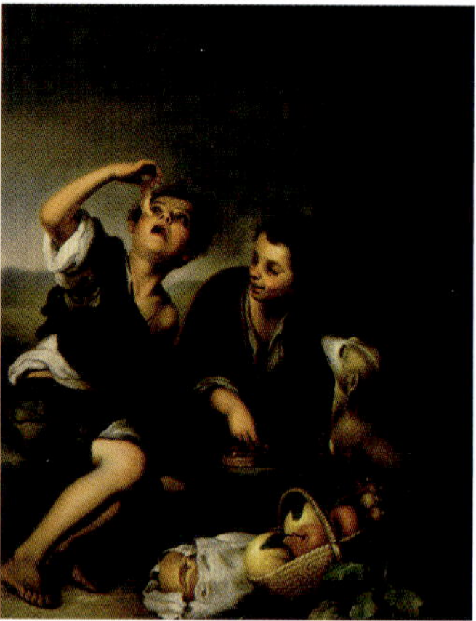

unknown artist 19th C
Children with Dog and a Basket of Fruit (after Bartolomé Esteban Murillo)
oil on canvas 80.5 x 63.5
1115

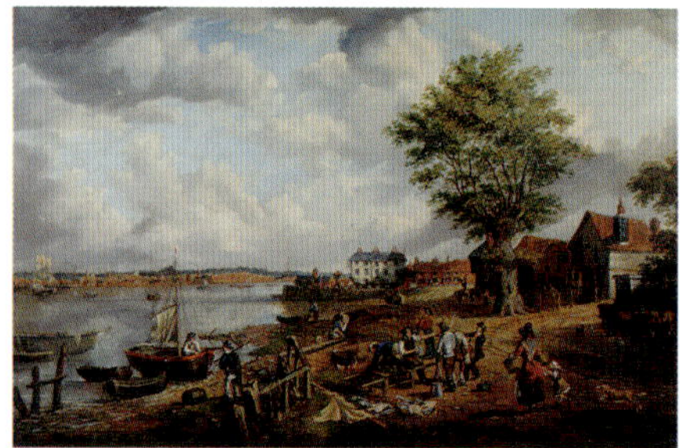

unknown artist 19th C
Floating Bridge
oil on canvas 61 x 95
658

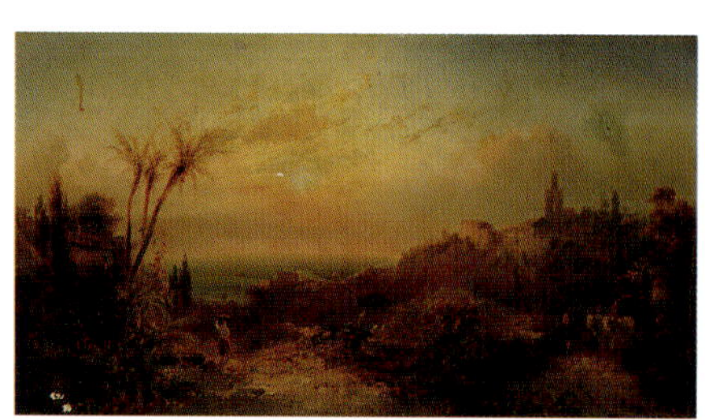

unknown artist 19th C
Landscape, Eastern Scene
oil on canvas 51 x 93.4
656

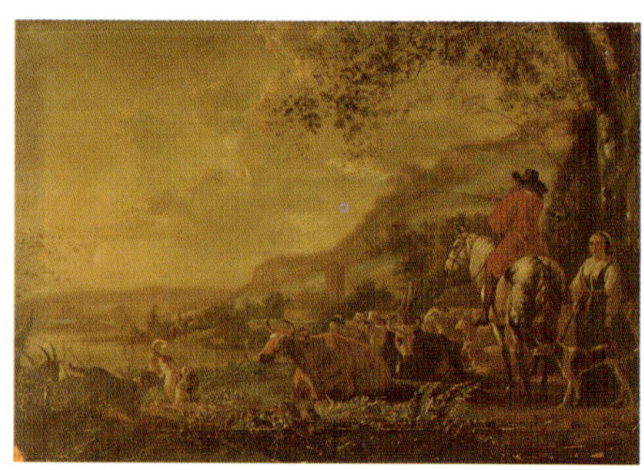

unknown artist 19th C
Lost Huntsman
oil on canvas 42.2 x 61
135

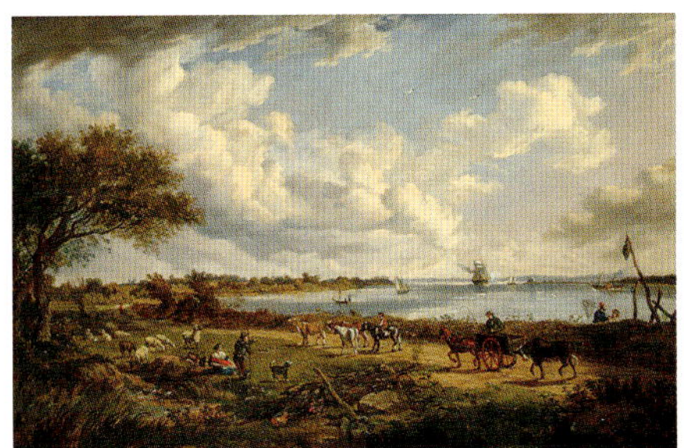

unknown artist 19th C
Netley Shore
oil on canvas 78.7 x 111.4
657

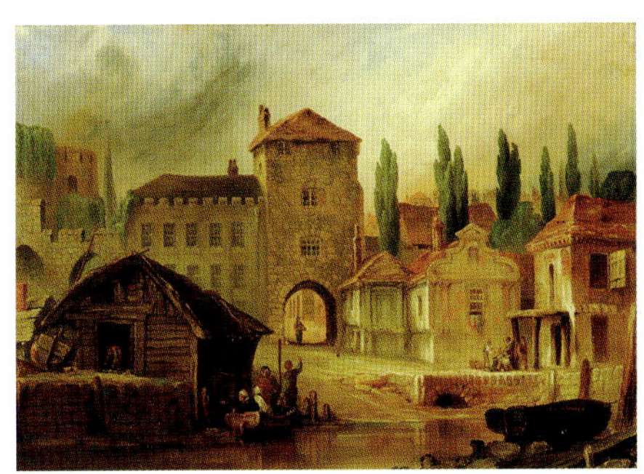

unknown artist 19th C
Old Boat House, West Quay, Southampton
oil on wood 36.5 x 52.1
664

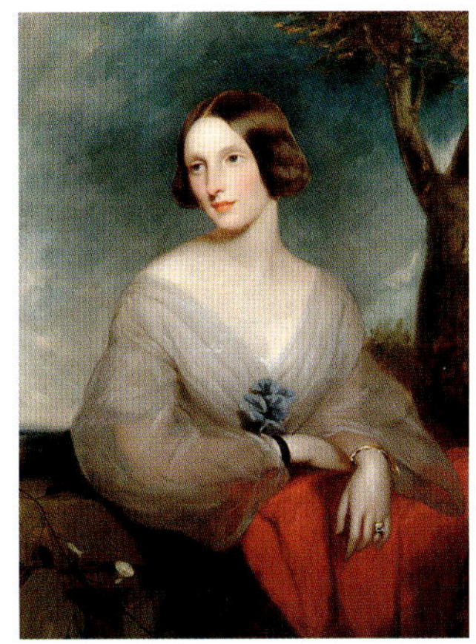

unknown artist 19th C
Portrait of a Lady
oil on canvas 101 x 75
872

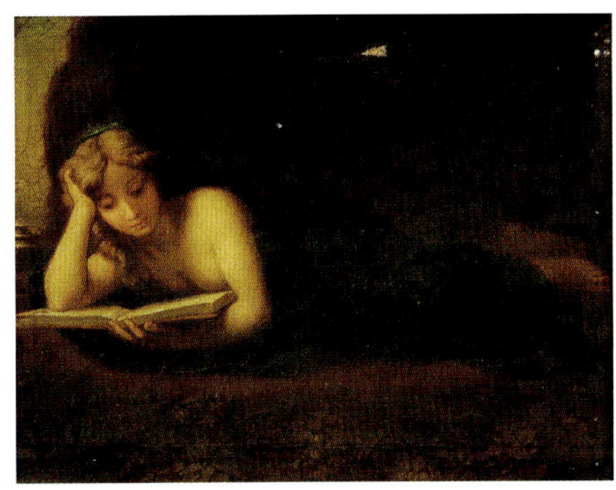

unknown artist 19th C
Reading Magdalene (after Correggio)
oil on canvas 23.2 x 29.3
122

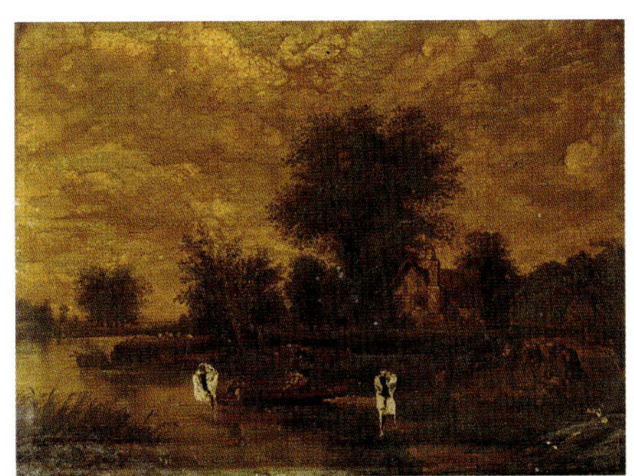

unknown artist 19th C
River Landscape with Cottage and Figures
oil on canvas 64 x 92.5
659

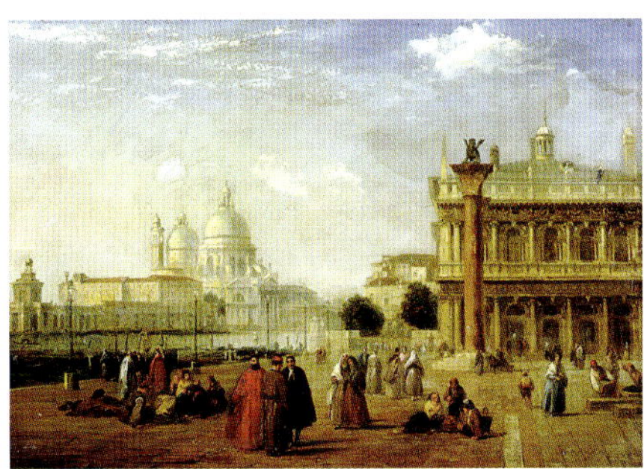

unknown artist 19th C
View of Venice
oil on canvas 43.2 x 63.5
90/1963

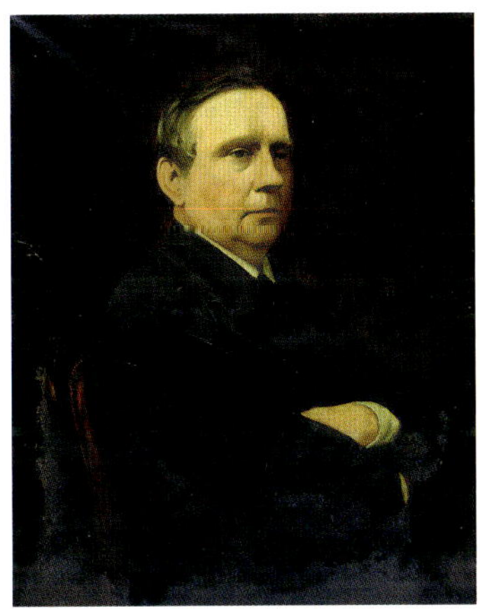

unknown artist
Councillor Timothy Falvey
oil on canvas 73.7 x 61
647

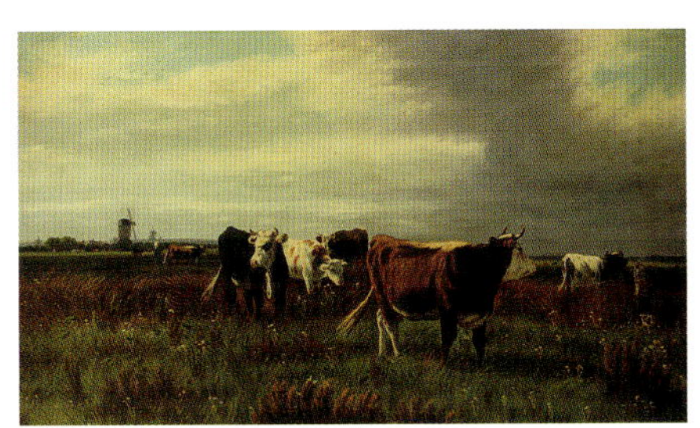

unknown artist
Cows in Pasture with Windmills
oil on canvas 76.2 x 127
660

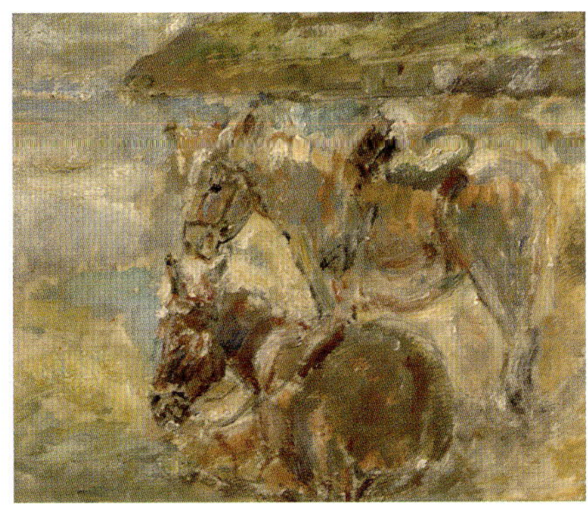

unknown artist
Donkeys by the Sea
oil on wood 28 x 36
2/1988

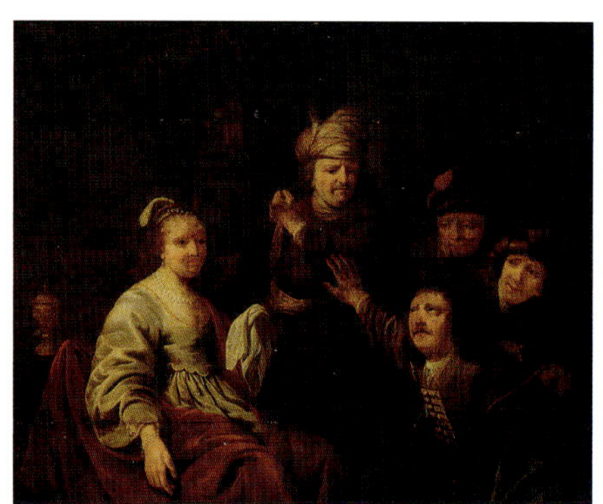

unknown artist
Five Figures in a Quarrel
oil on wood 90.9 x 111.1
669

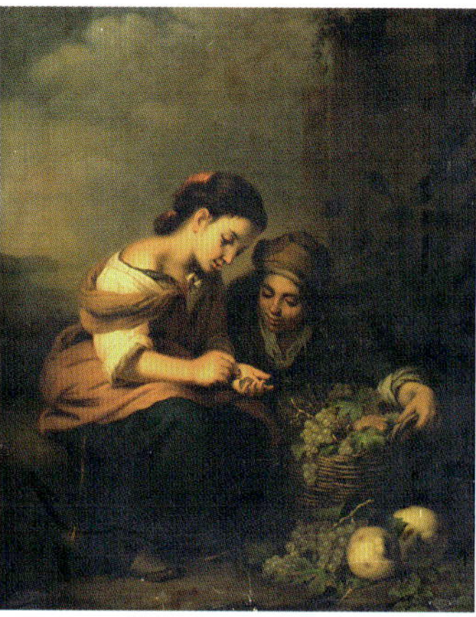

unknown artist
Girl and Boy with Basket of Grapes (after Bartolomé Esteban Murillo)
oil on canvas 80.7 x 63
1116

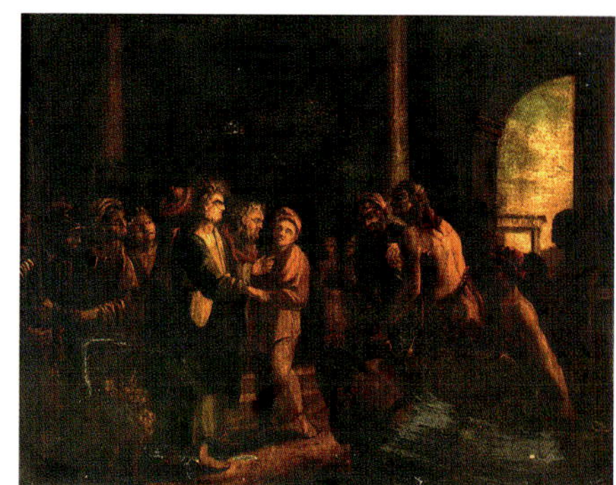

unknown artist
Group of Figures
oil on canvas 79.5 x 101
668

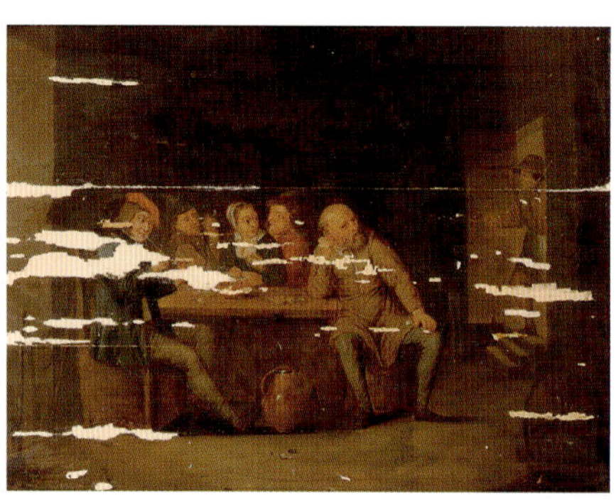

unknown artist
Group of Figures around a Table
oil on wood 48.5 x 63.8
1266

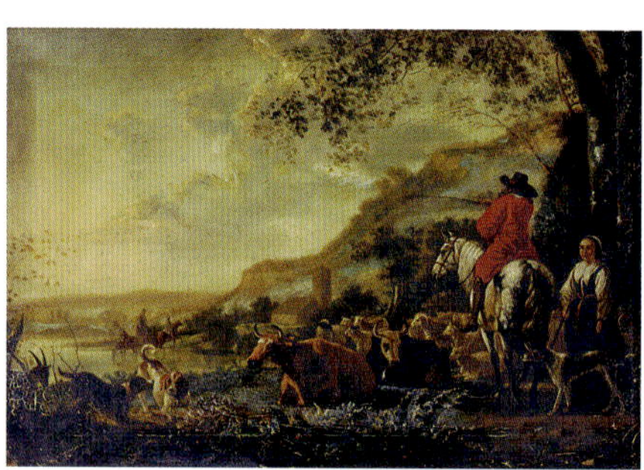

unknown artist
Lost Huntsman
oil on canvas 37.2 x 48.9
652

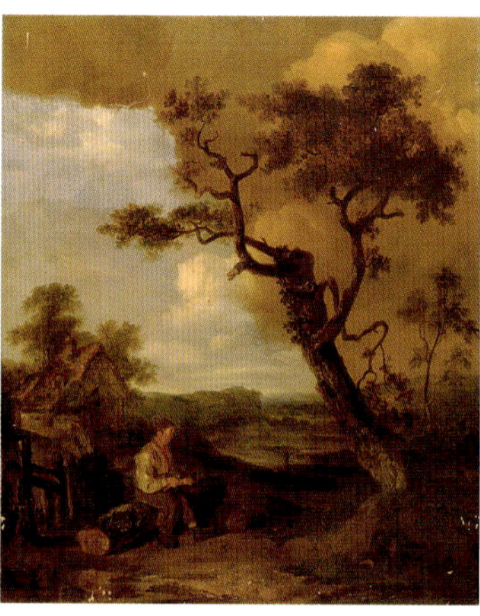

unknown artist
Pastoral Scene with Man Chopping Wood
oil on canvas 75.8 x 63.5
1277

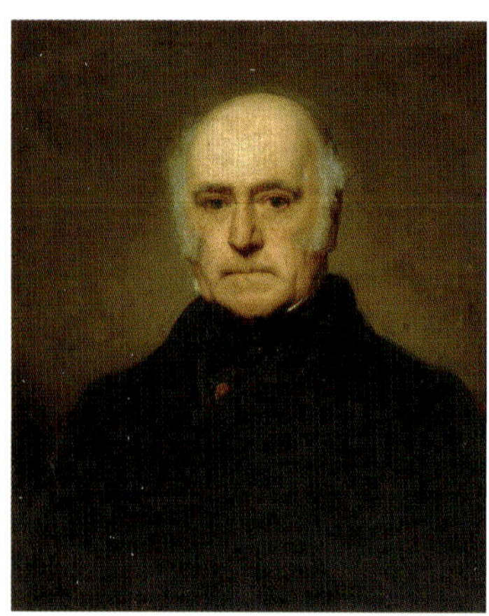

unknown artist
Portrait of a Minister
oil on canvas 73.3 x 59.6
648

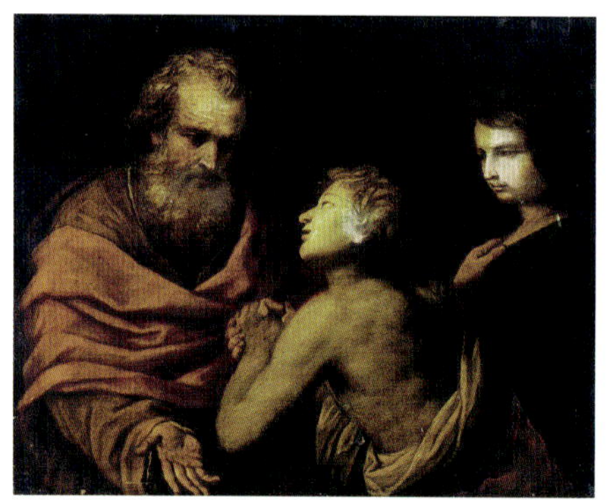

unknown artist
Return of the Prodigal Son
oil on canvas 76.3 x 95.3
907

unknown artist
Southampton, c.1810
oil on canvas 54.2 x 89.3
1381

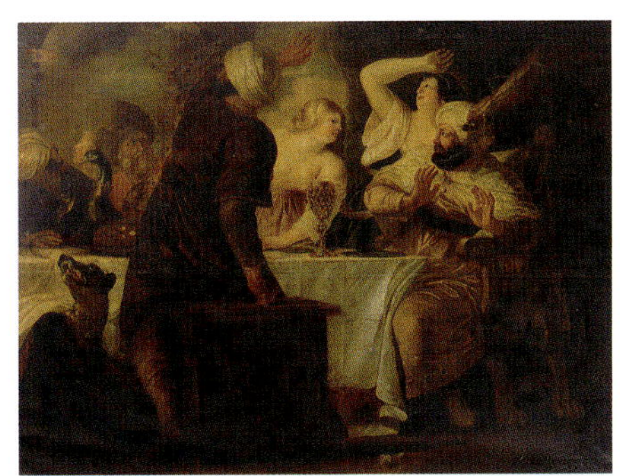

unknown artist
Writing on the Wall
oil on canvas 180.4 x 243.2
662

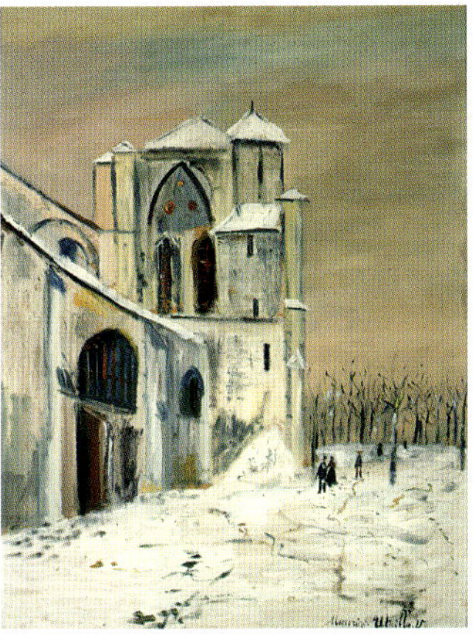

Utrillo, Maurice 1883–1955
The Church at Longpont 1919
oil on card 78.6 x 58.8
714

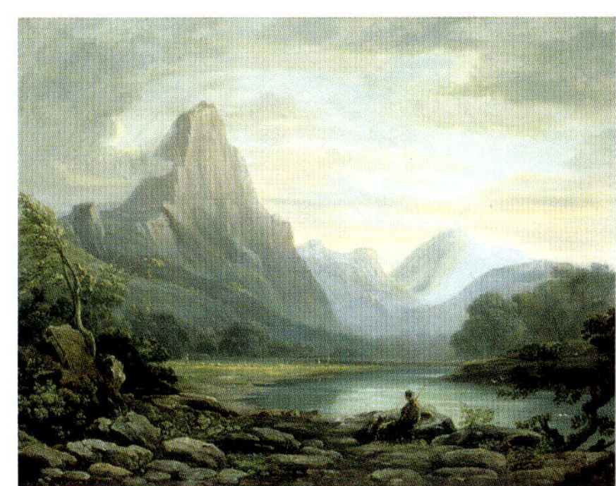

Varley, John I 1778–1842
A Welsh Valley 1819
oil on canvas 79.1 x 102.6
719

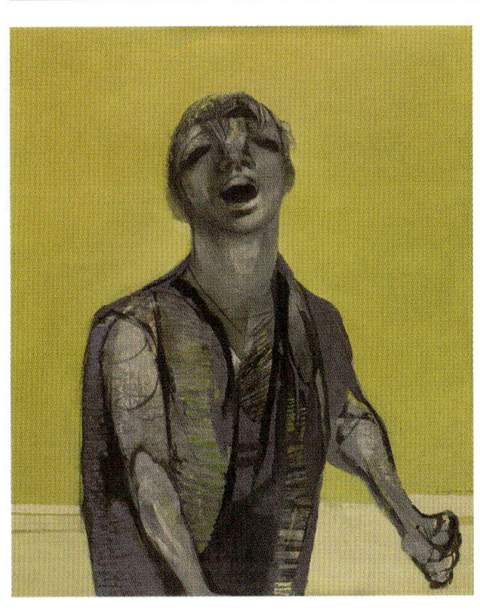

Vaughan, John Keith 1912–1977
The Singer
oil on canvas 83 x 72.8
L71

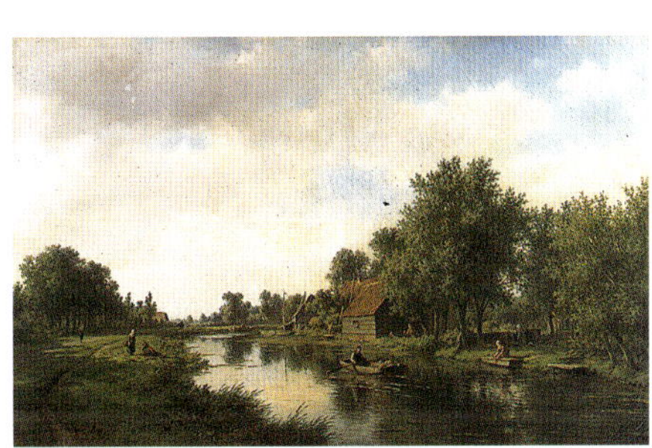

Velley, W.
River Scene
oil on canvas 74.6 x 112.4
1113

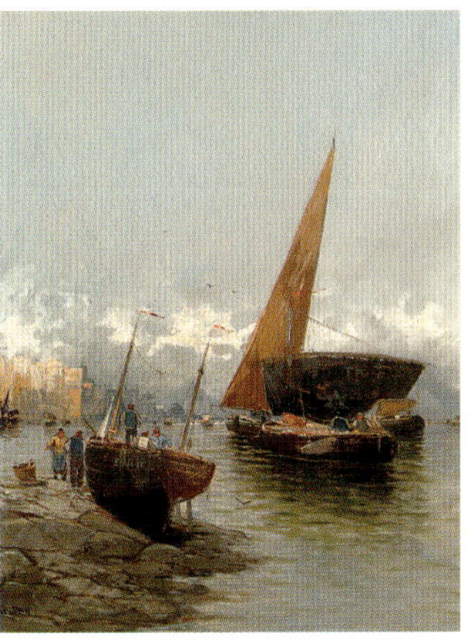

Velten, H.
French Harbour
oil on canvas 69 x 55
1268

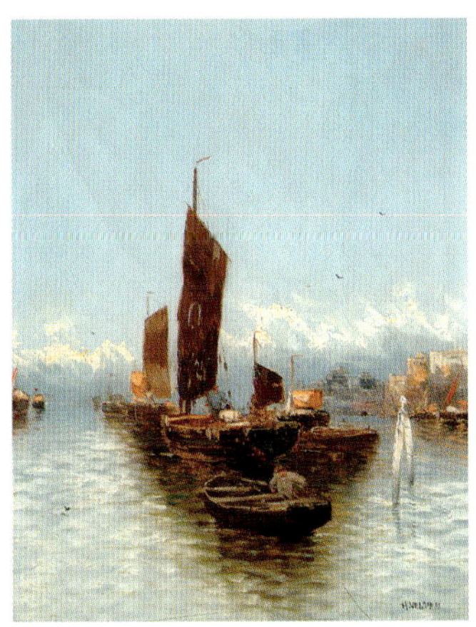

Velten, H.
Italian Harbour
oil on canvas 68.5 x 55.3
1267

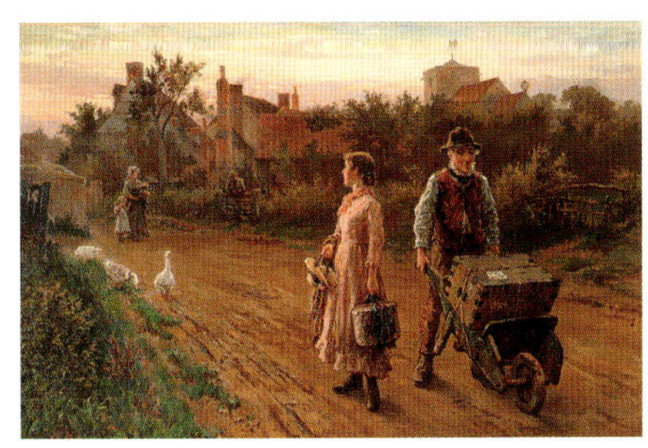

Verey, Arthur 1840–1915
Leaving Home
oil on canvas 83.9 x 127.3
721

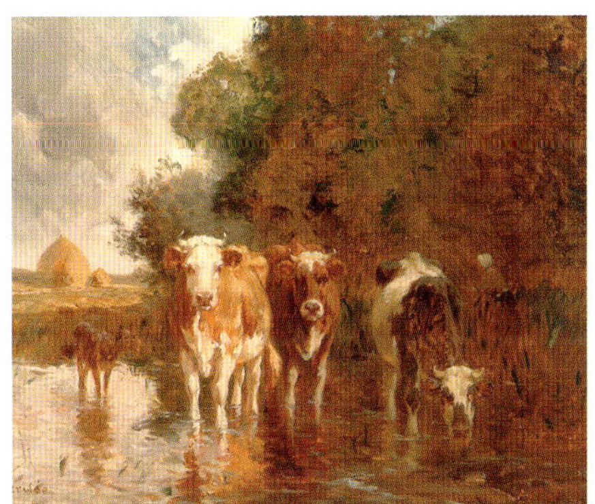

Verwee, Alfred Jacques 1838–1895
Cows in a Pool
oil on canvas 51 x 60.7
720

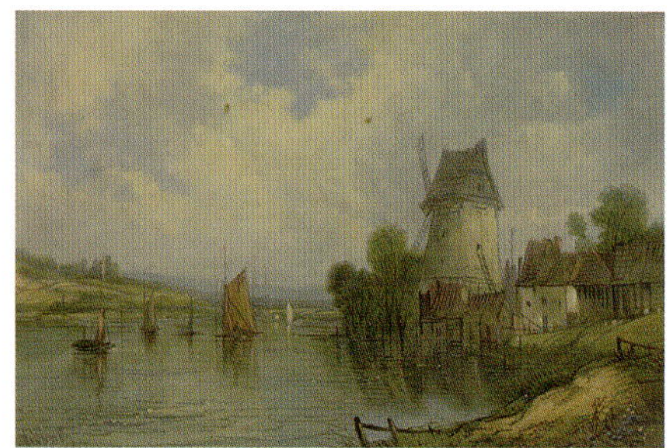

Vickers, Alfred H. 1849–1907
River Scene with a Windmill 1896
oil on canvas 20 x 30.4
1105

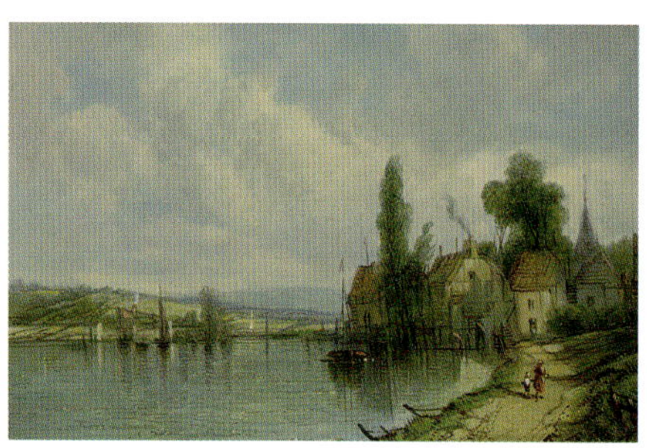

Vickers, Alfred H. 1849–1907
River Scene with Figures
oil on canvas 20.3 x 30.5
1106

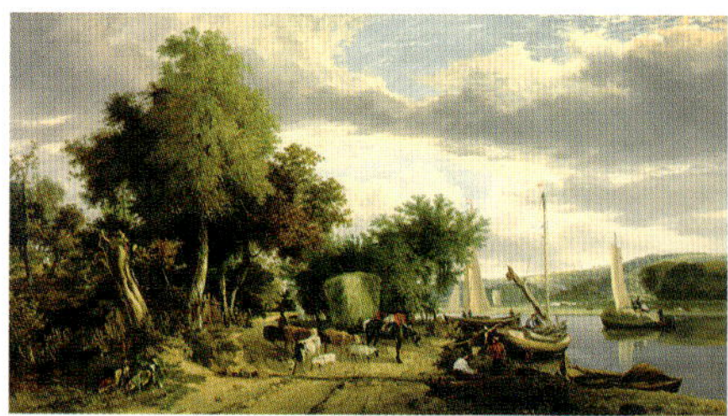

Vincent, George 1796–1831
View on the River Yare
oil on canvas 112.5 x 202
722

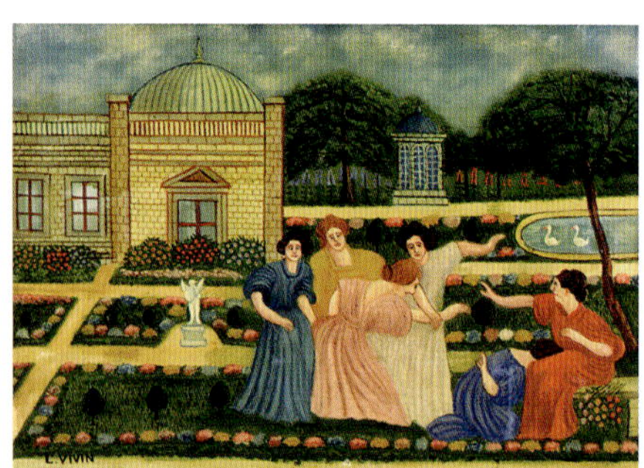

Vivin, Louis 1861–1936
La main chaude
oil on canvas 38 x 55.7
37/1963

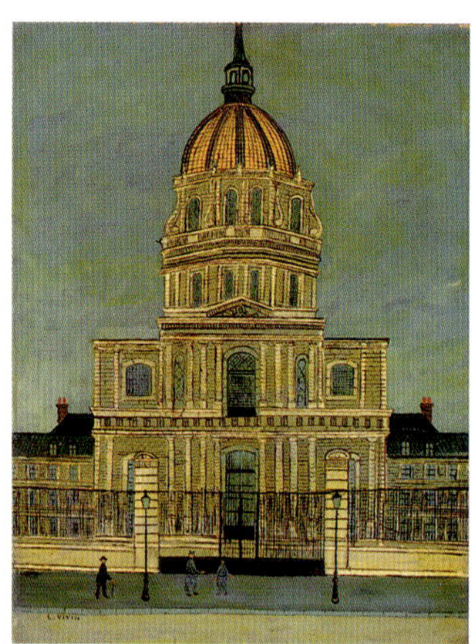

Vivin, Louis 1861–1936
Les Invalides
oil on canvas 61.3 x 46.5
75/1963

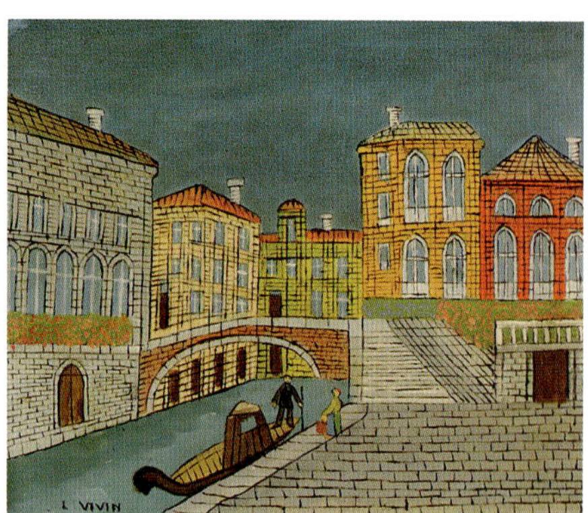

Vivin, Louis 1861–1936
Venice: Canal Scene with a Bridge
oil on canvas 37.7 x 45.7
38/1963

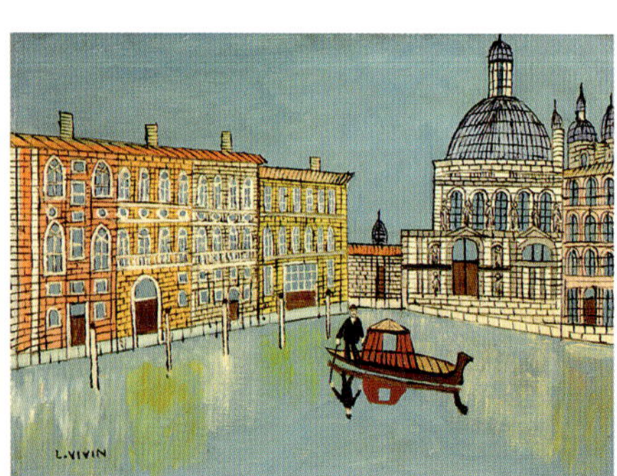

Vivin, Louis 1861–1936
Venice: Canal Scene with a Church
oil on canvas 33.3 x 46.4
77/1963

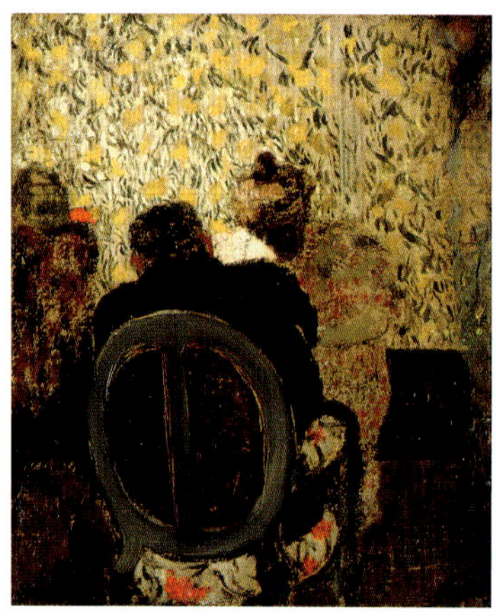

Vuillard, Jean Edouard 1868–1940
La manicure 1897
oil on board 33.5 x 30
2/1968

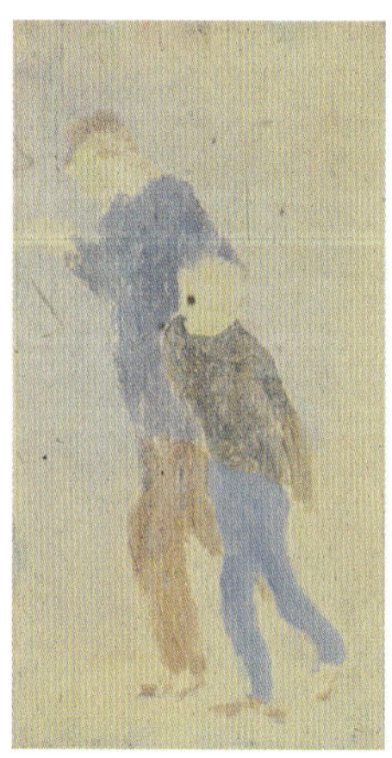

Vuillard, Jean Edouard 1868–1940
Two People
oil on wood 23.5 x 12.6
73/1963

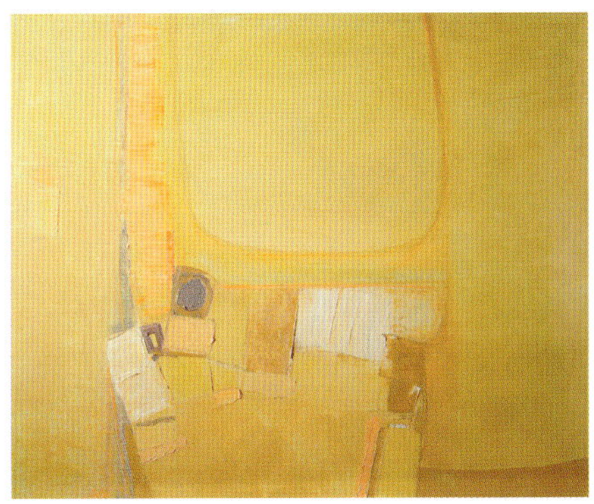

Wakefield, Larry 1925–1997
Yellow on Yellow (detail) 1966
oil on canvas 91.7 x 122
1/1990

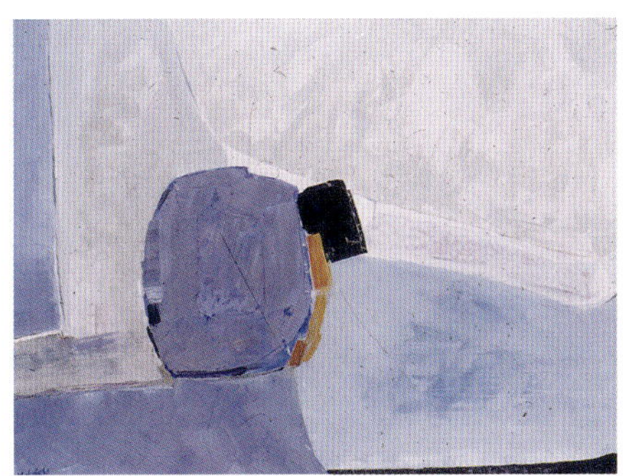

Wakefield, Larry 1925–1997
Solent
oil on board 91.2 x 121.5
1/1967

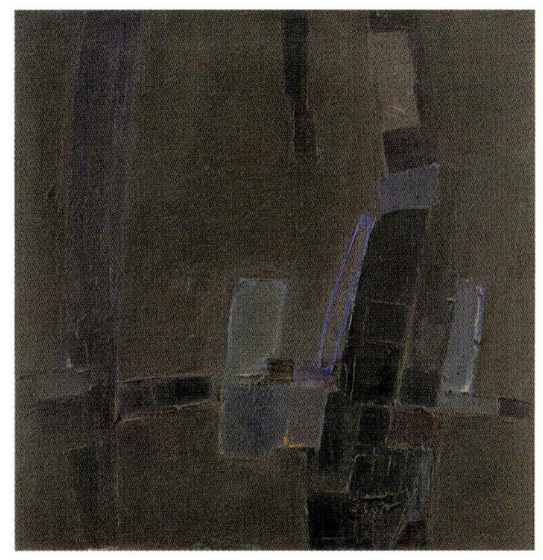

Wakefield, Larry 1925–1997
Untitled (Black with Blues)
oil on board 91 x 91.5
70/2006

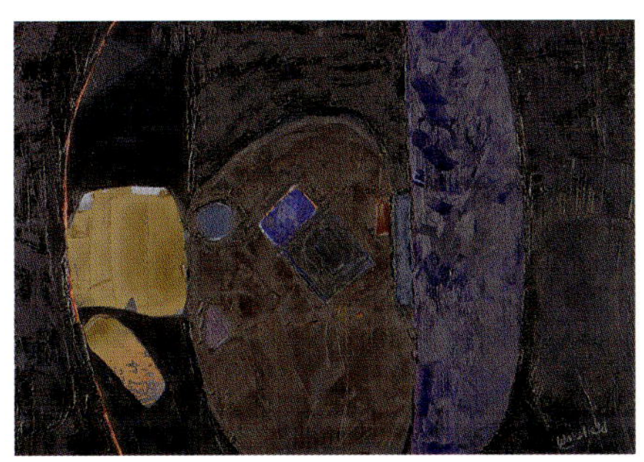

Wakefield, Larry 1925–1997
Untitled (Black with Brown, Blue and Purple)
oil on board 79.2 x 117.8
68/2006

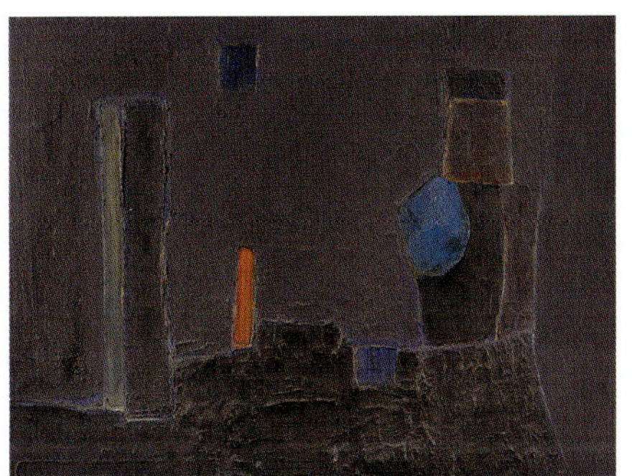

Wakefield, Larry 1925–1997
Untitled (Black with Red and Blue)
oil on board 91 x 201.5
69/2006

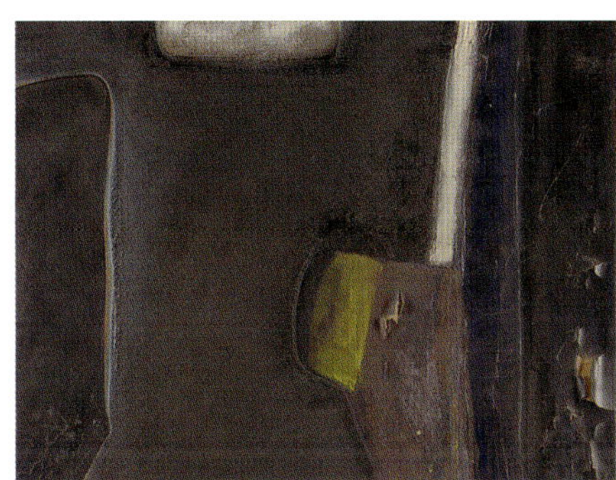

Wakefield, Larry 1925–1997
Untitled (Black with Yellow and White)
oil on board 91.5 x 122.2
72/2006

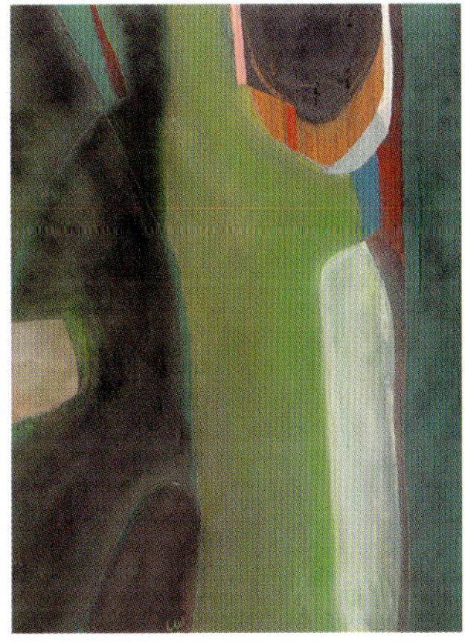

Wakefield, Larry 1925–1997
Untitled (Green with Red, White and Brown)
oil on board 122.4 x 92
71/2006

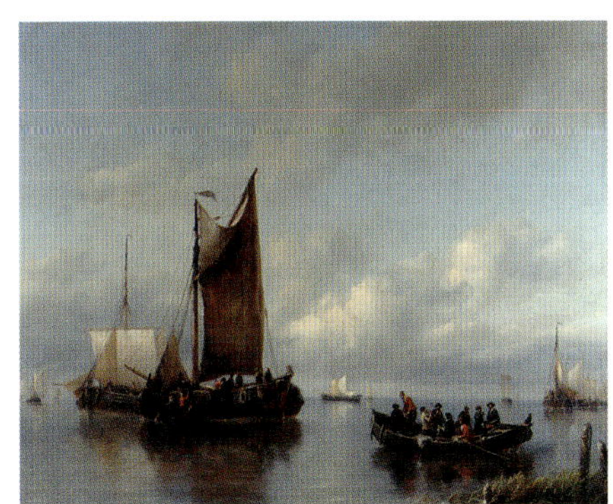

Waldorp, Antonie W. 1803–1866
Seascape 1846
oil on canvas 106.5 x 132.1
1112

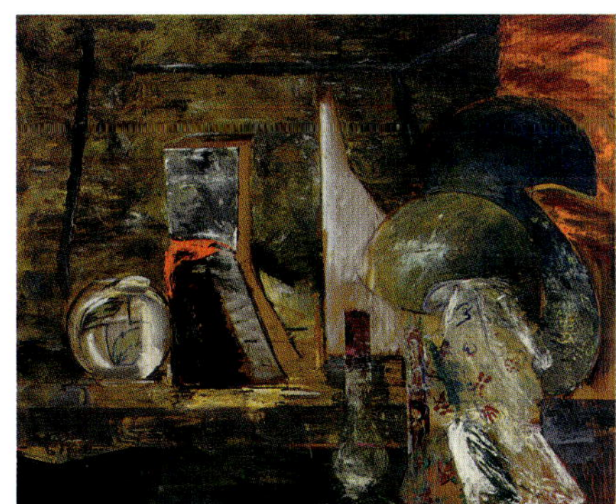

Walker, John b.1939
Labyrinth IV
oil on canvas 248 x 304
3/1980

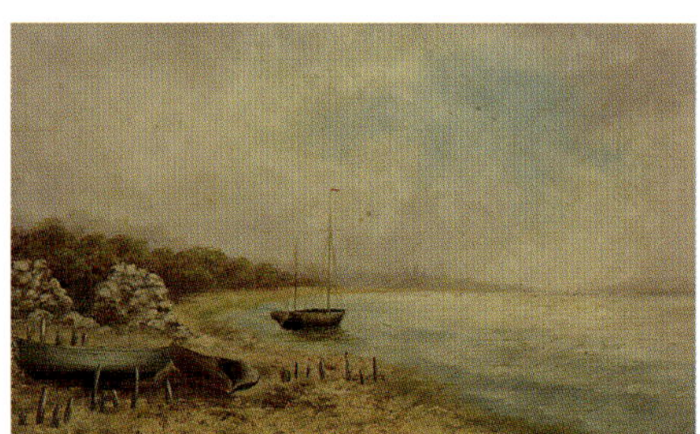
Wall, W. H.
Boats on a Beach
oil on canvas 25.5 x 41
723

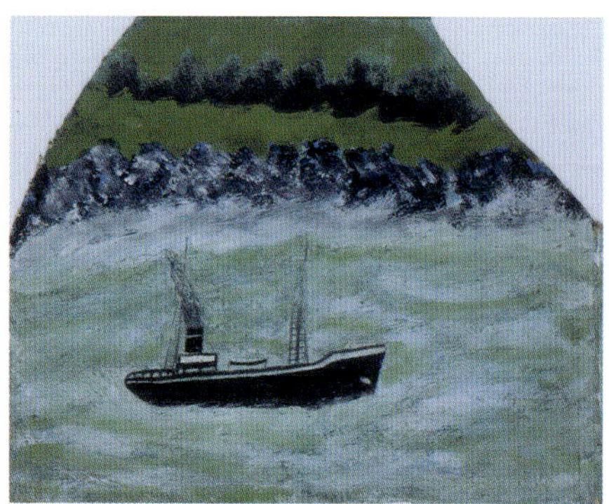
Wallis, Alfred 1855–1942
Boat on the Sea 1937
oil on card 48.6 x 57.2
19/2002

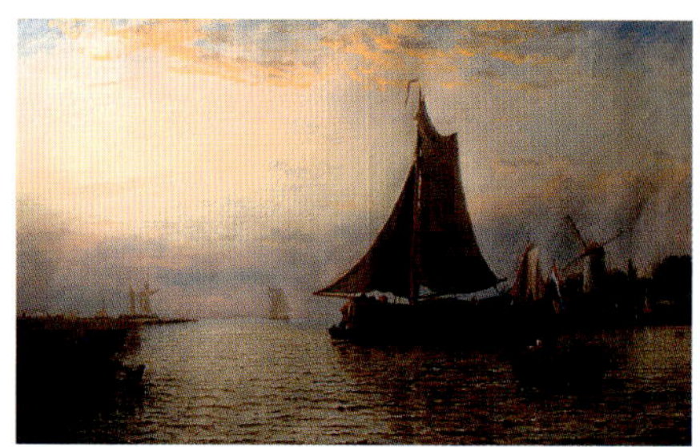
Walters, George Stanfield 1838–1924
'When the west with evening glows' 1881
oil on canvas 66 x 107
725

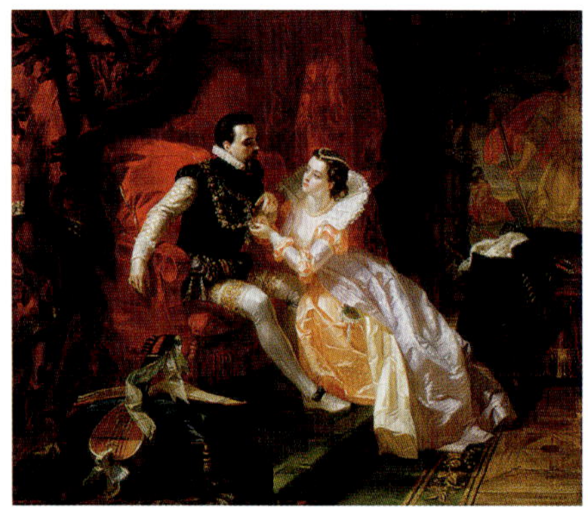
Ward, Edward Matthew 1816–1879
Leicester and Amy Robsart at Cumnor Hall 1866
oil on canvas 107 x 128.9
728

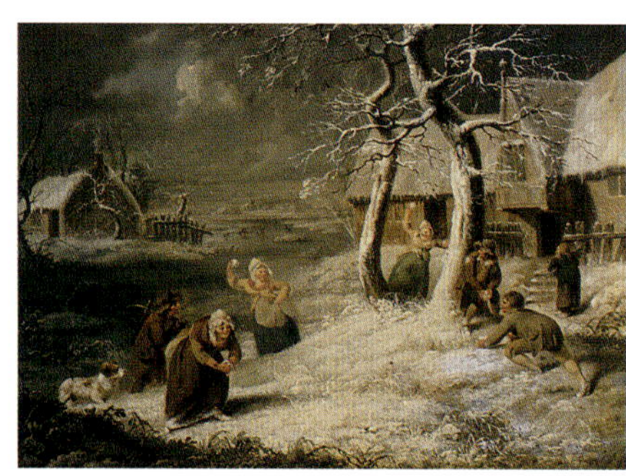
Ward, James (attributed to) 1769–1859
Peasants Snowballing
oil on canvas 72 x 89.8
730

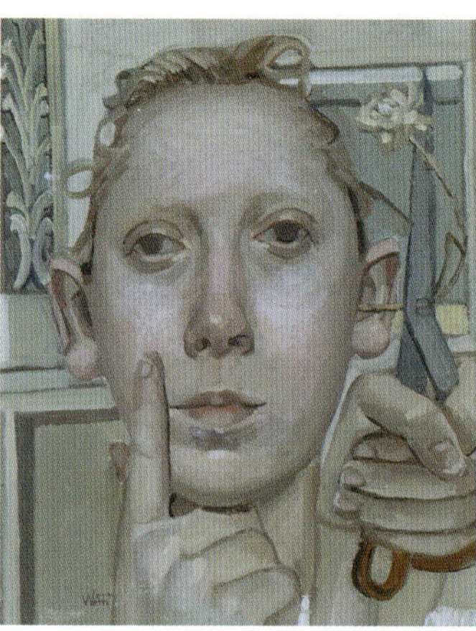
Watt, Alison b.1966
Study for 'Rosecutter' 1989
oil on board 47 x 42
62/2002

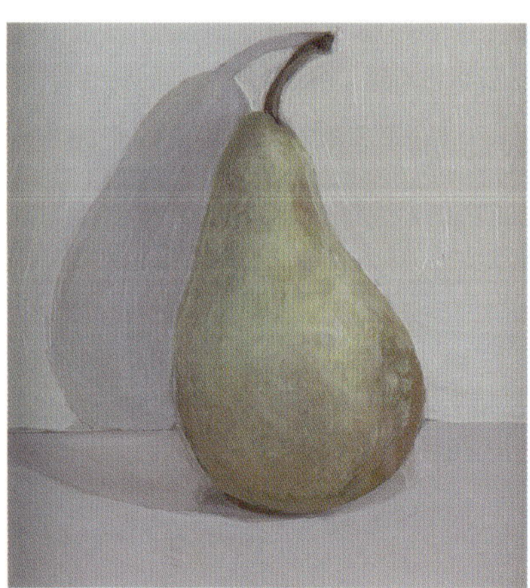
Watt, Alison b.1966
Pear
oil on board 34.2 x 34.2
24/2002

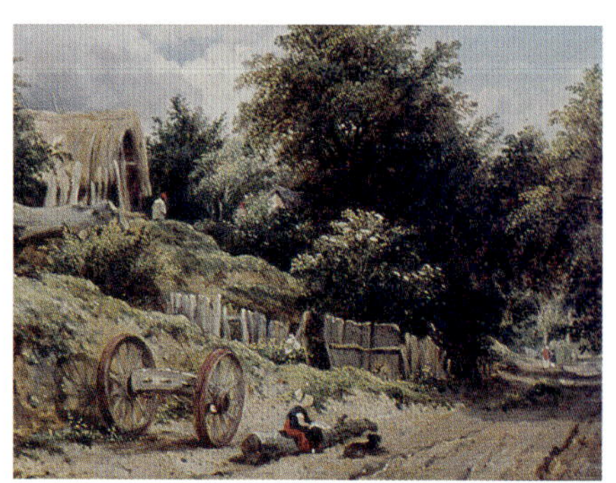
Watts, Frederick W. 1800–1862
Lane near Bishopstoke, Hampshire
oil on wood 21.6 x 29.5
1481

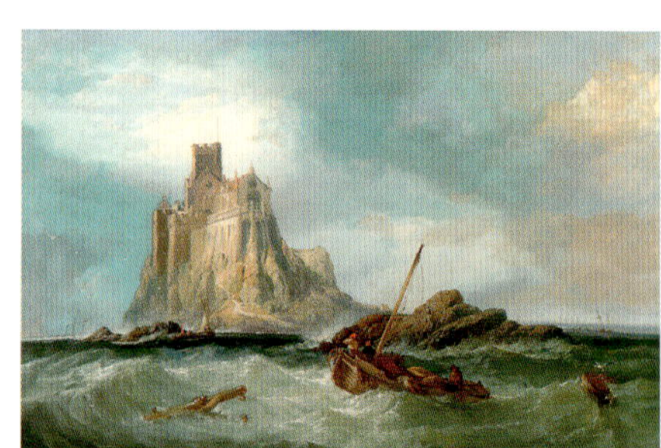
Webb, James c.1825–1895
St Michael's Mount 1861
oil on canvas 86.5 x 134
732

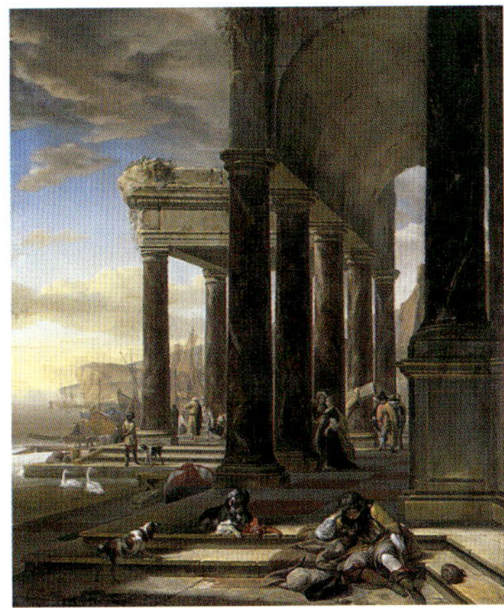

Weenix, Jan Baptist 1621–1660/1661
An Italian Port Scene
oil on canvas 87.6 x 73.7
3/1963

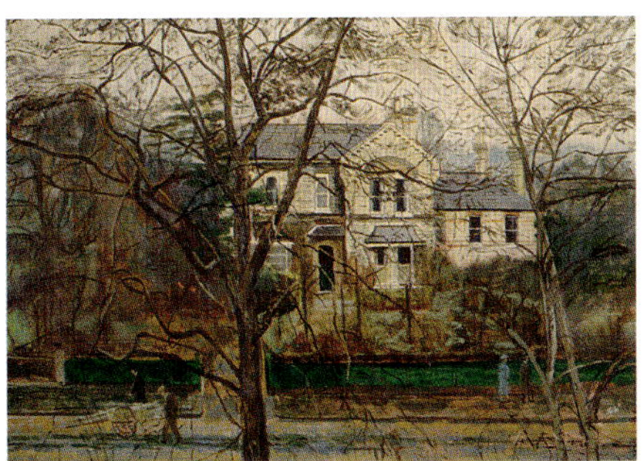

Weight, Carel Victor Morlais 1908–1997
The Builder's Mate
oil on canvas 60.6 x 91.5
1446

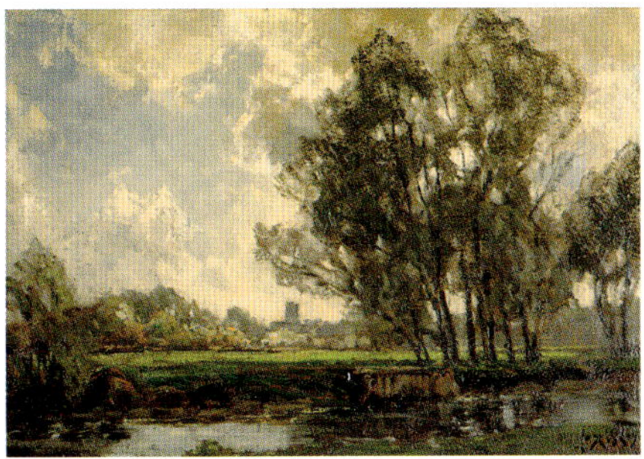

Weiss, José 1859–1919
Dedham Church
oil on canvas 40.5 x 61
733

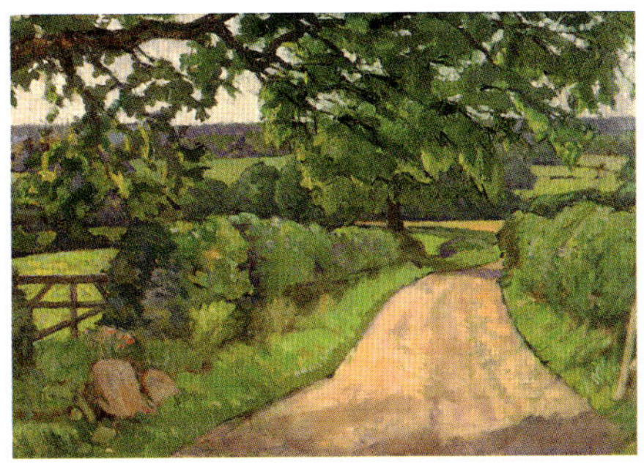

Wellington, Hubert Lindsay 1879–1967
Lane to Brockton, Staffordshire 1914
oil on canvas 41.2 x 61.2
4/1961

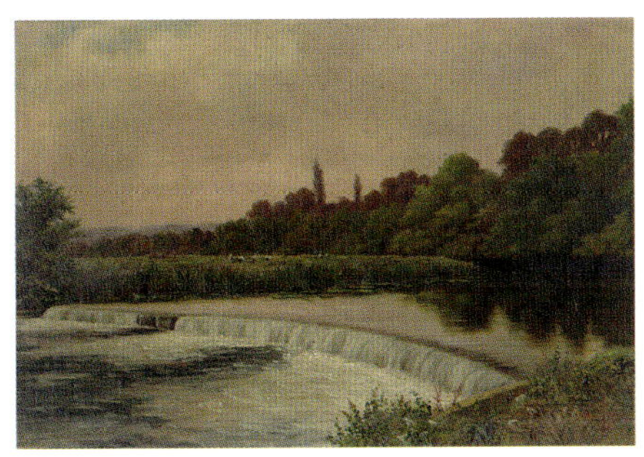

Wells, John T. active 1898–1902
Mill Dam on the Avon 1902
oil on canvas 30.5 x 45.9
735

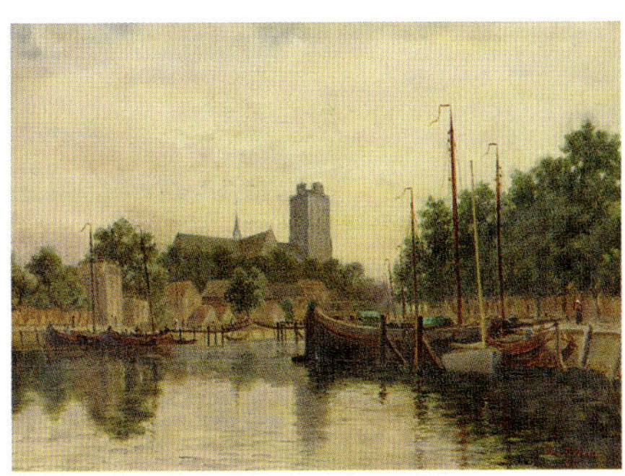

Wells, John T. active 1898–1902
Christchurch
oil on canvas 28 x 38.2
734

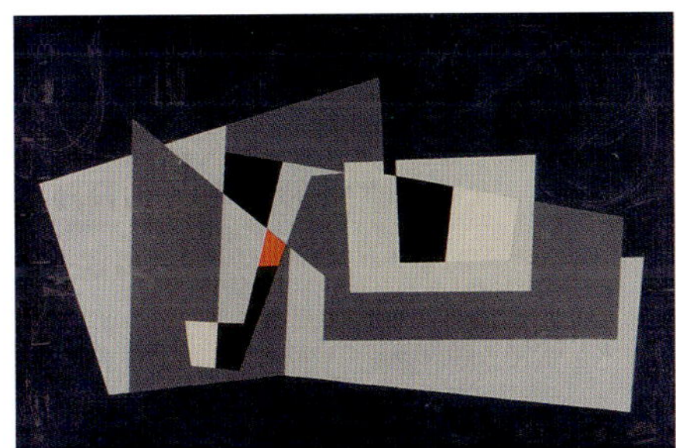

Wells, John 1907–2000
Air, Water, Stone 1955
oil on board 64 x 84.3 (E)
56/2006

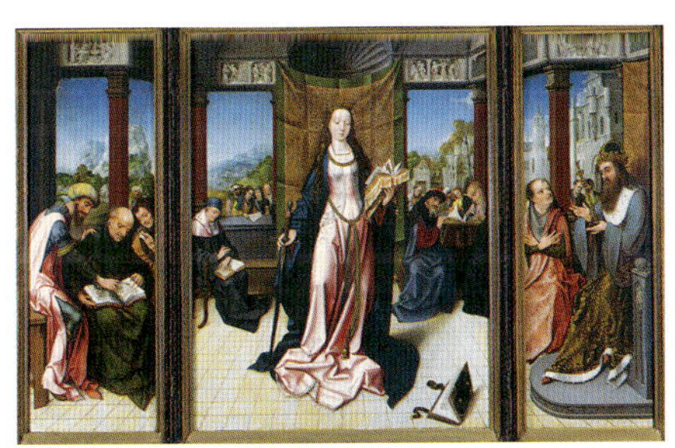

Weyden, Goswijn van der c.1465–after 1538
St Catherine and the Philosophers
oil on panel 108.6 x 157.2
1/1958

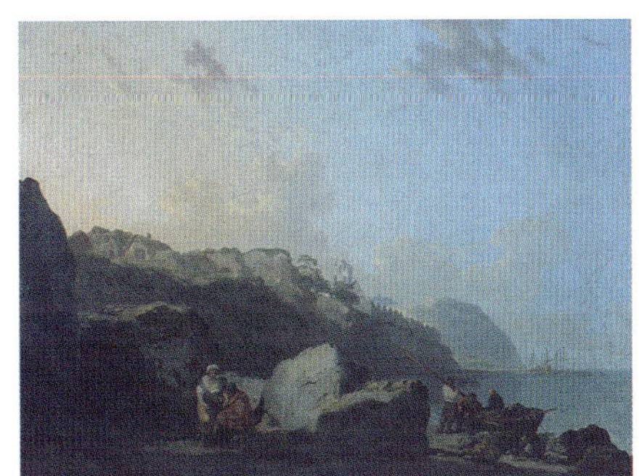

Wheatley, Francis 1747–1801
Seashore at Howth, Ireland 1782
oil on canvas 70.9 x 90.8
1333

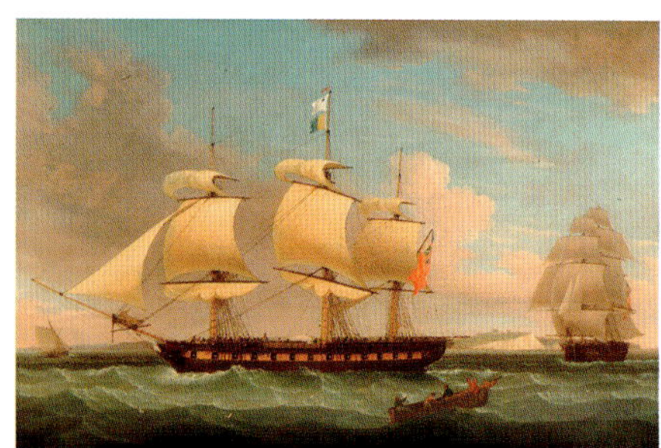

Whitcombe, Thomas c.1752–1824
Letter of Marque, 'Nelson'
oil on canvas 80.9 x 121.8
740

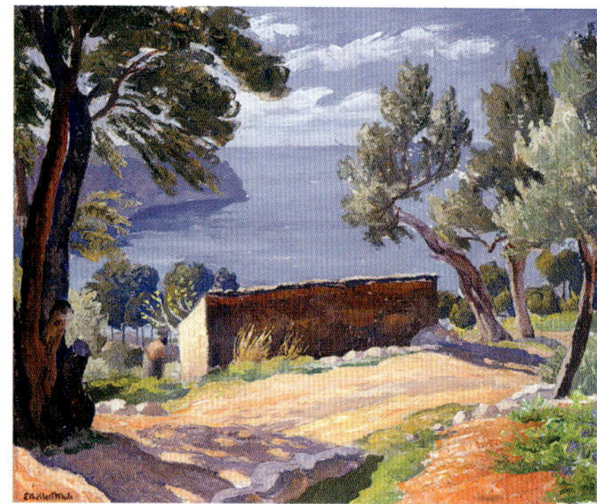

White, Ethelbert 1891–1972
Olives by the Sea
oil on canvas 46 x 55.2
741

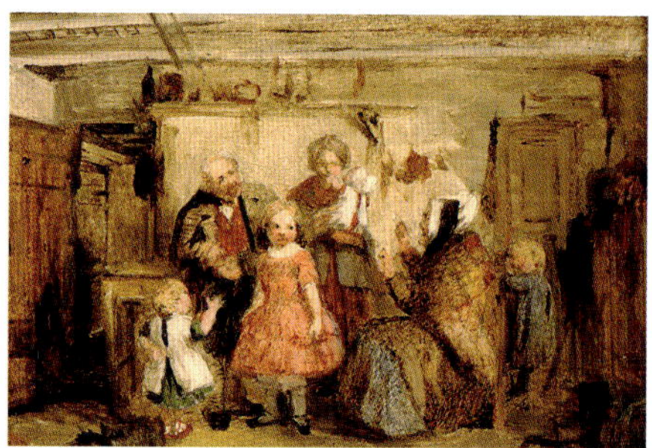

Wilkie, David (after) 1785–1841
A Study
oil on board 15 x 21.6
743

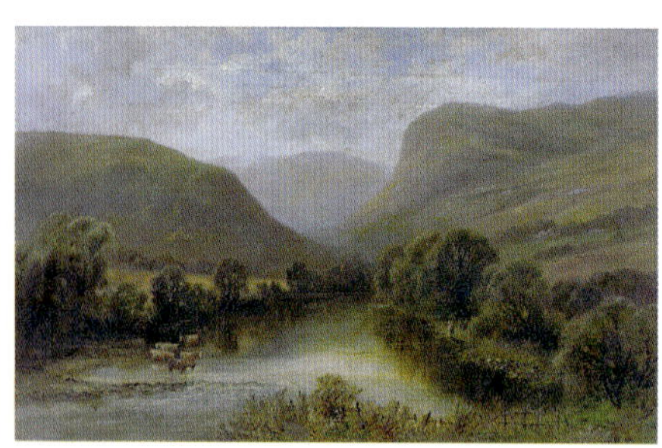

Wilkins, George active 1871–1885
Elan Valley, near Rhayader 1871
oil on canvas 35.5 x 56
744

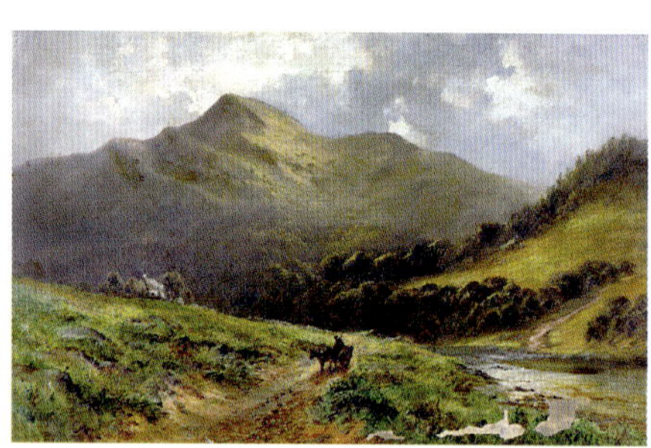

Wilkins, George active 1871–1885
Pass of Nantgwyllt
oil on canvas 35.5 x 56
745

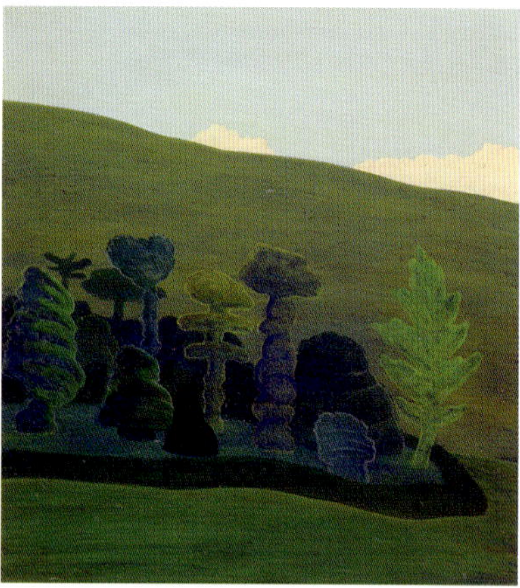

Willetts, David b.1939
Landscape 1976
acrylic on board 55 x 51.5
54/2002

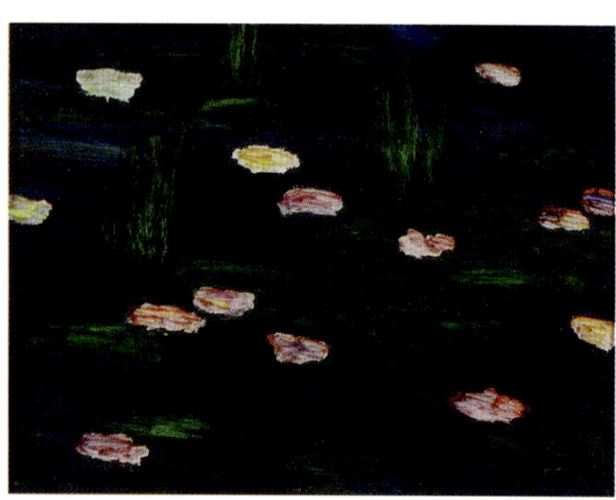

Willetts, David b.1939
Lilies 1976
acrylic on board 53.7 x 62.6
65/2002

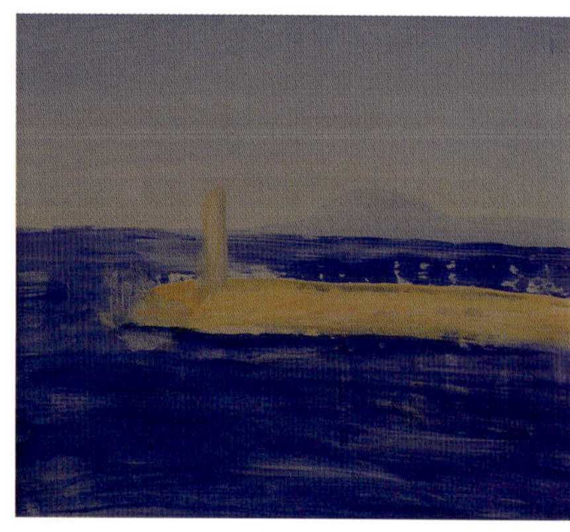

Willetts, David b.1939
On the Coast
acrylic on board 20.9 x 23.3
86/2002

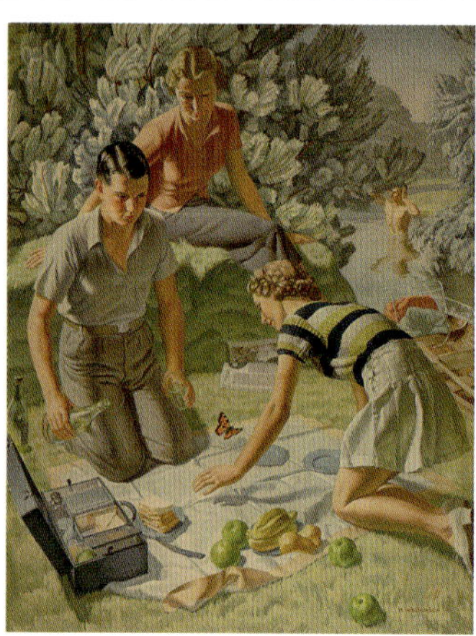

Williamson, Harold Sandys 1892–1978
Picnic
oil on canvas 116.8 x 91.4
1014

Facing Page: Power, Ronald, 1914–1989, *The Catch* (detail), Healing Arts, Isle of Wight NHS Primary Care Trust, (p. 251)

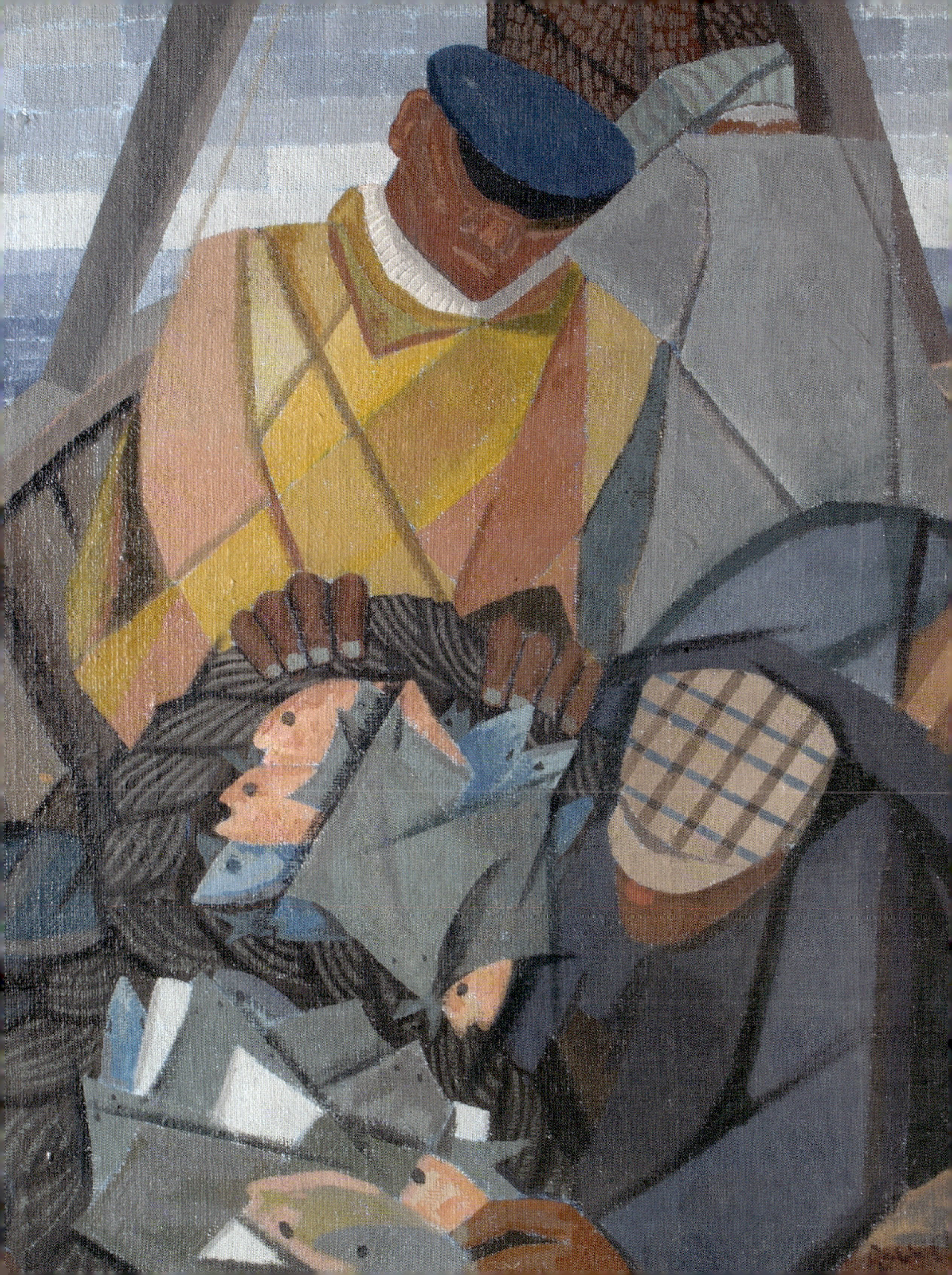

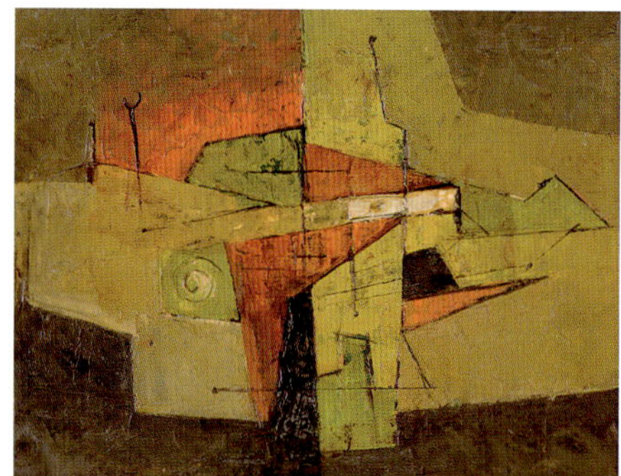

Wilson, Frank Avray b.1914
Composition
oil on canvas 36.5 x 48
1466

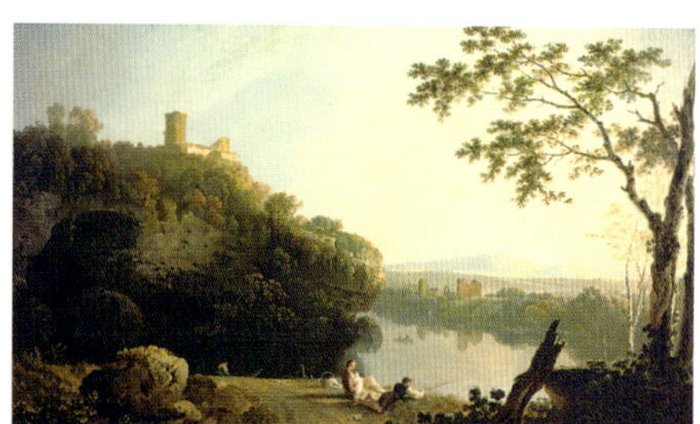

Wilson, Richard 1713/1714–1782
Classical Landscape
oil on canvas 126.4 x 209.5
1298

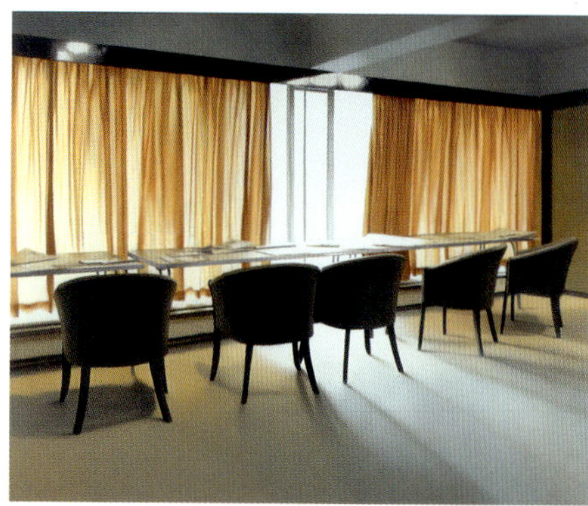

Winstanley, Paul b.1954
Nostalgia 1 1999
oil on linen 162.2 x 191.8
4/1999

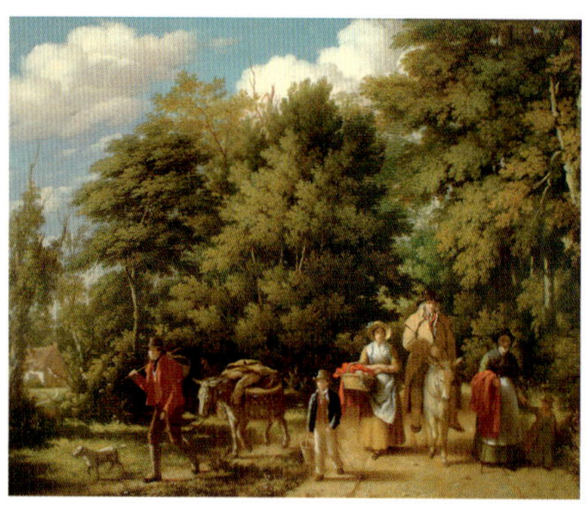

Witherington, Frederick William 1785–1865
Going to Market
oil on canvas 121.8 x 151.6
873

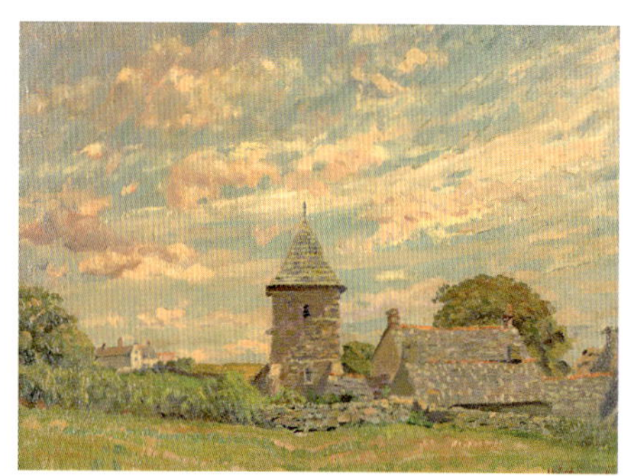

Withycombe, Joyce active 1928–1933
Worth Matravers 1928
oil on canvas 38.1 x 50.8
876

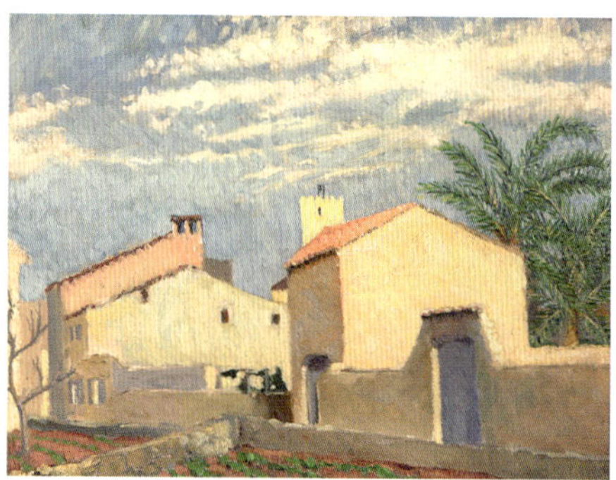

Withycombe, Joyce active 1928–1933
Majorca
oil on canvas 33 x 42
874

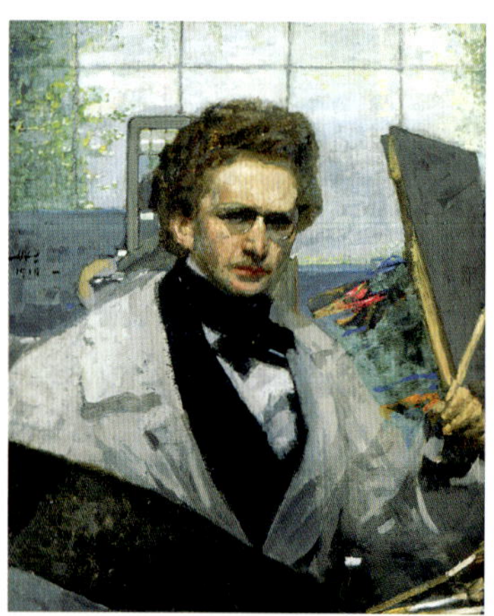

Wolmark, Alfred Aaron 1877–1961
Self Portrait 1910
oil on canvas 76.8 x 64.1
1485

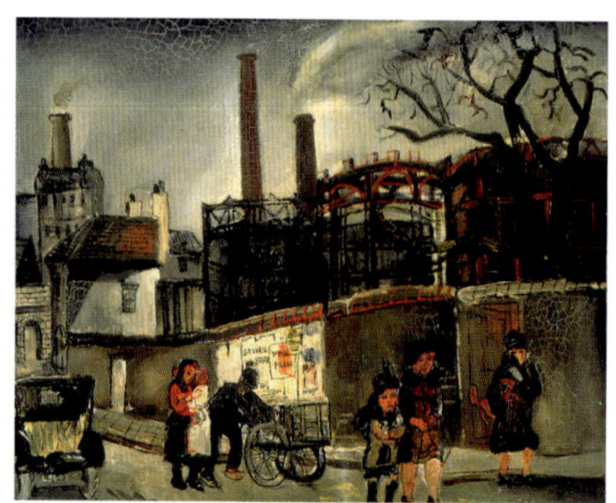

Wood, Christopher 1901–1930
Street in Paris 1926
oil on board 38.2 x 46.5
45/1977

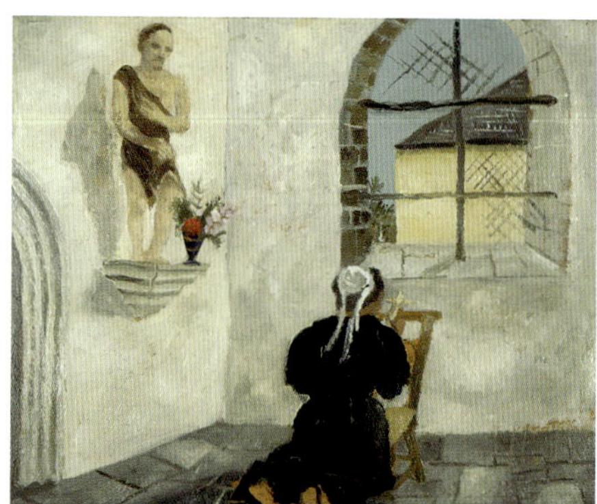

Wood, Christopher 1901–1930
Breton Woman at Prayer 1930
oil on card 53.6 x 64.5
1301

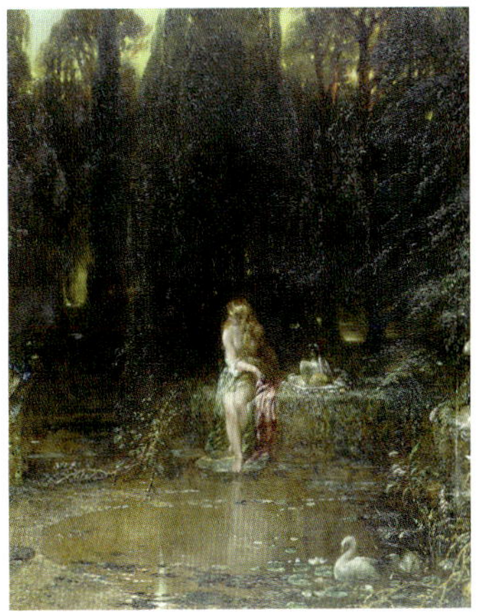

Woolmer, Alfred Joseph 1805–1892
Susannah at a Stream
oil on canvas 76.5 x 63.5
1249

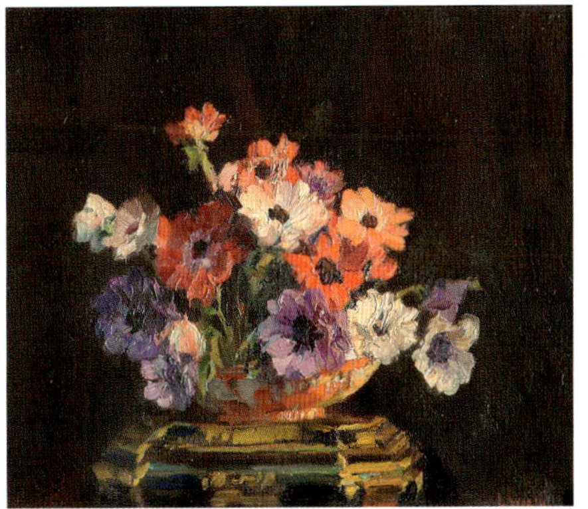

Worth, Laura active 1931–1932
Anemones
oil on canvas 42.7 x 48.8
892

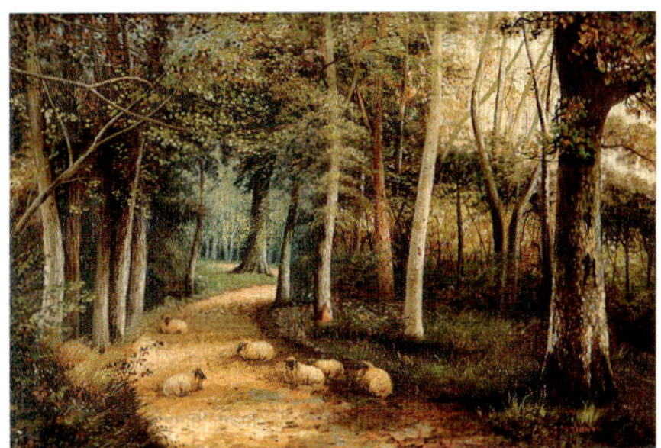

Wright, George 1860–1942
Flock of Sheep
oil on canvas 57.4 x 77
893

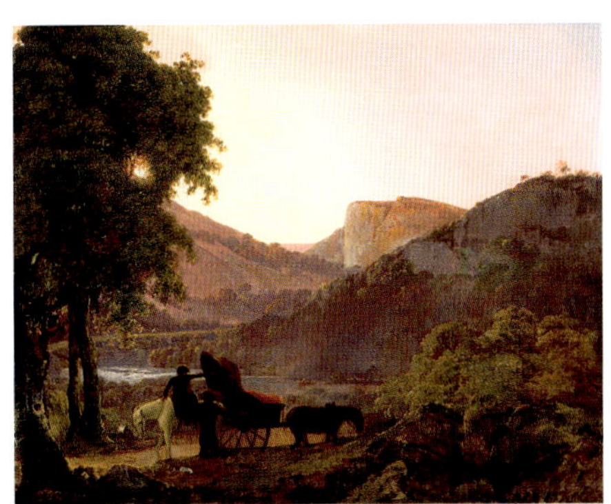

Wright, Joseph of Derby 1734–1797
Landscape 1780
oil on canvas 101.5 x 128.5
1416

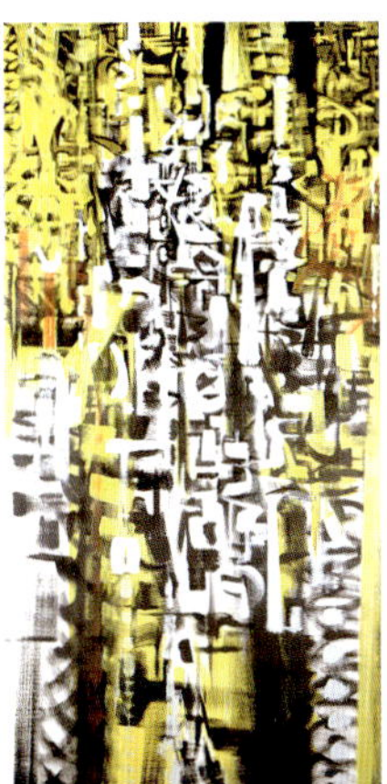

Wynter, Bryan 1915–1975
Monumental 1956
oil on canvas 202 x 101.5
15/2006

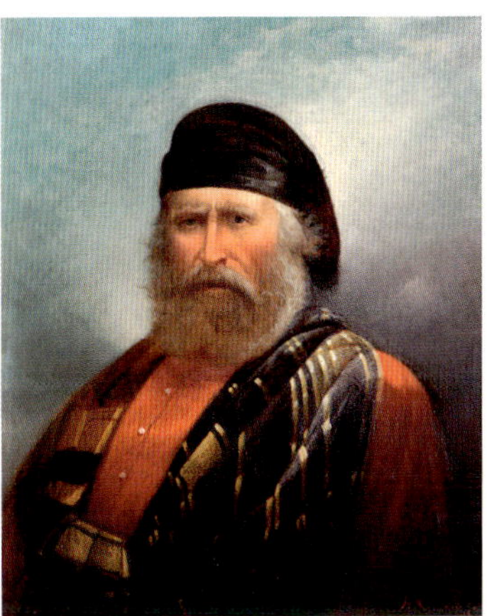

Ximenes, Antonio 1829–1896
Garibaldi (1807–1882) 1853
oil on canvas 76.5 x 63.2
1255

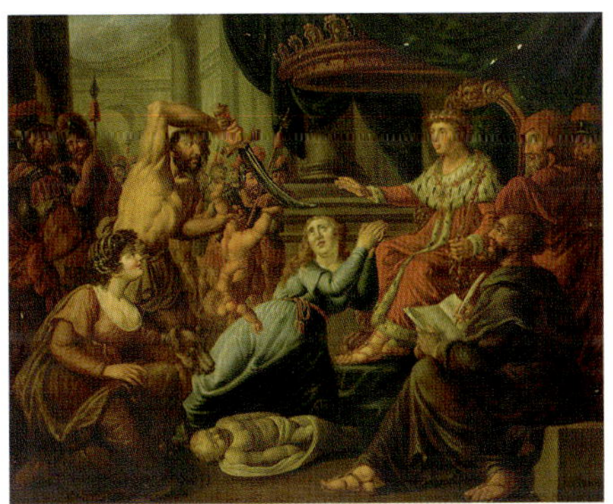

Young, John Tobias b.1790
The Judgement of Solomon 1810
oil on canvas 170 x 210.2
661

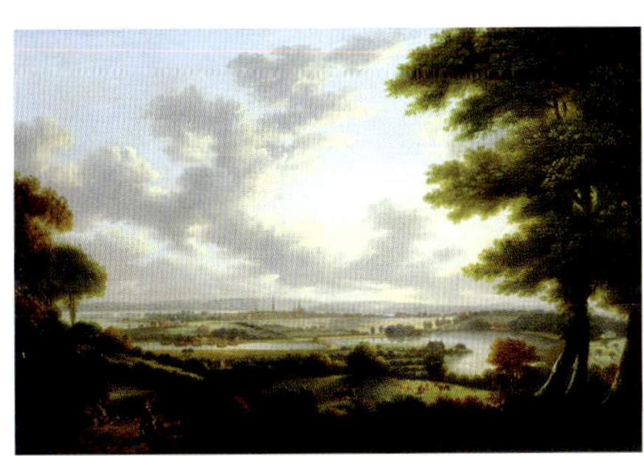

Young, Tobias c.1755–1824
Southampton from Bitterne
oil on canvas 41 x 62.8
1002

Southampton City Museums

Southampton's first municipal museum, Tudor House, was opened in 1912 and collected works of art, particularly paintings, prints and drawings, from the outset. As with other contemporary institutions, the collecting strategy lacked the focus that we would now expect, but this has been refined over the years so that with the coming of Southampton City Art Gallery there has been a harmonious division of interest.

The Museums have concentrated on Southampton – related works, which can primarily be divided into three categories: portraits of local people (known as Sotonians); portraits of ships that have had connections with our port (no matter what company or nationality); and topographical pictures. While our interest is more in the subject matter rather than the quality of the art, we have to remember that before the advent of photography it was only through these artistic depictions, however unsophisticated, that we could catch a glimpse of what Southampton looked like and understand how much it has changed since those times.

Nevertheless, there are significant works in the Museum collections. The ship paintings include works by the likes of Antonio Jacobsen. Topographical pictures of the eighteenth and early nineteenth centuries by Tobias Young and Thomas Gray Hart show what a rustic idyll the spa town of Southampton must have been, while the works of Philip Brannon are a little fanciful.

With Frederick Lee Bridell we have a local talent that was not fully developed at the time of his death at the age of 32. A critic commenting on his life remarked that his skies rivalled those of Turner. We are fortunate, then, to have his *View of Southampton* from 1855. Bridell mostly worked abroad, so it is rare to have a view of his home town, especially one which captures the moment of transition from spa town to bustling port and industrial centre and contains a wealth of detail.

Southampton City Museums pioneered the collection of material that reflects life on board the great passenger ships. Their collections of internal fittings, furnishings and murals that once graced saloons and public places creating the unique character and appeal of individual vessels includes works of art by well-known artists such as Anna Zinkeisen, Jan Juta and Norman Wilkinson.

A few of the marine paintings listed are by a talented amateur artist, Arthur Cozens. The bulk of Cozen's work, which was bequeathed to Southampton on his death in 1947, comprises watercolours and pencil drawings all of which are extremely accomplished. Unfortunately, he was not at his most confident when working in oils and neither the quality, nor the significance, of his main work is reflected in his paintings in this medium.

There are other themes and levels of interpretation that are woven into our pictures. Maria Spilsbury was an artist at a time when it was uncommon for a woman to pursue painting as a career. Maria, however, was married to John Taylor, a member of the highly talented, inventive and slightly unorthodox family of nonconformist manufacturers with a strong social conscience. Our one painting by Maria is the *New Year's Feast* which was painted in Walter

Taylor's Charity School, Portswood Green, toward the end of the eighteenth century. Amongst other points of note, it depicts the Taylor's black servant. The Taylors were friends of John Newton, one of the opponents of the slave trade in the late eighteenth century and whose views influenced Wilberforce, the man who led the movement that finally abolished slavery in Britain in 1807.

The Collection also contains a portrait of another member of the family, Walter Taylor, holding a circular saw blade which he is reputed to have invented. This new piece of technology led to the mass production in Southampton of ships' blocks for the Navy towards the end of the eighteenth century, an innovation that predated the work of Marc Brunel.

I could not finish this note without recording our gratitude to the Victoria & Albert Museum Purchase Grant Fund and our own Friends organisation for helping in the acquisition of some of our finest objects. Details appear in the Further Information section of this catalogue.

Alastair Arnott, Curator of Local Collections

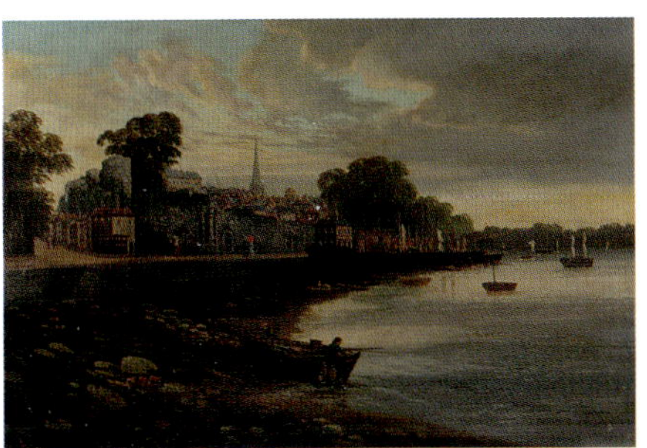

A. A.
Southampton Waters
oil on canvas 44 x 75
M158

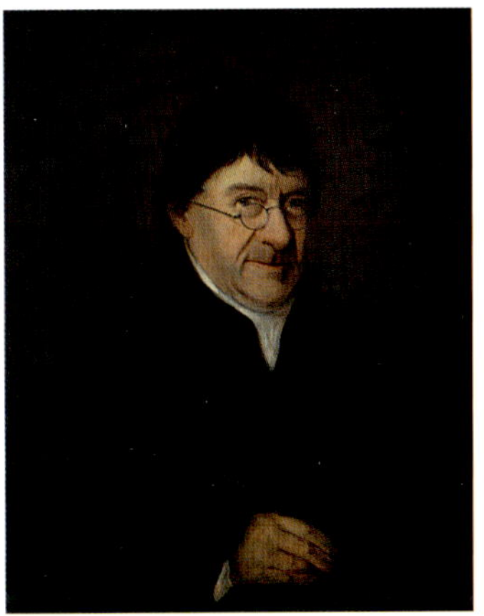

Ackerley, Chamberlayne
Mr James Chapman 1830
oil on canvas 74 x 61
M23468

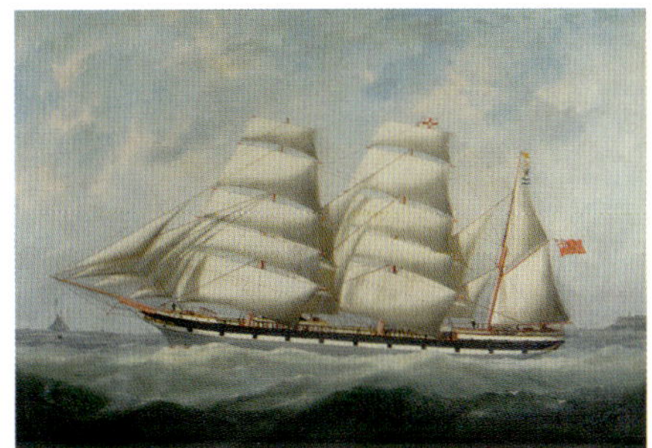

Adams, Edward
'SS Saraca' 1884
oil on canvas 61 x 90
M327

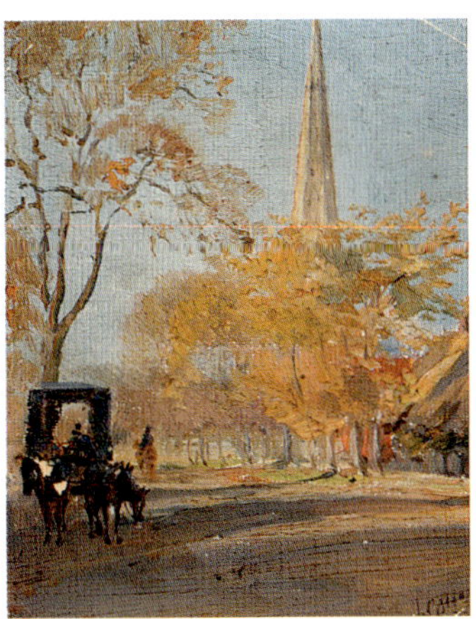

Alford, Leonard C. active 1883–1920
New Millbrook Church
oil on card 13.6 x 10.9
M5964

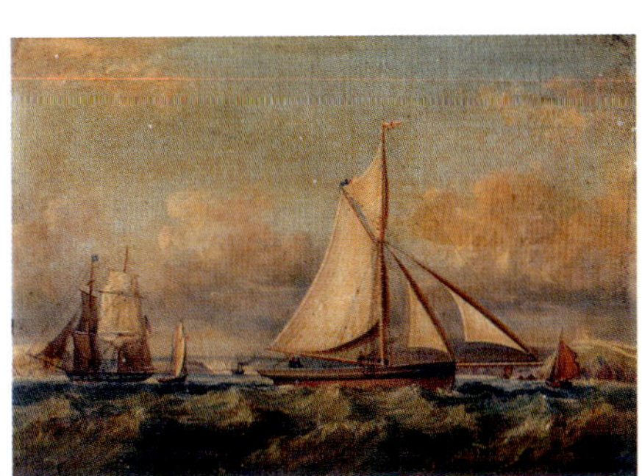

Atkinson, George 1806–1884
The Falmouth Pilot Cutter 1858
oil on canvas 30.5 x 43
M3040

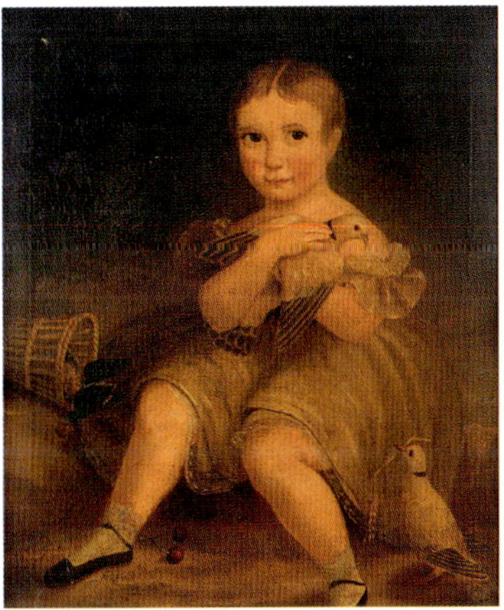

Baker March, F.
Mary Ann Potts c.1811
oil on canvas 74 x 63.5
M354

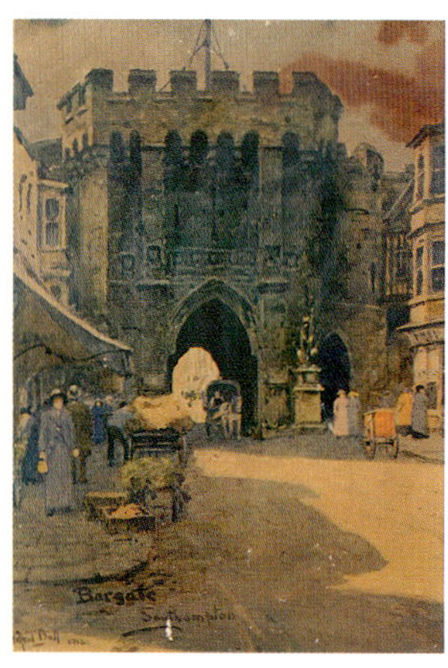

Ball, Wilfred Williams 1853–1917
Bargate 1912
oil on board 24 x 18
M1449

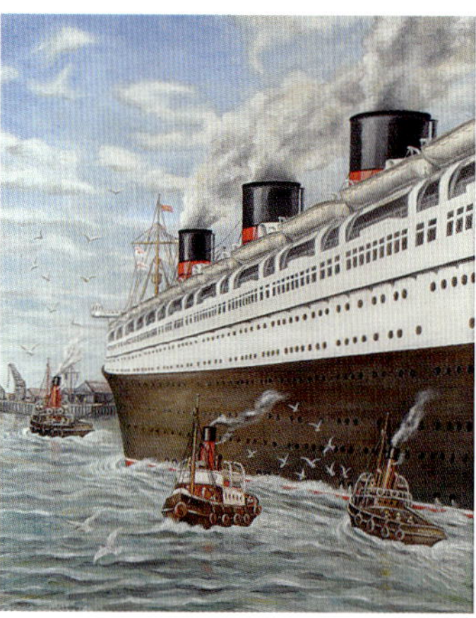

Bartlett, E. Reginald
'Queen Mary' 1960
oil on canvas 60 x 49.5
M11942

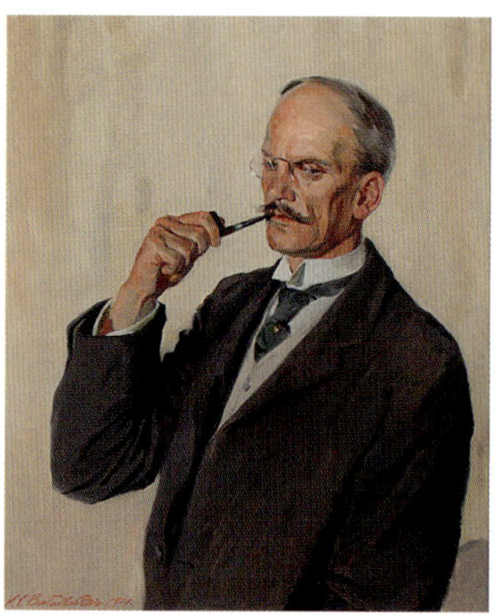

Batchelor Reis, V. I.
Edward Cooper Poole 1921
oil on canvas 75 x 62
M7063

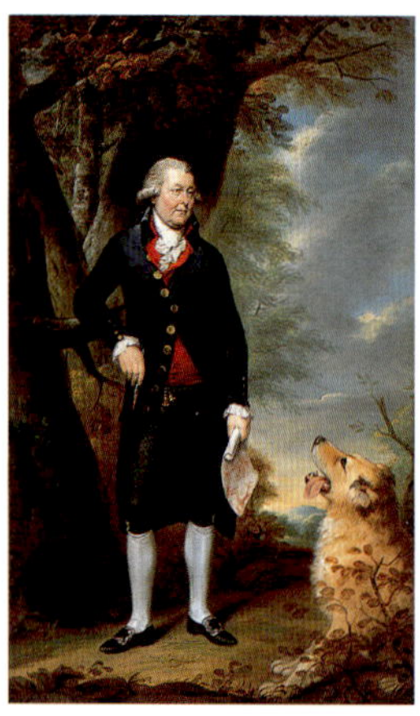

Beechey, William 1753–1839
George Rogers, an Artist
oil on canvas 236 x 146
M369

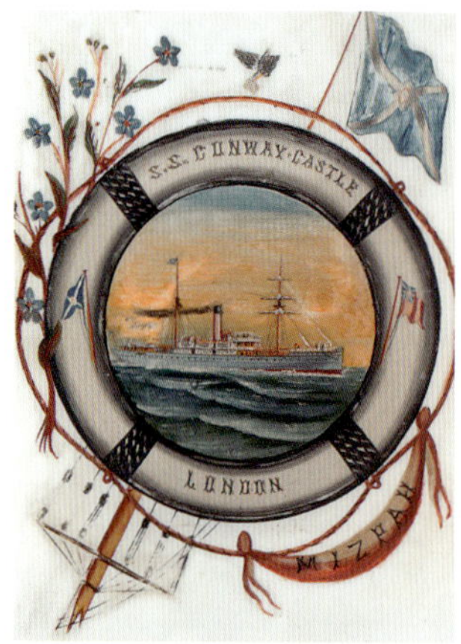

Bell, J.
'SS Conway Castle' 1885/1895
oil on glass 28 x 20.4
M6345

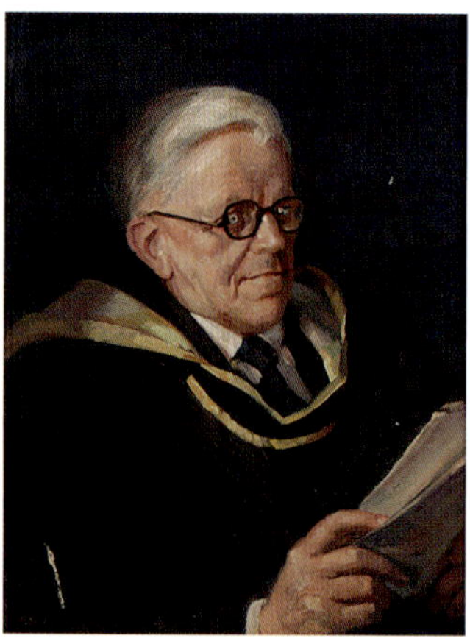

Bird, H.
Frederick James Hemmings, Headmaster of Tauntons School (1925–1948)
oil on canvas 68.2 x 54
M11617 (P)

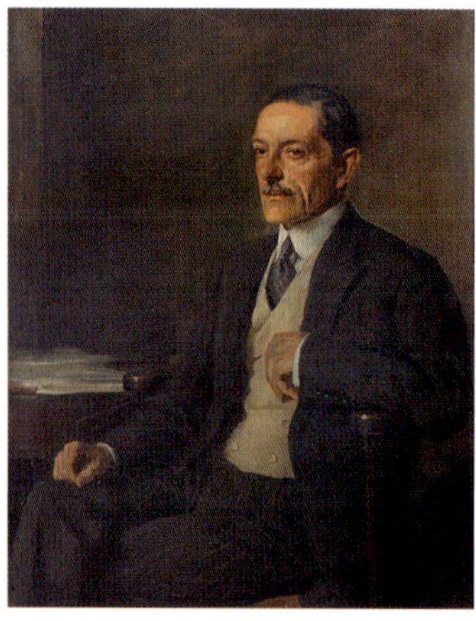

Birley, Oswald Hornby Joseph 1880–1952
Lord Royden 1951
oil on canvas 105 x 90
m12066 (P)

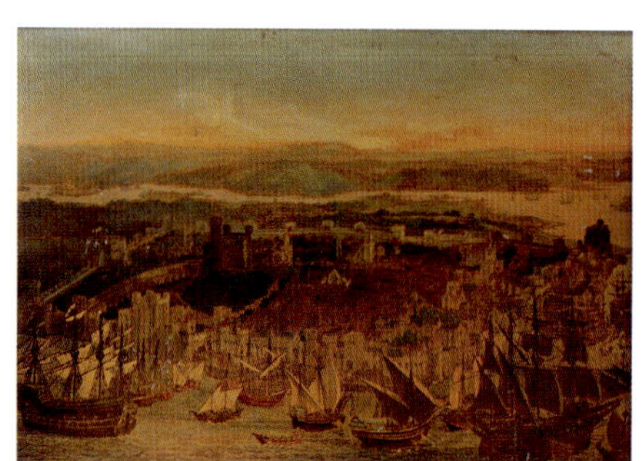

Brannon, Philip 1817–1890
Bird's Eye View of Southampton Showing Original Walls, Towers and Gates
oil on board 37 x 55
M161

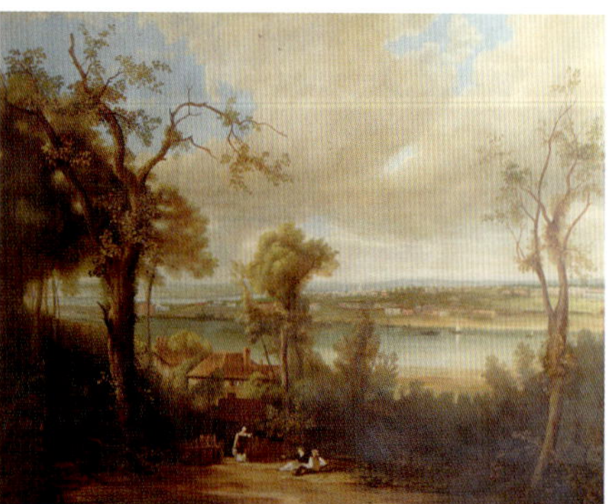

Brett, B. active c.1841–1918
Southampton from Peartree Green (after John Rawson Walker)
oil on canvas 98 x 124
M3383

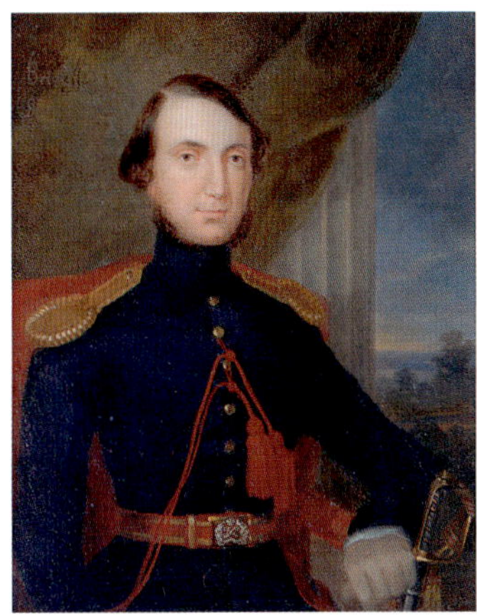

Bridell, Frederick Lee 1831–1863
Captain Lacey 1849
oil on canvas 17.9 x 15.3
M23357

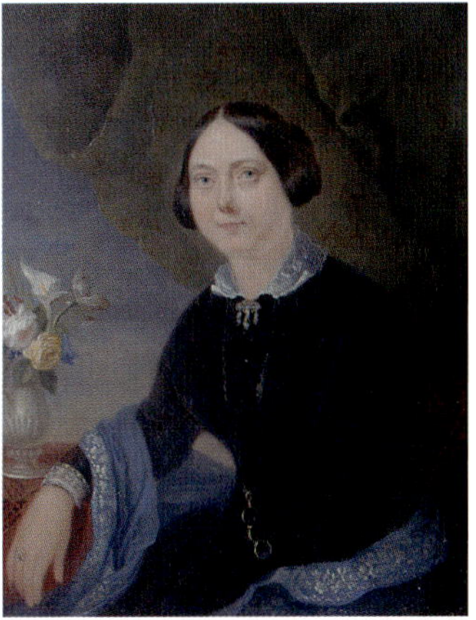

Bridell, Frederick Lee 1831–1863
Georgiana Lacey 1849
oil on canvas 17.9 x 15.3
M23358

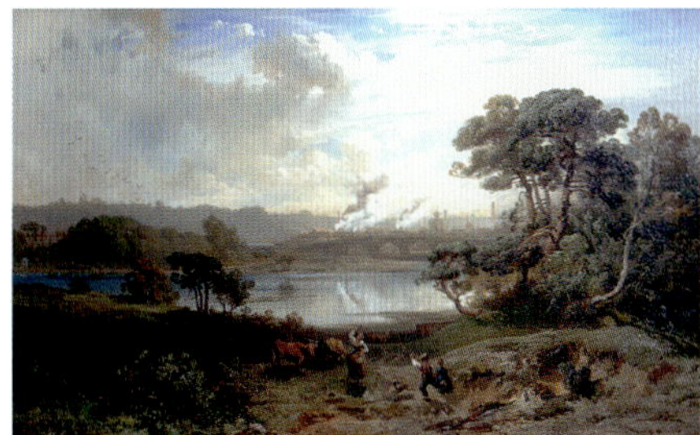

Bridell, Frederick Lee 1831–1863
View of Southampton 1855
oil on canvas 64 x 93
M23427

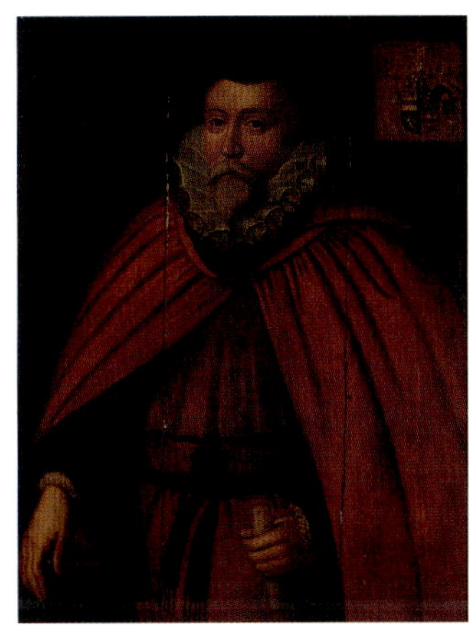

British (English) School 16th/17th C
Nicholas Fuller (1557–1623)
oil on wood 90 x 71
M373

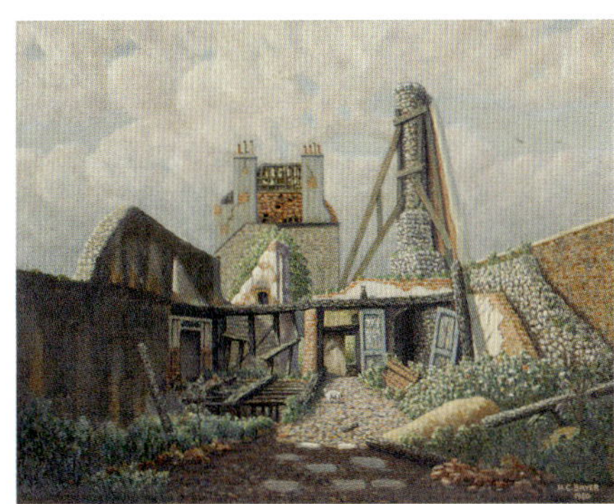

Bryer, H. C.
79 1–2 High Street, Southampton, with Norman Chimney, c.1200 1950
oil on board 34 x 44
M1440

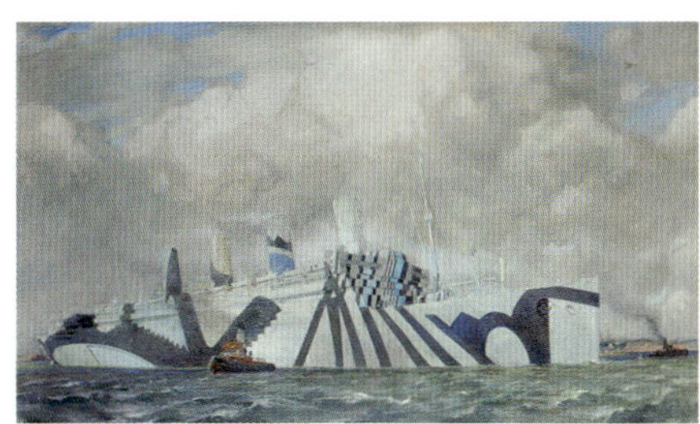

Clark, C.
'Aquitania' in Dazzle Paint 1919
oil on canvas 95 x 165
m12068 (P)

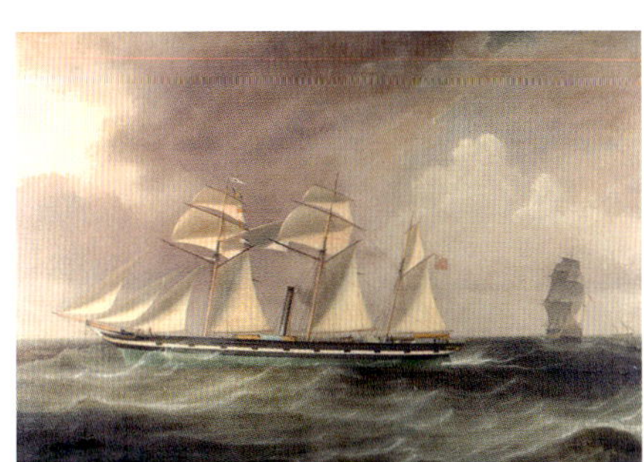

Clark, William 1803–1883
A Barque, 'Phoebe' 1851
oil on canvas 75 x 110
M335

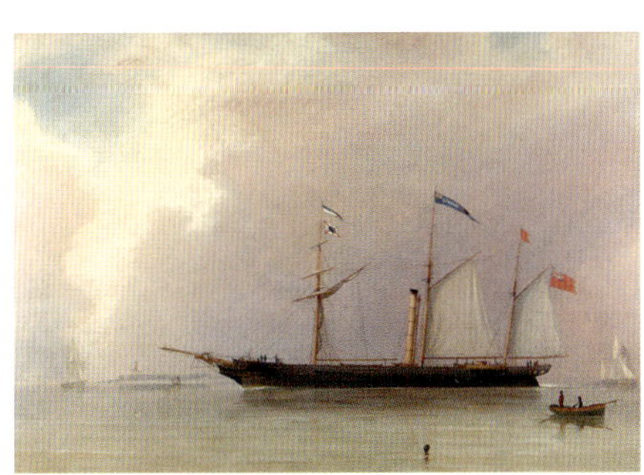

Clark, William 1803–1883
'SS Livorno'
oil on canvas 72 x 107
M316

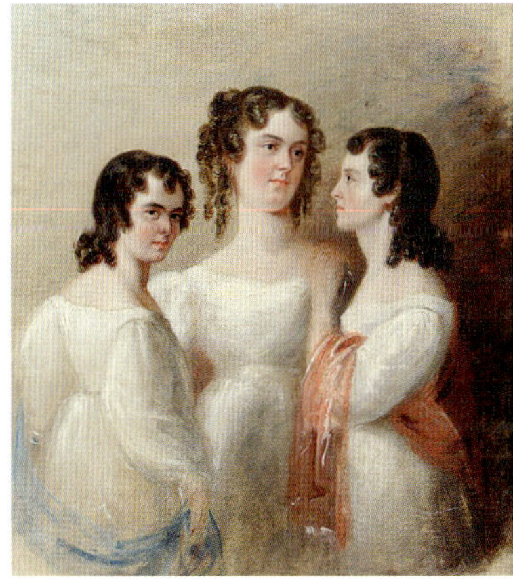

Cobbett, Ann b.1826
The Cobbett Sisters
oil on canvas 35.5 x 33
M4479

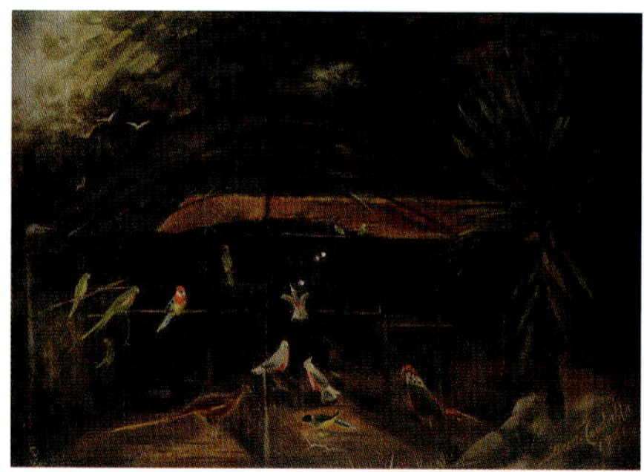

Constable, Bessie
The Aviary, Southampton 1921
oil on wood 24 x 35
M132

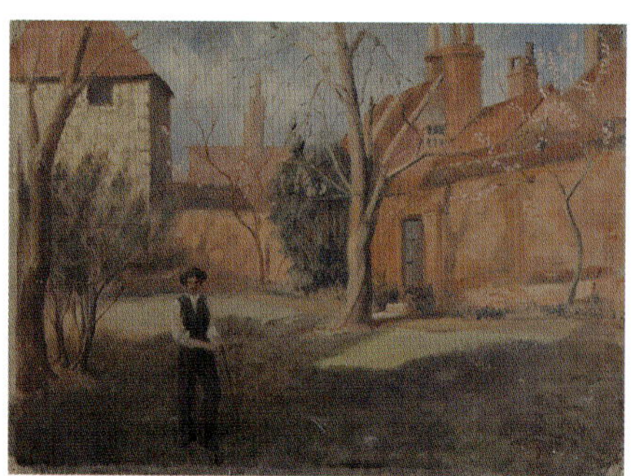

Cooksey, W. B. N
Garden of Madame Mae's House 1898
oil on canvas 25 x 35
M2069

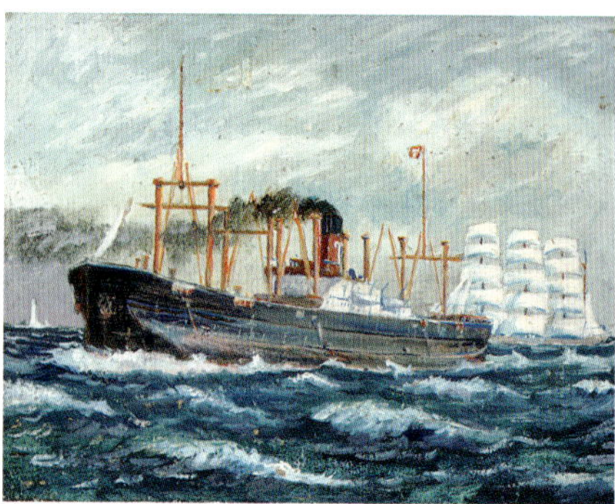

Cozens, Arthur 1880–1947
Turret Steamer and Clipper Bringing Home the Grain c.1910
oil on board 30 x 40
M12714

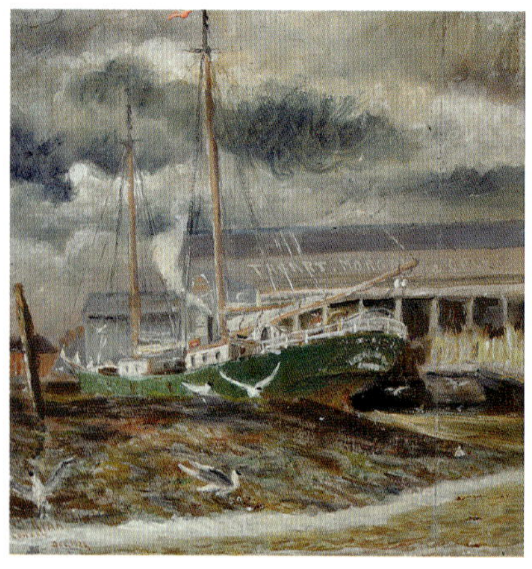

Cozens, Arthur 1880–1947
'Lock Ryan' of London 1928
oil on card 31 x 30
M13257

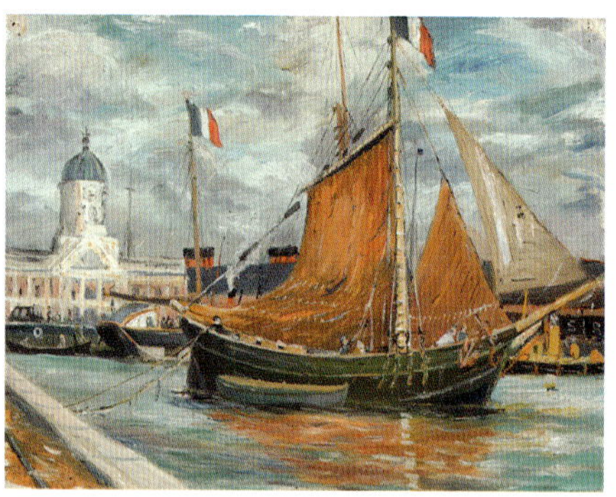

Cozens, Arthur 1880–1947
French Fishing Ketch off Town Quay c.1930
oil on paper 28.5 x 38
M13529

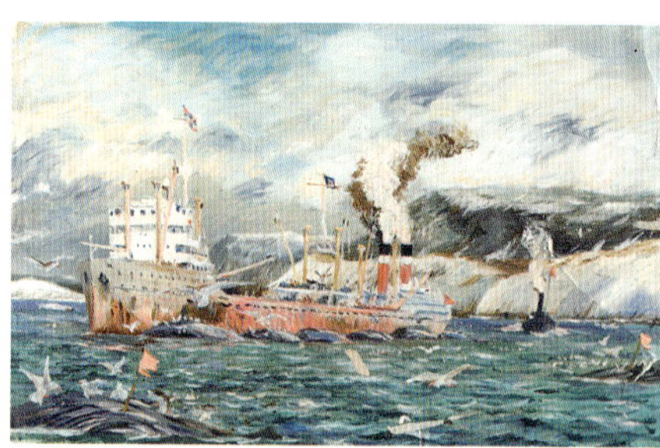

Cozens, Arthur 1880–1947
Whaling c.1930
oil on paper 38 x 56
M12713

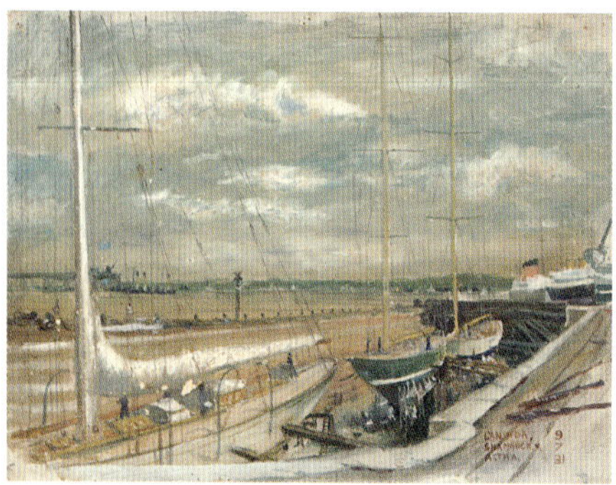

Cozens, Arthur 1880–1947
Yachts 'Candda', 'Shamrock' and 'Astra' in Dry Dock c.1930
oil on paper 28.5 x 38
M13528

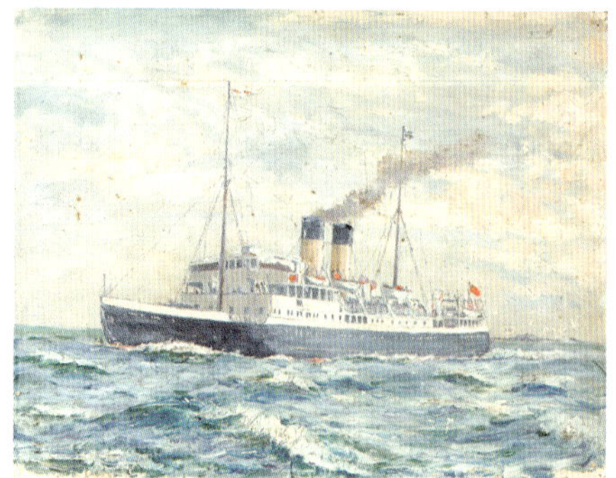

Cozens, Arthur 1880–1947
Southern Railway Steamer 1930s
oil on paper 28 x 38
M12466

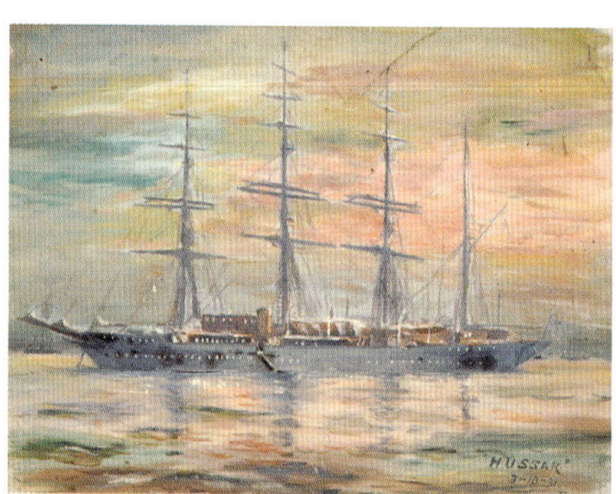

Cozens, Arthur 1880–1947
'Hussar' 1931
oil on paper 28.5 x 38
M13527

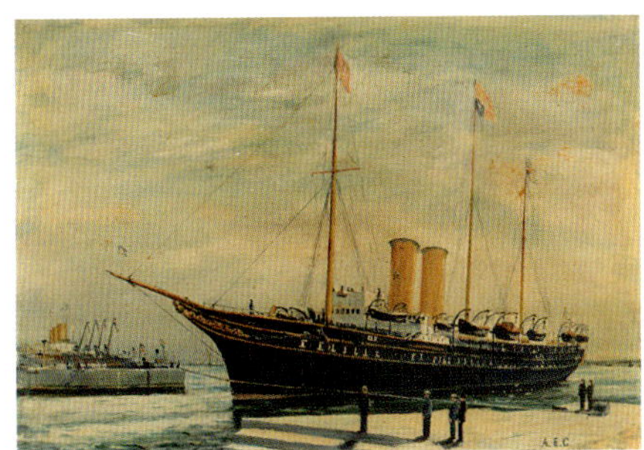

Cozens, Arthur 1880–1947
'HMY Victoria & Albert' Entering King George V Dock, Southampton 1933
oil on board 38.3 x 58
M4564

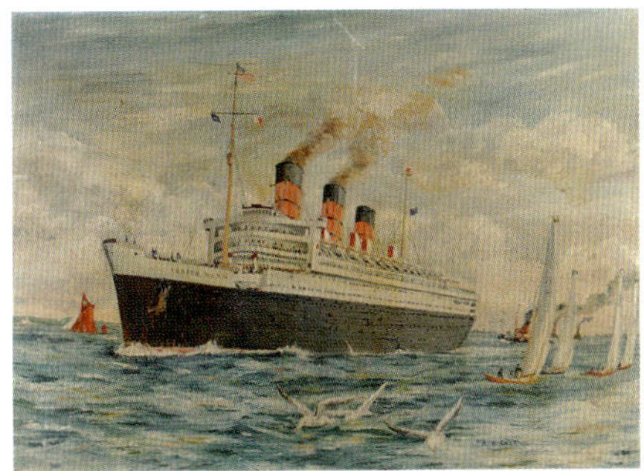

Cozens, Arthur 1880–1947
'Queen Mary' 1936
oil on board 50.2 x 70.6
M1460

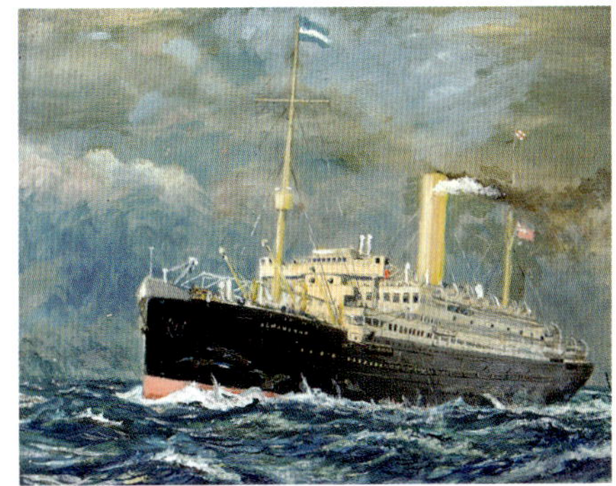

Cozens, Arthur 1880–1947
'Almanzora', Royal Mail
oil on card 33 x 42
M12649

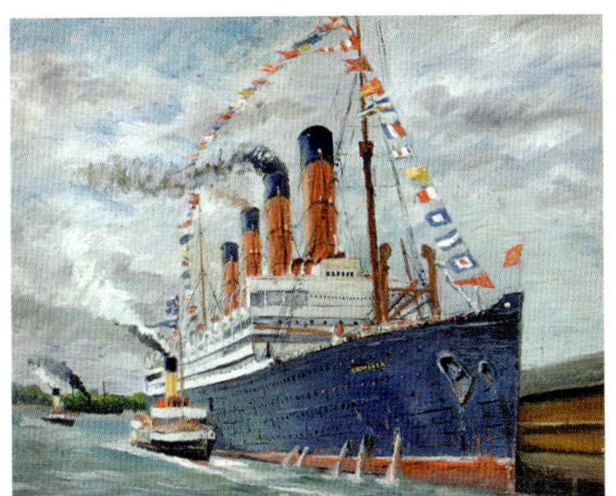

Cozens, Arthur 1880–1947
'Aquitania', Cunard
oil on board 35.5 x 45
M12648

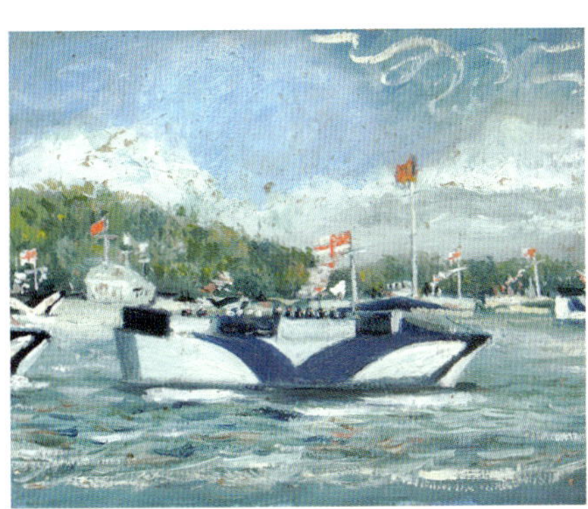

Cozens, Arthur 1880–1947
Camouflaged Naval Launch, World War II
oil on board 23 x 28
M13256

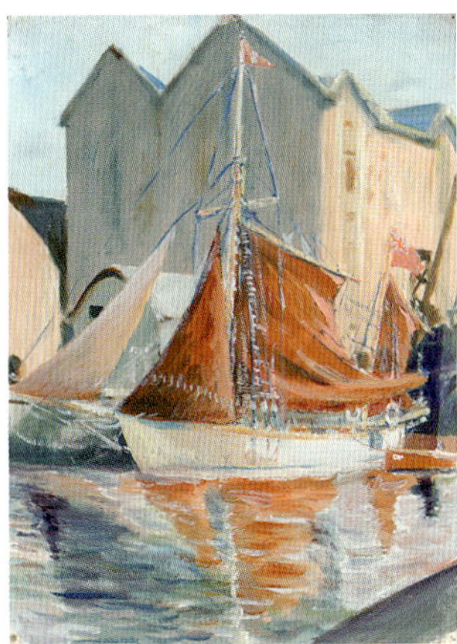

Cozens, Arthur 1880–1947
Coastal Vessel, Inner Dock
oil on paper 38 x 28.5
M13531

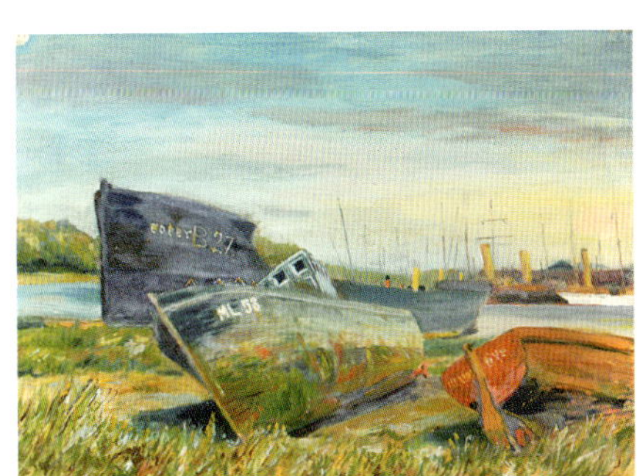

Cozens, Arthur 1880–1947
Derelict Fishing Boats
oil on paper 28 x 38
M13530

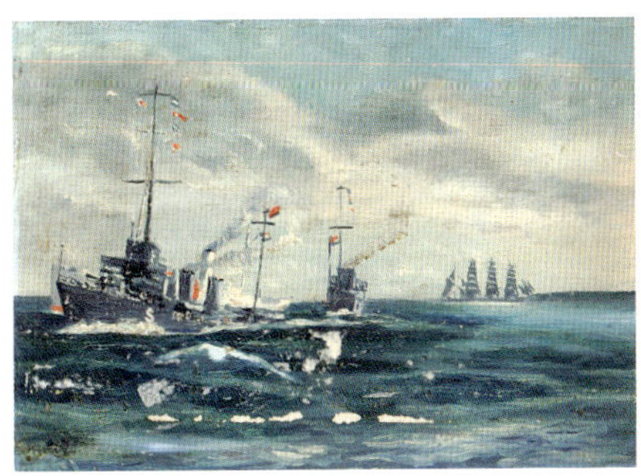

Cozens, Arthur 1880–1947
Destroyers Protecting Shipping
oil on card 25 x 35
M12601

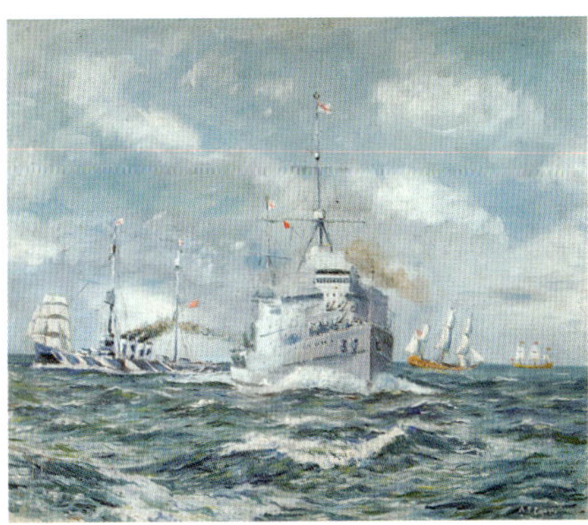

Cozens, Arthur 1880–1947
Sea Power
oil on board 50.2 x 60.3
M12640

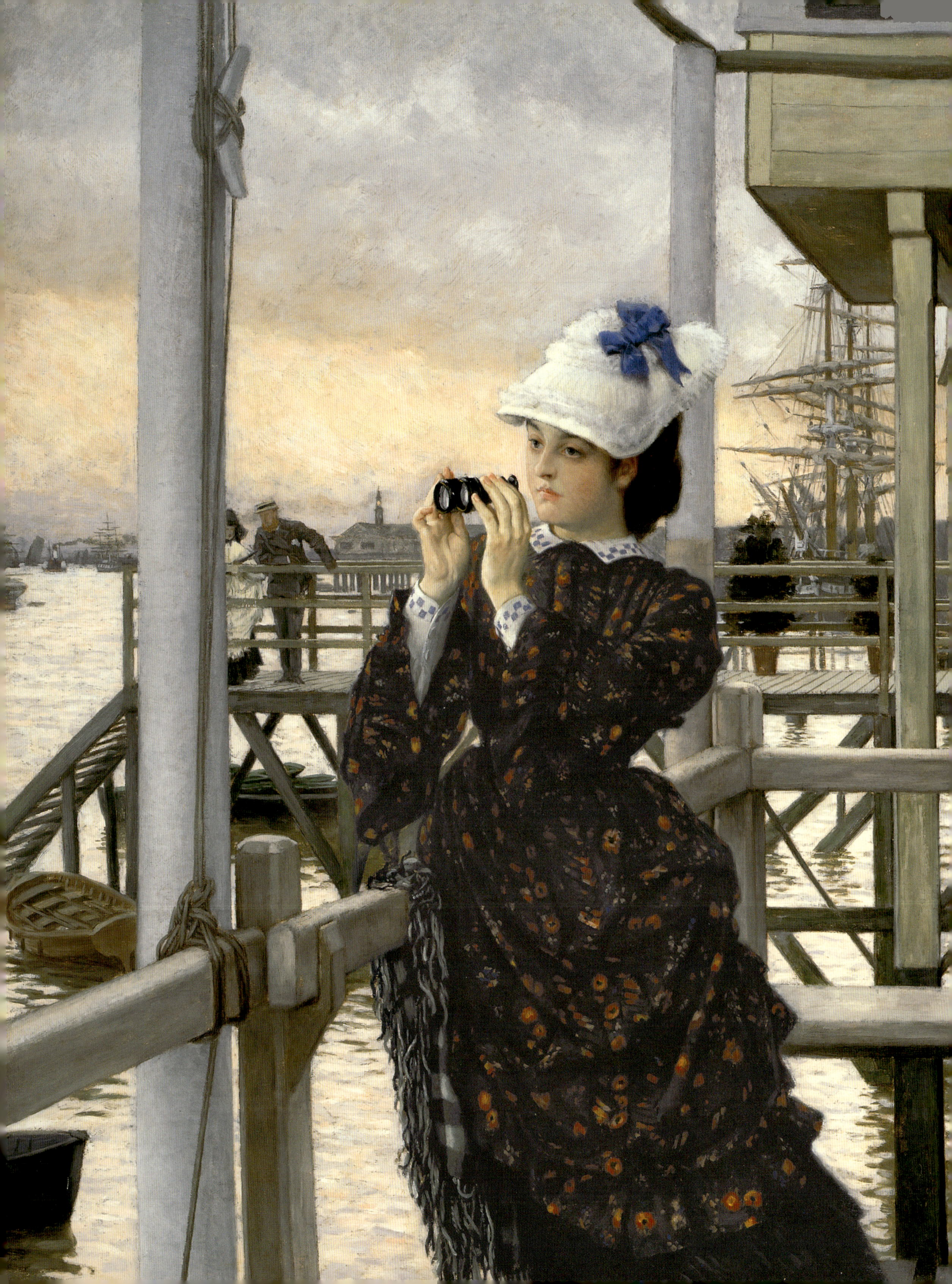

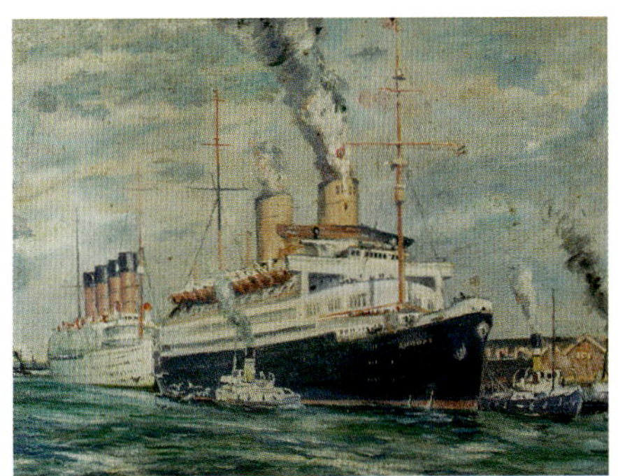

Cozens, Arthur 1880–1947
'SS Europa' Departing Southampton
oil on canvas 26.5 x 37
M152

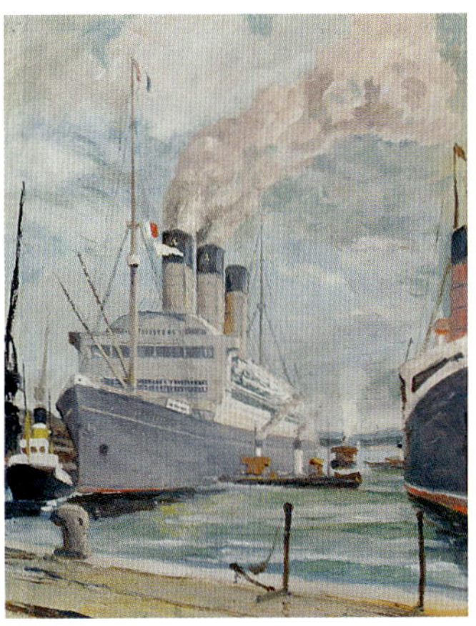

Cozens, Arthur 1880–1947
White Star Liner 'Majestic' (1922–1936)
oil on card 34.9 x 27.7
M1

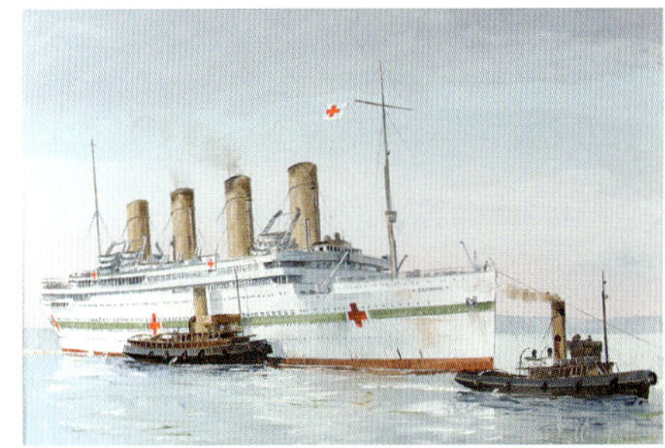

Crossley, Harley b.1936
'Britannic' as a Hospital Ship 1987
oil on canvas 48 x 74.3
M11983

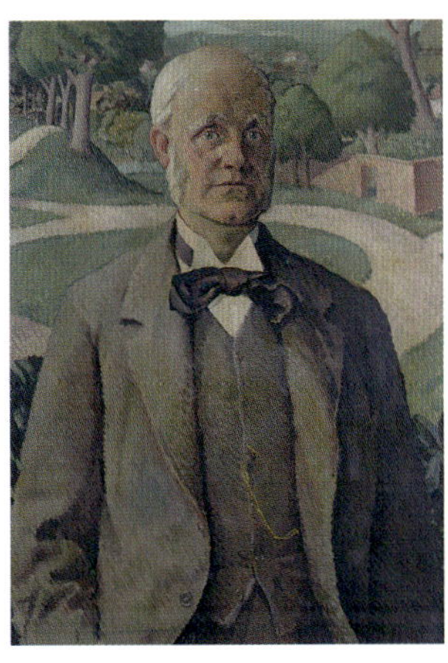

Daniels, Leonard 1909–1998
Portrait of an Unknown Man (possibly a headmaster of Tauntons School) 1936
acrylic on canvas 90 x 66
M11613

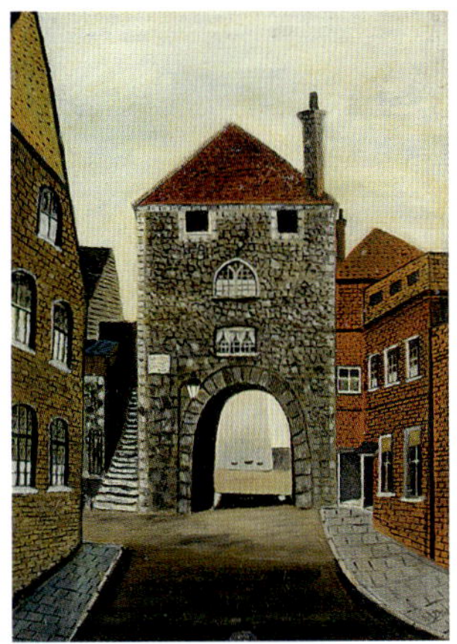

Dear, W.
Westgate, Southampton
oil on board 35.5 x 25.5
M6158

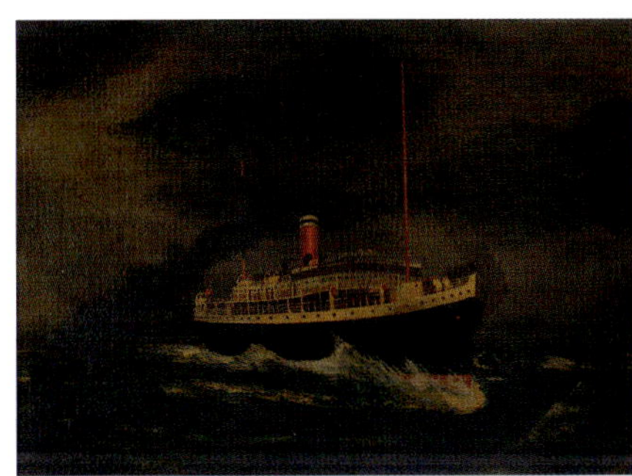

Dixon, J.
Steamship at Sea
oil on canvas 24.3 x 34.5
M216

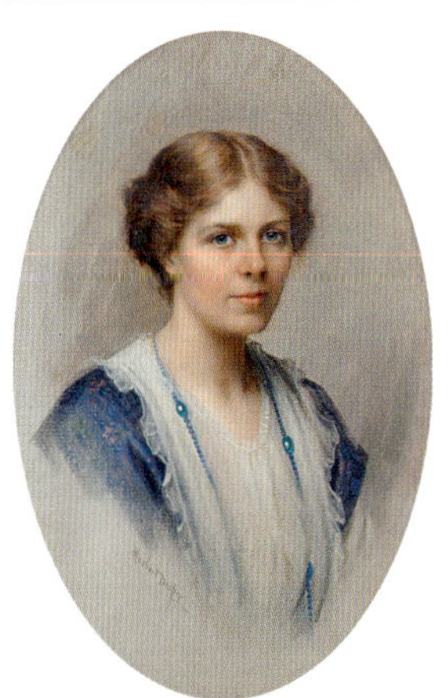

Draper, Herbert James 1864–1920
Mrs E. Milton
oil on canvas 70 x 49
M344

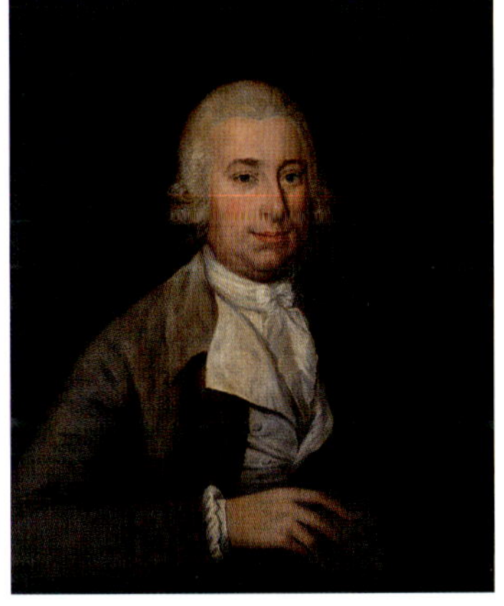

Dupont, Gainsborough (attributed to) 1754–1797
Walter Taylor (1734–1803) 1780
oil on canvas 73 x 61
M3041

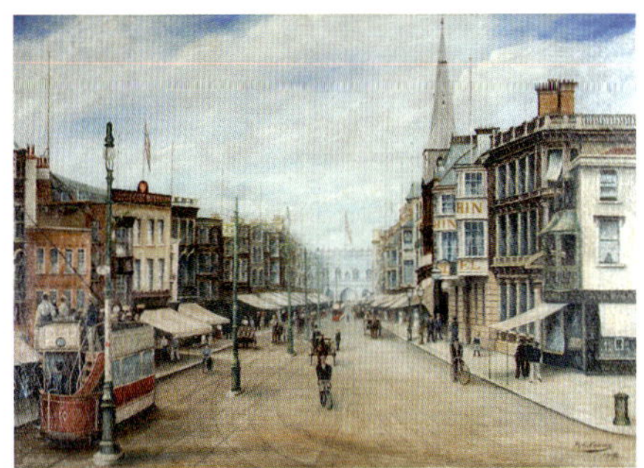

Fanner, R. E.
High Street, Southampton (detail) 1912
oil on canvas 73 x 119.6
M311

Facing page: Tissot, James, 1836–1902, *The Captain's Daughter (The Last Evening)* (detail), 1873, Southampton City Art Gallery, (p. 129)

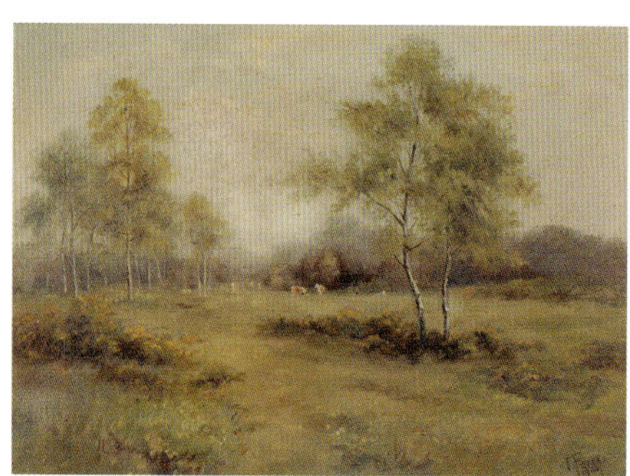

Ferry, John active 1897–1929
Springtime on the Common 1920
oil on canvas 24 x 34
M10178

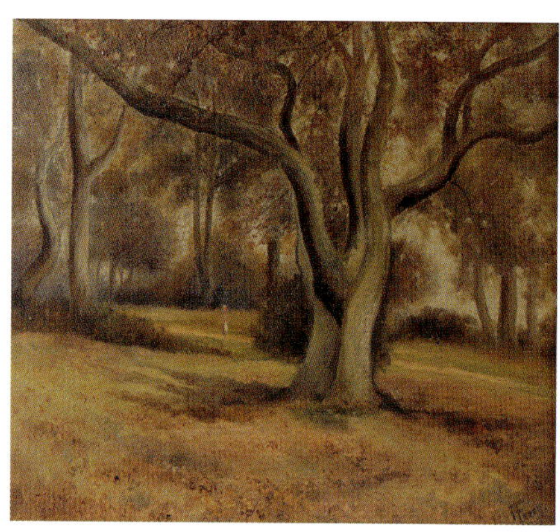

Ferry, John active 1897–1929
The Common 1929
oil on board 30 x 34 (E)
M10179

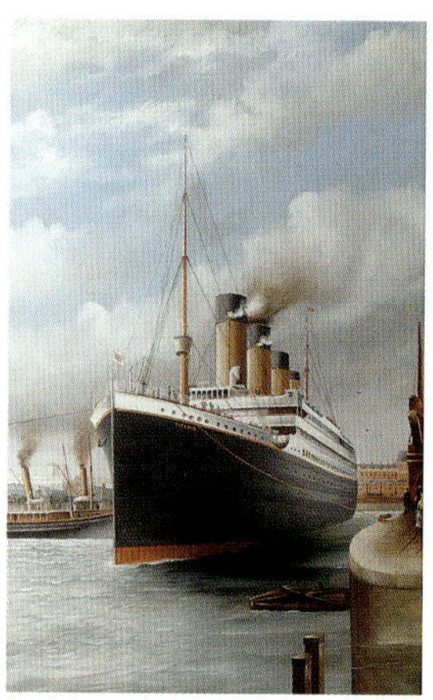

Fraser, George A.
'SS Titanic' 1912
oil on canvas 87.2 x 57.5
M54

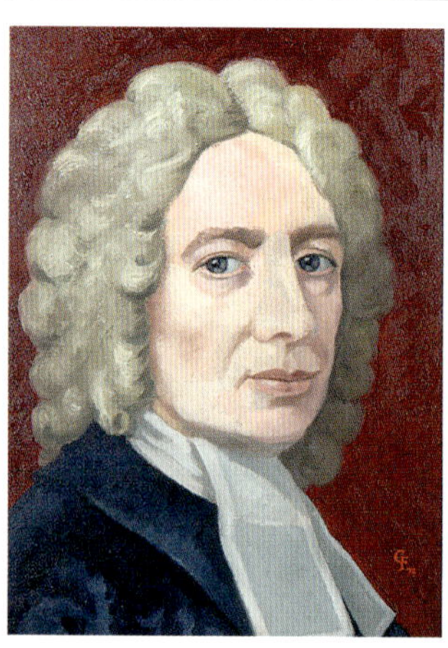

Fry, Gordon
Isaac Watts (1674–1748) 1974
oil on board 49 x 37
M367

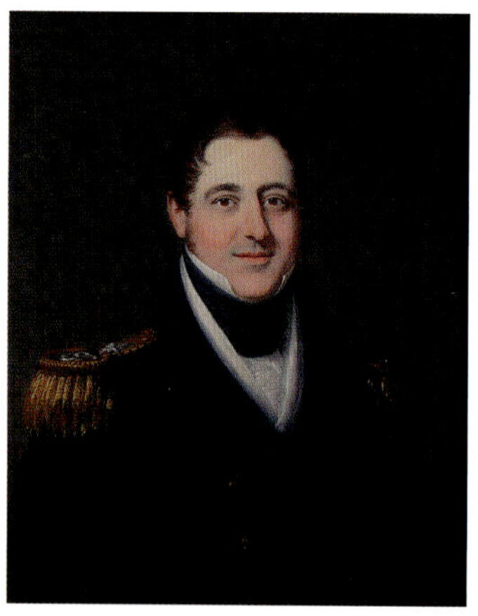

Gaugain, Philip A. active 1783–1847
Captain Pritchard 1824
oil on canvas 74 x 61.5
M358

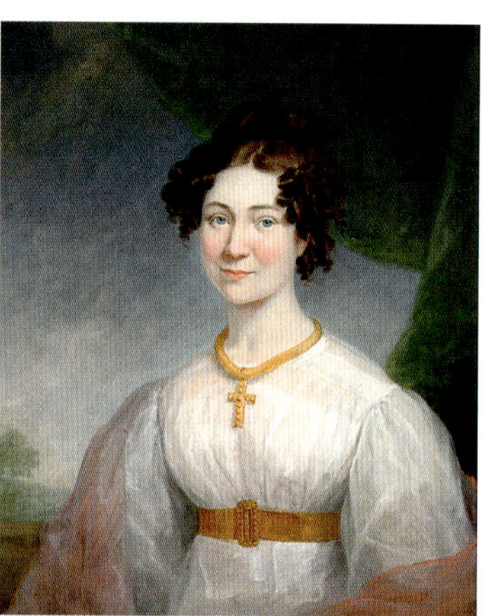

Gaugain, Philip A. active 1783–1847
Mary Ann Pritchard 1824
oil on canvas 76.5 x 63.5
M359

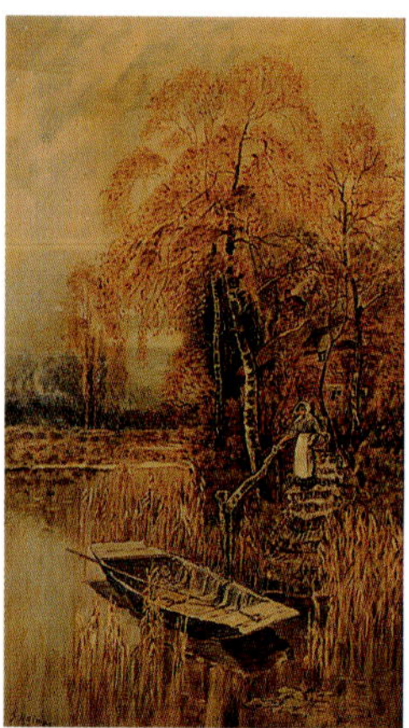

Haines, G. K.
River Scene 1915
oil on canvas 51 x 30.5
M153

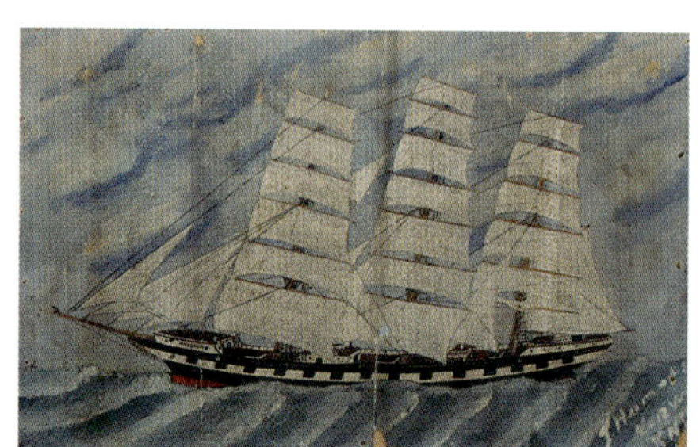

Hamoll, J.
'Hulda', a Schooner
oil on canvas 25.5 x 40
M5884

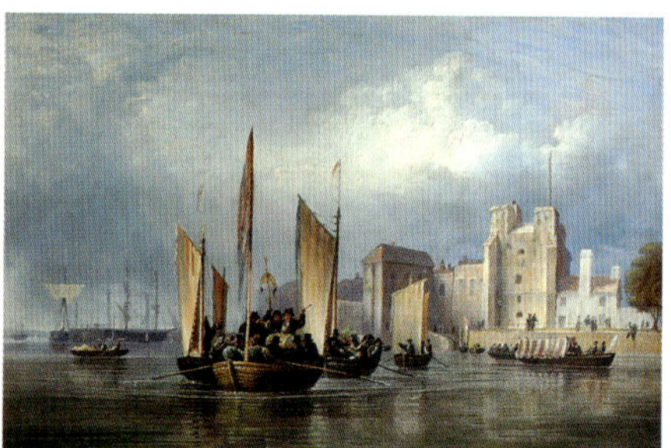

Hart, Thomas Gray 1797–1881
The Old Jail, Southampton 1832
oil on canvas 42.3 x 66
M8930

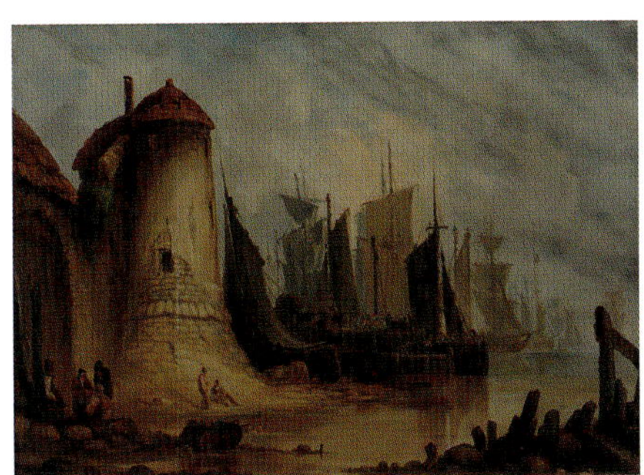

Hart, Thomas Gray 1797–1881
Canute Tower, Southampton
oil on canvas 35.3 x 51.8
M67

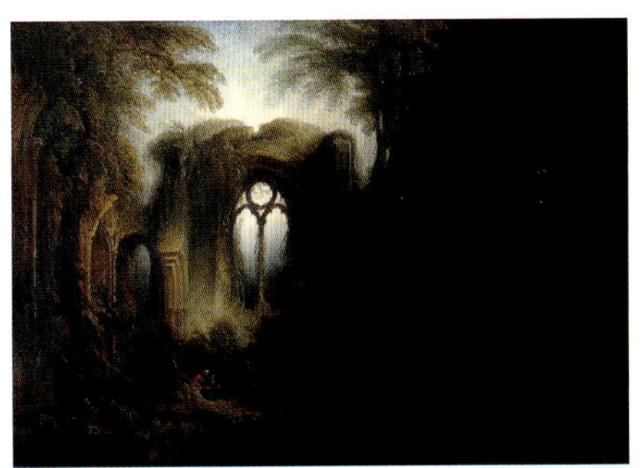

Hart, Thomas Gray 1797–1881
Netley Abbey, East Window
oil on canvas 92.5 x 133.7
M123

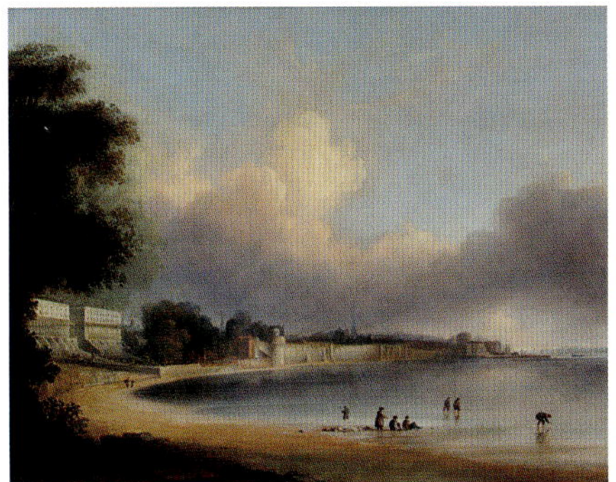

Hart, Thomas Gray 1797–1881
Western Walls Southampton
oil on wood 40.7 x 53
M4518

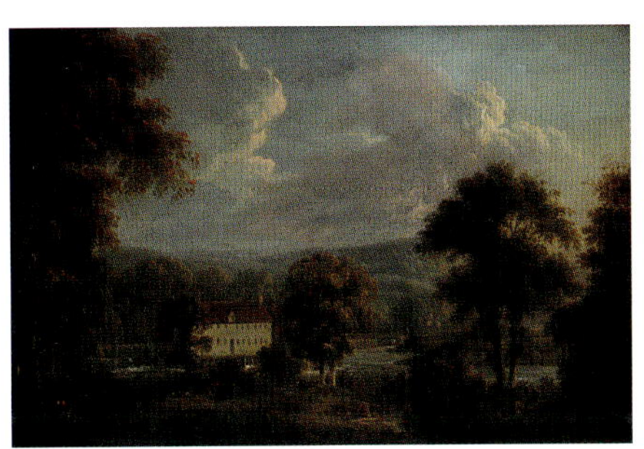

Havell, William (after) 1782–1857
Woodmill near Southampton 1809
oil on board 17 x 26
M11935

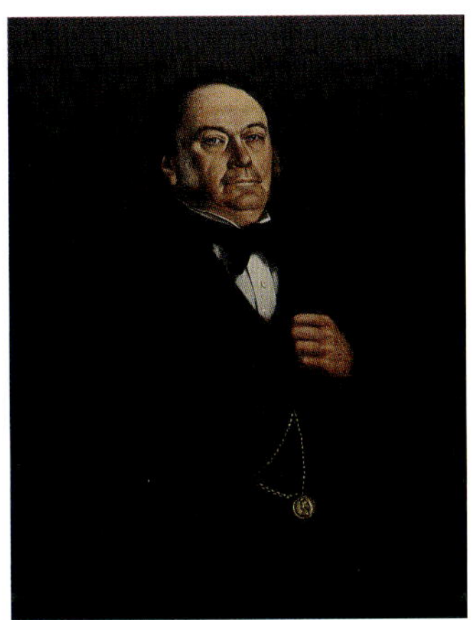

Heath
John Ransom 1865
oil on canvas 89 x 69
M136

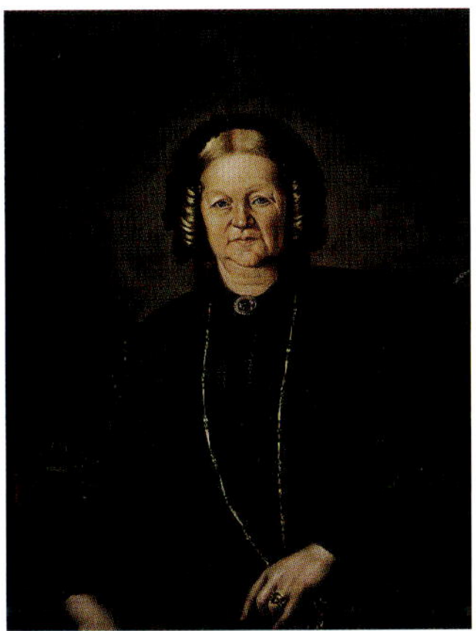

Heath
Mrs Hannah Ransom 1865
oil on canvas 88 x 69
M137

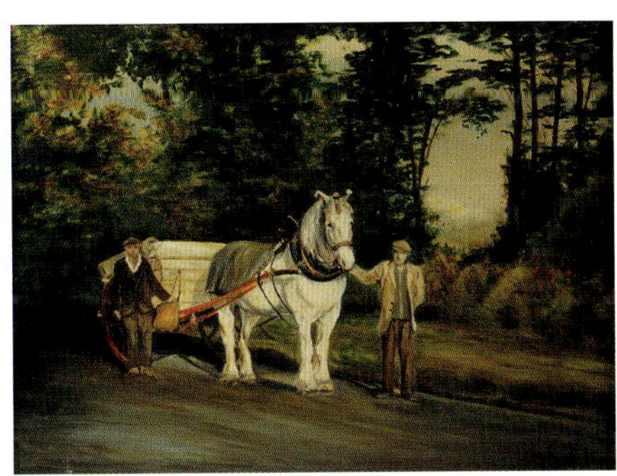

Henvest, Muriel
'Silver', an Aged Horse of the City of Southampton 1967
oil on board 39 x 55
M17595

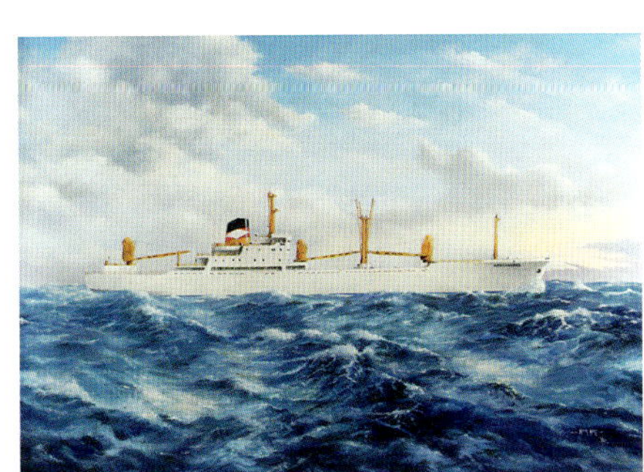

Hill, Noel
'Manzanares' 1980
oil on board 74 x 110
M10157 (P)

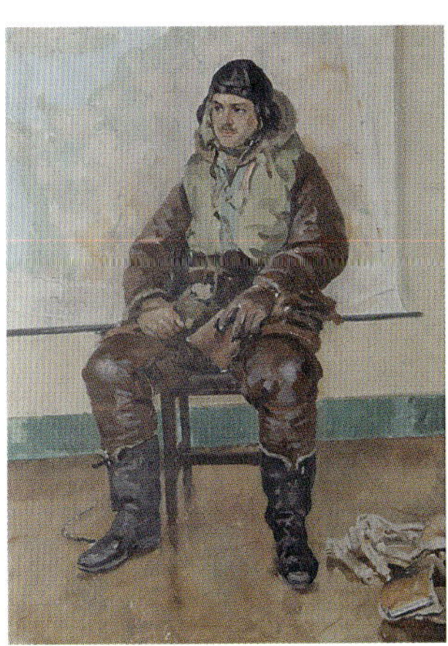

Hodge, Francis Edwin 1883–1949
Sergeant Pilot 1940
oil on board 40.5 x 30.3
M23606

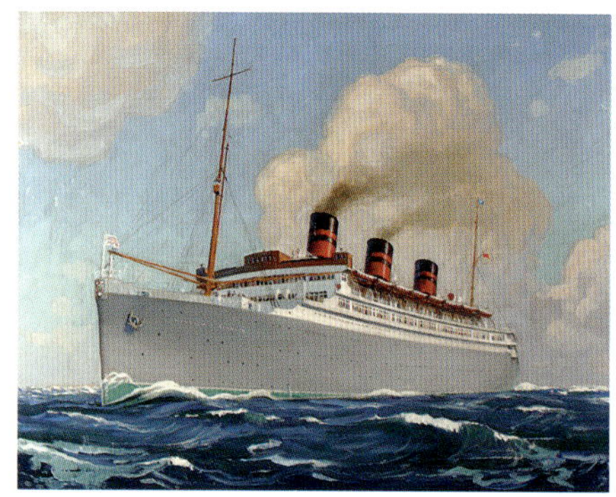

Houston, Robert 1891–1940
'Monarch of Bermuda'
oil on canvas 70.5 x 91.5
M11763

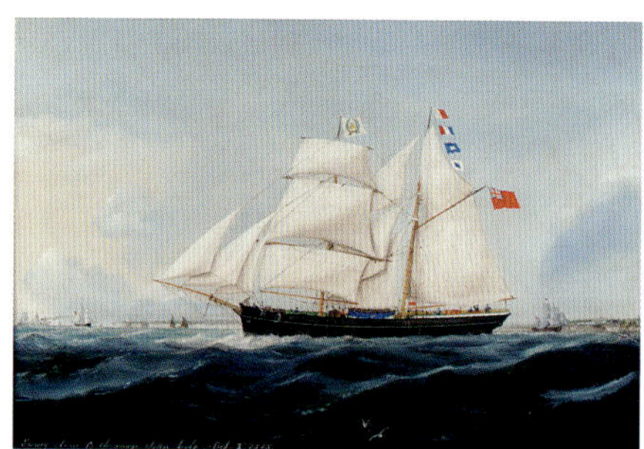

Hudson, John 1829–1879
'Emiely Anne' of Swanage 1868
oil on canvas 46 x 72.5
M321

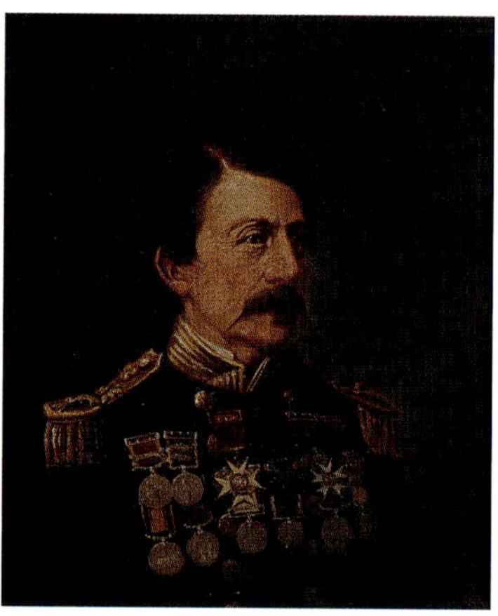

S. K. J. active 19th C
George Fiott Day, VC (1820–1876)
oil on canvas 36.5 x 31.5
M3447

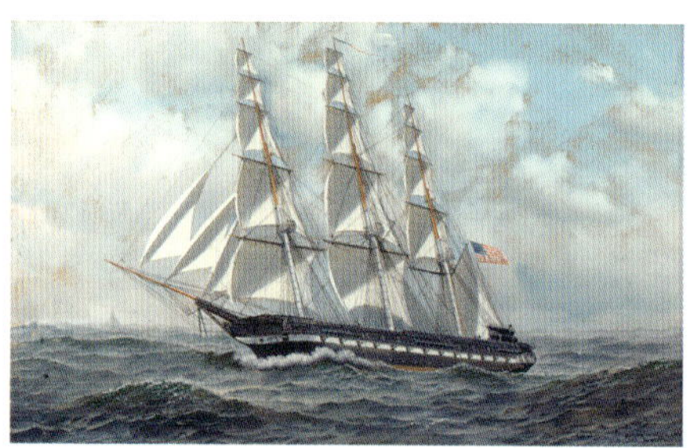

Jacobsen, Antonio 1849–1921
American Warship under Sail 1908
oil on board 54 x 88
M332

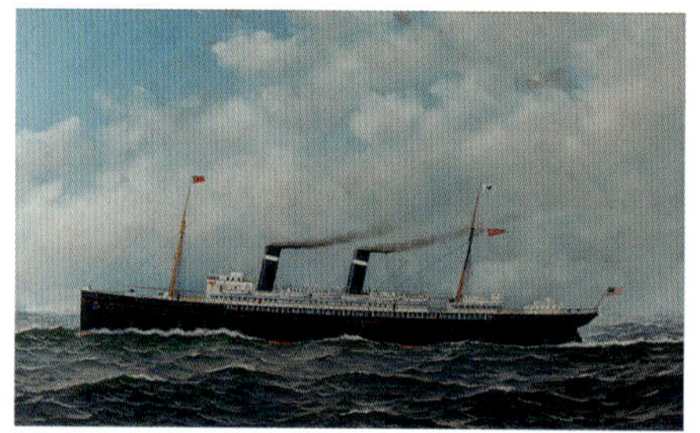

Jacobsen, Antonio 1849–1921
'SS St Louis' 1908
oil on board 53 x 88
M331

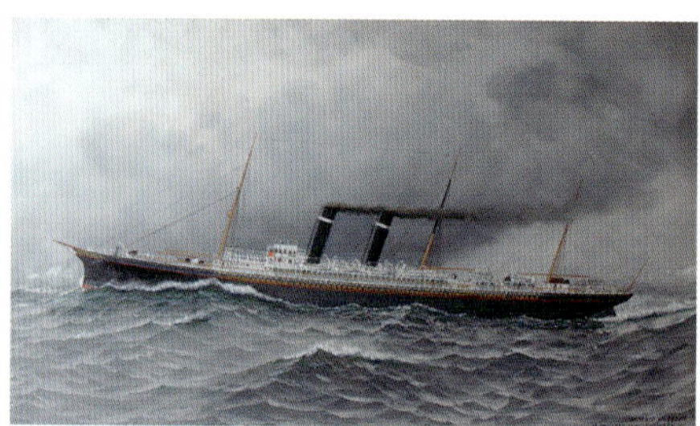

Jacobsen, Antonio 1849–1921
'SS New York' 1909
oil on board 43.1 x 75
M10523

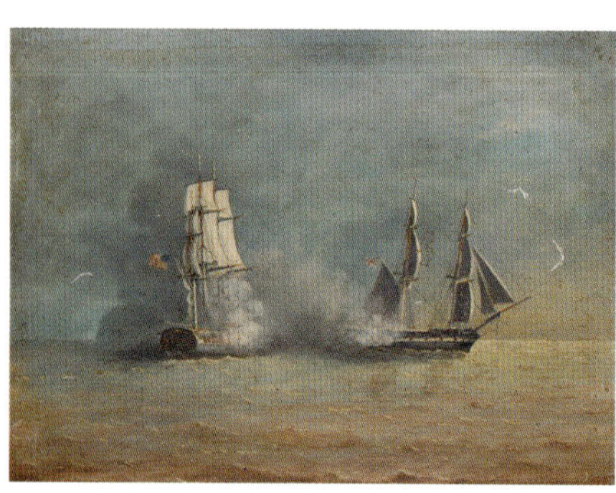

Jones, Montague
Naval Battle between 'HMS Peacock' and 'USS Hornet', 1873
oil on canvas 32 x 43.5
M22826

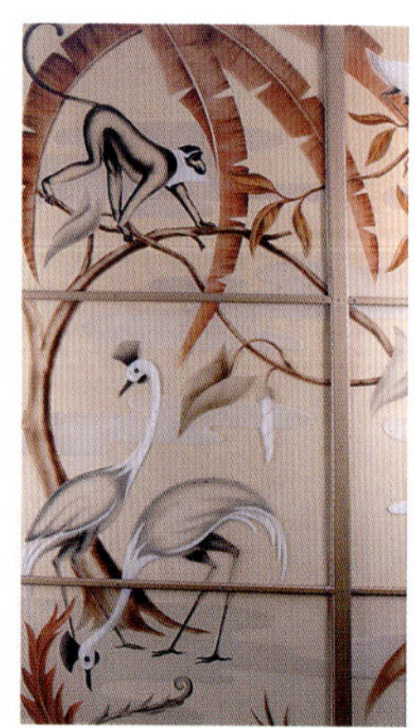

Juta, Jan active 1900–1939
Bermuda (panel from 'Queen Elizabeth') (detail) 1939
oil on glass 701 x 213
M23522

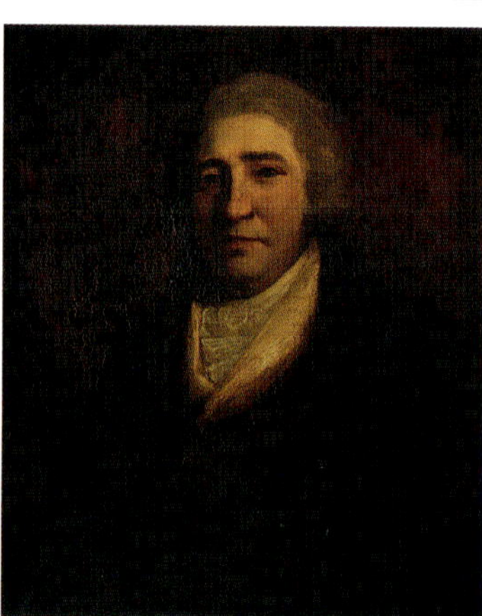

Kearsley, Thomas active 1792–1802
Charles Dibden c.1800
oil on canvas 74.5 x 62.5
M376

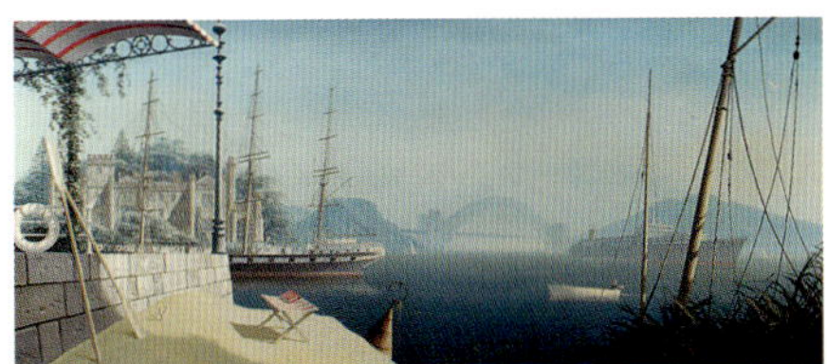

Kelly, Felix 1914–1994
View by Night, Port Side (panel from Shaw, Savill & Albion's 'Northern Star')
mixed media on board 27 x 125
M9294

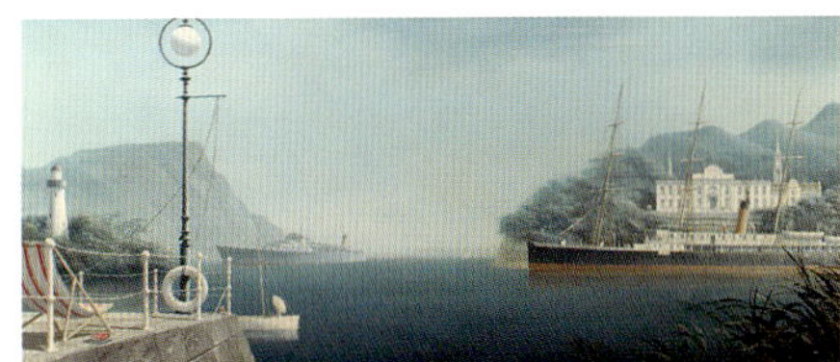

Kelly, Felix 1914–1994
View by Night, Starboard Side (panel from Shaw, Savill & Albion's 'Northern Star')
mixed media on board 125 x 278
M9295

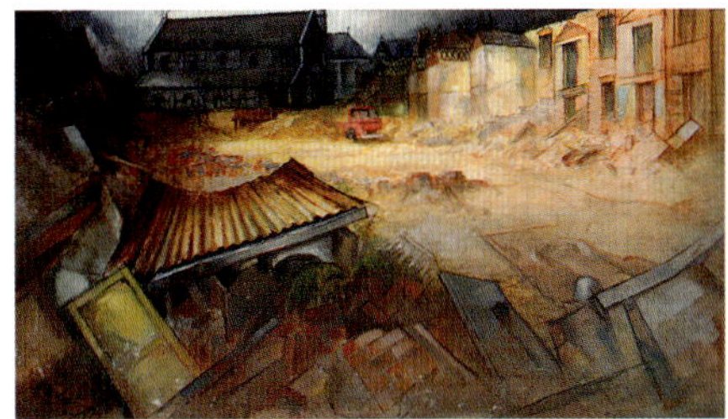

Legg, Henry George 1917–c.1995
Demolished Building, Six Dials, Southampton 1977
acrylic on board 53.4 x 94
M7994

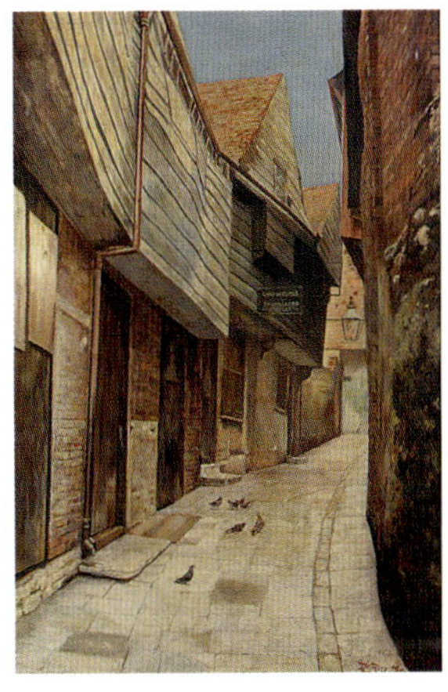

Lemare Jones, T.
Blue Anchor Lane, Southampton 1900
oil on canvas 90 x 60
M370

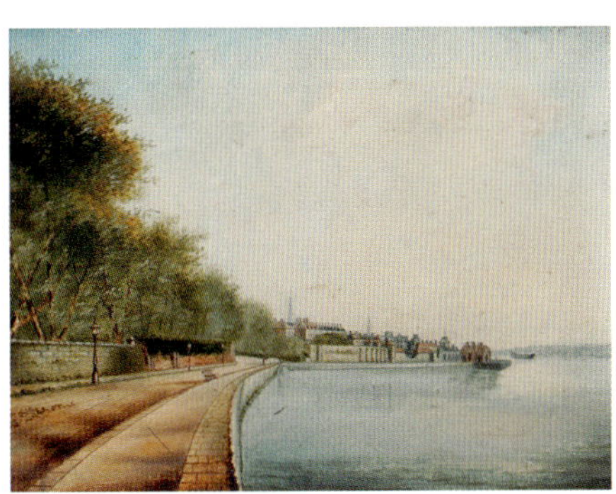

Locke, Henry Edward 1862–1925
Western Shore c.1880
oil on board 22 x 29
M2590

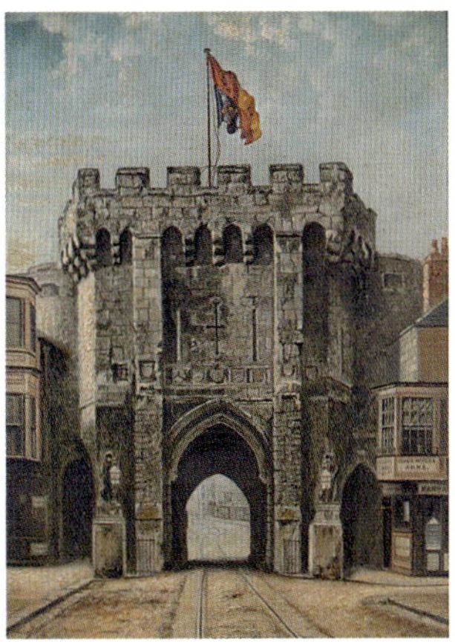

Locke, Henry Edward 1862–1925
Bargate 1888
oil on board 30 x 22
M2603

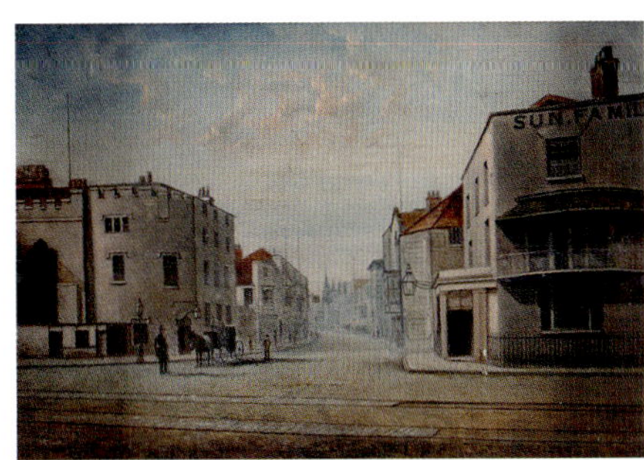

Locke, Henry Edward 1862–1925
High Street, Southampton, Looking from the Quay 1889
oil on wood 15 x 21.6
M387

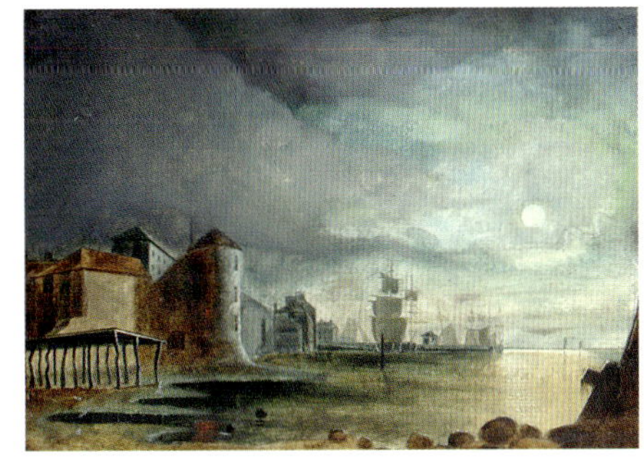

Locke, Henry Edward 1862–1925
Canute Tower and Town Quay 1890
oil on canvas 22.1 x 29.6
M2589

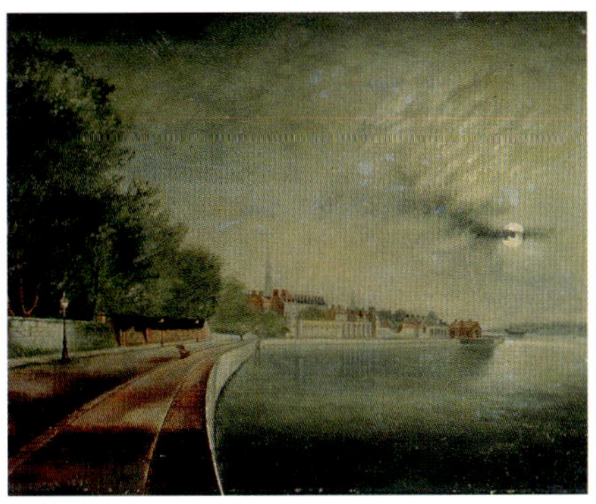

Locke, Henry Edward 1862–1925
Western Shore 1890
oil on cardboard 21.6 x 26.1
M5752

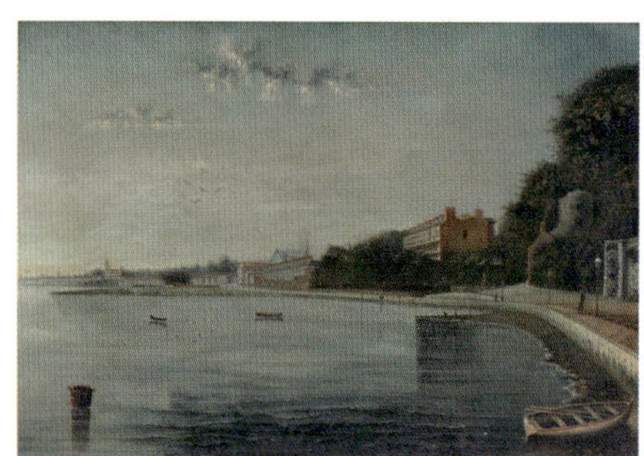

Locke, Henry Edward 1862–1925
Western Shore 1891
oil on canvas 39 x 59
M145

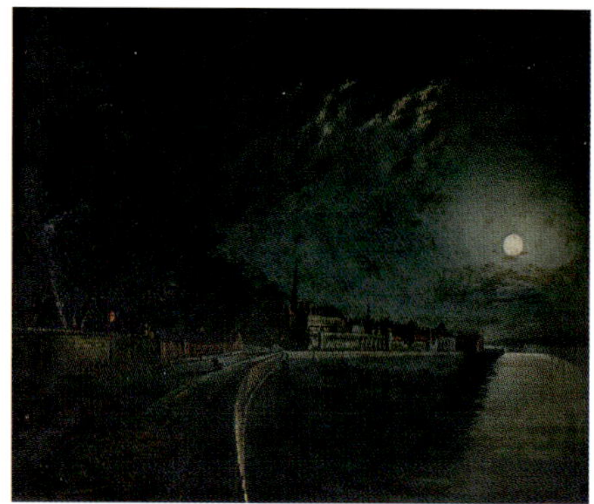

Locke, Henry Edward 1862–1925
Western Shore by Moonlight 1892
oil on board 21 x 30
M11639

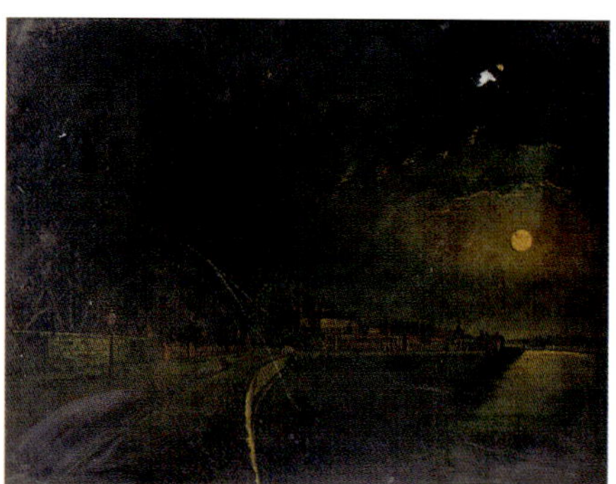

Locke, Henry Edward 1862–1925
Western Shore 1893
oil on board 22 x 29
M164

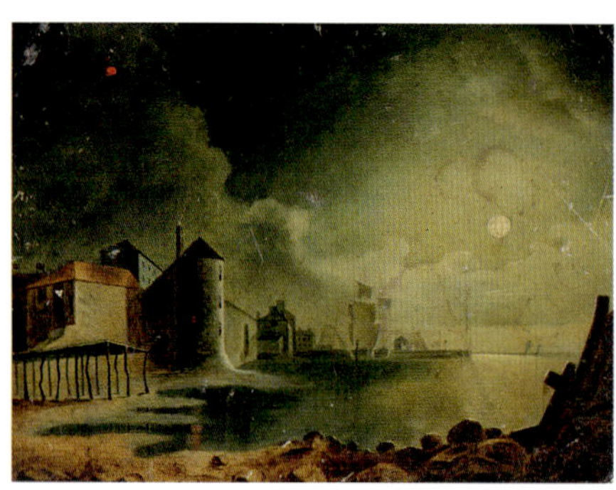

Locke, Henry Edward 1862–1925
Old Southampton around the Shore Looking East 1894
oil on board 23.2 x 31
M5750

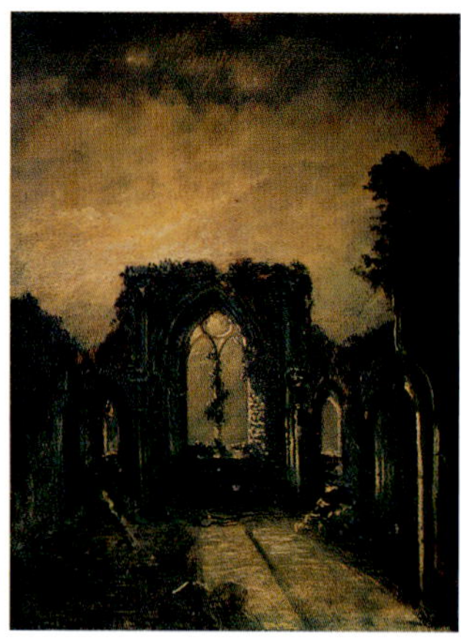

Locke, Henry Edward 1862–1925
Netley Abbey
oil on board 30 x 22
M4451

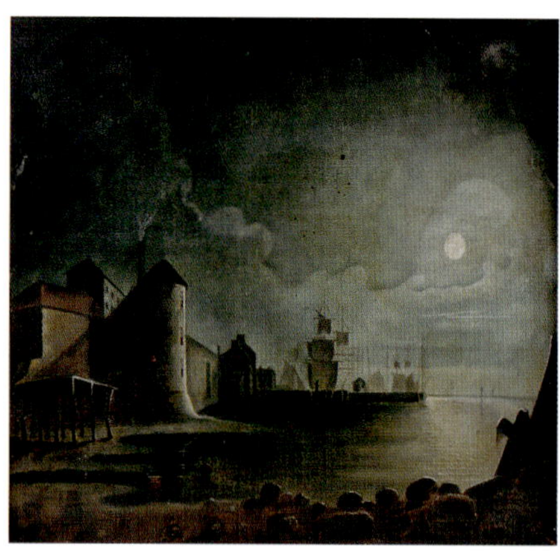

Locke, Henry Edward (after) 1862–1925
Canute Tower at Town Quay, Southampton by Moonlight 1894
oil on board 21 x 29
M1469

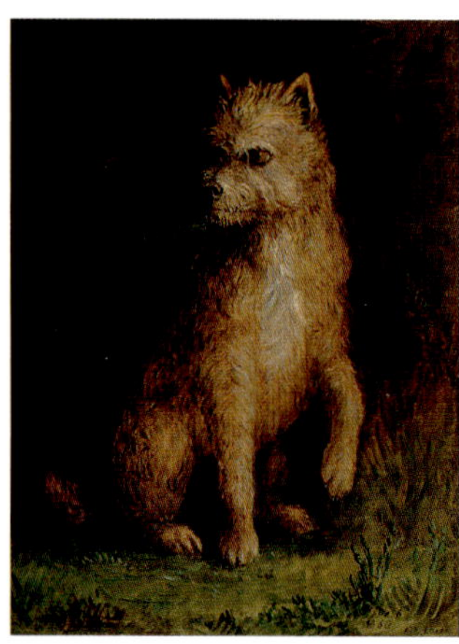

Lucas, Albert Durer 1828–1919
'Dash' 1860
oil on canvas 44 x 34
M21

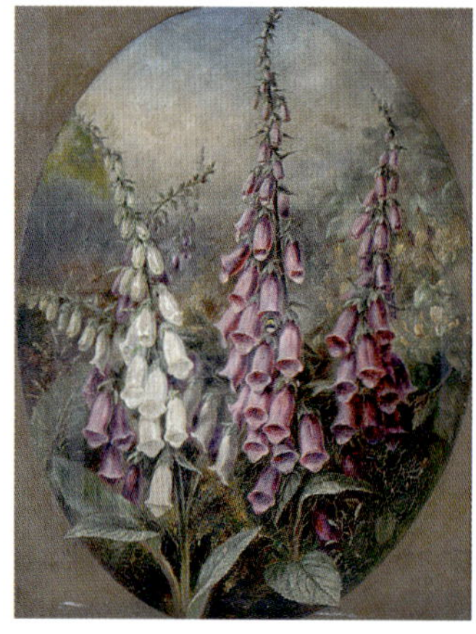

Lucas, Albert Durer 1828–1919
Foxgloves 1872
oil on canvas 42 x 33
M138

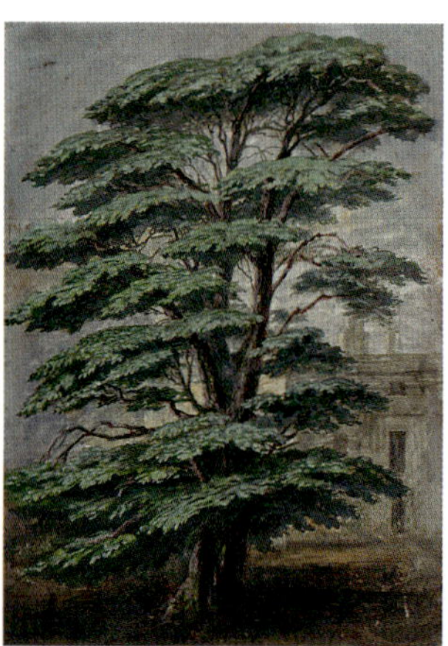

Lucas, Albert Durer 1828–1919
Cedar at Bevois Mount Where Pope Sat 1893
oil on board 20.3 x 15.2
M3328

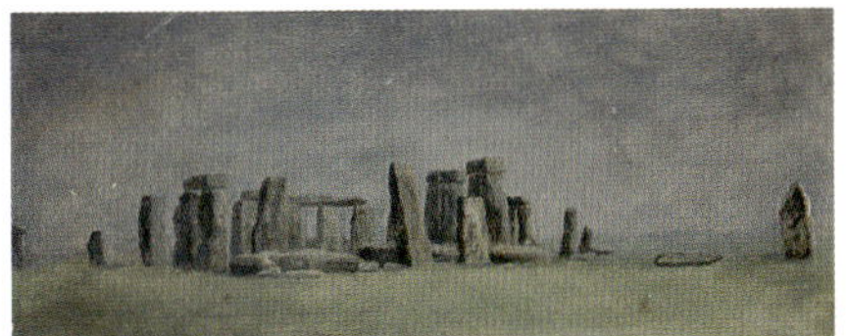

Lucas, Albert Durer 1828–1919
Stonehenge on Salisbury Plain 1904
oil on board 24.1 x 60.5
M5090

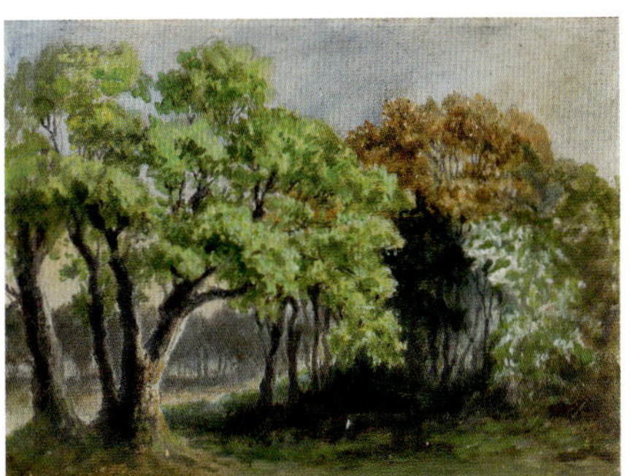

Lucas, Albert Durer 1828–1919
1 May 1894, on the Common
oil on board 15.4 x 21
M3327

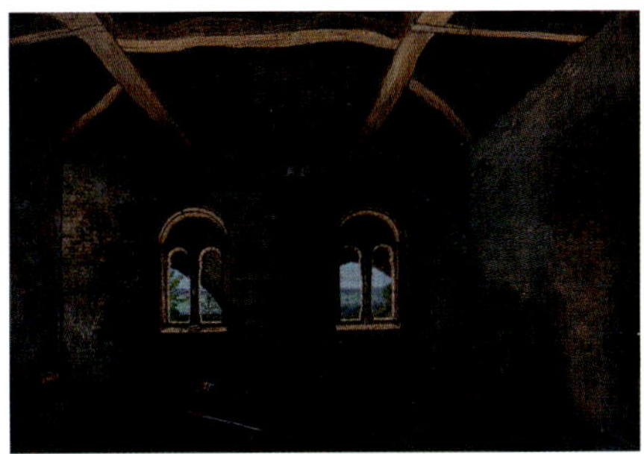

Lucas, Albert Durer 1828–1919
Interior of Norman Merchant House, Blue Anchor Lane, Southampton, 12th Century
oil on canvas 33 x 49.5
M355

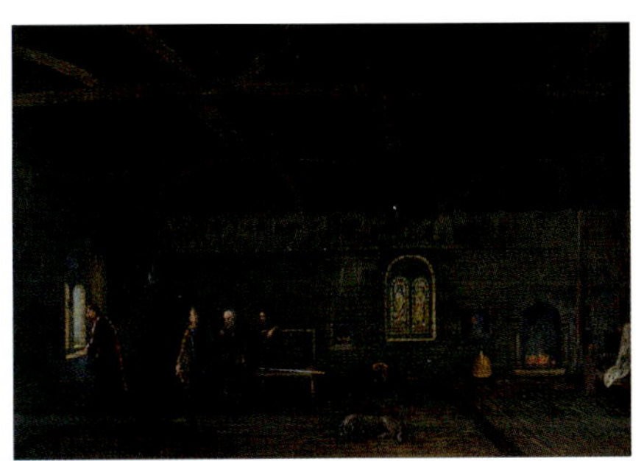

Lucas, Albert Durer 1828–1919
Interior of Norman Merchant House, Blue Anchor Lane, Southampton, 12th Century
oil on canvas 33 x 49.5
M356

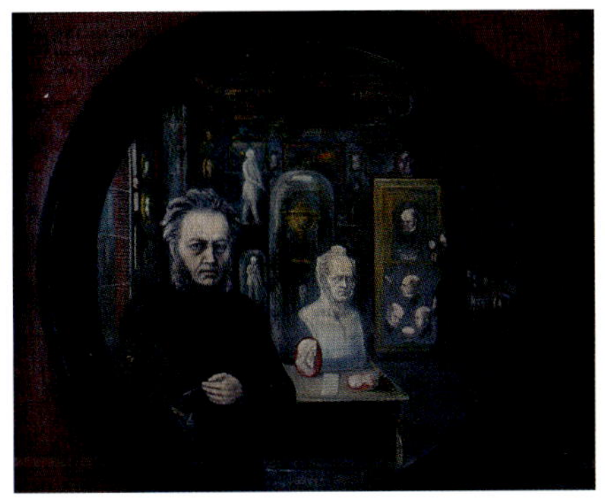

Lucas, Richard Cockle 1800–1883
Self Portrait
oil on canvas 42 x 52
M155

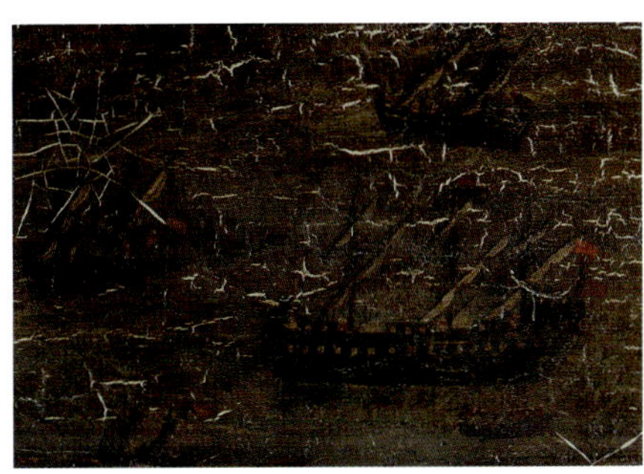

Lucas, Richard Cockle (attributed to)
1800–1883
View of Southampton in 1425 (detail)
oil on hempen cloth 50 x 94
M368

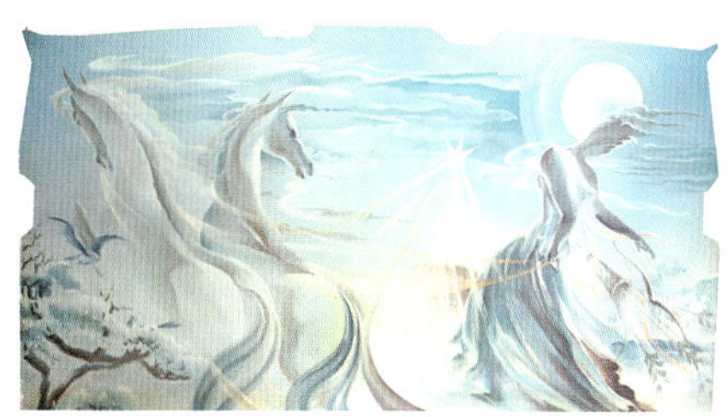

MacDermott, Beatrice
The Goddess Diana and Horses (from 'Caronia')
gesso & oil on wood 110.5 x 206.5
M23520

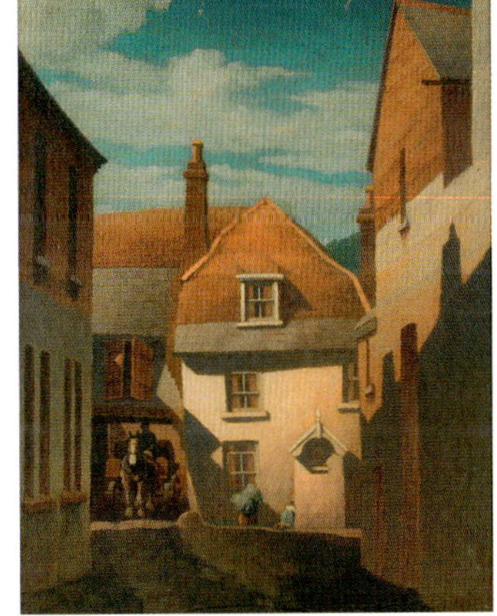

Mager, Frederick b.1882
Cooper's Yard
oil on board 60 x 50
M127

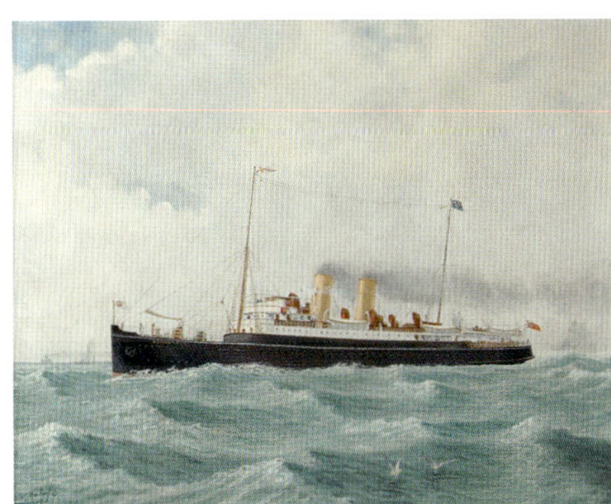

Marboeuf, V.
'SS Normannia' 1912
oil on canvas 49.5 x 64
M279

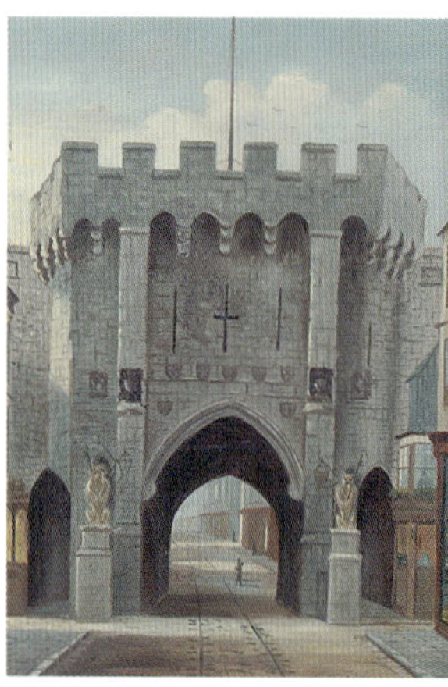

McKeown, H.
Bargate c.1900
oil on canvas 54 x 38
M1473

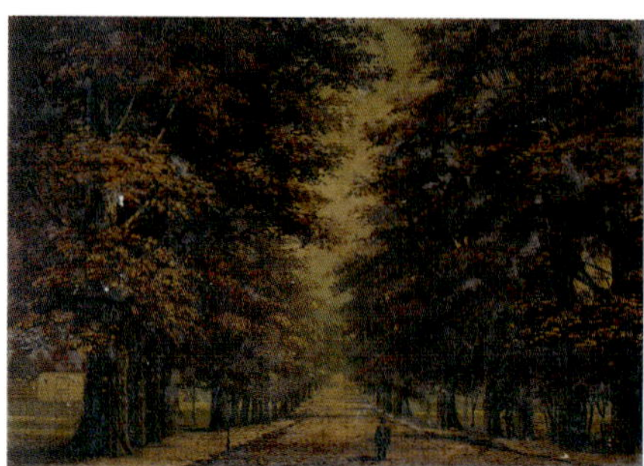

McKeown, H.
Common (Summer), the Avenue
oil on board 30.7 x 43.8
M39b

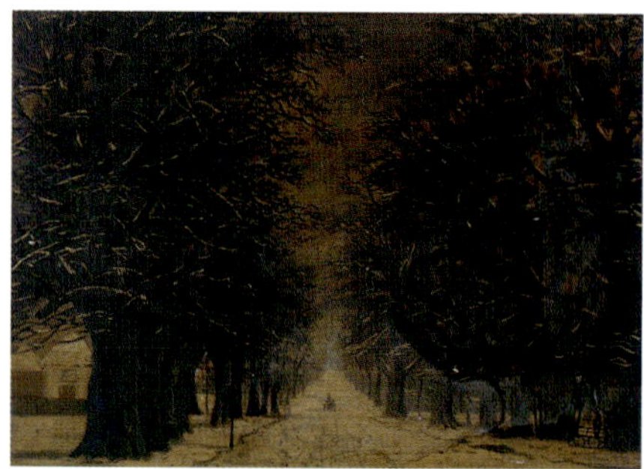

McKeown, H.
Common (Winter), the Avenue
oil on board 31 x 43.6
M39a

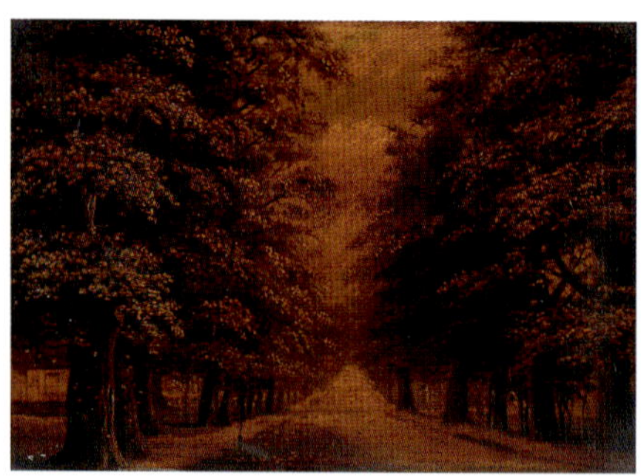

McKeown, H.
The Avenue, Southampton
oil on board 30 x 43
M162

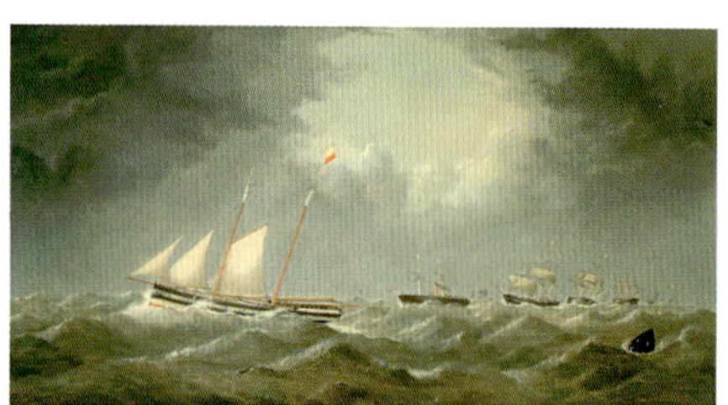

Mears, George 1826–1906
The Southampton Pilot 1871
oil on canvas 66.5 x 107.5
M3530

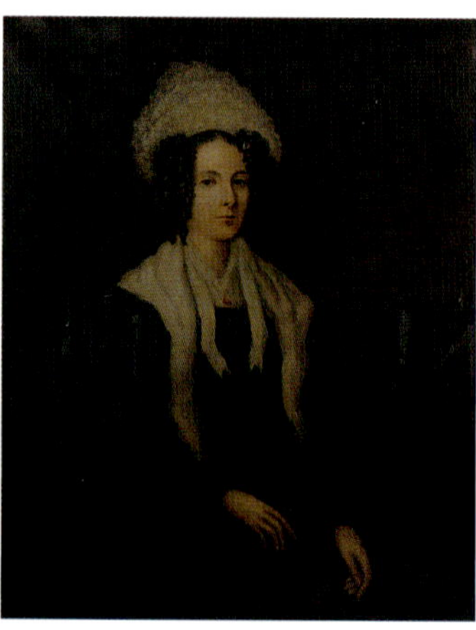

Meohorner, Hannah
Sarah Musgrave Payne
oil on canvas 75 x 63
M10217

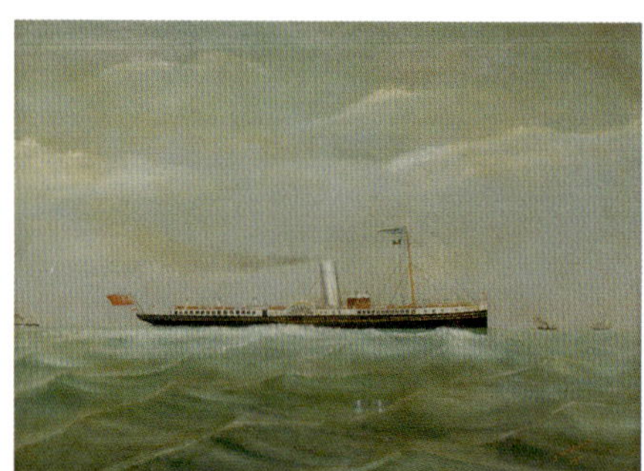

Moorman, J. W.
'PS Balmoral' 1901
oil on canvas 34 x 48.5
M1402

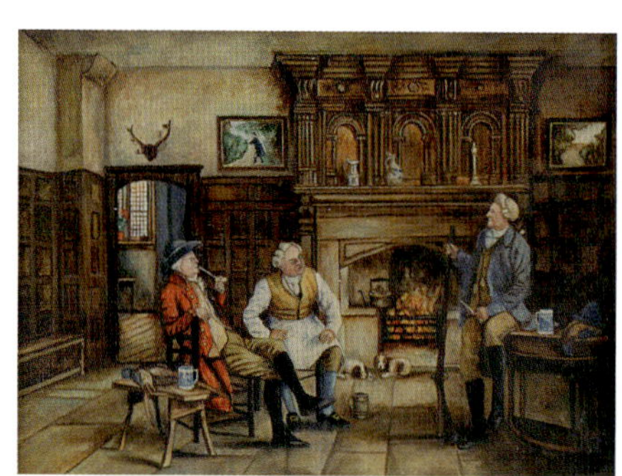

Nicholson, C.
A Tale of the Right and Left 1934
oil on board 16 x 24
M33

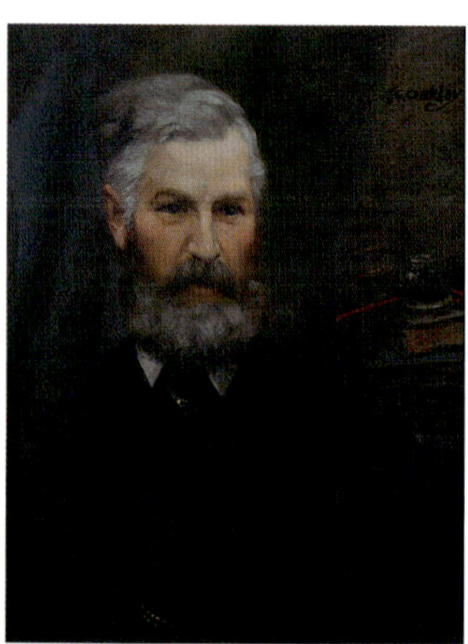

Oakley, Harold active 1904–1929
Penuel George Corbin, Headmaster of Tauntons School (1865–1892) 1909
oil on canvas 70 x 56
M11614 (P)

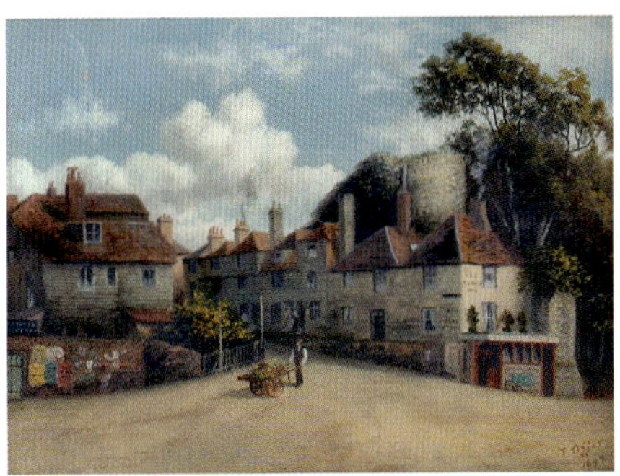

Offer, Frank Rawlings 1847–1932
Bargate Street 1897
oil on canvas 23 x 34
M5180

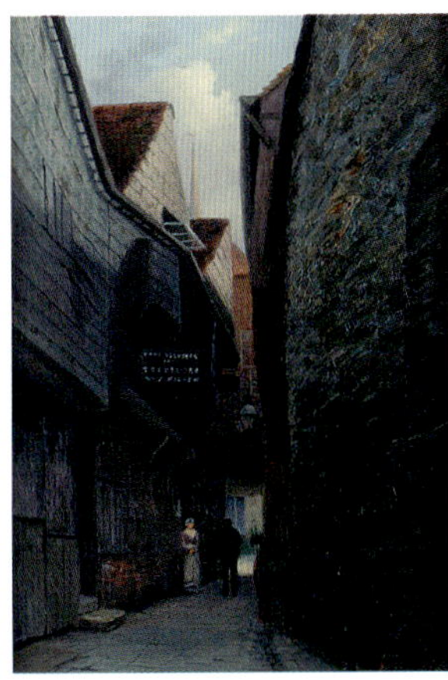

Offer, Frank Rawlings 1847–1932
Blue Anchor Lane, Southampton
oil on canvas 34.3 x 23.7
M130 (P)

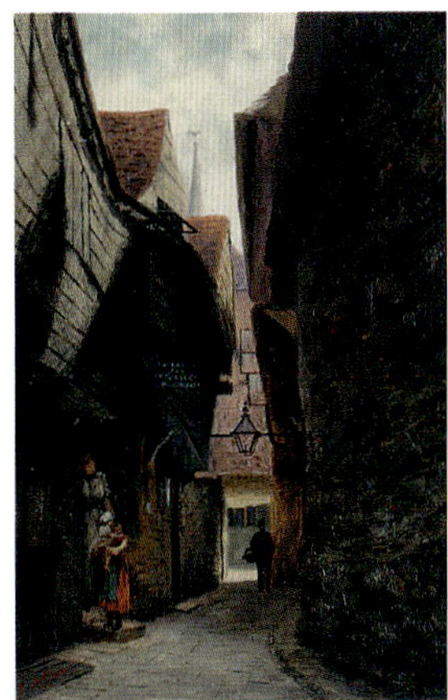

Offer, Frank Rawlings 1847–1932
Blue Anchor Lane, Southampton
oil on board 30.4 x 20.2
M1922

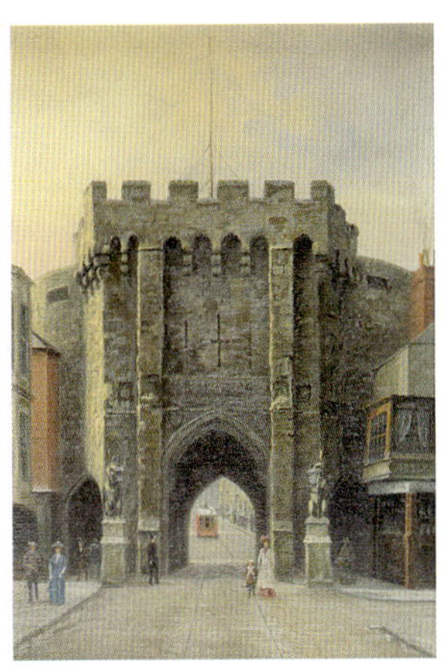

Offer, Frank Rawlings 1847–1932
The Bargate
oil on canvas 47.7 x 37.5
M163

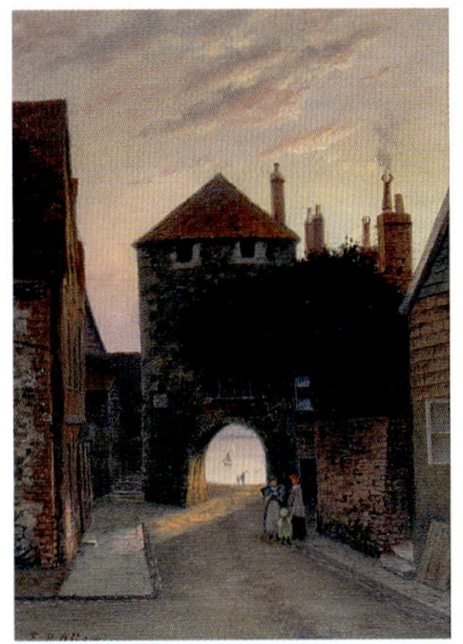

Offer, Frank Rawlings 1847–1932
The Westgate, Southampton
oil on canvas 33.7 x 24
M124

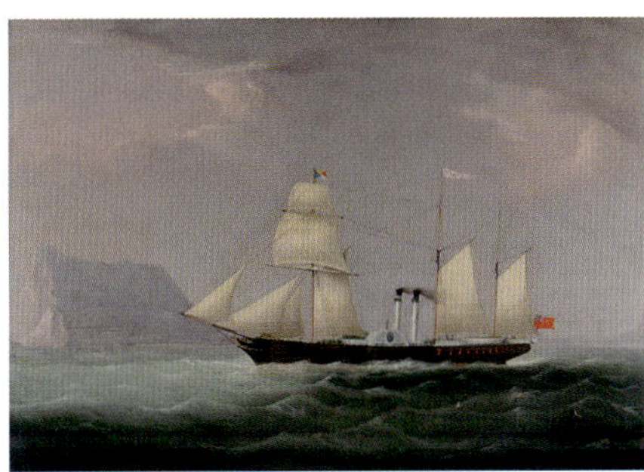

Owen, Samuel 1768–1857
'Tagus' Entering the Bay of Gibraltar 1844
oil on canvas 59 x 89
M159

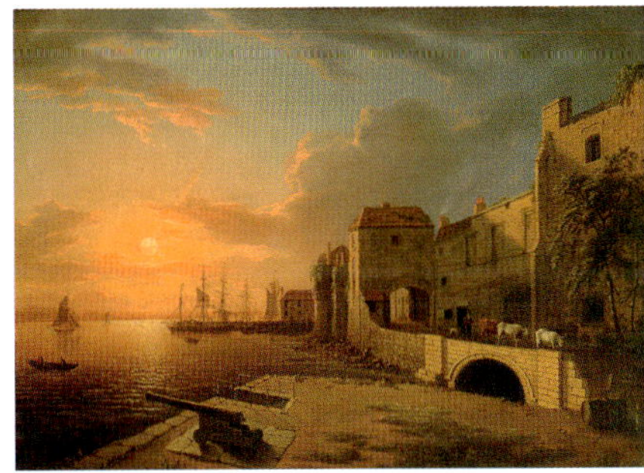

Pether, Henry active 1828–1865
Southampton Town Quay at Sunset
oil on canvas 65.2 x 84.2
M22

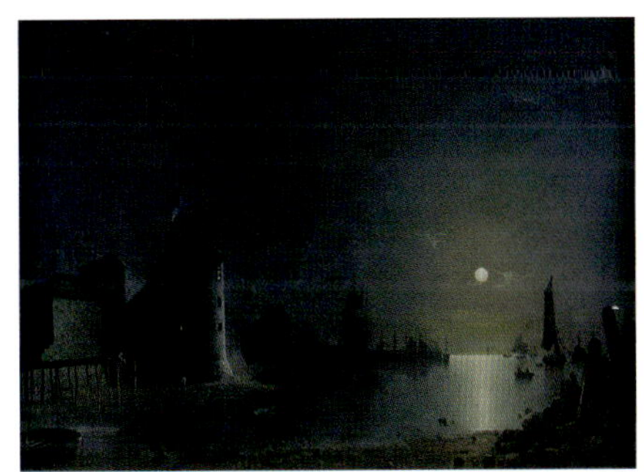

Pether, Henry active 1828–1865
Town Quay by Moonlight
oil on canvas 62 x 90
M313

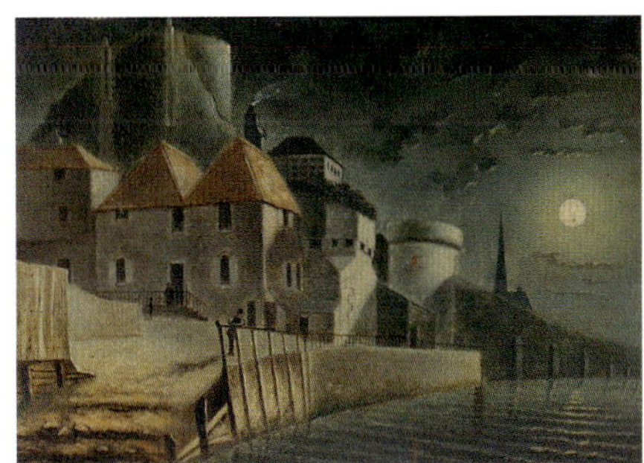

Pether, Henry (after) active 1828–1865
Northwest Corner of Town Walls 19th C
oil on board 14 x 22
M2252

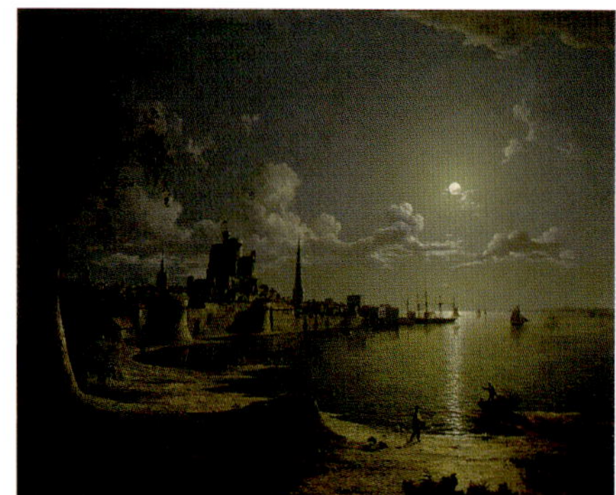

Pether, Sebastian 1790–1844
Moonlight Scene, Southampton
oil on canvas 129.8 x 150 (E)
Temp1

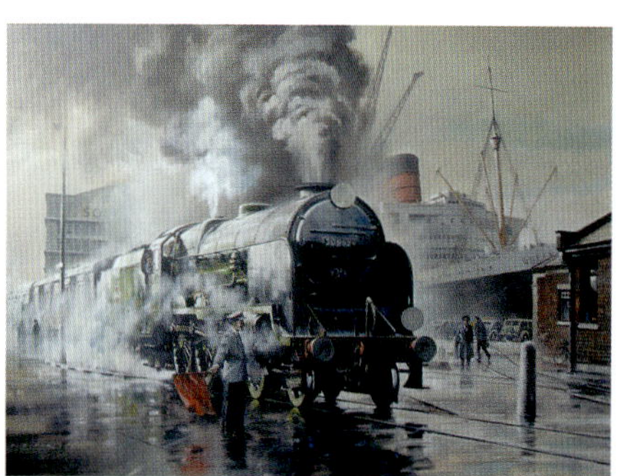

Petrie, James Wilson 1930–1997
Lord Nelson Class Locomotive, 'Sir Walter Raleigh' 1960
oil on canvas 76.2 x 101.6
M5729

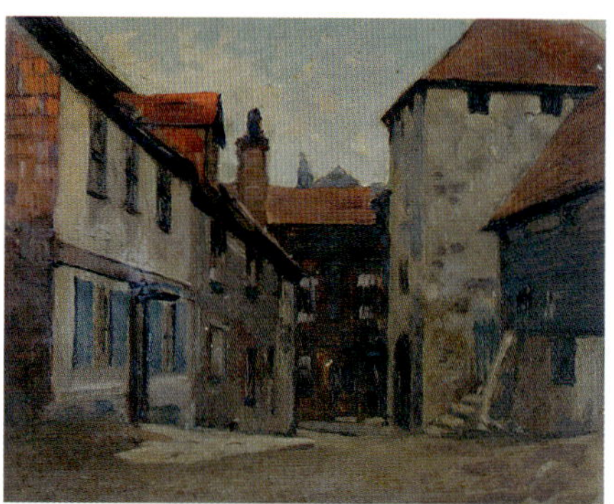

Pontin, George active 1893–1916
By the West Gate 1900
oil on paper 21 x 26.5
M3439(b)

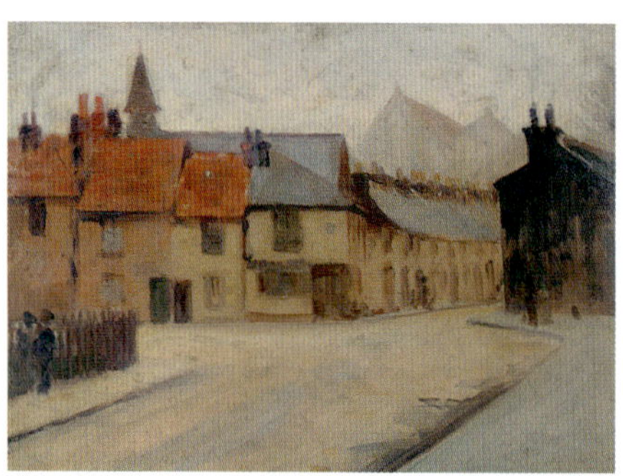

Pontin, George active 1893–1916
Cook Street and St Mary's 1900
oil on paper 20.2 x 28
M3439(e)

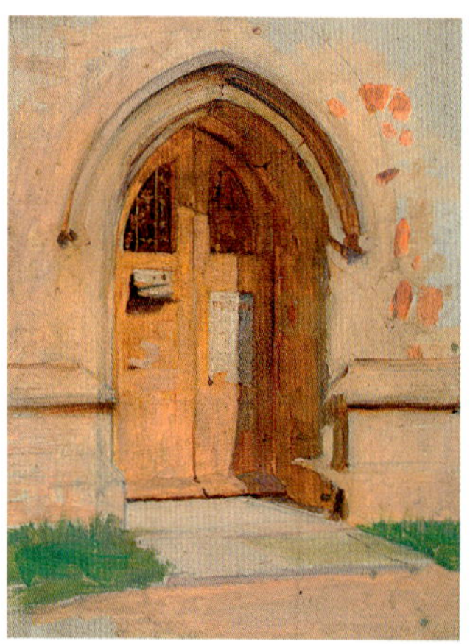

Pontin, George active 1893–1916
Doorway, Old Millbrook Church 1900
oil on paper 27 x 20.5
M3438(f)

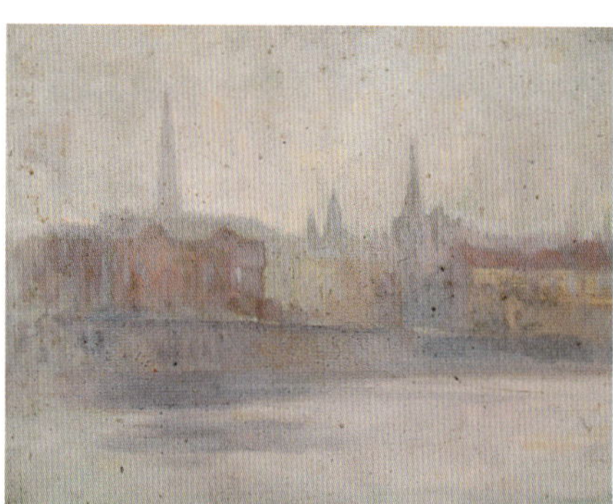

Pontin, George active 1893–1916
Early Morning 1900
oil on paper 20 x 25.6
M3439(k)

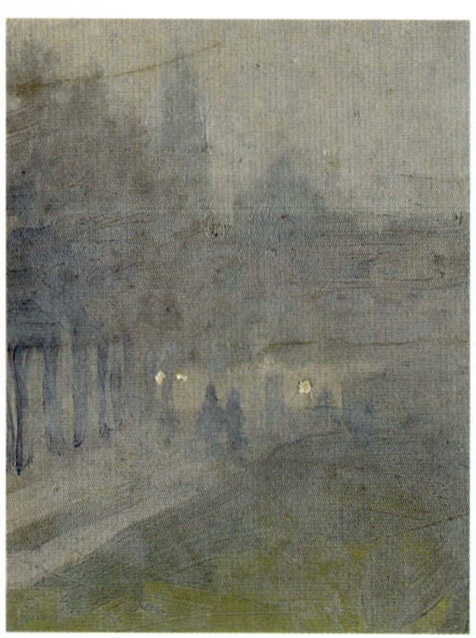

Pontin, George active 1893–1916
Evening, Grand Theatre 1900
oil on paper 13.5 x 10.4
M3439(a)

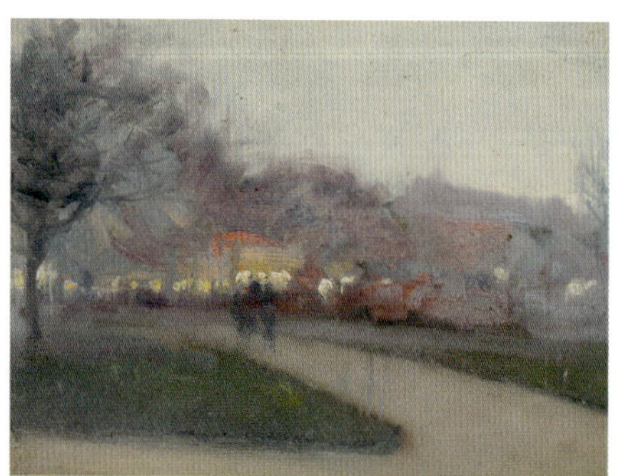

Pontin, George active 1893–1916
Evening, Marlands 1900
oil on paper 19.4 x 26.2
M3438(b)

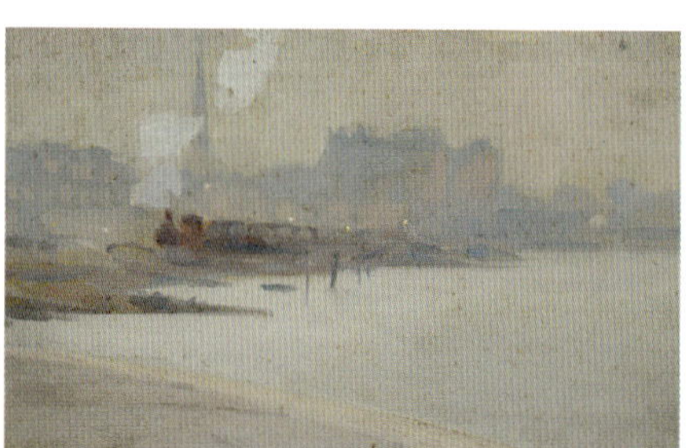

Pontin, George active 1893–1916
Filling in Western Shore near the Baths 1900
oil on paper 17.8 x 29
M3439(h)

Facing page: Spencer, Stanley, 1891–1959, *Patricia Preece* (detail), 1933, Southampton City Art Gallery, (p. 124)

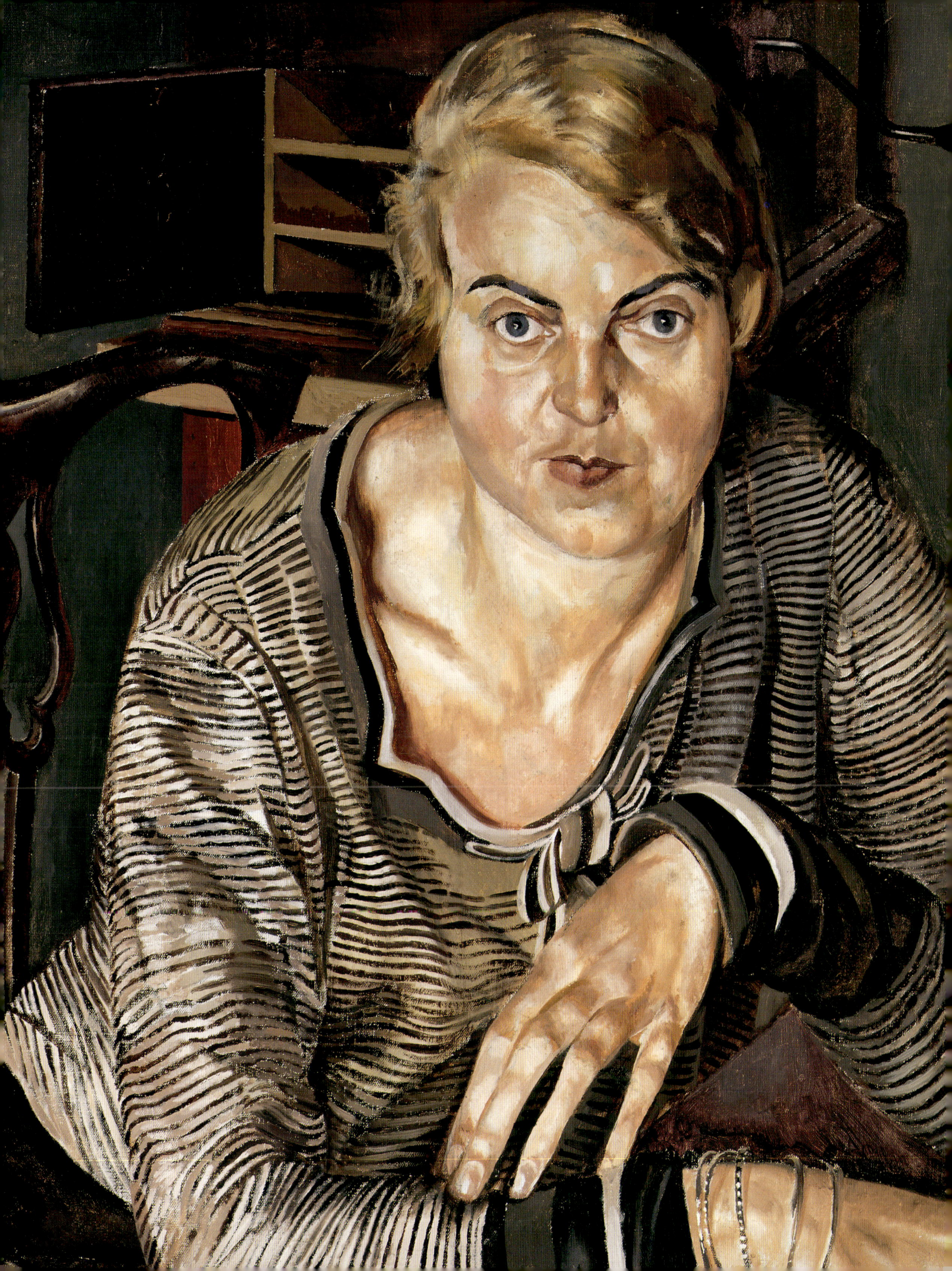

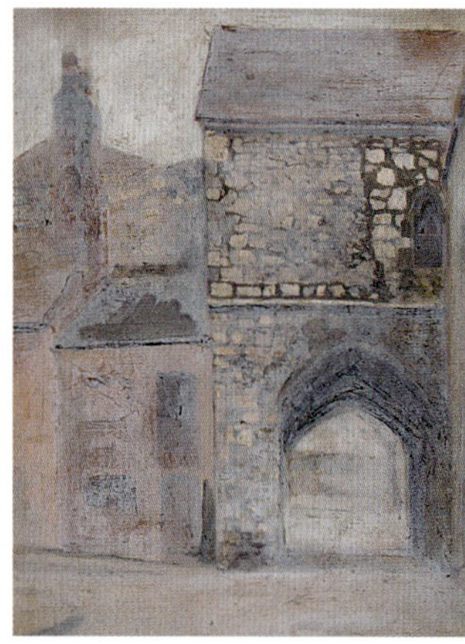

Pontin, George active 1893–1916
Gateway, Back of the Walls 1900
oil on paper 28.4 x 21.9
M3438(l)

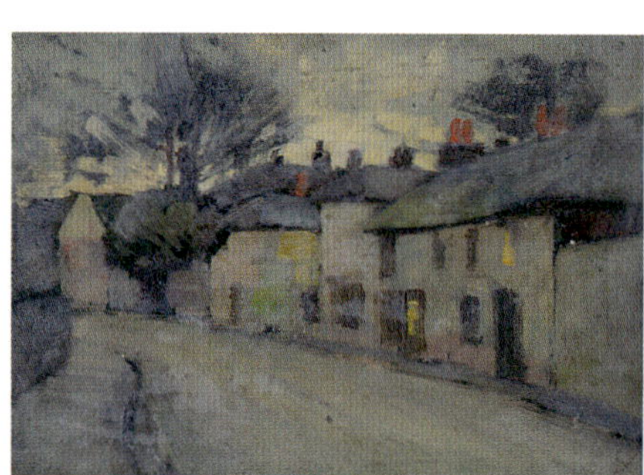

Pontin, George active 1893–1916
Hill Top, Millbrook Road 1900
oil on paper 18.2 x 26.1
M3438(h)

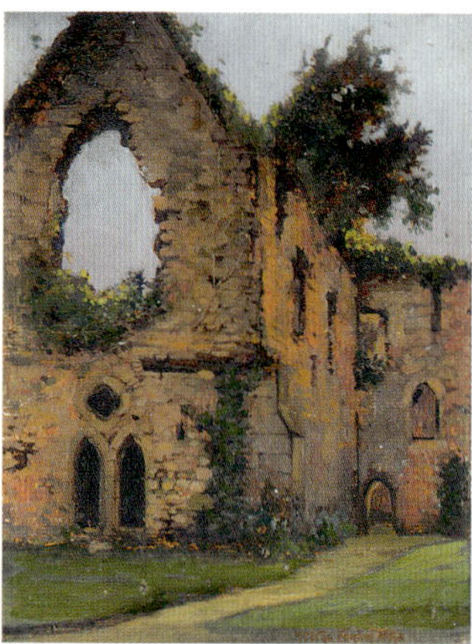

Pontin, George active 1893–1916
In Netley Abbey 1900
oil on paper 28 x 21.6
M3438(k)

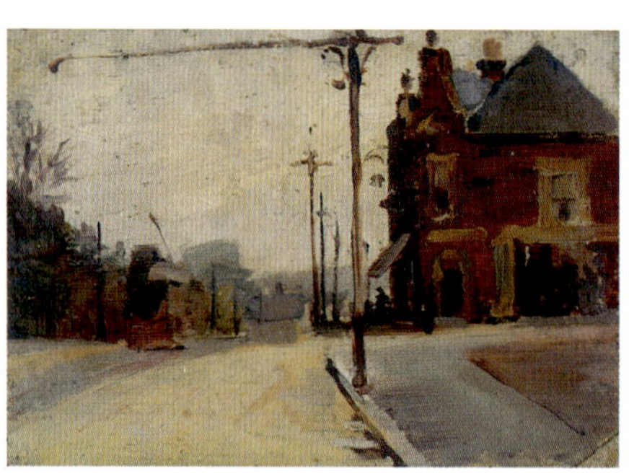

Pontin, George active 1893–1916
In Portswood Road 1900
oil on paper 14.8 x 20.9
M3439(l)

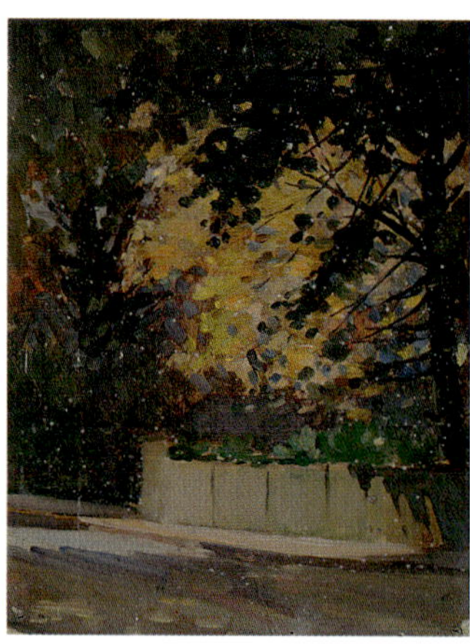

Pontin, George active 1893–1916
In Regent's Park 1900
oil on paper 24.3 x 18.8
M3438(e)

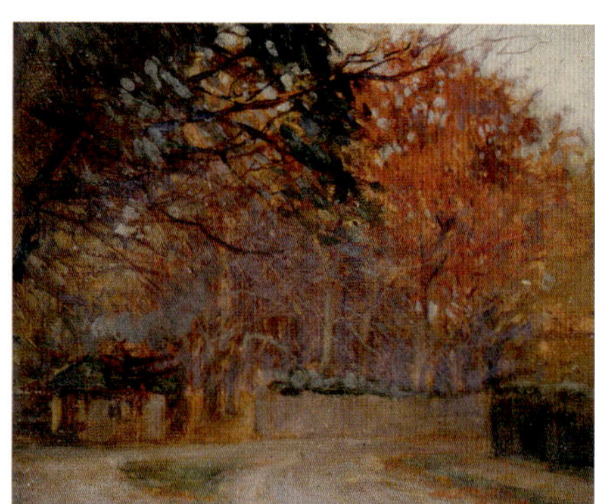

Pontin, George active 1893–1916
In Regent's Park 1900
oil on paper 23 x 28
M3439(d)

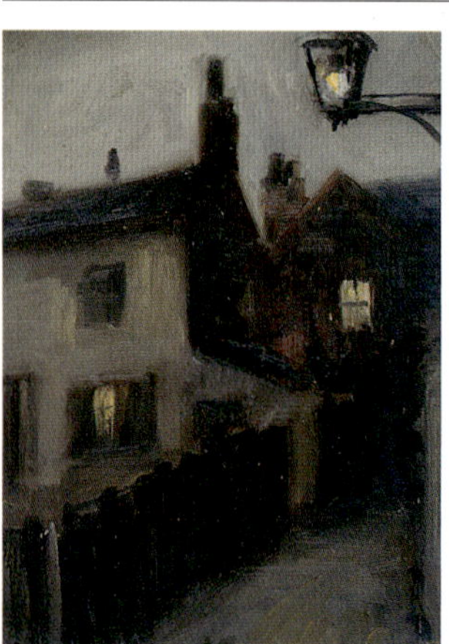

Pontin, George active 1893–1916
Lane at Hill Top 1900
oil on paper 28.2 x 21
M3438(i)

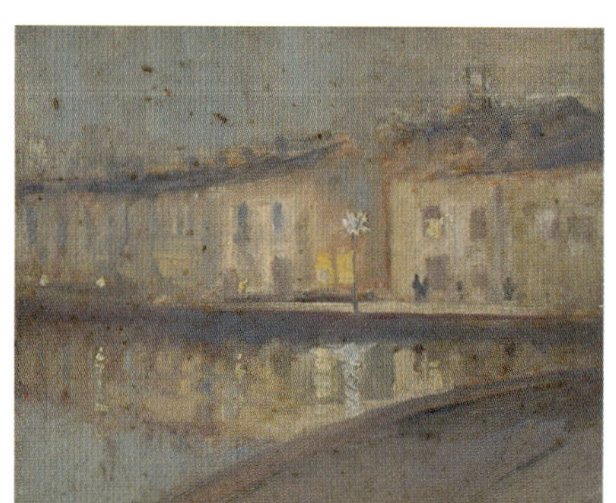

Pontin, George active 1893–1916
Near the Baths 1900
oil on paper 20 x 24.8
M3439(f)

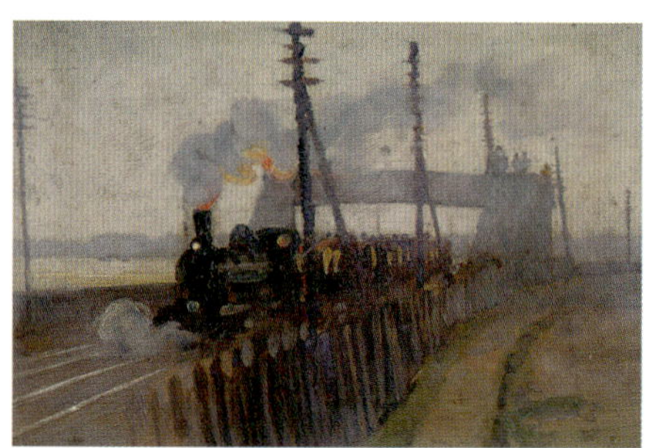

Pontin, George active 1893–1916
New Millbrook 1900
oil on paper 18.7 x 28.2
M3438(d)

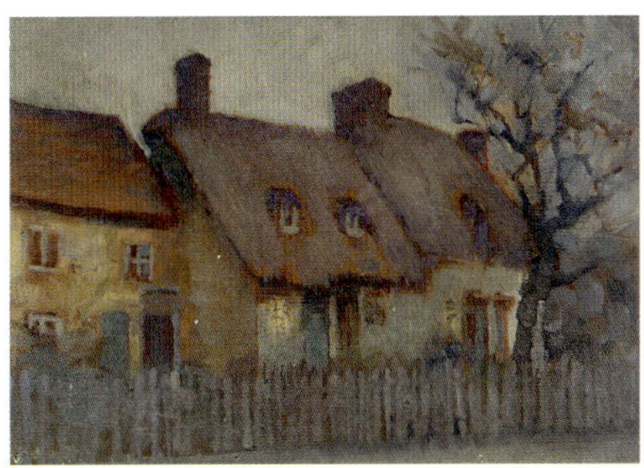

Pontin, George active 1893–1916
Old Cottages, Till Top 1900
oil on paper 20.3 x 27.9
M3439(g)

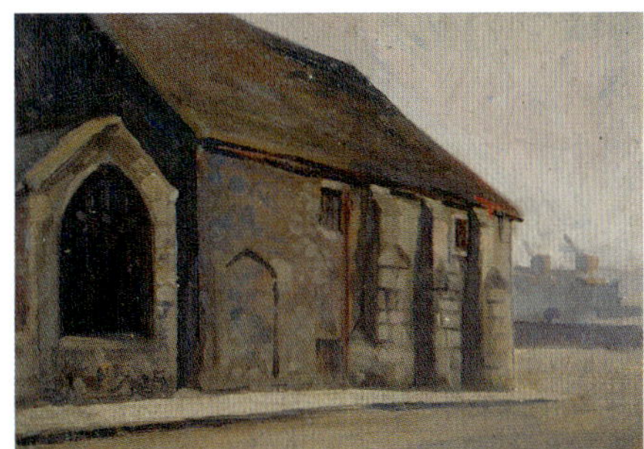

Pontin, George active 1893–1916
Old Prison, French Street 1900
oil on paper 19.9 x 28.5
M3439(i)

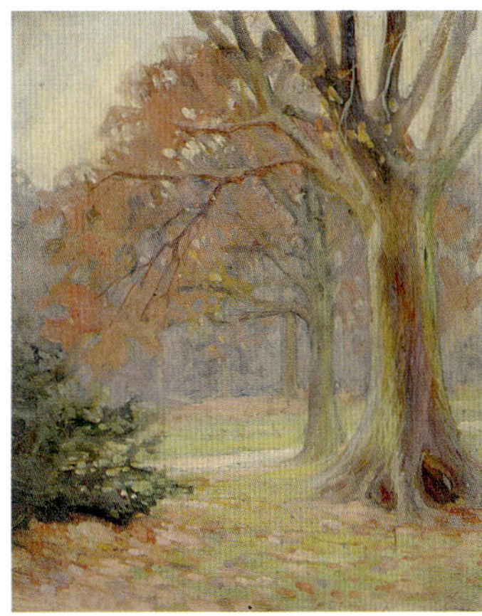

Pontin, George active 1893–1916
On the Common 1900
oil on paper 27.3 x 22.6
M3438(g)

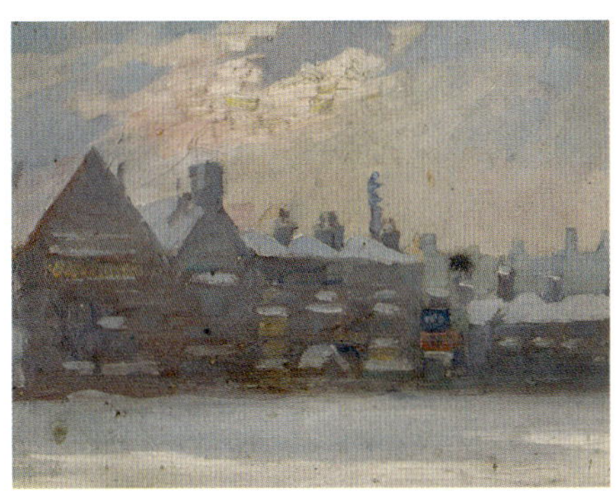

Pontin, George active 1893–1916
Snow Scene (back of East Street) 1900
oil on paper 21 x 26.2
M3439(c)

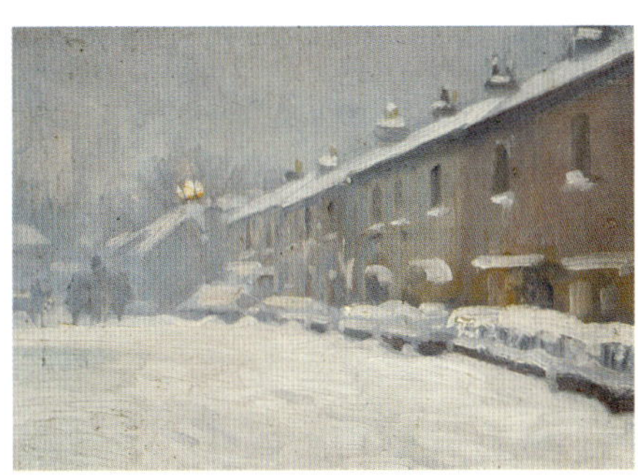

Pontin, George active 1893–1916
Snow Scene off Millbrook Road 1900
oil on paper 21 x 27.6
M3439(j)

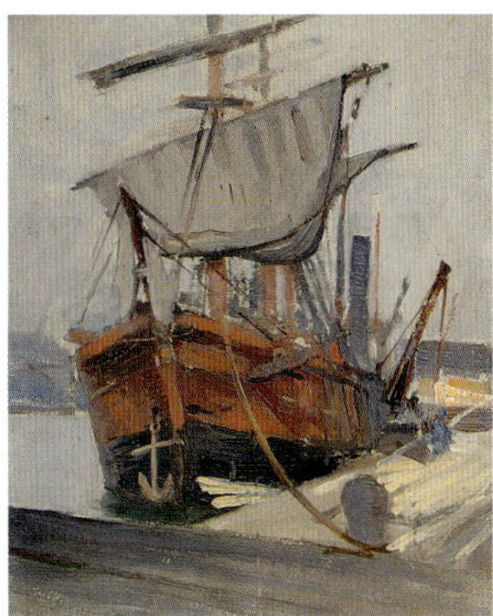

Pontin, George active 1893–1916
Timber in the Docks 1900
oil on paper 26 x 21.7
M3438(j)

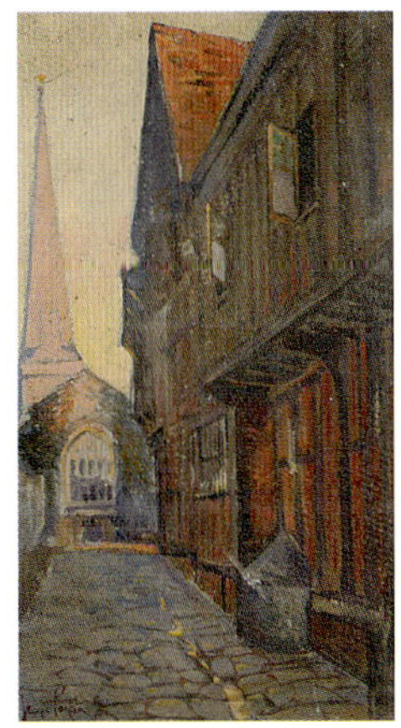

Pontin, George active 1893–1916
Tudor House and St Michael's 1900
oil on paper 22 x 12
M3438(a)

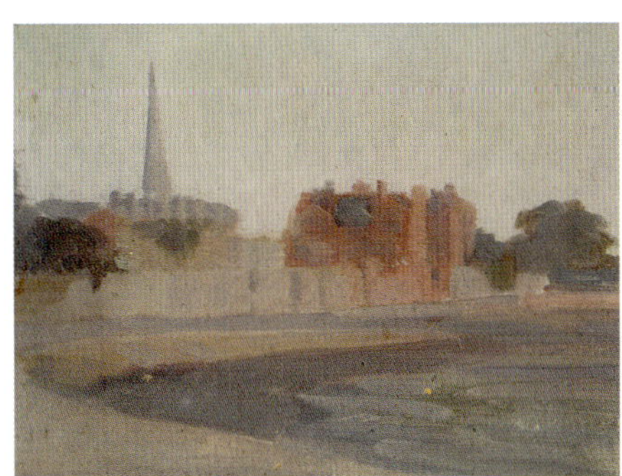

Pontin, George active 1893–1916
Western Shore 1900
oil on paper 19.3 x 26.3
M3438(c)

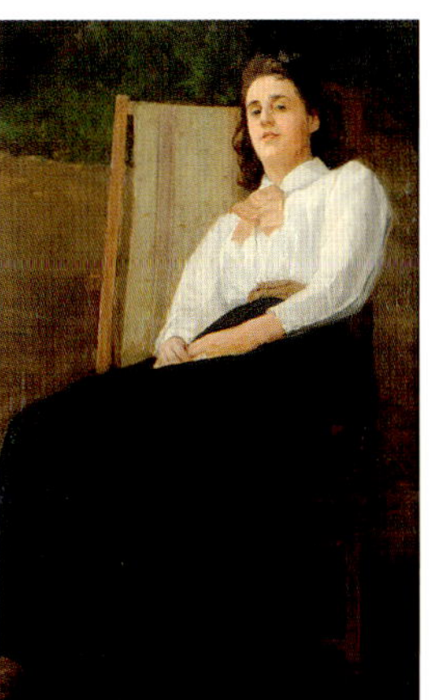

Poole, Victor
Ann Secunda Margaret Poole (1871–1950)
c.1900
oil on canvas 97 x 64
M315 (P)

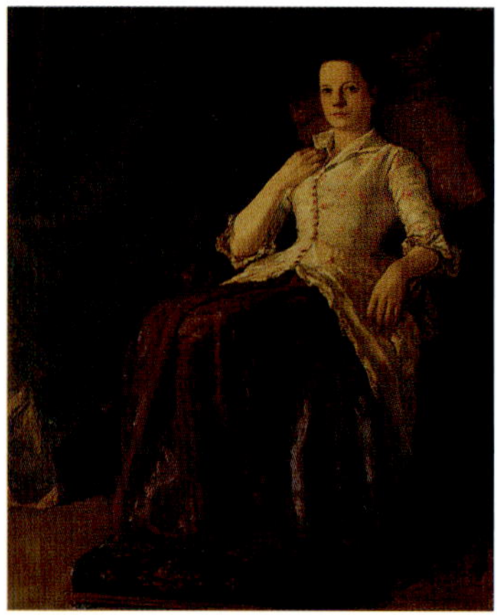

Poole, Victor
Emily Poole
oil on canvas 75 x 62
M129

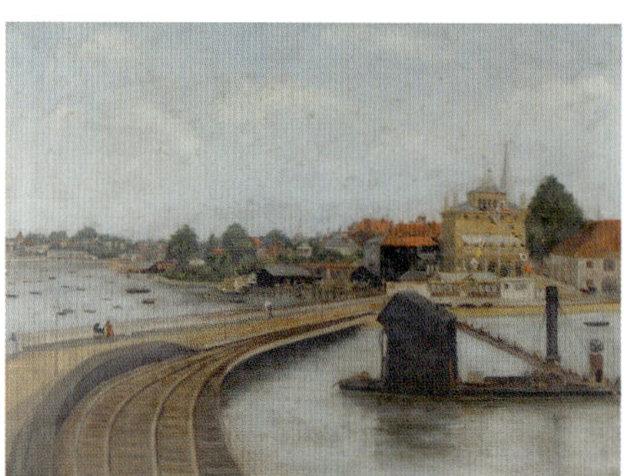

Powell, Lydia Sarah
Royal Pier (Yacht Club) c.1890
oil on canvas 39 x 54
M133

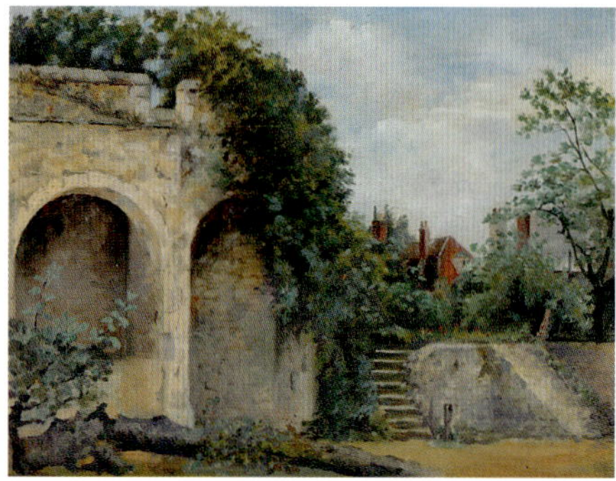

Powell, Lydia Sarah
Town Walls
oil on wood 24.3 x 32.7
M5758

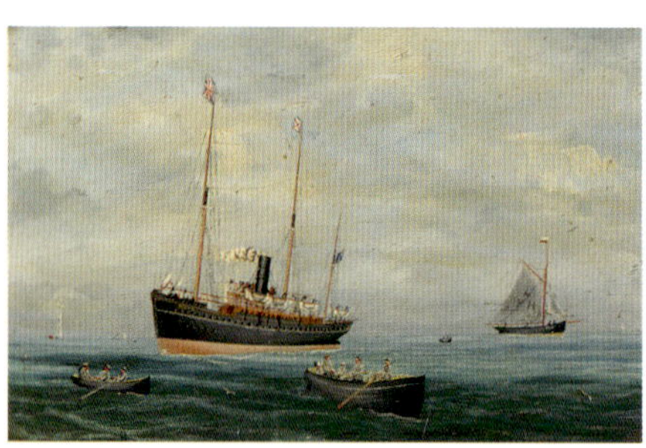

Raitt, J.
'SS Moor' off Coast with Plymouth Sailing Boat 1886
oil on card 15.3 x 23.1
M3408

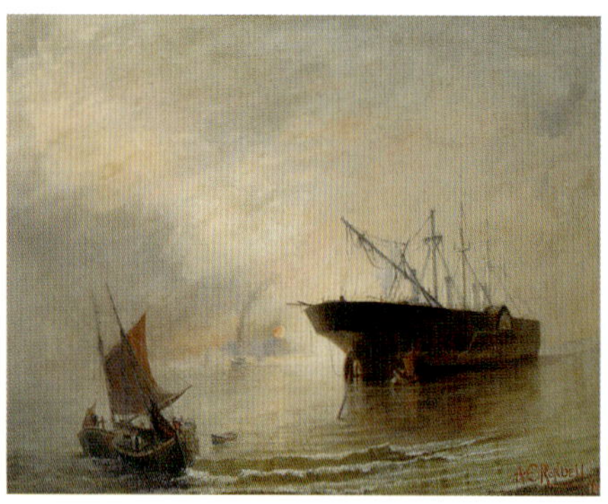

Rendell, A. E.
The Breaking up of the 'Great Eastern' 1889
oil on canvas 51.5 x 63.7
M322

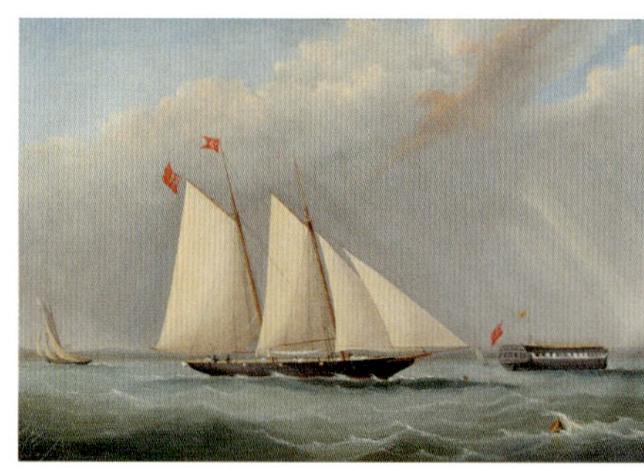

Rendell, A. E. (attributed to)
18th Century Schooner
oil on canvas 41.5 x 61
M59

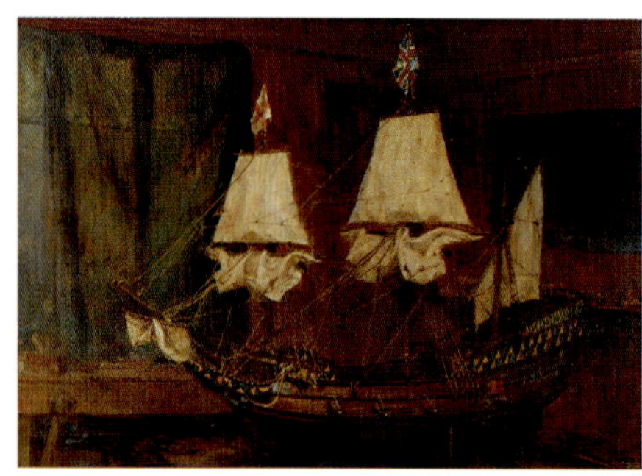

Robinson, Gregory 1876–1967
'Mayflower' Model 1925
oil on wood 49 x 74.5
M128 (P)

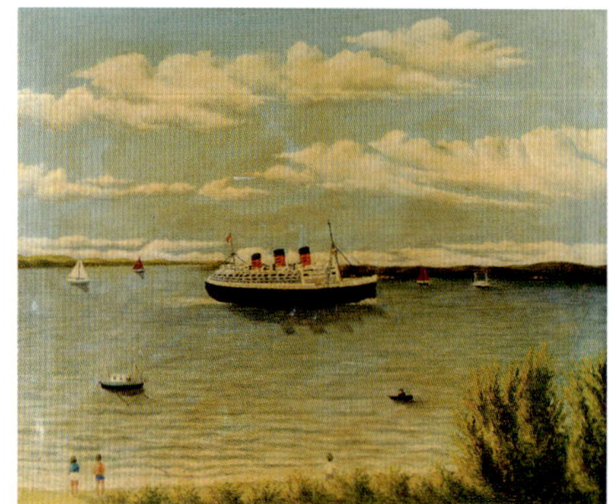

Rogers, A.
'Queen Mary' 1967
oil on canvas 55 x 65.5
M4563

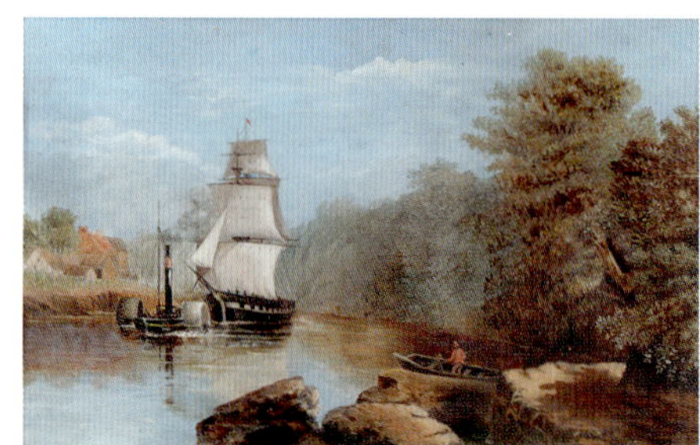

Sandell, George W. active 1881–1937
Ship up the Creek (after N. Green) 1881
oil on board 28 x 46.5
M16

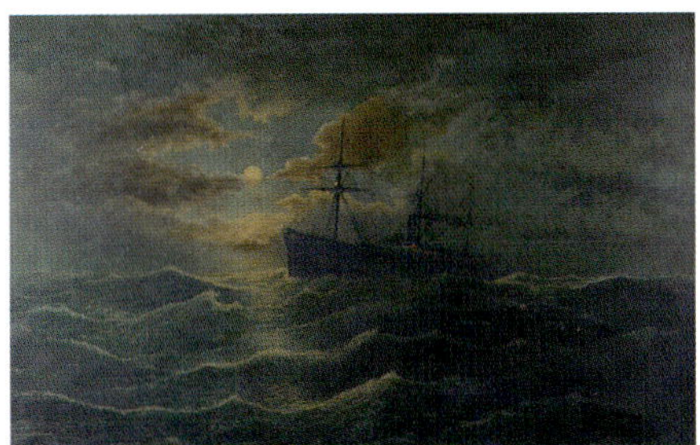

Sandell, George W. active 1881–1937
Steamship in Moonlight 1882
oil on canvas 45 x 72
M160

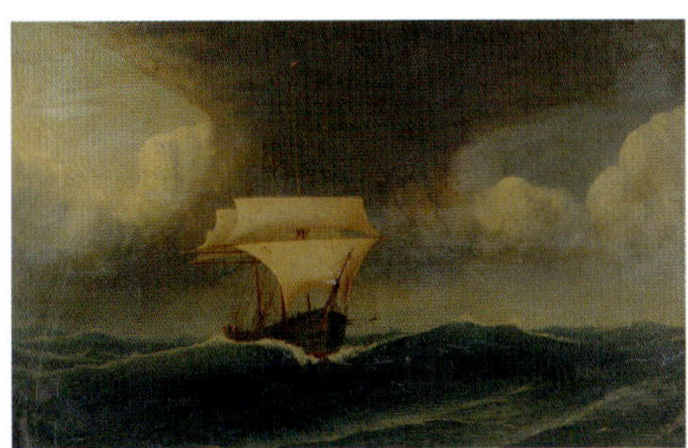

Sandell, George W. active 1881–1937
Sailing Ship under Reduced Sail (after Edward Hoyer) 1888
oil on board 45 x 73
M146

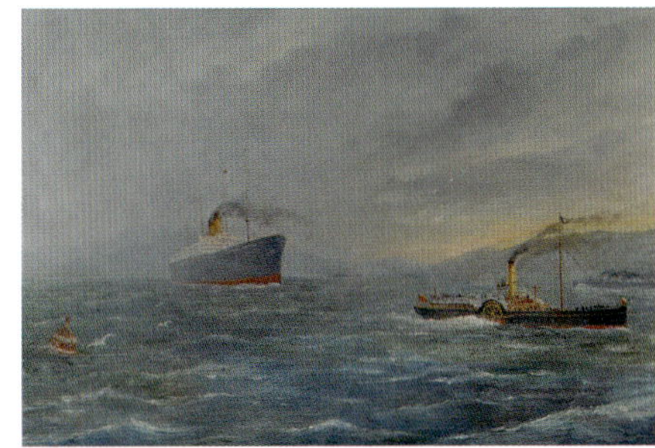

Sandell, George W. active 1881–1937
'SS Adriatic', the First White Star Liner to Come to Southampton Passing Down Cowes Roads, 31 May 1907 1907
oil on canvas 59 x 89.5
M328

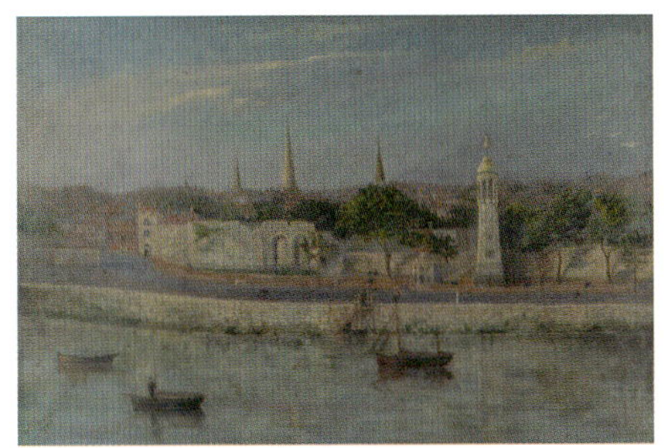

Sandell, George W. active 1881–1937
Western Esplanade, Southampton 1924
oil on canvas 62 x 92
M314

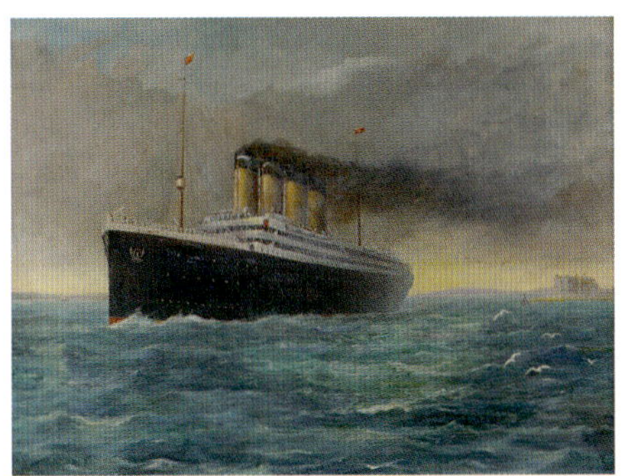

Sandell, George W. active 1881–1937
'SS Titanic'
oil on canvas 73 x 99
M334

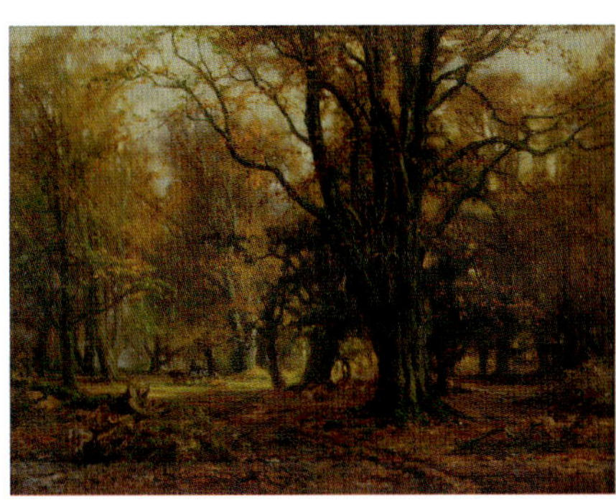

Short, Frederick Golden 1863–1936
New Forest 1898
oil on canvas 40 x 54
M11815

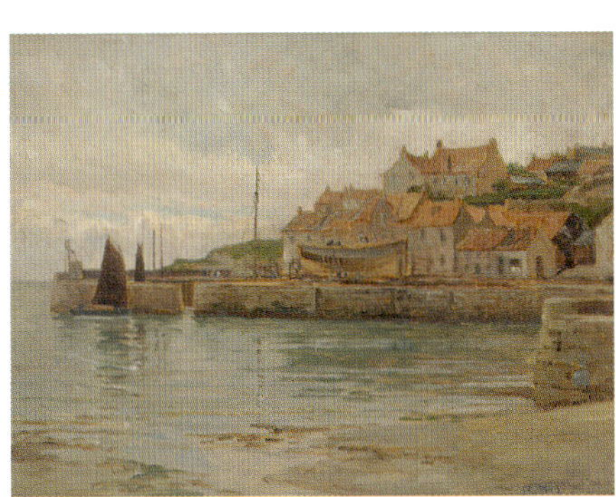

Short, Frederick Golden 1863–1936
Landscape 1912
oil on board 22 x 29
M4519

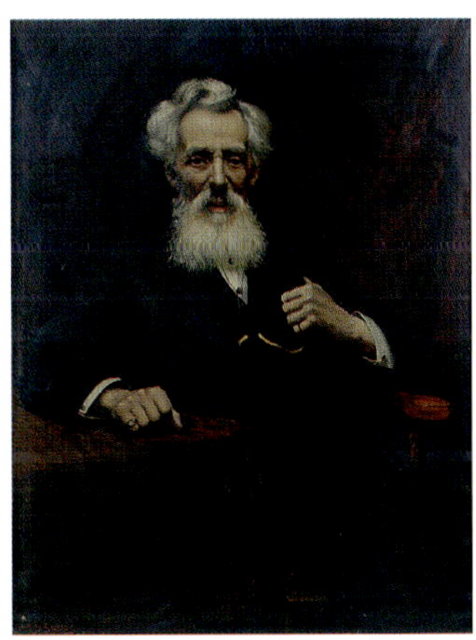

Skeats, Edward
Robert Chipperfield Esq., Chair of Tauntons School Governors (1877–1904)
oil on canvas 110 x 85
M11619

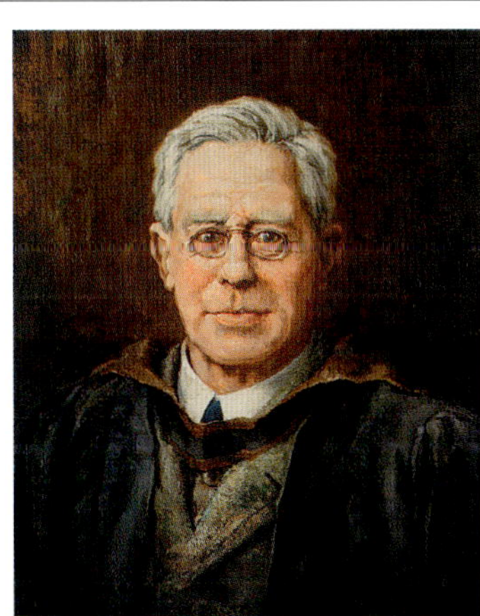

Smith, Percy John Delf 1882–1948
Seymour Jackson Gubb, Headmaster of Tauntons School (1892–1924)
oil on board 60 x 50
M11615

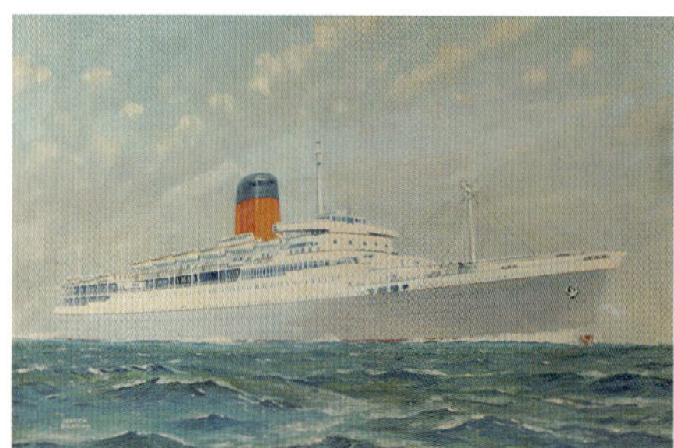

Smoothy, Derrick b.1923
'Pendennis Castle' (1959–1976)
oil on board 57 x 90
M7831 (P)

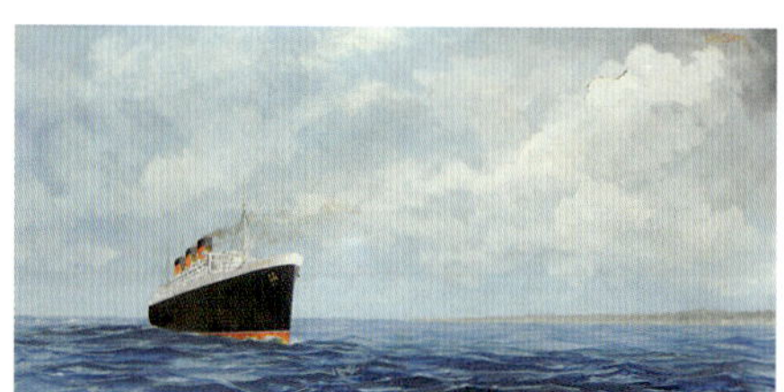

Sparkes, T. Roy
'Queen Mary' 1975
oil on canvas 49 x 101
M22934

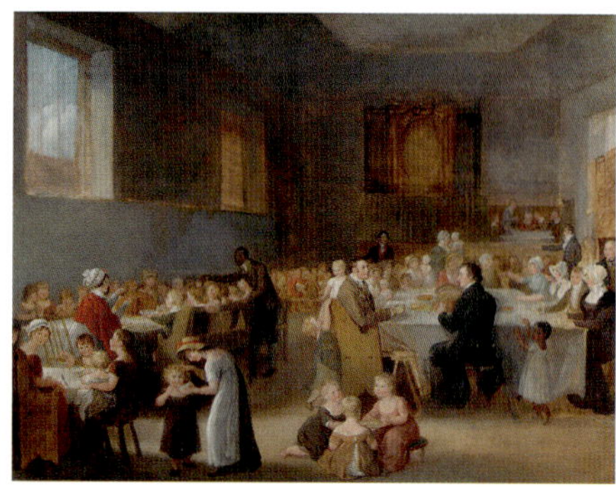

Spilsbury, Maria 1777–c.1823
New Year's Feast at Mr Walter Taylor's Charity School, Portswood Green, near Southampton
oil on canvas 62.5 x 84
M3042

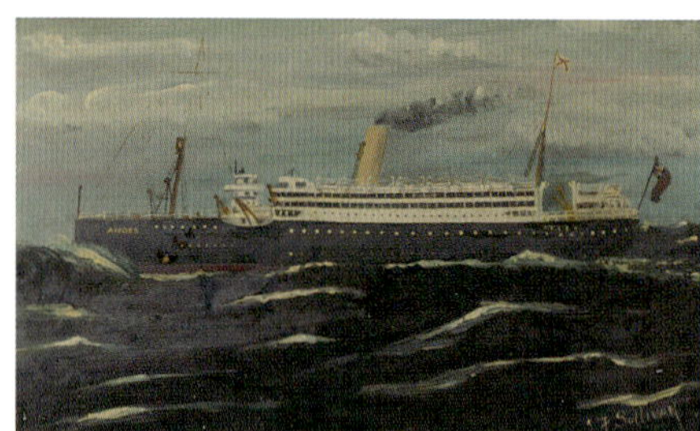

Sullivan, L. F.
'SS Andes'
oil on cardboard 29.5 x 49.5
M4653

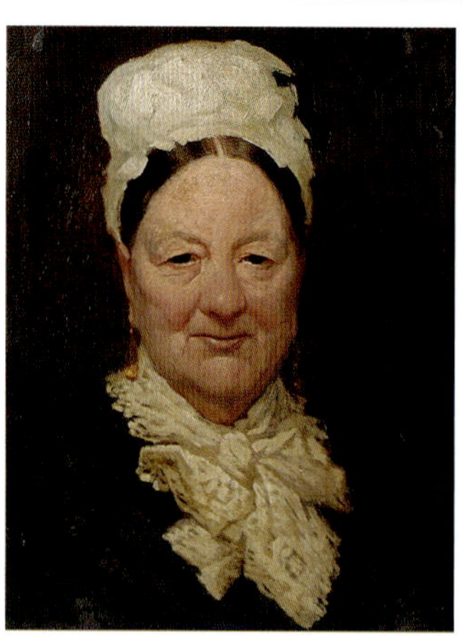

Taylor, S. M. Louisa active 1872–1890
Mrs A. E. White 1890
oil on board 51.5 x 41
M126

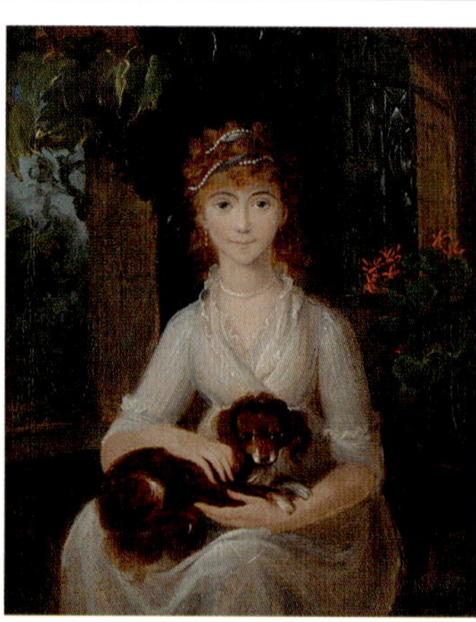

unknown artist
Mrs Walter Kingsbury 1821
oil on canvas 28.5 x 23
M4478

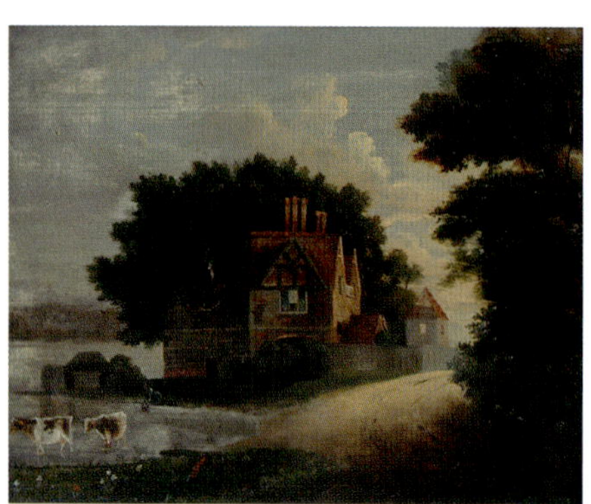

unknown artist
The Old Farmhouse at Northam 1830
oil on canvas 26.5 x 33.5
M1412

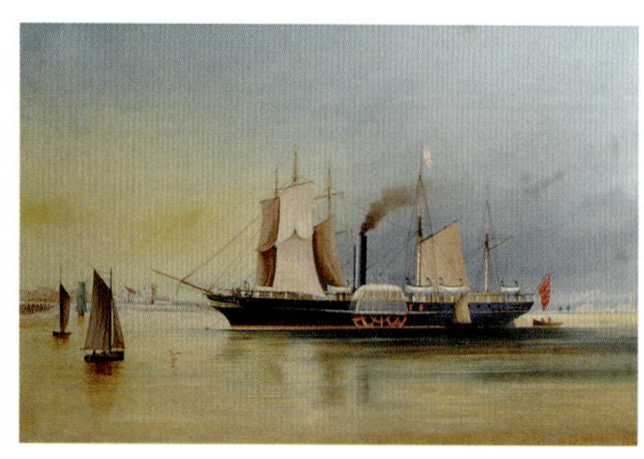

unknown artist
An Early Royal Mail Steam Packet Company Paddlesteamer (possibly 'Tweed') 1840s
oil on canvas 61 x 91.6
M329

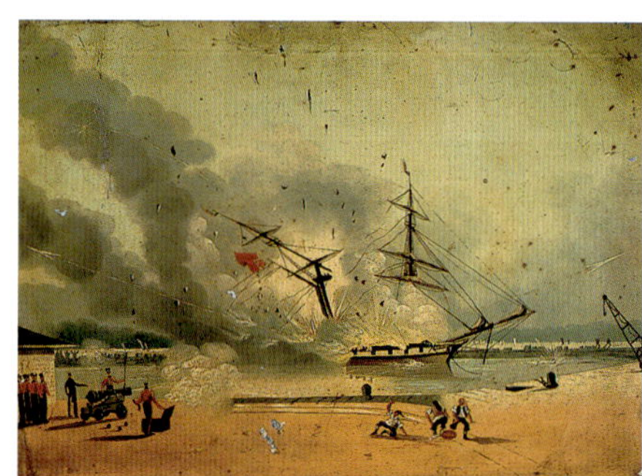

unknown artist
Brig 'Tartar' on Fire, Southampton Docks, 2 June 1842 1842
oil on tin 25 x 35
M11680

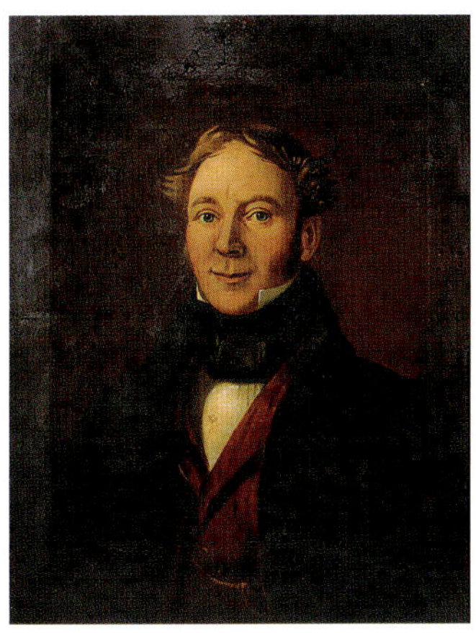

unknown artist
Portrait of an Unknown Gentleman c.1850
oil on canvas 75.5 x 60.5
M280

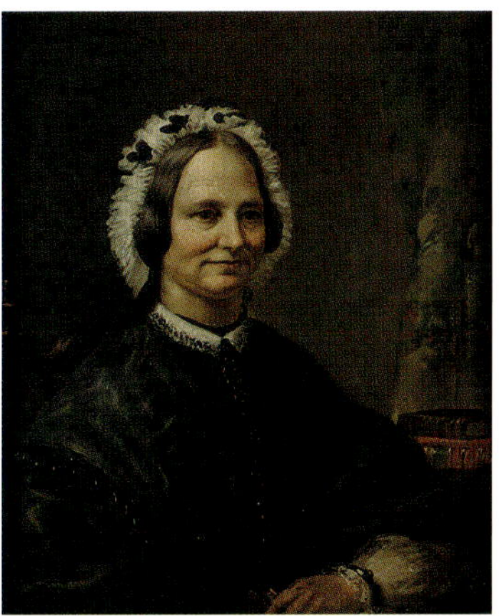

unknown artist
Portrait of an Unknown Woman c.1860
oil on board 74 x 62
M17617

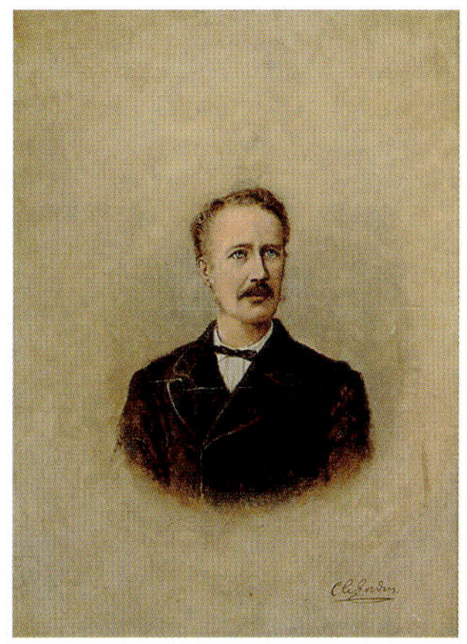

unknown artist
General Gordon 1880s
oil on board 31 x 23.6
M5928

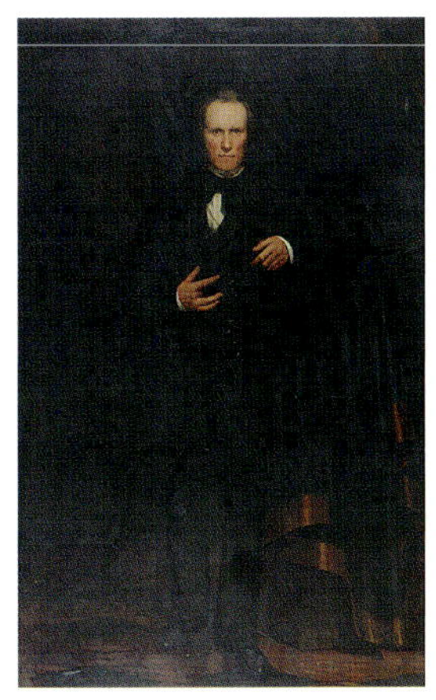

unknown artist 19th C
Andrew Lamb (1803–1881)
oil on canvas 236 x 145
M23519

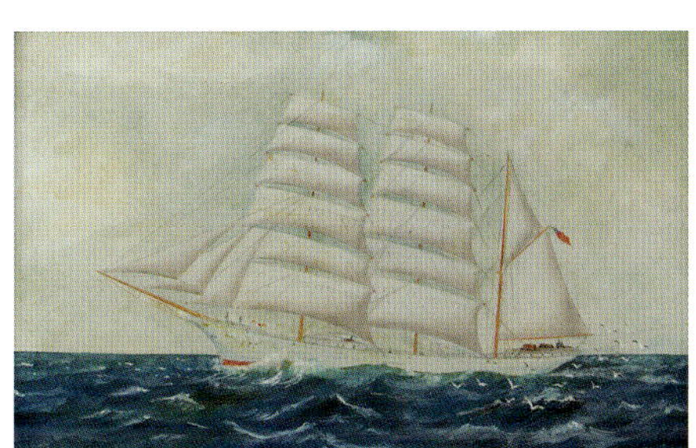

unknown artist 19th C
'Castle'
oil on board 27 x 44.5
M173

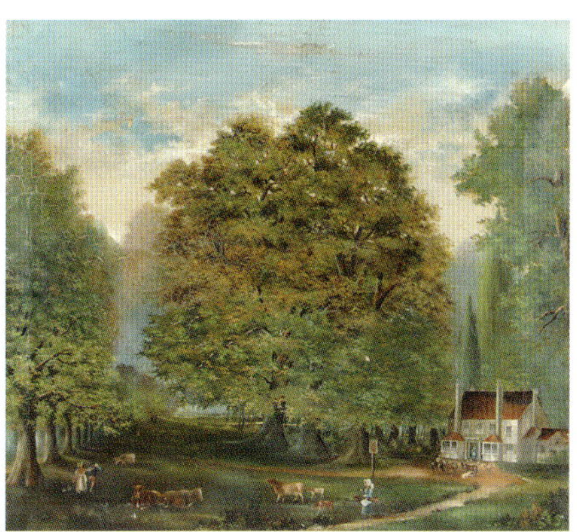

unknown artist 19th C
Cowherds, the Avenue
oil on canvas 76 x 86
M281

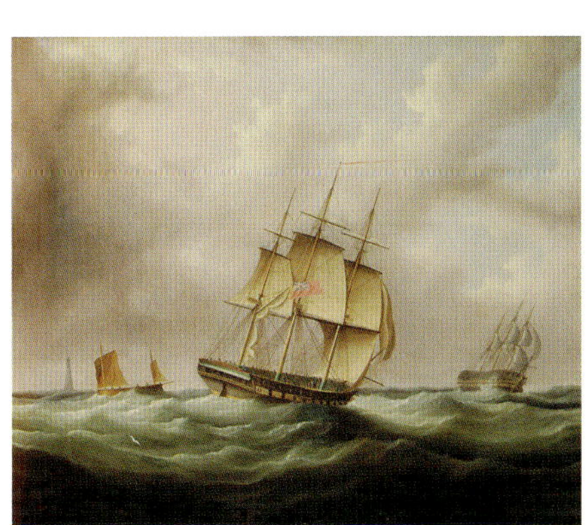

unknown artist 19th C
Early 19th Century Frigate
oil on canvas 62 x 74
M23521

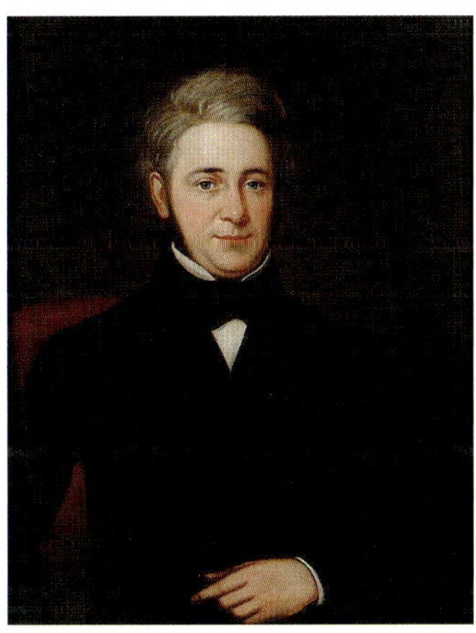

unknown artist 19th C
George Josiah Poole
oil on canvas 74 x 59
M326

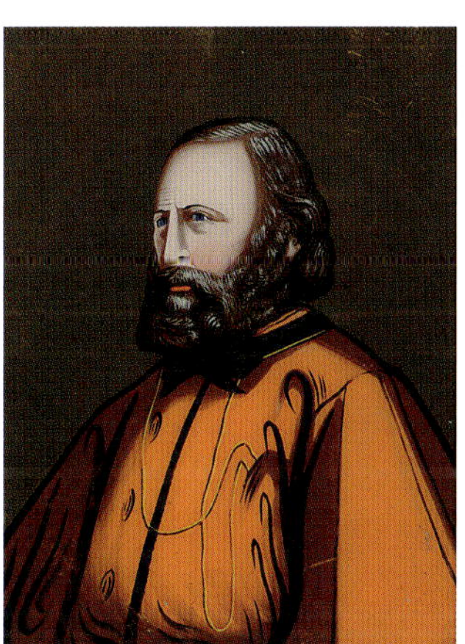

unknown artist 19th C
Portrait of an Unknown Gentleman
oil on glass 53.5 x 41
M156

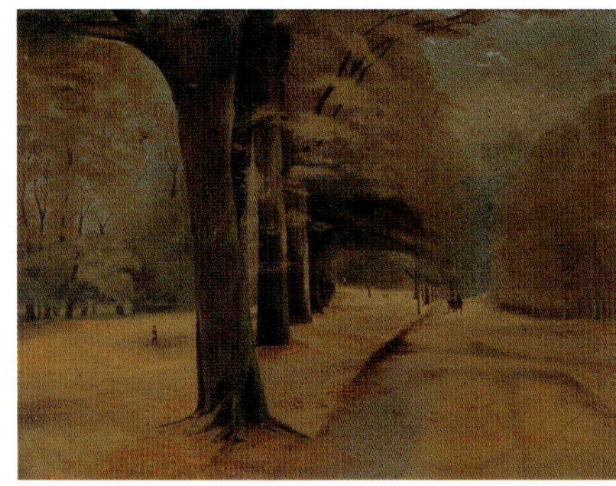

unknown artist 19th C
The Avenue, Southampton
oil on canvas 22 x 29
M379

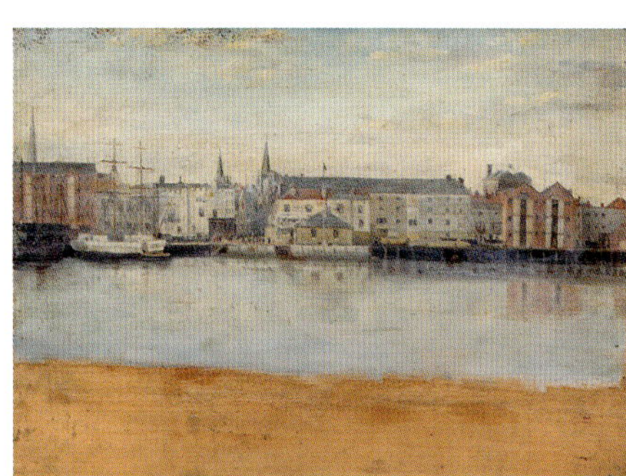

unknown artist 19th C
Town Quay (unfinished)
oil on board 24.3 x 32.5
M5759

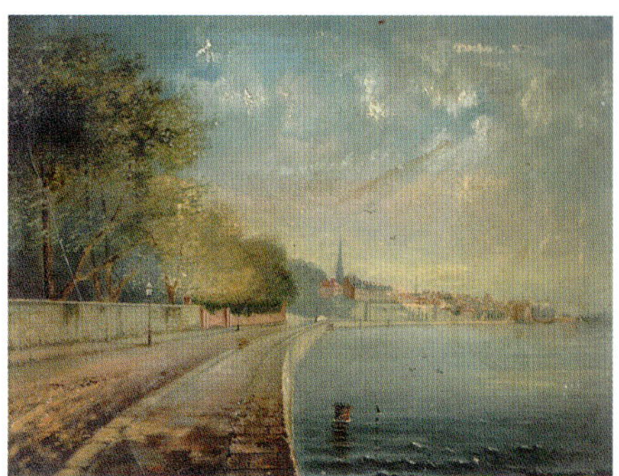

unknown artist 19th C
Western Shore
oil on board 22 x 29
M4323

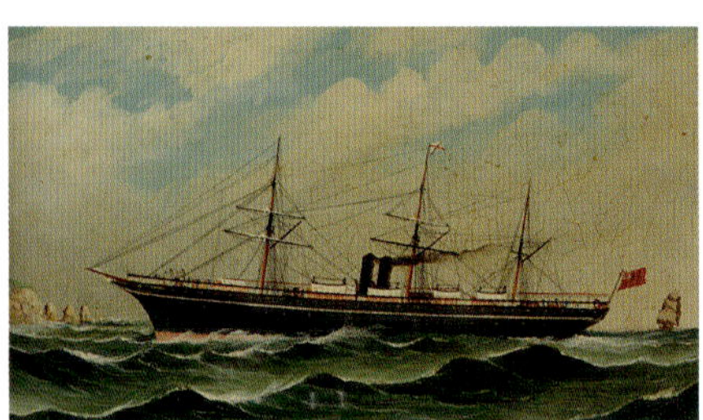

unknown artist late 19th C
Royal Mail Ship, 'Medway', 1877
oil on canvas 20.7 x 39.6
M3

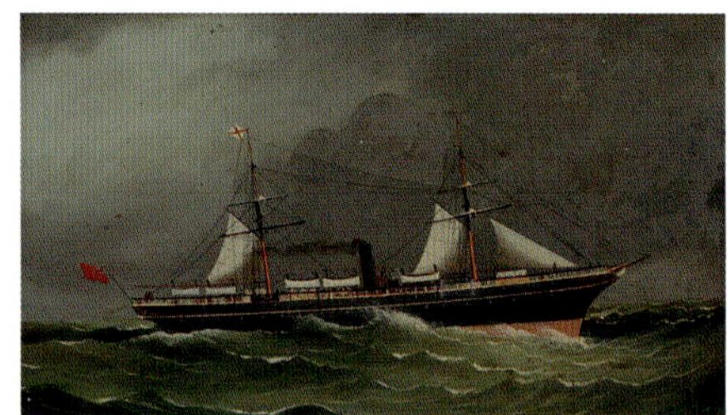

unknown artist late 19th C
Royal Mail Ship, 'Nile', 1869
oil on canvas 20.7 x 37
M17

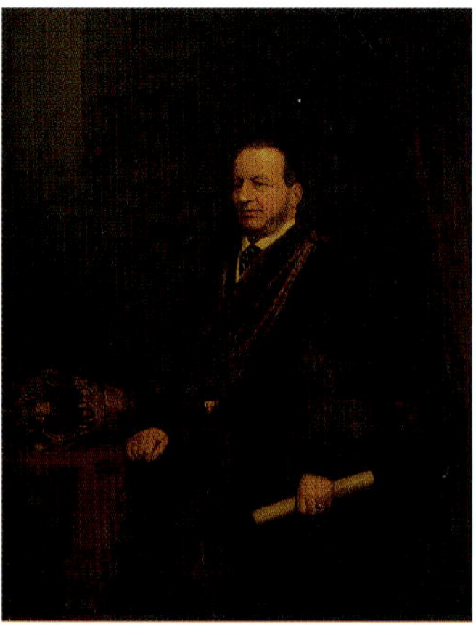

unknown artist
A Mayor of Southampton c.1900
oil on board 89 x 69
M366

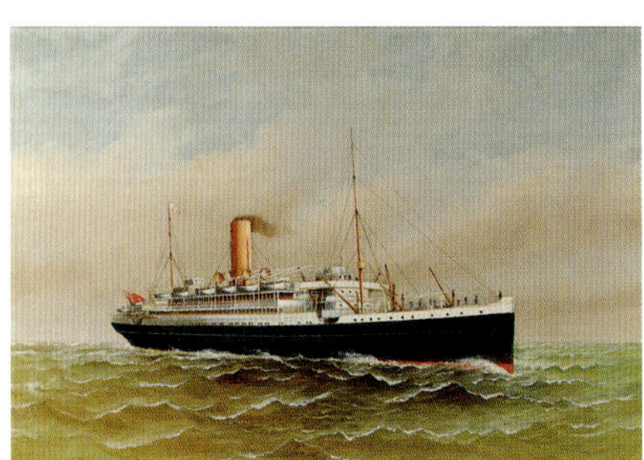

unknown artist
A Royal Mail Steamship 1900–1910
oil on canvas 59 x 89
M330

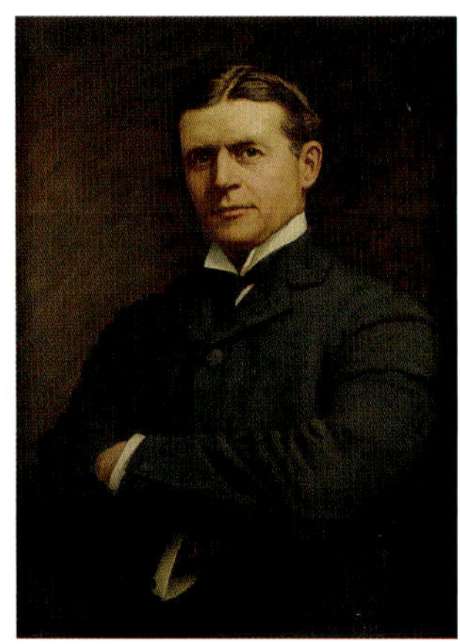

unknown artist
George Arbuthnot, Second Baron of Inverclyde (Chairman of Cunard) 1905
oil on canvas 81.3 x 61
M12058 (P)

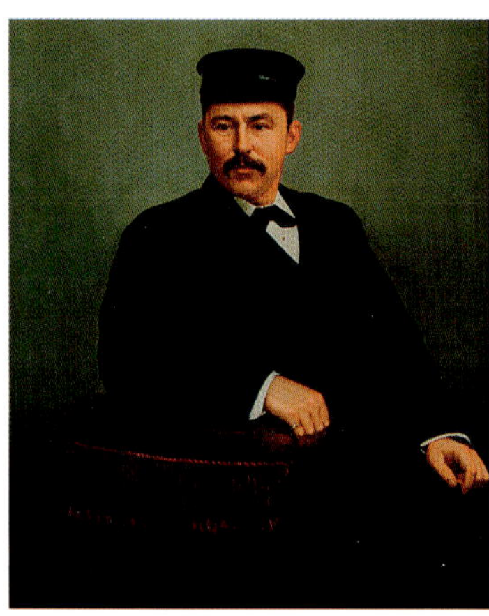

unknown artist
Captain Richard Norris Diaper 1912
oil on canvas 76 x 63
M22808

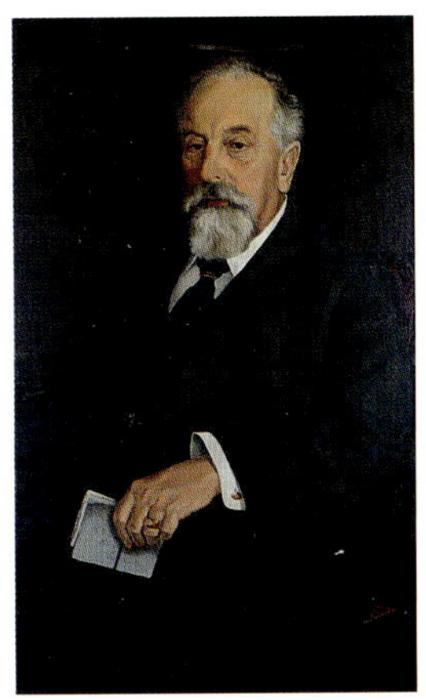

unknown artist
William Francis Summer Spranger Esq., JP (1848–1917) (detail) 1915
oil on canvas 118 x 94
M11618

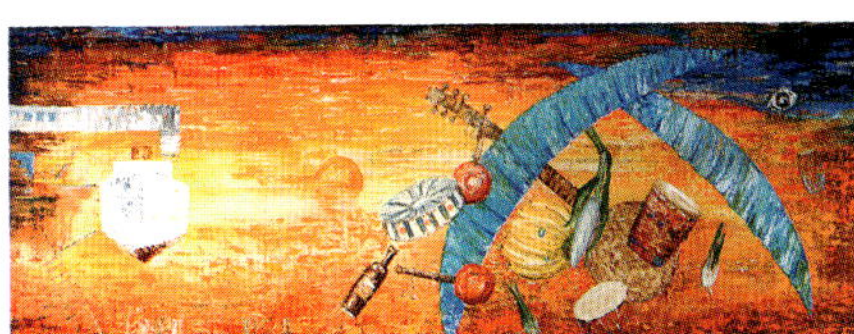

unknown artist
Panel from Banana Boat 'Golfito' 1949
oil on wood 120 x 330
M23603

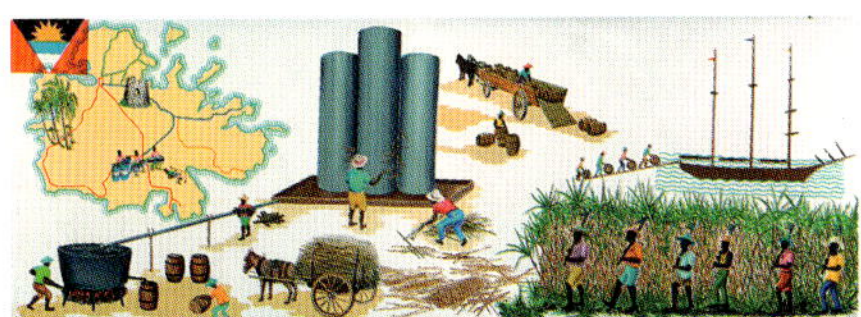

unknown artist
Panel from Banana Boat 'Golfito' 1949
oil on wood 117 x 330
M23604

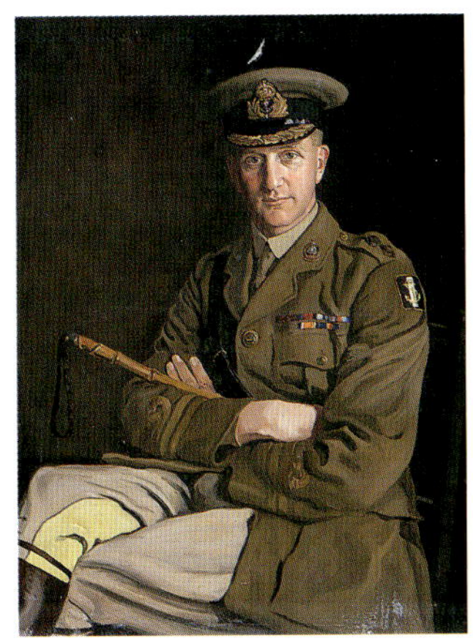

unknown artist 20th C
Daniel Beak, VC
oil on canvas 101.8 x 76.5
M11596 (P)

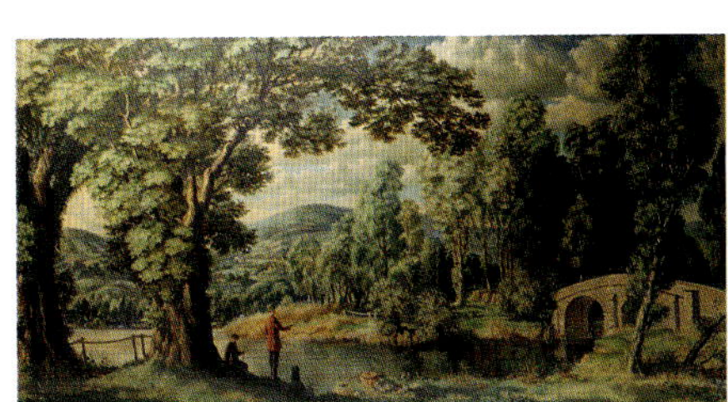

unknown artist 20th C
Rural Scene (from 'MV Britannic')
oil on canvas 86 x 165.5
M12076

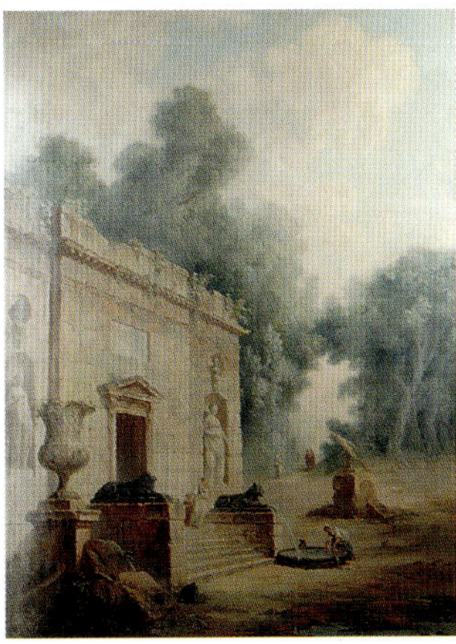

unknown artist 20th C
Smoking Room Panel from 'Aquitania' (panel 1)
oil on canvas 188.3 x 141
M12072

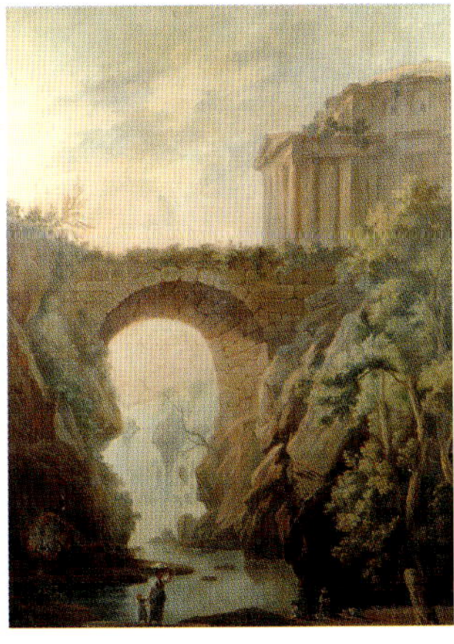

unknown artist 20th C
Smoking Room Panel from 'Aquitania' (panel 2)
oil on canvas 190 x 140
M12073

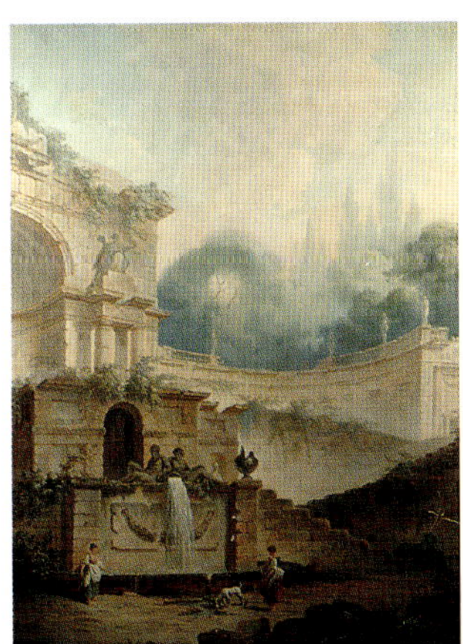

unknown artist 20th C
Smoking Room Panel from 'Aquitania' (panel 3)
oil on canvas 188.8 x 140.5
M12074

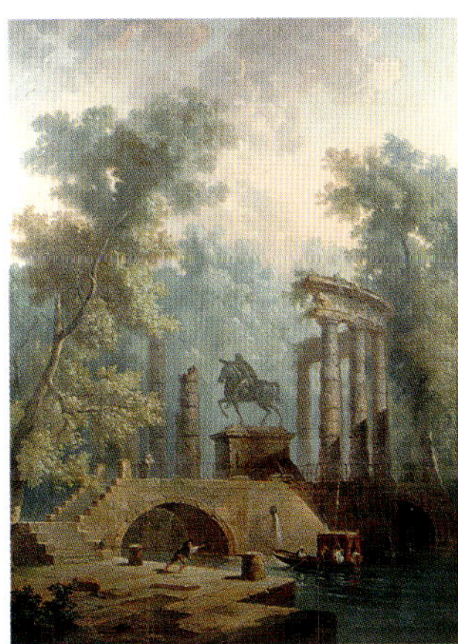

unknown artist 20th C
Smoking Room Panel from 'Aquitania' (panel 4)
oil on canvas 188.3 x 140.7
M12075

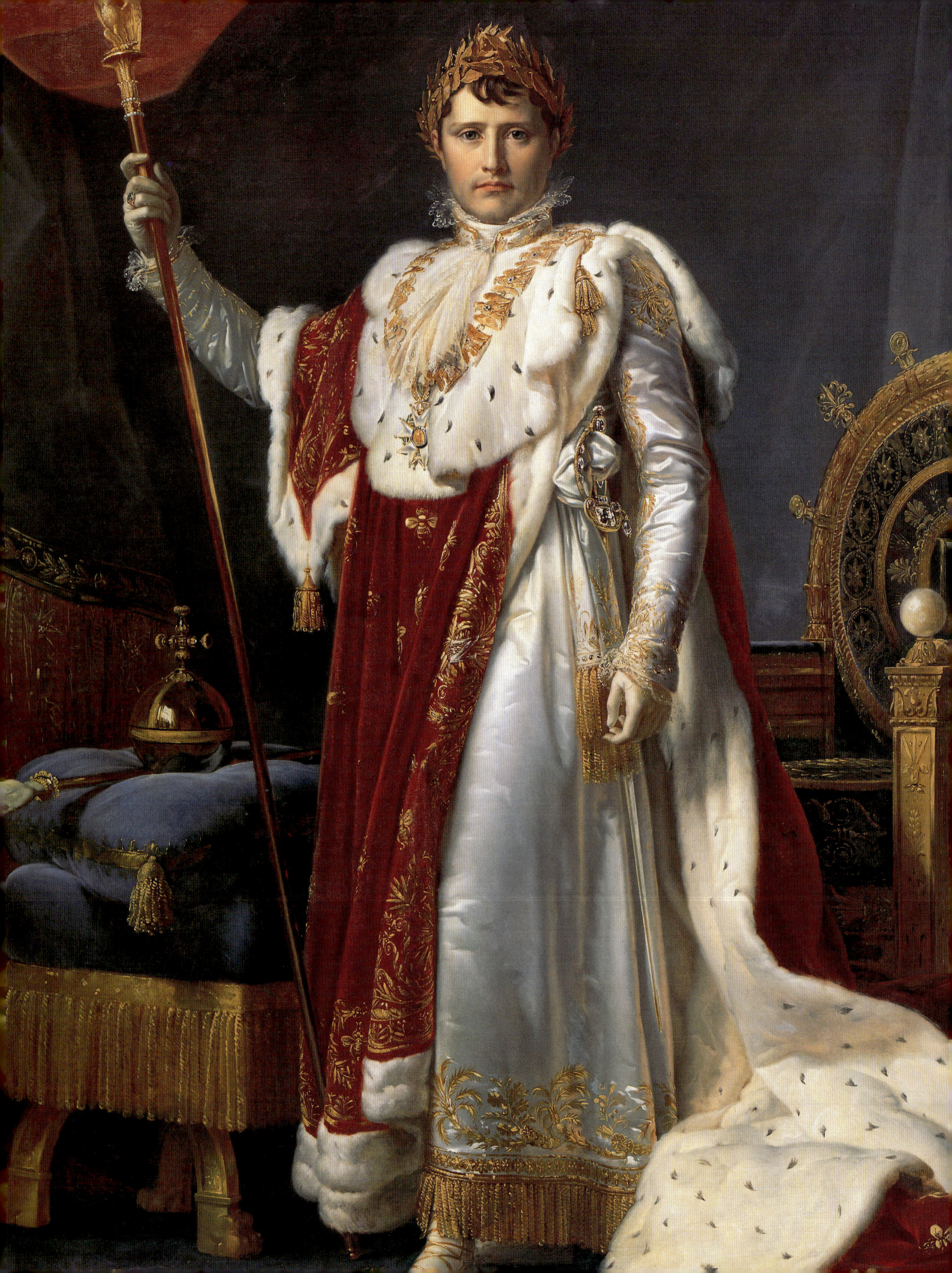

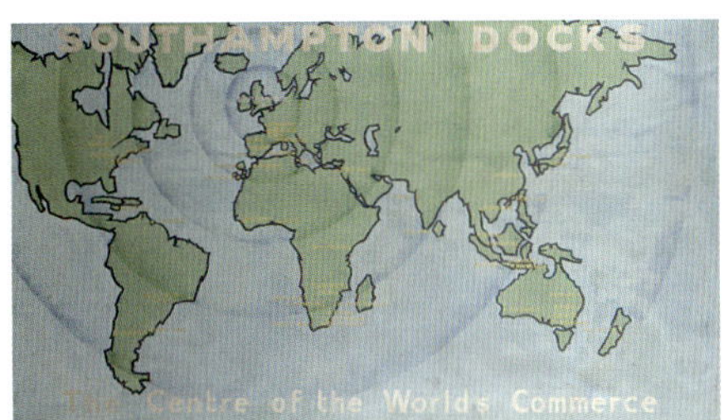

unknown artist 20th C
'Southampton Docks, Centre of the World's Commerce'
acrylic on canvas 101.5 x 179
M23605

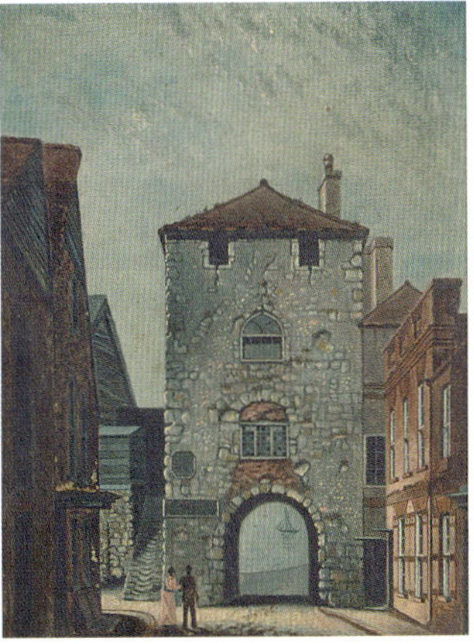

unknown artist 20th C
Westgate
oil on board 28 x 22
M2604

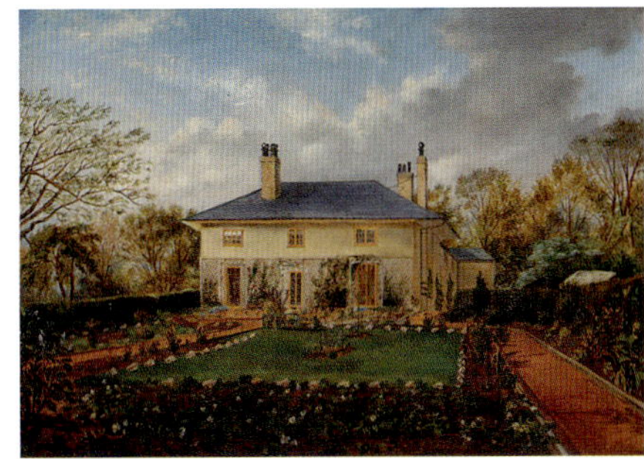

unknown artist
House and Garden (Hawthorn Cottage)
oil on canvas 40 x 58
M154

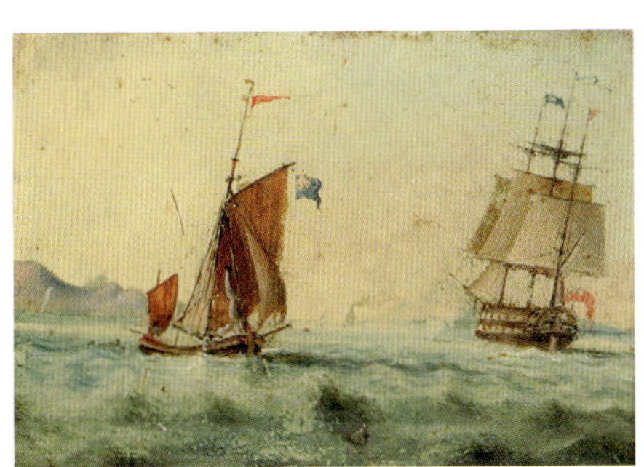

unknown artist
Ketch and Naval Man-o-War in Choppy Sea
oil on card 7.1 x 10.4
M6007

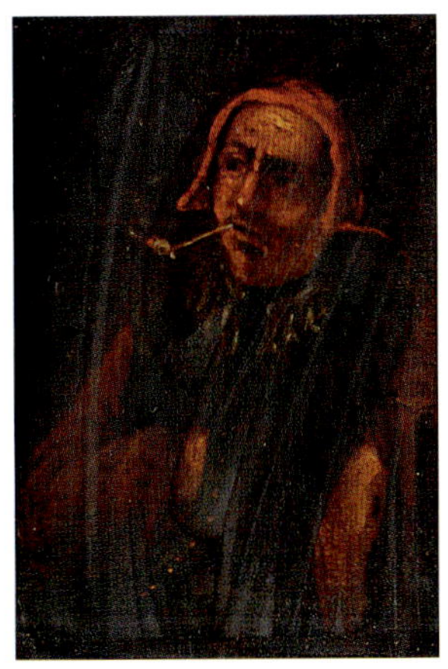

unknown artist
Man with Pipe
oil on wood 13.5 x 9.5
M15

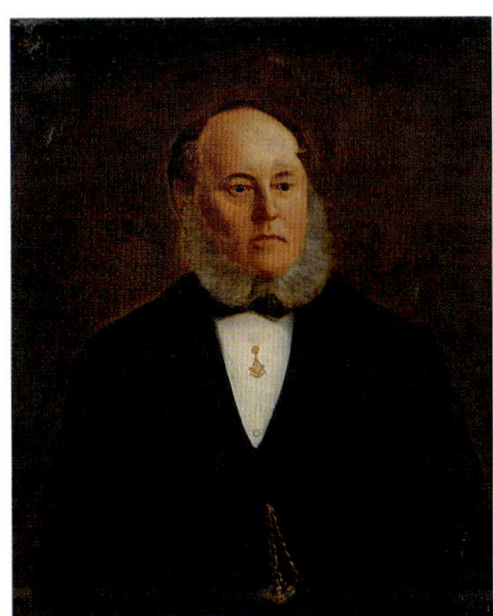

unknown artist
Portrait of an Unknown Gentleman
oil on canvas 72.5 x 61.5
M325

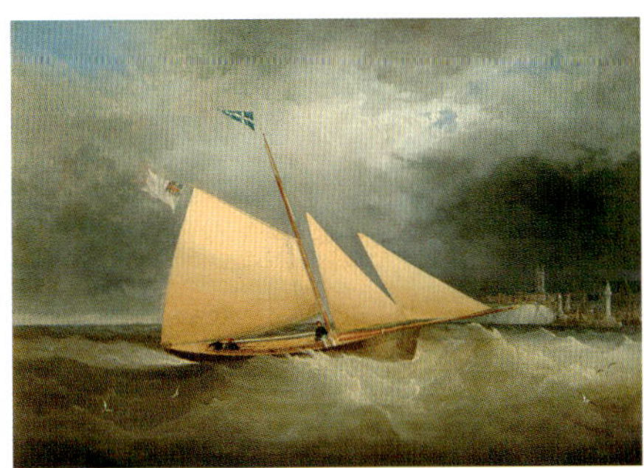

unknown artist
Sailing Ship
oil on canvas 56 x 78.8
M323

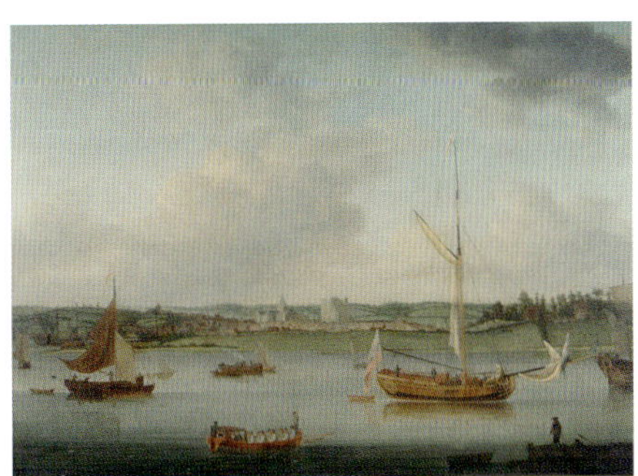

unknown artist
The Royal Barge at Rochester
oil on canvas 73 x 104
M333

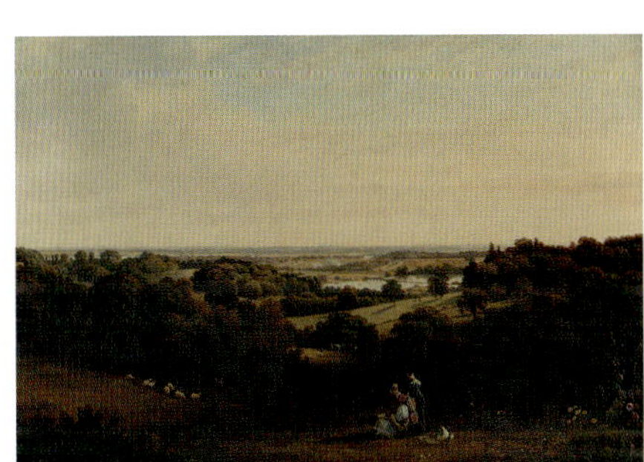

unknown artist
View of Southampton
oil on canvas 58 x 90
M1002

Facing page: Gérard, François, 1770–1837, *Napoleon (1769–1821)* (detail), Southampton City Art Gallery, (p. 48)

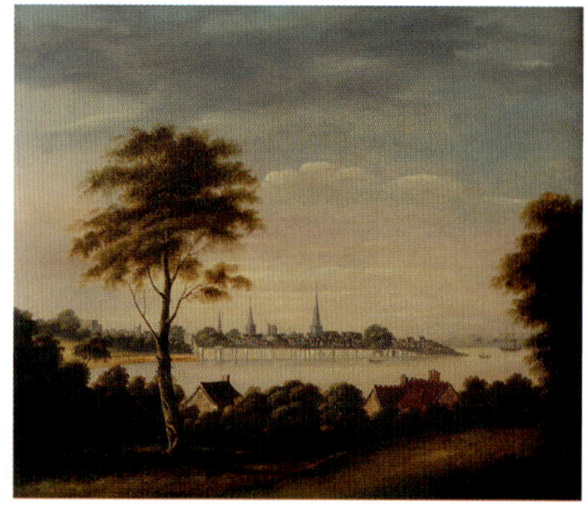

unknown artist
View of Southampton West Wall
oil on canvas 41 x 49
M11647

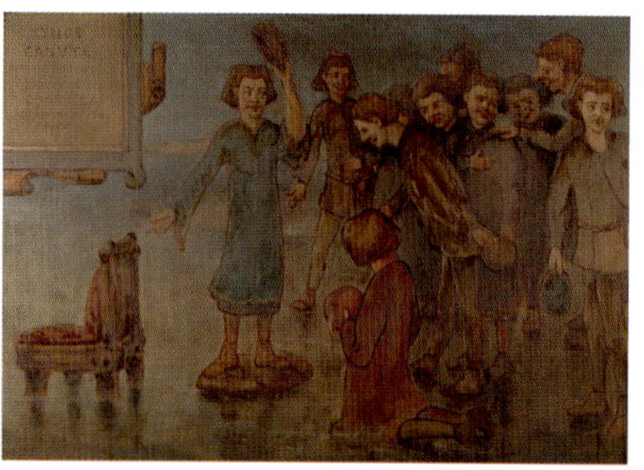

G. W.
'Kynge Canute Reprovynge Hys Foolishe Cortieres att Southampton, 1017 AD' 1913
oil on board 60 x 86.5
M139

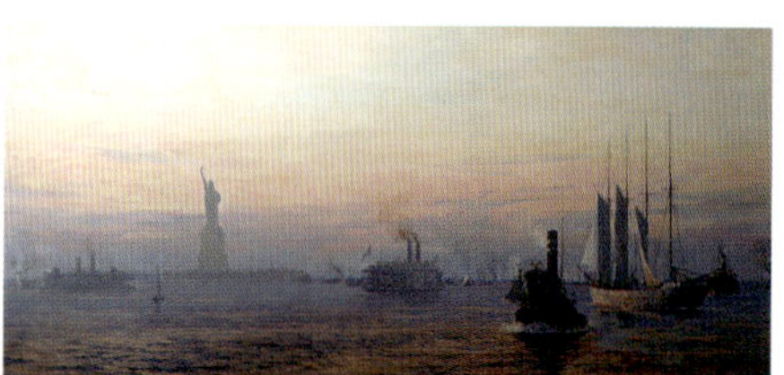

Wilkinson, Norman 1878–1971
Approach to the New World ('Olympic')
oil on canvas 83 x 179
M10159 (P)

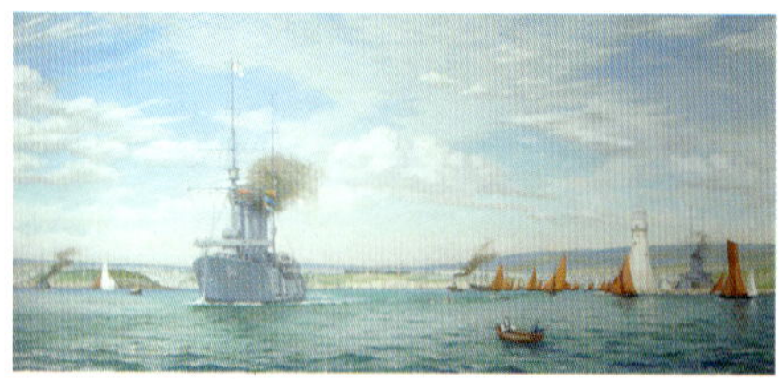

Wilkinson, Rodney 1924–2004
Plymouth Harbour (copy of original from the 'Titanic')
oil on canvas 83 x 178
Temp2 (P)

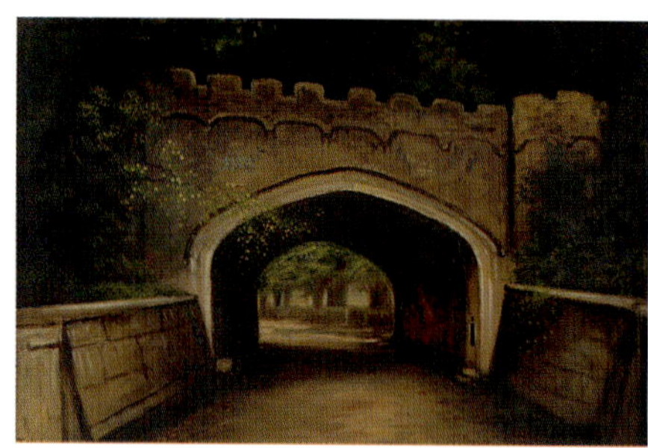

Wood, T.
The Lower Arch, Weston
oil on canvas 39 x 59
M3330 (P)

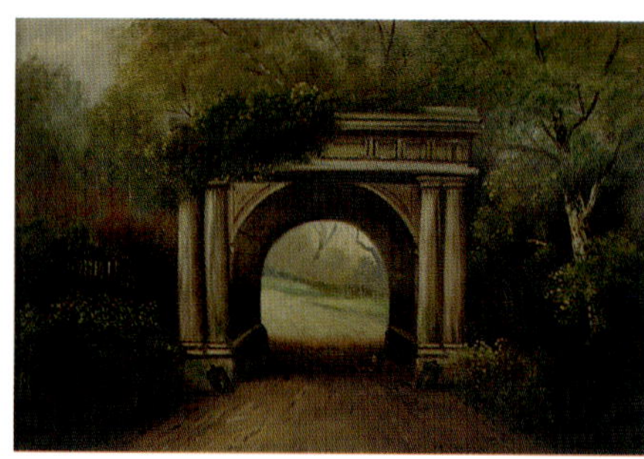

Wood, T.
Weston Arch
oil on canvas 39 x 59
M3329 (P)

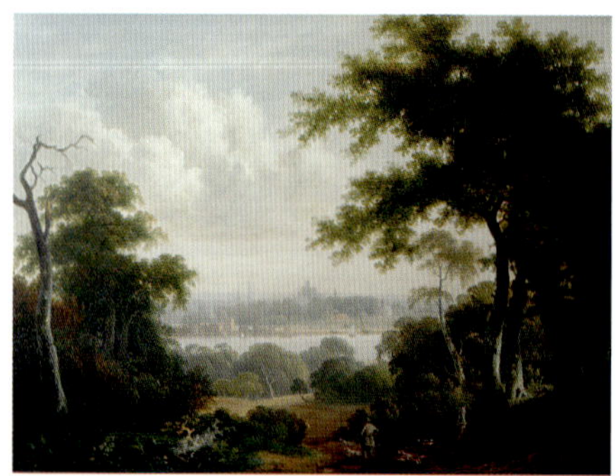

Young, Tobias c.1755–1824
Southampton from Bitterne, Peartree Green
c.1820
oil on panel 40.5 x 54.5
M349

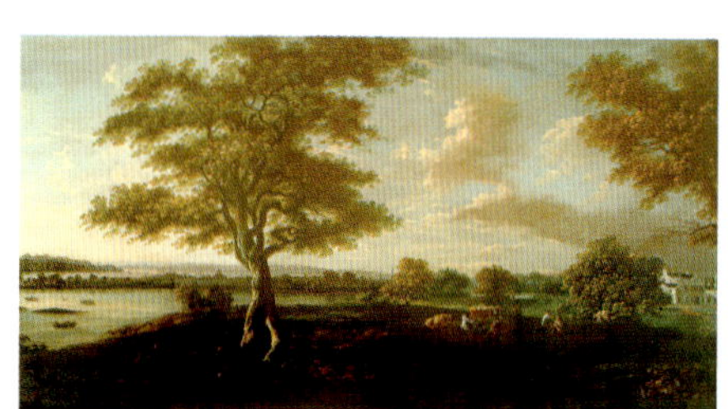

Young, Tobias c.1755–1824
Chessel House
oil on canvas 80.4 x 150
M361

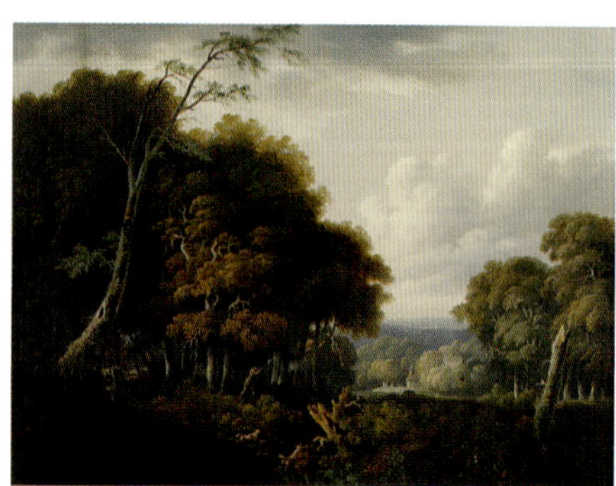

Young, Tobias c.1755–1824
Looking to Southampton from the New Forest
oil on board 39 x 53
M350

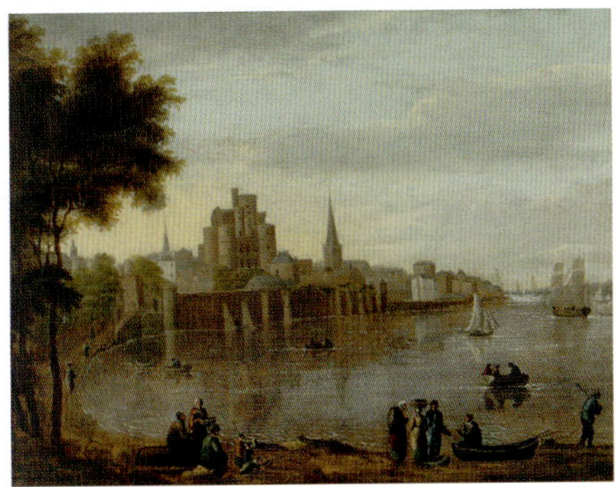

Young, Tobias c.1755–1824
'Old Southampton', Lansdowne Castle
oil on canvas 48 x 62
M371

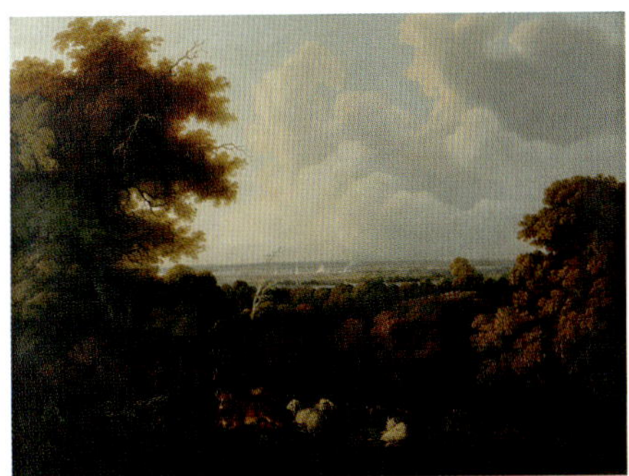

Young, Tobias c.1755–1824
Southampton from Peartree Green
oil on canvas 88 x 120
M13

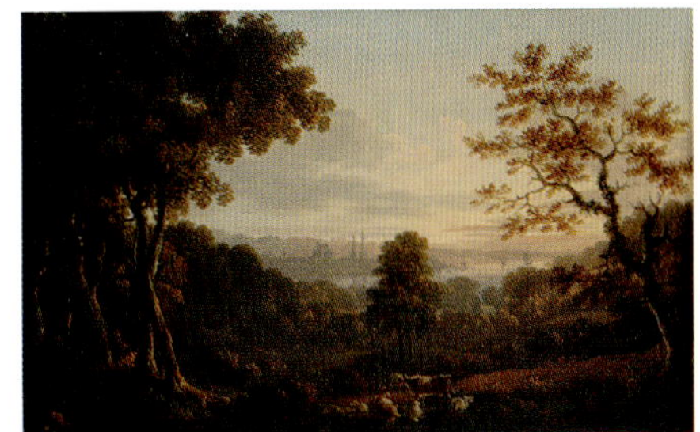

Young, Tobias c.1755–1824
Southampton from Peartree Green
oil on board 17 x 29
M14

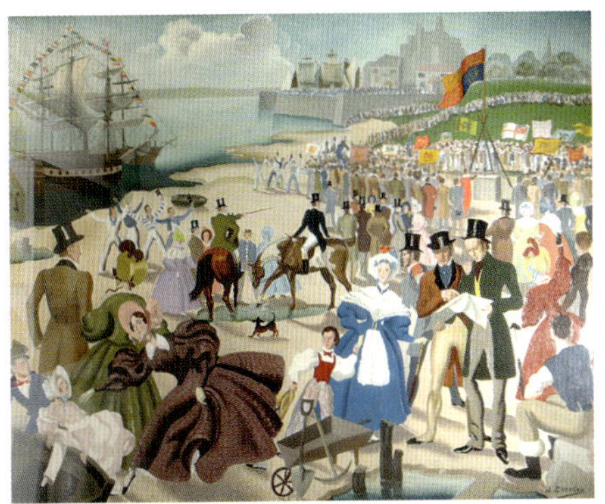

Zinkeisen, Anna Katrina 1901–1976
Laying of Foundation Stone of Southampton Docks, 1838 1938
oil on canvas 101.6 x 127
M8056

Southampton Mayor's Parlour

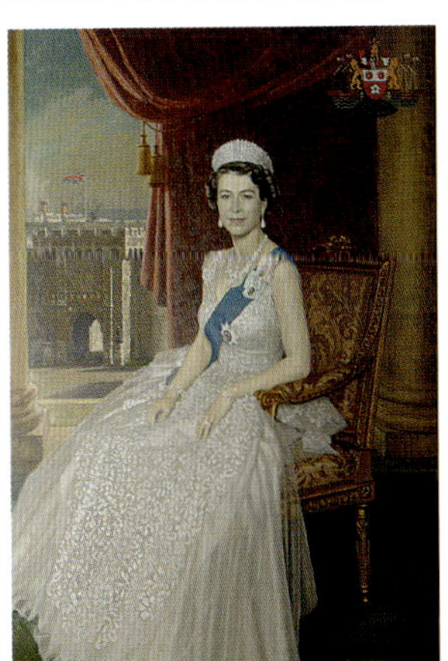

Halliday, Edward Irvine 1902–1984
Her Majesty the Queen (b.1926) 1966
oil on canvas 200 x 136 (E)
3

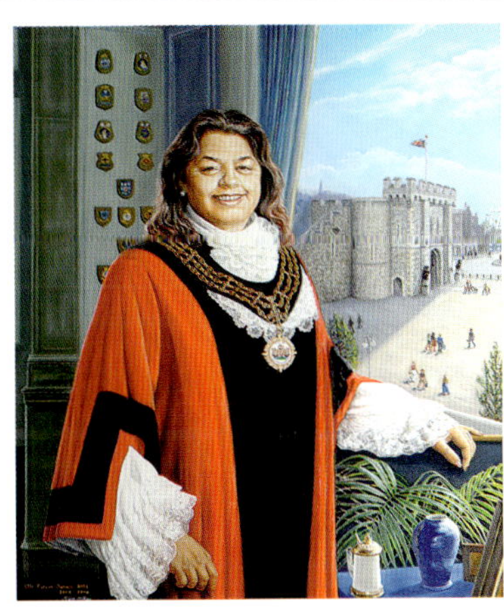

McKee, Alice b.1954
Councillor Parvin Damani, MBE 2003–2004
oil on canvas 150 x 120
2

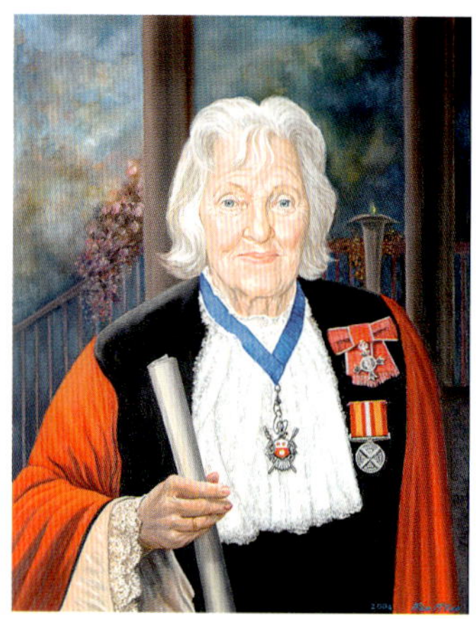

McKee, Alice b.1954
Councillor Kathy Johnson 2004
oil on canvas 76 x 60 (E)
1

Southampton Solent University

John Everett Millais was born in Southampton in 1829, and the building housing the former Southampton College of Art and currently all of the present university's art, design and media courses, was named after him. The British art school system has long been a fertile ground for creativity and artistic invention and its annual output has consistently impacted on all aspects of our cultural landscape from fashion to pop music, through design to television. Certain schools have been singularly influential, generating dynamic shifts in the visual and plastic arts with many of their students maturing into significant artists and even household names.

The precocious 11 year-old Millais was the youngest student ever to be admitted to the Royal Academy of Arts and at the age of 19 was one of the founders the highly influential Pre-Raphaelite Brotherhood in 1848. He produced many of his critically acclaimed paintings before the age of 25. Southampton has had an art school since 1856 producing such luminaries as Hubert von Herkomer, Edward John Gregory and Graham Ovenden from amongst its students.

Of course it is not always easy to predict from which direction or regional centre the next wave of Young British Artists will emerge, but we can be sure that the next decade will bring another unexpected development that will, in turn, surprise and challenge the establishment of the day. Undoubtedly, some of the current generation of artists emerging from Southampton will go on to stamp their mark on society. It was with this thought in mind, combined with a recognition of the creative invention presented in the annual degree shows at each of the British art schools, that the art collection at the newly incorporated Southampton Solent University was established. It is a rich and varied collection of which the painting works represented here form only a small part in an archive that embraces, sculpture, photography, illustration, embroidery and graphic design. The collection includes works by both students and staff together with other artists who have had a connection with the University, the former art school and more generally with Southampton and the South. Circumstances have dictated that the collection is largely contemporary comprising works dating from the 1980s onwards; nevertheless, we feel it will, with time, grow to form a significant reflection of the period. A developing theme is the reference to the larger Southampton and regional communities as seen in *Yachts in a Squall*, Richard Eurich's exquisite study of yachts racing in the Solent, and Dee Young's *The Quays* reflecting the recent prestigious retail development in the city centre.

The collection was first established in October 1998 to celebrate the formal dedication of the newly completed Sir Michael Andrews Building by HRH The Princess Royal. At that time, most of the works had been loaned by artists teaching at the University's predecessor, the Southampton Institute. The University also made its first purchase to commemorate the event with the acquisition of the sculptures *Shire I* and *Pony* by Amy Goodman. Despite limited funds the collection has steadily expanded with purchases being made at the annual student degree shows. It now comprises over 300 artworks. Many of the recently acquired works are by graduates of the Fine Art, Photography and Illustration degree courses in the Faculty of Media, Arts and Society. The pieces selected are characterised by their superb craftsmanship, vision, sensibility, social comment and, at times, humour. In quite a short time the collection has become a significant feature of the University's cultural landscape attracting favourable comments from students, staff and visitors alike. It is a tangible reflection of this new university's commitment to both the internal community of artists and to the wider community of which we form a part.

Southampton Solent University aims to contribute to the culture of the city and surrounding region through the promotion of the visual arts to a wider public and to its academic community of students and staff. It does this principally through the Millais Gallery, a substantial contemporary art space with a regular changing programme of events and exhibitions of regional and national standing. The work of students and staff is also celebrated through the University's art collection with artworks displayed throughout the campus in public areas, staff offices and meeting rooms. A feature of the policy has been the use of the main concourse in the Michael Andrews building as a gallery for occasional exhibitions. These exhibitions reflect the trends in art and design here in Southampton and promote the artists associated with the University. The exhibitions are a testament to the creativity of our students and staff and provide a constantly changing visual stimulus that inspires pleasure and controversy – sometimes in equal measure.

Ron McCormick, Custodian

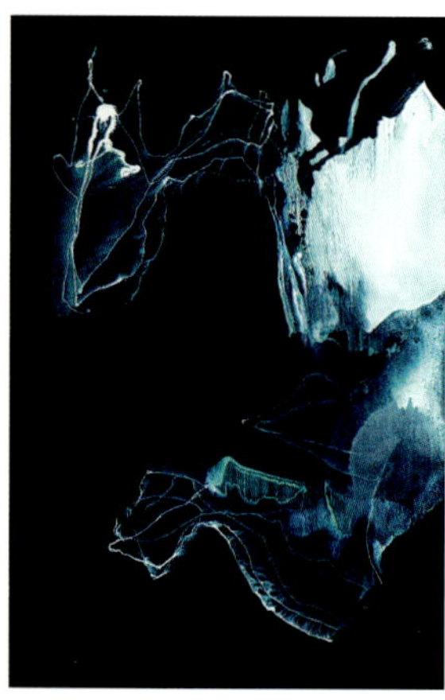

Adams, Elizabeth b.1982
Untitled (Green on Black) 2006
oil on board 182.5 x 120.9
SI/06/0679

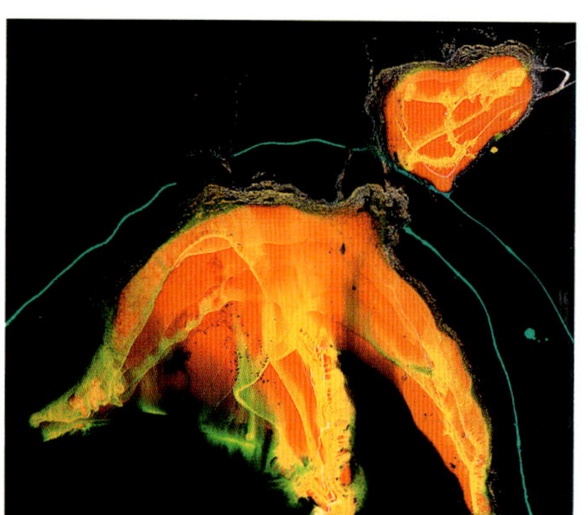

Adams, Elizabeth b.1982
Untitled (Orange on Brown) 2006
oil on board 56 x 66
SI/06/0680

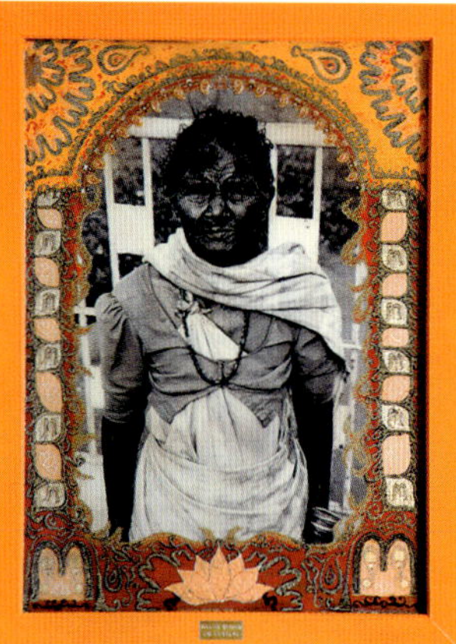

Baker, Sam b.1984
Beggar Woman of Ceylon 2006
mixed media on board 127.5 x 96.4
SI/06/0682

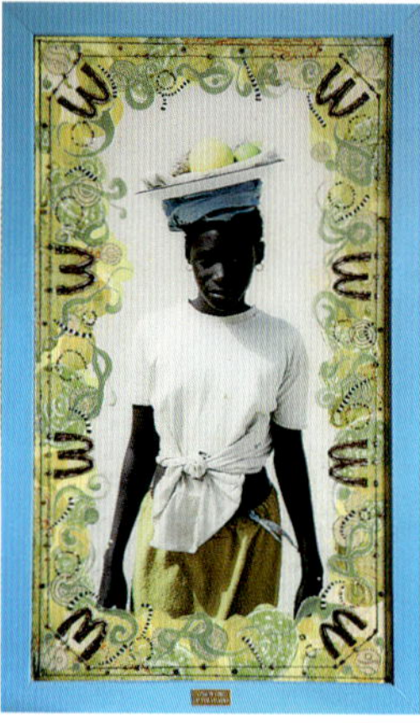

Baker, Sam b.1984
Lemon Girl of the Gambia 2006
mixed media on board 157.5 x 96.6
SI/06/0681

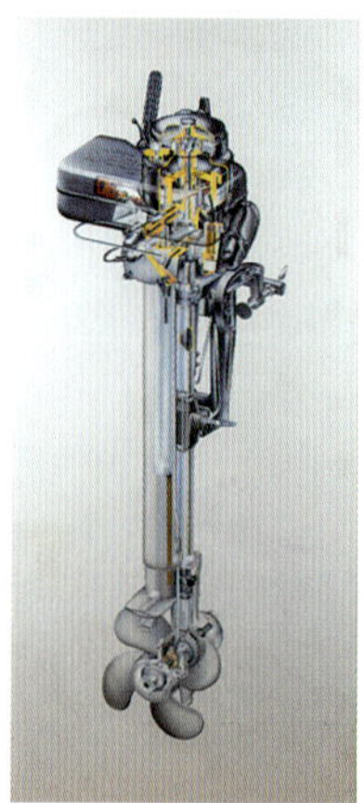

Barker, Mario b.1968
Outboard c.1990
acrylic on paper 140 x 68
SI/98/0002

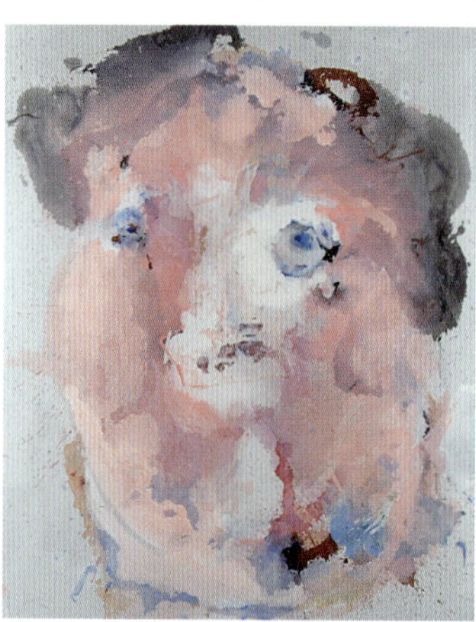

Bastick, Rosemary b.1948
Portrait 2003
oil on canvas 108 x 90
SI/03/0611

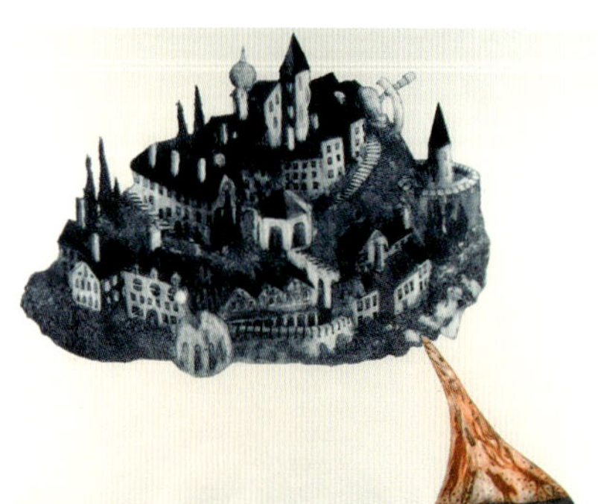

Cardall, Adam active 1998–2006
Castles in the Sky 2002
mixed media on paper 54 x 74
SI/02/0587

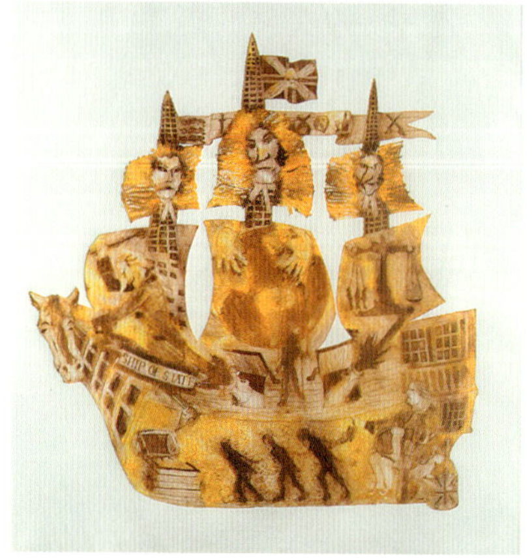

Cardall, Adam active 1998–2006
Ship of State 2002
mixed media on paper 75 x 55 (E)
SI/02/0588

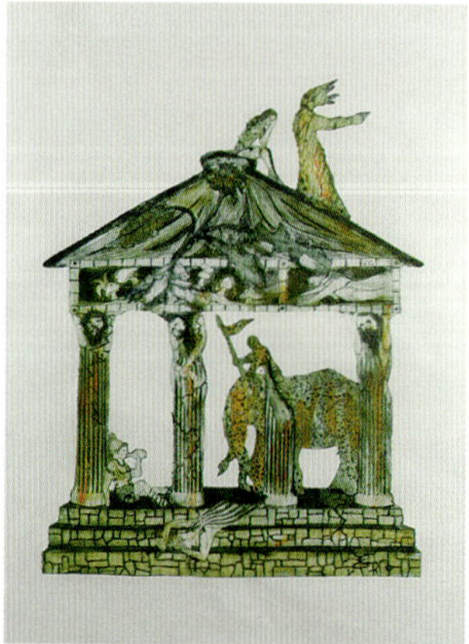

Cardall, Adam active 1998–2006
Standing on the Shoulders of Giants 2002
mixed media on paper 76 x 52
SI/02/0589

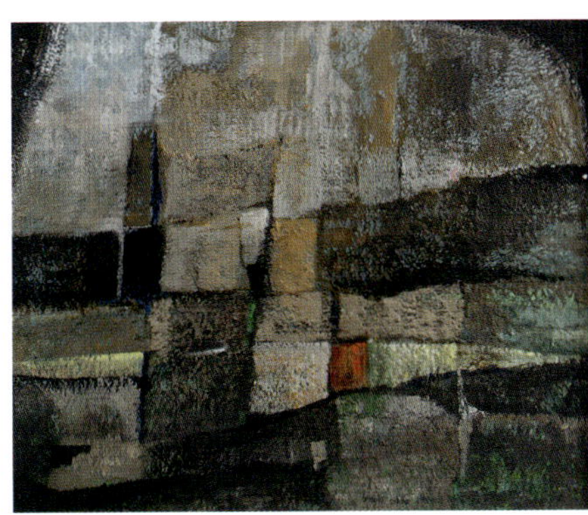

Chipp, John
Dorset Autumn c.1979
oil on linen over board 50.8 x 60.8
SI/05/0664

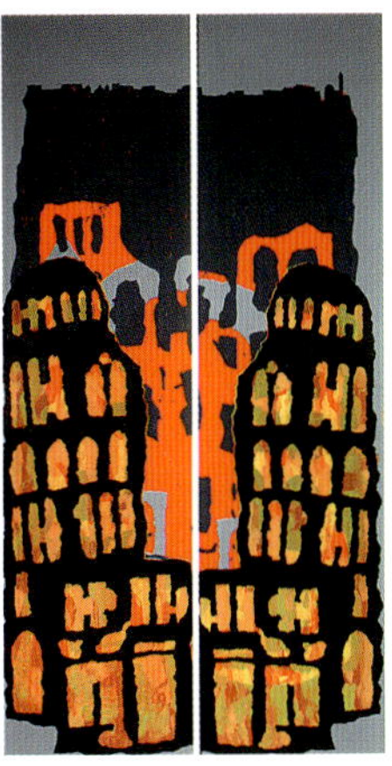

Cross, Steve active 1968–2006
The Fall of Mostar No. 1 & No.2 1995
oil on canvas 88 x 24.4; 88 x 24.4
SI/98/0060 (P)

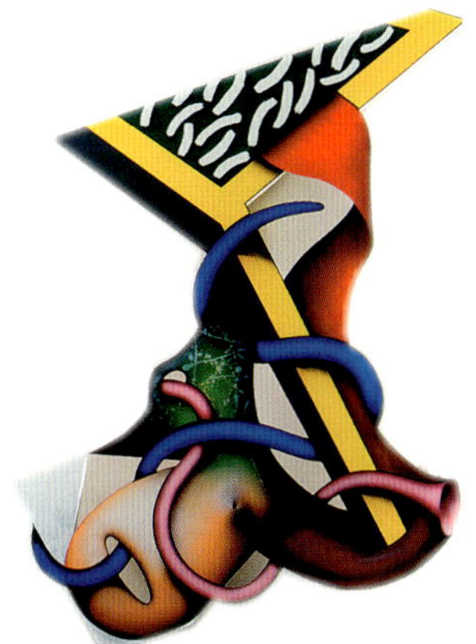

Curry, Rob b.1955
Visceral 1985
acrylic emulsion, ink & relief on board
150 x 120
SI/03/0629 (P)

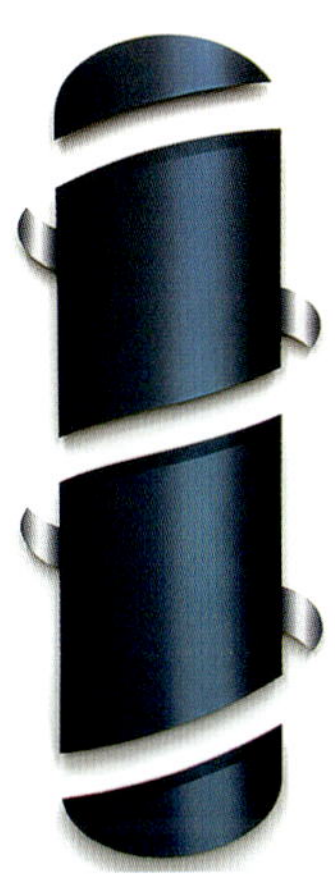

Curry, Rob b.1955
Twiss 1986
acrylic emulsion & ink on board 128 x 48
SI/03/0630 (P)

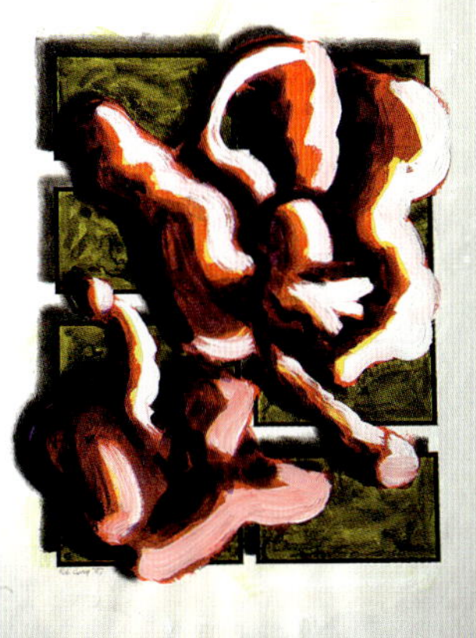

Curry, Rob b.1955
Augury 1987
mixed media on paper 74.9 x 49.5
SI/06/0673 (P)

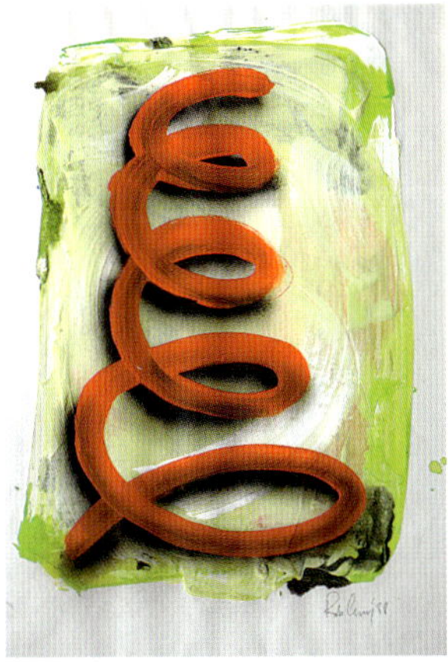

Curry, Rob b.1955
Axis 1988
mixed media on paper 74.9 x 49.5
SI/06/0676 (P)

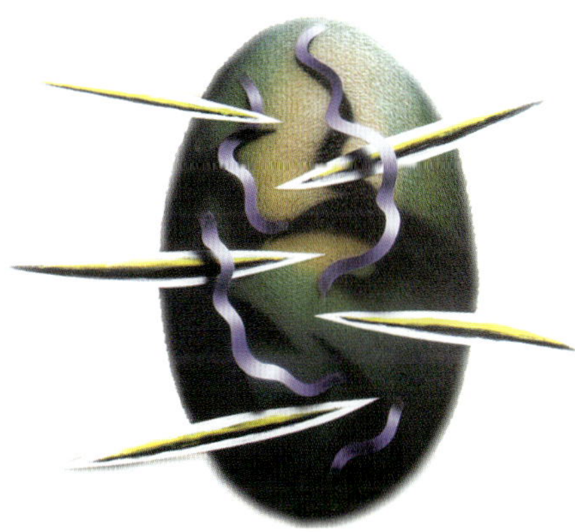

Curry, Rob b.1955
Maasai 1993
acrylic emulsion, ink & relief on board
117 x 157
SI/03/0627 (P)

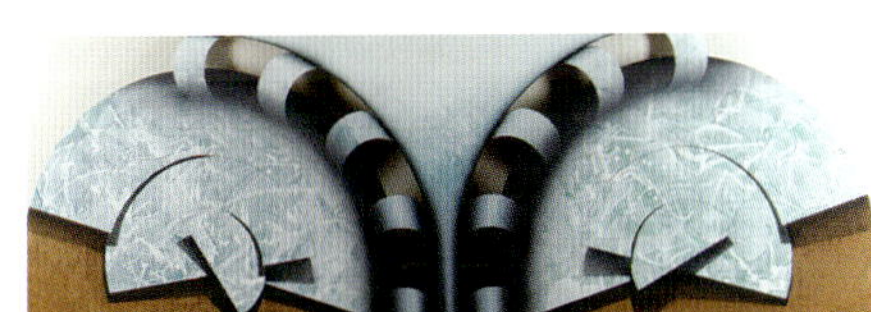

Curry, Rob b.1955
Lazarus 1994
acrylic emulsion & ink on board 24.4 x 81.6
SI/03/0626 (P)

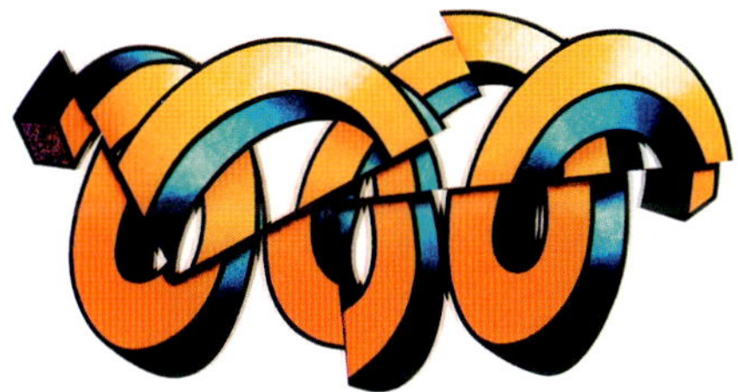

Curry, Rob b.1955
Under the Boardwalk 1994
acrylic emulsion with sand & ink on board
205 x 393
SI/03/0628 (P)

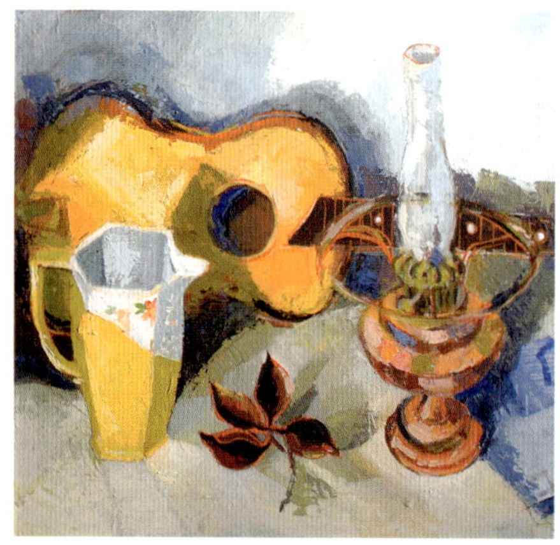

Davidson, Mary active 1985–1980
Still Life with Guitar 1988
oil on board 59.5 x 64
SI/88/0683

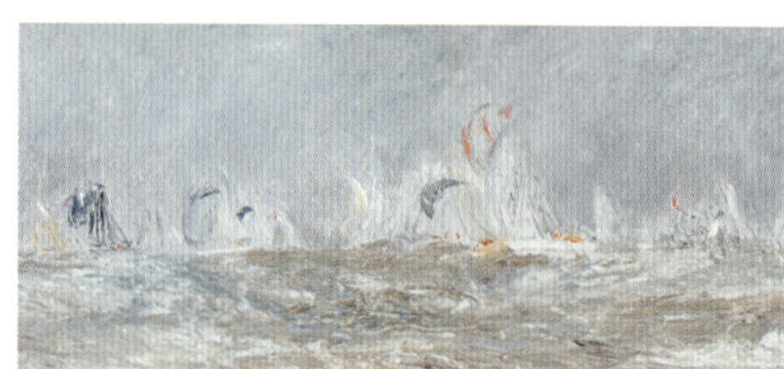

Eurich, Richard Ernst 1903–1992
Yachts in a Squall 1980
oil on board 29.2 x 64.8
SI/03/0596

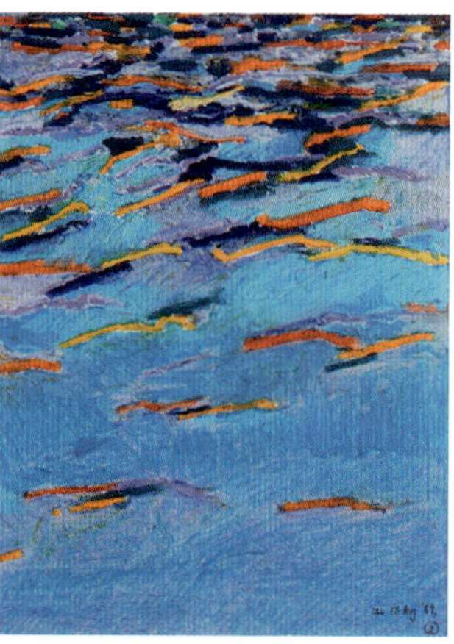

Fac
Textures 1989
oil & pastel on paper 30.3 x 23.8
SI/05/0665

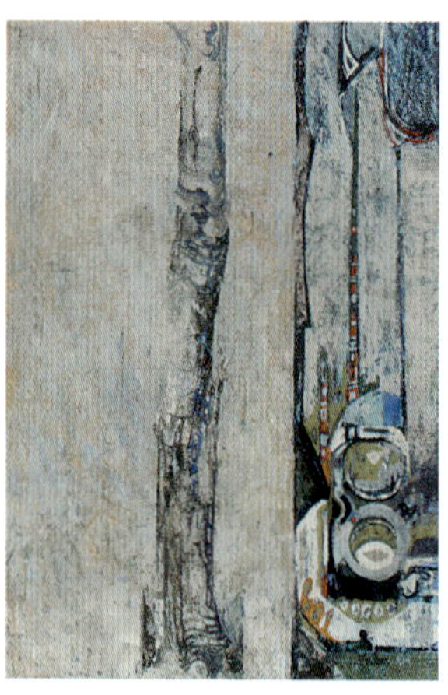

Folkes, Peter L. b.1923
Parked Car and Tree 1963
acrylic on paper 55 x 37.5
SI/05/0662

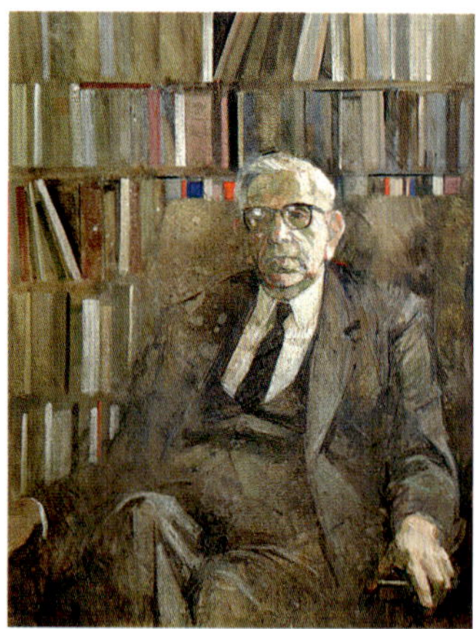

Folkes, Peter L. b.1923
Sir James Mathews, MA, LLD, JP 1994
oil on canvas 124.3 x 99.5
SI/06/0677

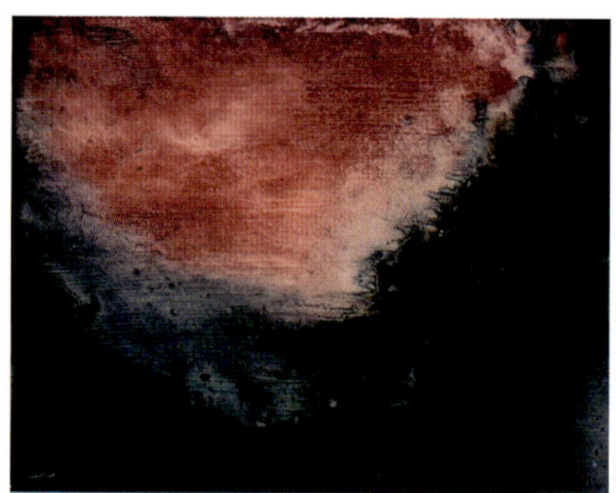

Francis, Emma b.1975
Bruiser 2004
oil on board 20 x 25.4
SI/04/0639

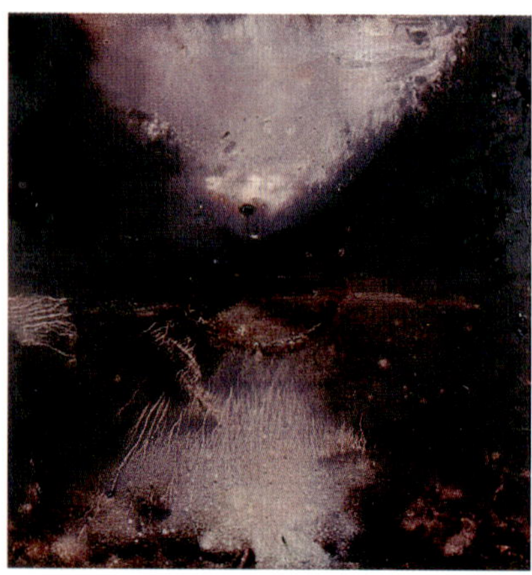

Francis, Emma b.1975
Crack 2004
oil on canvas 86 x 84
SI/04/0637

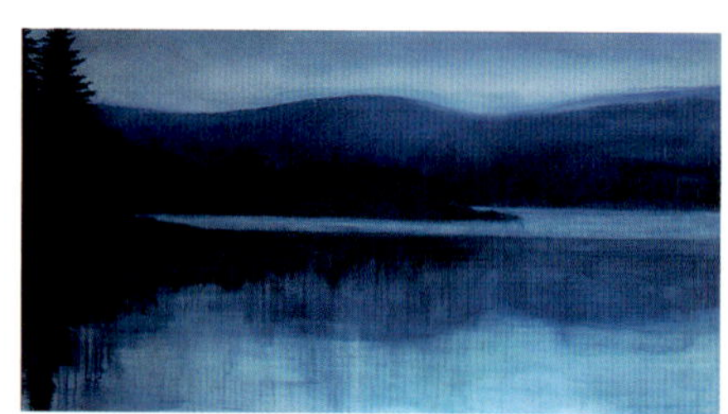

Francis, Emma b.1975
Divided 2004
oil on canvas 120.8 x 228
SI/04/0658

Francis, Emma b.1975
Lost 2004
oil on board 25.5 x 20
SI/04/0638

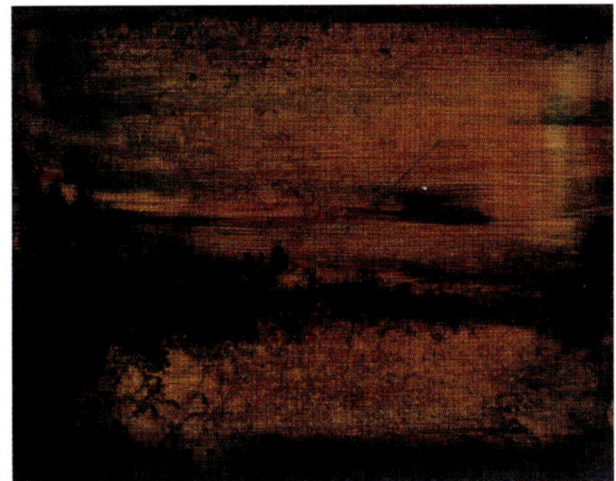

Francis, Emma b.1975
Umber 2004
oil on board 20 x 25.5
SI/04/0640

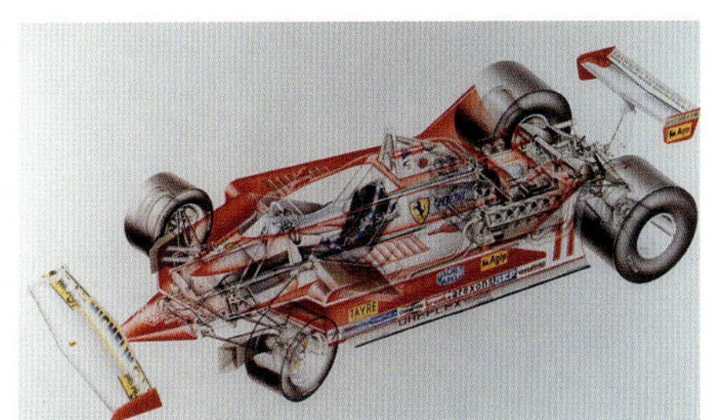

Garrod, Alistair active 1989–2006
Jody Scheckter's Ferrari 1992
acrylic on paper 43 x 73
SI/98/0213

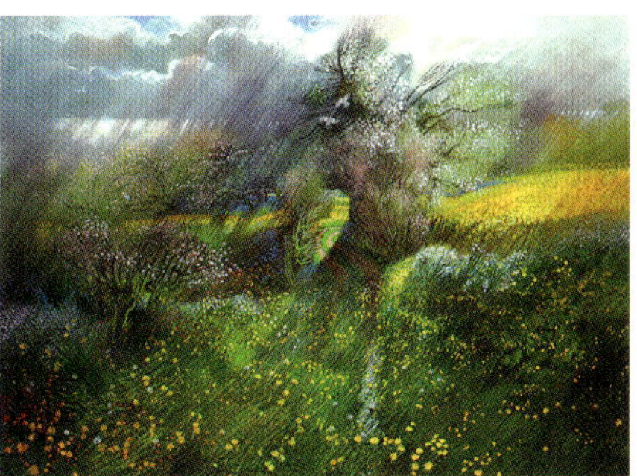

Griffin, John b.1944
Approaching Storm (Normandy) 1980s
tempera on paper 36 x 51.3
SI/06/0668 (P)

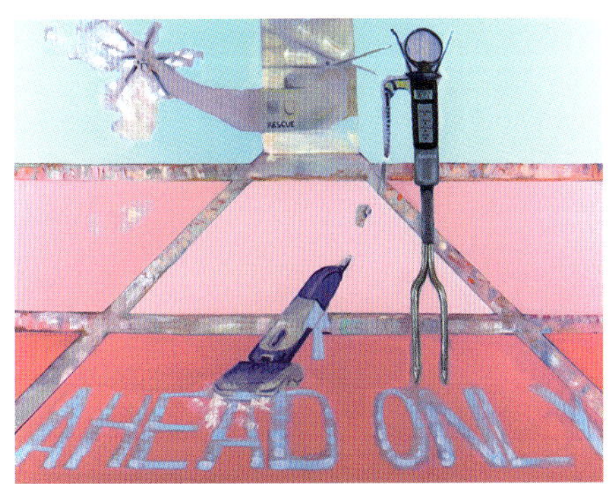

Janceva, Velika b.1980
Ahead Only 2001
oil on canvas 120 x 140
SI/01/0366 (P)

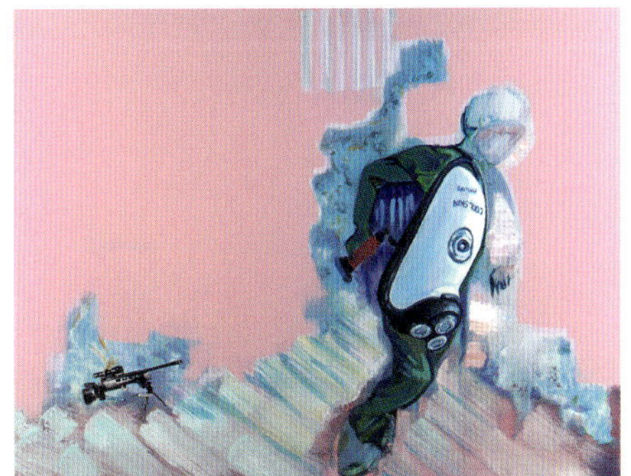

Janceva, Velika b.1980
Cool Skin 2001
oil & collage on canvas 60 x 80
SI/01/0368 (P)

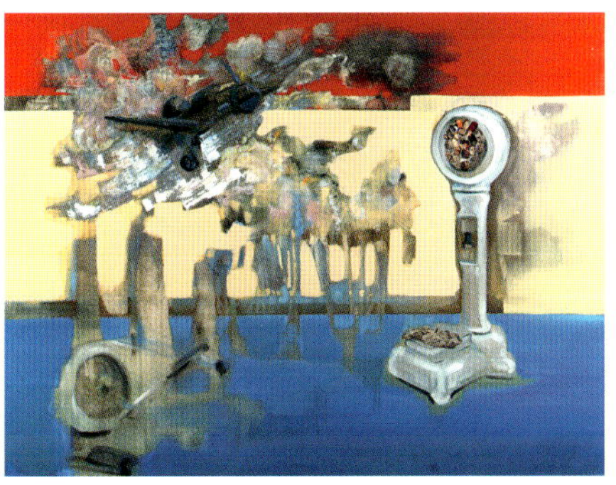

Janceva, Velika b.1980
Some Things We Simply Can't Measure 2001
oil & collage on canvas 119.5 x 159.5
SI/01/0349

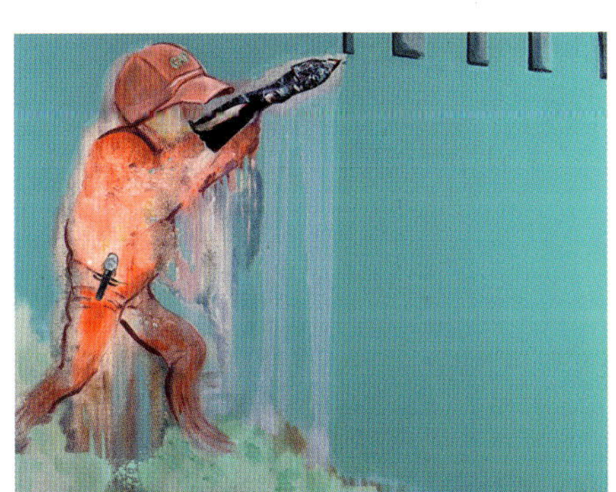

Janceva, Velika b.1980
The Gap Soldier 2001
oil & collage on canvas 60 x 80
SI/01/0367 (P)

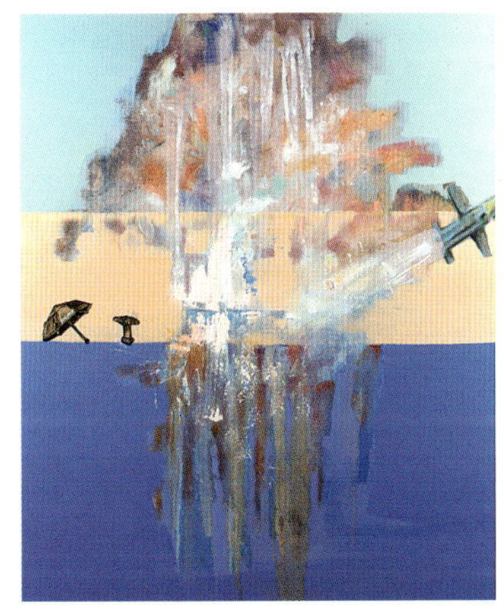

Janceva, Velika b.1980
Untitled 2001
oil on canvas 120 x 100
SI/01/0365 (P)

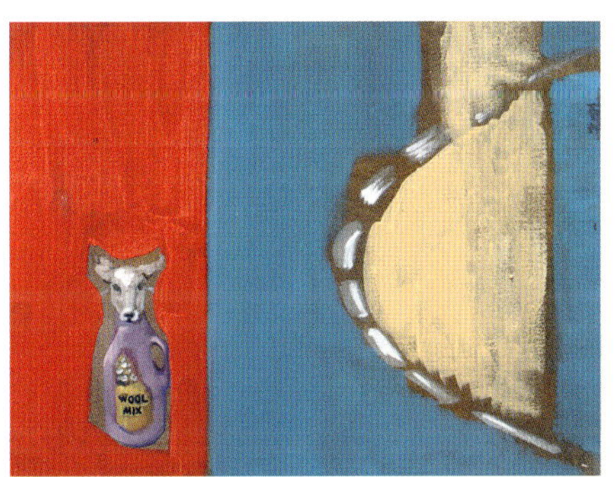

Janceva, Velika b.1980
Wool Mix 2001
oil on canvas 34 x 46
SI/01/0369 (P)

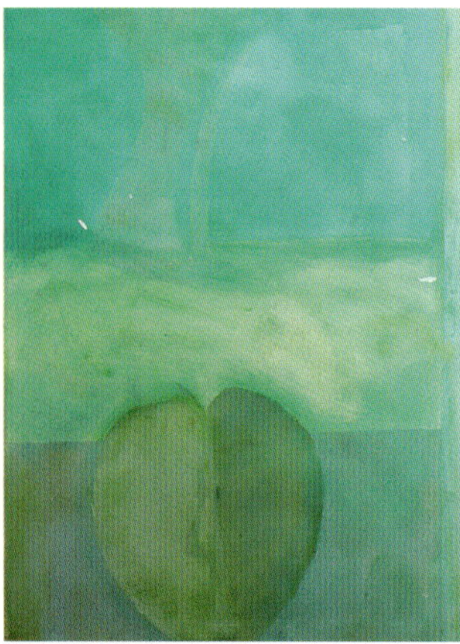

Jobe, Ngoneh b.1979
Apple 2001
oil on Somerset textured paper 81 x 60
SI/01/0347

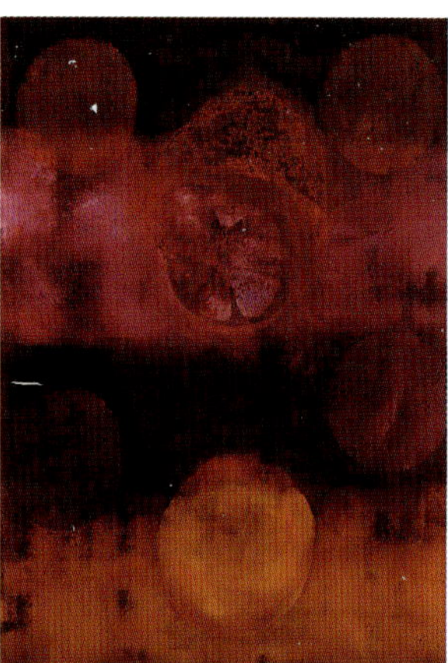

Jobe, Ngoneh b.1979
Grapefruit 2001
oil on Somerset textured paper 100.5 x 70.5
SI/01/0403

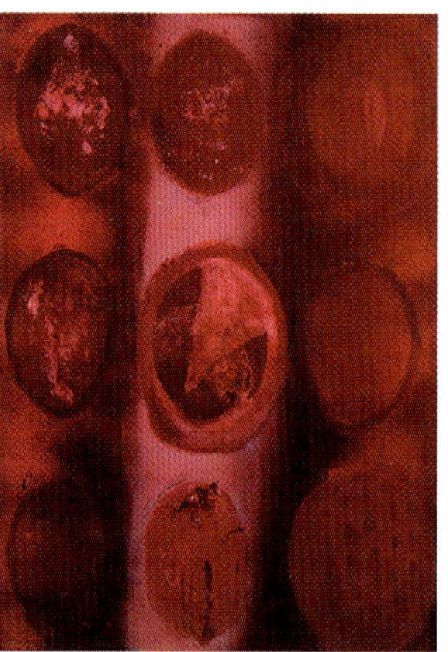

Jobe, Ngoneh b.1979
Strawberries 2001
oil on Somerset textured paper 100 x 71
SI/01/0398

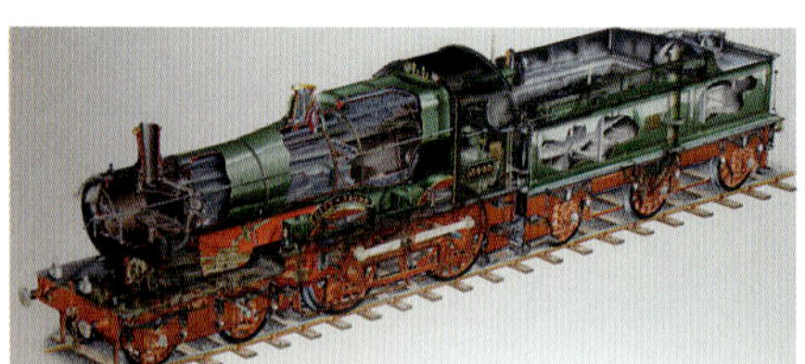

Jones, Anthony active 1986–2006
'City of Truro' 1988
acrylic on paper 76 x 169
SI/98/0001

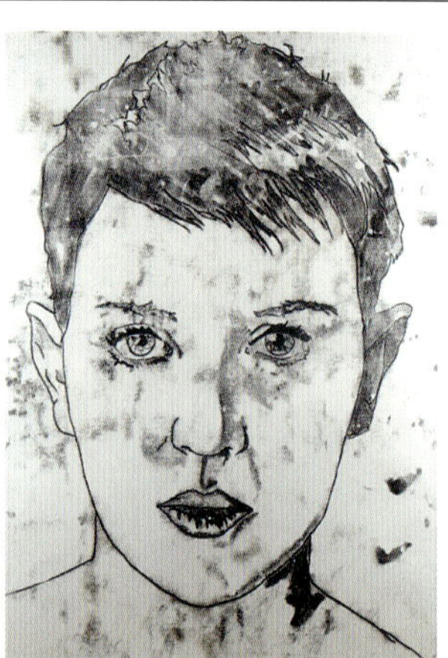

Kingston, Emma b.1983
Lucy Mono 1 2004
oil & ink on paper 135 x 100
SI/04/0634

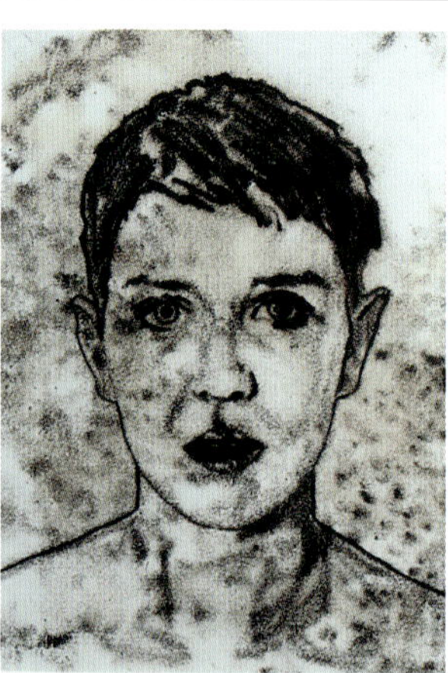

Kingston, Emma b.1983
Lucy Mono Black 2004
oil & ink on paper 38 x 28
SI/04/0635

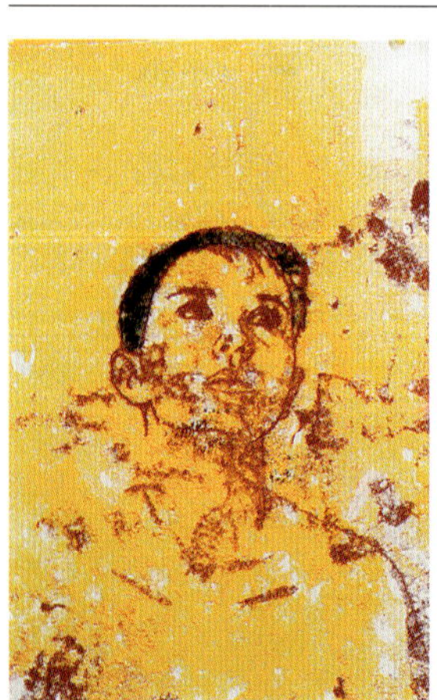

Kingston, Emma b.1983
Lucy Mono Yellow/Red/Black 2004
oil & ink on paper 30 x 20
SI/04/0636

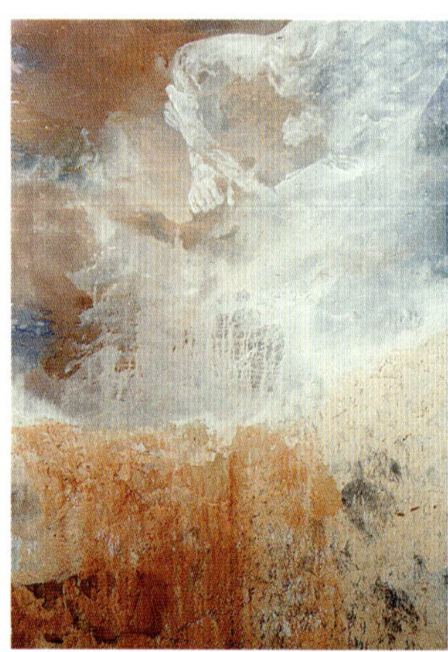

McDade, Steven b.1950
Fall 1992
oil on canvas 167.5 x 121.5
SI/98/0083 (P)

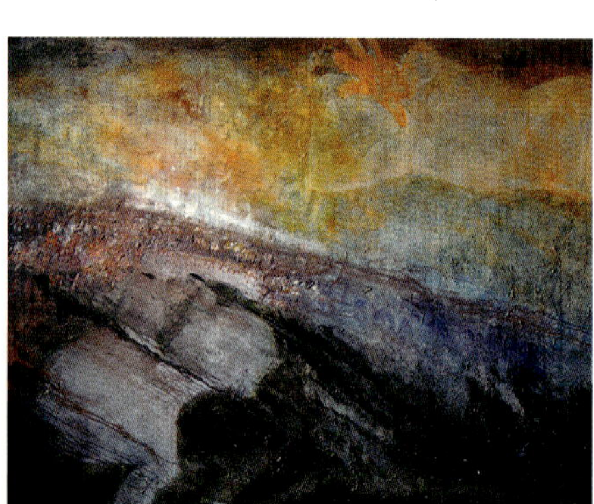

McDade, Steven b.1950
Language Flow 1992
oil on canvas 123.5 x 155
SI/98/0080 (P)

Facing page: Grant, Duncan, 1885–1978, *Angelica Playing the Violin* (detail), 1934, Southampton City Art Gallery, (p. 54)

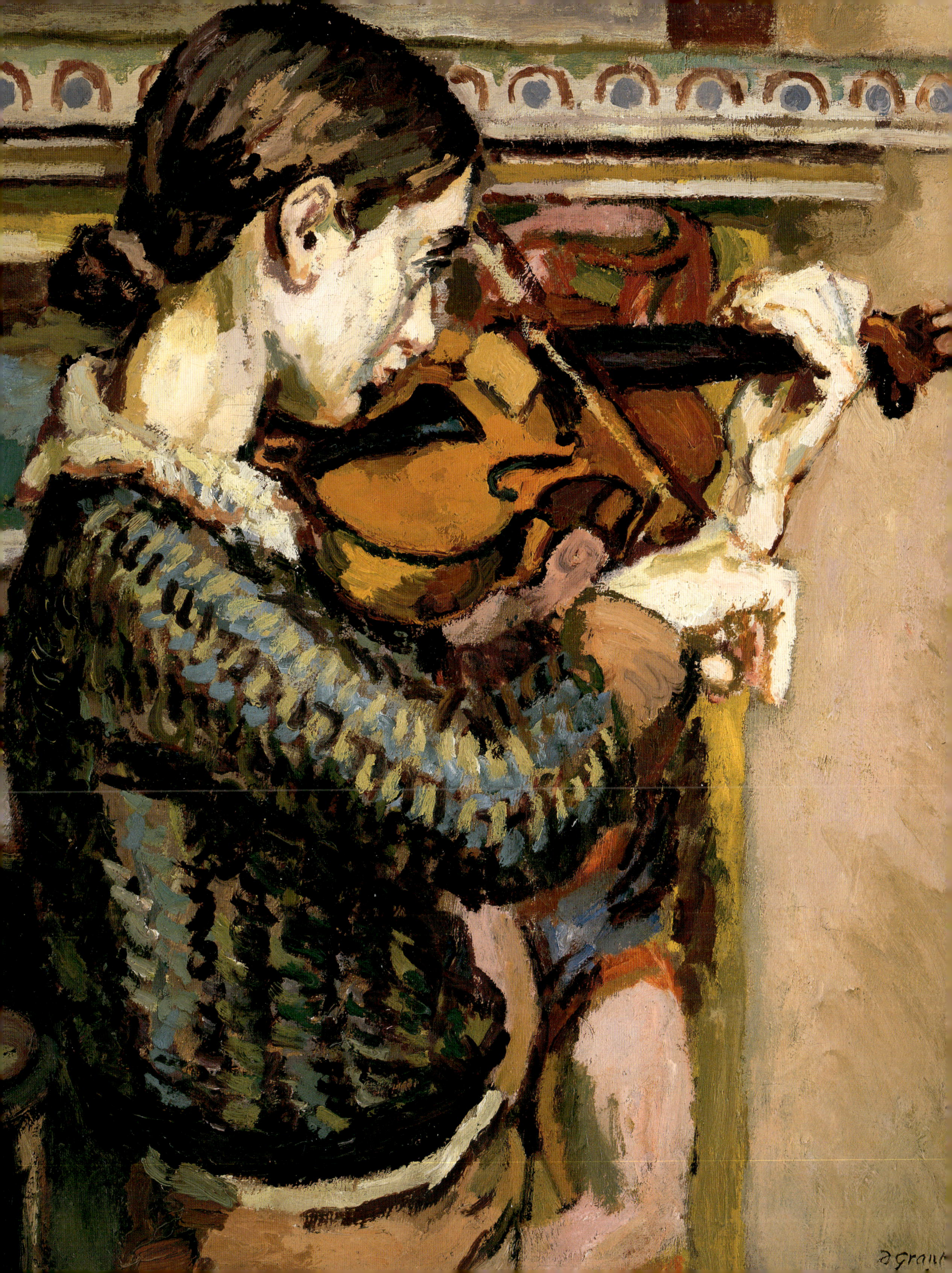
D Grant

McDade, Steven b.1950
Separate 1992
oil, acrylic & sand on canvas 121.5 x 99.5
SI/98/0082 (P)

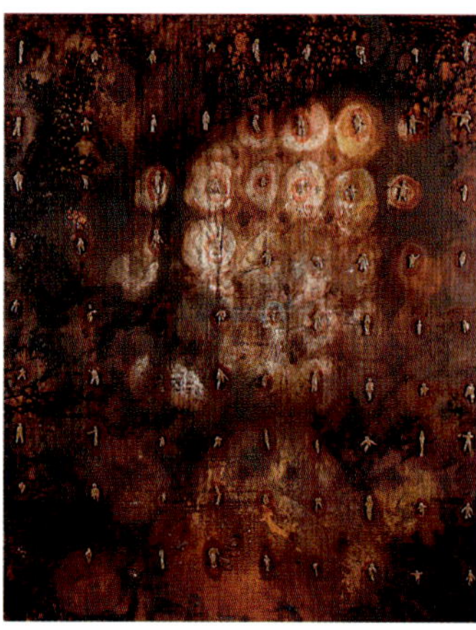

McDade, Steven b.1950
Descend 1994
oil & clay on canvas 152.4 x 122
SI/98/0088 (P)

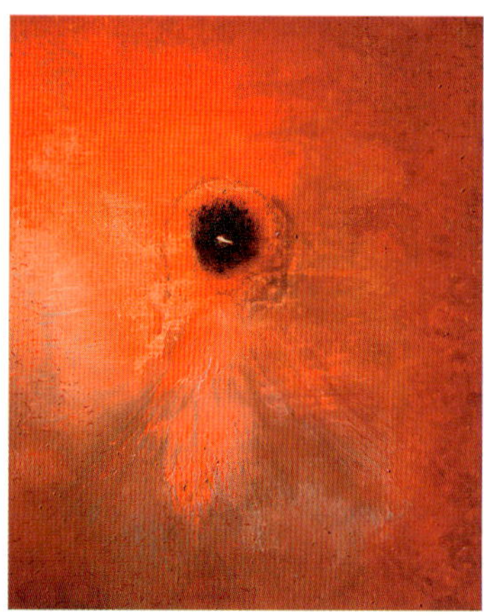

McDade, Steven b.1950
The Beginning of the World 1996
oil on canvas 144.6 x 119.5
SI/98/0089 (P)

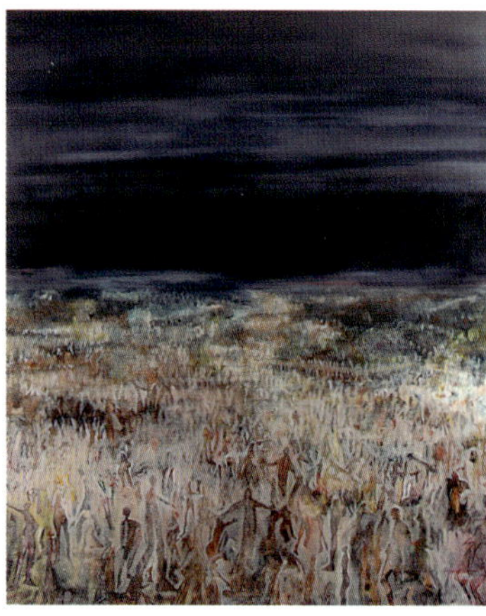

McDade, Steven b.1950
Network 1997
oil on canvas 182.8 x 152.4
SI/98/0086

McDade, Steven b.1950
Senate 1999
acrylic on perspex & paper 50 x 50
SI/00/0239 (P)

McDade, Steven b.1950
Spectre 1999
acrylic on board & perspex 50 x 50
SI/00/0240 (P)

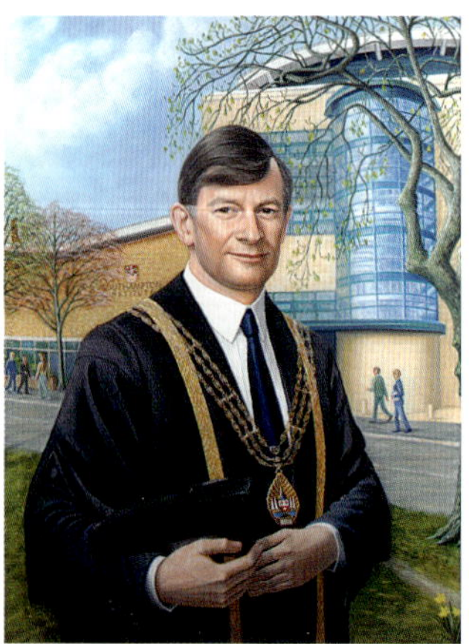

McKee, Alice b.1954
Michael Andrews 1999
acrylic on board 125 x 95
SI/99/0247

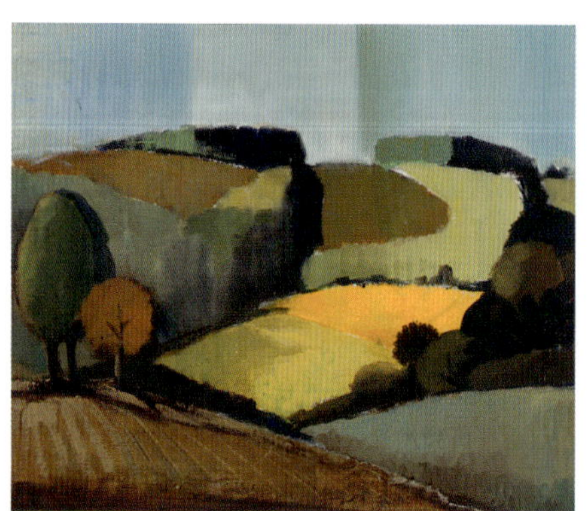

Miranda, C. active 1978–1990
Farley Landscape 1979
oil on linen over board 50.5 x 60.8
SI/05/0663

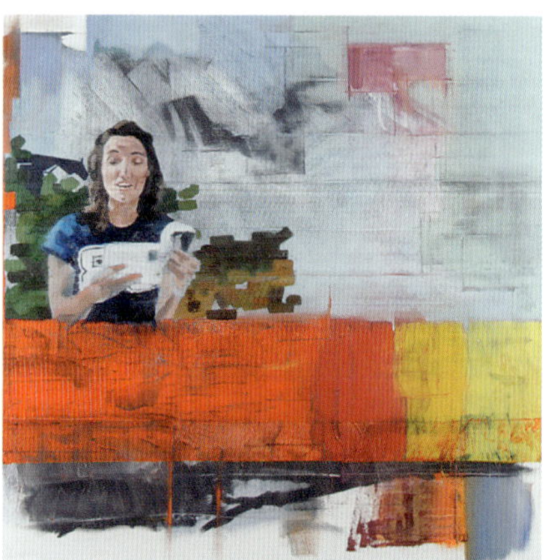

Murley, Tim active 2002–2006
Wish You Were Here No.1
oil on canvas 90 x 90
SI/03/0607

Oldfield, Michelle active 2002–2006
A Starscape: 50 Sci-Fi Films 2003
oil on canvas 169.5 x 120
SI/03/0609

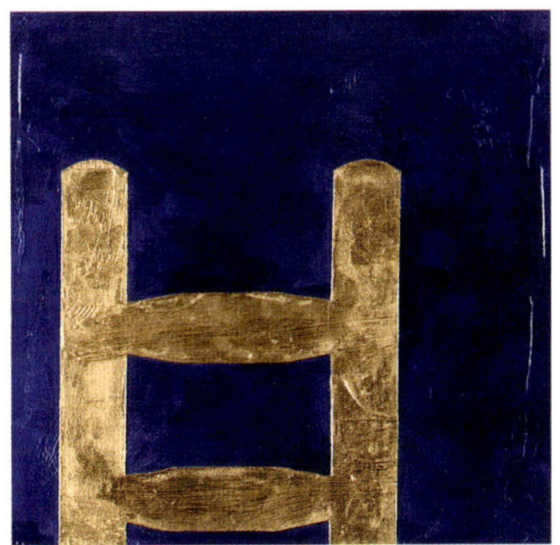

Palmer, Greg b.1959
A Spot of the Old (In and Out 1) 1999
oil on canvas & perspex 33 x 33 (E)
SI/00/0233 (P)

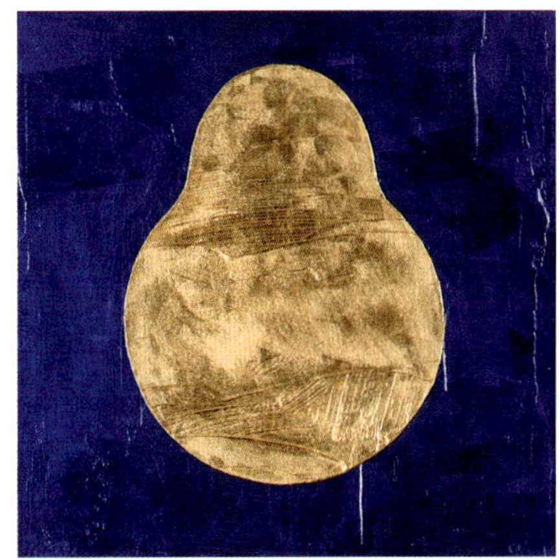

Palmer, Greg b.1959
A Spot of the Old (In and Out 2) 1999
oil on canvas & perspex 33 x 33 (E)
SI/00/0234 (P)

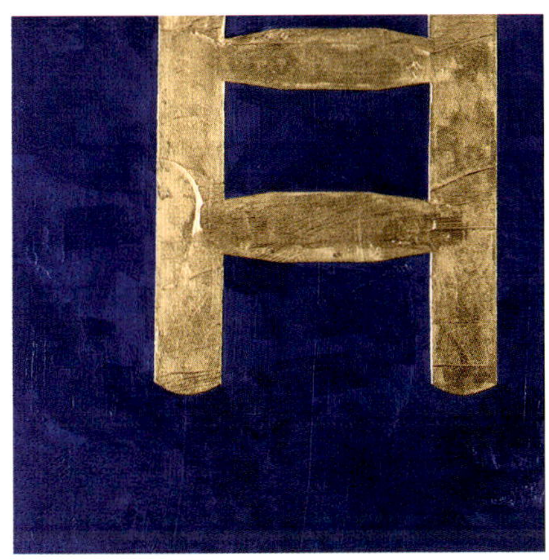

Palmer, Greg b.1959
A Spot of the Old (In and Out 3) 1999
oil on canvas & perspex 33 x 33 (E)
SI/00/0235 (P)

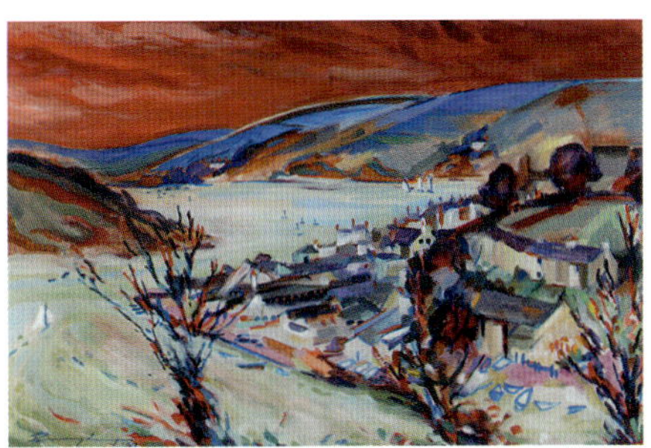

Perry, Lyon active 1986–1990
Island Quay, Salcombe 1987
acrylic on paper 36 x 54
SI/05/0660

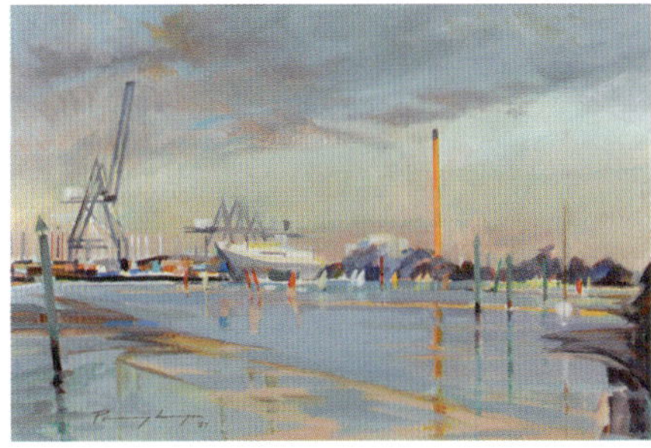

Perry, Lyon active 1986–1990
Southampton Docks 1987
acrylic on paper 36 x 54
SI/05/0661

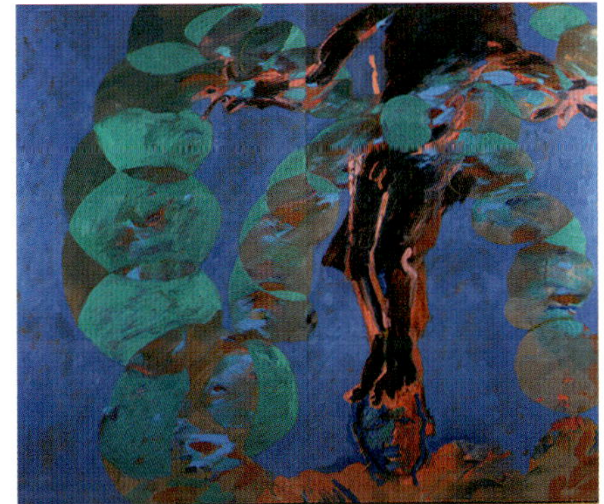

Powell, Stephen b.1955
Vertical Hold 1989
oil on canvas 178 x 214
SI/98/0052 (P)

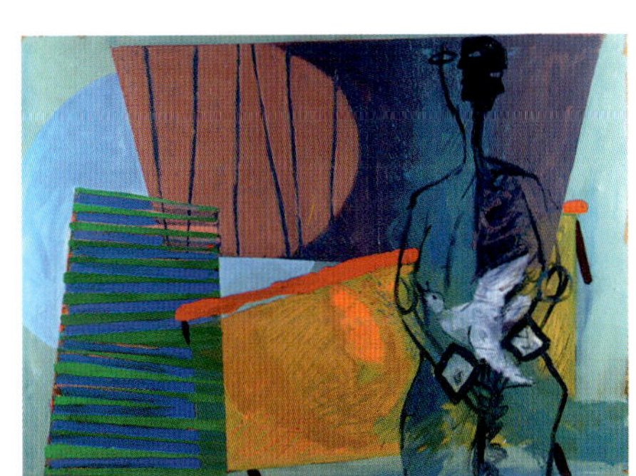

Powell, Stephen b.1955
Magician and Bird 1991
oil on canvas 107 x 146
SI/98/0048

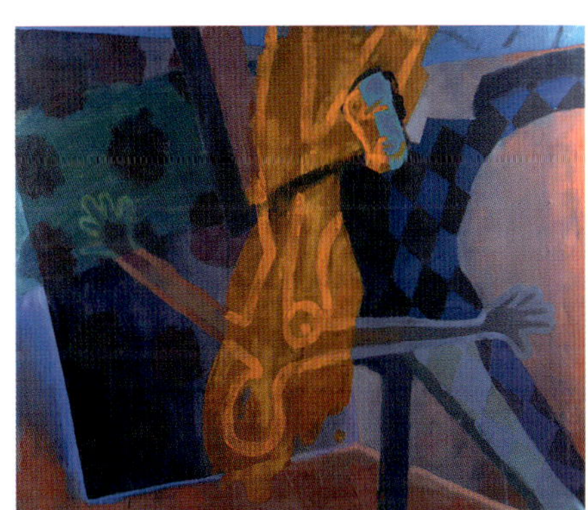

Powell, Stephen b.1955
Abracadabra 1992
oil on canvas 146 x 178
SI/98/0049 (P)

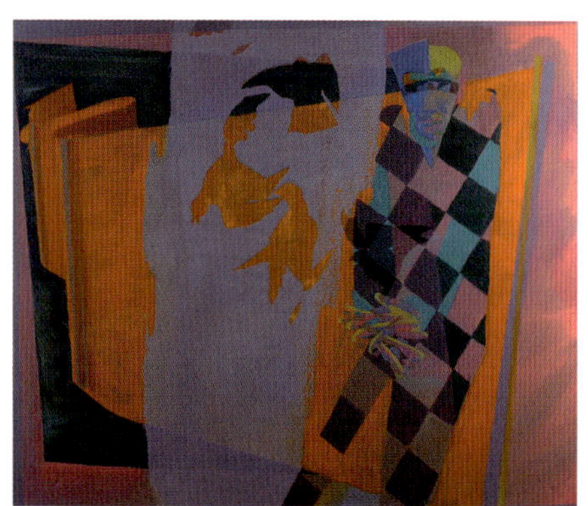

Powell, Stephen b.1955
None So Blind 1992
oil on canvas 142 x 170
SI/98/0054 (P)

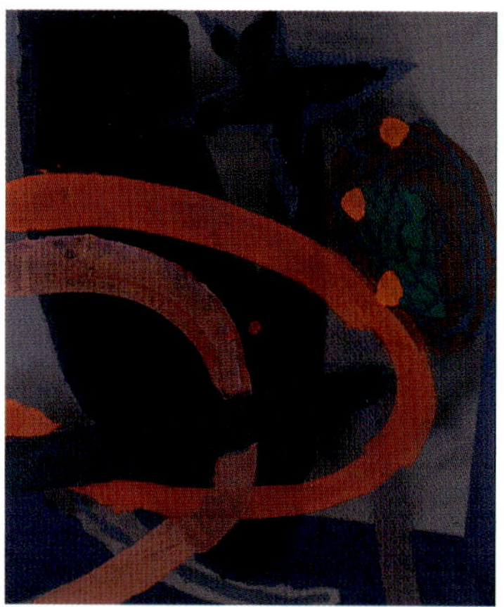

Powell, Stephen b.1955
Dance on the Edge 1996
oil on canvas 77.2 x 69.8
SI/98/0046 (P)

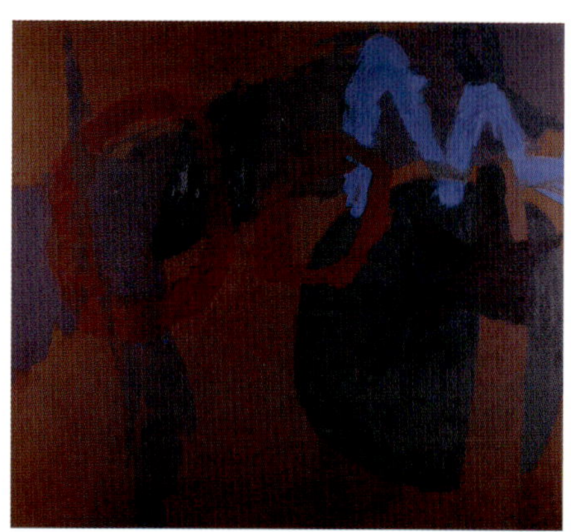

Powell, Stephen b.1955
Dizzy Heights 1997
oil on canvas 122.5 x 137.5
SI/98/0051 (P)

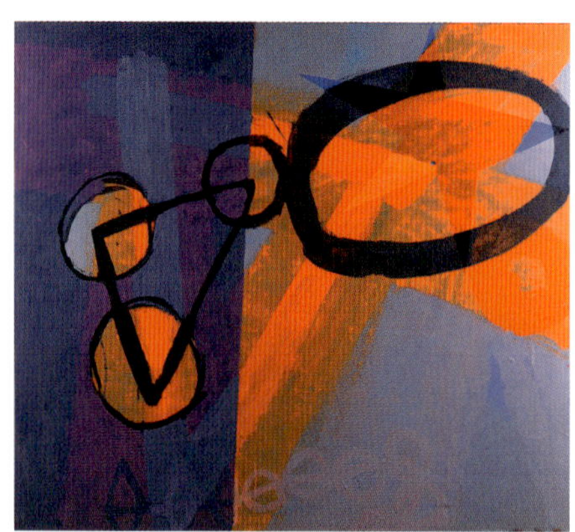

Powell, Stephen b.1955
Points to View 1997
oil on canvas 122 x 137
SI/98/0050 (P)

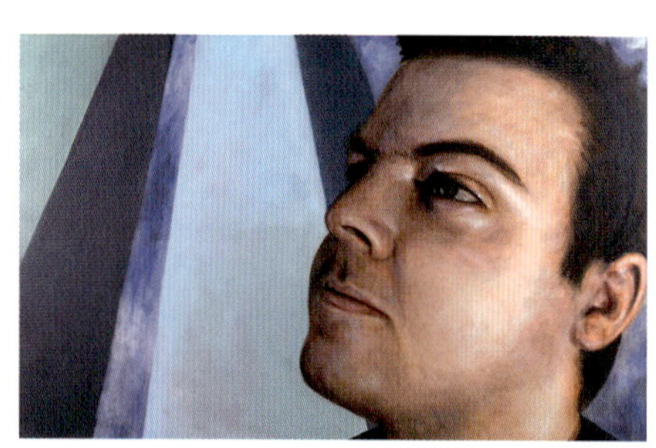

Talbert, Ryan active 2000–2006
A Tragedy in the Mind of the Living 2002
oil on canvas 112 x 173
SI/02/0581

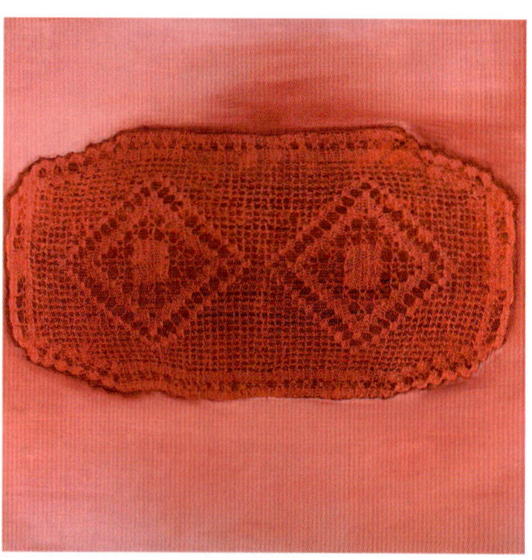

Taylor, Sarah b.1966
Still, Self, Life 1 1999
oil on board & perspex 50 x 50
SI/00/0236 (P)

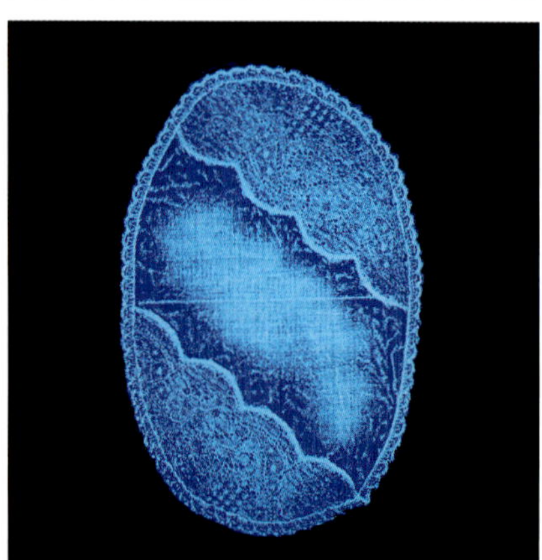

Taylor, Sarah b.1966
Still, Self, Life 2 1999
oil on board & perspex 50 x 50
SI/00/0237 (P)

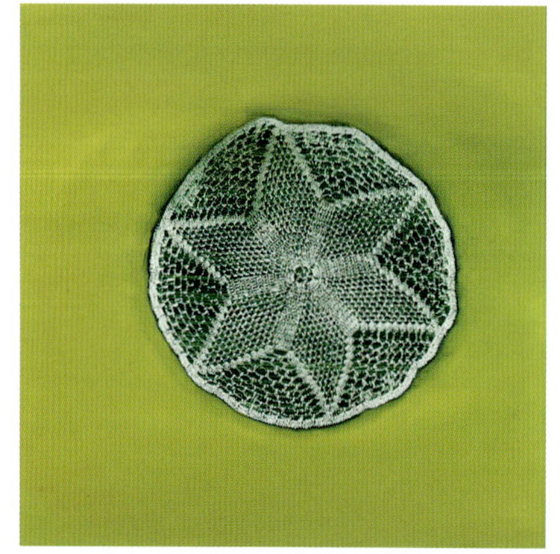

Taylor, Sarah b.1966
Still, Self, Life 3 1999
oil on board & perspex 50 x 50
SI/00/0238 (P)

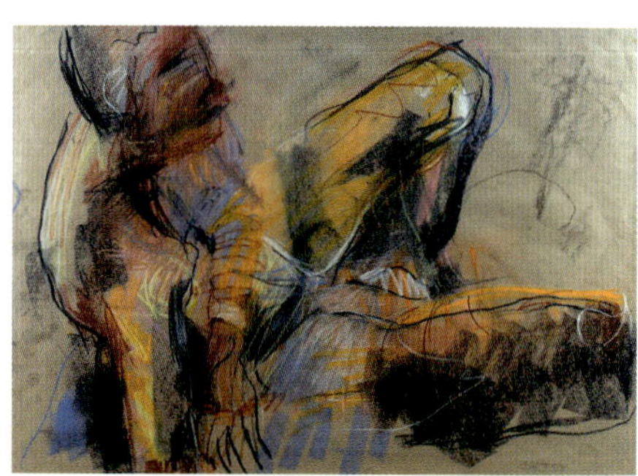

Thornton, Sue b.1952
Limbus 1998
mixed media on paper 59.3 x 84
SI/03/0608

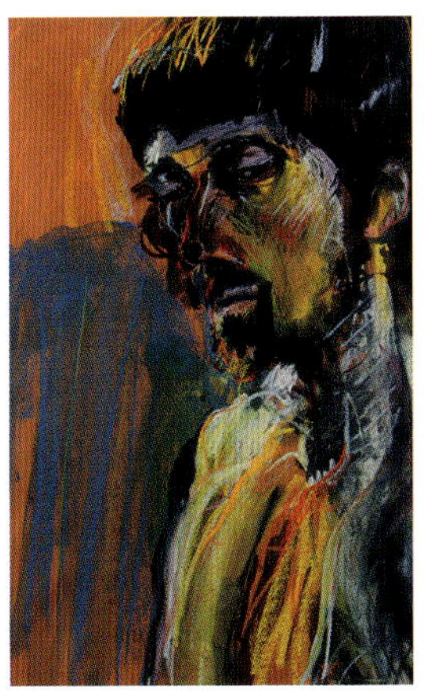

Thornton, Sue b.1952
Looking Sideways
mixed media on board 53 x 34
SI/03/0621

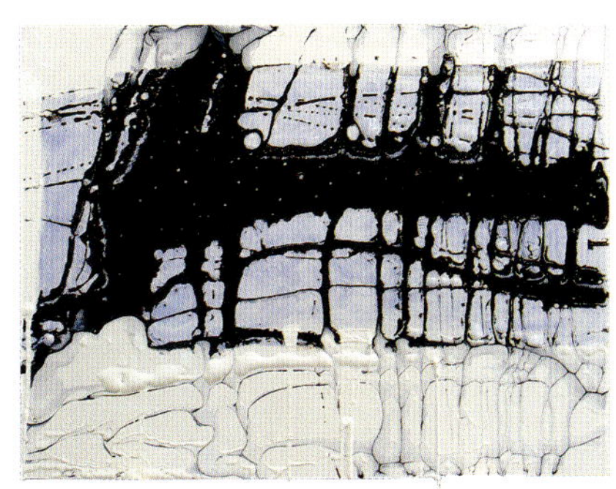

Wakelin, Tracy b.1965
Assemblage No.1 2005
oil & acrylic on board 90 x 120
SI/05/0666

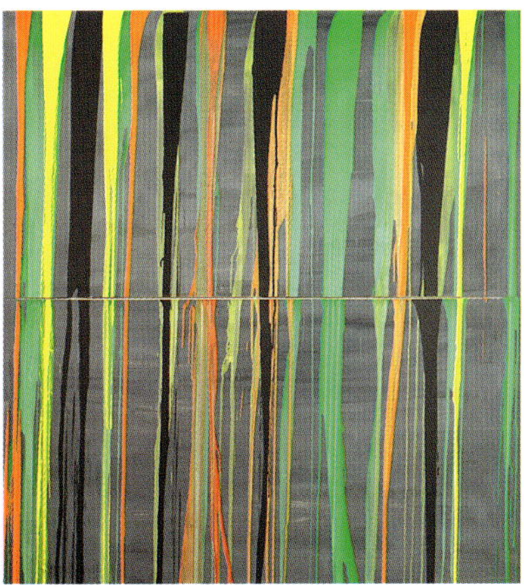

Wakelin, Tracy b.1965
Openings 2005
oil on canvas 143 x 134
SI/05/0667

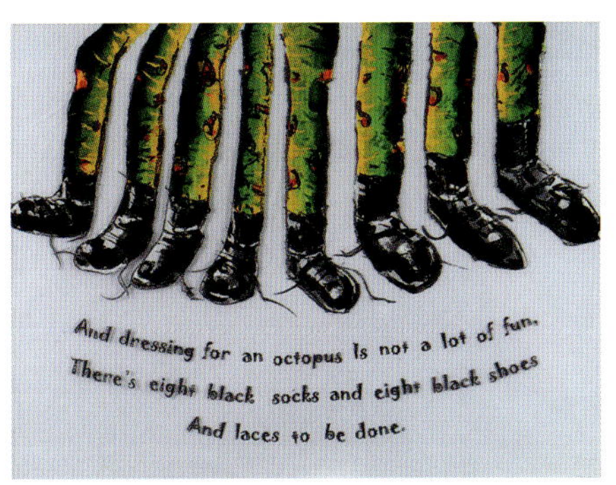

Watkins, Rhian b.1981
Octopus (Clive Riche-Boots) 2004
acrylic on acetate 29 x 39
SI/04/0649

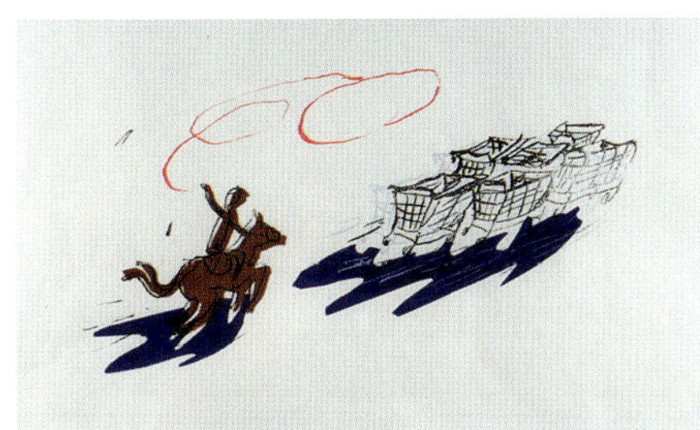

Watkins, Rhian b.1981
Shopping Trolleys (Jenny Boult) 2004
acrylic on paper 29 x 49
SI/04/0646

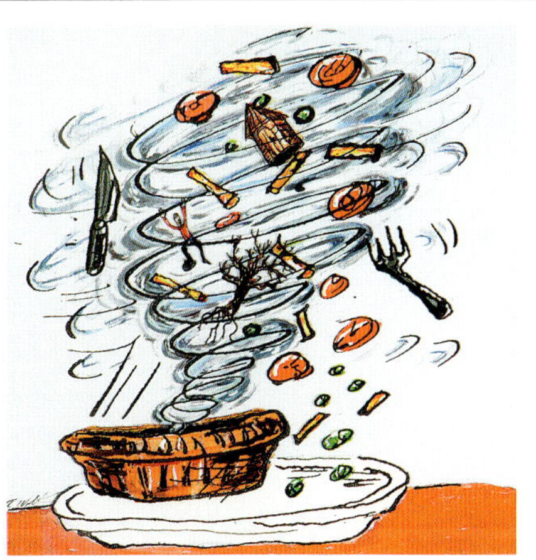

Watkins, Rhian b.1981
Sky in the Pie No.1 (Mcgough) 2004
acrylic on acetate 29 x 29
SI/04/0647

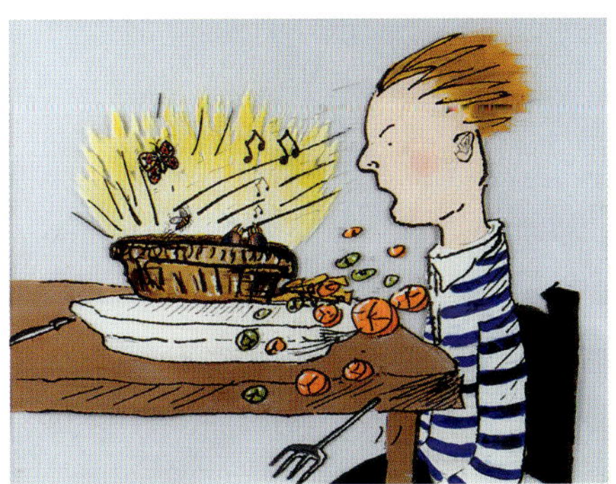

Watkins, Rhian b.1981
Sky in the Pie No.2 (Mcgough) 2004
acrylic on acetate 29 x 39
SI/04/0648

White, Jenna b.1979
Bow 2004
oil & plextol on canvas 127 x 300
SI/04/0653

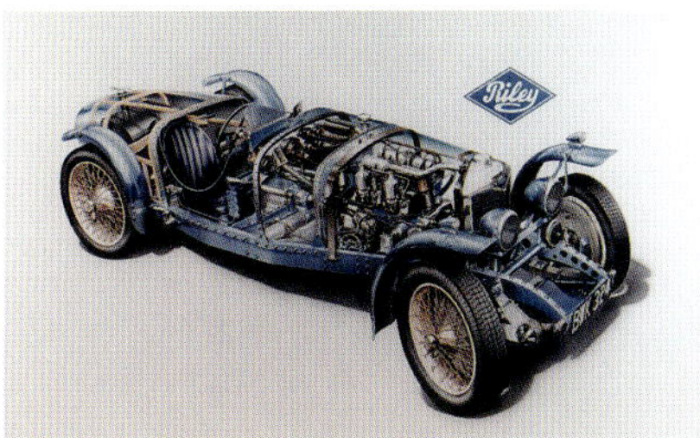

Whittington, Paul active 1994–2000
Riley Car 1995
acrylic on paper 40 x 69
SI/98/0214

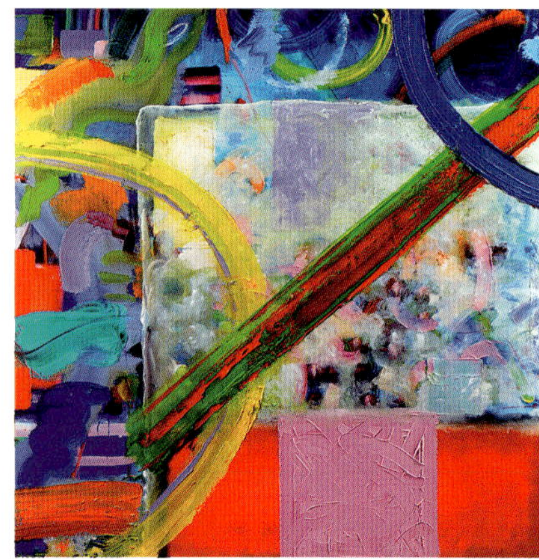

Young, Dee b.1959
The Quays 2000
oil on canvas 152 x 152
SI/01/ 0337

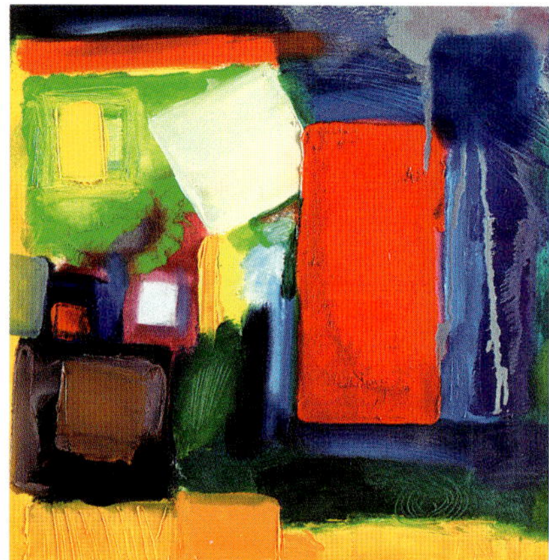

Young, Dee b.1959
Untitled No.10 2000
oil on canvas 49.5 x 49.5
SI/00/0407

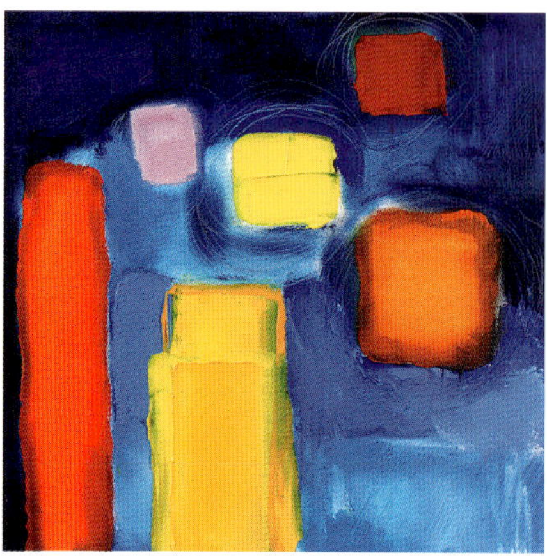

Young, Dee b.1959
Untitled No.11 2000
oil on canvas 49.5 x 49.5
SI/01/0232

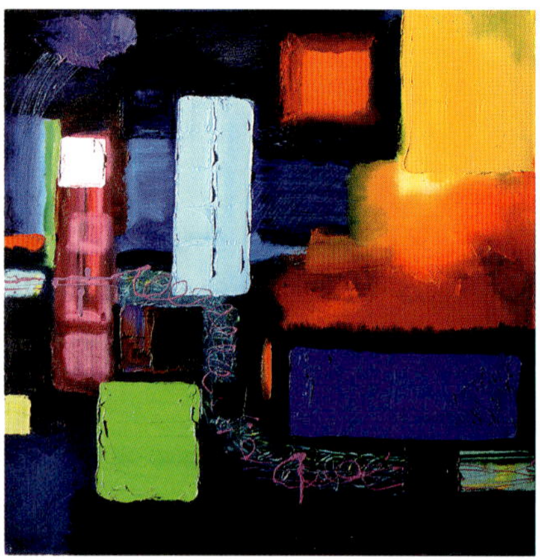

Young, Dee b.1959
Untitled No.12 2000
oil on canvas 65 x 66
SI/00/0406

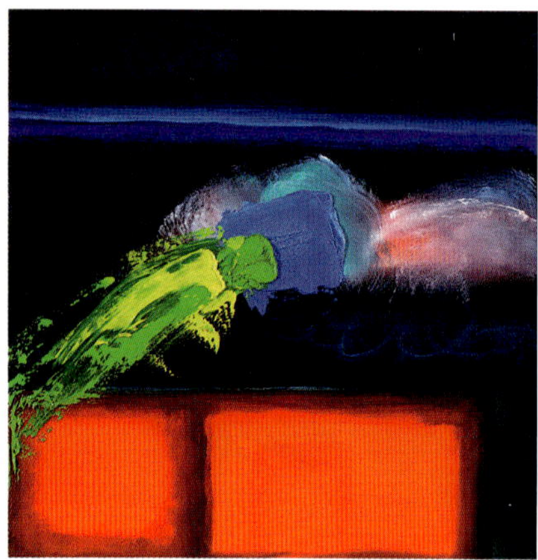

Young, Dee b.1959
Extreme Conditions 2001
oil on canvas 44.5 x 45
SI/01/0348

Southampton University Hospitals NHS Trust

Southampton University Hospitals NHS Trust has a well-established and successful arts programme with a proud history of professional arts activity in its hospitals for over 20 years. Our ongoing mission is to develop a high quality programme of integrated arts projects and commissions to change and improve the physical and social environment of Southampton's acute hospitals for the comfort, support and well-being of patients, visitors, staff and the local community.

The aims of the Trust's arts programme are: to promote and create high quality interior and exterior healthcare environments; enhance and complement patient care and other services through arts activities, events, workshops, placements and other projects; improve and finally to promote access to, participation in, and an understanding of, the role of the arts and artists in healthcare.

There has been increasing national and international recognition of the value and role of arts in healthcare. Research and documentation shows that the arts have a valuable contribution to make to promote healthy communities (through health prevention and education), in assisting recovery and rehabilitation, and by improving healthcare buildings. At a national level, the NHS plan identifies the quality of the environment and the patient experience as key areas of focus and development.

Over the past two decades, Southampton University Hospitals NHS Trust has commissioned a wide range of original artworks to enhance the healing environment of the Trust's hospital buildings and grounds. Although many of the artworks have been specifically commissioned for patient specialist treatment areas such as oncology, cardiology, intensive care and CT and MRI scanner suites, a wide selection of artwork is also on display in accessible patient and public spaces. In addition to the oil and acrylic paintings detailed in this catalogue, the Trust's collection encompasses many different art forms including printmaking, photography, textiles, sculpture, glazing, ceramics, stone, metal and woodwork. Patient artwork also features prominently in our collection, the result of stimulating and rewarding collaborative projects bringing together patients and local artists. Much of the work on display draws inspiration from nature or natural views with a strong emphasis on the Hampshire landscape.

The arts will continue to play a significant role in the future development of Southampton University Hospitals NHS Trust as a world-class specialist healthcare centre.

Abigail Dowell, Arts Coordinator

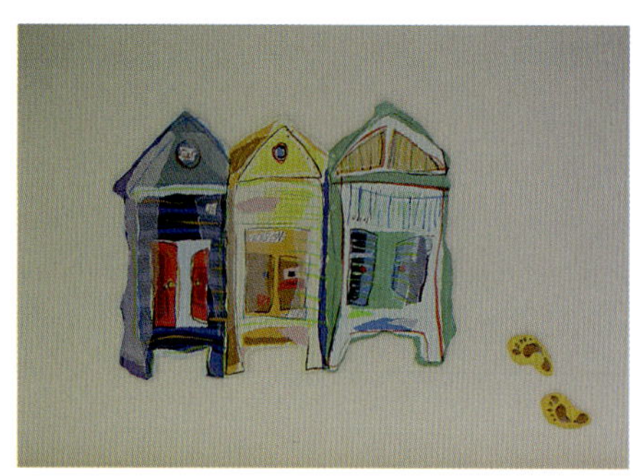

Alexander, Rachael b.1965 & **Muncaster, Jenny** b.1966
Beach Huts c.2001
acrylic on board 70 x 100
301

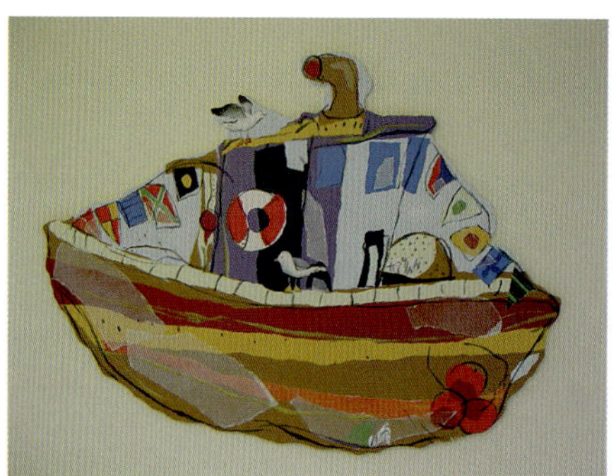

Alexander, Rachael b.1965 & **Muncaster, Jenny** b.1966
Fishing Boat c.2001
acrylic on board 100 x 150
300

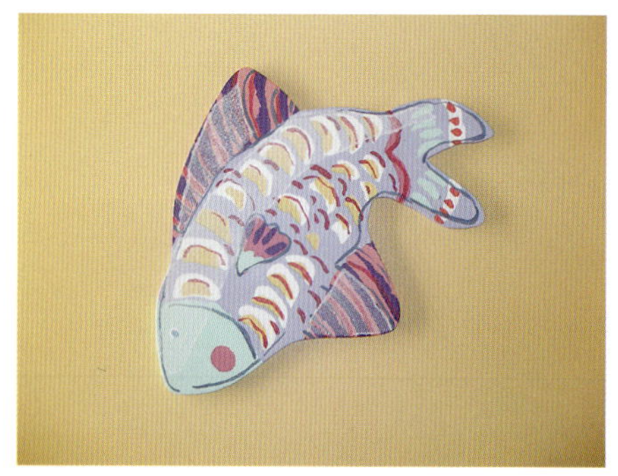

Alexander, Rachael b.1965 & **Muncaster, Jenny** b.1966
Ocean Theme Painting c.2001
acrylic on board
302

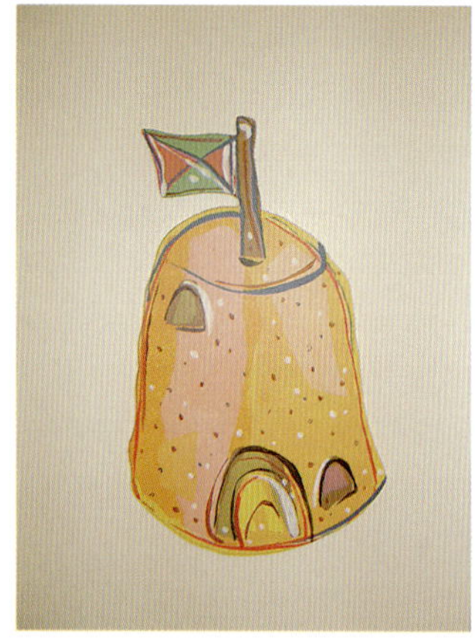

Alexander, Rachael b.1965 & **Muncaster, Jenny** b.1966
Ocean Theme Painting c.2001
acrylic on board
303

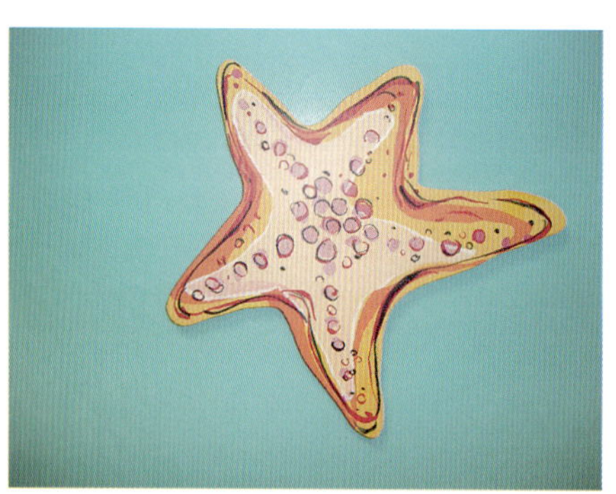

Alexander, Rachael b.1965 & **Muncaster, Jenny** b.1966
Ocean Theme Painting c.2001
acrylic on board
304

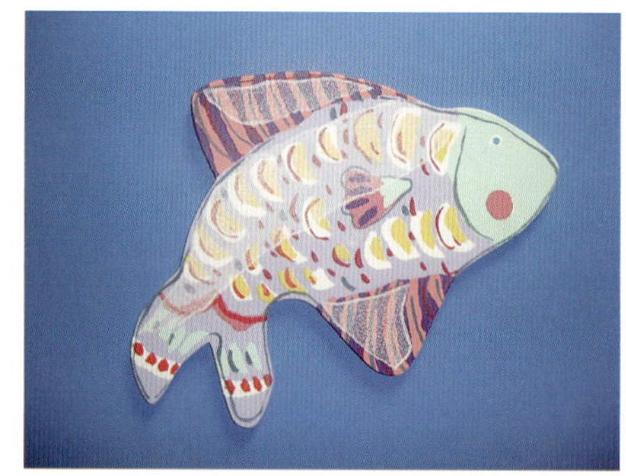

Alexander, Rachael b.1965 & **Muncaster, Jenny** b.1966
Ocean Theme Painting c.2001
acrylic on board
305

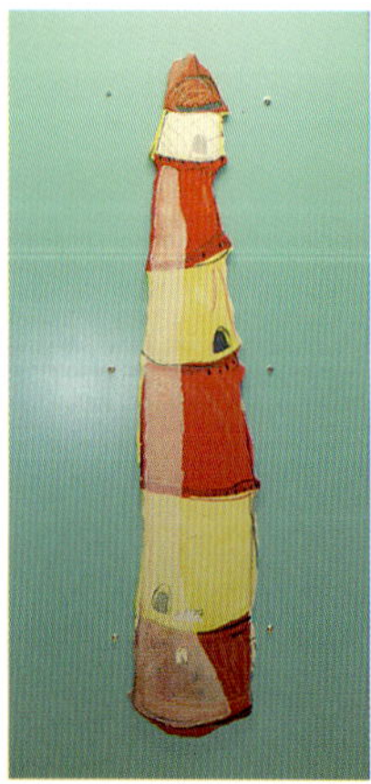

Alexander, Rachael b.1965 & **Muncaster, Jenny** b.1966
Ocean Theme Painting c.2001
acrylic on board
306

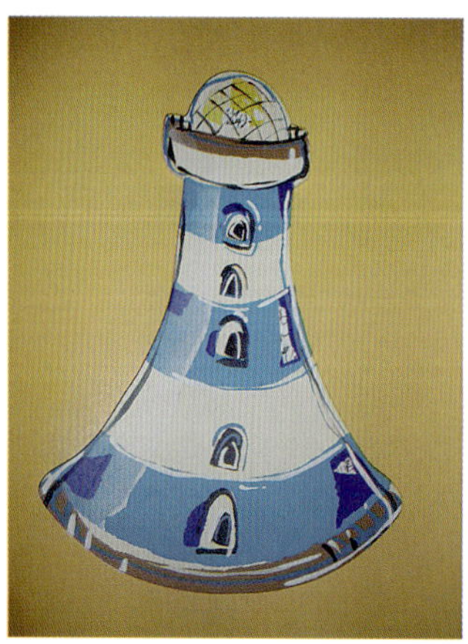

Alexander, Rachael b.1965 & **Muncaster, Jenny** b.1966
Ocean Theme Painting c.2001
acrylic on board
307

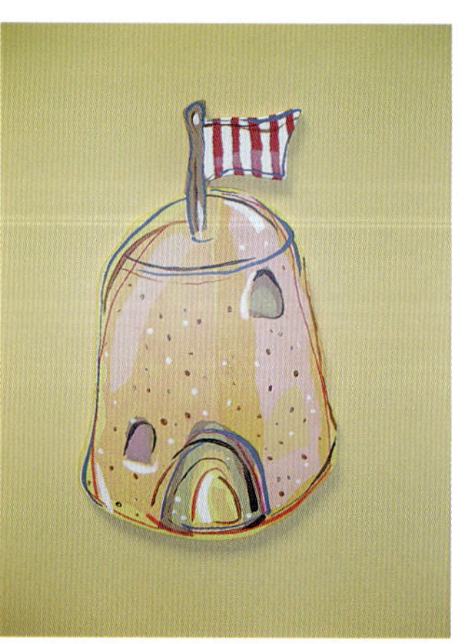

Alexander, Rachael b.1965 & **Muncaster, Jenny** b.1966
Ocean Theme Painting c.2001
acrylic on board
308

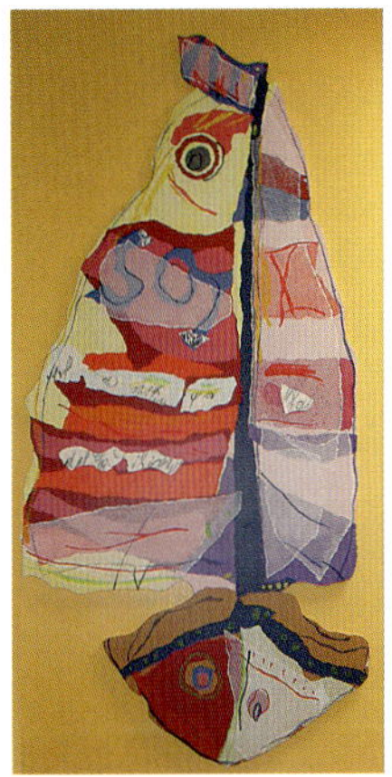

Alexander, Rachael b.1965 & **Muncaster, Jenny** b.1966
Ocean Theme Painting c.2001
acrylic on board
309

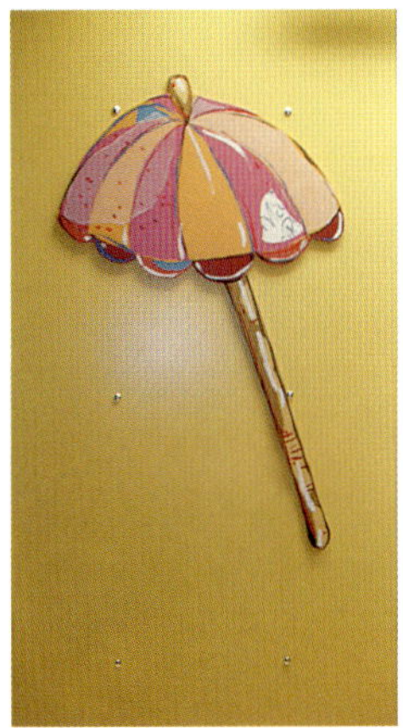

Alexander, Rachael b.1965 & **Muncaster, Jenny** b.1966
Ocean Theme Painting c.2001
acrylic on board
310

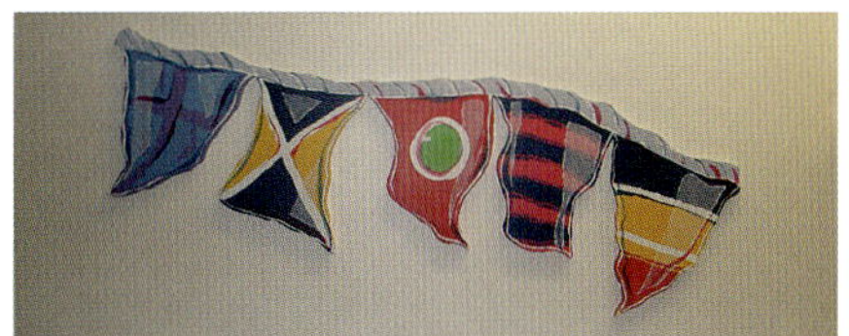

Alexander, Rachael b.1965 & **Muncaster, Jenny** b.1966
Ocean Theme Painting c.2001
acrylic on board
311

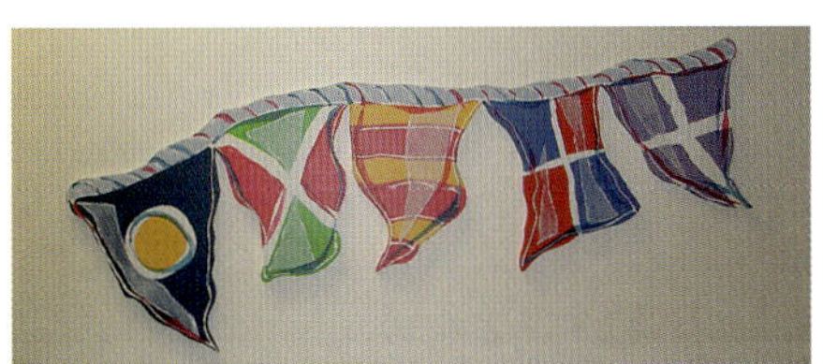

Alexander, Rachael b.1965 & **Muncaster, Jenny** b.1966
Ocean Theme Painting c.2001
acrylic on board
312

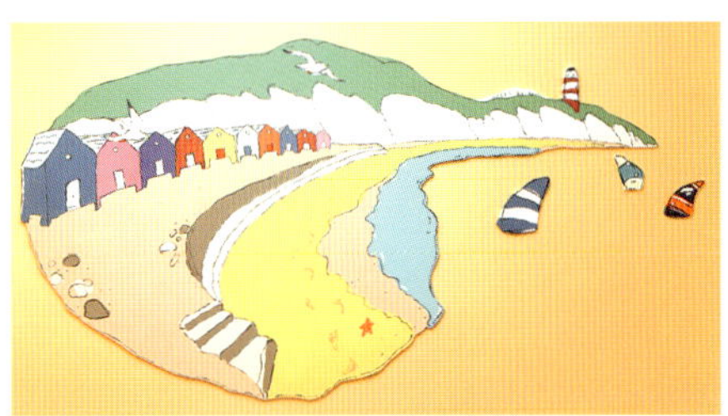

Alexander, Rachael b.1965 & **Muncaster, Jenny** b.1966
Seascapes: Beach Huts 2006
acrylic on board 100 x 200
31

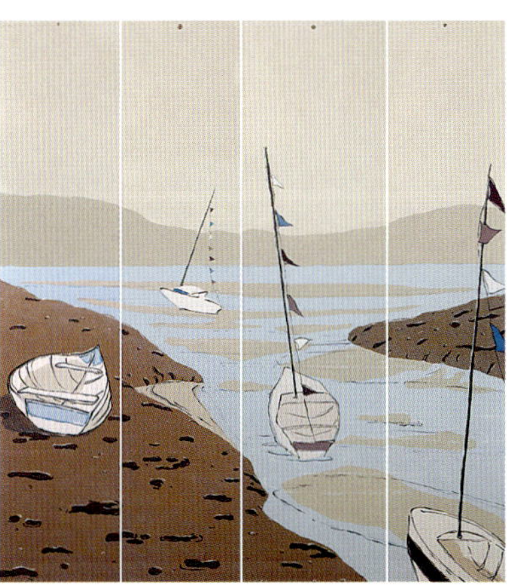

Alexander, Rachael b.1965 & **Muncaster, Jenny** b.1966
Seascapes: Estuary 2006
acrylic on board 120 x 100
28_P1

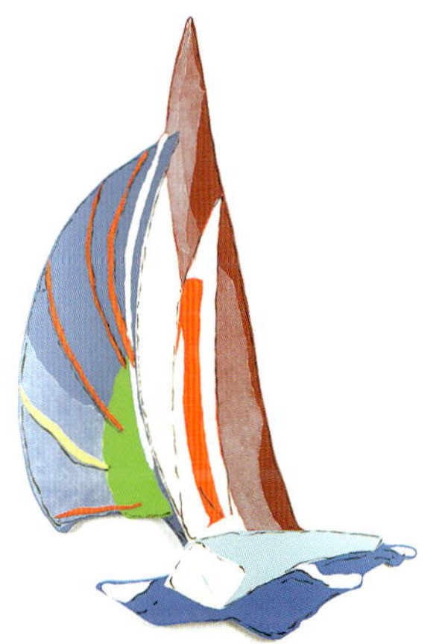

Alexander, Rachael b.1965 & **Muncaster, Jenny** b.1966
Seascapes: Sailing Boat 2006
acrylic on board 138 x 58
15

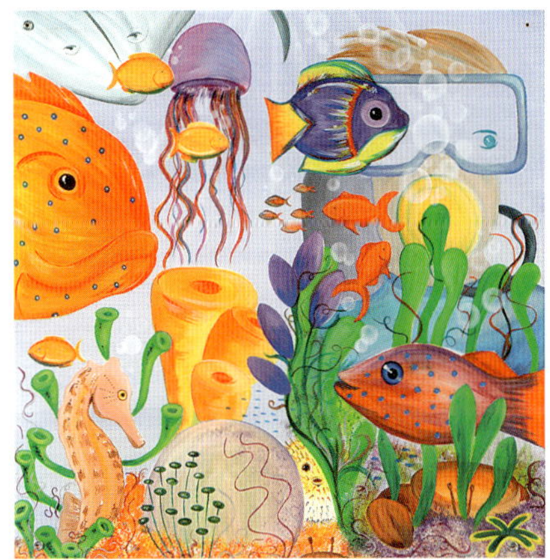

Cook, Lisa b.1973
Diver and Fish 2005
acrylic on board 75 x 75
69

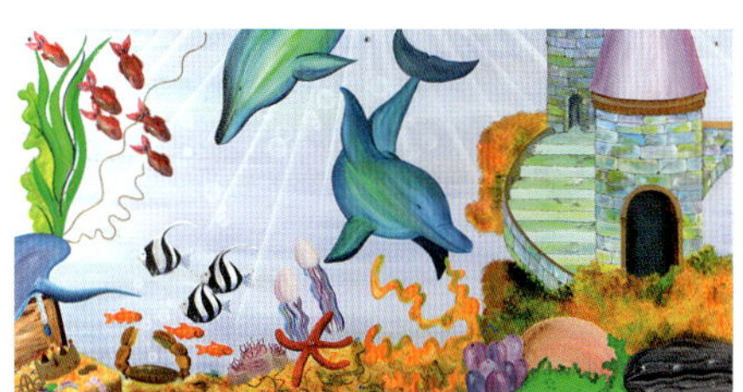

Cook, Lisa b.1973
Dolphin and Castle 2005
acrylic on board 100 x 200
68

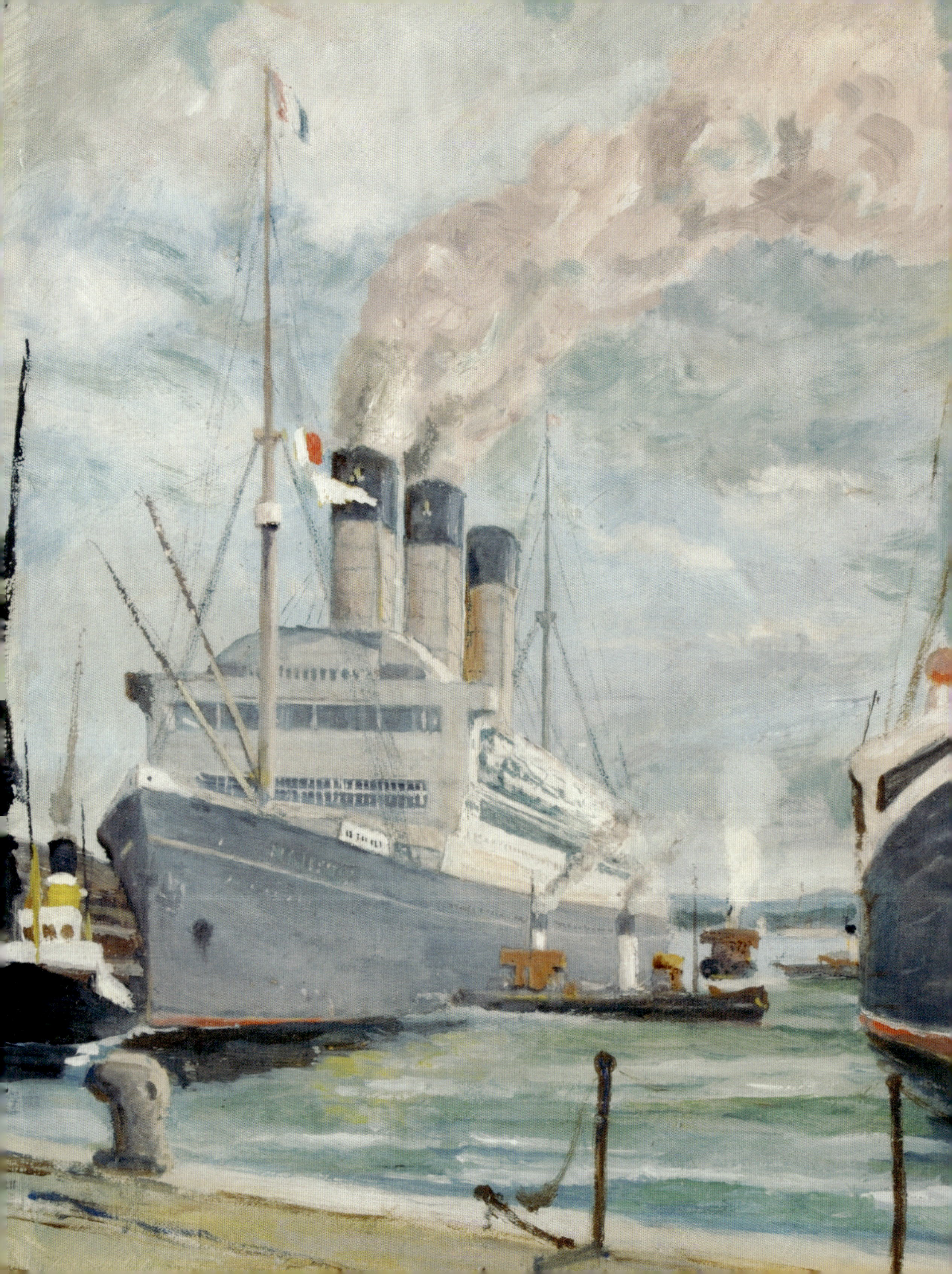

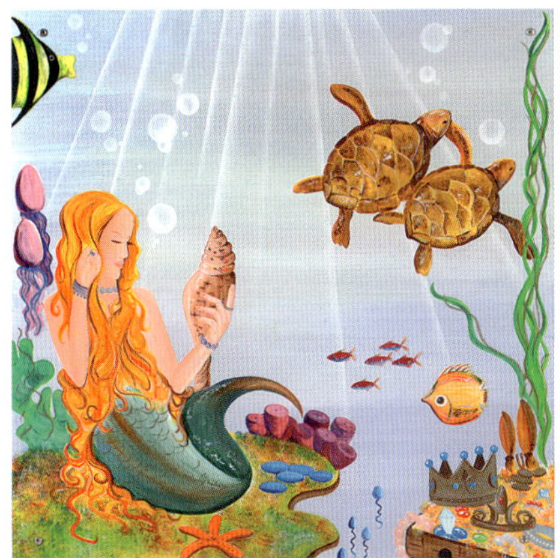

Cook, Lisa b.1973
Mermaid and Turtles 2005
acrylic on board 100 x 100
67

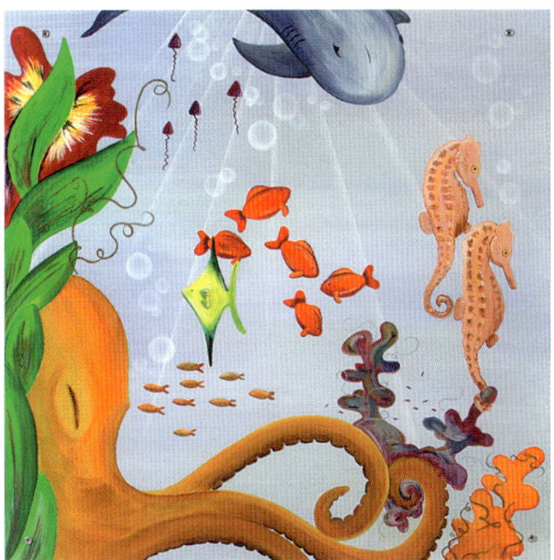

Cook, Lisa b.1973
Octopus and Seahorses 2005
acrylic on board 100 x 100
66

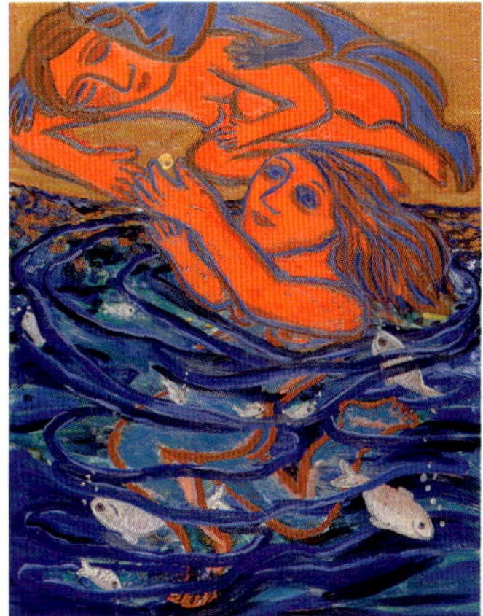

Cooper, Eileen b.1953
To Steal a Wedding Ring
oil on canvas 145 x 114
138

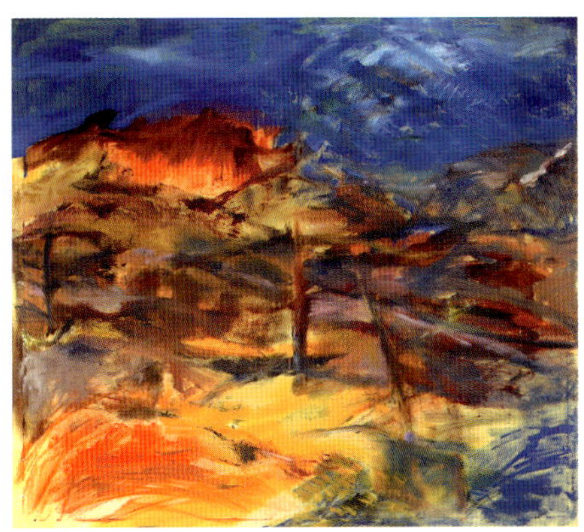

Gingell, Mary
Australian Outback 1987
acrylic on canvas 174 x 193
70

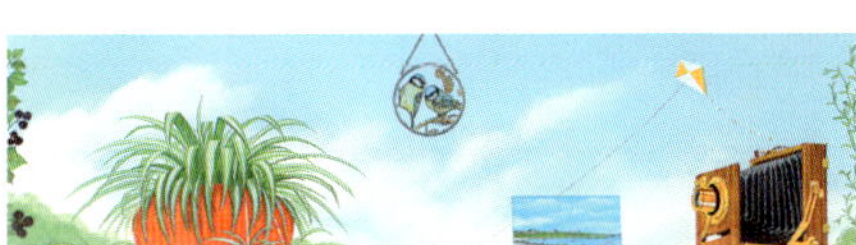

Gradidge, Daphne b.1953
Window with a Camera 1990
acrylic on panel 40 x 130
40

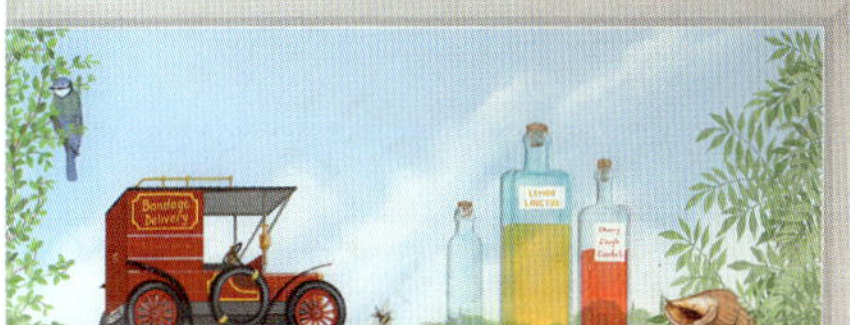

Gradidge, Daphne b.1953
Window with a Car 1990
acrylic on panel 40 x 105
34

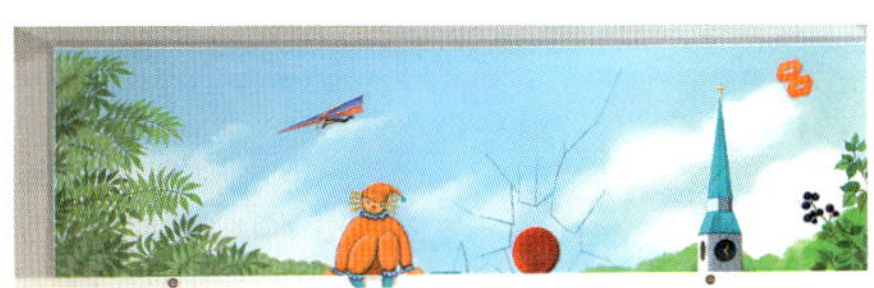

Gradidge, Daphne b.1953
Window with a Clown 1990
acrylic on panel 40 x 130
42

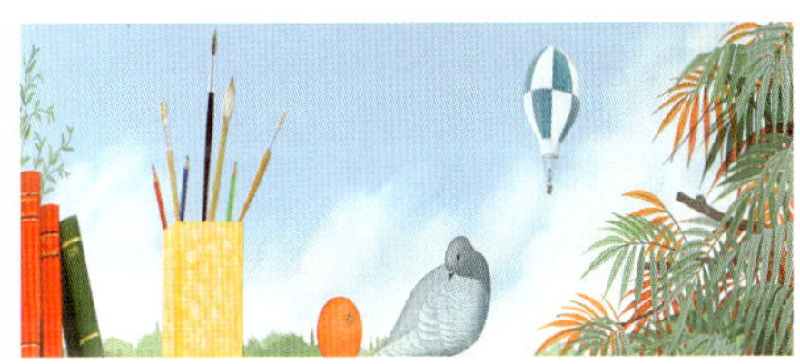

Gradidge, Daphne b.1953
Window with a Hot Air Balloon 1990
acrylic on panel 40 x 105
38

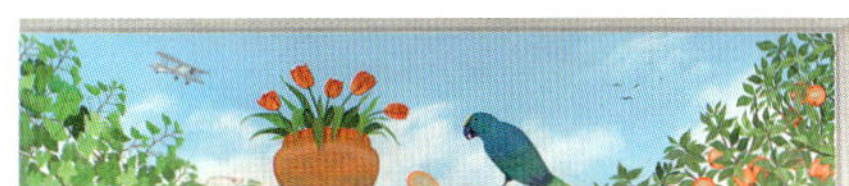

Gradidge, Daphne b.1953
Window with a Parrot 1990
acrylic on panel 40 x 180
62

Facing page: Cozens, Arthur, 1880–1947, *White Star Liner 'Majestic' (1922–1936)* (detail), Southampton City Museums, (p. 151)

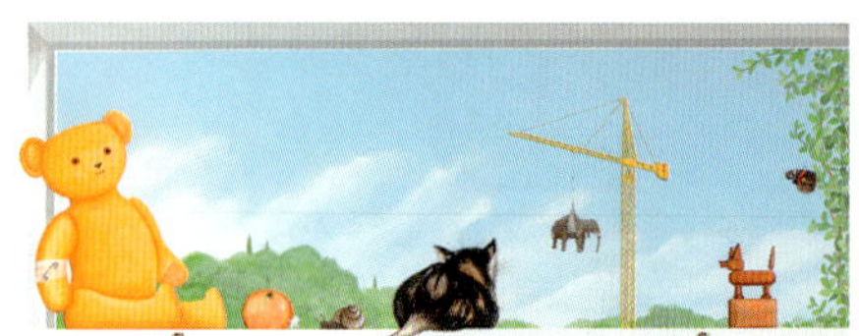

Gradidge, Daphne b.1953
Window with a Teddy Bear 1990
acrylic on panel 40 x 105
35

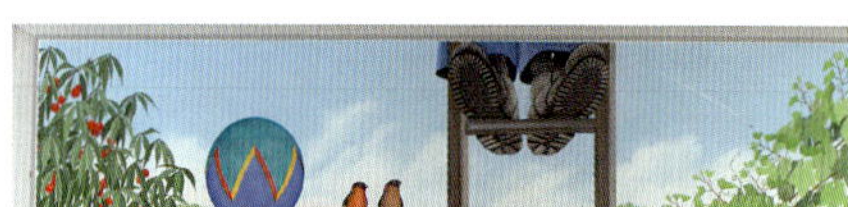

Gradidge, Daphne b.1953
Window with Feet 1990
acrylic on panel 40 x 180
63

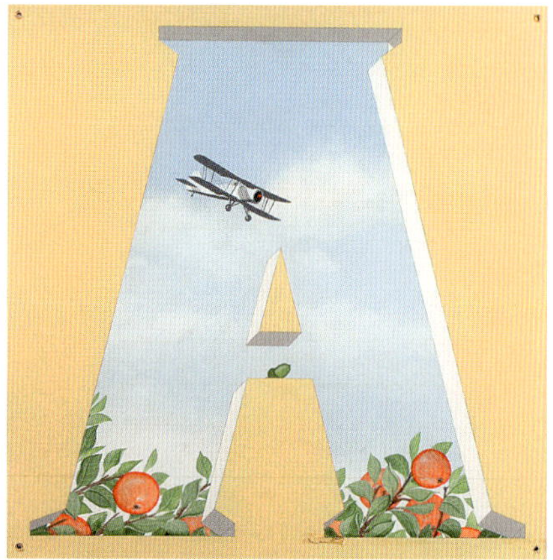

Gradidge, Daphne b.1953
A 1992
acrylic on MDF board 60.8 x 60.8
47

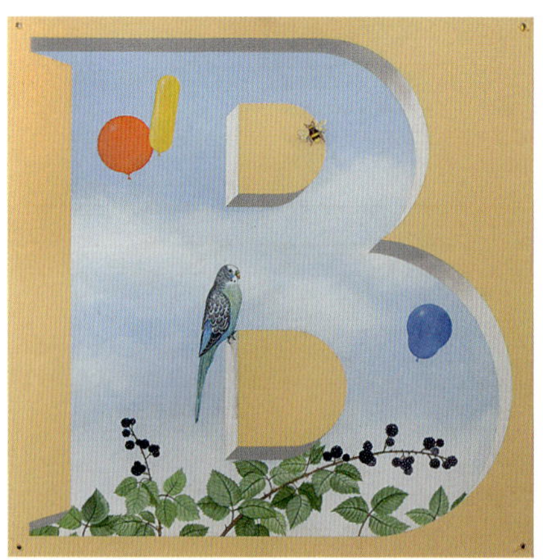

Gradidge, Daphne b.1953
B 1992
acrylic on MDF board 60.8 x 60.8
46

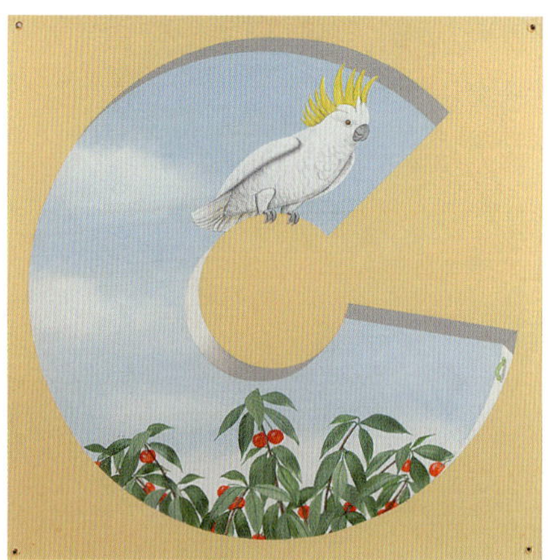

Gradidge, Daphne b.1953
C 1992
acrylic on MDF board 60.8 x 60.8
48

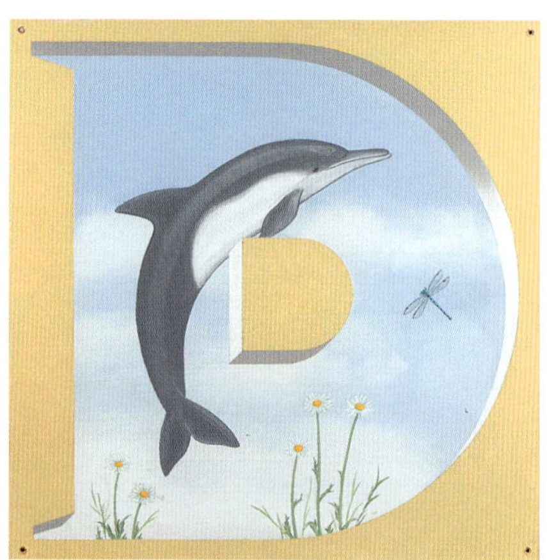

Gradidge, Daphne b.1953
D 1992
acrylic on MDF board 60.8 x 60.8
49

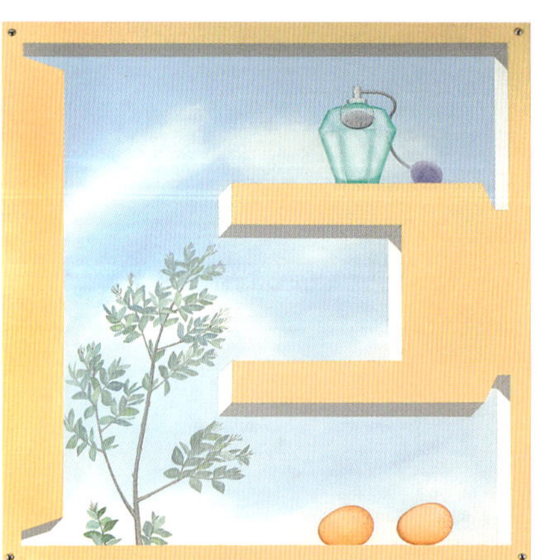

Gradidge, Daphne b.1953
E 1992
acrylic on MDF board 60.8 x 60.8
65

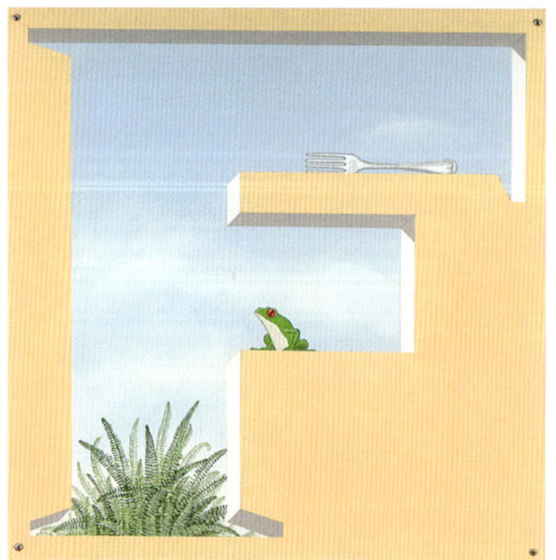

Gradidge, Daphne b.1953
F 1992
acrylic on MDF board 60.8 x 60.8
64

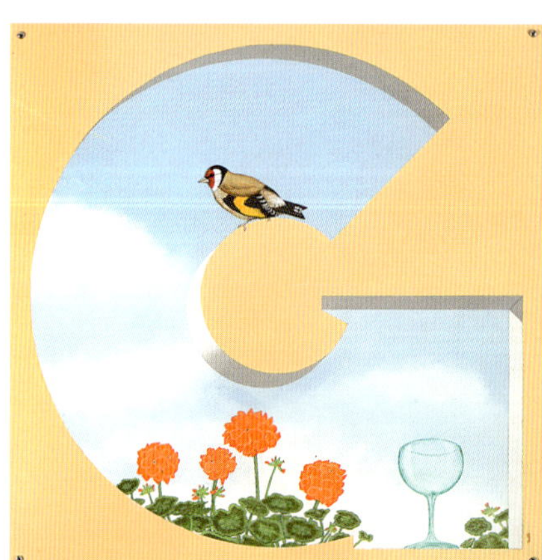

Gradidge, Daphne b.1953
G 1992
acrylic on MDF board 60.8 x 60.8
61

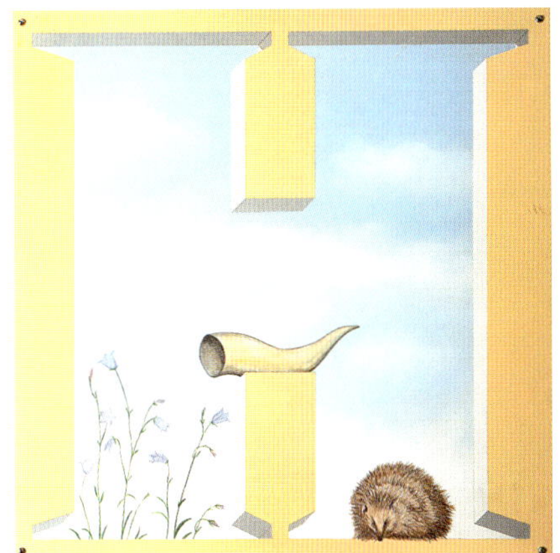

Gradidge, Daphne b.1953
H 1992
acrylic on MDF board 60.8 x 60.8
60

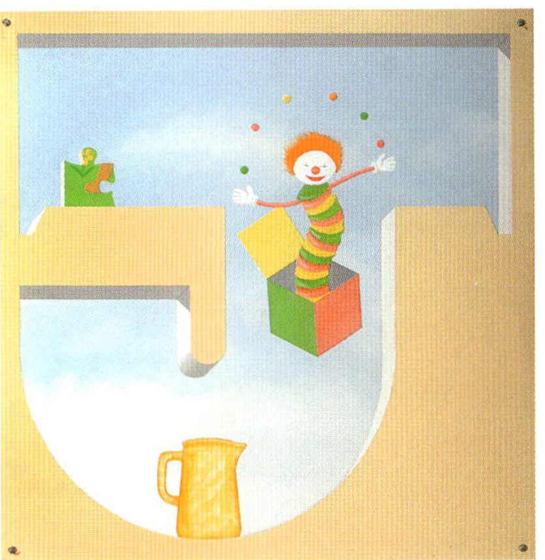

Gradidge, Daphne b.1953
J 1992
acrylic on MDF board 60.8 x 60.8
59

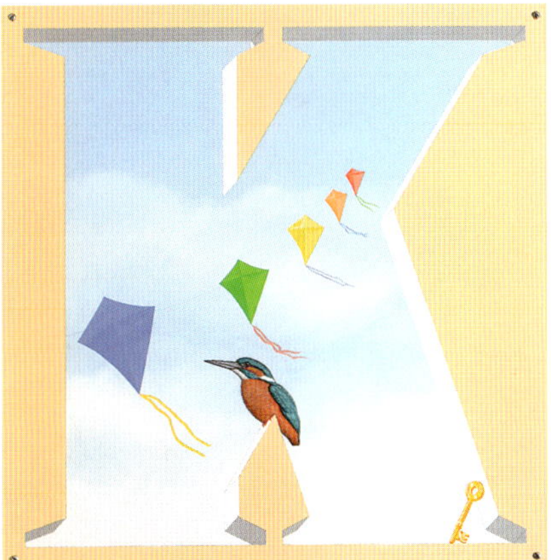

Gradidge, Daphne b.1953
K 1992
acrylic on MDF board 60.8 x 60.8
58

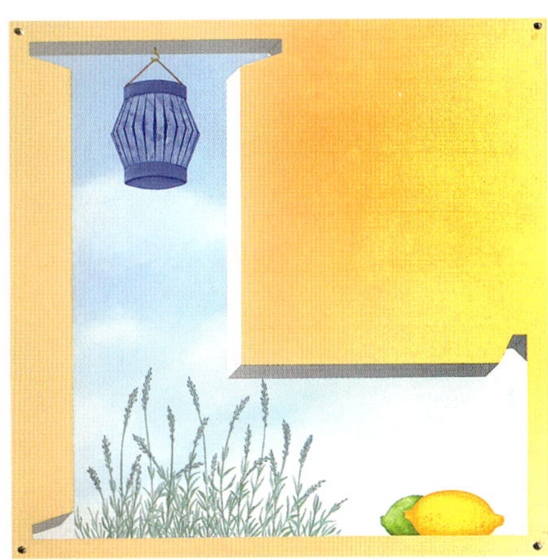

Gradidge, Daphne b.1953
L 1992
acrylic on MDF board 60.8 x 60.8
57

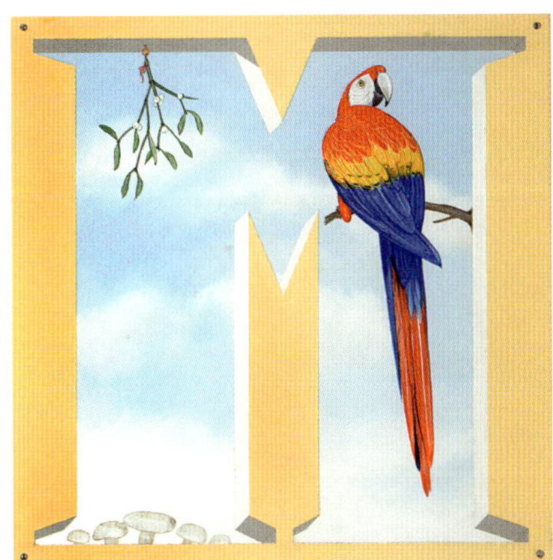

Gradidge, Daphne b.1953
M 1992
acrylic on MDF board 60.8 x 60.8
45

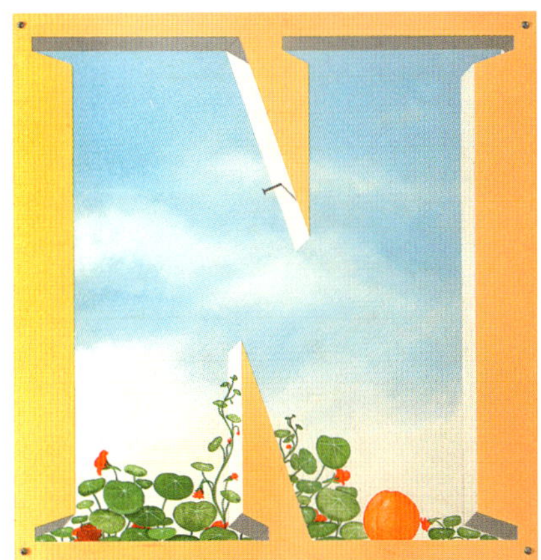

Gradidge, Daphne b.1953
N 1992
acrylic on MDF board 60.8 x 60.8
44

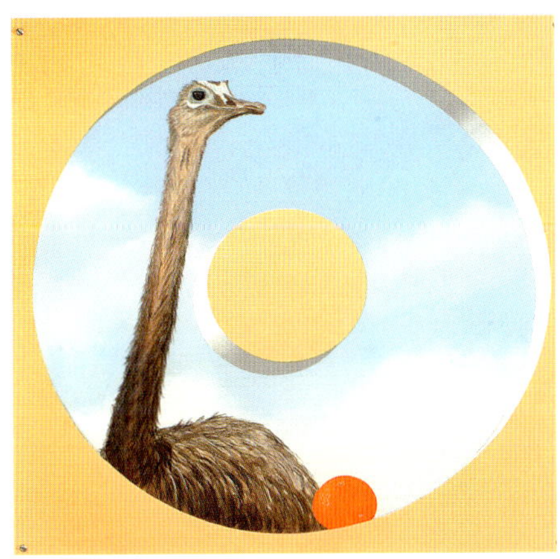

Gradidge, Daphne b.1953
O 1992
acrylic on MDF board 60.8 x 60.8
44b

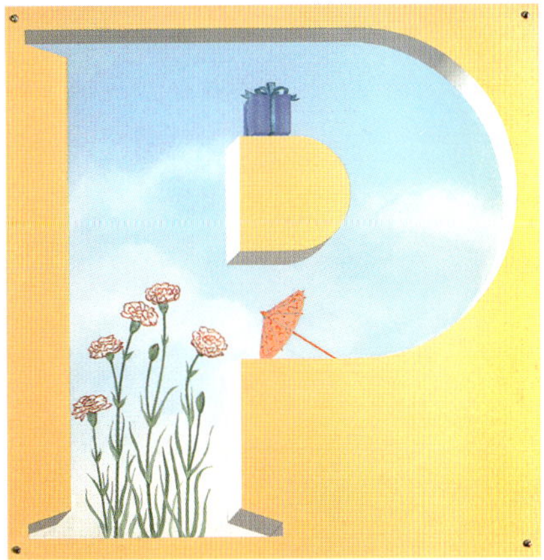

Gradidge, Daphne b.1953
P 1992
acrylic on MDF board 60.8 x 60.8
43

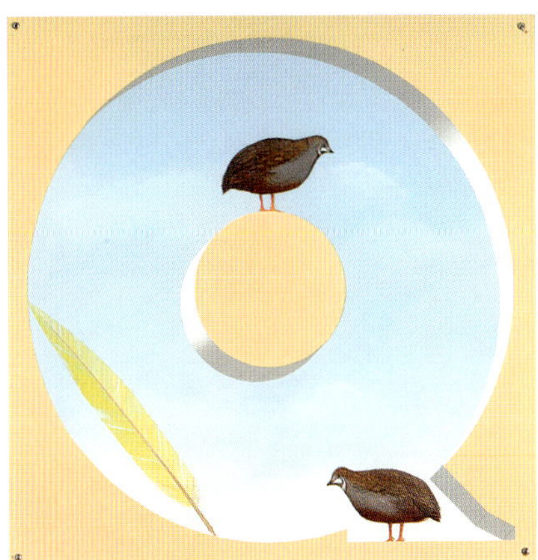

Gradidge, Daphne b.1953
Q 1992
acrylic on MDF board 60.8 x 60.8
41

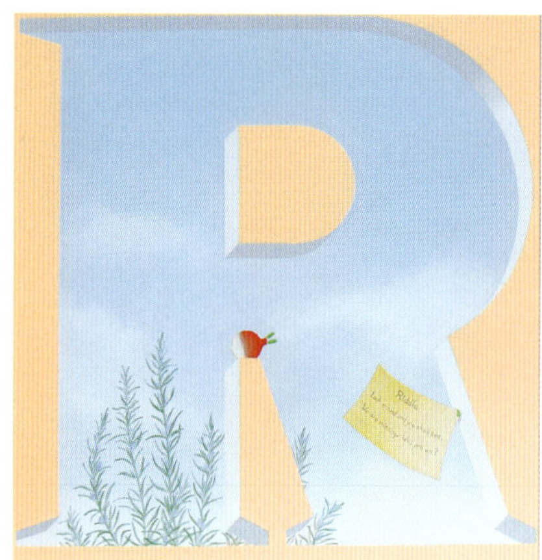

Gradidge, Daphne b.1953
R 1992
acrylic on MDF board 60.8 x 60.8
39

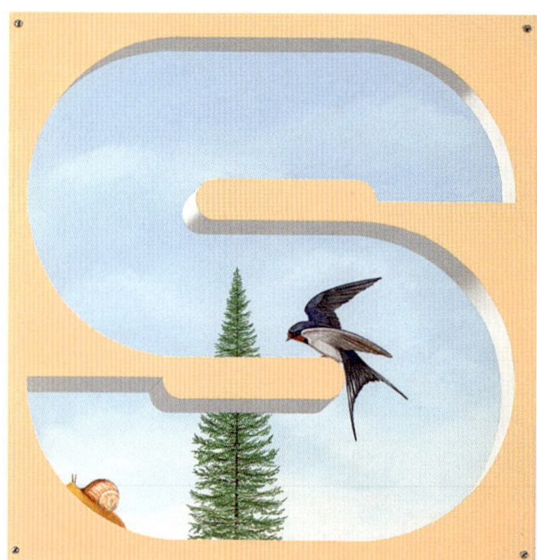

Gradidge, Daphne b.1953
S 1992
acrylic on MDF board 60.8 x 60.8
37

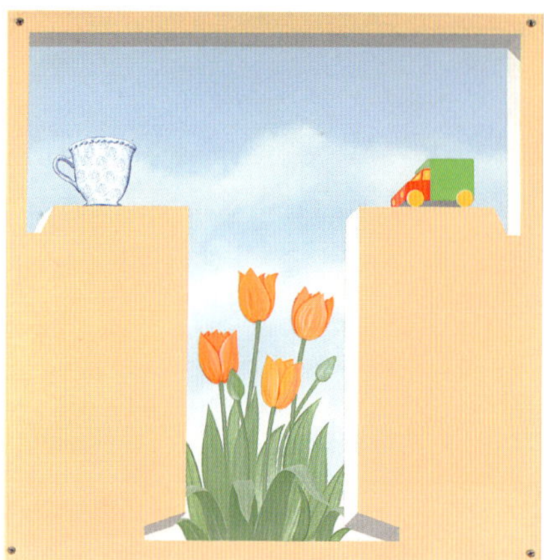

Gradidge, Daphne b.1953
T 1992
acrylic on MDF board 60.8 x 60.8
36

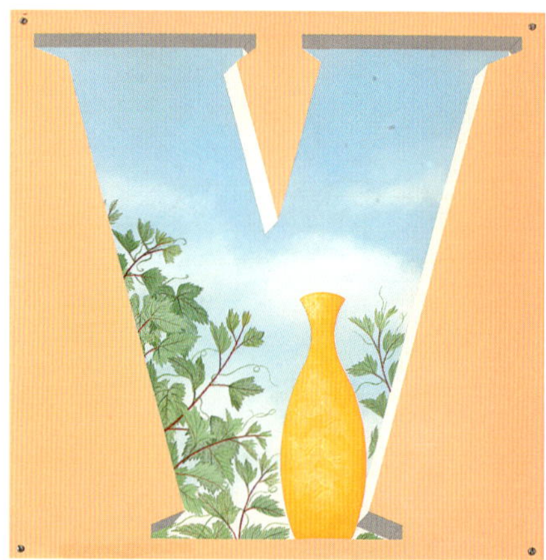

Gradidge, Daphne b.1953
V 1992
acrylic on MDF board 60.8 x 60.8
33

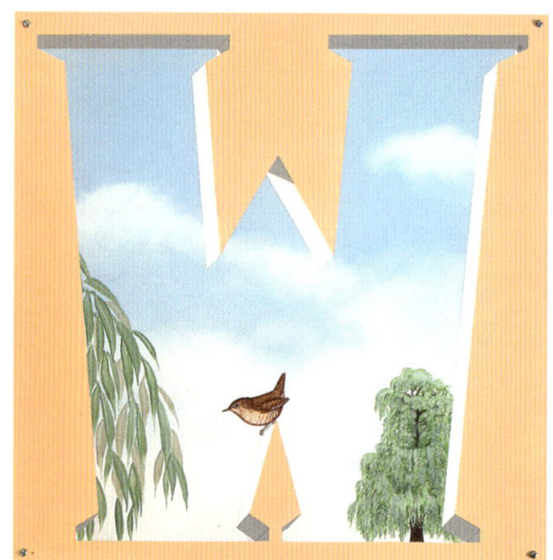

Gradidge, Daphne b.1953
W 1992
acrylic on MDF board 60.8 x 60.8
32

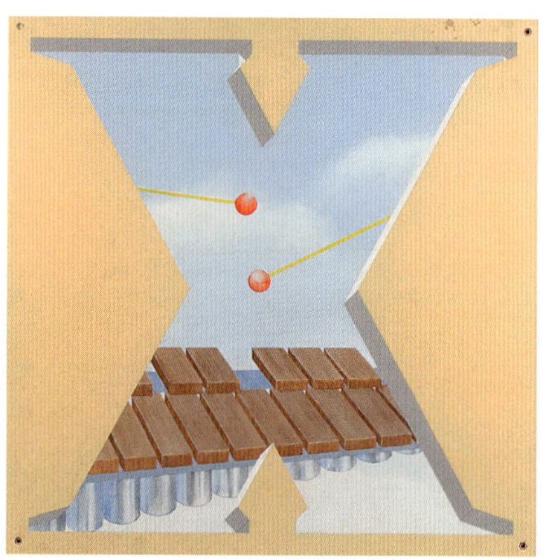

Gradidge, Daphne b.1953
X 1992
acrylic on MDF board 60.8 x 60.8
50

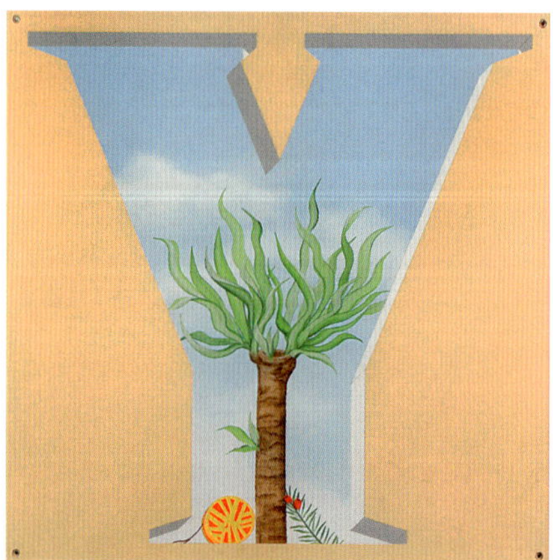

Gradidge, Daphne b.1953
Y 1992
acrylic on MDF board 60.8 x 60.8
51

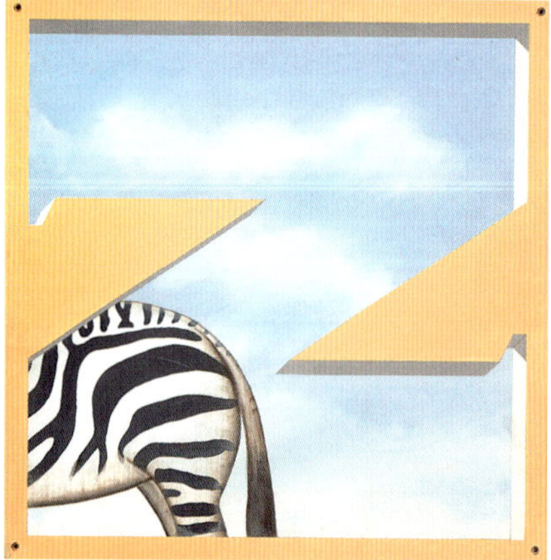

Gradidge, Daphne b.1953
Z 1992
acrylic on MDF board 60.8 x 60.8
56

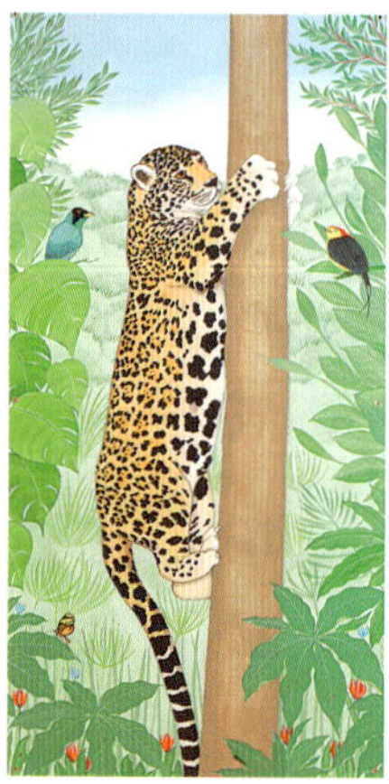

Gradidge, Daphne b.1953
Jaguar Climbing a Tree 1995
acrylic on board 122.5 x 60
24

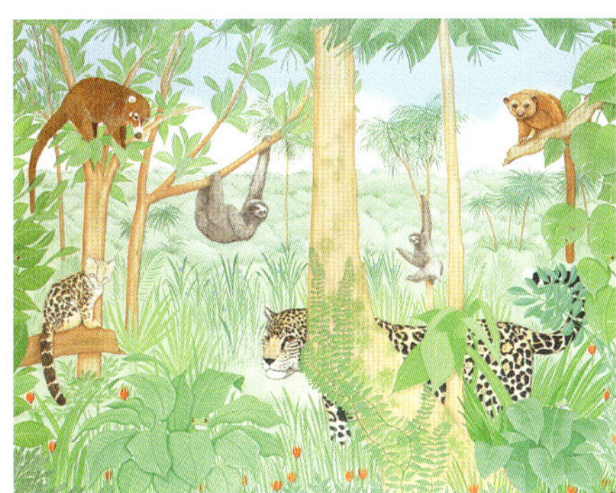

Gradidge, Daphne b.1953
Leopard with Sloths 1995
acrylic on board 122 x 160.4
22

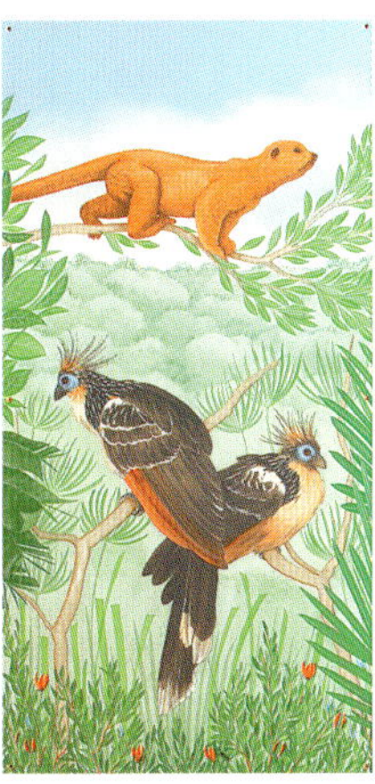

Gradidge, Daphne b.1953
Pair of Crested Birds 1995
acrylic on board 122.5 x 60
25

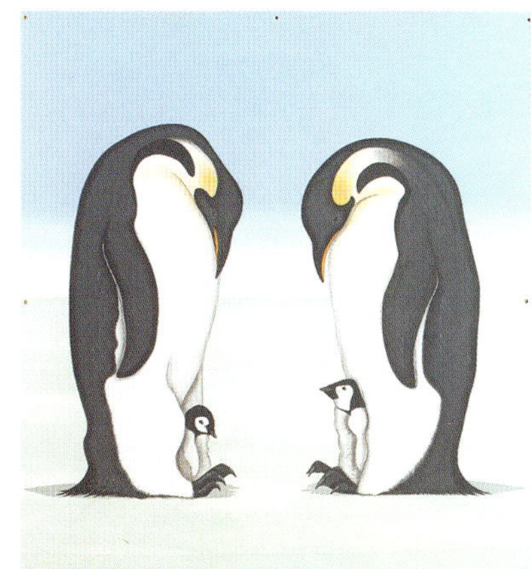

Gradidge, Daphne b.1953
Penguins 1995
acrylic on board 122.5 x 110
23

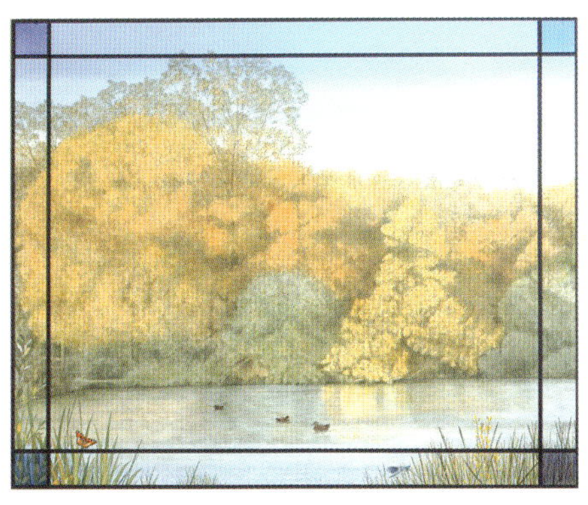

Gradidge, Daphne b.1953
Eyeworth Pond, Fritham 2004
acrylic on board 75 x 90
4

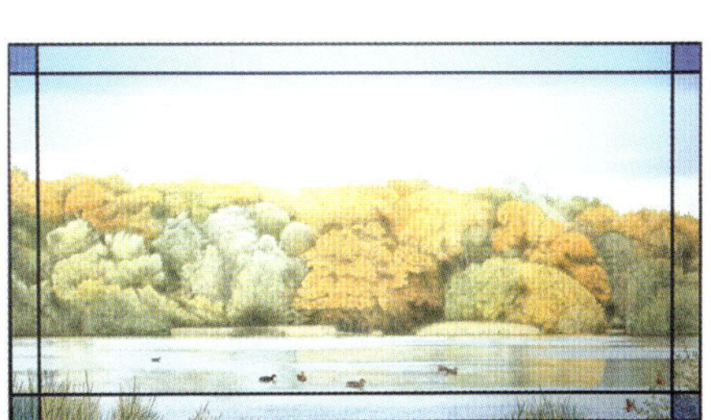

Gradidge, Daphne b.1953
Eyeworth Pond, Fritham 2004
acrylic on board 75 x 140
5

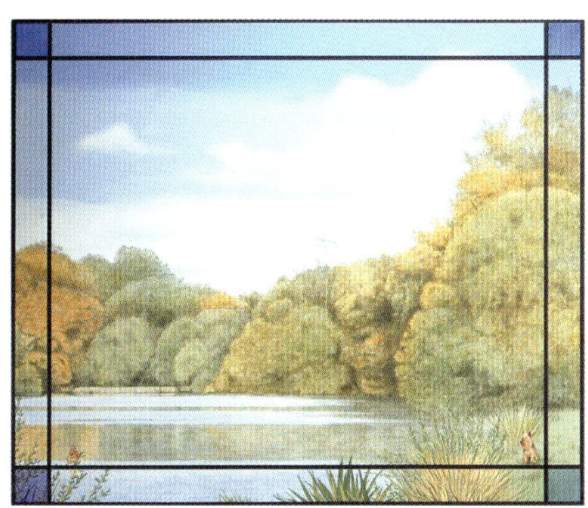

Gradidge, Daphne b.1953
Eyeworth Pond, Fritham 2004
acrylic on board 75 x 90
6

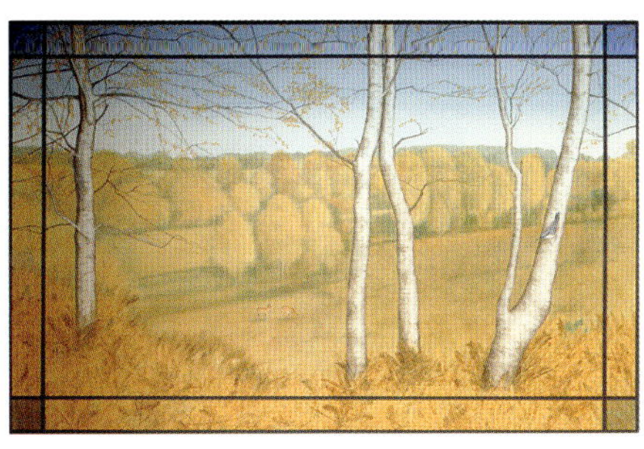

Gradidge, Daphne b.1953
Hale Purlieu 2004
acrylic on board 69.8 x 109.8 (E)
7

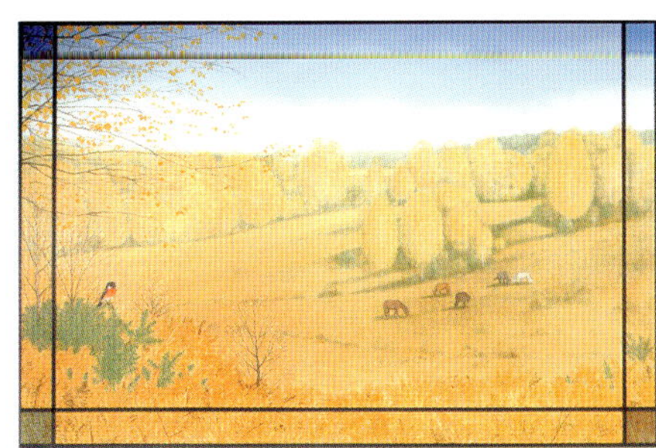

Gradidge, Daphne b.1953
Hale Purlieu 2004
acrylic on board 69.8 x 109.8 (E)
8

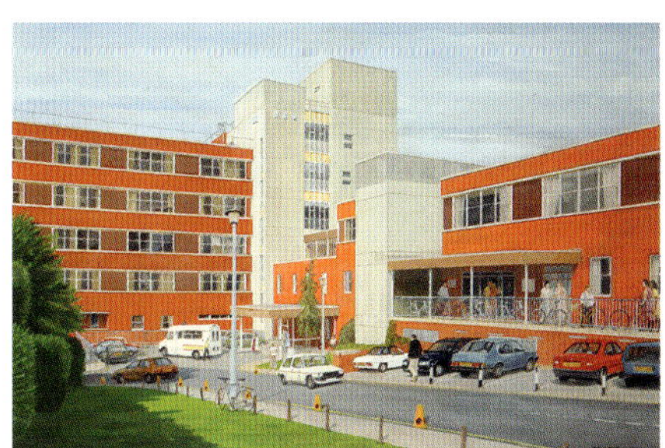

Hoskins, Brian
View of the Princess Anne Hospital 1995
oil on canvas 44.5 x 69
71

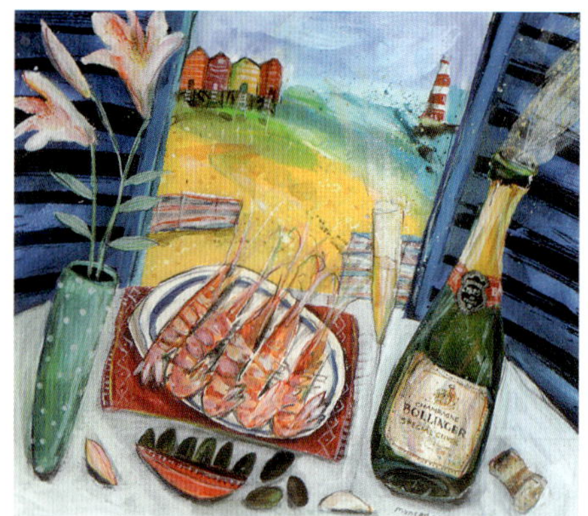

Muncaster, Jenny b.1966
Seafood and Champagne 2001
acrylic on paper 36 x 41
26

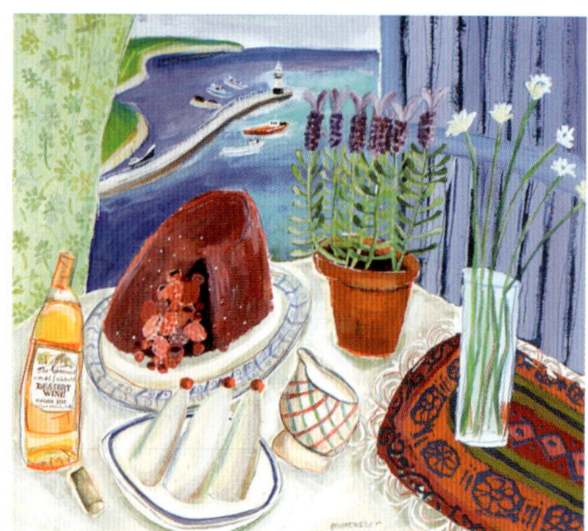

Muncaster, Jenny b.1966
Summer Pudding 2001
acrylic on paper 36 x 41
27

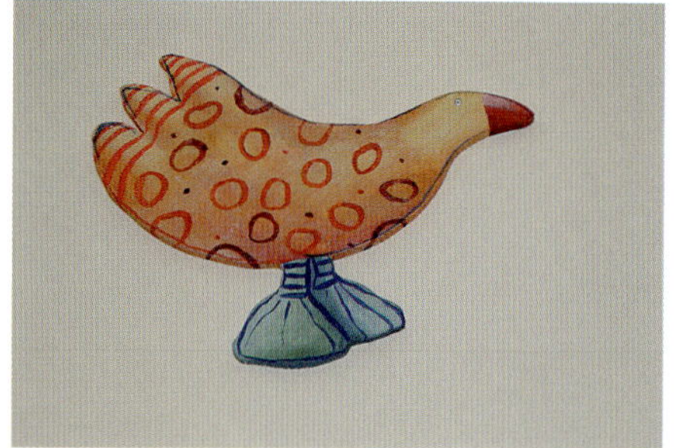

Muncaster, Jenny b.1966
Bird 2002
acrylic on board 50 x 70 (E)
270

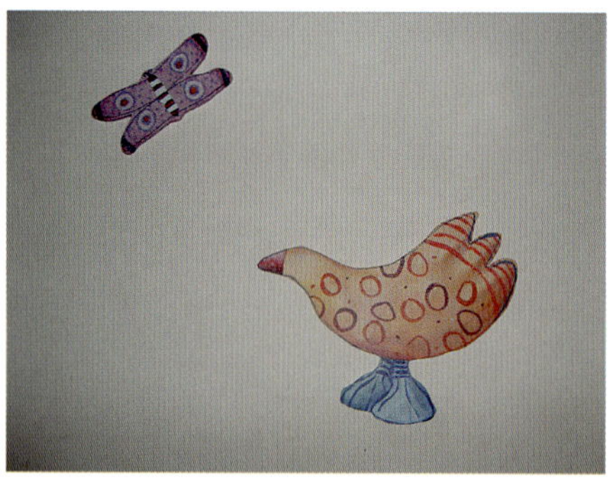

Muncaster, Jenny b.1966
Bird and Butterfly 2002
acrylic on board 75 x 100 (E)
263

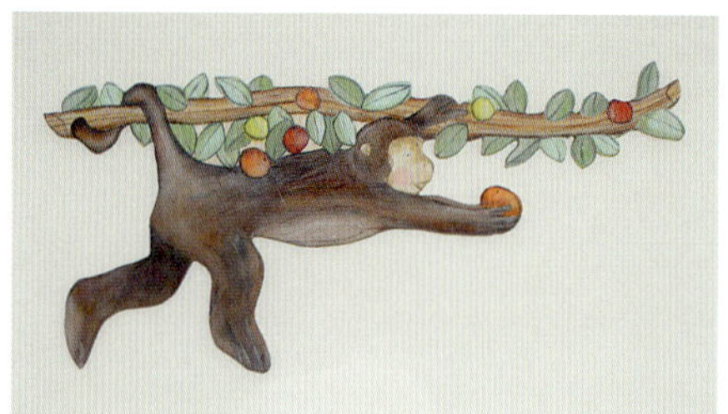

Muncaster, Jenny b.1966
Monkey 2002
acrylic on board 100 x 170 (E)
264

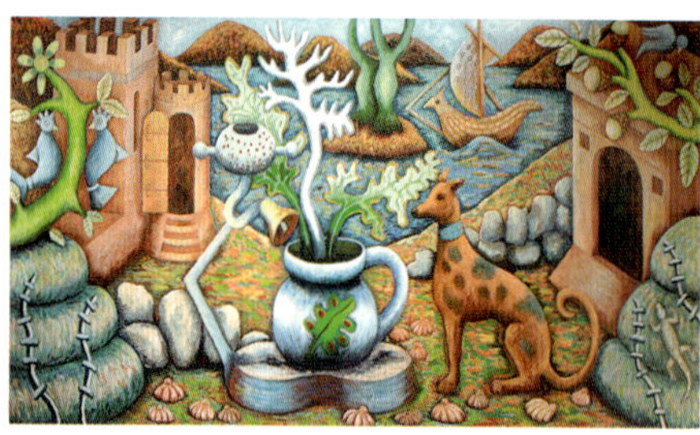

O'Driscoll, Suzanne b.1955
Cornerstones
acrylic on canvas 198 x 397
1

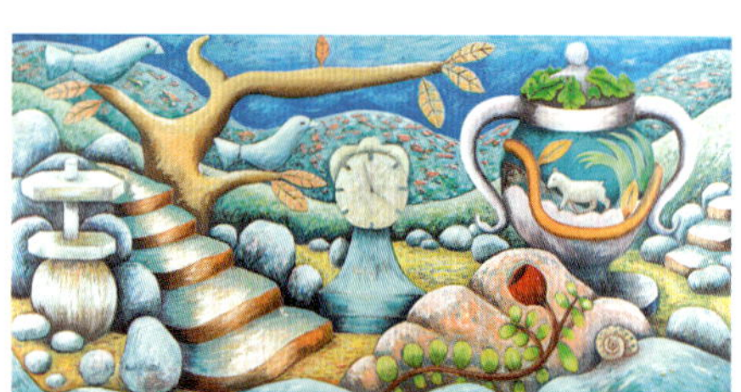

O'Driscoll, Suzanne b.1955
Tea at Four (part 1)
acrylic on canvas 121 x 244
2

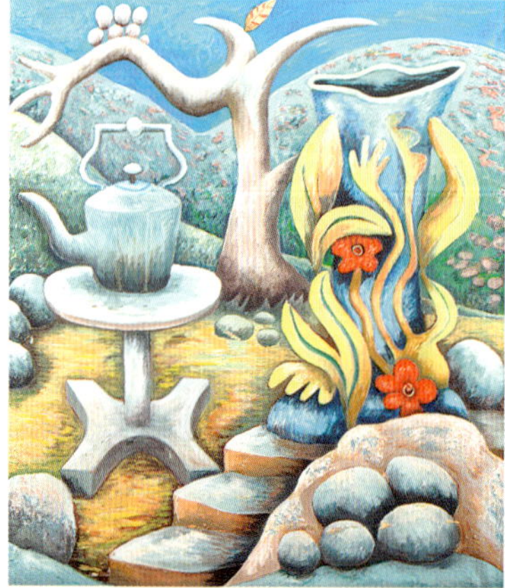

O'Driscoll, Suzanne b.1955
Tea at Four (part 2)
acrylic on canvas 121.7 x 106
3

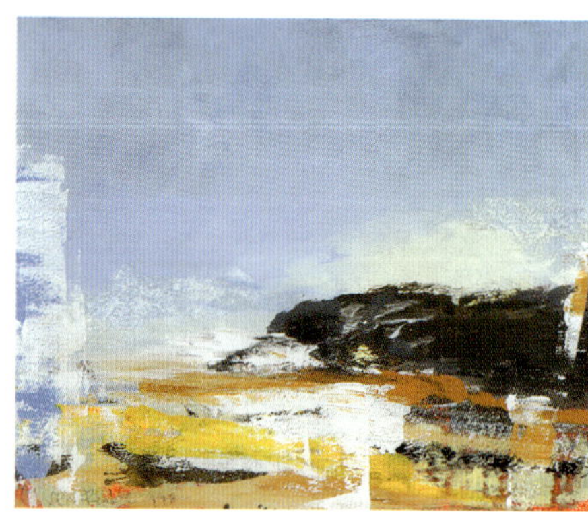

Rankle, Alan b.1952
Further Tales from the Beach House 1998
acrylic on paper 40 x 48.5
21

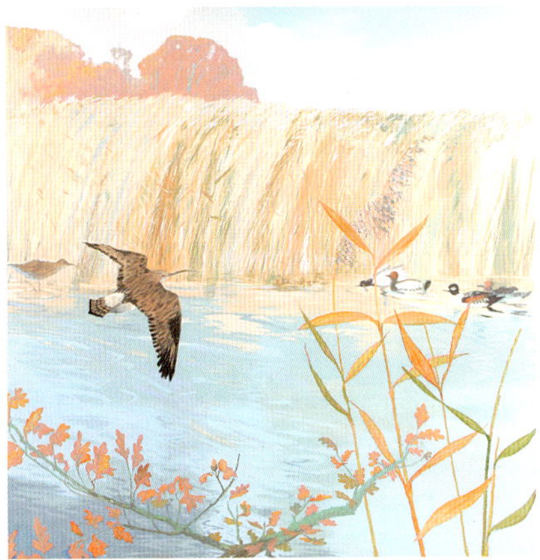

Toms, Anne b.1944
Bird in Flight 1994
acrylic on board 121 x 121
20

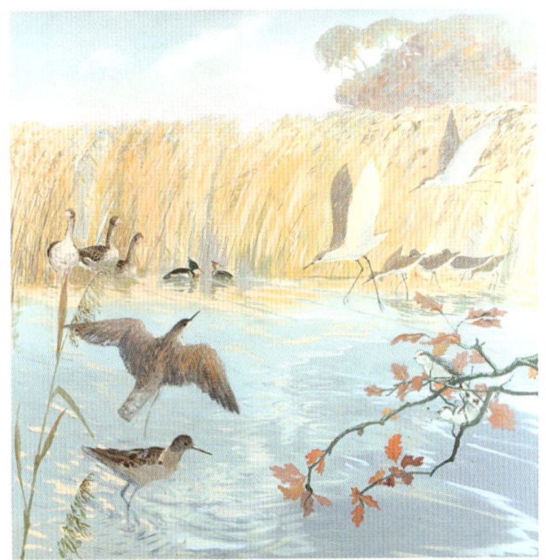

Toms, Anne b.1944
Curlews and Tufted Ducks 1994
acrylic on board 121 x 121
18

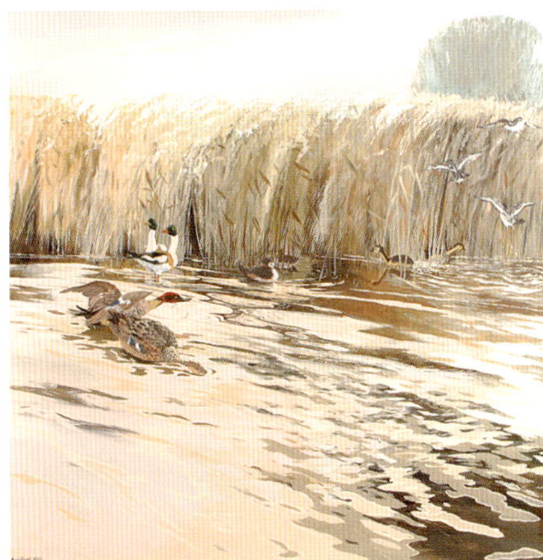

Toms, Anne b.1944
Ducks (triptych, left) 1994
acrylic on board 121 x 121
9

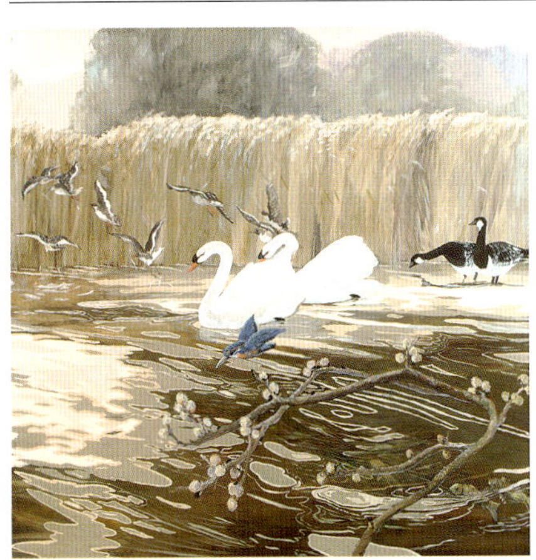

Toms, Anne b.1944
Swans and Kingfisher (triptych, centre) 1994
acrylic on board 121 x 121
10

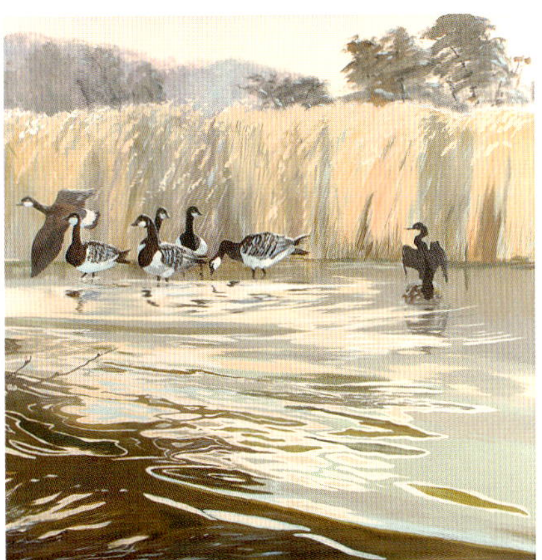

Toms, Anne b.1944
Geese and Cormorant (triptych, right) 1994
acrylic on board 121 x 121
11

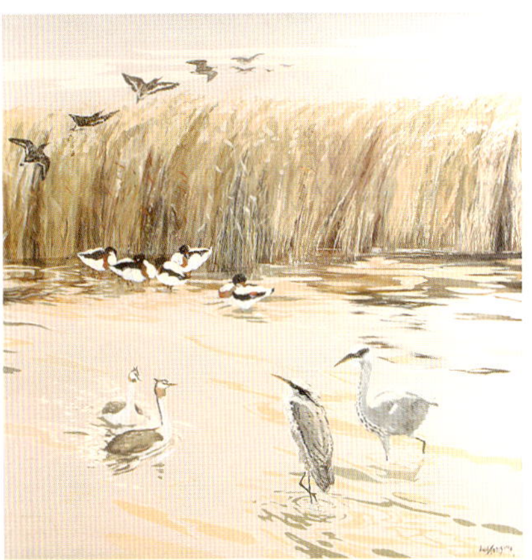

Toms, Anne b.1944
Herons 1994
acrylic on board 121 x 121
12

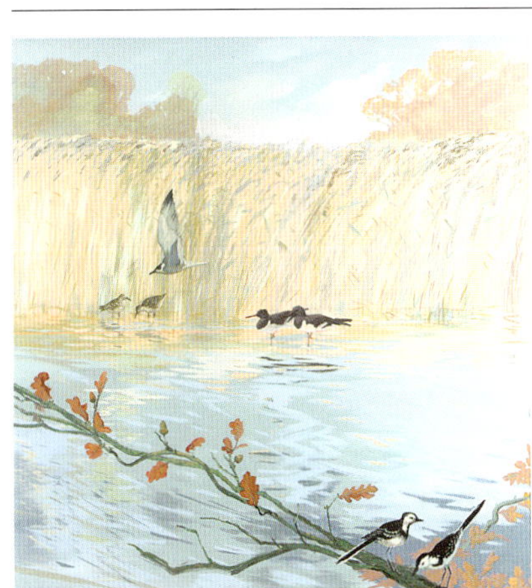

Toms, Anne b.1944
Oyster Catchers and Wagtails 1994
acrylic on board 121 x 121
19

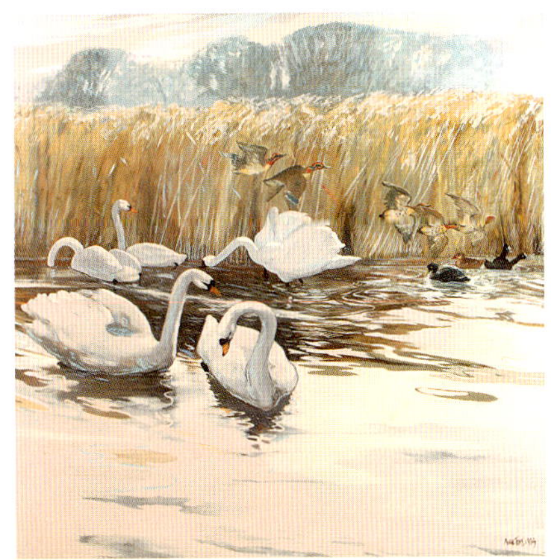

Toms, Anne b.1944
Swans and Ducks in Flight 1994
acrylic on board 121 x 121
13

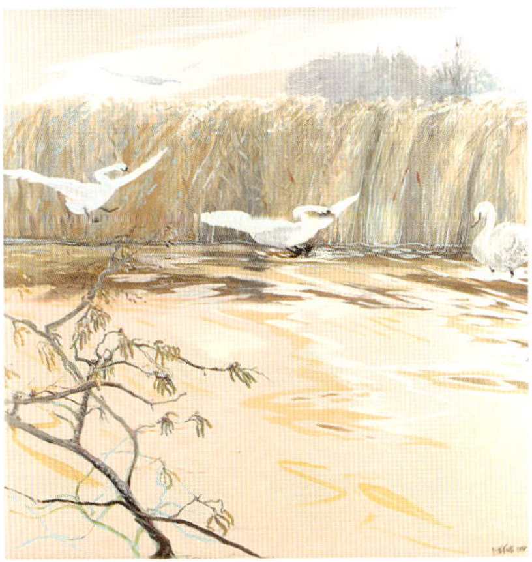

Toms, Anne b.1944
Swans Landing 1994
acrylic on board 121 x 121
17

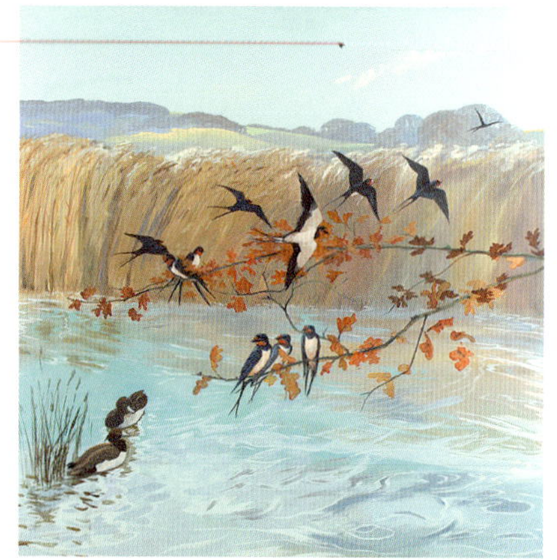

Toms, Anne b.1944
Swifts 1994
acrylic on board 121 x 121
16

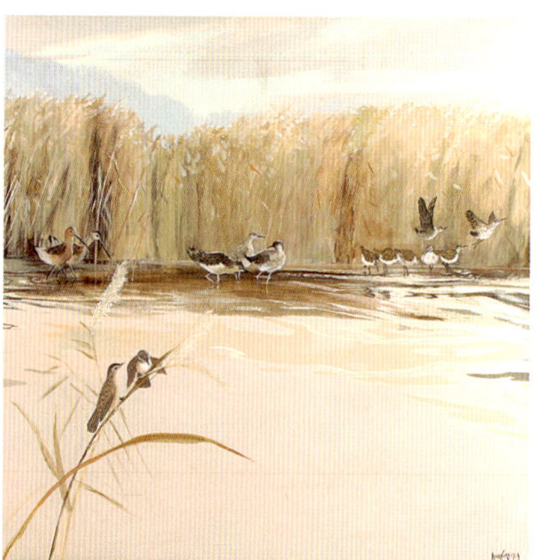

Toms, Anne b.1944
Wading Birds 1994
acrylic on board 121 x 121
14

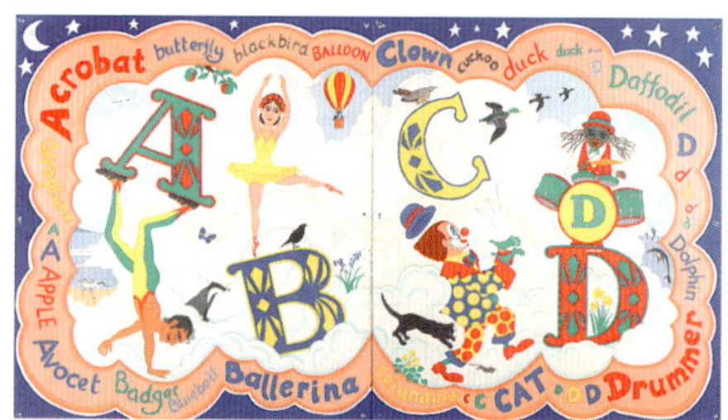

unknown artist
A, B, C, D 1993
acrylic on plasterboard 120 x 215.5
55

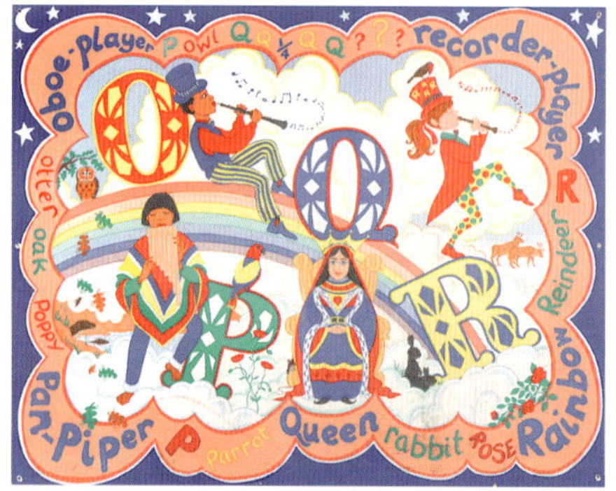

unknown artist
O, P, Q, R 1993
acrylic on plasterboard 120 x 152
54

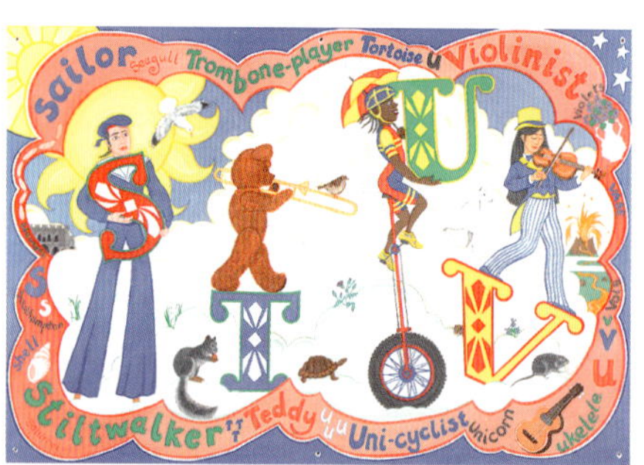

unknown artist
S, T, U, V 1993
acrylic on plasterboard 120 x 179
52

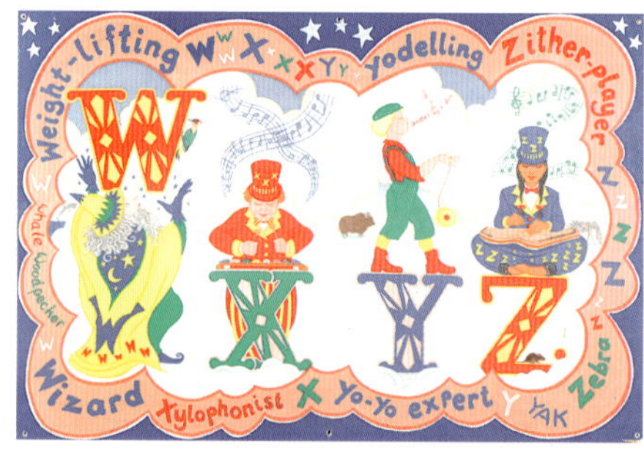

unknown artist
W, X, Y, Z 1993
acrylic on plasterboard 120 x 179
53

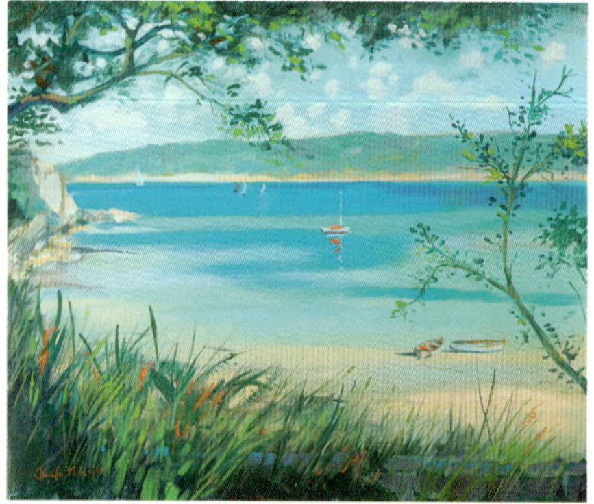

Wright, Jennifer b.1961
Southsands c.2005
oil on canvas 50.5 x 60.5
29

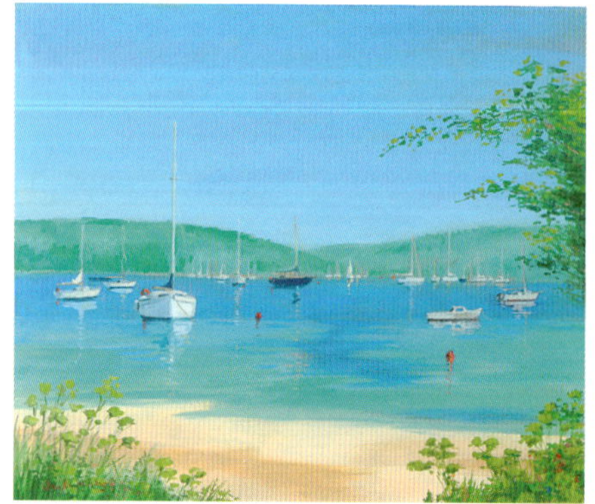

Wright, Jennifer b.1961
Estuary, Late Spring 2006
oil on canvas 50.5 x 60.5
30

University of Southampton

The University of Southampton holds and continues to develop a collection of largely modern and contemporary art that is displayed at various public and semi-public areas in and around the University campuses. The collection comprises approximately 350 works and began during the development of the Highfield campus, and under the direction of the then master-planner, Sir Basil Spence, in the 1960s and 1970s. The collection is overseen by the John Hansard Gallery, an Arts Council funded Gallery which is part of the University and is a temporary exhibitions gallery that does not house a collection itself.

At the core of the collection are a number of sculptural works that are permanently sited in fixed locations in the grounds of the University campus. These include works by David Nash, Barbara Hepworth, Justin Knowles, F. E. McWilliam and Nick Pope.

Within the buildings themselves are displayed a collection of largely two dimensional works that consist of paintings, drawings, prints and photographic works. Many of these are smaller works that hang in corridors, meeting rooms and other less accessible spaces. However, there are a number of more significant works that hang in major public spaces such as the University Library and the entrances to other main buildings. Amongst these are included significant paintings and a number of important works. Earlier works from the 1960s and 1970s are represented by the paintings by Richard Eurich, Richard Smith, Albert Irvin and Mark Lancaster. During the 1980s and 1990s works by Lucy Jones and Michael Kidner were added to the collection. Recent acquisitions include large paintings by the likes of Colin Crumplin.

A completely new University-wide policy is being developed with a more coherent approach being made to the further development of the collection. This will focus on bringing artists, architects and estates planners together by commissioning new work for permanent siting in new buildings or during major reconstruction or refurbishment. The Gallery is in the middle of creating a new database on the collection, which will be completed during 2007.

Stephen Foster, Director of the John Hansard Gallery

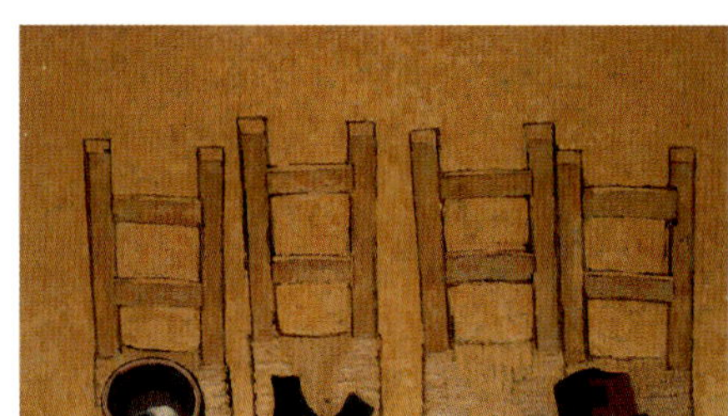

Barrett, Roderic 1920–2000
Waiting Chairs
oil on canvas 75 x 120
16

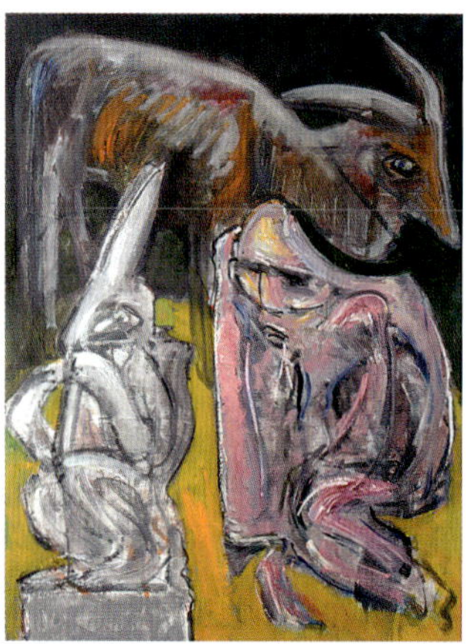

Bird, Philip b.1952
Deer, Ape and Hare 1982
oil on canvas 120 x 92
A1

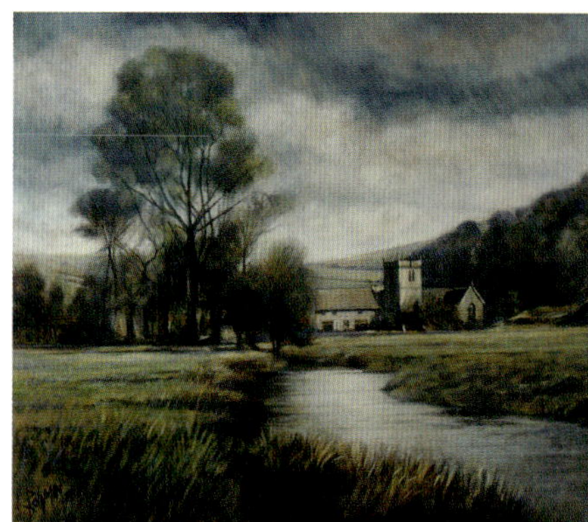

Bowman
River Landscape
oil on canvas 70 x 80
17

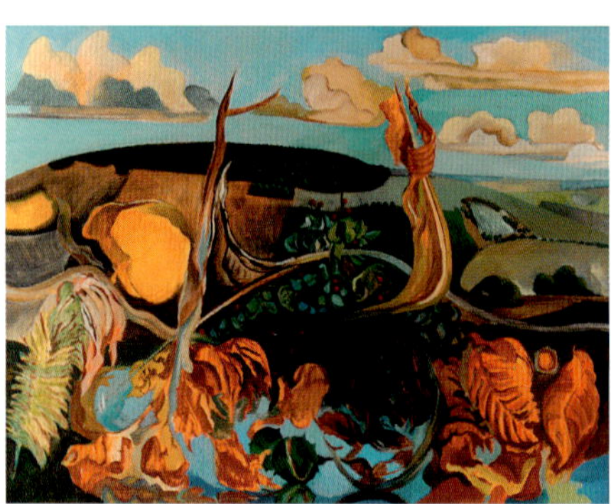

Bradshaw, Gordon b.1931
Landscape
oil on canvas 89 x 119
18

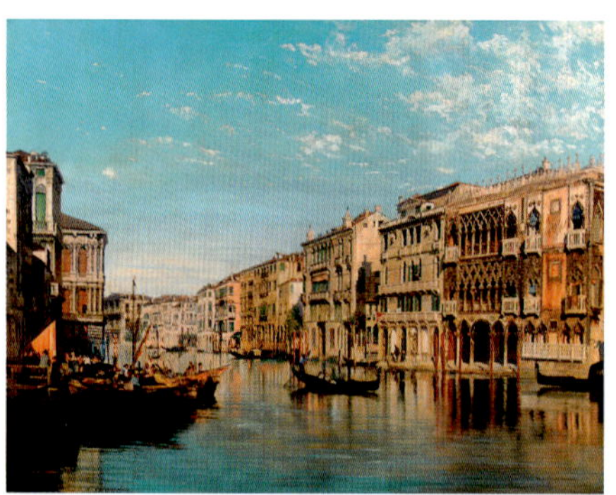

Brandeis, Antonietta 1849–1920
The Grand Canal, Venice 1882
oil on canvas 107 x 140
19

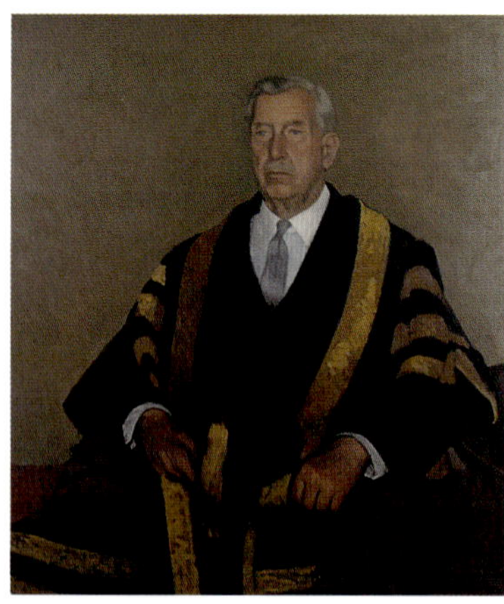

Buhler, Robert A. 1916–1989
Duke of Wellington 1964
oil on canvas 74 x 62
20

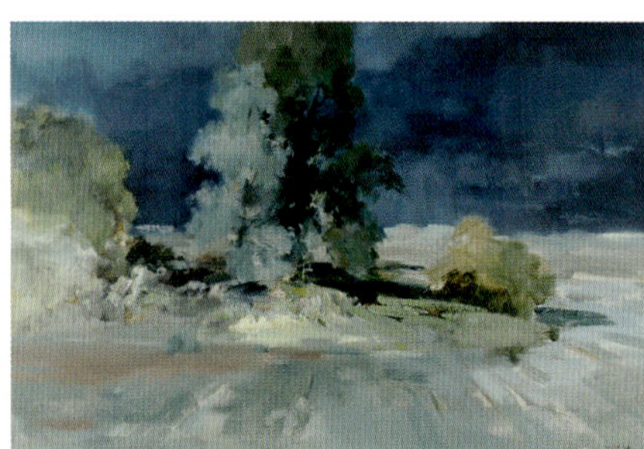

Burman, John b.1936
Trees in Light and Shade
oil on board 50 x 75 (E)
21

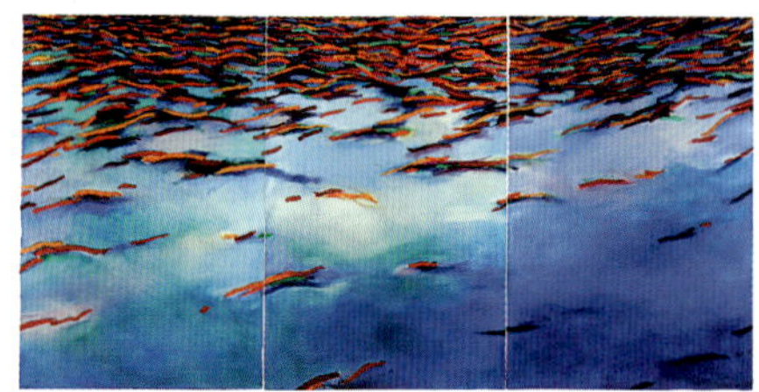

Chambers, Robert
Swarm 1990
acrylic on hardboard 166 x 324
1

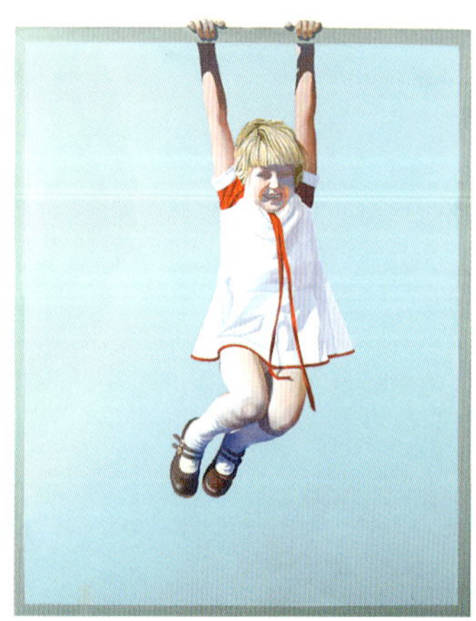

Charles, Mel
Hanging Figure (diptych, left panel) 1977
acrylic on canvas 216 x 143
2a

Facing page: Freud, Lucian, b.1922, *Bananas* (detail), 1952, Southampton City Art Gallery, (p. 47)

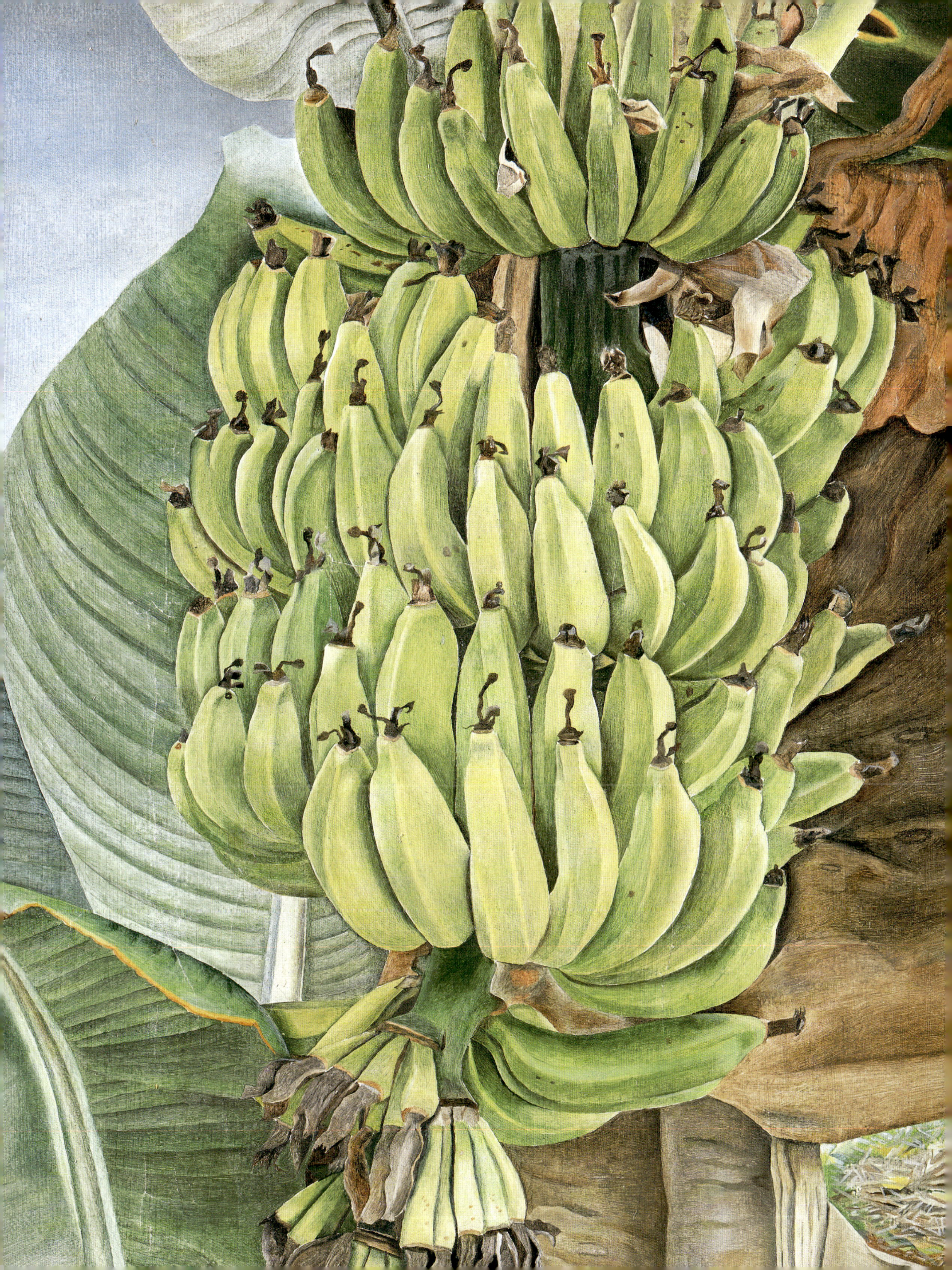

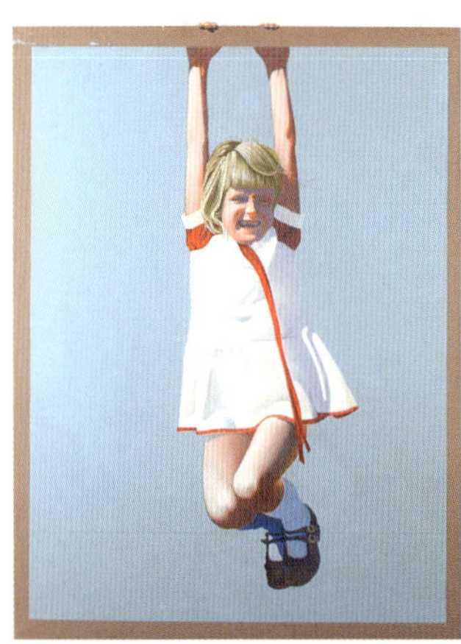

Charles, Mel
Hanging Figure (diptych, right panel) 1977
acrylic on canvas 216 x 143
2b

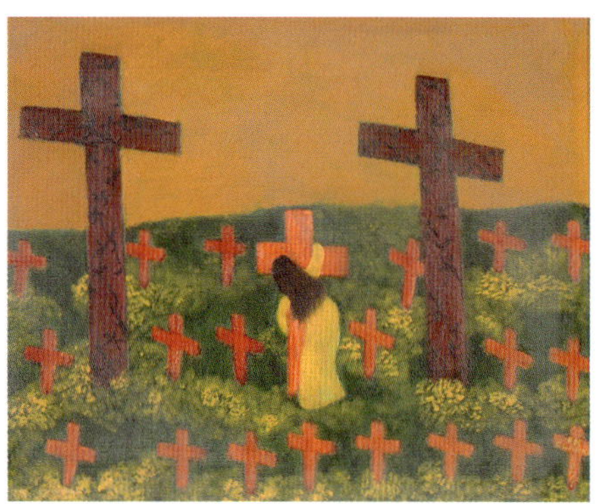

Clarke, Hilda Margery b.1926
Crosses
oil on canvas 30.5 x 38.1
23

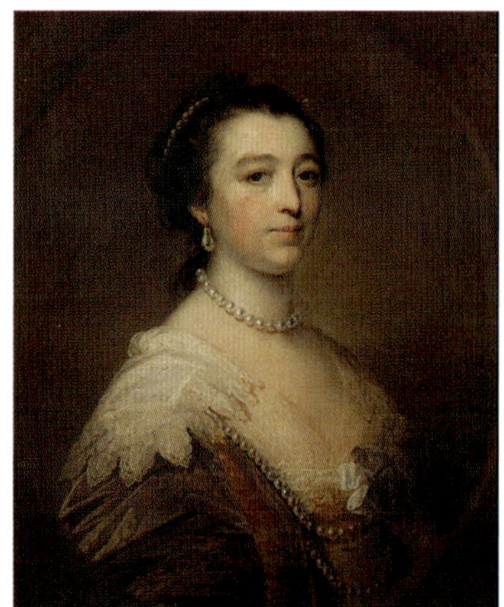

Cotes, Francis 1726–1770
Sarah Robinson 1761
oil on canvas 74 x 62
24

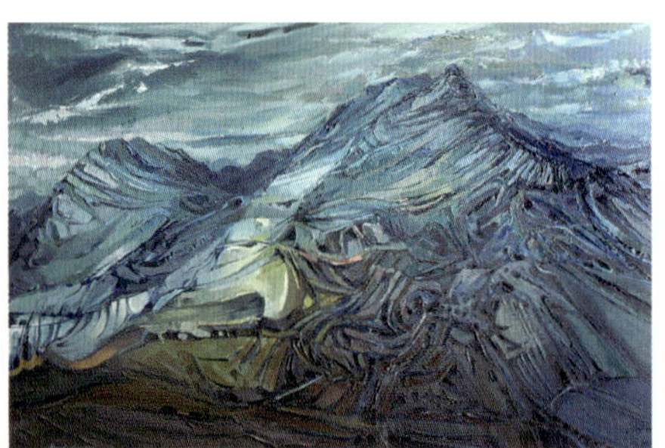

Cotton, Alan b.1938
Snowdonia
oil on board 90 x 120
25

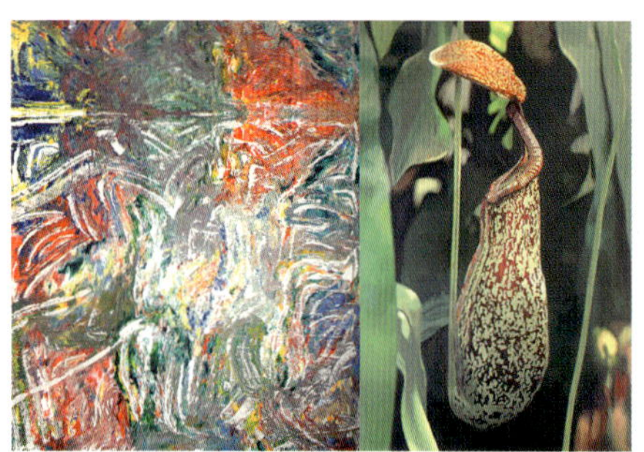

Crumplin, Colin b.1946
Pitcher Plant (Nepenthe) 1991
acrylic & oil on canvas 180 x 300
3

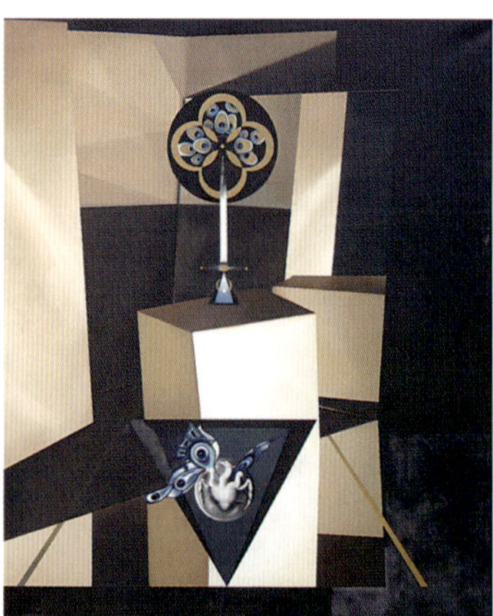

Drury, Judith b.1944
Peacock Mandala
oil on canvas 188 x 155
28

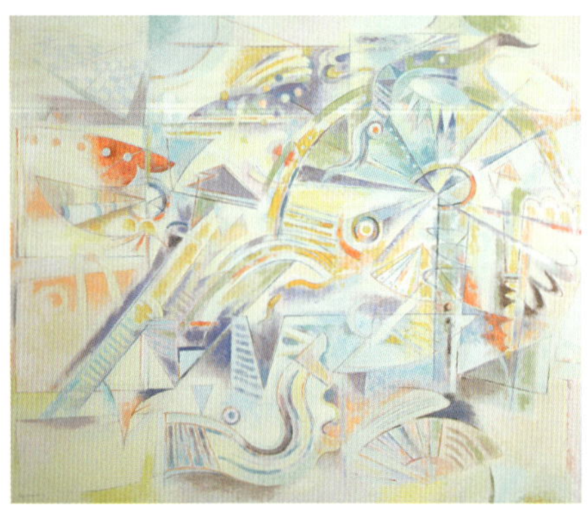

Elwell, Brian b.1938
Carnival 1975
oil on canvas 160 x 190
30

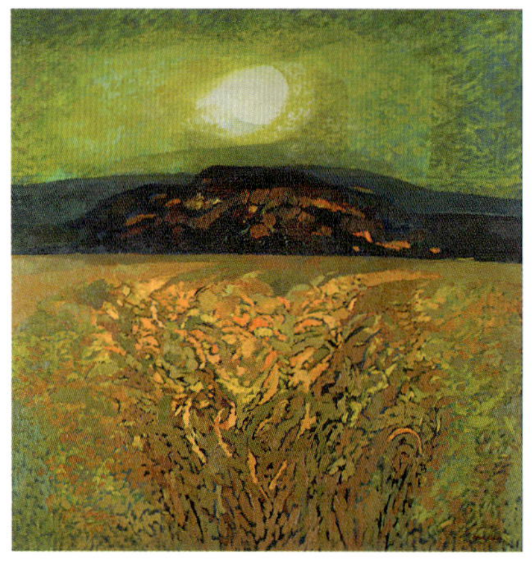

Elwyn, John 1916–1977
September
oil on canvas 90 x 90
31

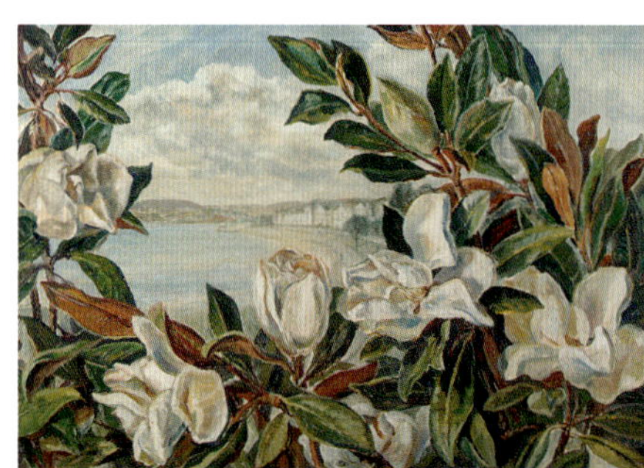

England, Muriel
The Pride of Devon
oil on board 50 x 76
A3

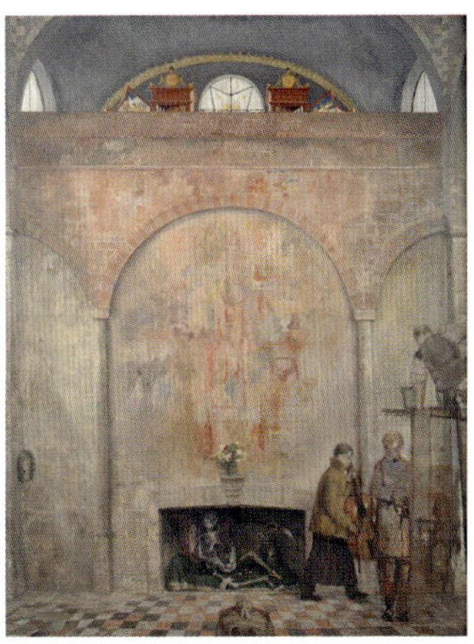

Eurich, Richard Ernst 1903–1992
The Rose 1960
oil on board 90 x 70
A2

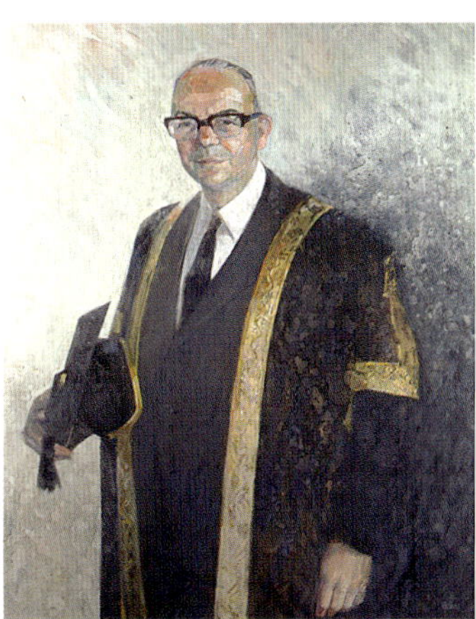

Folkes, Peter L. b.1923
Professor Kenneth Mather, Vice Chancellor (1965–1971)
oil on canvas 129 x 101
A6

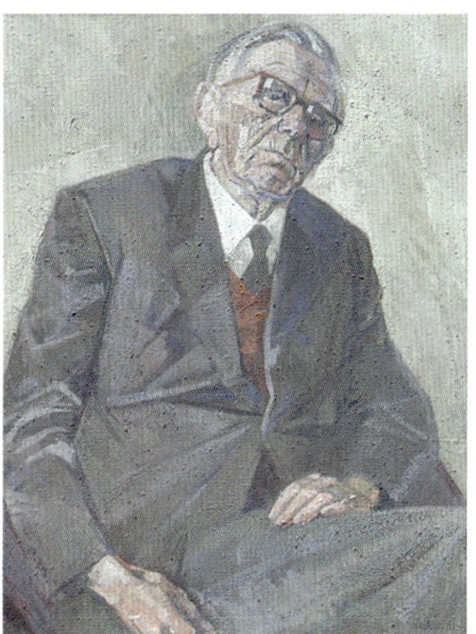

Folkes, Peter L. b.1923
Sir James Matthews
oil on canvas 115 x 93
32

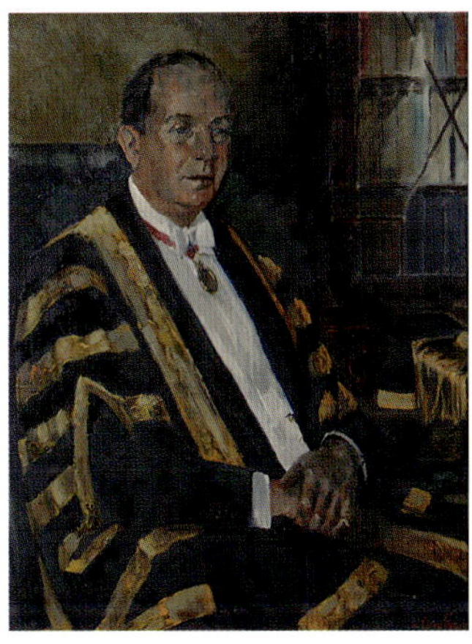

Fowle, LeClerc active 1950s–1982
Lord Murray
oil on canvas 90 x 74
34

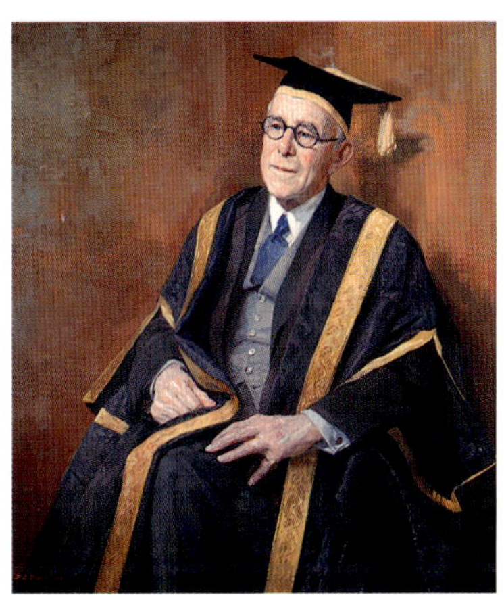

Freeth, Hubert Andrew 1913–1986
Sir Samuel Gurney Dixon
oil on canvas
35

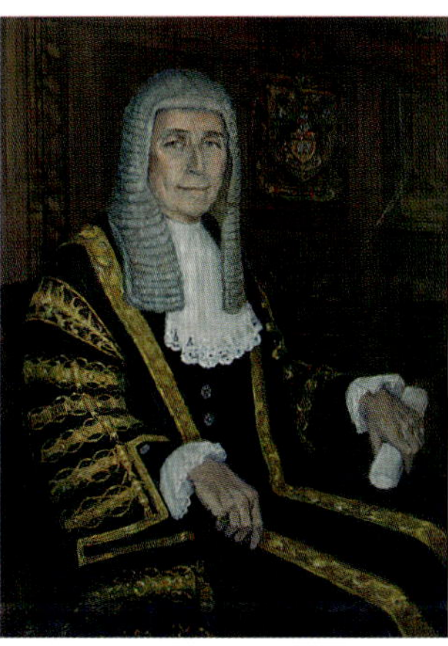

Gaussen Marks, Elena b.1938
Lord Tonypandy
oil on canvas 140 x 108 (E)
45

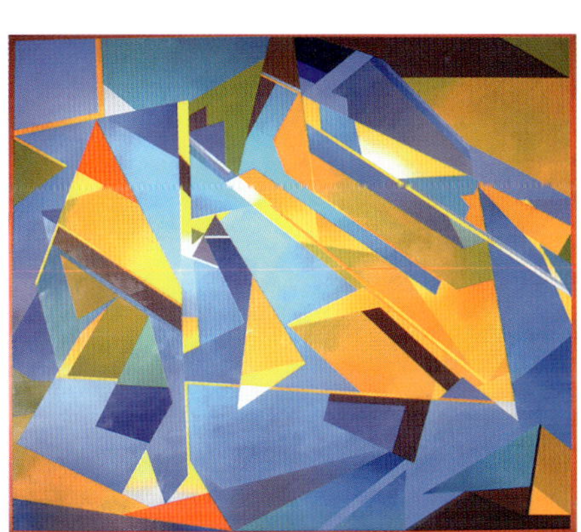

Hoskins, Ned b.1939
Aerial Conflict
acrylic on board 174 x 184 (E)
4

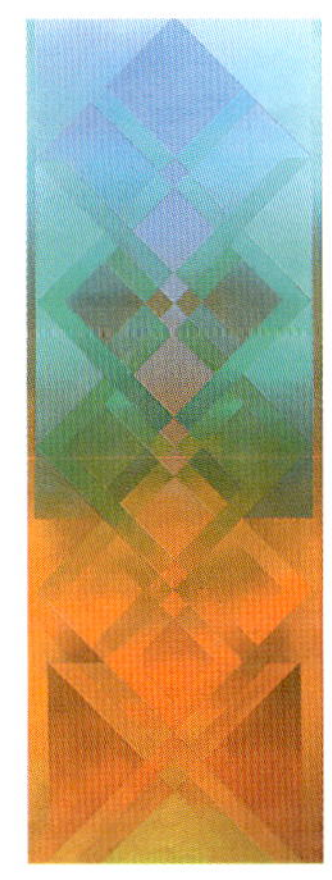

Hoskins, Ned b.1939
Convection
acrylic on canvas 120 x 50
5

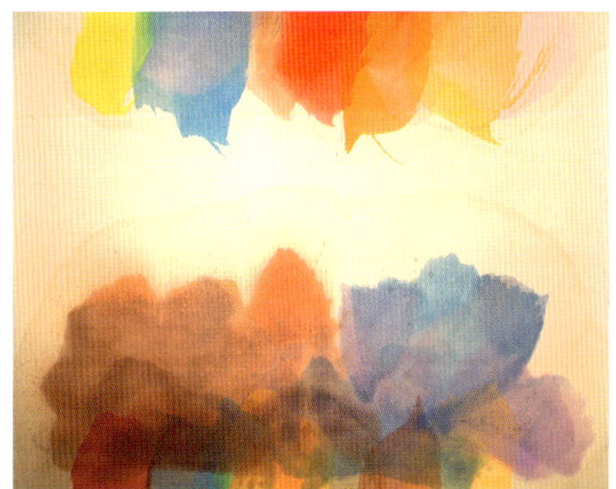

Irvin, Albert b.1922
Rite 1972
acrylic on canvas 210 x 310
6

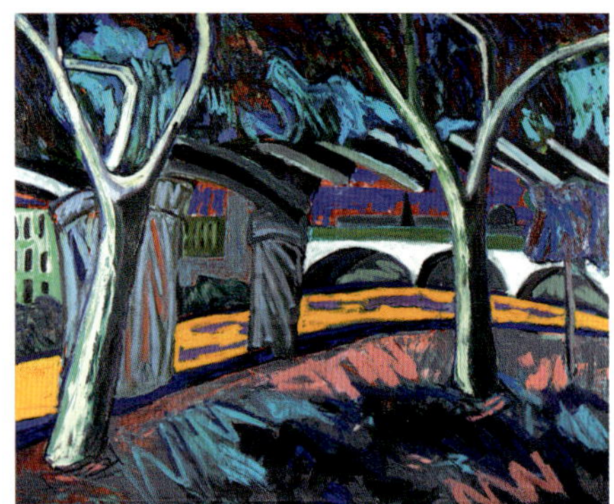

Jones, Lucy b.1955
River Bank
oil on canvas 175 x 240
39

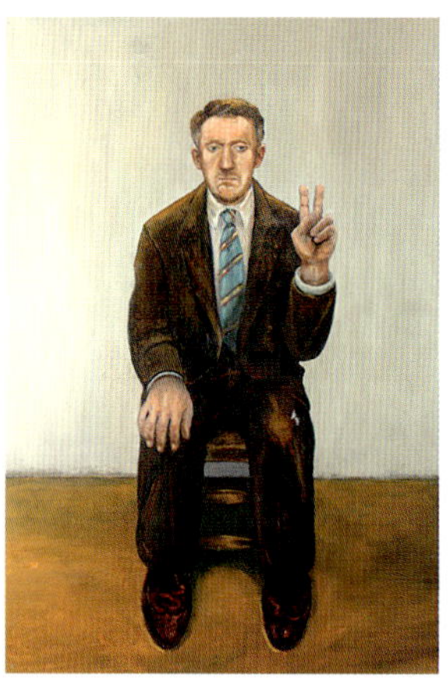

Kirby, John b.1949
Seated Man 1985
oil on canvas 140 x 100
41

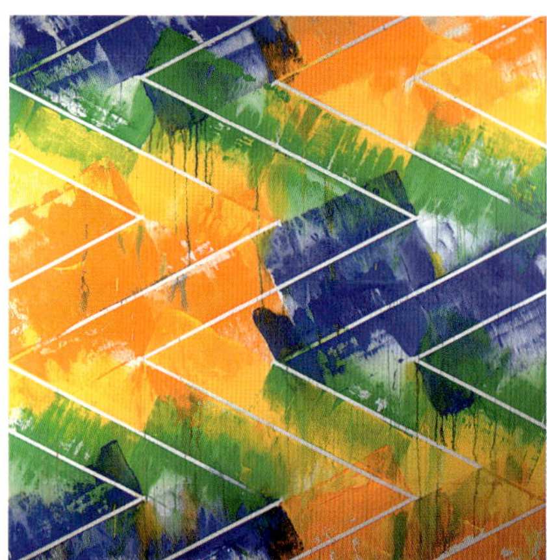

Lancaster, Mark b.1938
Henry VI Blue and Orange
acrylic on canvas 174 x 172
7

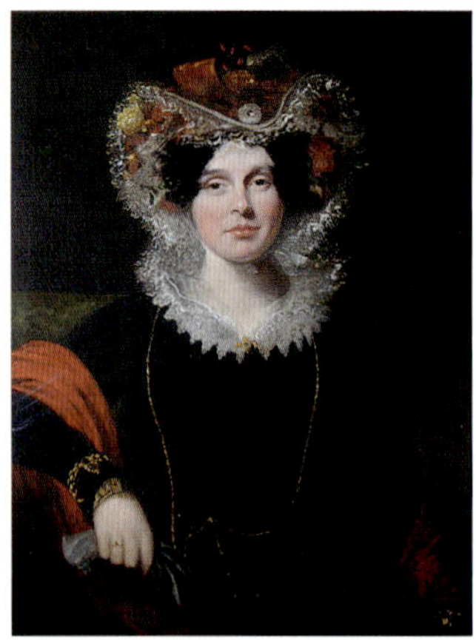

Lane, Samuel 1780–1859
Elizabeth Hobbes, Wife of Luke Groves Hansard
oil on canvas 88 x 70
42

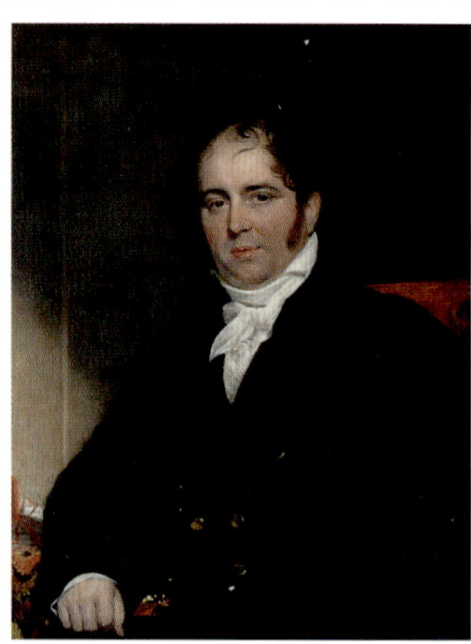

Lane, Samuel 1780–1859
Luke Groves Hansard
oil on canvas 88 x 70
43

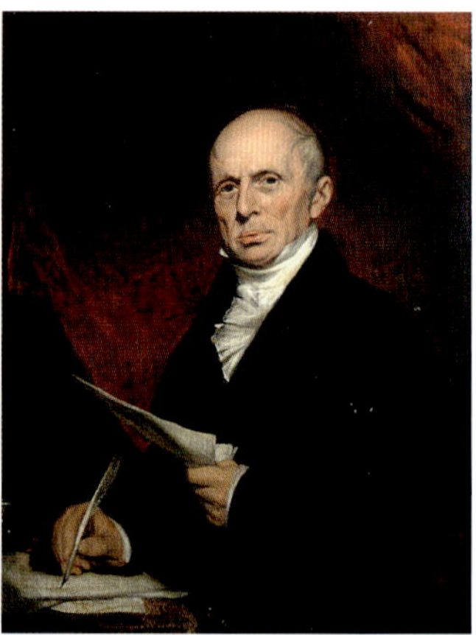

Lane, Samuel 1780–1859
Luke Hansard
oil on canvas 88 x 70
44

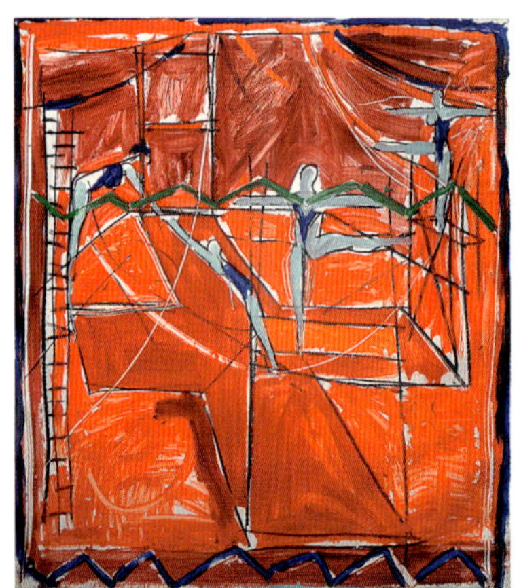

McLean, Bruce b.1944
Untitled
acrylic 152 x 145
8

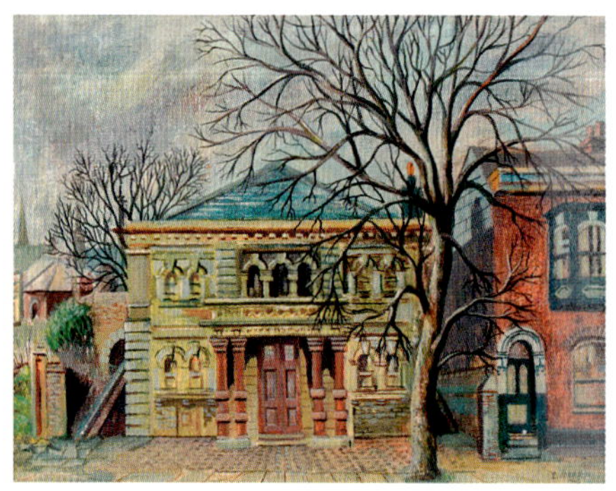

Merson, E.
Southampton Synagogue 1960
oil on canvas 37 x 51
47

Neiman, Oscar
Painting
oil on canvas 66 x 100
48

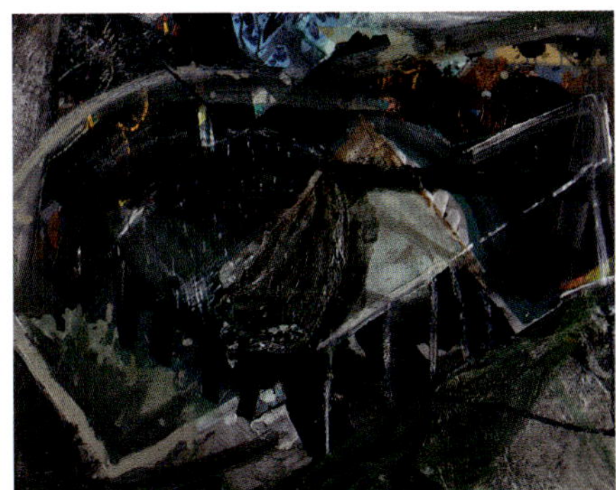

Olsen, Geoffrey b.1943
Running the White Tip (Merthyr) 1982–1983
acrylic on hardboard 76 x 100
11

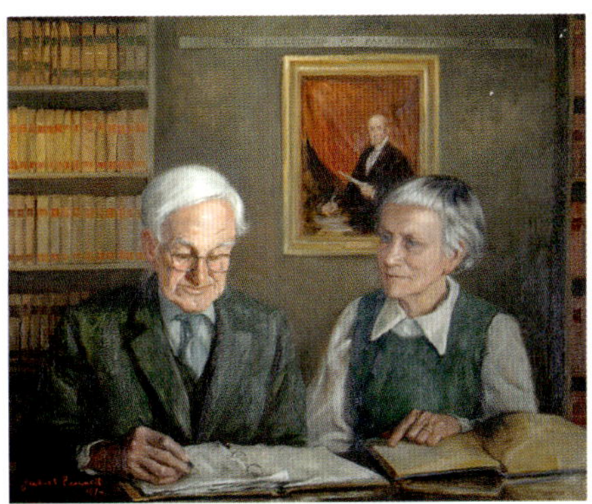

Pannett, Juliet 1911–2005
Professor and Doctor Ford 1974
oil on canvas 60 x 75
51

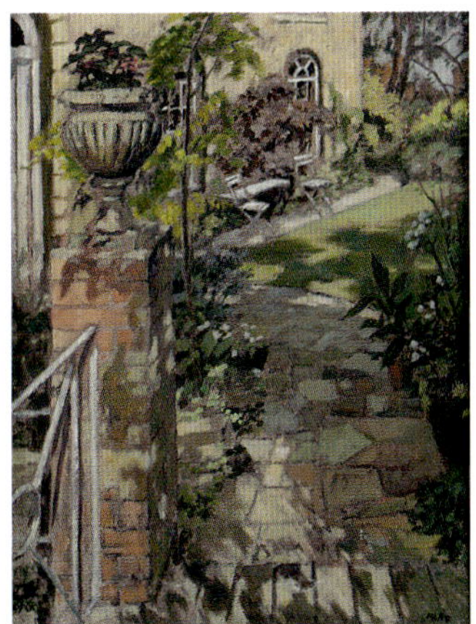

Pare, David 1911–1996
Mill Garden
oil on canvas 51 x 40
52

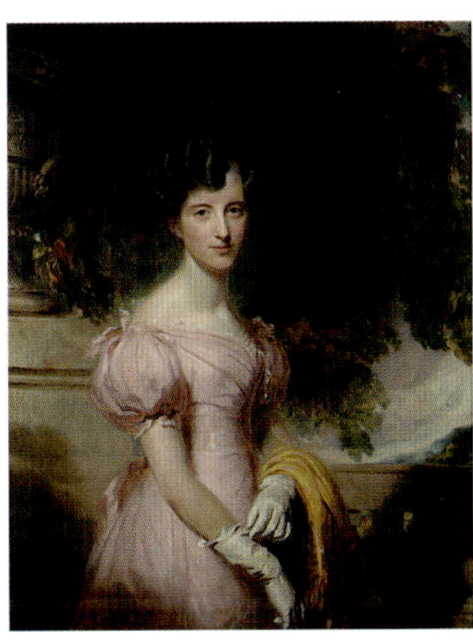

Patten, William d.1843
Portrait of a Lady 1828
oil on canvas 109 x 87
54

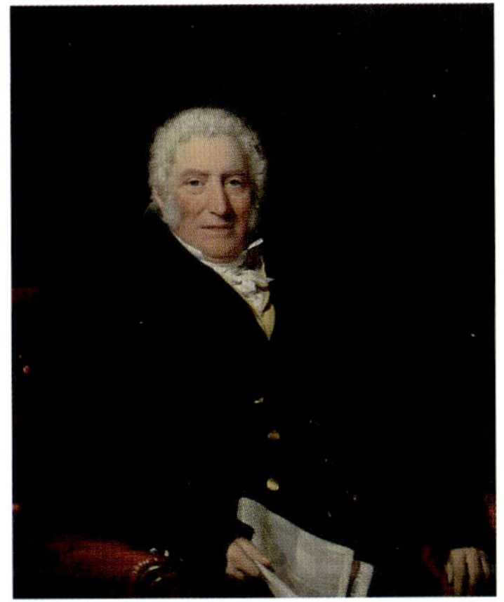

Patten, William d.1843
Portrait of a Gentleman 1831
oil on canvas 95 x 80
53

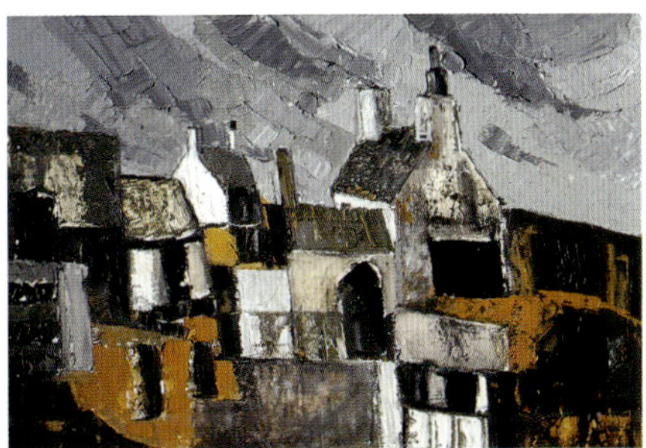

Pritchard, Gwilym b.1931
Buildings
oil on board 60 x 90
56

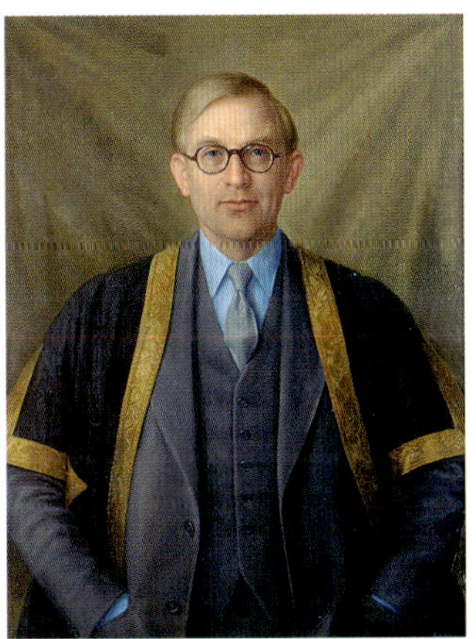

Ramos, Theodore b.1928
Doctor D. G. James, Vice Chancellor (1952–1965) 1953
oil on canvas 100 x 76
A5

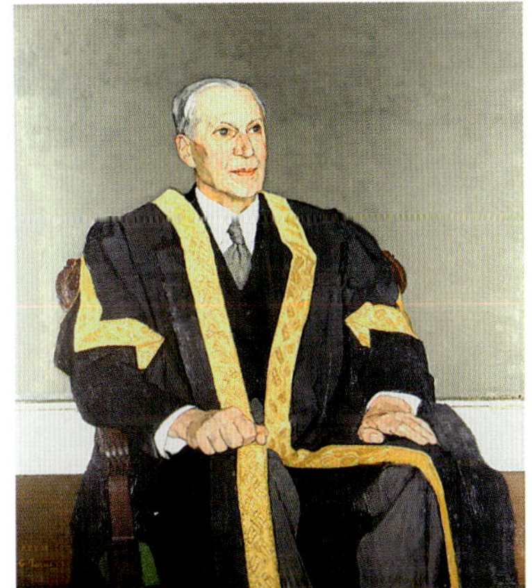

Rogers, Claude 1907–1979
Sir Robert Wood, Principal (1946–1952), Vice Chancelllor (1952) 1953
oil on canvas 120 x 100
A4

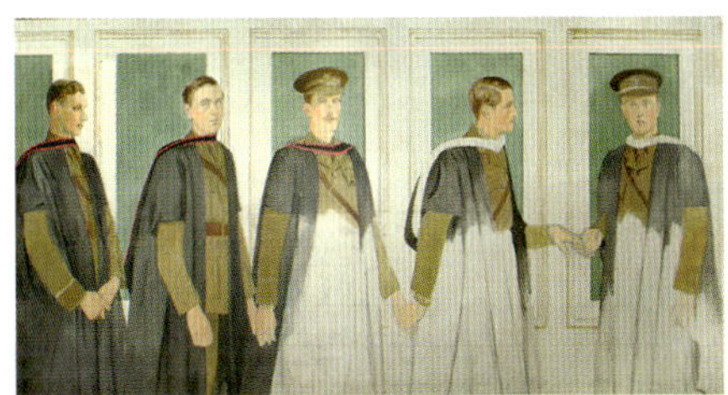

Rothenstein, William 1872–1945
War Cartoon (left panel) 1914–1918
oil on board 296 x 602.5
60

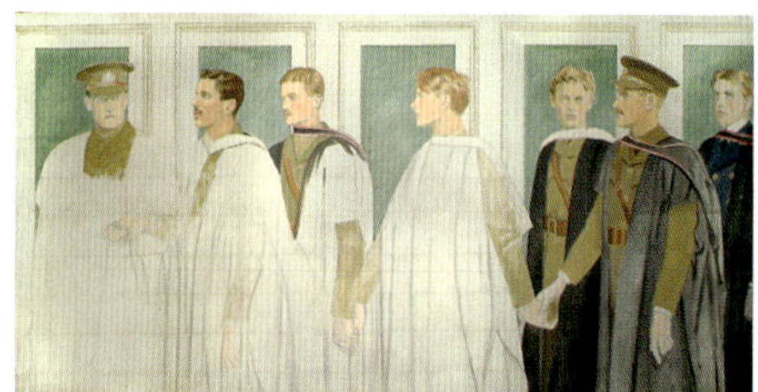

Rothenstein, William 1872–1945
War Cartoon (right panel) 1914–1918
oil on board 296 x 602.5
S2

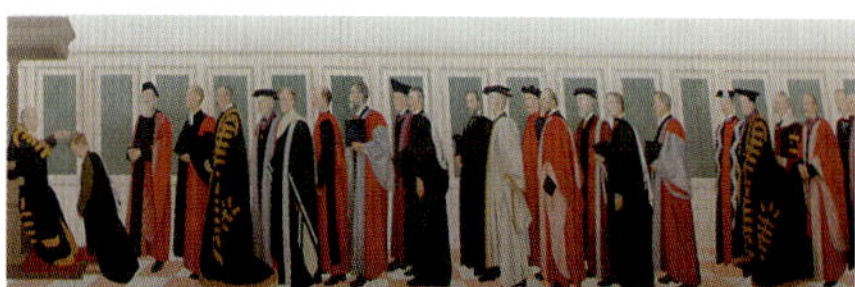

Rothenstein, William 1872–1945
Ceremony 1916
oil on canvas on board 305 x 1219
Temp1

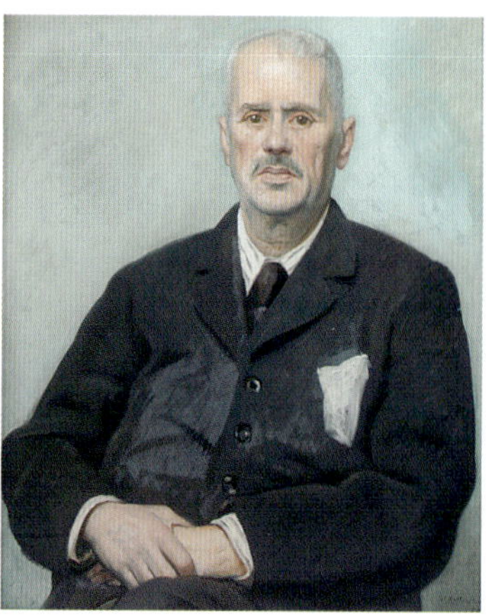

Rothenstein, William 1872–1945
Claude Montefiore 1935
oil on canvas 73 x 61
59

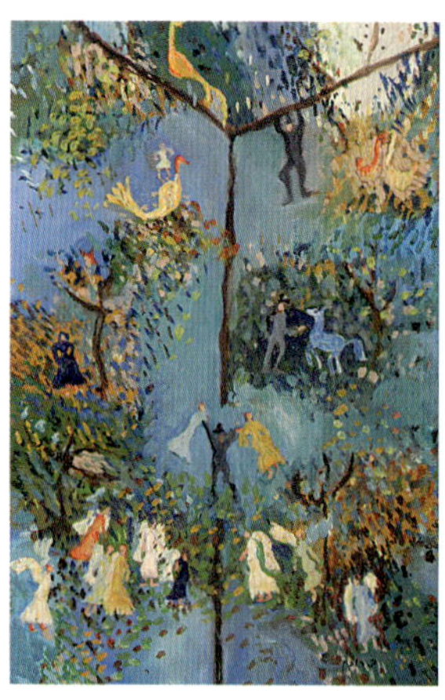

Rubin, Bina b.1942
Jerusalem
oil on board 60 x 45
62

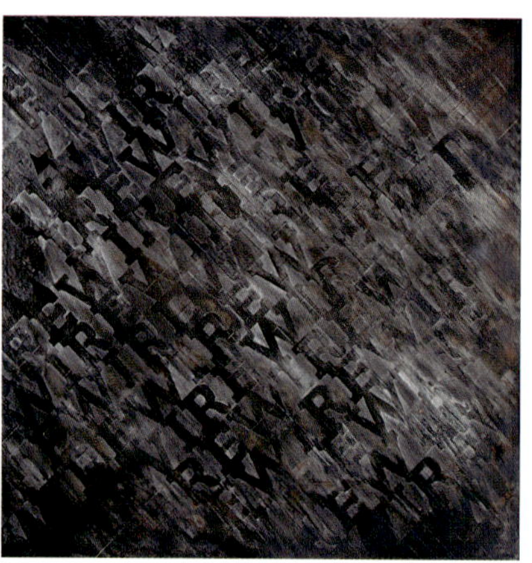

Sainsbury, Timothy active 1972–1981
Wire
oil on board 123 x 123
64

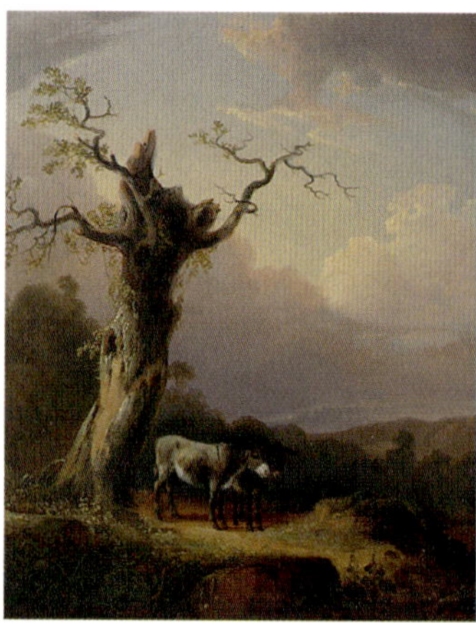

Shayer, William 1788–1879
Donkeys in Landscape
oil on panel 28 x 24
66

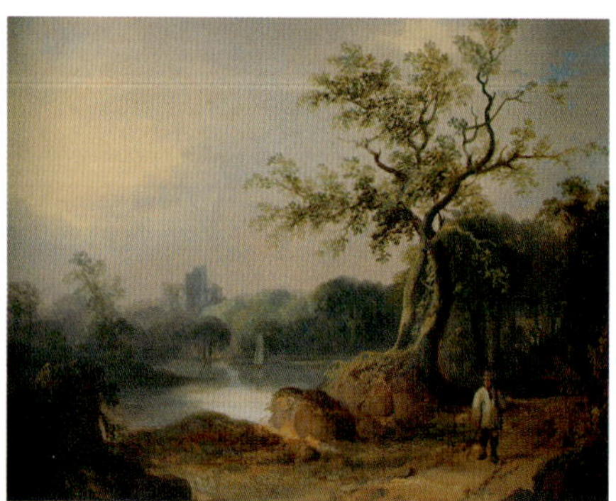

Shayer, William 1788–1879
Landscape with Figures on a Path
oil on panel 19 x 25
67

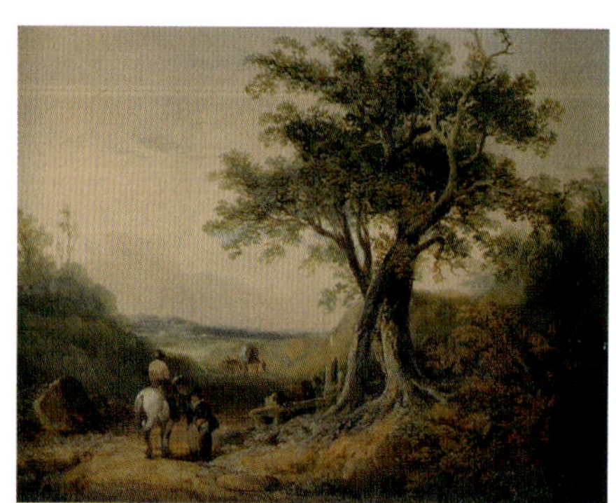

Shayer, William 1788–1879
Landscape with Travellers on a Road
oil on panel 19 x 25
68

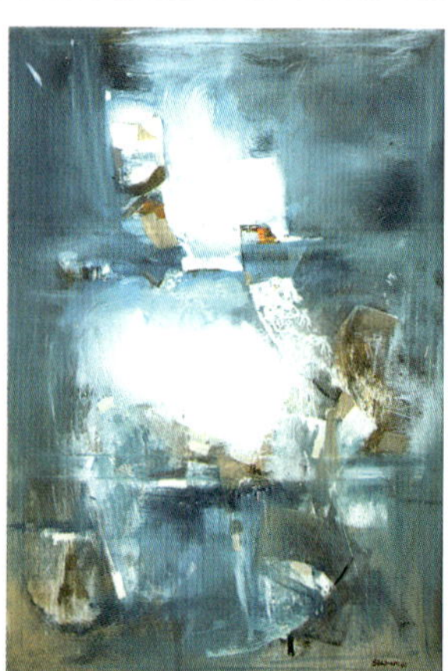

Sinkinson, Frederick active 1965–1992
Abstract 1965
oil 210 x 105
69

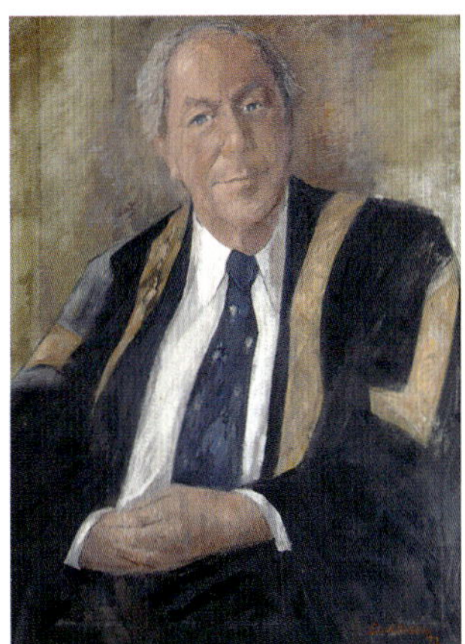

Sinkinson, Frederick active 1965–1992
Sir Gordon Higginson, Vice Chancellor (1985–1994) 1992
oil on canvas 95 x 70
A9

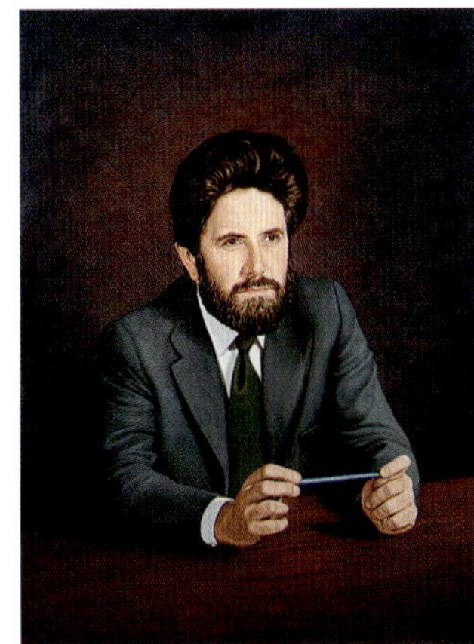

Smith, Ray b.1947
Kenneth Hilton 1991
oil on canvas 100 x 76
70

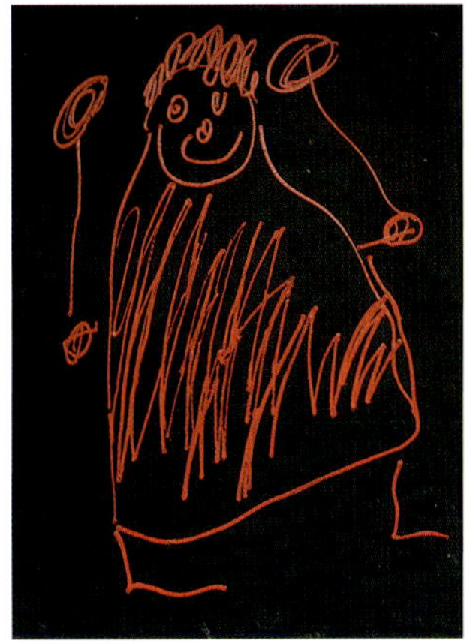

Smith, Ray b.1947
Balloon Man
acrylic 183 x 135
13

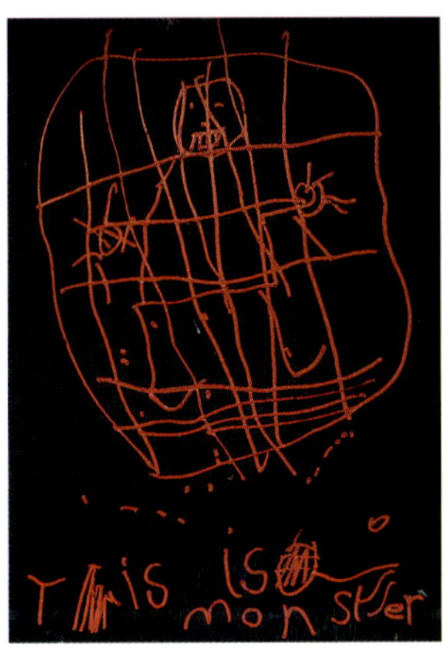

Smith, Ray b.1947
Monster
acrylic 183 x 135
14

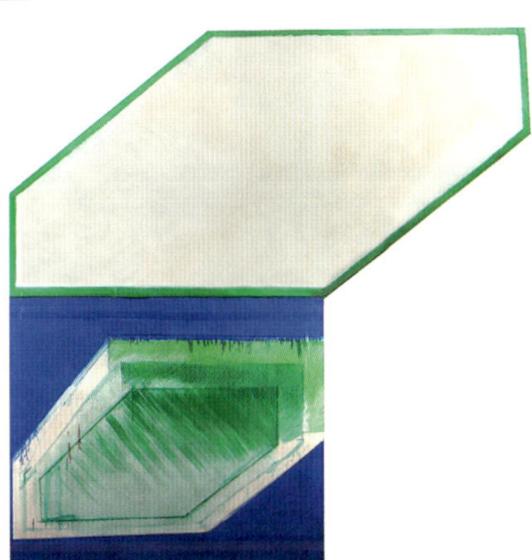

Smith, Richard b.1931
Fleetwood
acrylic 254 x 252
15

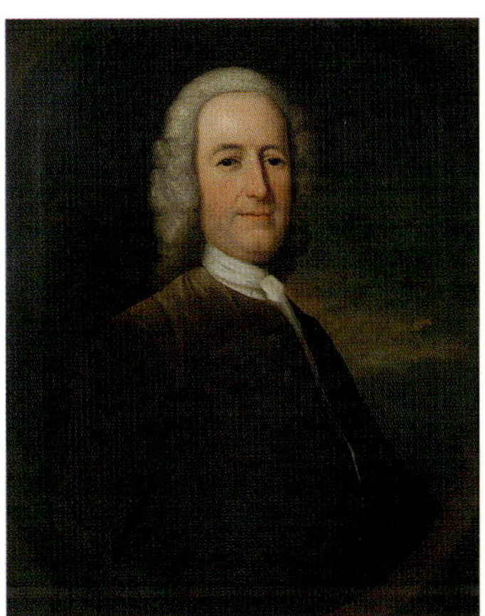

unknown artist
George Robinson 1746
oil on canvas 74 x 62
71

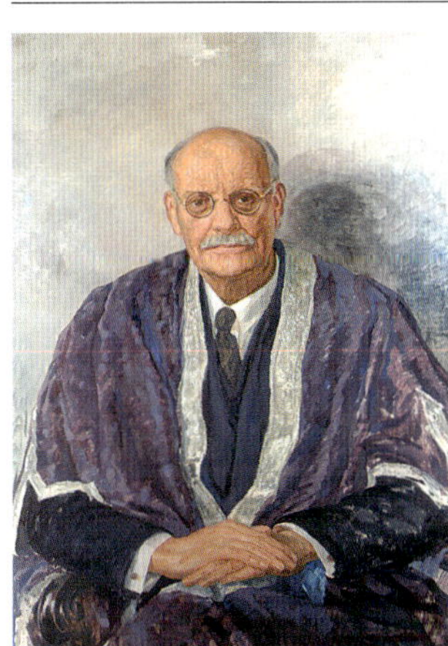

unknown artist
Doctor Kenneth Vickers, Principal (1922–1946)
oil on canvas 105 x 75
A11

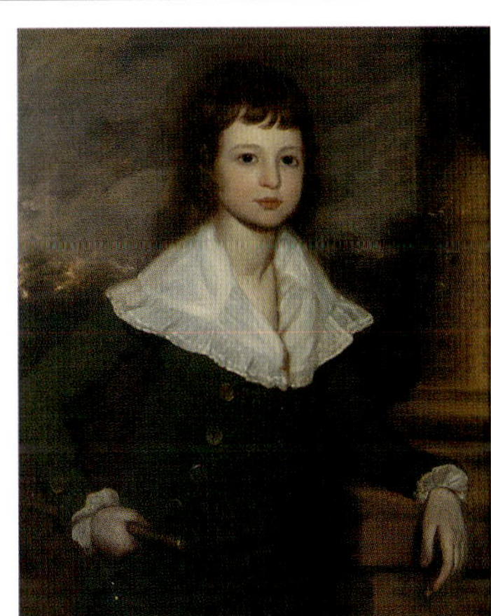

unknown artist
H. R. Hartley, Aged 9
oil on canvas 74 x 62
74

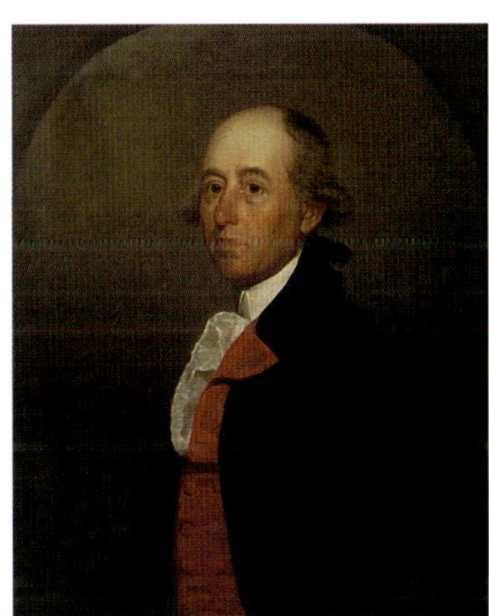

unknown artist
Henry Hartley
oil on canvas 74 x 62
72

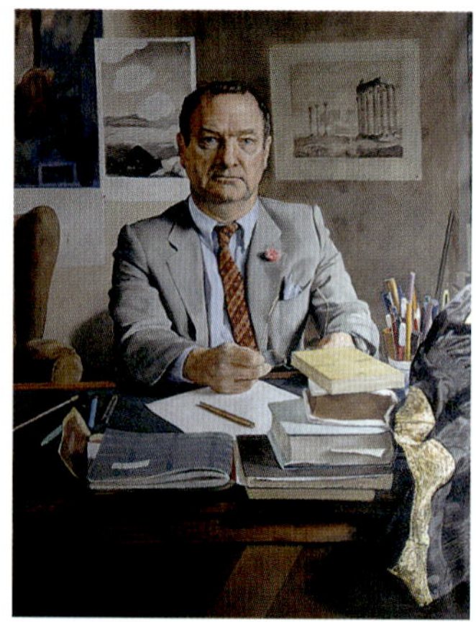

unknown artist
Professor John Roberts, Vice Chancellor (1979–1985)
oil on canvas 110 x 80
A8

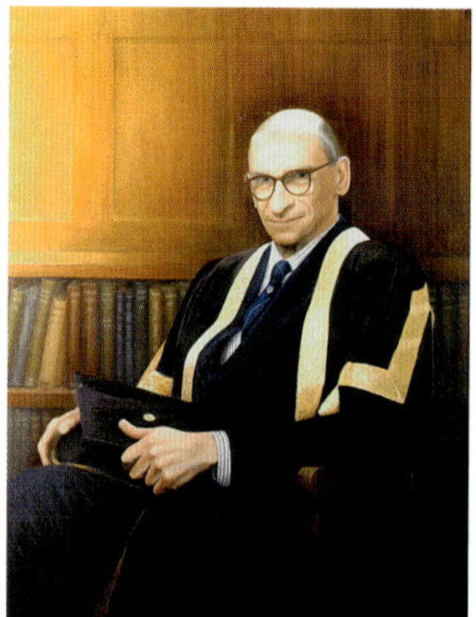

unknown artist
Professor Laurence Gower, Vice Chancellor (1971–1979)
oil on canvas 130 x 100
A7

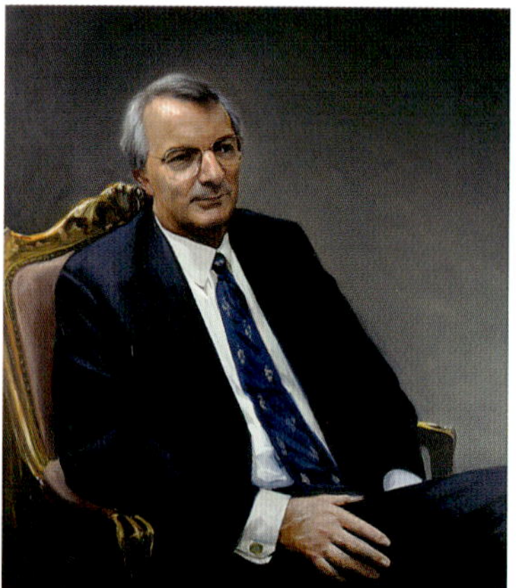

unknown artist
Sir Howard Newby, Vice Chancellor (1994–2001)
oil on canvas 103 x 89
A10

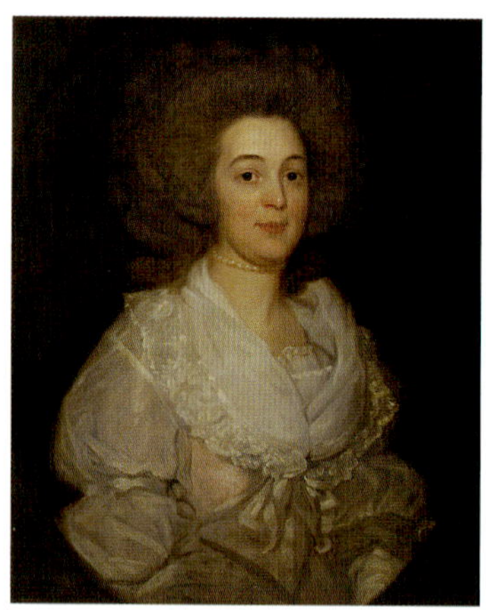

unknown artist
Susannah Hartley
oil on canvas 74 x 62
73

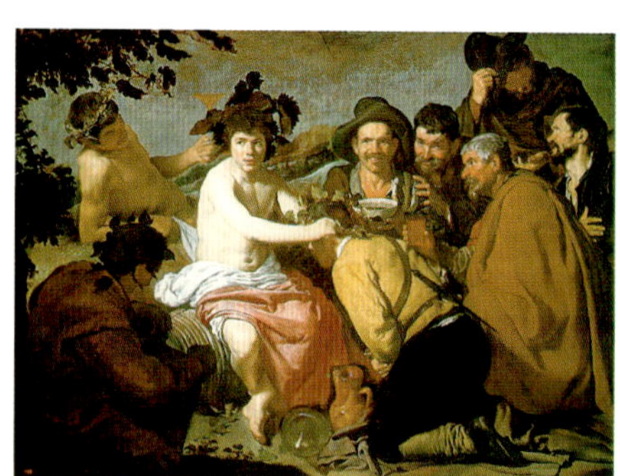

Velázquez, Diego (follower of) 1599–1660
Bacchus
oil on canvas 189 x 252
75

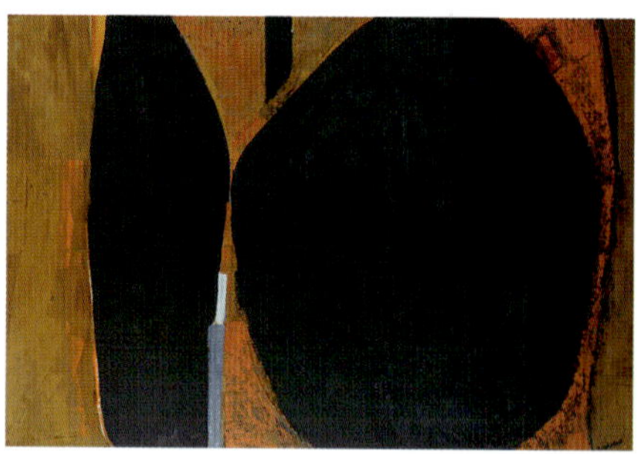

Wakefield, Larry 1925–1997
Brown Painting
oil on canvas 122 x 185
77

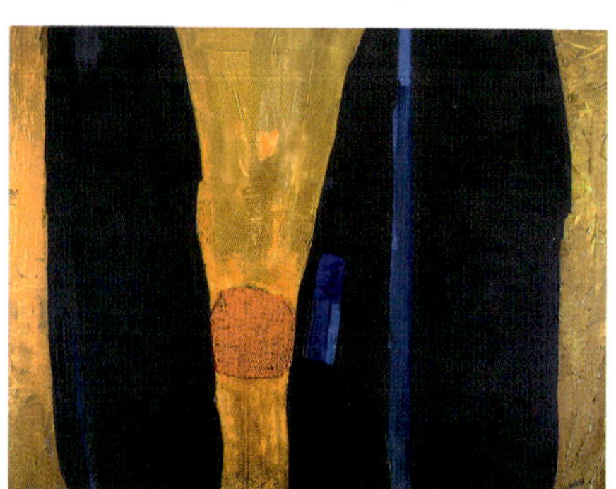

Wakefield, Larry 1925–1997
Painting
oil on canvas 120 x 183
78

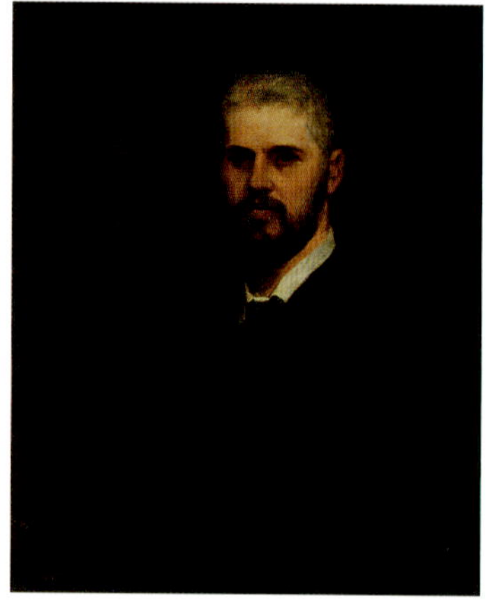

Watts, George Frederick 1817–1904
Claude Joseph Schmid Montefiore
oil on canvas 75 x 63
79

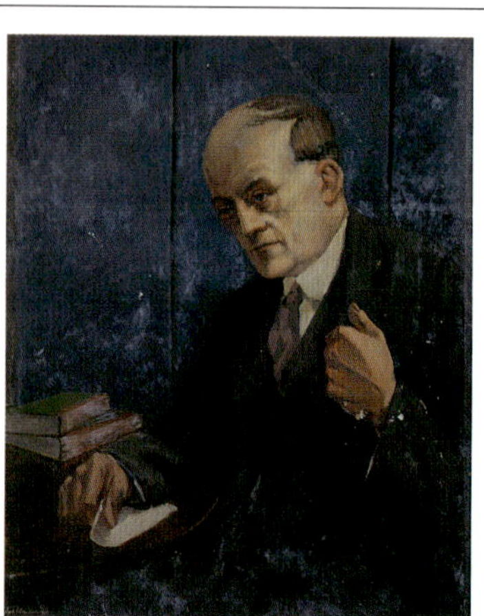

Withycombe, Joyce active 1928–1933
Doctor J. W. Horrocks
oil on canvas 74 x 62
A12

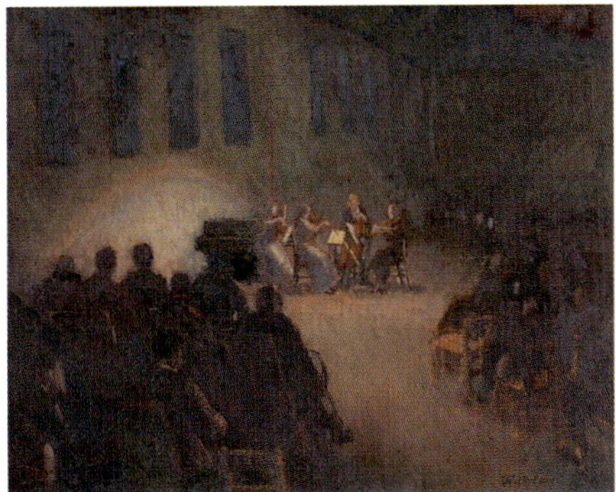

Withycombe, Joyce active 1928–1933
The Quartet
oil on canvas 34 x 44
81

Blackgang Sawmill and St Catherine's Quay

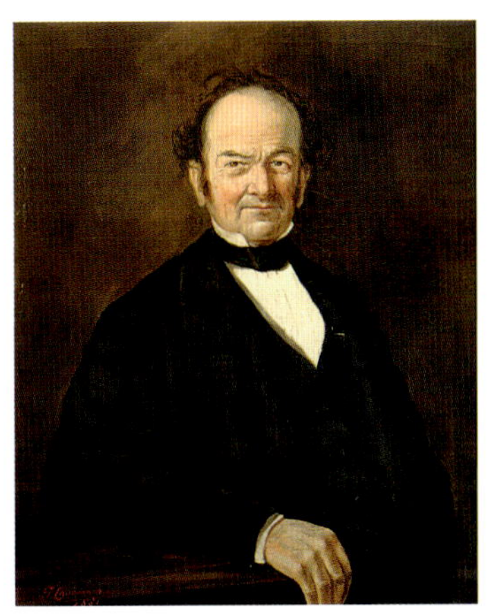

Charbonnier, Theodore active 1881–1894
Alexander Dabell (1809–1898) 1881
oil on canvas 73.5 x 61
1

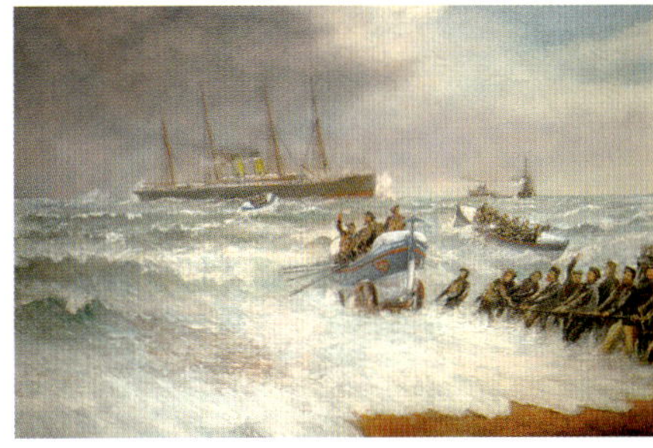

Edmunds
The Rescue of the German Steamer 'Eider' off Atherfield Ledge 1892
oil on canvas 38 x 57
6

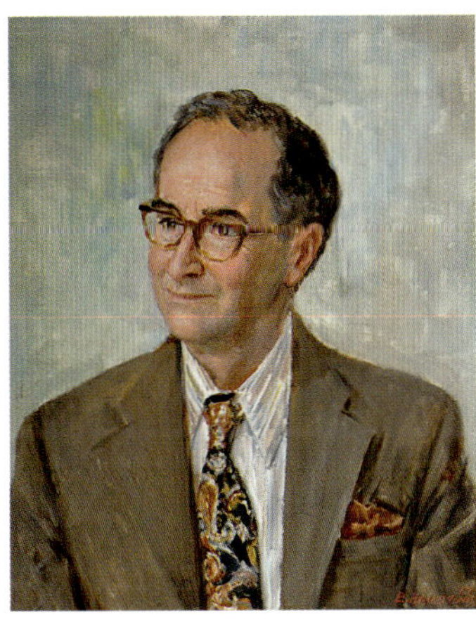

Hailstone, Bernard 1910–1987
Francis Dabell 1977
oil on canvas 59.6 x 49.2
4

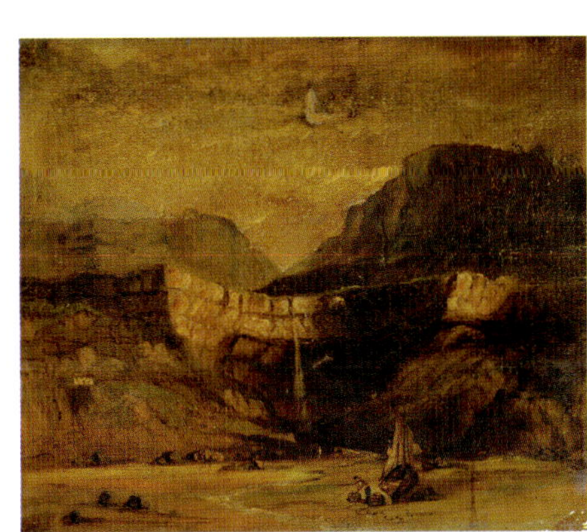

unknown artist
View of Blackgang Chine c.1800
oil on canvas 50 x 57
5

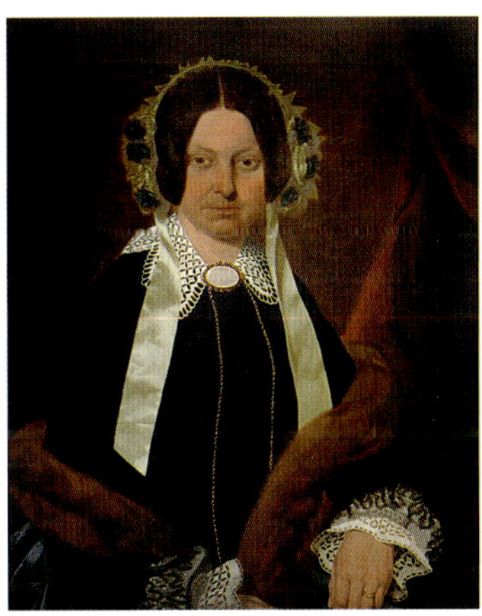

unknown artist
Amelia Dabell c.1881
oil on canvas 75 x 61.7
2

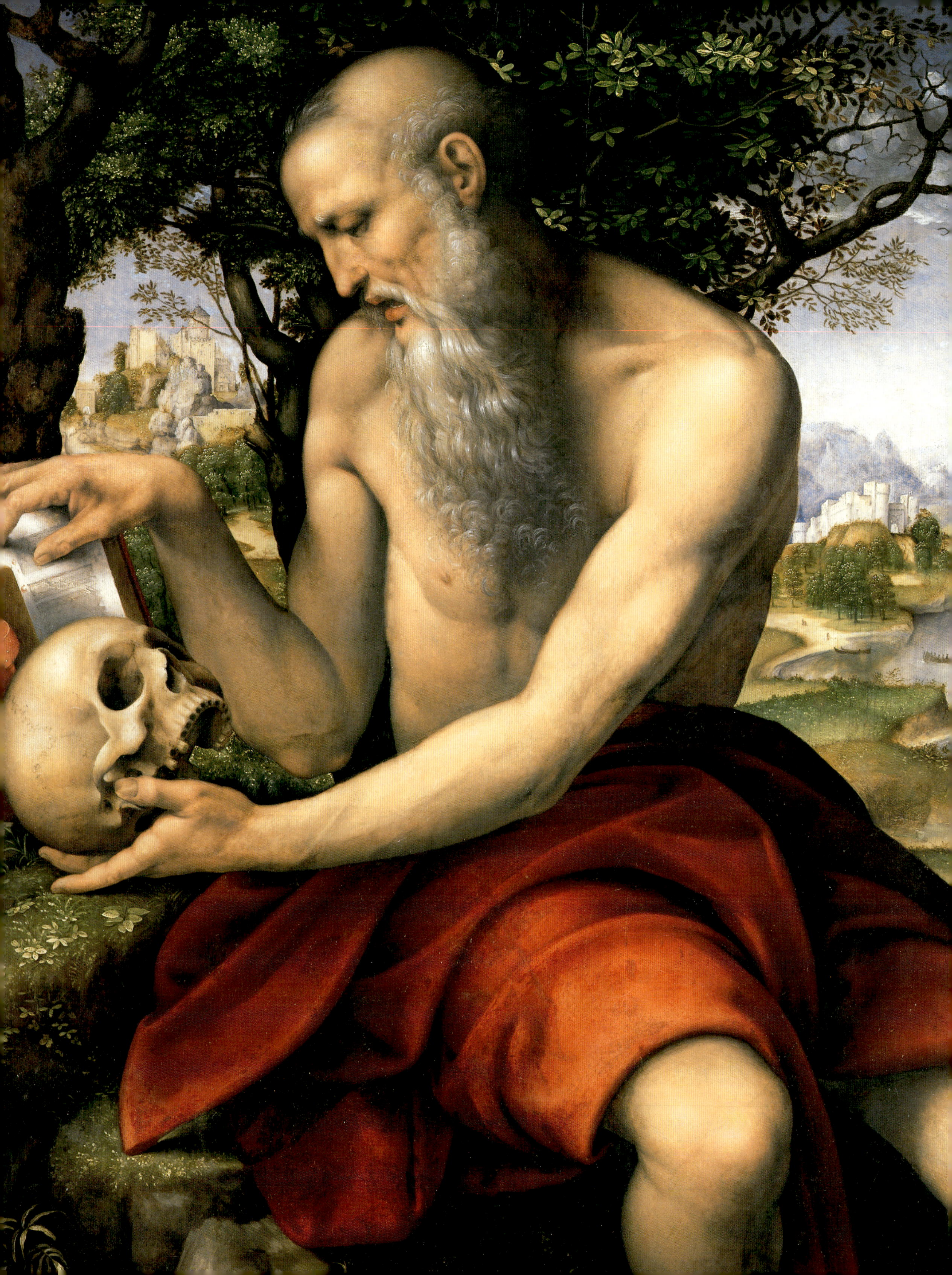

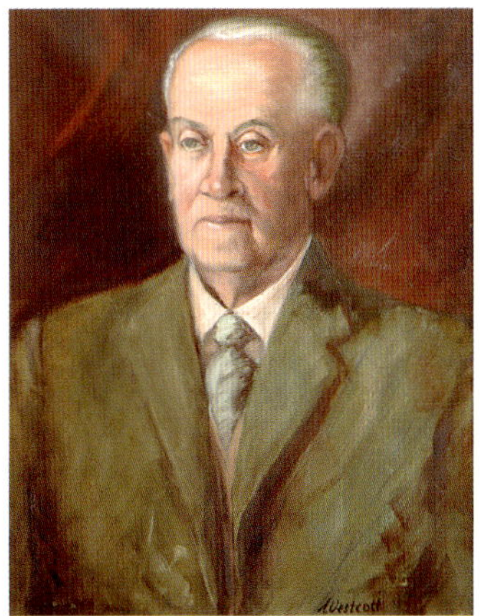

Westcott
Bruce Dabell c.1950
oil on canvas 58 x 47
3

Brading Roman Villa

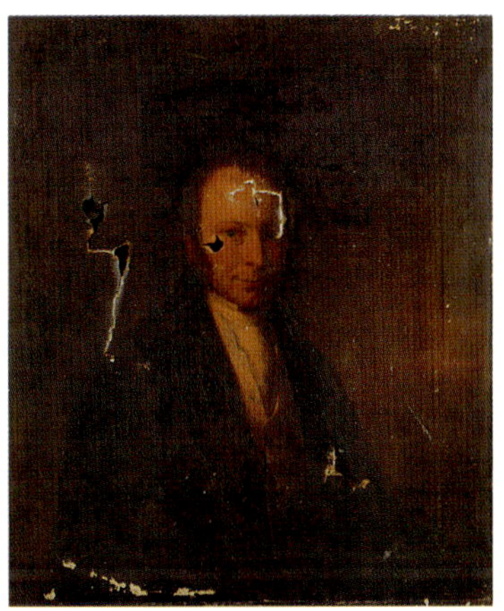

unknown artist 19th C
Portrait of a Gentleman (possibly Captain John Thorp of the 63rd Regiment of Foot or William Munns of Morton Farm)
oil on canvas 73 x 44 (E)
1

Cowes Maritime Museum

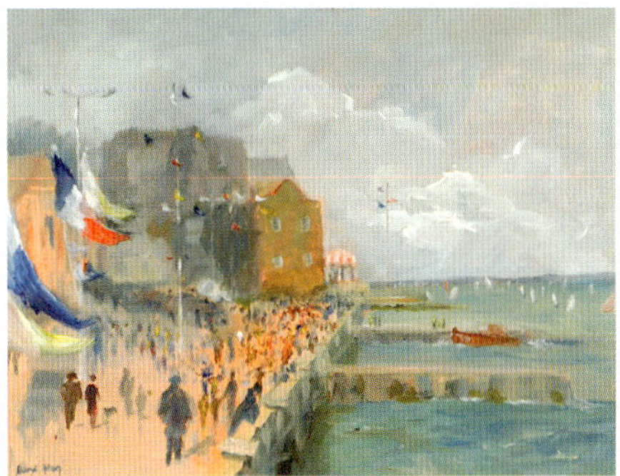

Allen, Beryl
Cowes Creek
oil on canvas 30 x 39.5 (E)
1993.96

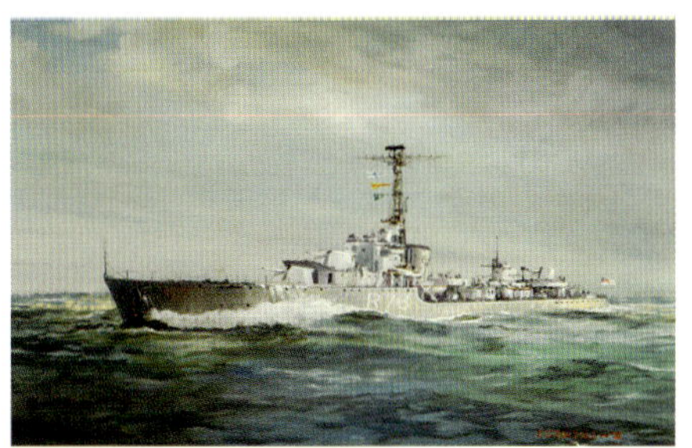

Burrows, E. G. active 20th C
'HMS Cavalier'
oil on board 29 x 39 (E)
1993.11

Facing page: Cesare da Sesto, 1477–1523, *St Jerome* (detail), 1520, Southampton City Art Gallery, (p. 29)

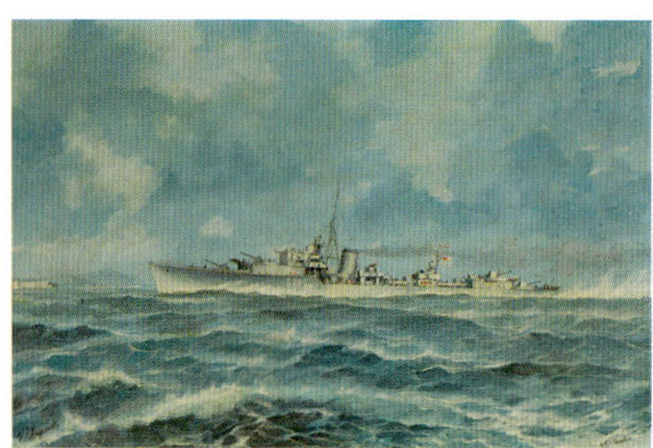

Colleypriest, Victor b.1901
'HMS Quentin' after 1942
oil on canvas 49 x 74.9 (E)
1993.95 (P)

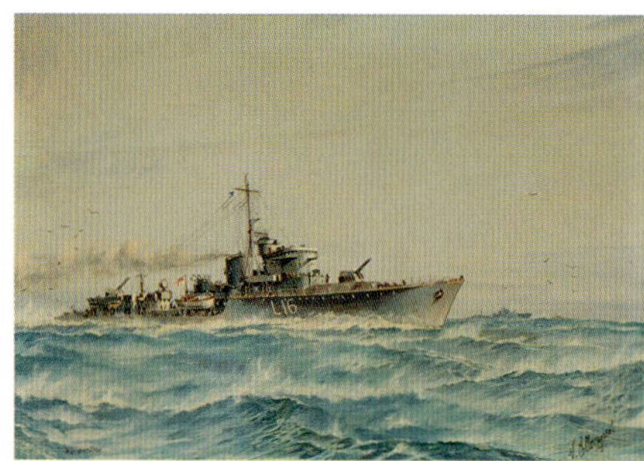

Colleypriest, Victor b.1901
'HMS Stevenstone' 1956
oil on canvas 49 x 74.1 (E)
1993.94 (P)

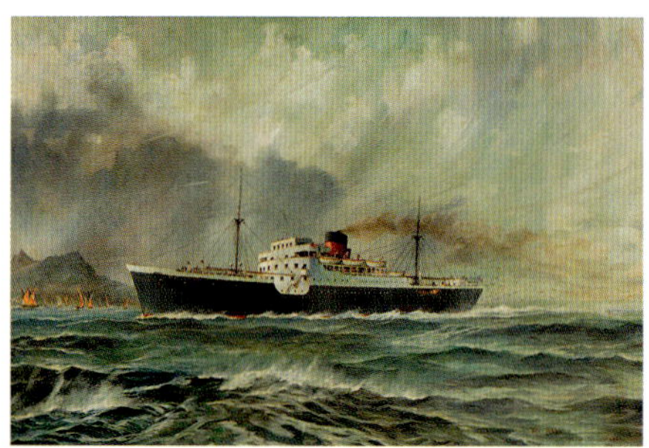

Colleypriest, Victor b.1901
'Sidi Mabrouk' 1956
oil on canvas 49 x 74.5 (E)
1993.968 (P)

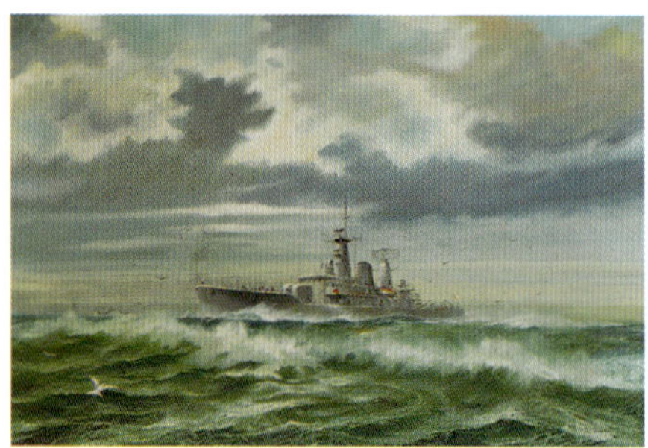

Colleypriest, Victor b.1901
'Arethusa' 1965
oil on canvas 59.3 x 90 (E)
1993.93 (P)

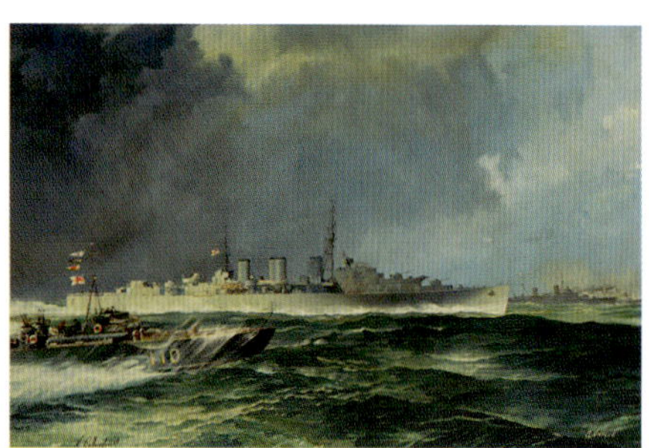

Colleypriest, Victor b.1901
HM Minelayer 'Abdiel' 1975
oil on canvas 49 x 74.5 (E)
1993.969 (P)

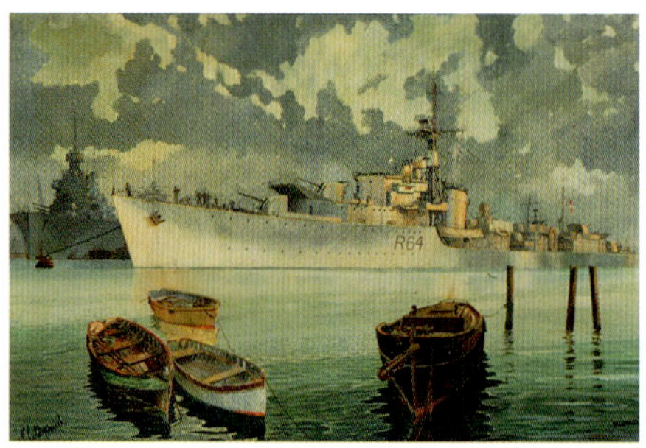

Colleypriest, Victor b.1901
'HMCS Sioux' 1975
oil on canvas 49 x 74.5 (E)
1993.965 (P)

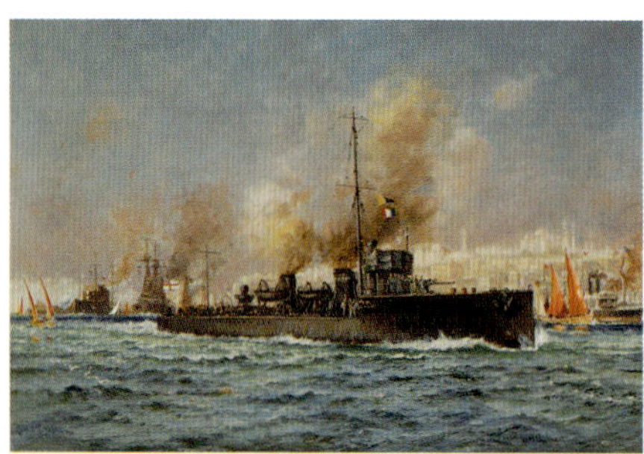

De Lacy, Charles John active 1885–1940
Destroyer 'Forester' off Constantinople
oil on canvas 39.2 x 60 (E)
1993.59 (P)

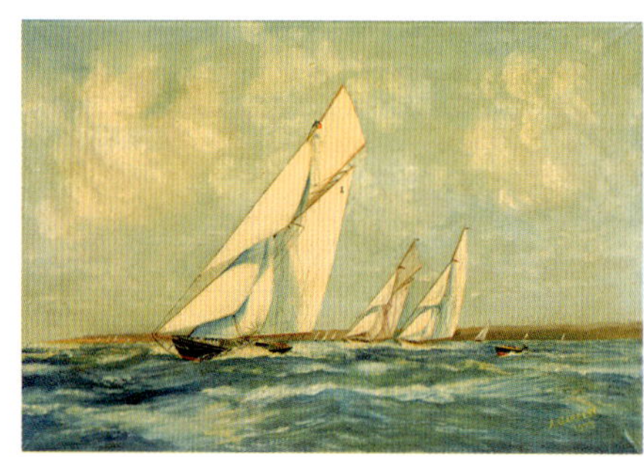

Garrett, A. (attributed to)
A Yacht Race 1973
oil on canvas 38 x 56 (E)
1993.12

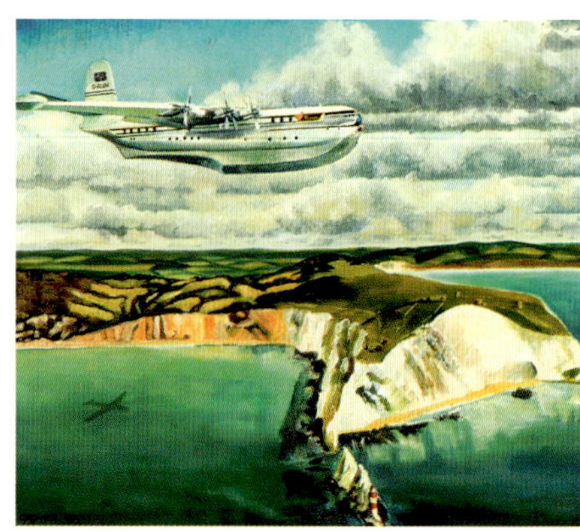

Groves
'Princess' and 'The Needles' 1983
oil on board 48.5 x 58.5 (E)
1993.85

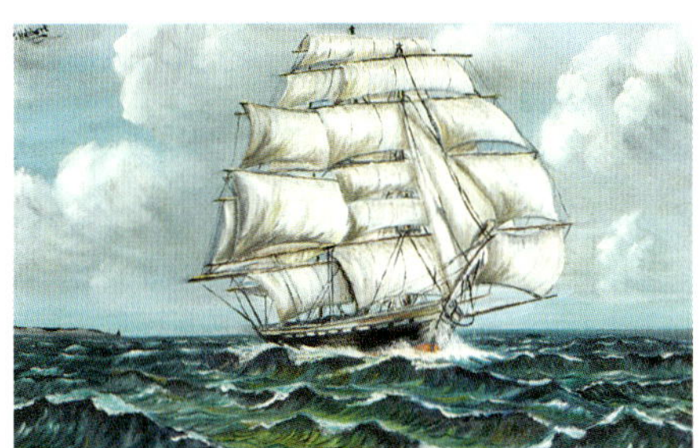

Hibbert, Phyllis I. b.1903
Schooner in Full Sail
oil on canvas 36.2 x 58.9 (E)
1993.973

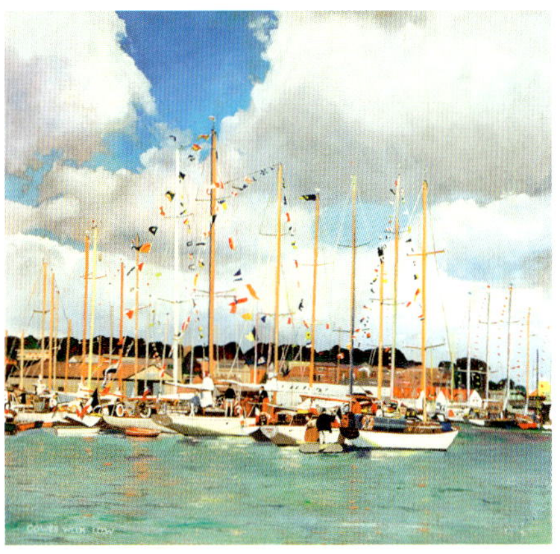

Holland, T.
Cowes Week, Isle of Wight 1981
oil on canvas 43 x 46 (E)
1993.971

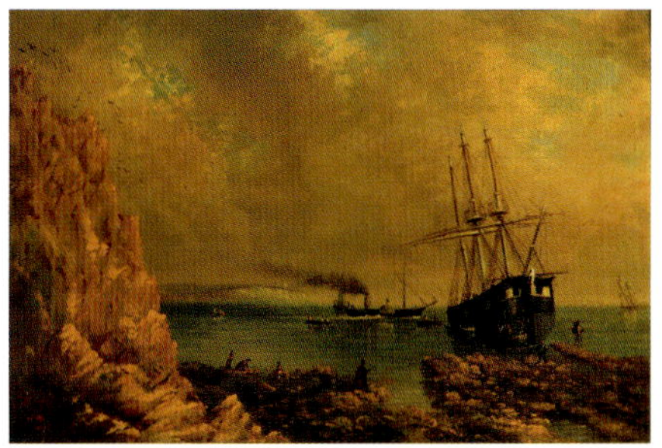

Marshall, John Frederick (circle of)
active 1875–1890
On Shanklin Rocks c.1866
oil on canvas 29.1 x 44.2 (E)
1993.54

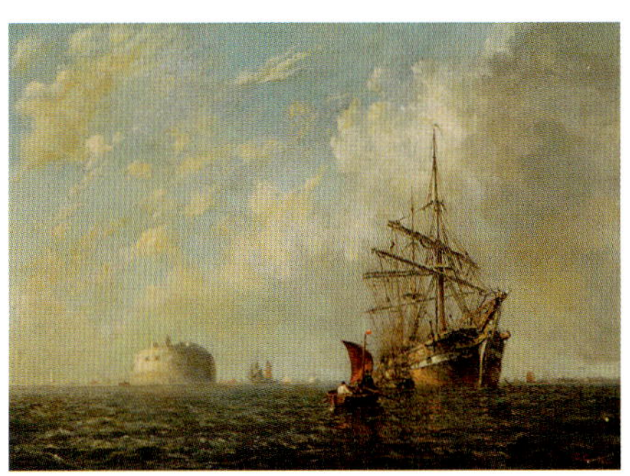

G. S.
Sailing Ship off Solent Fort 1901
oil on canvas 39.4 x 55 (E)
1993.97

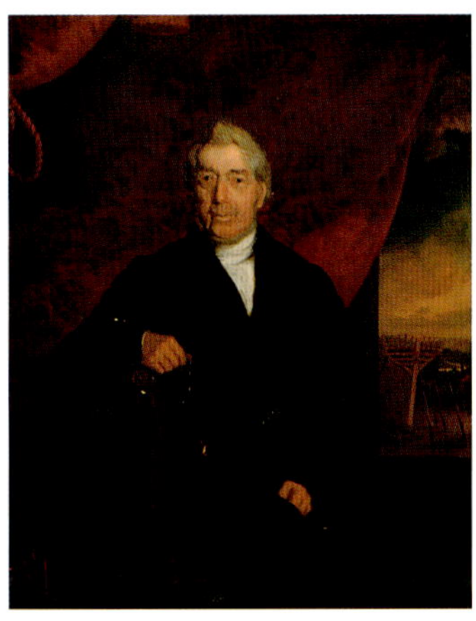

Steer, James (attributed to)
Thomas White (1773–1859) 1800–1850
oil on canvas 126 x 100.5 (E)
1993.106 (P)

English Heritage, Osborne House

Osborne House was built between 1845 and 1851 for Queen Victoria and Prince Albert. It was built in the Italianate style by the London speculative builder, Thomas Cubitt, under the personal supervision of Prince Albert.

Queen Victoria and Prince Albert were both 26 years old when they bought the Osborne estate. They had been married for 5 years and had 4 children. They wanted a country residence where they could enjoy private family life away from affairs of state. Osborne was the first home Queen Victoria and Prince Albert owned personally. Their other main residences (Buckingham Palace and Windsor Castle) were owned by the State.

Osborne House consists of a number of distinct, but connected, parts: the Pavilion where Queen Victoria, Prince Albert and the younger Princes and Princesses had their rooms; the Main Wing which housed the elder Princes and Princesses; the Household Wing which housed members of the Royal Household and the Durbar Wing which contains the Durbar Room and rooms used by Princess Beatrice, Queen Victoria's youngest child.

There are a number of service buildings at the rear of the house, all of which are contemporary with Queen Victoria's occupation. The stables however date from the eighteenth century and served the old house that the Queen and Prince demolished to make way for the new house. After a new stable building was built in the 1860s, these were altered to provide accommodation for servants.

The Swiss Cottage and Museum, built for the royal children in 1853 and 1862 respectively, are situated around a mile from the house. Here the Princesses learned the rudiments of housekeeping and cooking. The Princes learned the rudiments of warfare at the child-sized Victoria Fort and Barracks which are situated nearby. Both the Princes and Princesses learned how to garden and build up a museum collection.

After the death of Queen Victoria at Osborne in 1901, King Edward VII gave the house to the nation. In 1904 part of it opened to the public and in the same year the King Edward VII Convalescent Home for Officers (closed in 2001) occupied the remaining parts. Although the Pavilion was largely untouched the opening of the Convalescent Home did necessitate a number of alterations to other parts of the building.

Currently, Osborne gives a unique insight into the kind of life Queen Victoria and Prince Albert enjoyed at Osborne. The lives of the people who supported this lifestyle – the Royal Household and the 'below stairs' staff – are less evident, due to the Convalescent Home's later use of such areas.

The few paintings entered in this catalogue are but a fraction of those to be found at Osborne House. The vast majority of works on display belong to the Royal Collection and, as such, are in private ownership. Only those belonging to English Heritage are shown here.

Michael Hunter, Curator

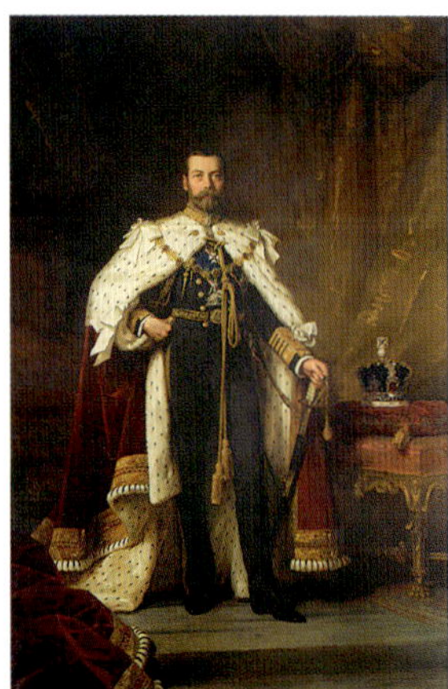

Fildes, Luke (after) 1844–1927
George V (1865–1936)
oil on canvas 261 x 170 (E)
79700124

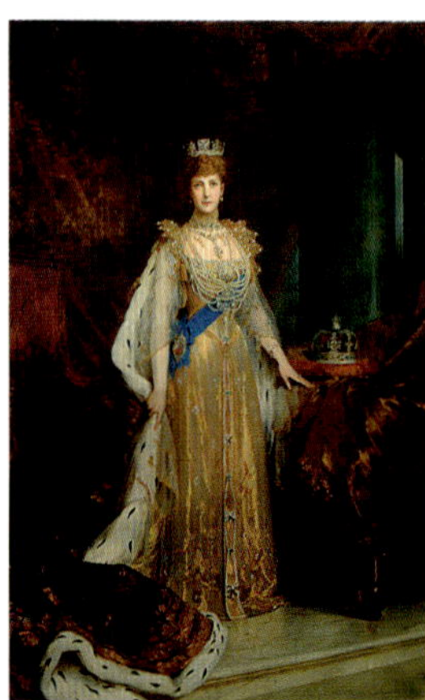

Fildes, Luke (after) 1844–1927
Queen Alexandra (1844–1925)
oil on canvas 277 x 170 (E)
79702163

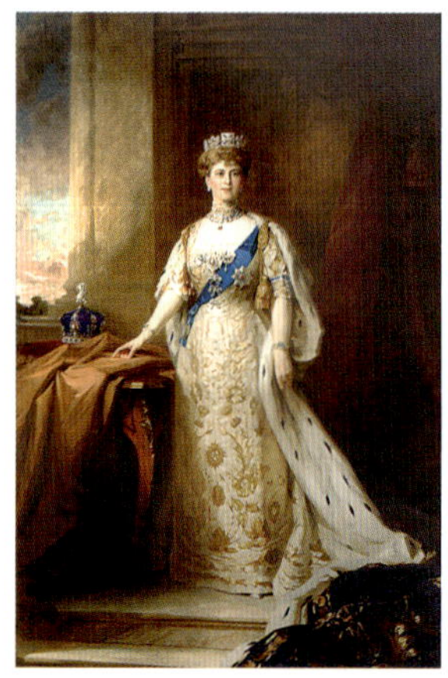

Fildes, Luke (after) 1844–1927
Queen Mary (1867–1953)
oil on canvas 266 x 170 (E)
79702164

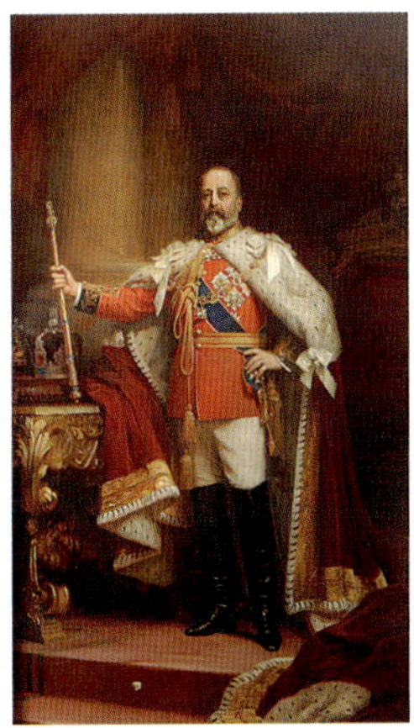

Fildes, Luke (copy of) 1844–1927
Edward VII (1841–1910)
oil on canvas 270 x 150 (E)
79700234

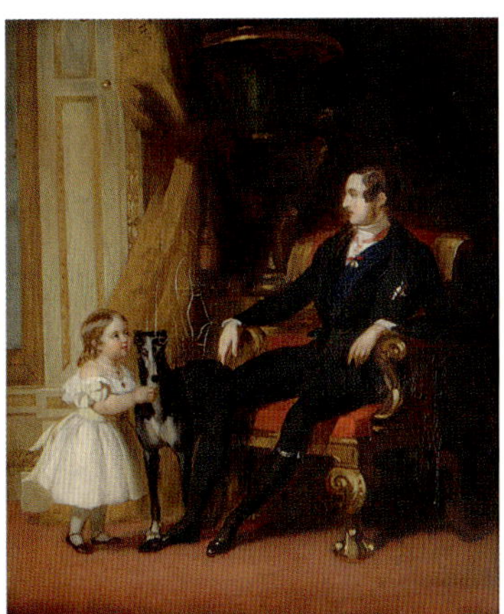

Lucas, John 1807–1874
Prince Albert (1819–1861), Princess Royal and Eos
oil on canvas 62 x 54 (E)
79705045

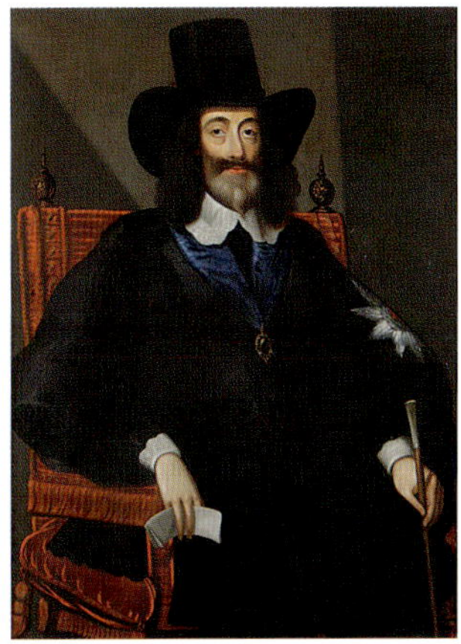

unknown artist
Charles I (1600–1649)
oil on canvas 124.3 x 95 (E)
79712473

Sir Max Aitken Museum

The Museum is housed in a magnificent eighteenth century sail maker's loft in Cowes High Street. This was acquired and restored by Sir Max Aitken in 1947 and for many years served as his base in Cowes and as a home for his very fine collection of marine paintings and marine artefacts. These include ship models, figureheads, cannons (of particular interest is a pair of sixteenth century Italian bronze cannons), furniture and other items from Royal Yachts, including the gaff from the J Class Yacht Britannia, and much else that is fascinating to all those interested in ships and the sea.

Sir Max Aitken Bt, DSO, DFC was well known in Cowes as a keen and very able yachtsman who successfully represented Great Britain in many offshore events, but he had many other claims to fame. Born in Canada in 1910, Sir Max has been acknowledged by his achievements as a newspaper magnate, a courageous fighter pilot in the Second World War, a Conservative MP, a racing powerboat pioneer, and the founder of the London Boat Show.

In 1979 he created a charitable trust to preserve his collection and to make this available to the public as a museum. Despite Sir Max's death in 1985, it remains a very personal museum and is much the same as he knew it, which serves as a lasting reminder of a truly remarkable man.

The very fine paintings in the Museum, which the Public Catalogue Foundation have kindly included in their records, include works by most of the better known British and Dutch marine artists. The majority date from the seventeenth, eighteenth, and nineteenth centuries, but there are, however, more recent works by the likes of Alfred Wallis (1855–1942) the increasingly sought after Cornish primitive painter, as well as Norman Wilkinson (1878–1971) and Montague Dawson (1895–1973).

Several of the paintings reflect Sir Max's interest in Nelson. There is a very fine painting of *The Battle of Trafalgar* by Thomas Buttersworth (1768–1842). Butterworth was almost certainly a sailor and there is a tradition in the family that he actually fought at Trafalgar. There are four companion canvases by an unidentified artist depicting the Battle of the Nile as well as a copy of Arthur William Devis's famous painting *The Death of Nelson* and numerous prints and other Nelson memorabilia.

A very popular painting with visitors to the Museum is a large canvas by Ludolf Backhuysen (1630–1708), *The Foundering of the 'Coronation', 90 Guns at Rame Head in 1691*, in which the Captain and 300 men were drowned. Although Backhuysen belongs to the Dutch school, he was German and first worked as a calligrapher in his native town of Emden.

Some of the paintings reflect a local interest. There is a very good painting by Peter Monamy (1681–1749), entitled *Shipping off Spithead.* Monamy was the most important artist of the first generation of British marine painters and was much influenced by the Van de Veldes. Also included is a Francis Swaine (c.1720–1782) of a man o' war and other shipping off the Isle of Wight, as well as *Shipping off Ryde* by John Wilson Carmichael (1800–1868).

Out of necessity, only a few of the paintings in the Museum are mentioned in this introduction, but it is hoped that this will encourage people to come and look at this very fine collection.

John A. N. Hoare, Trustee

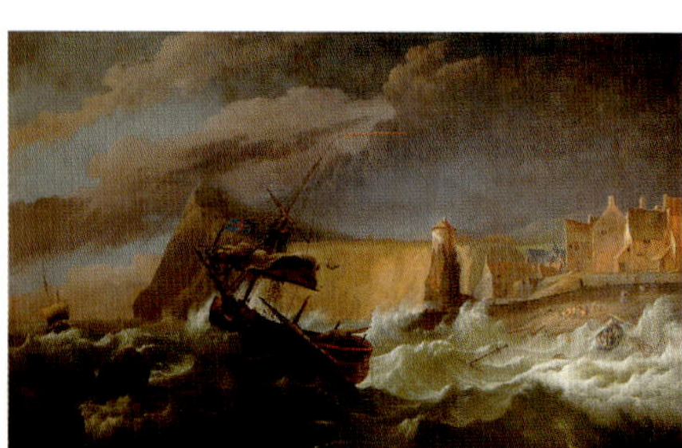

Backhuysen, Ludolf I 1630–1708
The Foundering of the 'Coronation' 90 Guns at Rame Head, 1691
oil on canvas 147.3 x 231.1
16

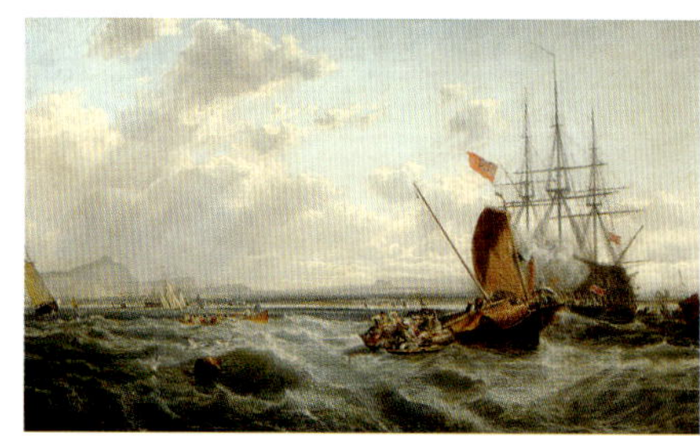

Bough, Samuel 1822–1878
British Emigrants Boarding a Merchant Vessel for Australia, Firth of Forth 1869
oil on canvas 91.4 x 152.4
24

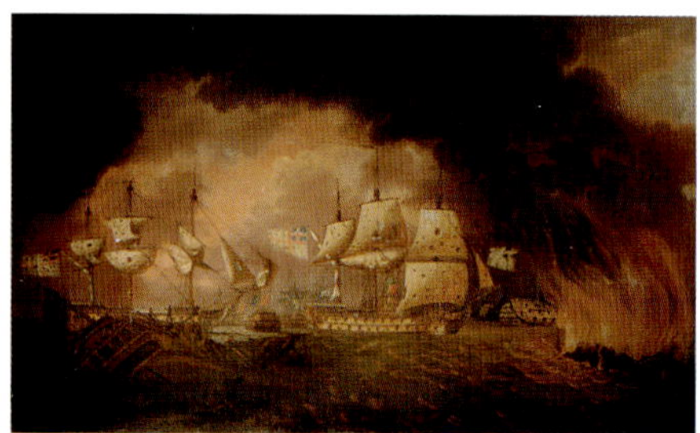

British (English) School
Scene from the Battle of the Nile, 1–2 August 1798 c.1820
oil on canvas 86.4 x 147.3
2

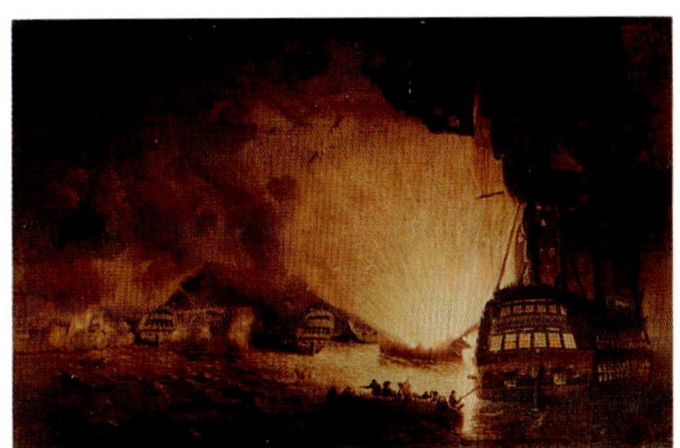

British (English) School
Scene from the Battle of the Nile, 1–2 August 1798 c.1820
oil on canvas 86.4 x 147.3
3

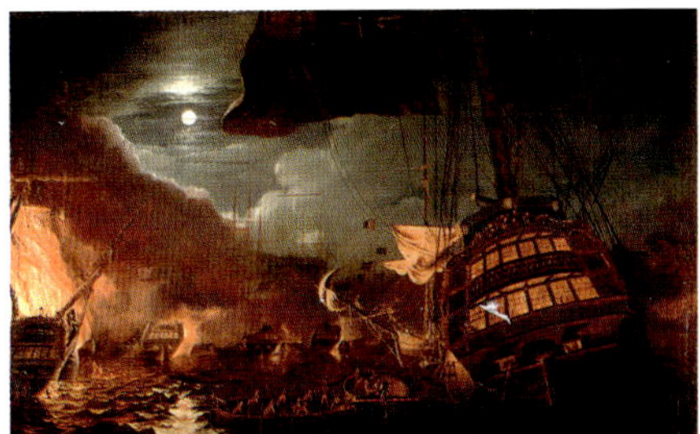

British (English) School
Scene from the Battle of the Nile, 1–2 August 1798 c.1820
oil on canvas 88.9 x 142.2
28

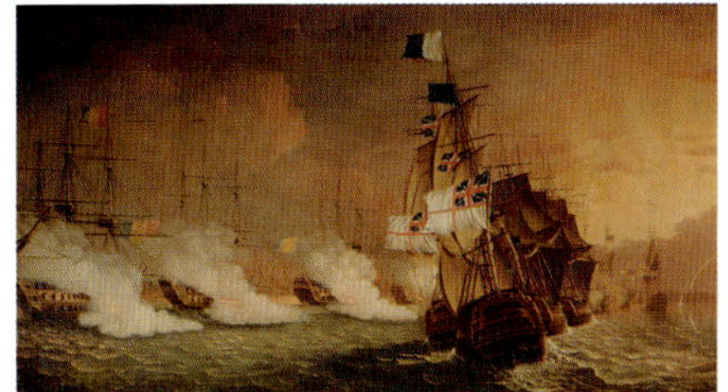

British (English) School
Scene from the Battle of the Nile, 1–2 August 1798 c.1820
oil on canvas 88.9 x 231.1
29

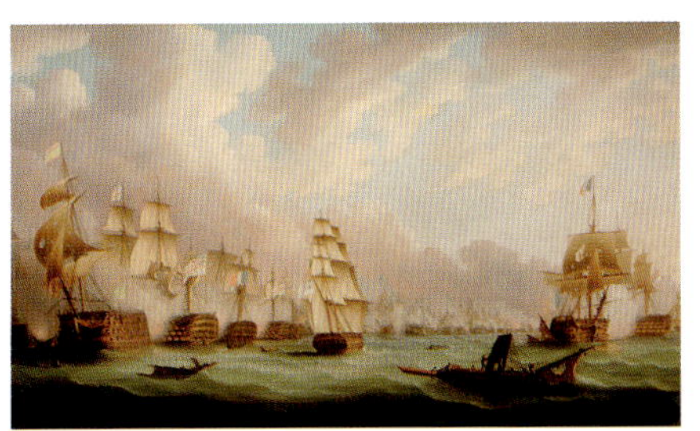

Buttersworth, Thomas 1768–1842
The Battle of Trafalgar, 21 October 1805 c.1820
oil on canvas 100.3 x 171.5
20

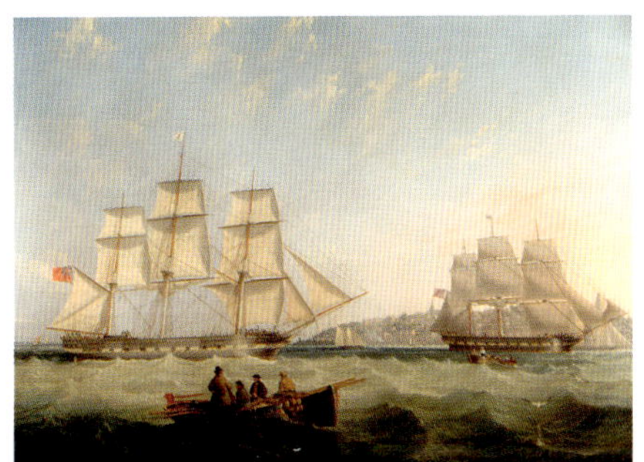

Carmichael, James Wilson 1800–1868
Shipping off Ryde 1854
oil on canvas 83.8 x 119.4
13

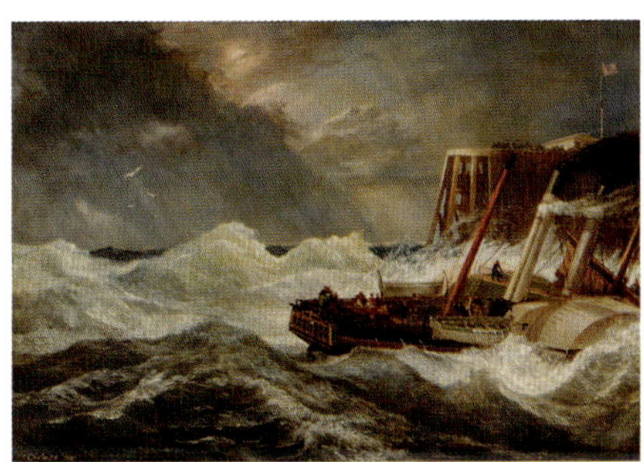

Chalon, John James 1778–1854
Arrival of a Steam Packet from Boulogne during a Gale, 1846 1847
oil on canvas 78.7 x 119.4
18

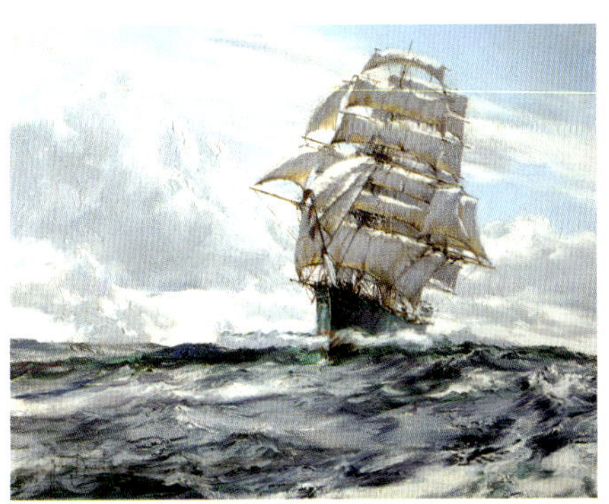

Dawson, Montague J. 1895–1973
'Thermopylae' Clipper
oil on panel 34.2 x 44.2
1

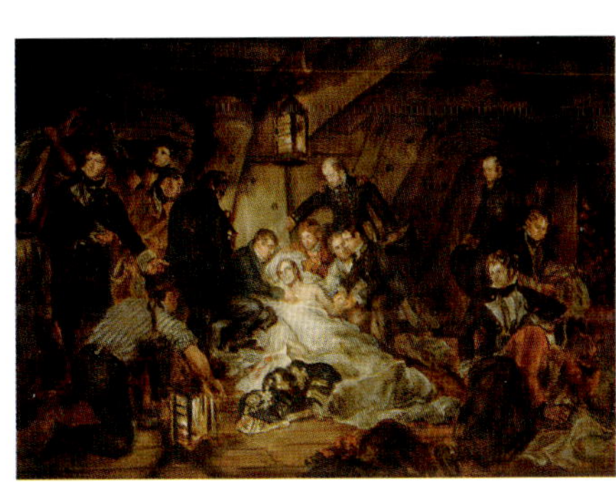

Devis, Arthur (copy after) 1712–1787
The Death of Nelson 18th C
oil on canvas 71.1 x 91.4
7

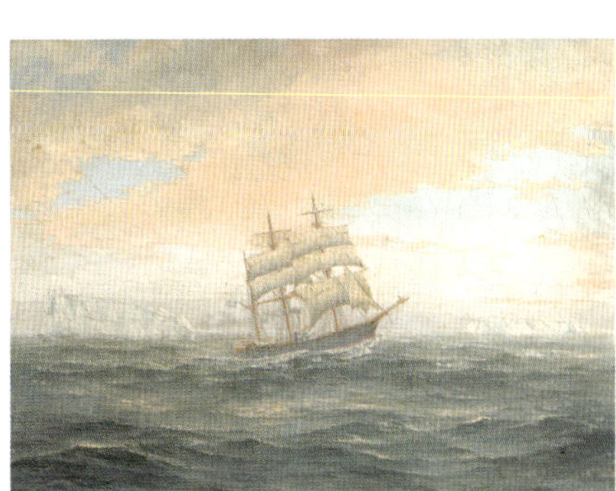

Engtoin, Quelelberge
The Argentine Corvette 'Uruguay' Searching for Nordenskjöld's Expedition in the Atlantic Ocean, 1903
oil on panel 45.7 x 63.5
21

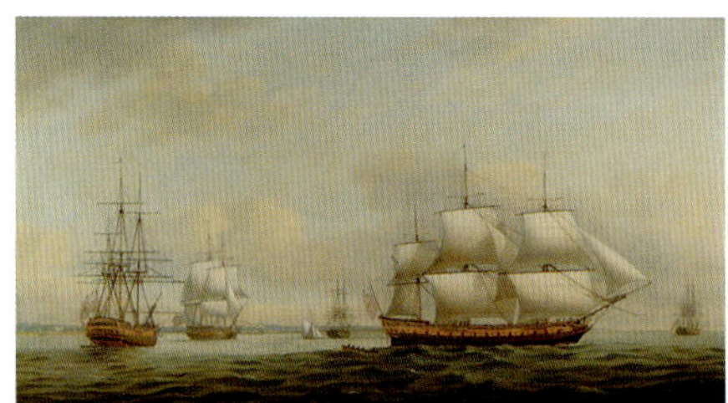

Luny, Thomas 1759–1837
The East Indiaman 'Ceres' off the Spithead Depicted in Four Different Views 1788
oil on canvas 86.4 x 147.3
27

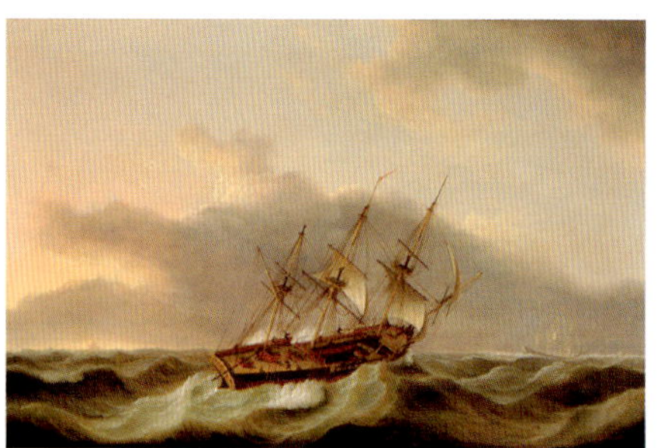

Luny, Thomas 1759–1837
Shipping in a Stiff Breeze 1807
oil on canvas 53.3 x 83.8
17

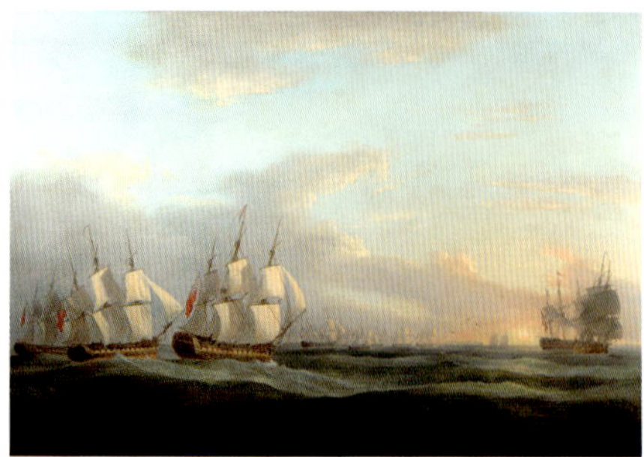

Luny, Thomas 1759–1837
Departure of the Fleet 1820
oil on canvas 100.3 x 149.9
5

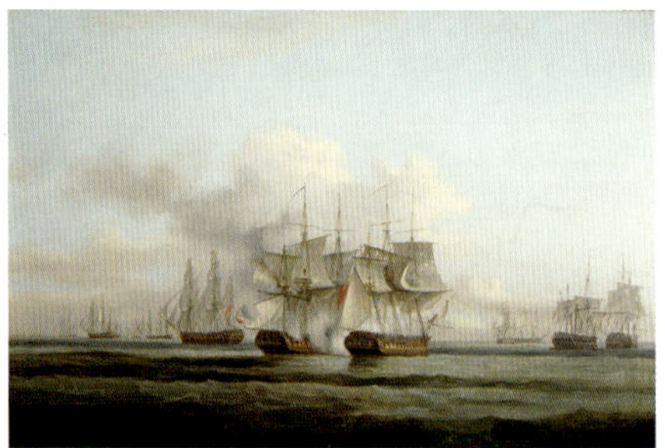

Luny, Thomas 1759–1837
The Engagement 1820
oil on canvas 100.3 x 149.9
8

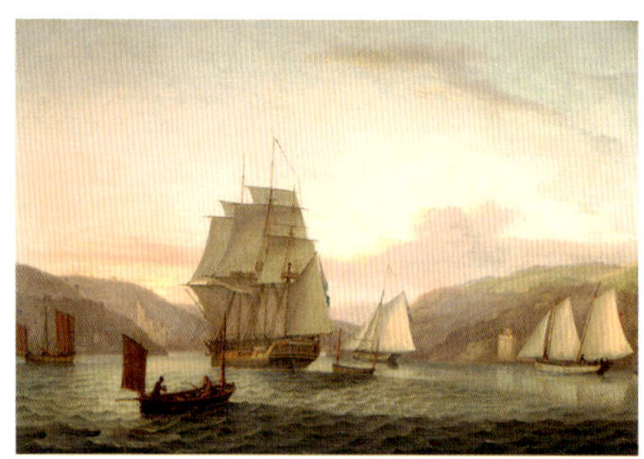

Luny, Thomas 1759–1837
Armed Merchantmen into Dartmouth
oil on canvas 72.4 x 108
23

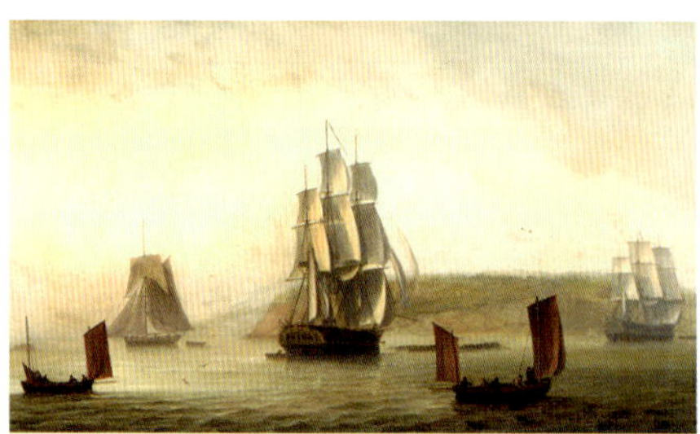

Luny, Thomas 1759–1837
Shipping Warping into Harbour off Berry Head
oil on canvas 63.5 x 99.1
11

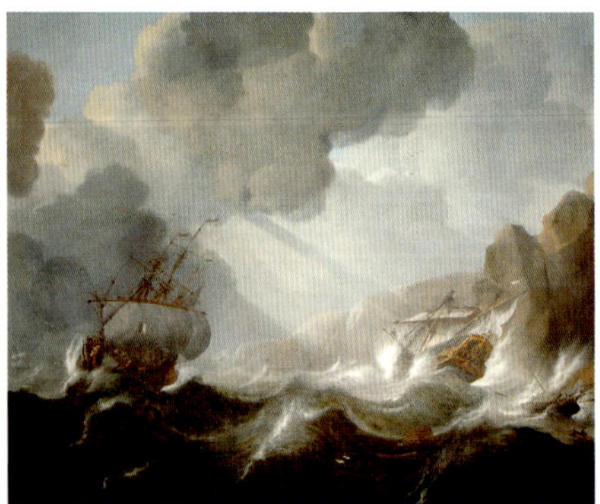

Macheren, Philip van d. after 1672
French Man of War 1685
oil on canvas 101.6 x 127
14

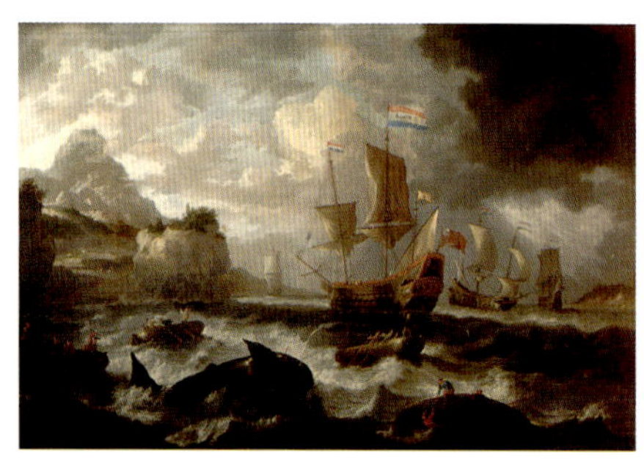

Minderhout, Hendrik van (attributed to) 1632–1696
Dutch Whalers
oil on canvas 110.5 x 165.1
15

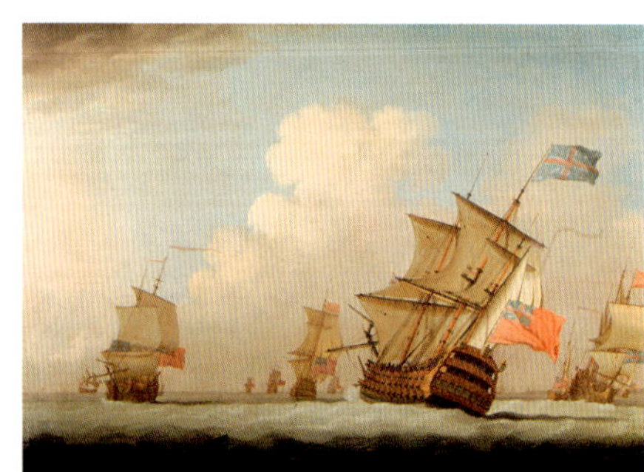

Monamy, Peter 1681–1749
Shipping off Spithead
oil on canvas 91.4 x 133.4
6

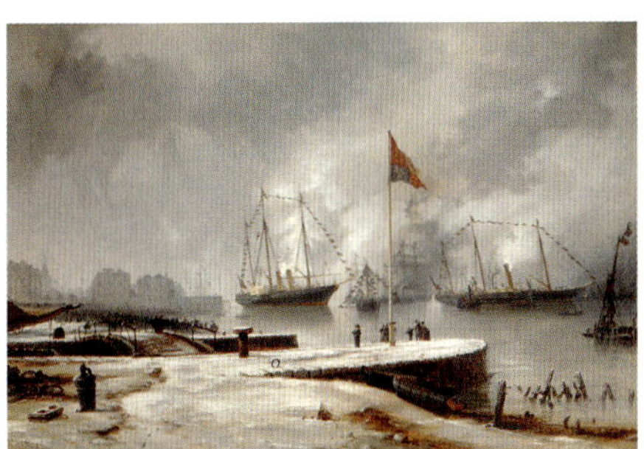

Nibbs, Richard Henry 1816–1893
The Departure from Gravesend of HRH Princess Royal on Her Marriage, 2 February 1858, to Prince Frederick, during a Snowstorm
oil on canvas 81.3 x 121.9
10

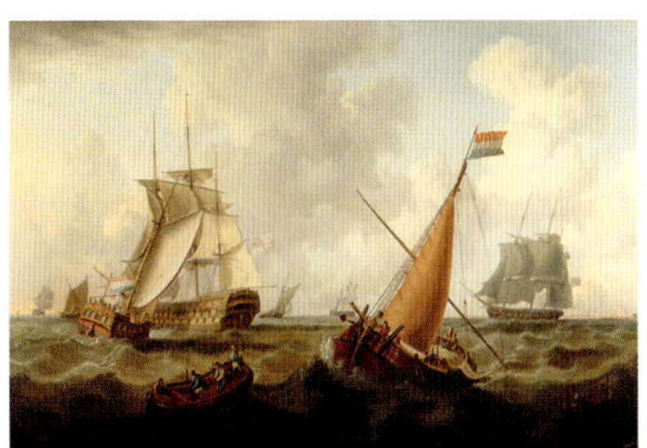

Powell, Charles Martin 1775–1824
Dutch and British Men O'War off the Coast, Dutch Boat in the Foreground
oil on canvas 81.3 x 121.9
26

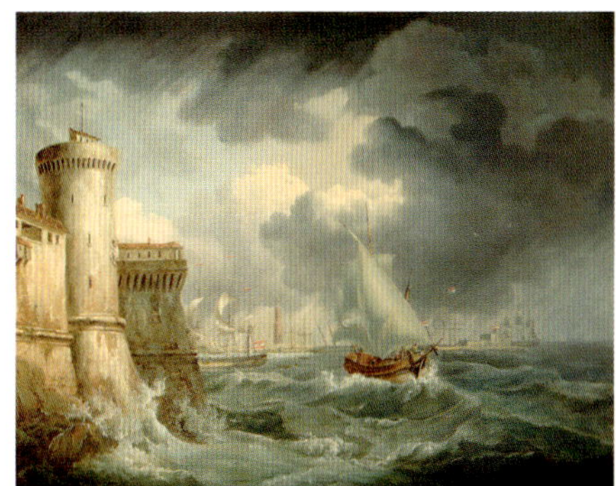

Serres, John Thomas 1759–1825
Shipping off Genoa 1823
oil on canvas 88.9 x 116.8
25

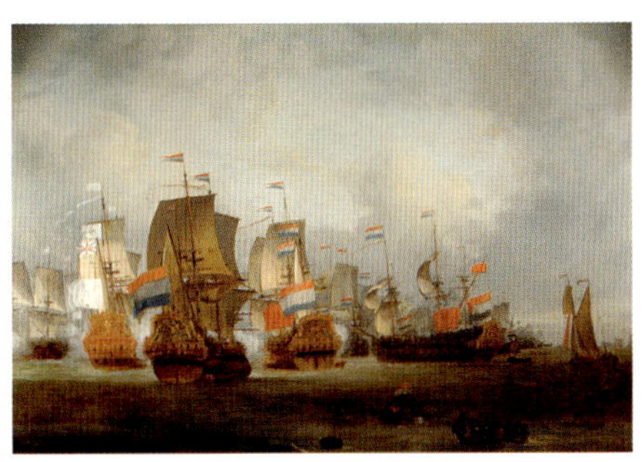

Storck, Abraham (attributed to) 1644–1708
British Men O'War and the Dutch Fleet Commanded by Admiral Tromp Fighting on the Thames
oil on canvas 101.6 x 172.7
22

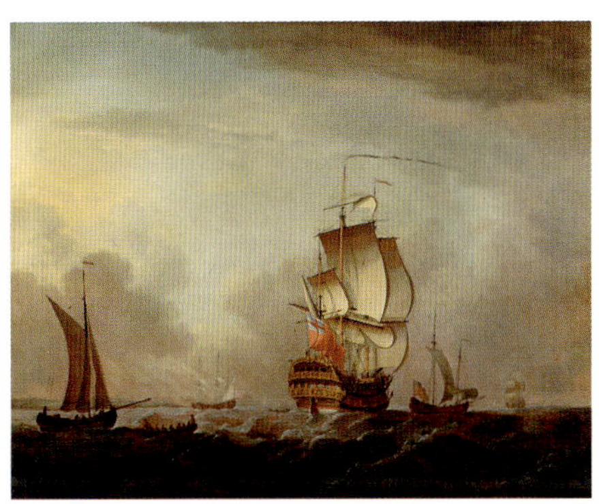

Swaine, Francis c.1720–1782
Shipping off the Isle of Wight
oil on canvas 99.1 x 124.5
12

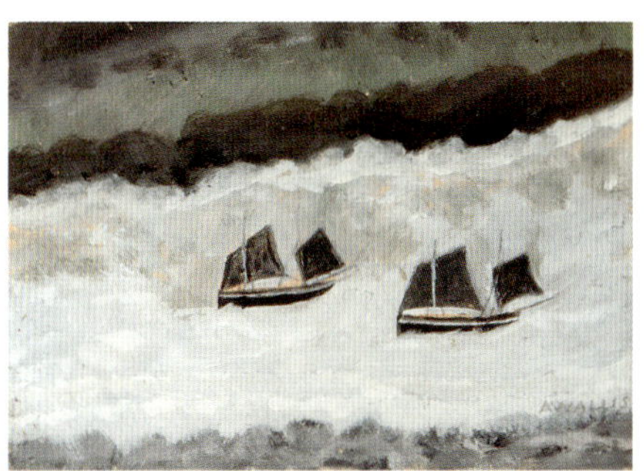

Wallis, Alfred 1855–1942
Sailing Boats
oil on board 21.6 x 29.2
4

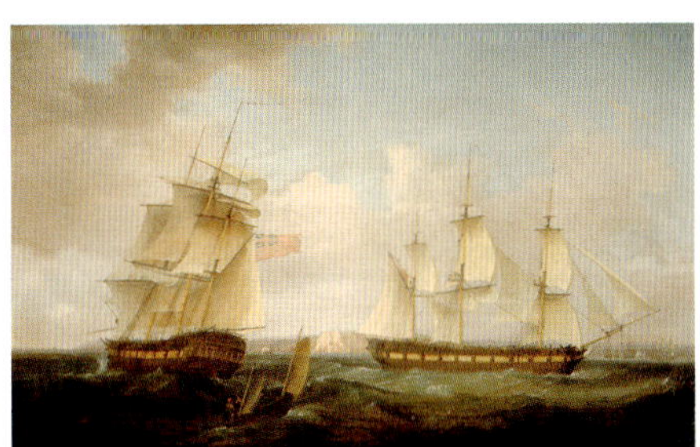

Whitcombe, Thomas c.1752–1824
Two Views of HM Frigate 'Amelia' off Berry Head 1808
oil on canvas 88.9 x 144.8
9

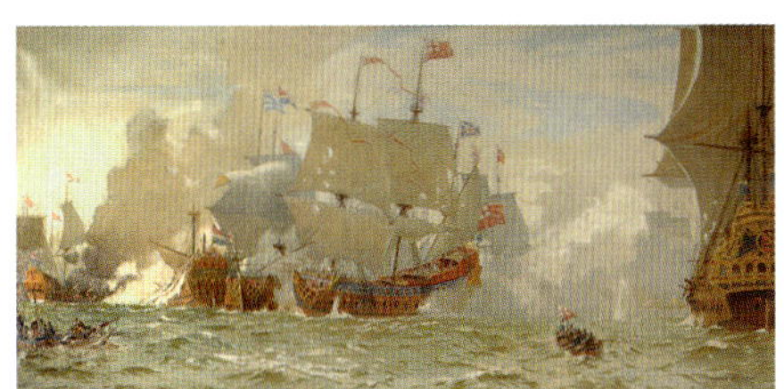

Wilkinson, Norman 1878–1971
Shipping Scene (St James's Fight, 5 July 1666) 1922
oil on canvas 91.4 x 193
19

Museum of Island Railway History

The Isle of Wight Steam Railway is a registered educational charity operated by paid staff and volunteers. Independent of the national rail system, it is one of Britain's heritage railways. Since 1971 the railway has operated from Havenstreet Station which was rebuilt by Southern Railway in 1926, the island platform and station building (comprising signal box, waiting room and toilets) still remain to this day. The line runs from Woolton through Havenstreet, and Ashey to Smallbrook where a rail link with island line's Ryde-Shanklin line connects on Isle of Wight steam railway running days. The major rail artefacts comprising steam and diesel locomotives, carriages and wagons among others are all owned by the railway. The buildings consist of an engine shed, carriage and wagon workshop, offices, café, station buildings and a former gas house which houses the shop, staff rest room, first aid room and a museum gallery of smaller Isle of Wight related railway artefacts. This building also houses the railway's collection of archives with plans, documents, photographs, paintings and books relating to Isle of Wight railway heritage.

Paddy Jardine, Curator

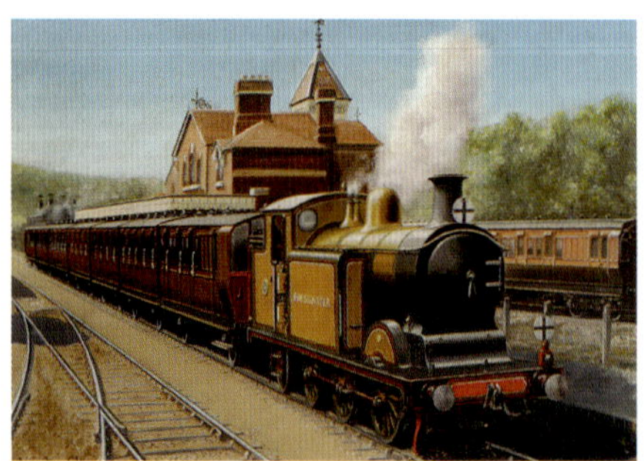

Ellis, Cuthbert Hamilton 1909–1987
Freshwater
oil on board 24.1 x 37.3 (E)
6

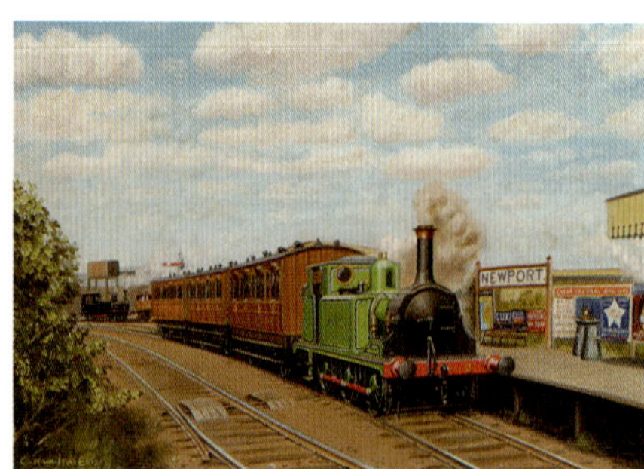

Ellis, Cuthbert Hamilton 1909–1987
Freshwater, Yamouth and Newport No.2
oil on board 25.2 x 37 (E)
1

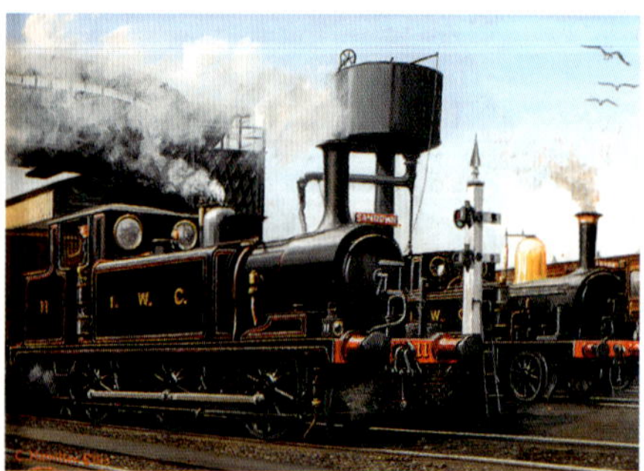

Ellis, Cuthbert Hamilton 1909–1987
Isle of Wight Central No.11 to Sandown at Ryde Pier
oil on board 24.5 x 35.3 (E)
10

Facing page: Eurich, Richard Ernst, 1903–1992, *The Rose* (detail), 1960, University of Southampton, (p. 203)

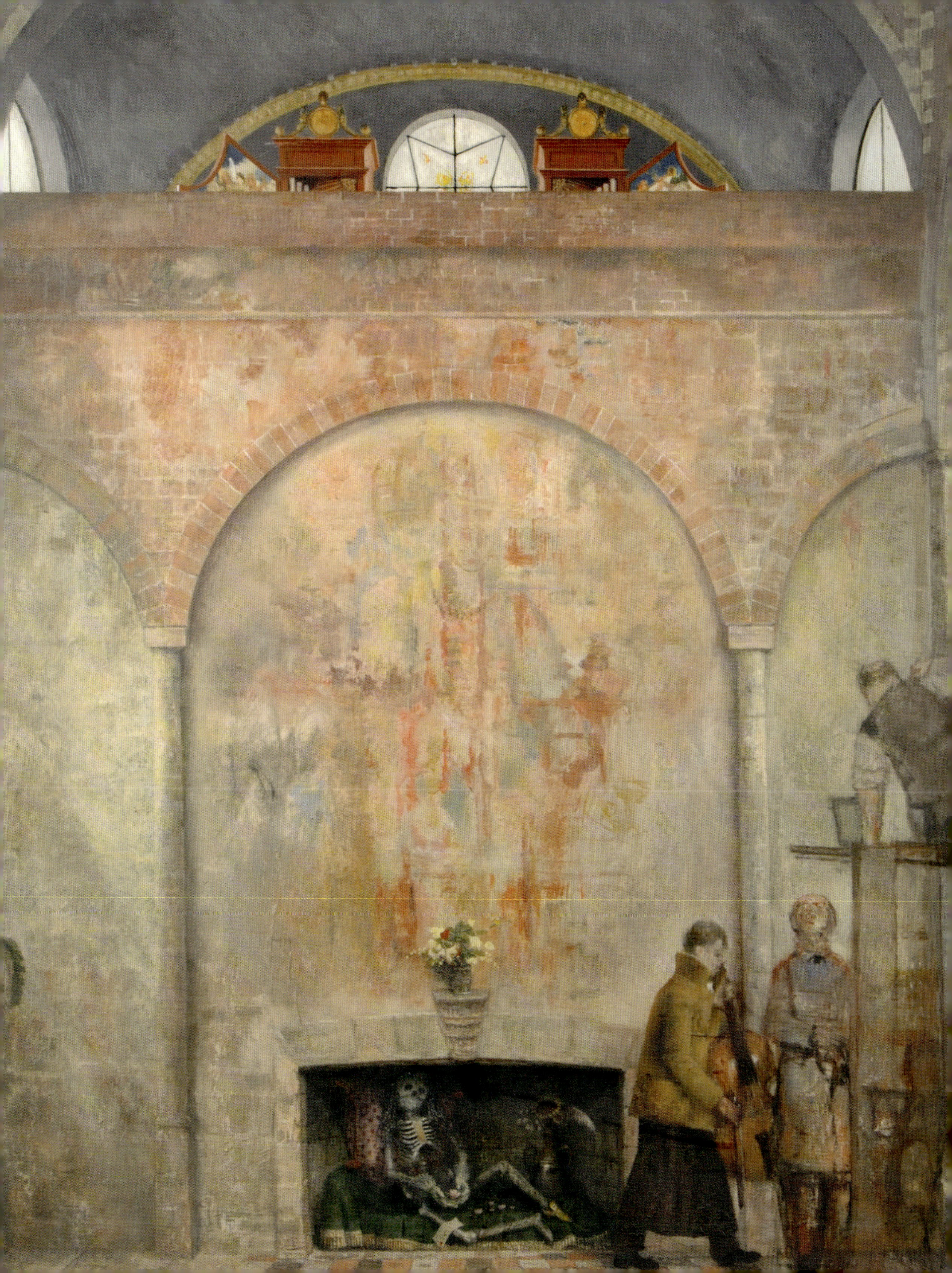

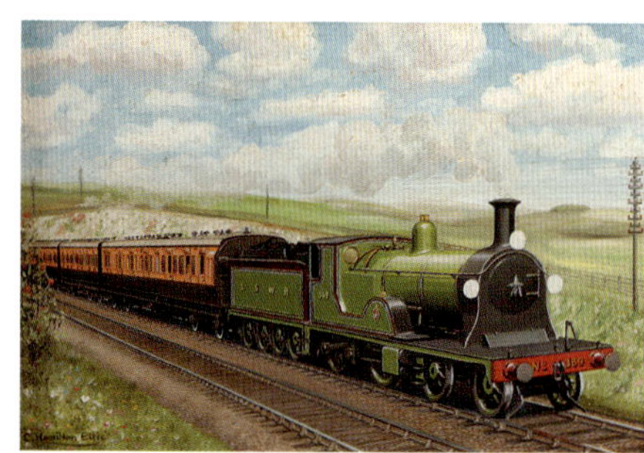

Ellis, Cuthbert Hamilton 1909–1987
London and South Western Railway No.369
oil on board 25.2 x 37.8 (E)
9

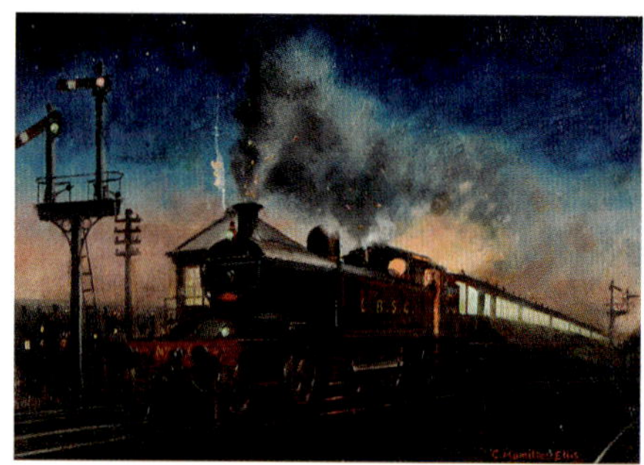

Ellis, Cuthbert Hamilton 1909–1987
London-Brighton South Coast at Night
oil on board 24.3 x 34.2 (E)
5

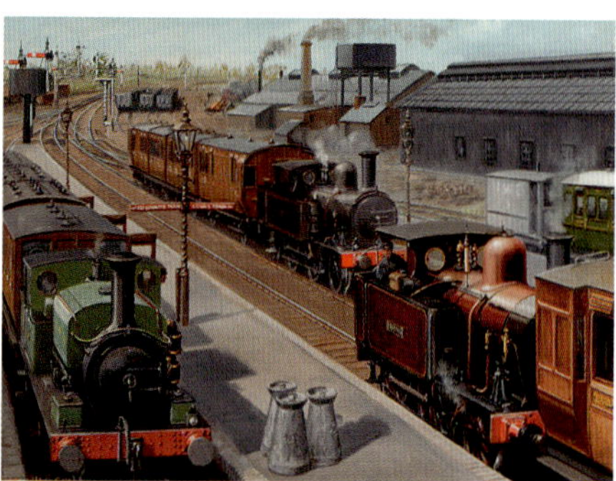

Ellis, Cuthbert Hamilton 1909–1987
Newport Station
oil on board 29.5 x 40 (E)
3

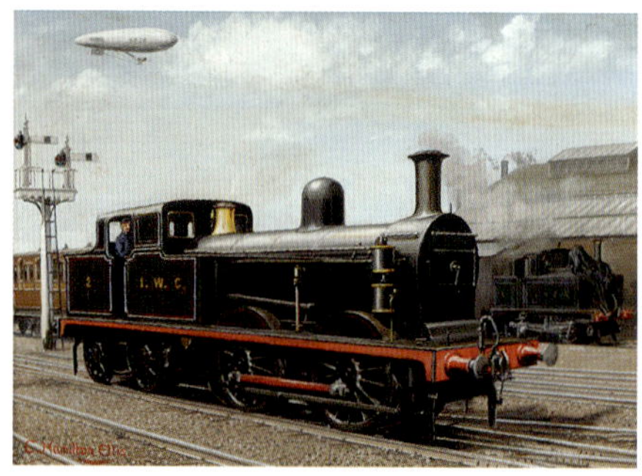

Ellis, Cuthbert Hamilton 1909–1987
No.2 'Isle of Wight Central' with No.1 'Isle of Wight Central' in the Background
oil on board 25.5 x 35.5 (E)
8

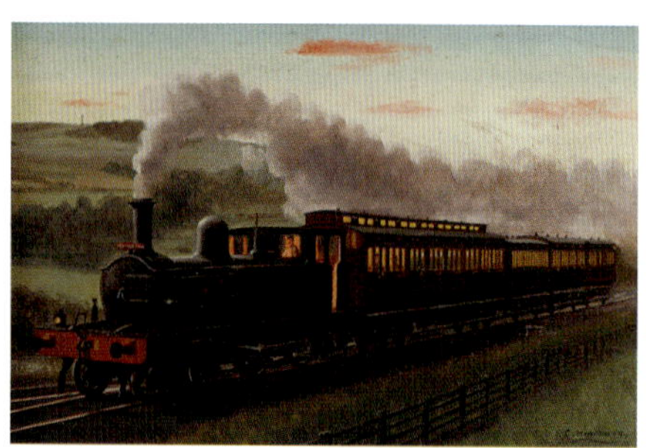

Ellis, Cuthbert Hamilton 1909–1987
No.6 'Ventnor Town' at Evening
oil on board 25 x 37.3 (E)
2

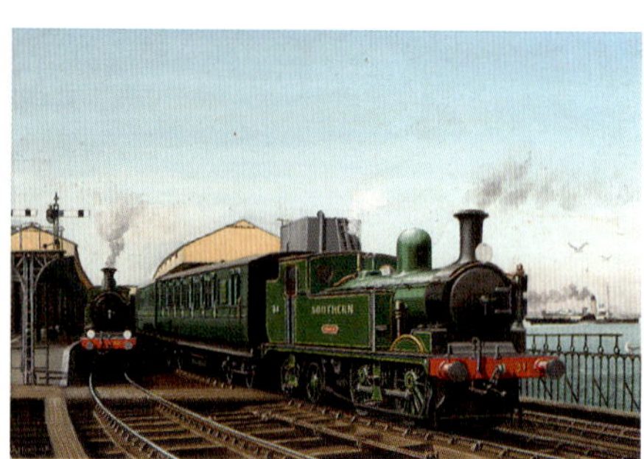

Ellis, Cuthbert Hamilton 1909–1987
No.31, 'Chale'
oil on board 24.2 x 37.8 (E)
7

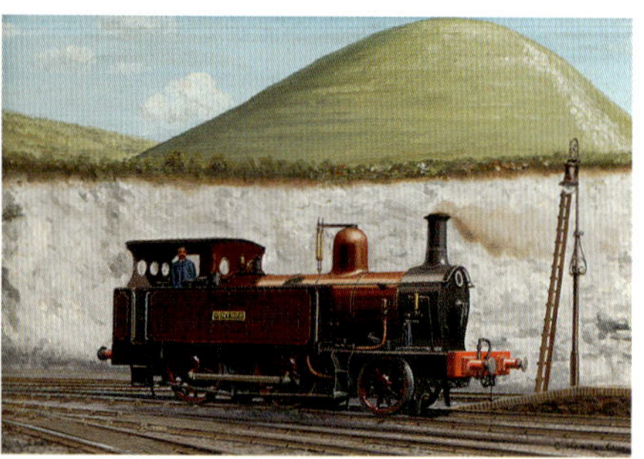

Ellis, Cuthbert Hamilton 1909–1987
'Ventnor'
oil on board 24.5 x 37.2 (E)
4

Carisbrooke Castle Museum

Carisbrooke Castle Museum is an unusual local history Museum. It was founded in 1898 by Queen Victoria's youngest daughter, Princess Beatrice, as a memorial to her husband, Prince Henry of Battenberg. Princess Beatrice's project of a museum devoted to Isle of Wight history was endorsed by Queen Victoria, who gave some of the most significant objects in the collections. The museum is now an independent trust based in an English Heritage castle.

The Museum cares for important and varied collections of Isle of Wight material, from objects excavated from the castle's medieval past, on loan from English Heritage, to recent watercolours of Island landscapes. People with local connections are represented: King Charles I, who was imprisoned in the castle; Queen Victoria, who bought Osborne on the Island as a family home; Princess Beatrice, who used Carisbrooke Castle as her summer residence; the poet Tennyson; and John Milne, the 'father of seismology'. There is local defence material, from a Tudor falcon owned by the village of Carisbrooke to Isle of Wight Rifle uniforms and Home Guard records. Other local collections include embroidered vestments from St Dominic's Priory in Carisbrooke, art pottery from Gunville, and Isle of Wight holiday souvenirs. Social history collections illustrate farming, crafts, smuggling, yachting and seaside holidays. There are collections of clothing and domestic objects. The evolution of the landscape and the development of towns and villages are shown by the large collections of paintings, engravings and photographs.

The oil paintings in our collections are linked with some of these themes. There are portraits of King Charles I, and of the Museum's other royal connections, Princess Beatrice and Prince Henry of Battenberg. Princess Beatrice and Prince Henry also held the Governorship of the Isle of Wight, a ceremonial position that had once played a significant role in national defence. The Duke of Bolton and Viscount Eversleigh, whose portraits feature in the collections, were also Governors of the Island.

Landscapes show rural activities, such as the transport of water from springs in Carisbrooke for sale in the town of Newport, and seascapes show the coastline and yachts. Not surprisingly, Carisbrooke Castle features in the collection, including the iconic image of the castle gatehouse. One of the most striking castle paintings is a Victorian interpretation of an event in the castle's history – the death of Princess Elizabeth, the daughter of King Charles I, at the age of 14, while a prisoner in the Castle in 1650.

The most unusual oil paintings in the collections comprise a miniature portrait of King Charles, and overlays painted on transparent mica (unfortunately miniatures are not included in the current series of catalogues). These overlays tell the story of the king: you can overlay his portrait with crown, robes and insignia of St George to represent his royal authority, with armour to represent the Civil War, and with bars to represent his imprisonment. Through the use of other overlays, Bishop Juxon can be added, the king's head can be removed, and he can be given a crown of laurels to represent his ultimate victory.

Rosemary Cooper, Curator

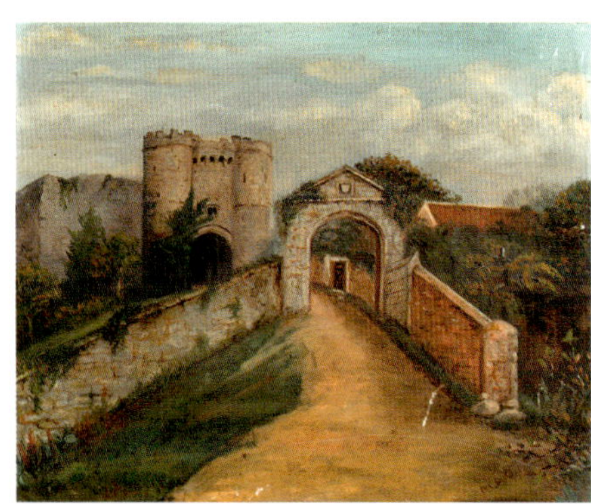

C. M. A.
Gateway and Gatehouse of Carisbrooke Castle
oil on canvas 35 x 42.5 (E)
P.1986.2046

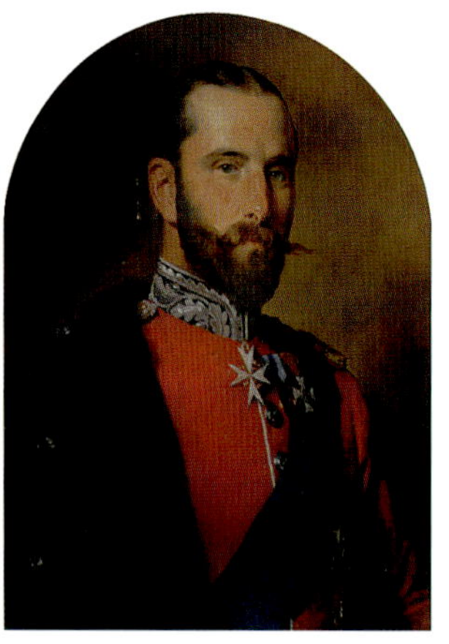

Angeli, Heinrich von 1840–1925
Prince Henry (1858–1896) in Military Uniform c.1896
oil on canvas 67 x 50 (E)
P.1986.2125

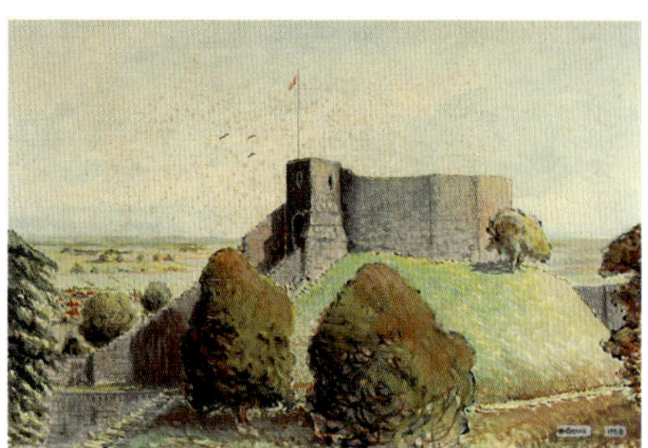

Banks, N.
The Keep at Carisbrooke Castle Painted from the Roof of the Residence 1958
oil on board 40.5 x 60.7
P.1986.1374

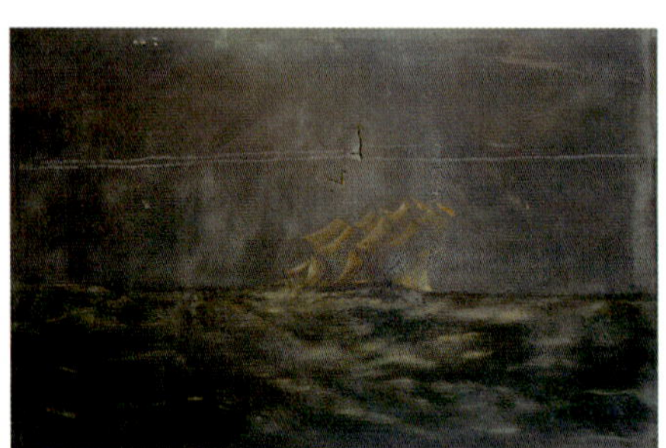

Beville, F. W.
Naval Ship off Freshwater Bay
oil on canvas 83 x 130 (E)
P.1986.2105

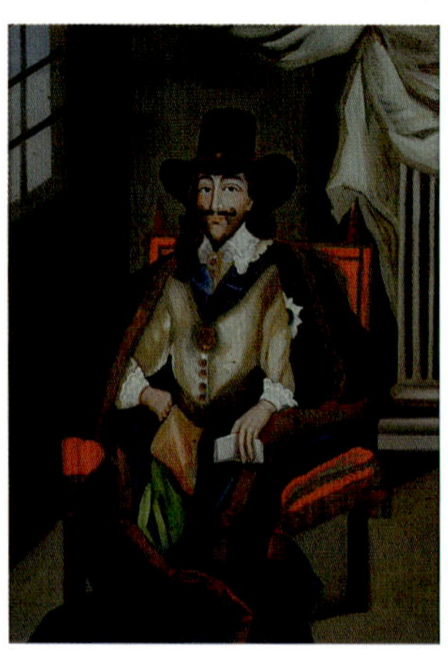

Bower, Edward (after) d.1666/1667
Charles I (1600–1649)
oil on glass 45.5 x 34.8 (E)
P.1986.2084

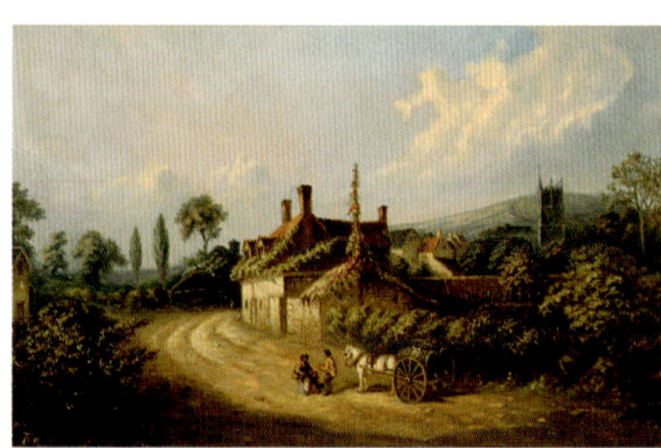

Cantelo, Ellen active c.1830–1859
Carisbrooke Village with Miss Sanders' Great-Grandparents and Their Water Cart c.1830
oil on canvas 39.5 x 60 (E)
2003.2

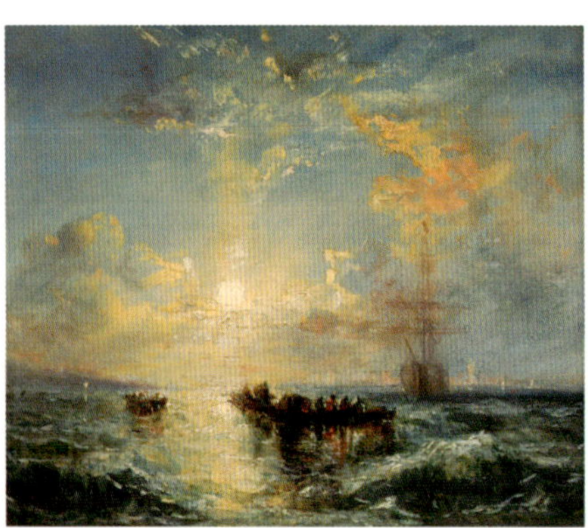

Collingwood-Smith, William 1815–1887
Sunset on Southampton Water Showing a Seascape with Shipping and the Isle of Wight
oil on canvas 24.5 x 30 (E)
P.1986.2045

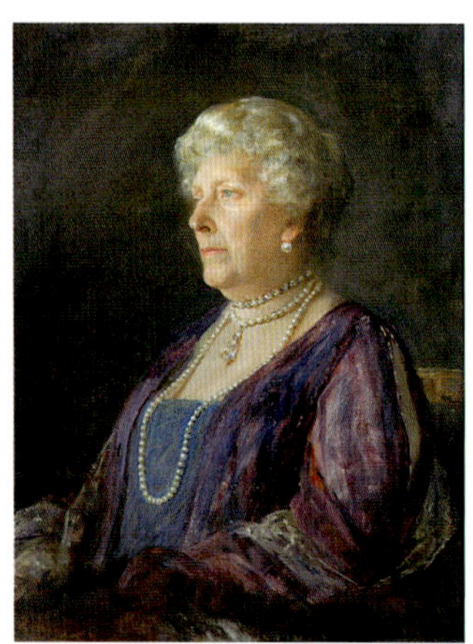

Cope, Arthur Stockdale 1857–1940
Princess Beatrice (1856–1944) 1928
oil on canvas 86.2 x 66.8 (E)
P.1986.2124

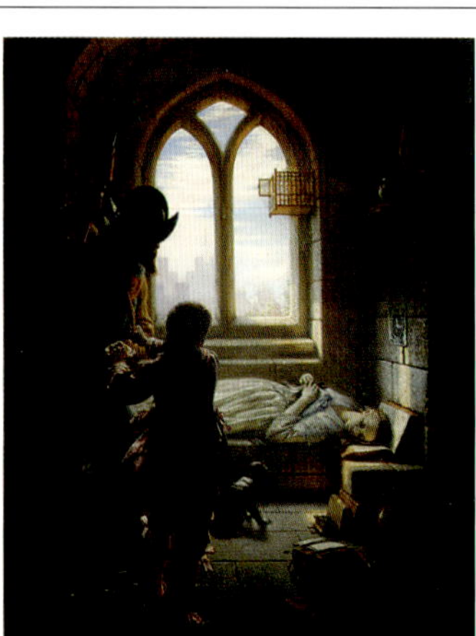

Cope, Charles West 1811–1890
The Royal Prisoners 1855
oil on canvas 89 x 71.5 (E)
P.1986.2082

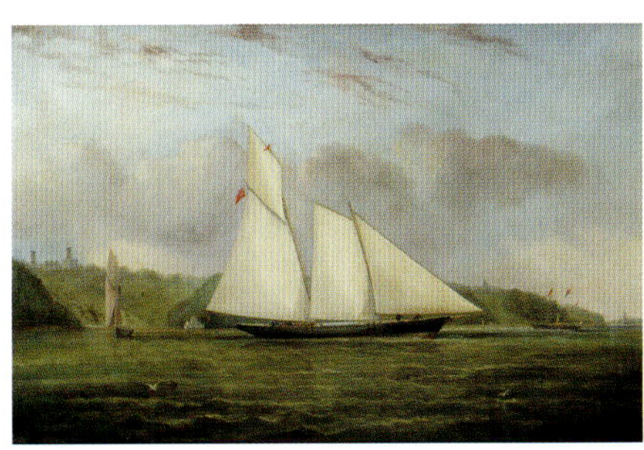

Fowles, Arthur Wellington c.1815–1883
Yacht Sailing off Osborne Bay 1866
oil on canvas 49 x 74 (E)
P.1986.2156

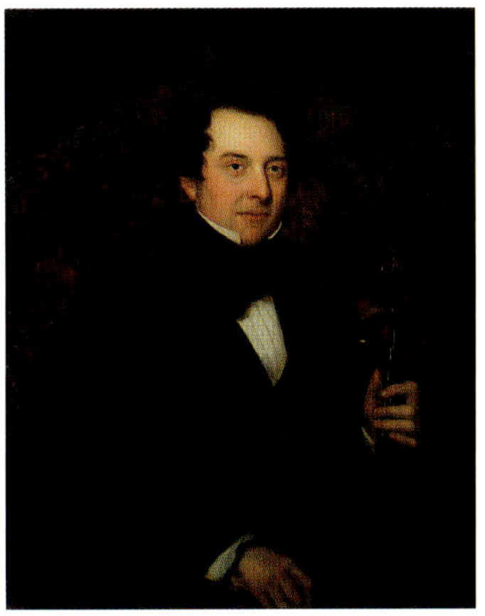

Gandy, Thomas active 1848–1859
Portrait of a Gentleman Holding a Cello (possibly William Turtle)
oil on canvas 90 x 69 (E)
1993.309

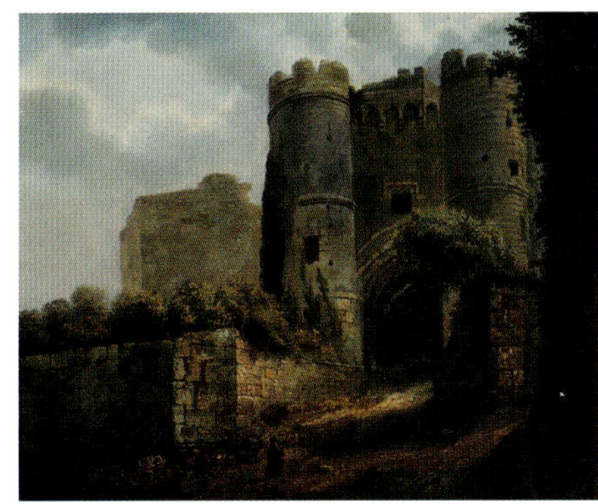

Ibbetson
The Gatehouse at Carisbrooke Castle 1887
oil on canvas 42 x 52.5 (E)
P.1986.2129

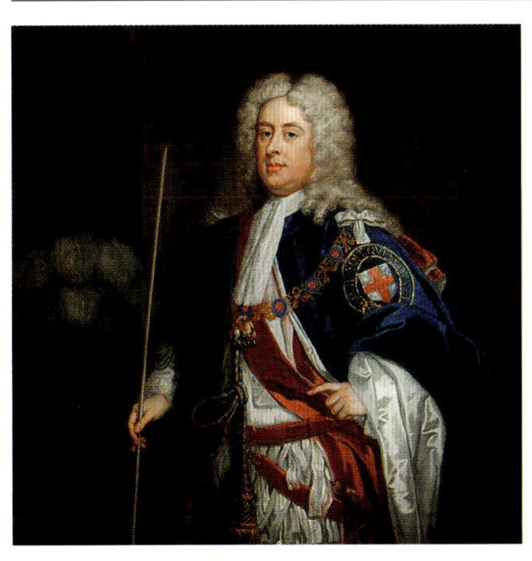

Kneller, Godfrey (after) 1646–1723
The Second Duke of Bolton Wearing the Robes of a Knight of the Garter with His Chamberlain's Wand
oil on canvas 123.5 x 124 (E)
P.1986.2182

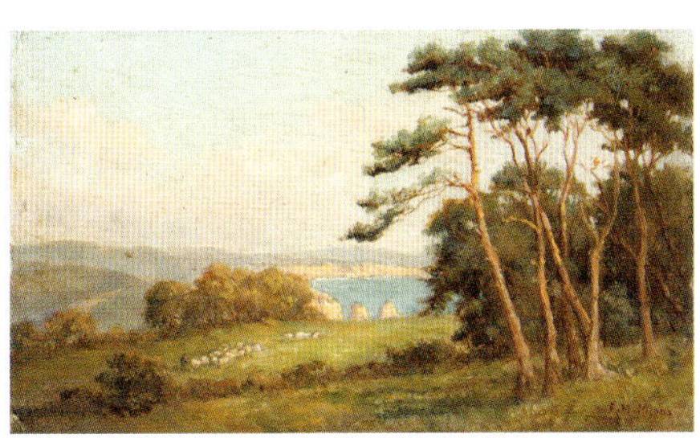

Minns, Fanny Mary active 1865–1905
Alum Bay Seen from Headon Hill
oil on board 14.2 x 25
P.1986.77

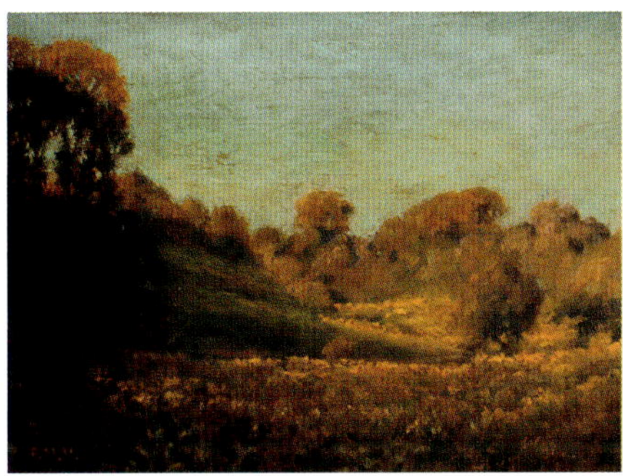

Minns, Fanny Mary active 1865–1905
Rural Scene near Arreton
oil on board 16.5 x 23.5
P.1986.2180

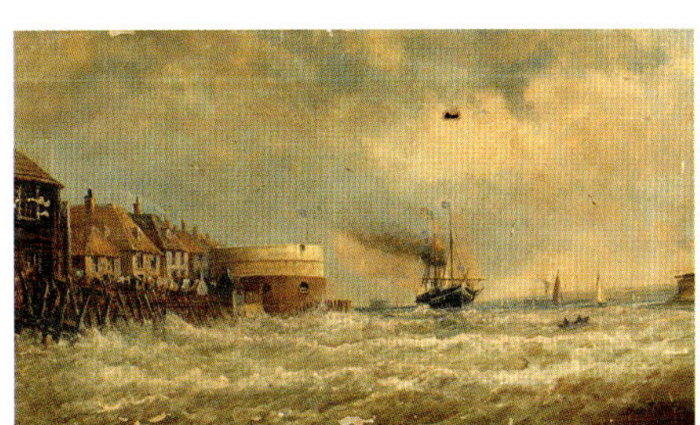

Robins, Henry 1820–1892
Large Ship Entering Portsmouth Harbour with the Isle of Wight in the Distance
oil on canvas 35.7 x 61
P.1986.2247

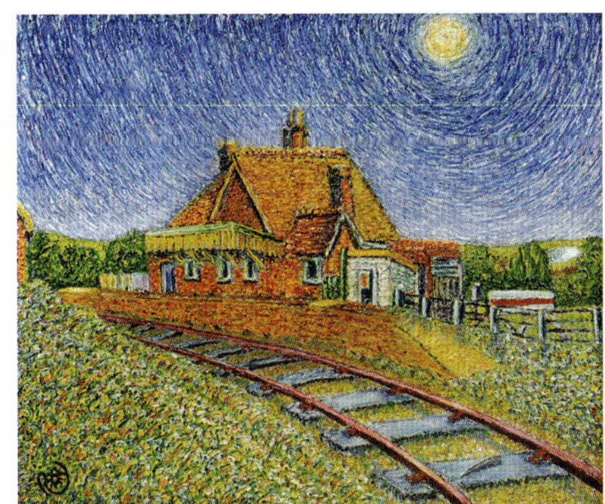

Roy, Michael
Station Building at Carisbrooke Halt 1957
oil on canvas 67 x 80 (E)
P.1986.2111 (P)

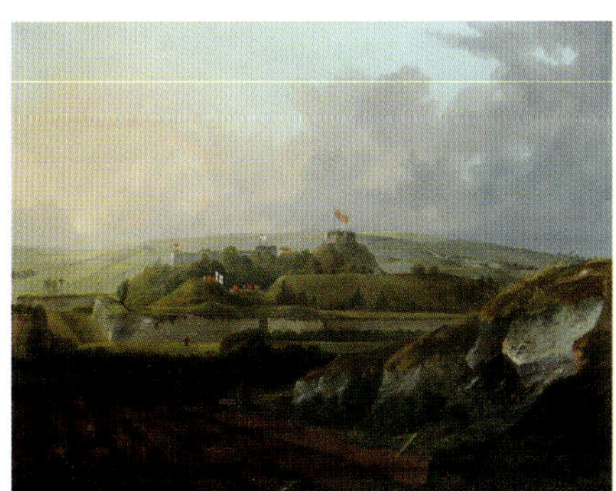

Stewart, F. A.
Carisbrooke Castle from Mount Joy as it Appeared on 23 August 1831, the Day the Duchess of Kent was there to View the Archery
oil on canvas 68.5 x 89 (E)
P.1986.2128

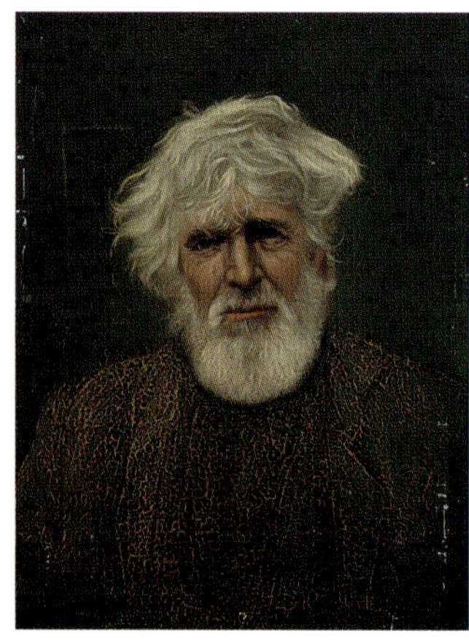

unknown artist
'Pound Hammer' Kingswell of Luccombe
1850–1900
oil on board 52 x 39.2
NETCC.1995.497

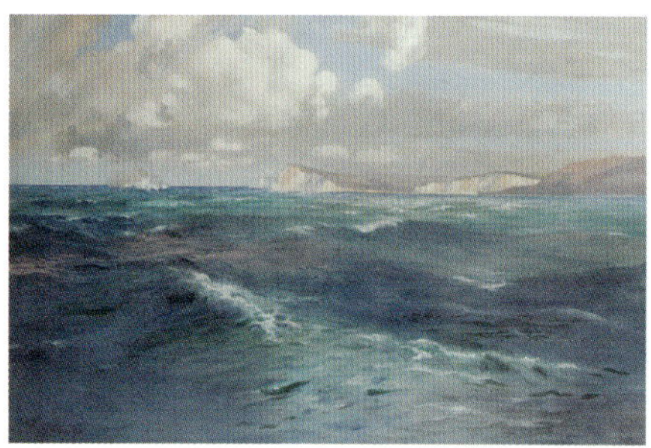

unknown artist
A Three-Masted Ship in a Rough Sea Passing a White Cliff, possibly Culver or Freshwater
oil on canvas 68 x 101 (E)
P.1986.2104

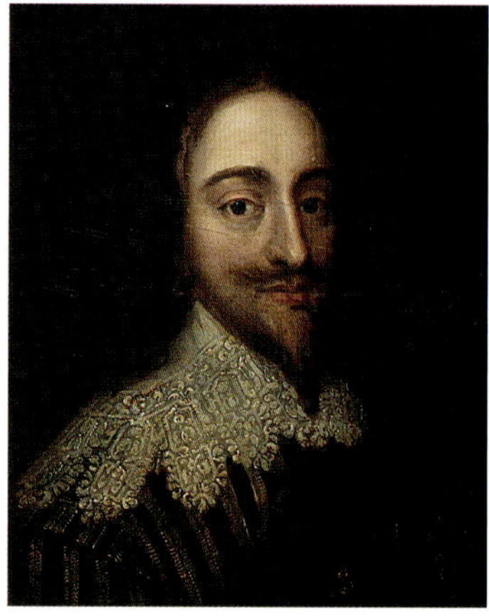

unknown artist
Charles I (1600–1649)
oil on board 30 x 24.5 (E)
P.1986.2164

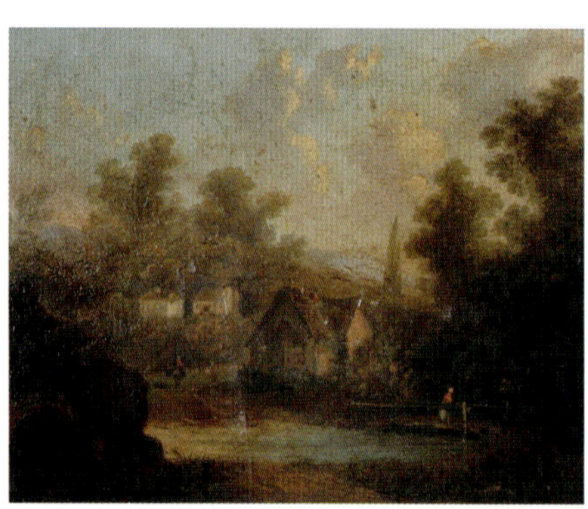

unknown artist
Clatterford Showing Cottages and Bridge
oil on board 15.4 x 20.5 (E)
P.1986.1992

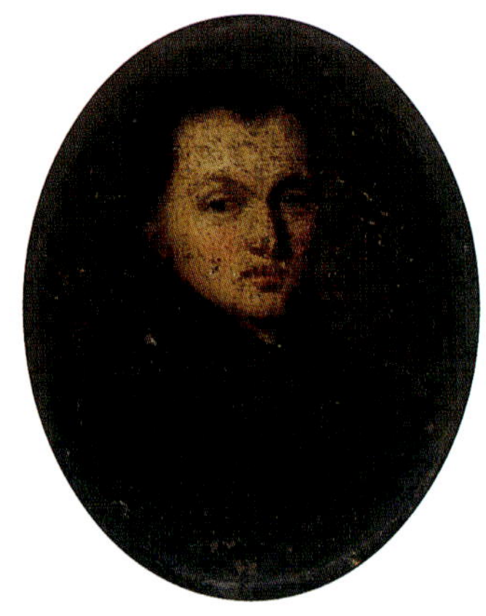

unknown artist
Portrait of a Man
oil on copper 9.5 x 8
P.1986.2888

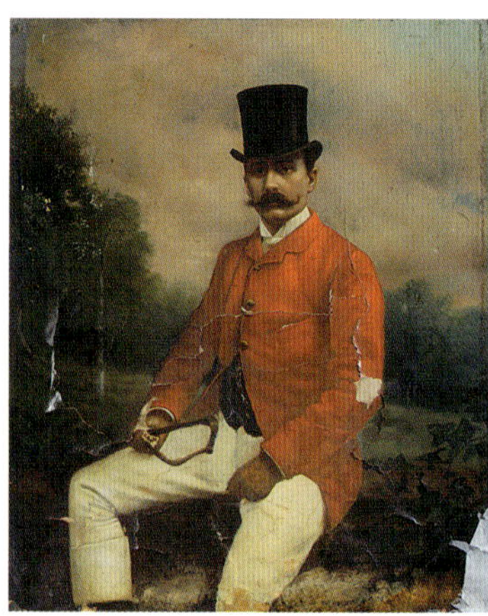

unknown artist
Portrait of an Unknown Gentleman in Hunting Pink
oil on canvas 60 x 50.5
netcc.P.1986.2085

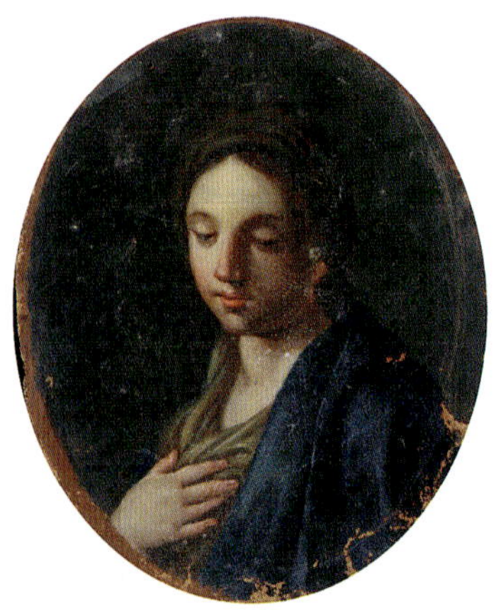

unknown artist
Portrait of a Lady (possibly the Madonna)
oil on canvas 16 x 13.5
P.1986.2889

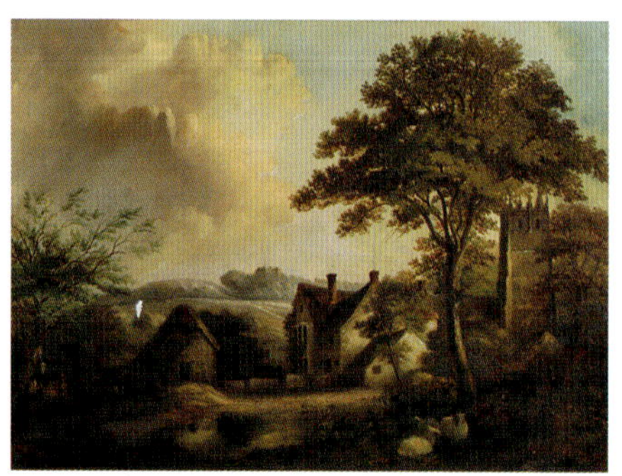

unknown artist
Priory Farm with Carisbrooke Church and Castle in the Background
oil on canvas 65 x 89 (E)
P.1986.2106

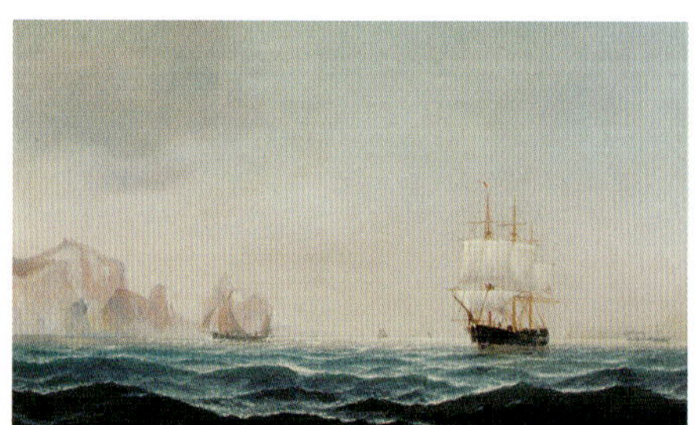

unknown artist
Ships Rounding 'The Needles'
oil on canvas 29 x 49.5 (E)
P.1986.2054

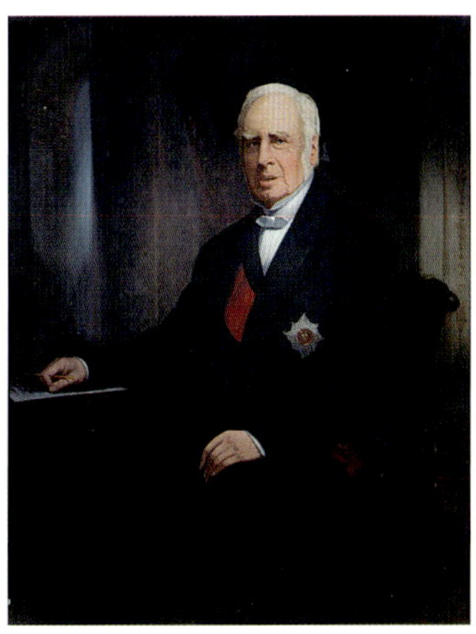

unknown artist
Viscount Eversley, First President of the Royal National Hospital at Ventnor
oil on canvas 141 x 111 (E)
P.1986.2183

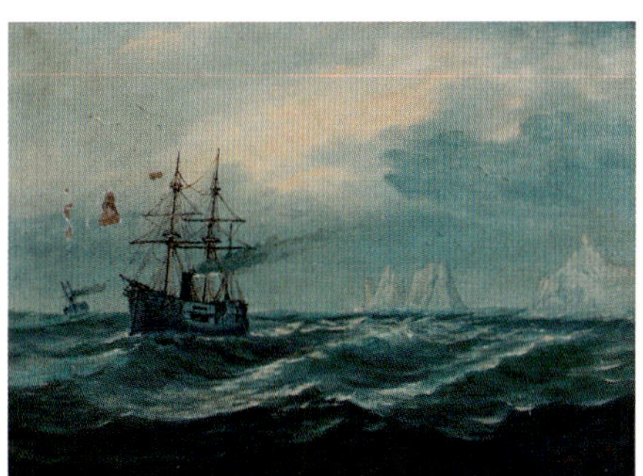

Wiber active 19th C
A Ship off 'The Needles' (possibly 'SS Sultan')
oil on board 16.3 x 23.1 (E)
NETCC.P.1986.1993

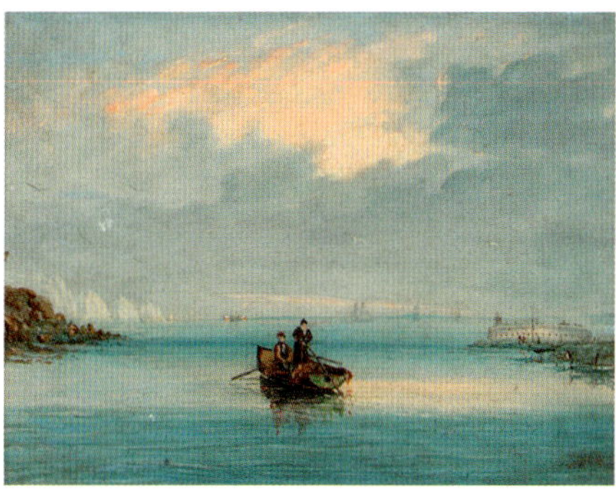

Wiber active 19th C
Rowing Boat in the Solent Looking West with 'The Needles' and Hurst Castle
oil on board 17 x 23 (E)
P.1986.1994

Healing Arts, Isle of Wight NHS Primary Care Trust

The NHS Trust for the Isle of Wight, through its arts in healthcare department, Healing Arts, delivers an extensive programme linking the arts with recovery from illness, maintenance of health and well-being, and the promotion of good health. This includes active participation in the arts by people receiving the therapy as part of their healthcare provision as referred by healthcare professionals.

The programme includes *An Environment for Healing*. Since 1985 the NHS on the Isle of Wight has been commissioning visual artists to contribute to the design and construction of its new capital building programme as well as the maintenance of its existing healthcare buildings, located at St Mary's Hospital, the District General Hospital at Newport, and at the health clinics and centres within the island's towns and community.

In the early 1980s the decision was made to build a new District General Hospital at St Mary's and to include the contribution of artists into its design and layout from its initial design stage. St Mary's was the first NHS hospital to undertake this commitment and policy in the UK. The premise has and continues to be (which has been backed up by many recent scientific studies) that an environment for the recovery from illness on wards, the treatment of illness and health conditions in clinics, and for healthcare staff to work in, gains substantial benefits from the considered and professional contribution of artists – be it visual artists, musicians, writers, poets, and dancers. The length of stay on a ward has been shown to be reduced, the level of pharmacies and pain-relief prescribed has seen a decline, and patients' blood pressure levels and other vital signs are made more stable as a consequence of the artwork. The other benefit is that hospitals themselves, as major public buildings, become an expression of the cultural values and civic pride of that community.

The visual artworks commissioned by the Isle of Wight NHS are all on public view, many of which are located in publicly accessible areas. However many are also in specialist treatment areas and wards such as cardiology, mental health or the paediatric centre. An advance appointment will need to be made in order to view these paintings.

Although our collection comprises a mixture of different mediums, including photographs, watercolours and textiles, it is necessary to include only oil, acrylic and tempera works for the purposes of this catalogue. There is a general theme behind the artworks – the natural world – with an emphasis on works where their inspiration has been drawn from the sea, coastline and the landscape of the Isle of Wight. Many of the artists on display have some connection with the Isle of Wight, either through living, working, or visiting the island, and this illustrates the level of skill and importance placed on the value of the arts in the island community.

The collection has been formed over the past 20 years, with a handful of works predating this. As a result, the collection, in the main, reflects the power the arts bring to the healing process. We hope that you will also experience this if you need to visit the island's healthcare services.

Guy Eades, Arts Director

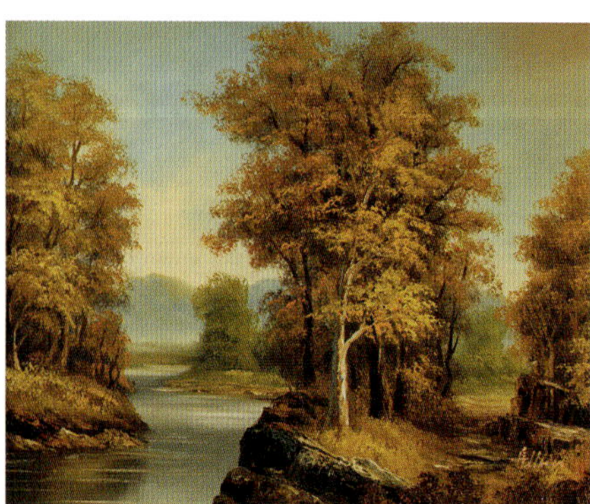

Allthus
Autumn Landscape
oil on canvas 39.5 x 49.7 (E)
862

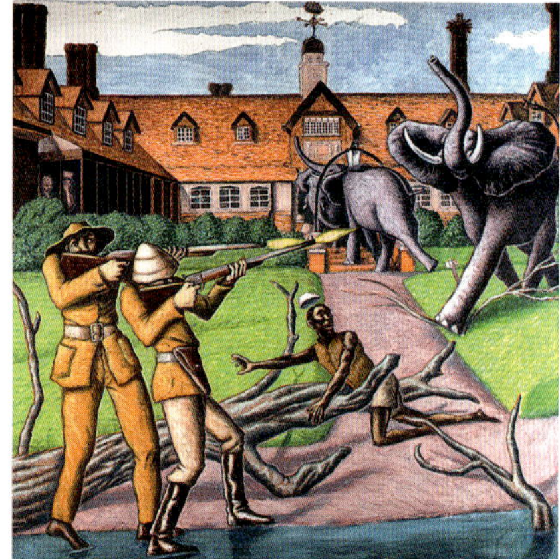

Anderson, M.
Frank James and Elephants
acrylic on canvas 122 x 122
335

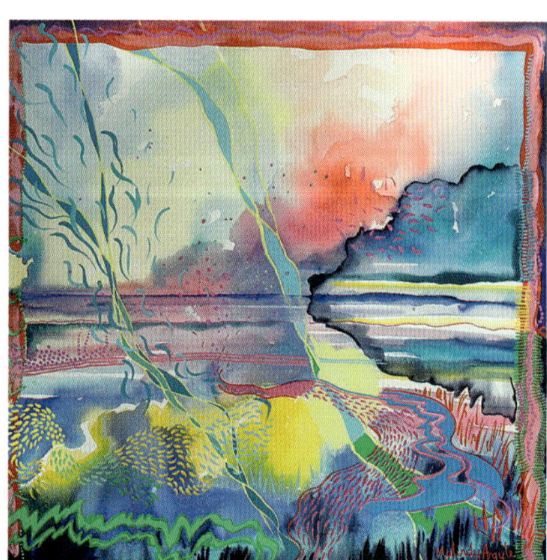

Argyle, Malindy b.1945
Lease of Life 2006
acrylic on paper 69 x 69
2060

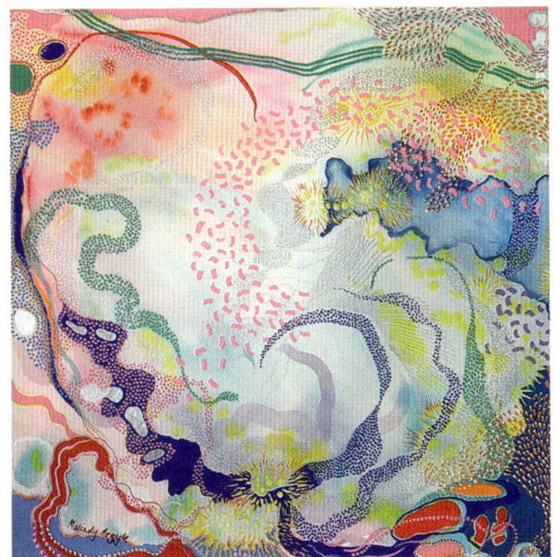

Argyle, Malindy b.1945
The Journey 2006
acrylic on paper 69 x 69
2062

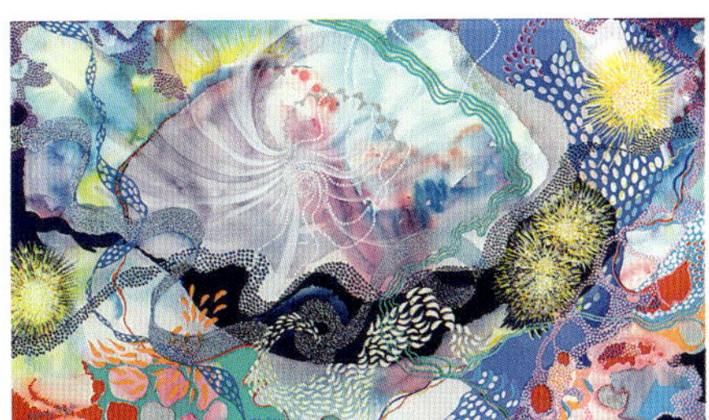

Argyle, Malindy b.1945
Water Ballet 2006
acrylic on paper 67 x 116
2063

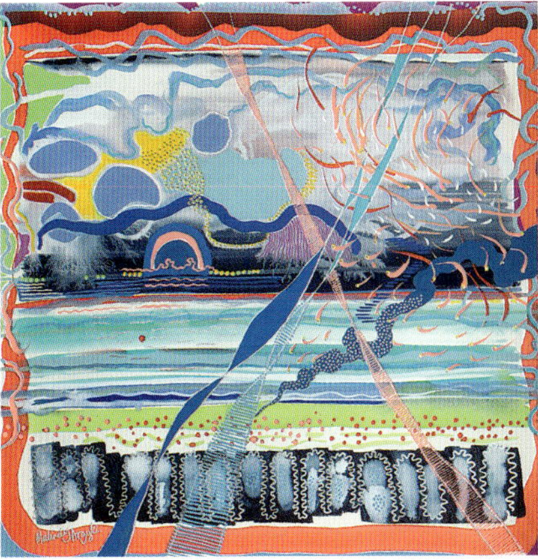

Argyle, Malindy b.1945
Winds of Change 2006
acrylic on paper 69 x 69
2061

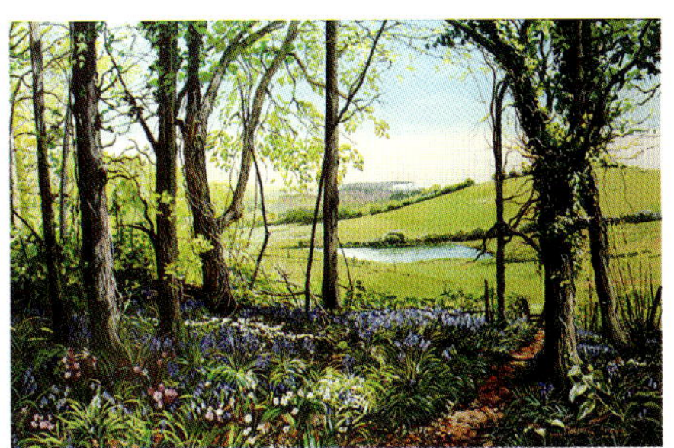

Argyle, Malindy b.1945
Borthwood Copse
acrylic on canvas 78.8 x 128
1928

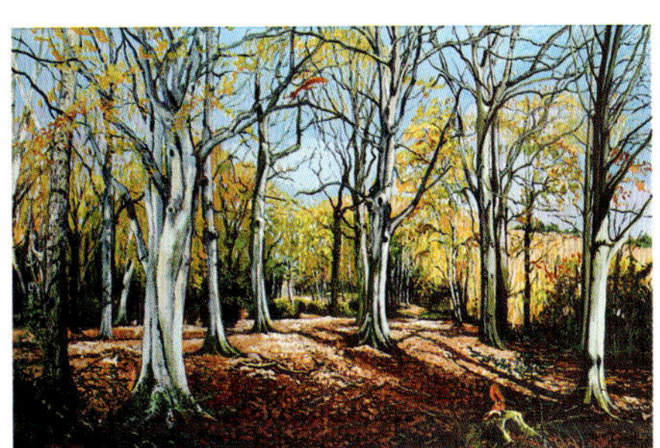

Argyle, Malindy b.1945
East Wight Downs
acrylic on canvas 78.8 x 128
1927

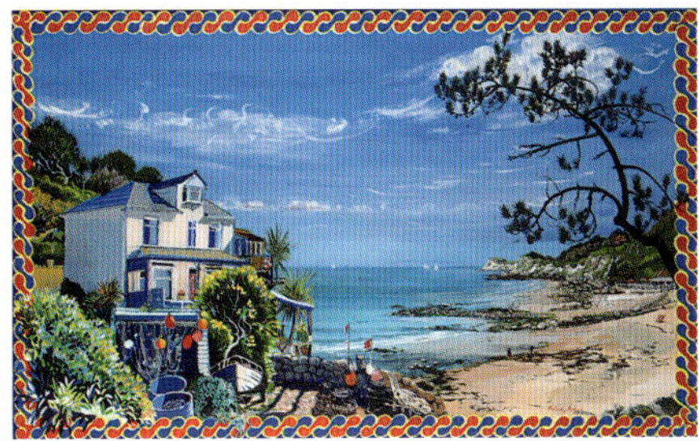

Argyle, Malindy b.1945
Pastoral: Steephill Cove
acrylic on panel 90 x 140
1925

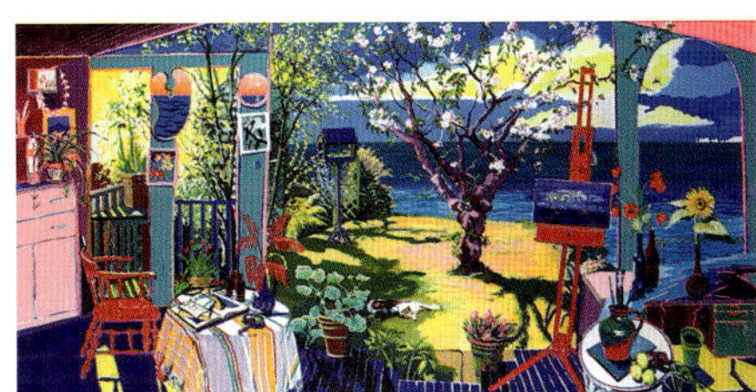

Argyle, Malindy b.1945
Still Life: Isle of Wight
acrylic on panel 98.8 x 200
1926

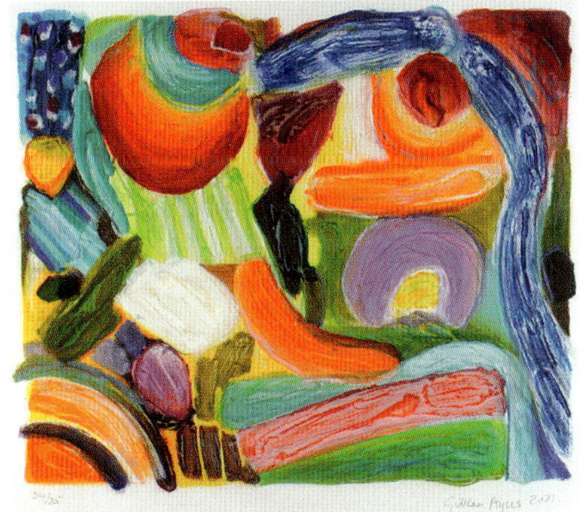

Ayres, Gillian b.1930
Matuka
mixed media on paper 25 x 60 (E)
2003

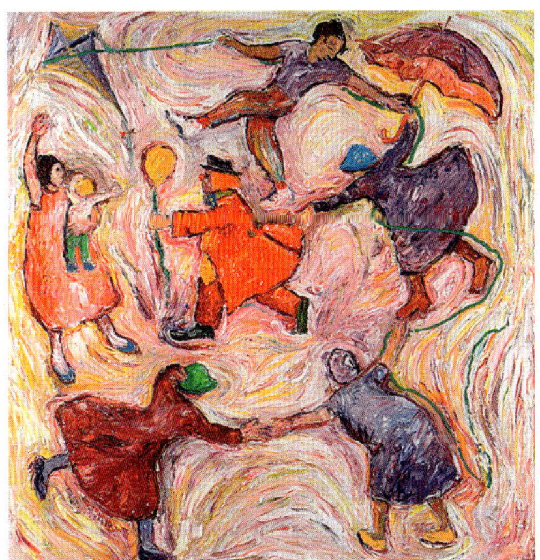

Banks, Mary
The Dance
oil on canvas 120 x 120 (E)
Temp35

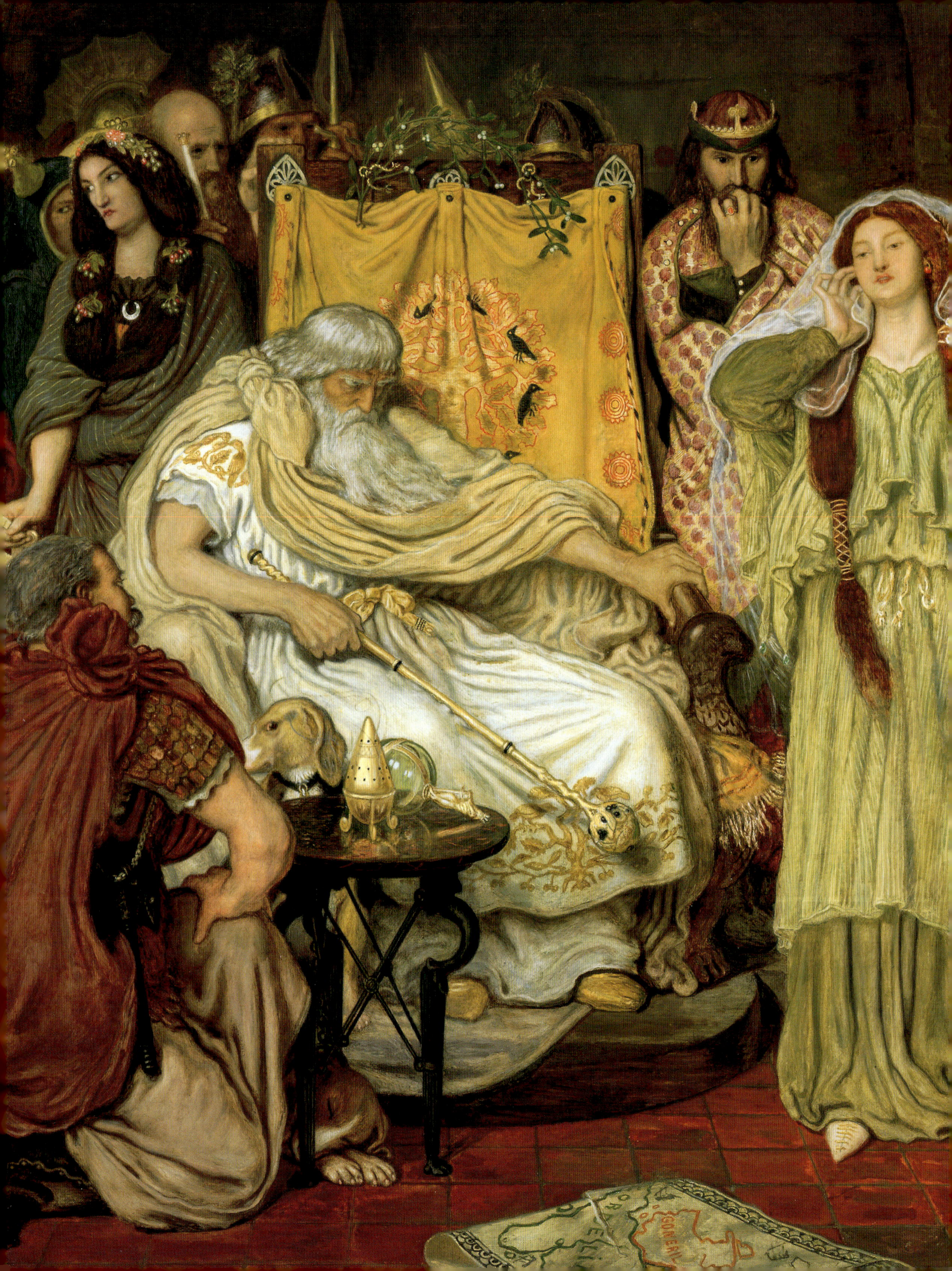
GONERIL

Barker
Winter Evening, Swansea Bay 1983
oil on canvas 51 x 75
344A

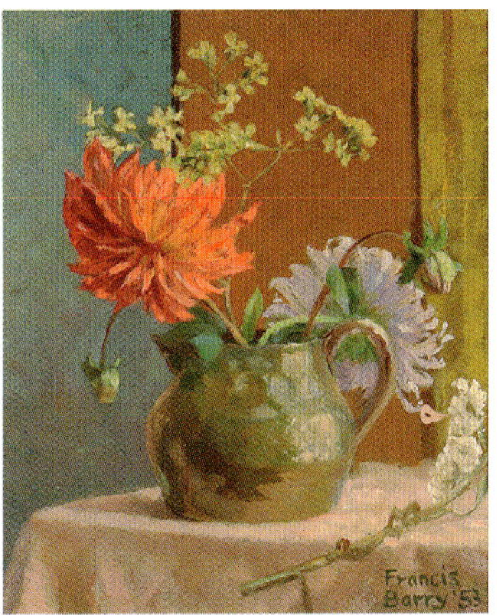

Barry, Francis
Chrysanthemums 1953
oil on canvas 34.2 x 29 (E)
91

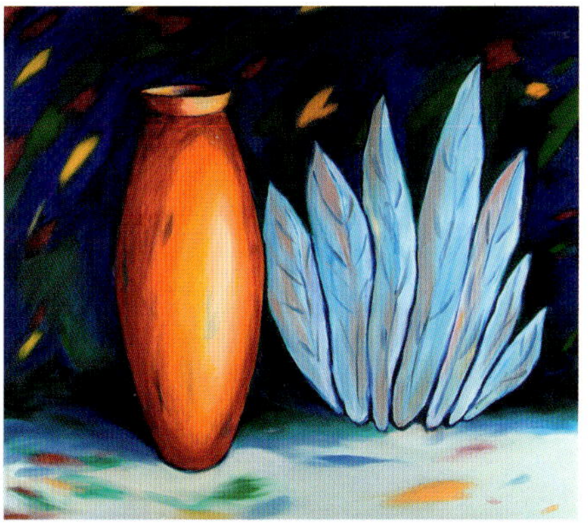

Blackett, Vivien b.1955
Jar and Wing 1986
oil on canvas 105.5 x 123.5 (E)
604

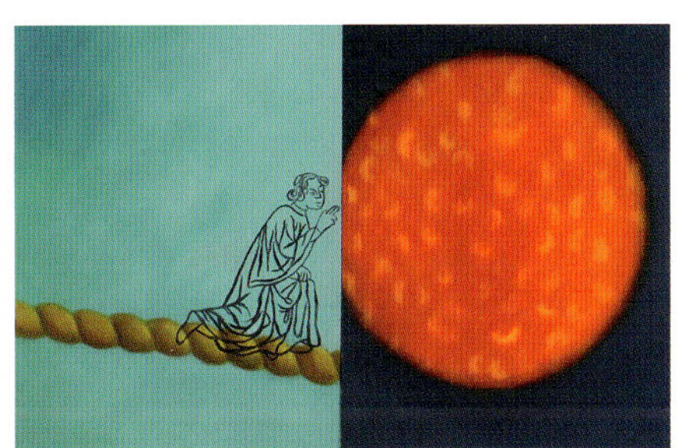

Blackett, Vivien b.1955
Inquire
oil on canvas 38 x 59.5
1880

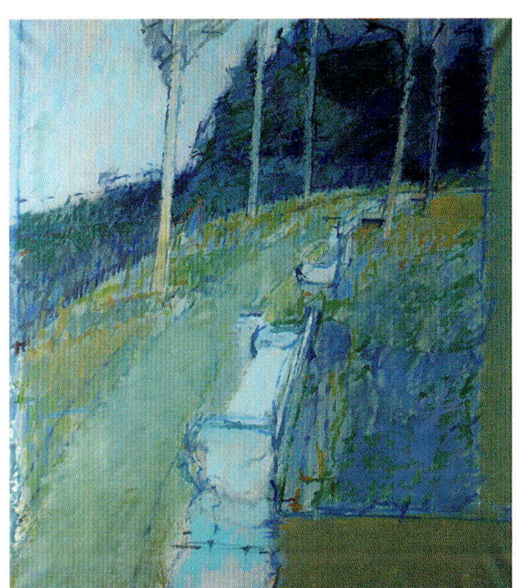

Boden, Richard active 1980–1986
Row of Benches 1980
oil on canvas 101 x 91.5
155

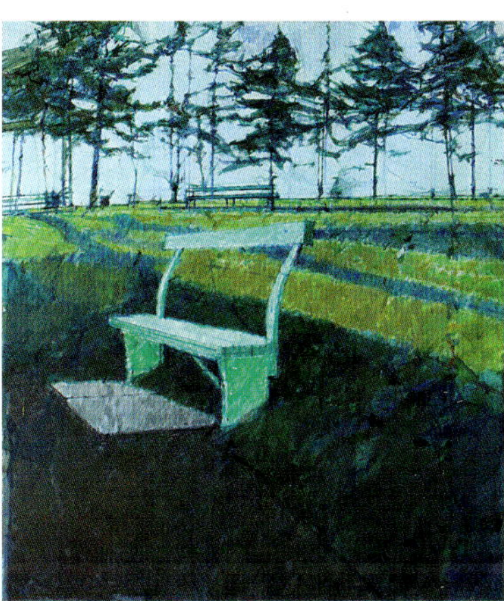

Boden, Richard active 1980–1986
Park Bench 1980–1982
oil on canvas 102 x 92
154

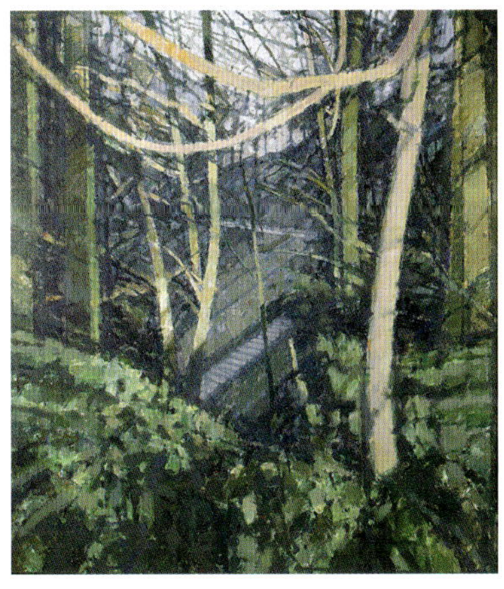

Boden, Richard active 1980–1986
St Giles' Hill 1983
oil on canvas 101.5 x 90
1118

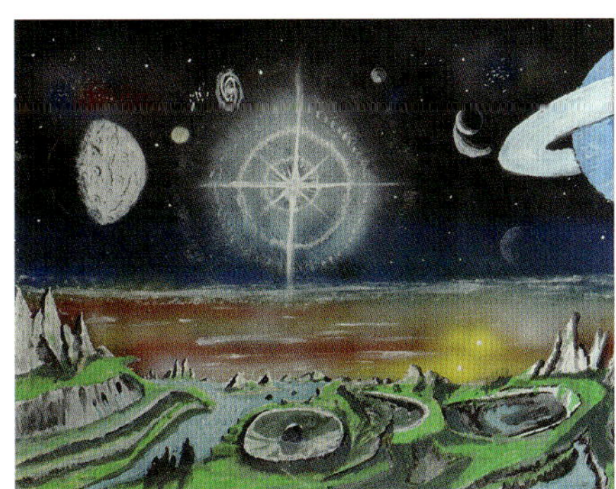

Boulter, Roger
Star and Planets
acrylic on board 44.7 x 59.5
2018

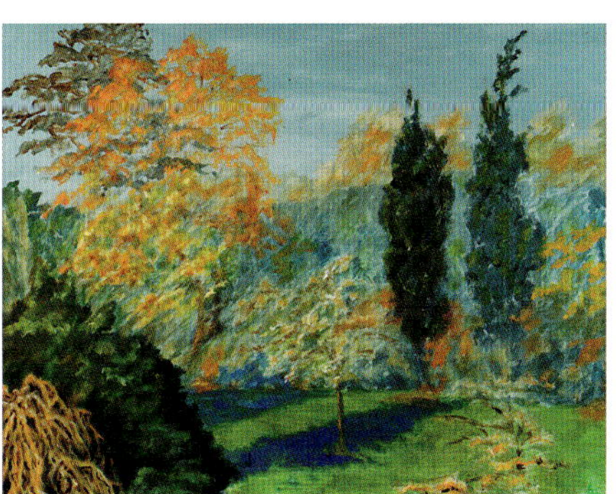

Bowyer, Elizabeth
Early Morning: Brook House
oil on board 42 x 57.2 (E)
Temp31

Facing page: Brown, Ford Madox, 1821–1893, *Cordelia's Portion* (detail), Southampton City Art Gallery, (p. 28)

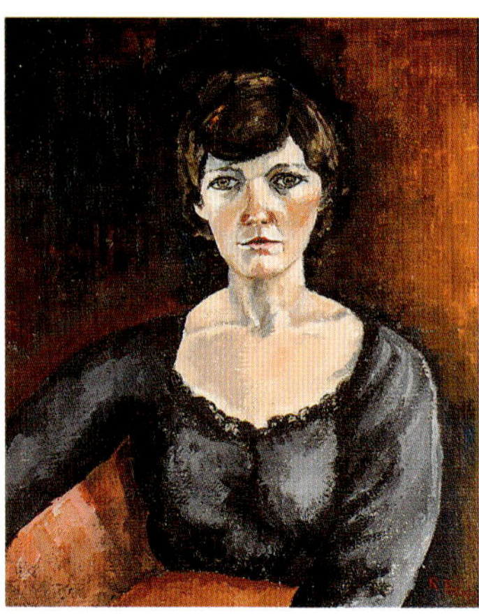

Bowyer, Robert
Mrs Shirley Cornelius
oil on canvas 60 x 49.5 (E)
Temp4

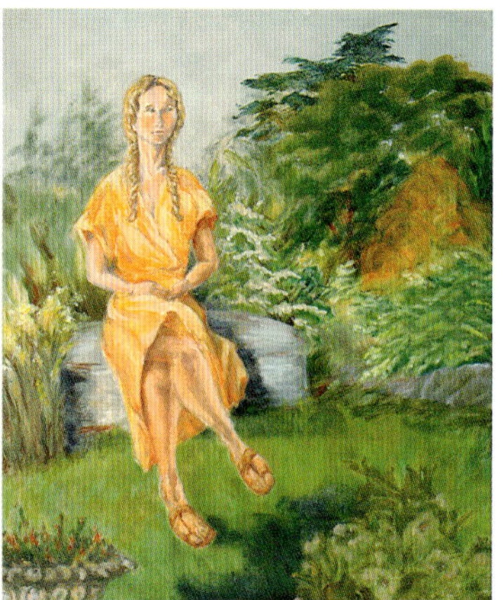

Bowyer, Robert
Seated Woman in a Garden
oil on board 61.2 x 51.4
Temp14

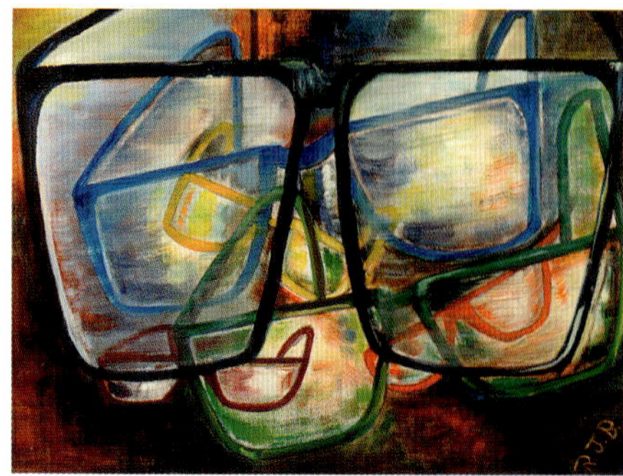

Bowyer, Robert
Spectacles
oil on canvas 29 x 39 (E)
Temp11

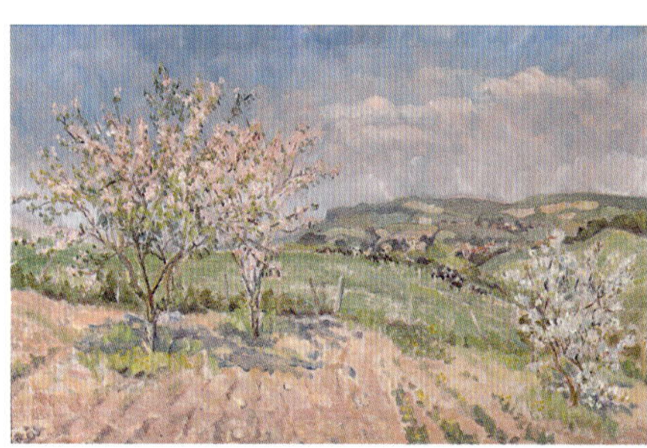

Burgess, Ria
Orchard near Niton
oil on canvas 50 x 75
temp622

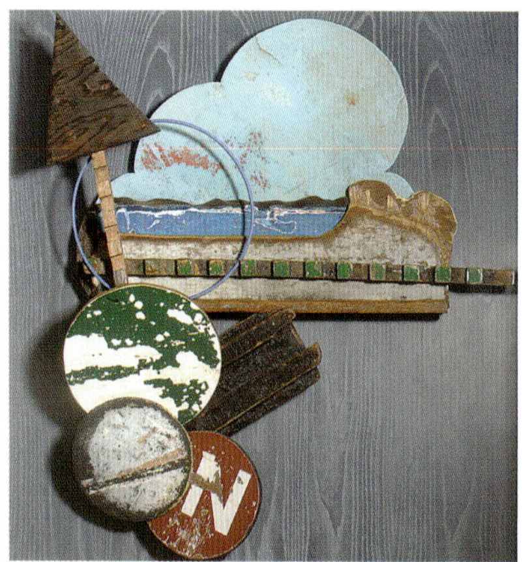

Butler, Roger b.1945
The Duver
oil on wood 83.5 x 83.5 (E)
1624

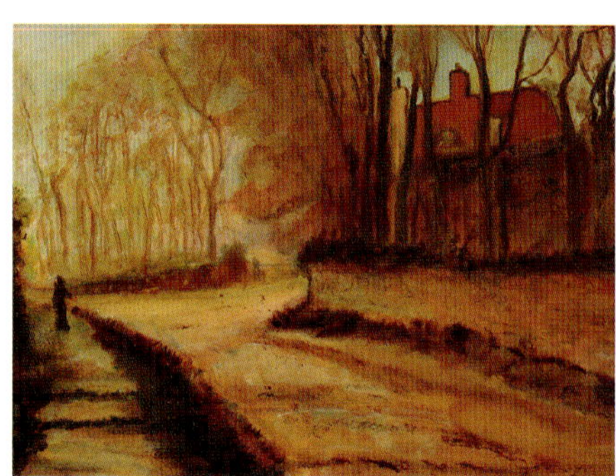

Campbell, Beatrice 1901–2000
Red House in the Wood
oil on canvas 26.5 x 35 (E)
Temp10

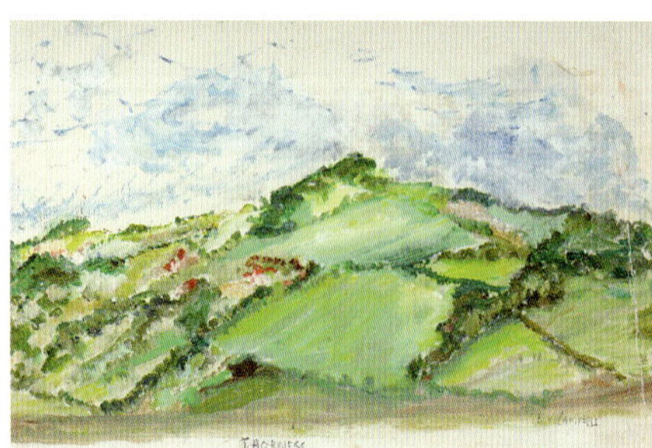

Campbell, Beatrice 1901–2000
Thorness
oil on paper 30.5 x 47.5 (E)
Temp13

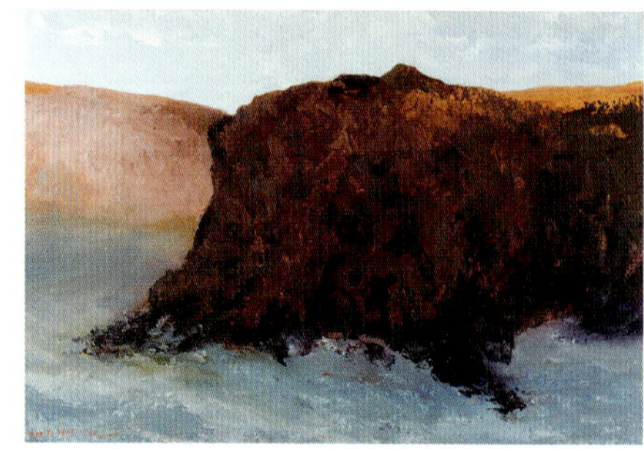

Clarke, Hilda Margery b.1926
Pembroke Promontory 1988
oil on canvas 49 x 73.5 (E)
1244

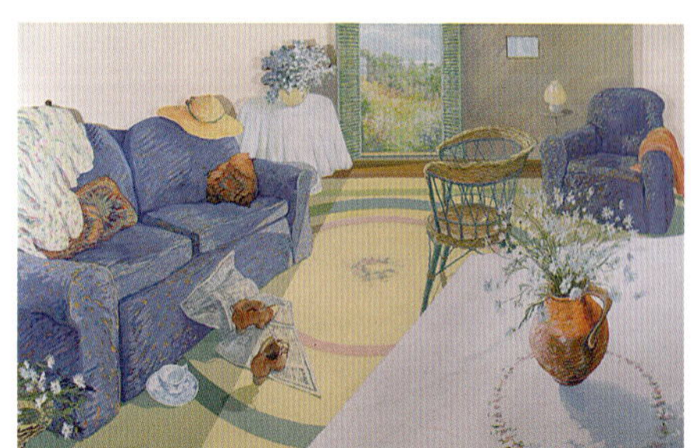

Court, Sally b.1948
Sitting Room, Garden and Seashore (detail, 1 of 3) c.1997
acrylic on board 155 x 305
Temp42A

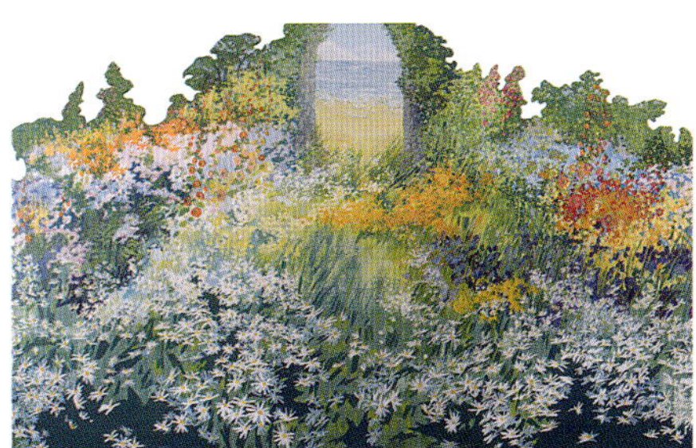

Court, Sally b.1948
Sitting Room, Garden and Seashore (detail, 2 of 3) c.1997
acrylic on board 155 x 305
temp42B

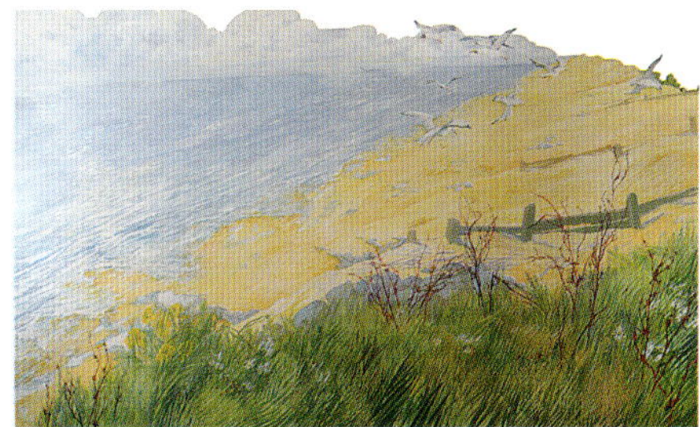

Court, Sally b.1948
Sitting Room, Garden and Seashore (detail, 3 of 3) c.1997
acrylic on board 155 x 305
temp42C

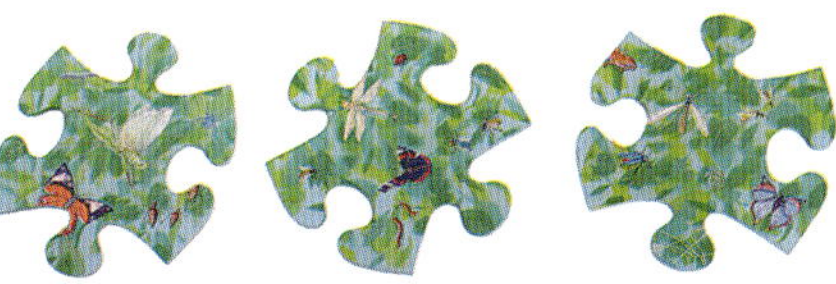

Court, Sally b.1948
Jungle Jigsaw 2002
acrylic on board 115 x 307
temp317

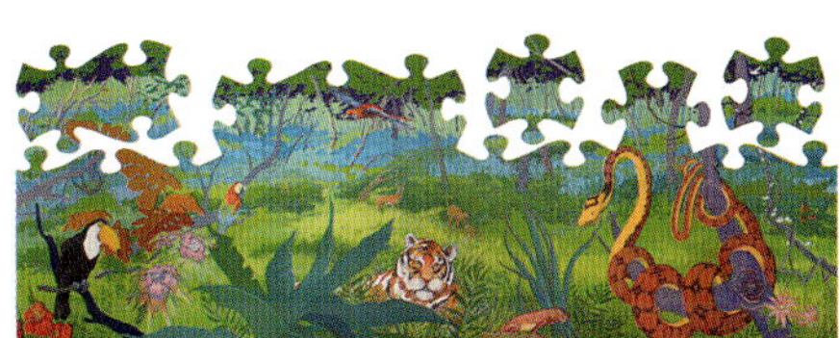

Court, Sally b.1948
Jungle Jigsaw 2002
acrylic on board 115 x 307
temp316

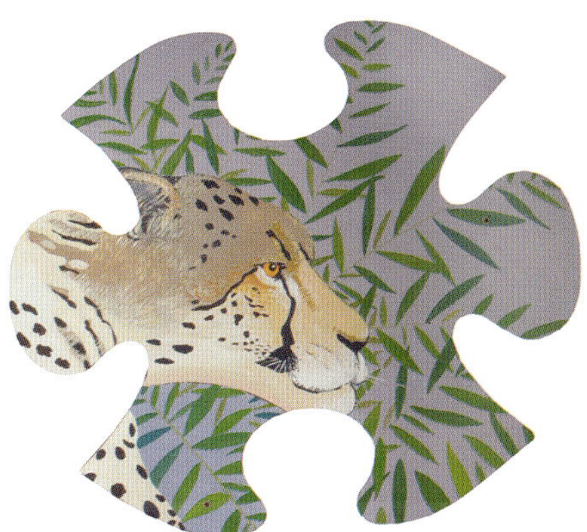

Court, Sally b.1948
Jungle Jigsaw: Cheetah (1 of 14) 2002
acrylic on board 54 x 61
temp303

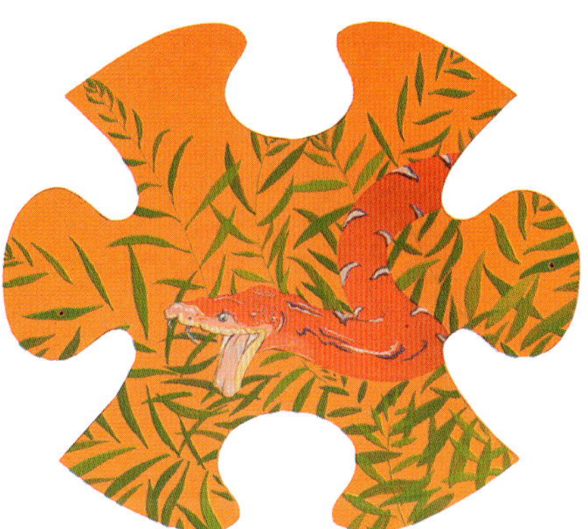

Court, Sally b.1948
Jungle Jigsaw: Snake Head (2 of 14) 2002
acrylic on board 54 x 61
temp304

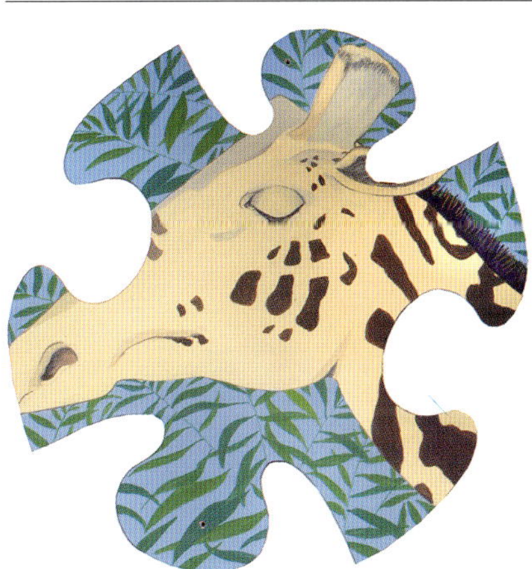

Court, Sally b.1948
Jungle Jigsaw: Giraffe Head (3 of 14) 2002
acrylic on board 54 x 61
temp305

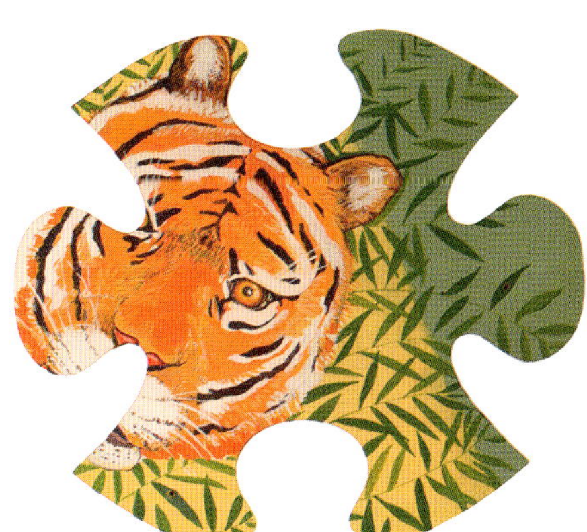

Court, Sally b.1948
Jungle Jigsaw: Tiger Head (4 of 14) 2002
acrylic on board 54 x 61
temp306

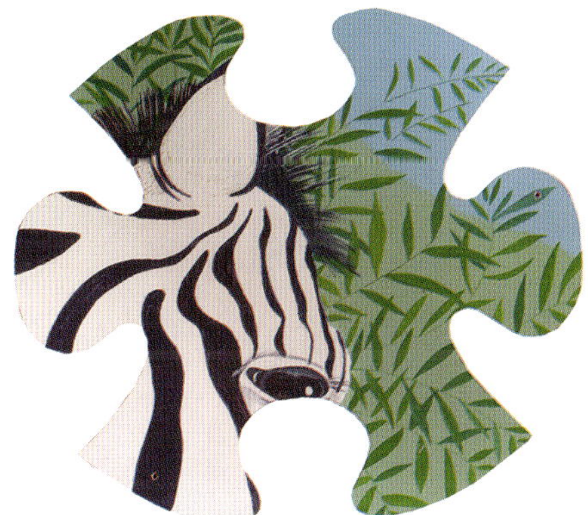

Court, Sally b.1948
Jungle Jigsaw: Zebra Head (5 of 14) 2002
acrylic on board 54 x 61
temp307

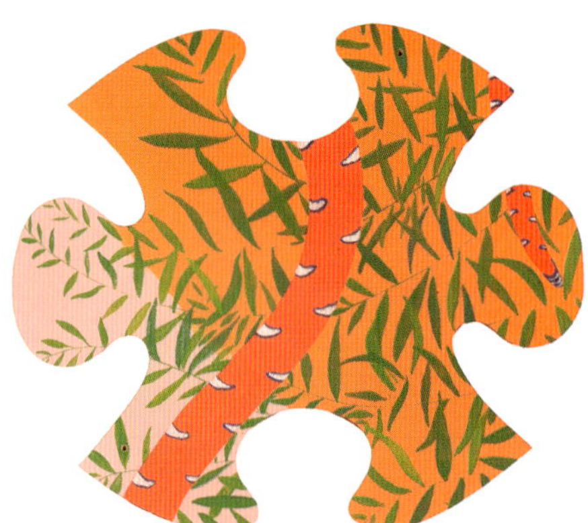

Court, Sally b.1948
Jungle Jigsaw: Snake Tail (6 of 14) 2002
acrylic on board 54 x 61
temp308

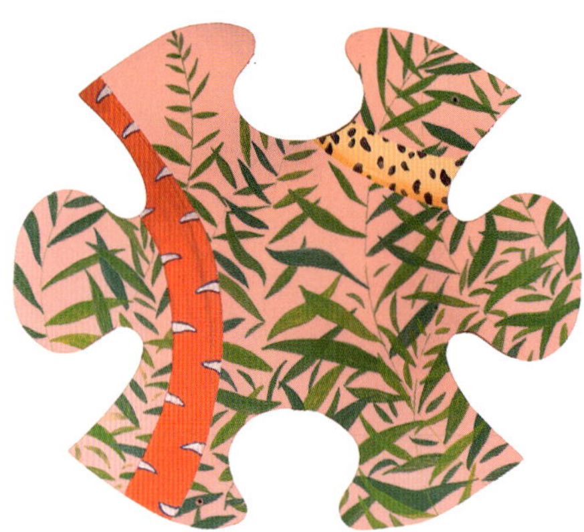

Court, Sally b.1948
Jungle Jigsaw: Snake Tail/ Cheetah Tail (7 of 14) 2002
acrylic on board 54 x 61
temp309

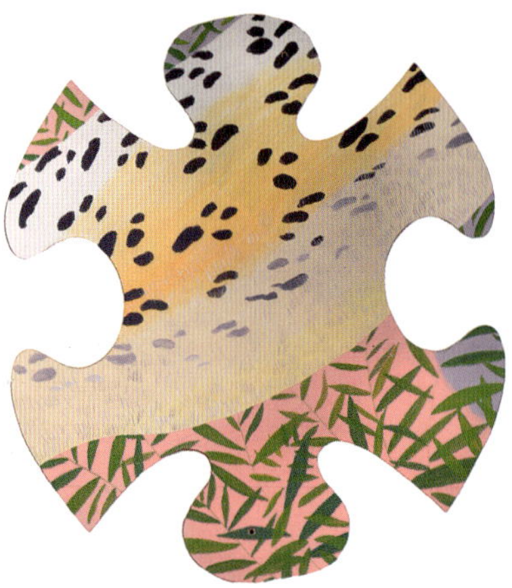

Court, Sally b.1948
Jungle Jigsaw: Cheetah Body (8 of 14) 2002
acrylic on board 54 x 61
temp310

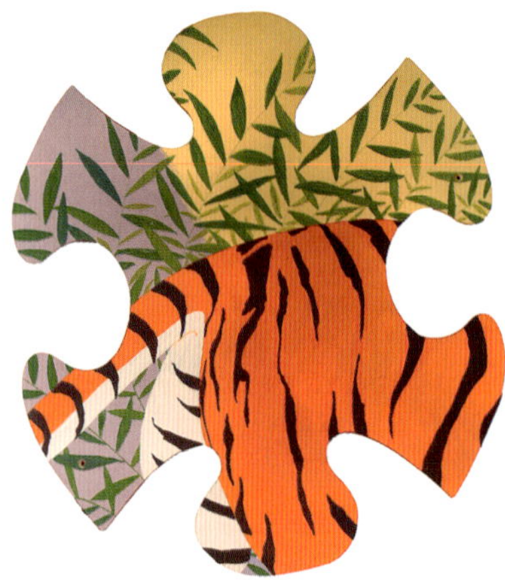

Court, Sally b.1948
Jungle Jigsaw: Tiger Tail (9 of 14) 2002
acrylic on board 54 x 61
temp311

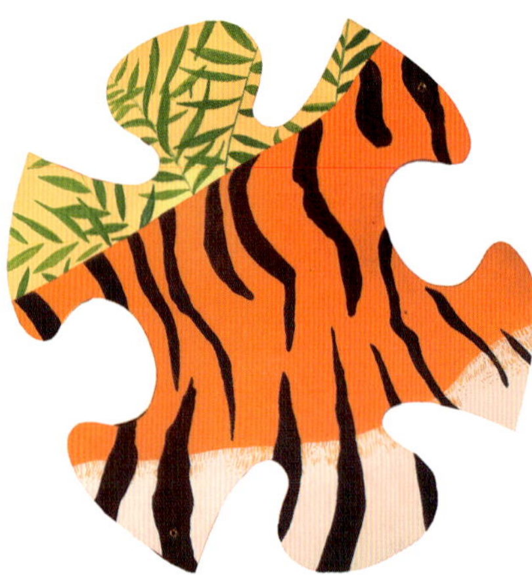

Court, Sally b.1948
Jungle Jigsaw: Tiger Body (10 of 14) 2002
acrylic on board 54 x 61
temp312

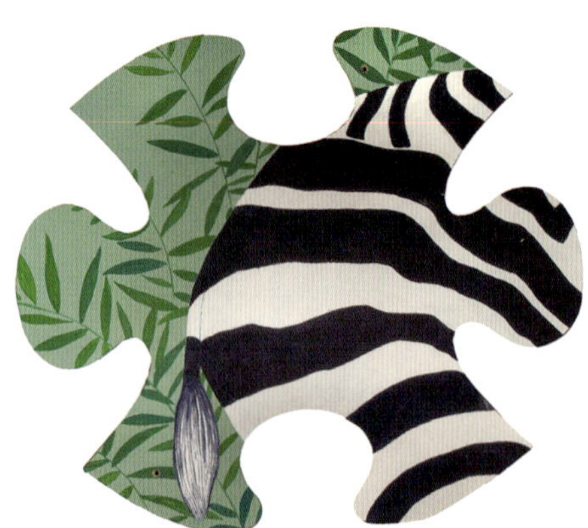

Court, Sally b.1948
Jungle Jigsaw: Zebra Tail (11 of 14) 2002
acrylic on board 54 x 61
temp313

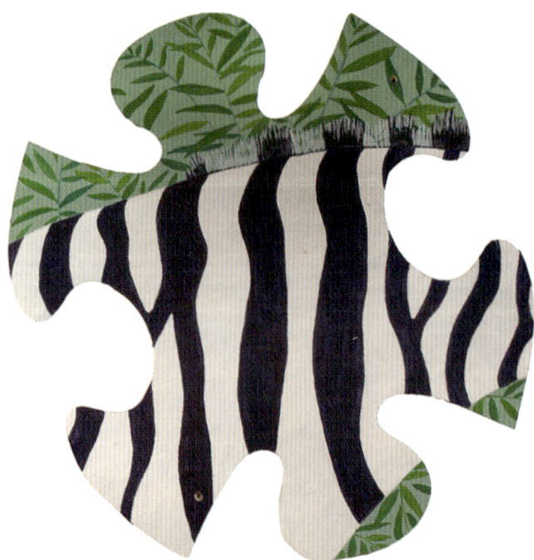

Court, Sally b.1948
Jungle Jigsaw: Zebra Neck (12 of 14) 2002
acrylic on board 54 x 61
temp314

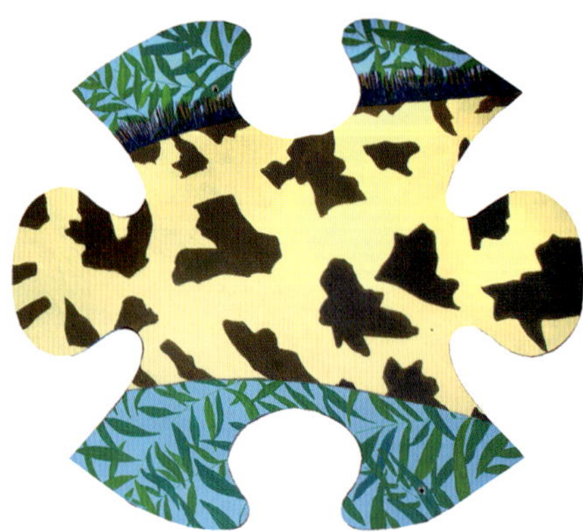

Court, Sally b.1948
Jungle Jigsaw: Giraffe Neck (13 of 14) 2002
acrylic on board 54 x 61
temp315

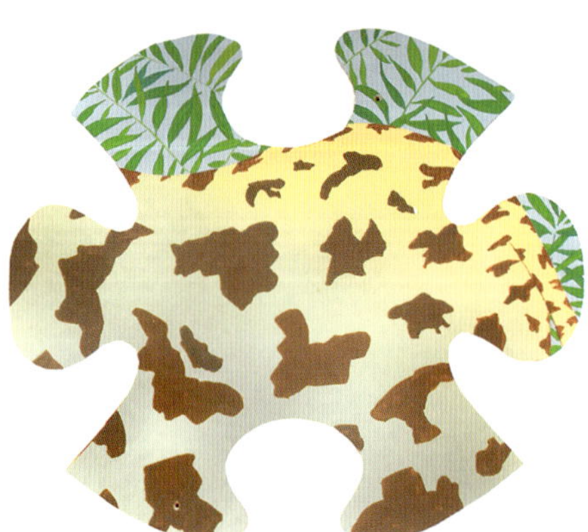

Court, Sally b.1948
Jungle Jigsaw: Giraffe Tail (14 of 14) 2002
acrylic on board 54 x 61
temp316

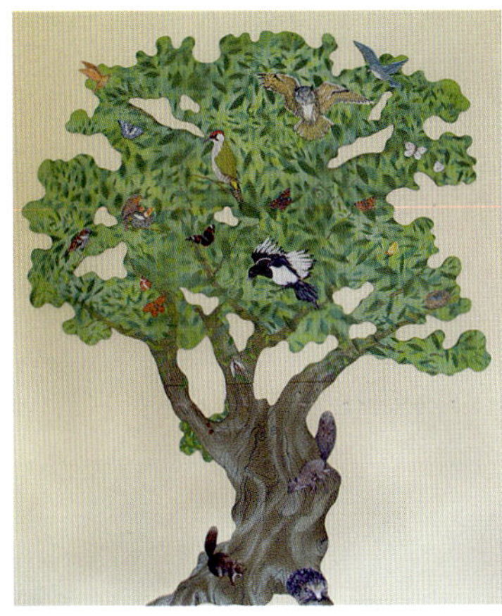

Court, Sally b.1948
Tree and Birds 2002
acrylic on board 200 x 150 (E)
1907

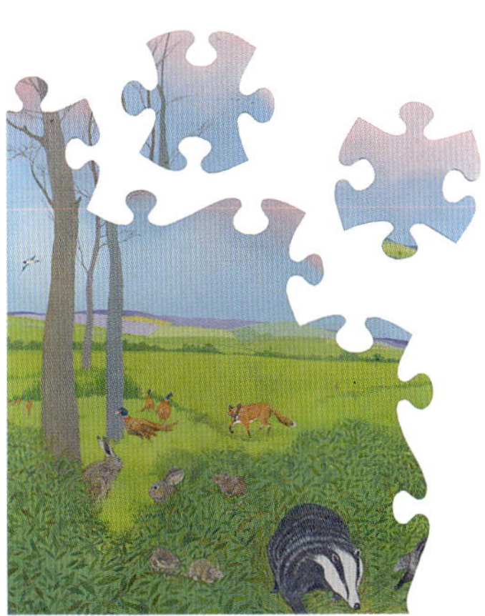

Court, Sally b.1948
Wildlife Jigsaw 2002
acrylic on board 137 x 110
temp324

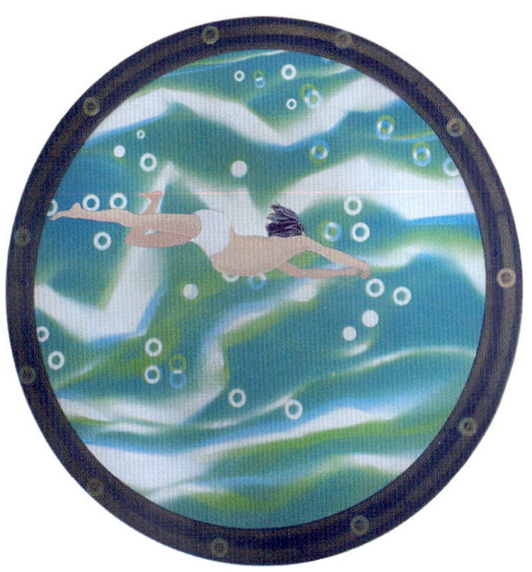

Court, Sally b.1948
Diver 1
acrylic on board 90
temp322A

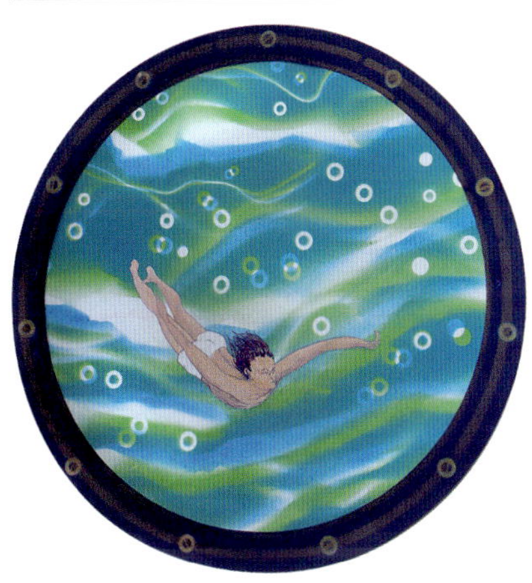

Court, Sally b.1948
Diver 2
acrylic on board 90
temp322B

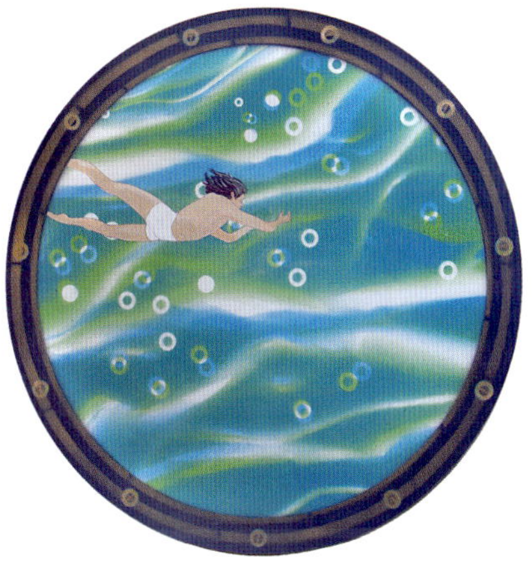

Court, Sally b.1948
Diver 3
acrylic on board 90
temp322C

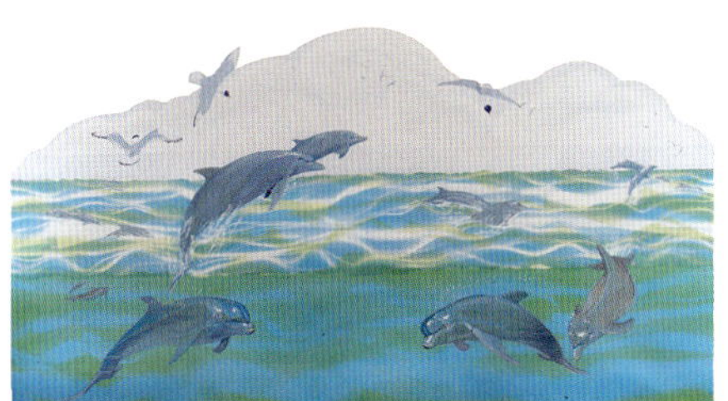

Court, Sally b.1948
Dolphin Scene
acrylic on board 125 x 250
temp323

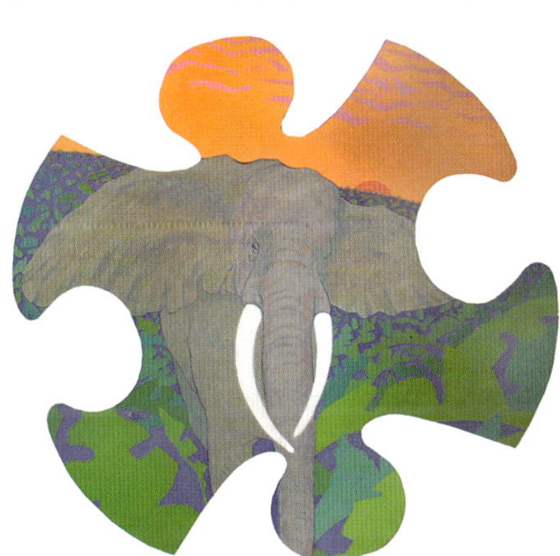

Court, Sally b.1948
Elephant
acrylic on board 115 x 120
temp300

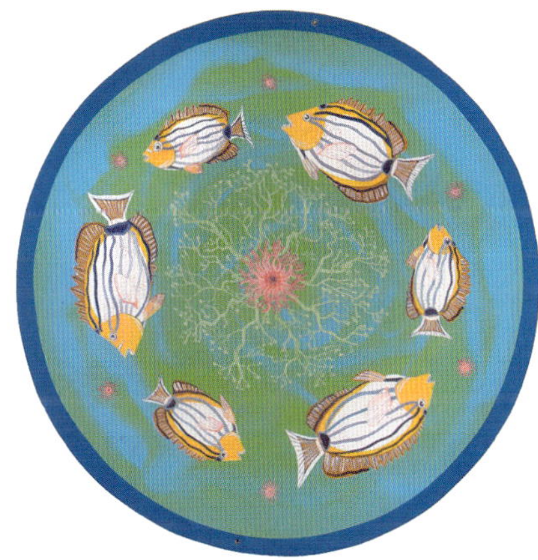

Court, Sally b.1948
Fish Roundel
acrylic on board 90
temp319

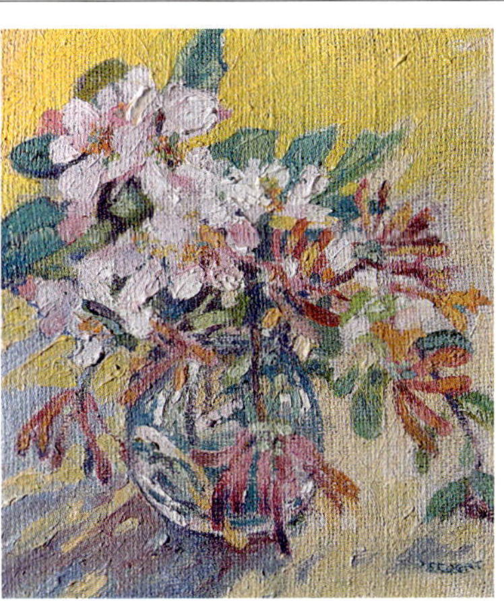

Court, Sally b.1948
Honeysuckle Blossom
oil on canvas 30 x 30 (E)
1626

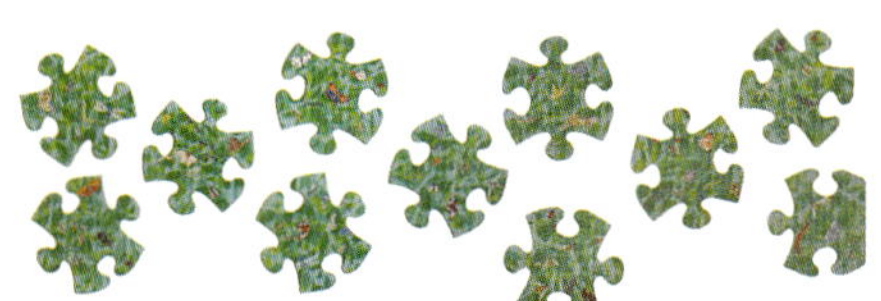

Court, Sally b.1948
Insect Jigsaw Installation
acrylic on board 115 x 292
temp602

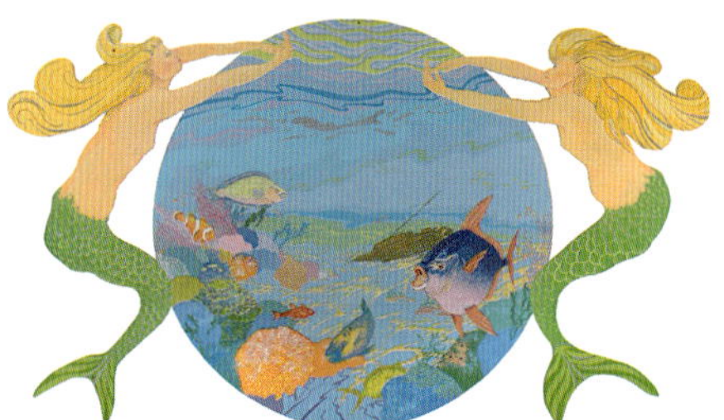

Court, Sally b.1948
Mermaid Roundel
acrylic on board 125 x 215
temp601

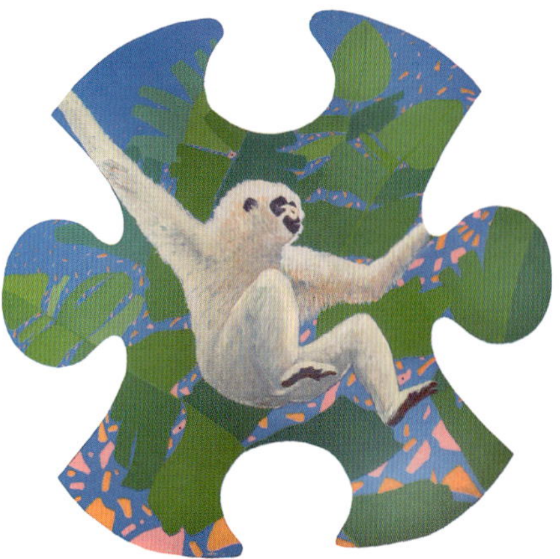

Court, Sally b.1948
Monkey
acrylic on board 115 x 120
temp302

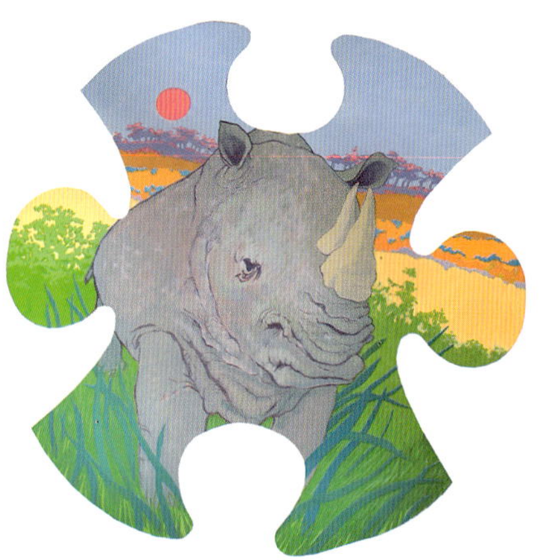

Court, Sally b.1948
Rhino
acrylic on board 115 x 120
temp301

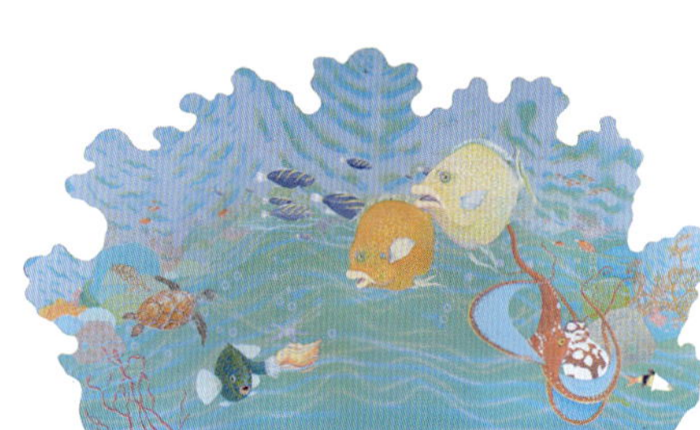

Court, Sally b.1948
Sea Scene
acrylic on board 122 x 238
temp318

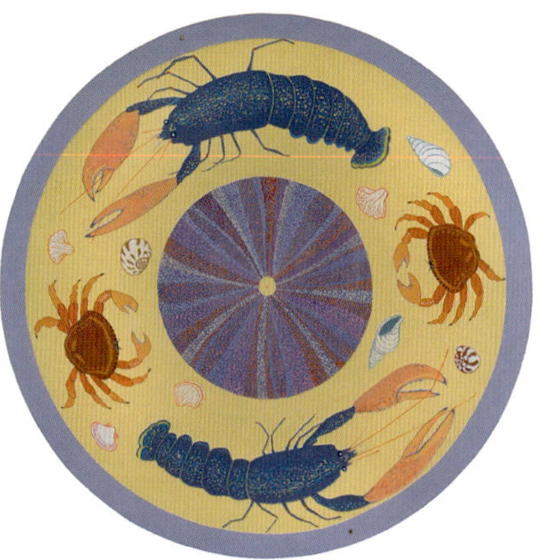

Court, Sally b.1948
Shellfish Roundel
acrylic on board 90
temp320

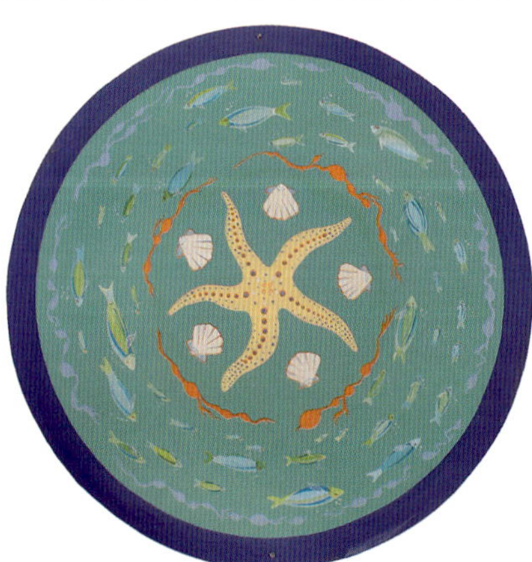

Court, Sally b.1948
Starfish Roundel
acrylic on board 90
temp321

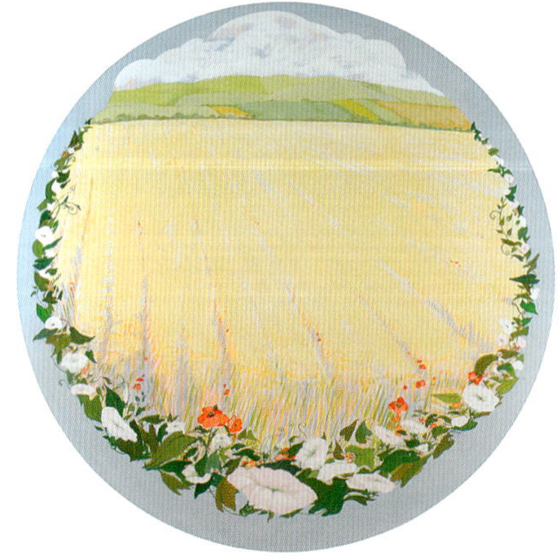

Court, Sally b.1948
Summer Field 2
acrylic on board 87
Temp88

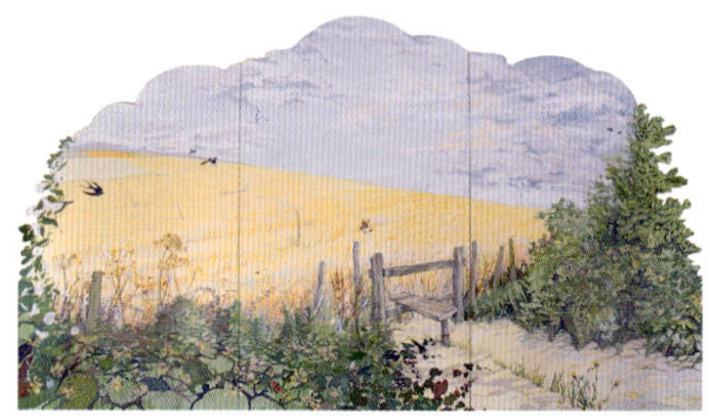

Court, Sally b.1948
The Cornfield
acrylic on board 216 x 367
Temp41

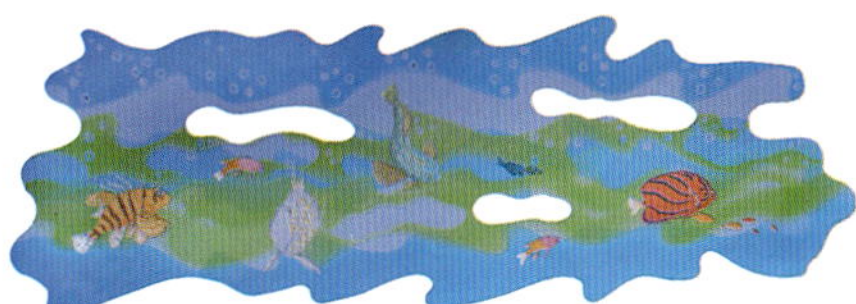

Court, Sally b.1948
The Sea (1 of 6)
acrylic on board 77 x 240
temp325

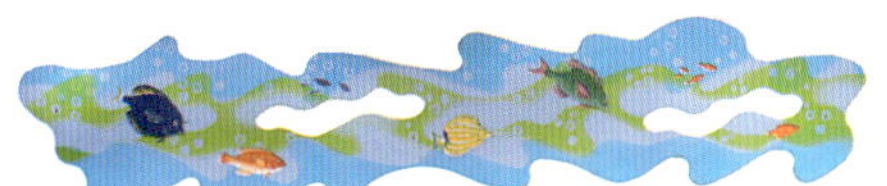

Court, Sally b.1948
The Sea (2 of 6)
acrylic on board 44 x 240
temp326

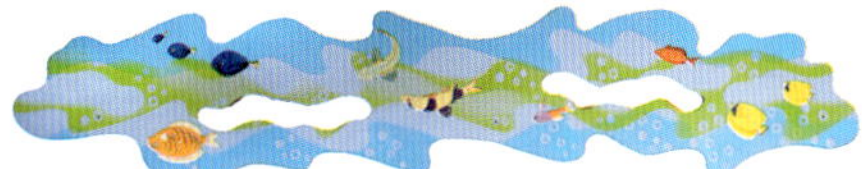

Court, Sally b.1948
The Sea (3 of 6)
acrylic on board 44 x 240
temp327

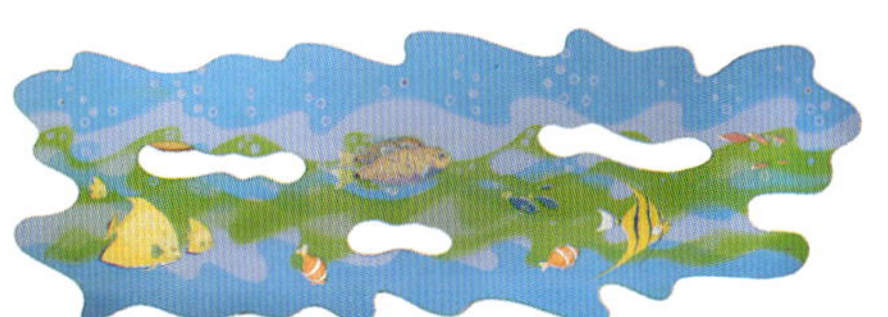

Court, Sally b.1948
The Sea (4 of 6)
acrylic on board 77 x 240
temp328

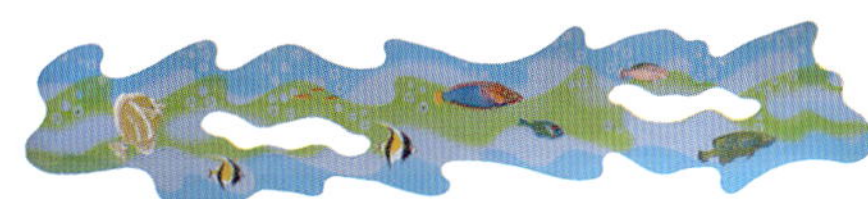

Court, Sally b.1948
The Sea (5 of 6)
acrylic on board 44 x 240
temp329A

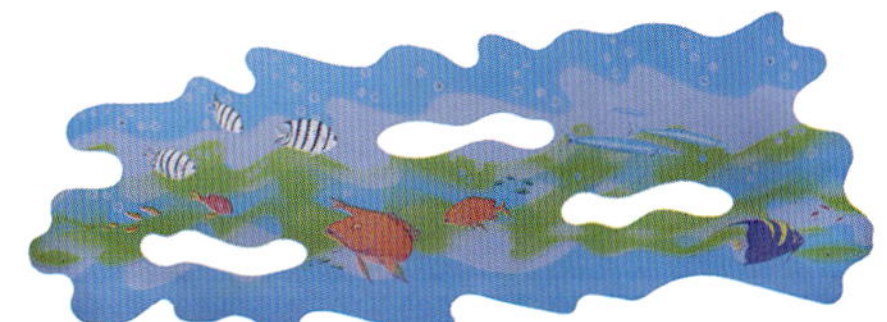

Court, Sally b.1948
The Sea (6 of 6)
acrylic on board 77 x 240
temp330

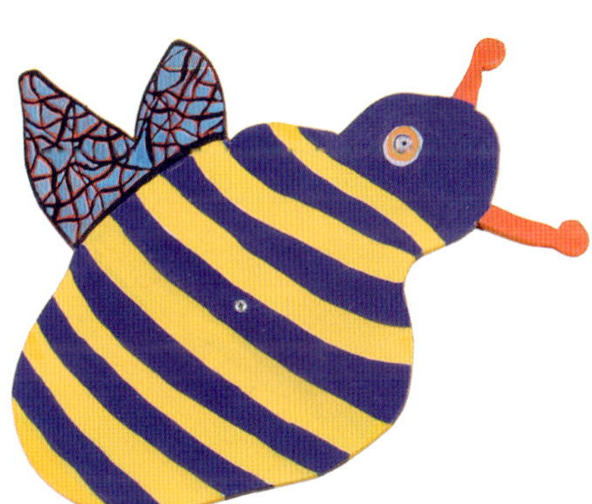

Court, Sally b.1948, **Eades, Carolanne** b.1945
& **Students of Watergate School**
Bee
acrylic on MDF board 40 x 50
temp28E

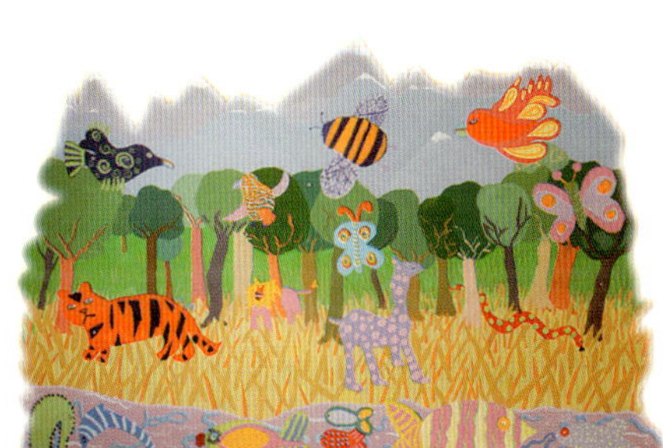

Court, Sally b.1948, **Eades, Carolanne** b.1945
& **Students of Watergate School**
Jungle Scene 1
acrylic on MDF board
temp28

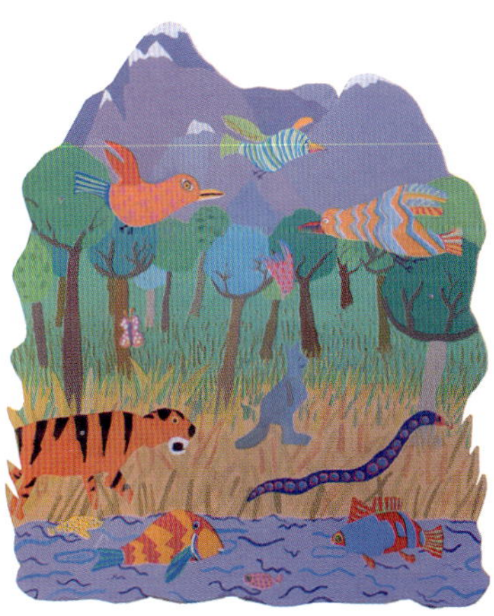

Court, Sally b.1948, **Eades, Carolanne** b.1945
& **Students of Watergate School**
Jungle Scene 2
acrylic on MDF board 115 x 100
temp28F

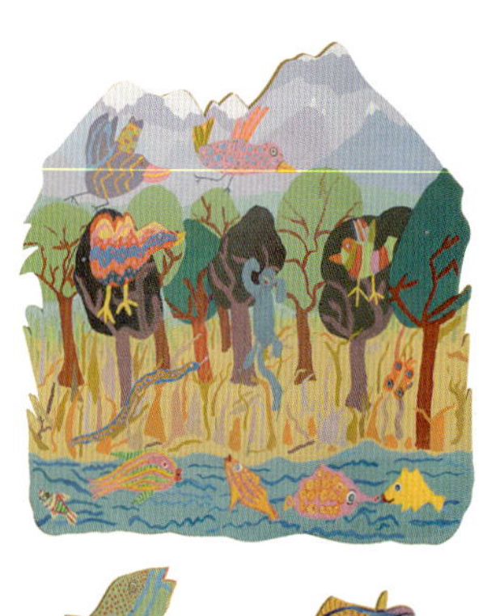
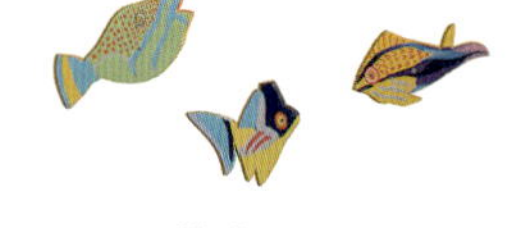

Court, Sally b.1948, **Eades, Carolanne** b.1945
& **Students of Watergate School**
Jungle Scene 3
acrylic on MDF board 150 x 125
temp28J

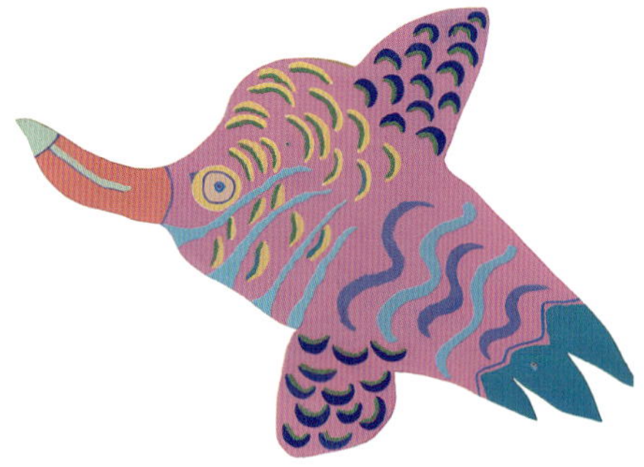

Court, Sally b.1948, **Eades, Carolanne** b.1945
& **Students of Watergate School**
Pink Bird
acrylic on MDF board 65 x 80
temp28G

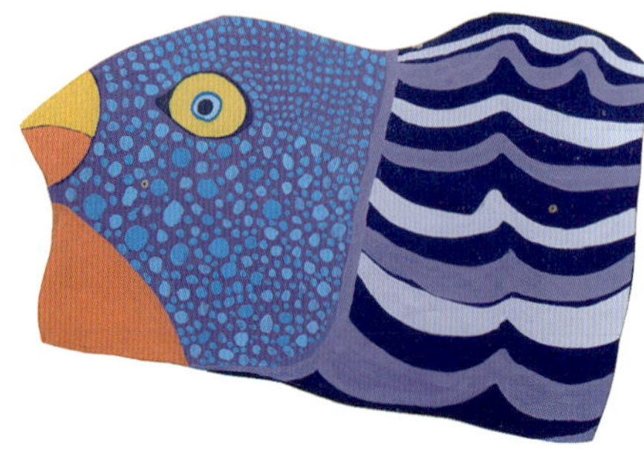

Court, Sally b.1948, **Eades, Carolanne** b.1945
& **Students of Watergate School**
Purple Fish
acrylic on MDF board 40 x 60
temp28C

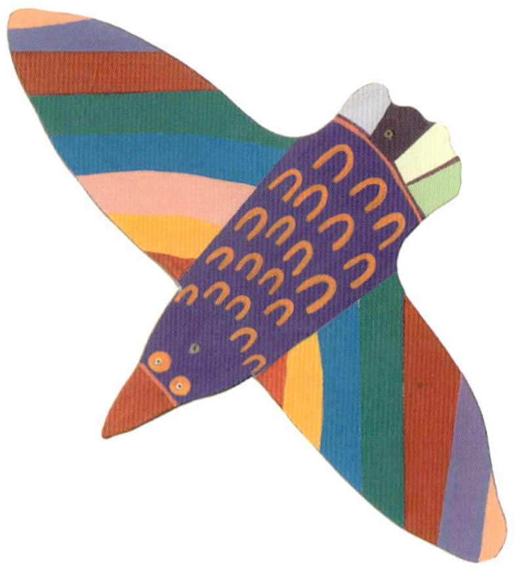

Court, Sally b.1948, **Eades, Carolanne** b.1945
& **Students of Watergate School**
Rainbow Bird
acrylic on MDF board 60 x 60
temp28B

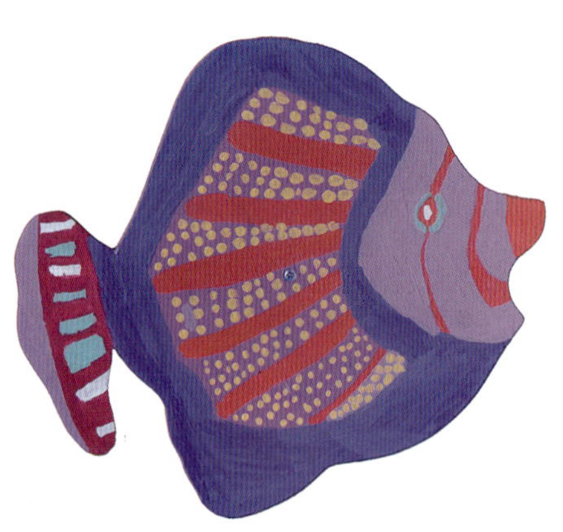

Court, Sally b.1948, **Eades, Carolanne** b.1945
& **Students of Watergate School**
Small Fish
acrylic on MDF board 35 x 40
temp28I

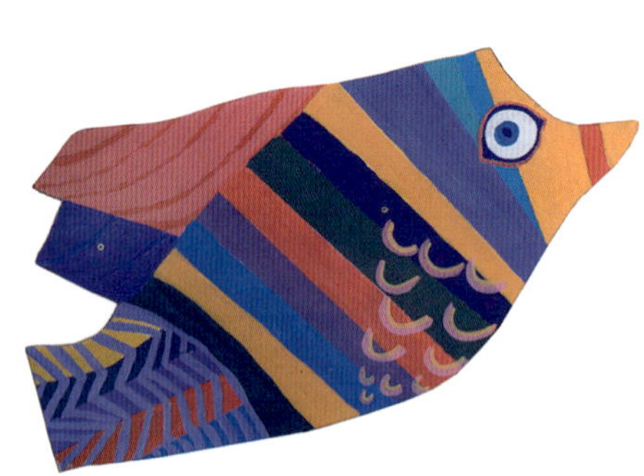

Court, Sally b.1948, **Eades, Carolanne** b.1945
& **Students of Watergate School**
Stripey Fish
acrylic on MDF board 60 x 70
temp28D

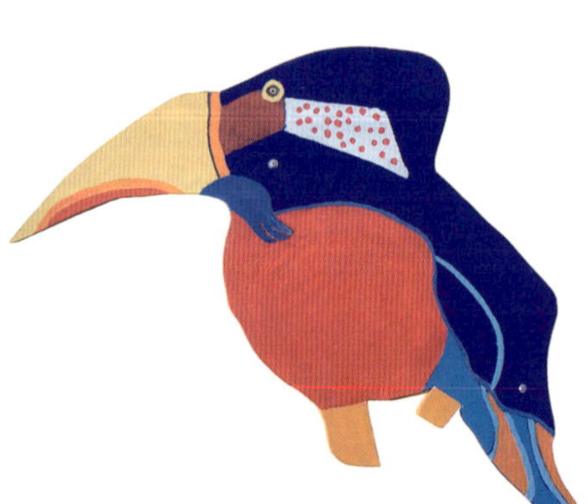

Court, Sally b.1948, **Eades, Carolanne** b.1945
& **Students of Watergate School**
Toucan
acrylic on MDF board 50 x 60
temp28H

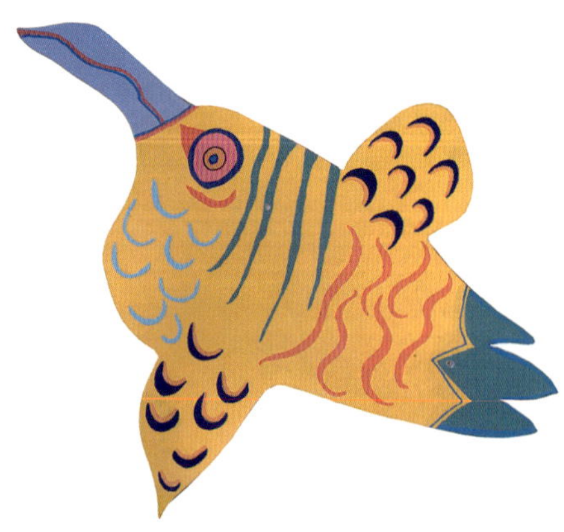

Court, Sally b.1948, **Eades, Carolanne** b.1945
& **Students of Watergate School**
Yellow Bird
acrylic on MDF board 70 x 70
temp28A

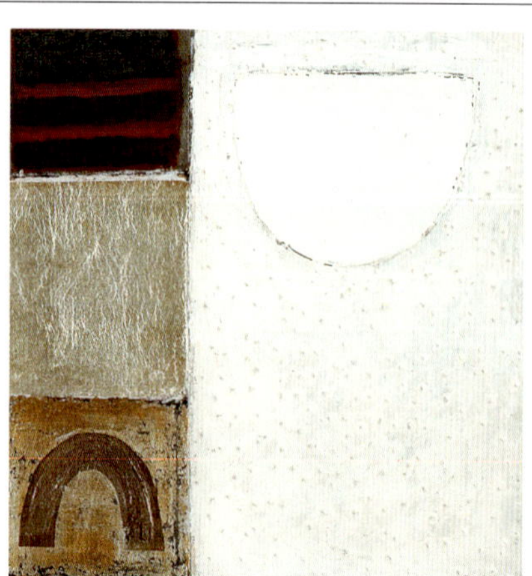

Crowther, Patricia b.1965
Winter Quay 2004
oil, oil pastel, silver & gold leaf on board
16.5 x 16.5 (E)
2044

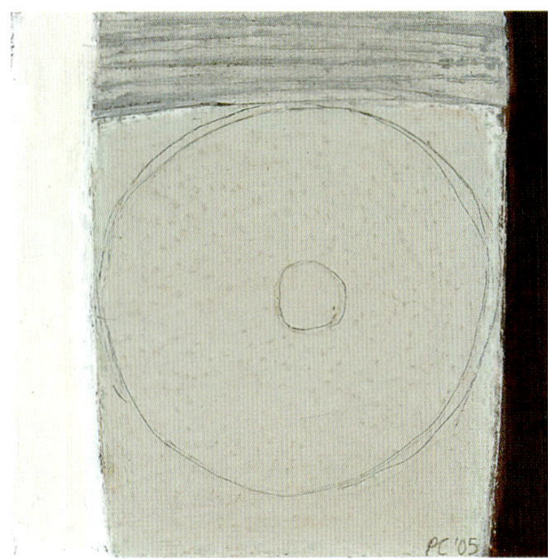

Crowther, Patricia b.1965
Mist Circle 2005
oil & oil pastel on board 16 x 16 (E)
2045

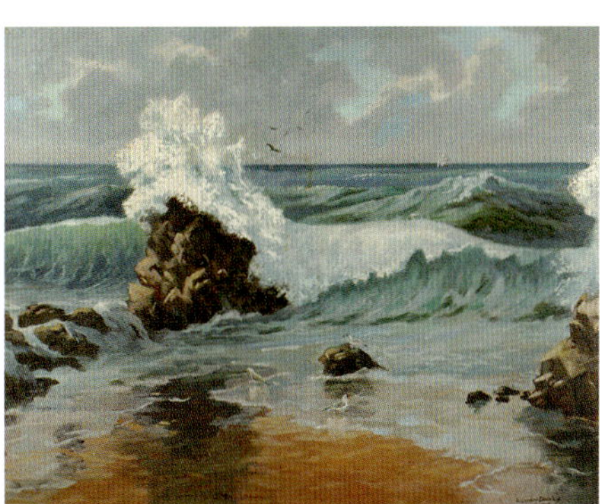

Davidge, E. Gordon
Breaking Wave
oil on canvas 58 x 75 (E)
1707

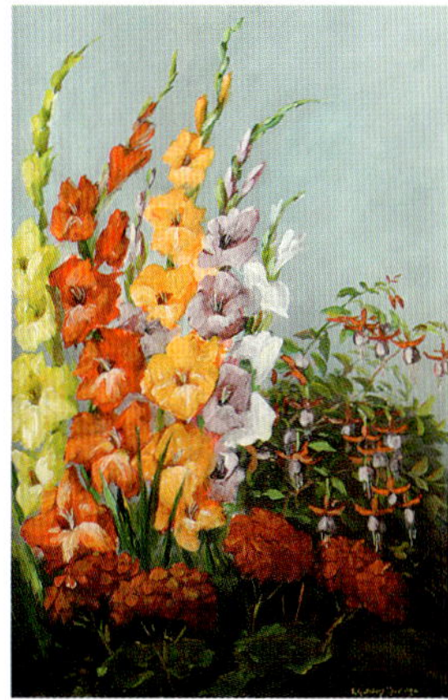

Davidge, E. Gordon
Flowers
oil on canvas 74.6 x 49.4 (E)
Temp1

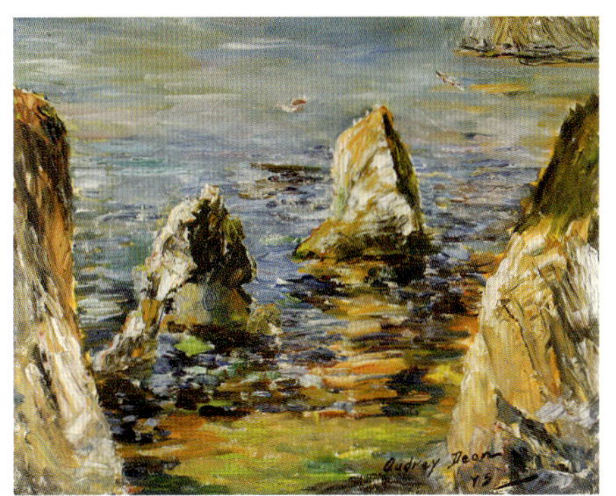

Dean, Audrey active 1973–1985
Arch Rock, Freshwater 1973
oil on canvas 59.5 x 75 (E)
1562

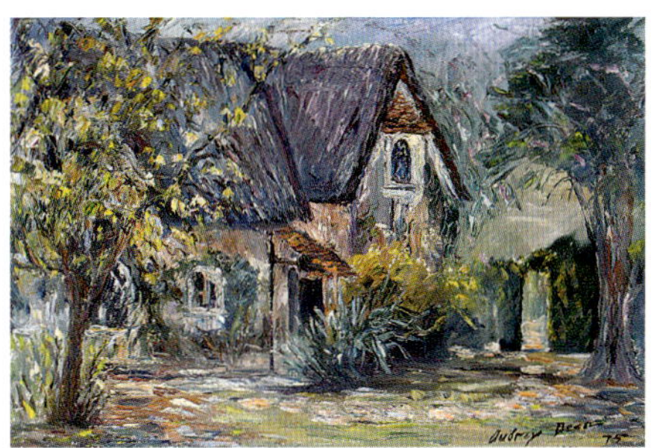

Dean, Audrey active 1973–1985
Cottages at Porchfield 1975
oil on canvas 50 x 75
1209

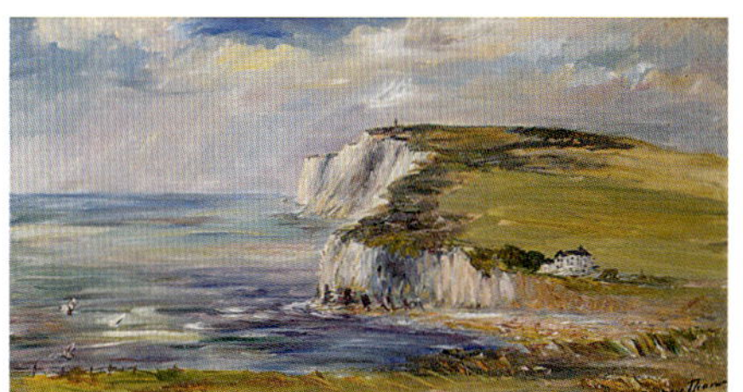

Dean, Audrey active 1973–1985
Freshwater Bay 1977
oil on canvas 39 x 75
Temp100

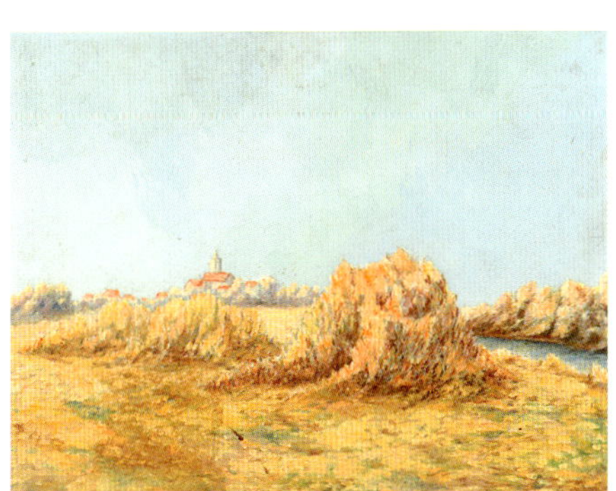

Dightam, Peter
Red-Roofed Landscape 1976
oil on board 37.5 x 49.7 (E)
344

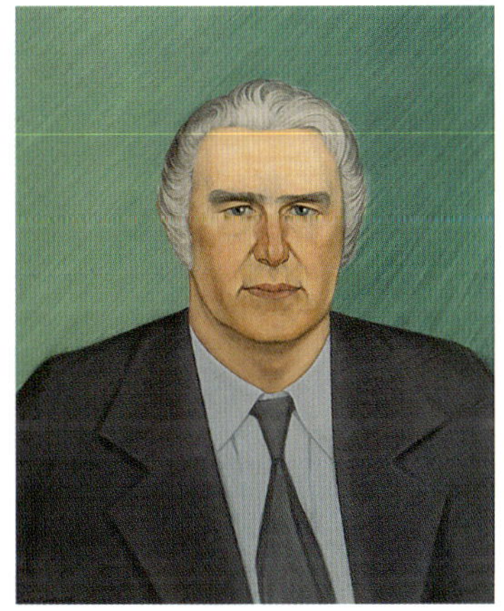

Fereday, Joseph 1917–2001
Portrait of a Gentleman
oil on canvas 59.5 x 50 (E)
Temp5

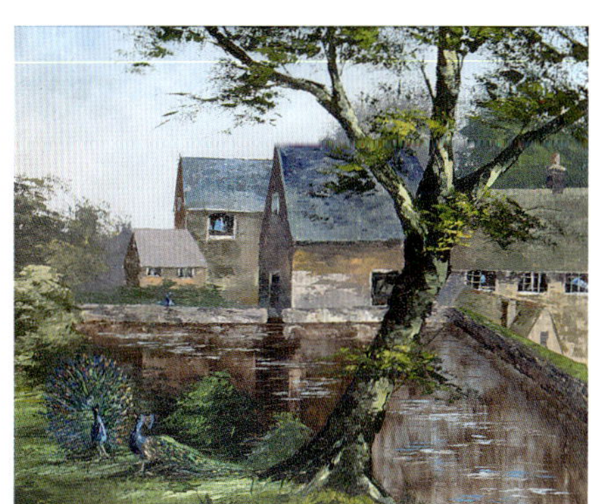

Fraser
Calbourne Mill
oil on board 49.5 x 59.5
temp600

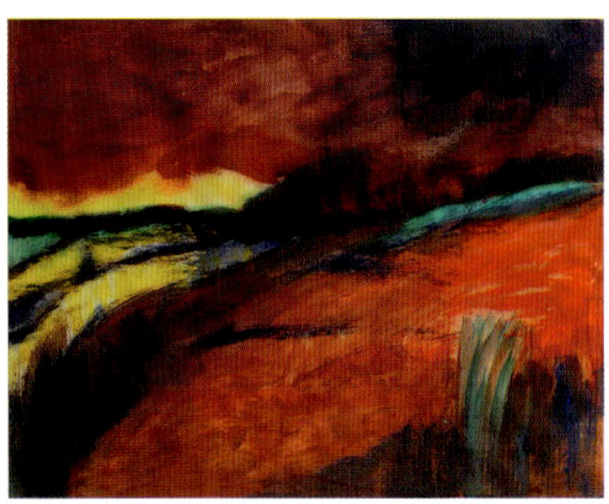

Gingell, Mary
Landscape 8: Dawn
acrylic on paper 72 x 98
937

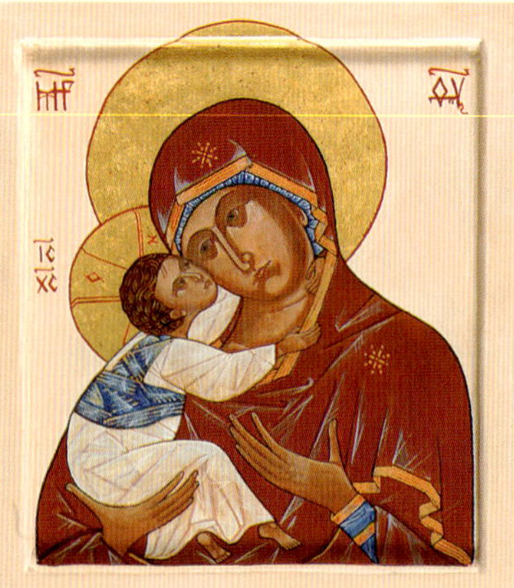

Graham, Melanie
Icon of Loving Tenderness 1993
acrylic on board 30.7 x 20.7
1036

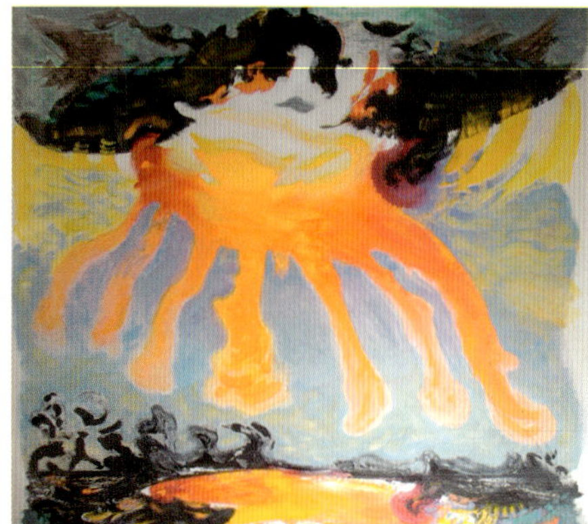

Hambling, Maggi b.1945
Dragon Sunrise
oil on canvas 148 x 170 (E)
Temp40

Hewitson, Eric
Artist Cracks the Mathematics of Chaos
acrylic on canvas 140 x 150 (E)
Temp26

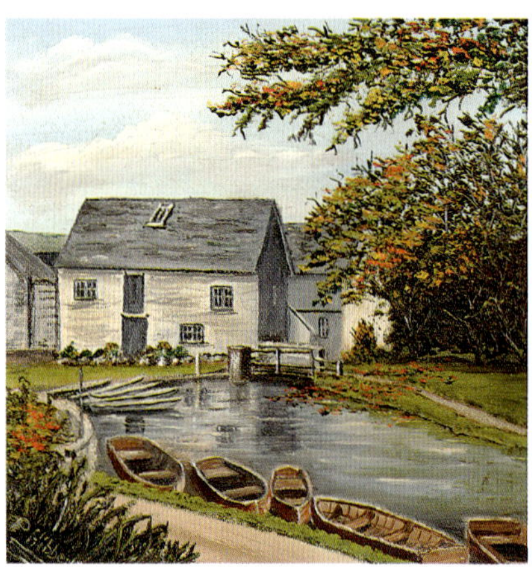

Hibbert, Phyllis I. b.1903
Alveston Mill 1957
oil on canvas 37 x 36.5 (E)
240

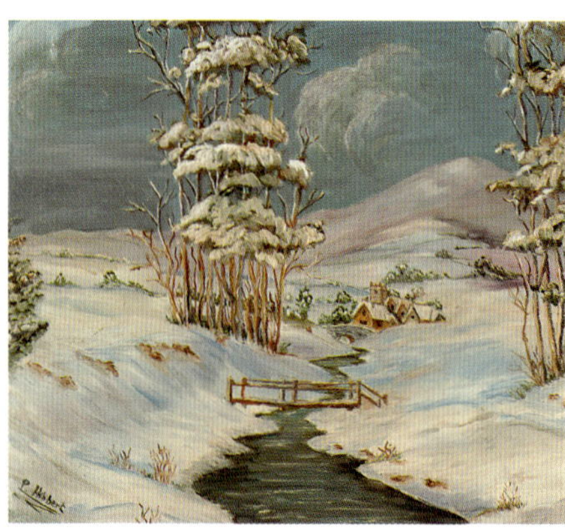

Hibbert, Phyllis I. b.1903
Bridge: Water
oil on canvas 36.2 x 42 (E)
237

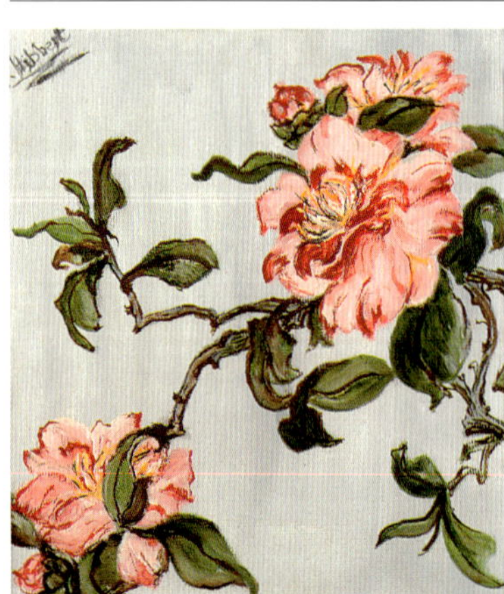

Hibbert, Phyllis I. b.1903
Camelias
oil on canvas 30 x 27.5 (E)
245

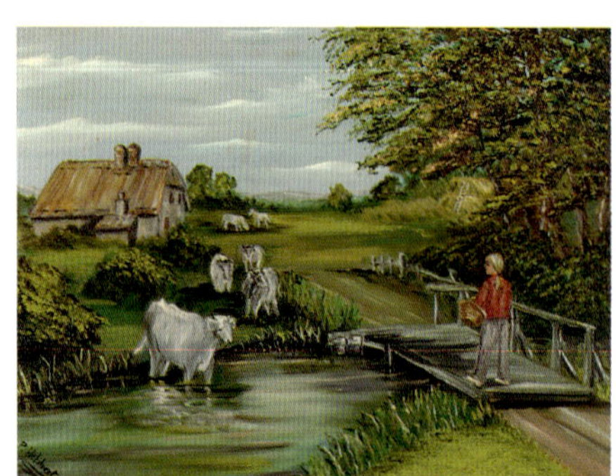

Hibbert, Phyllis I. b.1903
Devon Cows
oil on canvas 36.5 x 49.5 (E)
238

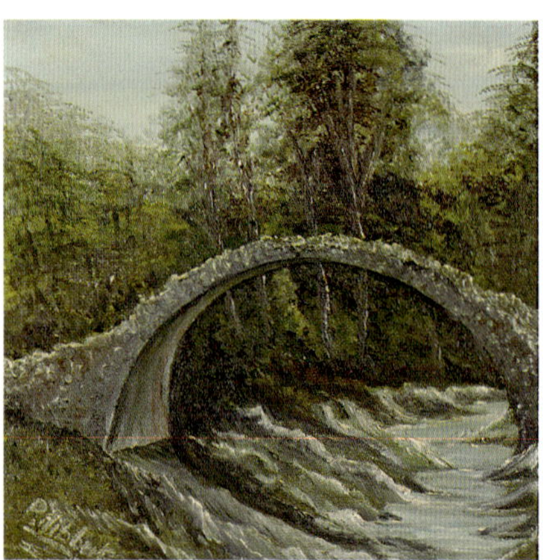

Hibbert, Phyllis I. b.1903
Stone Bridge, Scotland
oil on canvas 37.1 x 38 (E)
239

Facing page: Anguissola, Sofonisba, c.1532–1625, *The Artist's Sister in the Garb of a Nun* (detail), 1551, Southampton City Art Gallery, (p. 11)

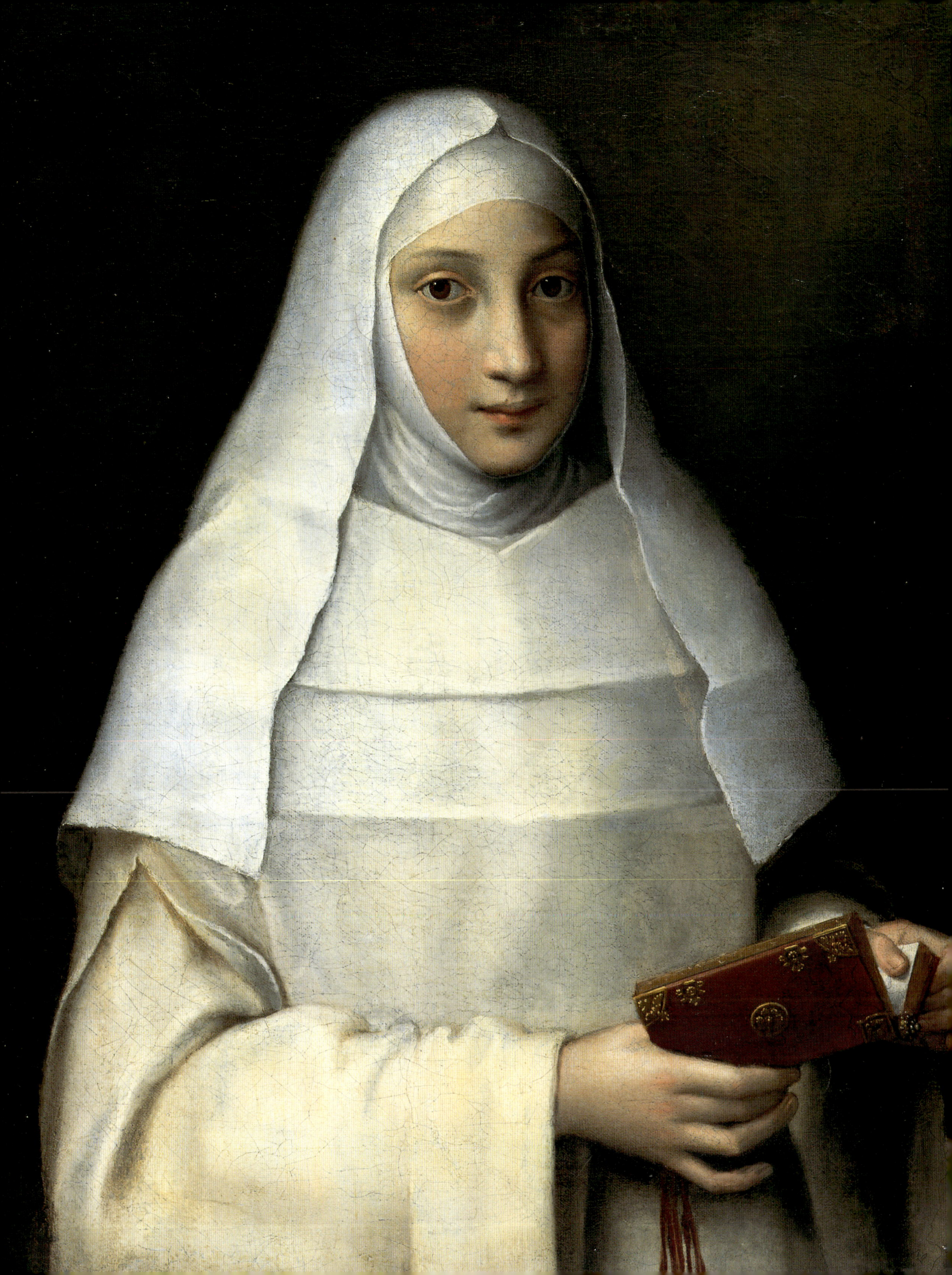

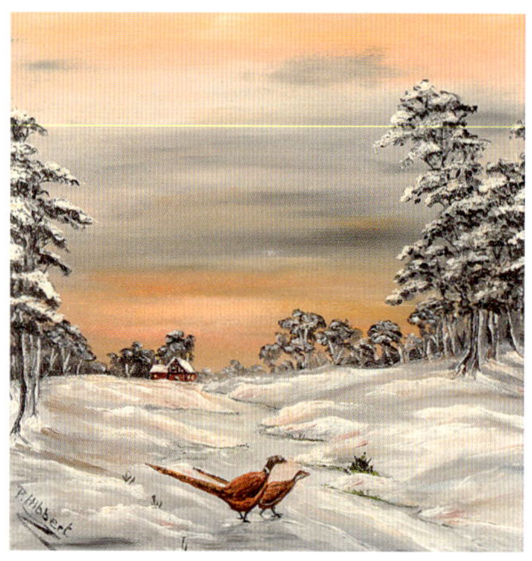

Hibbert, Phyllis I. b.1903
Two Pheasants
oil on canvas 37 x 36.5 (E)
236

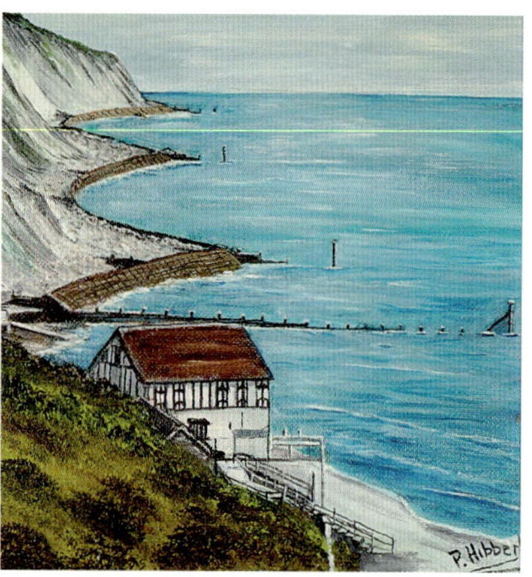

Hibbert, Phyllis I. b.1903
View of Ventnor to Bonchurch
oil on canvas 36.8 x 36.8 (E)
243

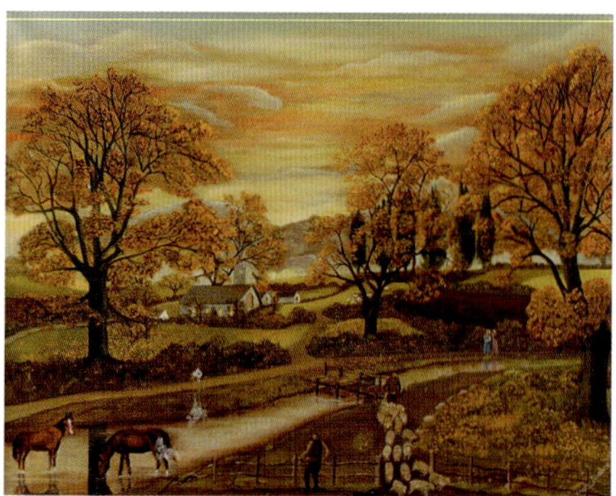

Hobden, George
Pastoral Scene with Horses
oil on canvas 70 x 90 (E)
1838

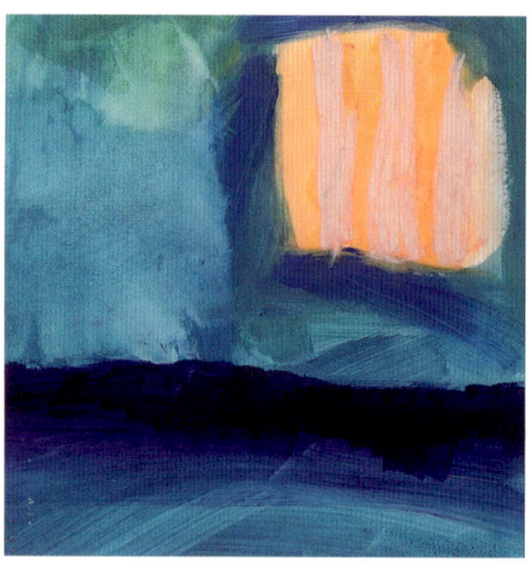

Hodge Thomas, Charlotte b.1968
Untitled (Abstract Orange & Turquoise) 1992
acrylic & watercolour on paper 43 x 43
1117

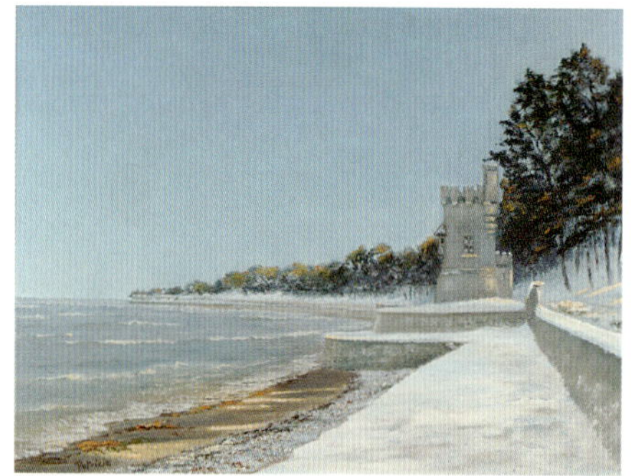

Hodges, P. J.
Appley in Winter
oil on board 42 x 57.5 (E)
351

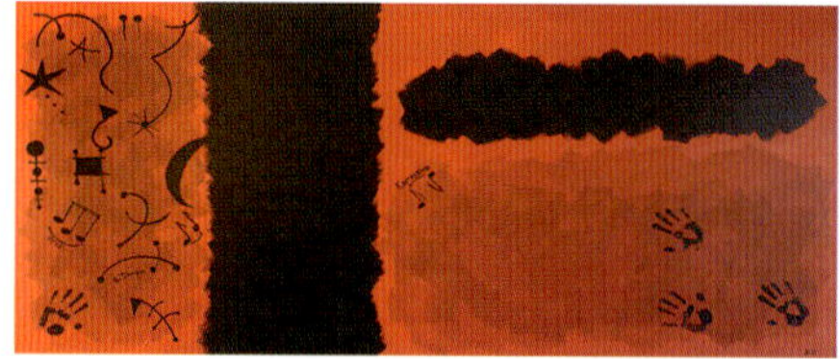

Hughes, Lucy
Noise
acrylic on board 122 x 244
Temp69

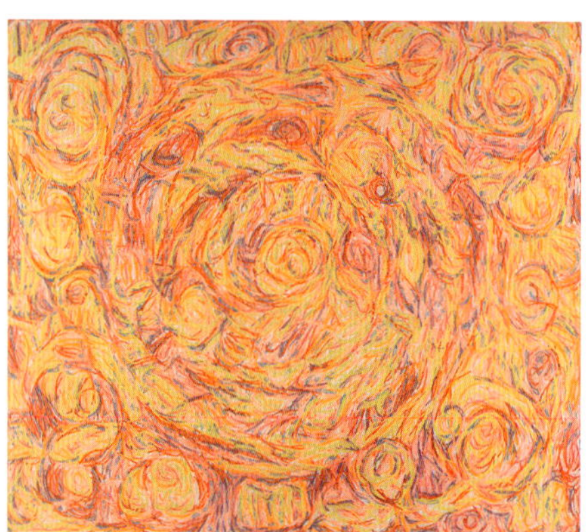

Johnson, Sara b.1957
Heartbeat 1991
acrylic on paper 63 x 73
979

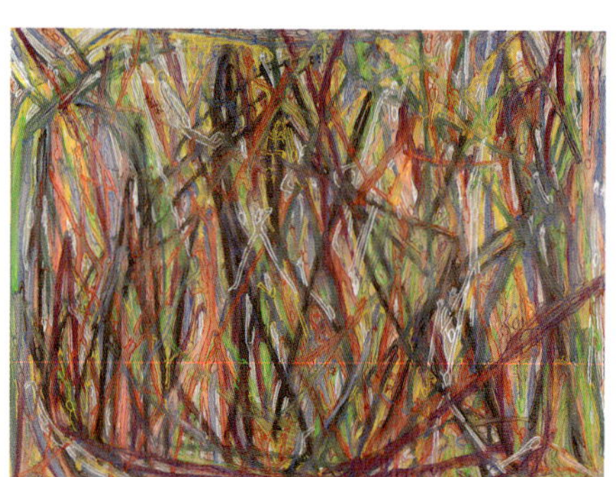

Johnson, Sara b.1957
Struggle c.1991
acrylic on paper 55 x 75
1719

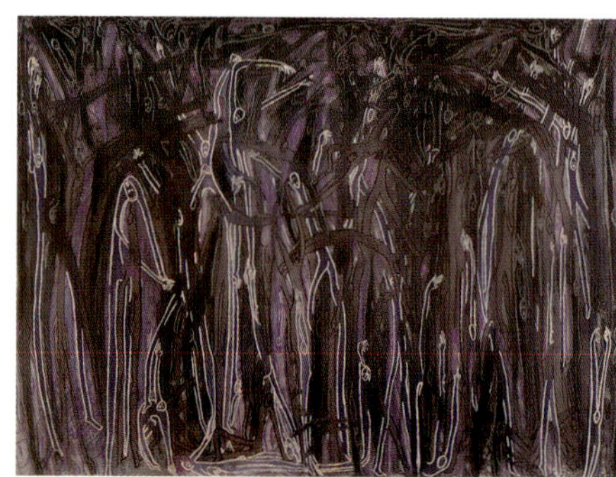

Johnson, Sara b.1957
Supplanter of Daylight c.1991
acrylic on paper 55 x 75
1353

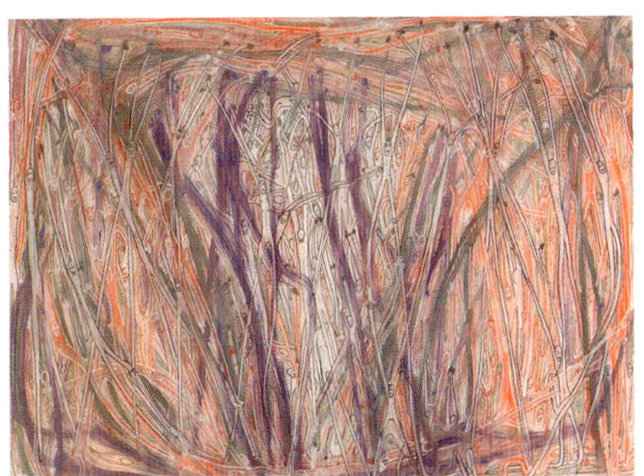

Johnson, Sara b.1957
White Cell Dreams c.1991
acrylic on paper 54 x 74
2017

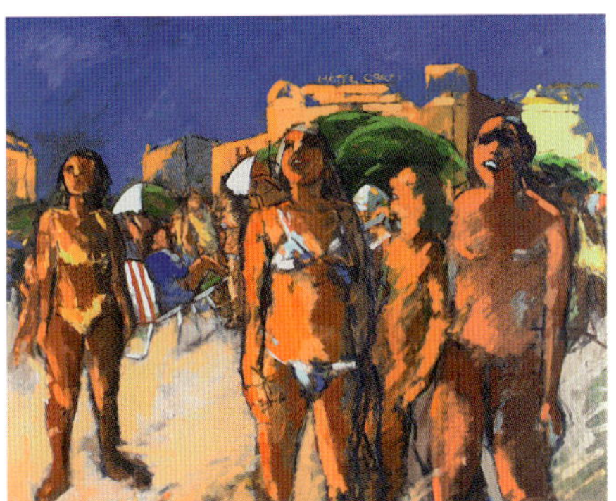

Joseph, S.
Beach Hotel
oil on canvas 96 x 121.2
157

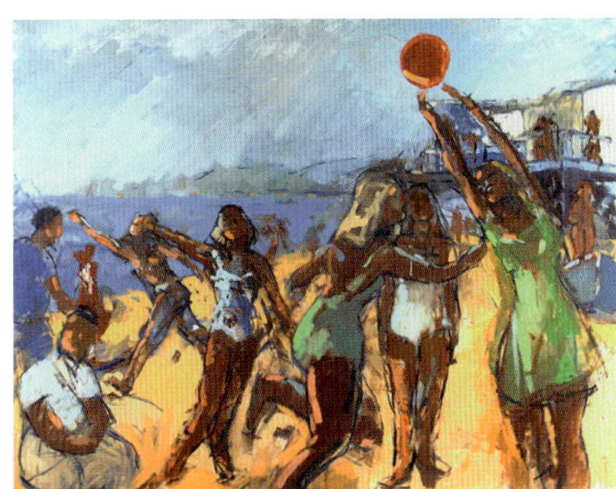

Joseph, S.
Red Ball
oil on canvas 95.5 x 127
156

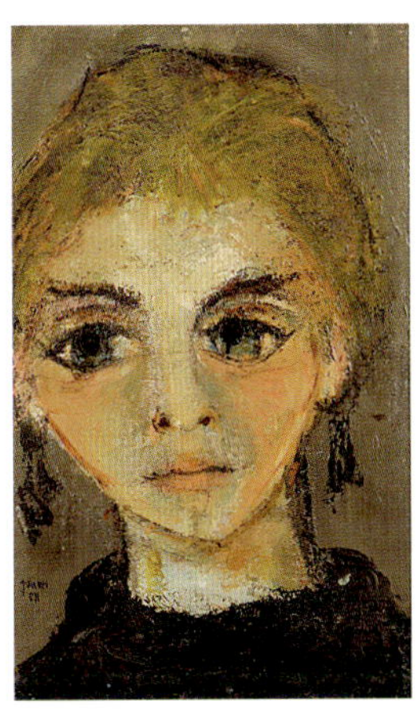

Julian, C. H.
Marguerite
oil on board 35 x 21.5
Temp32

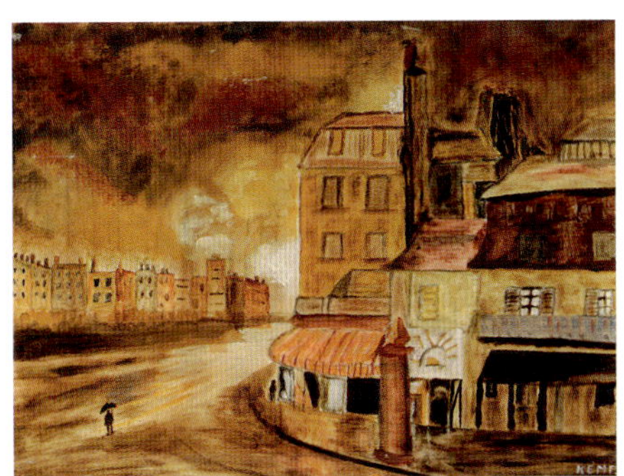

Kemp, S. J.
Storm in Paris
oil on canvas 35.5 x 48 (E)
508

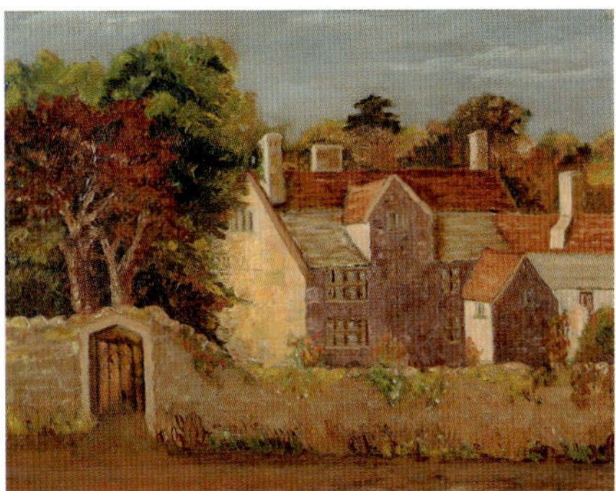

Kendrick, G.
Mottistone Manor
oil on board 30 x 40 (E)
333

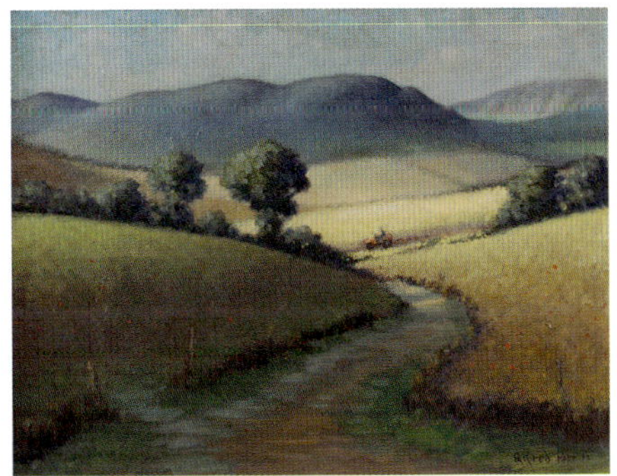

Kerr, Alfred active 1972–1985
Landscape 1972
oil on board 44.3 x 59.6 (E)
37

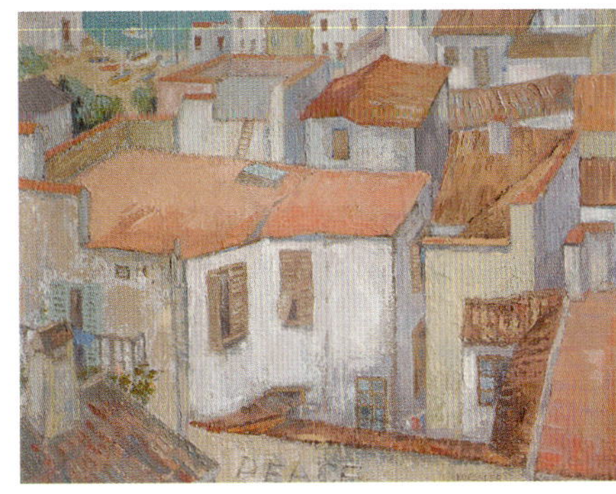

Koessler, Edith
Roofs at Gibraltar
oil on canvas 70 x 90
Temp77

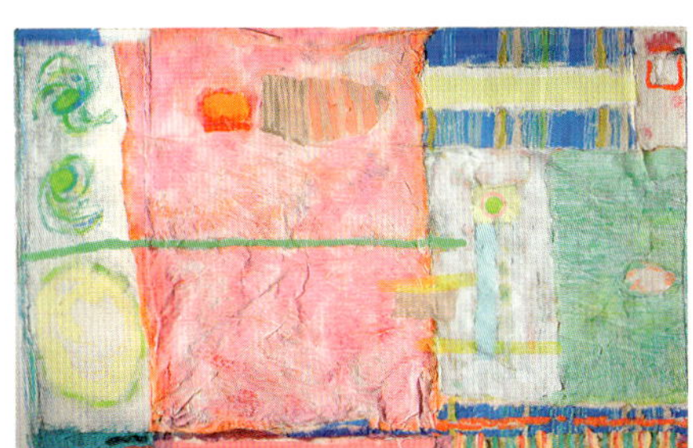

Kubisa, Seran b.1967
Connect 1 1994
mixed media 61 x 101
Temp17

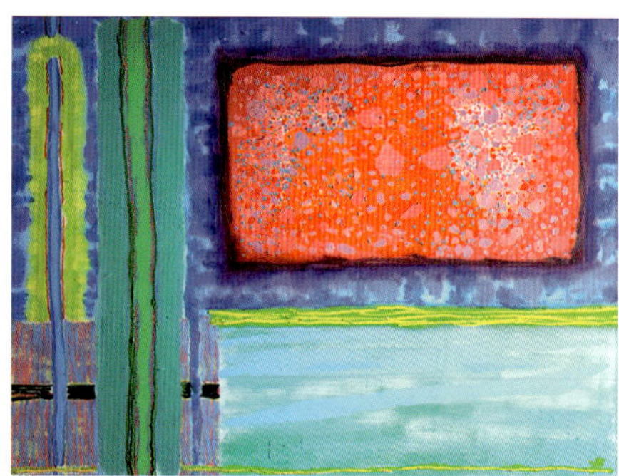

Kubisa, Seran b.1967
Star Cluster
oil on canvas 101 x 136
Temp18

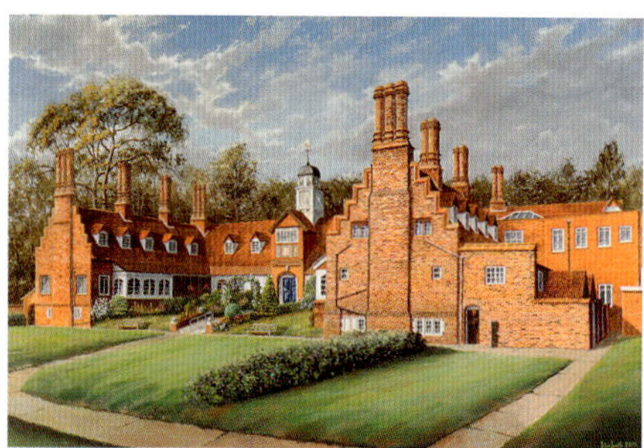

Leath, Peter active c.1995–2001
Frank James Hospital 2001
oil on board 49.5 x 74.5
Temp200

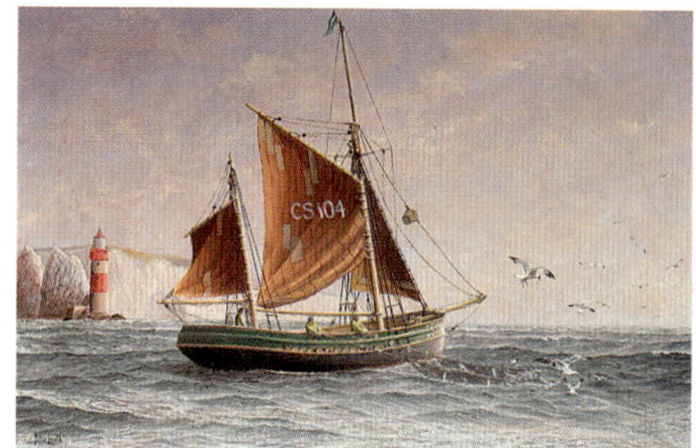

Leath, Peter active c.1995–2001
Thames Barge Fishing Off the Needles
oil on board 50 x 74
temp329

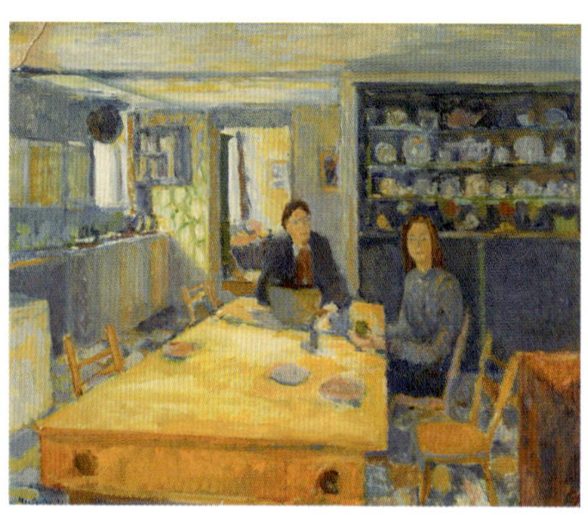

MacCarthy, C. active 1980–1985
Interior at Weedon 1980
oil on board 49 x 59.5 (E)
6

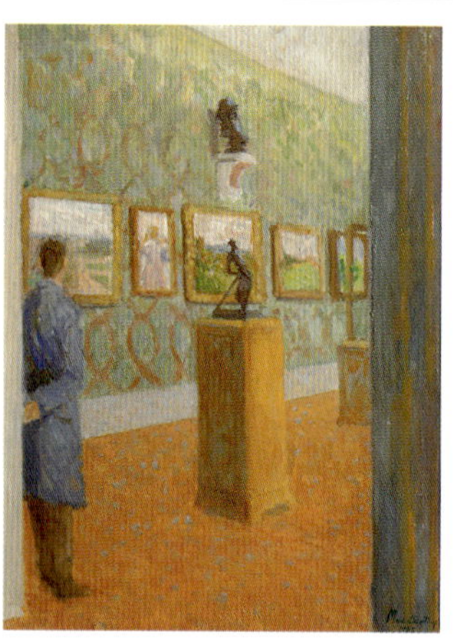

MacCarthy, C. active 1980–1985
In the Gallery 1985
oil on canvas 50 x 38
1998

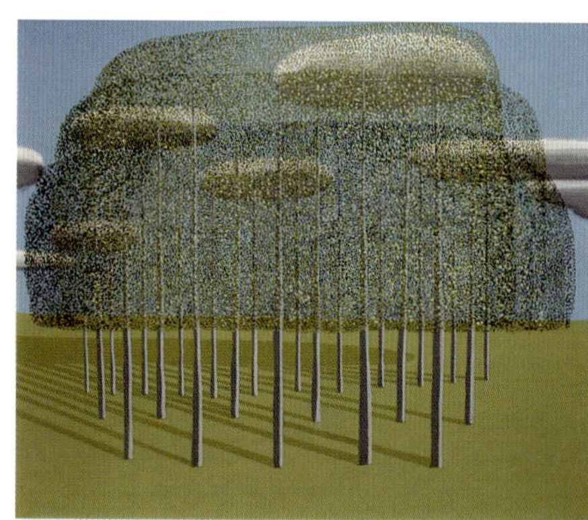

Markey, Peter b.1930
Copse 1990s
acrylic on board 60 x 69
1277

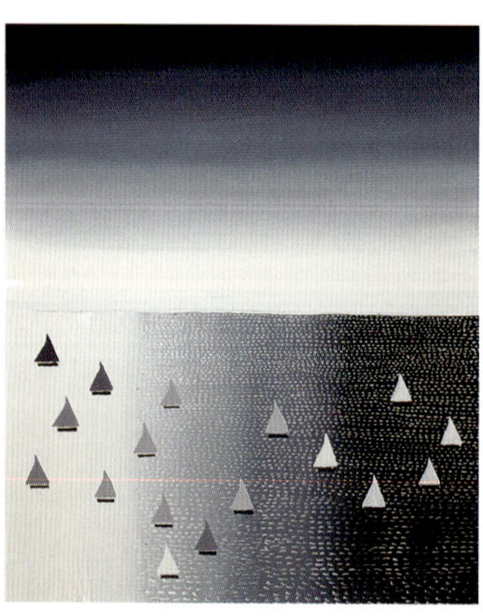

Markey, Peter b.1930
Yachts 1990s
oil on board 59 x 49.2
1278

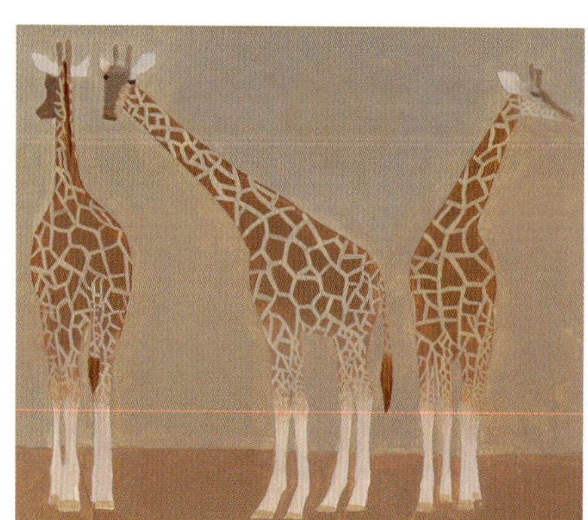

Markey, Peter b.1930
Three Giraffes 1993
oil on board 25 x 30 (E)
1362

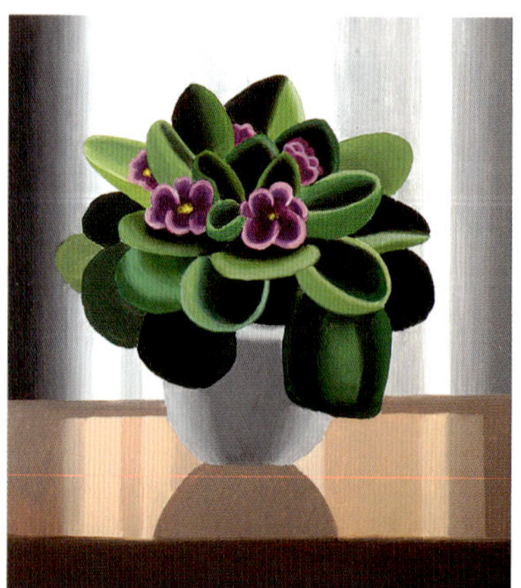

Markey, Peter b.1930
African Violets
oil on board 44.8 x 40
Temp79

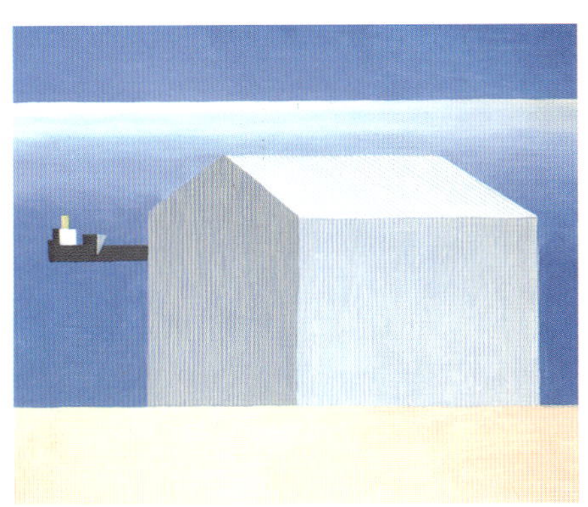

Markey, Peter b.1930
Boat and Building
acrylic on board 50 x 60 (E)
1666

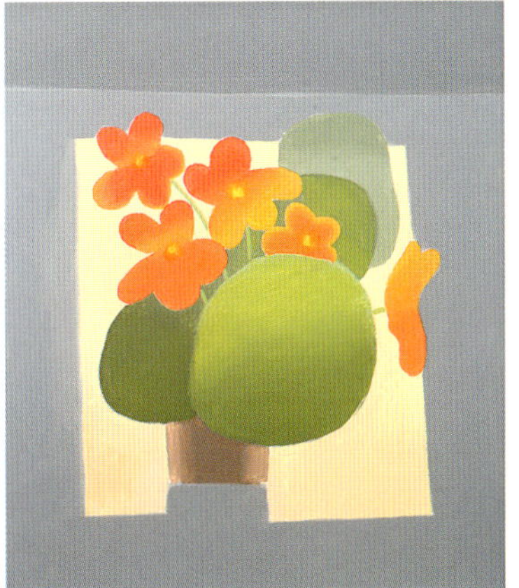

Markey, Peter b.1930
Geraniums
oil on board 43.7 x 38.5
Temp80

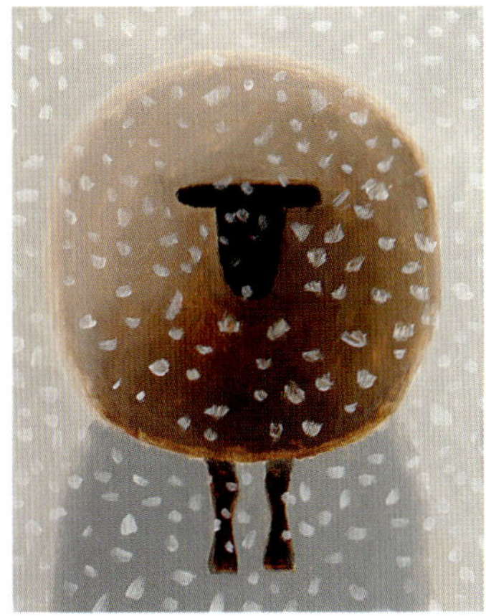

Markey, Peter b.1930
Sheep
acrylic on board 29.5 x 24 (E)
1685

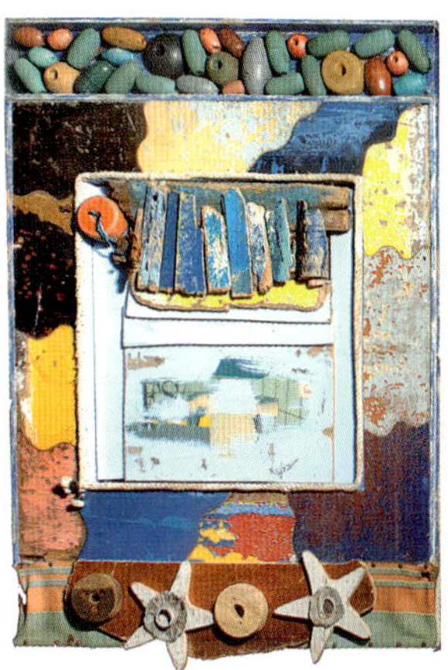

McLaren Clark, Lisa b.1973
Beachcomber
oil on wood 150 x 120
Temp75

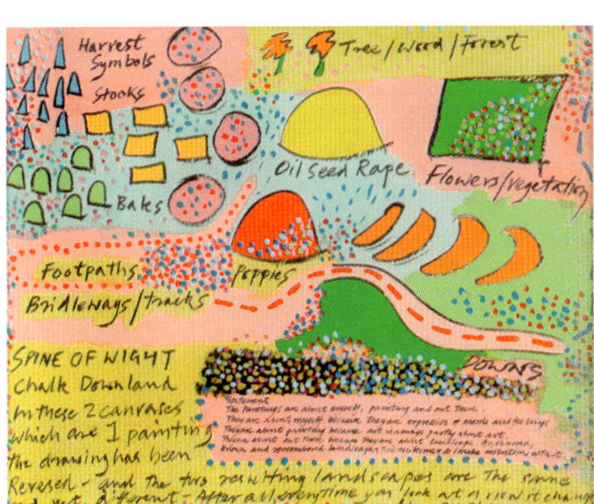

McPherson, Alan b.1943
Spine of Wight 1988
acrylic on paper 36 x 46 (E)
840

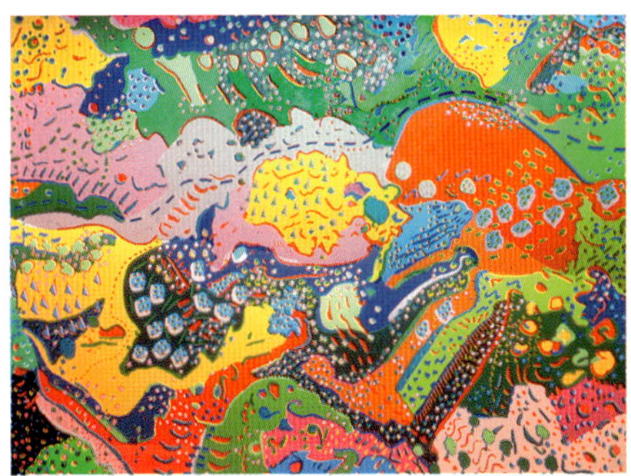

McPherson, Alan b.1943
Spine of Wight East 1988
acrylic on canvas 152.5 x 190
715

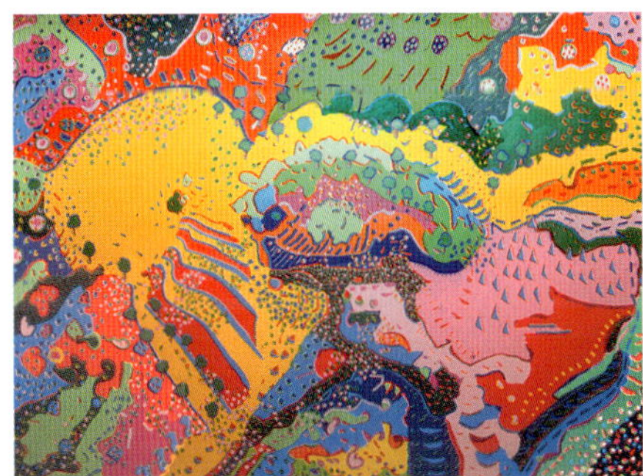

McPherson, Alan b.1943
Spine of Wight West 1988
acrylic on canvas 152.5 x 190
714

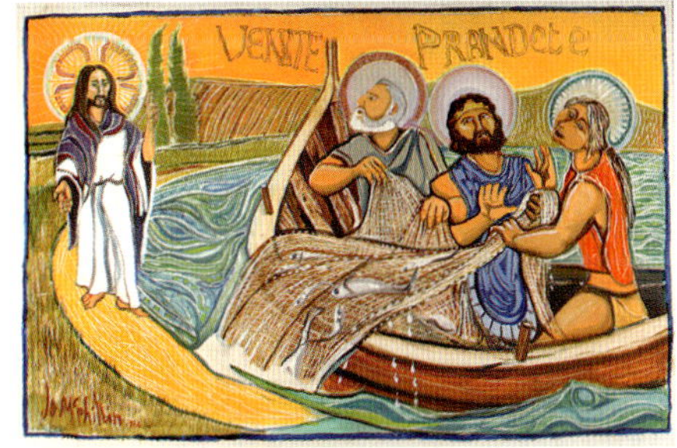

McPhilbin, Jo
Draught of Fishes 1986
oil on metal sheet 74.5 x 101.5 (E)
1048

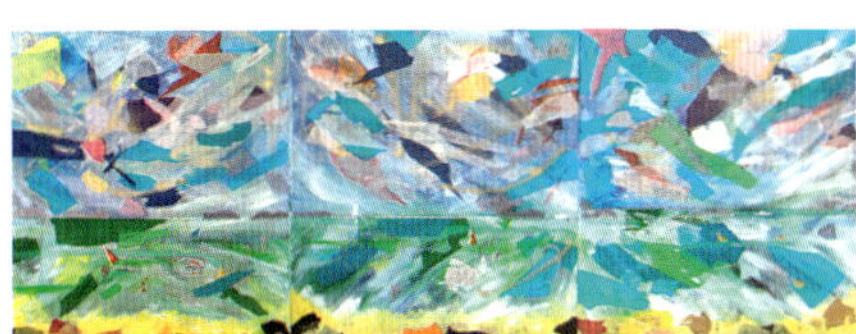

Mence, Marcia b.1948
Colour Storm Triptych
mixed media on canvas 150 x 350 (E)
Temp29

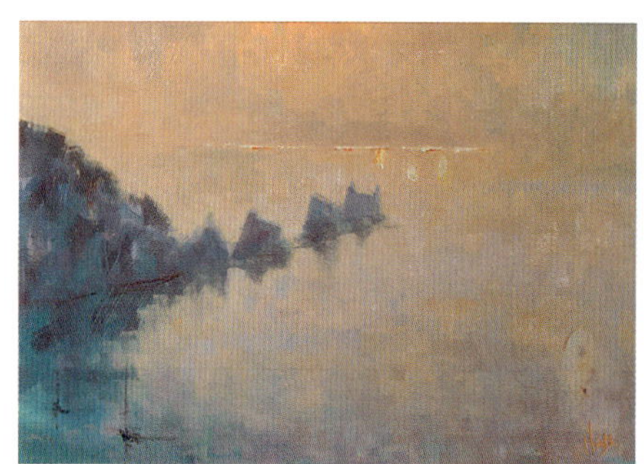

Mence, Myles b.1954
Needles and Bear of Britain
oil on board 38.5 x 59
2054

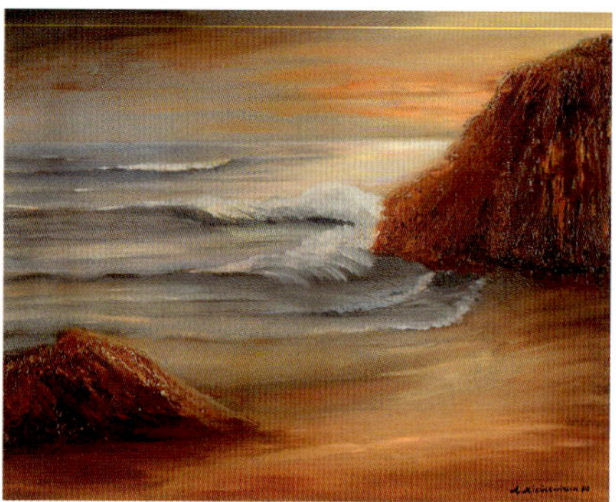

Mikulewitsch, A.
Sunset on the Isle of Wight 1980
oil on canvas 39.2 x 49.9 (E)
654

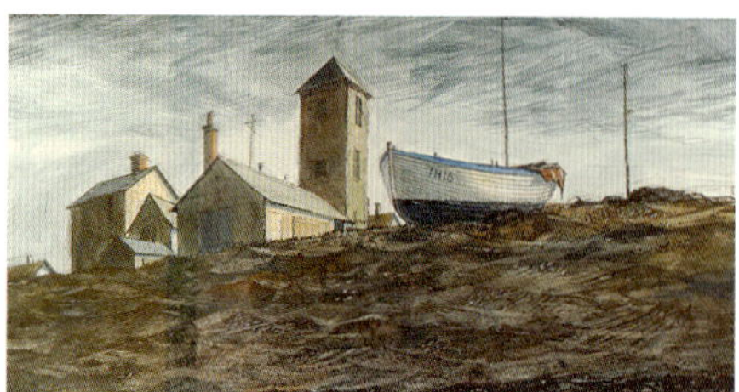

Morton, Cavendish b.1911
North Lookout Tower, Aldeburgh, Suffolk
mixed media on paper 31.5 x 60 (E)
2040

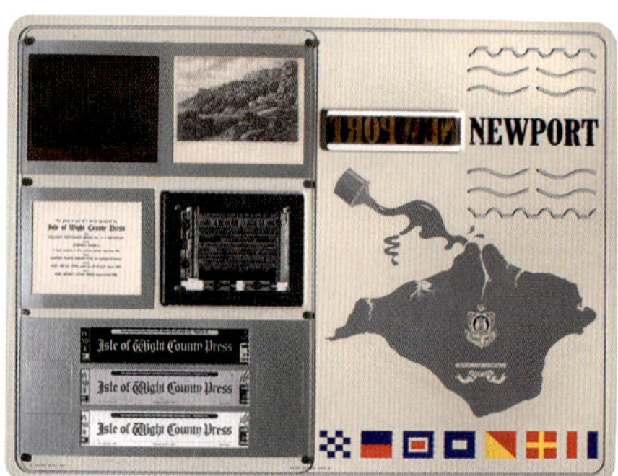

Nicoll, Stephen b.1946
Holiday Postcard Series 1: Newport (IOW county press) 1990
acrylic on lacquered MDF with woodblock letters and 'as found' material 86.5 x 122
Temp37

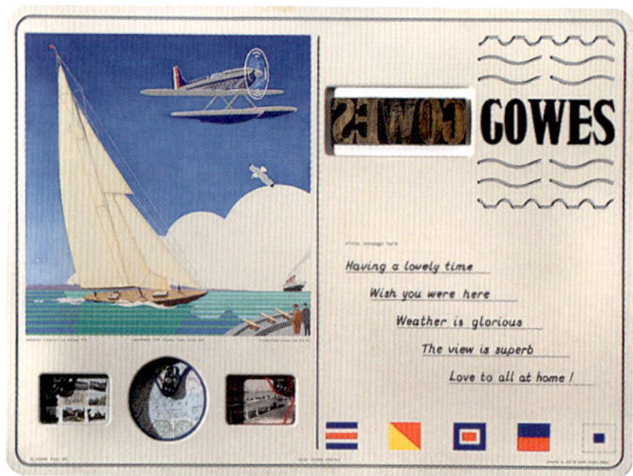

Nicoll, Stephen b.1946
Holiday Postcard Series 2: Cowes (postcard messages) 1990
acrylic on lacquered MDF with woodblock letters and 'as found' material 86.5 x 122
temp336

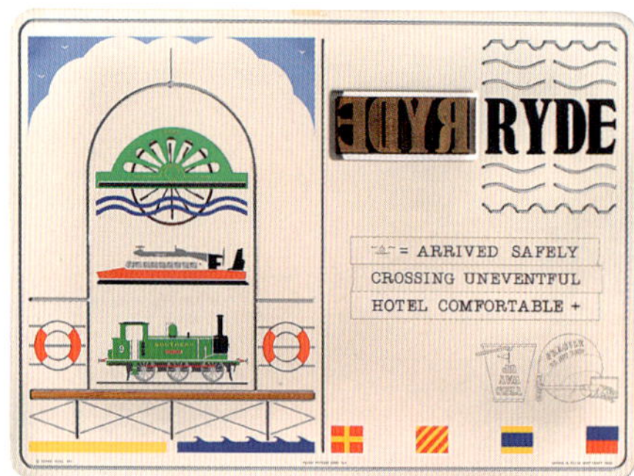

Nicoll, Stephen b.1946
Holiday Postcard Series 3: Ryde (telegrams and luggage) 1990
acrylic on lacquered MDF with woodblock letters and 'as found' material 86.5 x 122
temp331

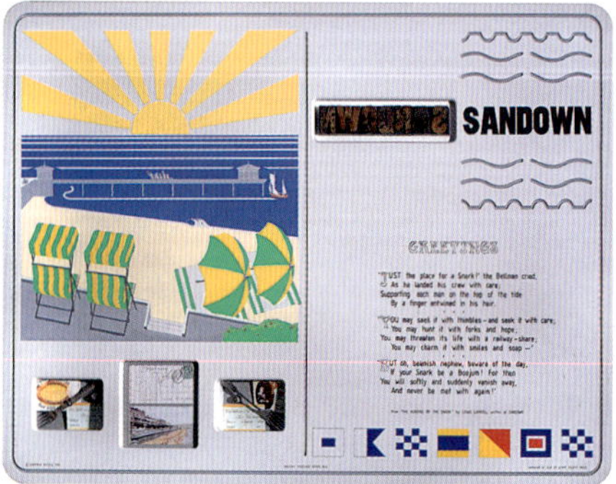

Nicoll, Stephen b.1946
Holiday Postcard Series 4: Sandown (poem and memorabilia 1990
acrylic on lacquered MDF with woodblock letters and 'as found' material 86.5 x 122
temp334

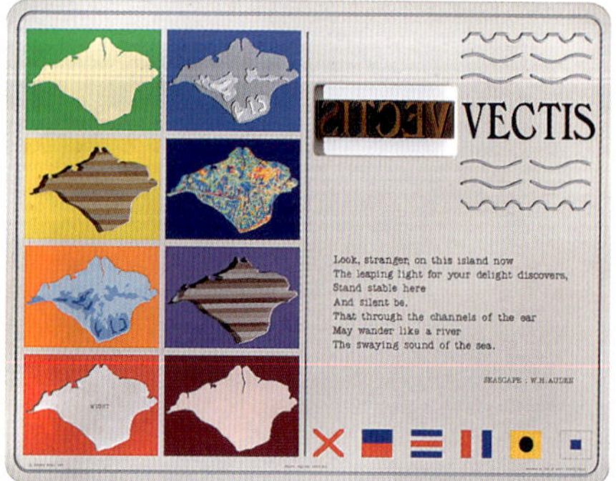

Nicoll, Stephen b.1946
Holiday Postcard Series 5: Vectis (poem and patterns) 1990
acrylic on lacquered MDF with woodblock letters and 'as found' material 86.5 x 122
temp337

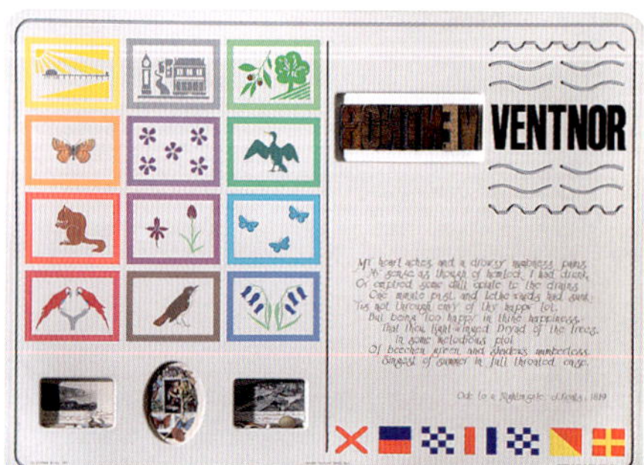

Nicoll, Stephen b.1946
Holiday Postcard Series 6: Ventnor (peom and postcards 1990
acrylic on lacquered MDF with woodblock letters and 'as found' material 86.5 x 122 (E)
temp335

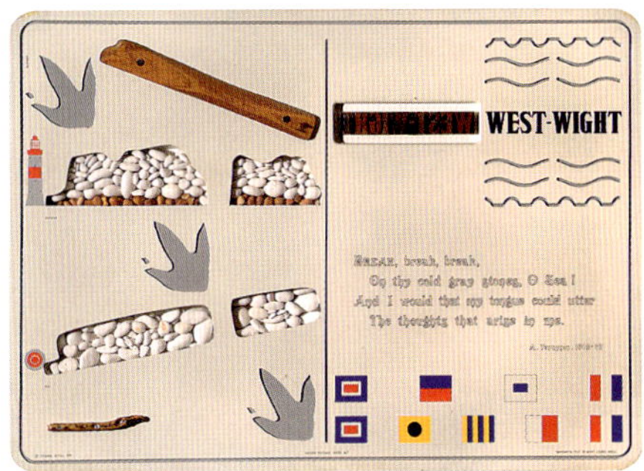

Nicoll, Stephen b.1946
Holiday Postcard Series 7: West Wight (poem and pebbles) 1990
acrylic on lacquered MDF with woodblock letters and as found material 86.5 x 122
temp332

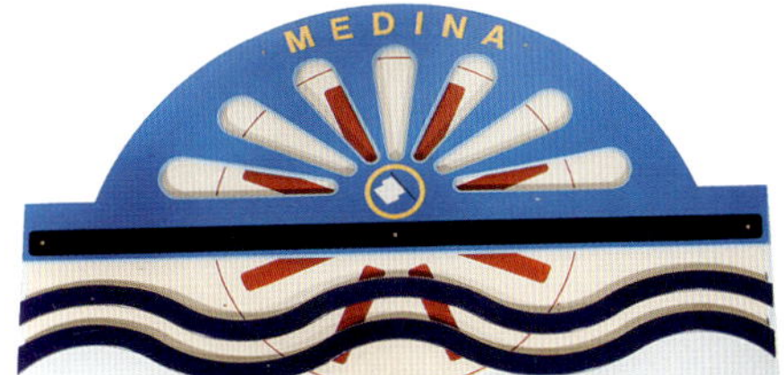

Nicoll, Stephen b.1946
Ward Sign: Medina (Paddle Steamer)
acrylic on lacquered MPF 100 x 180
Temp19

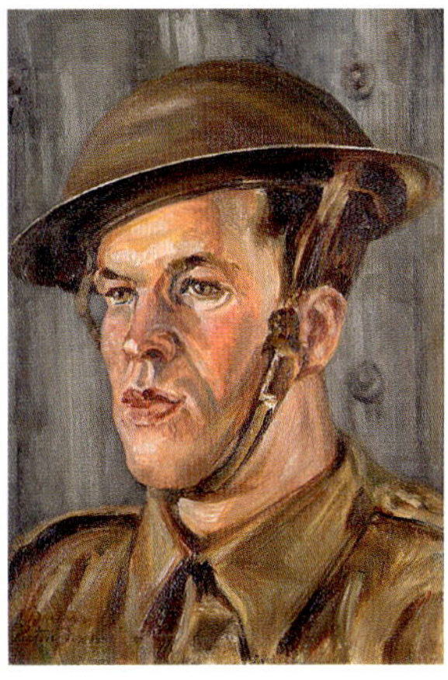

Picton Fox, Barbara d.1990
Portrait of a Soldier 1941
oil on canvas 35 x 25
1721

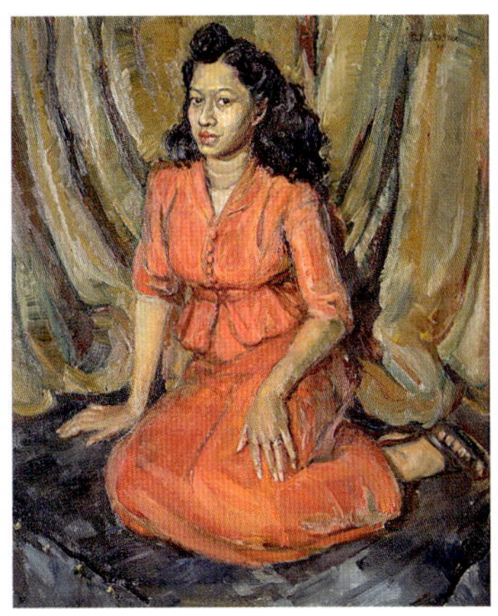

Picton Fox, Barbara d.1990
Burmese Woman 1949
oil on canvas 75 x 63
Temp103

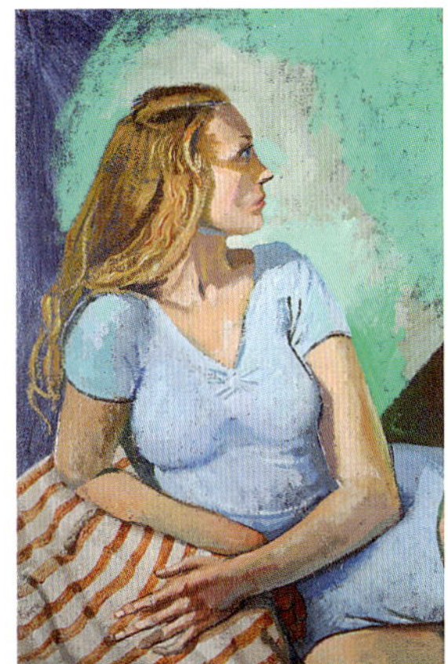

Power, Ronald 1914–1989
Blue Lady
oil on board 90.5 x 60.5 (E)
1308

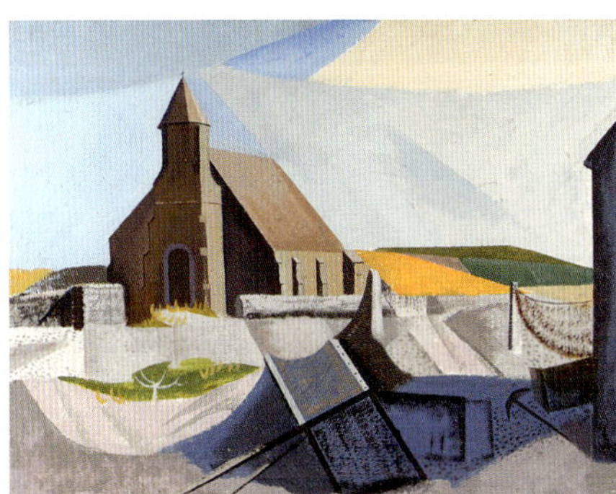

Power, Ronald 1914–1989
Church on Seashore
oil on board 56 x 75.5 (E)
1139

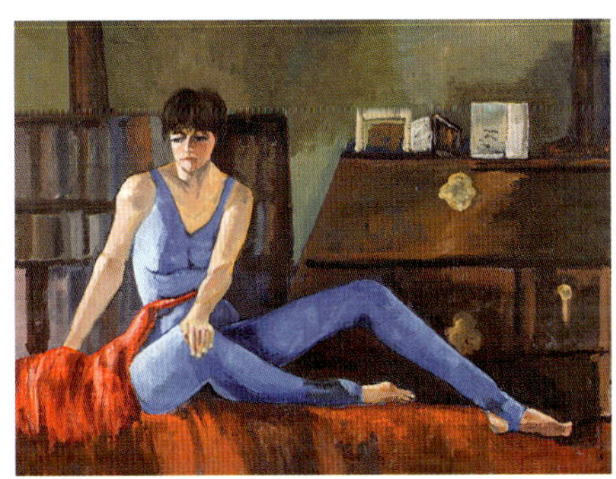

Power, Ronald 1914–1989
Dancer
oil on canvas 76 x 101.5 (E)
Temp8

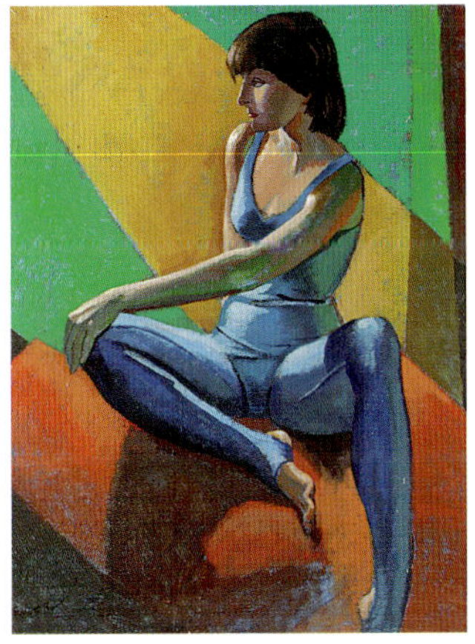

Power, Ronald 1914–1989
Dancer in Blue
oil on board 91 x 70 (E)
1304

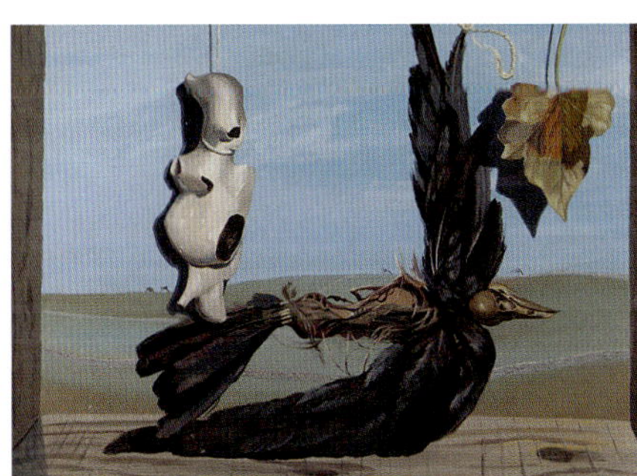

Power, Ronald 1914–1989
Dead Crow
oil on panel 40 x 59 (E)
35

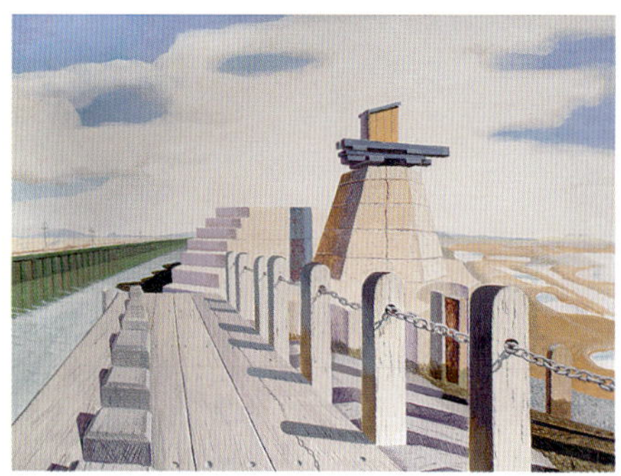

Power, Ronald 1914–1989
Estuary and Lock
oil on board 59 x 80
982

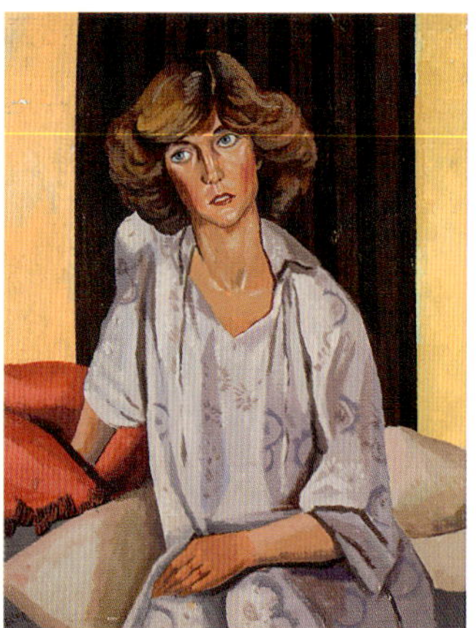

Power, Ronald 1914–1989
Lady in a Lilac Dress
oil on canvas 91 x 70.5 (E)
1305

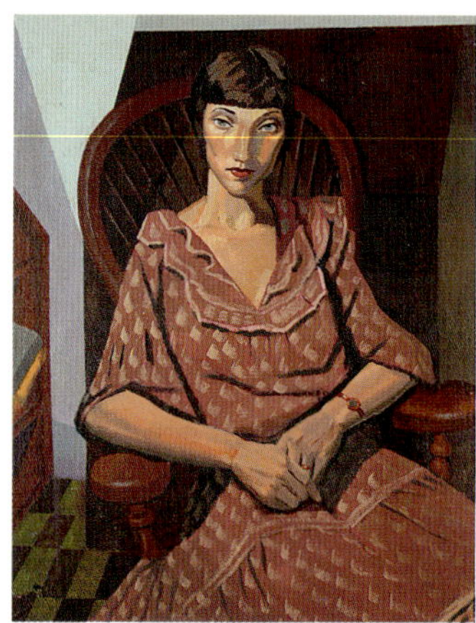

Power, Ronald 1914–1989
Lady in a Maroon Dress
oil on board 90 x 70 (E)
1306

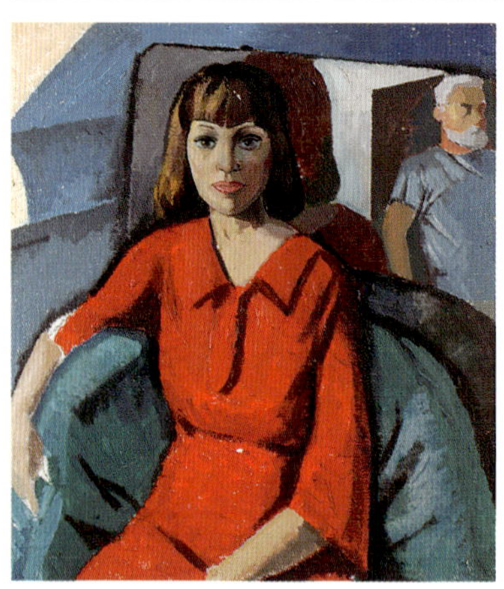

Power, Ronald 1914–1989
Lady in a Red Dress
oil on board 75.4 x 68 (E)
1312

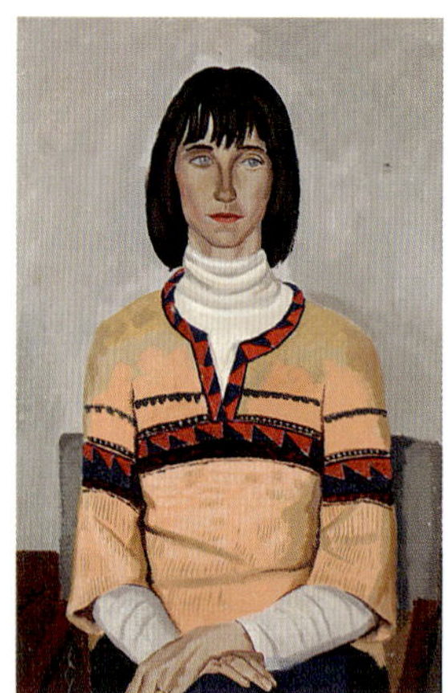

Power, Ronald 1914–1989
Lady in a Sawtooth Jumper
oil on board 82 x 54.5 (E)
1309

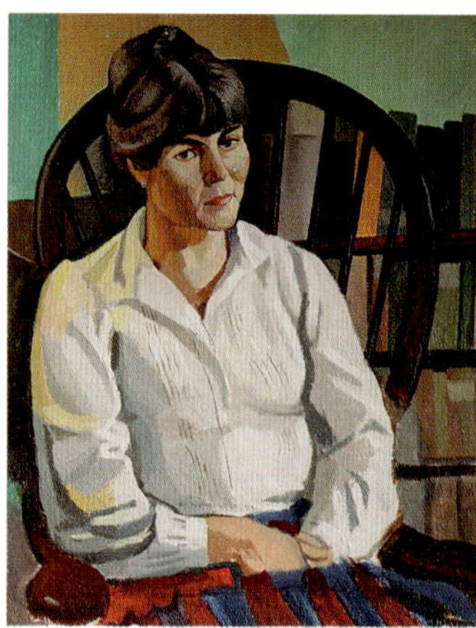

Power, Ronald 1914–1989
Lady in a White Blouse
oil on board 75 x 60.3 (E)
65

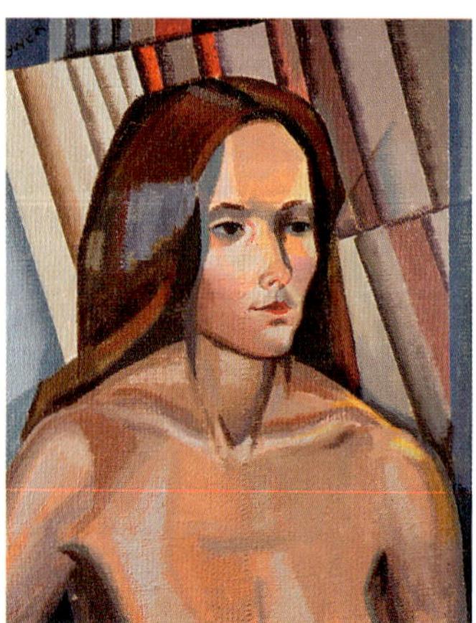

Power, Ronald 1914–1989
Lady with Auburn Hair
oil on hessian 62.4 x 42.7 (E)
1315

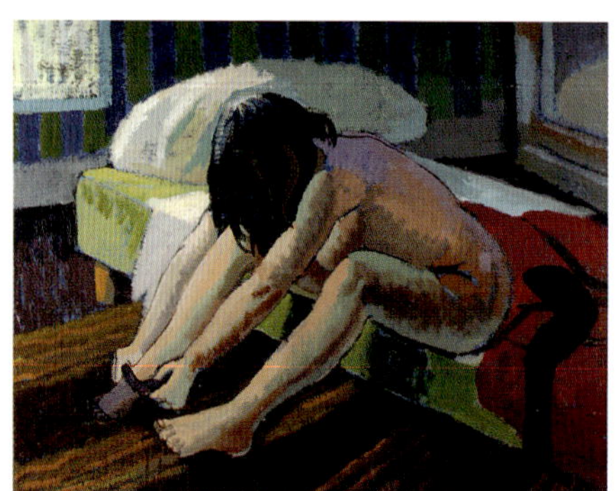

Power, Ronald 1914–1989
Nude: Dressing Morning
oil on board 69 x 90 (E)
1310

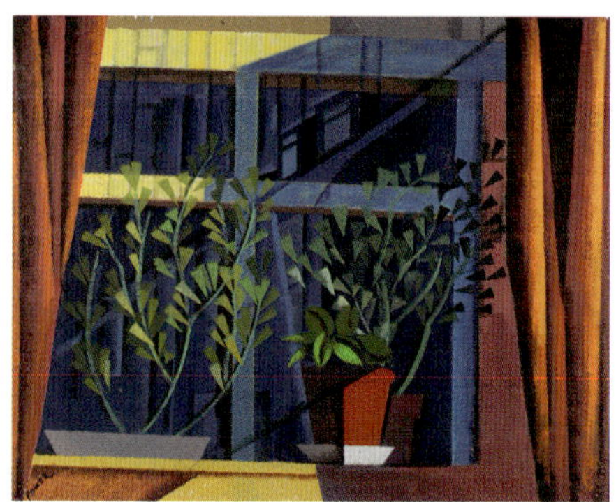

Power, Ronald 1914–1989
Plants on a Windowsill
oil on board 60 x 75.5 (E)
1137

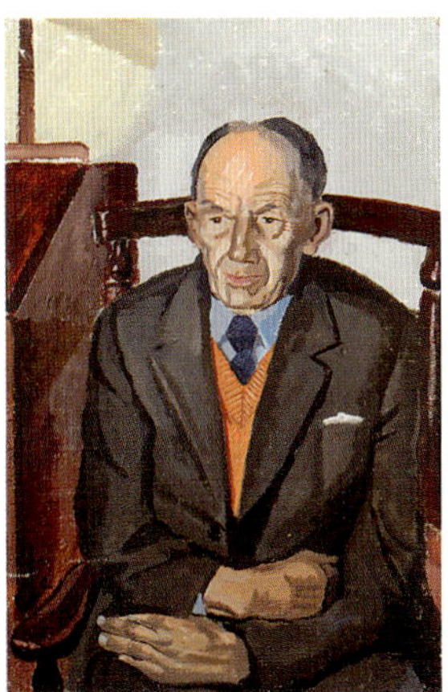

Power, Ronald 1914–1989
Portrait of a Gentleman
oil on hessian 76 x 51 (E)
Temp9

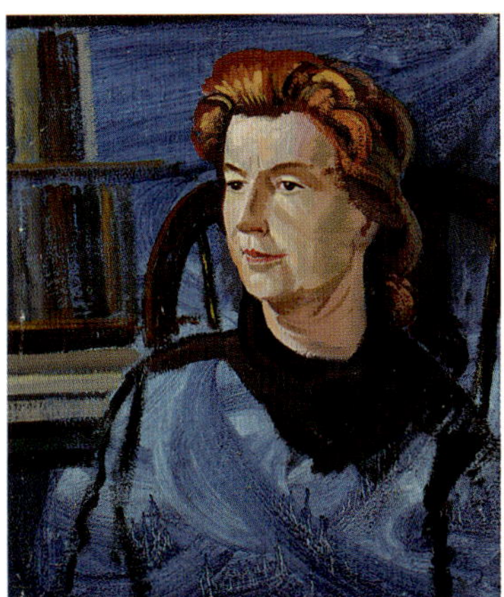

Power, Ronald 1914–1989
Portrait of a Lady in Blue
oil on board 63 x 55 (E)
1314

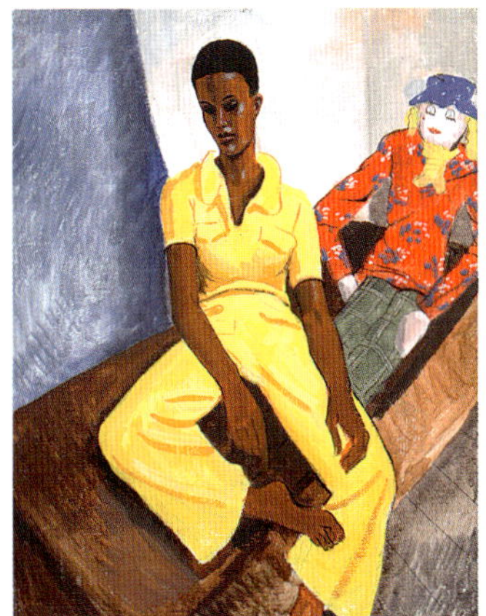

Power, Ronald 1914–1989
Portrait of a Lady in Yellow
oil on hessian 92 x 71 (E)
Temp6

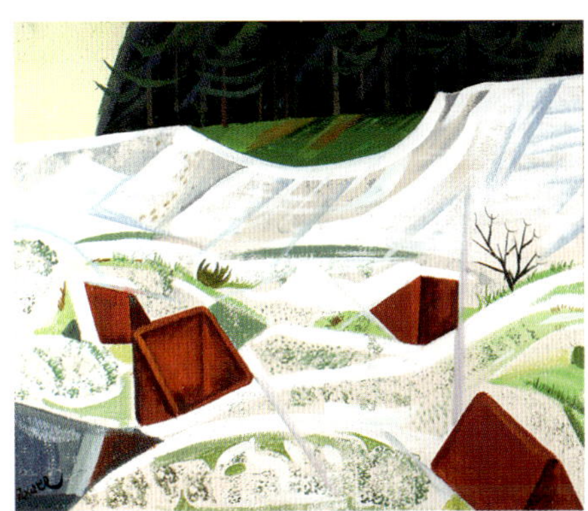

Power, Ronald 1914–1989
Quarry No.1
oil on hessian 62.5 x 76 (E)
1140

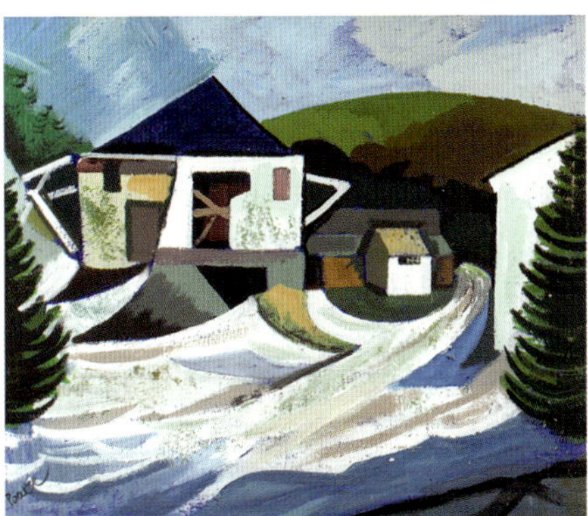

Power, Ronald 1914–1989
Quarry No.2
oil on board 60 x 70 (E)
1141

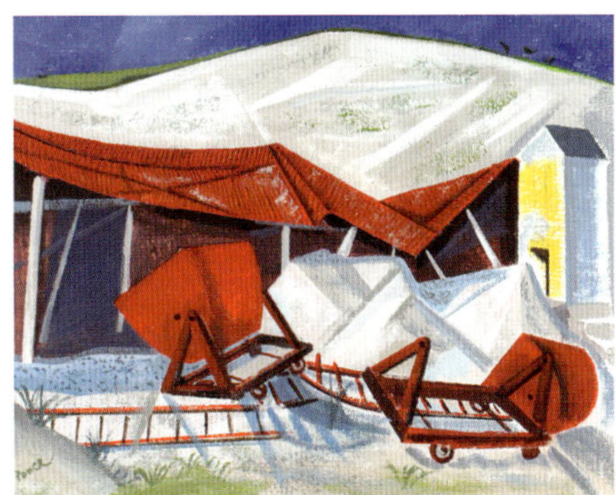

Power, Ronald 1914–1989
Quarry No.3
oil on board 69.5 x 90.5 (E)
1142

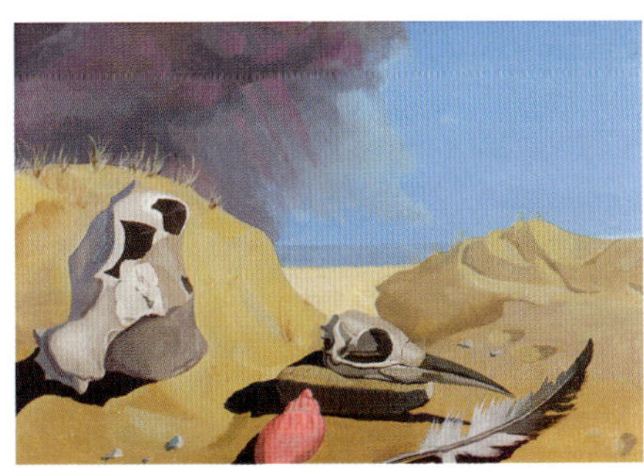

Power, Ronald 1914–1989
Seashore Finds
oil on panel 35 x 53 (E)
96

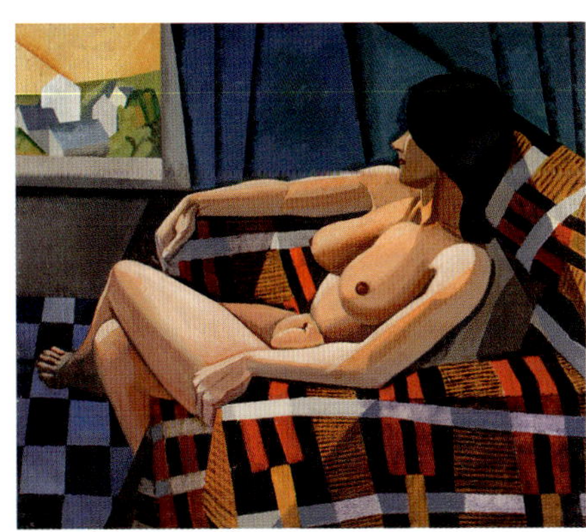

Power, Ronald 1914–1989
Seated Nude
oil on board 79.8 x 92.3 (E)
1303

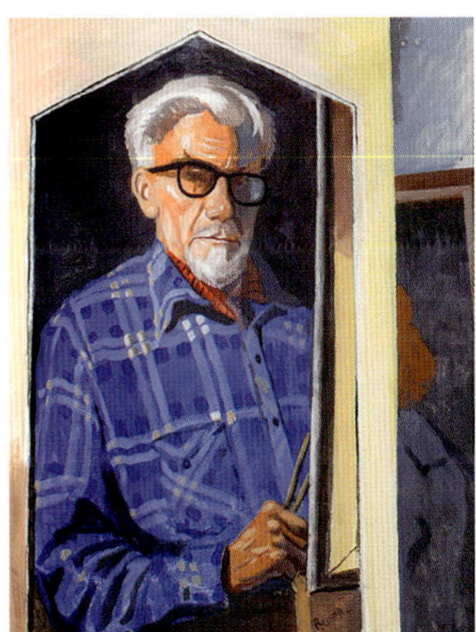

Power, Ronald 1914–1989
Self Portrait
oil on canvas 76 x 60.2 (E)
1313

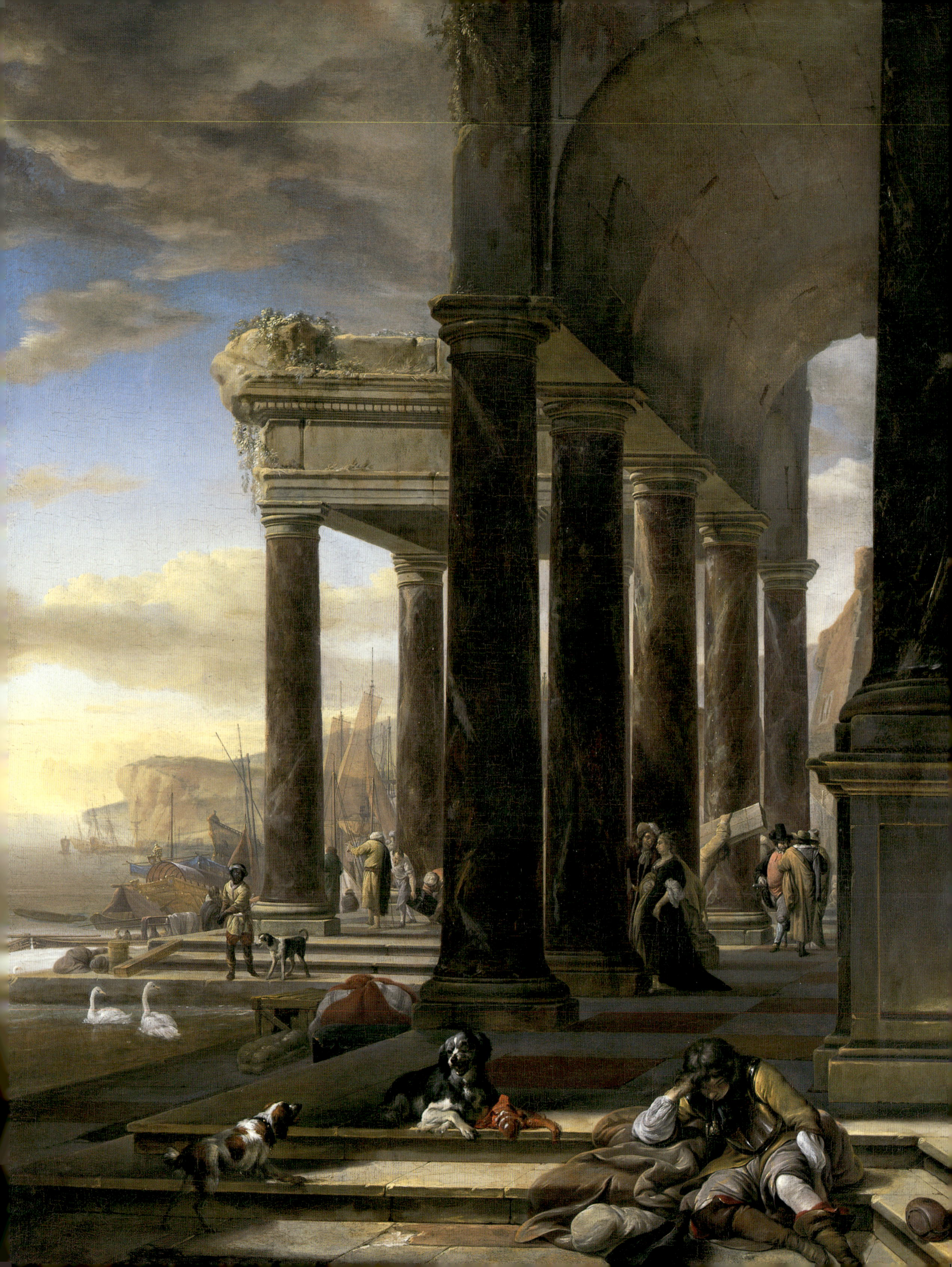

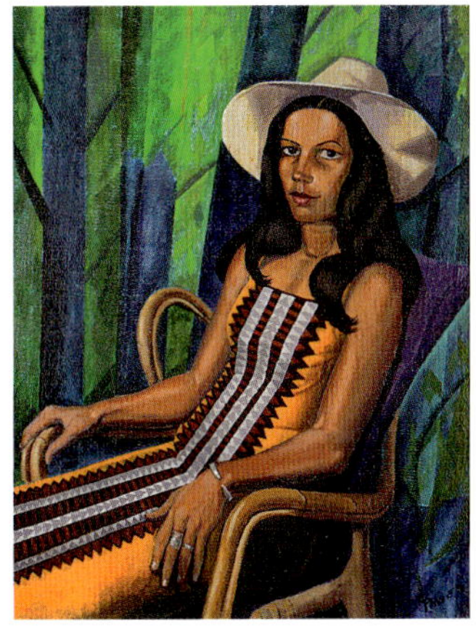

Power, Ronald 1914–1989
South American Woman
oil on board 90.5 x 70.5 (E)
1307

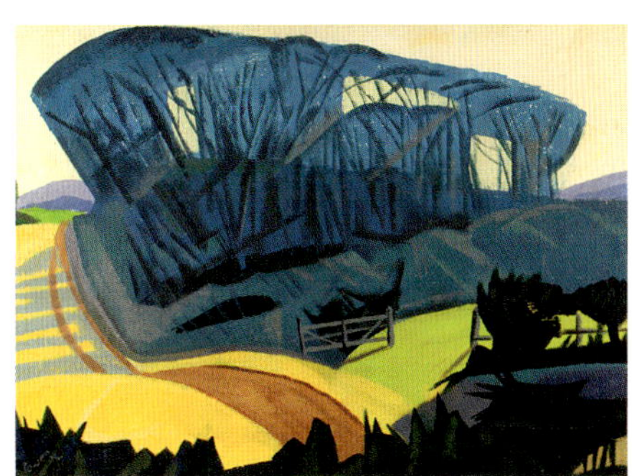

Power, Ronald 1914–1989
Spring Sun
oil on board 59 x 83 (E)
994A

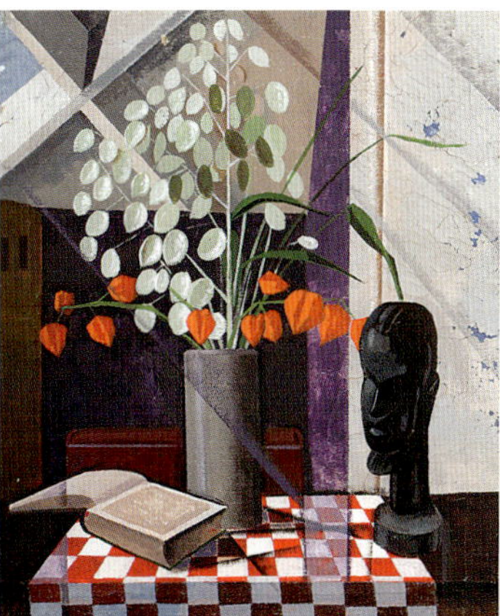

Power, Ronald 1914–1989
Still Life
oil on hessian 76 x 64 (E)
Temp7

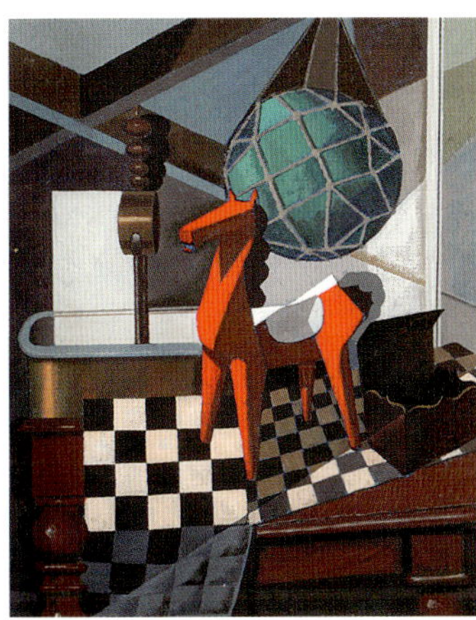

Power, Ronald 1914–1989
Still Life: Chequered Board
oil on canvas 76 x 61 (E)
1138

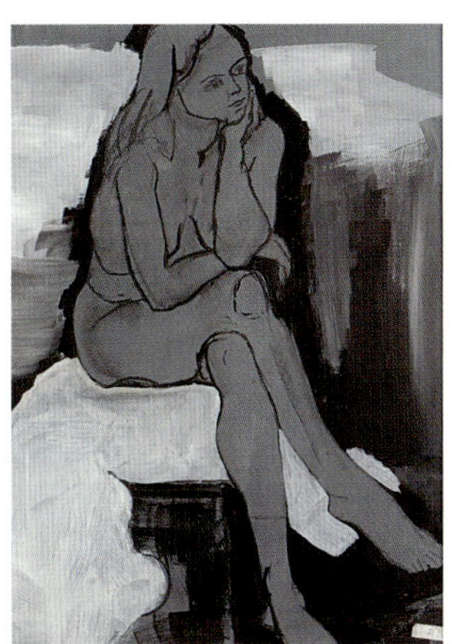

Power, Ronald 1914–1989
Study for Nude
acrylic on canvas 59.8 x 44 (E)
Temp3

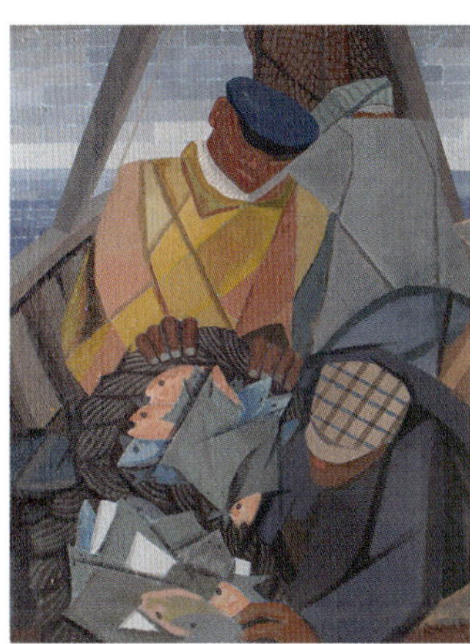

Power, Ronald 1914–1989
The Catch
oil on canvas 95 x 75
1662

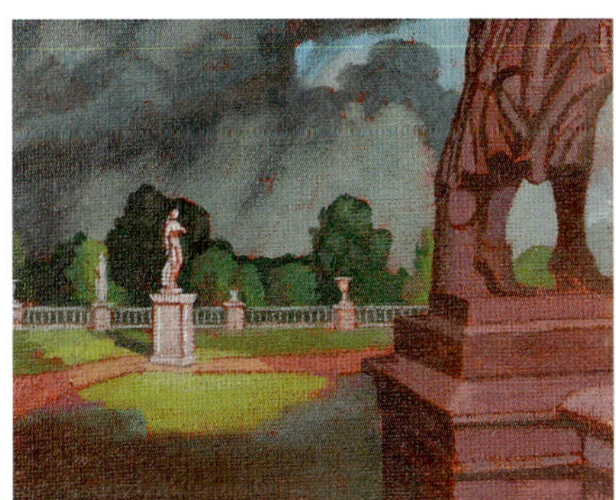

Power, Ronald 1914–1989
The Storm
oil on board 23.5 x 32.3 (E)
Temp12

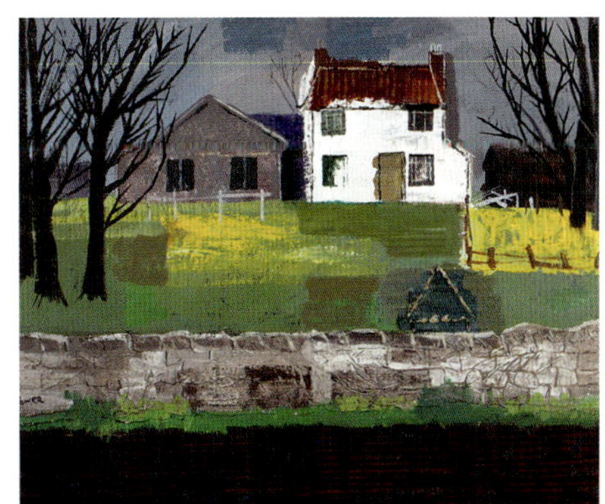

Power, Ronald 1914–1989
White Cottage
oil on board 63 x 75.5 (E)
1144

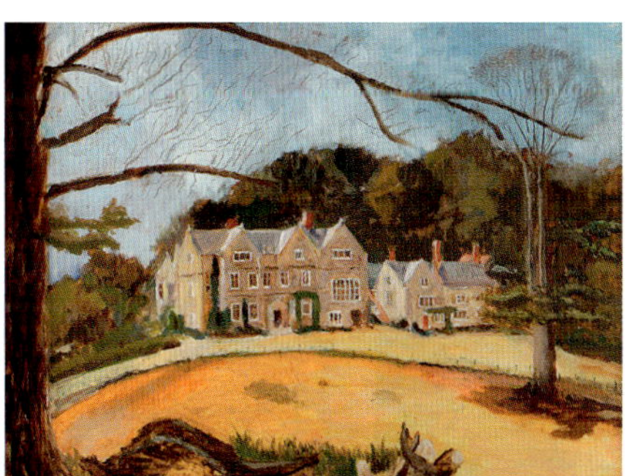

Robinson, N. W.
Northcourt Manor House 1976
oil on board 49 x 68 (E)
64

Facing page: Weenix, Jan Baptist, 1621–1660/1661, *An Italian Port Scene* (detail), Southampton City Art Gallery, (p. 139)

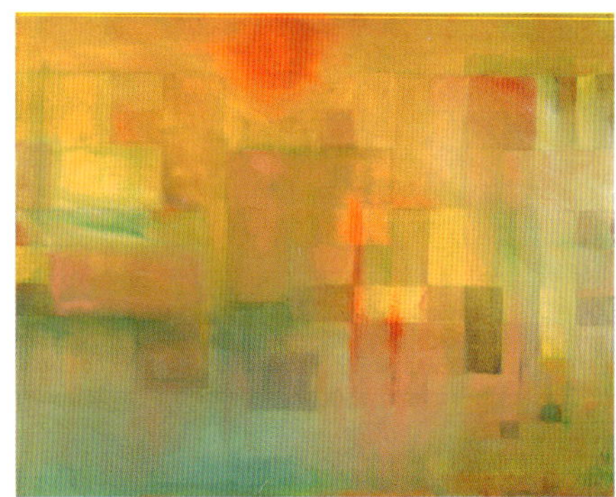

Seaward, L.
The Quay
oil on canvas 41 x 51.5 (E)
564

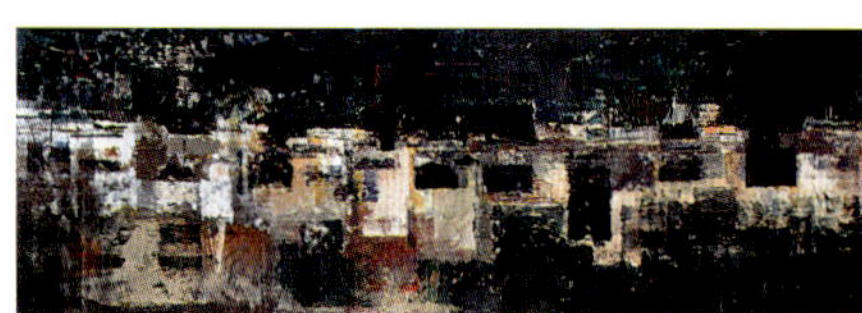

Simpson, Reg
City Waterfront
oil on panel 40 x 122
temp604

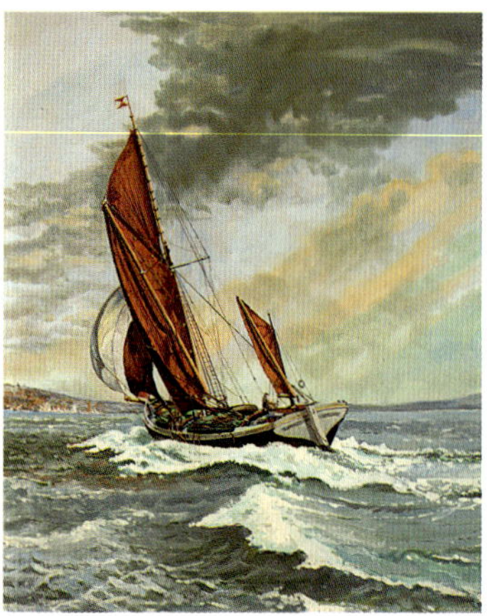

Squibb, Roy 1931–1992
Boat off Cowes 1967
oil on board 89 x 73.5 (E)
32

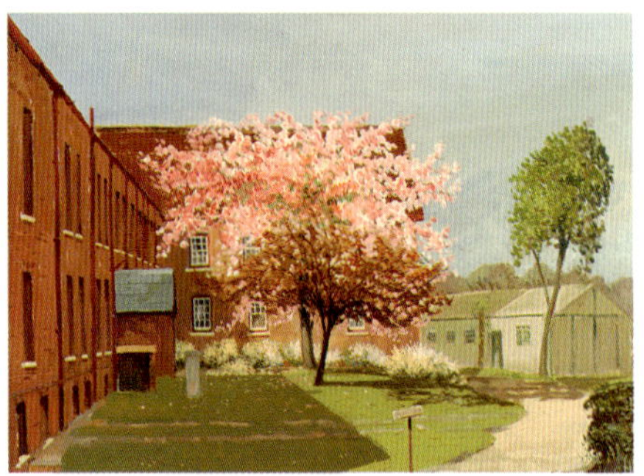

Squibb, Roy 1931–1992
Cherry Blossom: South Hospital, St Mary's
oil on canvas 40.7 x 57 (E)
1208

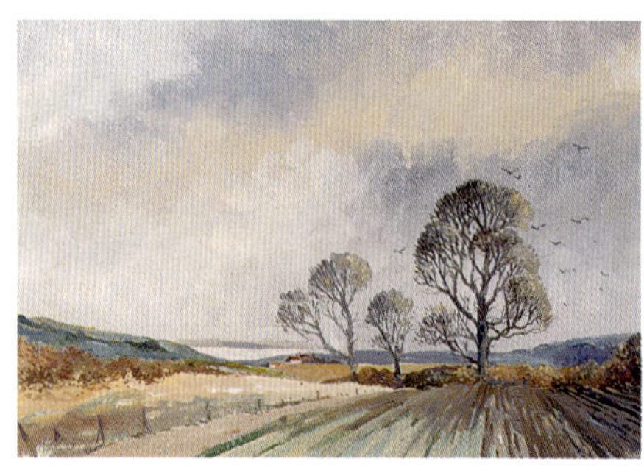

Squibb, Roy 1931–1992
Isle of Wight Landscape
oil on board 25 x 37.5
Temp71

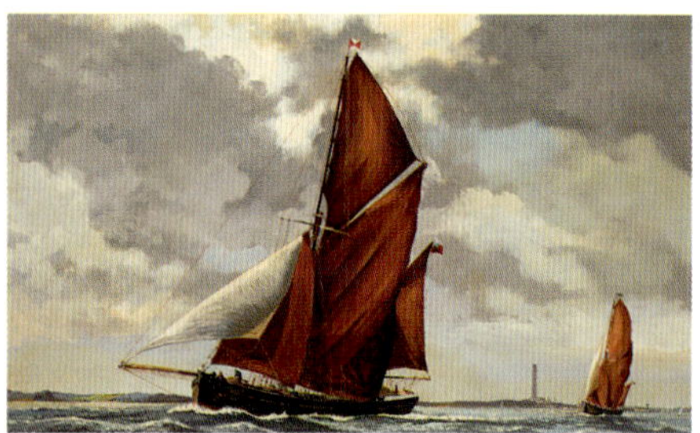

Squibb, Roy 1931–1992
Two Barges
oil on canvas 54 x 88 (E)
1211

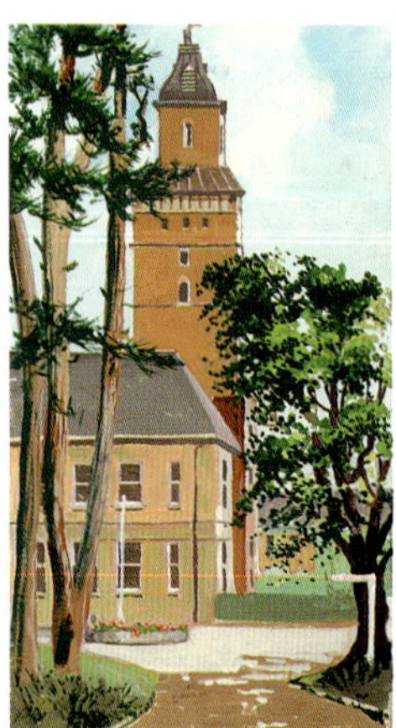

Squibb, Roy 1931–1992
Whitecroft: Clock Tower
oil on panel 37 x 20.5 (E)
1143

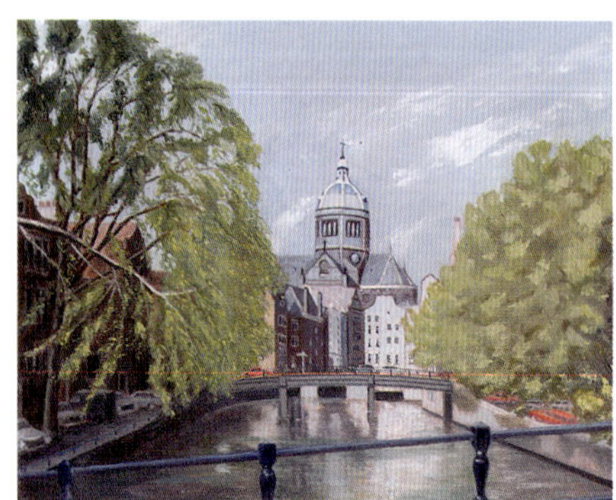

Stell
Amsterdam, St Nicholas' Church 1981
oil on board 39 x 49
temp603

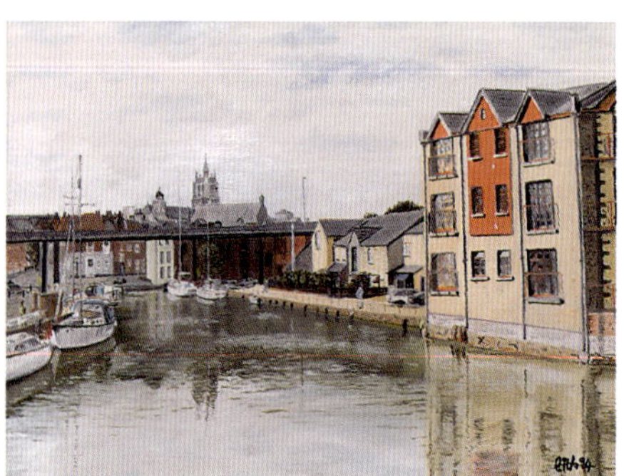

Stevenson, S.
Newport Harbour 1994
oil on board 30 x 39.5
temp605

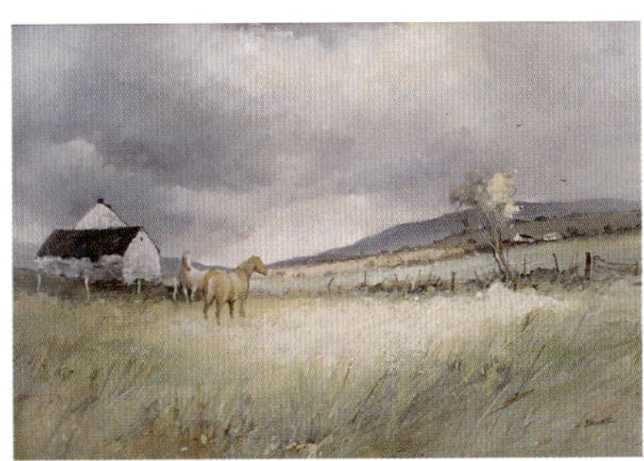

Stewart
Irish Landscape
oil on canvas 59.5 x 90.7
Temp70

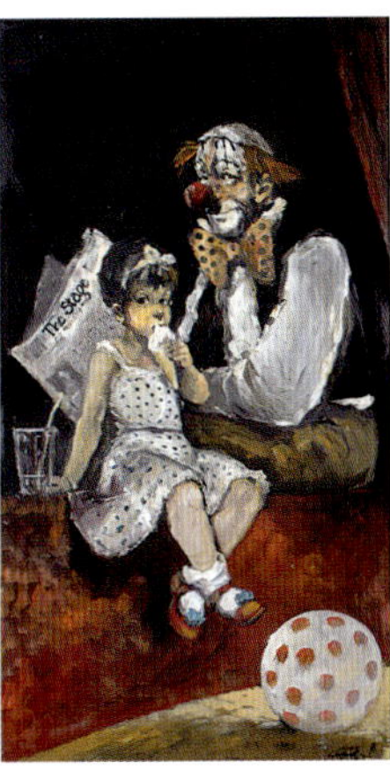

Stewart, Lorna
Clown
oil on canvas 113 x 60
Temp97

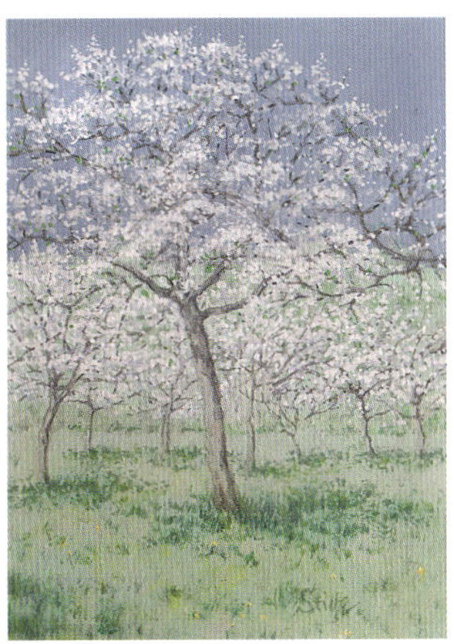

Stille Parker, Margareta active 1955–2002
Orchard 1955
acrylic on board 40 x 30
Temp62

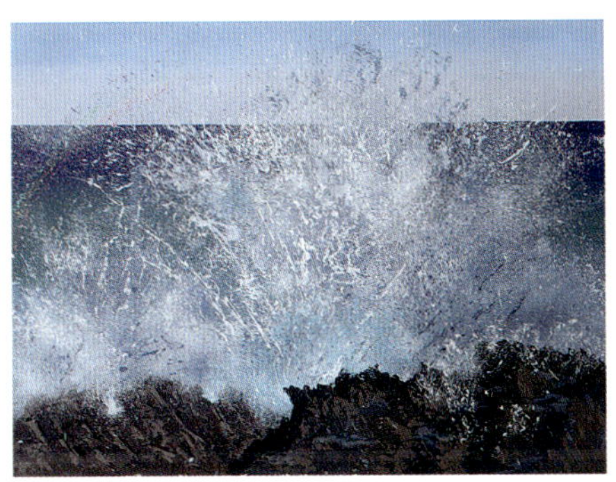

Thorpe, Hilary b.1959
The Wave 2001
acrylic on paper 57 x 75
Temp43

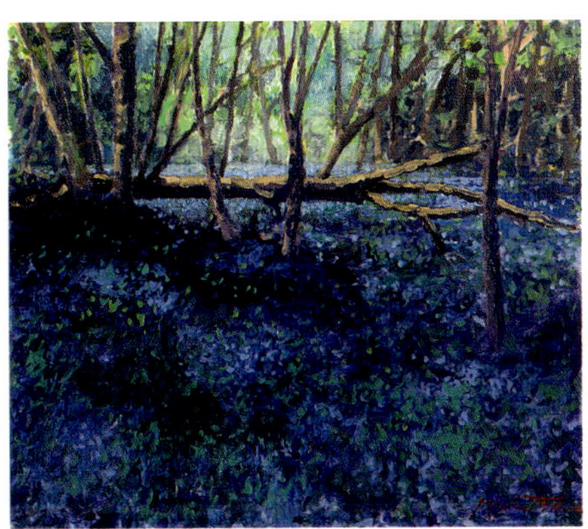

Till, Mike
Bluebell Wood 2001
oil on board 50 x 60.5
2056

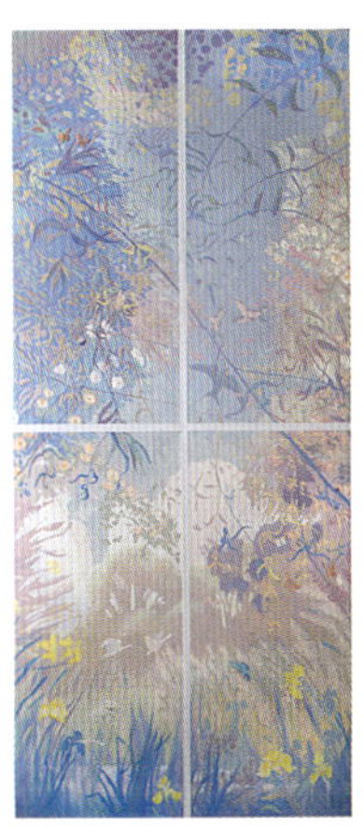

Toms, Anne b.1944
View across Lake (CT Scanner Ceiling)
acrylic on panel 240 x 120
Temp39

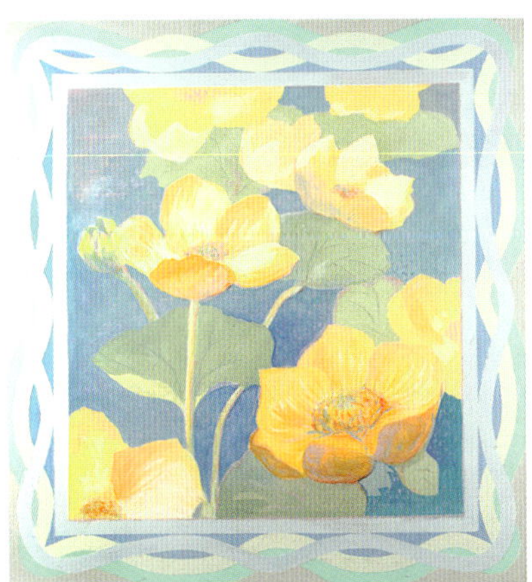

Toms, Anne b.1944
Water Buttercups
acrylic on canvas 74 x 70 (E)
1299

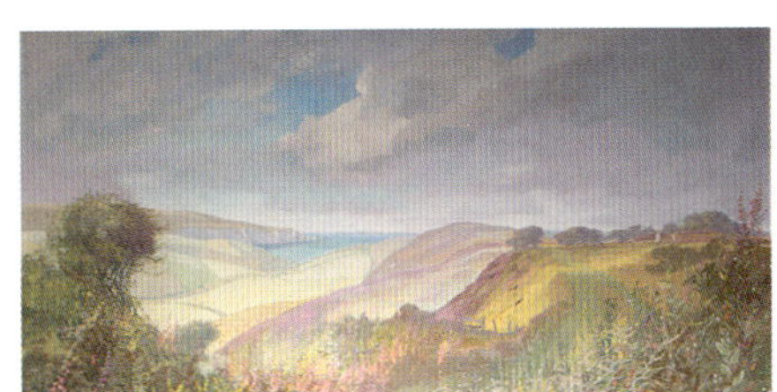

Toms, Anne b.1944
West Wight 1
oil on wood 117.5 x 238.5 (E)
Temp24/2

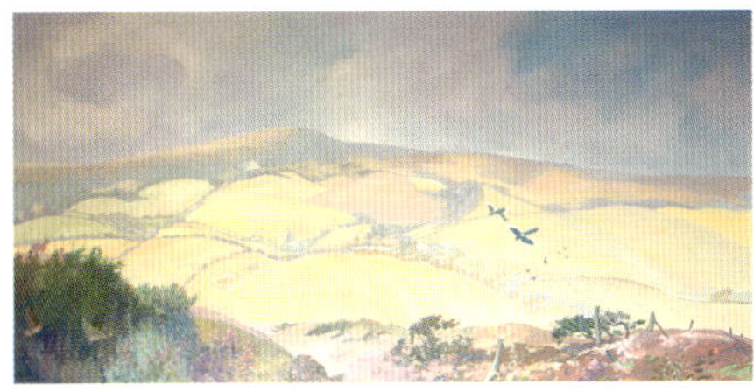

Toms, Anne b.1944
West Wight 2
oil on wood 117.5 x 238.5 (E)
Temp24/1

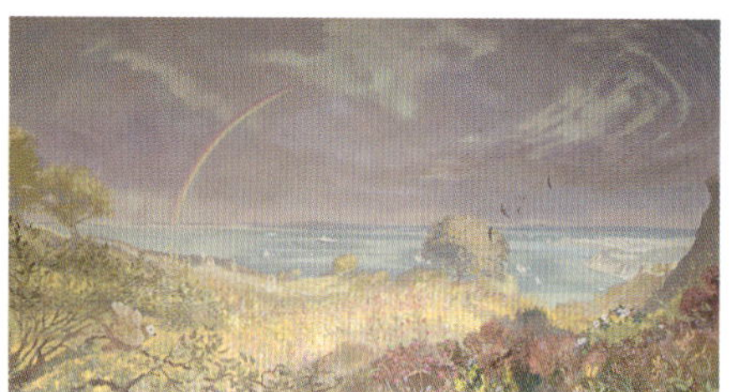

Toms, Anne b.1944
West Wight 3
oil on wood 117.5 x 238.5 (E)
Temp24/3

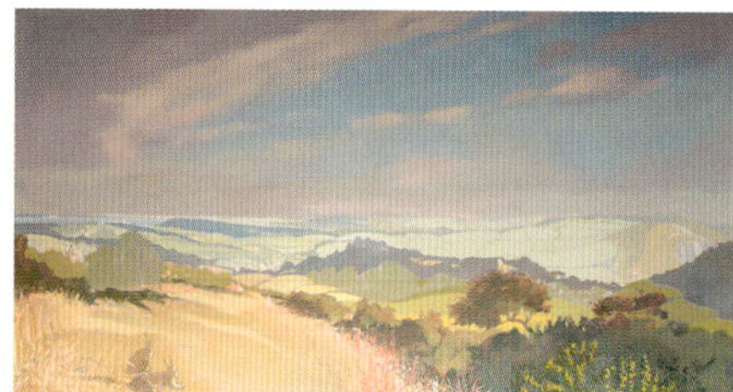

Toms, Anne b.1944
West Wight 4
oil on wood 117.5 x 238.5 (E)
Temp24/4

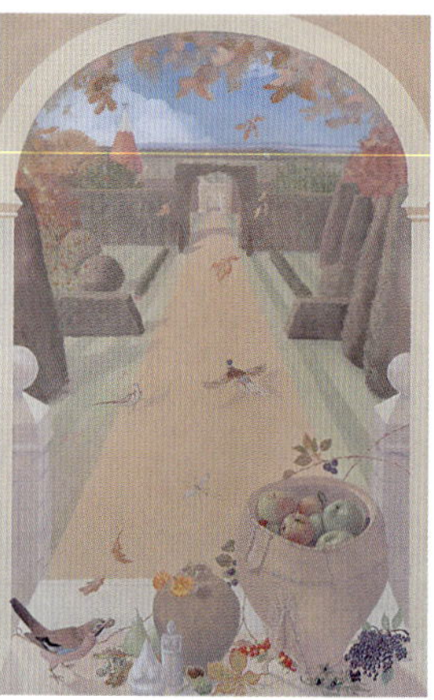

Toms, Anne b.1944
Four Seasons: Autumn 1985
oil on board 129 x 88
0010C

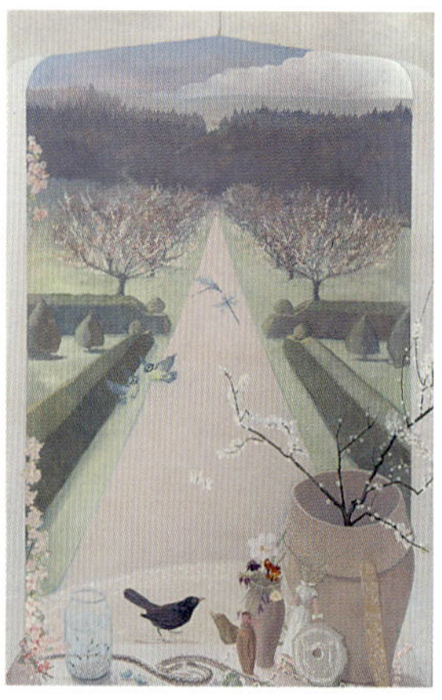

Toms, Anne b.1944
Four Seasons: Spring 1985
oil on board 129 x 88
0010A

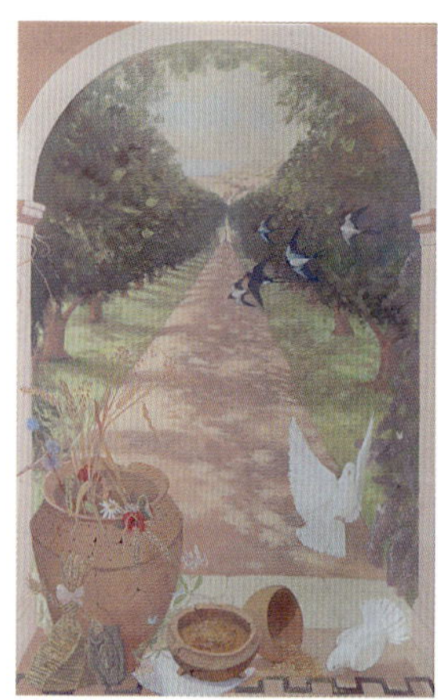

Toms, Anne b.1944
Four Seasons: Summer 1985
oil on board 129 x 88
0010B

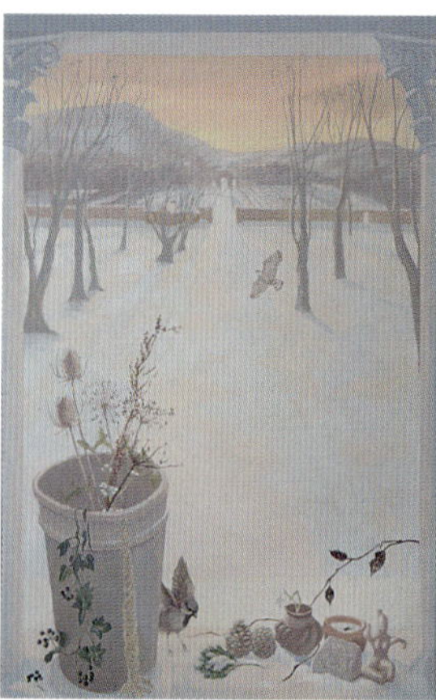

Toms, Anne b.1944
Four Seasons: Winter 1985
oil on board 129 x 88
0010D

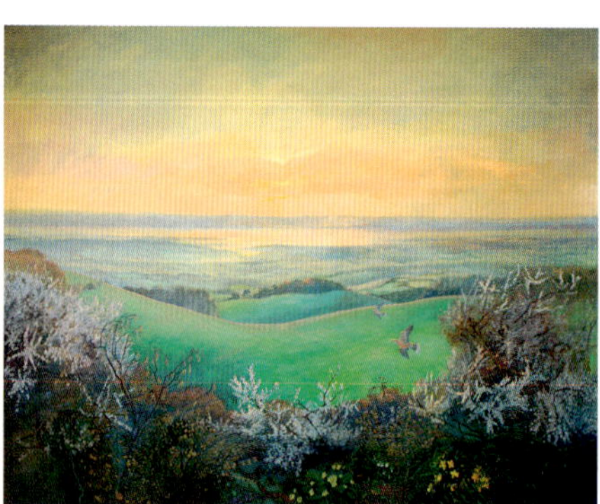

Toms, Anne b.1944
Dawn 1990s
oil on canvas 256 x 322.5
Temp44

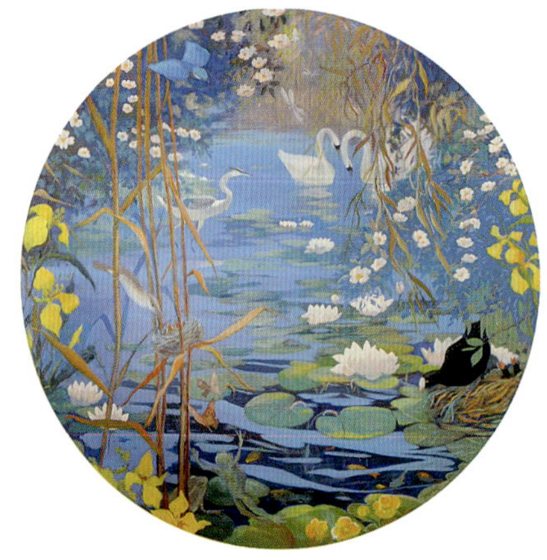

Toms, Anne b.1944
Lakeside 1991
oil on board 101.4
120

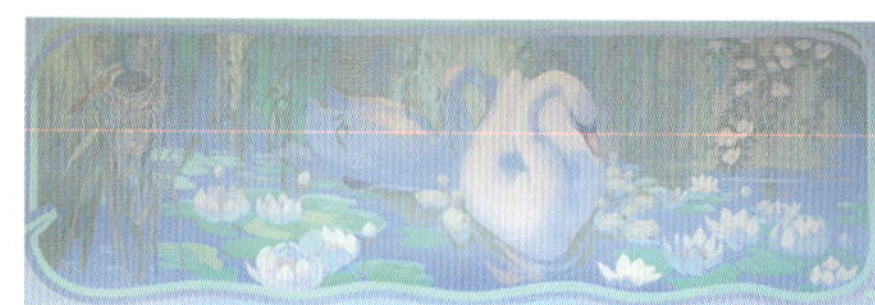

Toms, Anne b.1944
Bevy of Swans (detail) (part 1 of 8)
mid-1990s
oil on panel 71 x 216
2244

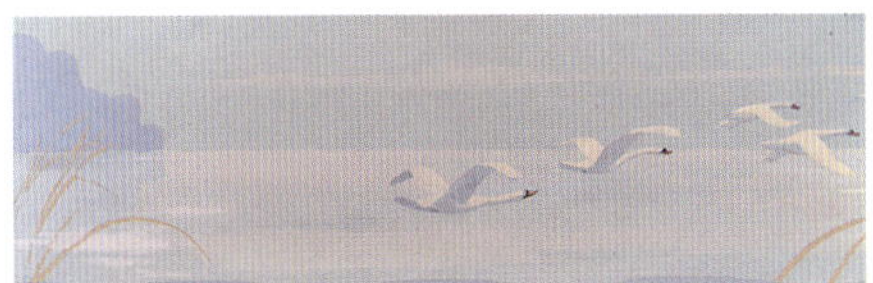

Toms, Anne b.1944
Bevy of Swans (detail) (part 2 of 8)
mid-1990s
oil on panel 53 x 328
temp343

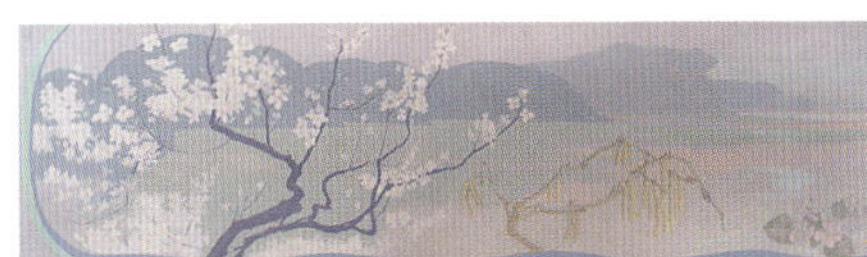

Toms, Anne b.1944
Bevy of Swans (detail) (part 3 of 8)
mid-1990s
oil on panel 57 x 465
temp344

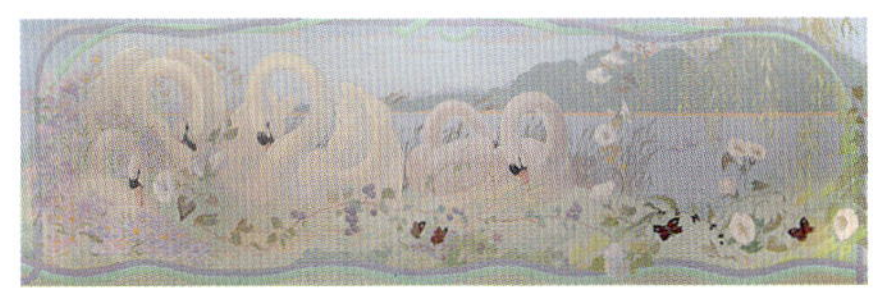

Toms, Anne b.1944
Bevy of Swans (detail) (part 4 of 8)
mid-1990s
oil on panel 71 x 236
temp345

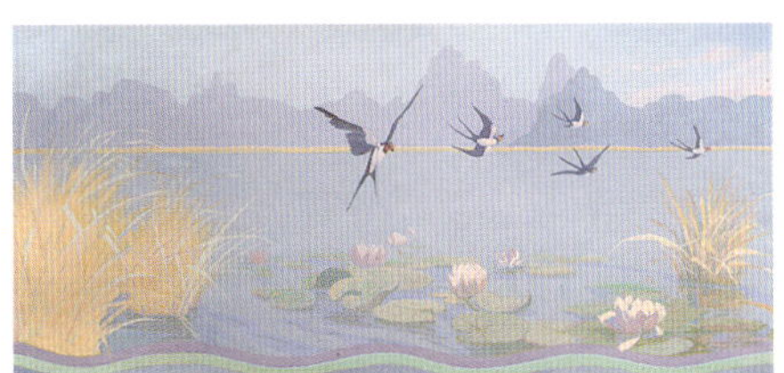

Toms, Anne b.1944
Bevy of Swans (detail) (part 5 of 8)
mid-1990s
oil on panel 71 x 316
temp346

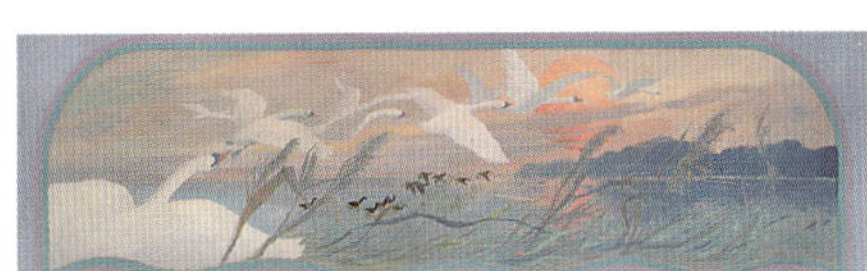

Toms, Anne b.1944
Bevy of Swans (detail) (part 6 of 8)
mid-1990s
oil on panel 71 x 237.5
temp347

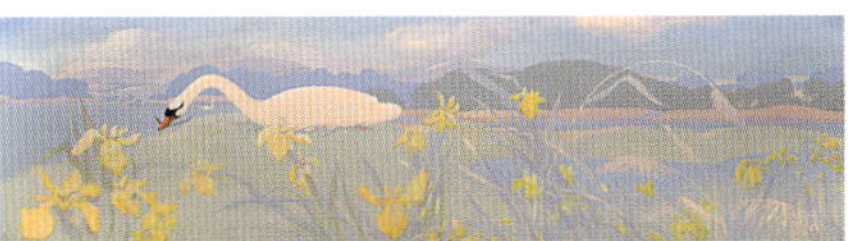

Toms, Anne b.1944
Bevy of Swans (detail) (part 7 of 8)
mid-1990s
oil on panel 57 x 219
temp348

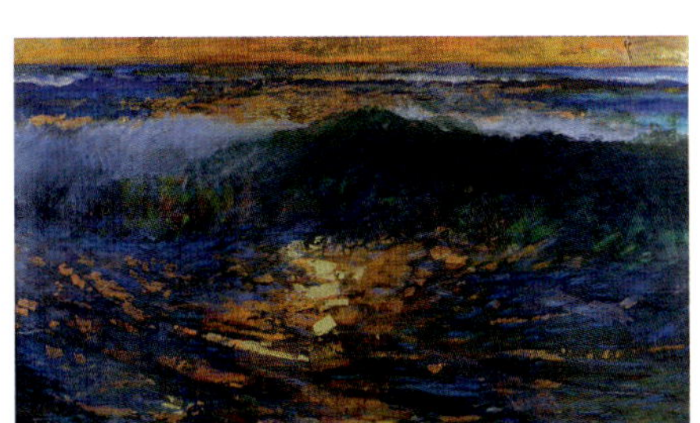

Toms, Anne b.1944
Beneath the Wave, under the Sky 2004
oil on canvas 70 x 119.5
1974

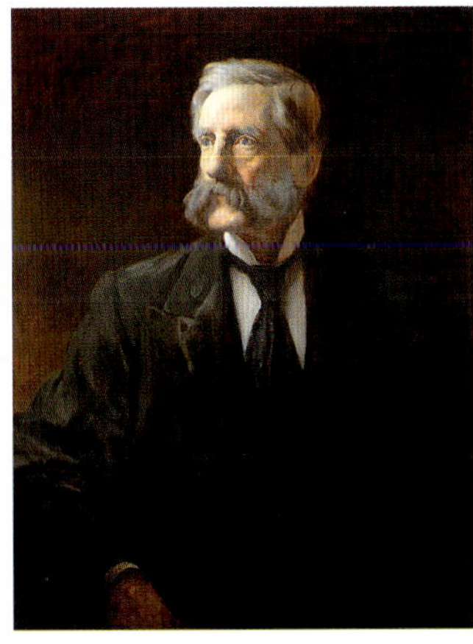

unknown artist 19th C
Arthur Hill Hassall, MD (1817–1894), Founder of the Royal National Hospital, Ventnor (1868)
oil on canvas 89.5 x 69.5 (E)
Temp30

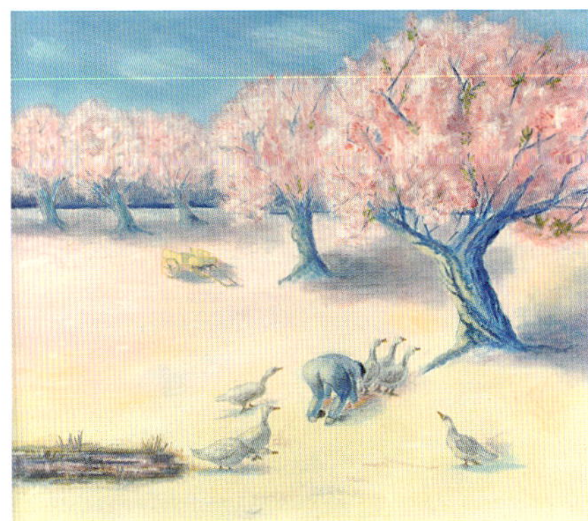

unknown artist 20th C
Ducks: French Orchard
oil on canvas 48.7 x 59.8 (E)
1625

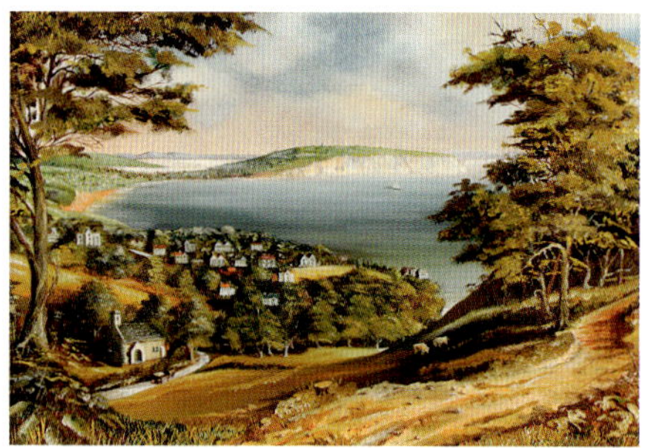

unknown artist 20th C
View to the Sea
oil on canvas 49 x 76 (E)
Temp2

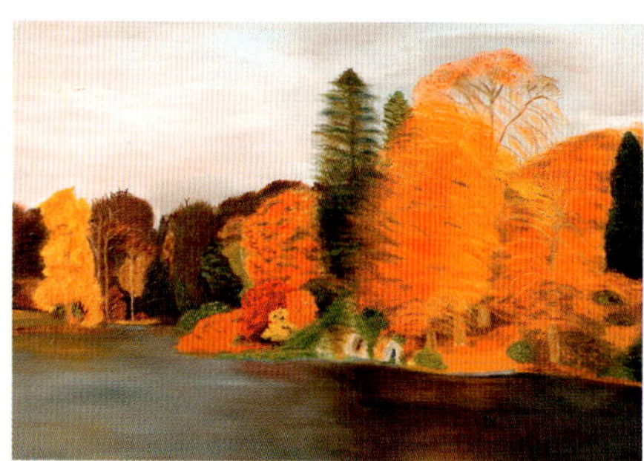

unknown artist 20th C
Wooded Lake
oil on canvas 55 x 74.5 (E)
Temp20

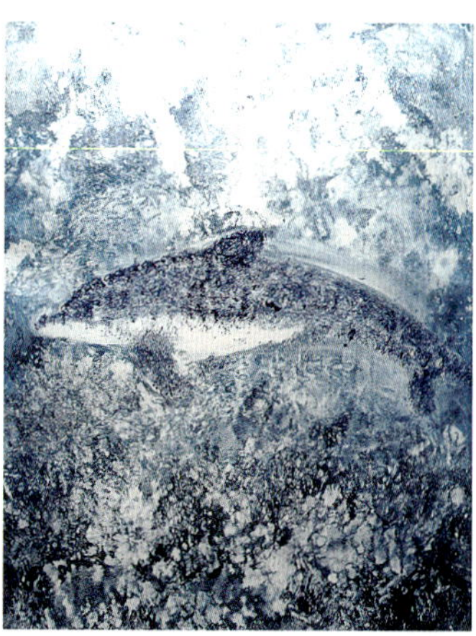

Vince, Dianne b.1966
Study for 'Dolphins No.1'
oil on board 37.5 x 29.5
1096

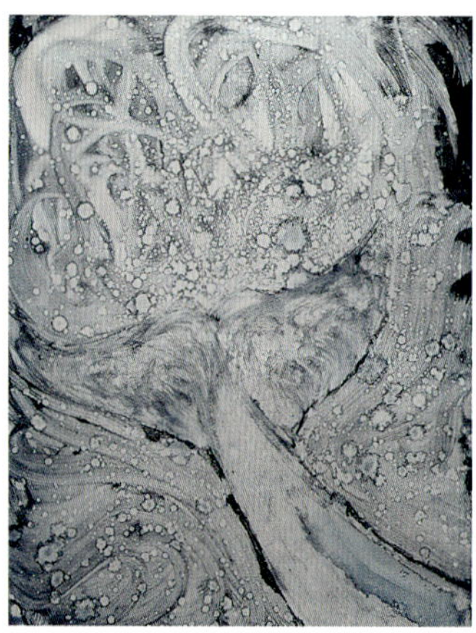

Vince, Dianne b.1966
Study for 'Dolphins No.2'
oil on paper 37.5 x 29.5
1097

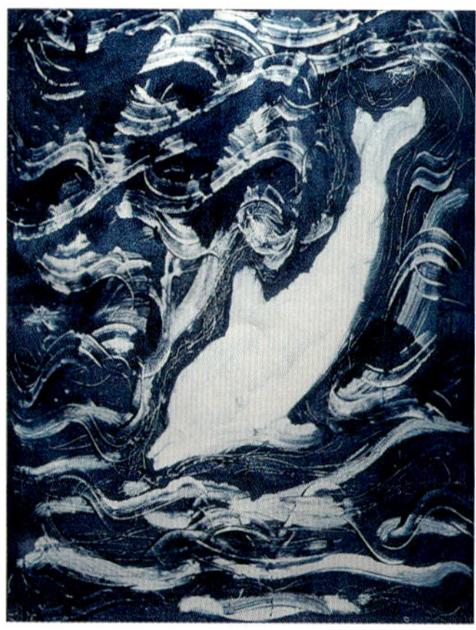

Vince, Dianne b.1966
Study for 'Dolphins No.3'
oil on paper 37.5 x 29.5
1098

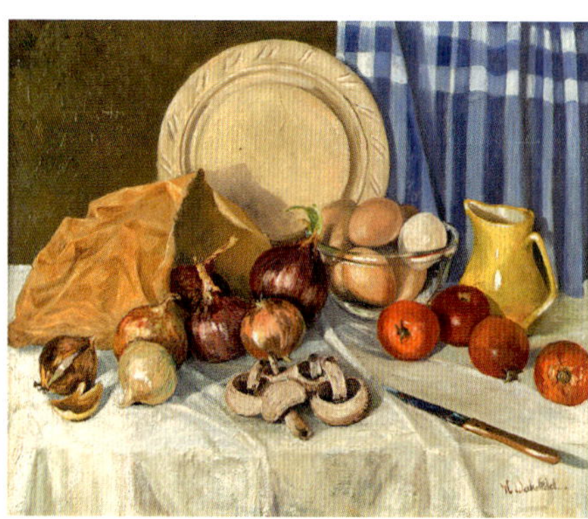

Wakefield, M. (Mrs)
Still Life
oil on board 44.5 x 54.5 (E)
500

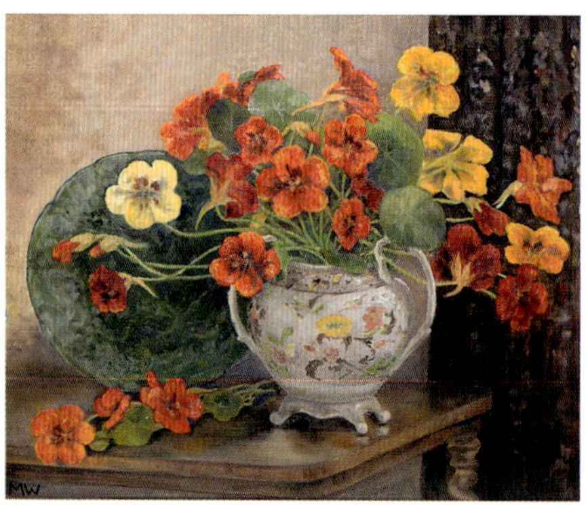

Wearn, Margery
Nasturtiums
oil on canvas 38 x 45
841

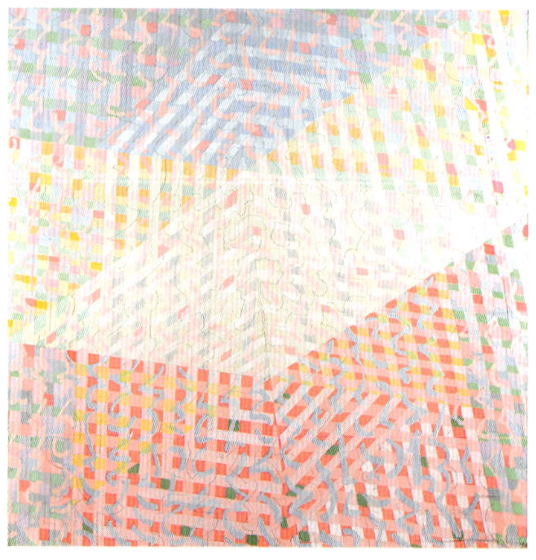

Wells, Peter 1938–1996
Chevron
oil on board 122 x 122
2002

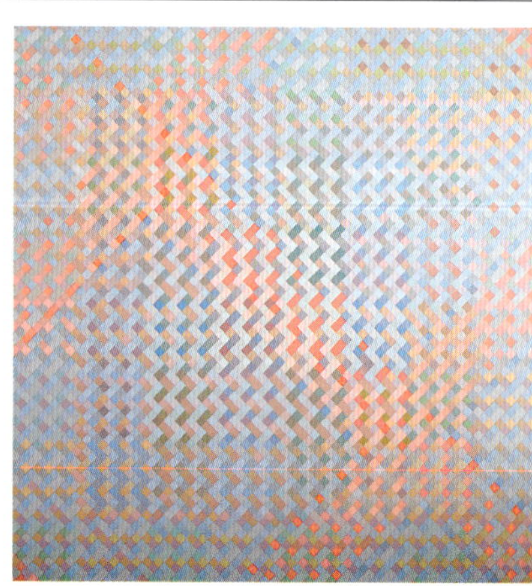

Wells, Peter 1938–1996
Coloured Squares
oil on board 122 x 122
2001

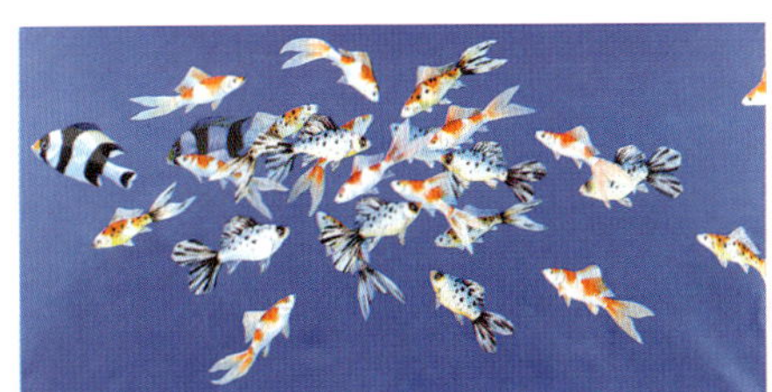

Wilkinson, Celia b.1963
Tropical Fish 1
oil on canvas 50.5 x 100
1973/1

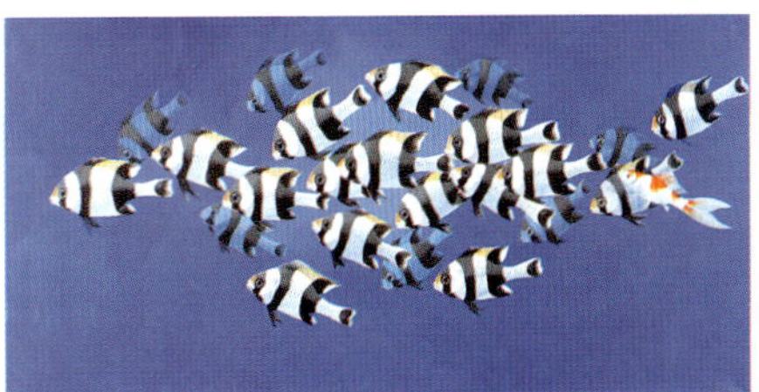

Wilkinson, Celia b.1963
Tropical Fish 2
oil on canvas 50.5 x 100
1973/2

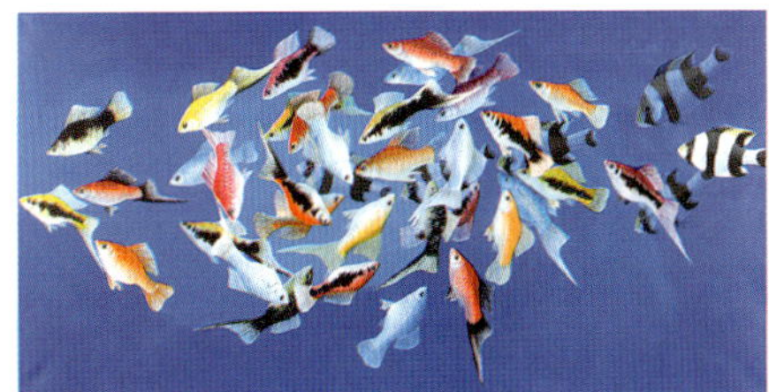

Wilkinson, Celia b.1963
Tropical Fish 3
oil on canvas 50.5 x 100
1973/3

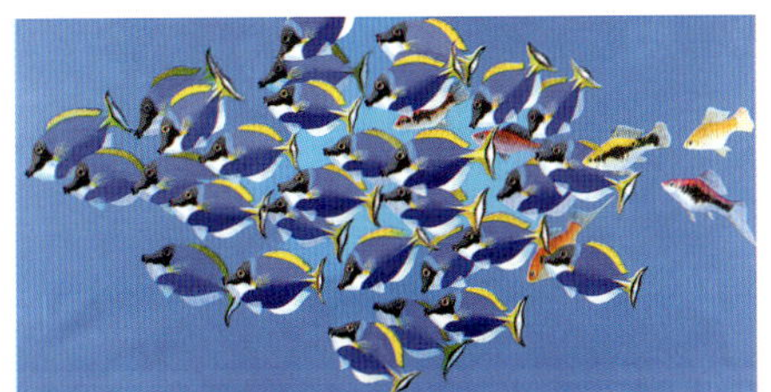

Wilkinson, Celia b.1963
Tropical Fish 4
oil on canvas 50.5 x 100
1973/4

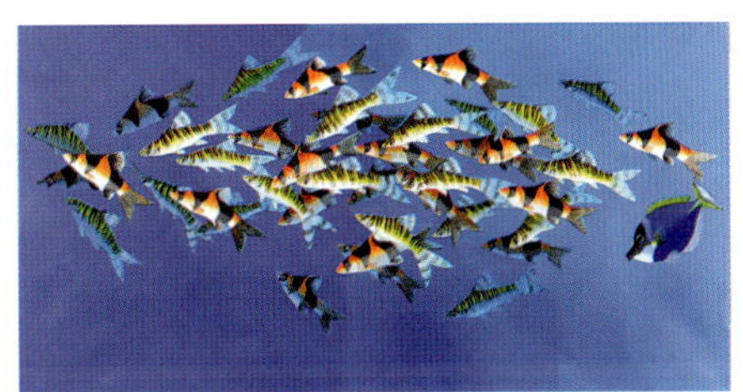

Wilkinson, Celia b.1963
Tropical Fish 5
oil on canvas 50.5 x 100
1973/5

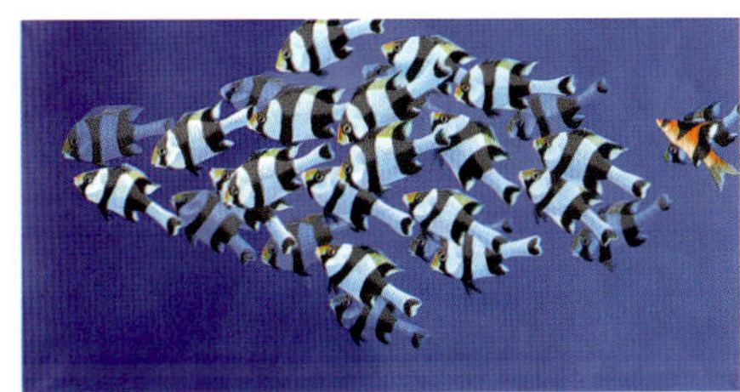

Wilkinson, Celia b.1963
Tropical Fish 6
oil on canvas 50.5 x 100
1973/6

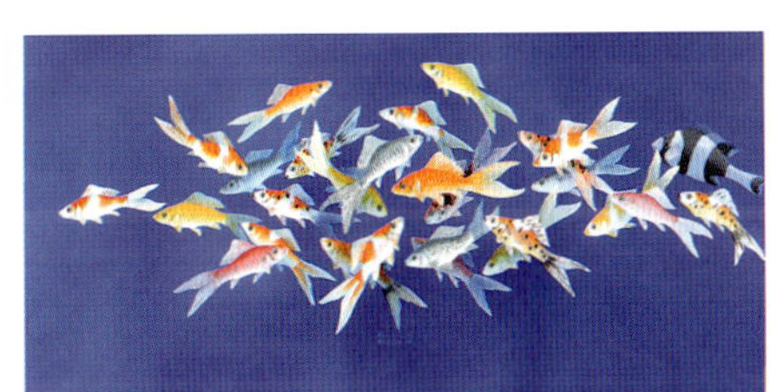

Wilkinson, Celia b.1963
Tropical Fish 7
oil on canvas 50.5 x 100
1973/7

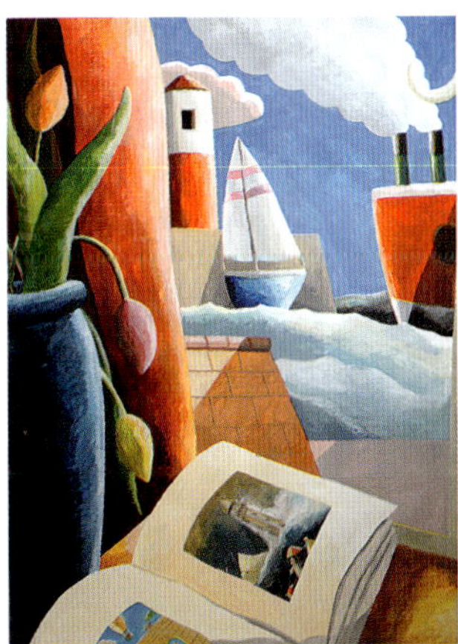

Williams, Emrys b.1958
Album 1997
acrylic on canvas 121 x 91 (E)
1695

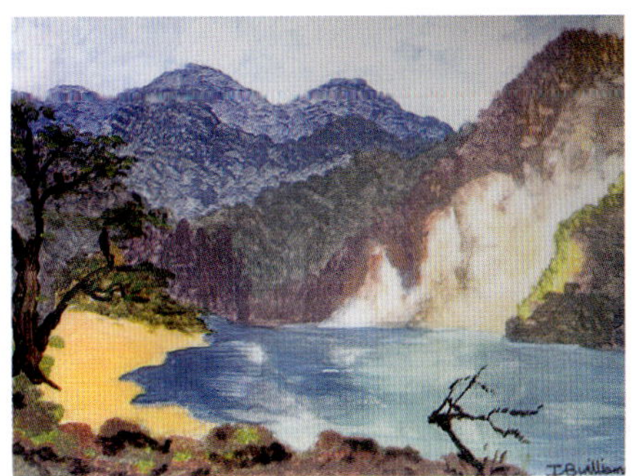

Williams, J. B.
Landscape
oil on canvas 28.5 x 39.2
Temp201

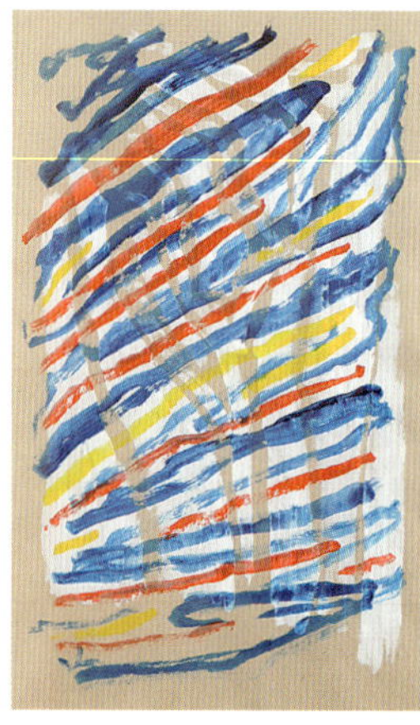

Wolton, Vidya b.1964
Red, Blue, White, Yellow
acrylic on paper 40 x 25
1390

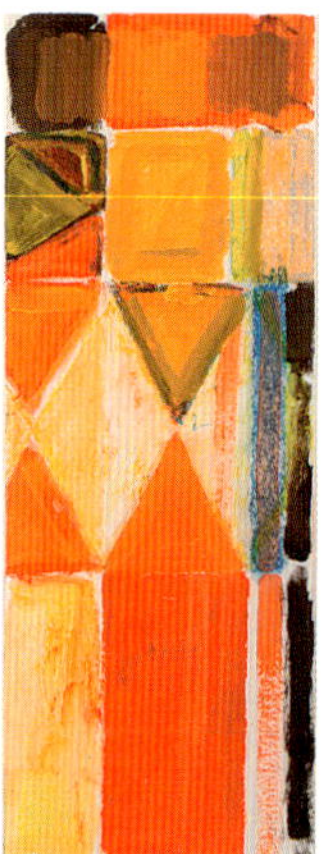

Wolton, Vidya b.1964
Untitled No.1
acrylic on paper 58 x 22.5
1262

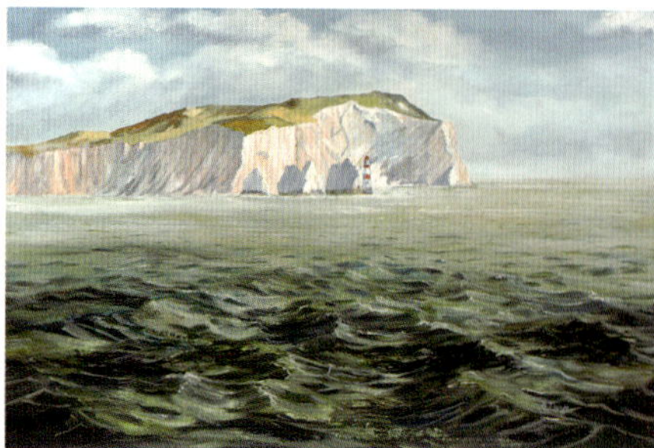

Wright, Barbara b.1944
Off 'The Needles'
oil on canvas 50 x 75 (E)
58

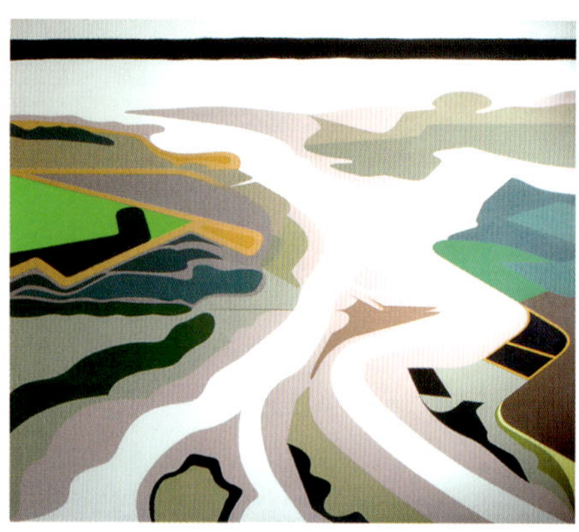

Wright, Peter b.1932
Estuary 1 1973
acrylic on canvas 168 x 168 (E)
1677 (P)

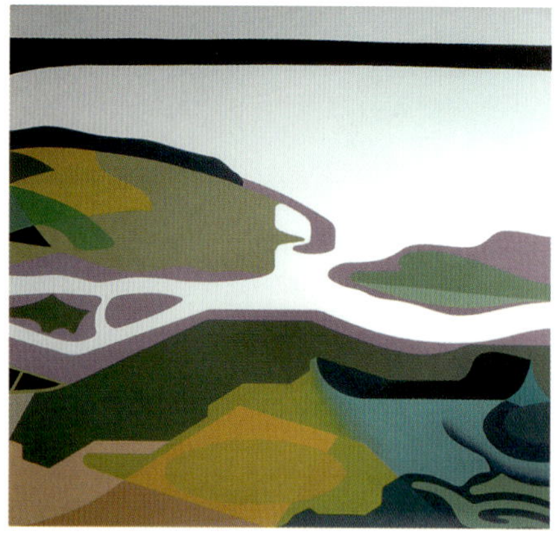

Wright, Peter b.1932
Estuary 2 1973
acrylic on canvas 129.5 x 129.5
1678 (P)

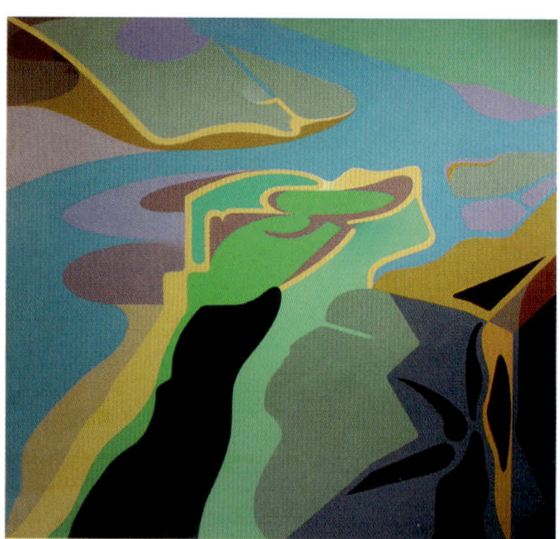

Wright, Peter b.1932
Estuary 3 1973
acrylic on canvas 167.2 x 168.4
Temp49 (P)

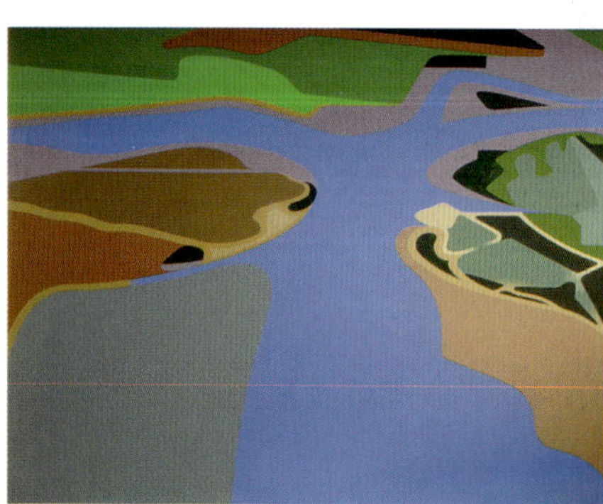

Wright, Peter b.1932
Estuary 4 1973
acrylic on canvas 135 x 150 (E)
Temp50 (P)

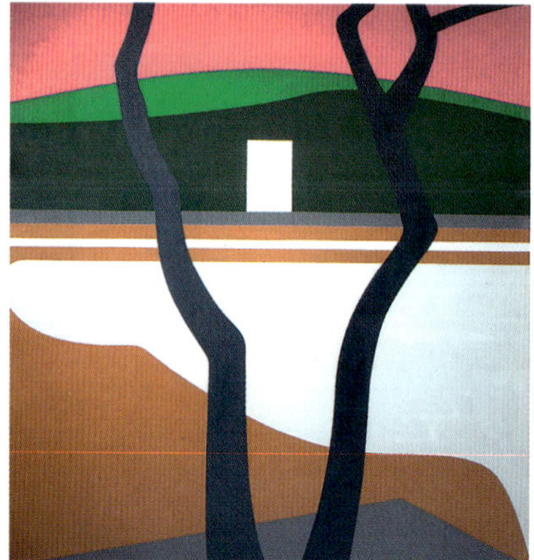

Wright, Peter b.1932
Bembridge Harbour 1975
oil on canvas 152 x 152 (E)
Temp21

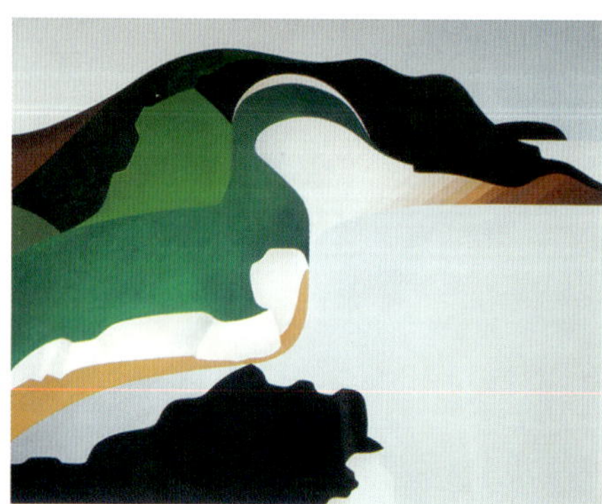

Wright, Peter b.1932
South West Coast 1979
oil on canvas 140 x 154 (E)
1877

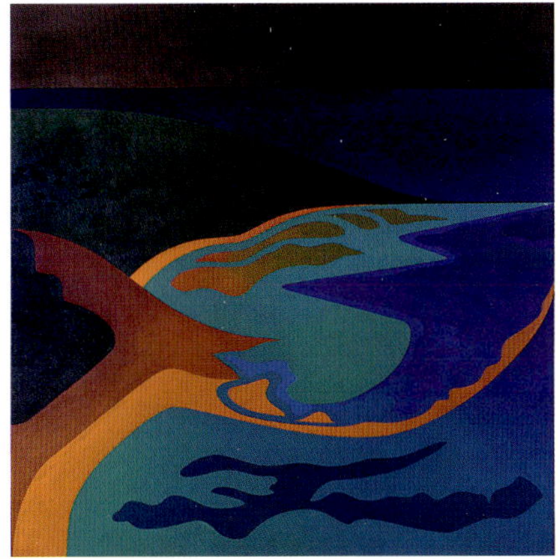

Wright, Peter b.1932
Whitecliff Bay 1980/1982
acrylic on canvas 152 x 152
Temp38

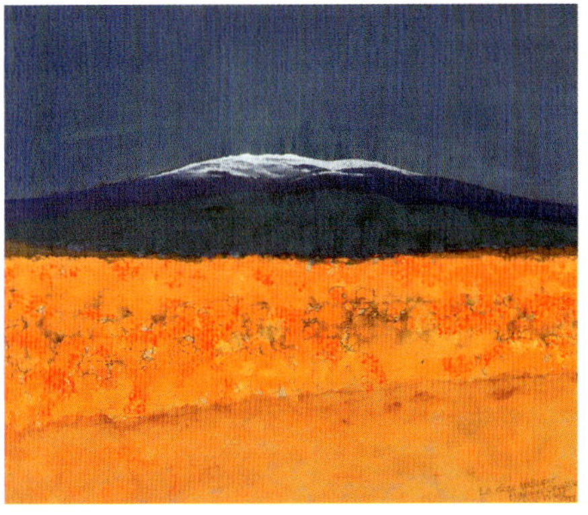

Wright, Peter b.1932
La serie Vallespir No.1 1993
acrylic on paper 40 x 48
1163

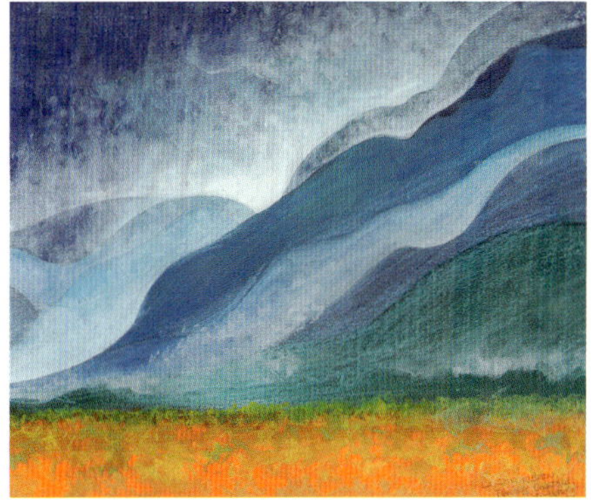

Wright, Peter b.1932
La serie Vallespir No.2 1993
acrylic on paper 40 x 48
1164

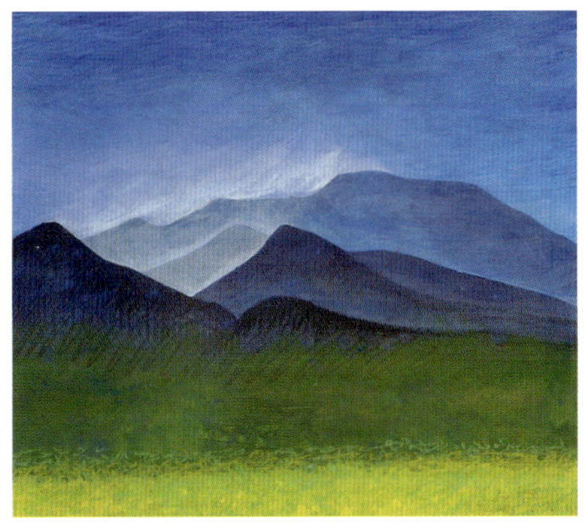

Wright, Peter b.1932
La serie Vallespir No.3 1993
acrylic on paper 40 x 48.2 (E)
1165

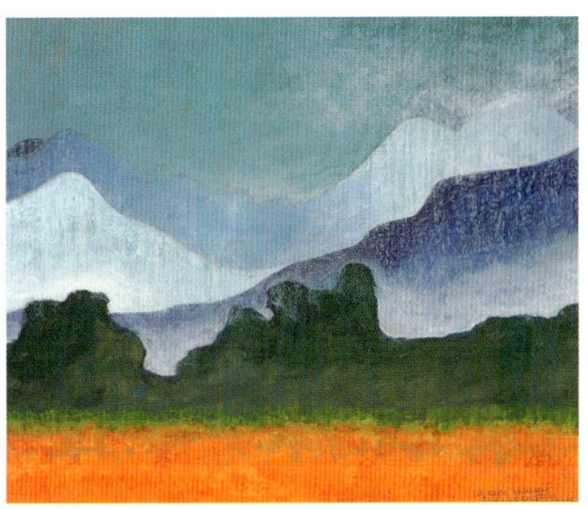

Wright, Peter b.1932
La serie Vallespir No.4 1993
acrylic on paper 39.3 x 47
1166

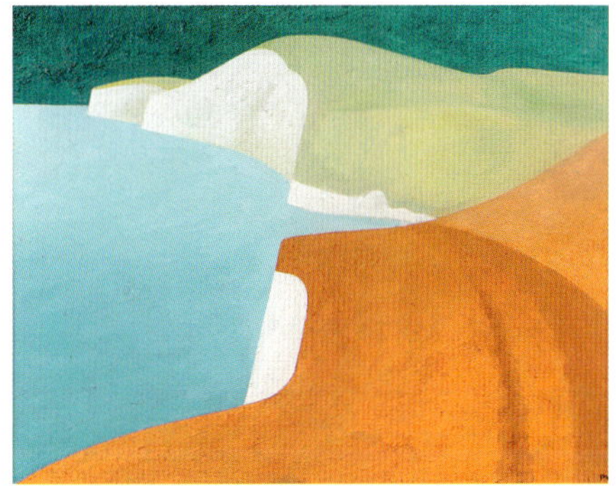

Wright, Peter b.1932
West Wight
oil on canvas 34.2 x 44.5 (E)
Temp23

Isle of Wight Bus Museum

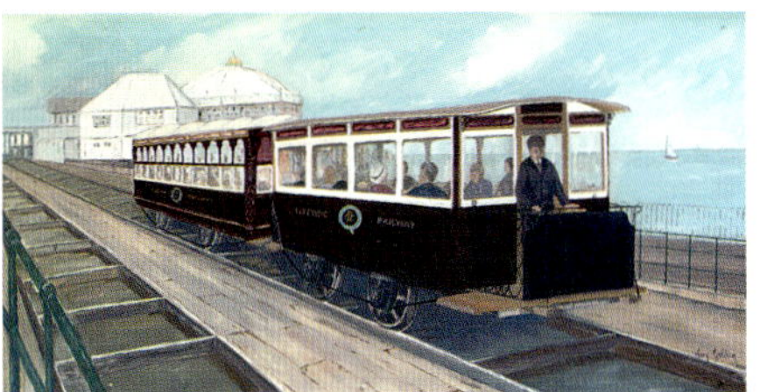

Golding, Mary b.1940
Ryde Pier Tram, c.1920 2000
acrylic & emulsion on board 122 x 245 (E)
1 (P)

Isle of Wight Council Museum Service

A museum service encompassing fine art and local history subjects came into being following Local Government re-organisation in 1974, when the Isle of Wight County Council assumed responsibilities for museum provision. One of the first initiatives was to provide a small maritime museum, attached to the Cowes Public Library, which still operates today. Opportunities arose at an early stage to acquire maritime art, in particular twentieth century depictions of naval vessels built by the firm of J. Samuel White, who were taken over in the 1970s, and left Cowes in 1981. Not unnaturally for a museum service based on an island, an art collection began to be formed which had a strong maritime bias.

Further Local Government re-organisation took place in 1995, which was to have an even greater impact upon the Museum Service in terms of its holdings of fine art collections. In this restructure, a unitary Local Authority was established (the Isle of Wight Council), which amalgamated the former Medina and South Wight Borough Councils. Medina Borough Council had inherited (through its predecessor Urban District Council) a miscellany of pictures, which had been located in various council buildings, and an immediate task from 1995 for the Isle of Wight Council was to make an inventory of the civic collections, and to physically care for pictures which had long been neglected in unsuitable locations, including damp cellars. From this point onwards, the Isle of Wight Council's responsibility for paintings included a number of important oils of the nineteenth century and earlier.

The present collection of pictures is only very modest in number. Of these, 90% of the subjects depicted relate to the Island in some way, and 60% are of local marine subjects. The greater strength in our fine art collections, however, is in watercolours, which include substantial numbers of sketches by Thomas Rowlandson, and a fine collection of nineteenth century coastal scenes. An inhibiting factor in displaying artwork presently is that the Museum Service has only a very modest space for exhibiting material under suitable conditions, which is in Newport at the Museum of Island History, but plans are being considered for establishing an art exhibition venue which could show more of the collection. Another constraint that applies in particular to the oils, is that a significant number require substantial remedial conservation work – a resource problem familiar to most owners of art collections!

Within the collection, a number of names and subjects stand out. Amongst the marine subjects are a fine series of large canvases by local artist Arthur Wellington Fowles (1815–1883); a number of oils attributed to Thomas Luny (1759–1837); and works by George Gregory (1849–1938). As with many art collections inherited from miscellaneous benefaction over the years, there are a few interesting oddities and surprises – notably William Simson's (1800–1847), *Columbus at the Door of the Convent of Santa Maria de la Rábida*, one of the first works he exhibited at the RA upon moving to London in 1838, and a move away from landscape to historical painting. Other interesting, if out of place items include a large canvas by David Bates (c.1840-1921) *Bedouin at an Oasis with Pyramids,* and a large eighteenth century *Venetian Canal Scene* of the school of Guardi. A couple of portraits stand out from the rest – a large full-length portrait of *Sir Leonard Thomas Worsley Holmes* 1816, by William Owen RA (1769–1825), and a late seventeenth century portrait, from the school of Kneller, believed to be the local philanthropist, *John Mann*.

The main work ahead for this collection is to find resources to conserve pictures, and to display more works of art when and where we are able. While we look forward to a future opportunity when a bespoke gallery can be provided to show our fine art collection, this catalogue provides an invaluable vehicle to make the entire picture collection visually accessible.

Michael Bishop, Museums Officer

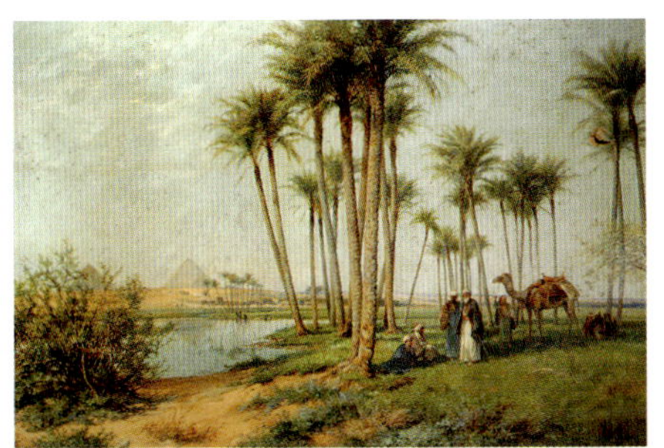

Bates, David c.1840–1921
Bedouin at an Oasis with Pyramids 1902
oil on canvas 99.5 x 149.5 (E)
1995.LG164

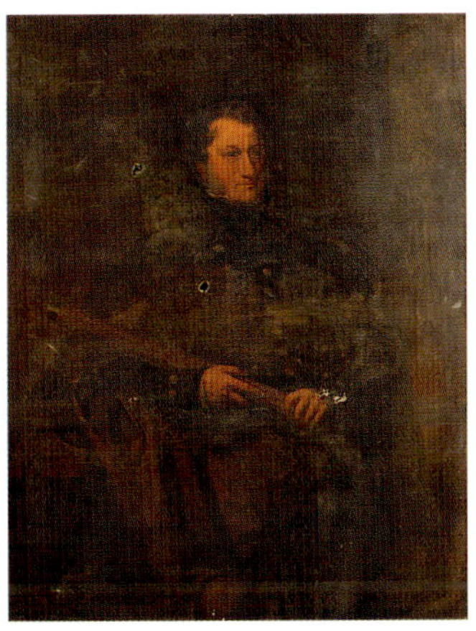

Briggs, Henry Perronet (attributed to)
1791/1793–1844
The Earl of Yarborough c.1820
oil on canvas 141 x 110.4 (E)
1995.LG160

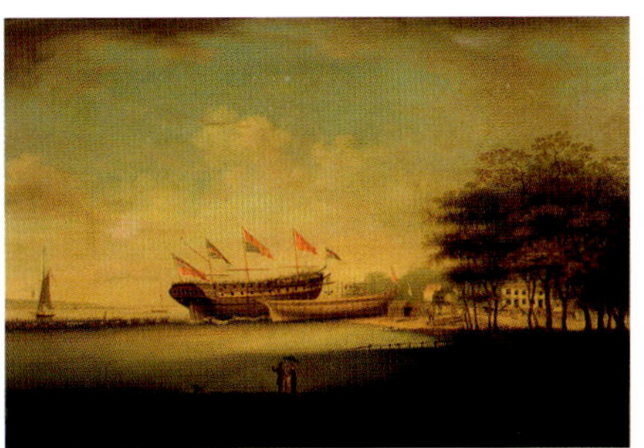

British (English) School
Launch of 'HMS Magicienne' at Fishbourne
c.1812
oil on canvas 59.5 x 90 (E)
1997.121

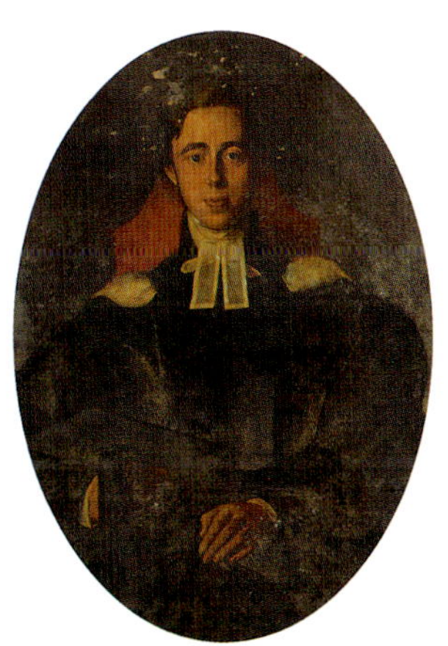

British (English) School
Reverend Thomas Binstead MacNamara, MA (1824–1910) 1848
oil on canvas 98.8 x 71.2 (E)
1995.LG161

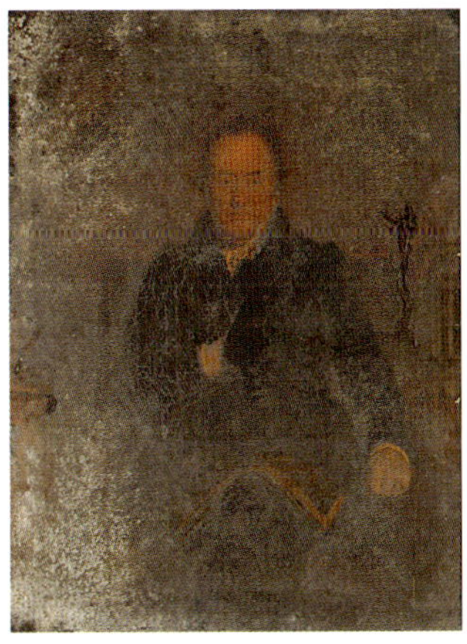

British (English) School 19th C
Portrait of a Gentleman
oil on canvas 140.4 x 110.3 (E)
1995.LG162

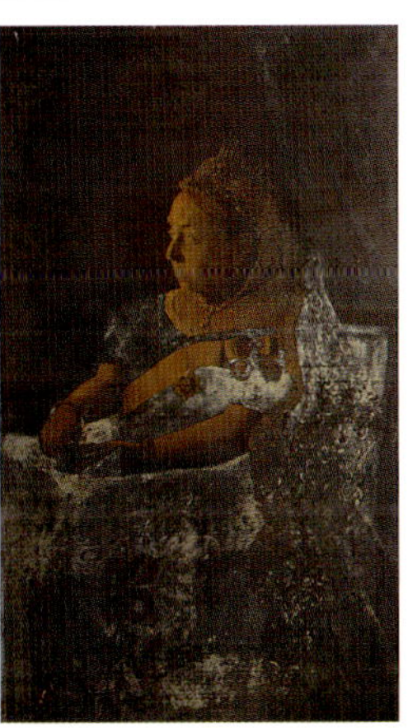

British (English) School late 19th C
Queen Victoria (1819–1901)
oil on canvas 141 x 88 (E)
1995.LG163

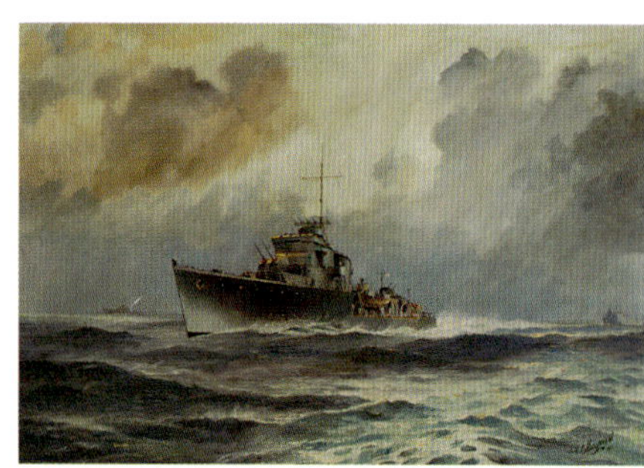

Colleypriest, Victor b.1901
'HMS Quorn' 1956
oil on canvas 48.3 x 74.3 (E)
1995.186 (P)

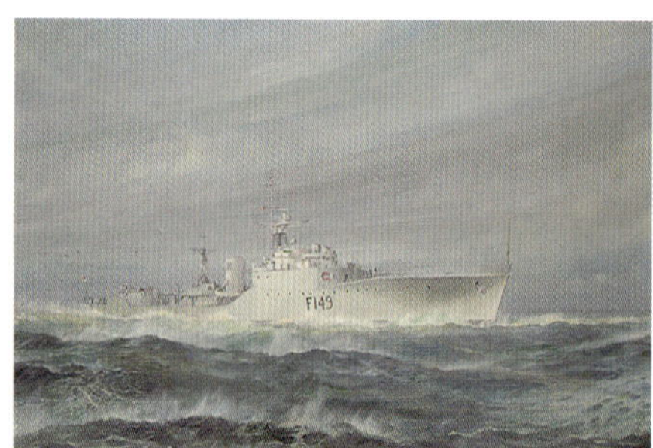

Colleypriest, Victor b.1901
'Kukai' 1958
oil on canvas 49 x 74.6 (E)
2005.4

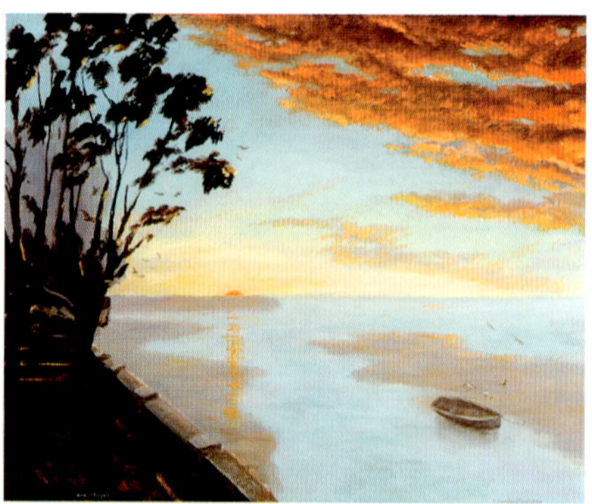

Davidge, E. Gordon
Buckingham Villa, Ryde, Sunset on the Solent from the Garden
oil on canvas 60 x 75 (E)
2006.73

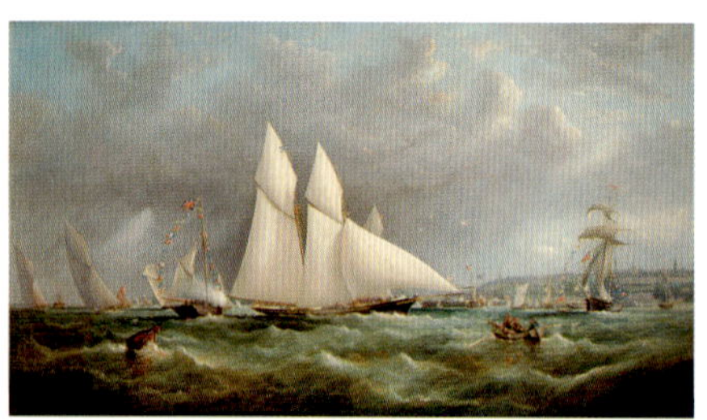

Fowles, Arthur Wellington 1815–1883
'The Cambria', Winner of the Town Cup RVYC Regatta, 1868 1869
oil on canvas 134.5 x 235.5 (E)
1995.LG147

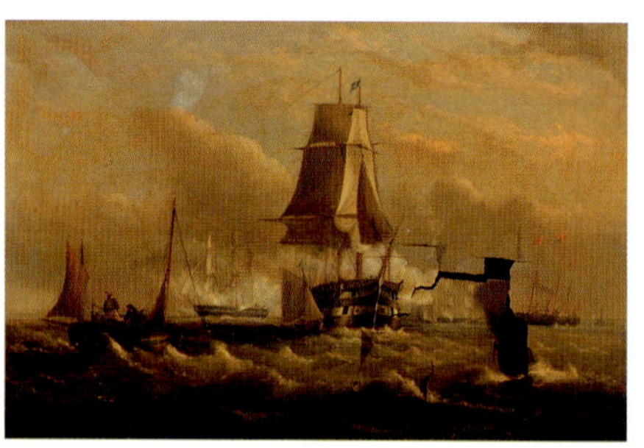

Fowles, Arthur Wellington 1815–1883
Royal Yacht 'Alberta' Approaching a Man of War, Solent 1870
oil on canvas 59.3 x 90.5 (E)
1995.LG4

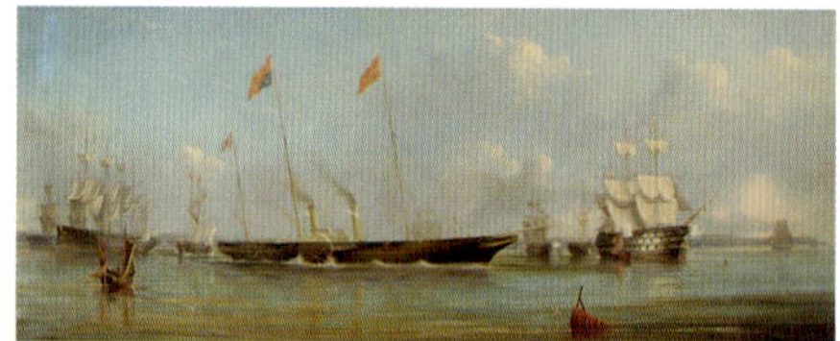

Fowles, Arthur Wellington 1815–1883
The Royal Yacht Reviews the Fleet at Spithead 1872
oil on canvas 132 x 335.5 (E)
1995.LG148

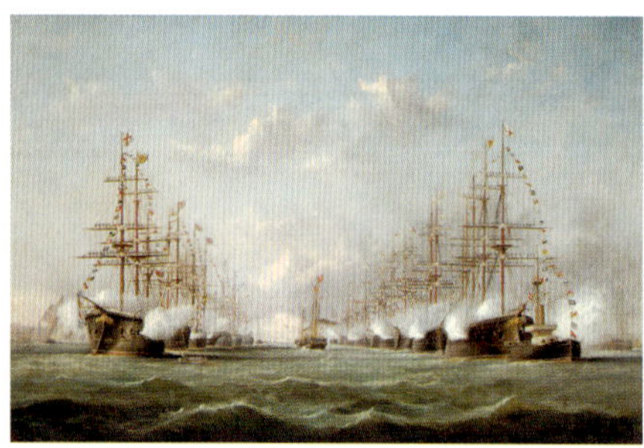

Fowles, Arthur Wellington 1815–1883
The Shah of Persia Reviewing the Fleet 1873
oil on canvas 147 x 223 (E)
1997.198

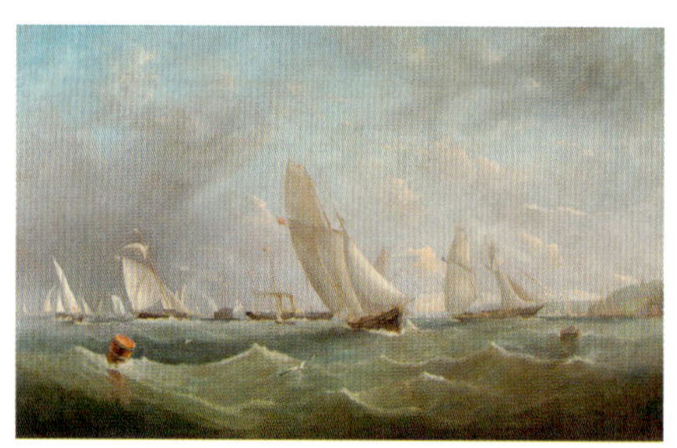

Fowles, Arthur Wellington 1815–1883
Yacht Racing in the Solent 1873
oil on canvas 165 x 258.5 (E)
1995.LG149

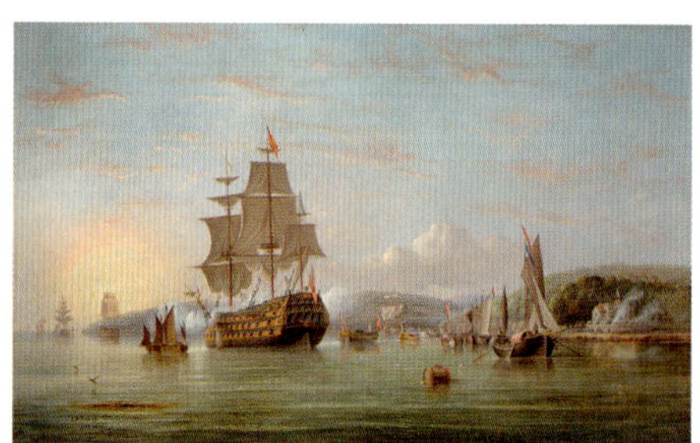

Fowles, Arthur Wellington 1815–1883
The Royal Barge off Cowes with the Royal Yacht Squadron Beyond 1879
oil on canvas 142 x 233 (E)
1995.LG146

Facing page: Gertler, Mark, 1892–1939, *Family Group* (detail), Southampton City Art Gallery, (p. 49)

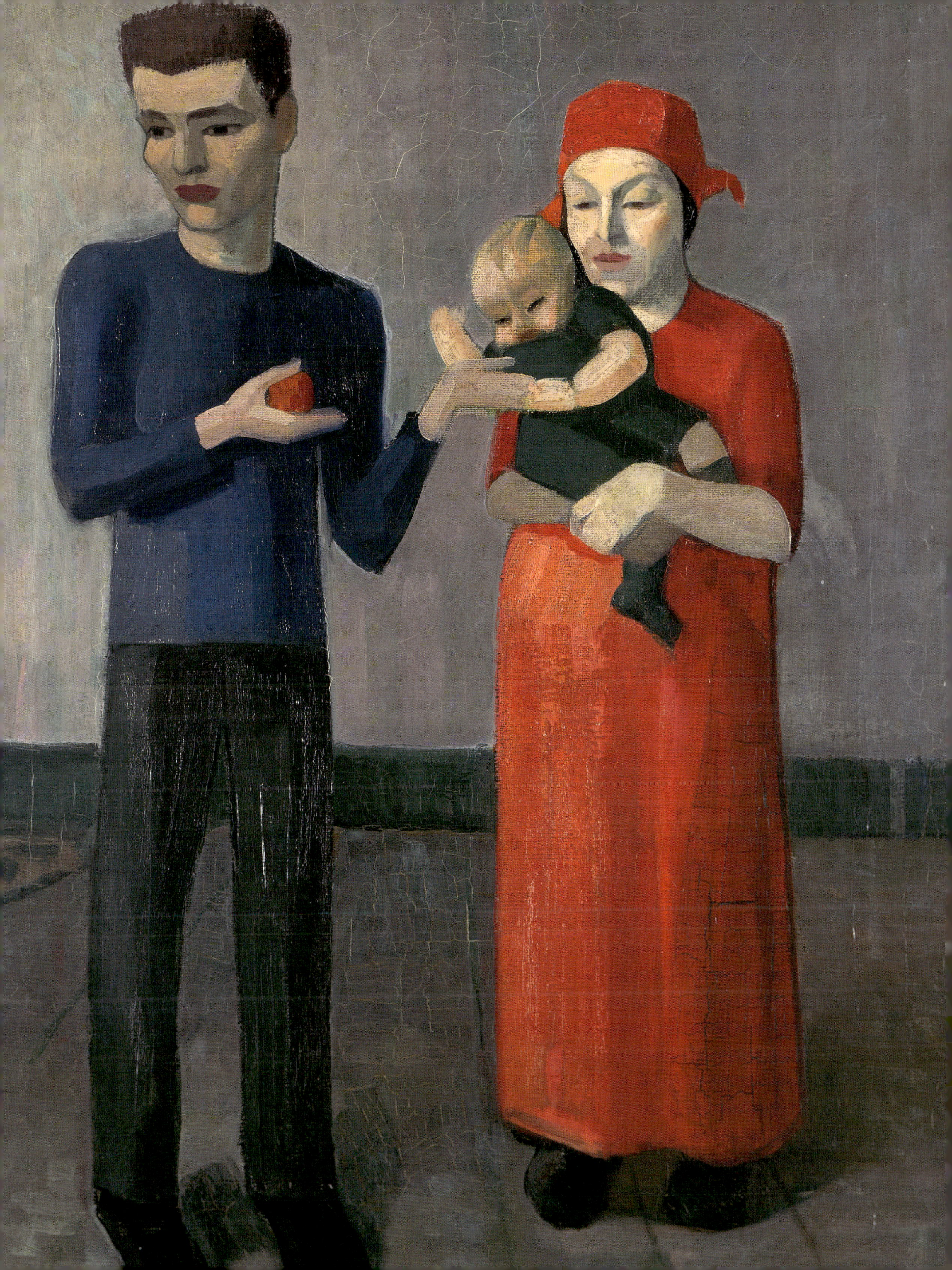

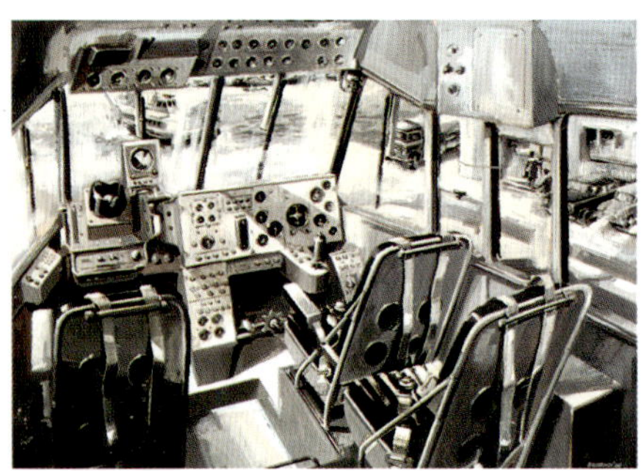

Goodburn
Interior of Cockpit of a Hovercraft 1969
acrylic on board 43.8 x 62 (E)
2001.10

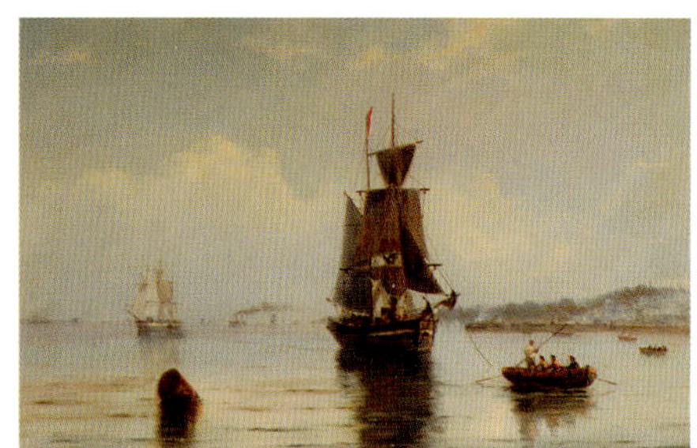

Gregory, George 1849–1938
Shipping off Ryde 1871
oil on canvas 55.5 x 85 (E)
1995.LG3

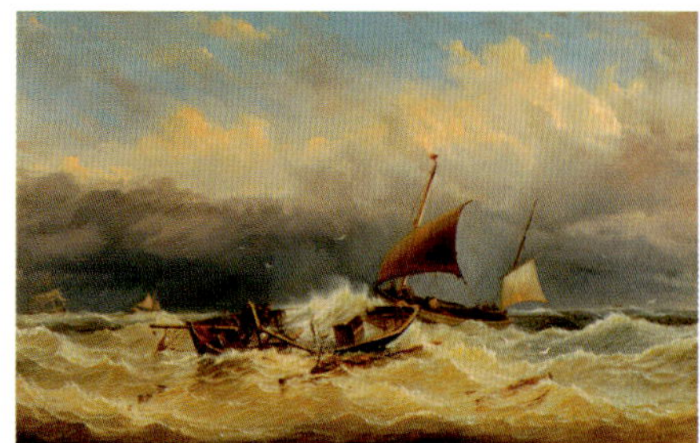

Gregory, George 1849–1938
Salvaging the Wreck 1895
oil on canvas 49.2 x 79.8
1995.718

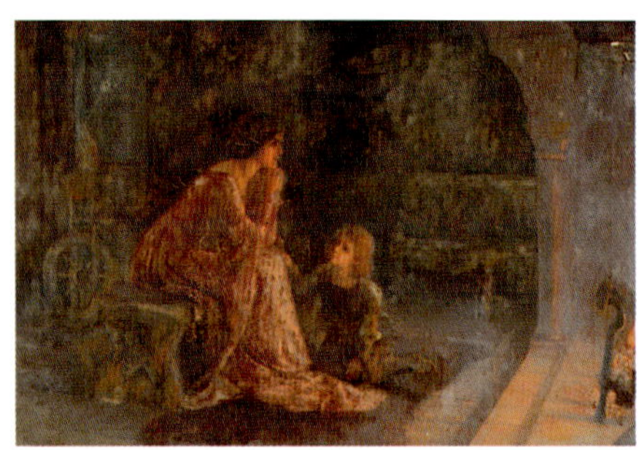

Groves, Mary active 1883–1933
Dethroned c.1933
oil on canvas 78 x 116.1 (E)
1995.LG157

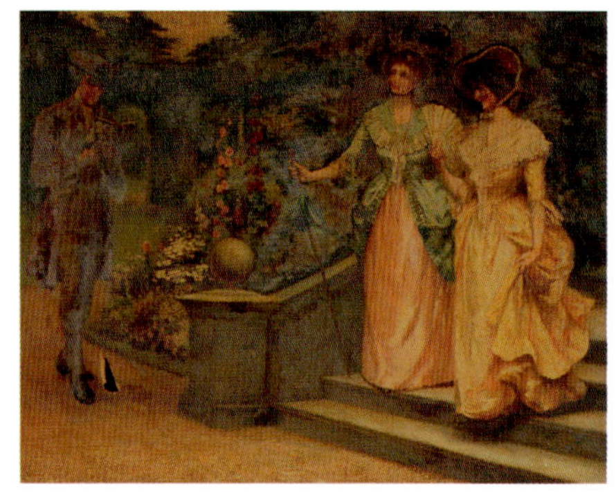

Groves, Mary active 1883–1933
The Bookworm and the Butterflies c.1933
oil on canvas 84.5 x 110 (E)
1995.LG158

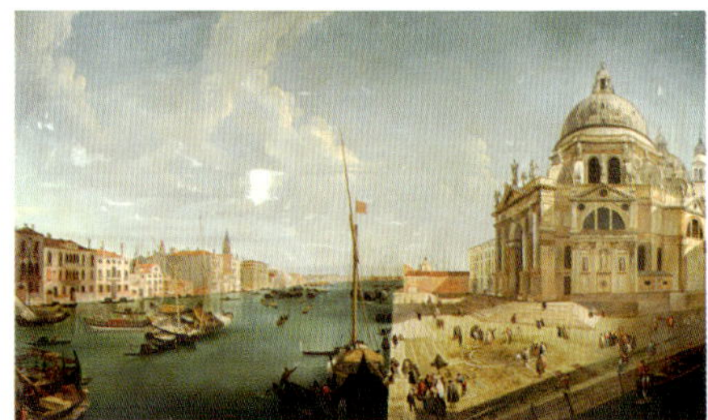

Guardi, Antonio (school of) 1699–1760 &
Guardi, Francesco (school of) 1712–1793
Venetian Canal Scene
oil on canvas 120.5 x 200 (E)
1995.LG61

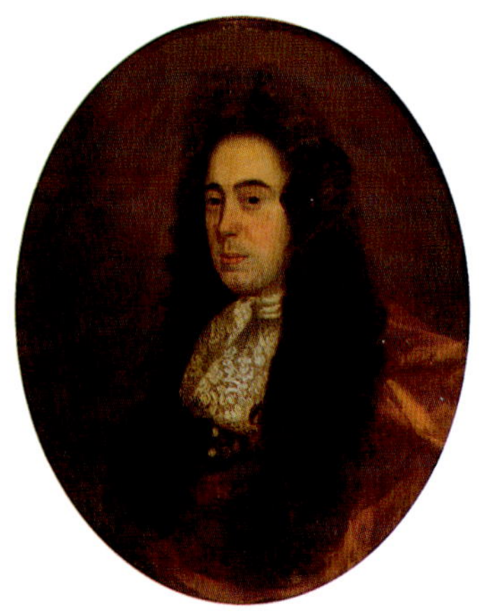

Kneller, Godfrey (school of) 1646–1723
John Mann
oil on canvas 74 x 62 (E)
1995.LG65

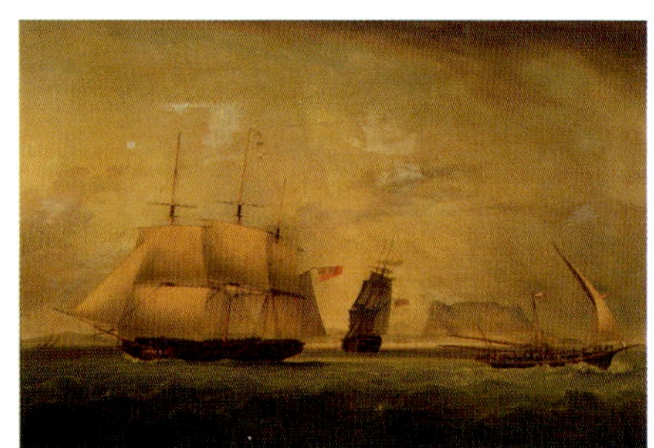

Luny, Thomas (attributed to) 1759–1837
'HMS Magicienne' off Table Top Mountain, South Africa
oil on canvas 59.8 x 89.8 (E)
1995.LG64

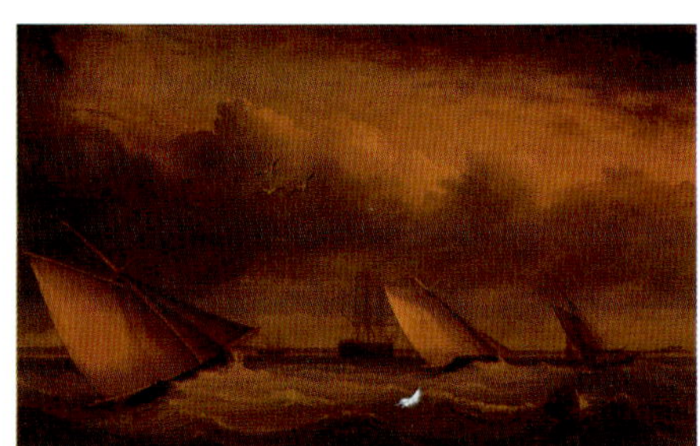

Luny, Thomas (attributed to) 1759–1837
Yacht Racing off Calshot
oil on canvas 31 x 49 (E)
1995.LG2

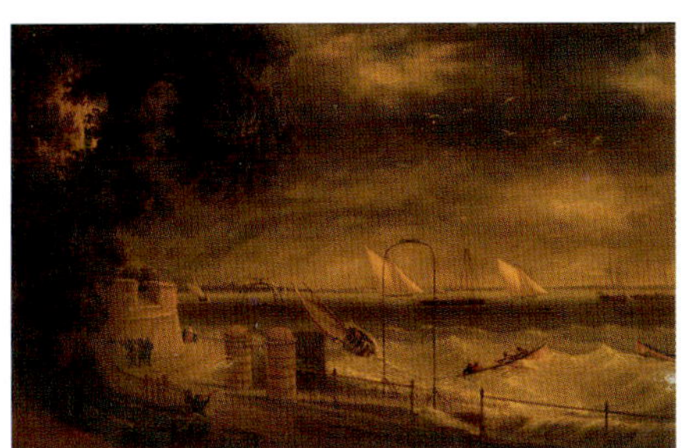

Luny, Thomas (attributed to) 1759–1837
Yachting off the Royal Yacht Squadron
oil on canvas 31.3 x 49.3 (E)
1995.LG1

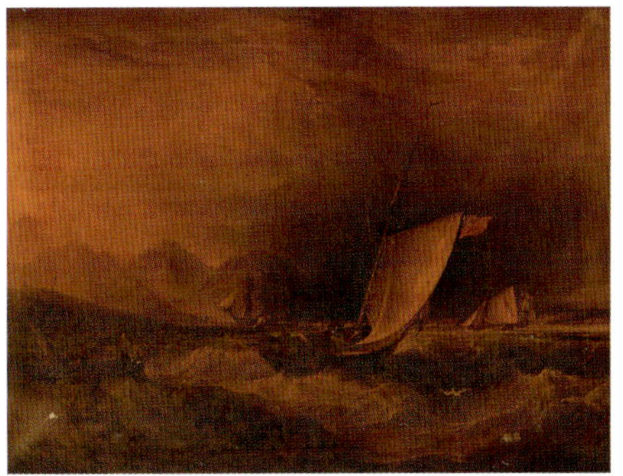

McEwen, William
Shipping off a Mountainous Coast 1841
oil on canvas 87.3 x 121 (E)
1995.LG156

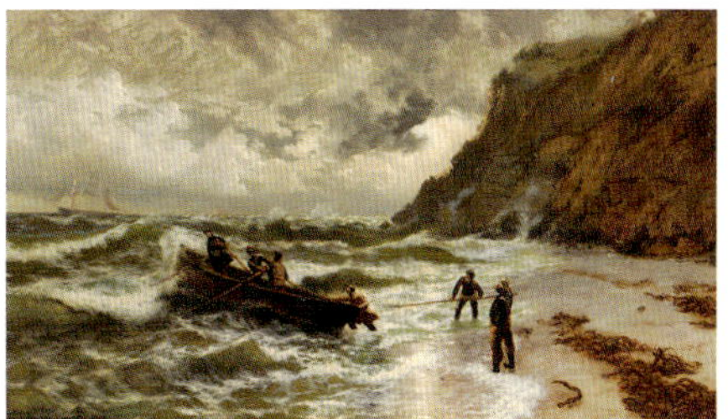

Miles, Thomas Rose 1869–1888
Signal for a Pilot, Shanklin Bay, Isle of Wight
oil on canvas 99 x 105 (E)
1995.601

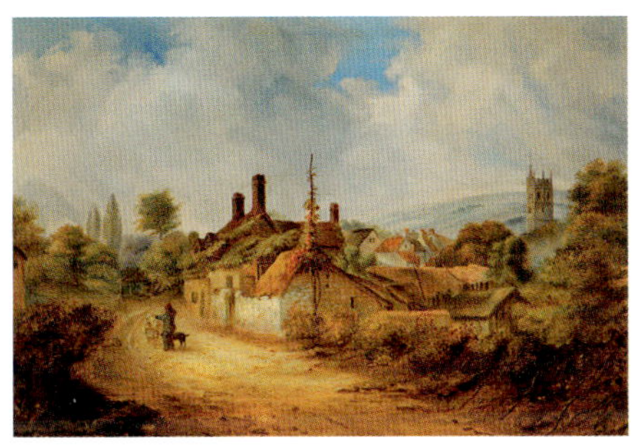

Minns, Fanny Mary active 1865–1905
Carisbrooke Village c.1865
oil on canvas 30.8 x 46 (E)
1995.LG21

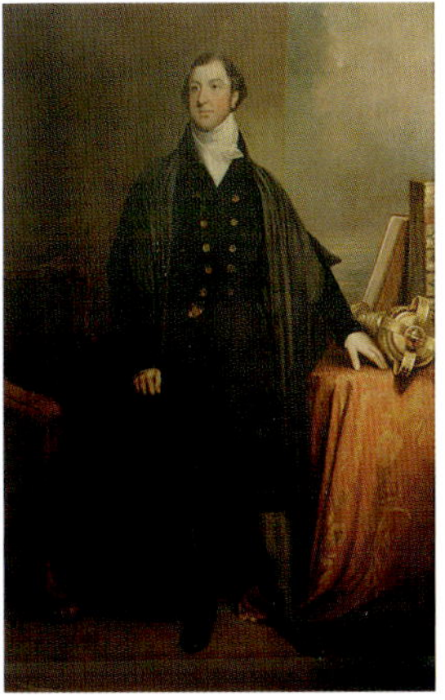

Owen, William 1769–1825
Sir Leonard Thomas Worsley Holmes 1816
oil on canvas 310 x 145 (E)
1995.LG63

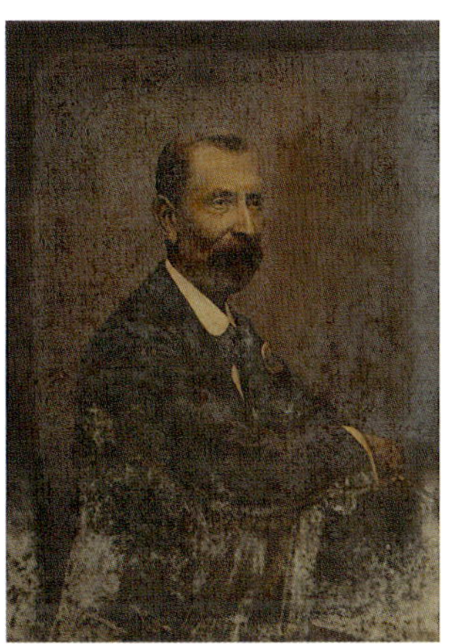

Priestly, J. T.
George Fellows, Esq. c.1907
oil on canvas 90 x 74 (E)
1995.LG159

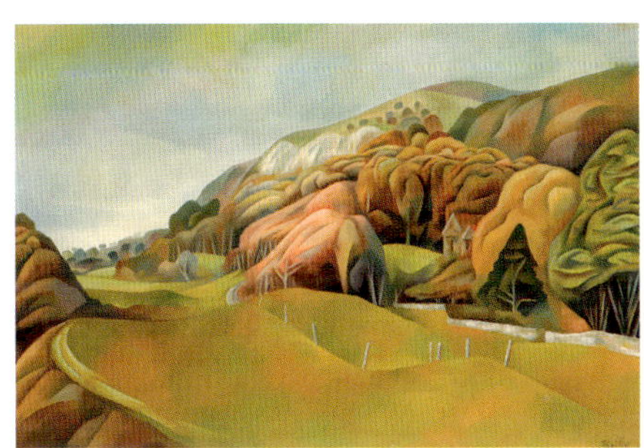

Reilly, John b.1928
The Undercliff 1980
oil on canvas 49.5 x 79.4 (E)
1999.53

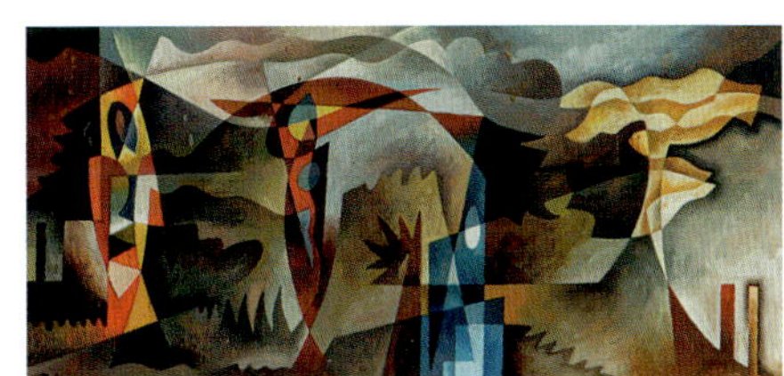

Reilly, John b.1928
Four in Harmony
acrylic on canvas 17.8 x 38 (E)
2006.75

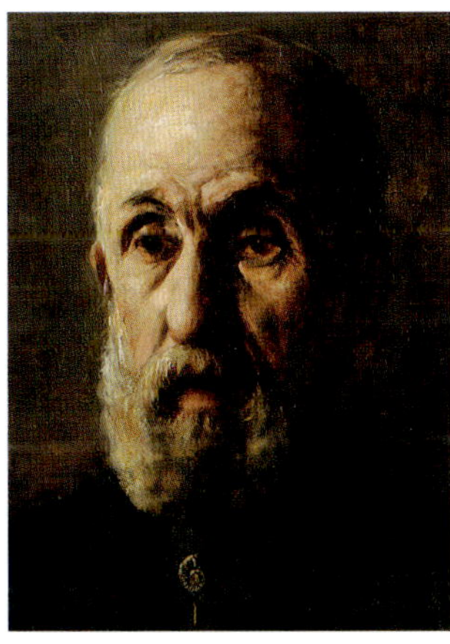

Ryan, Charles J. 1865–1949
Mark William Norman c.1893
oil on board 37 x 27.9 (E)
1997.292

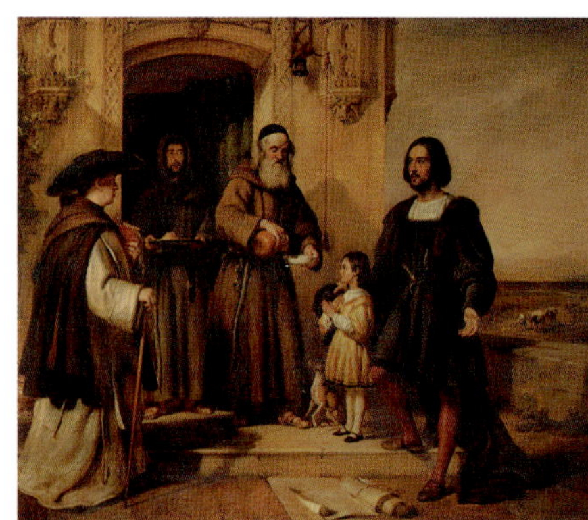

Simson, William 1800–1847
Columbus at the Door of the Convent of Santa Maria de la Rábida 1838
oil on canvas 110 x 141.7 (E)
1995.LG62

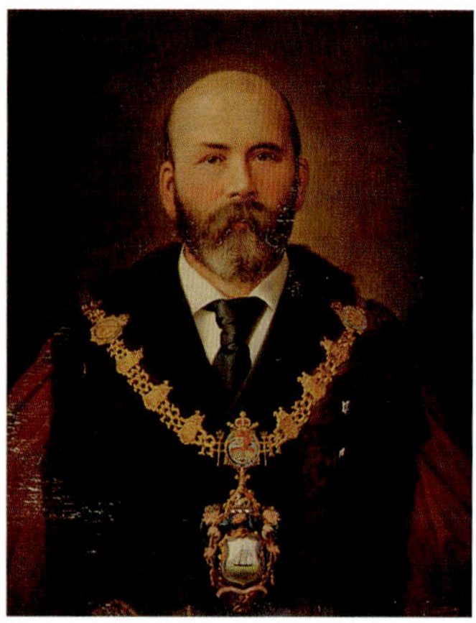

unknown artist
Ernest Groves, Mayor of Ryde (1895–1897)
1895–1900
oil on canvas 90 x 70 (E)
2006.74

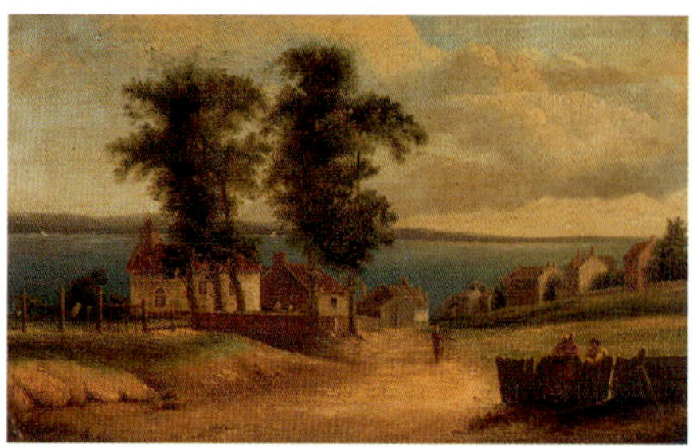

unknown artist early 19th C
View of Ryde
oil on board 27.7 x 45.5 (E)
2005.5

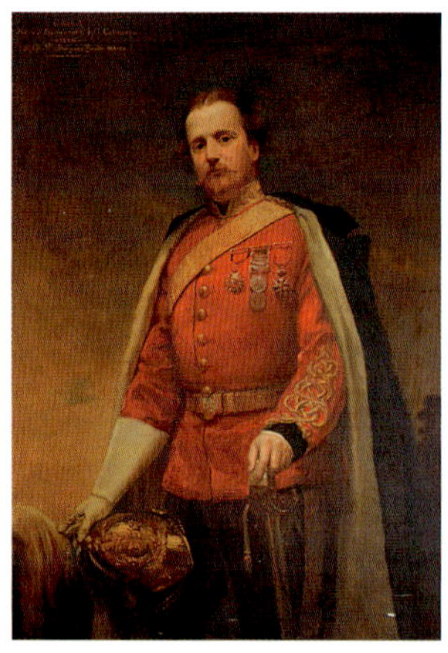

unknown artist late 19th C
Lieutenant General the Honourable Somerset J. Gough-Calthorpe
oil on canvas 140 x 99 (E)
OE 46 (P)

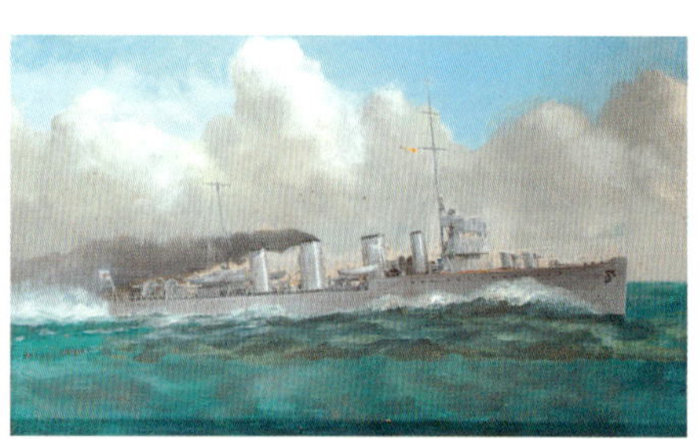

unknown artist late 20th C
Warship
oil on canvas 84.4 x 141 (E)
2005.3

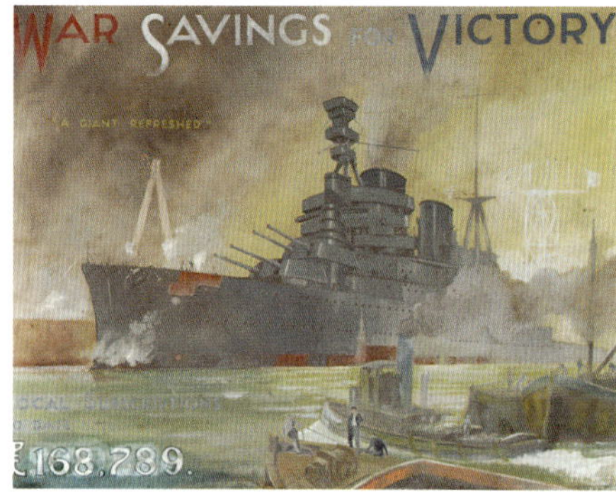

unknown artist
War Savings for Victory
oil on board 116 x 147.7 (E)
2006.76

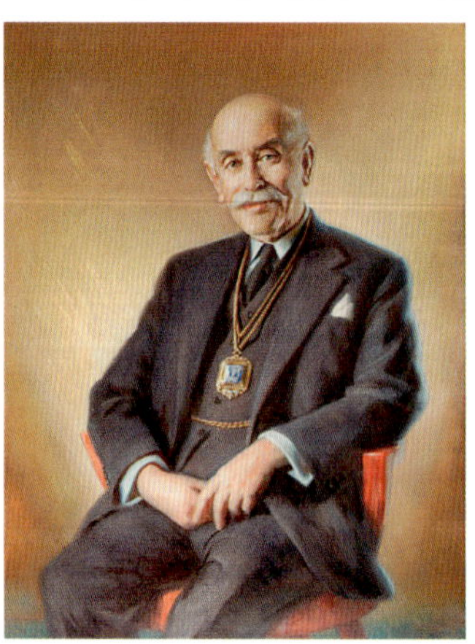

Voysey
Sir Godfrey Baring BT, KBE, JP, DL 1956
oil on canvas 120 x 70 (E)
1995.LG66

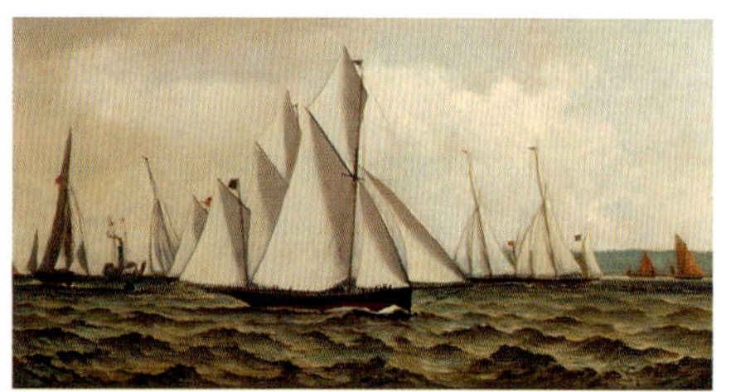

Webb, Geoffrey 1896–1981
Gaff Rigger Racing Yachts off the Isle of Wight
c.1980
oil on canvas 67.5 x 136 (E)
2005.1

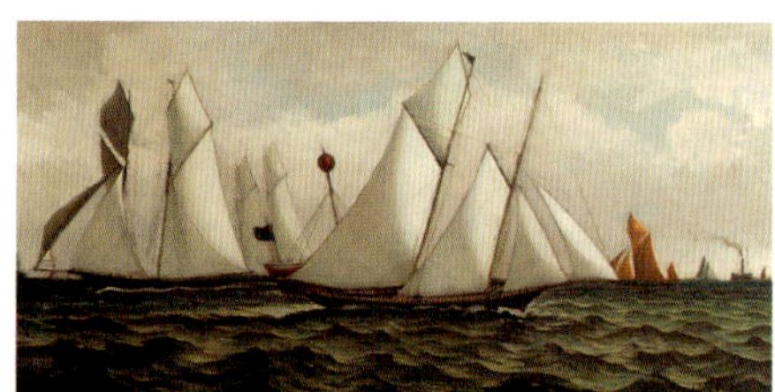

Webb, Geoffrey 1896–1981
Gaff Rigger Racing Yachts off the Isle of Wight
c.1980
oil on canvas 67.5 x 136 (E)
2005.2

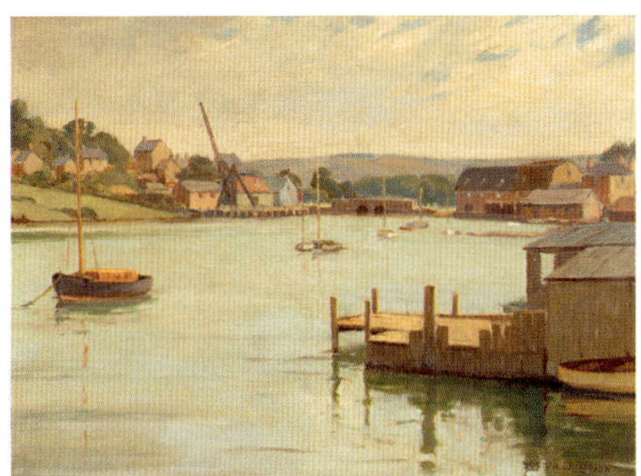

Wilkinson, Norman 1878–1971
Estuary Scene 1900–1950
oil on board 35 x 48.7 (E)
2005.6

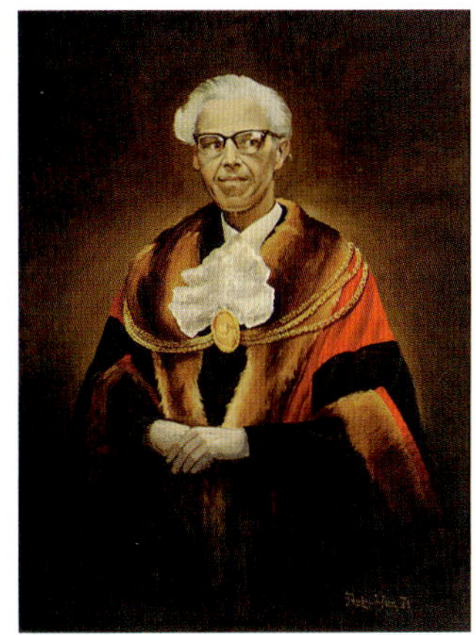

Young, R.
Patrick Bryan, Mayor of Newport (1970–1971)
1971
oil on canvas 122 x 91.4
1995.LG440

Quay Arts

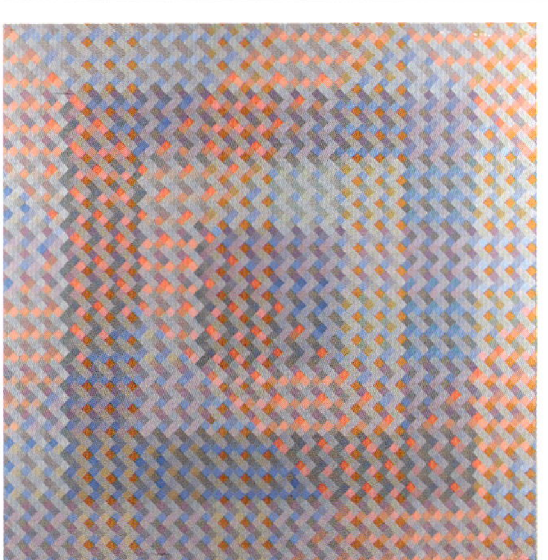

Wells, Peter 1938–1996
Untitled
oil on board 122 x 122
1

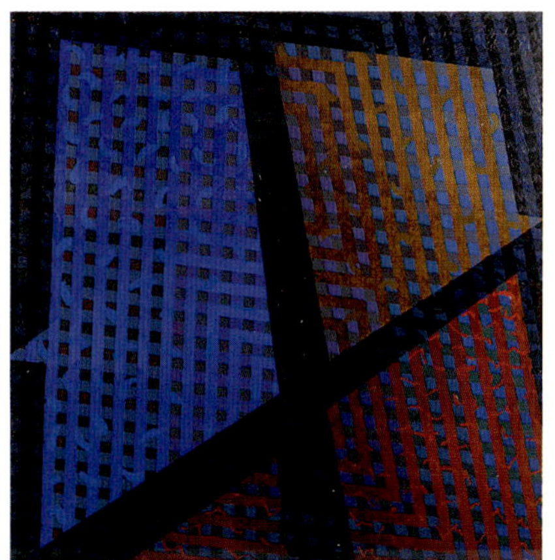

Wells, Peter 1938–1996
Untitled
oil on board 122 x 122
2

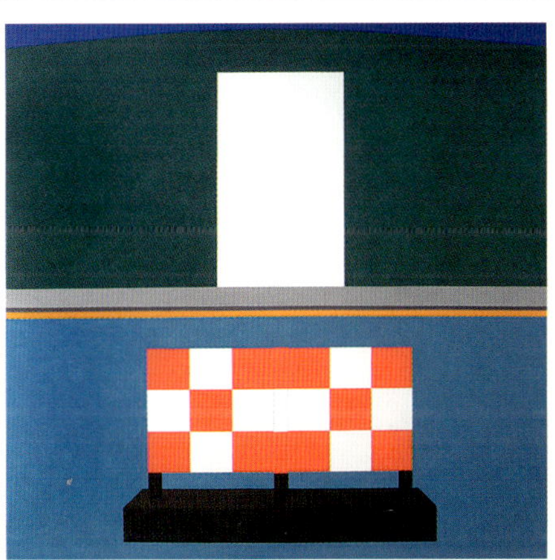

Wright, Peter b.1932
Port Marker 1975
oil on canvas 152 x 152
4 (P)

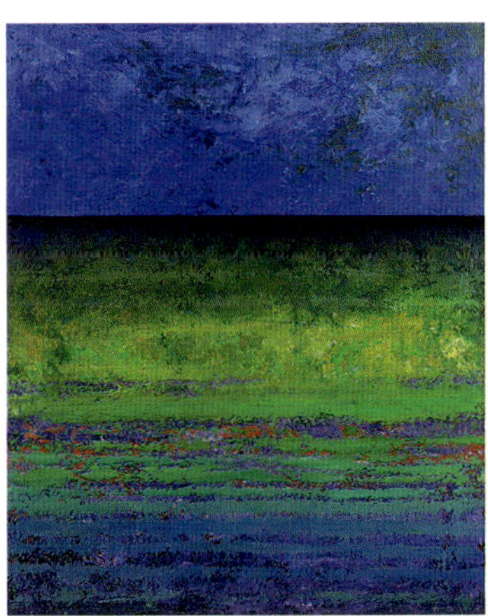

Wright, Peter b.1932
Blue, Green, Brown, Mauve 1997–1998
oil on board 122 x 102
3

Ryde Fire Station

This painting by William George Home Rosenberg, a painter of merit who exhibited paintings at the RA between 1871 and 1884, is one of the most important works owned by the Fire Service in this country. The painting recalls a family in the late nineteenth century being called away from the Opera because a fire had broken out at their home on London's Piccadilly. The scene shows the parents receiving their children who have been rescued by the Fire Brigade. The painting was presented to the Ryde Fire Brigade by George Henry Harrison in August 1925, a former Chief Fire Officer from Kingston-upon-Thames who retired to the Isle of Wight. It is well documented in the Ryde Council Records that it should hang in the town Fire Station. Over time however, conditions at the Fire Station caused severe damage to the painting and it was nearly lost forever. Thanks to the dedication of the Brigade, adequate funds were raised by sponsored events and it now hangs once again in Ryde Fire Station where members of the public may visit by appointment.

Ian Santini, Watch Manager

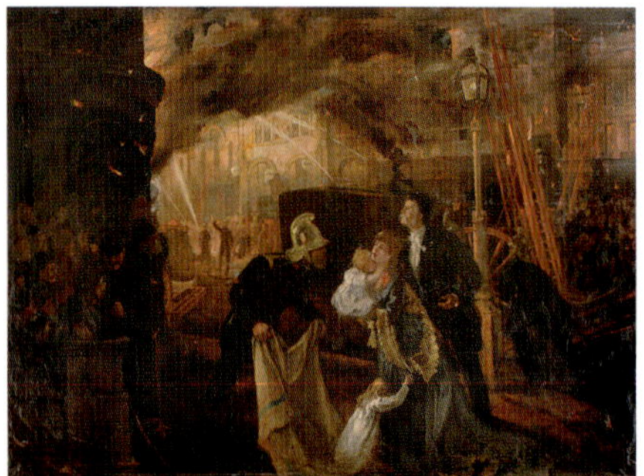

Rosenberg, William George Home
active 1871–1884
A Fire in London
oil on canvas 144 x 177.5 (E)
1

Ventnor Heritage Museum

During the Victorian era, Ventnor, and nearby Bonchurch, became a mecca for both writers and artists. Many well-known painters including Myles Birkett Foster, Thomas Leeson Rowbotham, Thomas Miles Richardson and Edward William Cooke, to name but a few, stayed at Seaside Cottage and other country houses in the area. The artist William Gray also lived in Ventnor, and many of his fine works depict the dramatic and beautiful scenery of the area.

Our museum cannot, unfortunately, expect to house originals from these masters, but our collection does still feature the scenic delights of the area, albeit by enthusiastic locals and visitors drawn here to paint throughout the years. Our painting detailing the capsizing of 'HMS Eurydice' in 1878 reminds us of the worst shipwreck ever to occur off our coast, when the vessel, struck by a sudden squall, capsized which resulted in the loss of over 300 lives. The disaster was witnessed by Sir Winston Churchill who was staying in Ventnor as a young boy.

The Museum holds extensive archives on all aspects of the history of Ventnor and the Undercliff. It is open from mid-May until the end of October. Membership of our Society is available and research questions are always welcome.

Graham Bennett, Curator

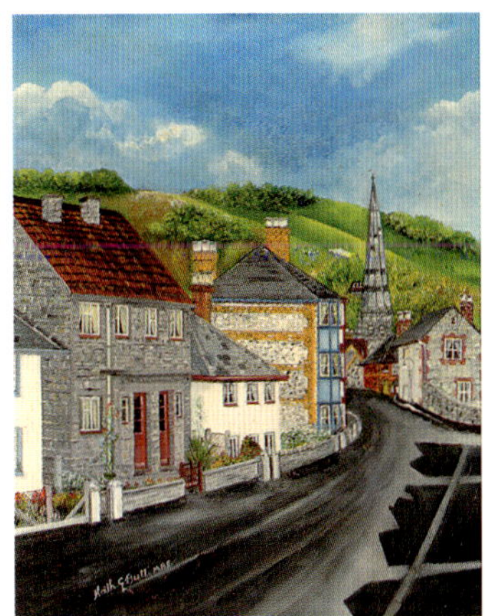

Bull, Keith G.
South Street, Ventnor 1995
oil on board 35.5 x 29
VENPR154

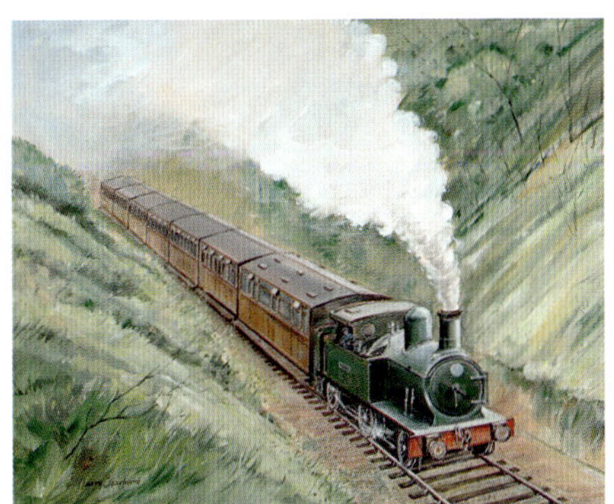

Charlwood, Harry 1924–2001
From Ryde Pierhead to Ventnor 1988
oil on board 39.3 x 49.6
VENPR170

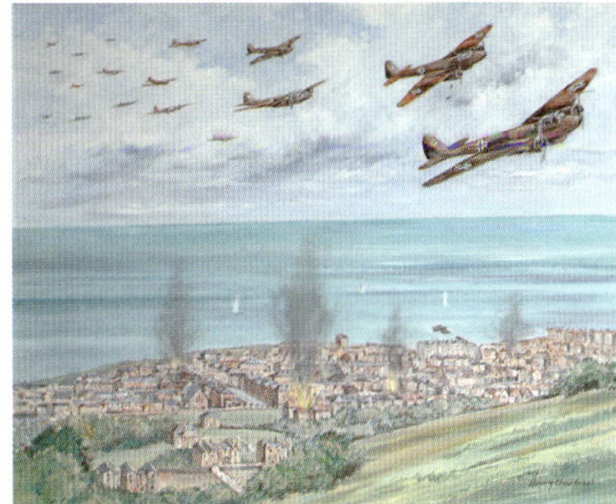

Charlwood, Harry 1924–2001
The Bombing of Ventnor, 1940 1990
oil on board 51 x 60
VENPR168

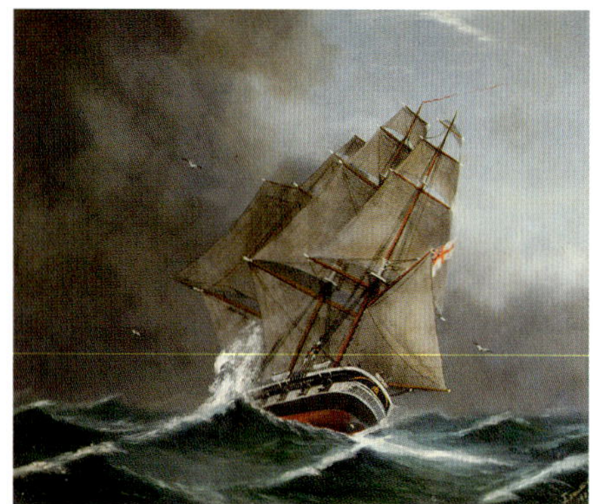

Edmunds, J. E.
The Capsizing of the 'Eurydice', 1878 1888
oil on canvas 43 x 54.5
VENPR167

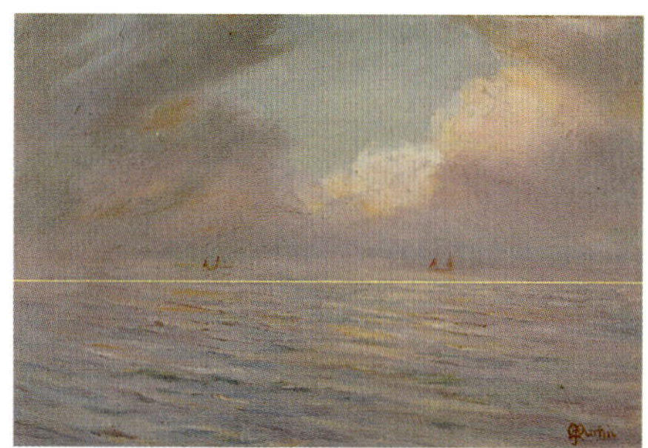

Martin, Harry James (attributed to)
c.1860–1944
Mackerel Boats c.1915
oil on board 20.5 x 30.5
VENPR23

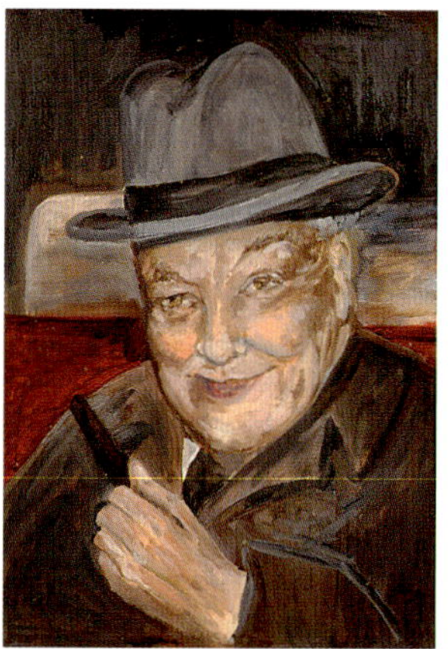

Pollard, Beatrice
Sir Winston Churchill (1874–1965) 1990
oil on board 40.6 x 30.7
VENPR173

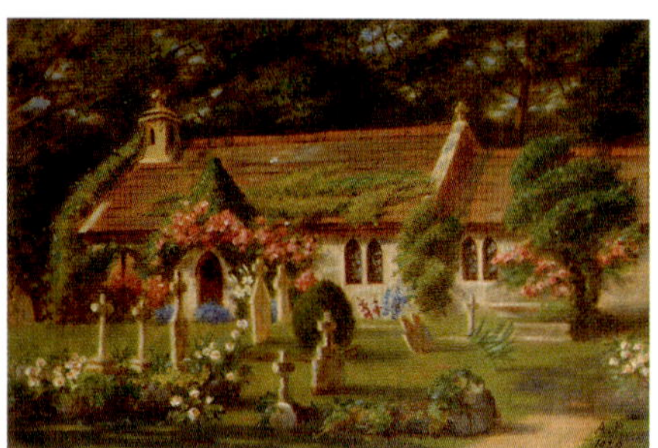

Poore, Adela active 1894–1929
Old Church, Bonchurch 1929
oil on canvas 28 x 37.4
VENPR52

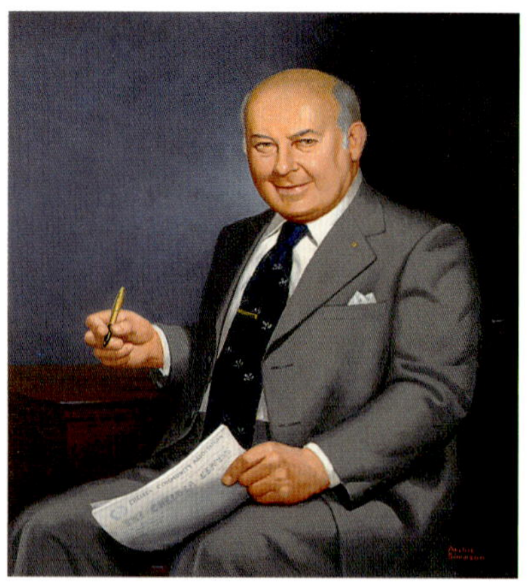

Simpson, Archie
Ernest Biggin 1980
oil on canvas 60.3 x 50.4
VH/2001/65

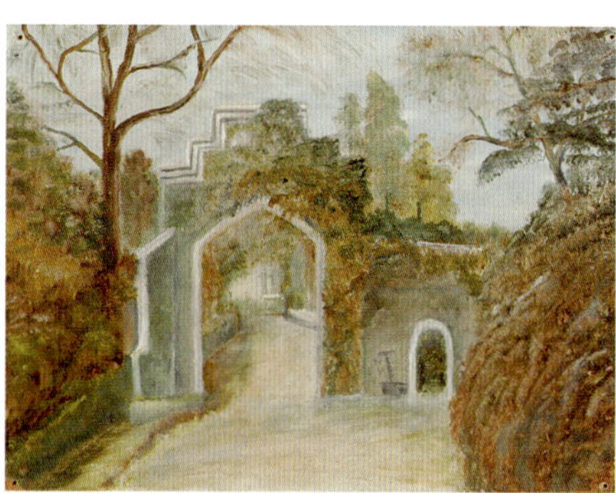

Stotesbury, Louise b.1919
Steephill Castle Entrance 1985
oil on board 23.1 x 31
VENPR179A

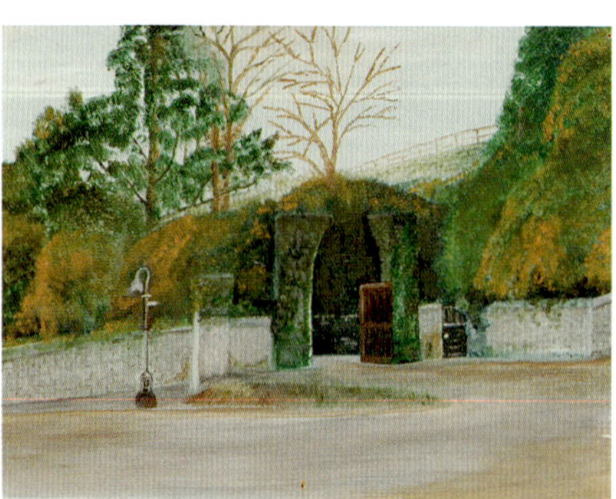

Stotesbury, Louise b.1919
Steephill Castle Entrance 1985
oil on board 23.3 x 31.4
VENPR179B

Yarmouth Isle of Wight Town Trust

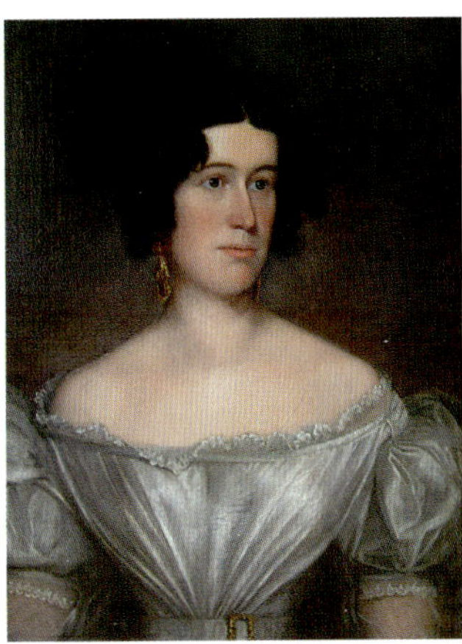

unknown artist
Lady Holmes c.1800
oil on canvas 77 x 64
1

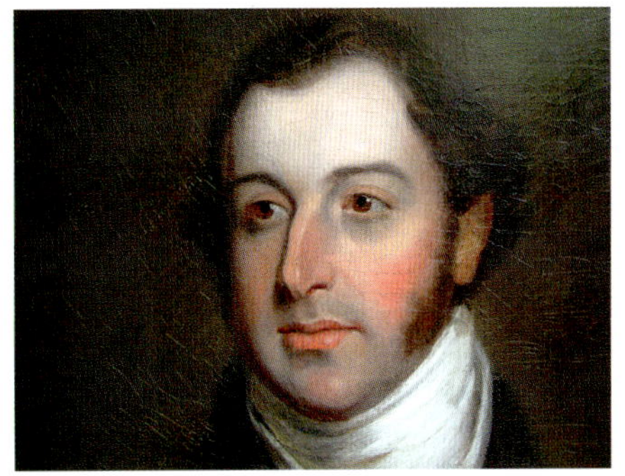

unknown artist
Leonard, Lord Holmes, Baron Holmes of Kilmallock, County Limerick (...) c.1800
oil on canvas 77 x 64
2

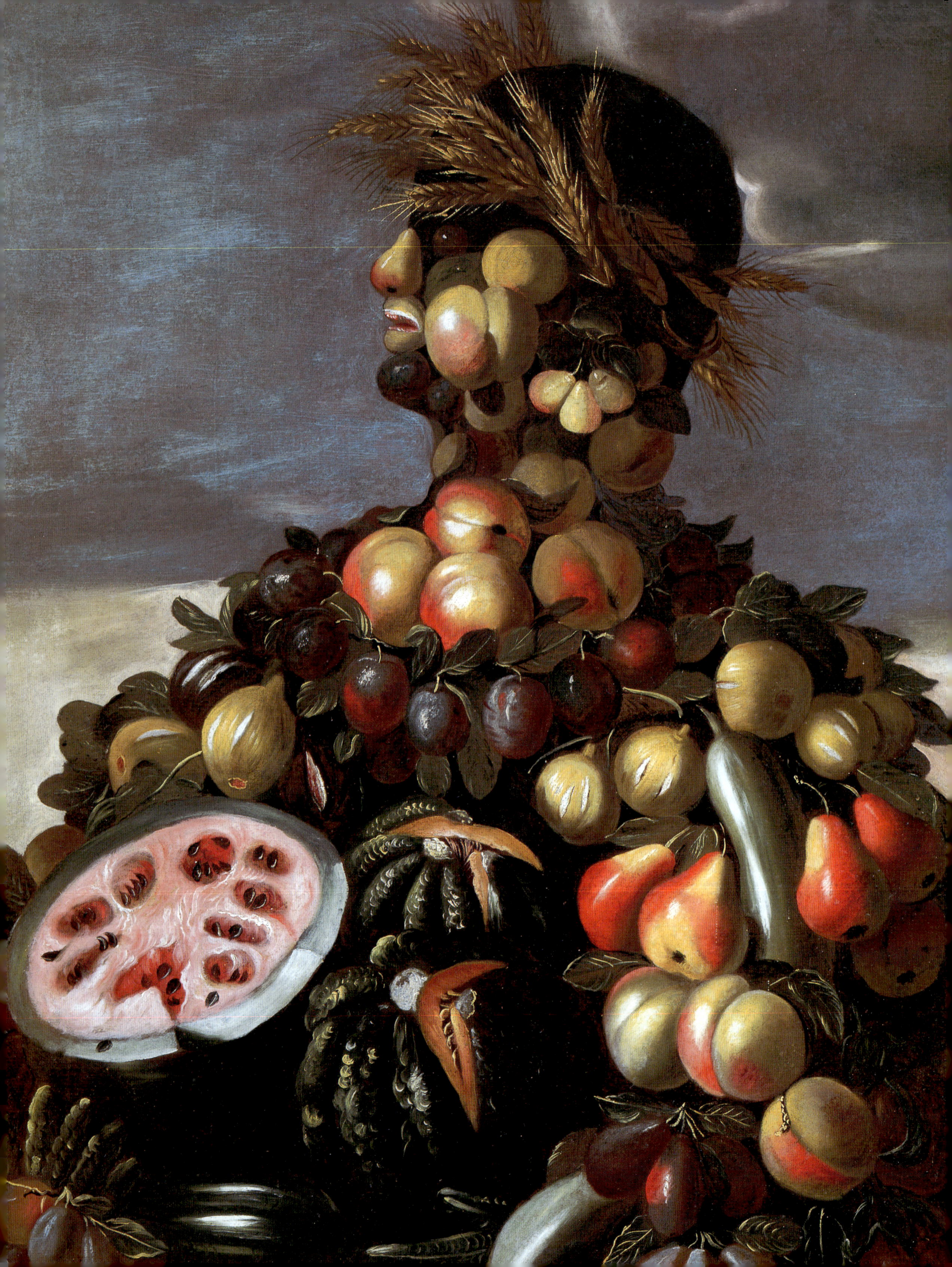

Paintings Without Reproductions

This section lists all the paintings that have not been included in the main pages of the catalogue. They were excluded as it was not possible to photograph them for this project. Additional information relating to acquisition credit lines or loan details is also included. For this reason the information below is not repeated in the Further Information section.

Southampton City Art Gallery

Batt, Arthur 1846–1911, *Calves and Ducks*, 1883, 50.8 x 68.8, oil on canvas, 21, purchased with the assistance of the Frederick William Smith Bequest Fund, 1936, not available at the time of photography

Locke, Henry Edward 1862–1925, *Western Shore*, c.1890, 22 x 30, oil on board, m141, gift, not available at the time of photography

Meadus, Eric 1931–1970, *Flowers against Yellow Background*, 1966, 51.7 x 55.5, oil on canvas, 17/1975, purchased with the assistance of the Frederick William Smith Bequest Fund, 1975, not available at the time of photography

Mills, David b.1947, *Phosphene Day*, 157 x 152.5, acrylic on canvas 8/1974 , purchased with the assistance of the Corporation Rate Fund, 1974, not available at the time of photography

Strutt, Arthur John 1819–1888, *Spanish Coach*, 1842, 76.4 x 119.7, oil on canvas, 1114, presented by Mr and Mrs W. J. Fernie, 1942, not available at the time of photography

Southampton City Museums

Stewart, R.W., *Figures in Street*, 51 x 61.2, oil on canvas, 17/2003, bequeathed, 2003, not available at the time of photography

Southampton University Hospitals NHS Trust

Alexander, Rachael b.1965 & **Muncaster, Jenny** b.1966, *Ocean Theme Painting* (15 paintings), 2002, acrylic on board, 313 to 327, commissioned by Southampton University Hospitals NHS Trust, c.2001, located in an area where access is not permitted in the interests of patient privacy and dignity

Gradidge, Daphne b.1953, *Animal Painting: Anteater*, 1995, 122.5 x 80, acrylic on board, 133, commissioned by Southampton University Hospitals NHS Trust, 1995, located in an area where access is not permitted in the interests of patient privacy and dignity

Gradidge, Daphne b.1953, *Animal Painting: Koala Bears and Parrot*, 1995, 122.5 x 150, acrylic on board, 131, commissioned by Southampton University Hospitals NHS Trust, 1995, located in an area where access is not permitted in the interests of patient privacy and dignity

Gradidge, Daphne b.1953, *Animal Painting: Monkey, Flamingo and Armadillo* (5 panels), 1995, 122.5 x 70 (panel 1), 122.5 x 60 (all other panels), acrylic on board, 124 to 128, commissioned by Southampton University Hospitals NHS Trust, 1995, located in an area where access is not permitted in the interests of patient privacy and dignity

Gradidge, Daphne b.1953, *Animal Painting: Parrots*, 1995, 122.5 x 150, acrylic on board, 130, commissioned by Southampton University Hospitals NHS Trust, 1995, located in an area where access is not permitted in the interests of patient privacy and dignity

Gradidge, Daphne b.1953, *Animal Painting: Tropical Birds*, 1995, 160 x 60, acrylic on board, 129, commissioned by Southampton University Hospitals NHS Trust, 1995, located in an area where access is not permitted in the interests of patient privacy and dignity

Gradidge, Daphne b.1953, *Animal Painting: Tropical Birds*, 1995, 122.5 x 70, acrylic on board, 132, commissioned by Southampton University Hospitals NHS Trust, 1995, located in an area where access is not permitted in the interests of patient privacy and dignity

Gradidge, Daphne b.1953, *Animal Painting: Tropical Birds and Parrots*, 1995, 122.5 x 80, acrylic on board, 134, commissioned by Southampton University Hospitals NHS Trust, 1995, located in an area where access is not permitted in the interests of patient privacy and dignity

Gradidge, Daphne b.1953, *Tropical View*, 1997, 140, acrylic on canvas, 238, commissioned by Southampton University Hospitals NHS Trust, 1997, located in an area where access is not permitted in the interests of patient privacy and dignity

Gradidge, Daphne b.1953, *Vines and a Pergola*, 1997, 140, acrylic on canvas, 239, commissioned by Southampton University Hospitals NHS Trust, 1997, located in an area where access is not permitted in the interests of patient privacy and dignity

Gradidge, Daphne b.1953, *Untitled*, acrylic on board, 159, located in an area where access is not permitted in the interests of patient privacy and dignity

Muncaster, Jenny b.1966, *Jungle Theme Painting* (series of 36 paintings), 2003, acrylic on board, 72 to 101, 265 to 269 & 271, commissioned by Southampton University Hospitals NHS Trust, 2002, located in an area where access is not permitted in the interests of patient privacy and dignity

Rome, Sally, *Untitled* (20 paintings in total), 1992, 116 x 202, 120 x 180, 120 x 190, 122 x 180, 108 x 117, 102 x 118, 125 x 202, 124 x 105,122 x 165, 122 x 116, all acrylic on board, 139 to 158, commissioned by Southampton University Hospitals NHS Trust, 1992, located in an area where access is not permitted in the interests of patient privacy and dignity

Toms, Anne b.1944, *Daytime River Scene*, c.1992, 155 x 350, acrylic on board, 110, commissioned by Southampton University Hospitals NHS Trust, c.1992, located in an area where access is not permitted in the interests of patient privacy and dignity

Toms, Anne b.1944, *River Bank*, c.1992, 130 x 300, acrylic on board, 111, commissioned by Southampton University Hospitals NHS Trust, c.1992, located in an area where access is not permitted in the interests of patient privacy and dignity

Toms, Anne b.1944, *Twilight on the River*, c.1992, 115 x 350, acrylic on board, 109, commissioned by Southampton University Hospitals NHS Trust, c.1992, located in an area where access is not permitted in the interests of patient privacy and dignity

Toms, Anne b.1944, *Untitled* (4 paintings in total), c.1992, all 60 x 60, all acrylic on board, 112 to 115, commissioned by Southampton University Hospitals NHS Trust, c.1992, located in an area where access is not permitted in the interests of patient privacy and dignity

unknown artist, *Teddy Bears at the Beach*, 1993, 120 x 120, acrylic on board, 116, located in an area where access is not permitted in the interests of patient privacy and dignity

unknown artist, *Teddy Bears in the Forest*, 1993, 120 x 120, acrylic on board, 117, located in an area where access is not permitted in the interests of patient privacy and dignity

unknown artist, *Teddy Bears' Picnic*, 1993, 120 x 120, acrylic on board, 118, located in an area where access is not permitted in the interests of patient privacy and dignity

unknown artist, *Teddy Bears with Umbrellas*, 1993, 120 x 120, acrylic on board, 119, located in an area where access is not permitted in the interests of patient privacy and dignity

unknown artist, *Tiger*, 68 x 122.5, acrylic on board, 135, located in an area where access is not permitted in the interests of patient privacy and dignity

unknown artist, *Tiger and Cheetah*, 68 x 122.5, acrylic on board, 136, located in an area where access is not permitted in the interests of patient privacy and dignity

unknown artist, *Underwater Scene*, 100 x 100, acrylic on panel, 137, located in an area where access is not permitted in the interests of patient privacy and dignity

unknown artist, *View from a Window: Bird Feeder*, c.1992, 50 x 200, acrylic on board, 104, commissioned by Southampton University Hospitals NHS Trust, 1992, located in an area where access is not permitted in the interests of patient privacy and dignity

unknown artist, *View from a Window: Hot Air Balloon*, c.1992, 50 x 200, acrylic on board, 103, commissioned by Southampton University Hospitals NHS Trust, 1992, located in an area where access is not permitted in the interests of patient privacy and dignity

unknown artist, *View from a Window: Plants*, c.1992, 50 x 200, acrylic on board, 105, commissioned by Southampton University Hospitals NHS Trust, 1992, located in an area where access is not permitted in the interests of patient privacy and dignity

University of Southampton

Chapman, Vivien, *Still Life*, oil on canvas, 22, not available at the time of photography

Dickens, Rosemary b.1943, *Orange Flower, Marrakesh*, oil on canvas, 26, not available at the time of photography

Donaldson, Antony b.1939, *Starr Queen for Jenny Davis*, 1962, 72 x 72, oil on board, 27, not available at the time of photography

Elwell, Brian b.1938, *Plant Improvisation*, oil on canvas, 29, not available at the time of photography

Facing page: Arcimboldo, Giuseppe, c.1527–1593, *Summer* (detail), Southampton City Art Gallery, (p. 11)

Gilt Mark, Mary, *An Extensive Frostly Landscape*, oil on board, 36, not available at the time of photography

Hay, Peter Alexander 1866–1952, *Reverend H. Livesey*, oil, 37, not available at the time of photography

Kidner, Michael b.1917, *Untitled*, oil on canvas, 40, not available at the time of photography

Mendez, Theo 1934–1997, *Pintura 302*, oil on canvas, 46, not available at the time of photography

Palmer, Garrick b.1933, *Painting 1*, oil on canvas, 49, not available at the time of photography

Palmer, Garrick b.1933, *Painting 2*, oil on canvas, 50, not available at the time of photography

Perry, Roy 1935–1993, *Winter Landscape*, 55 x 71, oil on board, 55, not available at the time of photography

Rydzewski, Pamela, *The Black Sun*, oil on canvas 63, not available at the time of photography

Saunders, Alasdair, *Nude Figure*, oil on board, 65, not available at the time of photography

Smith, Ray b.1947, *Mural Scheme*, acrylic, 12, not available at the time of photography

Wakefield, Larry 1925–1997, *Red Painting*, oil on canvas, 76, not available at the time of photography

Wilson, Frank Avray, b.1914, *Long Painting*, oil on canvas, 80, not available at the time of photography

Healing Arts, Isle of Wight NHS Primary Care Trust

Dean, Audrey active 1973–1985, *House in the Forest*, 50 x 75, oil on canvas, temp101, donated by the artist, 1985, not available at the time of photography

Heckford, Michael, *Harbour, Greek Island*, 1954, 101 x 306, oil on board, temp102, commissioned for Ryde Hospital Eye Clinic, 1950s, not available at the time of photography

Johnson, Sara b.1957, *Body Electric*, 1991, 56 x 75.5, acrylic on paper, 980, purchased from the artist, mid-1990s, not available at the time of photography

Kutzner, Frank, *Summer Flowers*, oil on board, temp98, purchased from the artist, 1987, not available at the time of photography

Miller, Stuart b.1964, *Book of Dreams*, oil on board, temp87, donated by the artist, not available at the time of photography

Nicoll, Stephen b.1946, *Ward Signs (6 paintings in total), 1. Binstead, 2. Whippingham, 3. Alverstone, 4. Luccombe, 5. Newport, 6. Kingston*, all 60 x 60, acrylic on MDF, not available at the time of photography

Power, Ronald 1914–1989, *Fen Dyke*, oil on board, temp93, bequeathed by the artist, late 1980s, not available at the time of photography

Power, Ronald 1914–1989, *The Fishermen*, 95 x 75, oil on canvas, temp94, bequeathed by the artist, late 1980s not available at the time of photography

Power, Ronald 1914–1989, *White Cliffs*, oil on canvas, temp86, bequeathed by the artist, late 1980s, not available at the time of photography

Sheath, John, *Coastal Scene*, oil on canvas, temp104, donated, 1985, not available at the time of photography

Toms, Anne b.1944, *Bevy of Swans (part 8 of 8)*, mid-1990s, oil on panel, temp349, commissioned with a grant, mid-1990s, not available at the time of photography

Toms, Anne b.1944, *Pair of Swans*, acrylic on board, temp72, commissioned, mid-1990s, not available at the time of photography

Wright, Peter b.1932, *Tennyson Down* , oil on canvas, temp59, donated, mid-1990s, not available at the time of photography

Further Information

The paintings listed in this section have additional information relating to one or more of the five categories outlined below. This extra information is only provided where it is applicable and where it exists. Paintings listed in this section follow the same order as in the illustrated pages of the catalogue.

I The full name of the artist if this was too long to display in the illustrated pages of the catalogue. Such cases are marked in the catalogue with a (...).

II The full title of the painting if this was too long to display in the illustrated pages of the catalogue. Such cases are marked in the catalogue with a (...).

III Acquisition information or acquisition credit lines as well as information about loans, copied from the records of the owner collection.

IV Artist copyright credit lines where the copyright owner has been traced. Exhaustive efforts have been made to locate the copyright owners of all the images included within this catalogue and to meet their requirements. Any omissions or mistakes brought to our attention will be duly attended to and corrected in future publications.

V The credit line of the lender of the transparency if the transparency has been borrowed. Bridgeman images are available subject to any relevant copyright approvals from the Bridgeman Art Library at www.bridgeman.co.uk

Solent Sky Aviation Museum

Appleton, Norman b.1926, *Spitfire MkIIa and Spitfire MkFXIVe*, © the artist
Bradbury, C. *DH Moth*
Bromley, Mark *Spirit of the Solent*
Brown, Stuart b.1966, *Spitfire over Suez*, © the artist
Cozens, G. A. *Supermarine Swift*
Davis, P. *Spitfire over Castle Bromwich, Birmingham*
Eastman, Mary active c.1932–1979, *Air Chief Marshall Sir John Boothman (1901–1957), KCB, KBE, DFC, ATC*
Gilbery, Michael 1913–2000, *Sir Alliott Verdon-Roe OBE (1877–1958)*, © the artist's estate
Green, W. A. *Spitfire 2 of 19 Squadron*
Green, W. A. *Imperial Airways Atalanta*
Green, W. A. *Moth*
Hatchard, David b.1945, *Vertical Take-off*, © the artist
Hatchard, David b.1945, *Up Close and Personal*, © the artist
Hatchard, David b.1945, *Spitfire Prototype over Southampton Airport*, © the artist
Mitchell, Jim *Aircraft Montage*
Pannell, J. P. M *Seaplane at the Pier*
Prub *Preparing for Action*
Prub *Spitfire VIII*
Toomer, A. J. *Spitfire*
Toomer, A. J. *Plane Crash*
unknown artist mid-20th C, *In Remembrance of 1940*
unknown artist *Bristol Freighter at Lydd Airfield*
Webb *Seaplane*
Wilson, Stanley active 1943–1944, *Australian Infantryman, Halifax*
Wilson, Stanley active 1943–1944, *A Devonshire Golly*
Wilson, Stanley active 1943–1944, *8th Army Gunner*
Young, John b.1930, *Spitfire Prototype Over the Needles*

Southampton City Art Gallery

Adams, Norman 1927–2005, *The Trumpet*, bequeathed through the National Art Collections Fund, 1991, © the artist's estate
Allegretto di Nuzio c.1315–1373, *The Coronation of the Virgin*, purchased with the assistance of the Frederick William Smith Bequest Fund, 1951
Allinson, Adrian Paul 1890–1959, *Zinnias*, presented by J. Vassell Adams, 1976
Anguissola, Sofonisba c.1532–1625, *The Artist's Sister in the Garb of a Nun*, purchased with the assistance of the Chipperfield Bequest Fund, 1936
Appleyard, Frederick 1874–1963, *Landscape*, donated by Ivor Williams, 1978
Arcimboldo, Giuseppe c.1527–1593, *Summer*, bequeathed by Arthur Tilden Jeffress, 1963
Arcimboldo, Giuseppe (follower of) c.1527–1593, *The Sense of Smell*, bequeathed by Arthur Tilden Jeffress, 1963
Armfield, Maxwell Ashby 1882–1972, *The Tower (Trees, Lucca)*, bequeathed by Dr David and Liza Brown, 2002, © the artist's estate/www.bridgeman.co.uk
Armfield, Maxwell Ashby 1882–1972, *Central Park, New York*, purchased with the assistance of the Victoria & Albert Museum/MGC Purchase Grant Fund, 1976, © the artist's estate/www.bridgeman.co.uk
Armfield, Maxwell Ashby 1882–1972, *Bunch of White*, bequeathed by Dr David and Liza Brown, 2002, © the artist's estate/www.bridgeman.co.uk
Armfield, Maxwell Ashby 1882–1972, *'Pacific Patterns', the Artist's House at Berkeley, California*, bequeathed by Dr David and Liza Brown, 2002, © the artist's estate/www.bridgeman.co.uk
Arthur, J. D. active 1909, *A Bit of Thun, Switzerland*, bequeathed by Robert Chipperfield, 1911
Arthur, J. D. active 1909, *A Bit of Thun, Switzerland*, bequeathed by Robert Chipperfield, 1911
Arthur, J. D. active 1909, *A River, Switzerland*, bequeathed by Robert Chipperfield, 1911
Arthur, J. D. active 1909, *Cottage at Studland*, bequeathed by Robert Chipperfield, 1911
Arthur, J. D. active 1909, *Landscape*, bequeathed by Robert Chipperfield, 1911
Arthur, J. D. active 1909, *Old Bay*, bequeathed by Robert Chipperfield, 1911
Atkinson, Lawrence 1873–1931, *Landscape*, purchased with the assistance of the Victoria & Albert Museum/MGC Purchase Grant Fund, 1979
Auerbach, Frank Helmuth b.1931, *JYM1*, purchased with the assistance of the Chipperfield Bequest Fund, 1982, © the artist
Austin, Samuel 1796–1834, *View of Southampton from near the Baths*, donated by the Libraries Department, 1969
Austin, Samuel 1796–1834, *View of Southampton from the End of the New Pier*, donated by the Libraries Department, 1969
Ayres, Gillian b.1930, *Hinba*, purchased with the assistance of the Victoria & Albert Museum/MGC Purchase Grant Fund, 1979, © the artist
Ayres, Gillian b.1930, *Kintraw*, bequeathed by Dr David and Liza Brown, 2002, © the artist
Ayres, Gillian b.1930, *Untitled*, bequeathed by Dr David and Liza Brown, 2002, © the artist
Ayrton, Michael 1921–1975, *Landscape with a Pig*, purchased with the assistance of the Chipperfield Bequest Fund, 1947, © the artist's estate
Bachmann, Adolphe b.c.1880, *Venice, Riva degli Schiavoni and the Doge's Palace*, bequeathed by Arthur Tilden Jeffress, 1963
Banting, John 1902–1972, *Time for Tea (Foliage Fantasy)*, purchased by the Friends of Southampton Museums and Galleries, 2002
Barker, Joseph (attributed to) 1782–1809, *Landscape*
Barker, Thomas 1769–1847, *Young Children*, purchased with the assistance of the Chipperfield Bequest Fund, 1936
Barker, Thomas 1769–1847, *Catching Colts*, purchased with the assistance of the Frederick William Smith Bequest Fund, 1936
Barker, Thomas 1769–1847, *Riderless Horse after the Battle of Sedan*, donated by Captain and Mrs N. F. H. Charlier, 1946
Barker, Thomas 1769–1847, *The Edge of the Common*, purchased with the assistance of the Chipperfield Bequest Fund, 1952
Barns-Graham, Wilhelmina 1912–2004, *Glacier Vortex*, bequeathed by Dr David and Liza Brown, 2002, © by courtesy of the Barns-Graham Charitable Trust
Bateman, James 1893–1959, *Haytime in the Cotswolds*, purchased with the assistance of the Chipperfield Bequest Fund, 1939
Batt, Arthur 1846–1911, *Good Companions*, bequeathed by Sir James Lemon, JP, 1923
Batt, Arthur 1846–1911, *Terrier Asleep and Collie Dozing before the Fire*, bequeathed by Miss A. B. Williamson, 1940
Batt, Arthur 1846–1911, *Terrier Watching Rabbit Trap*, bequeathed by Miss A. B. Williamson, 1940
Batt, Arthur 1846–1911, *The Empty Bucket*, bequeathed by Miss A. B. Williamson, 1940
Bauchant, André 1873–1958, *Lucretia*, bequeathed by Arthur Tilden Jeffress, 1963, © ADAGP, Paris and DACS, London 2007
Bayes, Walter 1869–1956, *Parisian Fountain*, purchased with the assistance of the Victoria & Albert Museum/MGC Purchase Grant Fund, 2000, © the artist's estate
Bell, Vanessa 1879–1961 & **Grant, Duncan** 1885–1978 *Bacchanale*,

purchased with the assistance of the Chipperfield Bequest Fund, 1972, © 1961 estate of Vanessa Bell courtesy Henrietta Garnett, © 1978 estate of Duncan Grant
Bell, Vanessa 1879–1961 & **Grant, Duncan** 1885–1978 *Children Arranging Flowers*, purchased with the assistance of the Chipperfield Bequest Fund, 1972, © 1961 estate of Vanessa Bell courtesy Henrietta Garnett, © 1978 estate of Duncan Grant
Bell, Vanessa 1879–1961 & **Grant, Duncan** 1885–1978 *Father and Child*, purchased with the assistance of the Chipperfield Bequest Fund, 1972, © 1961 estate of Vanessa Bell courtesy Henrietta Garnett, © 1978 estate of Duncan Grant
Bell, Vanessa 1879–1961 & **Grant, Duncan** 1885–1978 *The Toilet of Venus*, purchased with the assistance of the Chipperfield Bequest Fund, 1972, © 1961 estate of Vanessa Bell courtesy Henrietta Garnett, © 1978 estate of Duncan Grant
Bell, Vanessa 1879–1961 & **Grant, Duncan** 1885–1978 *Vase and Flowers*, purchased with the assistance of the Chipperfield Bequest Fund, 1972, © 1961 estate of Vanessa Bell courtesy Henrietta Garnett, © 1978 estate of Duncan Grant
Bellany, John b.1942, *Bethel*, purchased with the assistance of the Victoria & Albert Museum/ MGC Purchase Grant Fund, 1979, © the artist/www.bridgeman.co.uk
Bellini, Giovanni 1431–1436–1516, *Madonna and Child*, donated by HM Government, 1980
Beresford, Frank Ernest 1881–1967, *Reginald Joseph Mitchell, CBE (1895–1937) Aeronautical Engineer*, presented by Mr W. Naezer, 1951
Berman, Eugene 1899–1972, *Perspective Nocturne*, bequeathed by Arthur Tilden Jeffress, 1963
Bevan, Robert Polhill 1865–1925, *Mydlow Village, Poland*, purchased with the assistance of the Chipperfield Bequest Fund, 1952
Bevan, Robert Polhill 1865–1925, *A Sale at Tattersalls*, purchased with the assistance of the Chipperfield Bequest Fund, 1952
Bevan, Robert Polhill 1865–1925, *Cumberland Market, North Side*, purchased with the assistance of the Chipperfield Bequest Fund, 1947
Bigge, John Selby 1892–1973, *Composition*, purchased with the assistance of the National Art Collections Fund, 2005, © the artist's estate
Blackman, M. S. active c.1900, *Robert J. Chipperfield*
Blamey, Norman Charles 1914–1999, *Vesting Priest with Apparelled Amice*, purchased with the assistance of the Victoria & Albert Museum/MGC Purchase Grant Fund, 1993, © estate of Norman Blamey/Licensed by DACS 2007
Blanche, Jacques-Emile 1861–1942, *Yachts at Weymouth*, bequeathed by Arthur Tilden Jeffress, 1963, © ADAGP, Paris and DACS, London 2007
Boddington, Henry John 1811–1865, *Farm Scene*
Bomberg, David 1890–1957, *Interior of the Armenian Church*, bequeathed by Dr David and Liza Brown, 2002, © the artist's family
Bomberg, David 1890–1957, *Flower Group*, donated by the Contemporary Art Society, 1982, © the artist's family
Bomberg, David 1890–1957, *Cyprus*, purchased with the assistance of the Frederick William Smith Bequest Fund, 1960, © the artist's family
Bomberg, David 1890–1957, *Spanish Gypsy Woman*, bequeathed by Dr David and Liza Brown, 2002, © the artist's family
Bomberg, David 1890–1957, *Zahara Evening*, bequeathed by Dr David and Liza Brown, 2002, © the artist's family
Bone, Stephen 1904–1958, *Air-Sea Rescue Launch 'D' Type*, donated by the War Artists Advisory Committee, 1947
Bone, Stephen 1904–1958, *Trawler's Twelve Pounder*, donated by the War Artists Advisory Committee, 1947
Bone, Stephen 1904–1958, *Three Trawlers*, donated by the War Artists Advisory Committee, 1947
Bonnard, Pierre 1867–1947, *Deux chiens*, bequeathed by Arthur Tilden Jeffress, 1963, © ADAGP, Paris and DACS, London 2007
Bornfriend, Jacob 1904–1976, *Fruit*, purchased with the assistance of the Chipperfield Bequest Fund, 1954
Boudin, Eugène Louis 1824–1898, *Women Awaiting Fishing Boats on Berck Beach*, purchased with the assistance of the National Art Collections Fund, 1986
Boudin, Eugène Louis 1824–1898, *Marine effet de lune*, purchased with the assistance of the Frederick William Smith Bequest Fund, 1932
Boudin, Eugène Louis 1824–1898, *Port d'Honfleur*, presented by the National Art Collections Fund, 2003
Boudin, Eugène Louis 1824–1898, *Vessels and Horses on the Shoreline*, presented by the National Art Collections Fund, 2003
Box, Eden 1919–1988, *Stranger on the Shore*, donated by the artist, 1976
Boyd, Arthur Merric 1862–1940, *Australian Landscape*, bequeathed through the National Art Collections Fund, 2006
Brangwyn, Frank 1867–1956, *Yellow Dahlias*, purchased with the assistance of the Chipperfield Bequest Fund, 1932, © courtesy of the artist's estate/www.bridgeman.co.uk
Bratby, John Randall 1928–1992, *Jean and Still Life in front of a Window*, bequeathed by Arthur Tilden Jeffress, 1963, © the artist's estate/www.bridgeman.co.uk
Bratby, John Randall 1928–1992, *Canvas Reflected in a Window*, purchased with the assistance of the Frederick William Smith Bequest Fund, 1959, © the artist's estate/www.bridgeman.co.uk
Bratby, John Randall 1928–1992, *Swim Pool*, bequeathed by Arthur Tilden Jeffress, 1963, © the artist's estate/www.bridgeman.co.uk
Breanski, Alfred de 1852–1928, *Evening Repose, Burnham Beeches*, bequeathed by Sir James Lemon, JP, 1923
Breanski, Alfred de 1852–1928, *Golden Sunset, Loch Lubnaig*, donated by Mr E. H. Rose, 1936
Brent, Ralph Richard Angus b.1903, *Repairing the Bridge*, donated by the artist, 1977
Bridell, Frederick Lee 1831–1863, *Henry Rose*, presented by an anonymous donor
Bridell, Frederick Lee 1831–1863, *View of Southampton*, donated by Mrs A. N. Gannon, 1950
Bridell, Frederick Lee 1831–1863, *Autumn Evening*, donated by Richard Andrews, 1933
Bridell, Frederick Lee 1831–1863, *The Fisherman's House*, purchased with the assistance of the Frederick William Smith Bequest Fund, 1926
Bridell, Frederick Lee 1831–1863, *The Charcoal Burners*, donated by the Southampton Art Committee, 1920
Bridell, Frederick Lee 1831–1863, *The Lake of Constance*, purchased by an anonymous donor, 1950
Bridell, Frederick Lee 1831–1863, *The Coliseum at Rome by Moonlight*, purchased with the assistance of the Frederick William Smith Bequest Fund, 1932
Bridell, Frederick Lee 1831–1863, *The Temple of Vesta, Tivoli*, donated by the Frederick William Smith Bequest Fund, 1921
Bridell, Frederick Lee 1831–1863, *In the Austrian Tyrol*, donated by Sir Wyndham Dunstan, 1942
Bridell, Frederick Lee 1831–1863, *Lake Como, Sweet Chestnuts*, purchased by William Borrough Hill, 1910
Bridell, Frederick Lee 1831–1863, *Mountainside, Lake and Rocks*, purchased by William Borrough Hill, 1910
Bridell, Frederick Lee 1831–1863, *Mrs Gilroy of Southampton*, bequeathed by Edith Henstock, 1942
Bridell, Frederick Lee 1831–1863, *Quarry, Civita Castellana*, purchased by William Borrough Hill, 1906
Bridell, Frederick Lee 1831–1863, *Study of a Picture in the Collection of Sir Theodore Martin*, purchased by William Borrough Hill, 1910
Bridell, Frederick Lee 1831–1863, *The Forest on Fire*, donated by Harry Stratton Perkins, 1932
Bridell, Frederick Lee 1831–1863, *Tivoli*, purchased by William Borrough Hill, 1910
Bril, Paul 1554–1626, *Hilly Landscape with a Shepherd*, purchased by William Borrough Hill, 1910
British School *Isle of Wight*, bequeathed by Mayo-Porcelli, 1914
British School 18th C, *Boy with Cricket Bat*, presented by Mrs E. Bamforth, 1955
British School 18th C, *Classical Landscape with Cattle*, purchased with the assistance of the Frederick William Smith Bequest Fund, 1934
British School 18th C, *Farmyard Scene (The White Horse)*, bequeathed by Mayo-Porcelli, 1914
British School 18th C, *Portrait of a Man*
British School 18th C, *Portrait of a Man*, purchased with the assistance of the Chipperfield Bequest Fund, 1904
British School 18th C, *Portrait of a Man*, presented by David Minlore, 1942
British School 18th C, *The Setters*, bequeathed by Mayo-Porcelli, 1914
British School 19th C, *Alderman Samuel Michael Emanuel*, bequeathed, 1894
British School *Mrs Samuel Michael Emanuel*, bequeathed, 1894
British School 19th C, *After the Hunt*, bequeathed by Miss A. B. Williamson, 1940
British School 19th C, *Alderman Joseph Rankin Stebbing*, presented, 1903
British School 19th C, *Alderman Steptoe*
British School 19th C, *Alderman Thomas White Miles*
British School 19th C, *Charles Dickens (1812–1870)*, bequeathed by Sir James Lemon, JP, 1923
British School 19th C, *Children Roaming Heath*, bequeathed by Robert Chipperfield, 1911
British School 19th C, *Departure of the 'Mayflower', 1620*, presented by Councillor G. Waller, 1931
British School 19th C, *Diana Asleep in a Woodland Glade*, bequeathed by Arthur Tilden Jeffress, 1963
British School 19th C, *Fishing Boat Scene*, bequeathed by Robert Chipperfield, 1911
British School 19th C, *Fishing Scene, Early Morning*, presented by Mrs W. E. Sandell, 1950
British School 19th C, *Girl with Pigeons*, bequeathed by Robert Chipperfield, 1911
British School 19th C, *Horses in Stable*, presented by Lady Milner-White, 1939
British School 19th C, *Italian Landscape (Lake Como)*, bequeathed by Leonard William Lankester, 1939
British School 19th C, *John Henry Cooksey Esq.*, presented, 1895
British School 19th C, *John Joliffe Esq.*, presented, 1907
British School 19th C, *John Traffles Tucker Esq., Mayor (1853)*
British School 19th C, *Lake Como, Italy*, purchased with the assistance of the Frederick William Smith Bequest Fund, 1926
British School 19th C, *Landscape with Figure of a Woman*
British School 19th C, *Mr Andrews*, bequeathed by Richard Andrews, 1933
British School 19th C, *Mrs Andrews*, bequeathed by Richard Andrews, 1933
British School 19th C, *Old Shirley, Southampton*, presented by Lady Milner-White, 1939
British School 19th C, *Porchester Castle*, bequeathed by Robert Chipperfield, 1911
British School 19th C, *Portrait of a Lady*, bequeathed, 1979
British School 19th C, *River Itchen*, bequeathed by Robert Chipperfield, 1911
British School 19th C, *Samson Payne, Mayor of Southampton*, presented by Mr G. Maitland Payne, 1929
British School 19th C, *'San Jacinto' and 'Trent Affair'*, purchased with the assistance of the Frederick William Smith Bequest Fund, 1935
British School 19th C, *Ship Ashore*, bequeathed by Robert Chipperfield, 1911
British School 19th C, *Sir Frederick Perkins* (detail)
British School 19th C, *'The Bell' Inn*, bequeathed by Robert Chipperfield, 1911
British School 19th C, *The Fortune Teller*, bequeathed by Robert Chipperfield, 1911
British School 19th C, *The Round Pool, Kensington Gardens*, presented by Mrs Toomer, 1941
British School 19th C, *Three Monks*, bequeathed by Robert Chipperfield, 1911
British School 19th C, *William Charles Macready (1793–1873)*, bequeathed by Robert Chipperfield, 1911
Brockhurst, Gerald Leslie 1890–1978, *The Albert Bridge*, purchased with the assistance of the Frederick William Smith Bequest Fund, 1953
Brockhurst, Gerald Leslie 1890–1978, *Portrait of a Girl*, purchased with the assistance of the Chipperfield Bequest Fund, 1938
Brooks, Frank 1854–1937, *Alderman Mrs L. Foster Welch, JP*, presented by an anonymous donor, 1931
Brooks, Frank 1854–1937, *Misty Morning, Cader Idris*, purchased with the assistance of the Frederick

William Smith Bequest Fund, 1933
Brooks, Maria 1837–1913, *Out in the Rain*, bequeathed by Robert Chipperfield, 1911
Brown, Ford Madox 1821–1893, *Cordelia's Portion*, purchased with the assistance of the Frederick William Smith Bequest Fund, 1936
Brown, Jean *David Brown*, bequeathed by Dr David and Liza Brown, 2002
Brown, John Alfred Arnesby 1866–1955, *Spring*, purchased with the assistance of the Frederick William Smith Bequest Fund, 1934
Brundrit, Reginald Grange 1883–1960, *Autumn by the River*, purchased with the assistance of the Chipperfield Bequest Fund, 1931
Buckley, Stephen b.1944, *V S A*, © the artist
Buhler, Robert A. 1916–1989, *Robert Kitchener*, purchased with the assistance of the Chipperfield Bequest Fund, 1947, © the artist's estate/www.bridgeman.co.uk
Burcher, Frank P. *H. J. Buchan, Mayor of Southampton (1871)*, donated by Miss Alice Mary Buchan, 1932
Burne-Jones, Edward 1833–1898, *Lancelot at the Chapel of the Holy Grail*, bequeathed by Graham Robertson, 1958
Bylandt, Alfred Edouard Agenor van 1829–1890, *Wagon and Team*, bequeathed by Robert Chipperfield, 1911
Cameron, David Young 1865–1945, *Autumn Snows, Menteith*, purchased with the assistance of the Chipperfield Bequest Fund, 1936
Campbell, Steven b.1953, *The Fall of the House of Nook with Tree Blight*, purchased with the assistance of the Victoria & Albert Museum/MGC Purchase Grant Fund, 1985, © the artist
Campigli, Massimo 1895–1971, *Three Figures*, bequeathed by Arthur Tilden Jeffress, 1963, © DACS 2007
Carpenter, Patrick active 1939–1946, *Ammunition Column Moving out*, donated by the War Artists Advisory Committee, 1947
Carr, Henry Marvell 1894–1970, *Merchant Navy, the Bridge*, donated by the War Artists Advisory Committee, 1947
Carr, Thomas 1909–1999, *Wet Day*, purchased with the assistance of the Chipperfield Bequest Fund, 1947, © the estate of Thomas Carr
Cassana, Niccolò (copy after) 1659–1713, *Portrait of an Artist*
Cesare da Sesto 1477–1523, *St Jerome*, purchased with the assistance of the Chipperfield Bequest Fund, 1958
Chamberlain, Christopher 1918–1984, *Middlesborough*, purchased with the assistance of the Frederick William Smith Bequest Fund, 1953
Chambers, George 1803–1840, *Portsmouth*, donated by Mr F. J. Nettlefold, 1948
Chambers, H. P. (Mrs) *Antiques*, donated by Gilbert Mahon, 1939
Chambers, H. P. (Mrs) *Chrysanthemums*, donated by Gilbert Mahon, 1939
Chapman, George 1908–1993, *Old Woman Passing*, purchased with the assistance of the Gulbenkian Foundation, 1967, © Nicholas Chapman
Charlton, Alan b.1948, *Slot Painting*, presented by Gilbert and George, 1985, © the artist
Chubb, Ralph Nicholas 1892–1960, *The Bathers*, donated by the artist, 1954
Claes, Constant Guillaume 1826–1905, *Man Smoking*
Clare, George c.1830–c.1900, *Basket with Flowers*, bequeathed by Robert Chipperfield, 1911
Clare, George c.1830–c.1900, *Grapes*, bequeathed by Robert Chipperfield, 1911
Cleveley, John c.1712–1777, *'HMS Brune' Captures French Ship 'L'oiseau'*, purchased with the assistance of the Frederick William Smith Bequest Fund, 1935
Clough, Prunella 1919–1999, *Plinth*, purchased with the assistance of the Frederick William Smith Bequest Fund, 1996, © estate of Prunella Clough 2007. All rights reserved DACS
Coldstream, William Menzies 1908–1987, *E. A. Smith-Rewse*, purchased with the assistance of the Frederick William Smith Bequest Fund, 1969, © courtesy of the artist's estate/www.bridgeman.co.uk
Cole, George 1810–1883, *Still Life with Pheasant*, donated by Miss E. M. Welch, 1943
Cole, George 1810–1883, *Evening in Hampshire*, purchased with the assistance of the Frederick William Smith Bequest Fund, 1933
Cole, Leslie 1910–1976, *Naval Base: Women's Royal Naval Service Sick Bay*, donated by the War Artists Advisory Committee, 1947
Cole, Rex Vicat 1870–1940, *London from Waterloo Park, Highgate*, donated by Dr J. A. Danby, 1968
Collier, John 1850–1934, *Lady Darling*, donated by Mrs L. Pulteney, 1950
Collins, Cecil 1908–1989, *Flowers*, bequeathed by Dr David and Liza Brown, 2002, © TATE, London 2007
Collins, Cecil 1908–1989, *Portrait of the Artist*, bequeathed by Dr David and Liza Brown, 2002, © TATE, London 2007
Colquhoun, Ithell 1906–1988, *Rivières tièdes (Mediterranée)*, purchased with the assistance of the Frederick William Smith Bequest Fund, 1977, © the artist's estate
Conroy, Stephen b.1964, *The Australian*, bequeathed by Dr David and Liza Brown, 2002, © the artist
Conroy, Stephen b.1964, *Self Portrait*, bequeathed by Dr David and Liza Brown, 2002, © the artist
Cook, Richard 1784–1857, *High Street and Bargate, Southampton*, purchased with the assistance of the Chipperfield Bequest Fund, 1945
Cooper, Herbert *The Butcher's Van*, bequeathed by Dr David and Liza Brown, 2002
Copnall, Frank T. 1870–1949, *Sir Russell Bencraft, JP*, donated by Sir Russell Bencraft, 1943
Corot, Jean-Baptiste-Camille 1796–1875, *Ville d'Avray*, donated by the National Art Collections Fund, 1972
Corot, Jean-Baptiste-Camille 1796–1875, *Breakwater in Normandy*, purchased with the assistance of the Chipperfield Bequest Fund, 1947
Corot, Jean-Baptiste-Camille (after) 1796–1875, *Landscape*, bequeathed by Mrs W. Phillips, 1953
Courbet, Gustave 1819–1877, *La vague*, presented by Peter and Lies Askonas, 2004
Courbet, Gustave (imitator of) 1819–1877, *Seapiece at Honfleur*, purchased with the assistance of the Chipperfield Bequest Fund, 1938
Craft, Percy Robert 1856–1934, *Birds and Hare*, donated by the artist, 1934
Craig-Martin, Michael b.1941, *Untitled Painting No.1*, purchased with the assistance of the Frederick William Smith Bequest Fund, 1976, © the artist
Craxton, John b.1922, *Dark Landscape*, donated by the Contemporary Art Society, 1950, © John Craxton 2007. All rights reserved, DACS
Crook, Frederick *Villefranche*
Crumplin, Colin b.1946, *Cake*, donated by the artist, 1997, © the artist
Cundall, Charles Ernest 1890–1971, *Stevedores, Marseilles*, purchased with the assistance of the Frederick William Smith Bequest Fund, 1933, © courtesy of the artist's estate/www.bridgeman.co.uk
Cundall, Charles Ernest 1890–1971, *Barnet Fair*, purchased with the assistance of the Frederick William Smith Bequest Fund, 1939, © courtesy of the artist's estate/www.bridgeman.co.uk
Cundall, Charles Ernest 1890–1971, *Christmas Preparations at Beaulieu*, purchased with the assistance of the Frederick William Smith Bequest Fund, 1933, © courtesy of the artist's estate/www.bridgeman.co.uk
Cundall, Charles Ernest 1890–1971, *Repairing a Submarine*, donated by the War Artists Advisory Committee, 1947, © courtesy of the artist's estate/www.bridgeman.co.uk
Curradi, Francesco 1570–1661, *Tobias and the Angel*, donated by Mrs D. Villiers, 1953
Dalton, R. *Landscape*
Dalton, R. *River Scene*
Daniels, Leonard 1909–1998, *A British Restaurant at Winchester*, donated by the War Artists Advisory Committee, 1947
Dannatt, George b.1915, *Citadel No.5 (St Malo)*, presented by Mr and Mrs George Dannatt, 2006, © the artist
Daubigny, Charles-François 1817–1878, *On the Loire*, purchased with the assistance of the Frederick William Smith Bequest Fund, 1967
Davenport, Ian b.1966, *Poured Lines Painting*, purchased with the assistance of the Frederick William Smith Bequest Fund, 1996, © the artist, 2007
Davie, Alan b.1920, *Bird Singing*, bequeathed by Dr David and Liza Brown, 2002, © the artist
Davies, Peter b.1970, *Overlapping Grey Squares Painting*, purchased, 1998, © the artist
Davis, Peter b.1972, *0626-B01G Diamante*, presented by the artist, 1996
Davis, William 1812–1873, *Breakwater Scene*, bequeathed by Robert Chipperfield, 1911
Dawson, Montague J. 1895–1973, *'HMS Collingwood'*, purchased with the assistance of the Frederick William Smith Bequest Fund, 1939, © the artist's estate
Dawson, Montague J. 1895–1973, *The Forecastle Head*, purchased with the assistance of the Frederick William Smith Bequest Fund, 1934, © the artist's estate
De Karlowska, Stanislawa 1876–1952, *Polish Interior*, presented by Mr R. A. Bevan, 1968, © the artist's estate/www.bridgeman.co.uk
De Wint, Peter 1784–1849, *A Cornfield with Figures in Sunlight*, purchased with the assistance of the Chipperfield Bequest Fund, 1937
Deacon, George S. active 1860s–1879, *Charles Ewens, Esq., Town Clerk (1838–1870)*
Delaney, Barbara b.1941, *The Meeting of the Dragon, the Bull and the Anteater*, purchased with the assistance of the Orris Bequest, 2005, © the artist
Delvaux, Paul 1897–1994, *A Siren in Full Moonlight*, bequeathed by Arthur Tilden Jeffress, 1963, © Foundation P. Delvaux - St Idesbald, Belgium/DACS, London 2007
Delvaux, Paul 1897–1994, *Annunciation*, bequeathed by Arthur Tilden Jeffress, 1963, © Foundation P. Delvaux - St Idesbald, Belgium/DACS, London 2007
Denny, Robyn b.1930, *Time of Day III*, presented by the Arnolfini Collection Trust, 2001, © the artist
Desiderio, Monsù 1590–1644 or **Nomé, François de** c.1593–after 1644 or **Barra, Didier** c.1590–after 1652, *The Martyrdom of St Catherine*, purchased with the assistance of the Chipperfield Bequest Fund, 1948
Dicksee, Frank 1853–1928, *Romeo and Juliet*, bequeathed by Mr J. J. Crossfield, 1941
Dietrich, Gustave Otto b.1860, *Lake Scene*
Dingle, Thomas active 1846–1888, *The Nearest Way Home*, bequeathed by Robert Chipperfield, 1911
Dingwall, Kenneth b.1938, *Edinburgh Blue II*, purchased with the assistance of the Chipperfield Bequest Fund, 1979
Dodgson, John Arthur 1890–1969, *Still Life with Dessert*, presented by Stephen Dodgson, 1997, © the artist's estate
Dodgson, John Arthur 1890–1969, *Berkhampstead Garden*, bequeathed by Mrs Ann Valentine Harvey, 2005, © the artist's estate
Dodgson, John Arthur 1890–1969, *A Visit to the Studio*, presented by Stephen Dodgson, 1997, © the artist's estate
Dodgson, John Arthur 1890–1969, *Untitled*, presented by Stephen Dodgson, 1997, © the artist's estate
Doig, Peter b.1959, *Girl on Skis*, purchased with the assistance of the Chipperfield Bequest Fund, 1999
Doll, Anton Eduard 1826–1887, *Skating Scene*, presented by Mrs E. Schroeder, 1984
Dongen, Kees van 1877–1968, *Woman in Venice*, bequeathed by Arthur Tilden Jeffress, 1963, © ADAGP, Paris and DACS, London 2007
Douglas, Rose active 1893–1898, *Group by Rowing Boat*, donated by Mrs Lavington, 1945
Douglas, Rose active 1893–1898, *Pulling Rowboat Ashore*, donated by Mrs Lavington, 1945
Drew, Mary active 1880–1901, *I Cannot Play Alone*, bequeathed by Robert Chipperfield, 1911
Dring, William D. 1904–1990, *Self Portrait*, purchased with the assistance of the Victoria & Albert Museum/MGC Purchase Grant Fund, 2000, © courtesy of the artist's estate/www.bridgeman.co.uk
Dring, William D. 1904–1990, *Queen Mary (1867–1953) (after Luke Fildes)*, donated by the War Artists Advisory Committee, 1947, © courtesy of the artist's estate/www.bridgeman.co.uk
Drummond, Malcolm 1880–1945, *Charles Ginner (1878–1952)*, purchased with the assistance of the Frederick William Smith Bequest Fund, 1956, © the artist's estate
Drummond, Malcolm 1880–1945, *Girl Dressing*, purchased with the assistance of the Victoria & Albert Museum/MGC Purchase Grant

Fund, 1975, © the artist's estate
Drummond, Malcolm 1880–1945, *In the Park (St James' Park)*, purchased with the assistance of the Frederick William Smith Bequest Fund, 1953, © the artist's estate
Drummond, Malcolm 1880–1945, *Backs of Houses, Chelsea*, purchased with the assistance of the Frederick William Smith Bequest Fund, 1952, © the artist's estate
Drummond, Malcolm 1880–1945, *Fields and Road, Penn Street*, purchased with the assistance of the Victoria & Albert Museum/MGC Purchase Grant Fund, 1998, © the artist's estate
Drummond, Malcolm 1880–1945, *Wooded Pond*, purchased with the assistance of the Victoria & Albert Museum/MGC Purchase Grant Fund, 1998, © the artist's estate
Du Plessis, Enslin 1894–1978, *Mecklenburgh Square, Winter*, purchased with the assistance of the Chipperfield Bequest Fund, 1947
Dugdale, Thomas Cantrell 1880–1952, *Alderman Sir Sidney Kimber, JP*, presented by an anonymous donor, 1939, © Joanna Dunham
Dughet, Gaspard 1615–1675, *Landscape of the Roman Campagna*, purchased with the assistance of the Chipperfield Bequest Fund, 1959
Duncalf, Stephen b.1950, *The Workshop*, bequeathed by Dr David and Liza Brown, 2002, © the artist
Dutch School 18th C, *Dutch Wedding*, presented by Miss Smith, 1944
Dyce, William 1806–1864, *The Honourable Charlotte Noel*, purchased with the assistance of the Chipperfield Bequest Fund, 1933
Dyck, Anthony van 1599–1641, *Portrait of a Man*, purchased with the assistance of the Chipperfield Bequest Fund, 1953
Dyck, Anthony van 1599–1641, *Portrait of a Woman*, purchased with the assistance of the Chipperfield Bequest Fund, 1953
Eatwell, John b.1923, *Blue Mystery*, purchased with the assistance of the Chipperfield Bequest Fund, 1977
Eeckhout, Jacobus Josefus 1793–1861, *Man Writing*
Elk, Ger van b.1941, *Gilbert and George*, presented by Gilbert and George, 1985
Elleby, William Alfred active 1883–1903, *Early Summer*, bequeathed by Robert Chipperfield, 1911
Ellis, Paul H. active 1871–1908, *Eastern Sunset*, presented by Miss Morgan, 1906
Emms, John 1843–1912, *Girl with Two Hounds*, presented by Miss G. Emms, 1964
Emms, John 1843–1912, *Dogs Watching Bathers*, bequeathed by Mr H. L. Saltern, 1906
Emms, John 1843–1912, *George Primmer*, donated by Miss M. Emms, 1955
Emms, John 1843–1912, *Hounds Feeding*, bequeathed by Mr H. L. Saltern, 1906
Emms, John 1843–1912, *Hunting, New Forest*, bequeathed by Mr H. L. Saltern, 1906
Emms, John 1843–1912, *Portrait of a Lady*
Emms, John 1843–1912, *Portrait of a Man*
Emms, John 1843–1912, *Rest after Sport*, purchased with the assistance of the Frederick William Smith Bequest Fund, 1925
Emms, John 1843–1912, *Shepherd and Dogs*, bequeathed by Mr H. L. Saltern, 1906
Emms, John 1843–1912, *Stag Hunt, New Forest*, bequeathed by Mr H. L. Saltern, 1906
Emms, John 1843–1912, *Young Hounds Playing*, bequeathed by Mr H. L. Saltern, 1906
Emsley, Walter active 1883–1927, *Last of the Cottage Handloom Weavers of Lancashire*, presented by Mrs Emsley, 1945
Enness, Augustus William 1876–1948, *From a Lakeland Window: Hydrangeas*, purchased with the assistance of the Frederick William Smith Bequest Fund, 1935
Enness, Augustus William 1876–1948, *Langdale*, purchased with the assistance of the Frederick William Smith Bequest Fund, 1934
Enness, Augustus William 1876–1948, *Ludlow Castle*, purchased with the assistance of the Frederick William Smith Bequest Fund, 1934
Etty, William 1787–1849, *The World before the Flood*, purchased with the assistance of the Chipperfield Bequest Fund, 1937
Eurich, Richard Ernst 1903–1992, *Mrs Green*, bequeathed by Dr David and Liza Brown, 2002, © courtesy of the artist's estate/www.bridgeman.co.uk
Eurich, Richard Ernst 1903–1992, *Old Fawley Mill*, purchased with the assistance of the Chipperfield Bequest Fund, 1946, © courtesy of the artist's estate/www.bridgeman.co.uk
Eurich, Richard Ernst 1903–1992, *The Maze*, purchased with the assistance of the Victoria & Albert Museum/MGC Purchase Grant Fund, 1983, © courtesy of the artist's estate/www.bridgeman.co.uk
Eurich, Richard Ernst 1903–1992, *The Wreck of the 'Herzogin Cecilie'*, purchased with the assistance of the Frederick William Smith Bequest Fund, 1949, © courtesy of the artist's estate/www.bridgeman.co.uk
Evans, Richard 1784–1871, *Portrait of a Man*, donated by W. Frank Perkins, 1947
Everdingen, Cesar Boetius van c.1606–1678, *Allegory of Winter*, purchased with the assistance of the Chipperfield Bequest Fund, 1937
Everett, Edith M. Leeson b.1881, *Lady Swaythling*, donated by Lady Swaythling, 1927
Falkner, Anne L. active 1922, *The Lunch Hour*, donated by the artist
Fantin-Latour, Henri 1836–1904, *Yellow Roses*, donated by the National Art Collections Fund, 1973
Fantin-Latour, Henri 1836–1904, *Homage to Rubens*, purchased with the assistance of the Chipperfield Bequest Fund, 1938
Farquharson, Jean Boswell *Portrait of a Young Girl*, purchased with the assistance of the Chipperfield Bequest Fund, 1930
Fedden, Mary b.1915, *White Roses*, donated by Lady Bonham Carter, 1988, © the artist
Ferg, Franz de Paula 1689–1740, *Landscape*, bequeathed by Mayo-Porcelli, 1914
Ferg, Franz de Paula 1689–1740, *Landscape*, bequeathed by Mayo-Porcelli, 1914
Fergusson, John Duncan 1874–1961, *Street at Night*, purchased with the assistance of the Frederick William Smith Bequest Fund, 1967, © the Fergusson Gallery, Perth and Kinross Council, Scotland
Fergusson, John Duncan 1874–1961, *A Girl with Black Hair*, purchased with the assistance of the Frederick William Smith Bequest Fund, 1972, © the Fergusson Gallery, Perth and Kinross Council, Scotland
Ferry, John active 1897–1929, *Woodmill*, bequeathed by Robert Chipperfield, 1911
Fetti, Domenico c.1589–1623, *Rebecca at the Well*, purchased with the assistance of the Chipperfield Bequest Fund, 1936
Fielding, Anthony V. C. 1787–1855, *Vessels on Shore near Southampton*, donated by Mr F. J. Nettlefold, 1948
Fildes, Luke 1844–1927, *Annie Winifred Marsden-Smedley*, bequeathed by Miss A. A. Crossley, 1999
Flemish School 16th C, *Pietà*
Flemish School 17th C, *Winter Landscape with the Nativity*, purchased with the assistance of the Chipperfield Bequest Fund, 1951
Flint, William Russell 1880–1969, *Nomads' Rendezvous*, purchased with the assistance of the Chipperfield Bequest Fund, 1932
Forabosco, Girolamo c.1605–1679, *Portrait of a Lady*, purchased with the assistance of the Chipperfield Bequest Fund, 1934
Forain, Jean Louis 1852–1931, *The Fisherman*, purchased with the assistance of the Chipperfield Bequest Fund, 1936
Fox, George c.1816–1910, *'Many signs but nothing shown'*, bequeathed by Robert Chipperfield, 1911
Francis, Mark b.1962, *Growth Study*, purchased with the assistance of the Frederick William Smith Bequest Fund, 1999, © Mark Francis
Fraser, Donald Hamilton b.1929, *Beach with Cloud Banks and Cliffs*, presented by the Contemporary Art Society, 1957
French School *The Three Cupids*, purchased with the assistance of the Frederick William Smith Bequest Fund, 1933
Freud, Lucian b.1922, *Bananas*, bequeathed by Arthur Tilden Jeffress, 1963, © Lucian Freud
Friesz, Othon 1879–1949, *Rochers de Noron*, purchased with the assistance of the Frederick William Smith Bequest Fund, 1960, © ADAGP, Paris and DACS, London 2007
Frost, Terry 1915–2003, *Silver and Grey*, bequeathed by Dr David and Liza Brown, 2002, © the artist's estate
Froy, Martin b.1926, *Model Resting*, donated by the Contemporary Art Society, 1959, © the artist
Fry, Roger Eliot 1866–1934, *Fort Saint André, Villeneuve lez Avignon*, bequeathed by Dr David and Liza Brown, 2002
Fryer, Calvin W. 1871–1942, *Talbot Woods*, bequeathed by Robert Chipperfield, 1911
Fussell, Michael 1927–1974, *Still Life*, purchased with the assistance of the Corporation Rate Fund, 1979
Gainsborough, Thomas 1727–1788, *George Venables Vernon*, purchased with the assistance of the National Art Collections Fund, 1957
Gear, William 1915–1997, *Winter Landscape*, purchased with the assistance of the Frederick William Smith Bequest Fund, 1964, © the artist's estate
Gelb, Georg *Swiss Scene*, bequeathed by Robert Chipperfield, 1911
Gérard, François 1770–1837, *Napoleon (1769–1821)*, bequeathed by Arthur Tilden Jeffress, 1963
Gerrard, Kaff 1894–1970, *Corn Stooks*, presented by Professor Gerrard, 1991
Gerrard, Kaff 1894–1970, *Landscape with Pink Trees*, presented by Professor Gerrard, 1991
Gerrard, Kaff 1894–1970, *Seascape with Cliffs*, presented by Professor Gerrard, 1991
Gerrard, Kaff 1894–1970, *The Circumcision*
Gertler, Mark 1892–1939, *The Rabbi and His Grandchild*, purchased with the assistance of the Chipperfield Bequest Fund, 1954, © by permission of Luke Gertler
Gertler, Mark 1892–1939, *Seated Nude*, purchased with the assistance of the Chipperfield Bequest Fund, 1954, © by permission of Luke Gertler
Gertler, Mark 1892–1939, *Still Life with Bust*, purchased with the assistance of the Chipperfield Bequest Fund, 1953, © by permission of Luke Gertler
Gertler, Mark 1892–1939, *Family Group*, purchased with the assistance of the Frederick William Smith Bequest Fund, 1953, © by permission of Luke Gertler
Giaquinto, Corrado 1703–1765, *Virgin and Child with an Angel*, purchased with the assistance of the Victoria & Albert Museum/MGC Purchase Grant Fund, 1970
Gilbert, Joseph Marc *Queen Victoria (1819–1901)*, anonymous bequest
Gilman, Harold 1876–1919, *Interior*, purchased with the assistance of the Chipperfield Bequest Fund, 1937
Gilman, Harold 1876–1919, *The Breakfast Table*, purchased with the assistance of the Chipperfield Bequest Fund, 1948
Gilman, Harold 1876–1919, *Sylvia Gosse (1881–1968)*, purchased with the assistance of the Chipperfield Bequest Fund, 1950
Ginner, Charles 1878–1952, *The Barges, Leeds*, purchased with the assistance of the Victoria & Albert Museum/MGC Purchase Grant Fund, 1974
Ginner, Charles 1878–1952, *Early Morning*, purchased with the assistance of the Chipperfield Bequest Fund, 1969
Ginner, Charles 1878–1952, *The Albert Memorial*, purchased with the assistance of the Chipperfield Bequest Fund, 1967
Ginner, Charles 1878–1952, *Landscape*, donated by the Contemporary Art Society, 1964
Girvin, Joy b.1961, *Evening in the Borghese Gardens*, bequeathed by Dr David and Liza Brown, 2002, © the artist
Girvin, Joy b.1961, *Plas Brondanw*, bequeathed by Dr David and Liza Brown, 2002, © the artist
Glendening, Alfred Augustus I c.1840–c.1910, *Autumn, Arundel Park*, bequeathed by Robert Chipperfield, 1911
Glendening, Alfred Augustus I c.1840–c.1910, *In the Meadow, Youngsbury*, bequeathed by Robert Chipperfield, 1911
Glendening, Alfred Augustus I c.1840–c.1910, *Llyn Mymbyr, Capel Curig*, purchased with the assistance of the Chipperfield Bequest Fund, 1911
Golding, John b.1929, *Asphodel*, purchased with the assistance of the Gulbenkian Foundation, 1967, © the artist
Goodwin, William Sidney 1833–1916, *The Great Carbuncle*, bequeathed by W. S. Goodwin, 1916
Goodwin, William Sidney 1833–1916, *Landing of the Treasure*,

bequeathed by W. S. Goodwin, 1916
Goodwin, William Sidney 1833–1916, *The Rukh's Egg*, bequeathed by W. S. Goodwin, 1916
Goodwin, William Sidney 1833–1916, *Sinbad on the Raft*, bequeathed by W. S. Goodwin, 1916
Goodwin, William Sidney 1833–1916, *Stormy Sunset, New Forest*, bequeathed by W. S. Goodwin, 1916
Gore, Frederick b.1913, *Olive Trees, Les Baux*, purchased with the assistance of the Chipperfield Bequest Fund, 1948
Gore, Spencer 1878–1914, *Panshanger Park*, purchased with the assistance of the Frederick William Smith Bequest Fund, 1933
Gore, Spencer 1878–1914, *View from a Window*, purchased with the assistance of the Chipperfield Bequest Fund, 1938
Gore, Spencer 1878–1914, *Brighton Pier*, purchased with the assistance of the Frederick William Smith Bequest Fund, 1956
Gosse, Laura Sylvia 1881–1968, *Fountain, Saule*, bequeathed by Dr David and Liza Brown, 2002, © the artist's estate/www.bridgeman.co.uk
Gosse, Laura Sylvia 1881–1968, *From the Garden, Morning, Dieppe*, purchased with the assistance of the Frederick William Smith Bequest Fund, 1973, © the artist's estate/www.bridgeman.co.uk
Gosse, Laura Sylvia 1881–1968, *Street Scene, Dieppe*, purchased with the assistance of the Frederick William Smith Bequest Fund, 1973, © the artist's estate/www.bridgeman.co.uk
Gotlib, Henryk 1890–1966, *The Lake*, presented by the artist, © the artist's estate
Gotlib, Henryk 1890–1966, *Three Nudes*, donated by Janet Gotlib, 1996, © the artist's estate
Gotto, Basil 1866–1954, *Our Charlady*, purchased with the assistance of the Frederick William Smith Bequest Fund, 1940
Grace, Frances Lily active 1876–1909, *Watching the Birds*, bequeathed by Robert Chipperfield, 1911
Grant, Duncan 1885–1978, *Parrot Tulips*, presented by the Contemporary Art Society, 1954, © 1978 estate of Duncan Grant
Grant, Duncan 1885–1978, *Still Life*, purchased with the assistance of the Frederick William Smith Bequest Fund, 1972, © 1978 estate of Duncan Grant
Grant, Duncan 1885–1978, *Angelica Playing the Violin*, bequeathed by Lord Romilly, 1984, © 1978 estate of Duncan Grant
Grant, Duncan 1885–1978, *Thames Wharves*, purchased with the assistance of the Chipperfield Bequest Fund, 1937, © 1978 estate of Duncan Grant
Grant, Duncan 1885–1978, *Mrs Hammersley*, purchased with the assistance of the Chipperfield Bequest Fund, 1938, © 1978 estate of Duncan Grant
Grant, Duncan 1885–1978, *Still Life, Flowers in a Vase*, donated by Lady Bonham Carter, 1988, © 1978 estate of Duncan Grant
Grant, Duncan 1885–1978, *The White Jug*, bequeathed by Dr David and Liza Brown, 2002, © 1978 estate of Duncan Grant
Gray, H. Barnard active 1844–1871, *Lane near Kenilworth*, purchased by Robert Chipperfield, 1911
Greaves, Derrick b.1927, *Woman in a Red Hat with a Baby*, purchased with the assistance of the Frederick William Smith Bequest Fund, 1958, © the artist
Greaves, Walter 1846–1930, *Thames*, donated by Mr Benjamin Rhodes, 1979
Green, Anthony b.1939, *The Dinner Party*, purchased with the assistance of the Gulbenkian Foundation, 1967, © the artist
Greenham, Peter 1909–1992, *The Cheviots*, bequeathed by Dr David and Liza Brown, 2002, © the artist's estate/www.bridgeman.co.uk
Greenham, Peter 1909–1992, *Limeuil*, bequeathed by Dr David and Liza Brown, 2002, © the artist's estate/www.bridgeman.co.uk
Greenham, Peter 1909–1992, *Old Lady in Black*, bequeathed by Dr David and Liza Brown, 2002, © the artist's estate/www.bridgeman.co.uk
Greenham, Peter 1909–1992, *Portrait of an Old Lady*, purchased with the assistance of the Victoria & Albert Museum/MGC Purchase Grant Fund, 1982, © the artist's estate/www.bridgeman.co.uk
Gribble, Bernard Finegan 1873–1962, *A Well-Known Subject at Southampton*, purchased with the assistance of the Frederick William Smith Bequest Fund, 1940
Gribble, Bernard Finegan 1873–1962, *Poole Harbour*, purchased with the assistance of the Frederick William Smith Bequest Fund, 1933
Griffith, Frank 1889–1979, *Jaqueline*, donated, 1997
Grigg, Edgar P. active 1939–1940, *Flower Study*, presented by the artist, 1939
Grigg, Edgar P. active 1939–1940, *The Sculptor*, presented by the artist, 1939
Gross, Anthony 1905–1984, *Blue Rocks*, purchased with the assistance of the Gulbenkian Foundation, 1966, © Anthony Gross, RA, CBE - painter/etcher
Guthrie, Derek b.1936, *ICI Tanker*, presented by the Contemporary Art Society, 1965, © the artist
Gwynne-Jones, Allan 1892–1982, *Flowers in a Jam Jar*, bequeathed by Dr David and Liza Brown, 2002, © the artist's estate/www.bridgeman.co.uk
Gwynne-Jones, Allan 1892–1982, *Winter Landscape, Suffolk*, bequeathed by Dr David and Liza Brown, 2002, © the artist's estate/www.bridgeman.co.uk
Gwynne-Jones, Allan 1892–1982, *Still Life: A Jug, Teacup and Shells*, bequeathed by Dr David and Liza Brown, 2002, © the artist's estate/www.bridgeman.co.uk
Hackaert, Jan 1629–1699, *The Avenue*, purchased with the assistance of the Chipperfield Bequest Fund, 1934
Haile, Samuel 1909–1948, *Les automobilistes*, presented by Mrs Marianne Haile (the artist's widow), 1968
Hall, Frederick 1860–1948, *King Edward VII (1841–1910)*, presented by Alderman George Hussey, 1902, © the artist's estate/www.bridgeman.co.uk
Hambling, Maggi b.1945, *Untitled*, bequeathed by Dr David and Liza Brown, 2002, © the artist
Hambling, Maggi b.1945, *Mac with Shadows*, purchased from the artist, 1982, © the artist
Hambling, Maggi b.1945, *Catherine Parkinson*, bequeathed by Dr David and Liza Brown, 2002, © the artist
Hamnett, Nina 1890–1956, *Horace Brodzky*, presented by Denys Sutton, 1957, © the artist's estate/www.bridgeman.co.uk
Harcourt, George 1868–1947, *Sir Hubert von Herkomer, RA (1849–1914)*, purchased with the assistance of the Frederick William Smith Bequest Fund, 1934
Harmar, Fairlie 1876–1945, *La Bretonne*, presented by Mrs Cowlard (the artist's sister), 1950
Harper, Ed b.1970, *Sebert Road*, purchased with the assistance of the Orris Bequest, 2005, © the artist
Harpignies, Henri-Joseph 1819–1916, *Environs de Saint Pierre, Yonne*, purchased with the assistance of the Chipperfield Bequest Fund, 1954
Harris, Jane b.1956, *'Fandango'*, purchased with the assistance of the Chipperfield Bequest Fund, 2002
Hart, Thomas Gray 1797–1881, *Kilchurn Castle*
Hart, Thomas Gray 1797–1881, *South-East Tower, Town Quay*
Hartry, Edith active 1883–1919, *A Quiet Afternoon*, bequeathed by Robert Chipperfield, 1911
Hartry, Edith active 1883–1919, *Kitchen of a Dutch Barge*, presented by the artist, 1919
Hartry, Edith active 1883–1919, *The Catechism*, presented by the artist, 1919
Hayes, Edwin 1820–1904, *Howth Head*, presented by Captain and Mrs N. F. H. Charlier, 1946
Hayllar, James 1829–1920, *Rival Drinks*, bequeathed by Robert Chipperfield, 1911
Hayllar, James 1829–1920, *Old Fir Trees*, bequeathed by Robert Chipperfield, 1911
Hayllar, Mary active 1880–1885, *The Lawn Tennis Season*, bequeathed by Robert Chipperfield, 1911
Hayman, Francis c.1708–1776, *'Robert Lovelace Preparing to Abduct…'*, purchased with the assistance of the Chipperfield Bequest Fund, 1965
Hayman, Patrick 1915–1988, *Lovers by the Sea with a Hawk*, bequeathed by Dr David and Liza Brown, 2002, © DACS 2007
Hayman, Patrick 1915–1988, *The Heroes of Thermopylae*, bequeathed by Dr David and Liza Brown, 2002, © DACS 2007
Hayman, Patrick 1915–1988, *The Four Evangelists*, bequeathed by Dr David and Liza Brown, 2002, © DACS 2007
Hays, Dan b.1966, *Colorado Impression 12a (Sunrise, Beaver Creek, 11 September 2002)*, purchased with the assistance of the National Art Collections Fund, 2004
Hayward, Alfred Robert 1875–1971, *Château Gaillard*, purchased with the assistance of the Chipperfield Bequest Fund, 1931
Hayward, Alfred Robert 1875–1971, *St Mark's, Venice*, purchased with the assistance of the Frederick William Smith Bequest Fund, 1934
Heath, Adrian 1920–1992, *Composition 1952 (Rotating Forms)*, bequeathed by Dr David and Liza Brown, 2002, © the estate of Adrian Heath
Heath, Adrian 1920–1992, *Composition with Black and Purple*, purchased with the assistance of the Frederick William Smith Bequest Fund, 1976, © the estate of Adrian Heath
Heem, Jan Davidsz. de (attributed to) 1606–1683/1684, *Still Life*, purchased with the assistance of the Chipperfield Bequest Fund, 1959
Heintz, Joseph the elder 1564–1609, *The Four Elements*, presented by the National Art Collections Fund, 1975
Heintz, Joseph the younger c.1600–1678, *Venetian Regatta at the Rialto Bridge*, bequeathed by Arthur Tilden Jeffress, 1963
Herbert, Alfred c.1820–1861, *Hay Barges in the Thames Estuary*, presented by Lieutenant Colonel A. Stethe Wart Cox, RFA, 1942
Herkomer, Hubert von 1849–1914, *Portrait of a Boy*, donated by Mrs L. Herkomer, 1964
Herkomer, Hubert von 1849–1914, *Alderman Sir George Hussey*, presented by Alderman Sir George Hussey, 1901
Herkomer, Hubert von 1849–1914, *Souvenir of Watts*, purchased with the assistance of the Frederick William Smith Bequest Fund, 1935
Herkomer, Hubert von 1849–1914, *Farmyard*, purchased with the assistance of the Frederick William Smith Bequest Fund, 1935
Herkomer, Hubert von 1849–1914, *Lorenz Herkomer*, presented by Lady Herkomer, 1930
Herkomer, Hubert von 1849–1914, *Study of a Lord Mayor*, purchased with the assistance of the Frederick William Smith Bequest Fund, 1935
Herman, Josef 1911–2000, *The Bridge, Ystradgynlais*, purchased with the assistance of the Chipperfield Bequest Fund, 1948, © the artist's estate
Herman, Josef 1911–2000, *Miners*, bequeathed by Dr David and Liza Brown, 2002, © the artist's estate
Herman, Josef 1911–2000, *Reece Pemberton*, bequeathed by Mrs M. K. Pemberton, 2005, © the artist's estate
Heron, Patrick 1920–1999, *Black and Dull Green with Two Circles*, presented by the Contemporary Art Society, 1972, © estate of Patrick Heron 2007. All rights reserved, DACS
Herring, John Frederick I 1795–1865, *Wild Horses*
Hicks, George Elgar 1824–1914, *Self Portrait, Aged 22*, presented by Miss Annie Hicks, 1942
Hicks, George Elgar 1824–1914, *Portrait of Second Son*, presented by Miss Annie Hicks, 1942
Hicks, George Elgar 1824–1914, *Study of an Italian Man's Head*, presented by Miss Annie Hicks, 1942
Hicks, George Elgar 1824–1914, *Girl Seated*, presented by Miss Annie Hicks, 1942
Hicks, George Elgar 1824–1914, *Girl Seated by Shore*, presented by Miss Annie Hicks, 1942
Hicks, George Elgar 1824–1914, *Mother and Baby*, presented by Miss Annie Hicks, 1942
Hicks, George Elgar 1824–1914, *Boy in Sailor's Costume*, presented by Miss Annie Hicks, 1942
Hicks, George Elgar 1824–1914, *Seated Girl*, presented by Miss Annie Hicks, 1942
Hicks, George Elgar 1824–1914, *Seated Woman and Two Children*, presented by Miss Annie Hicks, 1942
Hicks, George Elgar 1824–1914, *Seated Woman Holding Dish*, presented by Miss Annie Hicks, 1942
Hicks, George Elgar 1824–1914, *Seated Woman in Chair*, presented by Miss Annie Hicks, 1942
Hicks, George Elgar 1824–1914, *Seated Woman in White Dress*, presented by Miss Annie Hicks, 1942
Hicks, George Elgar 1824–1914, *Sketch of Mrs Chas Rose's Two Boys*, presented by Miss Annie Hicks, 1942
Hicks, George Elgar 1824–1914,

Woman and Semi-Nude Child, presented by Miss Annie Hicks, 1942
Hicks, George Elgar 1824–1914, *Woman in White Dress with Red Sash*, presented by Miss Annie Hicks, 1942
Hicks, George Elgar 1824–1914, *Lady in White Dress Holding Flowers*, presented by Miss Annie Hicks, 1942
Hicks, George Elgar 1824–1914, *Mrs Park Yates*, presented by Miss Annie Hicks, 1942
Hicks, George Elgar 1824–1914, *Annie Hicks*, presented by Miss Annie Hicks, 1942
Hicks, George Elgar 1824–1914, *Miss Harrison*, presented by Miss Annie Hicks, 1942
Hicks, George Elgar 1824–1914, *Child's Head*, presented by Miss Annie Hicks, 1942
Hicks, George Elgar 1824–1914, *A Sussex Interior*, presented by Miss Annie Hicks, 1942
Hicks, George Elgar 1824–1914, *An Old Man's Head*, presented by Miss Annie Hicks, 1942
Hicks, George Elgar 1824–1914, *Baby*, presented by Miss Annie Hicks, 1942
Hicks, George Elgar 1824–1914, *Baby and Child Playing*, presented by Miss Annie Hicks, 1942
Hicks, George Elgar 1824–1914, *Biblical Study*, presented by Miss Annie Hicks, 1942
Hicks, George Elgar 1824–1914, *Boy in Sailor's Uniform*, presented by Miss Annie Hicks, 1942
Hicks, George Elgar 1824–1914, *Child in Red Costume*, presented by Miss Annie Hicks, 1942
Hicks, George Elgar 1824–1914, *Child with Ball*, presented by Miss Annie Hicks, 1942
Hicks, George Elgar 1824–1914, *Edward Hicks, DD, DCL*, presented by Miss Annie Hicks, 1942
Hicks, George Elgar 1824–1914, *Five Children Playing in the Forest*, presented by Miss Annie Hicks, 1942
Hicks, George Elgar 1824–1914, *Girl and Boy with Violin*, presented by Miss Annie Hicks, 1942
Hicks, George Elgar 1824–1914, *Group of Children by Seashore*, presented by Miss Annie Hicks, 1942
Hicks, George Elgar 1824–1914, *Group of Roses*, presented by Miss Annie Hicks, 1942
Hicks, George Elgar 1824–1914, *Group with Baby*, presented by Miss Annie Hicks, 1942
Hicks, George Elgar 1824–1914, *Group with Baby*, presented by Miss Annie Hicks, 1942
Hicks, George Elgar 1824–1914, *Lady in White Dress*, presented by Miss Annie Hicks, 1942
Hicks, George Elgar 1824–1914, *Lady in White Dress*, presented by Miss Annie Hicks, 1942
Hicks, George Elgar 1824–1914, *Lady in White Dress*, presented by an anonymous donor, 1942
Hicks, George Elgar 1824–1914, *Lady in White Dress with Blue Sash*, presented by Miss Annie Hicks, 1942
Hicks, George Elgar 1824–1914, *Lady in White Dress with Hat*, presented by Miss Annie Hicks, 1942
Hicks, George Elgar 1824–1914, *Lady in White Shawl*, presented by Miss Annie Hicks, 1942
Hicks, George Elgar 1824–1914, *Lady with Parasol*, presented by Miss Annie Hicks, 1942
Hicks, George Elgar 1824–1914, *Lady with Red Book*, presented by Miss Annie Hicks, 1942
Hicks, George Elgar 1824–1914, *Lady with Small Girl*, presented by an anonymous donor, 1942
Hicks, George Elgar 1824–1914, *Mother and Child*, presented by Miss Annie Hicks, 1942
Hicks, George Elgar 1824–1914, *Mother and Child*, presented by Miss Annie Hicks, 1942
Hicks, George Elgar 1824–1914, *Mother and Child*, presented by Miss Annie Hicks, 1942
Hicks, George Elgar 1824–1914, *Mother and Child*, presented by Miss Annie Hicks, 1942
Hicks, George Elgar 1824–1914, *Mother with Child in Pink Dress*, presented by Miss Annie Hicks, 1942
Hicks, George Elgar 1824–1914, *Mother with Child in White Dress*, presented by Miss Annie Hicks, 1942
Hicks, George Elgar 1824–1914, *Mrs Ridley*, presented by Miss Annie Hicks, 1942
Hicks, George Elgar 1824–1914, *Portrait of a Lady*, presented by Miss Annie Hicks, 1942
Hicks, George Elgar 1824–1914, *Rose Gordon Hicks*, presented by Miss Annie Hicks, 1942
Hicks, George Elgar 1824–1914, *Seated Figure in Red and Black*, presented by Miss Annie Hicks, 1942
Hicks, George Elgar 1824–1914, *Seated Girl*, presented by Miss Annie Hicks, 1942
Hicks, George Elgar 1824–1914, *Seated Girl*, presented by Miss Annie Hicks, 1942
Hicks, George Elgar 1824–1914, *Seated Girl*, presented by Miss Annie Hicks, 1942
Hicks, George Elgar 1824–1914, *Seated Girl in White Dress*, presented by Miss Annie Hicks, 1942
Hicks, George Elgar 1824–1914, *Seated Girl in Wood*, presented by Miss Annie Hicks, 1942
Hicks, George Elgar 1824–1914, *Seated Lady*, presented by Miss Annie Hicks, 1942
Hicks, George Elgar 1824–1914, *Seated Lady by Tree*, presented by Miss Annie Hicks, 1942
Hicks, George Elgar 1824–1914, *Seated Lady in White Dress*, presented by Miss Annie Hicks, 1942
Hicks, George Elgar 1824–1914, *Seated Lady in White Shawl*, presented by Miss Annie Hicks, 1942
Hicks, George Elgar 1824–1914, *Seated Lady with Flowers*, presented by Miss Annie Hicks, 1942
Hicks, George Elgar 1824–1914, *Seated Woman*, presented by Miss Annie Hicks, 1942
Hicks, George Elgar 1824–1914, *Seated Woman and Child*, presented by Miss Annie Hicks, 1942
Hicks, George Elgar 1824–1914, *Seated Woman in Black Dress*, presented by Miss Annie Hicks, 1942
Hicks, George Elgar 1824–1914, *Seated Woman in White Dress*, presented by Miss Annie Hicks, 1942
Hicks, George Elgar 1824–1914, *Seated Woman in Wood*, presented by Miss Annie Hicks, 1942
Hicks, George Elgar 1824–1914, *Self Portrait at the Age of 75*, presented by Miss Annie Hicks, 1942
Hicks, George Elgar 1824–1914, *Sketch for 'Entreat Me Not to Leave Thee'*, presented by Miss Annie Hicks, 1942
Hicks, George Elgar 1824–1914, *Sketch of Reclining Woman*, presented by Miss Annie Hicks, 1942
Hicks, George Elgar 1824–1914, *Standing Woman*, presented by Miss Annie Hicks, 1942
Hicks, George Elgar 1824–1914, *Standing Woman in White Dress*, presented by Miss Annie Hicks, 1942
Hicks, George Elgar 1824–1914, *Standing Woman with Fan*, presented by Miss Annie Hicks, 1942
Hicks, George Elgar 1824–1914, *Standing Woman with Red Cloak*, presented by Miss Annie Hicks, 1942
Hicks, George Elgar 1824–1914, *Three Children*, presented by Miss Annie Hicks, 1942
Hicks, George Elgar 1824–1914, *Three Children and Dog*, presented by Miss Annie Hicks, 1942
Hicks, George Elgar 1824–1914, *Three Young Cricketers*, presented by Miss Annie Hicks, 1942
Hicks, George Elgar 1824–1914, *Two Children*, presented by Miss Annie Hicks, 1942
Hicks, George Elgar 1824–1914, *Two Girls Standing*, presented by Miss Annie Hicks, 1942
Hicks, George Elgar 1824–1914, *Two Ladies*, presented by an anonymous donor, 1942
Hicks, George Elgar 1824–1914, *Two Seated Figures with Flowers*, presented by Miss Annie Hicks, 1942
Hicks, George Elgar 1824–1914, *Two Seated Ladies in White Dresses*, presented by Miss Annie Hicks, 1942
Hicks, George Elgar 1824–1914, *Two Women with Easel and Palette*, presented by Miss Annie Hicks, 1942
Hicks, George Elgar 1824–1914, *Woman and Three Children*, presented by Miss Annie Hicks, 1942
Hicks, George Elgar 1824–1914, *Woman in Black and White Dress*, presented by Miss Annie Hicks, 1942
Hicks, George Elgar 1824–1914, *Woman in Black Dress Holding Child*, presented by Miss Annie Hicks, 1942
Hicks, George Elgar 1824–1914, *Woman in Blue Dress with Fan*, presented by Miss Annie Hicks, 1942
Hicks, George Elgar 1824–1914, *Woman in White Dress*, presented by Miss Annie Hicks, 1942
Hicks, George Elgar 1824–1914, *Woman Standing by Balustrade*, presented by Miss Annie Hicks, 1942
Hicks, George Elgar 1824–1914, *Young Girl*, presented by Miss Annie Hicks, 1942
Hicks, George Elgar 1824–1914, *Young Lady in the Forest*, presented by an anonymous donor, 1942
Hicks, George Elgar 1824–1914, *Young Woman's Head*, presented by Miss Annie Hicks, 1942
Hill, Anthony b.1930, *Orthogonal/Diagonal Composition*, bequeathed by Dr David and Liza Brown, 2002, © 2007. All rights reserved, DACS
Hill, Anthony b.1930, *January 1956*, bequeathed by Dr David and Liza Brown, 2002, © 2007. All rights reserved, DACS
Hill, Anthony b.1930, *Untitled*, bequeathed by Dr David and Liza Brown, 2002, © 2007. All rights reserved, DACS
Hill, Derek 1916–2000, *Mrs Mary Miley Mangan*, purchased with the assistance of the Chipperfield Bequest Fund, 1947
Hillier, Tristram Paul 1905–1983, *Chapel of the Misericordia*, bequeathed by Arthur Tilden Jeffress, 1963, © the artist's estate
Hillier, Tristram Paul 1905–1983, *The Green Bottle*, purchased with the assistance of the Frederick William Smith Bequest Fund, 1950, © the artist's estate
Hillier, Tristram Paul 1905–1983, *Portuguese Farmhouse*, bequeathed by Arthur Tilden Jeffress, 1963, © the artist's estate
Hilton, Roger 1911–1975, *Ghislaine and Grey Nude*, bequeathed by Dr David and Liza Brown, 2002, © estate of Roger Hilton 2007. All rights reserved, DACS
Hilton, Roger 1911–1975, *Composition II*, bequeathed by Dr David and Liza Brown, 2002, © estate of Roger Hilton 2007. All rights reserved, DACS
Hilton, Roger 1911–1975, *August 1953*, bequeathed by Dr David and Liza Brown, 2002, © estate of Roger Hilton 2007. All rights reserved, DACS
Hilton, Roger 1911–1975, *October 1953*, bequeathed by Dr David and Liza Brown, 2002, © estate of Roger Hilton 2007. All rights reserved, DACS
Hilton, Roger 1911–1975, *October 1953*, bequeathed by Dr David and Liza Brown, 2002, © estate of Roger Hilton 2007. All rights reserved, DACS
Hilton, Roger 1911–1975, *Black on White, March 1954*, bequeathed by Dr David and Liza Brown, 2002, © estate of Roger Hilton 2007. All rights reserved, DACS
Hilton, Roger 1911–1975, *October 1956*, bequeathed by Dr David and Liza Brown, 2002, © estate of Roger Hilton 2007. All rights reserved, DACS
Hilton, Roger 1911–1975, *Grey Figure, February 1957*, purchased with the assistance of the Victoria & Albert Museum/MGC Purchase Grant Fund, 1962, © estate of Roger Hilton 2007. All rights reserved, DACS
Hilton, Roger 1911–1975, *May 1960*, bequeathed by Dr David and Liza Brown, 2002, © estate of Roger Hilton 2007. All rights reserved, DACS
Hilton, Roger 1911–1975, *December 1961*, bequeathed by Dr David and Liza Brown, 2002, © estate of Roger Hilton 2007. All rights reserved, DACS
Hilton, Roger 1911–1975, *Figure 61*, bequeathed by Dr David and Liza Brown, 2002, © estate of Roger Hilton 2007. All rights reserved, DACS
Hilton, Roger 1911–1975, *July 1961*, bequeathed by Dr David and Liza Brown, 2002, © estate of Roger Hilton 2007. All rights reserved, DACS
Hilton, Roger 1911–1975, *January 1962*, bequeathed by Dr David and Liza Brown, 2002, © estate of Roger Hilton 2007. All rights reserved, DACS
Hilton, Roger 1911–1975, *Figure and Bird*, bequeathed by Dr David and Liza Brown, 2002, © estate of Roger Hilton 2007. All rights reserved, DACS
Hitchens, Ivon 1893–1979, *Arched Trees No.7*, presented by Professor and Mrs C. A. Hackett, 1987, © Ivon Hitchens' estate/Jonathan Clark & Co
Hitchens, Ivon 1893–1979, *Oak Tree in Purple Woods*, purchased with the assistance of the Frederick William Smith Bequest Fund, 1959, © Ivon Hitchens' estate/Jonathan Clark & Co
Hitchens, Ivon 1893–1979, *Vase of Flowers*, presented by Constance Stallard, 1975, © Ivon Hitchens' estate/Jonathan Clark & Co
Hodgkin, Howard b.1932, *The*

Second Visit, presented by the Contemporary Art Society, 2001, © the artist
Hodgkin, Howard b.1932, *Simon Digby Talking, 1972–1975*, presented by the Contemporary Art Society, 1979, © the artist
Hodgkins, Frances 1869–1947, *Purbeck Courtyard Morning*, purchased with the assistance of the Chipperfield Bequest Fund, 1949
Hogley, Stephen E. active 1874–1893, *Going South*, bequeathed by Robert Chipperfield, 1911
Hogley, Stephen E. active 1874–1893, *In the Ogram Valley*, bequeathed by Robert Chipperfield, 1911
Holl, Frank 1845–1888, *Despair*, purchased with the assistance of the Frederick William Smith Bequest Fund, 1936
Holl, Frank 1845–1888, *Hope*, purchased with the assistance of the Frederick William Smith Bequest Fund, 1936
Hornibrook, George Farrington 1842–1882, *York Minster from the Foss*, bequeathed by Robert Chipperfield, 1911
Hoskins, Ned b.1939, *Double Sky Structure*, purchased with the assistance of the Corporation Rate Fund, 1974, © the artist
Hoyland, John b.1934, *16.10.68*, purchased with the assistance of the Frederick William Smith Bequest Fund, 1997, © the artist/www.bridgeman.co.uk
Hubbard, Eric Hesketh 1892–1957, *Eling Wharf*, purchased by the Friends of Southampton Museums and Galleries, 1989
Hughes-Stanton, Herbert Edwin Pelham 1870–1937, *Trépied, Pas de Calais*, purchased with the assistance of the Chipperfield Bequest Fund, 1933
Hunt, William Holman 1827–1910, *Afterglow in Egypt*, presented by Dr H. H. Clarke, 1946
Ibbetson, Julius Caesar 1759–1817, *Distant View of Anglesea*, purchased with the assistance of the Frederick William Smith Bequest Fund, 1949
Innes, Callum b.1962, *Repetition (Grey)*, purchased with the assistance of the Victoria & Albert Museum/MGC Purchase Grant Fund, 1996, © the artist, courtesy of the Sean Kelly Gallery, New York
Innes, Callum b.1962, *Resonance*, purchased with the assistance of the Frederick William Smith Bequest Fund, 1996, © the artist, courtesy of the Sean Kelly Gallery, New York
Innes, James Dickson 1887–1914, *Collioure*, purchased with the assistance of the Chipperfield Bequest Fund, 1951
Italian School 17th C, *Nativity: The Birth of Christ*, presented by E. A. Young, 1931
Italian School 18th C, *Cupid and Putto*, bequeathed by Lady Bonham Carter, 1990
Italian School 18th C, *Fantasy Architectural View*, bequeathed by Arthur Tilden Jeffress, 1963
Italian School 18th C, *Gladiators and Lions*, bequeathed by Arthur Tilden Jeffress, 1963
Italian School 18th C, *Oriental Scene with Figures*, bequeathed by Arthur Tilden Jeffress, 1963
Italian School 18th C, *View of Mole with San Giorgio*, bequeathed by Arthur Tilden Jeffress, 1963
Jackman, Paul active 1864–1878, *Fisherman's Cottage*, presented by Mrs Mary Martyn Collins, 1939
Jacque, Charles Émile 1813–1894, *Shepherd and His Flock*, purchased with the assistance of the Chipperfield Bequest Fund, 1935
James, Walter John 1869–1932, *Valley of the Rede*, presented by the Bliss Family, 1943
Jarman, Derek 1942–1994, *Trick*, presented, 2003
Jay, William Samuel 1843–1933, *Thicket Wood*, presented by Miss E. M. Welch, 1943
Jennings, Humphrey 1907–1950, *Untitled*, donated by the Elephant Trust, 1982, © DACS 2007
John, Augustus Edwin 1878–1961, *Port de Bouc*, purchased with the assistance of the Frederick William Smith Bequest Fund, 1955, © the artist's estate/www.bridgeman.co.uk
John, Augustus Edwin 1878–1961, *Brigit*, purchased with the assistance of the Chipperfield Bequest Fund, 1939, © the artist's estate/www.bridgeman.co.uk
John, Gwen 1876–1939, *Mère Poussepin*, purchased with the assistance of the Chipperfield Bequest Fund, 1954, © estate of Gwen John 2007. All rights reserved, DACS
John, Gwen 1876–1939, *Girl in Mulberry Dress*, purchased with the assistance of the Chipperfield Bequest Fund, 1962, © estate of Gwen John 2007. All rights reserved, DACS
Jones, Allen b.1937, *Pathway*, purchased with the assistance of the Corporation Rate Fund, 1967, © Allen Jones
Jones, Lizzie *The Couple*, purchased with the assistance of the Orris Bequest, 2006
Jones, Philip b.1971, *Orpheus at the Door of the Underworld*, donated by the artist, 1997, © the artist
Jones, Thomas 1742–1803, *View of Portsmouth from Portsdown Hill*, purchased with the assistance of the Chipperfield Bequest Fund, 1955
Jones, W. active before 1911, *Western Shore*, bequeathed by Robert Chipperfield, 1911
Jones, Zebedee b.1970, *Dark Green Gridiron*, purchased with the assistance of the Chipperfield Bequest Fund, 1996
Jordaens, Jacob 1593–1678, *The Holy Family*, purchased with the assistance of the Chipperfield Bequest Fund, 1935
Jordan, Rudolf (attributed to) 1810–1887, *The Engagement*, presented by Mr and Mrs W. J. Fernie, 1942
Joseph, Peter b.1929, *Dark Blue/Black Border No.37*, purchased with the assistance of the Chipperfield Bequest Fund, 1979, © the artist
Kemm, Robert 1837–1895, *At the Steps of the Altar*, bequeathed by Robert Chipperfield, 1911
Kemp-Welch, Lucy 1869–1958, *Timber Run in the Welsh Hills*, purchased with the assistance of the Chipperfield Bequest Fund, 1932, © David Messum
Kennaway, Charles Gray active 1860–1925, *James Patrick Muir*, presented by Captain and Mrs Paul Miller, 1942
Kidner, Michael b.1917, *Brown, Blue and Violet No.2*, purchased with the assistance of the Corporation Rate Fund, 1967, © the artist
Kinley, Peter 1926–1988, *Study for 'Three Houses'*, presented by Mr Jack Lancester, 2006
Knell, William Adolphus 1802–1875, *'HMS Victory'*, bequeathed by Robert Chipperfield, 1911
Knell, William Adolphus 1802–1875, *Lord Hood at Toulon*, purchased with the assistance of the Frederick William Smith Bequest Fund, 1935
Knell, William Adolphus 1802–1875, *Marine Subject*, bequeathed by Robert Chipperfield, 1911
Knell, William Adolphus 1802–1875, *Moonlight at Sea*, bequeathed by Robert Chipperfield, 1911
Knell, William Adolphus 1802–1875, *Moonlight Scene*, bequeathed by Robert Chipperfield, 1911
Knell, William Adolphus 1802–1875, *Seascape*, bequeathed, 1994
Knell, William Adolphus 1802–1875, *Sunset at Sea*, bequeathed by Robert Chipperfield, 1911
Knell, William Adolphus 1802–1875, *Sunset Scene*, bequeathed by Robert Chipperfield, 1911
Knight, John William Buxton 1842/1843–1908, *An English Port, Evening*, purchased with the assistance of the Frederick William Smith Bequest Fund, 1934
Knollys, Eardley 1902–1991, *Distant Spire*, donated by Lady Bonham Carter, 1988
Koekkoek, Barend Cornelis 1803–1862, *View over Heidelberg*, presented by Mr and Mrs W. J. Fernie, 1942
Koninck, Philips de 1619–1688, *An Extensive Landscape*, purchased with the assistance of the Victoria & Albert Museum/MGC Purchase Grant Fund, 1963
Lamb, Henry 1883–1960, *Edie McNeill*, purchased with the assistance of the Chipperfield Bequest Fund, 1938, © estate of Henry Lamb
Lamb, Henry 1883–1960, *Lady Mary Pakenham*, purchased with the assistance of the Chipperfield Bequest Fund, 1973, © estate of Henry Lamb
Lambert, B. *Landscape*, bequeathed by Sir James Lemon, JP, 1923
Lambert, B. *Landscape*, bequeathed by Sir James Lemon, JP, 1923
Laprade, Pierre 1875–1931, *Scene in a Garden*, purchased with the assistance of the Chipperfield Bequest Fund, 1938
Laurence, Sydney Mortimer 1865–1940, *Waves Breaking on Shore, Sunset (detail)*
Lavery, John 1856–1941, *The Countess of Rocksavage*, bequeathed by Arthur Tilden Jeffress, 1963, © the artist's estate
Lavery, John 1856–1941, *Monte Carlo, Afternoon*, purchased with the assistance of the Chipperfield Bequest Fund, 1932, © the artist's estate
Lavery, John 1856–1941, *Miss Betty Shaughnessy*, purchased with the assistance of the Chipperfield Bequest Fund, 1932, © the artist's estate
Lavery, John 1856–1941, *Miss Diana Chamberlain*, purchased with the assistance of the Chipperfield Bequest Fund, 1932, © the artist's estate
Lawrence, Thomas 1769–1830, *Dr John Moore, Archbishop of Canterbury*, purchased with the assistance of the Chipperfield Bequest Fund, 1937
Le Brun, Christopher b.1951, *Sir Tristram*, purchased with the assistance of the Chipperfield Bequest Fund, 1984, © the artist
Lecocq, Adrien Louis 1832–1887, *Landscape*, purchased with the assistance of the Frederick William Smith Bequest Fund, 1934
Lee, Dick 1923–2001, *Gillie*, purchased with the assistance of the Frederick William Smith Bequest Fund, 1958, © the artist's estate
Lee, Moses 1950–1995, *Untitled*, purchased, 1998
Lee, Sydney 1866–1949, *The Wine Store*, purchased with the assistance of the Frederick William Smith Bequest Fund, 1934
Lees, Derwent 1885–1931, *Banyuls*, purchased with the assistance of the Frederick William Smith Bequest Fund, 1949
Lefranc, Jules 1887–1972, *The Pretty Flowergirl*, bequeathed by Arthur Tilden Jeffress, 1963
Leme, Bella Paes b.1910, *Family Group*, presented, 1948
Lépine, Stanislas 1835–1892, *View of Paris*, donated by the Chipperfield Bequest Fund, 1936
Leslie, Clayton *River Scene*, bequeathed by Robert Chipperfield, 1911
Lines, Henry Harris 1801–1889, *Route of St Gotthard, Göschenen*, bequeathed by Miss H. Adams, 1921
Linke, Simon b.1958, *Anselm Kiefer*, bequeathed by Dr David and Liza Brown, 2002, © the artist
Linke, Simon b.1958, *The Estate of Tony Smith*, bequeathed by Dr David and Liza Brown, 2002, © the artist
Linnell, John 1792–1882, *Doctor Robert Walker*, purchased with the assistance of the Frederick William Smith Bequest Fund, 1956
Linnell, William 1826–1906, *The Old Mountain Road*
Lister, Edward d'Arcy b.1911, *Saturday Night*, presented by the John Lewis Partnership, 1958
Loutherbourg, Philip James de 1740–1812, *The Shipwreck*, purchased with the assistance of the Chipperfield Bequest Fund, 1949
Low, Charles c.1860–c.1920, *A Surrey Lane*, bequeathed by Robert Chipperfield, 1911
Lowry, Laurence Stephen 1887–1976, *The Canal Bridge*, purchased with the assistance of the Frederick William Smith Bequest Fund, 1951, © Southampton City Art Gallery
Lowry, Laurence Stephen 1887–1976, *The Floating Bridge, Southampton*, purchased with the assistance of the Chipperfield Bequest Fund, 1956, © the Lowry estate
Lucas, Albert Durer 1828–1919, *Blackberries*, bequeathed by Robert Chipperfield, 1911
Lucas, Albert Durer 1828–1919, *Forget-Me-Nots*, bequeathed by Robert Chipperfield, 1911
Lucas, Albert Durer 1828–1919, *Heather*, bequeathed by Robert Chipperfield, 1911
Lucas, Albert Durer 1828–1919, *Heather*, bequeathed by Robert Chipperfield, 1911
Lucas, Albert Durer 1828–1919, *Heather and Gorse*, bequeathed by Robert Chipperfield, 1911
Lucas, Albert Durer 1828–1919, *Landscape*, bequeathed by Robert Chipperfield, 1911
Lucas, Albert Durer 1828–1919, *Lilies of the Valley*, bequeathed by Robert Chipperfield, 1911
Lucas, Albert Durer 1828–1919, *Oak, Holly and Other Trees*, bequeathed by Robert Chipperfield, 1911
Lucas, Albert Durer 1828–1919, *Primroses*, bequeathed by Robert Chipperfield, 1911
Lucas, Albert Durer 1828–1919, *Vase of Flowers*, bequeathed by Robert Chipperfield, 1911
Lucas, Albert Durer 1828–1919, *Violets*, bequeathed by Robert Chipperfield, 1911
Luny, Thomas 1759–1837, *East Indian 'Cumberland' off Dover, 1803*, presented by Hugh and Colin Agnew, 1948
Lyoncourt, Hubert de *Château de Henat*, presented by Mrs M. J. Matthews, 1930
Maes, Nicolaes 1634–1693, *Portrait*

of a Man, purchased with the assistance of the Frederick William Smith Bequest Fund, 1934

Magill, Elizabeth b.1959, *Forest Edge I*, purchased with the assistance of the Victoria & Albert Museum/MGC Purchase Grant Fund, 2000, © the artist

Maitland, Paul Fordyce 1863–1909, *View on the Thames*, bequeathed by Dr David and Liza Brown, 2002

Makhoul, Bashir b.1963, *Al Hadara*, presented by Mrs Georgie Webb, 2005, © the artist

Manson, James Bolivar 1879–1945, *Self Portrait*, purchased with the assistance of the Frederick William Smith Bequest Fund, 1937

Manson, James Bolivar 1879–1945, *The Garden*, purchased with the assistance of the Chipperfield Bequest Fund, 1934

Marini, Antonio 1668–1725, *Italian Seascape*, purchased with the assistance of the Chipperfield Bequest Fund, 1967

Markó, András 1824–1895, *Swiss Scene*, bequeathed by Robert Chipperfield, 1911

Markó, András 1824–1895, *Swiss Scene*, bequeathed by Robert Chipperfield, 1911

Marshall, John Fitz 1859–1932, *Peaches*, purchased with the assistance of the Chipperfield Bequest Fund, 1911

Marshall, John Fitz 1859–1932, *Plums*, bequeathed by Robert Chipperfield, 1911

Martin, Étienne Philippe 1858–1945, *The Fountain*, purchased with the assistance of the Frederick William Smith Bequest Fund, 1936

Martin, Florence active 1876–1893, *The New Student*, purchased by Robert Chipperfield, 1911

Martin, John 1789–1854, *Sadak in Search of the Waters of Oblivion*, purchased with the assistance of the Chipperfield Bequest Fund, 1949

Martin, Kenneth 1905–1984, *Chance Order Change 10*, purchased with the assistance of the Frederick William Smith Bequest Fund, 1982, © the artist's estate

Maze, Paul Lucien 1887–1979, *The Harbour, Ostende*, purchased with the assistance of the Chipperfield Bequest Fund, 1937

McEvoy, Mary 1870–1941, *Audrey*, purchased with the assistance of the Chipperfield Bequest Fund, 1931

McFadden, Frank active 1879–1894, *Alderman Alfred Leighton McCalmont, JP*, presented by the artist

McFadden, Frank active 1879–1894, *Alderman Dunlop, JP*, presented by the artist

McFadden, Frank active 1879–1894, *R. S. Pearce Esq.*, presented by the artist

McIntyre, James active 1867–1909, *Not Married Yet*, purchased with the assistance of the Chipperfield Bequest Fund

McIntyre, James active 1867–1909, *Landscape*, bequeathed by Sir James Lemon, JP, 1923

McKenna, Stephen b.1939, *'Fourment'*, purchased with the assistance of the Victoria & Albert Museum/MGC Purchase Grant Fund, 1978, © the artist

McLean, Bruce b.1944, *Study for the Object of Exercise*, presented by the Contemporary Art Society, 1983

McLean, John b.1939, *Quadrillion*, purchased by Corporation Funds, 1967, © the artist

Meadus, Eric 1931–1970, *Summer, Swaythling*, purchased by Friends of Southampton Museums and Galleries, 1991, © the artist's estate

Meadus, Eric 1931–1970, *Portrait of a Nurse*, purchased with the assistance of the Frederick William Smith Bequest Fund, 1975, © the artist's estate

Meadus, Eric 1931–1970, *Untitled (May 1967)*, bequeathed by Mr John Gregory, 2006, © the artist's estate

Meadus, Eric 1931–1970, *Stockbridge*, purchased with the assistance of the Frederick William Smith Bequest Fund, 1975, © the artist's estate

Meadus, Eric 1931–1970, *Townscape*, purchased with the assistance of the Frederick William Smith Bequest Fund, 1975, © the artist's estate

Meadus, Eric 1931–1970, *Townscape by River*, purchased with the assistance of the Frederick William Smith Bequest Fund, 1975, © the artist's estate

Meadus, Eric 1931–1970, *Untitled (July 1968)*, bequeathed by Mr John Gregory, 2006, © the artist's estate

Meadus, Eric 1931–1970, *Wedding*, purchased with the assistance of the Frederick William Smith Bequest Fund, 1975, © the artist's estate

Meadus, Eric 1931–1970, *Portrait of a Spanish Soldier*, purchased with the assistance of the Frederick William Smith Bequest Fund, 1975, © the artist's estate

Meadus, Eric 1931–1970, *Choirboy*, purchased with the assistance of the Frederick William Smith Bequest Fund, 1975, © the artist's estate

Meadus, Eric 1931–1970, *Double/Inverted Landscape*, purchased with the assistance of the Frederick William Smith Bequest Fund, 1975, © the artist's estate

Meadus, Eric 1931–1970, *Park with Houses*, purchased with the assistance of the Frederick William Smith Bequest Fund, 1975, © the artist's estate

Meadus, Eric 1931–1970, *Self Portrait*, purchased with the assistance of the Frederick William Smith Bequest Fund, 1975, © the artist's estate

Meadus, Eric 1931–1970, *The Floating Bridge*, purchased with the assistance of the Frederick William Smith Bequest Fund, 1975, © the artist's estate

Meadus, Eric 1931–1970, *The January Landscape (Cowherds)*, purchased with the assistance of the Frederick William Smith Bequest Fund, 1975, © the artist's estate

Meadus, Eric 1931–1970, *The Red Church*, purchased with the assistance of the Frederick William Smith Bequest Fund, 1975, © the artist's estate

Meadus, Eric 1931–1970, *Townscape*, purchased with the assistance of the Frederick William Smith Bequest Fund, 1975, © the artist's estate

Medley, Robert 1905–1994, *Path to Cement Works near Gravesend*, purchased with the assistance of the Frederick William Smith Bequest Fund, 1962, © James Hyman Fine Art on behalf of the estate of Robert Medley

Medley, Robert 1905–1994, *The Ear*, presented, 1995, © James Hyman Fine Art on behalf of the estate of Robert Medley

Meert, Pieter c.1610–c.1669, *Portrait of a Man*, presented by Mr and Mrs W. J. Fernie, 1942

Meerts, Franz 1836–1896, *The Old Attorney*, bequeathed by Robert Chipperfield, 1911

Melland, Sylvia 1906–1993, *Thelma Hulbert*, donated by Christine Lyons and David Melland, 2000

Michaelson, Assur active 1895–1915, *Lord Swaythling in Moorish Costume*, presented by C. H. Wilkins Esq., 1931

Middleditch, Edward 1923–1987, *Night Sky*, donated by Ursula Milner-White, 2000

Millais, John Everett 1829–1896, *Flowing to the Sea*, purchased with the assistance of the Chipperfield Bequest Fund, 1937

Millet, Jean-François the elder 1642–1679, *Classical Landscape*, purchased with the assistance of the Chipperfield Bequest Fund, 1957

Mills, David b.1947, *Twist*, purchased with the assistance of the Chipperfield Bequest Fund, 1972

Mills, David b.1947, *Chocolate Suite No.1: Chocolate Orange*, presented by the artist, 1975

Mills, David b.1947, *Chocolate Suite No.2: Coffee Humbug*

Milroy, Lisa b.1959, *Melons*, purchased with the assistance of the Victoria & Albert Museum/MGC Purchase Grant Fund, 1986

Milroy, Lisa b.1959, *Togetherness*, purchased with the assistance of the Victoria & Albert Museum/MGC Purchase Grant Fund, 2005

Minton, John 1917–1957, *Rotherhithe from Wapping*, presented by the Contemporary Art Society, 1950, © Royal College of Art

Mitchell, W. B. active 1884–1902, *Near Ashford, Kent*, bequeathed by Robert Chipperfield, 1911

Mitchell, W. B. active 1884–1902, *Near Tonbridge, Kent*, bequeathed by Robert Chipperfield, 1911

Momper, Joos de the younger 1564–1635, *Landscape*, presented by G. F. Pitt Esq.

Monamy, Peter 1681–1749, *The 'Princesa' Action*, purchased with the assistance of the Frederick William Smith Bequest Fund, 1950

Monet, Claude 1840–1926, *The Church at Vétheuil*, purchased with the assistance of the Victoria & Albert Museum/MGC Purchase Grant Fund, 1975

Monkhouse, W. *A Mountain Stream in Yorkshire*, bequeathed by Robert Chipperfield, 1911

Moore, Henry 1831–1895, *Coming Storm*, purchased with the assistance of the Frederick William Smith Bequest Fund, 1936

Moore, Sidney active 1880–1911, *The Old Pedlar*, bequeathed by Robert Chipperfield, 1911

Moreelse, Johannes after 1602–1634, *The Young Poet*, purchased with the assistance of the Chipperfield Bequest Fund, 1936

Moret, Henry 1856–1913, *Landscape*, purchased with the assistance of the Frederick William Smith Bequest Fund, 1964

Morland, George 1763–1804, *The Wreckers*, purchased with the assistance of the Chipperfield Bequest Fund, 1947

Morland, George 1763–1804, *Interior of a Country Inn*, presented by the National Art Collections Fund, 1955

Morris, Cedric Lockwood 1889–1982, *The Jay*, donated by Lady Bonham Carter, 1988, © trustees of the Cedric Lockwood Morris Estate/Foundation

Morris, Desmond b.1928, *The Hermit Discovered*, purchased by the National Association of Decorative and Fine Arts Societies, 2002, © Desmond Morris

Morris, J. D. *Loch Aron*

Morris, John W. 1865–1924, *Cattle*, bequeathed by Sir James Lemon, JP, 1923

Morris, John W. 1865–1924, *Cattle*, presented by Mrs Lavington, 1945

Morris, John W. 1865–1924, *Highland Cattle in Mountain Scene*, presented by Mrs Lavington, 1945

Morrison, Paul b.1966, *Bast*, purchased with the assistance of the Frederick William Smith Bequest Fund, 2004, © Paul Morrison, courtesy of Alison Jacques Galllery, London

Morsberger, Philip b.1933, *Untitled*, presented by Mr Jack Lancester, 2006

Moseley, Richard S. active 1863–1912, *Telling His Big Brother*, presented, 1942

Munnings, Alfred James 1878–1959, *After the Race*, purchased with the assistance of the Chipperfield Bequest Fund, 1937, © the artist's estate

Mura, Francesco de 1696–1782, *The Adoration of the Shepherds*, presented by the National Art Collections Fund, 1975

Murray, David 1849–1933, *Cows in a Stream*, presented by Miss M. Chilcott, 1934

Nash, Paul 1889–1946, *Landscape of the Malvern Distance*, purchased with the assistance of the Chipperfield Bequest Fund, 1948, © TATE, London 2007

Nash, Paul 1889–1946, *The Archer*, purchased with the assistance of the Chipperfield Bequest Fund, 1942, © TATE, London 2007

Nesterova, Natalya b.1944, *Human Masks (left wing)*, donated, 1993, © DACS 2007

Nesterova, Natalya b.1944, *Human Masks (right wing)*, donated, 1993, © DACS 2007

Nevinson, Christopher 1889–1946, *Loading Timber at Southampton Docks*, purchased with the assistance of the Frederick William Smith Bequest Fund, 1962, © the artist's estate/www.bridgeman.co.uk

Nicholson, Ben 1894–1982, *Two Forms (1940–1942)*, purchased with the assistance of the Chipperfield Bequest Fund, 1966, © Angela Verren Taunt 2007. All rights reserved, DACS

Nicholson, Ben 1894–1982, *Greystone*, purchased with the assistance of the Chipperfield Bequest Fund, 1967, © Angela Verren Taunt 2007. All rights reserved, DACS

Nicholson, William 1872–1949, *The Morris Dancer*, purchased with the assistance of the Frederick William Smith Bequest Fund, 1939, © Elizabeth Banks

Nicholson, William 1872–1949, *Cliffs at Rottingdean*, purchased with the assistance of the Chipperfield Bequest Fund, 1962, © Elizabeth Banks

Nicholson, William 1872–1949, *A Glade near Midhurst*, purchased with the assistance of the Chipperfield Bequest Fund, 1938, © Elizabeth Banks

Nightingale, Leonard Charles active 1877–1913, *The Dipping Place*, bequeathed by Robert Chipperfield, 1911

Oakley, Herbert Colborne 1869–1944, *Alderman Edward Bance, DL, Mayor (1890–1904 & 1910)*, presented by Alderman Bance, 1906

Oakley, Herbert Colborne 1869–1944, *Bathers*

Oakley, Herbert Colborne 1869–1944, *Floral Piece*

Oakley, Herbert Colborne 1869–1944, *Neapolitan Boy*

Oakley, Herbert Colborne

1869–1944, *Welsh Gamin*
O'Dell, Alan Edmonds active c.1900, *The Hour before Sunset*, purchased with the assistance of the Frederick William Smith Bequest Fund, 1933
Offer, Frank Rawlings 1847–1932, *West Gate, Southampton*, bequeathed by Robert Chipperfield, 1911
Offer, Frank Rawlings 1847–1932, *Landscape*
Ofili, Chris b.1968, *Two Doo Voodoo*, purchased with the assistance of the Victoria & Albert Museum/MGC Purchase Grant Fund, 1998, © Chris Ofili - Afroco
Olsson, Albert Julius 1864–1942, *Silver Moonlight, St Ives Bay*, purchased with the assistance of the Frederick William Smith Bequest Fund, 1933
Ommanney, George active 1912–1917, *Reverend Ommaney*, presented by Mrs Tombleson, 1929
Opie, John 1761–1807, *Portrait of an Artist*, purchased with the assistance of the Chipperfield Bequest Fund, 1937
Orchardson, William Quiller 1832–1910, *The Flowers of the Forest*, purchased with the assistance of the Frederick William Smith Bequest Fund, 1935
Orlandi, Stefano 1681–1760, *A Church with Pagan Sacrifices at a Burning Altar*, bequeathed by Arthur Tilden Jeffress, 1963
Orlandi, Stefano 1681–1760, *Architectural Fantasy with Figures*, bequeathed by Arthur Tilden Jeffress, 1963
Ostade, Isack van 1621–1649, *Travellers at an Inn*, presented by the National Art Collections Fund, 1955
G. P. *Mexican Interior*, bequeathed by Arthur Tilden Jeffress, 1963
Pagliacci, Aldo 1913–1991, *Exterior of a Church in Flames*, bequeathed by Arthur Tilden Jeffress, 1963
Pagliacci, Aldo 1913–1991, *Interior of a Church in Flames*, bequeathed by Arthur Tilden Jeffress, 1963
Palamedesz., Palamedes I 1607–1638, *Battle Scene*, presented by Miss Smith, 1944
Palmer, Garrick b.1933, *Winchester Landscape*, presented by Charles Woolaston, 1975, © Garrick Palmer
Park, John Anthony 1880–1962, *Spring on the Stour*, purchased with the assistance of the Chipperfield Bequest Fund, 1937, © the artist's estate
Parsons, E. J. *West Gate, Southampton*, presented by Dr and Mrs H. E. Rawlence, 1936
Pascin, Jules 1885–1930, *Nude*, purchased with the assistance of the Chipperfield Bequest Fund, 1954
Pasmore, Victor 1909–1998, *Camberwell*, purchased with the assistance of the Frederick William Smith Bequest Fund, 1949, © the estate of Victor Pasmore, courtesy of Marlborough Fine Art (London) Limited
Pasmore, Victor 1909–1998, *Rectangular Motif: Red and Mustard*, purchased with the assistance of the Frederick William Smith Bequest Fund, 1952, © the estate of Victor Pasmore, courtesy of Marlborough Fine Art (London) Limited
Paterson, Emil Murray 1855–1934, *Bowl of Fruit*, presented by Mrs T. Stevens, 1936
Patterson, Richard b.1963, *Self Portrait*, purchased with the assistance of the Frederick William Smith Bequest Fund, 1996 © the artist, courtesy of Timothy Taylor Gallery, London
Payne, David d.1891, *An English Lane*, bequeathed by Robert Chipperfield, 1911
Peel, James 1811–1906, *Ford-on-Trent*, bequeathed by Robert Chipperfield, 1911
Peele, John Thomas 1822–1897, *Blackberrying, Isle of Man*, bequeathed by Robert Chipperfield, 1911
Peellaert, J. *The Forbidden Book*, presented by W. Day Esq., 1923
Penrose, Roland 1900–1984, *Good Shooting*, purchased with the assistance of the Frederick William Smith Bequest Fund, 1977, © Roland Penrose Estate, England 2007
Penrose, Roland 1900–1984, *The Conquest of the Air*, purchased with the assistance of the Frederick William Smith Bequest Fund, 1977, © Roland Penrose Estate, England 2007
Perfect, Dan b.1965, *Deerdog*, purchased with the assistance of the Orris Bequest Fund, 2005
Perrault, Léon Bazile (copy after) 1832–1908, *Cherub*
Pether, Henry active 1828–1865, *Venice by Moonlight*, bequeathed by Robert Chipperfield, 1911
Pike, Jack *Stream and Cattle*, bequeathed by Robert Chipperfield, 1911
Pike, Sidney active 1880–1907, *In Search of Food*, bequeathed by Robert Chipperfield, 1911
Pike, Sidney active 1880–1907, *Landscape with Cattle*, bequeathed by Robert Chipperfield, 1911
Pike, Sidney active 1880–1907, *Meadow with Sheep*, bequeathed by Robert Chipperfield, 1911
Pike, Sidney active 1880–1907, *Sheep*, bequeathed by Robert Chipperfield, 1911
Piper, John 1903–1992, *Ca' d'Oro*, bequeathed by Arthur Tilden Jeffress, 1963, © the artist's estate
Piper, John 1903–1992, *Portland Foreshore*, purchased with the assistance of the Chipperfield Bequest Fund, 1946, © the artist's estate
Pissarro, Camille 1830–1903, *Louveciennes*, purchased with the assistance of the Chipperfield Bequest Fund, 1936
Pissarro, Lucien 1863–1944, *Grey Weather, Finchingfield*, purchased with the assistance of the Victoria & Albert Museum/MGC Purchase Grant Fund, 1975, © the artist's estate
Pittoni, Giovanni Battista the younger 1687–1767, *The Sacrifice of Jephtha's Daughter*, purchased with the assistance of the Chipperfield Bequest Fund, 1969
Pontin, George active 1893–1916, *Town Quay, Southampton*, purchased with the assistance of the Frederick William Smith Bequest Fund, 1934
Potter, Mary 1900–1981, *Studio Window*, bequeathed by Dr David and Liza Brown, 2002, © 2007. All rights reserved, DACS
Potter, Mary 1900–1981, *Little Shadow*, bequeathed by Dr David and Liza Brown, 2002, © 2007. All rights reserved, DACS
Potter, Mary 1900–1981, *Frieze*, purchased with the assistance of the Chipperfield Bequest Fund, 1978, © 2007. All rights reserved, DACS
Potter, Mary 1900–1981, *Grasses and Shadows 2, 1973*, donated by Lady Bonham Carter, 1988, © 2007. All rights reserved, DACS
Potter, Mary 1900–1981, *Setting Sun*, donated by Lady Bonham Carter, 1988, © 2007. All rights reserved, DACS
Pride, James *Ruined Arch with Figure*, bequeathed by Dr David and Liza Brown, 2002
Priestman, Bertram 1868–1951, *Unseaworthy*, purchased with the assistance of the Chipperfield Bequest Fund, 1931
Pringle, John Quinton 1864–1925, *Springtime, Ardersier (village near Inverness)*, bequeathed by Dr David and Liza Brown, 2002
Pritchard, Edward F. D. 1809–1905, *Antwerp*, bequeathed by Robert Chipperfield, 1911
Procter, Dod 1892–1972, *Black and White*, purchased with the assistance of the Frederick William Smith Bequest Fund, 1933, © the artist's estate/www.bridgeman.co.uk
Protherore, Thomas active 1881–1904, *A Sad Case before the Bench*, presented by Mrs Mary Martyn Collins, 1939
Quinton, Clément 1851–1920, *Landscape with Sheep*, purchased with the assistance of the Frederick William Smith Bequest Fund, 1934
Rae, Fiona b.1963, *Untitled (Fast Breeder)*, purchased with the assistance of the Frederick William Smith Bequest Fund, 1998, © Fiona Rae, courtesy of Timothy Taylor Gallery, London
Randall, Michael 1947–2000, *Daydream*, purchased with the assistance of the Corporation Rate Fund, 1975
Ranken, William Bruce Ellis 1881–1941, *Blue Ante Room*, presented by the artist
Ranken, William Bruce Ellis 1881–1941, *Salon of Charles III*, presented by the artist
Ratcliffe, William Whitehead 1870–1955, *The Coffee House*, purchased with the assistance of the Frederick William Smith Bequest Fund, 1953, © the artist's estate
Ratcliffe, William Whitehead 1870–1955, *Clarence Gardens*, bequeathed by Dr David and Liza Brown, 2002, © the artist's estate
Rayworth, William *Still Life: Blue Grapes*, bequeathed, 1989
Rayworth, William *Still Life: White Grapes*, bequeathed, 1989
Redfern, David b.1947, *Work*, purchased with the assistance of the Victoria & Albert Museum/MGC Purchase Grant Fund, 1979, © the artist
Reed, William Thomas 1845–1881, *Continental Landscape*
Reed, William Thomas 1845–1881, *Early Morning, Epping Forest*, bequeathed by Robert Chipperfield, 1911
Reed, William Thomas 1845–1881, *In the Dolwyddelan Valley*, bequeathed by Robert Chipperfield, 1911
Rembrandt van Rijn (copy after) 1606–1669, *Lady Holding a Fan*, presented by C. A. Emanuel, 1944
Rembrandt van Rijn (copy after) 1606–1669, *Portrait of a Gentleman*, presented by C. A. Emanuel, 1944
Renoir, Pierre-Auguste 1841–1919, *The Boat on the Lake*, presented by Peter and Lies Askonas, 2006
Renoir, Pierre-Auguste 1841–1919, *Wilhelm Muhlfeld*, purchased with the assistance of the National Art Collections Fund, 1964
Revitt, E. M. *Fishers, Odiham*, bequeathed by Robert Chipperfield, 1911
Reynolds, Joshua 1723–1792, *Cornet Nehemiah Winter, 11th Dragoons*, purchased with the assistance of the Chipperfield Bequest Fund, 1956
Rhodes, Carol b.1959, *Factory Roof, Countryside*, purchased with the assistance of the Chipperfield Bequest Fund, 2004, © the artist
Richards, Ceri Geraldus 1903–1971, *Girl at Piano*, purchased with the assistance of the Frederick William Smith Bequest Fund, 1953, © estate of Ceri Richards 2007. All rights reserved, DACS
Ricketts, Charles S. 1866–1931, *The Death of Cleopatra*, purchased with the assistance of the Chipperfield Bequest Fund, 1972
Rieck, Hellmuth *Canaries*, bequeathed by Dr David and Liza Brown, 2002
Riley, Bridget b.1931, *Red Movement*, purchased through the Dr David and Liza Brown Bequest Fund, with the assistance of the Victoria & Albert Museum Purchase Grant Fund, the MLA and the National Art Collections Fund, 2006, © the artist
Robb, Brian 1913–1979, *Jugglers*, purchased with the assistance of the Frederick William Smith Bequest Fund, 1953
Roberts, David 1796–1864, *Interior of St Stephen's Church, Vienna*, bequeathed by Arthur Tilden Jeffress, 1963
Roberts, William Patrick 1895–1980, *Revolt in the Desert*, purchased with the assistance of the Frederick William Smith Bequest Fund, 1958, © William Roberts Society
Robertson, Walford Graham 1866–1948, *Fairyland, under Hindhead*, presented by Mrs Ernest Milton, 1953
Roe, Clarence 1850–1909, *Highland Landscape*, presented by E. M. Lowe Esq., 1941
Roe, Clarence 1850–1909, *Highland Landscape*, presented by E. M. Lowe Esq., 1941
Rogers, Claude 1907–1979, *Spiral Staircase*, purchased with the assistance of the Chipperfield Bequest Fund, 1936
Rogers, Claude 1907–1979, *Miss Lynn*, presented by the Arts Council of Great Britain, 1953
Romney, George 1734–1802, *Lord Ducie*, purchased with the assistance of the Chipperfield Bequest Fund, 1957
Romney, George 1734–1802, *Mrs Marton and Her Son Oliver*, purchased with the assistance of the Chipperfield Bequest Fund, 1953
Roos, Philipp Peter 1657–1706, *Landscape with Cattle*, presented by G. F. Pitt Esq.
Roos, Philipp Peter 1657–1706, *Landscape with Cattle*, presented by G. F. Pitt Esq.
Rosa, Salvator 1615–1673, *A Mountain Landscape*, presented by G. F. Pitt Esq.
Rothenstein, William 1872–1945, *Spring, the Morning Room*, purchased with the assistance of the Frederick William Smith Bequest Fund, 1939, © courtesy of the artist's estate/www.bridgeman.co.uk
Rothwell, Richard 1800–1868, *Portrait of a Lady*, purchased with the assistance of the Chipperfield Bequest Fund, 1934
Rousseau, Henri 1844–1910, *Child with a Doll in a Landscape*, purchased by Arthur Tilden Jeffress, 1963
Rousseau, Théodore 1812–1867, *Evening*, presented by Peter and Lies Askonas, 2004
Ruisdael, Jacob van 1628/1629–1682, *The Dunes near Haarlem*, purchased with the assistance of the Chipperfield Bequest Fund, 1964
Sant, James 1820–1916, *Enigma*, purchased with the assistance of the Frederick William Smith Bequest Fund, 1936

Sargent, John Singer 1856–1925, *Major E. C. Harrison*, purchased with the assistance of the National Art Collections Fund, 1935
Schetky, John Christian 1778–1874, *The Arrival of the King of France*, presented by Alderman Bance, 1930
Schlee, Nick b.1931, *The Ridgeway from Letcombe Basset*, presented by the artist, 2005, © the artist
Scholowei, M. *Family Group*, bequeathed by Sir James Lemon, JP, 1923
Scholowei, M. *The Cheat*, bequeathed by Sir James Lemon, JP, 1923
Scott, William George 1913–1989, *Kitchen Still Life*, bequeathed by Dr David and Liza Brown, 2002, © 2007 William Scott estate
Scott, William George 1913–1989, *Still Life: Coffee Pot I*, bequeathed by Dr David and Liza Brown, 2002, © 2007 William Scott estate
Scott Wilkie, Pamela b.1937, *Trio 1 No.1, Version 2 (from the series 'In Progress')*, bequeathed by Dr David and Liza Brown, 2002, © the artist
Seabrooke, Elliot 1886–1950, *Landscape in the South of France*, presented by Mr and Mrs Alan Lubbock, 1939
Seaward, Mary L. active 1903–1915, *Robert Chipperfield, JP*, presented by the artist, 1915
Seaward, Mary L. active 1903–1915, *Canon Basil Wilberforce*, presented by the artist, 1915
Seaward, Mary L. active 1903–1915, *The Reverend Thomas Atkins*, presented by the artist, 1915
Shayer, Charles Waller 1826–1914 & **Shayer, Henry Thring** 1825–1894 *Coast Scene*, purchased with the assistance of the National Art Collections Fund, 1955
Shayer, Charles Waller 1826–1914 & **Shayer, Henry Thring** 1825–1894 *The White Swan*, bequeathed by Henry Glasspool Esq., 1947
Shayer, William 1788–1879, *A Shady Corner*, presented by Mr F. J. Nettlefold, 1948
Shayer, William 1788–1879, *Mouth of the Old Canal*, presented, 1969
Shayer, William 1788–1879, *Coast Scene*, bequeathed by Robert Chipperfield, 1911
Shayer, William 1788–1879, *Coast Scene*, purchased with the assistance of the Frederick William Smith Bequest Fund, 1926
Shayer, William 1788–1879, *Gypsies in Wood*, purchased with the assistance of the Chipperfield Bequest Fund, 1933
Shayer, William 1788–1879, *Milking Time*, purchased with the assistance of the Chipperfield Bequest Fund, 1933
Shayer, William 1788–1879, *The Fish Stall*, presented by Miss E. M. Welch, 1943
Shayer, William 1788–1879, *The Gleaners*, presented by Miss E. M. Welch, 1943
Sheringham, George 1884–1937, *Flowers in a Teapot*, donated by Lady Bonham Carter, 1988
Short, Emily A. *Landscape with Cattle*, bequeathed by Mr H. L. Saltern, 1906
Short, Frederick Golden 1863–1936, *A Distant Forest Scene*, bequeathed by Miss A. B. Williamson, 1940
Short, Frederick Golden 1863–1936, *Autumn Leaves*, bequeathed by Miss A. B. Williamson, 1940
Short, Frederick Golden 1863–1936, *Seascape*, bequeathed by Robert Chipperfield, 1911
Short, Frederick Golden 1863–1936, *Trees and River, New Forest*, bequeathed by Morris Miles, 1908
Short, Frederick Golden 1863–1936, *Burley Road, New Forest*, bequeathed by Mr H. L. Saltern, 1906
Short, Frederick Golden 1863–1936, *New Forest*, bequeathed by Mr H. L. Saltern, 1906
Short, Frederick Golden 1863–1936, *Newquay, Cornwall*, bequeathed by Mr H. L. Saltern, 1906
Short, Frederick Golden 1863–1936, *Cloud Study, New Forest*, bequeathed by Mr H. L. Saltern, 1906
Short, Frederick Golden 1863–1936, *Lymington River*, bequeathed by Mr H. L. Saltern, 1906
Short, Frederick Golden 1863–1936, *New Forest*, bequeathed by Robert Chipperfield, 1911
Short, Frederick Golden 1863–1936, *Whitley Road*, purchased with the assistance of the Frederick William Smith Bequest Fund, 1936
Short, Frederick Golden 1863–1936, *Discharging Cargo, Lymington*, bequeathed by Mr H. L. Saltern, 1906
Sickert, Walter Richard 1860–1942, *A Red Sky at Night*, bequeathed by Arthur Tilden Jeffress, 1963, © estate of Walter R. Sickert 2007. All rights reserved, DACS
Sickert, Walter Richard 1860–1942, *The Mantelpiece*, purchased with the assistance of the Frederick William Smith Bequest Fund, 1932, © estate of Walter R. Sickert 2007. All rights reserved, DACS
Sickert, Walter Richard 1860–1942, *The Juvenile Lead*, purchased with the assistance of the Chipperfield Bequest Fund, 1951, © estate of Walter R. Sickert 2007. All rights reserved, DACS
Sickert, Walter Richard 1860–1942, *The Tichborne Claimant*, purchased with the assistance of the Chipperfield Bequest Fund, 1939, © estate of Walter R. Sickert 2007. All rights reserved, DACS
Simbari, Nicola b.1927, *Luna park a sera*, bequeathed by Arthur Tilden Jeffress, 1963
Simbari, Nicola b.1927, *Battistero*, bequeathed by Arthur Tilden Jeffress, 1963
Simbari, Nicola b.1927, *Processione al Flamino*, bequeathed by Arthur Tilden Jeffress, 1963
Sims, Charles 1873–1928, *The Bathers*, purchased with the assistance of the Frederick William Smith Bequest Fund, 1936
Sisley, Alfred 1839–1899, *Avenue of Chestnut Trees at La Celle-Saint-Cloud*, purchased with the assistance of the Chipperfield Bequest Fund, 1936
Skeats, Leonard Frank 1874–1943, *Alderman Frederick A. Dunsford, JP*
Skeats, Leonard Frank 1874–1943, *Brittany*, bequeathed by Robert Chipperfield, 1911
Skeats, Leonard Frank 1874–1943, *Robert Chipperfield, JP*
Skeats, Leonard Frank 1874–1943, *Sir James Lemon, JP*, presented, 1904
Skeats, Leonard Frank 1874–1943, *The Casualty List*, presented by Mrs Leonard Skeats, 1945
Skeats, Leonard Frank 1874–1943, *The Pedlar*, bequeathed by Sir James Lemon, JP, 1923
Smith, Bob & Roberta b.1963, *Winter then Autumn*
Smith, Edith Heckstall active 1884–1890, *Roses*, presented, 1943
Smith, Jack b.1928, *Various Activities No.4*, bequeathed through the National Art Collections Fund, 2006, © the artist
Smith, James Burrell 1822–1897, *Windermere*, bequeathed by Robert Chipperfield, 1911
Smith, Matthew Arnold Bracy 1879–1959, *Dulcie*, purchased with the assistance of the Frederick William Smith Bequest Fund, 1950, © by permission of the copyright holder
Smith, Matthew Arnold Bracy 1879–1959, *Landscape at Cagnes*, purchased with the assistance of the Chipperfield Bequest Fund, 1953, © by permission of the copyright holder
Smith, Matthew Arnold Bracy 1879–1959, *Roses and Lilies*, purchased with the assistance of the Chipperfield Bequest Fund, 1932, © by permission of the copyright holder
Smith, Matthew Arnold Bracy 1879–1959, *Still Life with Clay Figure*, purchased with the assistance of the Chipperfield Bequest Fund, 1947, © by permission of the copyright holder
Smith, Percy John Delf 1882–1948, *F. T. Murphy*, presented by Hothe Ward Murphy, 2006
Smith, Ray b.1947, *Compromise Formation*, presented by the artist, 1992, © the artist
Smith, Ray b.1947, *Secondary Revision*, presented by the artist, 1992, © the artist
Smith, Ray b.1947, *Transitional Object*, presented by the artist, 1992, © the artist
Smith, Richard b.1931, *Product*, bequeathed by Dr David and Liza Brown, 2002, © the artist
Smith, Richard b.1931, *Replace*, purchased with the assistance of the Victoria & Albert Museum/MGC Purchase Grant Fund, 1977, © the artist
Smith, Sam 1908–1983, *Bathers in Southampton Water*, purchased, 1982
Solomon, Abraham 1824–1862, *First Class, the Meeting*, purchased with the assistance of the Chipperfield Bequest Fund, 1939
Solomon, Abraham 1824–1862, *Second Class, the Parting*, purchased with the assistance of the Chipperfield Bequest Fund, 1939
Solomon, Simeon 1840–1905, *Aaron with the Scroll of the Law*, presented by the National Art Collections Fund, 1950
Sorolla y Bastida, Joaquín 1863–1923, *Estuary of the Nalón, Asturias*, purchased with the assistance of the Frederick William Smith Bequest Fund, 1933
Souter, John Bullloch 1890–1972, *A Kitchen Task*, purchased with the assistance of the Chipperfield Bequest Fund, 1931
Spear, Ruskin 1911–1990, *Winter*, purchased with the assistance of the Chipperfield Bequest Fund, 1947, © courtesy of the artist's estate/www.bridgeman.co.uk
Speed, Harold 1872–1957, *Old Tom*, presented by the artist, 1930
Spencer, Gilbert 1893–1979, *The Rat Catcher*, purchased with the assistance of the Frederick William Smith Bequest Fund, 1953, © courtesy of the artist's estate/www.bridgeman.co.uk
Spencer, Gilbert 1893–1979, *Melbury Beacon*, purchased with the assistance of the National Art Collections Fund, 1939, © courtesy of the artist's estate/www.bridgeman.co.uk
Spencer, Jean 1942–1998, *Four-Part Double-Square*, presented by Mrs Marion Waters, 2003, © the artist's estate
Spencer, Jean 1942–1998, *Four-Part Double-Square*, presented by Mrs Marion Waters, 2003, © the artist's estate
Spencer, Jean 1942–1998, *Four-Part Double-Square*, presented by Mrs Marion Waters, 2003, © the artist's estate
Spencer, Jean 1942–1998, *Four-Part Double-Square*, presented by Mrs Marion Waters, 2003, © the artist's estate
Spencer, Jean 1942–1998, *White Relief*, © the artist's estate
Spencer, Stanley 1891–1959, *Patricia Preece*, purchased with the assistance of the Frederick William Smith Bequest Fund, 1954, © estate of Stanley Spencer 2007. All rights reserved, DACS
Spencer, Stanley 1891–1959, *Pound Field, Cookham*, purchased with the assistance of the Frederick William Smith Bequest Fund, 1936, © estate of Stanley Spencer 2007. All rights reserved, DACS
Spencer, Stanley 1891–1959, *The Resurrection*, purchased with the assistance of the Frederick William Smith Bequest Fund, 1950, © estate of Stanley Spencer 2007. All rights reserved, DACS
Spreat, William active c.1820–1881, *Clifford Bridge on Teign*, bequeathed by Robert Chipperfield, 1911
Spreat, William active c.1820–1881, *Dedham Bridge on Tavy*, bequeathed by Robert Chipperfield, 1911
Stallard, Constance b.1870, *Black Lilies*, presented by the artist, 1954
Standing, W. *'Aquitania'*
Stanley, Amy *Church Passage, St Michael's*, bequeathed by Robert Chipperfield, 1911
Steel, George Hammond 1900–1960, *A Load from the Stack*, purchased with the assistance of the Chipperfield Bequest Fund, 1931
Steer, Philip Wilson 1860–1942, *Watching Cowes Regatta*, purchased with the assistance of the Frederick William Smith Bequest Fund, 1963, © TATE, London 2007
Steer, Philip Wilson 1860–1942, *Convalescent*, purchased with the assistance of the Chipperfield Bequest Fund, 1934, © TATE, London 2007
Steer, Philip Wilson 1860–1942, *Ludlow Walks*, purchased with the assistance of the Frederick William Smith Bequest Fund, 1932, © TATE, London 2007
Steer, Philip Wilson 1860–1942, *Digging for Bait, Shoreham*, purchased with the assistance of the Chipperfield Bequest Fund, 1930, © TATE, London 2007
Stevens, Alfred Emile Léopold Joseph Victor 1823–1906, *Off the Coast at Deauville*, bequeathed by Arthur Tilden Jeffress, 1963
Stewart, John I 1800–after 1865, *Fishing Scene*, presented by Mrs W. E. Sandell, 1950
Stokes, Adrian Durham 1902–1972, *Glass, Cup and Saucer with Two Wine Bottles*, bequeathed by Dr David and Liza Brown, 2002
Stokes, Adrian Durham 1902–1972, *Quarry at Evening, La Mortola*, bequeathed by Dr David and Liza Brown, 2002
Stokes, Adrian Durham 1902–1972, *Pots*, bequeathed by Dr David and Liza Brown, 2002
Stokes, Adrian Scott 1854–1935, *Heath Pond*, bequeathed by Dr David and Liza Brown, 2002
Stokes, Adrian Scott 1854–1935, *Near the Simplon Pass*, purchased with the assistance of the Frederick William Smith Bequest Fund, 1936
Stokes, Thomas active 1737, *Richard Taunton*
Stuart, Charles active 1880–1904, *A Gleam of Sunshine*, bequeathed by Robert Chipperfield, 1911
Stuart, Charles active 1880–1904, *Children on a Beach*, bequeathed

by Robert Chipperfield, 1911
Stuart, Charles active 1880–1904, *Fishing Boats*, bequeathed by Robert Chipperfield, 1911
Stuart, Charles active 1880–1904, *A Cumberland Lake*, bequeathed by Robert Chipperfield, 1911
Stuart, Charles active 1880–1904, *Criccieth, North Wales*
Suddaby, Rowland 1912–1972, *Window at No.5 Portland Place*, presented by Mrs Hazel King-Farlow, 1939, © the artist's estate
Sutherland, Graham Vivian 1903–1980, *Red Landscape*, purchased with the assistance of the Chipperfield Bequest Fund, 1949, © estate of Graham Sutherland
Sutherland, Graham Vivian 1903–1980, *Green Lane*, purchased with the assistance of the Chipperfield Bequest Fund, 1947, © estate of Graham Sutherland
Sutherland, Graham Vivian 1903–1980, *Sketch for 'Arthur Jeffress'*, bequeathed by Arthur Tilden Jeffress, 1963, © estate of Graham Sutherland
Sutherland, Graham Vivian 1903–1980, *Apple Orchard*, bequeathed by Arthur Tilden Jeffress, 1963, © estate of Graham Sutherland
Sutherland, Graham Vivian 1903–1980, *Arthur Jeffress*, bequeathed by Arthur Tilden Jeffress, 1963, © estate of Graham Sutherland
Sutherland, Graham Vivian 1903–1980, *Apples and Scales*, bequeathed by Arthur Tilden Jeffress, 1963, © estate of Graham Sutherland
Sutherland, Graham Vivian 1903–1980, *Santa Maria della Salute*, bequeathed by Arthur Tilden Jeffress, 1963, © estate of Graham Sutherland
Sutherland, Graham Vivian 1903–1980, *Path through Wood*, bequeathed by Arthur Tilden Jeffress, 1963, © estate of Graham Sutherland
Sutherland, Graham Vivian 1903–1980, *Hanging Form over Water*, bequeathed by Arthur Tilden Jeffress, 1963, © estate of Graham Sutherland
Sutherland, Graham Vivian 1903–1980, *Path through Woods*, bequeathed by Arthur Tilden Jeffress, 1963, © estate of Graham Sutherland
Sutton, Philip b.1928, *Nude with Hat*, purchased with the assistance of the Frederick William Smith Bequest Fund, 1962, © Philip Sutton RA
Taylor, Leonard Campbell 1874–1969, *Romsey Abbey*, purchased with the assistance of the Frederick William Smith Bequest Fund, 1933, © the artist's estate/www.bridgeman.co.uk
Thornbury, William Anslow active 1858–1906, *Sunset at Low Tide*, bequeathed by Sir James Lemon, JP, 1923
Thornbury, William Anslow active 1858–1906, *Sunset on the Thames*, bequeathed by Sir James Lemon, JP, 1923
Thors, Joseph (attributed to) c.1834–1898, *The Anglers*, bequeathed by Sir James Lemon, JP, 1923
Tibble, Geoffrey Arthur 1909–1952, *Hairdressing*, purchased with the assistance of the Chipperfield Bequest Fund, 1947
Tillier, Paul Prosper (copy after) 1834–1915, *Woman in Repose*
Timbrell, James Christopher 1807–1850, *Watching for Boats*, bequeathed by Robert Chipperfield, 1911
Tippett, Bruce b.1933, *Abstract*, bequeathed by Dr David and Liza Brown, 2002
Tippett, Bruce b.1933, *Abstract 3*, bequeathed by Dr David and Liza Brown, 2002
Tippett, Bruce b.1933, *Untitled*, bequeathed by Dr David and Liza Brown, 2002
Tippett, Bruce b.1933, *Mainly Blue*, bequeathed by Dr David and Liza Brown, 2002
Tissot, James 1836–1902, *In Church*, purchased with the assistance of the Frederick William Smith Bequest Fund, 1936
Tissot, James 1836–1902, *The Captain's Daughter (The Last Evening)*, purchased with the assistance of the Frederick William Smith Bequest Fund, 1936
Tomkins, Riduan b.1941, *Jacky*, presented by Mr Jack Lancester, 2006
Tonks, Henry 1862–1937, *The Torn Gown*, purchased with the assistance of the Chipperfield Bequest Fund, 1932, © family of the artist
Trevelyan, Julian 1910–1989, *'Siense Creti'*, purchased with the assistance of the Chipperfield Bequest Fund, 1958, © the artist's estate
Troostwyk, David b.1929, *The Funeral Cypress*, presented by the artist, 2005, © the artist
Turner, George II 1843–1910, *A Lane in Surrey*, bequeathed by Robert Chipperfield, 1911
Turner, George II 1843–1910, *Mountain Stream*, bequeathed by Robert Chipperfield, 1911
Turner, George II 1843–1910, *Watering Place*, bequeathed by Robert Chipperfield, 1911
Turner, Joseph Mallord William 1775–1851, *Fishermen upon a Lee Shore in Squally Weather*, purchased with the assistance of the Chipperfield Bequest Fund, 1951
Tyson, Kathleen 1898–c.1982, *Woodford*, purchased with the assistance of the Chipperfield Bequest Fund, 1937
Uglow, Euan 1932–2000, *Miss Benge*, purchased with the assistance of the Frederick William Smith Bequest Fund, 1962, © the artist's estate
unknown artist 18th C, *Coastal Town with Ruined Temple*, bequeathed by Arthur Tilden Jeffress, 1963
unknown artist *Couple Having Tea*, bequeathed by Arthur Tilden Jeffress, 1963
unknown artist *A Female Saint(?) in Ecstasy*, presented by the seventh Duke of Wellington, 1975
unknown artist *Figure of a Saint*
unknown artist *Martyrdom of a Saint in the Lion's Den*, bequeathed by Arthur Tilden Jeffress, 1963
unknown artist *St Jerome*, presented by E. A. Young, 1931
unknown artist 19th C, *Carnival Scene*, bequeathed by Arthur Tilden Jeffress, 1963
unknown artist 19th C, *Children with Dog and a Basket of Fruit (after Bartolomé Esteban Murillo)*, presented by Mr and Mrs W. J. Fernie, 1942
unknown artist 19th C, *Floating Bridge*
unknown artist 19th C, *Landscape, Eastern Scene*
unknown artist 19th C, *Lost Huntsman*, bequeathed by Robert Chipperfield, 1911
unknown artist 19th C, *Netley Shore*
unknown artist 19th C, *Old Boat House, West Quay, Southampton*
unknown artist 19th C, *Portrait of a Lady*, purchased with the assistance of the Frederick William Smith Bequest Fund, 1936
unknown artist 19th C, *Reading Magdalene (after Correggio)*
unknown artist 19th C, *River Landscape with Cottage and Figures*
unknown artist 19th C, *View of Venice*, bequeathed by Arthur Tilden Jeffress, 1963
unknown artist *Councillor Timothy Falvey*, presented by E. A. Young, 1931
unknown artist *Cows in Pasture with Windmills*
unknown artist *Donkeys by the Sea*, donated by Lady Bonham Carter, 1988
unknown artist *Five Figures in a Quarrel*
unknown artist *Girl and Boy with Basket of Grapes (after Bartolomé Esteban Murillo)*, presented by Mr and Mrs W. J. Fernie, 1942
unknown artist *Group of Figures*
unknown artist *Group of Figures around a Table*, presented by Mrs Lavington, 1945
unknown artist *Lost Huntsman*, bequeathed by Robert Chipperfield, 1911
unknown artist *Pastoral Scene with Man Chopping Wood*, presented by Charles P. Trippe, 1946
unknown artist *Portrait of a Minister*, presented by E. A. Young, 1931
unknown artist *Return of the Prodigal Son*, presented by E. A. Young, 1931
unknown artist *Southampton, c.1810*, purchased with the assistance of the Chipperfield Bequest Fund, 1950
unknown artist *Writing on the Wall*
Utrillo, Maurice 1883–1955, *The Church at Longpont*, purchased with the assistance of the Chipperfield Bequest Fund, 1939, © ADAGP, Paris and DACS, London 2007
Varley, John I 1778–1842, *A Welsh Valley*, purchased with the assistance of the Frederick William Smith Bequest Fund, 1936
Vaughan, John Keith 1912–1977, *The Singer*, bequeathed by Dr David and Liza Brown, 2002, © the estate of Keith Vaughan 2007. All rights reserved, DACS
Velley, W. *River Scene*, presented by Mr and Mrs W. J. Fernie, 1942
Velten, H. *French Harbour*, presented by Mrs Lavington, 1945
Velten, H. *Italian Harbour*, presented by Mrs Lavington, 1945
Verey, Arthur 1840–1915, *Leaving Home*, bequeathed by Robert Chipperfield, 1911
Verwee, Alfred Jacques 1838–1895, *Cows in a Pool*, purchased with the assistance of the Frederick William Smith Bequest Fund, 1934
Vickers, Alfred H. 1849–1907, *River Scene with a Windmill*, presented in memory of E. C. Knight Esq., 1942
Vickers, Alfred H. 1849–1907, *River Scene with Figures*, presented in memory of E. C. Knight Esq., 1942
Vincent, George 1796–1831, *View on the River Yare*, purchased with the assistance of the Chipperfield Bequest Fund, 1938
Vivin, Louis 1861–1936, *La main chaude*, bequeathed by Arthur Tilden Jeffress, 1963
Vivin, Louis 1861–1936, *Les Invalides*, bequeathed by Arthur Tilden Jeffress, 1963
Vivin, Louis 1861–1936, *Venice: Canal Scene with a Bridge*, bequeathed by Arthur Tilden Jeffress, 1963
Vivin, Louis 1861–1936, *Venice: Canal Scene with a Church*, bequeathed by Arthur Tilden Jeffress, 1963
Vuillard, Jean Edouard 1868–1940, *La manicure*, purchased with the assistance of the Chipperfield Bequest Fund, 1968, © ADAGP, Paris and DACS, London 2007
Vuillard, Jean Edouard 1868–1940, *Two People*, bequeathed by Arthur Tilden Jeffress, 1963, © ADAGP, Paris and DACS, London 2007
Wakefield, Larry 1925–1997, *Yellow on Yellow (detail)*, purchased, 1990, © the artist's estate
Wakefield, Larry 1925–1997, *Solent*, purchased with the assistance of the Gulbenkian Foundation, 1967, © the artist's estate
Wakefield, Larry 1925–1997, *Untitled (Black with Blues)*, bequeathed by Mr John Gregory, 2006, © the artist's estate
Wakefield, Larry 1925–1997, *Untitled (Black with Brown, Blue and Purple)*, bequeathed by Mr John Gregory, 2006, © the artist's estate
Wakefield, Larry 1925–1997, *Untitled (Black with Red and Blue)*, bequeathed by Mr John Gregory, 2006, © the artist's estate
Wakefield, Larry 1925–1997, *Untitled (Black with Yellow and White)*, bequeathed by Mr John Gregory, 2006, © the artist's estate
Wakefield, Larry 1925–1997, *Untitled (Green with Red, White and Brown)*, bequeathed by Mr John Gregory, 2006, © the artist's estate
Waldorp, Antonie W. 1803–1866, *Seascape*, presented by Miss Hills, 1942
Walker, John b.1939, *Labyrinth IV*, purchased with the assistance of the Victoria & Albert Museum/MGC Purchase Grant Fund, 1980, © the artist
Wall, W. H. *Boats on a Beach*, purchased with the assistance of the Chipperfield Bequest Fund, 1911
Wallis, Alfred 1855–1942, *Boat on the Sea*, bequeathed by Dr David and Liza Brown, 2002
Walters, George Stanfield 1838–1924, *'When the west with evening glows'*, bequeathed by Robert Chipperfield, 1911
Ward, Edward Matthew 1816–1879, *Leicester and Amy Robsart at Cumnor Hall*, purchased with the assistance of the Frederick William Smith Bequest Fund, 1934
Ward, James (attributed to) 1769–1859, *Peasants Snowballing*, purchased with the assistance of the Chipperfield Bequest Fund, 1937
Watt, Alison b.1966, *Study for 'Rosecutter'*, bequeathed by Dr David and Liza Brown, 2002, © the artist
Watt, Alison b.1966, *Pear*, bequeathed by Dr David and Liza Brown, 2002, © the artist
Watts, Frederick W. 1800–1862, *Lane near Bishopstoke, Hampshire*, purchased with the assistance of the National Art Collections Fund, 1955
Webb, James c.1825–1895, *St Michael's Mount*, purchased with the assistance of the Frederick William Smith Bequest Fund, 1934
Weenix, Jan Baptist 1621–1660/1661, *An Italian Port Scene*, purchased with the assistance of the Chipperfield Bequest Fund, 1963
Weight, Carel Victor Morlais 1908–1997, *The Builder's Mate*, purchased with the assistance of the Frederick William Smith Bequest Fund, 1954, © the estate of the artist
Weiss, José 1859–1919, *Dedham Church*, purchased with the

assistance of the Chipperfield Bequest Fund, 1935
Wellington, Hubert Lindsay 1879–1967, *Lane to Brockton, Staffordshire*, purchased with the assistance of the Chipperfield Bequest Fund, 1961, © the artist's estate
Wells, John T. active 1898–1902, *Mill Dam on the Avon*, bequeathed by Robert Chipperfield, 1911
Wells, John T. active 1898–1902, *Christchurch*, bequeathed by Robert Chipperfield, 1911
Wells, John 1907–2000, *Air, Water, Stone*, purchased with the assistance of the Orris Bequest Fund, 2006, © the estate of John Wells
Weyden, Goswijn van der c.1465–after 1538, *St Catherine and the Philosophers*, purchased with the assistance of the Chipperfield Bequest Fund, 1958
Wheatley, Francis 1747–1801, *Seashore at Howth, Ireland*, purchased with the assistance of the Chipperfield Bequest Fund, 1947
Whitcombe, Thomas c.1752–1824, *Letter of Marque, 'Nelson'*, purchased with the assistance of the Frederick William Smith Bequest Fund
White, Ethelbert 1891–1972, *Olives by the Sea*, purchased with the assistance of the Frederick William Smith Bequest Fund, 1933, © the Ethelbert White estate
Wilkie, David (after) 1785–1841, *A Study*, bequeathed by Mayo-Porcelli, 1914
Wilkins, George active 1871–1885, *Elan Valley, near Rhayader*, bequeathed by Robert Chipperfield, 1911
Wilkins, George active 1871–1885, *Pass of Nantgwyllt*, bequeathed by Robert Chipperfield, 1911
Willetts, David b.1939, *Landscape*, bequeathed by Dr David and Liza Brown, 2002
Willetts, David b.1939, *Lilies*, bequeathed by Dr David and Liza Brown, 2002
Willetts, David b.1939, *On the Coast*, bequeathed by Dr David and Liza Brown, 2002
Williamson, Harold Sandys 1892–1978, *Picnic*, purchased with the assistance of the Frederick William Smith Bequest Fund, 1940, © Paul Williamson
Wilson, Frank Avray b.1914, *Composition*, presented by the artist, 1955
Wilson, Richard 1713/1714–1782, *Classical Landscape*, purchased with the assistance of the Frederick William Smith Bequest Fund, 1946
Winstanley, Paul b.1954, *Nostalgia 1*, purchased with the assistance of the Victoria & Albert Museum/MGC Purchase Grant Fund, 1999, © the artist
Witherington, Frederick William 1785–1865, *Going to Market*, purchased with the assistance of the Frederick William Smith Bequest Fund, 1936
Withycombe, Joyce active 1928–1933, *Worth Matravers*, purchased with the assistance of the Frederick William Smith Bequest Fund, 1934
Withycombe, Joyce active 1928–1933, *Majorca*, purchased with the assistance of the Chipperfield Bequest Fund, 1933
Wolmark, Alfred Aaron 1877–1961, *Self Portrait*, purchased with the assistance of the Frederick William Smith Bequest Fund, 1956, © permission of Mrs Diana S. Hall
Wood, Christopher 1901–1930, *Street in Paris*, presented by Mr and Mrs Eurich, 1977
Wood, Christopher 1901–1930, *Breton Woman at Prayer*, purchased with the assistance of the Chipperfield Bequest Fund, 1947
Woolmer, Alfred Joseph 1805–1892, *Susannah at a Stream*, presented by Miss E. M. Welch, 1943
Worth, Laura active 1931–1932, *Anemones*, purchased with the assistance of the Chipperfield Bequest Fund, 1931
Wright, George 1860–1942, *Flock of Sheep*, bequeathed by Robert Chipperfield, 1911
Wright, Joseph of Derby 1734–1797, *Landscape*, purchased with the assistance of the Chipperfield Bequest Fund, 1952
Wynter, Bryan 1915–1975, *Monumental*, purchased with the assistance of the Dr David and Liza Brown Bequest Fund, 2006, © estate of Bryan Wynter 2007. All rights reserved, DACS
Ximenes, Antonio 1829–1896, *Garibaldi (1807–1882)*, presented by E. Tarry Esq., 1944
Young, John Tobias b.1790, *The Judgement of Solomon*
Young, Tobias c.1755–1824, *Southampton from Bitterne*

Southampton City Museums

A. A. *Southampton Waters*, gift
Ackerley, Chamberlayne *Mr James Chapman*, transferred from the City Record Office, 2005
Adams, Edward *'SS Saraca'*, on loan to Greenwich Maritime Museum
Alford, Leonard C. active 1883–1920, *New Millbrook Church*, gift
Atkinson, George 1806–1884, *The Falmouth Pilot Cutter*, bequeathed
Baker March, F. *Mary Ann Potts*, gift
Ball, Wilfred Williams 1853–1917, *Bargate*, gift
Bartlett, E. Reginald *'Queen Mary'*, gift, 1997
Batchelor Reis, V. I. *Edward Cooper Poole*, gift, 1969
Beechey, William 1753–1839, *George Rogers, an Artist*, purchased with the assistance of the Victoria & Albert Museum Purchase Grant Fund, 1966
Bell, J. *'SS Conway Castle'*, gift
Bird, H. *Frederick James Hemmings, Headmaster of Tauntons School (1925–1948)*, on long-term loan
Birley, Oswald Hornby Joseph 1880–1952, *Lord Royden*, on loan from Cunard, © the artist's estate
Brannon, Philip 1817–1890, *Bird's Eye View of Southampton Showing Original Walls, Towers and Gates*, gift
Brett, B. active c.1841–1918, *Southampton from Peartree Green (after John Rawson Walker)*, on loan to Training & Support
Bridell, Frederick Lee 1831–1863, *Captain Lacey*, gift, 2003
Bridell, Frederick Lee 1831–1863, *Georgiana Lacey*, gift, 2003
Bridell, Frederick Lee 1831–1863, *View of Southampton*, purchased with the assistance of the Victoria & Albert Museum Purchase Grant Fund and the Friends of Southampton Museums, Archives and Galleries, 2004
British (English) School *Nicholas Fuller (1557–1623)*
Bryer, H. C. *79 1–2 High Street, Southampton, with Norman Chimney, c.1200*, gift
Clark, C. *'Aquitania' in Dazzle Paint*, on loan from Cunard
Clark, William 1803–1883, *A Barque, 'Phoebe'*, gift, on loan to LMA
Clark, William 1803–1883, *'SS Livorno'*, gift, on loan to LMA
Cobbett, Ann b.1826, *The Cobbett Sisters*, gift, 1983
Constable, Bessie *The Aviary, Southampton*, gift
Cooksey, W. B. N *Garden of Madame Mae's House*, gift
Cozens, Arthur 1880–1947, *Turret Steamer and Clipper Bringing Home the Grain*, gift, 1947
Cozens, Arthur 1880–1947, *'Lock Ryan' of London*, gift, 1947
Cozens, Arthur 1880–1947, *French Fishing Ketch off Town Quay*, gift, 1947
Cozens, Arthur 1880–1947, *Whaling*, gift, 1947
Cozens, Arthur 1880–1947, *Yachts 'Candda', 'Shamrock' and 'Astra' in Dry Dock*, gift, 1947
Cozens, Arthur 1880–1947, *Southern Railway Steamer*, gift, 1947
Cozens, Arthur 1880–1947, *'Hussar'*, gift, 1947
Cozens, Arthur 1880–1947, *'HMY Victoria & Albert' Entering King George V Dock, Southampton*, gift, 1947
Cozens, Arthur 1880–1947, *'Queen Mary'*, purchased, c.1936
Cozens, Arthur 1880–1947, *'Almanzora', Royal Mail*, gift, 1947
Cozens, Arthur 1880–1947, *'Aquitania', Cunard*, gift, 1947
Cozens, Arthur 1880–1947, *Camouflaged Naval Launch, World War II*, gift, 1947
Cozens, Arthur 1880–1947, *Coastal Vessel, Inner Dock*, gift, 1947
Cozens, Arthur 1880–1947, *Derelict Fishing Boats*, gift, 1947
Cozens, Arthur 1880–1947, *Destroyers Protecting Shipping*, gift, 1947
Cozens, Arthur 1880–1947, *Sea Power*, gift, 1947
Cozens, Arthur 1880–1947, *'SS Europa' Departing Southampton*, gift, 1947
Cozens, Arthur 1880–1947, *White Star Liner 'Majestic' (1922–1936)*, purchased, c.1936
Crossley, Harley b.1936, *'Britannic' as a Hospital Ship*, gift, c.1998, © the artist/www.bridgeman.co.uk
Daniels, Leonard 1909–1998, *Portrait of an Unknown Man (possibly a headmaster of Tauntons School)*, gift, 1993
Dear, W. *Westgate, Southampton*, gift
Dixon, J. *Steamship at Sea*
Draper, Herbert James 1864–1920, *Mrs E. Milton*
Dupont, Gainsborough (attributed to) 1754–1797, *Walter Taylor (1734–1803)*, purchased
Fanner, R. E. *High Street, Southampton (detail)*, purchased, on loan to Wallienus & Wilhelm
Ferry, John active 1897–1929, *Springtime on the Common*
Ferry, John active 1897–1929, *The Common*
Fraser, George A. *'SS Titanic'*, gift, 1974
Fry, Gordon *Isaac Watts (1674–1748)*
Gaugain, Philip A. active 1783–1847, *Captain Pritchard*, bequeathed
Gaugain, Philip A. active 1783–1847, *Mary Ann Pritchard*, bequeathed, on loan to Theobalds
Haines, G. K. *River Scene*
Hamoll, J. *'Hulda', a Schooner*, gift
Hart, Thomas Gray 1797–1881, *The Old Jail, Southampton*, purchased with the assistance of the Victoria & Albert Museum Purchase Grant Fund, 1987, on loan to LMA
Hart, Thomas Gray 1797–1881, *Canute Tower, Southampton*, on loan to Chilworth
Hart, Thomas Gray 1797–1881, *Netley Abbey, East Window*, on loan to Chilworth
Hart, Thomas Gray 1797–1881, *Western Walls Southampton*, purchased
Havell, William (after) 1782–1857, *Woodmill near Southampton*, purchased
Heath *John Ransom*
Heath *Mrs Hannah Ransom*
Henvest, Muriel *'Silver', an Aged Horse of the City of Southampton*, gift, 1999
Hill, Noel *'Manzanares'*, on long-term loan from Fyffes Group Ltd
Hodge, Francis Edwin 1883–1949, *Sergeant Pilot*
Houston, Robert 1891–1940, *'Monarch of Bermuda'*, gift, 2005
Hudson, John 1829–1879, *'Emiely Anne' of Swanage*, gift
S. K. J. active 19th C, *George Fiott Day, VC (1820–1876)*, gift
Jacobsen, Antonio 1849–1921, *American Warship under Sail*, on loan to Greenwich Maritime Museum
Jacobsen, Antonio 1849–1921, *'SS St Louis'*
Jacobsen, Antonio 1849–1921, *'SS New York'*, purchased with a grant from the Prism Fund, 1991
Jones, Montague *Naval Battle between 'HMS Peacock' and 'USS Hornet', 1873*
Juta, Jan active 1900–1939, *Bermuda (panel from 'Queen Elizabeth') (detail)*, purchased with the assistance of the Victoria & Albert Museum Purchase Grant Fund, 1975
Kearsley, Thomas active 1792–1802, *Charles Dibden*
Kelly, Felix 1914–1994, *View by Night, Port Side (panel from Shaw, Savill & Albion's 'Northern Star')*, gift, 2005
Kelly, Felix 1914–1994, *View by Night, Starboard Side (panel from Shaw, Savill & Albion's 'Northern Star')*, gift, 2005
Legg, Henry George 1917–c.1995, *Demolished Building, Six Dials, Southampton*, gift
Lemare Jones, T. *Blue Anchor Lane, Southampton*, gift
Locke, Henry Edward 1862–1925, *Western Shore*, purchased
Locke, Henry Edward 1862–1925, *Bargate*, purchased
Locke, Henry Edward 1862–1925, *High Street, Southampton, Looking from the Quay*
Locke, Henry Edward 1862–1925, *Canute Tower and Town Quay*
Locke, Henry Edward 1862–1925, *Western Shore*, purchased
Locke, Henry Edward 1862–1925, *Western Shore*
Locke, Henry Edward 1862–1925, *Western Shore by Moonlight*
Locke, Henry Edward 1862–1925, *Western Shore*
Locke, Henry Edward 1862–1925, *Old Southampton around the Shore Looking East*
Locke, Henry Edward 1862–1925, *Netley Abbey*
Locke, Henry Edward (after) 1862–1925, *Canute Tower at Town Quay, Southampton by Moonlight*, purchased
Lucas, Albert Durer 1828–1919, *'Dash'*, gift
Lucas, Albert Durer 1828–1919, *Foxgloves*
Lucas, Albert Durer 1828–1919, *Cedar at Bevois Mount Where Pope Sat*
Lucas, Albert Durer 1828–1919, *Stonehenge on Salisbury Plain*, gift
Lucas, Albert Durer 1828–1919, *1 May 1894, on the Common*
Lucas, Albert Durer 1828–1919, *Interior of Norman Merchant House, Blue Anchor Lane,*

Southampton, 12th Century
Lucas, Albert Durer 1828–1919, *Interior of Norman Merchant House, Blue Anchor Lane, Southampton, 12th Century*
Lucas, Richard Cockle 1800–1883, *Self Portrait*
Lucas, Richard Cockle (attributed to) 1800–1883, *View of Southampton in 1425 (detail)*, gift
MacDermott, Beatrice *The Goddess Diana and Horses (from 'Caronia')*, purchased, c.1988
Mager, Frederick b.1882, *Cooper's Yard*, gift from the Public Libraries
Marboeuf, V. *'SS Normannia'*
McKeown, H. *Bargate*, gift
McKeown, H. *Common (Summer), the Avenue*
McKeown, H. *Common (Winter), the Avenue*
McKeown, H. *The Avenue, Southampton*
Mears, George 1826–1906, *The Southampton Pilot*, purchased with the assistance of the Victoria & Albert Museum Purchase Grant Fund, c.1980
Meohorner, Hannah *Sarah Musgrave Payne*, gift
Moorman, J. W. *'PS Balmoral'*, gift
Nicholson, C. *A Tale of the Right and Left*
Oakley, Harold active 1904–1929, *Penuel George Corbin, Headmaster of Tauntons School (1865–1892)*, on long-term loan, since 1993
Offer, Frank Rawlings 1847–1932, *Bargate Street*, purchased
Offer, Frank Rawlings 1847–1932, *Blue Anchor Lane, Southampton*, on loan from Chilworth
Offer, Frank Rawlings 1847–1932, *Blue Anchor Lane, Southampton*, purchased
Offer, Frank Rawlings 1847–1932, *The Bargate*, on loan to One Stop Shop
Offer, Frank Rawlings 1847–1932, *The Westgate, Southampton*, on loan to Hospital
Owen, Samuel 1768–1857, *'Tagus' Entering the Bay of Gibraltar*, gift, 2005
Pether, Henry active 1828–1865, *Southampton Town Quay at Sunset*, on loan to Horsley Towers
Pether, Henry active 1828–1865, *Town Quay by Moonlight*
Pether, Henry (after) active 1828–1865, *Northwest Corner of Town Walls*, purchased
Pether, Sebastian 1790–1844, *Moonlight Scene, Southampton*, on loan to Southampton University
Petrie, James Wilson 1930–1997, *Lord Nelson Class Locomotive, 'Sir Walter Raleigh'*, gift, © the artist's estate
Pontin, George active 1893–1916, *By the West Gate*, gift
Pontin, George active 1893–1916, *Cook Street and St Mary's*, gift
Pontin, George active 1893–1916, *Doorway, Old Millbrook Church*, gift
Pontin, George active 1893–1916, *Early Morning*, gift
Pontin, George active 1893–1916, *Evening, Grand Theatre*, gift
Pontin, George active 1893–1916, *Evening, Marlands*, gift
Pontin, George active 1893–1916, *Filling in Western Shore near the Baths*, gift
Pontin, George active 1893–1916, *Gateway, Back of the Walls*, gift
Pontin, George active 1893–1916, *Hill Top, Millbrook Road*, gift
Pontin, George active 1893–1916, *In Netley Abbey*, gift
Pontin, George active 1893–1916, *In Portswood Road*, gift
Pontin, George active 1893–1916, *In Regent's Park*, gift
Pontin, George active 1893–1916, *In Regent's Park*, gift
Pontin, George active 1893–1916, *Lane at Hill Top*, gift
Pontin, George active 1893–1916, *Near the Baths*, gift
Pontin, George active 1893–1916, *New Millbrook*, gift
Pontin, George active 1893–1916, *Old Cottages, Till Top*, gift
Pontin, George active 1893–1916, *Old Prison, French Street*, gift
Pontin, George active 1893–1916, *On the Common*, gift
Pontin, George active 1893–1916, *Snow Scene (back of East Street)*, gift
Pontin, George active 1893–1916, *Snow Scene off Millbrook Road*, gift
Pontin, George active 1893–1916, *Timber in the Docks*, gift
Pontin, George active 1893–1916, *Tudor House and St Michael's*, gift
Pontin, George active 1893–1916, *Western Shore*, gift
Poole, Victor *Ann Secunda Margaret Poole (1871–1950)*, on loan from a private individual, since 1969
Poole, Victor *Emily Poole*, gift, 1969
Powell, Lydia Sarah *Royal Pier (Yacht Club)*, gift
Powell, Lydia Sarah *Town Walls*
Raitt, J. *'SS Moor' off Coast with Plymouth Sailing Boat*
Rendell, A. E. *The Breaking up of the 'Great Eastern'*, on loan to LMA
Rendell, A. E. (attributed to) *18th Century Schooner*
Robinson, Gregory 1876–1967, *'Mayflower' Model*, on loan from R. C. Anderson, since 1925
Rogers, A. *'Queen Mary'*
Sandell, George W. active 1881–1937, *Ship up the Creek (after N. Green)*
Sandell, George W. active 1881–1937, *Steamship in Moonlight*, gift
Sandell, George W. active 1881–1937, *Sailing Ship under Reduced Sail (after Edward Hoyer)*, gift
Sandell, George W. active 1881–1937, *'SS Adriatic', the First White Star Liner to Come to Southampton Passing Down Cowes Roads, 31 May 1907*
Sandell, George W. active 1881–1937, *Western Esplanade, Southampton*, gift
Sandell, George W. active 1881–1937, *'SS Titanic'*
Short, Frederick Golden 1863–1936, *New Forest*, bequeathed
Short, Frederick Golden 1863–1936, *Landscape*, gift
Skeats, Edward *Robert Chipperfield Esq., Chair of Tauntons School Governors (1877–1904)*, gift, on long-term loan, since 1993
Smith, Percy John Delf 1882–1948, *Seymour Jackson Gubb, Headmaster of Tauntons School (1892–1924)*, gift, on long-term loan, since 1993
Smoothy, Derrick b.1923, *'Pendennis Castle' (1959–1976)*, on loan from Cayzen Irvine Shipping Ltd
Sparkes, T. Roy *'Queen Mary'*, gift
Spilsbury, Maria 1777–c.1823, *New Year's Feast at Mr Walter Taylor's Charity School, Portswood Green, near Southampton*
Sullivan, L. F. *'SS Andes'*
Taylor, S. M. Louisa active 1872–1890, *Mrs A. E. White*
unknown artist *Mrs Walter Kingsbury*
unknown artist *The Old Farmhouse at Northam*
unknown artist *An Early Royal Mail Steam Packet Company Paddlesteamer (possibly 'Tweed')*, gift, 2005
unknown artist *Brig 'Tartar' on Fire, Southampton Docks, 2 June 1842*, gift
unknown artist *Portrait of an Unknown Gentleman*
unknown artist *Portrait of an Unknown Woman*
unknown artist *General Gordon*
unknown artist 19th C, *Andrew Lamb (1803–1881)*, gift
unknown artist 19th C, *'Castle'*
unknown artist 19th C, *Cowherds, the Avenue*
unknown artist 19th C, *Early 19th Century Frigate*
unknown artist 19th C, *George Josiah Poole*, gift, 1969
unknown artist 19th C, *Portrait of an Unknown Gentleman*
unknown artist 19th C, *The Avenue, Southampton*, gift
unknown artist 19th C, *Town Quay (unfinished)*
unknown artist 19th C, *Western Shore*, bequeathed by Hector Young
unknown artist late 19th C, *Royal Mail Ship, 'Medway', 1877*, gift, 2005
unknown artist late 19th C, *Royal Mail Ship, 'Nile', 1869*, gift, 2005
unknown artist *A Mayor of Southampton*
unknown artist *A Royal Mail Steamship*, gift, 2005
unknown artist *George Arbuthnot, Second Baron of Inverclyde (Chairman of Cunard)*, on loan from Cunard, since 1998
unknown artist *Captain Richard Norris Diaper*, gift, 2000
unknown artist *William Francis Summer Spranger Esq., JP (1848–1917) (detail)*, on long-term loan, since 1993
unknown artist *Panel from Banana Boat 'Golfito'*, gift, c.1988
unknown artist *Panel from Banana Boat 'Golfito'*, gift, c.1988
unknown artist 20th C, *Daniel Beak, VC*, on long-term loan, since 1969
unknown artist 20th C, *Rural Scene (from 'MV Britannic')*, gift
unknown artist 20th C, *Smoking Room Panel from 'Aquitania' (panel 1)*, gift, 1998
unknown artist 20th C, *Smoking Room Panel from 'Aquitania' (panel 2)*, gift, 1998
unknown artist 20th C, *Smoking Room Panel from 'Aquitania' (panel 3)*, gift, 1998
unknown artist 20th C, *Smoking Room Panel from 'Aquitania' (panel 4)*, gift, 1998
unknown artist 20th C, *'Southampton Docks, Centre of the World's Commerce'*
unknown artist 20th C, *Westgate*, purchased
unknown artist *House and Garden (Hawthorn Cottage)*, gift
unknown artist *Ketch and Naval Man-o-War in Choppy Sea*
unknown artist *Man with Pipe*
unknown artist *Portrait of an Unknown Gentleman*
unknown artist *Sailing Ship*, on loan to Lilley Research
unknown artist *The Royal Barge at Rochester*, on loan to Greenwich Maritime Museum
unknown artist *View of Southampton*
unknown artist *View of Southampton West Wall*
G. W. *'Kynge Canute Reprovynge Hys Foolishe Cortieres att Southampton, 1017 AD'*
Wilkinson, Norman 1878–1971, *Approach to the New World ('Olympic')*, on loan from Rio Tinto Zinc, © the Norman Wilkinson estate
Wilkinson, Rodney 1924–2004, *Plymouth Harbour (copy of original from the 'Titanic')*, on loan from a private individual, © by kind permission of the Rodney Wilkinson estate
Wood, T. *The Lower Arch, Weston*, on loan from a private individual, since 1977
Wood, T. *Weston Arch*, on loan from a private individual, since 1977
Young, Tobias c.1755–1824, *Southampton from Bitterne, Peartree Green*, purchased, 1962
Young, Tobias c.1755–1824, *Chessel House*, on loan to Latimers
Young, Tobias c.1755–1824, *Looking to Southampton from the New Forest*
Young, Tobias c.1755–1824, *'Old Southampton', Lansdowne Castle*
Young, Tobias c.1755–1824, *Southampton from Peartree Green*
Young, Tobias c.1755–1824, *Southampton from Peartree Green*, gift
Zinkeisen, Anna Katrina 1901–1976, *Laying of Foundation Stone of Southampton Docks, 1838*, purchased, © the artist's estate

Southampton Mayor's Parlour

Halliday, Edward Irvine 1902–1984, *Her Majesty the Queen (b.1926)*, provided by public subscription to commemorate the granting of City status, 1964, © the artist's estate
McKee, Alice b.1954, *Councillor Parvin Damani, MBE*, gift from the Muslim Community, 2004, © the artist
McKee, Alice b.1954, *Councillor Kathy Johnson*, commissioned by the City, 2005, © the artist

Southampton Solent University

Adams, Elizabeth b.1982, *Untitled (Green on Black)*, purchased from the artist, 2006, © the artist
Adams, Elizabeth b.1982, *Untitled (Orange on Brown)*, purchased from the artist, 2006, © the artist
Baker, Sam b.1984, *Beggar Woman of Ceylon*, purchased from the artist, © the artist
Baker, Sam b.1984, *Lemon Girl of the Gambia*, purchased from the artist, 2006, © the artist
Barker, Mario b.1968, *Outboard*, acquired, before 1997, © the artist
Bastick, Rosemary b.1948, *Portrait*, purchased from the artist, 2003
Cardall, Adam active 1998–2006, *Castles in the Sky*, purchased from the artist, 2002
Cardall, Adam active 1998–2006, *Ship of State*, purchased from the artist, 2002
Cardall, Adam active 1998–2006, *Standing on the Shoulders of Giants*, purchased from the artist, 2002
Chipp, John *Dorset Autumn*, acquired, before 1990
Cross, Steve active 1968–2006, *The Fall of Mostar No.1 & No.2*, on long-term loan from the artist
Curry, Rob b.1955, *Visceral*, on long-term loan from the artist, © the artist
Curry, Rob b.1955, *Twiss*, on long-term loan from the artist, © the artist
Curry, Rob b.1955, *Augury*, on long-term loan from the artist, © the artist
Curry, Rob b.1955, *Axis*, on long-term loan from the artist, © the artist
Curry, Rob b.1955, *Maasai*, on long-term loan from the artist, © the artist
Curry, Rob b.1955, *Lazarus*, on long-term loan from the artist, © the artist
Curry, Rob b.1955, *Under the Boardwalk*, on long-term loan from the artist, © the artist
Davidson, Mary active 1985–1980, *Still Life with Guitar*, purchased by Southampton Institute, c.1990

Eurich, Richard Ernst 1903–1992, *Yachts in a Squall*, purchased from the Contemporary Art Society, 2003, © courtesy of the artist's estate/www.bridgeman.co.uk
Fac *Textures*, acquired, before 1990
Folkes, Peter L. b.1923, *Parked Car and Tree*, acquired, before 1990, © the artist
Folkes, Peter L. b.1923, *Sir James Mathews, MA, LLD, JP*, commissioned, 1994, © the artist
Francis, Emma b.1975, *Bruiser*, purchased from the artist, 2004, © the artist
Francis, Emma b.1975, *Crack*, purchased from the artist, 2004, © the artist
Francis, Emma b.1975, *Divided*, purchased from the artist, 2004, © the artist
Francis, Emma b.1975, *Lost*, purchased from the artist, 2004, © the artist
Francis, Emma b.1975, *Umber*, purchased from the artist, 2004, © the artist
Garrod, Alistair active 1989–2006, *Jody Scheckter's Ferrari*, acquired from the artist, before 1997
Griffin, John b.1944, *Approaching Storm (Normandy)*, on long-term loan from Dr Roger Brown, © the artist
Janceva, Velika b.1980, *Ahead Only*, on long-term loan from the artist, © the artist
Janceva, Velika b.1980, *Cool Skin*, on long-term loan from the artist, © the artist
Janceva, Velika b.1980, *Some Things We Simply Can't Measure*, purchased from the artist, 2001, © the artist
Janceva, Velika b.1980, *The Gap Soldier*, on long-term loan from the artist, © the artist
Janceva, Velika b.1980, *Untitled*, on long-term loan from the artist, © the artist
Janceva, Velika b.1980, *Wool Mix*, on long-term loan from the artist, © the artist
Jobe, Ngoneh b.1979, *Apple*, purchased from the artist, 2001, © the artist
Jobe, Ngoneh b.1979, *Grapefruit*, purchased from the artist, 2001, © the artist
Jobe, Ngoneh b.1979, *Strawberries*, purchased from the artist, 2001, © the artist
Jones, Anthony active 1986–2006, *'City of Truro'*, acquired from the artist, before 1997
Kingston, Emma b.1983, *Lucy Mono 1*, purchased from the artist, 2004
Kingston, Emma b.1983, *Lucy Mono Black*, purchased from the artist, 2004
Kingston, Emma b.1983, *Lucy Mono Yellow/Red/Black*, purchased from the artist, 2004
McDade, Steven b.1950, *Fall*, on long-term loan from the artist, © the artist
McDade, Steven b.1950, *Language Flow*, on long-term loan from the artist, © the artist
McDade, Steven b.1950, *Separate*, on long-term loan from the artist, © the artist
McDade, Steven b.1950, *Descend*, on long-term loan from the artist, © the artist
McDade, Steven b.1950, *The Beginning of the World*, on long-term loan from the artist, © the artist
McDade, Steven b.1950, *Network*, purchased from the artist, 2003, © the artist
McDade, Steven b.1950, *Senate*, on long-term loan from the artist, © the artist
McDade, Steven b.1950, *Spectre*, on long-term loan from the artist, © the artist
McKee, Alice b.1954, *Michael Andrews*, purchased from the artist, 1998, © the artist
Miranda, C. active 1978–1990, *Farley Landscape*, acquired, before 1990
Murley, Tim active 2002–2006, *Wish You Were Here No.1*, purchased from the artist, 2003
Oldfield, Michelle active 2002–2006, *A Starscape: 50 Sci-Fi Films*, purchased from the artist, 2003
Palmer, Greg b.1959, *A Spot of the Old (In and Out 1)*, on long-term loan from the artist
Palmer, Greg b.1959, *A Spot of the Old (In and Out 2)*, on long-term loan from the artist
Palmer, Greg b.1959, *A Spot of the Old (In and Out 3)*, on long-term loan from the artist
Perry, Lyon active 1986–1990, *Island Quay, Salcombe*, acquired, before 1990
Perry, Lyon active 1986–1990, *Southampton Docks*, acquired, before 1990
Powell, Stephen b.1955, *Vertical Hold*, on long-term loan from the artist, © the artist
Powell, Stephen b.1955, *Magician and Bird*, purchased from the artist, 2002, © the artist
Powell, Stephen b.1955, *Abracadabra*, on long-term loan from the artist, © the artist
Powell, Stephen b.1955, *None So Blind*, on long-term loan from the artist, © the artist
Powell, Stephen b.1955, *Dance on the Edge*, on long-term loan from the artist, © the artist
Powell, Stephen b.1955, *Dizzy Heights*, on long-term loan from the artist, © the artist
Powell, Stephen b.1955, *Points to View*, on long-term loan from the artist, © the artist
Talbert, Ryan active 2000–2006, *A Tragedy in the Mind of the Living*, purchased from the artist, 2002
Taylor, Sarah b.1966, *Still, Self, Life 1*, on long-term loan from the artist, © the artist
Taylor, Sarah b.1966, *Still, Self, Life 2*, on long-term loan from the artist, © the artist
Taylor, Sarah b.1966, *Still, Self, Life 3*, on long-term loan from the artist, © the artist
Thornton, Sue b.1952, *Limbus*, purchased from the artist, 2003, © the artist
Thornton, Sue b.1952, *Looking Sideways*, purchased from the artist, 2003, © the artist
Wakelin, Tracy b.1965, *Assemblage No.1*, purchased from the artist, 2005
Wakelin, Tracy b.1965, *Openings*, donated by the artist, 2006
Watkins, Rhian b.1981, *Octopus (Clive Riche-Boots)*, purchased from the artist, 2004, © the artist
Watkins, Rhian b.1981, *Shopping Trolleys (Jenny Boult)*, purchased from the artist, 2004, © the artist
Watkins, Rhian b.1981, *Sky in the Pie No.1 (Mcgough)*, purchased from the artist, 2004, © the artist
Watkins, Rhian b.1981, *Sky in the Pie No.2 (Mcgough)*, purchased from the artist, 2004, © the artist
White, Jenna b.1979, *Bow*, purchased from the artist, 2004
Whittington, Paul active 1994–2000, *Riley Car*, acquired from the artist, before 1997
Young, Dee b.1959, *The Quays*, purchased from the artist, 2001, © the artist
Young, Dee b.1959, *Untitled No.10*, purchased from the artist, 2000, © the artist
Young, Dee b.1959, *Untitled No.11*, purchased from the artist, 2000, © the artist
Young, Dee b.1959, *Untitled No.12*, purchased from the artist, 2000, © the artist
Young, Dee b.1959, *Extreme Conditions*, purchased from the artist, 2001, © the artist

Southampton University Hospitals NHS Trust

Alexander, Rachael b.1965 & **Muncaster, Jenny** b.1966 *Beach Huts*, commissioned by Southampton University Hospitals NHS Trust, c.2001, © the artists
Alexander, Rachael b.1965 & **Muncaster, Jenny** b.1966 *Fishing Boat*, commissioned by Southampton University Hospital NHS Trust, c.2001, © the artists
Alexander, Rachael b.1965 & **Muncaster, Jenny** b.1966 *Ocean Theme Painting*, commissioned by Southampton University Hospitals NHS Trust, c.2001, © the artists
Alexander, Rachael b.1965 & **Muncaster, Jenny** b.1966 *Ocean Theme Painting*, commissioned by Southampton University Hospitals NHS Trust, c.2001, © the artists
Alexander, Rachael b.1965 & **Muncaster, Jenny** b.1966 *Ocean Theme Painting*, commissioned by Southampton University Hospitals NHS Trust, c.2001, © the artists
Alexander, Rachael b.1965 & **Muncaster, Jenny** b.1966 *Ocean Theme Painting*, commissioned by Southampton University Hospitals NHS Trust, c.2001, © the artists
Alexander, Rachael b.1965 & **Muncaster, Jenny** b.1966 *Ocean Theme Painting*, commissioned by Southampton University Hospitals NHS Trust, c.2001, © the artists
Alexander, Rachael b.1965 & **Muncaster, Jenny** b.1966 *Ocean Theme Painting*, commissioned by Southampton University Hospitals NHS Trust, c.2001, © the artists
Alexander, Rachael b.1965 & **Muncaster, Jenny** b.1966 *Ocean Theme Painting*, commissioned by Southampton University Hospitals NHS Trust, c.2001, © the artists
Alexander, Rachael b.1965 & **Muncaster, Jenny** b.1966 *Ocean Theme Painting*, commissioned by Southampton University Hospitals NHS Trust, c.2001, © the artists
Alexander, Rachael b.1965 & **Muncaster, Jenny** b.1966 *Ocean Theme Painting*, commissioned by Southampton University Hospitals NHS Trust, c.2001, © the artists
Alexander, Rachael b.1965 & **Muncaster, Jenny** b.1966 *Seascapes: Beach Huts*, commissioned by Southampton University Hospitals NHS Trust, 2006, © the artists
Alexander, Rachael b.1965 & **Muncaster, Jenny** b.1966 *Seascapes: Estuary*, commissioned by Southampton University Hospitals NHS Trust, 2006, © the artists
Alexander, Rachael b.1965 & **Muncaster, Jenny** b.1966 *Seascapes: Sailing Boat*, commissioned by Southampton University Hospitals NHS Trust, 2006, © the artists
Cook, Lisa b.1973, *Diver and Fish*, commissioned by Southampton University Hospitals NHS Trust, 2004, © the artist
Cook, Lisa b.1973, *Dolphin and Castle*, commissioned by Southampton University Hospitals NHS Trust, 2004, © the artist
Cook, Lisa b.1973, *Mermaid and Turtles*, commissioned by Southampton University Hospitals NHS Trust, 2004, © the artist
Cook, Lisa b.1973, *Octopus and Seahorses*, commissioned by Southampton University Hospitals NHS Trust, 2004, © the artist
Cooper, Eileen b.1953, *To Steal a Wedding Ring*, acquired, c.1998, © Eileen Cooper 2007. All rights reserved, DACS
Gingell, Mary *Australian Outback*
Gradidge, Daphne b.1953, *Window with a Camera*, commissioned by Southampton University Hospitals NHS Trust, 1990, © the artist
Gradidge, Daphne b.1953, *Window with a Car*, commissioned by Southampton University Hospitals NHS Trust, 1990, © the artist
Gradidge, Daphne b.1953, *Window with a Clown*, commissioned by Southampton University Hospitals NHS Trust, 1990, © the artist
Gradidge, Daphne b.1953, *Window with a Hot Air Balloon*, commissioned by Southampton University Hospitals NHS Trust, 1990, © the artist
Gradidge, Daphne b.1953, *Window with a Parrot*, commissioned by Southampton University Hospitals NHS Trust, 1990, © the artist
Gradidge, Daphne b.1953, *Window with a Teddy Bear*, commissioned by Southampton University Hospitals NHS Trust, 1990, © the artist
Gradidge, Daphne b.1953, *Window with Feet*, commissioned by Southampton University Hospitals NHS Trust, 1990, © the artist
Gradidge, Daphne b.1953, *A*, commissioned by Southampton University Hospitals NHS Trust, 1992, © the artist
Gradidge, Daphne b.1953, *B*, commissioned by Southampton University Hospitals NHS Trust, 1992, © the artist
Gradidge, Daphne b.1953, *C*, commissioned by Southampton University Hospitals NHS Trust, 1992, © the artist
Gradidge, Daphne b.1953, *D*, commissioned by Southampton University Hospitals NHS Trust, 1992, © the artist
Gradidge, Daphne b.1953, *E*, commissioned by Southampton University Hospitals NHS Trust, 1992, © the artist
Gradidge, Daphne b.1953, *F*, commissioned by Southampton University Hospitals NHS Trust, 1992, © the artist
Gradidge, Daphne b.1953, *G*, commissioned by Southampton University Hospitals NHS Trust, 1992, © the artist
Gradidge, Daphne b.1953, *H*, commissioned by Southampton University Hospitals NHS Trust, 1992, © the artist
Gradidge, Daphne b.1953, *J*, commissioned by Southampton University Hospitals NHS Trust, 1992, © the artist
Gradidge, Daphne b.1953, *K*, commissioned by Southampton University Hospitals NHS Trust, 1992, © the artist
Gradidge, Daphne b.1953, *L*, commissioned by Southampton University Hospitals NHS Trust, 1992, © the artist
Gradidge, Daphne b.1953, *M*, commissioned by Southampton University Hospitals NHS Trust, 1992, © the artist
Gradidge, Daphne b.1953, *N*, commissioned by Southampton University Hospitals NHS Trust, 1992, © the artist

Gradidge, Daphne b.1953, *O*, commissioned by Southampton University Hospitals NHS Trust, 1992, © the artist
Gradidge, Daphne b.1953, *P*, commissioned by Southampton University Hospitals NHS Trust, 1992, © the artist
Gradidge, Daphne b.1953, *Q*, commissioned by Southampton University Hospitals NHS Trust, 1992, © the artist
Gradidge, Daphne b.1953, *R*, commissioned by Southampton University Hospitals NHS Trust, 1992, © the artist
Gradidge, Daphne b.1953, *S*, commissioned by Southampton University Hospitals NHS Trust, 1992, © the artist
Gradidge, Daphne b.1953, *T*, commissioned by Southampton University Hospitals NHS Trust, 1992, © the artist
Gradidge, Daphne b.1953, *V*, commissioned by Southampton University Hospitals NHS Trust, 1992, © the artist
Gradidge, Daphne b.1953, *W*, commissioned by Southampton University Hospitals NHS Trust, 1992, © the artist
Gradidge, Daphne b.1953, *X*, commissioned by Southampton University Hospitals NHS Trust, 1992, © the artist
Gradidge, Daphne b.1953, *Y*, commissioned by Southampton University Hospitals NHS Trust, 1992, © the artist
Gradidge, Daphne b.1953, *Z*, commissioned by Southampton University Hospitals NHS Trust, 1992, © the artist
Gradidge, Daphne b.1953, *Jaguar Climbing a Tree*, commissioned by Southampton University Hospitals NHS Trust, 1995, © the artist
Gradidge, Daphne b.1953, *Leopard with Sloths*, commissioned by Southampton University Hospitals NHS Trust, 1995, © the artist
Gradidge, Daphne b.1953, *Pair of Crested Birds*, commissioned by Southampton University Hospitals NHS Trust, 1995, © the artist
Gradidge, Daphne b.1953, *Penguins*, commissioned by Southampton University Hospitals NHS Trust, 1995, © the artist
Gradidge, Daphne b.1953, *Eyeworth Pond, Fritham*, commissioned by Southampton University Hospitals NHS Trust, 2003, © the artist
Gradidge, Daphne b.1953, *Eyeworth Pond, Fritham*, commissioned by Southampton University Hospitals NHS Trust, 2003, © the artist
Gradidge, Daphne b.1953, *Eyeworth Pond, Fritham*, commissioned by Southampton University Hospitals NHS Trust, 2003, © the artist
Gradidge, Daphne b.1953, *Hale Purlieu*, commissioned by Southampton University Hospitals NHS Trust, 2003, © the artist
Gradidge, Daphne b.1953, *Hale Purlieu*, commissioned by Southampton University Hospitals NHS Trust, 2003, © the artist
Hoskins, Brian *View of the Princess Anne Hospital*, acquired, c.1995
Muncaster, Jenny b.1966, *Seafood and Champagne*, gift, c.2001, © the artist
Muncaster, Jenny b.1966, *Summer Pudding*, gift, c.2001, © the artist
Muncaster, Jenny b.1966, *Bird*, commissioned by Southampton University Hospitals NHS Trust, 2002, © the artist
Muncaster, Jenny b.1966, *Bird and Butterfly*, commissioned by Southampton University Hospitals NHS Trust, 2002, © the artist
Muncaster, Jenny b.1966, *Monkey*, commissioned by Southampton University Hospitals NHS Trust, 2002, © the artist
O'Driscoll, Suzanne b.1955, *Cornerstones*, © the artist
O'Driscoll, Suzanne b.1955, *Tea at Four (part 1)*, © the artist
O'Driscoll, Suzanne b.1955, *Tea at Four (part 2)*, © the artist
Rankle, Alan b.1952, *Further Tales from the Beach House*, © the artist
Toms, Anne b.1944, *Bird in Flight*, commissioned by Southampton University Hospitals NHS Trust, c.1994, © the artist
Toms, Anne b.1944, *Curlews and Tufted Ducks*, commissioned by Southampton University Hospitals NHS Trust, c.1994, © the artist
Toms, Anne b.1944, *Ducks (triptych, left)*, commissioned by Southampton University Hospitals NHS Trust, c.1994, © the artist
Toms, Anne b.1944, *Swans and Kingfisher (triptych, centre)*, commissioned by Southampton University Hospitals NHS Trust, c.1994, © the artist
Toms, Anne b.1944, *Geese and Cormorant (triptych, right)*, commissioned by Southampton University Hospitals NHS Trust, c.1994, © the artist
Toms, Anne b.1944, *Herons*, commissioned by Southampton University Hospitals NHS Trust, c.1994, © the artist
Toms, Anne b.1944, *Oyster Catchers and Wagtails*, commissioned by Southampton University Hospitals NHS Trust, c.1994, © the artist
Toms, Anne b.1944, *Swans and Ducks in Flight*, commissioned by Southampton University Hospitals NHS Trust, c.1994, © the artist
Toms, Anne b.1944, *Swans Landing*, commissioned by Southampton University Hospitals NHS Trust, c.1994, © the artist
Toms, Anne b.1944, *Swifts*, commissioned by Southampton University Hospitals NHS Trust, c.1994, © the artist
Toms, Anne b.1944, *Wading Birds*, commissioned by Southampton University Hospitals NHS Trust, c.1994, © the artist
unknown artist *A, B, C, D*
unknown artist *O, P, Q, R*
unknown artist *S, T, U, V*
unknown artist *W, X, Y, Z*
Wright, Jennifer b.1961, *Southsands*, purchased with the assistance of the Wessex Cancer Trust, 2006, © the artist
Wright, Jennifer b.1961, *Estuary, Late Spring*, commissioned with the assistance of the Wessex Cancer Trust, 2005, © the artist

University of Southampton

Barrett, Roderic 1920–2000, *Waiting Chairs*, © the artist's estate
Bird, Philip b.1952, *Deer, Ape and Hare*
Bowman *River Landscape*
Bradshaw, Gordon b.1931, *Landscape*
Brandeis, Antonietta 1849–1920, *The Grand Canal, Venice*
Buhler, Robert A. 1916–1989, *Duke of Wellington*, acquired, 1964, © the artist's estate/www.bridgeman.co.uk
Burman, John b.1936, *Trees in Light and Shade*
Chambers, Robert *Swarm*, acquired, 1990
Charles, Mel *Hanging Figure (diptych, left panel)*, acquired, 1977
Charles, Mel *Hanging Figure (diptych, right panel)*, acquired, 1977
Clarke, Hilda Margery b.1926, *Crosses*, acquired, 1974, © the artist
Cotes, Francis 1726–1770, *Sarah Robinson*
Cotton, Alan b.1938, *Snowdonia*, acquired, 1975
Crumplin, Colin b.1946, *Pitcher Plant (Nepenthe)*, © the artist
Drury, Judith b.1944, *Peacock Mandala*, © the artist
Elwell, Brian b.1938, *Carnival*
Elwyn, John 1916–1977, *September*, © the artist's estate
England, Muriel *The Pride of Devon*
Eurich, Richard Ernst 1903–1992, *The Rose*, acquired, 1960, © courtesy of the artist's estate/www.bridgeman.co.uk
Folkes, Peter L. b.1923, *Professor Kenneth Mather, Vice Chancellor (1965–1971)*, © the artist
Folkes, Peter L. b.1923, *Sir James Matthews*, © the artist
Fowle, LeClerc active 1950s–1982, *Lord Murray*
Freeth, Hubert Andrew 1913–1986, *Sir Samuel Gurney Dixon*, © Freeth family
Gaussen Marks, Elena b.1938, *Lord Tonypandy*, acquired, 1984, © the artist
Hoskins, Ned b.1939, *Aerial Conflict*, © the artist
Hoskins, Ned b.1939, *Convection*, © the artist
Irvin, Albert b.1922, *Rite*
Jones, Lucy b.1955, *River Bank*
Kirby, John b.1949, *Seated Man*, acquired, 1985, © the artist
Lancaster, Mark b.1938, *Henry VI Blue and Orange*, © the artist
Lane, Samuel 1780–1859, *Elizabeth Hobbes, Wife of Luke Groves Hansard*
Lane, Samuel 1780–1859, *Luke Groves Hansard*
Lane, Samuel 1780–1859, *Luke Hansard*
McLean, Bruce b.1944, *Untitled*
Merson, E. *Southampton Synagogue*, acquired, 1960
Neiman, Oscar *Painting*
Olsen, Geoffrey b.1943, *Running the White Tip (Merthyr)*
Pannett, Juliet 1911–2005, *Professor and Doctor Ford*, acquired, 1974, © the artist's estate
Pare, David 1911–1996, *Mill Garden*
Patten, William d.1843, *Portrait of a Lady*
Patten, William d.1843, *Portrait of a Gentleman*
Pritchard, Gwilym b.1931, *Buildings*, © the artist
Ramos, Theodore b.1928, *Doctor D. G. James, Vice Chancellor (1952–1965)*, © the artist
Rogers, Claude 1907–1979, *Sir Robert Wood, Principal (1946–1952), Vice Chancelllor (1952)*
Rothenstein, William 1872–1945, *War Cartoon (left panel)*, © courtesy of the artist's estate/www.bridgeman.co.uk
Rothenstein, William 1872–1945, *War Cartoon (right panel)*, © courtesy of the artist's estate/www.bridgeman.co.uk
Rothenstein, William 1872–1945, *Ceremony*, presented to the University by the artist's son, 1959, © courtesy of the artist's estate/www.bridgeman.co.uk
Rothenstein, William 1872–1945, *Claude Montefiore*, © courtesy of the artist's estate/www.bridgeman.co.uk
Rubin, Bina b.1942, *Jerusalem*, © the artist
Sainsbury, Timothy active 1972–1981, *Wire*
Shayer, William 1788–1879, *Donkeys in Landscape*
Shayer, William 1788–1879, *Landscape with Figures on a Path*
Shayer, William 1788–1879, *Landscape with Travellers on a Road*
Sinkinson, Frederick active 1965–1992, *Abstract*
Sinkinson, Frederick active 1965–1992, *Sir Gordon Higginson, Vice Chancellor (1985–1994)*
Smith, Ray b.1947, *Kenneth Hilton*, © the artist
Smith, Ray b.1947, *Balloon Man*, © the artist
Smith, Ray b.1947, *Monster*, © the artist
Smith, Richard b.1931, *Fleetwood*, acquired, 1964, © the artist
unknown artist *George Robinson*
unknown artist *Doctor Kenneth Vickers, Principal (1922–1946)*
unknown artist *H. R. Hartley, Aged 9*
unknown artist *Henry Hartley*
unknown artist *Professor John Roberts, Vice Chancellor (1979–1985)*
unknown artist *Professor Laurence Gower, Vice Chancellor (1971–1979)*
unknown artist *Sir Howard Newby, Vice Chancellor (1994–2001)*
unknown artist *Susannah Hartley*
Velázquez, Diego (follower of) 1599–1660, *Bacchus*
Wakefield, Larry 1925–1997, *Brown Painting*, © the artist's estate
Wakefield, Larry 1925–1997, *Painting*, © the artist's estate
Watts, George Frederick 1817–1904, *Claude Joseph Schmid Montefiore*
Withycombe, Joyce active 1928–1933, *Doctor J. W. Horrocks*
Withycombe, Joyce active 1928–1933, *The Quartet*

Blackgang Sawmill and St Catherine's Quay

Charbonnier, Theodore active 1881–1894, *Alexander Dabell (1809–1898)*, commissioned by the family from a photograph
Edmunds *The Rescue of the German Steamer 'Eider' off Atherfield Ledge*
Hailstone, Bernard 1910–1987, *Francis Dabell*, commissioned by the family, © the artist's estate
unknown artist *View of Blackgang Chine*
unknown artist *Amelia Dabell*, commissioned by the family
Westcott *Bruce Dabell*, commissioned by the family

Brading Roman Villa

unknown artist 19th C, *Portrait of a Gentleman (possibly Captain John Thorp of the 63rd Regiment of Foot or William Munns of Morton Farm)*

Cowes Maritime Museum

Allen, Beryl *Cowes Creek*, unknown provenance
Burrows, E. G. active 20th C, *'HMS Cavalier'*, gift, 1993
Colleypriest, Victor b.1901, *'HMS Quentin'*, on loan from a private institution
Colleypriest, Victor b.1901, *'HMS Stevenstone'*, on loan from a private institution
Colleypriest, Victor b.1901, *'Sidi Mabrouk'*, on loan from a private institution
Colleypriest, Victor b.1901, *'Arethusa'*, on loan from a private institution
Colleypriest, Victor b.1901, *HM Minelayer 'Abdiel'*, on loan from a private institution
Colleypriest, Victor b.1901, *'HMCS Sioux'*, on loan from a private institution

De Lacy, Charles John active 1885–1940, *Destroyer 'Forester' off Constantinople*, on loan from a private institution
Garrett, A. (attributed to) *A Yacht Race*, purchased
Groves *'Princess' and 'The Needles'*, purchased, 1983
Hibbert, Phyllis I. b.1903, *Schooner in Full Sail*, unknown provenance
Holland, T. *Cowes Week, Isle of Wight*, purchased, 1983
Marshall, John Frederick (circle of) active 1875–1890, *On Shanklin Rocks*, unknown provenance
G. S. *Sailing Ship off Solent Fort*, gift, 1993
Steer, James (attributed to) *Thomas White (1773–1859)*, on loan from a private institution

English Heritage, Osborne House

Fildes, Luke (after) 1844–1927, *George V (1865–1936)*, transferred from the Vienna Legation, 1939
Fildes, Luke (after) 1844–1927, *Queen Alexandra (1844–1925)*, transferred from the Vienna Legation, 1939
Fildes, Luke (after) 1844–1927, *Queen Mary (1867–1953)*, transferred from the Vienna Legation, 1939
Fildes, Luke (copy of) 1844–1927, *Edward VII (1841–1910)*, transferred from the Vienna Legation, 1939
Lucas, John 1807–1874, *Prince Albert (1819–1861), Princess Royal and Eos*, purchased from Sotheby's British Paintings, 1992
unknown artist *Charles I (1600–1649)*, purchased at auction, 2002

Sir Max Aitken Museum

Backhuysen, Ludolf I 1630–1708, *The Foundering of the 'Coronation' 90 Guns at Rame Head, 1691*
Bough, Samuel 1822–1878, *British Emigrants Boarding a Merchant Vessel for Australia, Firth of Forth*
British (English) School *Scene from the Battle of the Nile, 1–2 August 1798*
British (English) School *Scene from the Battle of the Nile, 1–2 August 1798*
British (English) School *Scene from the Battle of the Nile, 1–2 August 1798*
British (English) School *Scene from the Battle of the Nile, 1–2 August 1798*
Buttersworth, Thomas 1768–1842, *The Battle of Trafalgar, 21 October 1805*
Carmichael, James Wilson 1800–1868, *Shipping off Ryde*
Chalon, John James 1778–1854, *Arrival of a Steam Packet from Boulogne during a Gale, 1846*
Dawson, Montague J. 1895–1973, *'Thermopylae' Clipper*, © the artist's estate
Devis, Arthur (copy after) 1712–1787, *The Death of Nelson*
Engtoin, Quelelberge *The Argentine Corvette 'Uruguay' Searching for Nordenskjöld's Expedition in the Atlantic Ocean, 1903*
Luny, Thomas 1759–1837, *The East Indiaman 'Ceres' off the Spithead Depicted in Four Different Views*
Luny, Thomas 1759–1837, *Shipping in a Stiff Breeze*
Luny, Thomas 1759–1837, *Departure of the Fleet*
Luny, Thomas 1759–1837, *The Engagement*
Luny, Thomas 1759–1837, *Armed Merchantmen into Dartmouth*
Luny, Thomas 1759–1837, *Shipping Warping into Harbour off Berry Head*
Macheren, Philip van d. after 1672, *French Man of War*
Minderhout, Hendrik van (attributed to) 1632–1696, *Dutch Whalers*
Monamy, Peter 1681–1749, *Shipping off Spithead*
Nibbs, Richard Henry 1816–1893, *The Departure from Gravesend of HRH Princess Royal on Her Marriage, 2 February 1858, to Prince Frederick, during a Snowstorm*
Powell, Charles Martin 1775–1824, *Dutch and British Men O'War off the Coast, Dutch Boat in the Foreground*
Serres, John Thomas 1759–1825, *Shipping off Genoa*
Storck, Abraham (attributed to) 1644–1708, *British Men O'War and the Dutch Fleet Commanded by Admiral Tromp Fighting on the Thames*
Swaine, Francis c.1720–1782, *Shipping off the Isle of Wight*
Wallis, Alfred 1855–1942, *Sailing Boats*
Whitcombe, Thomas c.1752–1824, *Two Views of HM Frigate 'Amelia' off Berry Head*
Wilkinson, Norman 1878–1971, *Shipping Scene (St James's Fight, 5 July 1666)*, © the Norman Wilkinson estate

Museum of Island Railway History

Ellis, Cuthbert Hamilton 1909–1987, *Freshwater*, bequeathed
Ellis, Cuthbert Hamilton 1909–1987, *Freshwater, Yamouth and Newport No.2*, bequeathed
Ellis, Cuthbert Hamilton 1909–1987, *Isle of Wight Central No.11 to Sandown at Ryde Pier*, bequeathed
Ellis, Cuthbert Hamilton 1909–1987, *London and South Western Railway No.369*, bequeathed
Ellis, Cuthbert Hamilton 1909–1987, *London-Brighton South Coast at Night*, bequeathed
Ellis, Cuthbert Hamilton 1909–1987, *Newport Station*, bequeathed
Ellis, Cuthbert Hamilton 1909–1987, *No.2 'Isle of Wight Central' with No.1 'Isle of Wight Central' in the Background*, bequeathed
Ellis, Cuthbert Hamilton 1909–1987, *No.6 'Ventnor Town' at Evening*, bequeathed
Ellis, Cuthbert Hamilton 1909–1987, *No.31, 'Chale'*, bequeathed
Ellis, Cuthbert Hamilton 1909–1987, *'Ventnor'*, bequeathed

Carisbrooke Castle Museum

C. M. A. *Gateway and Gatehouse of Carisbrooke Castle*
Angeli, Heinrich von 1840–1925, *Prince Henry (1858–1896) in Military Uniform*, gift from A. F. Covetti, 1898
Banks, N. *The Keep at Carisbrooke Castle Painted from the Roof of the Residence*, bequeathed by A. F. Maitland, 1950
Beville, F. W. *Naval Ship off Freshwater Bay*, bequeathed by A. F. Maitland, 1950
Bower, Edward (after) d.1666/1667, *Charles I (1600–1649)*, gift from P. Moore, 1969
Cantelo, Ellen active c.1830–1859, *Carisbrooke Village with Miss Sanders' Great-Grandparents and Their Water Cart*, bequeathed, 2003
Collingwood-Smith, William 1815–1887, *Sunset on Southampton Water Showing a Seascape with Shipping and the Isle of Wight*, bequeathed by A. F. Maitland, 1950
Cope, Arthur Stockdale 1857–1940, *Princess Beatrice (1856–1944)*
Cope, Charles West 1811–1890, *The Royal Prisoners*, gift, 1952
Fowles, Arthur Wellington c.1815–1883, *Yacht Sailing off Osborne Bay*, bequeathed by A. F. Maitland, 1950
Gandy, Thomas active 1848–1859, *Portrait of a Gentleman Holding a Cello (possibly William Turtle)*, gift from S. Turtle, 1993
Ibbetson *The Gatehouse at Carisbrooke Castle*
Kneller, Godfrey (after) 1646–1723, *The Second Duke of Bolton Wearing the Robes of a Knight of the Garter with His Chamberlain's Wand*, gift from C. W. L. Dashwood, 1957
Minns, Fanny Mary active 1865–1905, *Alum Bay Seen from Headon Hill*, gift from Lady K. M. Maybury, 1970
Minns, Fanny Mary active 1865–1905, *Rural Scene near Arreton*
Robins, Henry 1820–1892, *Large Ship Entering Portsmouth Harbour with the Isle of Wight in the Distance*, bequeathed by A. F. Maitland, 1950
Roy, Michael *Station Building at Carisbrooke Halt*, on loan from artist
Stewart, F. A. *Carisbrooke Castle from Mount Joy as it Appeared on 23 August 1831, the Day the Duchess of Kent was there to View the Archery*, bequeathed by A. F. Maitland, 1950
unknown artist *'Pound Hammer' Kingswell of Luccombe*, bequeathed, 1995
unknown artist *A Three-Masted Ship in a Rough Sea Passing a White Cliff, possibly Culver or Freshwater*
unknown artist *Charles I (1600–1649)*
unknown artist *Clatterford Showing Cottages and Bridge*
unknown artist *Portrait of a Man*
unknown artist *Portrait of an Unknown Gentleman in Hunting Pink*
unknown artist *Portrait of a Lady (possibly the Madonna)*
unknown artist *Priory Farm with Carisbrooke Church and Castle in the Background*, bequeathed by A. F. Maitland, 1950
unknown artist *Ships Rounding 'The Needles'*, bequeathed by A. F. Maitland, 1950
unknown artist *Viscount Eversley, First President of the Royal National Hospital at Ventnor*, gift from the Isle of Wight Hospital Management Committee, 1964
Wiber active 19th C, *A Ship off 'The Needles' (possibly 'SS Sultan')*, purchased
Wiber active 19th C, *Rowing Boat in the Solent Looking West with 'The Needles' and Hurst Castle*

Healing Arts, Isle of Wight NHS Primary Care Trust

Allthus *Autumn Landscape*, donated by the artist, 1985
Anderson, M. *Frank James and Elephants*, purchased, 1985
Argyle, Malindy b.1945, *Lease of Life*, commissioned, 2006, © the artist
Argyle, Malindy b.1945, *The Journey*, commissioned, 2006, © the artist
Argyle, Malindy b.1945, *Water Ballet*, commissioned, 2006, © the artist
Argyle, Malindy b.1945, *Winds of Change*, commissioned, 2006, © the artist
Argyle, Malindy b.1945, *Borthwood Copse*, commissioned, 2004, © the artist
Argyle, Malindy b.1945, *East Wight Downs*, commissioned, 2004, © the artist
Argyle, Malindy b.1945, *Pastoral: Steephill Cove*, commissioned, 2004, © the artist
Argyle, Malindy b.1945, *Still Life: Isle of Wight*, commissioned, 2004, © the artist
Ayres, Gillian b.1930, *Matuka*, purchased, 2005, © the artist
Banks, Mary *The Dance*, purchased, mid-1990s
Barker *Winter Evening, Swansea Bay*, donated by the artist, mid-1980s
Barry, Francis, *Chrysanthemums*, donated, 1985
Blackett, Vivien b.1955, *Jar and Wing*, purchased from an exhibition at Aspex Gallery, Portsmouth, 1988, © the artist
Blackett, Vivien b.1955, *Inquire*, purchased from an exhibition at Quay Arts, Isle of Wight, late 1990s, © the artist
Boden, Richard active 1980–1986, *Row of Benches*, donated by the artist, 1986
Boden, Richard active 1980–1986, *Park Bench*, donated by the artist, 1986
Boden, Richard active 1980–1986, *St Giles' Hill*, purchased
Boulter, Roger *Star and Planets*, donated by the artist, 2004
Bowyer, Elizabeth *Early Morning: Brook House*, bequeathed by the artist, 1991
Bowyer, Robert *Mrs Shirley Cornelius*, bequeathed by Elizabeth Bowyer, wife of the artist
Bowyer, Robert *Seated Woman in a Garden*, bequeathed by Elizabeth Bowyer, wife of the artist
Bowyer, Robert *Spectacles*, bequeathed by Elizabeth Bowyer, wife of the artist
Burgess, Ria *Orchard near Niton*
Butler, Roger b.1945, *The Duver*, purchased from the artist from an exhibition, late 1990s, © the artist
Campbell, Beatrice 1901–2000, *Red House in the Wood*, bequeathed by the artist, late 1990s
Campbell, Beatrice 1901–2000, *Thorness*, bequeathed by the artist, late 1990s
Clarke, Hilda Margery b.1926, *Pembroke Promontory*, purchased from the artist, mid-1990s, © the artist
Court, Sally b.1948, *Sitting Room, Garden and Seashore (detail, 1 of 3)*, donated by the artist, mid-1990s, © Sally Court, artist & designer
Court, Sally b.1948, *Sitting Room, Garden and Seashore (detail, 2 of 3)*, donated by the artist, mid-1990s, © Sally Court, artist & designer
Court, Sally b.1948, *Sitting Room, Garden and Seashore (detail, 3 of 3)*, donated by the artist, mid-1990s, © Sally Court, artist & designer
Court, Sally b.1948, *Jungle Jigsaw*, commissioned, 2002, © Sally Court, artist & designer
Court, Sally b.1948, *Tree and Birds*, commissioned, 2002, © Sally Court, artist & designer
Court, Sally b.1948, *Wildlife Jigsaw*, commissioned, 2002, © Sally Court, artist & designer
Court, Sally b.1948, *Jungle Jigsaw*, commissioned, 2000, © Sally Court, artist & designer
Court, Sally b.1948, *Jungle Jigsaw: Cheetah (1 of 14)*, commissioned, 2000, © Sally Court, artist & designer
Court, Sally b.1948, *Jungle Jigsaw: Snake Head (2 of 14)*,

commissioned, 2000, © Sally Court, artist & designer
Court, Sally b.1948, *Jungle Jigsaw: Giraffe Head (3 of 14)*, commissioned, 2000, © Sally Court, artist & designer
Court, Sally b.1948, *Jungle Jigsaw: Tiger Head (4 of 14)*, commissioned, 2000, © Sally Court, artist & designer
Court, Sally b.1948, *Jungle Jigsaw: Zebra Head (5 of 14)*, commissioned, 2000, © Sally Court, artist & designer
Court, Sally b.1948, *Jungle Jigsaw: Snake Tail (6 of 14)*, © Sally Court, artist & designer
Court, Sally b.1948, *Jungle Jigsaw: Snake Tail/ Cheetah Tail (7 of 14)*, commissioned, 2000, © Sally Court, artist & designer
Court, Sally b.1948, *Jungle Jigsaw: Cheetah Body (8 of 14)*, commissioned, 2000, © Sally Court, artist & designer
Court, Sally b.1948, *Jungle Jigsaw: Tiger Tail (9 of 14)*, commissioned, 2000, © Sally Court, artist & designer
Court, Sally b.1948, *Jungle Jigsaw: Tiger Body (10 of 14)*, commissioned, 2000, © Sally Court, artist & designer
Court, Sally b.1948, *Jungle Jigsaw: Zebra Tail (11 of 14)*, commissioned, 2000, © Sally Court, artist & designer
Court, Sally b.1948, *Jungle Jigsaw: Zebra Neck (12 of 14)*, commissioned, 2000, © Sally Court, artist & designer
Court, Sally b.1948, *Jungle Jigsaw: Giraffe Neck (13 of 14)*, commissioned, 2000, © Sally Court, artist & designer
Court, Sally b.1948, *Jungle Jigsaw: Giraffe Tail (14 of 14)*, commissioned, 2000, © Sally Court, artist & designer
Court, Sally b.1948, *Diver 1*, commissioned, 2000, © Sally Court, artist & designer
Court, Sally b.1948, *Diver 2*, commissioned, 2000, © Sally Court, artist & designer
Court, Sally b.1948, *Diver 3*, commissioned, 2000, © Sally Court, artist & designer
Court, Sally b.1948, *Dolphin Scene*, commissioned, 2000, © Sally Court, artist & designer
Court, Sally b.1948, *Elephant*, commissioned, 2000, © Sally Court, artist & designer
Court, Sally b.1948, *Fish Roundel*, commissioned, 2000, © Sally Court, artist & designer
Court, Sally b.1948, *Honeysuckle Blossom*, purchased from the artist, mid-1990s, © Sally Court, artist & designer
Court, Sally b.1948, *Insect Jigsaw Installation*, commissioned, 2000, © Sally Court, artist & designer
Court, Sally b.1948, *Mermaid Roundel*, commissioned, 2000, © Sally Court, artist & designer
Court, Sally b.1948, *Monkey*, commissioned, 2000, © Sally Court, artist & designer
Court, Sally b.1948, *Rhino*, commissioned, 2000, © Sally Court, artist & designer
Court, Sally b.1948, *Sea Scene*, commissioned, 2000, © Sally Court, artist & designer
Court, Sally b.1948, *Shellfish Roundel*, commissioned, 2000, © Sally Court, artist & designer
Court, Sally b.1948, *Starfish Roundel*, commissioned, 2000, © Sally Court, artist & designer
Court, Sally b.1948, *Summer Field 2*, commissioned, mid-1990s, © Sally Court, artist & designer
Court, Sally b.1948, *The Cornfield*, commissioned, mid-1990s, © Sally Court, artist & designer
Court, Sally b.1948, *The Sea (1 of 6)*, commissioned, 2000, © Sally Court, artist & designer
Court, Sally b.1948, *The Sea (2 of 6)*, commissioned, 2000, © Sally Court, artist & designer
Court, Sally b.1948, *The Sea (3 of 6)*, commissioned, 2000, © Sally Court, artist & designer
Court, Sally b.1948, *The Sea (4 of 6)*, commissioned, 2000, © Sally Court, artist & designer
Court, Sally b.1948, *The Sea (5 of 6)*, commissioned, 2000, © Sally Court, artist & designer
Court, Sally b.1948, *The Sea (6 of 6)*, commissioned, 2000, © Sally Court, artist & designer
Court, Sally b.1948, **Eades, Carolanne** b.1945 & **Students of Watergate School** *Bee*, commissioned, 2000, © Sally Court, artist & designer
Court, Sally b.1948, **Eades, Carolanne** b.1945 & **Students of Watergate School** *Jungle Scene 1*, commissioned, 2000, © Sally Court, artist & designer
Court, Sally b.1948, **Eades, Carolanne** b.1945 & **Students of Watergate School** *Jungle Scene 2*, commissioned, 2000, © Sally Court, artist & designer
Court, Sally b.1948, **Eades, Carolanne** b.1945 & **Students of Watergate School** *Jungle Scene 3*, commissioned, 2000, © Sally Court, artist & designer
Court, Sally b.1948, **Eades, Carolanne** b.1945 & **Students of Watergate School** *Pink Bird*, commissioned, 2000, © Sally Court, artist & designer
Court, Sally b.1948, **Eades, Carolanne** b.1945 & **Students of Watergate School** *Purple Fish*, commissioned, 2000, © Sally Court, artist & designer
Court, Sally b.1948, **Eades, Carolanne** b.1945 & **Students of Watergate School** *Rainbow Bird*, commissioned, 2000, © Sally Court, artist & designer
Court, Sally b.1948, **Eades, Carolanne** b.1945 & **Students of Watergate School** *Small Fish*, commissioned, 2000, © Sally Court, artist & designer
Court, Sally b.1948, **Eades, Carolanne** b.1945 & **Students of Watergate School** *Stripey Fish*, commissioned, 2000, © Sally Court, artist & designer
Court, Sally b.1948, **Eades, Carolanne** b.1945 & **Students of Watergate School** *Toucan*, commissioned, 2000, © Sally Court, artist & designer
Court, Sally b.1948, **Eades, Carolanne** b.1945 & **Students of Watergate School** *Yellow Bird*, commissioned, 2000, © Sally Court, artist & designer
Crowther, Patricia b.1965, *Winter Quay*, purchased, 2004, © the artist
Crowther, Patricia b.1965, *Mist Circle*, purchased, 2004, © the artist
Davidge, E. Gordon *Breaking Wave*, donated, 1985
Davidge, E. Gordon *Flowers*, donated, 1985
Dean, Audrey active 1973–1985, *Arch Rock, Freshwater*, donated by the artist, 1985
Dean, Audrey active 1973–1985, *Cottages at Porchfield*, donated by the artist, 1985
Dean, Audrey active 1973–1985, *Freshwater Bay*, donated by the artist, 1985
Dightam, Peter *Red-Roofed Landscape*, donated, 1985
Fereday, Joseph 1917–2001, *Portrait of a Gentleman*, donated
Fraser *Calbourne Mill*
Gingell, Mary *Landscape 8: Dawn*, purchased from the artist, 1988
Graham, Melanie *Icon of Loving Tenderness*, commissioned, 1990
Hambling, Maggi b.1945, *Dragon Sunrise*, purchased with a charitable grant from the artist after an exhibition at the Barbican Centre, London, 1990, © the artist
Hewitson, Eric *Artist Cracks the Mathematics of Chaos*, donated by the artist, 1996
Hibbert, Phyllis I. b.1903, *Alveston Mill*, donated, 1985
Hibbert, Phyllis I. b.1903, *Bridge: Water*, donated, 1985
Hibbert, Phyllis I. b.1903, *Camelias*, donated, 1985
Hibbert, Phyllis I. b.1903, *Devon Cows*, donated, 1985
Hibbert, Phyllis I. b.1903, *Stone Bridge, Scotland*, donated, 1985
Hibbert, Phyllis I. b.1903, *Two Pheasants*, donated,1985
Hibbert, Phyllis I. b.1903, *View of Ventnor to Bonchurch*, donated, 1985
Hobden, George *Pastoral Scene with Horses*, donated, 1985
Hodge Thomas, Charlotte b.1968, *Untitled (Abstract Orange & Turquoise)*, purchased
Hodges, P. J. *Appley in Winter*, donated, 1985
Hughes, Lucy *Noise*, donated by the artist, 2004
Johnson, Sara b.1957, *Heartbeat*, purchased from the artist, mid-1990s, © the artist
Johnson, Sara b.1957, *Struggle*, purchased from the artist, mid-1990s, © the artist
Johnson, Sara b.1957, *Supplanter of Daylight*, © the artist
Johnson, Sara b.1957, *White Cell Dreams*, purchased from the artist, mid-1990s, © the artist
Joseph, S. *Beach Hotel*, donated, 1985
Joseph, S. *Red Ball*, donated, 1985
Julian, C. H. *Marguerite*, bequeathed by Elizabeth Bowyer
Kemp, S. J. *Storm in Paris*, donated, 1985
Kendrick, G. *Mottistone Manor*, donated, 1985
Kerr, Alfred active 1972–1985, *Landscape*, donated by the artist, 1985
Koessler, Edith *Roofs at Gibraltar*, donated by the artist, c.1990
Kubisa, Seran b.1967, *Connect 1*, purchased from the artist from an exhibition at Aspex Gallery, Portsmouth, mid-1990s, © the artist
Kubisa, Seran b.1967, *Star Cluster*, purchased from the artist from an exhibition at Aspex Gallery, Portsmouth, mid-1990s, © the artist
Leath, Peter active c.1995–2001, *Frank James Hospital*
Leath, Peter active c.1995–2001, *Thames Barge Fishing Off the Needles*
MacCarthy, C. active 1980–1985, *Interior at Weedon*, donated by the artist, 1985
MacCarthy, C. active 1980–1985, *In the Gallery*, donated, 1985
Markey, Peter b.1930, *Copse*, purchased from the artist from an exhibition at Quay Arts, Isle of Wight, mid-1990s, © the artist
Markey, Peter b.1930, *Yachts*, purchased from the artist from an exhibition at Quay Arts, Isle of Wight, mid-1990s, © the artist
Markey, Peter b.1930, *Three Giraffes*, purchased from the artist from an exhibition at Quay Arts, Isle of Wight, mid-1990s, © the artist
Markey, Peter b.1930, *African Violets*, purchased from the artist from an exhibition at Quay Arts, Isle of Wight, mid-1990s, © the artist
Markey, Peter b.1930, *Boat and Building*, purchased from the artist from an exhibition at Quay Arts, Isle of Wight, mid-1990s, © the artist
Markey, Peter b.1930, *Geraniums*, purchased from the artist from an exhibition at Quay Arts, Isle of Wight, mid-1990s, © the artist
Markey, Peter b.1930, *Sheep*, purchased from the artist from an exhibition at Quay Arts, Isle of Wight, mid-1990s
McLaren Clark, Lisa b.1973, *Beachcomber*, purchased from the artist, 1990
McPherson, Alan b.1943, *Spine of Wight*, commissioned, 1988, © the artist
McPherson, Alan b.1943, *Spine of Wight East*, commissioned from the artist, 1988, © the artist
McPherson, Alan b.1943, *Spine of Wight West*, commissioned, 1988, © the artist
McPhilbin, Jo *Draught of Fishes*, donated by the artist, late 1980s
Mence, Marcia b.1948, *Colour Storm Triptych*, donated by the artist and Toby Beardsall, 2005, © the artist
Mence, Myles b.1954, *Needles and Bear of Britain*, donated, 2006
Mikulewitsch, A. *Sunset on the Isle of Wight*, donated, 1985
Morton, Cavendish b.1911, *North Lookout Tower, Aldeburgh, Suffolk*, purchased from the artist, 2004, © the artist
Nicoll, Stephen *Holiday Postcard Series 1: Newport (IOW county press)*, commissioned, 1989, © the artist
Nicoll, Stephen *Holiday Postcard Series 2: Cowes (postcard messages)*, commissioned, 1989, © the artist
Nicoll, Stephen *Holiday Postcard Series 3: Ryde (telegrams and luggage)*, commissioned, 1989, © the artist
Nicoll, Stephen *Holiday Postcard Series 4: Sandown (poem and memorabilia)*, commissioned, 1989, © the artist
Nicoll, Stephen *Holiday Postcard Series 5: Vectis (poem and patterns)*, commissioned, 1989, © the artist
Nicoll, Stephen *Holiday Postcard Series 6: Ventnor (poem and postcards)*, commissioned, 1989, © the artist
Nicoll, Stephen *Holiday Postcard Series 7: West Wight (poem and pebbles)*, commissioned, 1989, © the artist
Nicoll, Stephen *Ward Sign: Medina (Paddle Steamer)*, commissioned, 1989, © the artist
Picton Fox, Barbara d.1990, *Portrait of a Soldier*, donated by the artist
Picton Fox, Barbara d.1990, *Burmese Woman*, donated by the artist, 1985
Power, Ronald 1914–1989, *Blue Lady*, bequeathed by the artist, late 1980s, © the artist's estate
Power, Ronald 1914–1989, *Church on Seashore*, bequeathed by the artist, late 1980s, © the artist's estate
Power, Ronald 1914–1989, *Dancer*, donated, © the artist's estate
Power, Ronald 1914–1989, *Dancer in Blue*, bequeathed by the artist, late 1980s, © the artist's estate
Power, Ronald 1914–1989, *Dead Crow*, bequeathed by the artist, late 1980s, © the artist's estate
Power, Ronald 1914–1989, *Estuary and Lock*, bequeathed by the artist, late 1980s, © the artist's estate
Power, Ronald 1914–1989, *Lady in a Lilac Dress*, bequeathed by the artist, late 1980s, © the artist's estate
Power, Ronald 1914–1989, *Lady in a Maroon Dress*, bequeathed by

the artist, late 1980s, © the artist's estate
Power, Ronald 1914–1989, *Lady in a Red Dress*, bequeathed by the artist, late 1980s, © the artist's estate
Power, Ronald 1914–1989, *Lady in a Sawtooth Jumper*, bequeathed by the artist, late 1980s, © the artist's estate
Power, Ronald 1914–1989, *Lady in a White Blouse*, bequeathed by the artist, late 1980s, © the artist's estate
Power, Ronald 1914–1989, *Lady with Auburn Hair*, bequeathed by the artist, late 1980s, © the artist's estate
Power, Ronald 1914–1989, *Nude: Dressing Morning*, bequeathed by the artist, late 1980s, © the artist's estate
Power, Ronald 1914–1989, *Plants on a Windowsill*, bequeathed by the artist, late 1980s, © the artist's estate
Power, Ronald 1914–1989, *Portrait of a Gentleman*, bequeathed by the artist, late 1980s, © the artist's estate
Power, Ronald 1914–1989, *Portrait of a Lady in Blue*, bequeathed by the artist, late 1980s, © the artist's estate
Power, Ronald 1914–1989, *Portrait of a Lady in Yellow*, bequeathed by the artist, late 1980s, © the artist's estate
Power, Ronald 1914–1989, *Quarry No.1*, bequeathed by the artist, late 1980s, © the artist's estate
Power, Ronald 1914–1989, *Quarry No.2*, bequeathed by the artist, late 1980s, © the artist's estate
Power, Ronald 1914–1989, *Quarry No.3*, bequeathed by the artist, late 1980s, © the artist's estate
Power, Ronald 1914–1989, *Seashore Finds*, bequeathed by the artist, late 1980s, © the artist's estate
Power, Ronald 1914–1989, *Seated Nude*, bequeathed by the artist, late 1980s, © the artist's estate
Power, Ronald 1914–1989, *Self Portrait*, bequeathed by the artist, late 1980s, © the artist's estate
Power, Ronald 1914–1989, *South American Woman*, bequeathed by the artist, late 1980s, © the artist's estate
Power, Ronald 1914–1989, *Spring Sun*, bequeathed by the artist, late 1980s, © the artist's estate
Power, Ronald 1914–1989, *Still Life*, bequeathed by the artist, late 1980s, © the artist's estate
Power, Ronald 1914–1989, *Still Life: Chequered Board*, bequeathed by the artist, late 1980s, © the artist's estate
Power, Ronald 1914–1989, *Study for Nude*, donated, © the artist's estate
Power, Ronald 1914–1989, *The Catch*, bequeathed by the artist, late 1980s, © the artist's estate
Power, Ronald 1914–1989, *The Storm*, bequeathed by the artist, late 1980s, © the artist's estate
Power, Ronald 1914–1989, *White Cottage*, bequeathed by the artist, late 1980s, © the artist's estate
Robinson, N. W. *Northcourt Manor House*, donated, 1985
Seaward, L. *The Quay*, donated, 1985
Simpson, Reg *City Waterfront*, acquired, c.1985
Squibb, Roy 1931–1992, *Boat off Cowes*, bequeathed by the artist, early 1990s, © the artist's estate
Squibb, Roy 1931–1992, *Cherry Blossom: South Hospital, St Mary's*, bequeathed by the artist, early 1990s, © the artist's estate
Squibb, Roy 1931–1992, *Isle of Wight Landscape*, bequeathed by the artist, early 1990s, © the artist's estate
Squibb, Roy 1931–1992, *Two Barges*, bequeathed by the artist, early 1990s, © the artist's estate
Squibb, Roy 1931–1992, *Whitecroft: Clock Tower*, bequeathed by the artist, early 1990s, © the artist's estate
Stell *Amsterdam, St Nicholas' Church*
Stevenson, S. *Newport Harbour*
Stewart *Irish Landscape*, donated, 1985
Stewart, Lorna *Clown*, donated, 1985
Stille Parker, Margareta active 1955–2002, *Orchard*, donated by the artist, 2002
Thorpe, Hilary b.1959, *The Wave*, purchased from the artist, c.2001, © the artist
Till, Mike *Bluebell Wood*, donated, 2006
Toms, Anne b.1944, *View across Lake (CT Scanner Ceiling)*, commissioned, 1991, © Anne Toms
Toms, Anne b.1944, *Water Buttercups*, commissioned with a grant, mid-1990s, © Anne Toms
Toms, Anne b.1944, *West Wight 1*, commissioned, 1985, © Anne Toms
Toms, Anne b.1944, *West Wight 2*, commissioned, 1985, © Anne Toms
Toms, Anne b.1944, *West Wight 3*, commissioned, 1985, © Anne Toms
Toms, Anne b.1944, *West Wight 4*, commissioned, 1985, © Anne Toms
Toms, Anne b.1944, *Four Seasons: Autumn*, commissioned, 1985, © Anne Toms
Toms, Anne b.1944, *Four Seasons: Spring*, commissioned, 1985, © Anne Toms
Toms, Anne b.1944, *Four Seasons: Summer*, commissioned, 1985, © Anne Toms
Toms, Anne b.1944, *Four Seasons: Winter*, commissioned, 1985, © Anne Toms
Toms, Anne b.1944, *Dawn*, commissioned, 1995, © Anne Toms
Toms, Anne b.1944, *Lakeside*, commissioned with a grant, 1991, © Anne Toms
Toms, Anne b.1944, *Bevy of Swans (detail) (part 1 of 8)*, commissioned with a grant from the artist, mid-1990s, © Anne Toms
Toms, Anne b.1944, *Bevy of Swans (detail) (part 2 of 8)*, commissioned with a grant, mid-1990s, © Anne Toms
Toms, Anne b.1944, *Bevy of Swans (detail) (part 3 of 8)*, commissioned with a grant, mid-1990s, © Anne Toms
Toms, Anne b.1944, *Bevy of Swans (detail) (part 4 of 8)*, commissioned with a grant, mid-1990s, © Anne Toms
Toms, Anne b.1944, *Bevy of Swans (detail) (part 5 of 8)*, commissioned with a grant, mid-1990s, © Anne Toms
Toms, Anne b.1944, *Bevy of Swans (detail) (part 6 of 8)*, commissioned with a grant, mid-1990s, © Anne Toms
Toms, Anne b.1944, *Bevy of Swans (detail) part 7 of 8)*, commissioned with a grant, mid-1990s, © Anne Toms
Toms, Anne b.1944, *Beneath the Wave, under the Sky*, commissioned, 2003, © Anne Toms
unknown artist 19th C, *Arthur Hill Hassall, MD (1817–1894), Founder of the Royal National Hospital, Ventnor (1868)*, commissioned in the late nineteenth century by Ventnor Hospital trustees; beqeathed to the Isle of Wight NHS Trust, 1948
unknown artist 20th C, *Ducks: French Orchard*, donated
unknown artist 20th C, *View to the Sea*, donated
unknown artist 20th C, *Wooded Lake*, donated
Vince, Dianne b.1966, *Study for 'Dolphins No.1'*, commissioned, 1990, © the artist
Vince, Dianne b.1966, *Study for 'Dolphins No.2'*, commissioned, 1990, © the artist
Vince, Dianne b.1966, *Study for 'Dolphins No.3'*, commissioned, 1990, © the artist
Wakefield, M. (Mrs) *Still Life*, donated, 1985
Wearn, Margery *Nasturtiums*, donated, 1985
Wells, Peter 1938–1996, *Chevron*, bequeathed by the artist, 2000, © the artist's estate
Wells, Peter 1938–1996, *Coloured Squares*, bequeathed by the artist, 2000, © the artist's estate
Wilkinson, Celia b.1963, *Tropical Fish 1*, commissioned, 2003, © the artist
Wilkinson, Celia b.1963, *Tropical Fish 2*, commissioned, 2003, © the artist
Wilkinson, Celia b.1963, *Tropical Fish 3*, commissioned, 2003, © the artist
Wilkinson, Celia b.1963, *Tropical Fish 4*, commissioned, 2003, © the artist
Wilkinson, Celia b.1963, *Tropical Fish 5*, commissioned, 2003, © the artist
Wilkinson, Celia b.1963, *Tropical Fish 6*, commissioned, 2003, © the artist
Wilkinson, Celia b.1963, *Tropical Fish 7*, commissioned, 2003, © the artist
Williams, Emrys b.1958, *Album*, purchased from an exhibition at Quay Arts, Isle of Wight, 1998, © the artist
Williams, J. B. *Landscape*
Wolton, Vidya b.1964, *Red, Blue, White, Yellow*, © the artist, www.vidyaworks.co.uk
Wolton, Vidya b.1964, *Untitled No.1*, © the artist, www.vidyaworks.co.uk
Wright, Barbara b.1944, *Off 'The Needles'*, donated, © the artist
Wright, Peter b.1932, *Estuary 1*, on long-term loan from the artist, © the artist
Wright, Peter b.1932, *Estuary 2*, on long-term loan from the artist, © the artist
Wright, Peter b.1932, *Estuary 3*, on long-term loan from the artist, © the artist
Wright, Peter b.1932, *Estuary 4*, on long-term loan from the artist, © the artist
Wright, Peter b.1932, *Bembridge Harbour*, donated by the artist and residents of Bembridge, Isle of Wight, 1995, © the artist
Wright, Peter b.1932, *South West Coast*, donated by residents of Bembridge, Isle of Wight, 1998, © the artist
Wright, Peter b.1932, *Whitecliff Bay*, purchased from the artist, 1990, © the artist
Wright, Peter b.1932, *La serie Vallespir No.1*, purchased from the artist, 1995, © the artist
Wright, Peter b.1932, *La serie Vallespir No.2*, purchased from the artist, 1995, © the artist
Wright, Peter b.1932, *La serie Vallespir No.3*, purchased from the artist, 1995, © the artist
Wright, Peter b.1932, *La serie Vallespir No.4*, purchased from the artist, 1995, © the artist
Wright, Peter b.1932, *West Wight*, donated by the artist, 1988, © the artist

Isle of Wight Bus Museum

Golding, Mary b.1940, *Ryde Pier Tram, c.1920*, on long-term loan from the artist, © the artist

Isle of Wight Council Museum Service

Bates, David c.1840–1921, *Bedouin at an Oasis with Pyramids*, gift, 1995
Briggs, Henry Perronet (attributed to) 1791/1793–1844, *The Earl of Yarborough*, gift, 1995
British (English) School *Launch of 'HMS Magicienne' at Fishbourne*, gift, 1997
British (English) School *Reverend Thomas Binstead MacNamara, MA (1824–1910)*, gift, 1995
British (English) School 19th C, *Portrait of a Gentleman*, gift, 1995
British (English) School late 19th C, *Queen Victoria (1819–1901)*, gift, 1995
Colleypriest, Victor b.1901, *'HMS Quorn'*, on loan
Colleypriest, Victor b.1901, *'Kukai'*, on loan
Davidge, E. Gordon *Buckingham Villa, Ryde, Sunset on the Solent from the Garden*, gift, 2004
Fowles, Arthur Wellington 1815–1883, *'The Cambria', Winner of the Town Cup RVYC Regatta, 1868*, gift, 1995
Fowles, Arthur Wellington 1815–1883, *Royal Yacht 'Alberta' Approaching a Man of War, Solent*, gift, 1995
Fowles, Arthur Wellington 1815–1883, *The Royal Yacht Reviews the Fleet at Spithead*, gift, 1995
Fowles, Arthur Wellington 1815–1883, *The Shah of Persia Reviewing the Fleet*, acquired, 1995
Fowles, Arthur Wellington 1815–1883, *Yacht Racing in the Solent*, gift, 1995
Fowles, Arthur Wellington 1815–1883, *The Royal Barge off Cowes with the Royal Yacht Squadron Beyond*, gift, 1995
Goodburn *Interior of Cockpit of a Hovercraft*, gift
Gregory, George 1849–1938, *Shipping off Ryde*, gift, 1995
Gregory, George 1849–1938, *Salvaging the Wreck*, purchased, 1994
Groves, Mary active 1883–1933, *Dethroned*, gift, 1995
Groves, Mary active 1883–1933, *The Bookworm and the Butterflies*, gift, 1995
Guardi, Antonio (school of) 1699–1760 & **Guardi, Francesco (school of)** 1712–1793 *Venetian Canal Scene*, gift, 1995
Kneller, Godfrey (school of) 1646–1723, *John Mann*, gift, 1995
Luny, Thomas (attributed to) 1759–1837, *'HMS Magicienne' off Table Top Mountain, South Africa*, acquired, 1995
Luny, Thomas (attributed to) 1759–1837, *Yacht Racing off Calshot*, gift, 1995
Luny, Thomas (attributed to) 1759–1837, *Yachting off the Royal Yacht Squadron*, gift, 1995
McEwen, William *Shipping off a Mountainous Coast*, gift, 1995
Miles, Thomas Rose 1869–1888, *Signal for a Pilot, Shanklin Bay, Isle of Wight*, purchased, 1995
Minns, Fanny Mary active 1865–1905, *Carisbrooke Village*, gift, 1995
Owen, William 1769–1825, *Sir Leonard Thomas Worsley Holmes*, gift, 1995
Priestly, J. T. *George Fellows, Esq.*, gift, 1995
Reilly, John b.1928, *The Undercliff*, purchased, 1999, © the artist
Reilly, John b.1928, *Four in*

Harmony, unknown provenance, © the artist
Ryan, Charles J. 1865–1949, *Mark William Norman*, gift 1997
Simson, William 1800–1847, *Columbus at the Door of the Convent of Santa Maria de la Rábida*, gift, 1995
unknown artist *Ernest Groves, Mayor of Ryde (1895–1897)*, gift, 1995
unknown artist early 19th C, *View of Ryde*, gift
unknown artist late 19th C, *Lieutenant General the Honourable Somerset J. Gough-Calthorpe*, on loan
unknown artist late 20th C, *Warship*, unknown provenance
unknown artist *War Savings for Victory*, gift, 2004
Voysey *Sir Godfrey Baring BT, KBE, JP, DL*, gift, 1995
Webb, Geoffrey 1896–1981, *Gaff Rigger Racing Yachts off the Isle of Wight*, purchased, 1983
Webb, Geoffrey 1896–1981, *Gaff Rigger Racing Yachts off the Isle of Wight*, purchased, 1983
Wilkinson, Norman 1878–1971, *Estuary Scene*, purchased, 1983, © the Norman Wilkinson estate
Young, R. *Patrick Bryan, Mayor of Newport (1970–1971)*, gift, 1995

Quay Arts

Wells, Peter 1938–1996, *Untitled*, donated by Janet Wells, 2004, © the artist's estate
Wells, Peter 1938–1996, *Untitled*, donated by Janet Wells, 2004, © the artist's estate
Wright, Peter b.1932, *Port Marker*, acquired, 1997, on long-term loan from the artist, © the artist
Wright, Peter b.1932, *Blue, Green, Brown, Mauve*, acquired, 2002, © the artist

Ryde Fire Station

Rosenberg, William George Home active 1871–1884, *A Fire in London*, gift from George H. Harrison, JP, 1925

Ventnor Heritage Museum

Bull, Keith G. *South Street, Ventnor*, donated by Mr E. Biggin, 2001
Charlwood, Harry 1924–2001, *From Ryde Pierhead to Ventnor*, gift, 1991, © Ventnor Heritage Museum
Charlwood, Harry 1924–2001, *The Bombing of Ventnor, 1940*, gift, 1996, © Ventnor Heritage Museum
Edmunds, J. E. *The Capsizing of the 'Eurydice', 1878*, gift, 1995
Martin, Harry James (attributed to) c.1860–1944, *Mackerel Boats*, gift, 1993
Pollard, Beatrice *Sir Winston Churchill (1874–1965)*
Poore, Adela active 1894–1929, *Old Church, Bonchurch*
Simpson, Archie *Ernest Biggin*
Stotesbury, Louise b.1919, *Steephill Castle Entrance*, © the artist
Stotesbury, Louise b.1919, *Steephill Castle Entrance*, © the artist

Yarmouth Isle of Wight Town Trust

unknown artist *Lady Holmes*
unknown artist *Leonard, Lord Holmes, Baron Holmes of Kilmallock, County Limerick, Mayor of Yarmouth (1798, 1800 & 1803) (detail)*

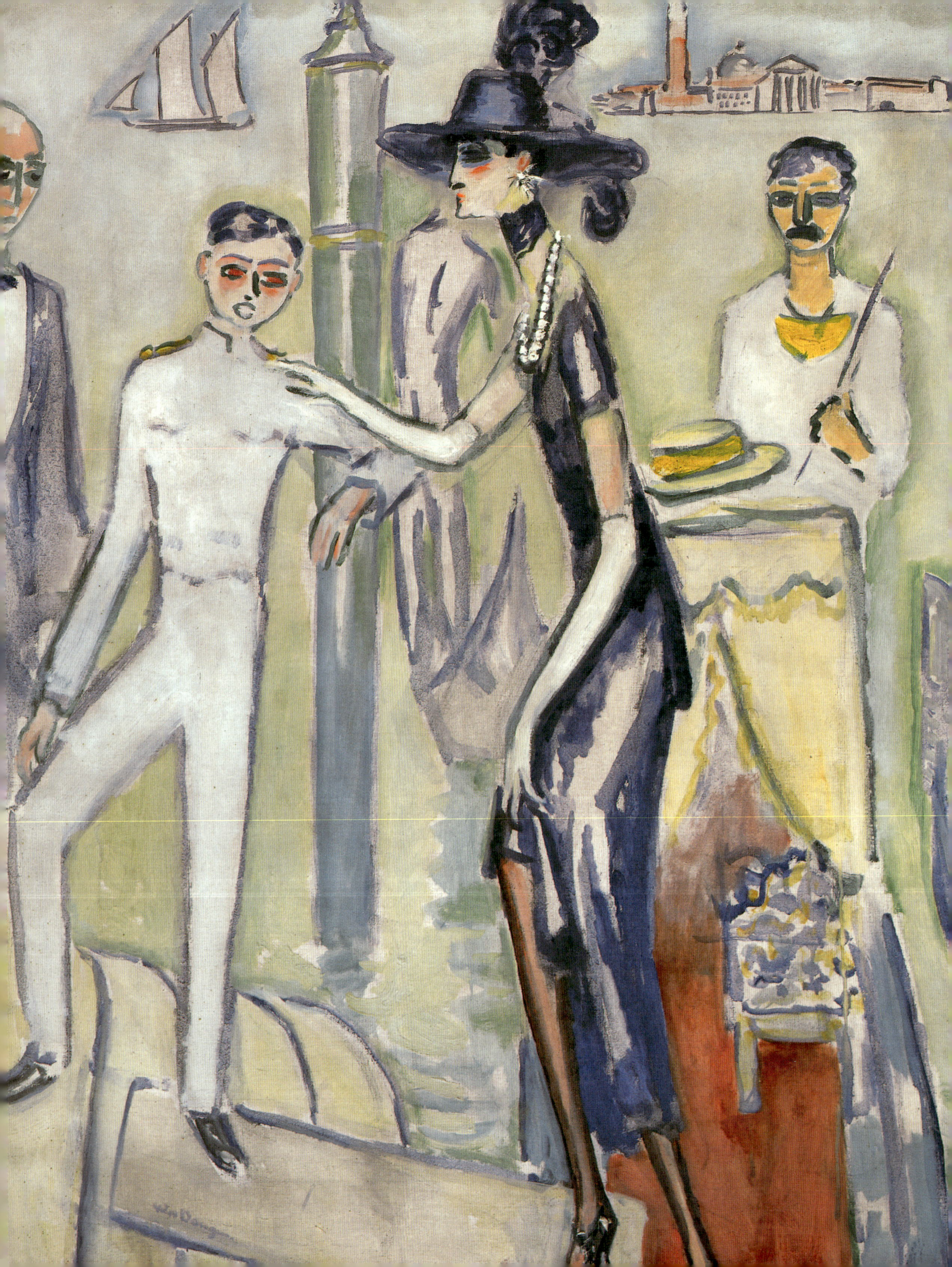

Collection Addresses

Southampton

Solent Sky Aviation Museum
Albert Road South, Southampton SO14 3FR
Telephone 02380 635830

Southampton City Art Gallery
Southampton City Council, Civic Centre
Southampton SO14 7LP
Telephone 02380 832277

Southampton City Museums:

Collections Management Centre
31 Industrial Park, Southern Road
Southampton SO15 1HG
Telephone 02380 237584

Southampton Maritime Museum
Wool House, Bugle Street
Southampton SO14 2AR
Telephone 02380 635904

Southampton Mayor's Parlour
Southampton City Council, Civic Centre
Southampton SO14 7LY
Telephone 02380 832434

Southampton Solent University
East Park Terrace, Southampton SO14 OYN
Telephone 02380 319000

Southampton University Hospitals NHS Trust
Southampton General Hospital, Tremona Road
Southampton SO16 6YD
Telephone 02380 795122

University of Southampton
Highfield, Southampton SO17 1BJ
Telephone 02380 592158

Isle of Wight

Blackgang Chine

Blackgang Sawmill and St Catherine's Quay
Blackgang Chine, near Ventnor, Isle of Wight PO38 2HN
Telephone 01983 730330

Brading

Brading Roman Villa
Morton Old Road, Brading, Isle of Wight PO36 OEN
Telephone 01983 406223

Cowes

Cowes Maritime Museum
Branch Library and Maritime Museum
Beckford Road, Cowes, Isle of Wight PO31 7SG
Telephone 01983 293394

English Heritage, Osborne House
York Avenue, East Cowes
Isle of Wight PO32 6JY
Telephone 01983 200022

Sir Max Aitken Museum
The Prospect, 83 High Street, West Cowes
Isle of Wight PO31 7AJ
Telephone 01983 295144

Havenstreet

Museum of Island Railway History
The Isle of Wight Railway Company Limited
The Railway Station, Havenstreet
Isle of Wight PO33 4DS
Telephone 01983 882204

Newport

Carisbrooke Castle Museum
Carisbrooke Castle, Newport
Isle of Wight PO30 IXY
Telephone 01983 523112

Facing page: Dongen, Kees van, 1877–1968, *Woman in Venice* (detail), Southampton City Art Gallery, (p. 38)

Healing Arts, Isle of Wight NHS Primary Care Trust
St Mary's Hospital, Parkhurst Road, Newport
Isle of Wight PO30 5TG
Telephone 01983 534253

Isle of Wight Bus Museum
Newport Harbour, Newport
Isle of Wight PO30 2EF
Telephone 01983 533352

Isle of Wight Council Museum Service:

Isle of Wight Council Museum Service
The Guildhall, High Street, Newport
Isle of Wight PO30 1TY
Telephone 01983 823847

Cothey Bottom Heritage Centre
The Guildhall, High Street, Newport
Isle of Wight PO30 1TY
Telephone 01983 823822

Museum of Island History
The Guildhall, High Street, Newport
Isle of Wight PO30 1TY
Telephone 01983 823366

Quay Arts
Sen Street, Newport Harbour
Isle of Wight PO30 5BG
Telephone 01983 822490

Ryde

Ryde Fire Station
Nicholson Road, Ryde
Isle of Wight PO33 1BE
Telephone 01983 812708

Ventnor

Ventnor Heritage Museum
11 Spring Hill, Ventnor
Isle of Wight PO38 1PE
Telephone 01983 855407

Yarmouth

Yarmouth Isle of Wight Town Trust
Town Hall, Yarmouth
Isle of Wight PO41 ONS
Telephone 01983 760690

Index of Artists

In this catalogue, artists' names and the spelling of their names follow the preferred presentation of the name in the Getty Union List of Artist Names (ULAN) as of February 2004, if the artist is listed in ULAN.

The page numbers next to each artist's name below direct readers to paintings that are by the artist; are attributed to the artist; or, in a few cases, are more loosely related to the artist being, for example, 'after', 'the circle of' or copies of a painting by the artist. The precise relationship between the artist and the painting is listed in the catalogue.

Supporters of the Public Catalogue Foundation

Master Patrons

The Public Catalogue Foundation is greatly indebted to the following Master Patrons who have helped it in the past or are currently working with it to raise funds for the publication of their county catalogues. All of them have given freely of their time and have made an enormous contribution to the work of the Foundation.

Peter Andreae *(Hampshire)*
Sir Henry Aubrey-Fletcher, Bt, Lord Lieutenant for Buckinghamshire *(Berkshire and Buckinghamshire)*
Sir Nicholas Bacon, DL, High Sheriff for Norfolk *(Norfolk)*
Peter Bretherton *(West Yorkshire: Leeds)*
Richard Compton *(North Yorkshire)*
George Courtauld, DL, Vice Lord Lieutenant for Essex *(Essex)*
The Marquess of Downshire *(North Yorkshire)*
Patricia Grayburn, MBE DL *(Surrey)*
Tommy Jowitt *(West Yorkshire)*
Sir Michael Lickiss *(Cornwall)*
Lord Marlesford, DL *(Suffolk)*
Phyllida Stewart-Roberts, OBE, Lord Lieutenant for East Sussex *(East Sussex)*
Leslie Weller, DL *(West Sussex)*

Financial Support

The Public Catalogue Foundation is particularly grateful to the following organisations and individuals who have given it generous financial support since the project started in 2003.

National Sponsor

Christie's

Benefactors (£10,000–£50,000)

City of Bradford Metropolitan District Council
Deborah Loeb Brice Foundation
The Bulldog Trust
A. & S. Burton 1960 Charitable Trust
The John S. Cohen Foundation
Christie's
Mr Lloyd Dorfman
The Foyle Foundation
Hampshire County Council
Peter Harrison Foundation
Hiscox plc
ICAP plc
Kent County Council
The Linbury Trust
The Manifold Trust
Robert Warren Miller
The Monument Trust
Miles Morland
National Gallery Trust
Stavros S. Niarchos Foundation
Norfolk County Council
Provident Financial
P. F. Charitable Trust
The Pilgrim Trust
RAB Capital plc
Renaissance West Midlands
Saga Group Ltd
University College, London
University of Leeds
Garfield Weston Foundation

Series Patrons (Minimum donation of £2,500)

Harry Bott
Janey Buchan
Dr Peter Cannon-Brookes
Mrs Greta Fenston
Glasgow Museums
Patricia Grayburn, MBE DL
G. Laurence Harbottle
Paul & Fiona Hart
Paul & Kathrine Haworth
Neil Honebon
The Keatley Trust
Michael A. Lambert
David & Amanda Leathers
Miles Morland
Adam Sedgwick
Sir Harry & Lady Soloman
Stuart M. Southall
University of Surrey
Chloe Teacher
David & Cissy Walker
Mr & Mrs Charles Wyvill

Catalogue Patrons (£1,000–£10,000)

ACE Study Tours
Adams & Remers
Marcus & Kate Agius
The AIM Foundation
John Alston, CBE
Amberley Castle
Archant Ltd
Mr Ian Askew
The Bacon Charitable Trust
Basingstoke and Deane Borough Council
Barlow Robbins LLP
Mr James & Lady Emma Barnard
Sir Christopher Bland
The Charlotte Bonham-Carter Charitable Trust
H. R. Pratt Boorman Family Foundation
The Bowerman Charitable Trust
Bramdean Asset Management LLP
Peter Bretherton
Mrs T. Brotherton-Ratcliffe
Mr & Mrs Patrick Burgess
Mr & Mrs Mark Burrell
Arnold J. Burton Charitable Trust
C. J. R. & Mrs C. L. Calderwood
Chichester District Council
The Timothy Colman Charitable Trust
Cornwall County Council
Mr S. J. D. Corsan
Graeme Cottam & Gloriana Marks de Chabris
Elaine Craven, Earl Street Employment Consultants Ltd
Harriett Cullen
De La Rue Charitable Trust
The Duke of Devonshire's Charitable Trust
Sir Harry Djanogly, CBE
Professor Patrick & Dr Grace Dowling
Marquess of Douro
East Sussex County Council
Eastbourne Borough Council
EEMLAC, through the Association for Suffolk Museums
Lord & Lady Egremont
Sir John & Lady Elliott
Andrew & Lucy Ellis
Essex County Council
Marc Fitch Fund
Elizabeth & Val Fleming
Christopher & Catherine Foyle
The Friends of Historic Essex
The Friends of the Royal Pavilion, Art Gallery & Museums, Brighton
The Friends of Southampton's Museums, Archives and Galleries
The Friends of York Art Gallery (E. J. Swift Bequest)
Deborah Gage (Works of Art) Ltd
Lewis & Jacqueline Golden
Gorringes
Charles Gregson
The Gulland Family
David Gurney
Philip Gwyn
The Hartnett Charitable Trust
Hazlitt, Gooden & Fox Ltd
Heartwood Wealth Management Ltd
Lady Hind Trust
Hobart Charitable Trust
David & Prue Hopkinson
The Isle of Wight Council
The J. and S. B. Charitable Trust
The Keatley Trust
Kent Messenger Group
Garrett Kirk, Jr
The Leche Trust

Leeds Art Collections Fund
Leeds City Council
Leeds Philosophical and Literary Society
Mark & Sophie Lewisohn
Maidstone Borough Council
The Marlay Group
The Mercers' Company
MLA East of England
Rupert Nabarro
Newcastle City Council
Oakmoor Trust
Sir Idris Pearce
The Pennycress Trust
Portsmouth City Council
Mr John Rank
Rathbone Investment Management Ltd
The Hans and Märit Rausing Charitable Trust
Roger & Jane Reed
Renaissance North East
Michael Renshall, CBE MA FCA
Sir Miles & Lady Rivett-Carnac
Rothschild Foundation
Royal Cornwall Museum
Russell New
Scarfe Charitable Trust
Shaftesbury PLC
The Shears Foundation
Smith & Williamson
South West of England Regional Development Agency
Caroline M. Southall
Stuart M. Southall
Southampton City Council
Mrs Andrew Stewart-Roberts, OBE
Mr Peter Stormonth Darling
Strutt and Parker
Suffolk County Council, through the Association for Suffolk Museums
The Bernard Sunley Charitable Foundation
Surrey County Council
The John Swire 1989 Charitable Trust
The Tanner Trust
Thistle Trust
Trusthouse Charitable Foundation
University College Falmouth
University of Essex
The Walland Trust Fund
John Wates Charitable Trust
Leslie Weller, DL
West Sussex County Council
Wilkin & Sons Ltd
Peter Wolton Charitable Trust
Michael J. Woodhall, FRICS